MACMILLAN COLOR
ATLAS OF THE STATES

STATES AND THEIR CAPITALS

Red number is page where state coverage begins

ALASKA 10
○ Juneau

WASHINGTON 329
○ Olympia
○ Salem
OREGON 258
○ Boise
IDAHO 83

MONTANA 181
○ Helena

NORTH DAKOTA 237
○ Bismarck

MINNESOTA 160
○ St. Paul

WISCONSIN 343
○ Madison

MICHIGAN 153
○ Lansing

MAINE 132
○ Augusta

NEW HAMPSHIRE 202
VERMONT 315
○ Montpelier
○ Concord
○ Boston
○ Providence
MASSACHUSETTS 146
RHODE ISLAND 272
CONNECTICUT 45
○ Hartford

NEW YORK 223
○ Albany
○ Trenton
NEW JERSEY 209
DELAWARE 52
○ Dover
WASHINGTON DC 59
○ Annapolis
MARYLAND 139
○ Richmond
VIRGINIA 322

PENNSYLVANIA 265
○ Harrisburg

OHIO 244
○ Columbus
WEST VIRGINIA 336
○ Charleston
○ Frankfort

INDIANA 97
○ Indianapolis

ILLINOIS 90
○ Springfield

IOWA 104
○ Des Moines

NEVADA 195
○ Carson City

CALIFORNIA 31
○ Sacramento

UTAH 308
○ Salt Lake City

WYOMING 350
○ Cheyenne

COLORADO 38
○ Denver

ARIZONA 17
○ Phoenix

NEW MEXICO 216
○ Santa Fe

SOUTH DAKOTA 286
○ Pierre

NEBRASKA 188
○ Lincoln

KANSAS 111
○ Topeka

MISSOURI 174
○ Jefferson City

OKLAHOMA 251
○ Oklahoma City

TEXAS 300
○ Austin

ARKANSAS 24
○ Little Rock

LOUISIANA 125
○ Baton Rouge

MISSISSIPPI 167
○ Jackson

KENTUCKY 118
○ Nashville
TENNESSEE 293

ALABAMA 3
○ Montgomery

GEORGIA 69
○ Atlanta

NORTH CAROLINA 230
○ Raleigh

SOUTH CAROLINA 279
○ Columbia

FLORIDA 62
○ Tallahassee

HAWAII 76
○ Honolulu

Scale

0   200   400 mi.

0   400 km

MACMILLAN COLOR ATLAS OF THE STATES

Mark T. Mattson

MACMILLAN LIBRARY REFERENCE USA
Simon & Schuster Macmillan
New York

Prentice Hall International
London   Mexico City   New Delhi   Singapore   Sydney   Toronto

Macmillan Library Reference USA
Simon & Schuster Macmillan
1633 Broadway
New York, NY 10019

Library of Congress Catalog Card Number: 96–10494

Printed in the United States of America

Printing Number
1 2 3 4 5 6 7 8 9 10

Library of Congress Cataloging-in-Publication Data

Mattson, Mark T.
    Macmillan color atlas of the states / Mark T. Mattson.
        p.   cm.
    Includes bibliographical references and index.
    ISBN 0–02–864659–2 (alk. paper)
    1. United States—Maps.   2. United States—Economic conditions—
Maps.   3. United States —Social conditions—Maps.   I. Title.
    G1200.M4   1996   <G&M>
    912.73—dc20   96–10494
                                                                         CIP
                                                                         MAP

This paper meets the requirements of ANSI/NISO Z39.48-1992 (Permanence of Paper).

TABLE OF CONTENTS

ACKNOWLEDGEMENTS

The list of those who contributed to this project is relatively small. Each person held many jobs and accepted various responsibilities. My deepest appreciation goes to Christopher Salvatico. Although his name is not on the title page, it belongs there because each page of this atlas is indelibly marked with his work. Chris provided organization, computer skills, design, words, and thought. Although he wasn't paid for it, he gave freely a generous dose of friendship, peace, and support over the two years that the Atlas of the States was in production.

My thanks also goes to Robert Greenbaum whose cartographic production over the period of at least one year is evident throughout this project. We must all thank Rob for the wonderful job that he did with the choropleth maps and the shaded relief for each state.

There are two people who must be thanked for their research and writing skills in the areas of physical geography and the environment. They are Gerry Krieg and Charlene Howard. On any given day, Gerry and Charlene would research a subject and write a summary which I would rewrite for publication. In reality, much of the writing that they did exists in its original form because it was done so well.

I would also like to thank Charles 'Bud' Boenecke who is currently serving as my graduate assistant at Temple University. Bud was responsible for organization of facts and research in the areas of soils and physical features. He careful input and all-around analysis adds considerably to the usefulness of this work.

Introduction

The information contained in this atlas is usable in a variety of ways. Origins of state names, locations of festivals, maps of cultural sites, lists of famous citizens, and descriptions of state flags constitute one level of information that needs no further interpretation and can be read for simple enjoyment or transferred to school reports.

Raw statistics, such as population figures, financial data, and ethnicity counts represent another class of information. Issues related to these data are more accessible when placed into either a national or regional context. Since the text of this work is an atlas of the states, a regional overview of the statistical data is presented in this introduction.

State Finances

The governmental structure of the United States contains not only federal and state components but thousands of local governmental authorities such as counties, municipalities, school districts, and special districts such as housing and port authorities. In 1992, 86,743 local governments were identified by the Census of Governments.

Common to all governmental units is the ability to tax or collect money to fund operating expenditures. In this atlas, finances for each state are elaborated. In brief, states collect money from four sources. Large sums come directly from federal government outlays, taxes of various kinds, and miscellaneous charges. Smaller sums come directly to the states from localities.

Finances for individual states vary. Sums attributable to one or all the aforementioned revenue sources can be compared with averages for all fifty states. In 1992, state governments collected an average of $3.2 billion from the federal government—26.3 percent of their total revenues. The average state collected $6.6 billion from its residents in taxes (54.2 percent of total state revenue). Miscellaneous sources, such as liquor taxes, licensing fees, and gasoline taxes, add $2.2 billion to revenues of the average state (17.8 percent). Local taxes accounted for 1.8 percent of revenues for the typical state ($217 million).

The average state spends $4.2 billion on education (34.6 percent of revenues), $3.1 billion on highways (25.6 percent), $974 million on welfare (8.0 percent), $962 million on health (7.9 percent), and $2.9 billion (24.0 percent) on other items such as corrections and the criminal and civil systems of justice. (U. S. Bureau of the Census, State Government Finances, series GF.)

Climate and Environment

Climate, soils, and landforms define the various ecoregions that spread across North America. Discussions of climate, typography, hydrology, and life forms are combined with facts about the weather to generate images of state environments. Added to this is information about environmental quality: States are ranked according to criteria such as air pollution, the generation of industrial solid wastes, landfill capacity, water usage, and the production of hazardous substances.

A list of endangered species concludes this section. Species have been divided into five classes—aquatic species, birds, mammals, other animals, and plants. In each list, numbers in parentheses indicate the number of species that are endangered within a class. The animal or plant name that follows identifies the specie that is most endangered.

Population Density

While the population of the United States increases from year to year, the space within which it is contained remains the same. The census of 1790 demonstrated a population of 4.5 persons per square mile. That figure has risen steady to 72.9 persons in 1993.

Currently, over 257 million people live in the United States. They are overwhelmingly concentrated in a belt that begins in Illinois and works its way east along the Great Lakes through New England and south along the Atlantic coast to Florida. Population is also concentrated in California.

The District of Columbia features the most highly concentrated population—9,482 people per square mile in 1993. The state with the most densely packed state is New Jersey. Many states in the Midwest and in the Mountain regions have few residents compared to their total land area. Alaska is the least dense state with only 1.1 residents per square mile.

Information used in this book to calculate population comes from the 1990 Census of Population and Housing, Population and Housing Unit Counts (CPH-2) and data published in the 1995 Statistical Abstract of the United States.

Population Distribution and Growth

The population of each state, regardless of its overall density, is located primarily in or around major urban centers. For the purpose of description and analysis of U. S. populations, the U.S. Office of Management and Budget designated 268 Metropolitan Areas (MSA's and CMSA's) in July of 1992. The concept of a metropolitan area is one in which surrounding communities are tied to a major metropolitan nucleus by a high degree of social and economic interaction. Within the United States, 79.7 percent of all persons (203,172,000) live within metropolitan areas. That figure is increasing: Between 1980 and 1992, metropolitan population increased by 14.9 percent.

In 1993, the most populous states were California and New York. The least populous states were Wyoming and Vermont. The greatest population increases between 1980 and 1993 have occurred in Nevada, Alaska, Arizona, and Florida. Several states have decreased in population, with West Virginia leading this category at –6.3 percent. Populations of North Dakota and Iowa have also declined. (1990 Census of Population and Housing, Population and Housing Unit Counts (CPH-2) and data published in the 1995 Statistical Abstract of the United States.)

The Middle Atlantic, East North Central, South Atlantic, and Pacific regions are the most populated in the country. The largest increases in population since 1980 have occurred in the Pacific (29.7 percent) and Mountain (29.3 percent) regions. The slowest regional growth rates were calculated for the East North Central (3.6 percent) and the Middle Atlantic (3.2 percent).

Components of Population Change

On a national scale, population has increased since 1960. The rate of increase, however, has slowed in recent years. This trend is expected to continue through the early decades of the twenty–first century. By 2025, U.S. population is expected to be increasing by a rate of only 0.2 percent per year. This is compared to a yearly rate of 1.6 percent in 1960. This trend is explained by an increase in deaths coupled with a decrease in births and the number of immigrants.

Population Projections

By the year 2010, the United States will have an estimated population of 300,430,000. Population growth will be extreme for African Americans and Hispanics, and will virtually come to a halt for Whites by year 2025. The fastest growing age groups between 1990 and year 2000 will be those 45 to 54 years old, and those 75 years old and over. In the first decade of the next century, the fastest growing group will be between 55 and 64 years of age. (U. S. Bureau of the Census, Current Population Reports, P25-1111.)

Components of Gender

Females outnumber males for all age groups except in the Hispanic population. The largest disparity in the sexes is demonstrated in the African American community, where there are barely nine males for every ten females. Given that women live longer than men (79.0 years as opposed to 72.1 in 1990), this disparity is more pronounced in later years. In 1992, only 95.3 men were alive for every 100 women for all ethnic groups. (U. S. Bureau of the Census, Current Population Reports, P25-1095 and P25-1104, 1992.)

Age of Population

The American population is growing older. In 1970, 18.9 percent of the population was over 55 years of age. This figure increased to 20.8 percent in 1992 and is expected to balloon to 29.3 percent by 2020.

Median age for the United States increased from 29.6 years in 1980 to 32.8 years in 1990. The states that are aging most quickly are also the states which are losing population. This would seem to indicate an out-migration of younger residents, resulting in a decreased rate of birth. Florida, a popular retirement state, has the oldest population. Utah, in the last two decennial censuses, has been America's youngest state. Population under 5 years of age and under 17 years of age has shown a steady decline since 1960. (U. S. Bureau of the Census, Current Population Reports, P25-1095 and data published in the 1995 Statistical Abstract of the United States.)

Immigration and Country of Origin

Most Americans acknowledge an ethnic heritage which is noted in the ethnicity section of this book. Many have parents, grandparents, or direct knowledge of relatives that left foreign lands to become citizens of the United States. This migration has happened over the entire history of the United States. Sometimes, it has happened in great waves due to economic and political circumstances.

A great wave of immigration started in 1840 and continued to 1920. Most of the immigrants of this era came from Europe. Today, immigrants from Central America, Mexico, South America, and many Asian countries overwhelmingly contribute to America's growth. Throughout the eighties, 86.5 percent of all new arrivals came from these areas. (U. S. Immigration and Naturalization Service, Statistical Yearbook, annual.)

African Americans

African Americans are the largest ethnic minority in the United States. In 1995 12.6 percent, or 33,117,000 U. S. citizens, were of African descent. By the year 2025, it is predicted that 14.2 percent of the population will be black (48.0 million). By the year 2050, the African American population is expected to grow to nearly twice its present size. (Estimates presented in the 1995 Statistical Abstract of the United States.)

America's African American population is spread across the country in a very distinct pattern. Reflecting the early days of slavery and emancipation, the large concentrations are located in a belt starting in North Carolina and winding south and west through Louisiana. Regional black populations of 20.5 percent in the South Atlantic and 19.6 percent in the East South Central confirm this observation. The state with the largest African American population is New York with 2,859,055, followed closely by California (2,208,801) and Texas (2,021,632). States where African Americans comprise the largest proportion of the population are Mississippi with 35.6 percent and Louisiana with 30.8 percent.

The African American population has been moving in two directions from its southern roots in recent decades. The first movement is northward and easterly. Blacks from Mississippi and Alabama have migrated to Michigan, Ohio, and New York in significant numbers. Blacks from Georgia, South Carolina, and North Carolina have move directly north to Maryland, New Jersey, and New York. The second major movement is westward. African Americans from Louisiana, Mississippi, and Texas have chosen to migrate in large numbers to southern California. (U. S. Bureau of the Census, Current Population Reports, P25-1095 and P25-1104, 1992.)

Hispanic Americans

Hispanic Americans are America's second largest ethnic group with 26,798,000 members in 1995 (10.2 percent of the country's population). They are also the second fastest growing component behind Asians and Pacific Islanders. America's Hispanic population is predicted to grow 26.8 percent in the nineties. A further increase of 22.1 percent is expected between 2000 and 2010. (Estimates presented in the 1995 Statistical Abstract of the United States.)

Like other ethnic groups, the Hispanic population has a distinct spatial distribution. The southwest corner of the United States, parts of the Middle Atlantic region, Florida, and Illinois have significant proportions of Hispanic citizens—59.5 percent of total Hispanic population lives in California, Arizona, New Mexico, and Texas. Most of these citizens are of Mexican or South American ancestry. Puerto Ricans have settled mainly in New York, New Jersey, and northward in Connecticut and Massachusetts. Smaller pockets of Puerto Rican Americans can be found in Dade County, Florida; and Chicago, Illinois. Cuban Americans are found primarily in Dade County, Florida (Miami). New York City has the largest Haitian population. Many Haitian Americans also live in Miami, Boston, and Chicago.

The migration of Puerto Rican Americans, from their heaviest concentration in New York City, has been primarily westward to southern California and southward to Florida.

Americans of Mexican descent have moved into the Midwestern and Western states from their origins along the Rio Grande and in New Mexico. The vast majority have moved to southern California. Very few have moved anywhere east of the Mississippi River. (U. S. Bureau of the Census, Current Population Reports, P25-1095 and P25-1104, 1992.)

Asian Americans

With the Refugee Acts of the past three decades, America's Asian population has become the most rapidly growing component of the nation's population. In 1995, 3.7 percent of the U. S. population is of Asian or Pacific Island descent. Most Asian Americans live on the coasts in three large cities—Los Angeles, San Francisco, and New York. Chicago also has a large Asian American community. Most migration of Asian Americans is westward from New York to northern California. A large number of migrants have also moved from southern to northern California and many have continued beyond into Washington State and Oregon. The Pacific Northwest will become a growth area for Asian Americans with Chinese from Hong Kong moving southward from western Canada. (U. S. Bureau of the Census, Current Population Reports, P25-1095 and P25-1104, 1992.)

Personal Income Per Capita

Per capita income varies from region to region in the United States. In 1993, the average income per capita (PCI) was $20,817. The South had the lowest PCI while the highest PCI was in the Northeast. (U.S. Bureau of Economic Analysis, Survey of Current Businesses, 1994.).

Personal per capita income increased 109.4 percent between 1980 and 1993 (current dollars). In constant 1987 dollars that figure is considerably lower—17.6 percent.

The rate of income growth is expected to decrease for the United States as a whole through the 1990s and into the next century. The Northeast will be most heavily hit by a scenario in which income remains the same or just slightly outdistances inflation. Incomes are expected to increase at only one third the rate at which they had between 1980 and 1993. (U.S. Bureau of Economic Analysis, Survey of Current Businesses, 1994.)

Employment

The largest job sector is manufacturing (19.6 million employees). Most manufacturing employees work in California, New York, Pennsylvania, and Ohio.

The number of employees in manufacturing has decreased and manufacturing establishments have moved south and west from their traditional bases in the Middle Atlantic and East North Central rust belt. Manufacturing firms and jobs have also moved out of the country in an effort to avoid unionization and to decrease employee wages.

Total receipts for firms engaged in manufacturing exceeded $1.0 trillion in 1991. Total payrolls exceeded $529.1 billion. (U. S. Bureau of the Census, Census of Manufacturers and Annual Survey of Manufacturing.)

The service sector is growing more quickly than any other sector of the U. S. economy. In 1982, 1.3 million service establishments employed 11.1 million U.S. workers. By 1991, those figures increased to 2.1 million establishments and 29.6 million employees.

Total receipts for firms engaged in services exceeded $1.1 trillion in 1987. Total payrolls exceeded $407.8 billion. (U. S. Bureau of the Census, 1987 Census of Service Industries, SC87-A-52, SC87-N-1, and SC87-S-4.)

Agriculture

The United States is a huge land area where suitability for farming changes dramatically from region to region. Most of the farming that is done in the United States is done in the Midwest. Iowa, Ohio, Minnesota, and Kansas, collectively known as America's agricultural heartland, produce nearly half of the goods grown in the United States. Western states produce less, confining their agricultural activities to herding and livestock grazing. California is the single exception to the rules of agricultural regionalization. Agricultural activities in California, the continent's most productive farm state, are supported through aggressive irrigation and fertilization.

Aside from where things grow and how land is put to use, three statements characterize American agriculture—the number of farms is decreasing, the average farm size is increasing, and agriculture is impacting the environment in serious ways.

In 1975, the United States had 2,521,000 farms compared with 2,068,000 in 1993. The average size of the American farm increased from 420 acres to 473 acres during the same time period. This is explained by an incorporation of agriculture where heavy equipment has taken the place of lone farming families.

The issue of corporate agriculture has important environmental considerations. In areas of the country where soil is rich and water is scarce, corporate farmers irrigate in increasing numbers. In 1960, thirty-three million acres were irrigated. In 1990, that number increased dramatically to 250 million acres.

Increased agricultural use of limited water resources has depleted water supplies in western states. It has also threatened water quality through chemical run-off and percolation.

Fast Facts

There are seventeen pages of tabular information at the end of this atlas. Readers will find this tabular information helpful when making direct comparisons of states and metropolitan areas. While space prohibits inclusion of every city, cities with populations of more than 25,000 are listed.

ALABAMA
The State of Alabama

Official State Seal

Originally used between 1819 and 1868, the Great Seal of Alabama was permanently adopted in 1939. The seal is a circle surrounding a map of the state. The map, which shows Alabama's largest rivers, also includes names and boundaries of surrounding states. The words "Alabama Great Seal" circle the state map within two rings of rope.

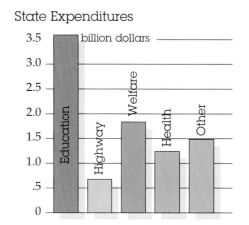

Legal Holidays

January: New Year's Day— 1st; Robert E. Lee Birthday—3rd Monday; Martin Luther King Birthday—3rd Monday; February: George Washington's Birthday—3rd Monday. February or March: Mardi Gras. April: Thomas Jefferson's Birthday—14th; Confederate Memorial Day—4th Monday; June: Jefferson Davis' Birthday—1st Monday. July: Independence Day—4th; September: Labor Day—1st Monday. October: Columbus Day—2nd Monday. November: Veterans' Day—11th; Thanksgiving Day—4th Thursday. December: Christmas Day—25th.

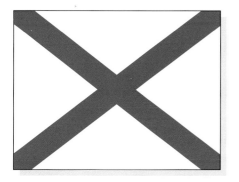

Official State Flag

Adopted in 1865, the Alabama state flag bears a strong resemblance to the colors and configuration of the Confederate flag. The red cross of St. Andrew rests dramatically on a pure white field in this simple scheme.

Festivals and Events

February or March: Mardi Gras. May: Winston 500, Talladega; Jubilee City Fest, Montgomery. June: Helen Keller Festival, Tuscumbia. July: Incident at Lonney's Tavern, Double Springs; BASS Masters Classic, Birmingham; World Championship Domino Tournament, Andalusia. August: Cherokee Pow Wow & Green Corn Festival, Gadsden. September: Old Time Festival at Old York USA, Oakman. October: Moundville Native American Festival, Moundville; National Peanut Festival, Dothan; National Shrimp Festival, Gulf Shores. December: Christmas on the River, Demopolis.

Alabama Compared to States in Its Region.

Resident Pop. in Metro Areas: 1st; Pop. Percent Increase: 2d; Pop. Over 65: 1st; Infant Mortality: 2d; School Enroll. Increase: 2d; High School Grad. and Up: 2d; Violent Crime: 1st; Hazardous Waste Sites: 3d; Unemployment: 2d; Median Household Income: 2d; Persons Below Poverty: 3d; Energy Costs Per Person: 1st.

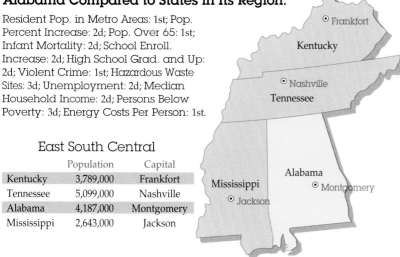

East South Central

	Population	Capital
Kentucky	3,789,000	Frankfort
Tennessee	5,099,000	Nashville
Alabama	4,187,000	Montgomery
Mississippi	2,643,000	Jackson

Alabama's Finances

Households: 1,444,000; Income Per Capita Current Dollars: $13,625; Change Per Capita Income 1980 to 1990: 13.4% (40th in U.S.); State Expenditures: $8,788,000,000; State Revenues: $8,910,000,000; Personal Income Tax: 2 to 5%; Average Taxes Paid Per Capita: $1,022; Sales Tax: None.

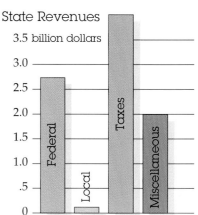

Location, Size, and Boundaries

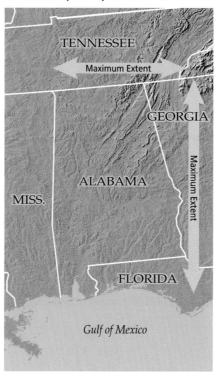

Location. Alabama is located in the southeastern United States in a region known as the East South Central. It is bounded on four sides by land with a small coast along the Gulf of Mexico in the south. The geographic center of Alabama is lat. 32° 50.5' N; long. 86° 38.0' W.

Size. Alabama is the 29th largest state in terms of size. Its area is 51,609 sq. mi. (133,667 km2). Inland water covers 938 sq. mi. (2,429 km2). Alabama touches the Gulf of Mexico along a 53-mile coastline.

Boundaries. Tennessee, 148 mi. (238 km); Georgia, 298 mi. (480 km); Florida, 219 mi. (352 km); Gulf of Mexico, 53 mi. (85 km); Mississippi, 326 mi. (525 km).

Geographic Extent. The north/south extent of Alabama is 329 mi. (530 km). The state extends 189 mi. (304 km) to the east/west.

Facts about Alabama. Origin of Name: After the *Alibamu* Indian tribe, which translates to "*I open* (or *I clear*) *the thicket*"; Nickname: Heart of Dixie; Motto: "We dare defend our rights" (*Audemus jura nostra defendere*); Abbreviations: Ala. (traditional), AL (postal); State Bird: yellowhammer; State Tree: southern pine; State Flower: camellia; State Song: "Alabama," words by Julia S. Tutwiler and music by Edna Goeckle Gussen.

Alabama Compared to Other States. Resident Pop. in Metro Areas: 29th; Pop. Percent Increase: 24th; Pop. Over 65: 23d; Infant Mortality: 5th; School Enroll. Increase: 32d; High School Grad. and Up: 46th; Violent Crime: 8th; Hazardous Waste Sites: 28th; Unemployment: 20th; Median Household Income: 41st; Persons Below Poverty: 7th; Energy Costs Per Person: 11th.

Sources of Information. Tourism: State of Alabama, Alabama Tourism and Travel, 401 Adams Ave., Montgomery, AL 36104. Economy: Alabama Development Office, State Capitol, Montgomery, AL 36130. Government: Office of the Secretary of State, Alabama State House Building, 11 So. Union St., Montgomery, AL 36130. History: State of Alabama, Alabama Tourism and Travel, 401 Adams Ave., Montgomery, AL 36104.

Map Labels

Russell Cave Nat'l Mon.
MADISON
JACKSON
Alabama Agricultural and Mechanical
Normal
Scottsboro
72
Joe Wheeler State Pk.
LAUDERDALE
Univ. of North Alabama
LIMESTONE
Monte Sano State Pk.
Sequoyah Caverns
Florence
Pope's Tavern
72
Athens
Huntsville
Ivy Green
U.S. Space & Rocket Center
Sheffield
Tuscumbia
COLBERT
2
431
Ft. Payne
DeSoto St. Pk.
Ringgo
Moulton
MORGAN
MARSHALL
Decatur
Russellville
Hartselle
Guntersville
Buck's Pocket State Pk.
Centre
FRANKLIN
43
LAWRENCE
Lake Guntersville State Pk.
DE KALB
Red Bay
Dismals Caverns
Ava Maria Grotto
CULLMAN
Cullman
Sardis Cty.
CHEROKEE
Rock Run
Shottsville
WINSTON
Double Springs
231
ETOWAH
Steele
Gadsden
Piedmont
Hamilton
Natural Bridge of Alabama
Rickwood Caverns State Pk.
Hanceville
278
Jacksonville State
Jacksonville
MARION
BLOUNT
Oneonta
Jacksonville
CLEBURNE
Sulligent
Jasper
Ragland
CALHOUN
Heflin
Winfield
WALKER
Warrior
Anniston
Vernon
Hubbertville
Fultondale
ST CLAIR
59
20
FAYETTE
Birmingham
Mtn. Brook
Pell City
Alabama Int'l Motor Speedway
Cheaha State Pk.
Wedowee
LAMAR
Fayette
Bessemer
Homewood
Talladega
Millport
Whitson
JEFFERSON
Hoover
Vestavia Hills
TALLADEGA
CLAY
RANDOLPH
Palmetto
Moores Bridge
Tannehill Hist. State Park
DeSoto Caverns
Ashland
Roanoke
Lake Lurleen State Pk.
TUSCALOOSA
Oak Mtn. State Pk.
Sylacauga
Carrollton
Northport
Univ. of Alabama
SHELBY
Columbiana
Horseshoe Bend Nat'l Military Park
Lafayette
PICKENS
Montevallo
Alexander City
CHAMBERS
Mantua
Tuscaloosa
West Blocton
Univ. of Montevallo
Rockford
Wind Creek State Pk.
280
Dadeville
Lanett
GREENE
Duncanville
BIBB
Clanton
COOSA
TALLAPOOSA
LEE
Opelika
Warsaw
Moundville Archaeological Park
Centreville
CHILTON
Auburn
Auburn
Chewacla State Pk.
Eutaw
HALE
Maplesville
Titus
ELMORE
Wetumpka
Phenix City
Greensboro
PERRY
Sprott
AUTAUGA
Tuskegee
Uchee
RUSSELL
Livingston
Marion
Paul M. Grist State Pk.
Prattville
Tuskegee
MACON
Holy Trinity
SUMTER
Livingston
Demopolis
80
Selma
Civil Rights Memorial
Montgomery
Hurtsboro
Whitfield
Linden
Beginning of Martin Luther King, Jr.'s march in 1965
Alabama State
MONTGOMERY
Union Springs
Central Mills
DALLAS
Hayneville
Ada
BULLOCK
Lakepoint Resort State Pk.
Chickasaw State Pk.
Catherine
LOUWNDES
Ramer
Blues Old Stand
Clayton
Butler
MARENGO
Roland Cooper State Pk.
Braggs
Troy State University
Eufaula
Bladen Springs State Pk.
Marengo
Camden
Oak Hill
Shady Grove
BARBOUR
CHOCTAW
Marvin
WILCOX
Ridgeville
Greenville
Troy
Blue Springs State Pk.
HENRY
Cullomburg
Lower Peach Tree
Midway
Georgiana
Luverne
PIKE
Grove Hill
MONROE
Victoria
Ozark
Abbeville
Shady Grove
Chatom
Pine Orchard
McKenzie
BUTLER
CRENSHAW
COFFEE
DALE
Jackson
Monroeville
Searight
Enterprise
Elba
Dothan
WASHINGTON
Frisco City
Evergreen
Andalusia
84
Chattahoochee St. Pk.
McIntosh
Barnett Crossroads
CONECUH
Frank Jackson State Pk.
Opp
Samson
Geneva
HOUSTON
Poarch
ESCAMBIA
COVINGTON
GENEVA
Deer Park
Fort Mims
Brewton
Florala State Pk.
Tensaw
Atmore
Claude D. Kelly State Pk.
MOBILE
Saraland
Bay Minette
Pritchard
Oakleigh Historic Complex
Mobile
10
Univ. of South Alabama
Daphne
Fairhope
Robertsdale
Bellingrath Gardens and Home
BALDWIN
Dauphin Island
Gulf State Pk.

Cultural Features List

■ **Alabama International Motor Speedway.** Stock car and sports car racing. Home of the Winston and Die Hard 500. (F-6)

■ **Ave Maria Grotto.** Located near St. Bernard Benedictine Abbey. Features famous religious buildings in miniature, including churches and shrines. (D-5)

■ **Bellingrath Gardens and Home.** Over 800 acres of flowers, trees, and sculptures. Also features the Delchamps Gallery of Boehm porcelain. (Q-2)

■ **Civil Rights Memorial.** Monument to those who died in the Civil Rights Movement between 1954 and 1968. Designed by Maya Lin, architect of the Vietnam Veterans Memorial in Washington D.C. (J-7)

■ **Dauphin Island.** Location of Fort Gaines and a French settlement dating from 1699. (Q-2)

■ **DeSoto Caverns.** The first officially recorded caves in the United States (1796). Named after the Spanish explorer Hernando de Soto. (F-6)

■ **Dismals Canyon.** Location of artifacts dating over 10,000 years; 100-foot-high rock walls. (D-2)

■ **Fort Mims.** Frontier fortification used during the Creek Indian War (1813-1814). (N-3)

■ **Horseshoe Bend National Military Park.** Location of the last battle of the Creek War (March 17, 1814). (G-8)

■ **Ivy Green.** Birthplace of Helen Keller (1880). (B-2)

■ **Moundville Archaeological Park.** Location of twenty prehistoric Indian mounds. (H-3)

■ **Natural Bridge of Alabama.** 60-foot-high sandstone bridge. Longest natural bridge east of the Rocky Mountains. (D-2)

■ **Oakleigh Historic Complex.** 1833 antebellum mansion and the Cox-Deasy House. (P-3)

■ **Pope's Tavern.** A Confederate hospital, now a museum. (B-2)

■ **Russell Cave National Monument.** Home of primitive people dating back 9,000 years. One of the oldest known site of humans in the United States. (A-7)

■ **Sequoyah Caverns.** Caverns that contain stalagmites and reflecting pools. (B-7)

■ **Tannehill Historic State Park.** National metallurgical engineering landmark. Includes the Iron and Steel Museum. (G-4)

■ **Tuskegee.** Location of museum dedicated to scientist and educator George Washington Carver; also has antebellum homes. (I-8)

■ **United States Space and Rocket Center.** Museum dedicated to space flight featuring NASA rocket and space shuttle exhibits. (B-5)

Scale

0   15   30   45 mi.

15   0   15   30   45   60 km

Legend

☆ State capitol

⊙ Cities over 35,000 population

○ Other significant cities

● County Seats

■ Major cultural attractions

□ State Parks

Ⓦ Welcome Centers

⚲ Major colleges and universities

Major Cities

City	Grid	City	Grid	City	Grid
Alexander City	G-7	Eufaula	K-10	Northport	G-3
Anniston	E-8	Florence	B-2	Opelika	H-10
Athens	B-4	Gadsden	D-7	Phenix City	I-10
Auburn	H-9	Homewood	F-5	Prattville	I-6
Bessemer	F-5	Hoover	F-5	Prichard	O-3
Birmingham	F-5	Huntsville	B-5	Scottsboro	B-7
Cullman	D-4	Jasper	E-4	Selma	J-5
Decatur	C-4	Mobile	P-2	Talladega	F-7
Dothan	M-10	Montgomery	J-7	Tuscaloosa	G-3
Enterprise	M-9	Mtn. Brook	F-5	Vestavia Hills	F-5

Alabama

Weather Facts

Record High Temperature: 112° F (44° C) on September 4, 1921, at Centreville; Record Low Temperature: -27° F (-33° C) on January 29, 1962, at New Market; Average January Temperature: 46° F (8° C); Average July Temperature: 81° F (27° C); Average Yearly Precipitation: 57 in. (145 cm).

Environmental Facts

Air Pollution Rank: 3d; Water Pollution Rank: 5th; Total Yearly Industrial Pollution: 106,145,301 lbs.; Industrial Pollution Rank: 6th; Hazardous Waste Sites: 12; Hazardous Sites Rank: 27th; Landfill Capacity: over-extended; Fresh Water Supply: large surplus; Daily Residential Water Consumption: 178 gals. per capita; Endangered Species: Aquatic Species (34)—cavefish, Alabama; Birds (4)—eagle, bald; Mammals (3)—bat, Indiana; Other Species (11)—riversnail, Anthony's; Plants (18)—amphianthus, little.

Environmental Quality

Alabama residents generate 4.4 million tons of solid waste each year, or approximately 2,200 pounds per capita. Landfill capacity in Alabama will be exhausted in only 5 to 10 years. The state has 12 hazardous waste sites. Annual greenhouse gas emissions in Alabama total 120.0 million tons, or 29.3 tons per capita. Industrial sources in Alabama release approximately 69.0 thousand tons of toxins, 954.0 thousand tons of acid precipitation-producing substances, and 2.2 million tons of smog-producing substances into the atmosphere each year.

The state has 6,600 acres in the National Park System, the largest area is the Little River Canyon National Preserve. State parks cover over 48,000 acres, attracting 6.0 million visitors per year.

Alabama spends approximately 1 percent of its budget, or approximately $16 per capita, on environmental and natural resources. Alabama representatives in the U.S. House voted in favor of national environmental legislation 39 percent of the time, while U.S. senators did so 17 percent of the time.

Average Monthly Weather

Birmingham	Jan	Feb	Mar	Apr	May	Jun	Jul	Aug	Sep	Oct	Nov	Dec	Yearly
Maximum Temperature °F	52.7	57.3	65.2	75.2	81.6	87.9	90.3	89.7	84.6	74.8	63.7	55.9	73.2
Minimum Temperature °F	33.0	35.2	42.1	50.4	58.3	65.9	69.8	69.1	63.6	50.4	40.5	35.2	51.1
Days of Precipitation	11.1	10.2	11.0	9.2	9.7	9.6	12.5	9.7	8.0	6.3	9.2	10.5	116.8
Mobile													
Maximum Temperature °F	60.6	63.9	70.3	78.3	84.9	90.2	91.2	90.7	87.0	79.4	69.3	63.1	77.4
Minimum Temperature °F	40.9	43.2	49.8	57.7	64.8	70.8	73.2	72.9	69.3	57.5	47.9	42.9	57.6
Days of Precipitation	10.6	9.7	10.5	7.4	8.4	11.4	16.2	14.0	10.2	5.7	7.8	10.4	122.3

Flora and Fauna

Alabama is approximately two-thirds covered by forests. Most forests contain conifer, or cone-bearing, trees such as pines. Other conifers in the state include the southern yellow pine and the red cedar. Alabama also has a number of deciduous trees, including sweet gum and hickory and many types of oak trees. Other plant life includes a variety of trees and shrubs, such as flowering dogwood and mountain laurel. Alabama is well known for its azalea flowers.

Alabama's fauna, or animal life, is perhaps even more diverse. Small mammals such as opossums, raccoons, skunks, and rabbits can be found throughout the state. Larger animals living in Alabama include bobcats and gray and red foxes. In the southern, swampy bayou parts of the state, alligators can even be seen. An abundance of fresh-water fish such as catfish, mullet, and buffalofish live in Alabama's rivers, lakes, and streams. Sea life along Alabama's Gulf Coast includes flounder, red snapper, crabs, and oysters. Many birds, including geese, migrate to Alabama for the winter.

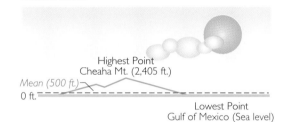

Physical Regions: (a) Interior Low Plateau; (b) Cumberland Plateau; (c) Appalachian Ridge and Valley; (d) Piedmont; (e) Black Belt; (f) East Gulf Coastal Plain.

Highest Point
Cheaha Mt. (2,405 ft.)
Mean (500 ft.)
0 ft.
Lowest Point
Gulf of Mexico (Sea level)

Land Use

Cropland: 13.5%; Pasture: 11.5%; Rangeland: 0.3%; Forest: 67.3%; Urban: 5.2%; Other: 2.2%.

For more information about Alabama's environment, contact the Commissioner of Conservation and Natural Resources, Room 702, 64 N. Union St., Montgomery, AL 36130-1901.

Topography

In the northern part of Alabama is the southernmost extension of the Appalachian Mountains, identified as the Appalachian Ridge and Valley Region. This is a series of sandstone ridges and limestone valleys that runs in a northeast-southwest direction. The soil is warm and moist and is mostly red and yellow clay. Also part of the Appalachian extension is the Cumberland Plateau region, found northwest of the ridges and valleys. The soil is similar to the type described above. In the northwest corner of the state lies the Interior Low Plateau, a fertile area for farming found in the Tennessee River valley, with warm moist clay, colored red to yellow.

In east-central Alabama is a region of low hills and valleys called the Piedmont. The soil found here is warm and moist. Here, iron or manganese concretions can be found. At the northern edge of this area, where it meets the Appalachian region, is Mt. Cheaha. This is the highest elevation in the state, rising 2,407 ft. (734 m) above sea level.

The lower half of Alabama is known as the East Gulf Coastal Plain. Some of this region, mostly a lowlands area, is covered primarily with pine forests. The most fertile portion of this region is known as the Black Belt, so called for its rich black clay soil. Cotton plantations can be found here.

Climate

The southern state of Alabama has a relatively mild climate. Warm, long summers and rather moderate winters characterize Alabama's weather patterns. Some temperature variation exists between northern and southern Alabama; however, only winter temperatures reflect this. January temperatures in the north, in cities such as Huntsville, average 46 degrees F. Mobile, at the southern tip of the state, has an average January temperature of 53 degrees F. However, both northern and southern Alabama have average July temperatures of 80 degrees F.

Alabama receives about 56 inches of precipitation annually. The southwest, where Mobile is located, receives the most rainfall, approximately 65 inches a year. Some places in central Alabama receive only 50 inches of precipitation a year.

Although Alabama usually has mild temperatures, the state has a frigid record low. In 1966, a -27 degree F temperature was recorded at New Market.

Hydrology

There are several major rivers in Alabama. The most prominent is the Tennessee, 164 miles long (264 km), which flows west in the northern part of the state. The Alabama and the Tombigbee flow north to south, and meet to form the Mobile River in the southwestern corner of the state. The Mobile River then flows into Mobile Bay. The Alabama River is formed from the junction of the Coosa and Tallapoosa rivers.

All Alabama lakes are man-made. Most of these were developed by the Tennessee Valley Authority (TVA) in the Tennessee River region in the northern part of the state. The largest of these is Guntersville Lake on the Tennessee River, covering about 109 sq. mi. (282 sq. km). Other large artificial lakes include the Wheeler, also on the Tennessee River, and the Martin, on the Tallapoosa River.

The Mobile River, along with several of its tributaries, flows into Mobile Bay, which itself drains into the Gulf of Mexico.

Alabama's History

Alabama's First People

Alabama was first occupied by cliff-dwellers between 8,000 and 10,000 years ago. Charcoal drawings found at an ancient campsite in a place called Russell Cave, provides evidence of their habitation.

The people from Russell Cave were hunters who took shelter for short periods before moving after game as it migrated seasonally. By A.D. 1000, agrarian groups called Mound Builders settled permanently in villages along Alabama's rivers. Mound Builders lived in huts and built earthen mounds that were used as temples. Thirty-four mounds exist today at a site called Moundville.

European explorers found more sophisticated native cultures when they began to arrive in the 16th century. Half of the Indians were Creek. Another group, the Cherokee, inhabited the northeast part of the state. The Chickasaw lived in the northwest and the Choctaw in the southwest.

European Exploration

Spanish explorer Alonso Alvarez de Pineda was the first to sail into Mobile Bay (1519). Hernando de Soto became the first white man to explore the interior of Alabama (1540). De Soto met and defeated a Choctaw tribe led by Chief Tuskalusa in Clarke County.

The first permanent settlements were French. Fort Louis was built along the Mobile River in 1702. This site was later moved farther south to what is now the city of Mobile.

At the conclusion of the French and Indian War, the Treaty of Paris (1763) forced the French to give up their holdings to the British. The area around Mobile was annexed into West Florida while northern Alabama became part of Illinois. In 1780, the Spanish took Mobile from the British. In 1795, the Spanish area north of Mobile was annexed by the United States with the signing of the Treaty of San Lorenzo. The Mobile area was later annexed during the War of 1812.

The massacre of several hundred pioneers at Fort Mims by the Creek Indians in 1813 led to the Battle of Horseshoe Bend in 1814. There, Andrew Jackson defeated the Creek forcing them to give up 40,000 square miles to the United States government. In 1817, the Alabama territory was established with its capital at Saint Stephens on the Tombigbee River.

Statehood

On December 14, 1819, Alabama became the twenty-second state. Huntsville served as the capital and William Wyatt Bibb served as the state's first governor. The capital was later moved to Cahaba in 1820 and then to Tuscaloosa in 1826.

Civil War

The 1840s brought turmoil to Alabama. Groups from northern states demanded that the United States outlaw slavery. In response, the 1848 Democratic state convention adopted the "Alabama Platform," which declared that the United States could not outlaw slavery.

Alabama seceded from the Union on January 11, 1861, and declared itself a republic. A convention was set up in Montgomery where southern states were sent delegates. On February 8, 1861, the convention established the Confederate States of America. Montgomery was made its first capital and came to be known as the Cradle of the Confederacy. The Confederate capitol was later moved to Richmond, Virginia on May 1861.

The Civil War brought hardship to the state. Union forces raided and looted many cities.

After the war, Reconstruction brought even greater hardship increasing the state's debt to more than $32 million by 1873. Alabama was readmitted the Union on June 2, 1868, and adopted a new constitution in 1875.

Industrialization

The end of the 19th century saw the build-ing of railroads as well as the creation of an iron and steel industry. Birmingham, Decatur, and Russellville became great manufacturing centers. In the 1880s, textile and lumber industries began to grow throughout the state.

Alabama prospered during World War I as Mobile became a center for shipbuilding.

Prosperity lasted until the Great Depression of the 1930s. Sixty banks in Alabama collapsed losing over $16 million.

The Tennessee Valley Authority, which was created by the federal government in 1933, built and maintained dams on Alabama rivers. These dams helped to provide power to area cities and factories.

World War II revived Alabama's factories and farms. Diversification resulted in a new set of industries—chemicals, rubber, and minerals.

Civil Rights

Agricultural modernization in the 1950s and 1960s eliminated many farm jobs. Many farmers moved into surrounding cities in search of work. They found urban areas that were being transformed by the civil rights movement. In Montgomery, a bus boycott was led by Rosa Parks and Dr. Martin Luther King, Jr. Schools were desegregated by order of the U.S. Supreme Court in 1954. Governor George C. Wallace tried personally to prevent school integration in 1963 resulting in the deployment of the National Guard to enforce the desegregation laws. Civil rights issues took on a violent side in Alabama. In 1963 four black children were killed when a bomb exploded in their church in Birmingham. This event helped persuade legislators to pass the Civil Rights Act of 1964.

Continued racial tensions led to further demonstrations. In March of 1965, Dr. Martin Luther King, Jr. led a march from Selma to Montgomery to protest discrimination in voting. This march led directly to the passing of the Voting Rights Act.

Important Events

1540 De Soto explores inland. Battles with Chief Tuskalusa at Mauvila.

1702 Jean Baptiste le Moyne, builds Fort Louis on Mobile River.

1711 Fort Louis is moved south to present day site of Mobile, Alabama.

1719 First slaves arrive at Dauphin Island.

1763 Treaty of Paris cedes Alabama to British from French.

1783 Great Britian cedes Alabama north of the 31st parallel to the United States.

1783 Mississippi Territory created and includes Alabama.

1802 Cotton gin invented and built in near Montgomery.

1813 Colonists massacred at Fort Mims.

1814 General Andrew Jackson defeats the Creeks at Horseshoe Bend in 1814.

1817 United States Congress creates Alabama Territory.

1819 Alabama becomes the twenty-second state with capital at Huntsville and William W. Bibb governor.

1851 State captiol built in Montgomery.

1861 Alabama secedes from Union. Jefferson Davis elected Confederate president.

1868 Alabama readmitted into Union June 2.

1901 Modern state constitution adopted.

1933 U.S. government creates Tennessee Valley Authority. TVA takes over the management of Wilson Dam at Muscle Shoals.

1954 U.S. Supreme Court rules that segregation of public schools is unconstitutional.

1956 Federal court orders desegregation of public busing programs in Alabama.

1963 George C. Wallace elected governor.

1965 Black voter registration drive starts with Martin Luther King's Freedom March from Selma to Montgomery.

1970 First Blacks elected to the state legislature since Reconstruction.

1986 First Republican Governor elected in 112 years.

Population Density

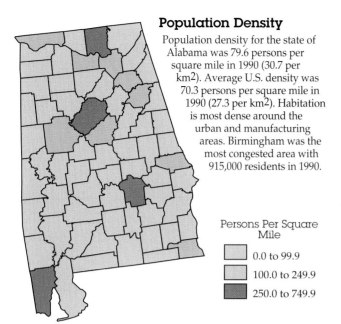

Population density for the state of Alabama was 79.6 persons per square mile in 1990 (30.7 per km^2). Average U.S. density was 70.3 persons per square mile in 1990 (27.3 per km^2). Habitation is most dense around the urban and manufacturing areas. Birmingham was the most congested area with 915,000 residents in 1990.

Persons Per Square Mile

- 0.0 to 99.9
- 100.0 to 249.9
- 250.0 to 749.9

Population Projections

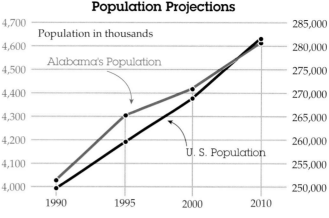

Population in thousands

Alabama's Population

U. S. Population

Population Change

Year	Population
1950	3,062,000
1960	3,274,000
1970	3,451,000
1980	3,893,888
1990	4,040,587
2000	4,410,000
2010	4,609,000

Period	Change
1950–1970	12.7%
1970–1980	12.8%
1980–1990	3.8%
1990–2000	9.1%

Population Change

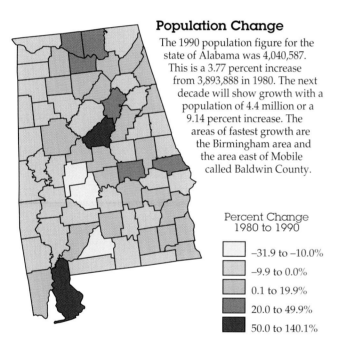

The 1990 population figure for the state of Alabama was 4,040,587. This is a 3.77 percent increase from 3,893,888 in 1980. The next decade will show growth with a population of 4.4 million or a 9.14 percent increase. The areas of fastest growth are the Birmingham area and the area east of Mobile called Baldwin County.

Percent Change 1980 to 1990

- –31.9 to –10.0%
- –9.9 to 0.0%
- 0.1 to 19.9%
- 20.0 to 49.9%
- 50.0 to 140.1%

Population Facts

State Population, 1993: 4,187,000
Rank: 22
Population 2000: 4,410,000 (Rank 23)
Density: 79.6 per sq. mi. (30.7 per km^2)
Distribution: 60.4% urban, 39.6% rural
Population Under 5 Years Old: 7.2%
Population Under 18 Years Old: 26.0%
Population Over 65 Years Old: 13.0%
Median Age: 33.0
Number of Households: 1,507,000
Average Persons Per Household: 2.62
Average Persons Per Family: 3.13
Female Heads of Households: 4.98%
Population That Is Married: 21.24%
Birth Rate: 15.7 per 1,000 population
Death Rate: 9.7 per 1,000 population
Births to Teen Mothers: 18.2%
Marriage Rate: 10.5 per 1,000 population
Divorce Rate: 6.1 per 1,000 population
Violent Crime Rate: 844 per 100,000 pop.
Population on Social Security: 17.7%
Percent Voting for President: 55.2%

Alabama's Famous Citizens

Aaron, Henry "Hank" (1934–). All-time home run king.

Black, Hugo (1886–1971). Supreme Court justice who championed civil liberties.

Carver, George Washington (1864–1943). Scientist and teacher.

Cole, Nat King (1919–1965). Singer and pianist.

Handy, William C. (1873–1958). Composer and performer.

Keller, Helen (1880–1968). Blind and deaf author and lecturer.

Lee, Harper (b. 1926). Writer. Author of *To Kill a Mockingbird*.

Louis, Joe (1914–1981). Heavyweight boxing champion from 1937 to 1949.

Mays, Willie (1931–). Considered by some to be the greatest baseball player who ever lived.

Owens, Jesse (1913–1980). Track and field star.

Parks, Rosa (b. 1913). Civil rights leader.

Wallace, George (b. 1919). Public official and governor of Alabama during civil rights movement.

Washington, Booker T. (1856–1915). Educator. Founded Tuskegee Institute.

Distribution of Income

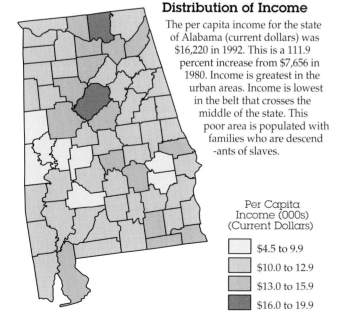

The per capita income for the state of Alabama (current dollars) was $16,220 in 1992. This is a 111.9 percent increase from $7,656 in 1980. Income is greatest in the urban areas. Income is lowest in the belt that crosses the middle of the state. This poor area is populated with families who are descend-ants of slaves.

Per Capita Income (000s) (Current Dollars)

- $4.5 to 9.9
- $10.0 to 12.9
- $13.0 to 15.9
- $16.0 to 19.9

Population Profile

Rank. Alabama ranks 22d among U.S. states in terms of population with 4,187,000 citizens.

Minority Population. The state's minority population is 26.8 percent. The state's male to female ratio for 1990 was 92 males for every 100 females. This figure is one of the lowest in the country with the District of Columbia being the lowest. It was below the national average of 95.22 males for every 100 females.

Government

Capital: Montgomery (established 1846).
Statehood: Became 22d state on Dec. 14, 1819.
Number of Counties: 67.
Supreme Court Justices: 9, 6-year term.
State Senators: 35, 4-year term.
State Legislators: 105, 4-year term.
United States Senators: 2.
United States Representatives: 7.
Electoral Votes: 9.
State Constitution: Adopted 1901.

Growth. Growing slightly faster than the projected national average, the state's population is expected to reach 4.6 million by the year 2010 *(see graph above)*.

Older Citizens. The state's population older than 65 was 522,989 in 1990. It grew 18.86% from 440,015 in 1980.

Younger Citizens. The number of children (under 18 years of age) was 1.1 million in 1990. This represents 26.2 percent of the state's popu-lation. The state's school aged population was 722 thousand in 1990. It is expected to increase to 762 thousand by the year 2000. This represents a 5.54% change.

Urban/Rural. 60.4% of the population of the state live in urban areas while 39.4% live in rural areas.

Largest Cities. Alabama has 10 cities with a population greater than 35,000. The populations of the state's largest centers are (starting from the most populous) Birmingham (265,968), Mobile (196,278), Montgomery (187,106), Huntsville (159,789), Tuscaloosa (77,759), Dothan (53,589), Decatur (48,761), Gadsden (42,523), Hoover (39,788), Florence (36,426), Prichard (34,311) Auburn (33,830), and Bessemer (33,497).

Native American

The Native American population in Alabama was 16,506 in 1990. This was an increase of 78.66 percent from 9,239 in 1980. There is a large concentration in Escambria County in the city of Poarch. This is where the Creek Indians have settled. A large concentration of Cherokee Indians can be found in the northeastern portion of the state.

Presence of Native Americans

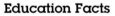 Minor

Nationalities 1990

African	4,572
American	705,907
Arab	4,795
Austrian	1,550
Czech	2,511
Dutch	45,830
English	375,853
Finnish	1,182
German	342,998
Greek	5,711
Hungarian	2,798
Irish	410,776
Italian	37,749
Norwegian	5,498
Polish	14,588
Portuguese	973
Russian	3,500
Scottish	52,538
Slovak	3,241
Swedish	11,612
Welsh	10,705
West Indian	2,383

African American

The African American population in Alabama was 1,020,705 in 1990. This was an increase of 2.45 percent from 996,283 in 1980. The African American population is centered around major urban areas such as Montgomery, Mobile, and Birmingham and in a belt that stretches across the southern half of the state.

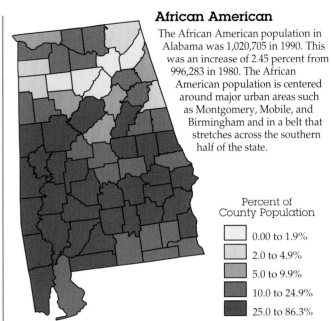

Percent of County Population

- 0.00 to 1.9%
- 2.0 to 4.9%
- 5.0 to 9.9%
- 10.0 to 24.9%
- 25.0 to 86.3%

Statewide Ethnic Composition

Three of every four people in Alabama are white. Most have ancestors from the British Isles. Slightly more than one half million people claim to be American and acknowledge no other nationality. Only 1,075 people claimed to have African roots in the 1990 Census despite the fact that the African American population was calculated at 1,020,705.

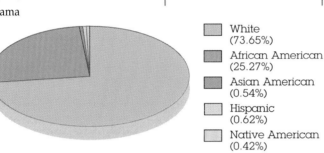

- White (73.65%)
- African American (25.27%)
- Asian American (0.54%)
- Hispanic (0.62%)
- Native American (0.42%)

Education Facts

Total Students 1990: 723,343
Number of School Districts: 129
Expenditure Per Capita on Education 1990: $624
Expenditure Per Capita K–12 1990: $550
Expenditure Per Pupil 1990: $3,648
Total School Enrollment 1990–1991: 726,158
Rank of Expenditures Per Student: 46th in the U.S.
African American Enrollment: 35.7%
Hispanic Enrollment: 0.2%
Asian/Pacific Islander Enrollment: 0.5%
Native American Enrollment: 0.7%

Mean SAT Score 1991 Verbal: 476
Mean SAT Score 1991 Math: 515
Average Teacher's Salary 1992: $27,000
Rank Teacher's Salary: 41st in U.S.
High School Graduates 1990: 41,400
Total Number of Public Schools: 1,292
Number of Teachers 1990: 40,119
Student/Teacher Ratio: 18.1
Staff Employed in Public Schools: 79,786
Pupil/Staff Ratio: 9.1
Staff/Teacher Ratio: 2

Hispanic[††]

The Hispanic population in Alabama was 24,629 in 1990. This is a decrease of 26.04 percent from 33,299 persons in 1980. The main concentration of Hispanics is in the city of Mobile. Other areas include Calhoun, Dale, and Coffee counties, which are homes to military bases. Baldwin County also has a concentration of Hispanics.

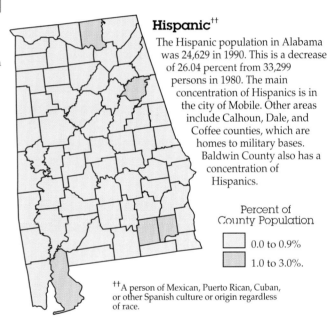

Percent of County Population

- 0.0 to 0.9%
- 1.0 to 3.0%.

[††]A person of Mexican, Puerto Rican, Cuban, or other Spanish culture or origin regardless of race.

Education

Attainment: 63.2 percent of population 25 years or older were high school graduates in 1989, earning Alabama a ranking of 50th in the United States; 11.6 percent of the state's population had completed college. Institutions of Higher Education: The largest universities and colleges in the state include the University of Alabama, at Tuscaloosa, with branch campuses in Birmingham and Huntsville; Auburn University, at Auburn, with a branch at Montgomery; Jacksonville State University, at Jacksonville. Expenditures per Student: Expenditure increased 75% between 1985 and 1990. Projected High School Graduations: 1998 (39,659), 2004 (37,305); Total Revenues for Education from Federal Sources: $257 million; Total Revenues for Education from State Sources: $1.4 billion; Total Revenues for Education from Local Sources: $516 million; Average Annual Salaries for Public School Principals: $33,500; Largest School Districts in State: Mobile County, Mobile, 67,553 students, 38th in the United States; Birmingham City, 42,240, 83d.

Asian American

The Asian American population in Alabama was 21,797 in 1990. This is an increase of 113.09 percent from 10,229 persons in 1980. Cities such as Huntsville, Montgomery, Birmingham, and Mobile are home to many Asian Americans. Asian Americans represent one of the fastest-growing groups in the state.

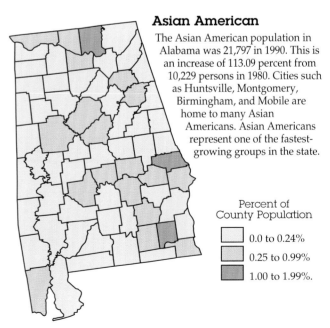

Percent of County Population

- 0.0 to 0.24%
- 0.25 to 0.99%
- 1.00 to 1.99%.

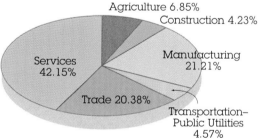

Major manufacturing areas
Major agricultural areas
Fish

Transportation

The state of Alabama has one of the nation's most extensive waterway systems, totaling approximately 1,350 miles. Included in the system is the Black Warrior-Tombigbee-Mobile River system, the longest navigable waterway in Alabama. The Tennessee-Tombigbee Waterway, completed in 1985, serves inland towns via Mobile, the only port in Alabama. Several towns, including Huntsville and Phenix City, are located along waterways.

Alabama is also served by the other usual transportation modes. The state has 97,000 miles of highways and roads. Passenger rail services pass through Alabama, stopping at major cities like Birmingham. Four freight railroads transport goods all over Alabama. Three larger airports at Mobile, Birmingham, and Huntsville handle most of Alabama's air traffic.

Energy and Transportation Facts

Energy. Yearly Consumption: 1,591 tril. BTUs (residential, 18.0%; commercial, 10.3%; industrial, 45.9%; transportation, 25.7%); Annual Energy Expenditures Per Capita: $2,029; Nuclear Power Plants Located in State: 5; Source of Energy Consumed: Petroleum— 29.4%; Natural Gas— 14.6%; Coal— 40.2%; Hydroelectric Power—6.3%; Nuclear Power—9.5%.

Transportation. Highway Miles: 92,201 (interstates, 900; urban, 19,366; rural, 72,835); Average Yearly Auto Insurance: $510 (30th); Auto Fatalities Rank: 9th; Registered Motor Vehicles: 3,304,064; Workers in Carpools: 19.4%; Workers Using Public Trans: 0.8%.

Agriculture

Alabama has 10 million farm acres. During the last 40 years, Alabama's farms have grown larger in size and fewer in number. In 1955, 177,000 farms were found in the state. Today, 47,000 remain.

Agriculture adds $2 billion to the state's gross product annually. The principal commodities in order of marketing receipts are broilers, cattle, greenhouse, and peanuts.

Boll weevil infestation in 1915 destroyed most cotton production. Today, only two percent of the state's agricultural income is derived from cotton. Acres once planted with cotton now are used as pasture lands to support livestock production and croplands to grow corn, peanuts, and soybeans. Forest products are also cultivated, providing raw materials for paper and furniture manufacturing.

Economic Sectors

Agriculture 6.85%
Construction 4.23%
Services 42.15%
Manufacturing 21.21%
Trade 20.38%
Transportation–Public Utilities 4.57%

Employment

Employment. Alabama employed 1.84 million people in 1993. Most work in manufacturing jobs (383,300 persons or 20.8% of the workforce). Wholesale and retail trade account for 20.5% or 376,300 workers. Government employs 341,000 workers (18.5%). Social and personal services employ 362,900 people (19.7%). Construction accounts for 4.2% or 77,900 workers. Transportation and utilities account for 4.6% or 84,700 persons. Agriculture employs 42,300 workers or 2.3%. Finance, real estate, and insurance account for 4.1% or 75,600 persons. Mining employs 10,700 people and accounts for only 0.6% of the workforce.

Unemployment. Unemployment has decreased to 7.5% in 1993 from a rate of 8.9% in 1985. Today's figure is higher than the national average of 6.8% as shown below.

Housing

Owner Occupied Units: 1,670,379; Average Age of Units: 25 years; Average Value of Housing Units: $53,700; Renter Occupied Units: 428,024; Median Monthly Rent: $325; Housing Starts: 20,100; Existing Home Sales: 77,900.

Economic Facts

Gross State Product: $68,000,000,000

Income Per Capita: $16,220

Disposable Personal Income: $14,533

Median Household Income: $23,597

Average Annual Pay, 1988: $21,287

Principal Industries: pulp, paper, chemicals, electronics, apparel, textiles, mining, timber, manufacturing, auto tires, ship building, commercial fishing, tourism

Major Crops: peanuts, cotton, soybeans, hay, corn, wheat, potatoes, pecans, sweet potatoes, cottonseed

Fish: Catfish, Shrimp, Crabs, Red Snapper, Oysters

Livestock: cattle, hogs, chickens

Non-Fuel Minerals: Cement, Clay, Gravel, Stone, Limestone, Iron Ore, Sulfur, Salt, Tin, Copper, Gold

Organic Fuel Minerals: Oil, Lignite Coal

Civilian Labor Force: 1,894,000 (Women: 854,000)

Total Employed: 1,758,000 (Women: 789,000)

Median Value of Housing: $53,700

Median Contract Rent: $325 per month

Manufacturing

Alabama's manufacturing sector is an important part of the state economy. Approximately one-fourth of Alabama's workers perform manufacturing jobs, and those manufacturing jobs provide almost one-fourth of the state gross product. The manufacture of paper products ranks as the number one manufacturing industry in Alabama. Chemical, clothing, steel, and rubber products are also produced in the state.

Manufacturing takes place in many parts of Alabama. Paper mills can be found in Mobile and Montgomery. Mobile is also a major chemical production center for Alabama. Clothing is mainly manufactured in small towns like Elba and Jasper. The steel industry, long a part of Alabama's economy, is centered in Birmingham.

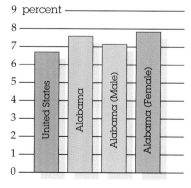

Unemployment Rate

9 percent
8
7
6
5
4
3
2
1
0

United States
Alabama
Alabama (Male)
Alabama (Female)

ALASKA
The State of Alaska

Official State Seal

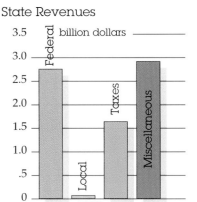

The Great Seal of Alaska was created in 1910. It was used as the territorial seal until statehood when it became the state seal. The seal contains the beauty and economic richness of the state. Above the mountains and the bay is the aurora borealis (northern lights). Around the bay are depictions of economic activities such as agriculture, fishing, railroading, and shipping.

Legal Holidays

January: New Year's Day—1st, Admission Day—3rd; Martin Luther King, Jr. Day—3rd Monday; February: Abraham Lincoln's Birthday—12th; Presidents' Day—3rd Monday; March: Seward's Day—30th; May: Memorial Day—4th Monday; July: Independence Day—4th; Alaska's Flag Day—4th; September: Labor Day—1st Monday; October: Columbus Day—2nd Monday; Alaska Day—18th; November: Veterans' Day—11th; Thanksgiving—4th Thursday; December: Christmas—25th.

Official State Flag

The official state flag of Alaska was adopted in 1927 as the territorial flag and as the state flag in 1959. It was designed by a thirteen-year-old Native American boy for a contest held in 1926. The North Star above the Big Dipper represents Alaska as being the northernmost state in the Union.

Alaska Compared to Other States. Resident Pop. In Metro Areas: 42d; Pop. Percent Increase: 2d; Pop. Over 65: 50th; Infant Mortality: 9th; School Enroll. Increase: 31st; High School Grad. and Up: 1st; Violent Crime: 21st; Hazardous Waste Sites: 43d; Unemployment: 2d; Median Household Income: 2d; Persons Below Poverty: 43d; Energy Costs Per Person: 1st.

Alaska Compared to States in Its Region.

Resident Pop. in Metro Areas: 5th; Pop. Percent Increase: 1st; Pop. Over 65: 5th; Infant Mortality: 1st; School Enroll. Increase: 4th; High School Grad. and Up: 1st; Violent Crime: 2d; Hazardous Waste Sites: 4th; Unemployment: 1st; Median Household Income: 1st; Persons Below Poverty: 4th; Energy Costs Per Person: 1st.

Pacific Region

	Population	Capital
Washington	5,255,000	Olympia
Oregon	3,032,000	Salem
California	31,211,000	Sacramento
Alaska	599,000	Juneau
Hawaii	1,172,000	Honolulu

Sources of Information. Tourism: Division of Tourism, P.O. Box E, Juneau, AK 99811. Economy: Alaska Employment Security Division, Department of Labor, P.O. Box 3-7000, Juneau, AK 99802. Government: Legislative Affairs Agency, Division of Public Services, P.O. Box Y, Juneau, AK 99811. History: Alaska State Library, Historical Library, P.O. Box G, Juneau, AK 99811.

Alaska's Finances

Households: 189,000; Income Per Capita Current Dollars: $21,603; Change Per Capita Income 1980 to 1992: 57.8% (49th in U.S.); State Expenditures: $4,788,000,000; State Revenues: $5,343,000,000; Personal Income Tax: 3.8 to 7%; Federal Income Taxes Paid Per Capita: $2,705; Sales Tax: N/A.

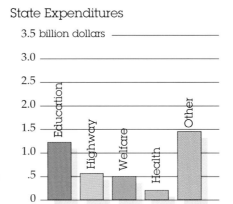

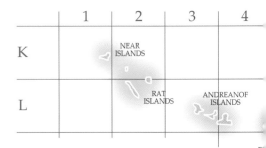

Facts about Alaska. Origin of Name: Aleutian Indian word meaning "*mainland*."; Nickname: The Last Frontier; Motto: "North to the Future"; Abbreviations: AK (postal); State Bird: Willow ptarmigan; State Tree: Sitka spruce; State Flower: Forget-me-not; State Song: "Alaska's Flag," words by Marie Drake, music by Elinor Dusenbury.

Location, Size, and Boundaries

Location. Alaska is located on the northwestern peninsula of the United States in a region known as the Pacific. It is bounded on three sides by water, the Pacific Ocean on the south, the Bering Sea on the west, and the Arctic Ocean on the north, and on the east by the Yukon Territory of Canada. The geographic center of Alaska is lat. 64° 43.9' N; long. 152° 28.2' W.

Size. Alaska is the largest state in terms of size. Its area is 615,230 sq. mi. (1,593,446 km2). Inland water covers 20,171 sq. mi. (52,243 km2). Alaska includes 33,904 miles (54,563 km.) of coastline.

Boundaries. Yukon Territory, Canada, c. 1,150 mi. (1,850 km).

Geographic Extent. The north/south extent of Alaska is 1,000 mi. (1,600 km). The state extends 2,400 mi. (3,840 km) to the east/west including the Aleutians.

Festivals and Events

January: Seward Polar Bear Jump Fest, Seward; February: Cordova Iceworm Festival, Cordova; Festival of the North, Ketchikan; Festival of Native Arts, Fairbanks; Nenana Tripod Racing Festival, Nenana; March: Comfish Alaska, Kodiak; Iditarod Trail Race, Anchorage; May: Kodiak Crab Festival, Kodiak; Little Norway Fest, Petersburg; Miners Day Celebration, Talkeetna; June: Midnight Sun Festival, Nome; Summer Music Fest, Sitka; July: Big Lake Regatta Water Festival, Big Lake; World Eskimo-Indian Olympics, Fairbanks; Talkeetna Moose Dropping Festival, Talkeetna; August: Blueberry Festival, Ketchikan; Seward Silver Salmon Derby, Seward; State Fair, Palmer; Tanana Valley Fair, Tanana; September: Willow Trading Post Potato Fest, Willow; Great Bathtub Race, Nome; November: Athabascan Fiddling Festival, Fairbanks; Great Alaska Shootout, Anchorage; December: Anvil Mountain Run, Nome; Christmas Festival of Lights, Ketchikan; Fireman's Carnival, Nome.

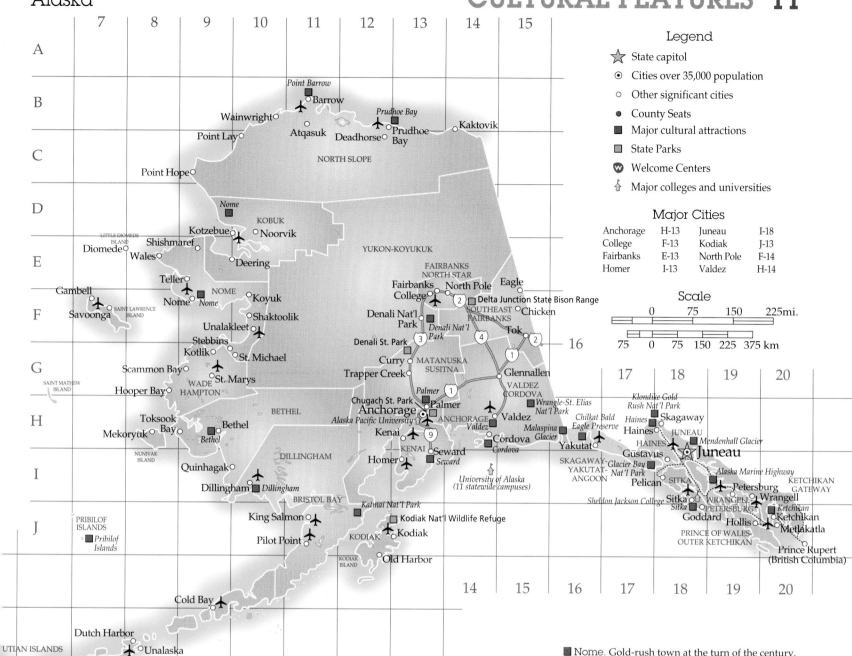

Legend

☆ State capitol
⊙ Cities over 35,000 population
○ Other significant cities
● County Seats
■ Major cultural attractions
☐ State Parks
ⓦ Welcome Centers
⚲ Major colleges and universities

Major Cities

Anchorage	H-13	Juneau	I-18
College	F-13	Kodiak	J-13
Fairbanks	E-13	North Pole	F-14
Homer	I-13	Valdez	H-14

Scale

0   75   150   225mi.

75   0   75   150   225   375 km

■ **Alaska Marine Highway.** Area between Prince Rupert and Skagway. Part of the Inside Passage and includes ferry service to visit beautiful fjords and abundant wildlife. (I-19)

■ **Bethel.** The largest town on the Bering Sea. Deep water port and commercial fishing center. Yupik Indian cultural center. (H-9)

■ **Chilkat Bald Eagle Preserve.** Over 3,500 bald eagles can be found here. (H-16)

■ **Cordova.** Former shipping depot for the old Kennecott Copper Mine. (H-14)

■ **Denali National Park.** Site of Mount McKinley, the highest peak in North America at 20,320 feet (6,194 meters). (F-13)

■ **Dillingham.** Sport and commercial fishing port in Bristol Bay. (I-10)

■ **Glacier Bay National Park and Preserve.** Sixteen glaciers flowing into Glacier Bay can be found in this park . (I-17)

■ **Haines.** Site of the annual Southeast Alaska State Fair in August. Nearby camping at Chilkat State Park. (H-17)

■ **Katmai National Park and Preserve.** Site of the Mount Katmai volcano which erupted last in 1912. Valley of Ten Thousand Smokes. (J-12)

■ **Ketchikan.** Historic Salmon Capital of the World. Salmon Capital of the World. Site of the world's largest collection of totem poles. (J-20)

■ **Klondike Gold Rush National Historic Park.** Dedicated to the 1898 gold rush. Site of the White Pass & Yukon Route mountain railway. (H-17)

■ **Malaspina Glacier.** Large glacier that reaches a height of 2,500 feet (760 meters). Larger than the state of Rhode Island. (H-16)

■ **Mendenhall Glacier.** Glacier that is 14 miles (23 km) long and 4 miles (6.4 km) wide. (H-18)

■ **Nome.** Gold-rush town at the turn of the century. Museums dedicated to the gold-rush era and Native American crafts. (D-9)

■ **Palmer.** Site of the state fair in August. Farming area made popular by a New Deal relief program in 1935. (H-13)

■ **Point Barrow.** The northernmost point of Alaska. Site of an Inupiat Eskimo community. (B-11)

■ **Pribilof Islands.** Breeding ground for seals and horned puffins. (J-7)

■ **Prudhoe Bay.** The largest oil field in North America. Beginning of the 800-mile Trans-Alaskan Pipeline. (B-13)

■ **Seward.** Fishing port marking the entrance to Resurrection Bay and Kenai Fjords National Park. (I-13)

■ **Sitka.** Russian-American capital. Russian Bishop's House and Saint Michael's Cathedral. (J-18)

■ **Valdez.** Southern end of the Trans-Alaskan Pipeline. (H-14)

■ **Wrangel–St. Elias National Park.** Fishing and rafting in the Copper River Basin; historic mining towns of McCarthy and Kennicott nearby. (H-15)

Weather Facts

Record High Temperature: 100° F (38° C) on June 11, 1926, at Fort Yukon; Record Low Temperature: -80° F (-62° C) on January 22, 1967, at Prospect Creek; Average January Temperature: 5° F (-15° C); Average July Temperature: 54° F (12° C); Average Yearly Precipitation: 56 in. (142 cm).

Environmental Facts

Air Pollution Rank: 35th; Water Pollution Rank: 8th; Total Yearly Industrial Pollution: 14,853,979 lbs.; Industrial Pollution Rank: 36th; Hazardous Waste Sites: 6; Hazardous Sites Rank: 43d; Landfill Capacity: adequate; Fresh Water Supply: large surplus; Daily Residential Water Consumption: 169 gals. per capita; Endangered Species: Birds (4)—curlew, Eskimo; Plants (1)—fern, Aleutian Shield.

Environmental Quality

Alaska residents generate 450,000 tons of solid waste each year, or approximately 1,800 pounds per capita. Landfill capacity in Alabama will be exhausted in more than 12 years. The state has 6 hazardous waste sites. Annual greenhouse gas emissions are not a problem in Alaska. Industrial sources in Alaska release approximately 18.0 thousand tons of toxins and 21.2 thousand tons of acid precipitation-producing substances into the atmosphere each year.

The state has 52.1 million acres within the National Park System; the largest area within the state is Wrangell-St. Elias. State parks cover just over 3.1 million acres, attracting 6.8 million visitors per year.

Alaska spends approximately 4 percent of its budget, or approximately $251 per capita, on environmental and natural resources. Alaska representatives in the U.S. House voted in favor of national environmental legislation at no time, while U.S. senators did so 13 percent of the time.

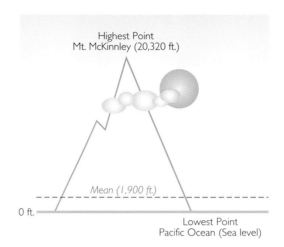

Highest Point
Mt. McKinnley (20,320 ft.)

Mean (1,900 ft.)

0 ft.

Lowest Point
Pacific Ocean (Sea level)

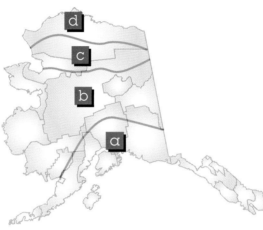

Physical Regions: (a) Pacific Mountain System; (b) Central Uplands & Lowlands; (c) Rocky Mountain System; (d) Arctic Coastal Plain.

For more information about Alaska's environment, contact the Department of Environmental Conservation, Juneau, AK 99811-1800.

Climate

Alaska has perhaps the most complex climate of all the states; four separate climatic types exist. Variable temperatures characterize the continental climate, while the maritime climate has relatively little temperature variation. Southern inland and western Alaska reflects the transitional climate that occurs when the other two climates meet. Anchorage, near this area, has average January and July temperatures of 7 degrees F and 57 degrees F. Arctic conditions can be found to the north, where temperatures remain frigid and sunlight stays to a minimum. Barrow, above the Arctic Circle, has average January and July temperatures of -16 degrees F and 40 degrees F.

Precipitation varies greatly in Alaska. The north-central panhandle receives over 220 inches of precipitation a year. However, the central plains often receive 10 inches or less.

Topography

There are several distinct physical regions in Alaska. The southernmost region is named the Pacific Mountain System. The panhandle in the southeast consists mainly of the Alexander Archipelago, with the St. Elias Mountains rising to the northwest. Southcentral Alaska is dominated by the Alaska Range, which includes Mt. McKinley, or Denali, the highest point in North America at 20,320 ft. (6,194 m). The coastal region in this area includes Prince William Sound and Cook Inlet. Southwest of the Alaska Range is the Alaskan Peninsula and the Aleutian Islands, the latter a long string of volcanic islands, some of which are still active. The soil in this and other regions of Alaska has evolved from volcanic ash, is gray in color, and is cool and moist to wet.

Much of Alaska between the Alaska Range in the south and the Brooks Range in the north is characterized by low hills and valleys, known as the Central Uplands and Lowlands topographic region. The western portion of this area is dominated by the Yukon and Kuskokwim river valleys and the Seward Peninsula. In the Rocky Mountain System topographic region, the Brooks Range—including the Endicott, Baird, and DeLong mountains—extends north to divide the northernmost topographic region, the Arctic Coastal Plain, a vast treeless tundra, from the rest of Alaska.

Hydrology

The major river in Alaska is the Yukon, which flows roughly 1,979 miles (3,185 km). It is the fifth longest river in North America. Its primary tributaries are the Porcupine and Tanana rivers. The Kuskokwim is the second longest river in Alaska at 550 miles (885 km). It flows southwest and drains into the Bering Sea at Kuskokwim Bay. The Meade, Kokolik, and Colville rivers flow north into the Arctic Ocean. In western Alaska, the Kobuk and Noatak rivers flow into the Chukchi Sea. In the southern portion of the state, the Susitna River flows into Cook Inlet, and the Copper River flows into the Gulf of Alaska. Alaska contains many lakes, the largest being Iliamna and Becharof lakes on the Alaskan Peninsula, and Seawik Lake near Kotzebue Sound. Others include Aleknagik, Minchumina, Selawik, and Teahekpuk.

Alaska is surrounded by water on three sides. To the south lies the Gulf of Alaska and Bristol Bay. The Bering Sea, Norton Sound, and the Chukchi Sea are to the west. The Arctic Ocean and the Beaufort Sea lie to the north.

Average Monthly Weather

Fairbanks	Jan	Feb	Mar	Apr	May	Jun	Jul	Aug	Sep	Oct	Nov	Dec	Yearly
Maximum Temperature °F	-3.9	7.3	21.7	40.8	59.2	70.1	71.8	66.5	54.4	32.6	12.4	-1.7	35.9
Minimum Temperature °F	-21.6	-15.4	-4.8	19.5	37.2	48.5	51.2	46.5	35.4	17.5	-4.6	-18.4	15.9
Days of Precipitation	7.2	6.4	5.9	4.9	7.0	10.5	12.4	12.5	9.5	10.8	10.0	8.7	106.0
Juneau													
Maximum Temperature °F	27.4	33.7	37.4	46.8	54.7	61.1	64.0	62.6	55.9	47.0	37.5	31.5	46.6
Minimum Temperature °F	16.1	21.9	25.0	31.3	38.1	44.2	47.4	46.6	42.3	36.5	28.0	22.1	33.3
Days of Precipitation	18.0	16.6	17.7	16.8	17.2	15.6	16.6	17.6	19.9	23.5	19.7	20.7	220.0

Flora and Fauna

Alaska's different climatic regions partially effect the state's different plant and animal species. In the northern, tundra-covered part of Alaska, only a limited number of plants such as lichens and mosses grow. Alaska wildflowers include asters, larkspurs, cowslips, and violets. About one-third of Alaska is covered by forests, found mainly in the southeastern and central parts of the state. Birch, aspen, tamarack, and several species of spruce can be found in Alaska forests. Two national forests, Chugach National Forest and Tongass National Forest, comprise one-sixth of all forested land in Alaska.

The southern part of Alaska is home to the world's largest carnivorous land mammal, the Alaskan brown bear. Other types of bear, in addition to deer, also live in the south. Arctic mammals such as the Arctic fox, caribou, and polar bear live in northern Alaska. Reindeer, moose, and even some domesticated musk oxen roam Alaska's landscape. Several types of fish and other sea life can be found off Alaska's coast, including salmon, shrimp, seals, and even whales.

Alaska's History

Alaska's First People

Between ten thousand and forty thousand years ago, aboriginal tribes arrived in Alaska. At that time, land connected northeastern Siberia with northwestern America, enabling people to cross over the Bering Strait to Alaska. These hunter-gatherers of Siberian origin fall into four main groups: Aleut, Eskimo, Tsimshian, and Tlingit.

The Aleut settled in western Alaska and became skilled hunters of sea mammals.

The Eskimo, or Inuit as they call themselves, are widely dispersed throughout Alaska. They are also skilled hunters of sea mammals, which they depend on for food, clothing, and shelter. Their shelters are made of caribou or seal skins (stronger structures of wood or stone are used in winter, though the igloo is rarely used).

Another native tribe, the Tsimshian, were also early settlers in Alaska. Subsisting largely on sea life like the others, today they live on a reservation, earning a living with fishing and forestry.

The Tlingit make up almost half of the Native American population in Alaska. They live on the panhandles and along the coast as well as on many of the islands. They are known for their bone and shell artwork as well as for their fishing skills.

European Exploration

In 1728, Peter the Great, czar of Russia, sponsored an expedition to find land opposite Siberia. Vitus Bering, a Dane in the employ of the Russians, sailed through what is now known as the Bering Strait and discovered St. Lawrence Island, though failing to reach the Alaskan mainland. Thirteen years later he and Aleksei Chirikov led different expeditions into Alaska, Bering landing at Mt. Elias. The sea otter pelts brought back from these expeditions spurred the establishment of a fur-trading business set up by Siberian merchants. The Russian settlers who followed established the first white outpost in 1784 at Three Saints Bay

on Kodiak Island for the purpose of hunting the region's fur-bearing animals. In 1799, the Russian-American Company was established to handle fur trading and govern the Russian colony near Sitka. In 1802, the Tlingit Indians attacked this station, killing most of the 450 defenders. Two years later, the Russians retaliated and set up a permanent post at Sitka.

Throughout the nineteenth century the Russians traded for fur, but the unpredictable nature of the trade and the depletion of the sea otter population frustrated their attempts to successfully settle the area. As a result, the Russians were only too willing to sell Alaska to the United States in 1867 for $7.2 million—a transaction known as Seward's Folly, after U.S. Secretary of State William H. Seward, who pressed for and signed the treaty.

Statehood

Various U.S. government branches, including the army, the navy, and the customs service, administered Alaska until 1884, when a civil government was established with the laws of the state of Oregon and a federally appointed governor.

Alaskans could elect a nonvoting delegate to Congress for the first time in 1906 and were granted territorial status, with limited self-rule, in 1912. In 1916, the first bill proposing statehood for Alaska was introduced in Congress.

With the building of the Alaska Highway and the Alaska Railroad in the following decades, the massive infusions of federal military spending during World War II, and Alaska's subsequent status as a Cold War outpost, the territory's population increased, as did the movement for statehood. Congress enacted the Alaska Statehood Act in June 1958 and Alaska voters approved it in a referendum that August by a five-to-one margin. On January 3, 1959, Alaska became the forty-ninth state in the union.

In 1971, the federal government passed the

Alaska Native Claims Settlement Act, which distributed 44 million acres of Alaskan territory to the Eskimo, Aleut, and other native Alaskan peoples.

Industrialization

While fishing and the fur trade dominated the Alaskan economy for the first century after the arrival of the Russians, the discovery of gold in Juneau in 1880 led to the first real development of Alaska. A major discovery of gold in Canada's Klondike region in 1896 led to the massive Yukon Gold Rush, which helped develop the interior for the first time.

Along with the continued development of the fishing and timber industries, Alaska's newfound mineral wealth helped it prosper for the next couple of decades.

After an economic downturn in the years preceding World War II, massive American investment in Alaska as a geographic resource led to the building of the Alaska Highway and extension of the Alaska Railroad, as well as other facilities. In 1989, oil production dropped and officials started looking to the Arctic National Wildlife Refuge for more sources. This remains an environmentally controversial proposition.

The Oil Industry

Alaska's present-day economy is dominated by the exploitation of natural gas and especially oil deposits, discovered in 1968 on the Arctic Slope near Prudhoe Bay. Despite opposition from environmentalists, the 789-mile Trans-Alaska Pipeline from Prudhoe Bay to Valdez was built, quickly making Alaska the nation's second leading oil producer. With this oil wealth, Alaskans were able to repeal their personal income tax.

On March 24, 1989, the Exxon Valdez oil tanker ran aground in Prince William Sound, spilling over ten million gallons of oil and upsetting the fragile ecosystem of bird and marine life there, perhaps for decades.

Important Events

1728 Vitus Bering, a Dane in the employ of the Russians, discovers St. Lawrence Island in the Bering Strait.

1741 Russian parties led by Bering and Aleksei Chirikov land on Alaska.

1799 The Russia-American Company sets up a furtrading station near Sitka.

1802 Tlingit Indians storm the Sitka outpost, killing most of the settlers.

1867 Seward's Folly: the United States buys Alaska from the Russians for $7.2 million on the

advice of Secretary of State William Seward.

1880 First major gold strike in Alaska is made by Joe Juneau and Dick Harris.

1896 The Yukon Gold Rush, spurred by the discovery of gold in the Klondike region of Canada, sees almost sixty thousand people pass through Alaska.

1900 Juneau is made the capital of Alaska; salmon canneries turn out a million cases.

1902 Fairbanks is founded at the site of Alaska's most productive gold field.

1912 Alaska becomes a U.S. territory.

1914 Anchorage is founded as a railroad construction camp.

1941-45 United States stations over 150,000 troops in Alaska.

1949 Alaska adopts a territorial income tax.

1959 Alaska becomes the forty-ninth state with capital at Juneau and William Egan as governor.

1964 Severe earthquake destroys Anchorage and a tsunami wipes out Valdez.

1971 Native Claims Settlement Act gives Alaska Natives title to 44 million acres for native land holdings.

1977 Trans-Alaska Pipeline from Prudhoe Bay to Valdez is completed.

1980 The personal income tax is repealed.

1989 Exxon Valdez oil tanker runs aground in Prince William Sound, spilling over ten million gallons of oil.

1991 A federal judge imposes a record $1.025 billion in fines on Exxon for the Exxon Valdez disaster.

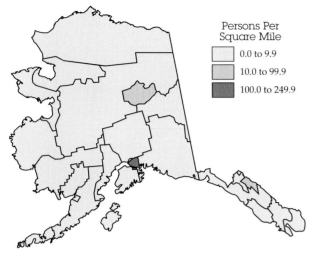

Persons Per Square Mile
- 0.0 to 9.9
- 10.0 to 99.9
- 100.0 to 249.9

Population Projections

Population in thousands

Alaska's Population

U. S. Population

(graph x-axis: 1990, 1995, 2000, 2010)
(left y-axis: 450, 500, 550, 600, 650, 700, 750, 800)
(right y-axis: 250,000; 255,000; 260,000; 265,000; 270,000; 275,000; 280,000; 285,000)

Population Change

Year	Population
1950	129,000
1960	229,000
1970	304,000
1980	401,851
1990	550,043
2000	687,000
2010	765,000

Period	Change
1950–1970	135.7%
1970–1980	32.2%
1980–1990	36.8%
1990–2000	24.9%

Population Density

Population density for the state of Alaska was 1.0 persons per square mile in 1990 (0.4 per km2). Average U.S. density was 70.3 persons per square mile in 1990 (27.3 per km2). Habitation is most dense in and around Anchorage and Fairbanks.

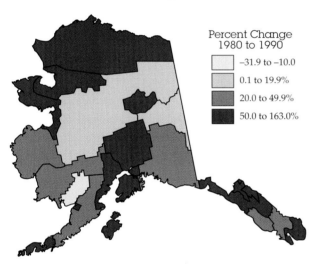

Percent Change 1980 to 1990
- –31.9 to –10.0
- 0.1 to 19.9%
- 20.0 to 49.9%
- 50.0 to 163.0%

Population Change

The 1990 population figure for the state of Alaska was 550,043. This is a 36.88 percent increase from 401,851 in 1980. The next decade will show growth with a population of 687 thousand or a 24.9 percent increase.

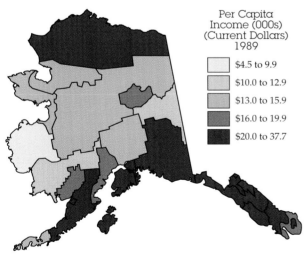

Per Capita Income (000s) (Current Dollars) 1989
- $4.5 to 9.9
- $10.0 to 12.9
- $13.0 to 15.9
- $16.0 to 19.9
- $20.0 to 37.7

Distribution of Income

The per capita income for the state of Alaska (current dollars) was $21,603 in 1992. This is a 57.8 percent increase from $13,692 in 1980. The oil industry provides many high–paying jobs for the residents of Alaska as can be seen in this map.

Population Facts

State Population, 1993: 599,000

Rank: 48

Population 2000: 687,000 (Rank 47)

Density: 1.0 per sq. mi. (0.4 per km2)

Distribution: 67.5% urban, 32.5% rural

Population Under 5 Years Old: 9.7%

Population Under 18 Years Old: 31.5%

Population Over 65 Years Old: 4.3%

Median Age: 29.4

Number of Households: 189,000

Average Persons Per Household: 2.80

Average Persons Per Family: 3.33

Female Heads of Households: 3.31%

Population That Is Married: 19.29%

Birth Rate: 21.6 per 1,000 population

Death Rate: 4.0 per 1,000 population

Births to Teen Mothers: 9.7%

Marriage Rate: 10.8 per 1,000 population

Divorce Rate: 5.5 per 1,000 population

Violent Crime Rate: 614 per 100,000 pop.

Population on Social Security: 6.1%

Percent Voting for President: 65.4%

Population Profile

Rank. Alaska ranks 48th among U.S. states in terms of population with 599,000 citizens.

Minority Population. The state's minority population is 26.5 percent. The state's male to female ratio for 1990 was 111.41 males for every 100 females. This figure is the highest in the country with Nevada, Hawaii, and California being the next highest. It was above the national average of 95.22 males for every 100 females.

Government

Capital: Juneau (established 1900).

Statehood: Became 49th state on Jan. 3, 1959.

Number of Counties: 15 boroughs.

Supreme Court Justices: N/A.

State Senators: 20, 4-year term.

State Legislators: 40, 2-year term.

United States Senators: 2.

United States Representatives: 1.

Electoral Votes: 3.

State Constitution: Adopted 1956.

Alaska's Famous Citizens

Baranov, Alexander (1746–1819). Russian merchant and fur trader who migrated to Alaska. Integral in founding of Russian-American Co.

Bartlett, E. L. (1904–1968). Fairbanks native and journalist active in the drive for statehood. Elected senator in 1958.

Bering, Vitus (1681–1741). Danish navigator who sought a land connection between Asia and America. Discovered Bering Strait.

Butcher, Susan (b. 1954). Sled-dog racer, who in 1988 became first to win Iditarod races three years in a row.

Egan, William (1919–1984). First governor of Alaska, also served one term as U.S. Senator.

Hickel, Walter (b. 1919). First Republican governor of Alaska (1966), also served as interior secretary.

Hubbard, Bernard (1888–1962). Jesuit scientist, explored and mapped Alaska region and studied Eskimo culture.

Jackson, Sheldon (1834–1909). Missionary, opened schools and churches in Alaska. Also introduced reindeer to the state.

Growth. Growing much faster than the projected national average, the state's population is expected to reach 765 thousand by the year 2010 (see graph above).

Older Citizens. The state's population older than 65 was 22,396 in 1990. It grew 93.96% from 11,547 in 1980.

Younger Citizens. The number of children (under 18 years of age) was 172 thousand in 1990. This represents 31.3 percent of the state's population. The state's school aged population was 112 thousand in 1990. It is expected to increase to 139 thousand by the year 2000. This represents a 24.11% change.

Urban/Rural. 67.5% of the population of the state live in urban areas while 32.5% live in rural areas.

Largest Cities. Alaska has one city with a population greater than 35,000. The populations of the state's largest centers are (starting from the most populous) Anchorage (226,338), Fairbanks (30,843), and Juneau (26,751).

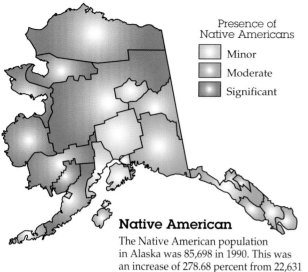

Presence of
Native Americans

- ☐ Minor
- ▨ Moderate
- ▩ Significant

Native American

The Native American population in Alaska was 85,698 in 1990. This was an increase of 278.68 percent from 22,631 in 1980. Native Americans represent the fastest-growing ethnic group in Alaska. Large groups of Eskimos as well as other Native Americans can be found along the coastal regions of the state.

Nationalities

African	430
American	23,000
Arab	454
Austrian	1,169
Czech	2,472
Dutch	8,223
English	51,658
Finnish	2,718
German	97,039
Greek	1,264
Hungarian	1,461
Irish	44,676
Italian	10,119
Norwegian	16,517
Polish	8,443
Portuguese	1,111
Russian	4,051
Scottish	11,480
Slovak	1,176
Swedish	11,469
Welsh	3,074
West Indian	400

Statewide Ethnic Composition

Over three-quarters of the Alaskan population is white. Of these many consider themselves of German, English, and Irish descent. Alaska also has a large Native American population. These people, the Eskimo and the Aleut, hug the coast and occupy the valleys of this rugged landscape. Many of these Native Americans continue traditional ways of life.

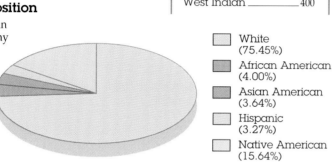

- ☐ White (75.45%)
- ▨ African American (4.00%)
- ▩ Asian American (3.64%)
- ☐ Hispanic (3.27%)
- ☐ Native American (15.64%)

Education Facts

Total Students 1990: 109,280

Number of School Districts: 54

Expenditure Per Capita on Education 1990: $1,568

Expenditure Per Capita K–12 1990: $1,321

Expenditure Per Pupil 1990: $6,952

Total School Enrollment 1990–1991: 112,161

Rank of Expenditures Per Student: 5th in the U.S.

African American Enrollment: 4.5%

Hispanic Enrollment: 1.9%

Asian/Pacific Islander Enrollment: 3.6%

Native American Enrollment: 22.4%

Mean SAT Score 1991 Verbal: 439

Mean SAT Score 1991 Math: 481

Average Teacher's Salary 1992: $44,700

Rank Teacher's Salary: 2d in U.S.

High School Graduates 1990: 5,700

Total Number of Public Schools: 495

Number of Teachers 1990: 6,676

Student/Teacher Ratio: 16.8

Staff Employed in Public Schools: 13,438

Pupil/Staff Ratio: 8.1

Staff/Teacher Ratio: 2.1

Education

Attainment: 86.9 percent of population 25 years or older were high school graduates in 1989, earning Alaska a ranking of 3d in the United States; 23.4 percent of the state's population had completed college. Institutions of Higher Education: The largest universities and colleges in the state include the University of Alaska (11 state wide campuses); Alaska Pacific University, Anchorage; Sheldon Jackson College, Sitka. Expenditures per Student: Expenditure increased 120% between 1985 and 1990. Projected High School Graduations: 1998 (9,271), 2004 (11,003); Total Revenues for Education from Federal Sources: $87 million; Total Revenues for Education from State Sources: $491 million; Total Revenues for Education from Local Sources: $198 million; Average Annual Salaries for Public School Principals: N/A; Largest School Districts in State Anchorage School District, 40,924 students, 88th in the United States.

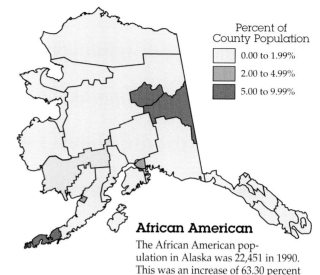

Percent of
County Population

- ☐ 0.00 to 1.99%
- ▨ 2.00 to 4.99%
- ▩ 5.00 to 9.99%

African American

The African American population in Alaska was 22,451 in 1990. This was an increase of 63.30 percent from 13,748 in 1980. The African American population is centered around the major cities in Alaska such as Anchorage and Fairbanks. There is also a sizable concentration on the Alaska Peninsula.

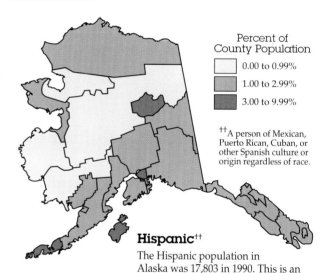

Percent of
County Population

- ☐ 0.00 to 0.99%
- ▨ 1.00 to 2.99%
- ▩ 3.00 to 9.99%

†† A person of Mexican, Puerto Rican, Cuban, or other Spanish culture or origin regardless of race.

Hispanic††

The Hispanic population in Alaska was 17,803 in 1990. This is an increase of 87.26 percent from 9,507 persons in 1980. The main concentration of Hispanics can be found in Anchorage, Fairbanks, Kodiak Island, and on the Alaska Peninsula. Like African Americans in Alaska, Hispanics reside mostly in urban areas.

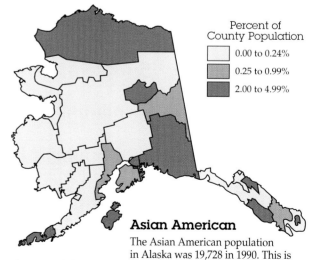

Percent of
County Population

- ☐ 0.00 to 0.24%
- ▨ 0.25 to 0.99%
- ▩ 2.00 to 4.99%

Asian American

The Asian American population in Alaska was 19,728 in 1990. This is an increase of 156.34 percent from 7,696 persons in 1980. The Asian American population in Alaska is not as concentrated as either the African American or Hispanic population. Large numbers can be found in the far north region as well as in the southeast. Anchorage and Fairbanks also are home to this group.

16 ECONOMY AND RESOURCES Alaska

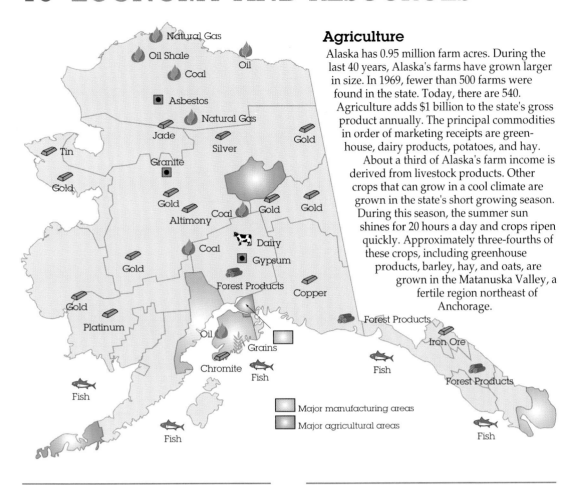

Agriculture

Alaska has 0.95 million farm acres. During the last 40 years, Alaska's farms have grown larger in size. In 1969, fewer than 500 farms were found in the state. Today, there are 540. Agriculture adds $1 billion to the state's gross product annually. The principal commodities in order of marketing receipts are greenhouse, dairy products, potatoes, and hay.

About a third of Alaska's farm income is derived from livestock products. Other crops that can grow in a cool climate are grown in the state's short growing season. During this season, the summer sun shines for 20 hours a day and crops ripen quickly. Approximately three-fourths of these crops, including greenhouse products, barley, hay, and oats, are grown in the Matanuska Valley, a fertile region northeast of Anchorage.

Transportation

Due to Alaska's terrain, road-building is difficult; hence, the state has only about 10,200 miles of roadway, including highways. Furthermore, only two-thirds of the 8,700 miles of roads are surfaced. Most of Alaska's transportation needs are served by sea or air. Alaska operates a ferry service that links many cities and towns in the coastal part of the state. Most of Alaska's trade with the 48 contiguous states is done by container ships. Major ports include Anchorage, Valdez, and Sitka. Small airplanes fly people, as well as supplies, throughout even the most desolate parts of Alaska. Large, modern airports can be found in Fairbanks and Juneau. A state-owned railroad carries freight and passengers between Alaska towns.

Energy and Transportation Facts

Energy. Yearly Consumption: 588 tril. BTUs (residential, 7.8%; commercial, 9.9%; industrial, 56.8%; transportation, 25.3%); Annual Energy Expenditures Per Capita: $3,249; Nuclear Power Plants Located in State: 0; Source of Energy Consumed: Petroleum— 33.7%; Natural Gas— 62.6%; Coal— 2.2%; Hydroelectric Power—1.5%; Nuclear Power—0.0%.

Transportation. Highway Miles: 13,634 (interstates, 1,088; urban, 1,648; rural, 11,986); Average Yearly Auto Insurance: $685 (12th); Auto Fatalities Rank: 2d; Registered Motor Vehicles: 486,095; Workers in Carpools: 24.4%; Workers Using Public Trans: 2.4%.

Housing

Owner Occupied Units: 232,608; Average Age of Units: 19 years; Average Value of Housing Units: $94,400; Renter Occupied Units: 81,927; Median Monthly Rent: $559; Housing Starts: 1,800; Existing Home Sales: N/A.

Economic Facts

Gross State Product: $20,000,000,000

Income Per Capita: $21,603

Disposable Personal Income: $19,093

Median Household Income: $41,408

Average Annual Pay, 1988: $30,830

Principal Industries: petroleum products, processed fish, wood products, paper products

Major Crops: eggs, milk, hay, greenhouse, potatoes, lumber

Fish: Salmon, Crabs, Shrimp, Scallops, Clams, Herring

Livestock: reindeer, sheep, cattle, horses

Non-Fuel Minerals: Gold, Zinc, Silver, Stone, Platinum, Lead, Gemstones

Organic Fuel Minerals: Petroleum, Coal

Civilian Labor Force: 258,000 (Women: 120,000)

Total Employed: 236,000 (Women: 111,000)

Median Value of Housing: $94,900

Median Contract Rent: $559 per month

Economic Sectors

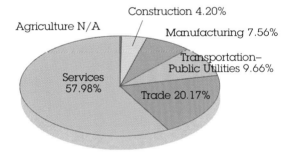

Agriculture N/A; Construction 4.20%; Manufacturing 7.56%; Transportation–Public Utilities 9.66%; Trade 20.17%; Services 57.98%

Manufacturing

The state of Alaska has a relatively small manufacturing base compared to other states. Manufactured products contribute only 5 percent to the state's gross product. In overall terms of added value, food processing leads all manufacturing ventures in Alaska. Petroleum, paper products, and wood products follow in value.

Major manufacturing centers in Alaska include the cities of Fairbanks, Anchorage, and Juneau. In the food processing industry, Kodiak and Kenai are important salmon-producing areas. The Prudhoe Bay area has petroleum refineries, as do Fairbanks and Kenai. Pulp mills in Ketchikan and Sitka produce Alaska's leading paper product, pulp. Most of the newspaper in the state is produced in Anchorage.

Employment

Employment. Alaska employed 0.28 million people in 1993. Most work in government jobs (74,400 persons or 27% of the workforce). Wholesale and retail trade account for 17.6% or 48,700 workers. Manufacturing employs 17,100 workers (6.2%). Social and personal services employ 56,800 people (20.6%). Construction accounts for 4.1% or 11,400 persons. Transportation and utilities account for 8.3% or 22,900 persons. Agriculture employs 9,700 workers or 3.5%. Finance, real estate, and insurance account for 4% or 11,100 workers. Mining employs 10,600 people and accounts for only 3.8% of the workforce.

Unemployment. Unemployment has decreased to 7.6% in 1993 from a rate of 9.7% in 1985. Today's figure is higher than the national average of 6.8% as shown below.

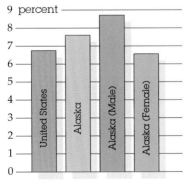

Unemployment Rate

ARIZONA
The State of Arizona

Official State Seal

The Great Seal of Arizona replaced the earlier seals of old territorial days in 1912. The words "The Great Seal of the State of Arizona" encircle the seal. The motto *Ditat Deus* is Latin for God Enriches. On the seal is a miner with his tools standing next to a quartz mill. In the background is a mountain range with a rising sun. Also shown are fields, orchards, and grazing cattle.

Legal Holidays

January: New Year's Day—1st, Martin Luther King, Jr., Day—3rd Monday; February: Lincoln Day—2nd Monday; Presidents' Day—3rd Monday; Admission Day—14th; May: Memorial Day—4th Monday; July: Independence Day—4th; September: Labor Day—1st Monday; October: Columbus Day—2nd Monday; November: Veterans' Day—11th; Thanksgiving—4th Thursday; December: Christmas—25th.

Official State Flag

The state flag of Arizona was adopted in 1917. The star represents the importance of minerals in the economy. The thirteen yellow and red rays represent the thirteen original states of the United States. The colors of the rays represent the period of Spanish control over the area.

Festivals and Events

January: Jazz Festival, Lake Havasu; Sonora Showcase, Yuma; February: Arizona Renaissance Fest, Apache Junction; Gold Rush Days, Wickenburg; La Fiesta de los Vaqueros, Tucson; Winter Visitor Snowbird Jamboree, Lake Havasu City; March: Old Town Tempe Fest of Arts, Tempe; April: San Xavier Pageant & Fiesta, Tucson; May: Cinco de Mayo Festival, Phoenix; Old Timer's Rodeo, Payson; June: Country Music Fest, Payson; Pine Country Pro Rodeo, Flagstaff; Territorial Days, Prescott; July: Oatman Sidewalk Egg Frying Contest, Oatman; September: Old-Timer's Fiddlers' Contest, Payson; October: Helldorado Days, Tombstone; Rex Allen Days, Willcox; Sedona Apple Fest, West Sedona; November: Four Corner States Bluegrass Fest, Wickenburg; December: Cowboy Christmas, Wickenburg; Indian Market, Phoenix; Tempe Fiesta Bowl Block Party, Tempe.

Arizona Compared to States in Its Region.

Resident Pop. in Metro Areas: 1st; Pop. Percent Increase: 5th; Pop. Over 65: 2d; Infant Mortality: 2d; School Enroll. Increase: 1st; High School Grad. and Up: 7th; Violent Crime: 3d; Hazardous Waste Sites: 4th; Unemployment: 1st; Median Household Income: 4th; Persons Below Poverty: 3d; Energy Costs Per Person: 6th.

Mountain Region

	Population	Capital
Montana	839,000	Helena
Wyoming	470,000	Cheyenne
Idaho	1,099,000	Boise
Nevada	1,389,000	Carson City
Utah	1,860,000	Salt Lake City
Colorado	3,566,000	Denver
Arizona	3,936,000	Phoenix
New Mexico	1,616,000	Santa Fe

Arizona's Finances

Households: 1,369,000; Income Per Capita Current Dollars: $17,119; Change Per Capita Income 1980 to 1992: 84.6% (41st in U.S.); State Expenditures: $8,236,000,000; State Revenues: $7,975,000,000; Personal Income Tax: 1 to 7%; Federal Income Taxes Paid Per Capita: $1,517; Sales Tax: 5% (food and prescription drugs exempt).

State Expenditures

7.0 billion dollars

- Education
- Highway
- Welfare
- Health
- Other

State Revenues

7.0 billion dollars

- Federal
- Local
- Taxes
- Miscellaneous

Location, Size, and Boundaries

Maximum Extent

Location. Arizona is located in the southwestern United States in what is known as the Mountain region. It is bounded on four sides by land. The geographic center of Arizona is lat. 34° 18.5' N; long. 111° 47.6' W.

Size. Arizona is the 6th largest state in terms of size. Its area is 113,909 sq. mi. (295,024 km2). Inland water covers 492 sq. mi. (1,274 km2).

Boundaries. Utah, 277 mi. (446 km); New Mexico, 389 mi. (626 km); Mexico, 373 mi. (600 km); California, 234 mi. (377 km); Nevada, 205 mi. (330 km).

Geographic Extent. The north/south extent of Arizona is 395 mi. (636 km). The state extends 340 mi. (547 km) to the east/west.

Facts about Arizona. Origin of Name: After an Indian word possibly meaning "*small spring*"; Nickname: The Grand Canyon State; Motto: "God Enriches" *(Ditat Deus)*; Abbreviations: Ariz. (traditional), AZ (postal); State Bird: cactus wren; State Tree: paloverde; State Flower: saguaro (giant cactus); State Song: "Arizona," words by Margaret Rowe Clifford, music by Maurice Blumenthal. "I Love You Arizona," words and music by Rex Allen, Jr.

Arizona Compared to Other States. Resident Pop. in Metro Areas: 10th; Pop. Percent Increase: 9th; Pop. Over 65: 19th; Infant Mort.: 27th; School Enroll. Increase: 3d; High School Grad. and Up: 20th; Violent Crime: 18th; Hazardous Waste Sites: 33d; Unemployment: 19th; Median Household Income: 27th; Persons Below Poverty: 12th; Energy Costs Per Person: 37th.

Sources of Information. Tourism: Arizona Office of Tourism, 1100 West Washington, Phoenix, AZ 85007. Government: Secretary of State, Publications, Capitol West Wing, 1700 West Washington, 7th Floor, Suite 706, Phoenix, AZ 85007. History: Arizona Hist. Soc. Museum, 1242 North Central Avenue, Phoenix, AZ 85004.

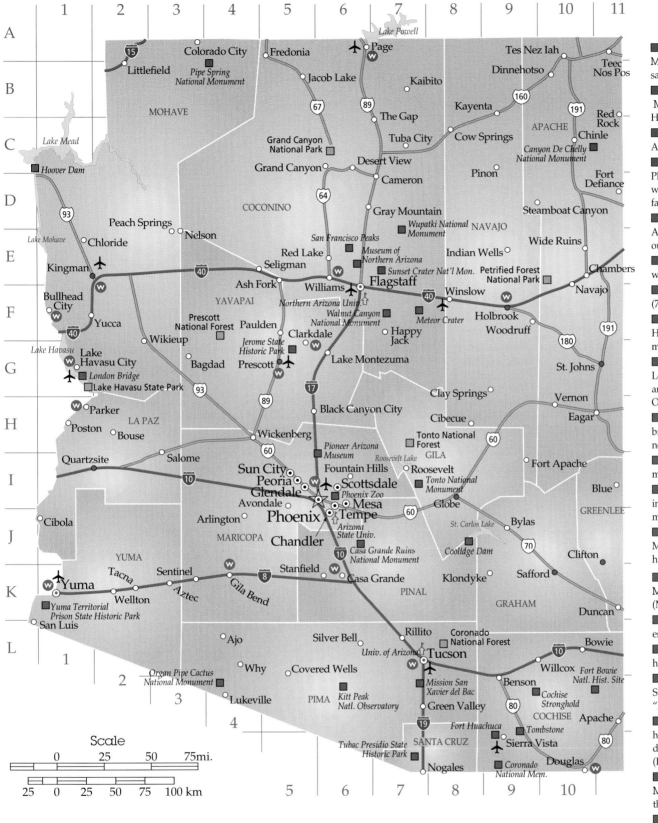

■ Canyon De Chelly National Monument. Scenic canyons and Anasazi ruins in Navajo country. (C-11)

■ Casa Grande Ruins National Monument. Four-story ruin of a Hohokam Indian structure. (J-6)

■ Cochise Stronghold. Hideout of the Apache chief Cochise. (M-9)

■ Coronado National Memorial. Place where Coronado first entered what is now the U.S. in search of the fabled Seven Cities of Cibola. (N-9)

■ Fort Bowie National Historic Site. Adobe ruin which was a military outpost during the Indian wars. (M-10)

■ Fort Huachuca. Territorial outpost with a historic museum. (N-9)

■ Hoover Dam. Highest concrete dam (727 ft.) in the United States. (C-1)

■ Jerome State Historic Park. Historic copper-mining town with museums, restaurants, and shops. (G-5)

■ Kitt Peak National Observatory. Location of the McMath solar telescope and the National Optical Astronomical Observatories. (M-6)

■ London Bridge. Site of famous bridge. English shops and village nearby. (G-1)

■ Meteor Crater. Impact site of a large meteor. Geologic wonder. (F-7)

■ Mission San Xavier del Bac. Built in 1700, it is one of the oldest Spanish missions in the Southwest . (L-7)

■ Museum of Northern Arizona. Museum dedicated to the art and history of northern Arizona. (E-6)

■ Organ Pipe Cactus National Monument. Site of organ pipe cacti. (M-4)

■ Phoenix Zoo. At 123 acres, the largest privately owned zoo in the U.S. (I-5)

■ Pioneer Arizona Museum. Living history museum of 1880s . (H-5)

■ Pipe Spring National Monument. Site of a Mormon fort built along the "Honeymoon Trail." (B-4)

■ San Francisco Peaks. The state's highest peak, including wilderness area downhill and cross-country ski trails. (E-6)

■ Sunset Crater National Monument. 1,000-foot cone volcano that erupted in 1064 and 1065. (E-7)

■ Tombstone. Sights include Boot Hill Cemetery, the O.K. Corral, and the Tombstone Courthouse State Park. (F-7)

■ Tonto National Monument. Cliff dwellings can be found at this site along the Apache Trail in Tonto National Forest. (I-7)

■ Tubac Presidio State Historic Park. Ruins of old adobe mission and Spanish fort. One of the oldest communities in the state. (N-7)

■ Walnut Canyon National Monument. Site of cliff dwellings. (F-7)

■ Wupatki National Monument. 35,000 acre reserve featuring prehistoric Indian ruins. (D-7)

■ Yuma Territorial Prison State Historic Park. Site of a prison that held many outlaws of the old West. Includes a museum. (K-1)

Legend

☆ State capitol

⊙ Cities over 35,000 population

○ Other significant cities

● County Seats

■ Major cultural attractions

▢ State Parks

Ⓦ Arizona Tourist Information

⚑ Major colleges and universities

Major Cities

Apache Jct.	M-4	Glendale	I-5	Phoenix	I-6
Avondale	I-5	Green Valley	M-7	Prescott	G-5
Bullhead City	F-1	Kingman	E-1	Scottsdale	I-6
Casa Grande	K-6	Lake Havasu-		Sierra Vista	N-9
Chandler	J-6	City	G-1	Sun City	I-5
Douglas	N-10	Mesa	I-6	Sun City West	I-5
Flagstaff	F-6	Nogales	L-7	Tempe	I-6
Fountain Hills	I-6	Paradise Valley	I-6	Tucson	L-7
Gilbert	J-6	Peoria	I-5	Yuma	K-1

Arizona

Weather Facts

Record High Temperature: 127° F (53° C) on July 6, 1901, at Parker; Record Low Temperature: -40° F (-40° C) on January 6, 1967, at Hawley Lake; Average January Temperature: 41° F (5° C); Average July Temperature: 80° F (27° C); Average Yearly Precipitation: 13 in. (33 cm).

Environmental Facts

Air Pollution Rank: 37th; Water Pollution Rank: 50th; Total Yearly Industrial Pollution: 46,114,093 lbs.; Industrial Pollution Rank: 20th; Hazardous Waste Sites: 10; Hazardous Sites Rank: 32d; Landfill Capacity: overextended; Fresh Water Supply: critical and current shortage; Daily Residential Water Consumption: 193 gals. per capita; Endangered Species: Aquatic Species (18)—catfish, Yaqui; Birds (9)—bobwhite, masked; Mammals (8)—bat, lesser (=Sanborn's) long-nosed; Other Species (4)—ambersnail, Kanab; Plants (18)—agave, Arizona.

Environmental Quality

Arizona residents generate 3.1 million tons of solid waste each year, or approximately 1,800 pounds per capita. Landfill capacity in Arizona will be exhausted in more than 12 years. The state has 11 hazardous waste sites. Annual greenhouse gas emissions in Arizona total 64.1 million tons, or 18.4 tons per capita. Industrial sources in Arizona release approximately 36.6 thousand tons of toxins, 753.3 thousand tons of acid precipitation-producing substances, and 1.2 million tons of smog-producing substances into the atmosphere each year.

The state has 2.7 million acres within the National Park System; the largest area within the state is Grand Canyon National Park.

Arizona spends approximately 1 percent of its budget, or approximately $13 per capita, on environmental and natural resources.

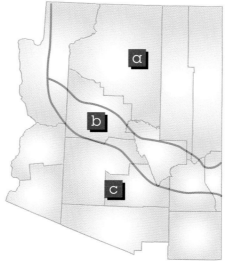

Physical Regions: (a) Colorado Plateau; (b) Transition Zone; (c) Basin and Range Region.

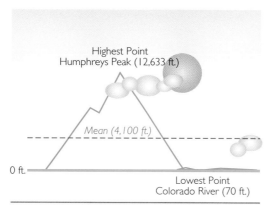

Highest Point
Humphreys Peak (12,633 ft.)

Mean (4,100 ft.)

0 ft.

Lowest Point
Colorado River (70 ft.)

Land Use

Cropland: 3.1%; Pasture: 0.2%; Rangeland: 75.9%; Forest: 11.7%; Urban: 2.6%; Other: 6.5%.

For more information about Arizona's environment, contact the Department of Environmental Quality, 2005 N. Central Ave., Phoenix, AZ 85004.

Average Monthly Weather

Flagstaff	Jan	Feb	Mar	Apr	May	Jun	Jul	Aug	Sep	Oct	Nov	Dec	Yearly
Maximum Temperature °F	41.7	44.5	48.6	57.1	66.7	77.6	81.9	78.9	74.1	63.7	51.0	43.6	60.8
Minimum Temperature °F	14.7	16.9	20.4	25.9	32.9	40.9	50.3	48.7	40.9	30.6	21.5	15.9	30.0
Days of Precipitation	7.4	6.7	8.3	5.7	4.3	2.8	11.6	11.4	6.3	4.8	5.3	6.2	80.7
Tuscon													
Maximum Temperature °F	64.1	67.4	71.8	80.1	88.8	98.5	98.5	95.9	93.5	84.1	72.2	65.0	81.7
Minimum Temperature °F	38.1	40.0	43.8	49.7	57.5	67.4	73.8	72.0	67.3	56.7	45.2	39.0	54.2
Days of Precipitation	4.4	3.6	4.1	2.1	1.4	1.7	10.6	9.3	4.7	3.4	3.0	4.4	52.7

Flora and Fauna

Arizona's contrasts in plant life follow the state's contrasts in elevation. Various cacti, including the large and famous saguaro cactus, are a common sight in Arizona's desert areas. Arizona also has many other distinctive plants such as mesquite, night-blooming cereus, and several types of yucca. Arizona's forested areas, which cover about one-fourth of the state, contain the largest area of ponderosa pines in the country. Other trees found in high-elevation forests include blue spruce, juniper, and Douglas and white fir. Many types of wildflowers, including poppies, phlox, and Indian

paintbrush, are found throughout Arizona.

In addition to having over 30 different types of lizards, Arizona also has many dangerous members of the animal kingdom. Rattlesnakes can be found in most parts of Arizona. The hotter desert areas are home to the deadly coral snake, scorpions, and even tarantulas. Arizona's large mammals include bear, elk, mountain lion, and deer. Smaller animals include foxes, badgers, weasels, and javelinas (wild pigs). Over 400 bird species, including wild turkeys and roadrunners, also live in Arizona. Trout, bass, and crappie swim in the state's waterways.

Topography

There are several distinct physical regions in Arizona. About two-fifths of northern Arizona is covered by the Colorado Plateau, a dry area dominated by high plateaus. In the northwestern part of this region lie the Coconino, Kanab, and Kaibab plateaus. They are bisected by the Colorado River, which carves the spectacular Grand Canyon through them. The Grand Canyon is over 200 miles (320 km) long and 1 mile (1.6 km) deep. In north-central Arizona is the Painted Desert, and east of this mountainous area is the Petrified Forest. The soil of this region has evolved from alluvial deposits, is predominantly loamy clay, and maintains a depth of 20 inches or less over the bedrock. Like all the soil of Arizona, it is considered warm and dry.

The Mogollon Rim serves as a border between the Northern Plateau Region and the Basin and Range Region in southern Arizona, and lies within the Transition Zone. This area has several mountain ranges, including the Santa Maria and White mountains. The soil is a dark clay rich in organic material.

Basins and ranges running northwest to southeast characterize southern Arizona. Ranges, mainly in the southeast, include the Chiricahua and the Pinaleno mountains. Southwestern Arizona contains the Sonora Desert and other arid stretches between sparse ranges. The soil is a distinctive red/brown desert type ranging from loamy clay to silica.

Climate

The Arizona climate varies greatly from the mountainous region to the state's deserts. About one-half of Arizona has a semiarid climate, and almost one third is considered arid. The remainder of the state has humid weather. Southwest Arizona, where Yuma is located, has hot weather; temperatures for January and July average 55 degrees F and 95 degrees F. Temperatures above 100 degrees F are common in the summer. The Colorado Plateau section of the state has significantly cooler weather. The average year-round temperature in Flagstaff is only 30 degrees F.

Southwestern Arizona receives virtually no precipitation at all—only about 3 inches a year. However, north-central Arizona receives an average of 18 inches of precipitation annually.

Many of Arizona's visitors come for the subtropical semiarid and arid conditions. The weather in these areas is often more comfortable than in the more humid regions.

Hydrology

The most important river in Arizona is the Colorado. It flows for about 675 miles (1,087 km) through the state. The Colorado enters Arizona from the north, then winds westward through the Grand Canyon to Hoover Dam at the Nevada border. It then flows southward, marking Arizona's western border with Nevada and California. The Gila and the Little Colorado are the largest tributaries of the Colorado in Arizona. Many of the smaller streams in the state flow only part of the year because of Arizona's dry climate.

All of the large lakes in the state are man-made, the result of damming. These include Lake Mead (partially in Nevada), created by Hoover Dam; Lake Havasu (partially in California), formed by Parker Dam; Lake Powell (partially in Utah), created by Glen Canyon Dam; and the Roosevelt Lake, created from Theodore Roosevelt Dam.

Arizona's History

Arizona's First People

The first humans to enter Arizona arrived over twelve thousand years ago by way of the Bering Strait. Their descendants evolved from hunters to a mostly agricultural lifestyle and settled in various parts of the state. The most well known of these tribes was the Anasazi, located in the northeastern part of the state (as well as in New Mexico). These basket-making people were cliff-dwellers, carving their homes out of the porous limestone mesas and mountains of the area. They and other tribes (such as the Hohokam) left significant evidence of an advanced culture, but by the time of the arrival of the first Europeans it and their populations were in serious decline—perhaps the effects of a severe drought.

The Indians encountered by the first Europeans belonged to many different tribes, the best known being the Hopi, Yuma, Navajo, Apache, Pima, and Papago.

European Exploration

Álvar Nuñez Cabeza de Vaca, a Spaniard, was the first European explorer to set foot in Arizona, in 1536. He was followed three years later by Friar Marcos de Niza and the African slave Estevan (or Estevánico), and in 1540 by Francisco Vásquez de Coronado, who was searching for the legendary Seven Cities of Cibola. Instead he discovered the Grand Canyon. Although the Spanish failed to find riches in their exploration of Arizona in the sixteenth century, they were soon followed by missionaries. The first mission was established by the Franciscans among the Hopi in 1629, and many others were founded by the end of the seventeenth century.

The first major European settlement in Arizona was constructed as a military garrison at Tubac in 1752. This was in response to the Pima and Papago Indians living in the area. In 1776, the garrison was moved to Tucson, which was the founding of that city. These settlements on the Santa Cruz River served mainly as stops for fortune-hunting expeditions on the way to California.

By the end of the eighteenth century, the Spanish had removed any threat from the Apaches by consigning them to a reservation and had begun mining and ranching activities. However, Mexico revolted against Spain in 1810, and by 1821, Arizona had fallen into Mexican hands.

Statehood

After the Mexican War of 1846-48, the lands north of the Gila River passed into U.S. hands. In 1850, this area became part of the new U.S. territory of New Mexico. The southern portion of Arizona became U.S. territory with the Gadsden Purchase of 1853. In 1860, some Arizonians joined with rebels in southern New Mexico who unsuccessfully tried to establish a new territory.

In 1862, a Confederate company briefly occupied Tucson, but Union forces soon took control. The next year, the new Territory of Arizona was created, with Ft. Whipple as the capital. Then the capital was moved to Prescott in 1864. It then moved to Tucson (1867), Prescott (1877), and finally to Phoenix (1889).

The 1860s and 1870s were a time of accelerated growth for Arizona. Settlements such as Gila Bend, Florence, and Tombstone were founded during this time. Mormons can in the 1870s and founded settlements of their own. The late 1870s brought the railroad into Arizona with a line to Yuma from California. About this time a movement for statehood began. After an initial refusal to grant statehood by Congress in 1906, enabling legislation was passed allowing Arizona to apply for statehood. On February 14, 1912, it was admitted to the Union as the forty-eighth state, the last of the conterminous states.

Industrialization

With the establishment of the first copper mine in 1854, silver mines around Tubac in 1856, and gold being mined at Gila City in the late 1850s, mining became a booming industry in Arizona. This activity attracted many people, and soon a cattle and agricultural industry had also developed. In 1880, the Southern Pacific Railroad from California reached Tucson, and three years later the Atlantic and Pacific Railroad crossed northern Arizona from Albuquerque to Flagstaff.

By 1907, Arizona was the leading copper producer in the nation, and in the first half of the twentieth century it continued to expand this capacity as well as its agriculture and livestock industries, boosted by the construction of Roosevelt Dam in 1911. Since World War II, manufacturing, spurred by the electronics industry (and a right-to-work state constitutional amendment), has come to dominate the state economy. With magnificent natural features such as the Grand Canyon and the Petrified Forest, Arizona tourism also ranks high on the economic ladder.

Water

With the arrival of agriculture in Arizona in the second half of the nineteenth century came the problem of supplying enough water to this arid region. Canal companies sprang up in Phoenix, but it wasn't until the construction of the Roosevelt Dam in 1911 that any serious action was taken. In the service of the Salt River Valley Project, the dam allowed the irrigation of 250,000 acres for agricultural development. Additional irrigation projects (including Hoover Dam, at the time the world's highest) were built in the 1930s after the shocks and dislocations of the Depression.

By 1977, Arizona was using 2.2 million acre-feet more water than could be replenished annually. The Central Arizona Project, which will divert 2.8 million acre-feet from the Colorado River to Phoenix and Tucson annually, is currently under construction.

Important Events

1536 First Spanish explorer, Cabeza de Vaca, enters Arizona.

1629 Franciscan missionaries establish a post among the Hopi.

1752 A military outpost is established at Tubac in response to tensions with the Pima and Papago Indians.

1776 Tucson is founded.

1821 Spanish lose Arizona to the Mexicans.

1848 Treaty of Guadalupe Hidalgo ending the Mexican War grants Arizona north of the Gila River to the United States.

1853 Gadsden Purchase adds the rest of Arizona to the United States.

1863 Arizona is declared a U.S. territory.

1868 Navajo Indians are transported to a reservation in the northeastern part of the state.

1871 Apaches are moved to White Mountain reservation.

1877 Major silver mine is discovered at Tombstone.

1881 Gunfight at the O.K. Corral in Tombstone, led by Wyatt Earp and Doc Holliday.

1886 Surrender of Geronimo ends twenty- five years of war with the Apaches.

1889 Capital is moved to Phoenix.

1911 Roosevelt Dam is constructed to irrigate the Salt River Valley.

1912 Arizona is admitted to the Union as the forty eighth state.

1919 Grand Canyon National Park is established.

1936 Boulder Dam (now Hoover Dam) is constructed on the Colorado River.

1942 Internment camp is established at Poston to hold Japanese Americans during World War II.

1948 Arizona Indians given the right to vote.

1964 Glen Canyon Dam constructed.

1985 Groundbreaking begins for the Central Arizona Project, a 330 mile pipeline designed to divert water from the Colorado River.

1988 Gov. Evan Meecham removed from office on misconduct charges.

1990 Arizona voters reject the creation of a paid holiday to remember Dr. Martin Luther King Jr.

Arizona

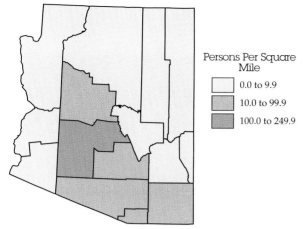

Population Density

Population density for the state of Arizona was 32.3 persons per square mile in 1990 (12.5 per km2). Average U.S. density was 70.3 persons per square mile in 1990 (27.3 per km2). Habitation is most dense around the city of Phoenix in Maricopa county. High density areas can also be found in the city of Tucson and in the southern counties of the state.

Persons Per Square Mile
- 0.0 to 9.9
- 10.0 to 99.9
- 100.0 to 249.9

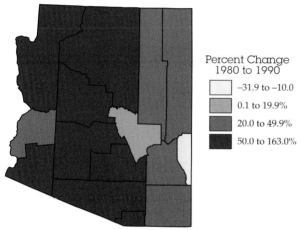

Percent Change 1980 to 1990
- −31.9 to −10.0
- 0.1 to 19.9%
- 20.0 to 49.9%
- 50.0 to 163.0%

Population Change

The 1990 population figure for the state of Arizona was 3,665,228. This is a 34.84 percent increase from 2,718,215 in 1980. The next decade will show growth with a population of 4.6 million or a 25.99 percent increase. Much of the state is growing rapidly. The only county with a decline in population is Greenlee County.

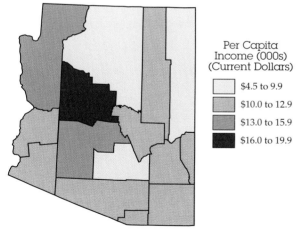

Per Capita Income (000s) (Current Dollars)
- $4.5 to 9.9
- $10.0 to 12.9
- $13.0 to 15.9
- $16.0 to 19.9

Distribution of Income

The per capita income for the state of Arizona (current dollars) was $17,119 in 1992. This is a 84.6 percent increase from $9,272 in 1980. Income is greatest in Yavapai County. Other high income counties include Maricopa County, where Phoenix is located, and Mohave County. The poorest counties are in areas where Indian reservations are located such as Coconino and Apache counties.

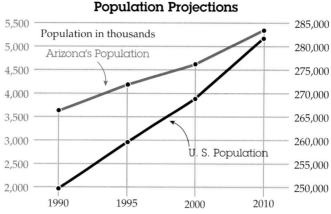

Population Projections

Population in thousands
Arizona's Population
U. S. Population

Population Change

Year	Population
1950	750,000
1960	1,321,000
1970	1,792,000
1980	2,718,215
1990	3,665,228
2000	4,618,000
2010	5,319,000

Period	Change
1950–1970	138.9%
1970–1980	51.7%
1980–1990	34.8%
1990–2000	26.0%

Population Facts

State Population, 1993: 3,936,000
Rank: 23
Population 2000: 4,618,000 (Rank 20)
Density: 32.3 per sq. mi. (12.5 per km2)
Distribution: 87.5% urban, 12.5% rural
Population Under 5 Years Old: 8.4%
Population Under 18 Years Old: 27.3%
Population Over 65 Years Old: 13.4%
Median Age: 32.2
Number of Households: 1,369,000
Average Persons Per Household: 2.62
Average Persons Per Family: 3.16
Female Heads of Households: 3.88%
Population That Is Married: 20.40%
Birth Rate: 18.8 per 1,000 population
Death Rate: 7.9 per 1,000 population
Births to Teen Mothers: 14.2%
Marriage Rate: 10.2 per 1,000 population
Divorce Rate: 6.9 per 1,000 population
Violent Crime Rate: 671 per 100,000 pop.
Population on Social Security: 16.2%
Percent Voting for President: 54.1%

Population Profile

Rank. Arizona ranks 23d among U.S. states in terms of population with 3,936,000 citizens.

Minority Population. The state's minority population is 28.9 percent. The state's male to female ratio for 1990 was 97.64 males for every 100 females. It was above the national average of 95.22 males for every 100 females.

Growth. Growing much faster than the projected national average, the state's population

Government

Capital: Phoenix (established 1889).
Statehood: Became 48th state on Feb. 14, 1912.
Number of Counties: 15.
Supreme Court Justices: 5, 6-year term.
State Senators: 30, 2-year term.
State Legislators: 60, 2-year term.
United States Senators: 2.
United States Representatives: 6.
Electoral Votes: 8.
State Constitution: Adopted 1911.

Arizona's Famous Citizens

Castro, Raul (b. 1916). Mexican-American elected governor in 1974. Also U.S. ambassador to El Salvador and Argentina.

Goldwater, Barry (b. 1909). U.S. senator from 1952 to 1986. Republican nominee for president in 1964.

Hayden, Carl (1877–1972). Set a record for time served in the U.S. Senate (from 1927 to 1969).

Jacobs, Helen Hull (b. 1908). Top tennis player. Won the U.S. women's singles title four years in a row (1932–1935).

Kay, Ulysses (b. 1917). Composer. Composed choral and orchestral works, and the score for the film *The Quiet One*.

Poston, Charles (1825–1902). Called the "Father of Arizona." Was first delegate to the U.S. Congress from Arizona.

Ronstadt, Linda (b. 1946). Country-rock singer. Had numerous hits in the 1970s, including "You're No Good."

Udall, Morris (b. 1922). Served in U.S. House from 1961 to 1991. Strong environmentalist, presidential candidate in 1976.

is expected to reach 5.3 million by the year 2010 *(see graph above)*.

Older Citizens. The state's population older than 65 was 478,774 in 1990. It grew 55.77% from 307,362 in 1980.

Younger Citizens. The number of children (under 18 years of age) was 981 thousand in 1990. This represents 26.8 percent of the state's population. The state's school–aged population was 615 thousand in 1990. It is expected to increase to 793 thousand by the year 2000. This represents a 28.94% change.

Urban/Rural. 87.5% of the population of the state live in urban areas while 12.5% live in rural areas.

Largest Cities. Arizona has 11 cities with a population greater than 35,000. The populations of the state's largest centers are (starting from the most populous) Phoenix (983,403), Tucson (405,390), Mesa (288,091), Glendale (148,134), Tempe (141,865), Scottsdale (130,069), Chandler (90,533), Yuma (54,923), Peoria (50,618), Flagstaff (45,857), Sun City (38,126), Sierra Vista (32,983), Gilbert (29,188), Prescott (26,455), and Lake Havasu City (24,363).

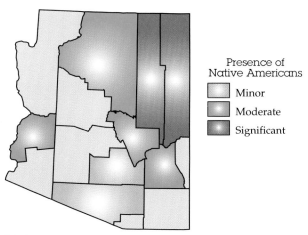

Presence of
Native Americans

- Minor
- Moderate
- Significant

Nationalities 1990

African	3,464
American	101,492
Arab	9,498
Austrian	7,544
Czech	14,817
Dutch	52,237
English	393,849
Finnish	7,406
German	684,857
Greek	10,025
Hungarian	14,475
Irish	297,014
Italian	118,108
Norwegian	46,816
Polish	69,773
Portuguese	4,895
Russian	24,457
Scottish	56,435
Slovak	13,996
Swedish	58,640
Welsh	20,233
West Indian	2,559

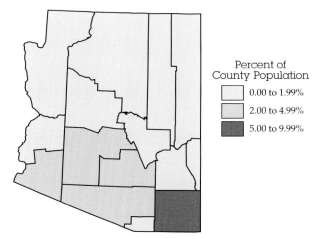

Percent of
County Population

- 0.00 to 1.99%
- 2.00 to 4.99%
- 5.00 to 9.99%

Native American

The Native American population in Arizona was 203,527 in 1990. This was an increase of 32.01 percent from 154,175 in 1980. The largest numbers of Native Americans in Arizona can be found in the numerious Indian reservations in the state, including the Navajo and the Hopi in the northeast, the Papago in the south, the Hualapai in the northwest, and the Fort Apache and the San Carlos in the east.

African American

The African American population in Arizona was 110,524 in 1990. This was an increase of 49.04 percent from 74,159 in 1980. The largest numbers of African Americans can be found in Phoenix, Tucson, Mesa, Glendale, Tempe, and Scottsdale. African Americans in Arizona tend to be concentrated in the southern regions of the state in counties such as Maricopa, Pinal, Cochise, Pima, and Yuma.

Statewide Ethnic Composition

Eighty percent of the population of Arizona is white. Of these the largest nationality is of German descent. There are also significant numbers of English, Irish, and Italians. The next largest ethnic group are the Hispanics, who make up almost 19 percent of the population. Many of these are of Mexican descent. Native Americans are also numerous.

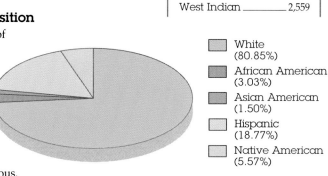

- White (80.85%)
- African American (3.03%)
- Asian American (1.50%)
- Hispanic (18.77%)
- Native American (5.57%)

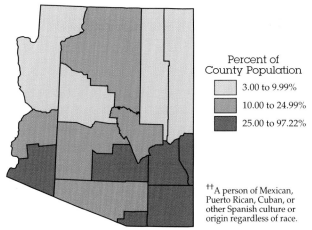

Percent of
County Population

- 3.00 to 9.99%
- 10.00 to 24.99%
- 25.00 to 97.22%

†† A person of Mexican, Puerto Rican, Cuban, or other Spanish culture or origin regardless of race.

Education Facts

Total Students 1990: 607,615	Mean SAT Score 1991 Verbal: 442
Number of School Districts: 238	Mean SAT Score 1991 Math: 490
Expenditure Per Capita on Education 1990: $867	Average Teacher's Salary 1992: $31,200
Expenditure Per Capita K–12 1990: $631	Rank Teacher's Salary: 25th in U.S.
Expenditure Per Pupil 1990: $4,196	High School Graduates 1990: 32,100
Total School Enrollment 1990–1991: 636,500	Total Number of Public Schools: 1,026
Rank of Expenditures Per Student: 38th in the U.S.	Number of Teachers 1990: 33,677
African American Enrollment: 4.1%	Student/Teacher Ratio: 18.9
Hispanic Enrollment: 23.7%	Staff Employed in Public Schools: 61,318
Asian/Pacific Islander Enrollment: 1.5%	Pupil/Staff Ratio: 9.9
Native American Enrollment: 6.6%	Staff/Teacher Ratio: 1.9

Hispanic††

The Hispanic population in Arizona was 688,338 in 1990. This is an increase of 56.19 percent from 440,701 persons in 1980. Hispanics represent the largest minority group in the state. The largest concentrations can be found in the southeastern and southwestern regions of Arizona. Many of these Hispanics are of Mexican descent.

Education

Attainment: 80.6 percent of population 25 years or older were high school graduates in 1989, earning Arizona a ranking of 21st in the United States; 22.2 percent of the state's population had completed college. Institutions of Higher Education: The largest universities and colleges in the state include Arizona State University, Tempe; Northern Arizona University, Flagstaff; University of Arizona, Tucson. Expenditures per Student: Expenditure increased 67% between 1985 and 1990. Projected High School Graduations: 1998 (41,944), 2004 (50,910); Total Revenues for Education from Federal Sources: $186 million; Total Revenues for Education from State Sources: $1.1 billion; Total Revenues for Education from Local Sources: $1 billion; Average Annual Salaries for Public School Principals: $45,542; Largest School Districts in State: Mesa Unified School District, Mesa 61,324 students, 52d in the United States; Tucson Unified District #1, Tucson 55,737, 83d.

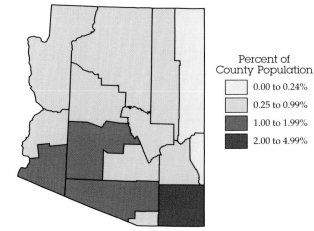

Percent of
County Population

- 0.00 to 0.24%
- 0.25 to 0.99%
- 1.00 to 1.99%
- 2.00 to 4.99%

Asian American

The Asian American population in Arizona was 55,206 in 1990. This is an increase of 141.20 percent from 22,888 persons in 1980. The Asian American population in Arizona is mainly concentrated in Cochise County. Large numbers can also be found in Phoenix and Tucson. Asian Americans represent the fastest-growing group in the state.

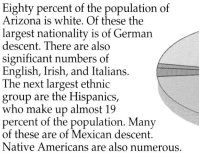

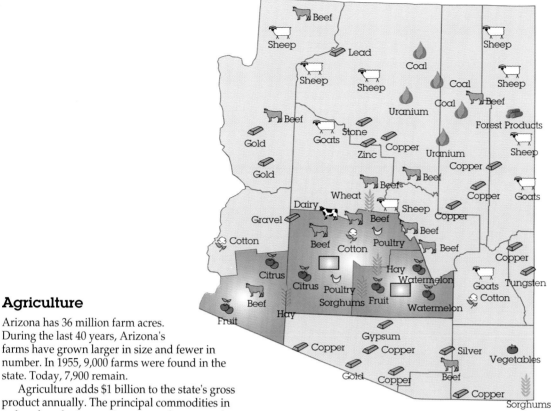

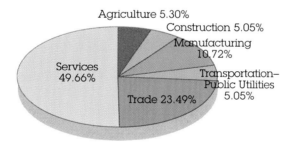

Major manufacturing areas
Major agricultural areas

Agriculture

Arizona has 36 million farm acres. During the last 40 years, Arizona's farms have grown larger in size and fewer in number. In 1955, 9,000 farms were found in the state. Today, 7,900 remain.

Agriculture adds $1 billion to the state's gross product annually. The principal commodities in order of marketing receipts are cattle, cotton, dairy products, and hay.

About 2 percent of Arizona's gross product is derived from agriculture. Crops account for 55 percent of this, and livestock products the rest. Cotton is the leading farm product, produced mainly in the south-central area of the state. Aside from cotton, Arizona is among the nation's leading producers of lettuce and citrus fruits. Beef cattle, raised south of the central mountains, are the largest source of farm income.

Housing

Owner Occupied Units: 1,659,430; Average Age of Units: 19 years; Average Value of Housing Units: $80,100; Renter Occupied Units: 485,781; Median Monthly Rent: $438; Housing Starts: 36,000; Existing Home Sales: 107,900.

Economic Facts

Gross State Product: $65,000,000,000

Income Per Capita: $17,119

Disposable Personal Income: $15,179

Median Household Income: $27,540

Average Annual Pay, 1988: $22,207

Principal Industries: electrical equipment, transportation equipment, machinery

Major Crops: cotton, lettuce, milk, hay, potatoes, citrus, maize, eggs

Fish: N/A

Livestock: cattle, sheep, hogs

Non-Fuel Minerals: Copper, Gold, Silver, Sand, Molybdenum, Stone, Pumice, Gemstones

Organic Fuel Minerals: Coal

Civilian Labor Force: 1,704,000 (Women: 786,000)

Total Employed: 1,608,000 (Women: 747,000)

Median Value of Housing: $80,100

Median Contract Rent: $438 per month

Economic Sectors

Agriculture 5.30%
Construction 5.05%
Manufacturing 10.72%
Transportation–Public Utilities 5.05%
Trade 23.49%
Services 49.66%

Manufacturing

Like many other southwestern states, Arizona's manufacturing sector has grown significantly since World War II. Of the $10 billion that is added value by manufacture, three-quarters occurs in the Phoenix area. Electronic equipment is the state's leading manufactured product. Other goods produced include transportation equipment and machinery.

Phoenix and Tucson lead Arizona's manufacturing sector in terms of goods produced. Factories in these two cities manufacture electronics (semiconductors and radios), transportation equipment (aircraft), and machinery (computers). Motorola, Arizona's largest manufacturing employer, is located in Phoenix. The city of Flagstaff and its surrounding area is becoming of increasing importance to Arizona's manufacturing sector.

Transportation

Arizona has a highly developed and accessible highway system that crosses the state both north-south and east-west. Even Arizona's remote areas are served by rural and Indian routes. Overall, the state has approximately 77,000 miles of highways and roads.

The Sky Harbor International Airport in Phoenix is Arizona's busiest airport. The southern city of Tucson had the nation's first municipal airport, built in 1919. Today, it is the second-busiest in Arizona. Many smaller cities have commuter airfields, serving a large business population. Many people have their own planes.

With many rivers dammed, water transportation in Arizona is virtually obsolete. Many railroads provide freight service to several Arizona cities. Passenger trains also run between larger cities.

Energy and Transportation Facts

Energy. Yearly Consumption: 924 tril. BTUs (residential, 22.2%; commercial, 22.1%; industrial, 19.9%; transportation, 35.8%); Annual Energy Expenditures Per Capita: $1,716; Nuclear Power Plants Located in State: 3; Source of Energy Consumed: Petroleum— 30.1%; Natural Gas— 10.9%; Coal— 29.6%; Hydroelectric Power—6.4%; Nuclear Power—23.0%.

Transportation. Highway Miles: 55,969 (interstates, 1,169; urban, 15,123; rural, 40,846); Average Yearly Auto Insurance: $667 (15th); Auto Fatalities Rank: 9th; Registered Motor Vehicles: 2,800,901; Workers in Carpools: 20.3%; Workers Using Public Trans: 2.1%.

Employment

Employment. Arizona employed 1.72 million people in 1993. Most work in social and personal services (448,000 persons or 26% of the workforce). Wholesale and retail trade account for 22.4% or 385,300 workers. Government employs 285,900 workers (16.6%). Manufacturing jobs employ 174,000 people (10.1%). Construction accounts for 5.1% or 88,500 workers. Transportation and utilities account for 4.5% or 77,600 persons. Agriculture employs 43,100 workers or 2.5%. Finance, real estate, and insurance account for 5.8% or 99,600 workers. Mining employs 12,300 people and accounts for only 0.7% of the work force.

Unemployment. Unemployment has decreased to 6.2% in 1993 from a rate of 6.5% in 1980. Today's figure is lower than the national average of 6.8% as shown below.

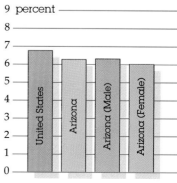

Unemployment Rate

percent

United States | Arizona | Arizona (Male) | Arizona (Female)

ARKANSAS
The State of Arkansas

Official State Seal

The seal of Arkansas in its present form was adopted in 1907. The state motto *"Regnat Populus"* (The People Rule) is printed on the scroll in the eagle's beak. The figure is surrounded by stars representing liberty. The word "Mercy" is printed on an angel on the left and the word "Justice" is printed on the sword on the right. The words "The Great Seal of Arkansas" surround the seal.

Legal Holidays

January: New Year's Day—1st, Robert E. Lee's Birthday—19th; Martin Luther King, Jr. Day—3rd Monday; February: Presidents' Day—3rd Monday; May: Memorial Day—4th Monday; June: Admission Day—15th; July: Independence Day—4th; September: Labor Day—1st Monday; October: Columbus Day—2nd Monday; November: Veterans' Day—11th; Thanksgiving—4th Thursday; December: Christmas—25th.

Official State Flag

Adopted in 1913, Arkansas's flag is made up of a red field with a white diamond. The large stars represent France, Spain, the United States, and the Confederacy. The blue bar and small stars mark Arkansas's order of admission to the Union.

Festivals and Events

February: Eagles Et Cetera, Bismarck; March: Jonquil Fest, Washington; April: Booneville Open Cow Pasture Pool, Booneville; Ozark UFO Conference, Eureka Springs; Spinach Fest, Alma; May: Armadillo Fest, Hamburg; Dermott's Annual Crawfish Festival, Dermott; Riverfest, Little Rock; Magnolia Blossom Fest, Magnolia; June: Bradley County Pink Tomato Fest, Warren; Johnson County Peach Festival, Clarksville; July: Chicken & Egg Festival, Prescott; Grape Festival, Altus; August: Great Arkansas Pig-Out, Morrilton; Mosquito Awareness Weekend, Prescott; Hope Watermelon Fest, Hope; September: Quadrangle Fest, Texarkana; October: Arkansas Oktoberfest, Hot Springs; Frontier Days, Washington; Livin' on the Levee, West Memphis; Wild Turkey Calling Festival, Yellville; November: Duck Calling Contest, Bismarck; December: Arkansas Craft Guild Christmas Show, Little Rock.

Arkansas Compared to States in Its Region.

Resident Pop. in Metro Areas: 4th; Pop. Percent Increase: 3d; Pop. Over 65: 1st; Infant Mortality: 2d; School Enroll. Increase: 1st; High School Grad. and Up: 4th; Violent Crime: 3d; Hazardous Waste Sites: 2d; Unemployment: 3d; Median Household Income: 4th; Persons Below Poverty: 2d; Energy Costs Per Person: 3d.

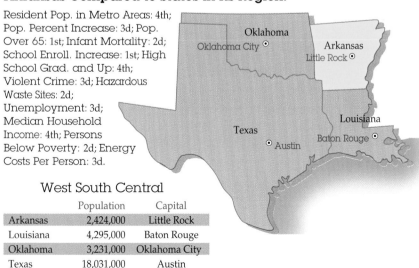

West South Central

	Population	Capital
Arkansas	2,424,000	Little Rock
Louisiana	4,295,000	Baton Rouge
Oklahoma	3,231,000	Oklahoma City
Texas	18,031,000	Austin

Arkansas's Finances

Households: 891,000; Income Per Capita Current Dollars: $15,439; Change Per Capita Income 1980 to 1992: 109.5% (18th in U.S.); State Expenditures: $5,062,000,000; State Revenues: $5,190,000,000; Personal Income Tax: N/A; Federal Income Taxes Paid Per Capita: $1,140; Sales Tax: 4.5% (Prescription drugs exempt).

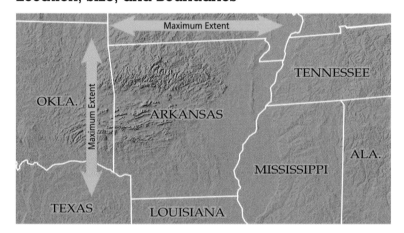

Location, Size, and Boundaries

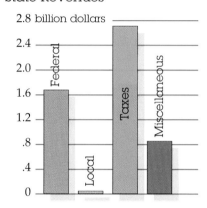

Location. Arkansas is located in the West South Central region of the United States. It is bounded on four sides by land. The geographic center of Arkansas is lat. 34° 48.9' N; long. 92° 18.1' W.

Size. Arkansas is the 27th largest state in terms of size. Its area is 53,104 sq. mi. (137,539 km2). Inland water covers 1,159 sq. mi. (3,002 km2).

Boundaries. Missouri, 331 mi. (533 km); Tennessee, 163 mi. (262 km); Mississippi, 208 mi. (335 km); Louisiana, 166 mi. (267 km); Texas, 102 mi. (164 km); Oklahoma, 198 mi. (319 km).

Geographic Extent. The north/south extent of Arkansas is 240 mi. (386 km). The state extends 275 mi. (443 km) to the east/west.

Facts about Arkansas. Origin of Name: French variant for the Quapaw Indians meaning "downstream people"; Nickname: The Land of Opportunity; Motto: "The People Rule" (*Regnat Populus*); Abbreviations: Ark. (Traditional), AR (postal); State Bird: mockingbird; State Tree: pine tree; State Flower: apple blossom; State Song: "Arkansas," words and music by Mrs. Eva Ware Barnett.

Arkansas Compared to Other States. Resident Pop. in Metro Areas: 39th; Pop. Percent Increase: 29th; Pop. Over 65: 6th; Infant Mort.: 22d; School Enroll. Increase: 34th; High School Grad. and Up: 47th; Violent Crime: 22d; Haz. Waste Sites: 28th; Unemployment: 21st; Median Household Income: 48th; Persons Below Poverty: 5th; Energy Costs Per Person: 15th.

Sources of Information. Tourism: Department of Parks and Tourism, 1 Capitol Mall, Little Rock, AR 72201. Economy, Government & History: Secretary of State's Office, Information Services, State Capitol, Little Rock, AR 72201.

Legend

⭐ State capitol

⊙ Cities over 35,000 population

○ Other significant cities

● County Seats

◼ Major cultural attractions

◻ State Parks

🆆 Welcome Centers

⛪ Major colleges and universities

Major Cities

Arkadelphia	I-5	Magnolia	L-4
Benton	H-6	North Little Rock	G-7
Bentonville	A-1	Paragould	C-12
Blytheville	C-13	Pine Bluff	I-7
Camden	K-5	Rogers	B-2
Conway	F-7	Russellville	E-5
El Dorado	J-7	Searcy	E-8
Fayetteville	C-1	Sherwood	G-7
Forrest City	F-11	Springdale	B-1
Fort Smith	E-1	Stuttgart	H-9
Hot Springs	H-5	Texarkana	L-2
Jacksonville	G-7	Van Buren	E-1
Jonesboro	D-11	West Memphis	F-13
Little Rock	G-7		

◼ **Arkansas Post National Memorial.** Site of first permanent settlement in lower Mississippi Valley, established by Henri de Tonti in 1686. (J-9)

◼ **Bauxite.** Once the center of U.S. aluminum production; museum with displays from early days of mining town. (H-6)

◼ **Blanchard Springs Caverns.** Underground river; crystalline formations; only cave system in the nation operated by the U.S. Forest Service. (C-7)

◼ **Confederate State Capitol.** In Washington; state capitol during American Civil War (1863–65); built in 1833. (K-3)

◼ **Crater of Diamonds State Park.** Only diamond-bearing field open to public in North America. (J-3)

◼ **Eureka Springs.** One of the fine art centers of the mid-South; antique and craft center; also a picturesque health resort, with more than 60 springs in city. (A-3)

◼ **Fort Smith National Historic Site.** United States military post from 1817–1871; "Hangin' Judge" Isaac C. Parker's courtroom, reproduction of the 1886 gallows, the "Hell on the Border" jail, and the 1846 Commissary Storehouse. (E-1)

◼ **Hampson Museum State Park.** Artifacts of the prehistoric Indian Mound Builders. (D-13)

◼ **Herman Davis Memorial.** One-acre state park and monument commemorates World War I hero Herman Davis. (C-13)

◼ **Hot Springs National Park.** Adjoins town of Hot Springs (boyhood home of Bill Clinton) in Ouachita Mountains; numerous therapeutic mineral hot springs and bathhouses. (H-5)

◼ **Jacksonport.** Early settlement on White River; old courthouse converted to museum. (D-9)

◼ **Lake Chicot State Park.** Popular fishing and birding park located on the shores of state's largest natural lake. (L-10)

◼ **Mammoth Spring.** One of world's largest springs; 10-million-gallon-per-hour outflow of 58-degree water; pour-off creates Spring River. (A-9)

◼ **Prairie Grove Battlefield.** Commemorates 1862 Civil War battle; 130 acres of battlefields, monuments, and a museum; battle reenactments. (C-1)

◼ **Wolf House.** Built in 1809; oldest two-story log structure in Arkansas; furnished with primitive antiques. (B-7)

Weather Facts

Record High Temperature: 120° F (49° C) on August 10,1936, at Ozark; Record Low Tem–perature: -29° F (-34° C) on February 13, 1905, in Benton County; Average January Temperature: 39° F (4° C); Average July Temperature: 82° F (28° C); Average Yearly Precipitation: 49 in. (124 cm).

Environmental Facts

Air Pollution Rank: 24th; Water Pollution Rank: 17th; Total Yearly Industrial Pollution: 31,772,497 lbs.; Industrial Pollution Rank: 25th; Hazardous Waste Sites: 10; Hazardous Sites Rank: 32d; Landfill Capacity: adequate; Fresh Water Supply: surplus; Daily Residential Water Consumption: 150 gals. per capita; Endangered Species: Aquatic Species (12)—crayfish, cave; Birds (3)—eagle, bald; Mammals (3)—bat, gray; Other Species

Environmental Quality

Arkansas residents generate 1.8 million tons of solid waste each year, or approximately 1,500 pounds per capita. Landfill capacity in Arkansas will be exhausted in 5 to 10 years. The state has 11 hazardous waste sites. Annual greenhouse gas emissions in Arkansas total 62.4 million tons, or 26.0 tons per capita. Industrial sources in Arkansas release approximately 40.4 thousand tons of toxins, 218 thousand tons of acid precipitation-producing substances, and 1.1 million tons of smog-producing substances into the atmosphere each year.

The state has 99,600 acres within the National Park System; the largest area within the state is Hot Springs National Park. State parks cover just over 44,000 acres, attracting 6.9 million visitors per year.

Arkansas spends approximately 1.2 percent of its budget, or approximately $18 per capita, on environmental and natural resources. Arkansas representatives in the U.S. House voted in favor of national environmental legislation 35 percent of the time, while U.S. senators did so 54 percent of the time.

Physical Regions: (a) Ozark Plateau; (b) Ouachita Mountains; (c) Arkansas Valley; (d) Mississippi Alluvial Plain; (e) West Gulf Coastal Plain.

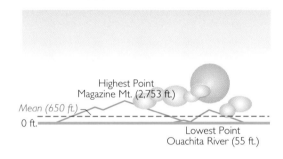

Land Use

Cropland: 27.4%; Pasture: 19%; Rangeland: 0.5%; Forest: 11.7%; Urban: 2.6%; Other: 6.5%.

For more information about Arkansas's environment, contact the Department of Pollution Control and Ecology, 8001 National Dr., P.O. Box 9538, Little Rock, AR 72219.

Topography

There are several distinct physical regions in Arkansas. The northwestern region of Arkansas consists of two highlands areas. In the northwest are the Boston Mountains, the southernmost reach of the heavily forested Ozark Plateau topographical region. The soil found here is warm and moist, as it is throughout Arkansas. Color is predominantly red/yellow, with low organic content. South of this region are the Ouachita Mountains, a range containing ridges and valleys and known for its hot springs (the town of Hot Springs is located on its eastern edge). These two mountainous areas are divided by the Arkansas River valley. Although this area is a lowland, it contains several mountain peaks, including the highest in the state: Magazine Mountain rises 2,753 ft. (839 m).

The rest of the state consists of lowlands. The Mississippi Alluvial Plain region is a mostly level plain that covers all of eastern Arkansas. It is a fertile area, fed by the Mississippi River and its tributaries, where much of Arkansas's agriculture is located. Soil here is considered warm and wet. Soil color ranges from light to black and is high in organic content. In south-central and southwestern Arkansas lies the West Gulf Coastal Plain. This is also a lowland area, and supports some of the state's agriculture. Soil in this region is a dark brown forest type.

Climate

Arkansas, one of the southern states, has a moist and mild climate. Warm to hot summers and cool winters characterize this climatic type. The highland region of the north is slightly cooler overall than more low-lying, southern areas. Little Rock, the capital, has average January and July temperatures of 40 degrees F and 81 degrees F. Farther north, in the Ozark Mountains area, temperatures for January and July average 38 degrees F and 79 degrees F.

Most of Arkansas's 49 inches of annual precipitation falls during the winter and spring. The Ouachita Mountain region receives the most rainfall—an average of 54 inches a year. The north-central region above Little Rock receives less than average precipitation—only 42 inches annually.

Tornadoes are fairly common in Arkansas, and usually occur in the spring. The extreme northwest and southeast parts of the state are most prone to these twisters.

Hydrology

The longest river within the state is the Arkansas. It flows southeast across the middle of the state for 1,485 miles (2,388 km) before emptying into the Mississippi River. The Mississippi forms Arkansas's entire eastern boundary with the states of Tennessee and Mississippi. The White River begins at Bull Shoals Lake in the north-central part of the state near its border with Missouri, and flows southeast into the Mississippi. Other important rivers include the Ouachita and Saline rivers, which join in south-central Arkansas, and the Red River in the southwestern corner of the state.

Lake Ouachita, the state's largest at about 60 sq. mi. (155 sq. km), is an artificial lake. There are also several large natural lakes. The largest of these is Lake Chicot, an oxbow of the Mississippi in southeastern Arkansas. Others include Lake Maumelle and Nimrod Lake.

Average Monthly Weather

Little Rock	Jan	Feb	Mar	Apr	May	Jun	Jul	Aug	Sep	Oct	Nov	Dec	Yearly
Maximum Temperature °F	49.8	54.5	63.2	73.8	81.7	89.5	92.7	92.3	85.6	75.8	62.4	53.2	72.9
Minimum Temperature °F	29.9	33.6	41.2	50.9	59.2	67.5	71.4	69.6	63.0	50.4	40.0	33.2	50.8
Days of Precipitation	9.4	9.1	10.1	10.1	10.0	8.3	8.2	7.0	7.3	6.7	8.2	9.1	103.6

Flora and Fauna

The state of Arkansas is approximately half covered with forests, the majority of which are hardwood forests. White elm, oak, and ash trees, all hardwoods, grow predominately in the Mississippi alluvial plain and the highlands. Softwood forests consisting chiefly of pine trees are found on the west Gulf coastal plain. Arkansas's flowering trees include the dogwood, red haw, and locust. Many types of wildflowers are native to the state. The Woodsia scopulina, a fern, only grows in the Rocky and Allegheny mountain ranges in Arkansas. Other wildflowers include yellow jasmine, passionflowers, water lilies, and orchids.

Arkansas has many different species of fauna living within its borders. Bobcats, deer, weasels, squirrels, and minks all live throughout the state. Arkansas is home for many different species of game birds, including the wild species of geese, ducks, and turkeys. Songbirds, such as the mockingbird and the whippoorwill, also live in Arkansas. Snakes, lizards, and other types of reptiles also call Arkansas home, as do turtles. Arkansas streams, rivers, and lakes host a variety of fish, including perch, drum, and sturgeon.

Arkansas's History

Arkansas's First People

The first human occupants of Arkansas were two early tribes dating back to about 10,000 B.C. The Bluff-Dwellers in the northwestern part of the state made their homes in caves and beneath the cliffs of the Boston and Ouachita mountains (the only mountains between the Appalachians and the Rockies) along the White River of the Ozark Plateau. A couple thousand years later and farther to the south, the Mound Builders, leaving Stone Age monuments (such as those of the Toltec group found near Little Rock), settled along the Mississippi River.

By the time the first Europeans arrived these tribes had disappeared and in their place were the agrarian Quapaw in the south; the warlike Caddo in the west and south; another tribe of warriors, the Ozark, who lived to the north of the Arkansas River; and the Chickasaw and Choctaw in the northeast.

European Exploration

The Spaniards arrived in Arkansas in 1541, led by Hernando de Soto. They explored the central and southern part of the state for about a year before the death of de Soto in 1542. In 1673, Jacques Marquette and Louis Jolliet traveled the Mississippi River as far south as the Arkansas River, and in 1682 René-Robert Cavelier, Sieur de La Salle, followed the Mississippi to its mouth. He claimed the Mississippi Valley for Louis XIV of France, calling the territory Louisiana. Four years later, Henri de Tonti established what became known as the Arkansas Post, the first permanent white settlement in Arkansas, near the mouth of the Arkansas River. In 1717, John Law founded a colony at Arkansas Post with the idea of developing the Mississippi Valley, but the scheme failed four years later as 1,300 colonists abandoned the experiment.

In 1762, France ceded the territory west of the Mississippi (including Arkansas) to the Spanish, who renamed Arkansas Post Fort Charles III. France reclaimed the territory in 1800 and three years later sold it to the United States as part of the Louisiana Purchase.

Statehood

Three years after the Louisiana Purchase, the District of Arkansas was created out of the Louisiana Territory. In 1812, it became part of the Missouri Territory (a subdivision of the Louisiana Territory). In 1819, Congress bestowed territorial status on Arkansas and established its boundaries. The capital was moved from Arkansas Post to Little Rock in 1821. Arkansas Territory acted as a trans–portation corridor during the 1830s. At this time, many Indian tribes living in the East were forced from their homes to make room for increased settlement. They were to be moved to lands west of Arkansas Territory to govern-ment-established Indian Territories. Peoples such as the Chickasaw and the Choctaw crossed through Arkansas on their way west. In 1836, Arkansas was admitted to the Union as the twenty-fifth state, a slave state.

On the eve of the Civil War (March 1861), a state convention voted against secession from the Union, but two months later (and one month after the beginning of the war), by a 69–1 vote, the convention decided to secede. Arkansas saw military action during the Civil War. One of the worst battles to take place in the state occurred at Elkhorn Tavern (Pea Ridge) on March 1862. Union forces were victorious over the Confederates in this battle. By 1864, Arkansas was split with the Union controlling the northern half with their capital at Little Rock and the Confederates controlling the southern half with their capital at Washington.

After the war a Unionist convention abolished slavery and wrote a new state constitution, but in 1866, a newly elected legislature comprised mainly of ex-secessionists passed laws denying rights and privileges to recently emancipated blacks. In reaction to this, Congress passed the Reconstruction Act in 1867, voiding the government of Arkansas and other southern states. After adopting a new state constitution reenfranchising blacks in 1868, Arkansas was readmitted to the Union.

Industrialization

Cotton was first commercially grown in Arkansas in 1800 and remained a primary component of the state's economy throughout the nineteenth century. Railroad construction during this period aided in the expansion of this and other agricultural endeavors. A severe flood of the Mississippi and Arkansas rivers in 1927 and droughts in the 1930s lowered prices for cotton and devastated the industry.

After the Depression there was a recovery in agriculture, and during World War II, with the establishment of military bases and manufacturing industries such as bauxite production, Arkansas was able to expand its economy. The chief industrial centers in the state are Little Rock, Pine Bluff, and Fort Smith. Although it continues to attract new industries, Arkansas remains one of the poorest states in the nation.

Civil Rights

In September 1957, Gov. Orval Faubus called out the National Guard to block the entrance of nine black students trying to integrate Little Rock's Central High School under the 1954 Supreme Court decision (*Brown v. Board of Education*) outlawing segregation. President Eisenhower responded by calling in federal troops to enforce a federal court order mandating the desegregation. The next year, Faubus attempted to close the public schools to prevent integration, but they reopened in 1959 with several black pupils. A decade later half the state's black pupils were attending public schools and by the end of the 1970s blacks had unrestricted access to all public school institutions.

Important Events

1541 De Soto explores the Mississippi region of Arkansas.

1673 Jolliet and Marquette explore the Mississippi River to the mouth of the Arkansas River.

1682 La Salle travels the Mississippi to its mouth and claims the territory for France.

1686 First white settlement is established at Arkansas Post.

1762 Arkansas, as part of the Louisiana Territory, is ceded to Spain.

1800 France wins back control of the territory.

1803 United States gains control of Arkansas with the Louisiana Purchase.

1819 Arkansas is made a territory by Congress.

1821 Little Rock is established as the capital.

1836 Arkansas enters the Union as the twenty-fifth state.

1861 Arkansas secedes from the Union.

1864 Union adopts a new constitution for the state, abolishing slavery.

1866 Ex Confederate legislature passes laws denying basic rights to the black population.

1867 United States takes control of the state government and passes a constitution enfranchising blacks.

1868 Arkansas is readmitted to the Union.

1874 Adoption of a new constitution guaranteeing full rights to all whites and blacks ends the period of Reconstruction.

1891 Jim Crow legislation is passed, segregating rail stations and coaches.

1921 Petroleum is discovered near El Dorado.

1928 The teaching of the theory of evolution is banned.

1930 Severe drought hits the state.

1931 The first woman in the U.S. Senate, Hattie Caraway, is elected.

1966 Winthrop Rockefeller becomes the first Republican governor since Reconstruction.

1992 Bill Clinton, former governor of Arkansas, is elected President of the United States.

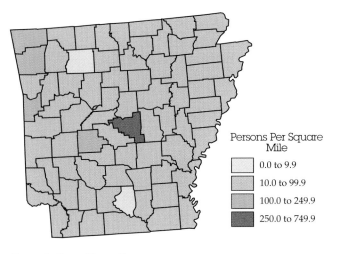

Persons Per Square Mile
- 0.0 to 9.9
- 10.0 to 99.9
- 100.0 to 249.9
- 250.0 to 749.9

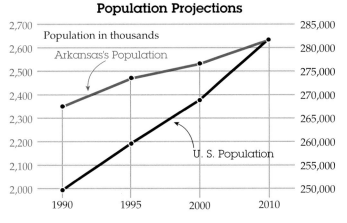

Population Projections

Population in thousands

Arkansas's Population

U. S. Population

Year	Population
1950	1,910,000
1960	1,789,000
1970	1,932,000
1980	2,286,435
1990	2,350,725
2000	2,529,000
2010	2,624,000

Population Change

Period	Change
1950–1970	1.2%
1970–1980	18.3%
1980–1990	2.8%
1990–2000	7.6%

Population Density

Population density for the state of Arkansas was 45.1 persons per square mile in 1990 (17.4 per km2). Average U.S. density was 70.3 persons per square mile in 1990 (27.3 per km2). Habitation is most dense around the urban areas with Little Rock being the most densely populated.

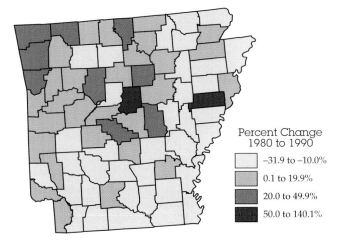

Percent Change 1980 to 1990
- −31.9 to −10.0%
- 0.1 to 19.9%
- 20.0 to 49.9%
- 50.0 to 140.1%

Population Change

The 1990 population figure for the state of Arkansas was 2,350,725. This is a 2.81 percent increase from 2,286,435 in 1980. The next decade will show growth with a population of 2.5 million or a 7.58 percent increase. The area of fastest growth is the northwestern corner of the state and the counties outside Memphis, Tennessee.

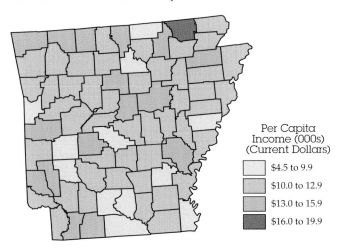

Per Capita Income (000s) (Current Dollars)
- $4.5 to 9.9
- $10.0 to 12.9
- $13.0 to 15.9
- $16.0 to 19.9

Distribution of Income

The per capita income for the state of Arkansas (current dollars) was $15,439 in 1992. This is a 109.5 percent increase from $7,371 in 1980. Income in Arkansas is distributed equally throughout the state with very few high-income areas that can be seen on the county level.

Population Facts

State Population, 1993: 2,424,000

Rank: 33

Population 2000: 2,529,000 (Rank 32)

Density: 45.1 per sq. mi. (17.4 per km²)

Distribution: 53.5% urban, 46.5% rural

Population Under 5 Years Old: 7.1%

Population Under 18 Years Old: 26.2%

Population Over 65 Years Old: 14.9%

Median Age: 33.8

Number of Households: 891,000

Average Persons Per Household: 2.57

Average Persons Per Family: 3.06

Female Heads of Households: 4.21%

Population That Is Married: 22.43%

Birth Rate: 15.5 per 1,000 population

Death Rate: 10.5 per 1,000 population

Births to Teen Mothers: 19.7%

Marriage Rate: 14.8 per 1,000 population

Divorce Rate: 6.9 per 1,000 population

Violent Crime Rate: 593 per 100,000 pop.

Population on Social Security: 19.9%

Percent Voting for President: 53.8%

Population Profile

Rank. Arkansas ranks 33d among U.S. states in terms of population with 2,424,000 citizens.

Minority Population. The state's minority population is 17.8 percent. The state's male to female ratio for 1990 was 93.05 males for every 100 females. It was below the national average of 95.22 males for every 100 females.

Growth. Growing slower than the projected national average, the state's population is

Government

Capital: Little Rock (established 1821).

Statehood: Became 25th state on Jun. 15, 1836.

Number of Counties: 75.

Supreme Court Justices: 7, 8-year term.

State Senators: 35, 4-year term.

State Legislators: 100, 2-year term.

United States Senators: 2.

United States Representatives: 4.

Electoral Votes: 6.

State Constitution: Adopted 1874.

Arkansas's Famous Citizens

Anthony, Katherine (1877–1965). Writer of biographies of famous women, including Catherine the Great and Dolley Madison.

Campbell, Glen (b. 1936). Country singer-songwriter. Had many hits in the 1960s and 1970s, including "Gentle on My Mind."

Caraway, Hattie (1878–1950). First woman ever elected to the U.S. Senate (initially appointed to finish her husband's term).

Clinton, William Jefferson (b. 1946). Democrat. Long time Arkansas governor elected 42d president of the United States on November 3, 1992.

Dean, Dizzy (1911–1974). Hall of Fame baseball pitcher. Helped the St. Louis Cardinals win the World Series in 1934.

Fulbright, J. William (1905–1995). U.S. senator from 1945 to 1975. Opposed the Vietnam War and established the Fulbright scholarship.

Johnson, John H. (b. 1918). Publisher. Founded *Ebony* magazine, aimed at an African-American audience, in 1945.

Rose, Uriah (1834–1913). Served as president of the Arkansas and American bar associations.

expected to reach 2.6 million by the year 2010 (*see graph above*).

Older Citizens. The state's population older than 65 was 350,058 in 1990. It grew 12.03% from 312,477 in 1980.

Younger Citizens. The number of children (under 18 years of age) was 621 thousand in 1990. This represents 26.4 percent of the state's population. The state's school aged population was 434 thousand in 1990. It is expected to increase to 441 thousand by the year 2000. This represents a 1.61% change.

Urban/Rural. 53.5% of the population of the state live in urban areas while 46.5% live in rural areas.

Largest Cities. Arkansas has six cities with a population greater than 35,000. The populations of the state's largest centers are (starting from the most populous) Little Rock (175,795), Fort Smith (72,798), North Little Rock (61,741), Pine Bluff (57,140), Jonesboro (46,535), Fayetteville (42,099), Hot Springs (32,462), Springdale (29,941), Jacksonville (29,101), Conway (26,481), Rogers (24,692), El Dorado (23, 146), Blytheville (22,906), Texarkana (22,631), and Russellville (21,260).

Arkansas

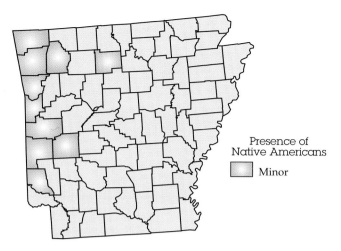

Native American

The Native American population in Arkansas was 12,773 in 1990. This was an increase of 0.47 percent from 12,713 in 1980. The Native American population, although growing slowly, is growing twice as fast as the African American population in the state.

Presence of Native Americans

☐ Minor

Nationalities 1990

African	2,096
American	314,204
Arab	1,501
Austrian	1,160
Czech	3,427
Dutch	41,661
English	213,211
Finnish	657
German	321,428
Greek	1,983
Hungarian	1,438
Irish	288,364
Italian	20,482
Norwegian	5,898
Polish	12,015
Portuguese	906
Russian	1,541
Scottish	23,630
Slovak	2,775
Swedish	10,510
Welsh	6,902
West Indian	1,938

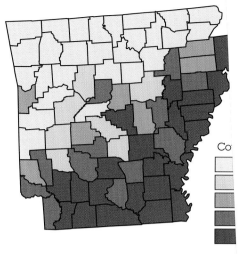

African American

The African American population in Arkansas was 3...
This was an increase of 0.24 percent from 373,025 in...
American population is concentrated in a band along...
River from West Memphis down to Texarkana on the...

Statewide Ethnic Composition

Over 80 percent of the population is white. Of these many consider themselves of German descent. Slightly more than 314,000 people claim to be American and acknowledge no other nationality. The next largest ethnic group is African Americans, of which only 2,000 consider themselves of African descent.

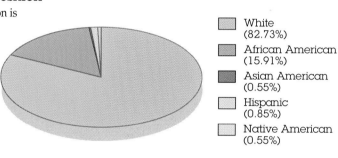

☐ White (82.73%)
☐ African American (15.91%)
☐ Asian American (0.55%)
☐ Hispanic (0.85%)
☐ Native American (0.55%)

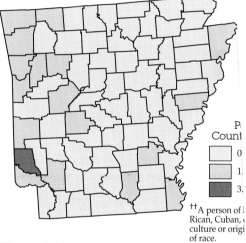

Hispanic ††

The Hispanic population in Arkansas was 19,876 in 199...
increase of 11.01 percent from 17,904 persons in 1980. Th...
concentration of Hispanics can be found in such areas s...
Memphis and Sevier County.

†† A person of ...
Rican, Cuban, ...
culture or origi...
of race.

Education Facts

Total Students 1990: 43,496	Mean SAT Score 1991 Verbal: 482
Number of School Districts: 329	Mean SAT Score 1991 Math: 523
Expenditure Per Capita on Education 1990: $621	Average Teacher's Salary 1992: $26,600
Expenditure Per Capita K–12 1990: $558	Rank Teacher's Salary: 44th in U.S.
Expenditure Per Pupil 1990: $3,419	High School Graduates 1990: 27,300
Total School Enrollment 1990–1991: 436,460	Total Number of Public Schools: 1,097
Rank of Expenditures Per Student: 47th in the U.S.	Number of Teachers 1990: 25,674
African American Enrollment: 24.0%	Student/Teacher Ratio: 17.0
Hispanic Enrollment: 0.4%	Staff Employed in Public Schools: 49,401
Asian/Pacific Islander Enrollment: 0.6%	Pupil/Staff Ratio: 8.8
Native American Enrollment: 0.2%	Staff/Teacher Ratio: 1.9

Education

Attainment: 67.6 percent of population 25 years or older were high school graduates in 1989, earning Arkansas a ranking of 47th in the United States; 14.8 percent of the state's population had completed college. Institutions of Higher Education: The largest universities and colleges in the state include the University of Arkansas, Fayetteville (other campuses at Little Rock, Monticello, and Pine Bluff). Expenditures per Student: Expenditure increased 76% between 1985 and 1990. Projected High School Graduations: 1998 (28,234), 2004 (26,032); Total Revenues for Education from Federal Sources: $133 million; Total Revenues for Education from State Sources: $682 million; Total Revenues for Education from Local Sources: $396 million; Average Annual Salaries for Public School Principals: $32,359; Largest School Districts in State Little Rock School District 26,057 students, 52d in the United States.

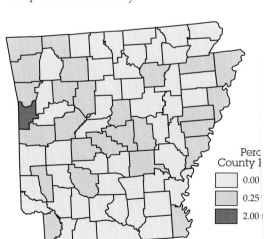

Asian American

The Asian American population in Arkansas was 12,530 in...
is an increase of 79.20 percent from 6,992 persons in 1980. T...
concentration of Asian Americans in Arkansas can be foun...
Sebastian County in and around the city of Fort Smith.

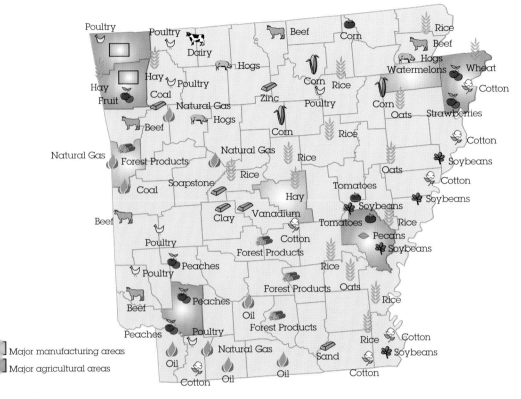

Poultry Poultry Dairy Beef Corn Rice Beef
Hogs Watermelons Hogs Wheat
Hay Poultry Corn Rice Cotton
Hay Fruit Coal Zinc Poultry Corn Oats Strawberries
Natural Gas Hogs Rice Cotton
Beef Natural Gas Rice Oats Soybeans
Natural Gas Forest Products Rice Cotton
Coal Soapstone Rice Tomatoes Soybeans
Hay Soybeans
Beef Clay Vanadium Tomatoes Rice Pecans
Poultry Cotton Soybeans
Forest Products Rice
Poultry Peaches Forest Products Oats Rice
Peaches Oil
Beef Peaches Forest Products
Poultry Rice Cotton
Natural Gas Sand Soybeans
Oil Oil Oil Cotton
Cotton

] Major manufacturing areas
] Major agricultural areas

riculture

insas has 15.4 million farm acres. During the last forty years, Arkansas farms have vn larger in size and fewer in number. In 1955, 145,000 farms were found in the ... Today, 46,000 remain.

\griculture adds $2 billion to the state's gross product annually. The principal modities in order of marketing receipts are broilers, soybeans, rice, and cotton. .ivestock products account for about two-thirds of the state's farm income.

insas leads the nation in the production of broilers (chickens between five and 12 ks old), chiefly in the northwestern part of the state. Soybeans, grown mainly in the , are the chief crop, followed by rice. Farmers sometimes raise fish in their flooded fields. Cotton and wheat are other leading crops.

using

ner Occupied Units: 1,000,667; Average Age Inits: 24 years; Average Value of Housing ts: $46,300; Renter Occupied Units: 258,065; dian Monthly Rent: $328; Housing Starts: 00; Existing Home Sales: 52,800.

onomic Facts

iss State Product: $38,000,000,000
ome Per Capita: $15,439
posable Personal Income: $13,879
dian Household Income: $21,147
erage Annual Pay, 1988: $19,008
icipal Industries: electrical equipment, food products, fabricated metal products, machinery, paper products, petroleum processing, clothing, metals, lumber products
jor Crops: rice, soybeans, eggs, cotton
h: Bass, Catfish, Crappies, Sturgeon, Trout
restock: chickens, cattle, turkeys, cattle, hogs
n-Fuel Minerals: Bromine, Stone, Bauxite, Vanadium, Clay, Lime, Gravel, Sand
ganic Fuel Minerals: Petroleum, Nat. Gas, Coal
vilian Labor Force: 1,118,000 (Women: 510,000)
tal Employed: 1,036,000 (Women: 472,000)
dian Value of Housing: $46,300
dian Contract Rent: $328 per month

Economic Sectors

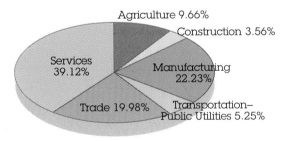

Agriculture 9.66%
Construction 3.56%
Services 39.12%
Manufacturing 22.23%
Trade 19.98%
Transportation–Public Utilities 5.25%

Manufacturing

Manufacturing employs more workers in the state of Arkansas than any other economic sector. Manufacturing industries account for approximately one-fourth of the state gross product. Food products comprise the majority of the goods produced in the state; however, Arkansas also manufactures electrical equipment, fabricated metal products, and printed materials.

Much of Arkansas's industry is concentrated in the Little Rock area. Food products, including canned vegetables and rice, are produced in this area, as well as in Fort Smith. Electrical equipment is produced in both Little Rock and Fort Smith, and also in Jonesboro and Jacksonville. Recently, chemical-processing industries have begun to develop in the state.

Transportation

Arkansas's earliest residents built settlements along rivers. Today, rivers still remain important transportation routes. A federal project begun in 1970 enables freight to move along the Mississippi River between Arkansas and Oklahoma. Arkansas river ports include Little Rock and Fort Smith. Arkansas has approximately 77,000 miles of roads and highways. An extensive system of federal, state, and county roads covers the state. Interstate highways 40 and 30 are Arkansas's most traveled highways.

At one time, freight railroads ran throughout Arkansas. However, since the 1940s, freight service has continually declined. Amtrak, the national passenger railroad, connects several Arkansas cities from Little Rock to Texarkana. Little Rock has Arkansas's main airport.

Energy and Transportation Facts

Energy. Yearly Consumption: 770 tril. BTUs (residential, 21.7%; commercial, 13.6%; industrial, 34.8%; transportation, 29.9%); Annual Energy Expenditures Per Capita: $1,975; Nuclear Power Plants Located in State: 2; Source of Energy Consumed: Petroleum— 31.0%; Natural Gas— 24.4%; Coal— 24.7%; Hydroelectric Power—4.2%; Nuclear Power—15.6%.

Transportation. Highway Miles: 77,162 (interstates, 542; urban, 7,691; rural, 69,471); Average Yearly Auto Insurance: $424 (43d); Auto Fatalities Rank: 2d; Registered Motor Vehicles: 1,501,480; Workers in Carpools: 20.0%; Workers Using Public Trans: 0.5%.

Employment

Employment. Arkansas employed 1.09 million people in 1993. Most work in manufacturing jobs (243,200 persons or 22.3% of the workforce). Wholesale and retail trade account for 20.1% or 219,500 workers. Government employs 169,400 workers (15.5%). Social and personal services employ 219,500 people (20.1%). Construction accounts for 3.4% or 37,300 workers. Transportation and utilities account for 5.2% or 56,800 persons. Agriculture employs 53,500 workers or 4.9%. Finance, real estate, and insurance account for 3.7% or 40,200 workers. Mining employs 3,600 people and accounts for only 0.3% of the workforce.

Unemployment. Unemployment has decreased to 6.2% in 1993 from a rate of 8.7% in 1985. Today's figure is lower than the national average of 6.8% as shown below.

Unemployment Rate

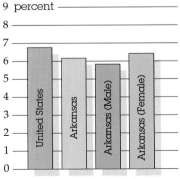

9 percent
8
7
6
5
4
3
2
1
0

United States
Arkansas
Arkansas (Male)
Arkansas (Female)

CALIFORNIA
The State of California

Official State Seal

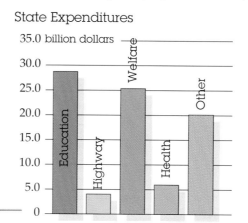

The Great Seal of California was adopted in 1849. The thirty-one stars along the top of the seal represent California's order of admission to the United States. The state motto "Eureka" is written beneath the stars. The goddess Minerva sits in the foreground with a grizzly bear (the state animal). Also included is a harbor surrounded by mountains and ships.

Legal Holidays

January: New Year's Day—1st; California Gold Discovery Anniversary—24th; Martin Luther King, Jr., Day—3d Monday; February: Presidents' Day—3d Monday; March: Bang Clang Day, Los Angeles—9th; April: Admission Day—9th; Cabrillo Day—28th; May: Memorial Day—4th Monday; July: Independence Day—4th; September: Labor Day—1st Monday; October: Columbus Day—2nd Monday; November: Veterans' Day—11th; Thanksgiving—4th Thursday; December: Christmas—25th.

Official State Flag

The state flag of California was adopted in 1911. The bear flag is based on the old flag of the California Republic that flew from June to July of 1846. The grizzly bear represents strength, while the single star represents sovereignty. The white background represents purity.

Festivals and Events

January: Chinese New Year Festival, San Francisco; February: Chinese New Year Golden Dragon Parade, Los Angeles; National Date Festival, Indio; March: Ocean Beach Kite Fest, San Diego; April: Cherry Blossom Festival, Lodi, San Francisco; Pier 39 Street Performers Festival, San Francisco; May: America's International Dixieland Jazz Festival, Sacramento; Jumping Frog Jubilee, Angel Camp; June: Jalapeño Eating Contest, Yreka; Napa Valley Wine Auction, Napa Valley; July: All-American Waterfest, Stockton; August: Old Adobe Festival, Petaluma; Venice Summer Arts & Crafts Fest, Venice; September: Cabrillo Fest, San Diego; Monterey Jazz Festival, Monterey; Vacaville Onion Fest, Vacaville; October: Brussels Sprout Fest, Santa Cruz; Heritage Parade & Festival, Placentia; November: Mother Goose Parade, El Cajon; Yosemite Winter's Holidays, Yosemite National Park; San Diego International Boat Show, San Diego; December: Flossie Beadle Week, Lakeside.

California Compared to States in Its Region.

Resident Pop. in Metro Areas: 1st; Pop. Percent Increase: 5th; Pop. Over 65: 4th; Infant Mortality: 3d; School Enroll. Increase: 2d; High School Grad. and Up: 5th; Violent Crime: 1st; Hazardous Waste Sites: 1st; Unemployment: 1st; Median Household Income: 3d; Persons Below Poverty: 1st; Energy Costs Per Person: 5th.

Pacific Region

	Population	Capital
Washington	5,255,000	Olympia
Oregon	3,032,000	Salem
California	31,211,000	Sacramento
Alaska	599,000	Juneau
Hawaii	1,172,000	Honolulu

California's Finances

Households: 10,381,000; Income Per Capita Current Dollars: $21,278; Change Per Capita Income 1980 to 1992: 82.2% (44th in U.S.); State Expenditures: $83,360,000,000; State Revenues: $79,399,000,000; Personal Income Tax: 1 to 11%; Federal Income Taxes Paid Per Capita: $2,129; Sales Tax: 6% (food and prescription drugs exempt).

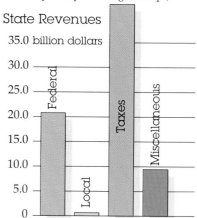

State Expenditures — bar chart (billion dollars): Education, Highway, Welfare, Health, Other

State Revenues — bar chart (billion dollars): Federal, Local, Taxes, Miscellaneous

Location, Size, and Boundaries

Location. California is located in the southwest Pacific region of the United States. It is bounded on three of four sides by land with a large coastline bordering the Pacific Ocean to the west. The geographic center of California is lat. 36° 57.9' N; long. 120° 4.9' W.

Size. California is the 3d largest state in terms of size behind Alaska and Texas. Its area is 158,869 sq. mi. (411,471 km2). Inland water covers 2,332 sq. mi. (6,040 km2).

Boundaries. Oregon, 220 mi. (354 km); Nevada, 612 mi. (985 km); Mexican state of Baja California, 144 mi. (232 km); Pacific Ocean, 840 mi. (1,352 km).

Geographic Extent. The north/south extent of California is 780 mi. (1,255 km). The state extends 350 mi. (560 km) to the east/west.

Facts about California. Origin of Name: Named by Spanish explorers after an island in a popular Spanish story; Nickname: The Golden State; Motto: "Eureka" (I Have Found It); Abbreviations: Calif. (traditional), CA (postal); State Bird: California valley quail; State Tree: California redwood; State Flower: Golden poppy; State Song: "I Love You, California," words by F. B. Silverwood, music by A. F. Frankenstein.

California Compared to Other States. Resident Pop. in Metro Areas: 2d; Pop. Percent Increase: 14th; Pop. Over 65: 45th; Infant Mortality: 41st; School Enroll. Increase: 8th; High School Grad. and Up: 28th; Violent Crime: 3d; Hazardous Waste Sites: 3d; Unemployment: 2d; Med. Household Income: 8th; Persons Below Poverty: 23d; Energy Costs Per Person: 45th.

Sources of Information. Tourism: California Office of Tourism, P.O. Box 9278, Van Nuys, CA 91409. Government & History: Secretary of the Senate, Room 3044, State Capitol, Sacramento, CA 95814.

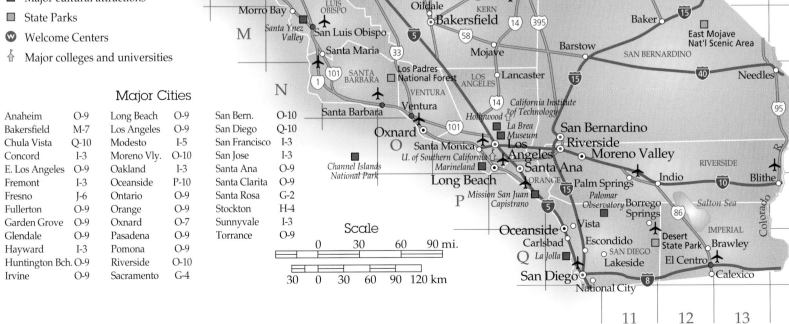

- **Alcatraz.** Island prison from which it was assumed no one could escape. Now a state park. (I-3)
- **Avenue of the Giants.** Route through Humboldt Redwoods State Park. (D-1)
- **Channel Islands National Park.** Home to sea lions, unique plants, and animals located on Santa Barbara and Anacapa islands. (O-6)
- **Death Valley National Park.** The lowest point in the Western Hemisphere, 282 feet (86 meters) below sea level. Site of desert life, salt beds, and borax formations. (J-10)
- **George C. Page La Brea Discoveries Museum.** Site of fossil remains of prehistoric animals trapped in tar pits. (O-9)
- **Golden Gate National Recreation Area.** The only United States national park located in a major metropolitan area. (H-2)
- **Hollywood.** Center of the motion picture industry in the United States. (O-9)
- **La Jolla.** Site of the Scripps Institution of Oceanography. (Q-10)
- **Lake Tahoe.** Resort with winter and summer sports and events. (F-6)
- **Lassen Volcanic National Park.** Site of Lassen Peak, which erupted from 1914 to 1921. (D-4)
- **Lava Beds National Monument.** Modoc Indian War was fought here in 1873. (A-4)
- **Marineland of the Pacific.** Oceanarium. (O-8)
- **Mission San Juan Capistrano.** Famous site where swallows return every March. (P-9)
- **Napa Valley.** Wine production region. (G-3)
- **Palomar Observatory.** One of the world's largest reflecting telescopes and most well known observatories. (P-11)
- **Santa Ynez Valley.** Pismo Beach and the site of Mission Santa Ynez built in 1804. (M-5)
- **Sequoia National Park.** Site of Mount Whitney, the highest point in the contiguous United States. Also the site of a large stand of sequoias. (K-8)
- **Yosemite National Park.** Glacial valley, waterfalls, and sequoia stands. (H-6)

Legend

- ☆ State capitol
- ⊙ Cities over 35,000 population
- ○ Other significant cities
- ● County Seats
- ■ Major cultural attractions
- ▢ State Parks
- Ⓦ Welcome Centers
- ⚲ Major colleges and universities

Major Cities

Anaheim	O-9	Long Beach	O-9	San Bern.	O-10
Bakersfield	M-7	Los Angeles	O-9	San Diego	Q-10
Chula Vista	Q-10	Modesto	I-5	San Francisco	I-3
Concord	I-3	Moreno Vly.	O-10	San Jose	I-3
E. Los Angeles	O-9	Oakland	I-3	Santa Ana	O-9
Fremont	I-3	Oceanside	P-10	Santa Clarita	O-9
Fresno	J-6	Ontario	O-9	Santa Rosa	G-2
Fullerton	O-9	Orange	O-9	Stockton	H-4
Garden Grove	O-9	Oxnard	O-7	Sunnyvale	I-3
Glendale	O-9	Pasadena	O-9	Torrance	O-9
Hayward	I-3	Pomona	O-9		
Huntington Bch.	O-9	Riverside	O-10		
Irvine	O-9	Sacramento	G-4		

Scale

0 30 60 90 mi.

30 0 30 60 90 120 km

California

Weather Facts

Record High Temperature: 134° F (57° C) on July 9, 1909, at Death Valley; Record Low Temperature: -45° F (-43° C) on January 19, 1933, at Boca; Average January Temperature: 45° F (7° C); Average July Temperature: 76° F (24° C); Average Yearly Precipitation: 22 in. (56 cm).

Environmental Facts

Air Pollution Rank: 14th; Water Pollution Rank: 3d; Total Yearly Industrial Pollution: 69,667,241 lbs.; Industrial Pollution Rank: 12th; Hazardous Waste Sites: 91; Hazardous Sites Rank: 3d; Landfill Capacity: overextended; Fresh Water Supply: surplus; Daily Residential Water Consumption: 199 gals. per capita; Endangered Species: Aquatic Species (27)—crayfish, Shasta; Birds (17)—condor, California; Mammals (12)—beaver, point arena mountain; Other Species (35)—frog, California red-legged; Plants (110)—aster, del mar sand.

Environmental Quality

California residents generate 44 million tons of solid waste each year, or approximately 3,100 pounds per capita. Landfill capacity in California will be exhausted in more than 12 years. The state has 91 hazardous waste sites. Annual greenhouse gas emissions in California total 443 million tons, or 15.7 tons per capita. Industrial sources in California release approximately 114,000 tons of toxins, 312,000 tons of acid precipitation-producing substances, and 8.9 million tons of smog-producing substances into the atmosphere each year.

The state has 4.5 million acres within the National Park System; the largest area within the state is Death Valley National Park.

State parks cover just over 1.2 million acres, attracting 70.5 million visitors per year.

California spends approximately 2.6 percent of its budget, or approximately $52 per capita, on environmental and natural resources.

Physical Regions: (a) Klamath Mountains; (b) Coast Ranges; (c) Central Valley; (d) Sierra Nevada; (e) Cascade Mountains; (f) Basin & Range Region; (g) Los Angeles Ranges; (h) San Diego Ranges.

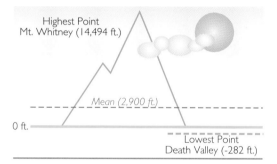

Highest Point Mt. Whitney (14,494 ft.)

Mean (2,900 ft.)

0 ft.

Lowest Point Death Valley (-282 ft.)

Land Use

Cropland: 19%; Pasture: 2.8%; Rangeland: 33%; Forest: 28.1%; Urban: 8.7%; Other: 8.4%.

For more information about California's environment, contact the Environmental Affairs Agency, P.O. Box 2815, Sacramento, CA 95812.

Average Monthly Weather

Eureka	Jan	Feb	Mar	Apr	May	Jun	Jul	Aug	Sep	Oct	Nov	Dec	Yearly
Maximum Temperature °F	53.4	54.6	54.0	54.7	57.0	59.1	60.3	61.3	62.2	60.3	57.5	54.5	57.4
Minimum Temperature °F	41.3	42.6	42.5	44.0	47.3	50.2	51.9	52.6	51.5	48.3	45.2	42.2	46.6
Days of Precipitation	16.0	14.2	15.5	11.7	8.3	5.3	2.1	2.5	4.5	8.7	13.3	15.5	117.5
San Diego													
Maximum Temperature °F	65.2	66.4	65.9	67.8	68.6	71.3	75.6	77.6	76.8	74.6	69.9	66.1	70.5
Minimum Temperature °F	48.4	50.3	52.1	54.5	58.2	61.2	64.9	66.8	65.1	60.3	53.6	48.7	57.0
Days of Precipitation	6.6	6.0	6.9	4.6	2.2	1.0	0.3	0.5	1.2	2.5	4.7	5.7	42.1

Flora and Fauna

The wide variation in California's topography and climate help contribute to the state's diverse flora and fauna. Forests cover slightly less than half (42 percent) of the state's land. The state of California is home to the coast redwood and the related, but rarer and older, giant sequoia. Some individual bristlecone pines, also found in California, are the oldest living trees. Besides these tree species, many others exist within the state's forests, such as varieties of oak, fir, hemlock, and cedar. The southeastern part of the state has desert-type plants, including cacti, Joshua trees, and indigo bushes. California wildflowers include fireweed, poppies, beardtongues, fiddle necks, and evening primroses.

The Sierra Nevada region is home to many large animals such as bears, cougars, and bighorn sheep. Other California animals include wolverines, bobcats, foxes, and rabbits. Animals that are adapted to desert conditions, such as coyotes and rattlesnakes, can also be found in California. North America's largest bird, the California condor, is native to the state, as are grouse and geese. California's rivers, lakes, and streams contain many kinds of fish from salmon and trout to catfish and bass.

Topography

Much of eastern California is dominated by the Sierra Nevada topological region, a mountainous area broken only by the Yosemite Valley. It contains several peaks over 14,000 ft. (4,270 m), including Mt. Whitney, the highest point in the contiguous United States at 14,494 ft. (4,418 m). The soil is warm and dry, red/brown in color, and high in organic content. To the west of the Sierra Nevada is the Central Valley, a low fertile region that runs northwest to southeast for more than 400 miles (640 km). It is fed by the San Joaquin and Sacramento rivers and supports much of California's agriculture. The soil is a gray/brown loamy fine sand, 20 inches or less over bedrock in places.

The Coastal Range regions form the western boundary of the Central Valley. This extended area of mountain ranges includes the Tehachapi and Diablo ranges. Low-lying fertile valleys can be found between the various ranges, including the Napa Valley in the north, famous for its vineyards, with warm and dry soil gray/brown in color.

Southern California contains the Basin and Range region that includes the vast Mojave Desert and Death Valley, the latter featuring the lowest point in the United States, Badwater, at 282 ft. (86 m) below sea level. The Los Angeles and San Diego Range topographic regions are also in the south and share the same brown alluvial fine loamy sand.

Climate

The combination of a wide latitudinal range and complex topography results in California's varied climatic pattern. The southernmost part of California, where San Diego is located, has a hot and dry climate. Otherwise, the majority of California has two recognizable seasons: a dry season from May to September, and a wet season for the rest of the year. Los Angeles, in southern California, has January and July temperatures of 56 degrees and 72 degrees F. Farther north, in San Francisco, January and July temperatures average 50 degrees F and 59 degrees F. The northern California coast receives the most precipitation, about 80 inches annually. Precipitation decreases from north to south; San Diego averages only 10 inches a year. California's deserts receive virtually no rain.

The highest temperature ever recorded in the United States occurred in California. In 1937, Greenland Ranch in Death Valley recorded a 134 degree F temperature.

Hydrology

The longest rivers in California are the Sacramento, flowing south for 307 miles (494 km), and the San Joaquin, flowing 368 miles (592 km) northwest. The two rivers meet northeast of San Francisco, eventually draining into San Francisco Bay. The most important river in California may be the Colorado, which forms the eastern border with Arizona. Water from the Colorado is diverted for farm irrigation and for some of the cities of southern California, most of which is semiarid or desert. Other significant rivers include the Owens, Kern, Salinas, and the Feather.

The Salton Sea, created in the early 1900s by Colorado River floodwaters, is the state's largest lake at 190 sq. mi. (492 sq. km). Lake Tahoe, on the border with Nevada, is the deepest lake in the state. Other large lakes include Clear, Honey, Eagle, Mono, and Shasta, all in northern California. The state's portion of the Pacific coast contains many bays and inlets, including San Diego and San Francisco bays.

California's History

California's First People

The California region has been inhabited for tens of thousands of years. At the time of European contact, there were so many different tribes in the California culture area that over one hundred distinct dialects were spoken. Like native people in the neighboring Great Basin, Southwest, and Columbia Plateau culture areas, these Indians were primarily hunter-gatherers. The abundant flora and fauna (acorns and other wild food, deer and shellfish) of the land rendered agriculture unnecessary. The people organized themselves into fairly small "tribelets" that were socially isolated.

Some of the tribes inhabiting the region included the Wintun, Patwin, Shasta, Pomo, Karok, Maidu, and Yana in the north; the Miwok, Yokuts, Tubatulabal, Costanoan, and Salinan in the central region; and the Chumash, Mohave, Ipai, Tipai, and Cahuilla in the south.

European Exploration

In 1533, Fortun Jimenez, sent on an expedition by Hernando Cortes up the western coast of Mexico, came upon Baja California (now part of Mexico). Cortes himself established a settlement two years later, but it was soon abandoned. In 1542, Juan Rodríguez Cabrillo, in search of the Northwest Passage, became the first European to sight Alta (upper) California. Several decades later, Sir Francis Drake, in 1579, explored the California coast, landed at Drake's Bay (near San Francisco) and claimed the area for England, calling it New Albion. In 1602, Sebastián Vizcaíno explored the coast, primarily around Monterey.

More than a century and a half passed before permanent settlement was attempted. An expedition in 1769 led by Capt. Gaspar de Portolá and Father Junípero Serra established outposts at San Diego and Monterey. These also served as missions, which were used in the successful conversion of much of the Indian population. A few forts were also built during this period, but the Spanish presence remained sparse.

With the conclusion of Mexican independence in 1822, Spain lost control of California. Mexico annexed the region in 1825. By the peace treaty ending the Mexican War of 1846-1848, Mexico ceded California to the United States.

Statehood

U.S. citizens began to migrate to California during the period of Mexican control. Captain John C. Frémont led expeditions to the area in the early 1840s. In 1846, after a group of American immigrants had revolted and declared the "Bear Flag Republic" of California, Commodore John Sloat raised the U.S. flag at Sonoma. The Mexican War had already begun in Texas, and California would afterward remain in American hands.

After the discovery of gold in 1848, a mass influx of prospectors helped triple the white population to more than ninety thousand by 1850. These gold-hunters were referred to as the "forty-niners," and they came looking for their fortunes. San Francisco became the staging-ground for thousands of prospectors in search of supplies for their journeys into the hills. With no administrative structure to deal with the burgeoning population, quick action was needed to institute a government of law. In 1849, delegates met in Monterey to draw up a state constitution and begin the process of applying for statehood. In 1850, California was admitted into the Union as the thirty-first state. The capital was moved to Sacramento in 1854.

Despite some pro slavery sentiment in the state, it remained with the Union during the Civil War. In 1869, completion of the trans-continental railroad to Sacramento linked California with the rest of the country. Over 30,000 Chinese were brought in to complete the railroad. After a riot occurred in 1877 the federal government prohibited further Chinese immigration.

Industrialization

When Mexico took control of California, it granted large plots of land (ranchos) to Mexicans, who established cattle raising and agriculture (mostly grains) as commercial enterprises. Despite the gold rush of 1849, gold production fizzled quickly, with the peak year being 1852.

The second half of the nineteenth century saw the state's agricultural production diversify. Southern California, with the aid of irrigation, became the country's citrus capital, cultivating oranges, lemons, and other citrus fruits. North of San Francisco, the soil was favorable for the development of wine vineyards.

The twentieth century witnessed the discovery of oil in the 1920s, and during the same period Hollywood became the center of the film industry. There was a large increase in military installations during World War II, and defense, aerospace, and other industries contributed to California's healthy economic mix.

Water

The enormous water needs of California for agricultural, industrial, and residential purposes have been met only with the development of large-scale water projects. The Imperial Valley is irrigated by almost 4.5 million acre-feet of water diverted from the Colorado River. The San Joaquin River contributes significant amounts to the Central Valley, and the Feather River delivers water to the San Francisco and San Joaquin Valley areas. With the doubling of the population between 1960 and 1990 (fifteen million to thirty million), and the accompanying increase in population in neighboring states (also dry), careful regional planning will be needed to assure that a sufficient quantity of this precious natural resource is available.

Important Events

1533 Baja California sighted by Fortun Jimenez.

1535 Baja California named "Santa Cruz" by Hernando Cortes.

1542 Juan Rodríguez Cabrillo enters San Diego Bay in search of the Northwest Passage.

1579 Sir Francis Drake claims area north of San Francisco for England, naming it New Albion.

1602 Sebastián Vizcaíno explores and maps the Monterey area.

1769 A joint military missionary expedition, led by Gaspar de Portolá and Father Junípero Serra, establishes a settlement at San Diego.

1821 Mexican independence frees California from Spanish control.

1825 California territory claimed by Mexico.

1848 California ceded to United States by Mexico in aftermath of the Mexican War.

1849 California Gold Rush.

1850 California admitted to the Union as the thirty-first state.

1890 Creation of Yosemite National Park.

1906 San Francisco earthquake and fires.

1928 Herbert Hoover elected thirty-first President of the United States.

1957 Brooklyn Dodgers move to Los Angeles and the New York Giants move to San Francisco.

1965 Thirty-four killed in race riots in Watts.

1968 Sen. Robert Kennedy is assassinated; Californian Richard Nixon elected thirty seventh President of the United States.

1971 Major earthquake in Los Angeles.

1980 Former governor Ronald Reagan elected fortieth President of the United States.

1989 Major earthquake in San Francisco Oakland area.

1992 Riots break out in East L.A. after police are acquitted of beating motorist Rodney King.

1994 The trial of OJ Simpson for the murders of Nicole Brown-Simpson and Ronald Goldman begins.

1995 OJ Simpson is acquitted for the murders of Nicole Brown-Simpson and Ronald Goldman.

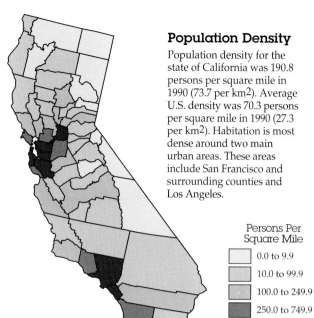

Population Density

Population density for the state of California was 190.8 persons per square mile in 1990 (73.7 per km2). Average U.S. density was 70.3 persons per square mile in 1990 (27.3 per km2). Habitation is most dense around two main urban areas. These areas include San Francisco and surrounding counties and Los Angeles.

Persons Per Square Mile

- 0.0 to 9.9
- 10.0 to 99.9
- 100.0 to 249.9
- 250.0 to 749.9
- 750.0 to 15,999.9

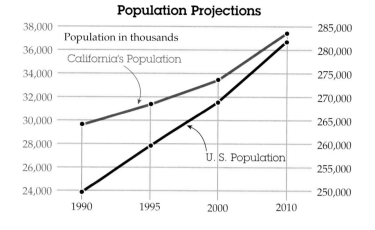

Population Projections

Population in thousands

California's Population

U. S. Population

Population Change

Year	Population
1950	10,586,000
1960	15,870,000
1970	20,007,000
1980	23,667,902
1990	29,760,021
2000	33,500,000
2010	37,347,000

Period	Change
1950–1970	89.0%
1970–1980	18.3%
1980–1990	25.7%
1990–2000	12.6%

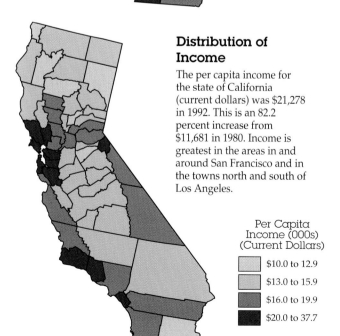

Population Change

The 1990 population figure for the state of California was 29,760,021. This is a 25.74 percent increase from 23,667,902 in 1980. The next decade will show growth with a population of 33.5 million or a 12.57 percent increase. The areas of fastest growth are in the central portion of the state extending to the south.

Percent Change 1980 to 1990

- 0.1 to 19.9%
- 20.0 to 49.9%
- 50.0 to 163.0%

Population Facts

State Population, 1993: 31,211,000

Rank: 1

Population 2000: 33,500,000 (Rank 1)

Density: 190.8 per sq. mi. (73.7 per km²)

Distribution: 92.6% urban, 7.4% rural

Population Under 5 Years Old:

Population Under 18 Years Old:

Population Over 65 Years Old: 10.5%

Median Age: 31.5

Number of Households: 10,381,000

Average Persons Per Household:

Average Persons Per Family: 3.32

Female Heads of Households: 4.01%

Population That Is Married: 18.38%

Birth Rate: 20.6 per 1,000 population

Death Rate: 7.2 per 1,000 population

Births to Teen Mothers: 11.6%

Marriage Rate: 7.9 per 1,000 population

Divorce Rate: 4.3 per 1,000 population

Violent Crime Rate: 1,090 per 100,000 pop.

Population on Social Security: 12.3%

Percent Voting for President: 49.1%

California's Famous Citizens

Boitano, Brian (b. 1963). Figure skater. Won an Olympic Gold Medal in 1988 and the U.S. Title from 1985 to 1988.

Robert Duvall (b. 1931). Actor. Won an Academy Award for his role in the 1982 film *Tender Mercies*.

Feinstein, Dianne (b. 1933). Mayor of San Francisco from 1978 to 1988. Elected to the U.S. Senate in 1992.

Hayakawa, Samuel (1906–1992). President of San Francisco State College from 1968 to 1973. U.S. senator from 1977-1983.

Jobs, Steven (b. 1955). Co-founded the Apple Computer Corporation in 1975. The company's Macintosh made computers more user friendly.

Saroyan, William (1908–1981). Author and playwright. Won the Pulitzer Prize in 1940 for *The Time of Your Life*.

Stanford, Leland (1824–1893). Governor, 1861-1863 and U.S. senator, 1885-1893. Founded Stanford University in 1885.

Stone, Irving (b. 1903). Author of biographical novels about, among others, Vincent Van Gogh, Clarence Darrow, and Sigmund Freud.

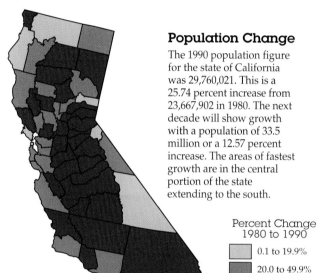

Distribution of Income

The per capita income for the state of California (current dollars) was $21,278 in 1992. This is an 82.2 percent increase from $11,681 in 1980. Income is greatest in the areas in and around San Francisco and in the towns north and south of Los Angeles.

Per Capita Income (000s) (Current Dollars)

- $10.0 to 12.9
- $13.0 to 15.9
- $16.0 to 19.9
- $20.0 to 37.7

Population Profile

Rank. California ranks 1st among U.S. states in terms of population with 31,211,000 citizens.

Minority Population. The state's minority population is 43.6 percent. The state's male to female ratio for 1990 was 100.24 males for every 100 females. It was above the national average of 95.22 males for every 100 females.

Growth. Growing faster than the projected national average, the state's population is

Government

Capital: Sacramento (established 1854).

Statehood: Became 31st state on Sep. 9, 1850.

Number of Counties: 58.

Supreme Court Justices: 7, 12-year term.

State Senators: 40, 4-year term.

State Legislators: 80, 2-year term.

United States Senators: 2.

United States Representatives: 52.

Electoral Votes: 54.

State Constitution: Adopted 1879.

expected to reach 37.3 million by the year 2010 *(see graph above)*.

Older Citizens. The state's population older than 65 was 3,135,552 in 1990. It grew 29.88% from 2,414,250 in 1980.

Younger Citizens. The number of children (under 18 years of age) was 7.8 million in 1990. This represents 26.0 percent of the state's population. The state's school aged population was 4.9 million in 1990. It is expected to increase to 5.7 million by the year 2000. This represents a 16.38% change.

Urban/Rural. 92.6% of the population of the state live in urban areas while 7.4% live in rural areas.

Largest Cities. California has 183 cities with a population greater than 35,000. The populations of the state's largest centers are (starting from the most populous) Los Angeles (3,485,398), San Diego (1,110,549), San Jose (782,248), San Francisco (723,959), Long Beach (429,433), Oakland (372,242), Sacramento (369,365), Fresno (354,202), Santa Ana (293,742), Anaheim (266,406), Riverside (226,505), Stockton (210,943), Huntington Beach (181,519), and Glendale (180,038).

Native American

The Native American population in California was 242,164 in 1990. This was an increase of 6.33 percent from 227,757 in 1980. Indian reservations are located throughout the state, especially in the southern regions in San Diego County. Indian reservations can also be found in Mono, Tulare, Humboldt, and Mendocino counties, among others.

Presence of
Native Americans

 Minor

Moderate

Nationalities

African	59,327
American	709,442
Arab	123,933
Austrian	65,852
Czech	77,973
Dutch	335,739
English	2,370,828
Finnish	44,316
German	3,676,049
Greek	102,178
Hungarian	104,722
Irish	1,951,628
Italian	1,079,022
Norwegian	263,646
Polish	378,077
Portuguese	275,492
Russian	327,675
Scottish	393,809
Slovak	66,016
Swedish	370,470
Welsh	119,081
West Indian	47,164

Statewide Ethnic Composition

Almost 69 percent of the population of the state of California is white. Of these the largest numbers consider themselves to be of German, English, Irish, or Italian descent. The next largest ethnic group are the Hispanics, who make up a little over 25 percent of the California population. Asian Americans make up only 9.5 percent.

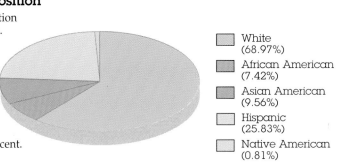

White (68.97%)

African American (7.42%)

Asian American (9.56%)

Hispanic (25.83%)

Native American (0.81%)

Education Facts

Total Students 1990: 4,771,978

Number of School Districts: 1,074

Expenditure Per Capita on Education 1990: $811

Expenditure Per Capita K–12 1990: $750

Expenditure Per Pupil 1990: $4,826

Total School Enrollment 1990–1991: 4,950,474

Rank of Expenditures Per Student: 27th in the U.S.

African American Enrollment: 8.7%

Hispanic Enrollment: 33.0%

Asian/Pacific Islander Enrollment: 10.4%

Native American Enrollment: 0.8%

Mean SAT Score 1991 Verbal: 415

Mean SAT Score 1991 Math: 482

Average Teacher's Salary 1992: $40,200

Rank Teacher's Salary: 6th in U.S.

High School Graduates 1990: 267,900

Total Number of Public Schools: 7,433

Number of Teachers 1990: 221,003

Student/Teacher Ratio: 22.4

Staff Employed in Public Schools: 419,673

Pupil/Staff Ratio: 11.4

Staff/Teacher Ratio: 2.0

Education

Attainment: 78.6 percent of population 25 years or older were high school graduates in 1989, earning California a ranking of 20th in the United States; 26.4 percent of the state's population had completed college. Institutions of Higher Education: The largest universities and colleges in the state include the University of California, Berkeley, (and 8 other campuses); The California State University system (19 campuses); Stanford University, Stanford; The University of San Francisco and Golden Gate University, San Francisco; the University of Santa Clara, Santa Clara; University of the Pacific, Stockton; Whittier College, Whittier; The Art Center College of Design and the California Institute of Technology, Pasadena. Expenditures per Student: Expenditure increased 75% between 1985 and 1990. Projected High School Graduations: 1998 (330,463), 2004 (410,265); Total Revenues for Education from Federal Sources: $1.3 billion; Total Revenues for Education from State Sources: $12.5 billion; Total Revenues for Education from Local Sources: $4 billion; Average Annual Salaries for Public School Principals: $52,325; Largest School Districts in State Los Angels Unified School District , Los Angeles, 609,746 students, 3d in the United States; San Diego Unified School District , San Diego 119,314 students, 14th.

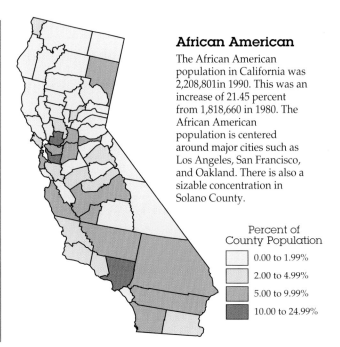

African American

The African American population in California was 2,208,801in 1990. This was an increase of 21.45 percent from 1,818,660 in 1980. The African American population is centered around major cities such as Los Angeles, San Francisco, and Oakland. There is also a sizable concentration in Solano County.

Percent of
County Population

0.00 to 1.99%

2.00 to 4.99%

5.00 to 9.99%

10.00 to 24.99%

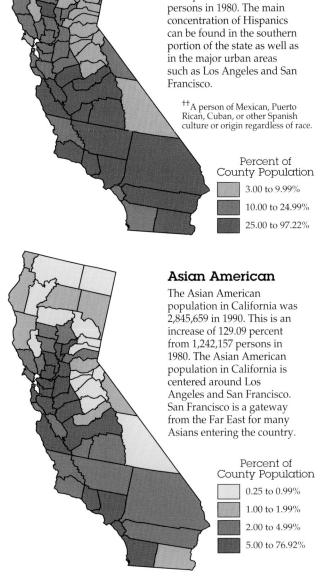

Hispanic[++]

The Hispanic population in California was 7,687,938 in 1990. This is an increase of 69.18 percent from 4,544,331 persons in 1980. The main concentration of Hispanics can be found in the southern portion of the state as well as in the major urban areas such as Los Angeles and San Francisco.

[++]A person of Mexican, Puerto Rican, Cuban, or other Spanish culture or origin regardless of race.

Percent of
County Population

3.00 to 9.99%

10.00 to 24.99%

25.00 to 97.22%

Asian American

The Asian American population in California was 2,845,659 in 1990. This is an increase of 129.09 percent from 1,242,157 persons in 1980. The Asian American population in California is centered around Los Angeles and San Francisco. San Francisco is a gateway from the Far East for many Asians entering the country.

Percent of
County Population

0.25 to 0.99%

1.00 to 1.99%

2.00 to 4.99%

5.00 to 76.92%

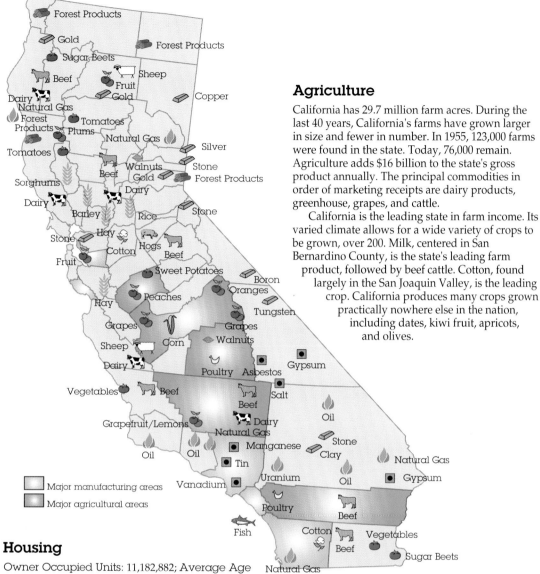

Major manufacturing areas

Major agricultural areas

Housing

Owner Occupied Units: 11,182,882; Average Age of Units: 28 years; Average Value of Housing Units: $195,500; Renter Occupied Units 4,553,387; Median Monthly Rent: $620; Housing Starts: 90,000; Existing Home Sales: 437,700.

Economic Facts

Gross State Product: $697,000,000,000

Income Per Capita: $21,278

Disposable Personal Income: $18,495

Median Household Income: $35,798

Average Annual Pay, 1988: $27,499

Principal Industries: electronics, computers, aerospace, motor vehicles, ships, meat processing, fruit-processing, wine-making, plastic products, textiles, chemicals, printing products, metal products, wood products, communications

Major Crops: milk, cotton, grapes, wheat, barley, maize, lettuce, tomatoes, carrots, celery, apples, figs, strawberries, almonds, walnuts

Fish: Tuna, Salmon, Halibut, Herring, Swordfish, Shark

Livestock: cattle

Non-Fuel Minerals: Borax, Potash, Boron, Gold, Asbestos, Diatomite, Pumice, Feldspar

Organic Fuel Minerals: Petroleum, Nat. Gas

Civilian Labor Force: 14,833,000 (Women: 6,369,000)

Total Employed: 13,714,000 (Women: 5,916,000)

Median Value of Housing: $195,500

Median Contract Rent: $620 per month

Agriculture

California has 29.7 million farm acres. During the last 40 years, California's farms have grown larger in size and fewer in number. In 1955, 123,000 farms were found in the state. Today, 76,000 remain. Agriculture adds $16 billion to the state's gross product annually. The principal commodities in order of marketing receipts are dairy products, greenhouse, grapes, and cattle.

California is the leading state in farm income. Its varied climate allows for a wide variety of crops to be grown, over 200. Milk, centered in San Bernardino County, is the state's leading farm product, followed by beef cattle. Cotton, found largely in the San Joaquin Valley, is the leading crop. California produces many crops grown practically nowhere else in the nation, including dates, kiwi fruit, apricots, and olives.

Economic Sectors

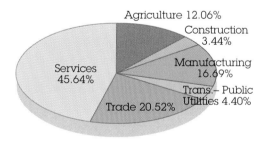

Agriculture 12.06%
Construction 3.44%
Manufacturing 16.69%
Trans.– Public Utilities 4.40%
Trade 20.52%
Services 45.64%

Manufacturing

California leads the nation as the top manufacturing state. Throughout the 20th century, California industry has grown and diversified. Today, electrical equipment is the leading type of manufactured product. However, California also has transportation equipment, food processing, and printing industries across the state.

The electronics industry is concentrated in the Santa Clara area, also known as the Silicon Valley; however, Los Angeles and Sacramento also manufacture electronic equipment. Southern California is the leading aircraft manufacturing center in the country. Food processing takes place in both northern and southern California, in the San Francisco and Los Angeles areas. Furthermore, California wines are some of the best in the world.

Transportation

The California freeway system is perhaps the most well-known transportation mode in the state. California's first major freeway, the Pasadena Freeway, opened in 1940. Today, California has more registered automobile drivers than any other state, partially due to the massive highway system.

California's two busiest airports are across the state from each other, in San Francisco and Los Angeles. However, other major airports can be found throughout the state in San Diego, Sacramento, and Fresno. About 34 freight railways operate in California. Approximately 40 cities are served by passenger railroads. Although California does not have inland water transportation routes, it does have several important ports, such as Oakland, Eureka, and Richmond.

Energy and Transportation Facts

Energy. Yearly Consumption: 7,162 tril. BTUs (residential, 17.6%; commercial, 17.8%; industrial, 26.8%; transportation, 37.7%); Annual Energy Expenditures Per Capita: $1,562; Nuclear Power Plants Located in State: 4; Source of Energy Consumed: Petroleum— 54.8%; Natural Gas— 33.8%; Coal— 1.1%; Hydroelectric Power—4.7%; Nuclear Power—5.7%.

Transportation. Highway Miles: 168,378 (interstates, 2,402; urban, 79,986; rural, 88,392); Average Yearly Auto Insurance: $800 (7th); Auto Fatalities Rank: 40th; Registered Motor Vehicles: 22,202,300; Workers in Carpools: 20.4%; Workers Using Public Trans: 4.9%.

Employment

Employment. California employed 13.85 million people in 1993. Most work in social and personal services (3,460,000 persons or 25.1% of the workforce). Manufacturing accounts for 13.0% or 1,803,000 workers. Wholesale and retail trade account for 20.1% or 2,787,000 workers. Government employs 2,078,000 workers (15.0%). Construction employs 446,000 workers (3.2%). Transportation and utilities account for 4.3% or 602,000 persons. Agriculture employs 429,000 workers or 3.1%. Finance, real estate, and insurance account for 5.7% or 786,000 workers. Mining employs 34,000 people and accounts for only 0.2% of the work force.

Unemployment. Unemployment has increased to 9.2% in 1993 from a rate of 7.2% in 1985. Today's figure is higher than the national average of 6.8% as shown below.

Unemployment Rate

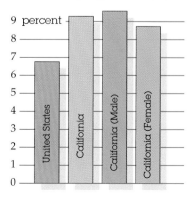

percent — United States, California, California (Male), California (Female)

COLORADO
The State of Colorado

Official State Seal

The Great Seal of Colorado bears the words *"Nil Sine Numine"* (Nothing Without Providence) on a white ribbon. Also included on the seal is an eye that represents the eye of God. Below the eye is a Roman fasces, which represents authority. On the fasces is a banner with the words Union and Constitution. Three mountains and a miner's pick and hammer complete the design.

Legal Holidays

January: New Year's Day—1st; February: Abraham Lincoln's Birthday—12th; Presidents' Day—3d Monday; April: Alfred E. Packer Day (Boulder)—23d; May: Memorial Day—4th Monday; July: Independence Day—4th; August: Colorado Day—2nd; September: Labor Day—1st Monday; October: Columbus Day—2nd Monday; November: Veterans' Day—11th; Thanksgiving—4th Thursday; December: Christmas—25th.

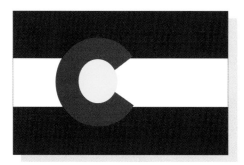

Official State Flag

The state flag of Colorado was adopted in 1911 and was revised in 1929 and 1964. The blue, gold, and white are the colors of columbine (state flower). The C represents Colorado, while the red represents the meaning of the state's name in Spanish. Gold and silver tassels must accompany the flag.

Festivals and Events

January: Aspen/Snowmass Winterskol, Snowmass; National Western Stock Show & Rodeo, Denver; February: Snowmass Mardi Gras, Snowmass; March: NCAA Skiing Championships, Steamboat Springs; May: Mountain Film, Telluride; Original Cinco de Mayo Celebration, Denver; June: Aspen Music Festival, Aspen; Colorado Shakespeare Fest, Boulder; Telluride Country/Bluegrass Music Festival, Telluride; July: Leadville Summer Music Fest, Leadville; Wildflower Festival, Crested Butte; August: Hometown Days, Strasburg; No Man's Land Celebration, Breckenridge; Great Pike's Peak Cowboy Poetry Gathering, Colorado Springs; Telluride Mushroom Fest, Telluride; September: Fest of Mountain & Plain, Denver; Longs Peak Scottish Highland Festival, Estes Park; Oktoberfest, Denver; October: Great American Beer Fest, Denver; Harvest Festival, Monte Vista.

Colorado Compared to States in Its Region.

Resident Pop. in Metro Areas: 3d; Pop. Percent Increase: 3d; Pop. Over 65: 7th; Infant Mortality: 2d; School Enroll. Increase: 4th; High School Grad. and Up: 2d; Violent Crime: 4th; Hazardous Waste Sites: 1st; Unemployment: 6th; Median Household Income: 2d; Persons Below Poverty: 6th; Energy Costs Per Person: 8th.

Mountain Region

	Population	Capital
Montana	839,000	Helena
Wyoming	470,000	Cheyenne
Idaho	1,099,000	Boise
Nevada	1,389,000	Carson City
Utah	1,860,000	Salt Lake City
Colorado	3,566,000	Denver
Arizona	3,936,000	Phoenix
New Mexico	1,616,000	Santa Fe

Colorado's Finances

Households: 1,282,000; Income Per Capita Current Dollars: $20,124; Change Per Capita Income 1980 to 1992: 89.6% (38th in U.S.); State Expenditures: $6,494,000,000; State Revenues: $7,016,000,000; Personal Income Tax: N/A; Federal Income Taxes Paid Per Capita: $1,896; Sales Tax: 3% (food and prescription drugs exempt).

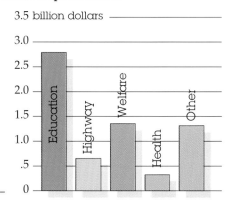

State Expenditures

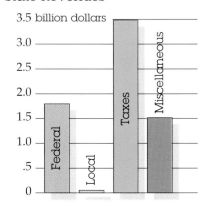

State Revenues

Location, Size, and Boundaries

Location. Colorado is located in the West Central United States in what is known as the Mountain region. It is bounded on four sides by land. The geographic center of Colorado is lat. 38° 59.9' N; long. 105° 38.5' W.

Size. Colorado is the 8th largest state in terms of size. Its area is 104,247 sq. mi. (270,000 km2). Inland water covers 481 sq. mi. (1,246 km2).

Boundaries. Wyoming, 260 mi. (419km); Nebraska, 173 mi. (278 km); Kansas, 207 mi. (333 km); Oklahoma, 58 mi. (93 km); New Mexico, 333 mi. (536 km); Utah, 276 mi. (444 km).

Geographic Extent. The north/south extent of Colorado is 276 mi. (444 km). The state extends 387 mi. (623 km) to the east/west.

Facts about Colorado. Origin of Name: From the Spanish word *colorado* meaning *"colored red"*; Nickname: The Centennial State; Motto: "Nothing Without Providence" *(Nil sine Numine)*; Abbreviations: Colo. (traditional), CO (postal); State Bird: lark bunting; State Tree: blue spruce; State Flower: Rocky Mountain columbine; State Song: "Where the Columbines Grow," words and music by A. J. Fynn.

Colorado Compared to Other States. Resident Pop. in Metro Areas: 17th; Pop. Percent Increase: 5th; Pop. Over 65: 48th; Infant Mort.: 27th; School Enroll. Increase: 23d; High School Grad. and Up: 3d; Violent Crime: 25th; Hazardous Waste Sites: 22d; Unemployment: 36th; Median Household Income: 18th; Persons Below Poverty: 28th; Energy Costs Per Person: 48th.

Sources of Information. Tourism: Colorado Tourism Board, 1625 Broadway, Suite 1700, Denver, CO 80202. Government: Legislative Council, State Capitol Building, Denver, CO 80203. History: Colorado Historical Society, 1300 Broadway, Denver, CO 80203.

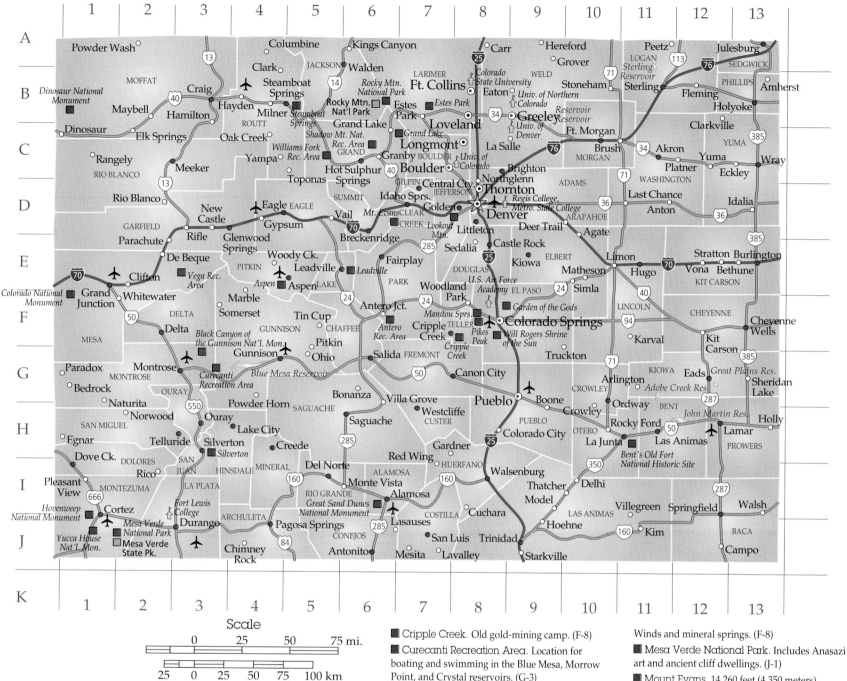

Scale

0   25   50   75 mi.

25   0   25   50   75   100 km

Legend

⭐ State capitol

⊙ Cities over 35,000 population

○ Other significant cities

● County Seats

■ Major cultural attractions

▪ State Parks

Ⓦ Welcome Centers

⚑ Major colleges and universities

Major Cities

Arvada	D-8	Golden	D-8
Aurora	D-8	Grand Junction	E-1
Boulder	C-7	Greeley	B-9
Brighton	C-8	Lafayette	C-8
Broomfield	C-8	Lakewood	D-8
Canon City	G-7	Littleton	D-8
Clifton	E-2	Longmont	C-8
Colorado Spr.	F-8	Louisville	C-8
Columbine	A-4	Loveland	B-8
Commerce City	D-8	Northglenn	C-8
Denver	D-8	Pueblo	G-9
Durango	J-3	Thornton	D-8
Englewood	D-8	Westminster	D-8
Fort Collins	B-8	Wheat Ridge	D-8

■ Aspen. Skiing resort as well as a cultural center. (E-4)

■ Bent's Old Fort National Historic Site. 1834 trading post. (H-11)

■ Black Canyon of the Gunnison National Monument. Sheer-walled 12 mile canyon. (G-3)

■ Cripple Creek. Old gold-mining camp. (F-8)

■ Curecanti Recreation Area. Location for boating and swimming in the Blue Mesa, Morrow Point, and Crystal reservoirs. (G-3)

■ Colorado National Monument. Sandstone monoliths as well as canyons. (F-1)

■ Dinosaur National Monument. Dinosaur fossils and remains of other prehistoric life. (B-1)

■ Estes Park. Gateway to the Rocky Mountain National Park. (B-7)

■ Garden of the Gods. Red sandstone formations can be found at this site. (F-8)

■ Grand Lake. Site of the Alva B. Adams Tunnel, world's largest irrigation tunnel. Also a resort area. (B-6)

■ Great Sand Dunes National Monument. Site of multicolored sands. (I-6)

■ Hovenweep National Monument. Site of ancient cliff dwellings, towers, and pueblos. (J-1)

■ Leadville. Highest incorporated city in the United States. (E-6)

■ Lookout Mountain. Location of the Buffalo Bill Tomb as well as Sky High Drive. (D-8)

■ Manitou Springs. Location of the Cave of the Winds and mineral springs. (F-8)

■ Mesa Verde National Park. Includes Anasazi art and ancient cliff dwellings. (J-1)

■ Mount Evans. 14,260 feet (4,350 meters). Scenic area. (D-6)

■ Pikes Peak. Rising 14,100 feet (4,300 meters), Pikes Peak provides a scenic view of the area. (F-8)

■ Rocky Mountain National Park. World's highest suspension bridge as well as 115 peaks over 10,000 feet (3,050 meters) high. (B-6)

■ Shadow Mountain National Recreation Area. Boating, swimming, and scenic views. (C-6)

■ Silverton. Mining town. (H-3)

■ Steamboat Springs. Area that includes skiing and hot springs. (B-5)

■ Vega Recreation Area. Boating, swimming, and fishing. (E-3)

■ Will Rogers Shrine of the Sun. Memorial to Will Rogers located on Cheyenne Mountain. (F-8)

■ Williams Fork Recreation Area. Boating, swimming, and fishing. (E-3)

■ Yucca House National Monument. Site of a prehistoric Indian pueblo. (J-1)

Weather Facts

Record High Temperature: 118° F (48° C) on July 11, 1888, at Bennett; Record Low Temperature: -61° F (-52° C) on January 31, 1981, at Maybell; Average January Temperature: 27° F (-3° C); Average July Temperature: 74° F (23° C); Average Yearly Precipitation: 16 in. (41 cm).

Environmental Facts

Air Pollution Rank: 40th; Water Pollution Rank: 37th; Total Yearly Industrial Pollution: 5,508,388 lbs.; Industrial Pollution Rank: 42d; Hazardous Waste Sites: 16; Hazardous Sites Rank: 23d; Landfill Capacity: overextended; Fresh Water Supply: surplus; Daily Residential Water Consumption: 193 gals. per capita; Endangered Species: Aquatic Species (5)—chub, bonytail; Birds (4)—crane, whooping; Mammals (1)—ferret, black-footed; Other Species (2)—butterfly, uncompahgre fritillary; Plants (13)—beardtongue, penland.

Environmental Quality

Colorado residents generate 2.0 million tons of solid waste each year, or approximately 1,200 pounds per capita. Landfill capacity in Colorado will be exhausted in 5 to 10 years. The state has 16 hazardous waste sites. Annual greenhouse gas emissions in Colorado total 72.3 million tons, or 21.89 tons per capita. Industrial sources in Colorado release approximately 10.3 thousand tons of toxins, 254.8 thousand tons of acid precipitation-producing substances, and 1.7 million tons of smog-producing substances into the atmosphere each year.

The state has over 588,000 acres within the National Park System; the largest area within the state is Rocky Mountain National Park. State parks cover just over 159,000 acres, attracting 8.6 million visitors per year.

Colorado spends approximately 1.7 percent of its budget, or approximately $23 per capita, on environmental and natural resources.

Average Monthly Weather

Colorado Springs	Jan	Feb	Mar	Apr	May	Jun	Jul	Aug	Sep	Oct	Nov	Dec	Yearly
Maximum Temperature °F	41.4	45.3	49.3	59.5	68.9	79.9	84.9	82.3	74.9	64.6	50.4	43.9	62.1
Minimum Temperature °F	16.2	19.6	23.8	32.9	42.5	51.5	57.4	55.6	47.2	37.0	25.0	18.9	35.6
Days of Precipitation	5.0	4.9	7.5	7.3	10.4	9.4	13.1	12.0	6.7	5.1	4.0	4.6	89.9
Grand Junction													
Maximum Temperature °F	35.7	44.5	54.1	65.2	76.2	87.9	94.0	90.3	81.9	68.7	51.0	38.7	65.7
Minimum Temperature °F	15.2	22.4	29.7	38.2	48.0	56.6	63.8	61.5	52.2	41.1	28.2	17.9	39.6
Days of Precipitation	7.0	6.0	7.7	6.4	6.3	4.2	5.3	6.6	5.7	5.5	5.5	6.2	72.3

Flora and Fauna

As in other areas, Colorado's flora and fauna vary across the state's different climatic and topographic zones. These differences in altitude and amount of moisture allow for a large variety of plant and animal life. The higher altitudes have trees such as fir, spruce, aspen, and different species of pine. Colorado's plains region, in the east, is mainly covered with grasses. Important plants in the transition areas between plains and mountains include sagebrush, mountain mahogany, and juniper. Colorado has many kinds of wildflowers as well, such as dogtooth violets and irises.

Mountain wildlife includes an assortment of big game such as elk and deer. Several species, including lynx, bison, and wolverines, that were once plentiful in the Colorado mountains are either extinct there or very rare. Other smaller animals including beaver, porcupine, and marmot also live in Colorado. Antelope, jackrabbits, and many kinds of burrowing animals live on Colorado's plains. Several different species of quail, pheasants, and grouse inhabit the Colorado landscape. Rivers and lakes in the state are filled with game fish such as trout, perch, and catfish.

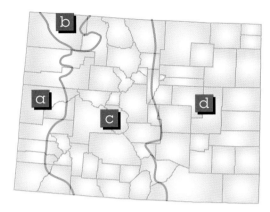

Physical Regions: (a) Colorado Plateau; (b) Intermontane Basin; (c) Rocky Mountains; (d) Great Plains.

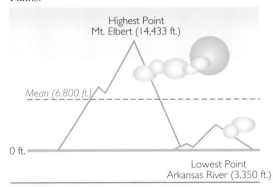

Highest Point Mt. Elbert (14,433 ft.)

Mean (6,800 ft.)

0 ft.

Lowest Point Arkansas River (3,350 ft.)

Land Use

Cropland: 25.9%; Pasture: 3%; Rangeland: 55.4%; Forest: 9.6%; Urban: 2.9%; Other: 3.2%.

For more information about Colorado's environment, contact the Department of Environmental Resources, 1313 Sherman, Room 718, Denver, CO 80203.

Topography

There are several distinct physical regions in Colorado. The eastern part of the state marks the westernmost extent of the Great Plains physical region of the United States. All soil in this region is classified as warm and dry, either loamy clay or sand, and its color ranges from brown to desert red. This area has the lowest elevation in Colorado and rises gradually to the base of the Rocky Mountains. The Rocky Mountain physical region covers much of the middle of the state and is known for many towering peaks that surpass 14,000 ft. (4,270 m). Soil in the mountains is cool and moist, and primarily a gray/brown clay. The Continental Divide separates the Rockies into eastern and western ranges, and also marks the dividing line between rivers that drain into the Atlantic, and those that flow west to the Pacific. The Front and the Laramie are two of the ranges of the eastern Rockies. The Sangre de Cristo Range in the south crosses into New Mexico.

The San Luis Valley is a large flatlands that separates the Sangre de Cristos from the San Juan Mountains in the southwest. The Colorado Plateau physical region covers much of western Colorado. This area contains many mesas, including Uncompahgre Plateau and White River Plateau, as well as gorges and valleys, where some crops are grown. The soil is a warm and dry very fine loamy sand.

Climate

Colorado has a continental climate that is significantly affected by the state's physical features. Differences in altitude around the state make for sudden changes in temperature. Generally, as elevation increases, temperature decreases. In Colorado's mountains, in places such as Boulder, January and July temperatures average 18 degrees F and 55 degrees F. Down in the plains region, average January and July temperatures are noticeably warmer at 28 degrees F and 74 degrees F.

In Colorado, precipitation increases with elevation; this directly contrasts temperature patterns. Statewide, Colorado averages 15 inches of annual precipitation. The western mountain slopes receive the most precipitation. Snow falls in the highland areas, attracting many skiers.

Chinook winds sometimes blow over the Colorado plains in winter. These warm winds can raise temperature, often 20 degrees F, in only a short time.

Hydrology

Several important river systems originate in Colorado, most from the north-central part of the state. The North Platte flows north into Wyoming, while the South Platte winds northeast into Nebraska. The Colorado, which drains one-twelfth of all U.S. land, flows southwest into Utah. The Arkansas travels eastward through the state into Kansas. The Rio Grande begins in the south-central part of the state, and flows south into New Mexico. Other rivers drain every part of the state, including the Apishapa, the Gunnison, and Big Sandy Creek.

The largest lake in Colorado is John Martin Reservoir, a result of a damming project on the Arkansas River. It covers 31 sq. mi. (78 sq. km). There are many other man-made bodies of water, including the Prewitt, Green Mountain, and Blue Mesa reservoirs. Grand Lake is the largest natural lake in the state.

Colorado's History

Colorado's First People

There is evidence of hunting tribes existing in Colorado as much as twenty thousand years ago, though who they were remains a mystery. About A.D. 100, the Basket Makers settled in southwestern Colorado. They were eventually absorbed into the Pueblo Indian culture starting around 800. These Anasazi Indians (or Cliff Dwellers, for the intricate homes they constructed in canyons and cliffs) developed advanced agricultural techniques and pottery-making skills. Their civilization flourished from the eleventh through the thirteenth centuries. By the time of the arrival of the first white men, Colorado was home to Plains Indians (mainly Arapaho and Cheyenne) in the eastern part of the state and to Great Basin tribes (mainly Utes) in the western regions.

European Exploration

The Spanish were the first European explorers in Colorado, though there is some question as to exactly when they set foot in the state. Francisco Vásquez de Coronado in 1541 and Juan de Oñate in 1601 led probable early expeditions. In 1706, Juan de Uribarri claimed part of Colorado for Spain, which joined it with New Mexico to the south.

The French ceded the Louisiana Territory to Spain in 1762 and reclaimed it in 1800. In the selling of this territory under the Louisiana Purchase in 1803, Colorado east of the Rockies became U.S. territory, while the rest of the state was still claimed by Spain. Since the boundaries between the French and Spanish areas of Colorado had never been formally defined, the United States decided to explore the area, sending out Lt. Zebulon M. Pike (who attempted but failed to scale Pike's Peak) in 1806 and several others in subsequent years. Finally, in 1819, the United States and Spain agreed to set the boundary along the Arkansas River and north along the Continental Divide.

The Spanish part of Colorado passed to the Mexicans after their war of independence from the Spanish in 1821. Twenty-seven years later, in the treaty that ended the Mexican War, the rest of Colorado came under U.S. control.

Statehood

The decade following the Mexican War was troubled by U.S. government disputes with various Indian tribes. A gold rush in 1859 pressed the various Indian tribes to the limit by trying to force them off lands given to them in 1851. The Southern Cheyenne and Arapaho, some of whose chiefs had ceded the majority of their land to the United States in 1861, shortly afterward resumed hunting and raiding over a wider area in response to perceived duplicity on the part of the U.S. government In 1864, as many as four hundred Indians were massacred at Sand Creek, which led to five years of intensified fighting between the Indians and the government. This massacre at Sand Creek was referred to as the "Chivington Massacre" after Col. J. M. Chivington who was in command of the Colorado militia during the engagement. Col. Chivington and his men scalped, knifed, shot, and clubbed Indian women, children, and men. It was regarded as one of the worst criminal acts in American history at the time. By 1880, under various treaties, most of the Indian tribes had been defeated and removed to reservations in Oklahoma.

In 1866, President Andrew Johnson vetoed the first bill to grant Colorado statehood. Denver became the capital of the Colorado Territory in 1867, and the state was finally admitted to the Union as the thirty-eighth state in 1876.

Industrialization

The fur trade was the predominant industry through the middle of the nineteenth century. Agriculture, mainly cattle and some crops, began to develop in the second half of the century, but the largest impact on the economy was the discovery of silver and gold (the latter first found along Cherry Creek, present site of Denver, in 1858).

Silver production eventually took over as the leading industry, reaching its peak by 1880. However, in the 1890s, a depression reduced demand for silver and the U.S. government changed from silver to the gold standard, forcing many mines to close.

Colorado turned to agriculture in the twentieth century, growing sugar beets, wheat, and other crops made possible only by massive irrigation efforts. The Great Depression of the 1930s, accompanied by droughts, took a toll on the state's economy, but a renewed interest in Colorado's mineral reserves during World War II helped revive the state. Since the war, the defense and aerospace industries have helped fuel a boom that has seen Colorado's economy emerge as one of the healthiest in the nation.

Tourism

Colorado's many mineral springs attracted tourists as early as the 1860s. Colorado Springs, founded as a spa, was a major tourist stop, and Denver saw over 200,000 visitors a year by the mid-1880s. The extension of rail lines through much of Colorado in the 1870s also made the state's many scenic natural features accessible to tourists.

Rocky Mountain National Park and Mesa Verde National Park are two of Colorado's most beautiful areas. Mesa Verde National Park contains Indian Cliff Dwellings that are some of the best-preserved in the United States. Rocky Mountain National Park is a scenic wonder with majestic mountains that seem to reach to the sky. Another attraction, Dinosaur National Monument is a vast area of preserved fossils attesting to a time when dinosaurs ruled the Earth.

For those who enjoy winter sports, Colorado has two of the best ski areas in the world—Aspen and Vail. These areas provide beginner trails as well as professional courses for the more experienced.

Important Events

1541 Coronado is the first Spanish explorer in the state.

1601 Juan de Oñate explores the southeastern part of the state.

1706 Juan de Uribarri claims this area for Spain.

1779 Juan Bautista de Anza defeats Comanche Indians near present day Pueblo.

1806 Lt. Zebulon Pike attempts unsuccessful scaling of mountain that would bear his name.

1819 Eastern Colorado is established as a U.S. territory under the AdamsOnís Treaty.

1848 The remaining Colorado territory is given to the U.S. by Mexico in the Treaty of Guadalupe Hidalgo.

1858 Gold is found at Cherry Creek.

1861 The Colorado Territory is established by Congress with the state's present day boundaries.

1864 On November 29, as many as two hundred Southern Cheyenne and Arapaho under Black Kettle are massacred at their village on Sand Creek.

1867 Treaty of Medicine Lodge resettles Cheyenne and Arapaho on reservations in Oklahoma.

1872 Denver and Pueblo are linked by the Rio Grande Railroad.

1876 Colorado admitted to the Union as the thirty-eighth state.

1881 The Ute tribe is deported to reservations.

1891 Gold is discovered at Cripple Creek.

1924 Many Ku Klux Klan members are elected to statewide office.

1946 Uranium is discovered near Grand Junction.

1967 Colorado is the first state to liberalize abortion laws.

1974 Shale oil boom on the Western Slope.

1988 Rocky Flats weapons plant almost shut down due to accumulation of nuclear wastes.

1992 Colorado elects the first Native American U.S. senator, Ben Nighthorse Campbell (Democrat).

1995 Colorado Senator Ben Nighthorse Campbell switches to the Republican party and causes an uproar.

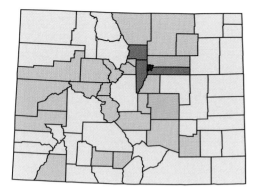

Population Density

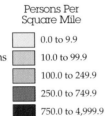

Population density for the state of Colorado was 31.8 persons per square mile in 1990 (12.3 per km2). Average U.S. density was 70.3 persons per square mile in 1990 (27.3 per km2). Habitation is most dense in and around the urban areas of Denver and Boulder in the counties of Boulder, Jefferson, Adams, and Arapahoe.

Persons Per Square Mile

	0.0 to 9.9
	10.0 to 99.9
	100.0 to 249.9
	250.0 to 749.9
	750.0 to 4,999.9

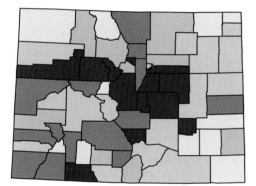

Population Change

The 1990 population figure for the state of Colorado was 3,294,394 in 1990. This is a 13.99 percent increase from 2,889,964 in 1980. The next decade will show growth with a population of 3.8 million or a 15.74 percent increase. The areas of fastest growth are the center of the state and in urban areas such as Colorado Springs and the Denver vicinity.

Percent Change 1980 to 1990

	-31.9 to -10.0%
	-9.9 to 0.0%
	0.1 to 19.9%
	20.0 to 49.9%
	50.0 to 163.0%

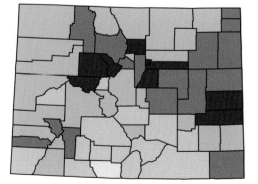

Distribution of Income

The per capita income for the state of Colorado (current dollars) was $20,124 in 1992. This is an 89.6 percent increase from $10,616 in 1980. Income is greatest in the urban areas. Much of the state shows a healthy increase in incomes. Urban areas such as Denver, Colorado Springs, and Boulder also show promising growth.

Per Capita Income (000s) (Current Dollars)

	$4.5 to 9.9
	$10.0 to 12.9
	$13.0 to 15.9
	$16.0 to 19.9
	$20.0 to 37.7

Population Projections

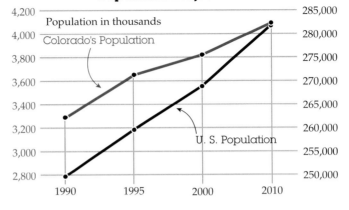

Population Change

Year	Population
1950	1,325,000
1960	1,769,000
1970	2,223,000
1980	2,889,964
1990	3,294,394
2000	3,813,000
2010	4,098,000

Period	Change
1950–1970	67.8%
1970–1980	30.0%
1980–1990	14.0%
1990–2000	15.8%

Population Facts

State Population, 1993: 3,566,000

Rank: 26

Population 2000: 3,813,000 (Rank 25)

Density: 31.8 per sq. mi. (12.3 per km²)

Distribution: 82.4% urban, 17.6% rural

Population Under 5 Years Old: 7.6%

Population Under 18 Years Old: 26.2%

Population Over 65 Years Old: 10.0%

Median Age: 32.5

Number of Households: 1,282,000

Average Persons Per Household: 2.51

Average Persons Per Family: 3.07

Female Heads of Households: 3.78%

Population That Is Married: 20.95%

Birth Rate: 16.2 per 1,000 population

Death Rate: 6.6 per 1,000 population

Births to Teen Mothers: 11.3%

Marriage Rate: 9.4 per 1,000 population

Divorce Rate: 5.5 per 1,000 population

Violent Crime Rate: 559 per 100,000 pop.

Population on Social Security: 12.8%

Percent Voting for President: 62.7%

Population Profile

Rank. Colorado ranks 26th among U.S. states in terms of population with 3,566,000 citizens.

Minority Population. The state's minority population is 19.6 percent. The state's male to female ratio for 1990 was 98.09 males for every 100 females. It was above the national average of 95.22 males for every 100 females.

Growth. Growing faster than the projected national average, the state's population is

Government

Capital: Denver (established 1876).

Statehood: Became 38th state on Aug. 1, 1876.

Number of Counties: 63.

Supreme Court Justices: 7, 10-year term.

State Senators: 35, 4-year term.

State Legislators: 65, 2-year term.

United States Senators: 2.

United States Representatives: 6.

Electoral Votes: 8.

State Constitution: Adopted 1876.

Colorado's Famous Citizens

Chase, Mary Coyle (1907-1981). Playwright. Won the Pulitzer Prize in 1944 for *Harvey*, about a drunk with a six-foot invisible rabbit.

Denver, John (b. 1943). Singer-songwriter. Biggest hit was "Rocky Mountain High," which went platinum.

Gossage, Richard (Goose) (b. 1951). Baseball pitcher. Holds NL record for most strikeouts by a relief pitcher in a season (1977).

Guggenheim, Simon (1867–1941). U.S. senator from 1907 to 1913. Established the John Simon Guggenheim Memorial Foundation (1925).

Jackson, Helen Hunt (1830–1885). Writer. Portrayed Native Americans in a sympathetic light in novels such as *Ramona* (1884).

Libby, Willard (1908–1980). Chemist. Won the Nobel Prize in 1960 for his work with radiocarbon.

Sabin, Florence (1871–1953). Anatomist. Became the first woman to become a full professor at Johns Hopkins University in 1925.

expected to reach 4.1 million by the year 2010 (*see graph above*).

Older Citizens. The state's population older than 65 was 329,443 in 1990. It grew 33.20% from 247,325 in 1980.

Younger Citizens. The number of children (under 18 years of age) was 861 thousand in 1990. This represents 26.1 percent of the state's population. The state's school-aged population was 573 thousand in 1990. It is expected to increase to 652 thousand by the year 2000. This represents a 13.79% change.

Urban/Rural. 82.4% of the population of the state live in urban areas while 17.6% live in rural areas.

Largest Cities. Colorado has 14 cities with a population greater than 35,000. The populations of the state's largest centers are (starting from the most populous) Denver (467,610), Colorado Springs (281,140), Aurora (222,103), Lakewood (126,481), Pueblo (98,640), Arvada (89,235), Fort Collins (87,758), Boulder (83,312), Westminster (74,625), Greeley (60,536), Thornton (55,031), Longmont (51,555), Southglenn (43,087), Loveland (37,352), Littleton (33,685), and Wheat Ridge (29,419).

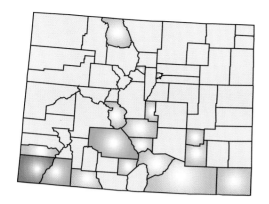

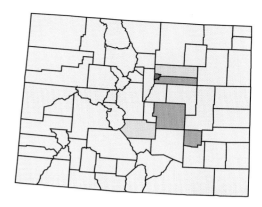

Nationalities

African	3,178
American	96,610
Arab	5,960
Austrian	10,246
Czech	19,254
Dutch	53,877
English	363,136
Finnish	5,729
German	840,255
Greek	9,288
Hungarian	10,589
Irish	290,800
Italian	112,147
Norwegian	48,300
Polish	51,609
Portuguese	3,045
Russian	22,653
Scottish	60,833
Slovak	15,193
Swedish	77,709
Welsh	20,840
West Indian	1,637

Native American

The Native American population in Colorado was 27,776 in 1990. This was an increase of 34.30 percent from 20,682 in 1980. Native Americans can be found in the Indian reservations, the largest of which is the Ute Mountain Indian Reservation located in the southwestern corner in Montezuma and La Plata counties.

Presence of Native Americans
- Minor
- Moderate
- Significant

African American

The African American population in Colorado was 133,146 in 1990. This was an increase of 30.93 percent from 101,695 in 1980. The largest concentration of African Americans can be found in the Denver area. Other pockets include Colorado Springs, and Arapahoe, Crowley, Adams, and Fremont counties.

Percent of County Population
- 0.00 to 1.99%
- 2.00 to 4.99%
- 5.00 to 9.99%
- 10.00 to 24.99%

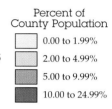

Statewide Ethnic Composition

Over 88 percent of the population of Colorado is white. Many of these people consider themselves of German, English, or Irish descent. The next largest ethnic group are the Hispanics. Hispanics can be of any ethnic group, but are mainly of Mexican origin. African Americans make up 4 percent of the population.

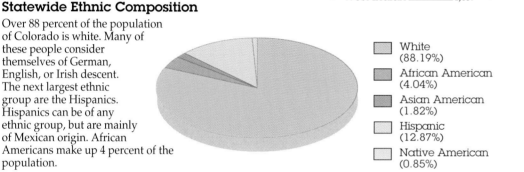

- White (88.19%)
- African American (4.04%)
- Asian American (1.82%)
- Hispanic (12.87%)
- Native American (0.85%)

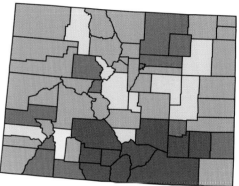

†† A person of Mexican, Puerto Rican, Cuban, or other Spanish culture or origin regardless of race.

Hispanic††

The Hispanic population in Colorado was 424,302 in 1990. This is an increase of 24.90 percent from 339,717 persons in 1980. The main concentration of Hispanics can be found in the southern portion of the state in counties bordering Mexico.

Percent of County Population
- 0.00 to 0.99%
- 1.00 to 2.99%
- 3.00 to 9.99%
- 10.00 to 24.99%
- 25.00 to 97.22%

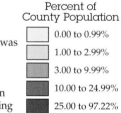

Education Facts

Total Students 1990: 562,755

Number of School Districts: 176

Expenditure Per Capita on Education 1990: $787

Expenditure Per Capita K–12 1990: $716

Expenditure Per Pupil 1990: $4,702

Total School Enrollment 1990–1991: 569,792

Rank of Expenditures Per Student: 29th in the U.S.

African American Enrollment: 5.1%

Hispanic Enrollment: 16.1%

Asian/Pacific Islander Enrollment: 2.2%

Native American Enrollment: 0.9%

Mean SAT Score 1991 Verbal: 453

Mean SAT Score 1991 Math: 506

Average Teacher's Salary 1992: $33,100

Rank Teacher's Salary: 23d in U.S.

High School Graduates 1990: 32,000

Total Number of Public Schools: 1,337

Number of Teachers 1990: 32,375

Student/Teacher Ratio: 17.6

Staff Employed in Public Schools: 60,603

Pupil/Staff Ratio: 9.3

Staff/Teacher Ratio: 1.9

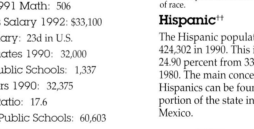

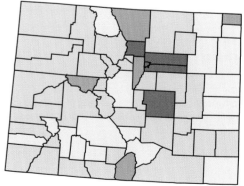

Asian American

The Asian American population in Colorado was 59,862 in 1990. This is an increase of 82.80 percent from 32,747 persons in 1980. The Asian American population can be found mostly in urban areas and the counties surrounding them, such as Denver and Colorado Springs.

Percent of County Population
- 0.00 to 0.24%
- 0.25 to 0.99%
- 1.00 to 1.99%
- 2.00 to 4.99%

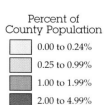

Education

Attainment: 83.2 percent of population 25 years or older were high school graduates in 1989, earning Colorado a ranking of 10th in the United States; 27 percent of the state's population had completed college. Institutions of Higher Education: The largest universities and colleges in the state include the University of Colorado (founded 1861), Boulder; Colorado School of Mines (founded 1869), Golden; University of Northern Colorado, Greeley; University of Southern Colorado, Pueblo; Colorado State University, Fort Collins; University of Denver, Denver; United States Air Force Academy, Colorado Springs. Expenditures per Student: Expenditure increased 83% between 1985 and 1990. Projected High School Graduations: 1998 (39,159), 2004 (42,469); Total Revenues for Education from Federal Sources: $123 million; Total Revenues for Education from State Sources: $991 million; Total Revenues for Education from Local Sources: $1.4 billion; Average Annual Salaries for Public School Principals: N/A; Largest School Districts in State Jefferson County R-1 School District , Golden, 75,164 students, 32d in the United States; Denver County School District , Denver, 58,299 students, 56th.

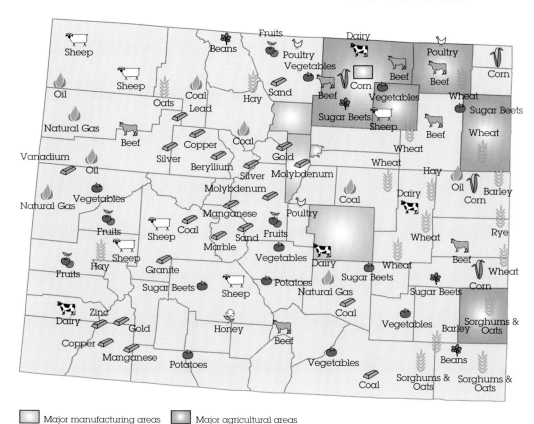

Major manufacturing areas　　Major agricultural areas

Agriculture

Colorado has 32.8 million farm acres. During the last 40 years, Colorado's farms have grown larger in size and fewer in number. In 1955, 41,000 farms were found in the state. Today, 25,500 remain.

Agriculture adds $2 billion to the state's gross product annually. The principal commodities in order of marketing receipts are cattle, corn, wheat, and dairy products.

Livestock products account for about 71 percent of the state's farm income, with beef cattle being the leading product. Some of these cattle are fattened in special feed lots to increase their value on the market. Greeley is the center of this activity.

Hay is the principal crop, in part because of its importance as cattle feed. Other important crops include wheat, corn, and greenhouse carnations.

Housing

Owner Occupied Units: 1,477,349; Average Age of Units: 24 years; Average Value of Housing Units: $82,700; Renter Occupied Units: 472,590; Median Monthly Rent: $418; Housing Starts: 29,500; Existing Home Sales: 82,100.

Economic Facts

Gross State Product: $66,000,000,000

Income Per Capita: $20,124

Disposable Personal Income: $17,517

Median Household Income: $30,140

Average Annual Pay, 1988: $23,981

Principal Industries: machinery, scientific instruments, food products, electrical equipments, fabricated metal products, printing

Major Crops: wheat, hay, corn, milk, sugar beets, alfalfa

Fish: Bass, Catfish, Crappie, Perch, Trout

Livestock: cattle, sheep

Non-Fuel Minerals: Gold, Molybdenum, Sand, Gravels, Uranium

Organic Fuel Minerals: Petroleum, Coal, Nat. Gas

Civilian Labor Force: 1,755,000 (Women: 820,000)

Total Employed: 1,667,000 (Women: 780,000)

Median Value of Housing: $82,700

Median Contract Rent: $418 per month

Economic Sectors

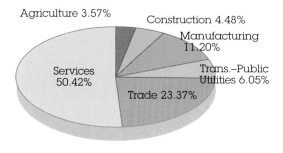

Agriculture 3.57%
Construction 4.48%
Manufacturing 11.20%
Services 50.42%
Trans.–Public Utilities 6.05%
Trade 23.37%

Manufacturing

The manufacturing sector in Colorado has grown considerably in the last 50 years following World War II. Currently, 13 percent of Colorado's state gross product comes from the state's manufacturing industries. In terms of added value by manufacture, scientific instruments are the number one manufactured product, followed by processed foods, transportation equipment, and machinery.

Almost all manufacturing industries, including computers and newspapers, are located in the Denver metropolitan area. However, other Colorado cities and towns have manufacturing industries as well. Factories in Colorado Springs manufacture medical equipment. Coors, a major beer brewery, has its headquarters in Golden. Other plants around the state manufacture luggage, clothing, and plastics.

Transportation

Colorado's mountains cause transportation problems for the state. But despite the natural barriers, Colorado has approximately 77,000 miles of highways and roads. Many of these roads have to be continually snowplowed in the winter. Colorado has the highest road tunnel, the 1.7-mile-long Eisenhower Memorial Tunnel.

Railroad track in Colorado has decreased from 5,000 miles in the 1930s to only 3,600 miles today. However, 11 freight lines operate on these tracks, and at least 10 Colorado cities receive passenger rail service. The Stapleton International Airport in Denver is Colorado's busiest airport. Denver is a popular stopover for flights to and from the West Coast. More than 175 public and private airports exist throughout the state.

Energy and Transportation Facts

Energy. Yearly Consumption: 964 tril. BTUs (residential, 22.5%; commercial, 24.6%; industrial, 24.3%; transportation, 28.7%); Annual Energy Expenditures Per Capita: $1,603; Nuclear Power Plants Located in State: 0; Source of Energy Consumed: Petroleum— 36.2%; Natural Gas— 28.2%; Coal— 33.8%; Hydroelectric Power—1.8%; Nuclear Power—0.0%.

Transportation. Highway Miles: 78,043 (interstates, 951; urban, 12,777; rural, 65,266); Average Yearly Auto Insurance: $653 (17th); Auto Fatalities Rank: 23d; Registered Motor Vehicles: 2,915,285; Workers in Carpools: 17.3%; Workers Using Public Trans: 2.9%.

Employment

Employment. Colorado employed 1.81 million people in 1993. Most work in social and personal services (468,100 persons or 25.9% of the workforce). Manufacturing accounts for 10.4% or 188,200 workers. Wholesale and retail trade account for 22.3% or 403,000 workers. Government employs 297,100 workers (16.5%). Construction employs 83,600 workers (4.6%). Transportation and utilities account for 5.7% or 103,700 persons. Agriculture employs 50,500 workers or 2.8%. Finance, real estate, and insurance account for 5.9% or 106,000 workers. Mining employs 15,900 people and accounts for only 0.9% of the work force.

Unemployment. Unemployment has decreased to 5.2% in 1993 from a rate of 5.9% in 1985. Today's figure is lower than the national average of 6.8% as shown below.

Unemployment Rate

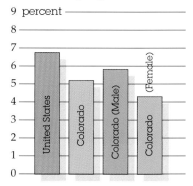

CONNECTICUT
The State of Connecticut

Official State Seal

The seal of Connecticut has evolved throughout the state's history. The state motto, *"Qui Transtulit Sustinet"* (He Who Transplanted Still Sustains), is printed on a blue ribbon. The inscription encircling the seal translates to "Seal of the Commonwealth of Connecticut." Centered in the seal are three grape vines that represent a modern addition to the seal.

Legal Holidays

January: New Year's Day—1st; Connecticut Ratification Day—9th; February: Abraham Lincoln's Birthday—12th; Presidents' Day—3rd Monday; May: Memorial Day—4th Monday; July: Independence Day—4th; September: Labor Day—1st Monday; October: Columbus Day—2nd Monday; November: Veterans' Day—11th; Thanksgiving—4th Thursday; December: Christmas—25th.

Official State Flag

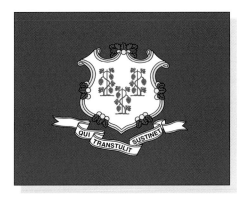

The state flag of Connecticut has been through many changes since Revolutionary times. It originated from regimental flags and was standardized in 1931 to be similar to the state seal. The military squarelike shape was adopted in 1897. The state motto appears on a white ribbon below three grape vines on a white field.

Festivals and Events

January: Janubeary, Granby; Winter Fun Fest, New Preston; February: Kids Liberty Days, Mystic; March: Maple Sugaring Fest, New Preston; April: Connecticut Storytelling Fest, New London; May: Lobsterfest, Mystic; June: Sea Music Fest, Mystic; Levitt Pavilion Performing Arts/Music Fest, Westport; July: Riverfest, Hartford; Horse & Carriage Weekend, Mystic; August: Scottish Bagpipe & Highland dance Fest, New Preston; September: Woodstock Fair, Woodstock; Huckleberry Finn Raft Race, New Preston; October: Great Teddy Bear Jamboree Show/Sale, Bristol; Chowderfest, Mystic; November: New England Field Days, Mystic; Live Turkey 'Olimpiks', New Preston; December: Lantern Light Tours, Mystic.

Connecticut Compared to Its Region.

Resident Pop. in Metro Areas: 2d; Pop. Percent Increase: 5th; Pop. Over 65: 2d; Infant Mortality: 2d; School Enroll. Increase: 2d; High School Grad. and Up: 4th; Violent Crime: 2d; Hazardous Waste Sites: 3d; Unemployment: 3d; Median Household Income: 1st; Persons Below Poverty: 5th; Energy Costs Per Person: 3d.

New England Region

	Population	Capital
Maine	1,239,000	Augusta
New Hampshire	1,125,000	Concord
Vermont	576,000	Montpelier
Massachusetts	6,012,000	Boston
Rhode Island	1,000,000	Providence
Connecticut	3,277,000	Hartford

Connecticut's Finances

Households: 1,230,000; Income Per Capita Current Dollars: $26,979; Change Per Capita Income 1980 to 1992: 121.7% (5th in U.S.); State Expenditures: $9,957,000,000; State Revenues: $10,137,000,000; Personal Income Tax: 1.5%; Federal Income Taxes Paid Per Capita: $3,067; Sales Tax: 8% (food and prescription drugs exempt).

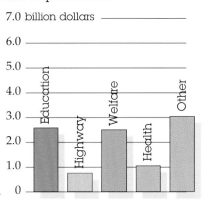

State Expenditures

7.0 billion dollars

Bars: Education, Highway, Welfare, Health, Other

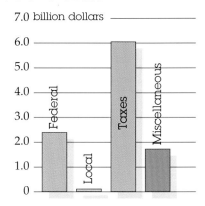

State Revenues

7.0 billion dollars

Bars: Federal, Local, Taxes, Miscellaneous

Location, Size, and Boundaries

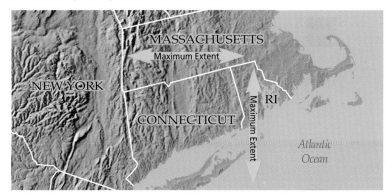

Location. Connecticut is located in the northeastern United States in the New England region. It is bounded on four sides by land with a small coastline bordering Long Island Sound in the south. The geographic center of Connecticut is lat. 41° 35.7' N; long. 72° 42.4' W.

Size. Connecticut is the 48th largest state in terms of size. Its area is 5,009 sq. mi. (12,973 km²). Inland water covers 147 sq. mi. (381 km²).

Boundaries. Massachusetts, 94 mi. (151 km); Rhode Island, 54 mi. (87 km); New York, 180 mi. (290 km).

Geographic Extent. The north/south extent of Connecticut is 55 mi. (89 km). The state extends 90 mi. (145 km) to the east/west.

Facts about Connecticut. Origin of Name: From the *Algonquian* Indian word meaning *"on the long tidal river"*; Nickname: The Constitution State; Motto: "He Who Transplanted Still Sustains"; Abbreviations: Conn. (traditional), CT (postal); State Bird: robin; State Tree: white oak; State Flower: mountain laurel; State Song: "Yankee Doodle," composer unknown.

Connecticut Compared to Other States. Resident Pop. in Metro Areas: 4th; Pop. Percent Increase: 48th; Pop. Over 65: 11th; Infant Mortality: 41st; School Enroll. Increase: 11th; High School Grad. and Up: 17th; Violent Crime: 26th; Hazardous Waste Sites: 24th; Unemployment: 12th; Median Household Income: 1st; Persons Below Poverty: 49th; Energy Costs Per Person: 31st.

Sources of Information. Tourism: State Department of Economic Development, Tourism Division, 865 Brook Street, Rocky Hill, CT 06067. Government: Office of the Secretary of State, Administrative Legislative Division, 30 Trinity Street, Hartford, CT 06106. History: Connecticut State Library, History and Genealogy Unit, Capitol Avenue, Hartford, CT 06106.

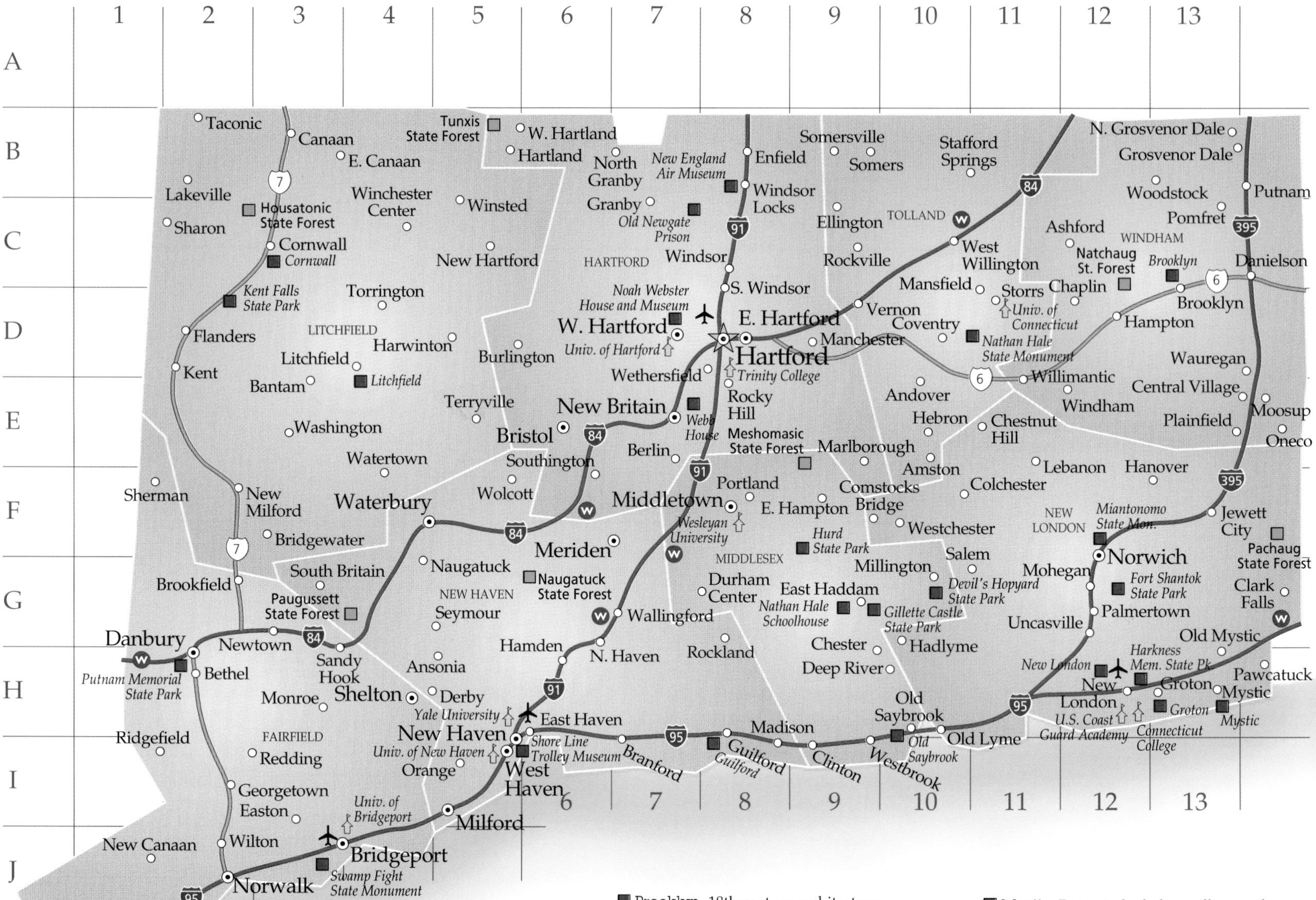
1
2
3
4
5
6
7
8
9
10
11
12
13
A
B
C
D
E
F
G
H
I
J
K
Taconic
Canaan
E. Canaan
Tunxis State Forest
W. Hartland
Hartland
North Granby
New England Air Museum
Enfield
Somersville
Somers
Stafford Springs
N. Grosvenor Dale
Grosvenor Dale
Lakeville
Sharon
Housatonic State Forest
Winchester Center
Winsted
Granby
Old Newgate Prison
Windsor Locks
Ellington
TOLLAND
Woodstock
Putnam
Pomfret
Ashford
WINDHAM
Cornwall
New Hartford
HARTFORD
Windsor
Rockville
West Willington
Natchaug St. Forest
Brooklyn
Danielson
Kent Falls State Park
Torrington
Noah Webster House and Museum
S. Windsor
Mansfield
Storrs
Univ. of Connecticut
Chaplin
Vernon
Coventry
Nathan Hale State Monument
Hampton
Flanders
LITCHFIELD
Harwinton
W. Hartford
Univ. of Hartford
E. Hartford
Hartford
Manchester
Litchfield
Burlington
Wauregan
Kent
Bantam
Wethersfield
Trinity College
Willimantic
Andover
Windham
Central Village
Terryville
New Britain
Webb House
Rocky Hill
Hebron
Chestnut Hill
Moosup
Plainfield
Washington
Bristol
Meshomasic State Forest
Marlborough
Oneco
Watertown
Southington
Berlin
Amston
Lebanon
Hanover
Sherman
New Milford
Waterbury
Wolcott
Middletown
Portland
E. Hampton
Comstocks Bridge
Colchester
NEW LONDON
Miantonomo State Mon.
Jewett City
Wesleyan University
Westchester
Pachaug State Forest
Bridgewater
Meriden
Hurd State Park
MIDDLESEX
Salem
Norwich
Brookfield
South Britain
Naugatuck
Naugatuck State Forest
Millington
Mohegan
Fort Shantok State Park
Clark Falls
Paugussett State Forest
NEW HAVEN
Durham Center
East Haddam
Devil's Hopyard State Park
Seymour
Wallingford
Nathan Hale Schoolhouse
Gillette Castle State Park
Palmertown
Uncasville
Danbury
Newtown
Old Mystic
Sandy Hook
Hamden
Chester
Hadlyme
Harkness Mem. State Pk.
Putnam Memorial State Park
Bethel
Ansonia
N. Haven
Rockland
Deep River
New London
Groton
Pawcatuck
Monroe
Shelton
Derby
Yale University
Old Saybrook
Mystic
East Haven
Madison
U.S. Coast Guard Academy
Connecticut College
Ridgefield
FAIRFIELD
New Haven
Shore Line Trolley Museum
Branford
Guilford
Clinton
Westbrook
Old Lyme
Redding
Univ. of New Haven
Orange
West Haven
Georgetown
Easton
Univ. of Bridgeport
Milford
New Canaan
Wilton
Bridgeport
Swamp Fight State Monument
Norwalk
Stamford
Darien
Greenwich
7
84
91
395
6
95

Scale

0 5 10 15 mi.

5 0 5 10 15 20 km

Legend

- ☆ State capitol
- ⊙ Cities over 35,000 population
- ○ Other significant cities
- ● County Seats
- ■ Major cultural attractions
- □ State Parks
- Ⓦ Welcome Centers
- ⇧ Major colleges and universities

Major Cities

Ansonia	H-5	Middletown	F-8	Shelton	H-4
Bridgeport	J-3	Milford	I-5	Stamford	K-1
Bristol	I-6	Naugatuck	G-4	Storrs	D-11
Danbury	H-2	New Britain	E-7	Torrington	D-4
Darien	K-1	New Haven	H-5	Waterbury	F-4
Derby	H-4	New London	H-12	West Haven	I-5
East Hartford	D-8	North Haven	G-6	West Hartford	D-7
East Haven	H-6	Norwalk	J-2	Wethersfield	D-8
Hartford	D-8	Norwich	F-12	Willimantic	E-11
Meriden	F-7	Orange	I-5	Windsor Locks	B-8

■ Brooklyn. 18th century architecture. Restored farmhouses furnished with antiques. (C-13)

■ Cornwall. Restored historic homes furnished with antiques. Location of Mohawk Mountain Ski Area. (C-3)

■ Devil's Hopyard State Park. Scenic views and waterfalls. (G-10)

■ Fort Shantok State Park. Historic fort and stockade. (G-12)

■ Gillette Castle State Park. Home of the actor William Gillette, built in 1919. (G-9)

■ Groton. Site of Fort Griswold where in 1781 the British defeated colonial militiamen. Also the location of the USS *Nautilus* nuclear-powered submarine. (H-12)

■ Guilford. Location of the oldest stone house in New England, built in 1639. (I-8)

■ Harkness Memorial State Park. Mansion, museum, and formal gardens. (H-12)

■ Hurd State Park. Location of many interesting geological formations. (F-9)

■ Kent Falls State Park. Waterfalls. (D-2)

■ Litchfield. Site of the first law school in United States (1744). (D-4)

■ Miantonomo State Monument. Burial place of the Narraganset chief (1643). (F-12)

■ Mystic. Recreated whaling village and a Marinelife Aquarium. (H-13)

■ Nathan Hale Schoolhouse. The colonial patriot taught here in 1773–74. (G-9)

■ Nathan Hale State Monument. Burial place of Nathan Hale. (D-10)

■ New England Air Museum. History of flight museum. (B-8)

■ New London. Site of the United States Coast Guard Academy and Ocean Beach Park. (H-12)

■ Noah Webster House and Museum. Home of the lexicographer. (D-7)

■ Old Newgate Prison. The first chartered copper mine; prison in American Revolution. (B-7)

■ Old Saybrook. Original site of Yale University. (H-10)

■ Putnam Memorial State Park. Revolutionary War campground (1778–79) and museum. (H-1)

■ Shore Line Trolley Museum. Museum dedicated to classic trolleys. (I-6)

■ Swamp Fight State Monument. Pequot War with Indians ended here in 1637. (J-3)

■ Webb House. Washington and French General Rochambeau planned Yorktown campaign in this historic home. (E-7)

Connecticut

Weather Facts

Record High Temperature: 105° F (41° C) on July 21, 1922, at Waterbury; Record Low Temperature: -32° F (-36° C) on February 15, 1939, at Falls Village; Average January Temperature: 25° F (-4° C); Average July Temperature: 70° F (21° C); Average Yearly Precipitation: 47 in. (119 cm).

Environmental Facts

Air Pollution Rank: 32d; Water Pollution Rank: 11st; Total Yearly Industrial Pollution: 16,580,924 lbs.; Industrial Pollution Rank: 34th; Hazardous Waste Sites: 15; Hazardous Sites Rank: 24th; Landfill Capacity: overextended; Fresh Water Supply: large surplus; Daily Residential Water Consumption: 128 gals. per capita; Endangered Species: Aquatic Species (1)—sturgeon, shortnose; Birds (3)—eagle, bald; Mammals (1)—bat, Indiana; Other Species (1)—beetle, puritan tiger; Plants (1)—pogonia, small whorled.

Environmental Quality

Connecticut residents generate 2.9 million tons of solid waste each year, or approximately 1,800 pounds per capita. Landfill capacity in Connecticut will be exhausted in less than 5 years. The state has 15 hazardous waste sites. Annual greenhouse gas emissions in Connecticut total 42.3 million tons, or 14.63 tons per capita. Industrial sources in Connecticut release approximately 30.9 thousand tons of toxins, 123.8 thousand tons of acid precipitation–producing substances, and 900 thousand tons of smog-producing substances into the atmosphere each year.

The state has 3,300 acres within the National Park System; a significant area within the state is Weir Farm National Historic Site. State parks cover just over 180,000 acres, attracting 6.7 million visitors per year.

Connecticut spends less than 1 percent (0.77%) of its budget, or approximately $19 per capita, on environmental and natural resources.

Average Monthly Weather

Hartford	Jan	Feb	Mar	Apr	May	Jun	Jul	Aug	Sep	Oct	Nov	Dec	Yearly
Maximum Temperature °F	33.6	36.3	45.5	60.0	71.4	80.1	84.8	82.6	74.8	63.9	50.6	37.3	60.1
Minimum Temperature °F	16.7	18.8	28.0	37.6	47.3	57.0	61.9	60.0	51.7	40.9	32.5	20.9	39.5
Days of Precipitation	10.6	10.2	11.3	11.1	11.8	11.5	9.7	9.8	9.4	8.3	11.2	11.9	126.8

Flora and Fauna

Slightly over two-thirds of Connecticut's land is covered by forests. However, the vast majority of these wooded areas are controlled by private ownership. A variety of both hardwood and softwood trees grow in Connecticut. Hardwoods include trees such as beech, maple, hickory, and elm; softwoods include hemlock and red and white pines. The state flower, the mountain laurel, is referred to by residents as "flowering shrub ivy." The mountain laurel, dogwood, bayberry, and sheep laurel all grow throughout the state. Connecticut's flowering plants include cowslips and hepatica.

The only abundant large animal living in Connecticut is the white-tailed deer; its population has risen considerably since the 1970s. Other animals, seen as hunting and trapping targets to some people, include muskrat, fox, hare, and raccoon. Many game birds live throughout Connecticut; the freshwater duck is the most common. Other Connecticut birds include orioles and sparrows. Along the Long Island Sound, clams, mussels, and lobsters can still be found, despite pollution of the area. Connecticut's waterways contain fish such as trout and shad.

Physical Regions: (a) Taconic Section; (b) Western New England Upland; (c) Connecticut Valley Lowland; (d) Eastern New England Upland; (e) Coastal Lowlands.

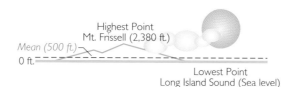

Highest Point
Mt. Frissell (2,380 ft.)

Mean (500 ft.)

0 ft.

Lowest Point
Long Island Sound (Sea level)

Land Use

Cropland: 7.8%; Pasture: 3.6%; Rangeland: 0%; Forest: 58.8%; Urban: 22.7%; Other: 7.1%.

For more information about Connecticut's environment, contact the Department of Environmental Protection, State Office Bldg., 165 Capitol Ave., Hartford, CT 06106.

Topography

Connecticut can be divided into several different physical regions. The Coastal Lowland region, an area of several miles in width, runs along Connecticut's coast. This area is generally flat, with rocky ridges and some harbors and beaches. The Connecticut Valley Lowlands region, formed by the Connecticut River, divides the state in half running north to south.

The eastern part of the state is covered by the Eastern New England Upland physical region, an area consisting of hills and valleys. Elevations of 1,100 to 1,200 ft. (335 to 366 m) are found in the northwest section of this area. The land gently slopes toward the southeast, with elevations in the southeast corner rising no higher than 500 ft. (150 m).

Most of western Connecticut is covered by the Western New England Upland physical region, which is the southernmost extension of the Berkshire Hills. In the far northwest corner, separated from the Berkshire Hills by the Housatonic River, is the edge of the Taconic Range. Mt. Frissell, the highest point in Connecticut, is located here. The soil throughout Connecticut is cool and moist, brown in color, and high in organic matter, iron, and aluminum.

Climate

Connecticut's climate can be best described as moderate; weather becomes neither too hot nor too cold. Like other New England states, Connecticut has four distinguishable seasons. A coastal city like Bridgeport has average January and July temperatures of 30 degrees F and 74 degrees F. Hartford, in central Connecticut, has an average July temperature of 74 degrees F as well, but a cooler 25 degrees F for January.

The state of Connecticut receives an average of 47 inches of precipitation a year. Although much of the precipitation falls equally over the entire state, some minor differences exist. Overall, interior areas receive slightly more precipitation than coastal areas. Connecticut also receives snowfall, the heaviest falling in the northwest.

For a small state, Connecticut's climate can vary considerably over a short distance. While the northern part of the state may be receiving snowfall, a close coastal area may have only light rainfall.

Hydrology

The most important river in the state is the Connecticut. It flows south through the middle of the state before draining into Long Island Sound. Its entire length is 390 miles (628 km), about a fifth of this in Connecticut. Other important rivers include the Quinebaug, the Thames, and the Natchaug in the east; and the Farmington, the Housatonic, and the Naugatuck in the west. There are many waterfalls along these waterways, the largest being Kent Falls on the Housatonic River.

The largest lake in Connecticut is Lake Candlewood, near the western border with New York. It is an artificial lake that covers about 8 sq. miles (21 sq. km). There are several other man-made reservoirs in the state, including Nepaug, Hancock Brook, and Mansfield Hollow reservoirs. There are thousands of natural lakes, including Bolton Lake, Twin Lakes, and Crystal Pond.

Connecticut's History

Connecticut's First People

Some Native Americans are believed to have occupied Connecticut as long as ten thousand years ago. By the time Europeans arrived in the early seventeenth century, there were but six thousand or so Algonquian Indians split into several groups. The Pequot, a warlike tribe that had migrated from the Hudson Valley after confrontations with the Mohawk, settled along the coast. Other tribes included the Mohegan, the Niantic, the Quinnipiac, and the Wanguk. Apparently fear of the Mohawk kept most of these tribes from adopting the inland area of Connecticut as their homeland. It also led several of the tribes to develop friendly relations with the white settlers, selling land and trading and teaching the colonists about the New World.

European Exploration

In 1614, Adrian Block, a Dutch navigator, sailed into the Connecticut River and claimed the region for the Dutch. Nineteen years later, the Dutch purchased some land from the Pequot Indians and established a trading post at the site of present-day Hartford. However, four years later, in 1637, the Pequot War was fought by the Pequot against the colonists; the Indians were defeated.

In 1639, the Fundamental Orders of Connecticut was adopted by the Puritan settlements of Windsor, Wethersfield, and Hartford (collectively known as the Connecticut Colony).

In 1654, the Dutch fort at Hartford was taken over by English colonists, and in 1662 the Connecticut Colony was granted a royal charter of self-government by Charles II. However, in the 1687, when James II dispatched Sir Edmund Andros to seize the charter, colonists hid it in an oak tree in Hartford, which then became the landmark Charter Oak.

By the time of the American Revolution, most of Connecticut's roughly 200,000 population, accustomed to autonomy and independence from England, supported the War of Independence. The state supplied over 30,000 troops and became known as the "arsenal of the nation" for its production of gunpowder and munitions.

The Revolution saw a few skirmishes on Connecticut soil. The most notable battles took place at Danbury (1777), New Haven (1779), and New London (1781). One famous fighter was Nathan Hale who, in 1776, was hung as a spy by the British. Hale, who was a school teacher, was attached to Washington's army as an intelligence-gatherer. He was apprehended around Harlem Heights in New York by a Loyalist. Before his execution, Hale was noted as saying, "I only regret that I have but one life to lose for my country."

Statehood

The Connecticut delegation to the Constitutional Convention played an instrumental role in the writing of the U.S. Constitution, and in 1787, Connecticut became the fifth state to ratify it. Disagreeing with much of the foreign policy of the early republic, Connecticut opposed the War of 1812, providing a meeting place at the Hartford Convention in 1814-15 for those opposed to the war.

Connecticut established itself early on as an antislavery state, the state legislature abolishing slavery in 1784 and the state acting as a major conduit for escaped slaves fleeing the South via the Underground Railroad. The state also played a major role in the Civil War, providing over 57,000 men and many provisions to the Union cause.

Connecticut adopted a new state constitution in 1818 that effectively ended the Federalists' early domination of state government. This constitution was in effect until 1964, when the federal courts ordered the state to redistrict its legislature.

In 1974, Ella Grasso was elected governor of Connecticut, becoming the first woman elected governor of a U.S. state in her own right.

Industrialization

In 1795, the Mutual Assurance Company of Norwich was founded and Hartford quickly became the insurance capital of the United States. About the same time, Eli Whitney (better known for his cotton gin) standardized production by using interchangeable parts in the manufacture of muskets at Whitneyville. This was the beginning of mass production and led to the establishment of Connecticut as a leading manufacturing state. By the beginning of the twentieth century, Connecticut was a leading producer of hats, typewriters, machine tools, and other goods. Manufacturing is still the dominant industry in the state today, with some poultry and dairy farming and tourism adding to the economic mix. Machinery, metals, precision instruments, textiles, and cutlery are among the manufactured goods that provide Connecticut with the highest per capita income in the United States.

The Defense Industry

It was during the Revolutionary War, when Connecticut produced much of the gunpowder and arms for the colonists, that the state became known as the "arsenal of the nation." It has maintained its status as a major defense state ever since. During the Civil War, Colt and Winchester produced arms for the Union soldiers, and in World War I state industry churned out rifles and bayonets. By war's end, over 75 percent of the state's production went toward defense products.

Connecticut's highly industrialized economy was hit hard by the Depression, but recovered during World War II as it became engaged in the production of submarines, airplane engines, shell cases, and other products important to the war effort.

Important Events

1614 Dutch navigator Adrian Block claims the region around the Connecticut River for the Dutch.

1633 House of Hope built by the Dutch on the site of present-day Hartford.

1637 Pequot War in which Pequot Indians were unsuccessful in stopping the tide of colonial settlement.

1639 The Fundamental Orders of Connecticut, considered the first written constitution, is adopted.

1642 A free school is opened in New Haven.

1662 The Connecticut Colony receives a charter of self-rule from Charles II.

1665 New Haven assimilated into the Connecticut Colony.

1687 Colonists hide self-rule charter from the king's envoy in the Charter Oak.

1701 Collegiate School, later renamed Yale, is founded.

1755 The *Connecticut Gazette*, the state's first paper, is founded in New Haven.

1776 Nathan Hale is executed as a spy by the British.

1788 Connecticut becomes the fifth state to ratify the constitution.

1795 Hartford becomes the center of the U.S. insurance industry.

1806 First American dictionary published in New Haven by Noah Webster.

1812 Strong opposition to the War of 1812 in Connecticut.

1818 New state constitution ratified, weakening the Federalists.

1848 Slavery is abolished throughout the state.

1878 New Haven becomes the site of the first commercial telephone exchange.

1917 A submarine station is established at Groton.

1922 Hartford becomes location of Connecticut's first radio station.

1954 First atomic submarine is launched at Groton.

1974 Ella Grasso is elected governor—the first woman in the country elected without succeeding her husband.

1991 City of Bridgeport files for bankruptcy.

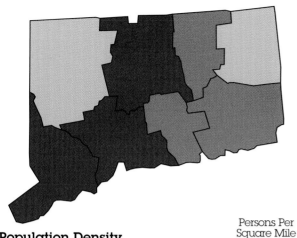

Population Density

Population density for the state of Connecticut was 678.4 persons per square mile in 1990 (262.0 per km2). Average U.S. density was 70.3 persons per square mile in 1990 (27.3 per km2). Habitation is most dense around the urban and manufacturing areas which include Stamford, New Haven, Waterbury, and Hartford.

Persons Per Square Mile
- 100.0 to 249.9
- 250.0 to 749.9
- 750.0 to 4,999.9

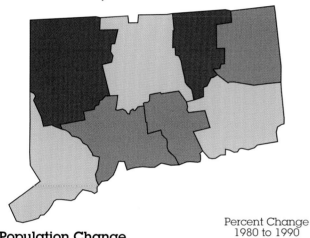

Population Change

The 1990 population figure for the state of Connecticut was 3,287,116 in 1990. This is a 5.78 percent increase from 3,107,576 in 1980. The next decade will show growth with a population of 3.5 million or a 4.8 percent increase. Connecticut has seen moderate growth throughout the decade.

Percent Change 1980 to 1990
- 0.1 to 5.0%
- 5.1 to 12.0%
- 12.1 to 14.0%

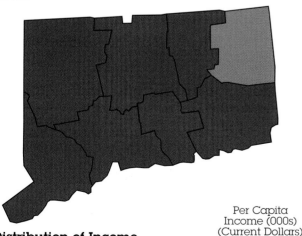

Distribution of Income

The per capita income for the state of Connecticut (current dollars) was $26,979 in 1992. This is a 121.7 percent increase from $12,170 in 1980. Much of the state is well within the highest incomes in the country.

Per Capita Income (000s) (Current Dollars)
- $16.0 to 19.9
- $20.0 to 35.2

Population Projections

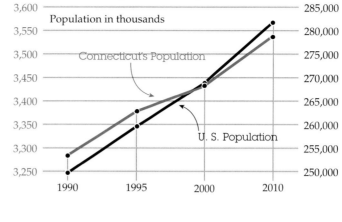

Population in thousands

Connecticut's Population

U. S. Population

(x-axis: 1990, 1995, 2000, 2010)
(left y-axis: 3,250 to 3,600; right y-axis: 250,000 to 285,000)

Population Change

Year	Population
1950	2,007,000
1960	2,544,000
1970	3,041,000
1980	3,107,576
1990	3,287,116
2000	3,445,000
2010	3,532,000

Period	Change
1950–1970	51.5%
1970–1980	2.2%
1980–1990	5.8%
1990–2000	4.8%

Population Facts

State Population, 1993: 3,277,000

Rank: 27

Population 2000: 3,445,000 (Rank 27)

Density: 678.4 per sq. mi. (262.0 per km²)

Distribution: 79.1% urban, 20.9% rural

Population Under 5 Years Old: 7.3%

Population Under 18 Years Old: 23.5%

Population Over 65 Years Old: 13.9%

Median Age: 34.4

Number of Households: 1,230,000

Average Persons Per Household: 2.59

Average Persons Per Family: 3.10

Female Heads of Households: 4.27%

Population That Is Married: 20.83%

Birth Rate: 15.2 per 1,000 population

Death Rate: 8.4 per 1,000 population

Births to Teen Mothers: 8.2%

Marriage Rate: 8.6 per 1,000 population

Divorce Rate: 3.2 per 1,000 population

Violent Crime Rate: 540 per 100,000 pop.

Population on Social Security: 16.2%

Percent Voting for President: 63.8%

Connecticut's Famous Citizens

Allen, Ethan (1738–1789). Revolutionary War figure. Leader of the "Green Mountain Boys," who defeated the British at Fort Ticonderoga on May 10, 1775.

Arnold, Benedict (1741–1801). Revolutionary War figure. Fought bravely in the American Revolution until he committed treason by selling military documents and conspiring to turn over West Point to British forces.

Benton, William (1900–1973). Public official, businessman. Owner and publisher of the *Encyclopaedia Britannica*. Elected to the United States Senate in 1949. Appointed U.S. ambassador to the United Nations Educational, Scientific, and Cultural Organization in 1963.

Calder, Alexander (1898–1976). Sculptor. Created a new art style of abstract forms known as "stabiles" and "mobiles."

Putnam, Israel (1718–1790). Military leader. Famous for the saying, "Don't fire until you see the whites of their eyes."

Webster, Noah (1758–1843). Publisher. He started the *American Dictionary of the English Language* in 1807. It contained 12,000 words and was the most complete work of its time.

Population Profile

Rank. Connecticut ranks 27th among U.S. states in terms of population with 3,277,000 citizens.

Minority Population. The state's minority population is 16.6 percent. The state's male to female ratio for 1990 was 94.02 males for every 100 females. It was below the national average of 95.22 males for every 100 females.

Growth. Growing more slowly than the projected national average, the state's population is expected to reach 3.5 million by the year 2010 *(see graph above)*.

Older Citizens. The state's population older than 65 was 445,907 in 1990. It grew 22.21% from 364,864 in 1980.

Younger Citizens. The number of children (under 18 years of age) was 750 thousand in 1990. This represents 22.8 percent of the state's population. The state's school aged population was 476 thousand in 1990. It is expected to increase to 520 thousand by the year 2000. This represents a 9.24% change.

Urban/Rural. 79.1% of the population of the state live in urban areas while 20.9% live in rural areas.

Largest Cities. Connecticut has 18 cities with a population greater than 35,000. The populations of the state's largest centers are (starting from the most populous) Bridgeport (141,686), Hartford (139,739), New Haven (130,474), Waterbury (108,961), Stamford (108,056), Norwalk (78,331), New Britain (75,491), Danbury (65,585), Bristol (60,640), West Hartford (60,110), Meriden (59,479), West Haven (54,021), East Hartford (50,452), Stratford (49,389), and Middletown (42,762).

Government

Capital: Hartford (established as sole capital 1875).

Statehood: Became 5th state on Jan. 9, 1788.

Number of Counties: 8.

Supreme Court Justices: 7, 8-year term.

State Senators: 36, 2-year term.

State Legislators: 151, 2-year term.

United States Senators: 2.

United States Representatives: 6.

Electoral Votes: 8.

State Constitution: Adopted 1965.

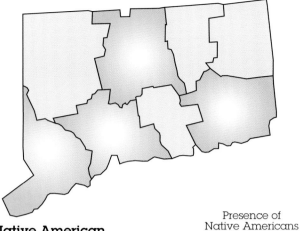

Native American

The Native American population in Connecticut was 6,654 in 1990. This was an increase of 37.99 percent from 4,822 in 1980. Large groups of Native Americans can be found in Hartford, Bridgeport, New Haven, and Waterbury.

Presence of Native Americans

 Minor

Nationalities

African	7,465
American	76,487
Arab	9,876
Austrian	11,815
Czech	9,571
Dutch	19,151
English	292,593
Finnish	4,996
German	306,666
Greek	22,290
Hungarian	31,631
Irish	393,577
Italian	510,713
Norwegian	11,628
Polish	224,811
Portuguese	35,523
Russian	55,723
Scottish	48,161
Slovak	31,284
Swedish	48,015
Welsh	9,306
West Indian	30,495

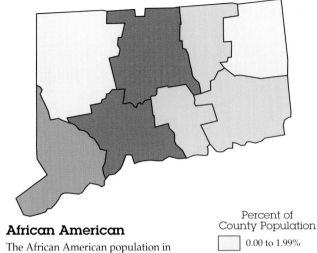

African American

The African American population in Connecticut was 274,269 in 1990. This was an increase of 26.60 percent from 216,641 in 1980. Most of the African American population can be found in cities such as Hartford, Waterbury, and New Haven.

Percent of County Population

- 0.00 to 1.99%
- 2.00 to 4.99%
- 10.00 to 24.99%

Statewide Ethnic Composition

Over 86 percent of the population of Connecticut is white. The largest numbers consider themselves of Italian, Irish, German, or English descent. African Americans made up the next largest ethnic group. Only 7,465 people claimed to have African roots despite the fact that the African American population was calculated at 274,269 in 1990.

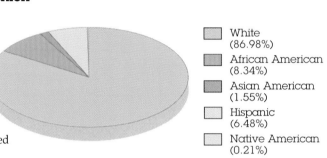

- White (86.98%)
- African American (8.34%)
- Asian American (1.55%)
- Hispanic (6.48%)
- Native American (0.21%)

Education Facts

Total Students 1990: 461,560	Mean SAT Score 1991 Verbal: 429
Number of School Districts: 166	Mean SAT Score 1991 Math: 468
Expenditure Per Capita on Education 1990: $1,129	Average Teacher's Salary 1992: $47,000
Expenditure Per Capita K–12 1990: $1,067	Rank Teacher's Salary: 1st in U.S.
Expenditure Per Pupil 1990: $8,455	High School Graduates 1990: 31,800
Total School Enrollment 1990–1991: 472,970	Total Number of Public Schools: 983
Rank of Expenditures Per Student: 2d in the U.S.	Number of Teachers 1990: 36,105
African American Enrollment: 12.5%	Student/Teacher Ratio: 13.1
Hispanic Enrollment: 9.7%	Staff Employed in Public Schools: 57,423
Asian/Pacific Islander Enrollment: 2.0%	Pupil/Staff Ratio: 8.0
Native American Enrollment: 0.2%	Staff/Teacher Ratio: 1.6

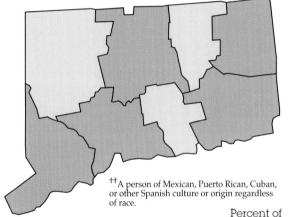

††A person of Mexican, Puerto Rican, Cuban, or other Spanish culture or origin regardless of race.

Hispanic††

The Hispanic population in Connecticut was 213,116 in 1990. This is an increase of 71.18 percent from 124,499 persons in 1980. The Hispanic population is spread evenly throughout the state with most Hispanics living in urban areas.

Percent of County Population

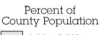
- 1.00 to 2.99%
- 3.00 to 9.99%

Education

Attainment: 80.6 percent of population 25 years or older were high school graduates in 1989, earning Connecticut a ranking of 22d in the United States; 27.5 percent of the state's population had completed college. Institutions of Higher Education: The largest universities and colleges in the state include the University of Connecticut, Storrs; University of Hartford, West Hartford; Yale University, New Haven; University of Bridgeport, Bridgeport; Trinity College, Hartford; Wesleyan University, Middletown; United States Coast Guard Academy, New London. Expenditures per Student: Expenditure increased 59% between 1985 and 1990. Projected High School Graduations: 1998 (32,232), 2004 (36,429); Total Revenues for Education from Federal Sources: $105 million; Total Revenues for Education from State Sources: $1.2 billion; Total Revenues for Education from Local Sources: $1.6 billion; Average Annual Salaries for Public School Principals: $51,262; Largest School Districts in State: Hartford School District, 24,682 students, 187th in the United States.

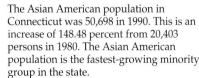

Asian American

The Asian American population in Connecticut was 50,698 in 1990. This is an increase of 148.48 percent from 20,403 persons in 1980. The Asian American population is the fastest-growing minority group in the state.

Percent of County Population
- 0.25 to 0.99%
- 1.00 to 1.99%
- 2.00 to 4.99%

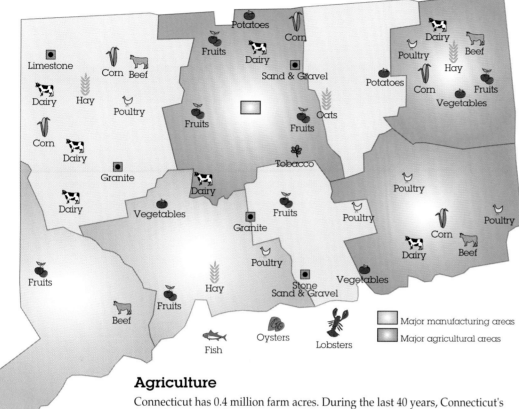

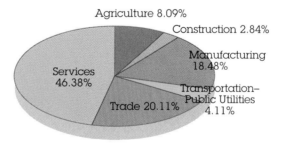

Major manufacturing areas
Major agricultural areas

Fish   Oysters   Lobsters

Transportation

For a small state, Connecticut has a relatively good transportation network. Several ports are located along Connecticut's coast, including New Haven, New London, and Bridgeport. Ships also use the Connecticut River as far as Hartford, in the middle of the state.

Virtually all of the 19,000 miles of highways and roads are surfaced. The state turnpike runs the length of Connecticut, from Greenwich to Killingly. Passenger railroads are especially important to Connecticut commuters, especially commuters going to and from New York City. About 45 Connecticut cities are served by passenger rail lines. In addition, four major freight lines operate throughout the state. Approximately 100 airports exist throughout Connecticut; Bradley International in Windsor Locks is one of the busiest airports.

Energy and Transportation Facts

Energy. Yearly Consumption: 732 tril. BTUs (residential, 30.2%; commercial, 23.5%; industrial, 18.4%; transportation, 27.9%); Annual Energy Expenditures Per Capita: $1,885; Nuclear Power Plants Located in State: 4; Source of Energy Consumed: Petroleum— 61.2%; Natural Gas— 15.3%; Coal— 3.4%; Hydroelectric Power—0.9%; Nuclear Power—19.3%.

Transportation. Highway Miles: 20,280 (interstates, 341; urban, 11,496; rural, 8,784); Average Yearly Auto Insurance: $878 (4th); Auto Fatalities Rank: 48th; Registered Motor Vehicles: 2,569,164; Workers in Carpools: 14.4%; Workers Using Public Trans: 3.9%.

Employment

Employment. Connecticut employed 1.68 million people in 1993. Most work in social and personal services (443,300 persons or 26.4% of the workforce). Manufacturing accounts for 17.5% or 293,600 workers. Wholesale and retail trade account for 19.6% or 328,600 workers. Government employs 206,700 workers (12.3%). Construction employs 47,200 workers (2.8%). Transportation and utilities account for 4.1% or 69,200 persons. Agriculture employs 20,100 workers or 1.2%. Finance, real estate, and insurance account for 8.3% or 139,400 workers. Mining employs 900 people and accounts for only 0.1% of the work force.

Unemployment. Unemployment has increased to 6.2% in 1993 from a rate of 4.9% in 1985. Today's figure is lower than the national average of 6.8% as shown below.

Agriculture

Connecticut has 0.4 million farm acres. During the last 40 years, Connecticut's farms have grown larger in size and fewer in number. In 1955, 13,000 farms were found in the state. Today, 4,000 remain.

Agriculture adds $1 billion to the state's gross product annually. The principal commodities in order of marketing receipts are greenhouse, dairy products, eggs, and tobacco.

Egg production is the leading agricultural activity in Connecticut, located mainly in the eastern portion of the state. Milk and dairy cattle are also found in many rural areas. Ornamental shrubs and flowers are the primary products of Connecticut's greenhouse industry. The leading crops are tobacco and hay. The tobacco is grown to provide the wrapping for cigars.

Housing

Owner Occupied Units: 1,320,850; Average Age of Units: 36 years; Average Value of Housing Units: $177,800; Renter Occupied Units: 418,520; Median Monthly Rent: $598; Housing Starts: 9,300; Existing Home Sales: 45,900.

Economic Facts

Gross State Product: $89,000,000,000

Income Per Capita: $26,979

Disposable Personal Income: $22,891

Median Household Income: $41,721

Average Annual Pay, 1988: $30,689

Principal Industries: transportation equipment, scientific instruments, machinery, printing, fabricated metal products, firearms, chemicals, cutlery, silverware

Major Crops: milk, eggs, greenhouse products, shade tobacco

Fish: Shellfish, Flounder, Shad

Livestock: Broilers

Non-Fuel Minerals: Stone, Traprock, Feldspar, Sand, Gravel, Lime, Clay

Organic Fuel Minerals: N/A

Civilian Labor Force: 1,801,000 (Women: 850,000)

Total Employed: 1,679,000 (Women: 798,000)

Median Value of Housing: $177,800

Median Contract Rent: $598 per month

Economic Sectors

Agriculture 8.09%
Construction 2.84%
Manufacturing 18.48%
Services 46.38%
Transportation-Public Utilities 4.11%
Trade 20.11%

Manufacturing

The state of Connecticut is highly industrialized. In recent years, many foreign businesses have located or expanded their enterprises in Connecticut. Manufacturing industries contribute 24 percent to the state's gross product. Transportation equipment is, by far, the most important manufactured product. However, machinery, fabricated metal products, and chemicals are all significant industries.

Much of the transportation equipment made in Connecticut is used by the military. Helicopter factories can be found in Stratford, East Hartford, and Bridgeport. Most of the state's machinery is made in either Bridgeport or Hartford. New Haven, along the coast, is one of Connecticut's major hardware centers.

Unemployment Rate

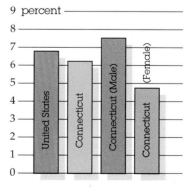

9 percent
8
7
6
5
4
3
2
1
0

United States | Connecticut | Connecticut (Male) | Connecticut (Female)

DELAWARE
The State of Delaware

Official State Seal

The Great Seal of Delaware was designed in 1777. Pictures of wheat, corn, and livestock appear on a crest. This depicts the importance of agriculture in Delaware's economy. A ship appears above the crest, representing the importance of shipping. The banner with the motto "Liberty and Independence" is placed below a farmer and a hunter.

Legal Holidays

January: New Year's Day—1st; February: Abraham Lincoln Birthday Observance—1st; Presidents' Day—3rd Monday; May: Memorial Day—4th Monday; July: Independence Day—4th; September: Labor Day—1st Monday; October: Columbus Day—2nd Monday; November: Veterans' Day—11th; Thanksgiving—4th Thursday; December: Delaware Day—7th; Christmas—25th.

Official State Flag

The state flag of Delaware was adopted in 1913. It is similar to the flag used by troops during the Civil War. The date "December 7, 1787" is the day Delaware ratified the U.S. Constitution. Symbols from the state seal are placed in front of a field of colonial blue with a buff diamond.

DECEMBER 7, 1787

Festivals and Events

April/ May: Old Dover Days, Dover; May: Greek Festival, Wilmington; June: Italian Festival, Wilmington; July: Old-Fashioned Ice Cream Festival, Wilmington; August: Sandcastle Contest, Rehoboth Beach; September: Nanticoke Native American Pow Wow, Millsboro; October: Sea Witch Weekend Fest, Rehoboth/ Dewey Beaches.

Delaware Compared to States in Its Region.

Resident Pop. in Metro Areas: 3d; Pop. Percent Increase: 3d; Pop. Over 65: 4th; Infant Mortality: 5th; School Enroll. Increase: 4th; High School Grad. and Up: 2d; Violent Crime: 5th; Hazardous Waste Sites: 5th; Unemployment: 8th; Median Household Income: 2d; Persons Below Poverty: 7th; Energy Costs Per Person: 2d.

South Atlantic Region

	Population	Capital
Delaware	700,000	Dover
Maryland	4,965,000	Annapolis
Washington DC	578,000	—
Virginia	6,491,000	Richmond
West Virginia	1,820,000	Charleston
North Carolina	6.,945,000	Raleigh
South Carolina	3,643,000	Columbia
Georgia	6,917,000	Atlanta
Florida	13,679,000	Tallahassee

Delaware's Finances

Households: 247,000; Income Per Capita Current Dollars: $21,451; Change Per Capita Income 1980 to 1992: 107.1% (20th in U.S.); State Expenditures: $2,241,000,000; State Revenues: $2,456,000,000; Personal Income Tax: 3.2 to 7.7%; Federal Income Taxes Paid Per Capita: $2,128; Sales Tax: N/A.

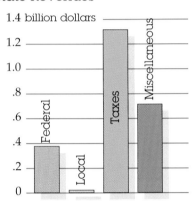

State Expenditures

State Revenues

Location, Size, and Boundaries

Location. Delaware is located on the Eastern Seaboard of the United States in a region known as the South Atlantic. It is bounded on three of four sides by land with a general coastline along the Atlantic Ocean in the east. The geographic center of Delaware is lat. 38° 58.8' N; long. 75° 30.7' W.

Size. Delaware is the 49th largest state in terms of size. Its area is 2,057 sq. mi. (5,328 km2). Inland water covers 75 sq. mi. (194 km2). Delaware touches the Atlantic Ocean along a 28 mi. (45 km) coastline.

Boundaries. Pennsylvania, 23 mi. (37 km); New Jersey, 27 mi. (44 km); Atlantic Ocean, 28 mi. (45 km); Maryland, 122 mi. (196 km).

Geographic Extent. The north/south extent is 96 mi. (154 km). The state extends 35 mi. (56 km) to the east/west.

Facts about Delaware. Origin of Name: Named after Lord De La Warr, an early governor of Virginia; Nickname: The First State; Motto: "Liberty and independence"; Abbreviations: Del. (traditional), DE (postal); State Bird: blue hen chicken; State Tree: American holly; State Flower: peach blossom; State Song: "Our Delaware," words by George B. Hynson and music by William M. S. Brown.

Delaware Compared to Other States. Resident Pop. in Metro Areas: 14th; Pop. Percent Increase: 15th; Pop. Over 65: 31st; Infant Mort.12th; School Enroll. Increase: 9th; High School Grad. and Up: 23d; Violent Crime: 16th; Hazardous Waste Sites: 20th; Unemployment: 41st; Median Household Income: 9th; Persons Below Poverty: 45th; Energy Costs Per Person: 9th.

Sources of Information. Tourism/Economy: Delaware Tourism Office, 99 Kings Highway, Box 1401, Dover, DE 19903. Government/History: Delaware Tourism Office, 99 Kings Highway, Box 1401, Dover, DE 19903.

Map labels:

A

Henry Francis du Pont
Winterthur Museum
Brandywine Creek
State Park
Nemours Mansion
and Gardens
Brandywine Coll. of Widener Univ.

B

Brandywine Springs Park
Fort Christina
Monument
Eleutherian Mills- Hagley Foundation
Cooch's Bridge
Holy Trinity
Wilmington
Univ. of
Delaware
Newark
Goldey Beacom
College
Grand Opera House
Wilmington Maritime Center

C

Welsh Tract
Baptist Church
New Castle

D

Glasgow
Red Lion
Fort Delaware
State Park
Wrangle Hill
Lums Pond
State Park
Kirkwood
Delaware City
Chesapeake and
Delaware Canal

E

Summit
Bridge
NEW
CASTLE
Biddles
Creek
Port Penn
McDonough
Bay View
St. Anne's
Episcopal Church

F

Middletown
Odessa
Odessa
Taylors
Bridge
Old Drawyer's
Presb. Church

G

Townsend
Blackbird
Flemings
Landing
Blackbird
State Forest
Prices
Corners
Bombay Hook
National Wildlife Refuge
Clayton
Smyrna

H

Kenton
Magnolia
Cheswold
Seven Hickories

I

Fords Corner
KENT
Leipsic
Bombay Hook
National Wildlife
Refuge
Dover
State House
Little Creek
Hartly
Wesley College
Delaware State College

J

Bethesda
Camden
Wyoming
Bowers Beach
Woodside
Magnolia
Willow Grove

K

Petersburg
Viola
Frederica
Felton
Barratt's Chapel
Hollandsville
Killen Pond
State Park

L

Whiteleysburg
Houston
Milford
Valley Gardens
Goldey Beacom
College
Harrington
Greenville
Lincoln
Slaughter
Beach
Farmington

M

Oakley
Prime Hook National
Wildlife Refuge
Greenwood
Ellendale
Milton
Bridgeville
Ellendale
State Forest
Univ. of
Delaware
Lewes
Atlanta
Redden
State Forest
Lewes
Cape Henlopen
State Park
Henlopen
Acres

N

Seaford
Sussex Co.
Court House
Georgetown
Craigs Mill
Delaware Tech. &
Community College
Rehoboth Beach
Rehoboth
Beach
Blades
Univ. of
Delaware

O

Woodland
SUSSEX
Dewey Beach
Indian River
Inlet Park

P

Broad Creek
Millsboro
Masseys
Landing
Delaware Seashore
State Park
Bethel
Christ Episcopal Church
Ocean
View
Bethany Beach
Mt. Pleasant
Church
Laurel
Prince George's Chapel
Dagsboro
Bethany Bch.
Millville
South
Bethany

Q

Packing House
Corner
Bacons
Frankford
Roxana
Trap Pond
State Park
Gumboro
Selbyville
Fenwick
Island
Delmar

Scale

0 5 10 15 mi.

5 0 5 10 15 20 km

Major Cities

City	Grid
Dover	I-3
Newark	C-1
Wilmington	B-3

Cultural features list:

■ Barratt's Chapel. First Methodist service in 1784. (K-4)

■ Bethany Beach. Resort on Atlantic Ocean. (P-8)

■ Bombay Hook National Wildlife Refuge. Waterfowl sanctuary. (G-2)

■ Brandywine Springs Park. Family park. (B-3)

■ Cape Henlopen State Park. Marks entrance to Delaware Bay. (N-7)

■ Chesapeake and Delaware Canal. Wildlife area. Connects Chesapeake Bay and Delaware River. (D-2)

■ Christ Episcopal Church, Broad Creek Hundred. Church built in 1771. (P-3)

■ Cooch's Bridge. Site of only battle of American Revolution fought in Delaware (1777). (B-1)

■ Delaware Seashore State Park. Fishing, seashore park. (P-8)

■ Eleutherian Mills-Hagley Foundation. Du Pont Company began here in 1802. Also the site of the Hagley Museum. (B-3)

■ Fort Christina Monument. Commemorates landing of Swedish colonists at The Rocks in 1638. (B-3)

■ Fort Delaware State Park. A fortress built in 1848–60. Used as a Civil War prison. (D-3)

■ Grand Opera House. Built in 1871 as part of Masonic Temple. (B-3)

■ Henry Francis du Pont Winterthur Museum. Museum dedicated to the period between 1640 and 1840. (A-2)

■ Holy Trinity (Old Swedes Church). The oldest church in United States. (B-3)

■ Indian River Inlet Park. Park with swimming and sunbathing. (O-8)

■ Lewes. Resort town with fishing, swimming, picnicking. (N-7)

■ Lums Pond State Park. Fishing, swimming, picnicking. (D-1)

■ Nemours Mansion and Gardens. Scenic grounds with period mansion and landscaped gardens. (B-3)

■ Odessa. Historic homes from the 1800s. (F-2)

□ Old Drawyers' Presbyterian Church. Dating from 1773. (F-2)

■ Prince George's Chapel. Church erected in 1757. (P-6)

■ Rehoboth Beach. Resort town with beach and a boardwalk. (O-8)

■ St. Anne's Episcopal Church. Church erected in 1768. (F-1)

■ State House. The second oldest state house in the United States. (I-3)

■ Sussex County Court House on the Square. Court house built in 1839. (N-5).

■ Trap Pond State Park. Lake, beaches; camping, boating, and picnicking. (Q-4)

■ Valley Garden. Landscaped gardens. (L-2)

■ Welsh Tract Baptist Church. Built in 1746 on land purchased from William Penn in 1703. (C-1)

■ Wilmington Maritime Center. Museum dedicated to maritime art, maps, and memorabilia. (B-3)

Legend

☆ State capitol

⊙ Cities over 35,000 population

○ Other significant cities

● County Seats

■ Major cultural attractions

□ State Parks

Ⓦ Welcome Centers

⚲ Major colleges and universities

Weather Facts

Record High Temperature: 110° F (43° C) on July 20, 1926, at Millsboro; Record Low Temperature: -17° F (-27° C) on January 17, 1893, at Millsboro; Average January Temperature: 34° F (1° C); Average July Temperature: 76° F (24° C); Average Yearly Precipitation: 36 in. (91 cm).

Environmental Facts

Air Pollution Rank: 41st; Water Pollution Rank: 35th; Total Yearly Industrial Pollution: 5,383,898 lbs.; Industrial Pollution Rank: 43d; Hazardous Waste Sites: 20; Hazardous Sites Rank: 18th; Landfill Capacity: adequate; Fresh Water Supply: large surplus; Daily Residential Water Consumption: 139 gals. per capita; Endangered Species: Aquatic Species (1)—sturgeon, shortnose; Birds (3)—eagle, bald; Mammals (1)—squirrel, Delmarva peninsula fox; Other Species (3)—turtle, hawksbill sea; Plants (3)—achyranthes splendens var. rotundata.

Environmental Quality

Delaware residents generate 600,000 tons of solid waste each year, or approximately 1,850 pounds per capita. Landfill capacity in Delaware will be exhausted in more than 12 years. The state has 20 hazardous waste sites. Annual greenhouse gas emissions in Delaware total 14.2 million tons, or 21.5 tons per capita. Industrial sources in Delaware release approximately 8.2 thousand tons of toxins, 158.6 thousand tons of acid precipitation-producing substances, and 300 thousand tons of smog-producing substances into the atmosphere each year.

The state has no national parks. State parks cover just over 10,725 acres, attracting 3.2 million visitors per year.

Delaware spends approximately 1.8 percent of its budget, or approximately $50 per capita, on environmental and natural resources. Delaware representatives in the U.S. House voted in favor of national environmental legislation 75 percent of the time, while U.S. senators did so 71 percent of the time.

Average Monthly Weather

Wilmington	Jan	Feb	Mar	Apr	May	Jun	Jul	Aug	Sep	Oct	Nov	Dec	Yearly
Maximum Temperature °F	39.2	41.8	50.9	63.0	72.7	81.2	85.6	84.1	77.8	66.7	54.8	43.6	63.5
Minimum Temperature °F	23.2	24.6	32.6	41.8	51.7	61.2	66.3	65.4	58.0	45.9	36.4	27.3	44.5
Days of Precipitation	10.8	9.6	10.8	10.9	11.5	9.6	9.2	8.9	8.0	7.7	9.5	9.7	116.2

Flora and Fauna

In the small state of Delaware, forests cover approximately 620 square miles, which is close to one-third of the land. In northern Delaware, near Wilmington, beech, maple, and walnut trees grow. Farther south, forested areas are mixed with holly, sweet gum, black tupelo, and a few different kinds of pine trees. Swampy areas of Delaware are home to red cedar and bald cypress trees. Several kinds of flowers are common in all parts of the state. Both pink lady's-slippers and magnolias grow in Delaware swamps. Water lilies and floating hearts can be found in and along waterways.

Since Delaware lies within the path of many migratory birds, its marsh lands provide a haven for several species, both migrating and resident. Birds living in the state include herons, ducks, wrens, and sandpipers. Delaware also is home to many mammals such as deer, rabbit, fox, and otter. A plethora of sea life can be found in waterways in and around Delaware. Some examples of this wildlife include crabs, eels, and diamond terrapins.

Physical Regions: (a) Atlantic Coastal Plain; (b) Piedmont.

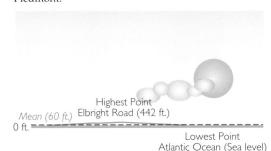

Mean (60 ft.) Highest Point Elbright Road (442 ft.)
0 ft.
Lowest Point Atlantic Ocean (Sea level)

Land Use

Cropland: 43%; Pasture: 2.4%; Rangeland: 0%; Forest: 29.4%; Urban: 13.6%; Other: 11.6%.

For more information about Delaware's environment, contact the Chief Environmental Officer, 89 Kings Highway, P.O. Box 1401, Dover, DE 19903.

Topography

Delaware is divided into only two distinct physical regions. Most of the state occupies the Atlantic Coastal Plain, which is a region that stretches along the east coast of the United States from New York to Florida. This area is mainly flatlands, with low hills and pastures. Marshlands are found in the southern portion of the state. The Cypress Swamp, in the far south, covers more than 25,000 acres (10,000 hectares). The soil is characterized as warm and wet, as it is throughout Delaware, derived from clay, and colored light to almost black. The consistently low elevations in this region give Delaware the distinction of having the lowest mean elevation in the United States at 60 ft. (18 m).

In the northeast corner of Delaware lies a small section of the Piedmont physical region, an area of gentle hills and valleys that stretch as far south as Alabama. This is a very fertile region, with rich farmland. The highest elevation in the state, 442 ft. (135 m), is found in this northeast region bordering Pennsylvania and Maryland. The soil of this region varies from red/yellow to gray/brown in color and is mostly clay.

Climate

Delaware has a humid continental climate, characterized by long summers and rather mild winters. Pennsylvania's mountains protect Delaware from severe winter weather. The state lies directly in the path of storms from the Gulf of Mexico and the continental West. However, the influences of the Atlantic Ocean and the Chesapeake Bay mitigate the stormy weather. Average temperatures vary by about 4 degrees across the state. In Wilmington, average January and July temperatures are 32 degrees F and 75 degrees F. Breezes from the Atlantic Ocean cool the Delaware coast in the summer.

Delaware receives approximately 45 inches of precipitation a year. The state also receives some snowfall, though not an abundance. Even the coast receives snowfall, only about 12 inches. Millsboro, in southeastern Delaware, has recorded both the state's highest and lowest temperatures. A 110-degree temperature was recorded in 1930, and a -17 degree temperature in 1893.

Hydrology

The most important river in the state is the Delaware. It forms the boundary between northern Delaware and New Jersey, before emptying into the Delaware Bay. Other rivers that empty into the Delaware River or Bay include the Christina (at Wilmington), the Smyrna, the Leipsic, the St. Jones, the Murderkill, the Mispillion, and the Broadkill. Some rivers in Delaware, especially in the southern part of the state, flow westward into Maryland before emptying into the Chesapeake Bay. Among these are the Pocomoke, Nanticoke, and Choptank rivers, and Marshyhope Creek.

Delaware's entire eastern boundary is water. The Delaware River and Bay make up most of this border. In the southern part of the state are Rehoboth Bay and Indian River Bay, south of Cape Henlopen.

The Chesapeake and Delaware Canal, built in the 1820s, is a man-made water passage between the northern Chesapeake Bay and the Delaware River just below Delaware City.

Delaware's History

Delaware's First People

There is evidence of human occupation of Delaware as long as ten thousand years ago. A variety of different peoples probably inhabited the state early on, though we know little of who they were.

In the early seventeenth century, when the first Europeans arrived, the Lenni Lenape (or Delaware) Indians were the dominant tribe, controlling most of the northern part of the state. Some other tribes, including the Nanticoke and Assateague, occupied the southern portion. These tribes were generally friendly with the first Dutch settlers, though by the middle of the seventeenth century some animosity had developed between the Indians and the Dutch. When a Dutch farmer killed a Lenni Lenape woman in 1655, several of the tribes joined in attacks on Dutch settlements.

European Exploration

In 1609, Henry Hudson discovered Delaware Bay while sailing for the Dutch East Indies. The first land was bought by the Dutch West India Company in 1630 to be used as a whaling community. In 1631, The Dutch set up a settlement at a site called Zwaanendael, now present-day Lewes, but it was destroyed by Indians a year later. Seven years later the Swedes, led by Peter Minuit, succeeded, establishing Fort Christina at the site of present-day Wilmington in 1638. This area was renamed New Sweden. Here, the first log cabins in the New World were constructed. The Dutch, under Peter Stuyvesant, took the settlement from the Swedes in 1655, and nine years later the British seized control.

In 1682, the territory was ceded by the English to William Penn by the duke of York. The land became a Pennsylvania province, but was administered independently of Pennsylvania. Although Delaware did gain an elected assembly in 1704, it did not fully gain independence from the Penn family and Pennsylvania until 1776.

Statehood

After establishing independence from Pennsylvania in 1776 and resolving border disputes with Maryland around the same period, Delaware adopted its first constitution of four on September 21, 1776. Other constitutions were adopted in 1792, 1831, and 1897. New Castle was the capitol until 1777 when it was moved to Dover. Delaware, soon after, became the first state in the Union to ratify the Constitution on December 7, 1787. During the Revolutionary War, the Delaware River was blockaded around Delaware by the British fleet.

During the Civil War, although Delaware was still a slave state, it did not secede from the Union and indeed even supplied soldiers to the cause, though it was not really trusted by the other northern states. Delaware slaves were not freed until the ratification of the Thirteenth Amendment in 1865, but even then opposition to black rights in the form of measures such as poll taxes (1873) and literacy tests (1893) proliferated.

Industrialization

Delaware's industrial history began in 1802 with the Dupont family. The Dupont family immigrated from France at the beginning of the nineteenth century, opening a gunpowder plant on the Brandywine River that launched an industrial regime that still dominates Delaware today. Such things as the steam engine, nylon, and other items were developed with sponsorship from the Duponts.

Buoyed by a railroad connecting Philadelphia and Baltimore, industry (mills, shipyards, foundries, etc.) fueled Delaware's economy throughout the nineteenth century. Wilmington, which experienced explosive growth during this period, became a leading center for the chemical industry in the twentieth century— primarily due to the E. I. DuPont de Nemours Company. Agricultural products, such as poultry and soybeans, also contributed to the state's economy, which continued to thrive even during the recession of the early 1980s. This was largely a result of the favorable atmosphere in Delaware for corporations to do business.

To support this growing industrial base, new modes of transportation were built. The Chesapeake and Delaware canal was completed in 1829 and was 15 miles long. The first railroad in the state, the New Castle—Frenchtown Railroad, was completed in the early 1830s. The Delaware Memorial Bridge, which connects the state with New Jersey, was completed in 1951 and was 3.5 miles (5.6 kilometers) long.

America's Corporate Headquarters

A tax law passed by the state legislature in 1899, attracted corporations to the city of Wilmington. As a result, Wilmington grew in both prominence and in population. Delaware has become a haven for corporations to locate their headquarters. Dubbed the "corporate state" by some consumer groups during the 1970s, today Delaware is the state of incorporation for more than half of the Fortune 500 companies.

DuPont, the state's largest corporation, reflects the varied corporate portfolio with its interests in banking, real estate, and media as well as its traditional role in chemical and other industries.

The late 1960s and the 1970s saw a decline in the economy and many areas of the state, especially in the cities, saw many workers lose their jobs. In 1968, riots broke out amongst unemployed African American workers in Wilmington. The National Guard had to be called in to quell hostilities. The 1980s saw an upturn in the economy with the passing of new banking and corporate laws, however, it has not yet recovered enough.

Important Events

1609 Henry Hudson first discovers Delaware Bay.

1631 Dutch attempt first settlement at Zwaanendael (present-day Lewes).

1638 Swedes establish first permanent settlement at Fort Christina (present-day Wilmington).

1655 Dutch capture New Sweden from the Swedes.

1682 Delaware is turned over to William Penn by the duke of York.

1700 Blackbeard and his pirates 'visit' the townspeople of Lewes.

1787 Delaware becomes the first state in the Union to ratify the Constitution.

1802 E I. DuPont de Nemours & Co. is founded as a gunpowder manufacturing firm.

1829 Chesapeake and Delaware Canal is opened.

1838 Construction is competed on a railroad linking Philadelphia and Baltimore through Wilmington.

1855 Delaware passes state prohibition law which is repealed two years later.

1873 Delaware enacts legislation levying poll taxes, effectively disenfranchising blacks.

1897 Delaware's present constitution is adopted.

1934 Delaware withdraws its unemployment insurance at the height of the Great Depression.

1948 Pea Patch Island is returned to the state by the federal government (which had controlled it for over 100 years).

1962 East coast dock workers' strike shuts down Delaware's shipping industry.

1971 Delaware's legislature enacts the Coastal Zone Act, intended to protect the environment from any new heavy industry.

1978 Court-ordered school busing is instituted in northern Delaware to achieve integration.

1989 A tanker from Uruguay runs aground near Claymont, spilling up to 1.6 million gallons of industrial fuel in the Delaware river.

1993-1994 Paramount/QVC buyout bid is acted out in a Delaware court.

Population Density

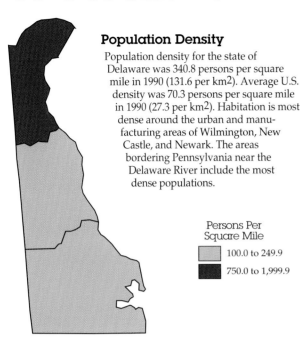

Population density for the state of Delaware was 340.8 persons per square mile in 1990 (131.6 per km^2). Average U.S. density was 70.3 persons per square mile in 1990 (27.3 per km^2). Habitation is most dense around the urban and manu-facturing areas of Wilmington, New Castle, and Newark. The areas bordering Pennsylvania near the Delaware River include the most dense populations.

Persons Per Square Mile

- 100.0 to 249.9
- 750.0 to 1,999.9

Population Projections

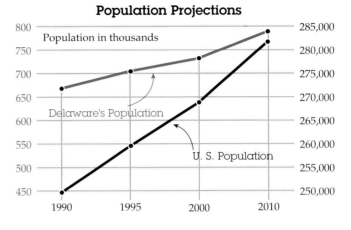

Population in thousands

Delaware's Population

U. S. Population

Population Change

Year	Population
1950	318,000
1960	449,000
1970	551,000
1980	594,338
1990	666,168
2000	734,000
2010	790,000

Period	Change
1950–1970	73.3%
1970–1980	7.8%
1980–1990	12.1%
1990–2000	10.2%

Population Change

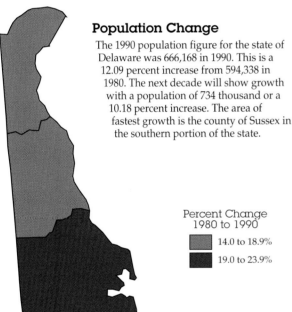

The 1990 population figure for the state of Delaware was 666,168 in 1990. This is a 12.09 percent increase from 594,338 in 1980. The next decade will show growth with a population of 734 thousand or a 10.18 percent increase. The area of fastest growth is the county of Sussex in the southern portion of the state.

Percent Change 1980 to 1990

- 14.0 to 18.9%
- 19.0 to 23.9%

Population Facts

State Population, 1993: 700,000

Rank: 46

Population 2000: 734,000 (Rank 45)

Density: 340.8 per sq. mi. (131.6 per km^2)

Distribution: 73.0% urban, 27.0% rural

Population Under 5 Years Old: 7.5%

Population Under 18 Years Old: 25.0%

Population Over 65 Years Old: 12.3%

Median Age: 32.9

Number of Households: 247,000

Average Persons Per Household: 2.61

Average Persons Per Family: 3.09

Female Heads of Households: 4.40%

Population That Is Married: 20.71%

Birth Rate: 16.7 per 1,000 population

Death Rate: 8.7 per 1,000 population

Births to Teen Mothers: 11.9%

Marriage Rate: 8.2 per 1,000 population

Divorce Rate: 4.4 per 1,000 population

Violent Crime Rate: 714 per 100,000 pop.

Population on Social Security: 15.9%

Percent Voting for President: 55.2%

Delaware's Famous Citizens

Clayton, John (1796–1856). Chief justice of the state supreme court (1837–1839). Also served three terms as U.S. senator.

Davies, Samuel (1723–1761). Religious leader in the Great Awakening movement and president of the College of New Jersey.

Evans, Oliver (1755–1819). Invented a machine that carded wool and a steam-powered river dredge.

Macdonough, Thomas (1783–1825). Naval officer. Instrumental in defeating the British at Plattsburgh in the War of 1812.

Marquand, J. P. (1893–1960). Writer. Noted for his short stories featuring Mr. Moto, a Japanese detective.

Redding, Jay Saunders (1906–1988). Wrote about the experience of being an African-American in America. Professor of English.

Ridgely, Mabel Lloyd (1872–1962). First president of the Delaware League of Women Voters.

Squibb, Edward R. (1819–1900). Started chemical laboratory in 1858, which became E. R. Squibb & Sons in 1892.

Distribution of Income

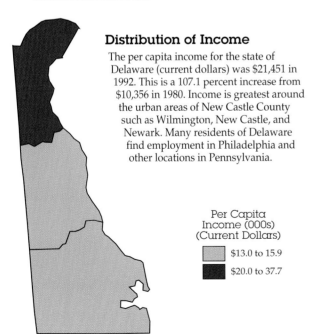

The per capita income for the state of Delaware (current dollars) was $21,451 in 1992. This is a 107.1 percent increase from $10,356 in 1980. Income is greatest around the urban areas of New Castle County such as Wilmington, New Castle, and Newark. Many residents of Delaware find employment in Philadelphia and other locations in Pennsylvania.

Per Capita Income (000s) (Current Dollars)

- $13.0 to 15.9
- $20.0 to 37.7

Population Profile

Rank. Delaware ranks 46th among U.S. states in terms of population with 700,000 citizens.

Minority Population. The state's minority population is 20.9 percent. The state's male to female ratio for 1990 was 94.10 males for every 100 females. It was below the national average of 95.22 males for every 100 females.

Growth. Growing faster than the projected national average, the state's population is

expected to reach 790 thousand by the year 2010 (*see graph above*).

Older Citizens. The state's population older than 65 was 80,735 in 1990. It grew 8.68% from 74,287 in 1980.

Younger Citizens. The number of children (under 18 years of age) was 163 thousand in 1990. This represents 24.5 percent of the state's population. The state's school aged population was 99 thousand in 1990. It is expected to increase to 112 thousand by the year 2000. This represents a 13.13% change.

Urban/Rural. 73.0% of the population of the state live in urban areas while 27.0% live in rural areas.

Largest Cities. Delaware has one city with a population greater than 35,000. The populations of the state's largest centers are (starting from the most populous) Wilmington (71,529), Dover (27,630), Newark (25,098), Brookside (15,307), and Pike Creek (10,163).

Government

Capital: Dover (established 1777).

Statehood: Became 1st state on Dec. 7, 1787.

Number of Counties: 3.

Supreme Court Justices: 5, 12-year term.

State Senators: 21, 4-year term.

State Legislators: 41, 2-year term.

United States Senators: 2.

United States Representatives: 1.

Electoral Votes: 3.

State Constitution: Adopted 1897.

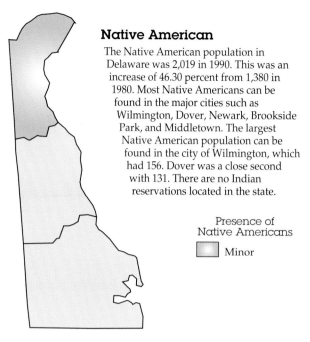

Native American

The Native American population in Delaware was 2,019 in 1990. This was an increase of 46.30 percent from 1,380 in 1980. Most Native Americans can be found in the major cities such as Wilmington, Dover, Newark, Brookside Park, and Middletown. The largest Native American population can be found in the city of Wilmington, which had 156. Dover was a close second with 131. There are no Indian reservations located in the state.

Presence of Native Americans

☐ Minor

Nationalities

African	1,074
American	29,084
Arab	1,052
Austrian	1,433
Czech	1,385
Dutch	7,741
English	84,317
Finnish	571
German	101,318
Greek	2,527
Hungarian	2,010
Irish	88,552
Italian	48,156
Norwegian	1,926
Polish	28,137
Portuguese	735
Russian	4,934
Scottish	10,081
Slovak	2,857
Swedish	4,510
Welsh	4,666
West Indian	1,834

African American

The African American population in Delaware was 112,460 in 1990. This was an increase of 16.95 percent from 96,157 in 1980. Large concentrations of African Americans can be found in the major cities such as Wilmington, Dover, Newark, Brookside Park, and Middletown. African Americans are spread evenly thoughout the state with no county holding an overwhelming majority.

Percent of County Population

■ 10.0 to 15.99%
■ 16.0 to 17.99%

Statewide Ethnic Composition

Over 80 percent of the population of Delaware is white. Of these numbers the largest nationality is German, followed by Irish and English. There is also a large number of Polish residents living in the state. The next largest group is the African Americans, with a little over 16 percent of the population.

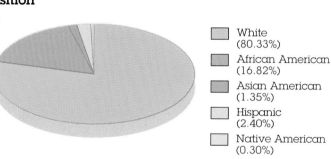

☐ White (80.33%)
☐ African American (16.82%)
☐ Asian American (1.35%)
☐ Hispanic (2.40%)
☐ Native American (0.30%)

Education Facts

Total Students 1990: 97,808

Number of School Districts: 19

Expenditure Per Capita on Education 1990: $835

Expenditure Per Capita K–12 1990: $782

Expenditure Per Pupil 1990: $6,016

Total School Enrollment 1990–1991: 99,658

Rank of Expenditures Per Student: 9th in the U.S.

African American Enrollment: 26.9%

Hispanic Enrollment: 2.6%

Asian/Pacific Islander Enrollment: 1.5%

Native American Enrollment: 0.1%

Mean SAT Score 1991 Verbal: 428

Mean SAT Score 1991 Math: 464

Average Teacher's Salary 1992: $34,500

Rank Teacher's Salary: 15th in U.S.

High School Graduates 1990: 5,600

Total Number of Public Schools: 170

Number of Teachers 1990: 6,077

Student/Teacher Ratio: 16.4

Staff Employed in Public Schools: 10,842

Pupil/Staff Ratio: 9.0

Staff/Teacher Ratio: 1.8

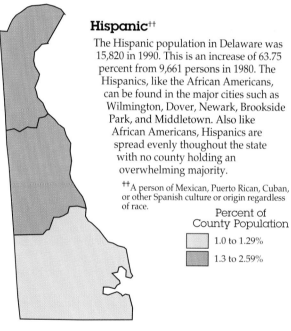

Hispanic[††]

The Hispanic population in Delaware was 15,820 in 1990. This is an increase of 63.75 percent from 9,661 persons in 1980. The Hispanics, like the African Americans, can be found in the major cities such as Wilmington, Dover, Newark, Brookside Park, and Middletown. Also like African Americans, Hispanics are spread evenly thoughout the state with no county holding an overwhelming majority.

[††]A person of Mexican, Puerto Rican, Cuban, or other Spanish culture or origin regardless of race.

Percent of County Population

☐ 1.0 to 1.29%
■ 1.3 to 2.59%

Education

Attainment: 80.6 percent of population 25 years or older were high school graduates in 1989, earning Delaware a ranking of 18th in the United States; 19 percent of the state's population had completed college. Institutions of Higher Education: The largest universities and colleges in the state include Delaware State College, Dover; Delaware Technical and Community College, (4 campuses); University of Delaware, Newark (and 2 other campuses); Wesley College, Dover; Brandywine College of Widener University, Wilmington. Expenditures per Student: Expenditure increased 76% between 1985 and 1990. Projected High School Graduations: 1998 (8,096), 2004 (7,658); Total Revenues for Education from Federal Sources: $35 million; Total Revenues for Education from State Sources: $318 million; Total Revenues for Education from Local Sources: $110 million; Average Annual Salaries for Public School Principals: $49,506.

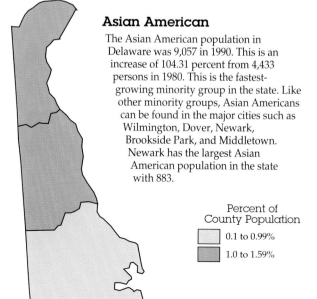

Asian American

The Asian American population in Delaware was 9,057 in 1990. This is an increase of 104.31 percent from 4,433 persons in 1980. This is the fastest-growing minority group in the state. Like other minority groups, Asian Americans can be found in the major cities such as Wilmington, Dover, Newark, Brookside Park, and Middletown. Newark has the largest Asian American population in the state with 883.

Percent of County Population

☐ 0.1 to 0.99%
■ 1.0 to 1.59%

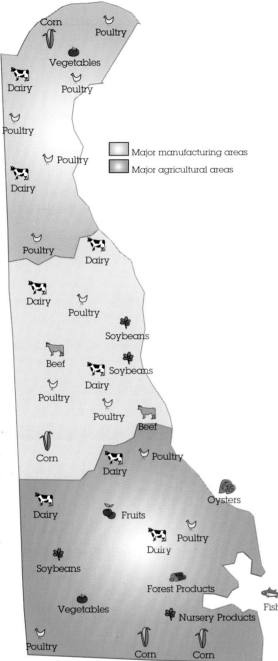

Major manufacturing areas
Major agricultural areas

Transportation

Before paved roads, Delaware's transportation needs were almost entirely served by water routes. Even today, water transportation is important to the state. The Chesapeake and Delaware Canal, in northern Delaware, provides an easier way for ships to go between Baltimore and Philadelphia. The Lewes and Rehoboth Canal links Lewes and Rehoboth Bay. A ferry also operates between Lewes and Cape May, New Jersey.

Delaware has approximately 5,300 miles of highways and roads, nearly all of which are surfaced. The state's highway system began in 1911. Only a few Delaware cities are served by a passenger rail line. However, four different freight lines provide service throughout the state. The Greater Wilmington Airport is the main airport for Delaware.

Energy and Transportation Facts

Energy. Yearly Consumption: 237 tril. BTUs (residential, 19.8%; commercial, 14.8%; industrial, 38.0%; transportation, 27.0%); Annual Energy Expenditures Per Capita: $2,040; Nuclear Power Plants Located in State: 0; Source of Energy Consumed: Petroleum— 57.6%; Natural Gas— 18.2%; Coal— 24.2%; Hydroelectric Power—0.0%; Nuclear Power—0.0%.

Transportation. Highway Miles: 5,524 (interstates, 41; urban, 1,855; rural, 3,669); Average Yearly Auto Insurance: $745 (9th); Auto Fatalities Rank: 17th; Registered Motor Vehicles: 544,982; Workers in Carpools: 16.6%; Workers Using Public Trans: 2.4 %.

Agriculture

Delaware has 0.55 million farm acres. During the last 40 years, Delaware's farms have grown larger in size and fewer in number. In 1955, 6,000 farms were found in the state. Today, 2,500 remain. Agriculture adds less than $500 million to the state's gross product annually. The principal commodities in order of marketing receipts are broilers, soy-beans, corn, and greenhouse.

Livestock products account for about 80 percent of the state's farm income, with broilers being the leading product. Sussex County is the center of broiler production. Hogs are raised on farms in the southern portion of the state. Delaware's leading crop is soybeans, found on about two-fifths of the state's farmland. Corn is ranked second in crop production. Other crops produced include wheat, potatoes, and peas.

Housing

Owner Occupied Units: 289,919; Average Age of Units: 28 years; Average Value of Housing Units: $100,100; Renter Occupied Units: 72,176; Median Monthly Rent: $495; Housing Starts: 6,300; Existing Home Sales: 9,400.

Economic Sectors

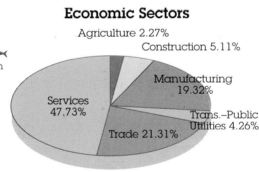

Agriculture 2.27%
Construction 5.11%
Manufacturing 19.32%
Services 47.73%
Trans.–Public Utilities 4.26%
Trade 21.31%

Employment

Employment. Delaware employed 354,000 people in 1993. Most work in social and personal services (89,400 persons or 25.3% of the workforce). Manufacturing accounts for 18.4% or 65,300 workers. Wholesale and retail trade account for 21.4% or 75,700 workers. Government employs 297,100 workers (16.5%). Construction employs 18,200 workers (5.1%). Transportation and utilities account for 4.2% or 14,800 persons. Agriculture employs 7,400 workers or 2.1%. Finance, real estate, and insurance account for 9.8% or 34,700 workers. Mining employs 100 people and accounts for less than 0.1% of the workforce.

Unemployment. Unemployment remained the same between 1985 and 1993 at a rate of 5.3%. Today's figure is lower than the national average of 6.8% as shown below.

Economic Facts

Gross State Product: $16,000,000,000

Income Per Capita: $21,451

Disposable Personal Income: $18,300

Median Household Income: $34,875

Average Annual Pay, 1988: $25,647

Principal Industries: chemicals, transportation equipment, food products, metals, printing, publishing, textiles, machinery

Major Crops: soybeans, greenhouse products, corn, forest products, milk

Fish: Bass, Carp, Catfish, Eels, Trout, Clams, Crabs, Oysters

Livestock: broiler chickens

Non-Fuel Minerals: Clay, Sand, Gravel, Brandywine Blue Granite

Organic Fuel Minerals: N/A

Civilian Labor Force: 364,000 (Women: 168,000)

Total Employed: 342,000 (Women: 159,000)

Median Value of Housing: $100,100

Median Contract Rent: $495 per month

Manufacturing

Since colonial times, manufacturing has taken place in Delaware, especially in the Wilmington area. Today, manufacturing still centers around Wilmington, but factories have also been built farther south. Chemical production is Delaware's most important industry. However, the manufacture of processed foods and automobiles also contributes to the state economy.

Wilmington has been dubbed the Chemical Capital of the World. Chemical research and management, and not manufacturing, give it this distinction. DuPont and ICI, two major chemical firms, are located in Wilmington. The capital of Dover is a leading producer of prepared desserts such as pudding. Surprisingly, Delaware is considered a leading automobile production state, with plants in Newark and Newport.

Unemployment Rate

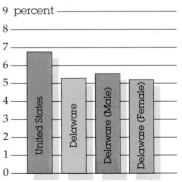

percent

United States
Delaware
Delaware (Male)
Delaware (Female)

WASHINGTON D.C. The District of Columbia

Official City Seal

The Great Seal of Washington, D.C., was adopted in 1871. It is a simple yet elegant scheme depicting a statue of George Washington. A woman representing Justice is seen placing a wreath at the statue. She is holding the Constitution in her arms. Included in the background is the Capitol.

Legal Holidays

January: New Year's Day—1st; Martin Luther King, Jr. Day—3rd Monday; February: Abraham Lincoln's Birthday—12th; President's Day—3rd Monday; May: Memorial Day—4th Monday; July: Independence Day—4th; September: Labor Day—1st Monday; October: Columbus Day—2d Monday; November: Veteran's Day—11th; Thanksgiving—4th Thursday; December: Christmas—25th

Official Flag

The official flag of Washington, D.C., was adopted in 1938. It is based on the coat of arms of George Washington and composed of three red stars above two red bars on a white field.

District of Columbia's Finances

Households: 250,000; Income Per Capita Current Dollars: $26,360; Change Per Capita Income 1980 to 1992: 110.7% (Rank N/A); City Expenditures: $4,803,000,000; City Revenues: $4,743,000,000; Personal Income Tax: 6 to 9.5%; Federal Income Taxes Paid Per Capita: $2,491; Sales Tax: 6% (food and prescription drugs exempt).

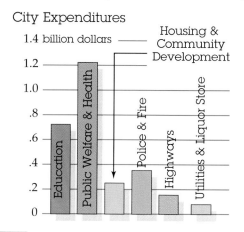

City Expenditures

City Revenues

Washington, D.C. in Its Region.

South Atlantic Region

	Population	Capital
Delaware	700,000	Dover
Maryland	4,965,000	Annapolis
Washington DC	578,000	—
Virginia	6,491,000	Richmond
West Virginia	1,820,000	Charleston
North Carolina	6,945,000	Raleigh
South Carolina	3,643,000	Columbia
Georgia	6,917,000	Atlanta
Florida	13,679,000	Tallahassee

Location, Size, and Boundaries

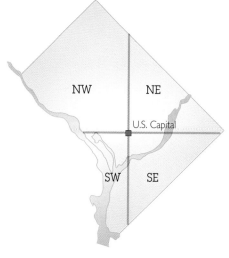

Four Regions of Washington, D.C. The city of Washington, D.C., is divided into four regions: NW, NE, SW, and SE. North Capitol, South Capitol, East Capitol, and West Capitol streets and the U.S. Capitol building define the axis and center point for this division.

Location. Washington, D.C., is located on the Eastern Seaboard of the United States in what is known as the South Atlantic region. It is bounded on three sides by land and on one side by the Potomac River. The geographic center of Washington D.C. is lat. 39° 10.0' N; long. 76° 51.0' W.

Size. Washington, D.C., is the 51st largest area in terms of size. Its area is 69 sq. mi. (179 km2). Inland water covers 6 sq. mi. (15.5 km2).

Boundaries. Maryland, 26 mi. (42 km); Virginia, 12 mi. (19 km).

Geographic Extent. The north/south extent of Washington, D.C., is 14 mi. (22 km). The city extends 11.5 mi. (18.4 km) to the east/west.

Facts about District of Columbia. Origin of Name: Named after Christopher Columbus in 1791; Nickname: Washington or DC; Abbreviations: DC (postal).

Sources of Information. Tourism: Washington Visitor Information Center, 1455 Pennsylvania Ave. NW, Washington, DC 20004. Economy: Washington, DC, Convention and Visitors Association, 1212 New York Ave. NW, Suite 600, Washington, DC 20005. Government: Washington, DC, Convention and Visitors Association, 1212 New York Ave. NW, Suite 600, Washington, DC, 20005. History: Washington Visitor Information Center, 1455 Pennsylvania Ave. NW, Washington, DC, 20004. For More Information: DC Committee to Promote Washington, 1212 New York Ave., NW, 2d floor, Washington, DC 20005.

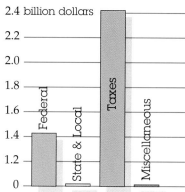

Washington, D.C.

Washington, D.C., is the capital of the United States. The city of Washington originally existed within the boundaries of the District of Columbia, but now has grown to include the entire District. The District of Columbia or D.C. is a federally owned area on the Potomac river located between Maryland and Virginia.

Washington, D.C., proper is 69 square miles (179 square kilometers) in size with an entire metropolitan area in excess of 400 square miles (1,000 square kilometers). This metropolitan area extends into adjacent counties of Maryland and Virginia.

The main industry in the city is government. In addition to the federal government (which employs approximately one-third of the workforce) there are over one hundred embassies and several major international organizations located in the city. Some of the major institutions include the World Bank and the Organization of American States. Law, medicine, printing, construction, and retailing also employ many people in the city.

History

The site for the capital of the fledgling United States was selected by George Washington in 1791. The area was chosen because it was approximately the geographic center of the original thirteen colonies.

George Washington appointed Pierre Charles L'Enfant to design the city in 1791. L'Enfant based the city on a grid street system with broad radial avenues. In 1793, Washington laid the cornerstone for the new capital. Seven years later, in 1800, the government was moved to the new city from Philadelphia. In 1802 the city was chartered.

The unfinished capital experienced its first taste of war in 1814, when the British captured

and burned it in the War of 1812. The capital was rebuilt, and by the 1860s the population of the city had grown to over sixty thousand residents. Its next wartime experience was the Civil War (1861–1865), in which Washington, D.C., was continually threatened by Confederate troops. During this period Washington, D.C., was the staging ground for thousands of Union soldiers preparing to go off to war as well as an area where wounded soldiers returned for treatment. The city was also the site of the assassination of President Abraham Lincoln by John Wilkes Booth in 1865.

Growth of the city exploded after the Civil War. Population increased as thousands of newly freed slaves swarmed to the capital. The boundaries grew when in 1895 Georgetown, Maryland, was annexed by Washington. African Americans continued to relocate to the city to the point where the lack of housing became a problem and the excess population crowded into alleys. To combat the housing shortage, Congress passed the Alley Dwelling Act in 1914. The African-American population averaged between one-quarter and one-third of the population of the city between 1870 and 1950, until 1970 when it reached almost three-quarters of the population.

Federal jobs provided continued growth during and after World War II. Population expanded to more than a million residents during this time.

During the latter half of the twentieth century, Washington, D.C., suffered the same fate as many other American cities. As the inner city deteriorated and jobs became scarce, people moved out to the many suburbs in the neighboring counties in Maryland and Virginia. Some growth was achieved with the opening of a new subway and the implementation of downtown renovation projects. The 1990 population of Washington,

D.C., was approximately 606,900. The 1990 metropolitan population was 3,923,574.

Washington, D.C., unfortunately has been the scene of violent events such as the 1968 riots that were set off by the assassination of Dr. Martin Luther King, Jr. The city has also seen a large increase in crime, especially homicide, with record rates in the late 1980s and early 1990s. Even government officials are not immune, as evidenced by the arrest and conviction of Mayor Marion Barry on drug charges in 1990.

Government

The city is the home of the federal government. The government of Washington, D.C., itself is based on the Home Rule Act of 1974, which provides for the election of a mayor and city council. Before this time (1874–1967) the city was led by a board of commissioners. The residents have nonvoting representation in Congress and have the right to vote in presidential elections even though the District of Columbia is not a state. There is, however, a movement under way to persuade Congress and the president to make the District of Columbia a state.

Culture and Education

Cultural institutions in the city include the National Gallery of Art, the National Zoo, the Library of Congress, and the John F. Kennedy Center for the Performing Arts. The city is also home to the Smithsonian Institution, a series of museums devoted to history, science, art, and nature. The city's institutions of higher learning include the George Washington , Howard , Georgetown, and American Universities.

Important Events in Washington D.C.'s History

1791 George Washington selects site for the new capital.

1793 George Washington lays the cornerstone for the new capital.

1800 The United States government is moved to the new capital from Philadelphia.

1802 Washington D.C., receives its charter.

1814 The capital is captured and burned by the British in the War of 1812.

1865 President Abraham Lincoln is assassinated at Ford's Theatre by John Wilkes Booth.

1895 Georgetown, Maryland, is annexed by Washington D.C.

1968 Riots occur in the aftermath of the assassination of Dr. Martin Luther King, Jr.

1974 The Home Rule Act is enacted permitting the election of a mayor and city council.

1976 Subway opens.

1990 Washington D.C., mayor Marion Barry is arrested and convicted on drug charges.

1994 Marion Barry is reelected mayor.

Energy and Transportation Facts

Energy. Yearly Consumption: 175 tril. BTUs (residential, 19.4%; commercial, 46.3%; industrial, 19.4%; transportation, 15.4%); Annual Energy Expenditures Per Capita: $1,899; Nuclear Power Plants: 0; Electricity by Nuclear: 0.0%; Energy

Produced by Coal: 0.0%; Energy Produced by Petroleum: 0.0%; Energy Produced by Natural Gas: 0.0%.

Transportation. Highway Miles: 1,104 (interstates, 12; urban, 1,104; rural, 0);

Average Yearly Auto Insurance: $880 (3d); Auto Fatalities Rank: N/A; Registered Motor Vehicles: 256,406; Workers in Carpools: 34.3%; Workers Using Public Trans: 36.6%.

Housing. Owner Occupied Units: 278,489; Average Age of Units: 48 years; Average

Value of Housing Units: $123,900; Renter Occupied Units: 152,069; Median Monthly

Rent: $479; Housing Starts: 100; Existing Home Sales: 12,300.

Economic Facts. Gross State Product: $39,000,000,000 (1989); Income Per Capita: $26,360; Disposable Personal Income: $22,101;

Median Household Income: $30,727; Principal Industries: government, communication; Civilian Labor Force: 282,000 (Women: 141,000); Total

Employed: 260,000 (Women: 130,000); Average Annual Pay, 1988: $35,570; Median Value of Housing: $123,900; Med. Contract Rent: $479

Employment

Employment. The District of Columbia employed 670,000 people in 1993. Most work in government (287,300 persons or 42.9% of the workforce). Manufacturing accounts for 2.1% or 13,900 workers. Wholesale and retail trade account for 7.9% or 52,700 workers. Services industries employ 255,100 workers (38.1%). Construction employs 8,400 workers (1.3%). Transportation and utilities account for 3.2% or 21,300 persons. Agriculture employs 3,400 workers or 0.5%. Finance, real estate, and insurance account for 4.7% or 31,400 workers. Mining employs 100 people and accounts for less than 0.1% of the work force.

Unemployment. Unemployment has increased to 8.5% in 1993 from a rate of 8.4% in 1985. Today's figure is higher than the national average of 6.8%.

Nationalities

African	8,864	Irish	22,738
American	11,651	Italian	8,881
Arab	2,406	Norwegian	1,693
Austrian	1,557	Polish	6,303
Czech	1,005	Portuguese	627
Dutch	2,145	Russian	9,019
English	23,318	Scottish	4,969
Finnish	324	Slovak	883
German	27,824	Swedish	2,354
Greek	2,069	Welsh	1,286
Hungarian	1,507	West Indian	6,363

Education Facts

Total Students 1990: 81,301
Number of School Districts: 1
Expenditure Per Capita on Education 1990: $945
Expenditure Per Capita K–12 1990: $884
Expenditure Per Pupil 1990: $8,221
Total School Enrollment 1990–1991: 80,694
Rank of Expenditures Per Student: N/A
African American Enrollment: 90.7%
Hispanic Enrollment: 4.6%
Asian/Pacific Islander Enrollment: 0.9%
Native American Enrollment: 0.0%

Mean SAT Score 1991 Verbal: 405
Mean SAT Score 1991 Math: 435
Average Teacher's Salary 1992: $41,300
Rank Teacher's Salary: N/A
High School Graduates 1990: 3,700
Total Number of Public Schools: 184
Number of Teachers 1990: 6,022
Student/Teacher Ratio: 13.4
Staff Employed in Public Schools: 10,619
Pupil/Staff Ratio: 7.7
Staff/Teacher Ratio: 1.8

Population Facts

City Population, 1990: 606,900
Population 2000: 634,000 (Rank N/A)
Density: 9,884.4 per sq. mi. (3,841.1 per km²)
Distribution: 100% urban, 0% rural
Population Under 5 Years Old: 7.0%
Population Under 18 Years Old: 19.9%
Population Over 65 Years Old: 13.1%
Median Age: 33.5
Number of Households: 250,000
Average Persons Per Household: 2.26
Average Persons Per Family: 3.15

Female Heads of Households: 8.00%
Population That Is Married: 10.40%
Birth Rate: 19.5 per 1,000 population
Death Rate: 12.0 per 1,000 population
Births to Teen Mothers: 17.8%
Marriage Rate: 7.9 per 1,000 population
Divorce Rate: 4.5 per 1,000 population
Violent Crime Rate: 2,453 per 100,000 pop.
Population on Social Security: 13.1%
Percent Voting for President: 49.6%

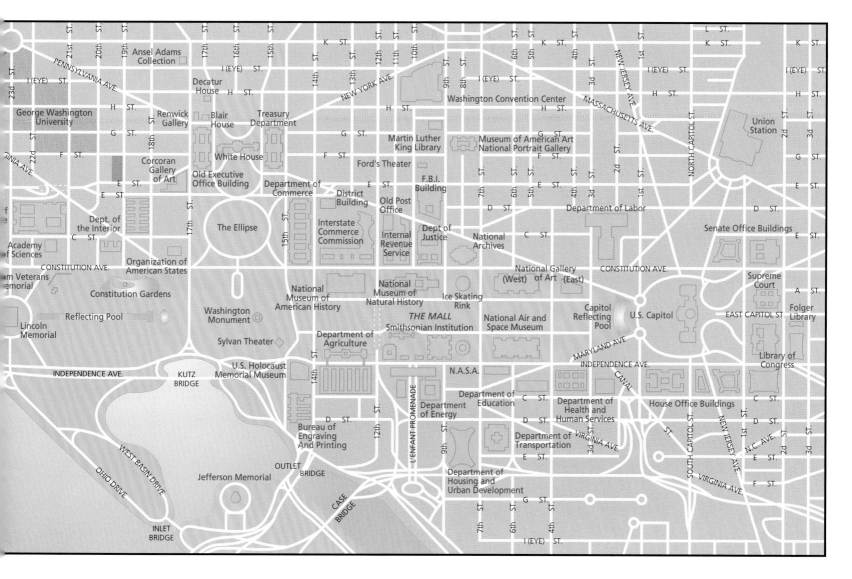

FLORIDA
The State of Florida

Official State Seal

The Great Seal of Florida was designed in 1868. The motto "In God We Trust" was taken from the silver dollar. Included on the seal is a sabal palm tree (a cocoa tree before 1970). Also included is a depiction of a Seminole Indian woman spreading flowers along the shore. A steamboat rides the blue waters in front of a shining sun on the horizon.

Legal Holidays

January: New Year's Day—1st, Admission Day—3rd; Martin Luther King, Jr., Day—3rd Monday; Robert E. Lee's birthday—19th; February: Abraham Lincoln's Birthday—12th; Susan B. Anthony's Birthday—15th; Presidents' Day—3rd Monday; March: Admission Day—3rd; April: Pascua Florida Day—2d; Confederate Memorial Day—26th; May: Memorial Day—4th Monday; June: Jefferson Davis' Birthday—3rd; July: Independence Day—4th; September: Labor Day—1st Monday; October: Columbus Day—2d Monday; Farmer's Day—12th; November: Veterans' Day—11th; Thanksgiving—4th Thursday; December: Christmas—25th.

Official State Flag

This flag was one of many to be flown over Florida. After the Civil War the state seal was placed in the center of the flag. Later, the red crosses were added to distinguish it from a flag of truce. Modifications were made in 1970.

Festivals and Events

January: Zora Neale Hurston Fest, Eatonville; February: Edison Festival of Lights, Ft. Myers; Gasparilla Pirate Fest, Tampa; Strawberry Fest, Plant City; March: Medieval Fair, Sarasota; Spiffs International Folk Fair, St. Petersburg; April: SunFest, W. Palm Beach; May: Florida Folk Festival, White Springs; Holy Trinity's British Fest, Pensacola; Sweet Corn Fest, Zellwood; June: Fiesta of Five Flags, Pensacola; Miami/Bahamas Goombay Fest, Miami; July: Hemingway Days Fest, Key West; Sandblast, Ft. Lauderdale; August: Surfside's International Fiesta, Surfside; September: Pensacola Beach Seafood Fest, Pensacola Beach; October: Baynanza, Miami; November: New Star Rising Bluegrass Fest, Live Oak, Harvest Festival, Miami; December: Palm Harbor Arts/Crafts/Music Festival, Palm Harbor.

Florida Compared to States in Its Region.

Resident Pop. in Metro Areas: 1st; Pop. Percent Increase: 1st; Pop. Over 65: 1st; Infant Mortality: 7th; School Enroll. Increase: 2d; High School Grad. and Up: 4th; Violent Crime: 1st; Hazardous Waste Sites: 1st; Unemployment: 2d; Median Household Income: 5th; Persons Below Poverty: 5th; Energy Costs Per Person: 8th.

South Atlantic Region

	Population	Capital
Delaware	700,000	Dover
Maryland	4,965,000	Annapolis
Washington DC	578,000	—
Virginia	6,491,000	Richmond
West Virginia	1,820,000	Charleston
North Carolina	6,945,000	Raleigh
South Carolina	3,643,000	Columbia
Georgia	6,917,000	Atlanta
Florida	13,679,000	Tallahassee

Florida's Finances

Households: 5,135,000; Income Per Capita Current Dollars: $19,397; Change Per Capita Income 1980 to 1992: 97.2% (27th in U.S.); State Expenditures: $24,851,000,000; State Revenues: $23,652,000,000; Personal Income Tax: N/A; Federal Income Taxes Paid Per Capita: $1,982; Sales Tax: 6% (food and prescription drugs exempt).

State Expenditures

14.0 billion dollars

- Education
- Highway
- Welfare
- Health
- Other

State Revenues

14.0 billion dollars

- Federal
- Local
- Taxes
- Miscellaneous

Location, Size, and Boundaries

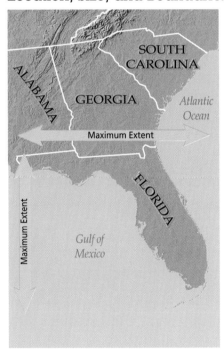

Location. Florida is located in the extreme southeastern United States in what is known as the South Atlantic region. It is bounded on three of four sides by water. The geographic center of Florida is lat. 28° 8' N; long. 81° 37.9' W.

Size. Florida is the 22d largest state in terms of size. Its area is 58,560 sq. mi. (151,670 km2). Inland water covers 4,470 sq. mi. (11,577 km2). Florida touches the Atlantic Ocean with a 580–mile coastline.

Boundaries. Alabama, 219 mi. (353 km); Georgia, 230 mi. (370 km); Atlantic Ocean, 580 mi. (933 km); Gulf of Mexico, 770 mi. (1,239 km).

Geographic Extent. The north/south extent of Florida is 447 mi. (719 km). The state extends 361 mi. (581 km) to the east/west.

Facts about Florida. Origin of Name: Named by Juan Ponce de León, possibly for the Spanish word *florida*, for *"flowery"*; Nickname: The Sunshine State; Motto: "In God we trust" (unofficial); Abbreviations: Fla. (traditional), FL (postal); State Bird: mockingbird; State Tree: Sabal palm; State Flower: orange blossom; State Song: "Old Folks at Home" (*"Swanee River"*), words and music by Stephen Foster.

Florida Compared to Other States. Resident Pop. in Metro Areas: 6th; Pop. Percent Increase: 11th; Pop. Over 65: 1st; Infant Mortality: 16th; School Enroll. Increase: 6th; High School Grad. and Up: 37th; Violent Crime: 1st; Hazardous Waste Sites: 6th; Unemployment: 9th; Med. Household Income: 28th; Persons Below Poverty: 22d; Energy Costs Per Person: 46th.

Sources of Information. Tourism: Dept. of Commerce, Division of Tourism, Direct Mail, 126 Van Buren Street, Tallahassee, FL 32399. Government: Governor's Office, Plaza Level, The Capitol, Tallahassee, FL 32399. History: Museum of Florida History, R. A. Gray Building, 500 S. Bronough St., Tallahassee, FL 32399.

ATLANTIC OCEAN

GULF OF MEXICO

■ Alligator Safari Zoo. Nine mile zoo with 2,000 alligators and 100 reptile species. (G-11)

■ Biscayne National Park. Offshore reefs and keys with mangroves and wildlife. (M-13)

■ Bok Tower Gardens. One of Florida's oldest attractions featuring 57-bell tower and gardens. (H-10)

■ Busch Gardens, Tampa. African theme park with wildlife and rides. (H-9)

■ Canaveral National Seashore. Wildlife refuge with beaches, marshes, and lagoons. (G-12)

■ Castillo de San Marcos National Monument. Old masonry fort. (C-11)

■ Cypress Gardens. Botanical and zoological gardens with over 8,000 varieties of plants. (H-10)

■ De Soto National Memorial. Site of the landing of the Spanish explorer in 1539. (I-9)

■ Everglades National Park. Wildlife with cypress and mangrove swamps. (M-12)

■ Florida Caverns State Park. Site of limestone caverns and rock gardens. (A-4)

■ Fort Caroline National Memorial. French Huguenot fort built in 1564. (C-10)

■ Fort Jefferson National Monument. Masonry fort built in 1846. (O-11)

■ Fort Matanzas National Monument. Fort built by the Spanish in 1740. (D-10)

■ Fountain of Youth. Site of Ponce de León 1513 landing. Original colony of St. Augustine (D-11)

■ Gulf Islands National Seashore. Offshore islands with historical forts. (B-1)

■ Hillsborough River State Park. Fort used during Second Seminole War. (G-9)

■ Homosassa Springs. Natural aquarium containing both freshwater and saltwater fish. (F-9)

■ John Pennekamp Coral Reef State Park. Living coral formations. (N-13)

■ Kennedy Space Center. Space launch and missile center. (G-12)

■ Key West. Island resort with wildlife. (O-10)

■ Maclay State Gardens. Landscaped gardens. (B-6)

■ Miami Metrozoo. Zoological gardens. (L-13)

■ Monkey Jungle. Monkey colony. (M-12)

■ Orchid Jungle. Orchid varieties from varied regions of the world. (M-12)

■ Parrot Jungle and Gardens. Parrots, and other exotic birds. Petting zoo. (M-13)

■ St. Augustine. Oldest city in the United States. (D-11)

■ Sarasota. Museums featuring Spanish architecture. (I-9)

■ Sea World. The world's largest marine-life park with shows and rides. (G-10)

■ Silver Springs. One of the world's largest springs. (E-10)

■ Stephen Foster State Folk Culture Center. Museum. (C-9)

■ Thomas A. Edison's Winter Home. Laboratory, museum, and gardens of the famous inventor. (K-10)

■ U.S. Astronaut Hall of Fame. Space hardware and personal mementos. (F-12)

■ Universal Studios Florida. Largest film studio outside Hollywood. Shows and rides. (F-11)

■ Walt Disney World, EPCOT Center, and MGM Studios. Theme parks, international and technological exhibits, and movie sets. (G-11)

Legend

⭐ State capitol
⊙ Cities over 35,000 population
○ Other significant cities
● County Seats
■ Major cultural attractions
▢ State Parks
Ⓦ Welcome Centers
🏛 Major colleges and universities

Major Cities

Boca Raton	K-13	Lakeland	G-10	Pensacola	B-1
Cape Coral	J-10	Largo	N-12	Plantation	L-13
Clearwater	H-8	Lauderhill	L-13	Pomp. Beach	K-13
Coral Springs	K-13	Melbourne	H-12	Port St. Lucie	I-13
Daytona Beach	E-11	Miami Beach	L-13	Sarasota	I-9
Fort Lauderdale	L-13	Miami	L-13	St. Petersburg	H-9
Gainesville	D-9	North Miami	L-13	Sunrise	L-13
Hialeah	L-13	Orlando	F-11	Tallahassee	B-6
Hollywood	L-13	Palm Bay	H-12	Tampa	H-9
Jacksonville	C-10	Pembr. Pines	L-13	W. Palm Beach	J-13

Scale

0 25 50 75 mi.

25 0 25 50 75 100 km

Weather Facts

Record High Temperature: 109° F (43° C) on June 28, 1927, at Monticello; Record Low Temperature: -2° F (-19° C) on February 13, 1899, at Tallahassee; Average January Temperature: 60° F (16° C); Average July Temperature: 80° F (27° C); Average Yearly Precipitation: 55 in. (140 cm).

Environmental Facts

Air Pollution Rank: 21st; Water Pollution Rank: 10th; Total Yearly Industrial Pollution: 70,679,931 lbs.; Industrial Pollution Rank: 11th; Hazardous Waste Sites: 52; Hazardous Sites Rank: 6th; Landfill Capacity: overextended; Fresh Water Supply: large surplus; Daily Residential Water Consumption: 165 gals. per capita; Endangered Species: Aquatic Species (4)—shrimp, squirrel chimney cave; Birds (10)—caracara, audubon's crested; Mammals (14)—bat, gray; Other Species (12)—crocodile, American; Plants (52)—aster, Florida golden.

Environmental Quality

Florida residents generate 16.0 million tons of solid waste each year, or approximately 2,600 pounds per capita. Landfill capacity in Florida will be exhausted in 5 to 10 years. The state has 51 hazardous waste sites. Annual greenhouse gas emissions in Florida total 167.4 million tons, or 13.6 tons per capita. Industrial sources in Florida release approximately 151.9 thousand tons of toxins, 1.1 million tons of acid precipitation-producing substances and 4.1 million tons of smog-producing substances into the atmosphere each year.

The state has 2.1 million acres within the National Park System; the largest area within the state is Everglades National Park. State parks cover just over 254,200 acres, attracting 13.1 million visitors per year.

Florida spends approximately 2.5 percent of its budget, or approximately $38 per capita, on environmental and natural resources.

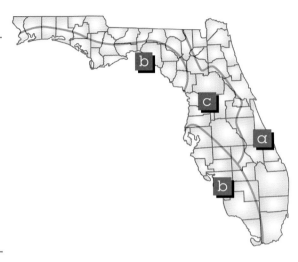

Physical Regions: (a) Atlantic Coastal Plain; (b) East Gulf Coastal Plain; (c) Florida Uplands.

Highest Point
Mean (100 ft.) Walton County (345 ft.)
0 ft.
Lowest Point
Atlantic Ocean (Sea level)

Land Use

Cropland: 11.7%; Pasture: 13.6%; Rangeland: 11.7%; Forest: 39.2%; Urban: 12.2%; Other: 11.6%.

For more information about Florida's environment, contact the Department of Environmental Regulation, 2600 Blair Stone Rd., Tallahassee, FL 32399-2400.

Average Monthly Weather

Miami	Jan	Feb	Mar	Apr	May	Jun	Jul	Aug	Sep	Oct	Nov	Dec	Yearly
Maximum Temperature °F	75.0	75.8	79.3	82.4	85.1	87.3	88.7	89.2	87.8	84.2	79.8	76.2	82.6
Minimum Temperature °F	59.2	59.7	64.1	68.2	71.9	74.6	76.2	76.5	75.7	71.6	65.8	60.8	68.7
Days of Precipitation	6.5	5.9	5.9	5.8	10.3	14.8	16.1	17.2	17.3	14.1	8.5	6.5	128.8
Orlando													
Maximum Temperature °F	71.9	72.9	78.3	83.6	88.3	90.6	91.7	91.6	89.7	84.4	78.2	73.1	82.8
Minimum Temperature °F	49.3	50.0	55.3	60.3	66.2	71.2	73.0	73.4	72.5	65.4	56.8	50.9	62.0
Days of Precipitation	6.2	7.0	7.6	5.4	8.5	13.7	17.2	15.9	13.7	8.4	5.6	6.0	115.3

Flora and Fauna

Florida has a large selection of trees: approximately 350 different kinds grow in the state. Forests cover almost one-half of Florida's land. One of the most famous wooded areas is the Everglades, where cypress and mangrove trees grow. Elsewhere in Florida, ash, hickory, pine, and exotic palm trees can be found. The state's wet regions have plants such as sea grass, Spanish moss, air plants (epiphytes), and various vines. Both wild (lupines and sunflowers) and domesticated (camellias and hibiscus) flowers can be found in all parts of Florida.

Perhaps the most famous animal living in Florida is the alligator. However, more common animals such as black bears, bobcats, foxes, squirrels, and white-tailed deer also live in the state. Florida's great diversity of wildlife is best reflected in its aquatic creatures. Freshwater fish include bream (or bluegill) and black bass; ocean species include mackerel and marlin. Water mammals such as dolphins and manatees live off Florida's coast. Florida also has the largest colonies of birds such as pelicans, egrets, and ibises found north of the Caribbean Sea.

Topography

Most of Florida is a flat plain, but distinctive geographical areas are evident. The entire eastern part of Florida is defined by the Atlantic Coastal Plain physical region, which stretches north to New York. The soil is considered warm and wet, high in organic content. Just off the Atlantic coast can be found a series of sandbars and barrier islands. The southern portion of the peninsula is covered by the Everglades and Big Cypress Swamp. These areas, which together cover more than 7,000 sq. miles (18,130 sq. km), are covered in shallow water for much of the year. Hammocks, which are wooded dry elevations, are found scattered throughout the Everglades. The Florida Keys, a string of islands curving southwest off the peninsula, is the southernmost point in the continental United States.

The East Gulf Coastal Plain on Florida's Gulf shore is similar to that of the Atlantic Coastal Plain; soil runs from a fine gray sand to black with high organic content. Barrier islands parallel much of the peninsula. Most of the Florida panhandle is at a higher elevation than the rest of Florida, although not much more than 300 ft. (91 m). This region of low hills, known as the Florida Uplands physical region, is interrupted by swampy areas near the coast. The soil is warm and moist loamy fine sand made of quartz.

Climate

Florida's weather pattern is influenced by several factors- its southern location, shape, and many water bodies. No place in the state is more than 70 miles away from some type of water body. Florida, like other southern states, has a warm, humid climate. The southern tip of Florida has a tropical climate similar to that of Central America. Temperatures vary slightly throughout the state. January and July temperatures for Tallahassee, the capital, average 54° F and 81° F. In Miami, in southern Florida, temperatures in January and July average 67° F and 82° F.

Northwest and southeast Florida receive the most annual precipitation–64 in. North central Florida receives slightly less, about 52 in. of precipitation a year.

Florida lies directly in the path of hurricanes. One of the most destructive hurricanes in recent history was Hurricane Andrew, which struck in August 1992.

Hydrology

The longest river in the state is the St. Johns, located in the east-central part of the state. It flows northward about 265 miles (427 km) and empties into the Atlantic Ocean near Jacksonville. The Apalachicola, Ochlockonee, and Suwannee rivers enter northwestern Florida and drain into the Gulf of Mexico. The Kissimmee River in central Florida drains into Lake Okeechobee.

Lake Okeechobee is the largest lake in the state, covering about 690 sq. miles (1,787 sq. km). There are numerous other sizable lakes in Florida, including Lake George, Lake Apopka, and Cypress Lake. Most of these lakes are not deep, because of Florida's extensive network of underground streams and caverns.

The Everglades, Florida's most unique aquatic feature, is really a river 6 inches (15 cm) deep and 50 miles (81 km) wide that flows from Lake Okeechobee to the Florida Bay.

Florida's History

Florida's First People

The first evidence of human habitation in Florida dates back more than ten thousand years. Caribbean peoples and Indians from the north had migrated to the Florida peninsula in search of large game animals. By about 5000 B.C. the northern tribes had become less nomadic, developing some agriculture and settling in villages. Southern tribes subsisted on wild vegetation and land and aquatic animals, not adopting agriculture until around 450 B.C.

By the time Europeans began to arrive in the sixteenth century, there were several Indian tribes settled around Florida. There were the Apalachee in the northwest; the Timucua in the north central area; the Tocobaga on Tampa Bay; the Calusa in the southwest; and the Tekesta on the southeast coast.

European Exploration

In 1513, Juan Ponce de León landed on Florida's northeast shore, named the area and claimed it for Spain. Eight years later he returned to found a colony but was rebuffed by the Indians, sustaining a wound that would kill him that year.

In 1539, Hernando de Soto explored the area around Tampa Bay, and twenty years later Tristan de Tuna attempted to establish a settlement for the Spanish on Pensacola Bay but was forced to abandon the project after two trying years.

In 1564, the French Huguenots built a colony at Fort Caroline, near present-day Jacksonville. In 1565, the Spanish, led by Pedro Menendez de Aviles, attacked and killed most of the colonists, after establishing their own colony at St. Augustine.

Over the next two centuries, the Spanish established many forts and missions across northern Florida. However, their conflicts with the native peoples and the diseases they brought with them from Europe decimated a great number of the Indian population.

Around 1750, Creek Indians from Georgia began to move into Florida and became known as the Seminole (refugee).

In 1763, Spain traded Florida for Cuba with the British. British settlers moved into the area with the Seminole. During the Revolutionary War, the settlers remained loyal to the British and shortly afterward, in 1781, the Spanish drove the British out. Two years later, the British ceded Florida to the Spanish.

Statehood

The United States gained control of the western part of Florida as part of the Louisiana Purchase in 1810. In 1819, Spain ceded Florida to the United States, which took formal control two years later.

In 1822, the territory of Florida was created, and two years later Tallahassee became the capital. An influx of settlers resulted in friction with the Seminole. In 1835, a seven-year war resulted in the forced removal of most of the Seminole to Oklahoma.

In 1845, Florida was admitted to the Union as the twenty-seventh state, a slave state paired with Iowa, a free state. However, in 1861, the state seceded from the Union to join the Confederacy. Although much of Florida was under Union control during the Civil War, Tallahassee remained Confederate throughout the war. In 1868, Florida was readmitted to the Union after adopting a new constitution, though there was much conflict during the next decade of Reconstruction. In 1885, yet another constitution was adopted and, with revisions added in 1968, remains Florida's present constitution.

Industrialization

In the early part of the nineteenth century, soon after U.S. control of Florida was established, cotton plantations worked by slaves became the first industry in Florida. These plantations thrived in the first half of the century, but were affected by recession and the

Civil War and never really recovered.

After the war Florida's economy boomed, fueled by the discovery of phosphate, the development of citrus groves and other farming made possible by the filling in of swampland, and eventually by tourism.

The first part of the twentieth century saw a continuing expansion of the economy as real estate speculation drove land prices skyward. With the crash of these land prices in 1926 and the Great Depression a few years later, Florida suffered economically with the rest of the nation.

After World War II, the aerospace industry and increased tourism led to a robust recovery. In 1971, Walt Disney opened his second theme park, Walt Disney World. Walt Disney World is a 27,000 acre (10,800 ha) theme park near Orlando. The park is broken up into theme areas such as a turn-of-the-century American Main Street, a western world, and the Magic Kingdom to name a few. Not long after the opening of the main park, the Disney company expanded to include EPCOT Center, Disney-MGM Studios, Discovery Island, and many other sites and attractions.

The Everglades

This unique natural feature, often thought of as a large swamp, is actually a very shallow river measuring about fifty miles wide with an average depth of only six inches. Indeed it has been nicknamed the "River of Grass" for the many types of grasses that are prominent throughout its course.

Established as a national park in 1947, the area is home to a rich mixture of tropical and temperate plant and wildlife species, some of which are on the endangered species list.

Overpopulation and agricultural and other development have threatened to disrupt the delicate balance of this natural ecosystem, but in the 1990s legislation has been passed to prevent any further damage and to restore parts of the area to its former condition.

Important Events

1513 Ponce de León lands on the northeast coast of Florida.

1539 De Soto explores Tampa Bay.

1559 Spanish attempt to establish a colony at Pensacola Bay, but abandon it two years later.

1564 French Huguenots establish a colony at Fort Caroline.

1565 Spanish attack and conquer the Huguenot settlement and establish their own colony at St. Augustine.

1750 Some Creek Indians from Georgia enter Florida and become known as Seminoles.

1763 Spain trades Florida to the British for Cuba.

1776 Settlers remain loyal to the British during the Revolutionary War.

1783 Spanish regain control of Florida.

1819 Spain cedes control of Florida to the U.S.

1822 Territory of Florida is established.

1835–1842 War between the Seminole Indians and the U.S., ending in the Seminoles' forced removal.

1845 Florida is admitted to the Union as the twenty seventh state.

1861 Florida secedes from the Union.

1868 Florida readmitted to the Union.

1906 State commences the draining of the Everglades for development.

1912 Final link to Key West by overseas railroad is completed.

1938 Overseas highway to Key West is completed.

1947 Everglades National Park is established.

1950 Cape Canaveral launches its first rocket.

1968 Florida adopts a new state constitution.

1980 Mariel boat lift of Cuban refugees into Florida strains social service network.

1986 Space shuttle Challenger explodes on liftoff at Kennedy Space Center, killing all crew members.

1988 Amendment is approved by the state's voters establishing English as the official state language.

1992 Hurricane Andrew devastates southern Florida, killing 38 people and causing over $20 billion in damages.

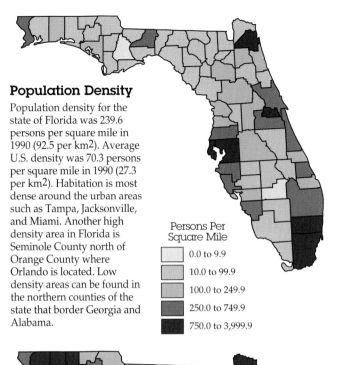

Population Density

Population density for the state of Florida was 239.6 persons per square mile in 1990 (92.5 per km2). Average U.S. density was 70.3 persons per square mile in 1990 (27.3 per km2). Habitation is most dense around the urban areas such as Tampa, Jacksonville, and Miami. Another high density area in Florida is Seminole County north of Orange County where Orlando is located. Low density areas can be found in the northern counties of the state that border Georgia and Alabama.

Persons Per Square Mile
- 0.0 to 9.9
- 10.0 to 99.9
- 100.0 to 249.9
- 250.0 to 749.9
- 750.0 to 3,999.9

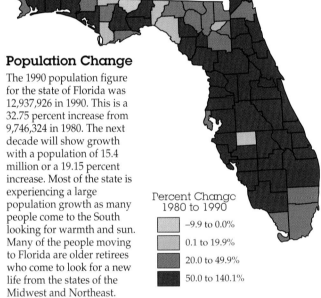

Population Change

The 1990 population figure for the state of Florida was 12,937,926 in 1990. This is a 32.75 percent increase from 9,746,324 in 1980. The next decade will show growth with a population of 15.4 million or a 19.15 percent increase. Most of the state is experiencing a large population growth as many people come to the South looking for warmth and sun. Many of the people moving to Florida are older retirees who come to look for a new life from the states of the Midwest and Northeast.

Percent Change 1980 to 1990
- –9.9 to 0.0%
- 0.1 to 19.9%
- 20.0 to 49.9%
- 50.0 to 140.1%

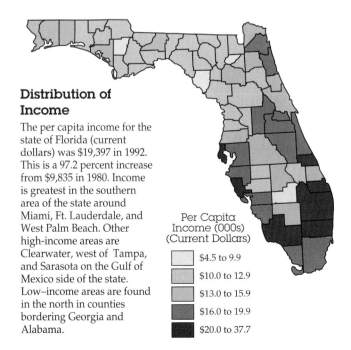

Distribution of Income

The per capita income for the state of Florida (current dollars) was $19,397 in 1992. This is a 97.2 percent increase from $9,835 in 1980. Income is greatest in the southern area of the state around Miami, Ft. Lauderdale, and West Palm Beach. Other high-income areas are Clearwater, west of Tampa, and Sarasota on the Gulf of Mexico side of the state. Low–income areas are found in the north in counties bordering Georgia and Alabama.

Per Capita Income (000s) (Current Dollars)
- $4.5 to 9.9
- $10.0 to 12.9
- $13.0 to 15.9
- $16.0 to 19.9
- $20.0 to 37.7

Population Projections

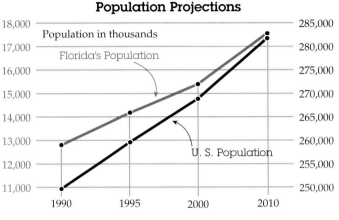

Population in thousands

Florida's Population

U. S. Population

Population Change

Year	Population
1950	2,771,000
1960	5,004,000
1970	6,848,000
1980	9,746,324
1990	12,937,926
2000	15,415,000
2010	17,530,000

Period	Change
1950–1970	147.1%
1970–1980	42.3%
1980–1990	32.8%
1990–2000	19.1%

Population Facts

State Population, 1993: 13,679,000

Rank: 4

Population 2000: 15,415,000 (Rank 4)

Density: 239.6 per sq. mi. (92.5 per km²)

Distribution: 84.8% urban, 15.2% rural

Population Under 5 Years Old: 7.0%

Population Under 18 Years Old: 23.0%

Population Over 65 Years Old: 18.4%

Median Age: 36.4

Number of Households: 5,135,000

Average Persons Per Household: 2.46

Average Persons Per Family: 2.95

Female Heads of Households: 4.24%

Population That Is Married: 21.58%

Birth Rate: 15.4 per 1,000 population

Death Rate: 10.4 per 1,000 population

Births to Teen Mothers: 13.9%

Marriage Rate: 10.9 per 1,000 population

Divorce Rate: 6.3 per 1,000 population

Violent Crime Rate: 1,184 per 100,000 pop.

Population on Social Security: 20.6%

Percent Voting for President: 50.2%

Population Profile

Rank. Florida ranks 4th among U.S. states in terms of population with 13,679,000 citizens.

Minority Population. The state's minority population is 27.0 percent. The state's male to female ratio for 1990 was 93.79 males for every 100 females. It was below the national average of 95.22 males for every 100 females.

Growth. Growing much faster than the projected national average, the state's population

Government

Capital: Tallahassee (established 1824).

Statehood: Became 27th state on Mar. 3, 1845.

Number of Counties: 67.

Supreme Court Justices: 7, 6-year term.

State Senators: 40, 4-year term.

State Legislators: 120, 2-year term.

United States Senators: 2.

United States Representatives: 23.

Electoral Votes: 25.

State Constitution: Adopted 1968.

Florida's Famous Citizens

Askew, Reubin (b. 1928). Served as Democratic governor for two terms (1971–1979). Sought and lost the Democratic presidential nomination in 1984 to Walter F. Mondale.

Capriati, Jennifer (b. 1976). The youngest American tennis player ever to turn professional (at 13 years, 11 months old).

Hurston, Zora Neale (1903–1960). Folklorist, anthropologist, and fiction writer. Interpreted black folktales in collections like *Mules and Men*.

Narvaez, Panfilo de (1480–1528). Attempted to colonize the territory of Florida for the Spanish in 1528.

Rawlings, Marjorie Kinnan (1896–1953). Wrote about the people and countryside of Florida in such books as *The Yearling*.

Ringling, John (1866–1936). With his brothers, established the Ringling Brothers and Barnum and Bailey Circus in Sarasota.

Suarez, Xavier (b. 1949). Elected the first Cuban-American mayor of Miami in 1985.

Vereen, Ben (b. 1946). Broadway entertainer. Won a Tony Award in 1973 for his role in *Pippin*.

is expected to reach 17.5 million by the year 2010 (*see graph above*).

Older Citizens. The state's population older than 65 was 2,369,431 in 1990. It grew 40.40% from 1,687,573 in 1980.

Younger Citizens. The number of children (under 18 years of age) was 2.9 million in 1990. This represents 22.2 percent of the state's population. The state's school aged population was 1.8 million in 1990. It is expected to increase to 2.2 million by the year 2000. This represents a 20.58% change.

Urban/Rural. 84.8% of the population of the state live in urban areas while 15.2% live in rural areas.

Largest Cities. Florida has 56 cities with a population greater than 35,000. The populations of the state's largest centers are (starting from the most populous) Jacksonville (635,230), Miami (358,548), Tampa (280,015), St. Petersburg (238,629), Hialeah (188,004), Orlando (164,693), Fort Lauderdale (149,377), Tallahassee (124,773), Hollywood (121,697), Clearwater (98,784), Miami Beach (92,639), Kendall (87,271), Gainsville (84,770), Coral Springs (74,991), and Pompano Beach (72,411).

Native American

The Native American population in Florida was 36,335 in 1990. This was an increase of 47.02 percent from 24,714 in 1980. A large number of Native Americans can be found in Jacksonville as well as in Tampa and St. Petersburg. There are also three Indian reservations located in the southern part of the state: the Brighton, Big Cypress, and Miccosukee Indian reservations.

Presence of Native Americans

☐ Minor
☐ Moderate

Nationalities

African	18,896
American	724,919
Arab	40,919
Austrian	44,490
Czech	33,835
Dutch	157,554
English	1,287,805
Finnish	19,233
German	1,870,001
Greek	56,416
Hungarian	68,049
Irish	1,153,099
Italian	620,739
Norwegian	59,386
Polish	295,037
Portuguese	23,975
Russian	183,244
Scottish	203,811
Slovak	50,553
Swedish	111,989
Welsh	55,457
West Indian	226,854

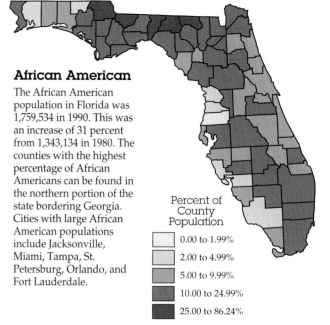

African American

The African American population in Florida was 1,759,534 in 1990. This was an increase of 31 percent from 1,343,134 in 1980. The counties with the highest percentage of African Americans can be found in the northern portion of the state bordering Georgia. Cities with large African American populations include Jacksonville, Miami, Tampa, St. Petersburg, Orlando, and Fort Lauderdale.

Percent of County Population

☐ 0.00 to 1.99%
☐ 2.00 to 4.99%
☐ 5.00 to 9.99%
☐ 10.00 to 24.99%
☐ 25.00 to 86.24%

Statewide Ethnic Composition

Over 83 percent of the population of Florida is white. Many of these consider themselves of German, English, or Irish descent. A large proportion claim to be American and acknowledge no other nationality. African Americans and Hispanics make up approximately the same proportion of the state population.

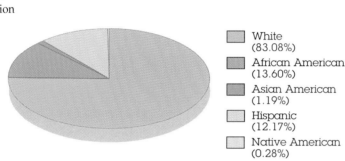

☐ White (83.08%)
☐ African American (13.60%)
☐ Asian American (1.19%)
☐ Hispanic (12.17%)
☐ Native American (0.28%)

Education Facts

Total Students 1990: 1,772,349

Number of School Districts: 67

Expenditure Per Capita on Education 1990: $787

Expenditure Per Capita K–12 1990: $654

Expenditure Per Pupil 1990: $5,003

Total School Enrollment 1990–1991: 1,861,592

Rank of Expenditures Per Student: 24th in the U.S.

African American Enrollment: 23.8%

Hispanic Enrollment: 11.9%

Asian/Pacific Islander Enrollment: 1.4%

Native American Enrollment: 0.2%

Mean SAT Score 1991 Verbal: 416

Mean SAT Score 1991 Math: 466

Average Teacher's Salary 1992: $31,100

Rank Teacher's Salary: 26th in U.S.

High School Graduates 1990: 95,600

Total Number of Public Schools: 2,505

Number of Teachers 1990: 109,505

Student/Teacher Ratio: 17.0

Staff Employed in Public Schools: 206,351

Pupil/Staff Ratio: 8.6

Staff/Teacher Ratio: 2.0

Hispanic††

The Hispanic population in Florida was 1,574,143 in 1990. This is an increase of 83.43 percent from 858,158 persons in 1980. By far the largest concentration of Hispanics can be found in and around Miami. This is partially due to the large numbers of immigrants coming in from places like Cuba, which lies a short 90 miles offshore.

††A person of Mexican, Puerto Rican, Cuban, or other Spanish culture or origin regardless of race.

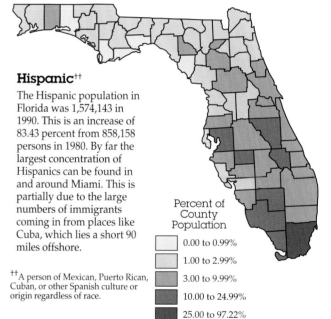

Percent of County Population

☐ 0.00 to 0.99%
☐ 1.00 to 2.99%
☐ 3.00 to 9.99%
☐ 10.00 to 24.99%
☐ 25.00 to 97.22%

Education

Attainment: 77.9 percent of population 25 years or older were high school graduates in 1989, earning Florida a ranking of 27th in the United States; 20 percent of the state's population had completed college. Institutions of Higher Education: The largest universities and colleges in the state include the University of Florida, Gainesville; Florida State University Tallahassee; Florida Agricultural and Mechanical University, Tallahassee; the University of South Florida, Tampa; University of Miami, Coral Gables. Expenditures per Student: Expenditure increased 75% between 1985 and 1990. Projected High School Graduations: 1998 (115,512), 2004 (151,090); Total Revenues for Education from Federal Sources: $498 million; Total Revenues for Education from State Sources: $4.1 billion; Total Revenues for Education from Local Sources: $2.8 billion; Average Annual Salaries for Public School Principals: $45,711; Largest School Districts in State: Dade County School District, Miami, 279,357 students, 5th in the United States; Broward County School District, Ft. Lauderdale, 10th.

Asian American

The Asian American population in Florida was 154,302 in 1990. This is an increase of 167.61 percent from 57,660 persons in 1980. Asian Americans are not as concentrated in Florida as African Americans and Hispanics. However, large numbers of Asian Americans can be found in the cities of Orlando and Gainesville. There is also a concentration in the northern panhandle in Okaloosa County.

Percent of County Population

☐ 0.00 to 0.24%
☐ 0.25 to 0.99%
☐ 1.00 to 1.99%
☐ 2.00 to 4.99%

Transportation

The state of Florida has an extensive transportation network. Its Miami International Airport has often been called the "Gateway to Latin America," as many flights originate or stop in Miami on their way to and from Central and South America. Other cities such as Jacksonville, Tampa, and Fort Lauderdale have airports as well.

Florida has about 93,000 miles of highways and roads. Included in this total are interstate and turnpike systems that link most Florida cities. Two passenger railroad lines also connect Florida cities with cities in neighboring states. Seven freight rail lines ship cargo across Florida. Florida also has several ports, which serve as points of entry into the country. Tampa's port is the busiest in the state.

Agriculture

Florida has 10.3 million farm acres. During the last 40 years, Florida's farms have grown larger in size and fewer in number. In 1955, 58,000 farms were found in the state. Today, 39,000 remain.

Agriculture adds $6 billion to the state's gross product annually. The principal commodities in order of marketing receipts are oranges, greenhouse, tomatoes, and sugar cane.

Crops account for about 80 percent of the state's farm income, with oranges being the leading product. Oranges, as well as grapefruit, limes, tangerines, and other citrus fruits, are grown mainly in south-central Florida. Tomatoes are ranked second in crop production. Other vegetables, supplied to northern states in colder months, include cabbage, peppers, lettuce, and squash. Sugar cane is also an important crop.

Housing

Owner Occupied Units: 6,100,262; Average Age of Units: 20 years; Average Value of Housing Units: $77,100; Renter Occupied Units: 1,669,618; Median Monthly Rent: $481; Housing Starts: 128,400; Existing Home Sales: 208,900.

Economic Facts

Gross State Product: $227,000,000,000

Income Per Capita: $19,397

Disposable Personal Income: $17,246

Median Household Income: $27,483

Average Annual Pay, 1988: $21,991

Principal Industries: printing, food products, electrical equipment, scientific instruments, machinery, tourism, chemicals

Major Crops: citrus, greenhouse products, tobacco, sugarcane, soybeans, watermelons, peanuts, pecans, strawberries, cantaloupes

Fish: Bass, Catfish, Crappies, Red Snapper, Bluefish

Livestock: cattle, hogs, broiler chickens, horses

Non-Fuel Minerals: Limestone, Phosphate, Dolomite, Sand, Gravel, Stone, Clay

Organic Fuel Minerals: Petroleum, Nat. Gas

Civilian Labor Force: 6,431,000 (Women: 2,999,000)

Total Employed: 5,961,000 (Women: 2,771,000)

Median Value of Housing: $77,100

Median Contract Rent: $481 per month

Energy and Transportation Facts

Energy. Yearly Consumption: 3,022 tril. BTUs (residential, 27.3%; commercial, 23.2%; industrial, 13.8%; transportation, 35.7%); Annual Energy Expenditures Per Capita: $1,533; Nuclear Power Plants Located in State: 5; Source of Energy Consumed: Petroleum— 56.0%; Natural Gas— 12.9%; Coal— 23.1%; Hydroelectric Power—0.1%; Nuclear Power—7.9%.

Transportation. Highway Miles: 110,640 (interstates, 1,474; urban, 48,637; rural, 62,003); Average Yearly Auto Insurance: $684 (13th); Auto Fatalities Rank: 17th; Registered Motor Vehicles: 10,232,336; Workers in Carpools: 18.3%; Workers Using Public Trans: 2.0%.

Economic Sectors

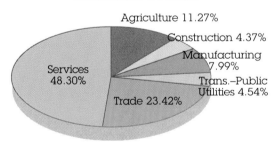

Agriculture 11.27%
Construction 4.37%
Manufacturing 7.99%
Trans.–Public Utilities 4.54%
Trade 23.42%
Services 48.30%

Manufacturing

Many states have manufacturing sectors based on heavy industry; however, this is not the case with Florida. Florida's manufacturing industries, primarily based on food products, are continually growing. In terms of value added by manufacture, however, electrical equipment is Florida's top manufacturing industry. Other state industries include the manufacture of transportation equipment, printed materials, and chemicals.

Much of Florida's manufacturing takes place in and around its major cities. Fort Lauderdale and Tampa produce the bulk of the electrical equipment, including communication equipment. Florida's food industry is mainly centered on citrus fruits grown throughout the state. One of the world's largest publishers, Harcourt Brace Jovanovich, is headquartered near Orlando, in central Florida.

Major manufacturing areas

Major agricultural areas

Employment

Employment. Florida employed 6.16 million people in 1993. Most work in social and personal services (1,814,300 persons or 29.4% of the workforce). Manufacturing accounts for 7.9% or 484,200 workers. Wholesale and retail trade account for 23.6% or 1,452,200 workers. Government employs 881,500 workers (14.3%). Construction employs 286,700 workers (4.6%). Transportation and utilities account for 4.6% or 285,600 persons. Agriculture employs 178,800 workers or 2.9%. Finance, real estate, and insurance account for 5.8% or 356,600 workers. Mining employs 6,300 people and accounts for only 0.1% of the workforce.

Unemployment. Unemployment has increased to 7.0% in 1993 from a rate of 6.0% in 1985. Today's figure is higher than the national average of 6.8% as shown below.

Unemployment Rate

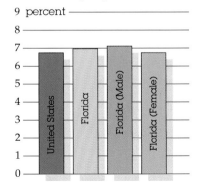

9 percent
8
7
6
5
4
3
2
1
0

United States | Florida | Florida (Male) | Florida (Female)

GEORGIA

The State of Georgia

Official State Seal

The Great Seal of Georgia was adopted in 1798. The seal is two-sided, with one side showing an arch and three pillars with the words "Wisdom," "Justice," and "Moderation." The pillars represent the three branches of government, while the soldier stands prepared to defend these principles. The other side of the seal contains the state motto, "Agriculture and Commerce."

Legal Holidays

January: New Year's Day—1st, Ratification Day—2nd; Martin Luther King, Jr., Day—3rd Monday; Robert E. Lee's birthday—19th; February: Oglethorpe Day—2nd; Georgia Day—12th; Presidents' Day—3rd Monday; April: Confederate Memorial Day—26th; May: Memorial Day—4th Monday; June: Jefferson Davis's Birthday—3rd; July: Independence Day—4th; September: Labor Day—1st Monday; October: Columbus Day—2nd Monday; November: Veterans' Day—11th; Thanksgiving—4th Thursday; December: Christmas—25th.

Georgia's Finances

Households: 2,367,000; Income Per Capita Current Dollars: $18,130; Change Per Capita Income 1980 to 1992: 117.0% (9th in U.S.); State Expenditures: $12,781,000,000; State Revenues: $12,379,000,000; Personal Income Tax: 1 to 6%; Federal Income Taxes Paid Per Capita: $1,651; Sales Tax: 4% (prescription drugs exempt).

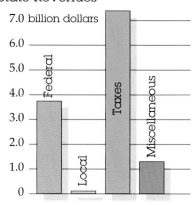

State Expenditures

State Revenues

Official State Flag

The Georgia flag was created in 1879 and was based on the Stars and Bars. It originally had one vertical blue stripe and two red and one white horizontal stripe. The coat of arms was added in 1905. The horizontal stripes were replaced by the Confederate battle flag in 1956.

Festivals and Events

January: Augusta Futurity, Augusta; March: Antebellum Jubilee, Stone Mountain; Macon Cherry Blossom Festival, Macon; April: Georgia Renaissance Festival, Atlanta; May: Prater's Mill Country Fair, Dalton; Spring Music Fest, Hiawassee; Wildflower Festival of the Arts, Dahlonega; June: Bluegrass Fest, Dahlonega; Country-by-the-Sea Music Fest, Jekyll Island; July: Family Day Celebration, Dahlonega; August: Fairy Tale Festival, Lookout Mountain; September: Yellow Daisy Festival, Stone Mountain; October: Heritage Holidays, Rome; Scottish Tattoo /Highland Games Fest, Stone Mountain; November: Legends of Christmas, Lookout Mountain; December: New Year's Bluegrass Festival, Jekyll Island.

Georgia Compared to States in Its Region.

Resident Pop. in Metro Areas: 6th; Pop. Percent Increase: 2d; Pop. Over 65: 8th; Infant Mortality: 1st; School Enroll. Increase: 5th; High School Grad. and Up: 5th; Violent Crime: 4th; Hazardous Waste Sites: 6th; Unemployment: 3d; Median Household Income: 4th; Persons Below Poverty: 3d; Energy Costs Per Person: 3d.

South Atlantic Region

	Population	Capital
Delaware	700,000	Dover
Maryland	4,965,000	Annapolis
Washington DC	578,000	—
Virginia	6,491,000	Richmond
West Virginia	1,820,000	Charleston
North Carolina	6,945,000	Raleigh
South Carolina	3,643,000	Columbia
Georgia	6,917,000	Atlanta
Florida	13,679,000	Tallahassee

Location, Size, and Boundaries

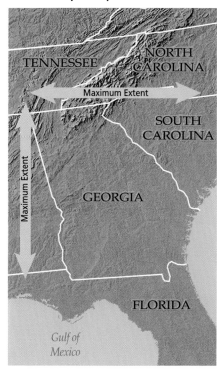

Location. Georgia is located in the South Atlantic region of the United States. It is bounded on three of four sides by land with a small coast along the Atlantic Ocean in the southeast. The geographic center of Georgia is lat. 32° 42.8' N; long. 83° 29.7' W.

Size. Georgia is the 21st largest state in terms of size. Its area is 58,876 sq. mi. (152,489 km2). Inland water covers 803 sq. mi. (2,080 km2). Georgia touches the Atlantic Ocean along a 100 mile coastline.

Boundaries. Tennessee, 73 mi. (118 km); North Carolina, 70 mi. (113 km); South Carolina, 266 mi. (428 km); Atlantic Ocean, 100 mi. (161 km); Florida, 242 mi. (389 km); Alabama, 288 mi. (463 km).

Geographic Extent. The north/south extent is 320mi. (515 km). The state extends 254 mi. (409 km) to the east/west.

Facts about Georgia. Origin of Name: Named for King George II of England; Nickname: The Empire State of the South; Motto: "Wisdom, Justice and Moderation"; Abbreviations: Ga. (traditional), GA (postal); State Bird: brown thrasher; State Tree: live oak; State Flower: Cherokee rose; State Song: "Georgia on My Mind," words by Stuart Gorrell and music by Hoagy Carmichael.

Georgia Compared to Other States. Resident Pop. in Metro Areas: 30th; Pop. Percent Increase: 12th; Pop. Over 65: 47th; Infant Mortality: 1st; School Enroll. Increase: 10th; High School Grad. and Up: 41st; Violent Crime: 13th; Haz. Waste Sites: 26th; Unemployment: 24th; Med. Household Income: 23d; Persons Below Poverty: 15th; Energy Costs Per Person: 18th.

Sources of Information. Tourism/Economy: Georgia Dept. of Industry, Trade and Tourism, P.O. Box 1776, Atlanta, GA 30301. Government/History: Office of the Secretary of State, 214 State Capitol, Atlanta, GA 30334.

Georgia

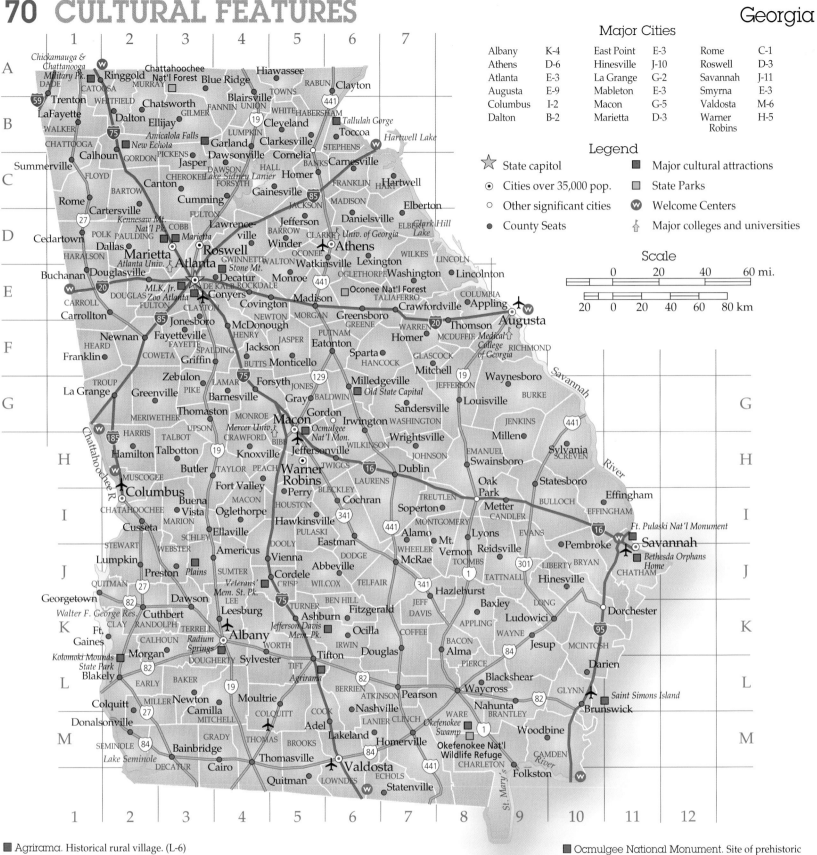

Legend

⭐ State capitol
⊙ Cities over 35,000 pop.
○ Other significant cities
● County Seats

■ Major cultural attractions
▫ State Parks
Ⓦ Welcome Centers
⚑ Major colleges and universities

Scale

0   20   40   60 mi.

20   0   20   40   60   80 km

■ **Agrirama.** Historical rural village. (L-6)

■ **Amicalola Falls State Park.** Highest falls in the state (729 feet; 222 meters). (B-3)

■ **Bethesda Orphans Home.** Oldest orphanage in the United States. (1740). (J-11)

■ **Chickamauga and Chattanooga National Military Park.** Civil War battlefields and memorials. (A-1)

■ **Fort Pulaski National Monument.** Fort built from 1829 to 1847. (I-11)

■ **Georgia Veterans' Memorial State Park.** Museum dedicated to World Wars I and II. (J-4)

■ **Jefferson Davis Memorial Park.** Confederate museum. (K-6)

■ **Kennesaw Mountain National Battlefield Park.** Site where Gen. William Tecumseh Sherman fought during his "March to the Sea" in 1864. (D-3)

■ **Kolomoki Mounds State Park.** Site of Indian mounds. (L-2)

■ **Marietta.** Site of Confederate cemetery. (D-3)

■ **Martin Luther King, Jr., Center for Non-Violent Social Change.** Burial place of the civil rights leader. Many of the leader's writings can also be seen. (E-3)

■ **New Echota Historic Site.** Site of last Cherokee capital. (B-2)

■ **Ocmulgee National Monument.** Site of prehistoric Indian mounds. (G-5)

■ **Okefenokee Swamp.** Wilderness sites with scenic views and wildlife. (M-8)

■ **Old State Capitol.** State capitol from 1807 to 1868. (G-6)

■ **Plains.** Birthplace of President Jimmy Carter. (J-3)

■ **Radium Springs.** Vacation resort with spring. (K-3)

■ **St. Simons Island.** Site of Christ Church (1736). Beaches. (L-10)

■ **Stone Mountain.** Confederate Civil War memorial. (E-4)

■ **Tallulah Gorge.** Site of a deep canyon. (B-6)

■ **Zoo Atlanta.** Zoological gardens. (E-3)

Weather Facts

Record High Temperature: 113° F (45° C) on May 26, 1974, at Greenville; Record Low Temperature: -17° F (-27° C) on January 26, 1936, in Floyd County; Average January Temperature: 48° F (9° C); Average July Temperature: 81° F (27° C); Average Yearly Precipitation: 50 in. (127 cm).

Environmental Facts

Air Pollution Rank: 17th; Water Pollution Rank: 9th; Total Yearly Industrial Pollution: 55,415,410 lbs.; Industrial Pollution Rank: 18th; Hazardous Waste Sites: 13; Hazardous Sites Rank: 26th; Landfill Capacity: overextended; Fresh Water Supply: large surplus; Daily Residential Water Consumption: 157 gals. per capita; Endangered Species: Aquatic Species (22)—acornshell, southern; Birds (9)—crane, whooping; Mammals (5)—bat, gray; Other Species (7)—beetle, American burying; Plants (23)—amphianthus, little.

Environmental Quality

Georgia residents generate 4.4 million tons of solid waste each year, or approximately 1,400 pounds per capita. Landfill capacity in Georgia will be exhausted in more than 12 years. The state has 13 hazardous waste sites. Annual greenhouse gas emissions in Georgia total 145.4 million tons, or 22.9 tons per capita. Industrial sources in Georgia release approximately 72.3 thousand tons of toxins, 1.4 million tons of acid precipitation-producing substances, and 3.0 million tons of smog-producing substances into the atmosphere each year.

The state has 40,100 acres within the National Park System; the largest area within the state is Kennesaw Mountain National Battlefield Park. State parks cover just over 60,200 acres, attracting 16.2 million visitors per year.

Georgia spends approximately 1.1 percent of its budget, or approximately $15 per capita, on environmental and natural resources.

Average Monthly Weather

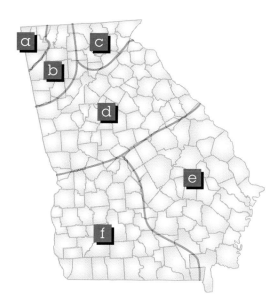

Physical Regions: (a) Appalachian Plateau; (b) Appalachian Ridge and Valley Region; (c) Blue Ridge; (d) Piedmont; (e) Atlantic Coastal Plain; (f) East Gulf Coastal Plain.

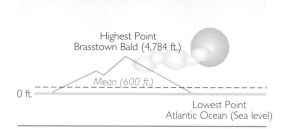

Land Use

Cropland: 18.2%; Pasture: 8.8%; Rangeland: 0%; Forest: 63.1%; Urban: 6.8%; Other: 3.1%.

For more information about Georgia's environment, contact the Department of Natural Resources, Floyd Towers East, 205 Butler St. S.W., Atlanta, GA 30334-1794.

Atlanta	Jan	Feb	Mar	Apr	May	Jun	Jul	Aug	Sep	Oct	Nov	Dec	Yearly
Maximum Temperature °F	51.2	55.3	63.2	73.2	79.8	85.6	87.9	87.6	82.3	72.9	62.6	54.1	71.3
Minimum Temperature °F	32.6	34.5	41.7	50.4	58.7	65.9	69.2	68.7	63.6	51.4	41.3	34.8	51.1
Days of Precipitation	11.4	10.1	11.4	9.0	9.1	9.9	11.9	9.4	7.6	6.4	8.5	10.2	115.0
Savannah													
Maximum Temperature °F	60.3	63.1	69.9	77.8	84.2	88.6	90.8	90.1	85.6	77.8	69.5	62.5	76.7
Minimum Temperature °F	37.9	40.0	46.8	54.1	62.3	68.5	71.5	71.4	67.6	55.9	45.5	39.4	55.1
Days of Precipitation	9.3	8.8	9.4	6.8	8.7	11.0	13.8	12.7	10.1	5.9	6.5	8.2	111.1

Flora and Fauna

In a country where many states continually lose forest lands, Georgia is an exception; over the past 60 years, the state has increased its forested land. Today, over two-thirds of Georgia's area is covered by woods. Different types of pine trees grow along the Coastal Plain as well as in the Piedmont region. Hickory trees grow in Georgia's more mountainous areas. The forest floor in the coastal area is home to a variety of vines, palmettos, and shrubs. Wildflowers such as Cherokee roses and violets are found throughout the state.

Many species of animals live in all parts of the state, including opossums, rabbits, and raccoons. Black bears live mainly in the highlands, but also around the Okefenokee Swamp. Some of Georgia's birds include doves, wild turkeys, grouse, and ducks. Mockingbirds, brown thrashers, and other songbirds also live in the state. The Okefenokee Swamp is one of the largest bird refuges in the United States. Georgia's lakes, rivers, and streams have bass, shad, and eels. Crabs, oysters, and turtles live along coastal areas.

Topography

There are several distinct topographic regions in Georgia. The northern part of the state is divided between two mountain ranges. In the northwest corner lies part of the Appalachian Plateau physical region, with mountains situated northeast-southwest and interspersed with fertile valleys used for agriculture. Soil type is characterized as a warm and moist red/yellow clay. East of this region lies the southernmost part of the Blue Ridge Mountain physical region. Soil is typically warm and moist with color running from red/yellow to gray. These mountains contain the highest elevations in the state, with some peaks rising above 4,000 ft. (1200 m). South and east of the Appalachian-Blue Ridge Range lies the Piedmont physical region. This region gradually slopes southward from an elevation of between 1,500 and 2,000 ft. (457 to 610 m) to an area about 300 to 400 ft. (90 to 120 m) above sea level. The soil is warm and moist red clay in this area of gently rolling hills that contains major cities such as Atlanta and Augusta.

The East Gulf Coastal Plain physical region covers most of the southeastern part of the state. Soil type ranges from red clay to fine loamy sand. There is much farmland in this region. The southeastern portion of the Coastal Plain is mostly marshland, much of it covered by the Okefenokee Swamp.

Climate

Most of Georgia has a humid, subtropical climate that brings mild winter weather, and moist and hot summers. The more mountainous north has cooler summers and somewhat cold winters. In Atlanta, in the northwestern part of the state, January and July temperatures average 45 degrees F and 80 degrees F. Temperatures rarely fall below 15 degrees F. In Savannah, near the Georgia-South Carolina border, temperatures average 52 degrees F and 82 degrees F. As a state, Georgia receives approximately 50 inches of precipitation a year. Much of the precipitation falls in the summer months, especially July and August. October and November are Georgia's driest months. Northeastern Georgia receives more average precipitation (75 inches) than the central part of the state (40 inches).

Georgia's winter weather varies significantly from day to day. This is because of the confrontation between subtropical and polar air masses.

Hydrology

Georgia has several important rivers. The Savannah begins in the northeast corner of the state and flows southeast to form Georgia's eastern boundary with South Carolina. The Chattahoochee starts in the central part of the state and flows southwest, forming the bottom half of the western boundary with Alabama. The Flint River winds its way south, meeting the Chattahoochee at the Florida border. The Ogeechee and the Altamaha, as well as the Savannah, are the major rivers draining into the Atlantic Ocean.

There are many large lakes in Georgia, mostly man-made as a result of hydroelectric projects. The largest of these include Hartwell and Clark Hill lakes on the Savannah; Lake Sinclair on the Oconee; Lake Sidney Lanier on the Chattahoochee and Lake Seminole at the junction of the Chattahoochee and the Flint; and Lake Blackshear on the Flint.

Georgia's History

Georgia's First People

Human occupation of Georgia began over twelve thousand years ago by nomadic hunting tribes. About A.D. 700, the Mississippian or Temple Mound Builder culture began to flourish. These Mound Builders sustained themselves with improved agricultural techniques that allowed them time to develop their distinctive legacy. They built burial as well as ceremonial temple mounds and fashioned pottery and sculpture to symbolize their beliefs. They have left major mounds at Etowah and Ocmulgee.

When the Europeans arrived, the Creek and the Cherokee occupied Georgia. These tribes were able to coexist or assimilate with the white man until gold was discovered and the Indians were expelled in the 1830s.

European Exploration

Hernando de Soto of Spain passed through Georgia in 1540 in search of gold in the Mississippi region. The French Huguenots settled on part of the Georgia coast in 1562, but were displaced three years later by the Spanish under Pedro Menendez Aviles. By the dawn of the eighteenth century, the Spanish had established numerous missions along the Georgia coast. Due to skirmishes with pirates, Indians, and the British, they soon abandoned most of these outposts.

In 1721, the British established their first settlement in Georgia on the Altamaha River. Eleven years later James Oglethorpe was granted a charter by King George II to found a colony for the working poor of England. In 1733, Oglethorpe and the colonists arrived at Yamacraw Bluff and establish what was to become Savannah. In 1752, control of the colony was put back in the hands of Parliament, thus establishing Georgia as a royal colony.

During the Revolutionary War, Savannah and Augusta stayed mostly under the control of the British, with the exception of some backwoods settlers who tried to resist. It wasn't until 1781 that the British were defeated at Augusta, and a year later that they were driven from Savannah.

Statehood

Shortly after the war, in 1788, Georgia became the fourth state to ratify the Constitution; Augusta was its capital. Settlers migrated south from the Carolinas and Virginia into Georgia's interior, but it was several decades before the area was settled due to conflicts with the Creek and Cherokee peoples who were native to the area.

The Creek were gradually pushed westward until by 1826 all their lands had been taken. The discovery of gold in 1829 attracted more white people to the lands of the Cherokee. The U.S. Supreme Court supported removal laws passed to seize Cherokee lands for homesteaders, and the Cherokee people lost many of their number on the forced march to the Oklahoma Territory, which became known as the Trail of Tears.

Georgia seceded from the Union in 1861 and was the scene of much destruction during the Civil War. Apart from Virginia, Georgia was one of the most battered states during the Civil War. The most pressing time was 1864 when Union General William Tecumseh Sherman raced out of Tennessee after the Union victory at Chattanooga into the northwestern region of the state. Sherman's "March to the Sea" was a costly one for Georgia. The "scorched earth" policy which Sherman followed left little of economic value behind him. Rails were ripped up, fields were burned, and cattle slaughtered. Three main engagements took place at this time. Kennesaw Mountain (June), Atlanta (September), and Savanna (December) were all Union victories, and costly defeats for Rebel forces.

After the war, the state was put under military rule for failing to ratify the Fourteenth Amendment. In 1868, Georgia finally ratified the amendment but a year later was again placed under military rule for failing to implement the Reconstruction Acts. The state was finally readmitted to the Union in 1870.

Industrialization

With the introduction of the cotton gin in the late eighteenth century, Georgia quickly became a leading cotton producer, resulting in increased settlement in the state, displacement of the native Creek and Cherokee, and the widespread institution of slavery. The planter system that developed in the production of cotton established certain social and economic structures, primarily a tenancy system introduced after slavery that kept ex-slaves and the poor in poverty, and that lasted into the twentieth century.

The cotton industry was hard hit by a major boll weevil infestation in the 1920s and then by the Depression in the 1930s. The industry never really recovered, and Georgia's postwar economy has been more diversified. Poultry is now the leading agricultural product, and textile and paper manufacturing are other major components of the state's economy.

Civil Rights

Georgia, like many other southern states, experienced much tumult in race relations in the 1950s and 1960s. Gov. Herman Talmadge was elected in 1948 after promising to preserve segregation at any cost. Succeeding governors followed suit, with Lester Maddox organizing boycotts of stores that changed segregation policies in 1960. The state attempted to interfere in the court-ordered admission of two black students to the University of Georgia the following year. Martin Luther King, Jr., based his civil rights crusade in Georgia and was buried in Atlanta after his assassination. Federal civil rights legislation, enacted in the mid-1960s due partly to King's influence, guaranteed Georgia's blacks the right to vote.

Important Events

1540 Hernando de Soto is the first European to explore Georgia.

1586 Santa Catalina de Gaule mission is established on St. Catherine's Island.

1702 British succeed in replacing the Spaniards on the Georgia coast.

1732 James Edward Oglethorpe is granted a charter by George II to establish a colony in the territory of Georgia for the poor of England.

1733 Oglethorpe and colonists establish settlement at present-day Savannah.

1752 Britain takes control of Georgia from colonists.

1782 British surrender control of Savannah to the Colonists.

1788 Georgia becomes the fourth state to ratify the Constitution.

1802 Land west of Chattahoochee River ceded to federal government by the Creek.

1825 Creek Indians cede their remaining land to the state.

1838 Cherokee forcibly removed from Georgia to walk the "Trail of Tears" to Oklahoma

1861 Georgia secedes from the Union.

1870 Georgia readmitted to the Union after several years under federal military rule.

1921 Beginning of serious boll weevil infestation that would devastate the cotton industry.

1937–1947 Governors Eurith D. Rivers and Ellis Arnall mirror Franklin Roosevelt's federal policies by passing progressive social legislation.

1948 New Governor Herman Talmadge vows to oppose integration.

1965 The first African American, Julian Bond, is elected to the state legislature.

1968 Martin Luther King, Jr., is assassinated.

1973 Maynard Jackson is elected mayor of Atlanta— the first black mayor of a major southern city.

1976 Former Governor Jimmy Carter is elected President of the United States.

1995 Newt Gingrich becomes first Republican Speaker of the U.S. House of Representatives in forty years.

Population Density

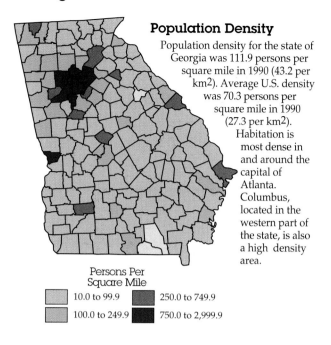

Population density for the state of Georgia was 111.9 persons per square mile in 1990 (43.2 per km2). Average U.S. density was 70.3 persons per square mile in 1990 (27.3 per km2). Habitation is most dense in and around the capital of Atlanta. Columbus, located in the western part of the state, is also a high density area.

Persons Per Square Mile

☐	10.0 to 99.9	☐	250.0 to 749.9
☐	100.0 to 249.9	■	750.0 to 2,999.9

Population Projections

Population in thousands

Georgia's Population

U. S. Population

9,000	285,000
8,500	280,000
8,000	275,000
7,500	270,000
7,000	265,000
6,500	260,000
6,000	255,000
5,500	250,000

1990   1995   2000   2010

Population Change

Year	Population
1950	3,445,000
1960	3,956,000
1970	4,607,000
1980	5,463,105
1990	6,478,216
2000	7,957,000
2010	9,045,000

Period	Change
1950–1970	33.7%
1970–1980	18.6%
1980–1990	18.6%
1990–2000	22.8%

Population Change

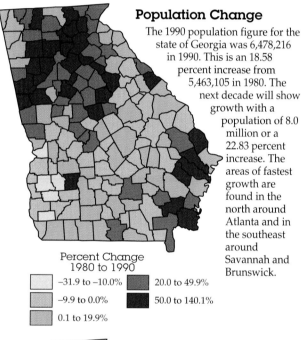

The 1990 population figure for the state of Georgia was 6,478,216 in 1990. This is an 18.58 percent increase from 5,463,105 in 1980. The next decade will show growth with a population of 8.0 million or a 22.83 percent increase. The areas of fastest growth are found in the north around Atlanta and in the southeast around Savannah and Brunswick.

Percent Change 1980 to 1990

☐	−31.9 to −10.0%	☐	20.0 to 49.9%
☐	−9.9 to 0.0%	■	50.0 to 140.1%
☐	0.1 to 19.9%		

Population Facts

State Population, 1993: 6,917,000

Rank: 11

Population 2000: 7,957,000 (Rank 10)

Density: 111.9 per sq. mi. (43.2 per km²)

Distribution: 63.2% urban, 36.8% rural

Population Under 5 Years Old: 7.9%

Population Under 18 Years Old: 26.7%

Population Over 65 Years Old: 10.1%

Median Age: 31.6

Number of Households: 2,367,000

Average Persons Per Household: 2.66

Average Persons Per Family: 3.16

Female Heads of Households: 5.09%

Population That Is Married: 20.17%

Birth Rate: 17.4 per 1,000 population

Death Rate: 8.0 per 1,000 population

Births to Teen Mothers: 16.7%

Marriage Rate: 9.8 per 1,000 population

Divorce Rate: 5.5 per 1,000 population

Violent Crime Rate: 738 per 100,000 pop.

Population on Social Security: 13.7%

Percent Voting for President: 46.9%

Georgia's Famous Citizens

Berry, Martha McChesney (1866–1942). Educator. Founded a Sunday school for illiterate families that evolved into Berry College.

Candler, Asa Griggs (1851–1929). Philanthropist-businessman. Launched Coca-Cola and made it the best-selling soft drink.

Carter, James Earl (b. 1924). Served as governor of Georgia (1971-1975). Elected 39th president of the United States (1976).

Hope, John (1868–1936). Educator. Became president of Atlanta University, the first graduate school for blacks, in 1929.

Nabrit, James M. Jr. (b. 1900). Lawyer-educator. President of Howard University (1961-69) and civil-rights activist.

O'Connor, Flannery (1925–1964). Wrote about the religious and violent undercurrents in southern culture in such books as *Wise Blood*.

Wheeler, Joseph (1836–1906). Soldier. Wrote a Confederate cavalry manual and resisted Sherman's March through Georgia.

Woodward, Joanne (b. 1930). Actress. Won an Academy Award in 1957 for her role in *The Three Faces of Eve*.

Distribution of Income

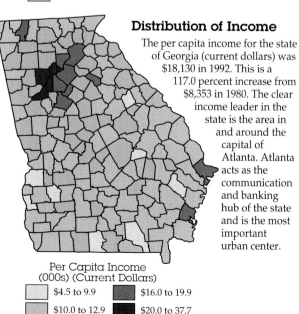

The per capita income for the state of Georgia (current dollars) was $18,130 in 1992. This is a 117.0 percent increase from $8,353 in 1980. The clear income leader in the state is the area in and around the capital of Atlanta. Atlanta acts as the communication and banking hub of the state and is the most important urban center.

Per Capita Income (000s) (Current Dollars)

☐	$4.5 to 9.9	☐	$16.0 to 19.9
☐	$10.0 to 12.9	■	$20.0 to 37.7
☐	$13.0 to 15.9		

Population Profile

Rank. Georgia ranks 11th among U.S. states in terms of population with 6,917,000 citizens.

Minority Population. The state's minority population is 30.0 percent. The state's male to female ratio for 1990 was 94.32 males for every 100 females. It was below the national average of 95.22 males for every 100 females.

Growth. Growing much faster than the projected national average, the state's population is expected to reach 9.0 million by the year 2010 *(see graph above)*.

Older Citizens. The state's population older than 65 was 654,270 in 1990. It grew 26.62% from 516,731 in 1980.

Younger Citizens. The number of children (under 18 years of age) was 1.7 million in 1990. This represents 26.7 percent of the state's population. The state's school aged population was 1.1 million in 1990. It is expected to increase to 1.4 million by the year 2000. This represents a 20.09% change.

Urban/Rural. 63.2% of the population of the state live in urban areas while 36.8% live in rural areas.

Largest Cities. Georgia has 13 cities with a population greater than 35,000. The populations of the state's largest centers are (starting from the most populous) Atlanta (394,017), Columbus (178,681), Savannah (137,560), Macon (106,612), Albany (78,122), Sandy Springs (67,842), South Augusta (55,998), Roswell (47,923), Athens (45,734), Augusta (44,639), Marietta (44,129), Warner Robins (43,726), Valdosta (39,806), East Point (34,402), Martinez (33,731), Smyrna (30,981), and Rome (30,326).

Government

Capital: Atlanta (established 1868).

Statehood: Became 4th state on Jan. 2, 1788.

Number of Counties: 159.

Supreme Court Justices: 7, 6-year term.

State Senators: 56, 2-year term.

State Legislators: 180, 2-year term.

United States Senators: 2.

United States Representatives: 11.

Electoral Votes: 13.

State Constitution: Adopted 1982.

Native American

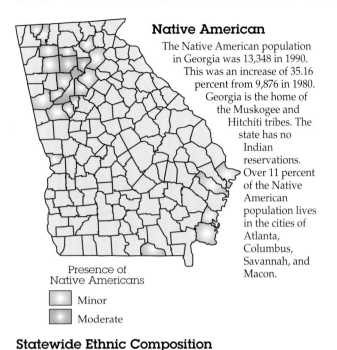

The Native American population in Georgia was 13,348 in 1990. This was an increase of 35.16 percent from 9,876 in 1980. Georgia is the home of the Muskogee and Hitchiti tribes. The state has no Indian reservations. Over 11 percent of the Native American population lives in the cities of Atlanta, Columbus, Savannah, and Macon.

Presence of
Native Americans

Minor

Moderate

Nationalities

African	19,154
American	837,184
Arab	8,790
Austrian	5,754
Czech	6,238
Dutch	67,199
English	683,423
Finnish	3,357
German	634,529
Greek	12,026
Hungarian	8,598
Irish	628,660
Italian	77,544
Norwegian	12,880
Polish	43,886
Portuguese	3,184
Russian	20,083
Scottish	95,252
Slovak	8,040
Swedish	24,152
Welsh	22,283
West Indian	10,769

Statewide Ethnic Composition

Seventy-one percent of the population of Georgia is white. Slightly more than three quarters of a million people claim to be American and acknowledge no other nationality. Over one quarter of the pop-ulation is African American. Only 19,154 people claimed to have African roots in the 1990 Census despite the fact that African Americans were calculated at 1,746,565.

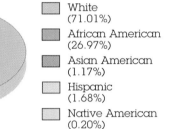

White (71.01%)

African American (26.97%)

Asian American (1.17%)

Hispanic (1.68%)

Native American (0.20%)

Education Facts

Total Students 1990: 1,126,535

Number of School Districts: 186

Expenditure Per Capita on Education 1990: $796

Expenditure Per Capita K–12 1990: $729

Expenditure Per Pupil 1990: $4,852

Total School Enrollment 1990–1991: 1,151,687

Rank of Expenditures Per Student: 26th in the U.S.

African American Enrollment: 37.9%

Hispanic Enrollment: 0.6%

Asian/Pacific Islander Enrollment: 0.8%

Native American Enrollment: 0.05%

Mean SAT Score 1991 Verbal: 400

Mean SAT Score 1991 Math: 444

Average Teacher's Salary 1992: $29,500

Rank Teacher's Salary: 31st in U.S.

High School Graduates 1990: 53,400

Total Number of Public Schools: 1,732

Number of Teachers 1990: 62,934

Student/Teacher Ratio: 18.3

Staff Employed in Public Schools: 125,939

Pupil/Staff Ratio: 8.9

Staff/Teacher Ratio: 2.0

Education

Attainment: 71 percent of population 25 years or older were high school graduates in 1989, earning Georgia a ranking of 42d in the United States; 20 percent of the state's population had completed college. Institutions of Higher Education: The largest universities and colleges in the state include the University of Georgia (founded 1785), Athens; Georgia Institute of Technology (founded 1888), Atlanta; Emory University, Atlanta. Expenditures per Student: Expenditure increased 61% between 1985 and 1990. Projected High School Graduations: 1998 (75,677), 2004 (82,040); Total Revenues for Education from Federal Sources: $272 million; Total Revenues for Education from State Sources: $2.1 billion; Total Revenues for Education from Local Sources: $1.3 billion; Average Annual Salaries for Public School Principals: $45,124; Largest School Districts in State, Dekalb County School District, Decatur, 72,824 students 33d in the United States; Cobb County School District , Marietta, 66,971 41st.

African American

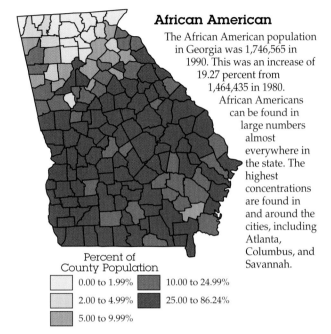

The African American population in Georgia was 1,746,565 in 1990. This was an increase of 19.27 percent from 1,464,435 in 1980. African Americans can be found in large numbers almost everywhere in the state. The highest concentrations are found in and around the cities, including Atlanta, Columbus, and Savannah.

Percent of
County Population

0.00 to 1.99%

2.00 to 4.99%

5.00 to 9.99%

10.00 to 24.99%

25.00 to 86.24%

Hispanic[††]

The Hispanic population in Georgia was 108,922 in 1990. This is an increase of 77.80 percent from 61,260 persons in 1980. The largest numbers of Hispanics can be found in and around Columbus. Other concentrations include a group of four counties in the southeastern portion of the state. Gainesville is also a site where high numbers can be found.

Percent of
County Population

0.00 to 0.99%

1.00 to 2.99%

3.00 to 9.99%

10.00 to 24.99%

[††]A person of Mexican, Puerto Rican, Cuban, or other Spanish culture or origin regardless of race.

Asian American

The Asian American population in Georgia was 75,781 in 1990. This is an increase of 207.67 percent from 24,631 persons in 1980. Asian Americans are the fastest-growing minority group in the state. The Asian American pattern is very similar to the Hispanic pattern in Georgia in that there are enclaves of counties with high numbers of Asian residents.

Percent of
County Population

0.00 to 0.24%

0.25 to 0.99%

1.00 to 1.99%

2.00 to 4.99%

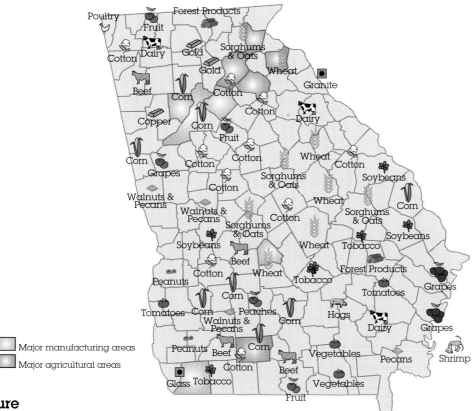

Major manufacturing areas

Major agricultural areas

Agriculture

Georgia has 12.1 million farm acres. During the last 40 years, Georgia's farms have grown larger in size and fewer in number. In 1955, 166,000 farms were found in the state. Today, 45,000 remain. Agriculture adds $2 billion to the state's gross product annually. The principal commodities in order of marketing receipts are broilers, peanuts, cattle, and eggs.

Georgia's leading farm product is broilers, produced mainly in the area north of Atlanta. The most important crop in the state is peanuts, found primarily in the southwestern portion of the state. Georgia leads the nation in producing peanuts, as well as pecans. The state is also the nation's number one peach producer, with orchards centered in Peach County. Cotton, once the leading product, today accounts for only 2 percent of farm income.

Housing

Owner Occupied Units: 2,638,418; Average Age of Units: 22 years; Average Value of Housing Units: $71,300; Renter Occupied Units: 808,365; Median Monthly Rent: $433; Housing Starts: 51,600; Existing Home Sales: N/A.

Economic Facts

Gross State Product: $130,000,000,000

Income Per Capita: $18,130

Disposable Personal Income: $15,943

Median Household Income: $29,021

Average Annual Pay, 1988: $23,164

Principal Industries: textiles, transportation equipment, paper products, chemicals, food products, clothing, carpet production

Major Crops: peanuts, eggs, milk, corn, soybeans, tobacco, orchard crops

Fish: Shrimp, Crab

Livestock: hogs, cattle, chickens

Non-Fuel Minerals: Kaolin, Granite, Limestone, Marble

Organic Fuel Minerals: N/A

Civilian Labor Force: 3,166,000 (Women: 1,500,000)

Total Employed: 3,008,000 (Women: 1,421,000)

Median Value of Housing: $71,300

Median Contract Rent: $433 per month

Economic Sectors

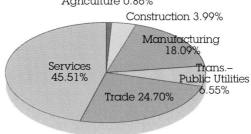

Agriculture 0.86%
Construction 3.99%
Manufacturing 18.09%
Services 45.51%
Trans.–Public Utilities 6.55%
Trade 24.70%

Manufacturing

Georgia's industrial base did not develop until after the Civil War. Throughout the 19th century, manufacturing industries, especially textiles, flocked to the state. The post-World War II era saw even more industrial growth. Today, textiles still ranks as a leading manufacturing industry in Georgia. Transportation equipment and processed foods are also important products.

Georgia trails only North Carolina in textile production. Carpet, the leading textile product, is produced in Cartersville, Calhoun, and Dalton, the nation's leading carpet-producing city. Many small towns in Georgia have apparel factories. The Atlanta region has large automobile and aircraft facilities, as does Doraville. The town of Chamblee is an important peanut butter producer.

Transportation

After years of continuing decline, Georgia's water transportation network is once again gaining in importance. Savannah is the leading port of Georgia. However, inland cities like Augusta and Columbus are served by the Savannah and Chattahoochee rivers, respectively.

Construction of the state highway system began in the early 1900s. Out of Georgia's 105,000 miles of roads and highways, approximately three-quarters are surfaced. Railroad service is also included in Georgia's transportation network. Two freight lines move goods across the state. Five Georgia cities have passenger rail service. Atlanta is the railroad center for the Southeast. Atlanta is also home to Georgia's busiest airport, Hartsfield International. This airport handles the most airplane takeoffs and landings in the world.

Energy and Transportation Facts

Energy. Yearly Consumption: 2,057 tril. BTUs (residential, 21.4%; commercial, 15.7%; industrial, 30.6%; transportation, 32.2%); Annual Energy Expenditures Per Capita: $1,884; Nuclear Power Plants Located in State: 4; Source of Energy Consumed: Petroleum— 37.7%; Natural Gas— 15.8%; Coal— 30.8%; Hydroelectric Power—2.3%; Nuclear Power—13.3%.

Transportation. Highway Miles: 110,790 (interstates, 1,243; urban, 26,147; rural, 84,643); Average Yearly Auto Insurance: $514 (29th); Auto Fatalities Rank: 23d; Registered Motor Vehicles: 5,899,437; Workers in Carpools: 19.7%; Workers Using Public Trans: 2.8%.

Employment

Employment. Georgia employed 3.27 million people in 1993. Most work in wholesale and retail trade (772,600 persons or 23.6% of the workforce). Manufacturing accounts for 17.0% or 554,600 workers. Social and personal services account for 22.3% or 729,100 workers. Government employs 546,900 workers (16.7%). Construction employs 127,700 workers (3.9%). Transportation and utilities account for 6.2% or 201,700 persons. Agriculture employs 78,400 workers or 2.4%. Finance, real estate, and insurance account for 5.1% or 165,600 workers. Mining employs 7,500 people and accounts for only 0.2% of the workforce.

Unemployment. Unemployment has decreased to 5.8% in 1993 from a rate of 6.5% in 1985. Today's figure is lower than the national average of 6.8% as shown below.

Unemployment Rate

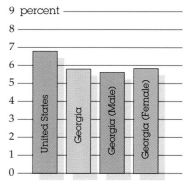

percent — United States, Georgia, Georgia (Male), Georgia (Female)

HAWAII
The State of Hawaii

Official State Seal

The Great Seal of Hawaii was adopted in 1894. However, the legend was changed from "The Republic of Hawaii" to "The State of Hawaii." The motto, *"Ua Mau ke Ea o ka Aina i ka Pono,"* translates to "The Life of the Land Is Perpetuated in Righteousness." Included on the seal is a coat of arms supported by Kamehameha I and the goddess of liberty.

Legal Holidays

January: New Year's Day—1st, Martin Luther King, Jr., Day—3rd Monday; February: Presidents' Day—3rd Monday; March: Prince Jonah Kalanianaole Day—26th; May: Lei Day—1st; Memorial Day—4th Monday; June: Kamehameha Day—11th; July: Independence Day—4th; Hawaii Flag Day—4th; August: Admission Day—Third Friday; September: Labor Day—1st Monday; October: Columbus Day—2nd Monday; Discovers Day—13th; November: Veterans' Day—11th; Thanksgiving—4th Thursday; December: Christmas—25th.

Official State Flag

The Hawaiian flag originated with a British explorer of the islands. In 1845 the number of stripes was changed to eight to represent the main islands of the Hawaiian chain.

Festivals and Events

January: Narcissus Festival, Honolulu (through February); February: Cherry Blossom Festival, Honolulu (through April); March: Highland Gathering & Games, Honolulu; April: Merrie Monarch Festival, Hilo; July: Honomu Village Fair, Honomu; August: Hula Festival, Honolulu; Honolulu Toro Nagashi, Honolulu; September: Hawaiian Ocean Fest, Oahu; Bankoh Na Wahine O Kai, Waikiki, Oahu; October: Bankoh Molokai Hoe, Molokai, Oahu; November: Artists of Hawaii, Honolulu; December: Hawaiian Christmas Rough Water Swim, Honolulu.

Hawaii Compared to States in Its Region.

Resident Pop. in Metro Areas: 3d; Pop. Percent Increase: 4th; Pop. Over 65: 3d; Infant Mortality: 5th; School Enroll. Increase: 1st; High School Grad. and Up: 4th; Violent Crime: 5th; Hazardous Waste Sites: 5th; Unemployment: 3d; Median Household Income: 2d; Persons Below Poverty: 5th; Energy Costs Per Person: 2d.

Pacific Region

	Population	Capital
Washington	5,255,000	Olympia
Oregon	3,032,000	Salem
California	31,211,000	Sacramento
Alaska	599,000	Juneau
Hawaii	1,172,000	Honolulu

Hawaii's Finances

Households: 356,000; Income Per Capita Current Dollars: $21,218; Change Per Capita Income 1980 to 1992: 96.9% (29th in U.S.); State Expenditures: $4,903,000,000; State Revenues: $4,568,000,000; Personal Income Tax: 2 to 10%; Federal Income Taxes Paid Per Capita: $2,224; Sales Tax: 4% (prescription drugs exempt).

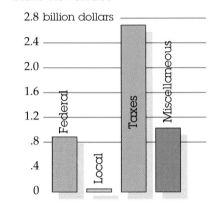

Location, Size, and Boundaries

Location. Hawaii is located in the Pacific region of the United States. It is bounded on four sides by water. The geographic center of Hawaii is lat. 20° 57.1' N; long. 157° 16.6' W.

Size. Hawaii is the 47th largest state in terms of size. Its area is 6,450 sq. mi. (16,706 km2). Inland water covers 25 sq. mi. (65 km2).

Boundaries. Pacific Ocean, 750 mi. (1,207 km).

Geographic Extent. The north/south extent of Hawaii is 220 mi. (352 km). The state extends 1,647 mi. (2,635 km) to the east/west.

Facts about Hawaii. Origin of Name: *Hawaiki* or *Owhyhee* native words for "homeland"; Nickname: The Aloha State; Motto: "The Life of the Land Is Perpetuated in Righteousness" *(Ua mau ke ea o ka aina i ka pono)*; Abbreviations: HI (postal); State Bird: nene; State Tree: kukui; State Flower: yellow hibiscus; State Song: "Hawaii Ponoi," words by King Kalakaua, music by Henry Berger.

Hawaii Compared to Other States. Resident Pop. in Metro Areas: 21st; Pop. Percent Increase: 8th; Pop. Over 65: 38th; Infant Mortality: 48th; School Enroll. Increase: 4th; High School Grad. and Up: 13th; Violent Crime: 43d; Haz. Waste Sites: 47th; Unemployment: 47th; Med. Household Income: 5th; Persons Below Poverty: 46th; Energy Costs Per Person: 22d.

Sources of Information. Tourism: Hawaii Visitors Bureau, P.O. Box 8527, Honolulu, HI 96830. Economy: Hawaii Department of Business and Economic Development, P.O. Box 2359, Honolulu, HI 96804. Government: Hawaii Department of Business, Economic Development, and Tourism, P.O. Box 2359, Honolulu, HI 96804. History: Hawaii State Library, Hawaii and Pacific Room, 478 South King Street, Honolulu, HI 96813.

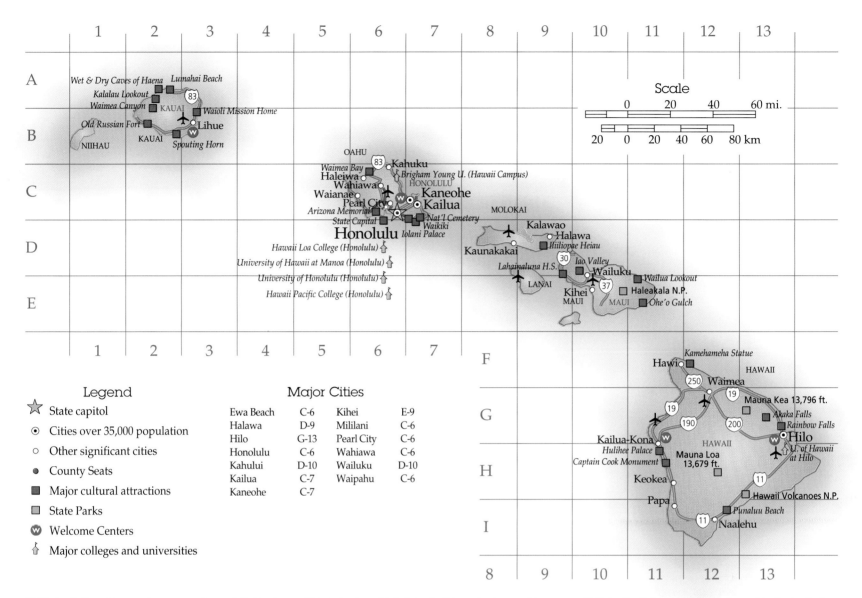

Legend

⭐ State capitol

⊙ Cities over 35,000 population

○ Other significant cities

● County Seats

■ Major cultural attractions

□ State Parks

Ⓦ Welcome Centers

⚐ Major colleges and universities

Major Cities

Ewa Beach	C-6	Kihei	E-9
Halawa	D-9	Mililani	C-6
Hilo	G-13	Pearl City	C-6
Honolulu	C-6	Wahiawa	C-6
Kahului	D-10	Wailuku	D-10
Kailua	C-7	Waipahu	C-6
Kaneohe	C-7		

■ Akaka Falls. Falling 420 feet over a volcanic cliff. (G-13)

■ Arizona Memorial. Memorial to the USS *Arizona* sunk at Peal Harbor on December 7, 1941. (C-6)

■ Captain Cook Monument. The site where the British navigator was killed in 1779. (H-11)

■ Hulihee Palace. Summer palace used by Hawaiian royalty, now a museum. (H-11)

■ Iao Valley. Site of an unusual rock formation called the Iao Needle. (D-10)

■ Iliiliopae Heiau. One of the largest heiaus in Hawaii (320 feet long and 120 feet wide). (D-9)

■ Iolani Palace. Palace where the kings and queens of Hawaii lived. (C-6)

■ Kalalau Lookout. Scenic view into a 4,000-foot valley. (A-2)

■ Kamehameha Statue. The original statue which was lost at sea. (F-12)

■ Lahainaluna High School. Oldest school west of the Rocky Mountains, established in 1831. (D-9)

■ Lumahai Beach. The beach featured in South Pacific. Photographic beach. (A-2)

■ National Memorial Cemetery of the Pacific. Resting place of World War II, Korean, and Vietnam War veterans. (C-7)

■ Ohe'o Gulch (Seven Pools). Site of pools of water where Hawaiian women bathed. (E-11)

■ Old Russian Fort. Built by the Russian Fur Company in 1817. (B-2)

■ Punaluu Beach. Black sand beach which was possibly the site of the first landing of the Polynesians. (I-12)

■ Rainbow Falls. Named after the rainbows that form in the waterfall. (G-13)

■ Spouting Horn. Water rushing into lava tubes forms fountains of spray. (B-2)

■ State Capitol. Site of Hawaii's lawmaking body. (C-6)

■ Waikiki. Resort area with scenic beaches with surfing and other water sports. (D-7)

■ Wailua Lookout. Scenic view of the Keanae Peninsula. (E-11)

■ Waimea Bay. Fine beach for sunning and picnicking. (C-6)

■ Waimea Canyon. Said to be the "Grand Canyon of the Pacific." (B-2)

■ Waioli Mission Home. Mission built in 1834 and recently restored. (B-3)

■ Wet and Dry Caves of Haena. Caverns where one is dry and one is wet. Said to be a meeting place for Hawaiian chiefs. (A-2)

Weather Facts

Record High Temperature: 100° F (38° C) on Apr 26, 1927, at Pahala; Record Low Temperature: 14° F (-10° C) on January 1, 1957, at Haleakala; Average January Temperature: 69° F (21° C); Average July Temperature: 75° F (24° C); Average Yearly Precipitation: 111 in. (282 cm).

Environmental Facts

Air Pollution Rank: 50th; Water Pollution Rank: 47th; Total Yearly Industrial Pollution: 604,706 lbs.; Industrial Pollution Rank: 50th; Hazardous Waste Sites: 2; Hazardous Sites Rank: 47th; Landfill Capacity: overextended; Fresh Water Supply: large surplus; Daily Residential Water Consumption: 214 gals. per capita; Endangered Species: Birds (31)—'akepa, Hawaii; Mammals (2)—bat, Hawaiian hoary; Other Species (4)—snail, Oahu tree; Plants (159)—'ahinahina (mauna kea silversword).

Environmental Quality

Hawaii residents generate 1.0 million tons of solid waste each year, or approximately 1,800 pounds per capita. Landfill capacity in Hawaii will be exhausted in 5 to 10 years. The state has 7 hazardous waste sites. Annual greenhouse gas emissions in Hawaii are insignificant. Industrial sources in Hawaii release approximately 1.6 thousand tons of toxins and 54.4 thousand tons of acid precipitation-producing substances into the atmosphere each year.

The state has 245,000 acres within the National Park System; the largest area within the state is Hawaii Volcanoes National Park. State parks cover just over 25,400 acres, attracting 19.1 million visitors per year.

Hawaii spends less than 1 percent (about 0.9%) of its budget, or approximately $25 per capita, on environmental and natural resources. Hawaii representatives in the U.S. House voted in favor of national environmental legislation 63 percent of the time, while U.S. senators did so 59 percent of the time.

Island Regions: (a) Niihau; (b) Kauai; (c) Oahu; (d) Lanai; (e) Molokai; (f) Kahoolawe; (g) Maui; (h) Hawaii.

Topography

The 132 islands that constitute the Hawaiian Islands have all been formed by volcanic activity. Of these islands, all but eight are minor outcroppings of rock or isles of sand. Some of the volcanoes that formed Hawaii's distinctive topography are still active. The largest active volcano in the world is located on the island of Hawaii; Mauna Loa reaches to 13,680 ft. (4,170 m) above sea level.

The eight main islands are Niihau, Kauai, Oahu, Lanai, Molokai, Kahoolawe, Maui, and Hawaii. The coastlines of these islands consist mainly of white sandy beaches, although other beaches have a black appearance from the lava residue of volcanic activity. Some areas of coastline have no beach at all, but only a sudden wall of rock that juts out from the sea. The largest of the islands is Hawaii, which also has the highest peaks. The highest point in the state is Mauna Kea, on Hawaii, which rises 13,796 ft. (4,205 m) above sea level.

Much of the islands consist of lush tropical forest or woodland, with flora and fauna that is found nowhere else in the world.

Land Use

Cropland: 9.5%; Pasture: 0.9%; Rangeland: 24.4%; Forest: 38.8%; Urban: 4.2%; Other: 22.2%.

For more information about Hawaii's environment, contact the Chief Environment Officer, Department of Health, 1250 Punchbowl St., Honolulu, HI 96813

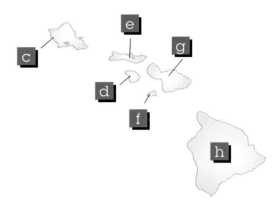

Climate

The climate of Hawaii is not as hot as one may perceive it to be. Hawaii has a mild climate all year round, with little temperature variation between months. Cooling trade winds from the northeast blow over Hawaii during the summer, keeping the weather pleasantly mild. Honolulu, on the island of Oahu, has January and July average temperatures of 72 degrees F and 80 degrees F. Hilo, on the big island of Hawaii, averages 70 degrees F and 75 degrees F for January and July.

Precipitation falls very unevenly throughout Hawaii. Mount Waialeale, on the island of Kauai, averages over 480 inches of rain a year. Conversely, the lowlands only average less than 10 inches of precipitation. Snowfall only occurs in the mountains with elevations usually over 9,000 feet.

Hawaii does not have any real temperature extremes. The state's highest recorded temperature is only 100 degrees.

Hydrology

The longest river on the island of Hawaii is the Wailuku, which flows eastward for about 30 miles (48 km) to the Pacific Ocean. On Oahu, the Kuakonahua Stream runs for about the same distance in the northern part of the island.

Each of the islands, being surrounded by water, has many bays. Hilo Bay is located on Hawaii's eastern shore. Kiholo Bay can be found on the western shore, and Pohue and Kaalualu bays in the south. The largest bays on Oahu are Kaneohe Bay on the eastern shore, and Pearl Harbor (near Honolulu) in the south. Prominent bays on Maui are Kahului in the north and Maalaea in the south.

A series of channels separates the major islands. The Alenuihaha divides Hawaii and Maui. The Kaiwi separates Maui and Oahu, and the Kauai divides Oahu and Kauai. Numerous smaller channels and bays are scattered throughout the islands.

Average Monthly Weather

Hilo	Jan	Feb	Mar	Apr	May	Jun	Jul	Aug	Sep	Oct	Nov	Dec	Yearly
Maximum Temperature °F	79.5	79.0	79.0	79.7	81.0	82.5	82.8	83.3	83.6	83.0	80.9	79.5	81.2
Minimum Temperature °F	63.2	63.2	63.9	64.9	66.1	67.1	68.0	68.4	68.0	67.5	66.3	64.3	65.9
Days of Precipitation	17.3	17.3	23.4	25.4	25.4	24.2	27.4	26.4	23.4	23.9	23.0	21.1	278.1
Honolulu													
Maximum Temperature °F	79.9	80.4	81.4	82.7	84.8	86.2	87.1	88.3	88.2	86.7	83.9	81.4	84.2
Minimum Temperature °F	65.3	65.3	67.3	68.7	70.2	71.9	73.1	73.6	72.9	72.2	69.2	66.5	69.7
Days of Precipitation	9.8	9.3	8.9	9.1	7.3	5.8	7.4	6.4	7.0	8.8	9.2	10.1	99.0

Flora and Fauna

Hawaii has some of the most exotic plant life in the entire world. Approximately 2,500 species of flora can be found only in the state of Hawaii. Hawaii is approximately 40 percent covered by forests, and most of the trees in these forests are tropical hardwoods. Various shrubs can also be found growing near wooded areas. In addition to forests, Hawaii has an abundance of flowering plants, some 1,400 different species. Orchids, gardenias, poinsettias, and bougainvillea all grow in the state.

Hawaii is also home to a number of unusual species of birds. Among the most well-known are the Hawaiian goose and nene. As a result of its remote location, few animals are considered native to Hawaii. When the first people inhabited the islands, only a few types of mammals, including a bat and a seal, existed there. Polynesian and European settlers brought animals such as dogs, cattle, horses, cats, and sheep to Hawaii. Hawaii's marine life consists of dolphins, tuna, marlin, and many other sea creatures.

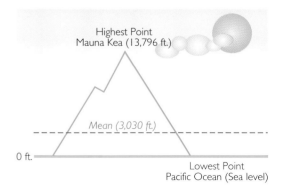

Hawaii's History

Hawaii's First People

Polynesians arrived in the islands known as Hawaii from the Marquesas Group, which is north of Tahiti, between 300 and 600 A.D. Little is known of these seafaring people. During later centuries, other immigrants from Tahiti came to Hawaii and mixed with the older population. This created a new people that are known today as "original" or "native" Hawaiians.

European Exploration

In 1778, Capt. James Cook became the first European to have contact with the Hawaiian Islands. He named them the Sandwich Islands after the earl of Sandwich, but was killed in an incident with the islanders the following year.

Over the next several decades after Cook's arrival, Kamehameha I consolidated power by gaining control of the various islands. He completed this mission by about 1810, helped considerably by weapons introduced by the white men.

A year after Kamehameha I's death in 1819, missionaries from Boston came to the Hawaiian Islands to spread Christianity and other Western ideas and established newspapers and public schools. By the mid-1820s, the native population of the islands had been halved (300,000 to 140,000) in the roughly fifty years since Captain Cook first landed, primarily due to the diseases the white man brought with him for which the islanders had no natural immunity. Under the rule of Kamehameha III (1825-54) there was a continuation of the westernization of the islands. Hawaiian religion had been abolished a couple of years before he took power, and by 1840, with the encouragement of the United States, Kamehameha III introduced the first written constitution for the islands, incorporating many Western notions of government.

Statehood

By the end of Kamehameha III's reign, the monarchy was recognized by the United States, Britain, and France. Gerrit Judd, a medical missionary, had served as prime minister for the final twelve years of his rule, and this increased U.S. presence led to calls for U.S. annexation. After Kalakaua assumed the throne in 1873 he attempted to increase the powers of the monarch, resulting in conflicts with the legislature. When he was succeeded by his sister, Liliuokalani, in 1891, the power struggles continued and she was overthrown in 1893 by a coalition of Hawaiians and American business interests.

The following year, a new constitution was drawn up and the Republic of Hawaii was established with Sanford Dole, an American born in Hawaii, as president. With Americans now in control of the new republic, they pushed for annexation. The United States complied four years later. In 1900, Congress officially declared Hawaii a U.S. territory.

Hawaii was the site of war when Pearl Harbor, on Oahu island, was attacked by Japanese warplanes on December 7, 1941, touching off the United States' full involvement in World War II. Pearl Harbor was the home port for the U.S. Navy's Pacific Fleet. On the day of the attack there were over seventy-five warships in port ranging from battleships to auxiliaries. The Pacific Fleet's carrier force was out at sea at the time. The attack lasted a little more than two hours, but had a devastating effect. When the attack was over eighteen warships and 200 airplanes were destroyed. The cost in human life was equally as staggering with 2,400 dead and 2,300 wounded or missing.

Although the House passed a statehood bill in 1947, the Senate did not immediately follow suit. Hawaii was finally admitted to the Union as the fiftieth state in 1959.

Industrialization

In the early part of the nineteenth century, sandalwood was the chief Hawaiian trade item. Whaling was another important industry in the islands in this era. However, in 1835, Ladd & Co. established the first large commercial plantation for growing sugarcane, which would come to dominate the economy. Chinese and Japanese immigrants were used to work the sugar fields, and in 1876 the United States signed a treaty with Hawaii guaranteeing most goods to be duty free at Customs, a further boon to the sugar industry.

By the beginning of the twentieth century, pineapples came to vie with sugar as the leading industry in the state. These two agricultural products remained the primary economic force in Hawaii until World War II. Since then the defense industry, spurred by military spending, and tourism have fueled the economy.

The Islands State and the Monarchy

Hawaii is the only state that is not a part of the North American continent. In addition, it is the only state that consists of a group of islands. These islands, about 125 in number, were formed some 25 million years ago by a fissure in the ocean floor. The creation of the islands in this manner has left numerous volcanoes, including Mauna Kea, a huge extinct volcano, and Mauna Loa, a large active volcano in Hawaii Volcanoes National Park—both on the island of Hawaii.

The islands are surrounded by coral reefs and enjoy a temperate climate year-round that has contributed to the islands' appeal as a tourist destination.

Hawaii is the only state in the United States which was once a kingdom ruled by native royalty. There were eight monarchs who ruled the united Hawaiian islands from 1795 to 1893. The most famous was Kamehameha I who was the first to rule over a united Hawaii. Another famous monarch was Queen Liliuokalani who was the last ruler before the United States took control of the islands in 1893.

Important Events

1778 Captain James Cook discovers the Hawaiian Islands, which he names the Sandwich Islands.

1790s Kamehameha I consolidates control of the various Hawaiian Islands.

1819 Kamehameha II replaces his father and abolishes Hawaiian religion.

1820 Missionaries from New England arrive to spread the Christian faith.

1830 Sandalwood, which had been the primary trade item for Hawaiians, is depleted.

1840 First constitution for Hawaii is implemented.

1848 Great Mahele is implemented—land reform that abolished the feudal land holding system

1875 Treaty allowing the exchange of duty-free goods between Hawaii and the U.S.

1893 Queen Liliuokalani is overthrown by American-led business interests.

1894 Republic of Hawaii is formed under a new constitution.

1898 Hawaii is annexed by the U.S.

1900 Hawaii becomes a U.S. territory with Sanford Dole as governor.

1911 United States constructs a military base at Pearl Harbor.

1924 During a strike by Filipino sugar workers on Kauai, twenty people are killed.

1928 Lei Day is established in honor of the aloha spirit.

1941 Japanese launch air strike on Pearl Harbor, initiating U.S. entry into World War II; islands are put under martial law.

1942 Japanese Americans are interred into camps by Executive Order 9066.

1944 Martial law is lifted in Hawaii.

1946 Supreme Court finds that the imposition of martial law had been unconstitutional.

1959 Hawaii is admitted to the Union as the fiftieth state.

1988 The Senate votes to apologize for interring Japanese Americans during World War II.

1992 Hurricane Iniki hits Hawaii and causes $1.4 billion in damages.

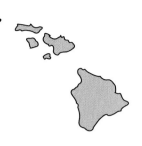

Population Density

Population density for the state of Hawaii was 172.5 persons per square mile in 1990 (66.6 per km2). Average U.S. density was 70.3 persons per square mile in 1990 (27.3 per km2). Habitation is most dense on the island of Oahu. Oahu is the home of the capital, Honolulu. Other cities on the island include Kaneohe and Kailua. The Pearl Harbor military base is also located on the island.

Persons Per Square Mile

	10.0 to 99.9
	750.0 to 1,499.9

Population Projections

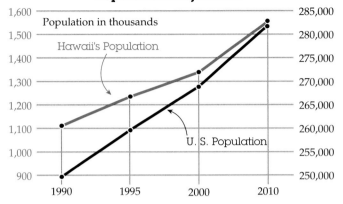

Population Change

Year	Population
1950	500,000
1960	642,000
1970	774,000
1980	964,691
1990	1,108,229
2000	1,345,000
2010	1,559,000

Period	Change
1950–1970	54.8%
1970–1980	24.7%
1980–1990	14.8%
1990–2000	21.4%

Population Change

The 1990 population figure for the state of Hawaii was 1,108,229. This is a 14.88 percent increase from 964,691 in 1980. The next decade will show growth with a population of 1.4 million or a 21.36 percent increase. All of the main islands of the Hawaiian chain have seen significant growth ranging from small increases upward to 50 percent of 1980 figures. The next decade promises to continue this trend as more people flock to this warm, sunny state.

Percent Change 1980 to 1990

	0.1 to 19.9%
	20.0 to 49.9%

Population Facts

State Population, 1993: 1,172,000

Rank: 40

Population 2000: 1,345,000 (Rank 38)

Density: 172.5 per sq. mi. (66.6 per km²)

Distribution: 89.0% urban, 11.0% rural

Population Under 5 Years Old: 7.8%

Population Under 18 Years Old: 25.3%

Population Over 65 Years Old: 11.4%

Median Age: 32.6

Number of Households: 356,000

Average Persons Per Household: 3.01

Average Persons Per Family: 3.48

Female Heads of Households: 3.38%

Population That Is Married: 18.99%

Birth Rate: 18.5 per 1,000 population

Death Rate: 6.1 per 1,000 population

Births to Teen Mothers: 10.5%

Marriage Rate: 16.1 per 1,000 population

Divorce Rate: 4.6 per 1,000 population

Violent Crime Rate: 242 per 100,000 pop.

Population on Social Security: 13.3%

Percent Voting for President: 41.9%

Hawaii's Famous Citizens

Bingham, Hiram (1789–1869). Missionary. Helped translate the Hawaiian language into writing, devising a 12 letter alphabet.

Bishop, Bernice (1831–1884). Last direct descendant of King Kamehameha I.

Damien, Father (1840–1889). Priest. Improved conditions at the leper colony on Molokai Island before himself succumbing to the disease.

Dole, James (1877–1958). Founded the Hawaiian pineapple industry and established the Hawaiian Pineapple Co. (now Dole) in 1901.

Fong, Hiram (b. 1907). First U.S. senator of Asian ancestry. Served from 1959 to 1977.

Inouye, Daniel K. (b. 1924). U.S. senator since 1962. Served on committees investigating the Watergate and Iran-contra scandals.

Kahanamoku, Duke (1890–1968). Won the 100 meter freestyle in the 1912 and 1920 Olympics. Sheriff of Honolulu from 1932 to 1961.

Midler, Bette (b. 1945). Singer-actress. Nominated for an Academy Award for her role in the film The Rose.

Distribution of Income

The per capita income for the state of Hawaii (current dollars) was $21,218 in 1992. This is a 96.9 percent increase from $10,774 in 1980. Income is greatest on the islands of Oahu, Molokai, Lanai, and Maui. Much of this income is derived from the tourist trade, which brings millions of dollars to the local economy. Most banking, communications, and other business takes place in the capital of Honolulu.

Per Capita Income (000s) (Current Dollars)

	$13.0 to 15.9
	$16.0 to 21.9

Population Profile

Rank. Hawaii ranks 40th among U.S. states in terms of population with 1,172,000 citizens.

Minority Population. The state's minority population is 72.1 percent. The state's male to female ratio for 1990 was 103.59 males for every 100 females. It was above the national average of 95.22 males for every 100 females.

Growth. Growing much faster than the projected national average, the state's population is expected to reach 1.5 million by the year 2010 (see graph above).

Older Citizens. The state's population older than 65 was 125,005 in 1990. It grew 64.16% from 76,150 in 1980.

Younger Citizens. The number of children (under 18 years of age) was 280 thousand in 1990. This represents 25.3 percent of the state's population. The state's school aged population was 174 thousand in 1990. It is expected to increase to 192 thousand by the year 2000. This represents a 10.34% change.

Urban/Rural. 89% of the population of the state live in urban areas while 11% live in rural areas.

Largest Cities. Hawaii has four cities with a population greater than 35,000. The populations of the state's largest centers are (starting from the most populous) Honolulu (365,272), Hilo (37,808), Kailua (36,818), Kaneohe (35,448), Waipahu (31,435), Pearl City (30,993), Waimalu (29,967), Mililani Town (29,359), Schofield Barracks (19,597), Wahiawa (17,386), Kahului (16,889), Ewa Beach (14,315), Halawa (13,408), Waipio (11,812), Kaneohe Station (11,662), Kihei (11,107), and Wailuku (10,668).

Government

Capital: Honolulu (established 1959).

Statehood: Became 50th state on Aug 21, 1959.

Number of Counties: 5.

Supreme Court Justices: 5, 10-year term.

State Senators: 25, 4-year term.

State Legislators: 51, 2-year term.

United States Senators: 2.

United States Representatives: 2.

Electoral Votes: 4.

State Constitution: Adopted 1950.

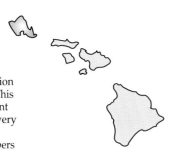

Native American

The Native American population in Hawaii was 5,099 in 1990. This was an increase of 79.99 percent from 2,833 in 1980. There are very few Native Americans in the Hawaiian Islands. Their numbers have, however, been rising steadily since the 1980s. About one-fifth of the Native American population lives in and around the city of Honolulu.

Presence of
Native Americans

☐ Minor

Nationalities

African	422
American	7,572
Arab	880
Austrian	1,115
Czech	1,396
Dutch	5,106
English	44,581
Finnish	942
German	74,978
Greek	1,195
Hungarian	1,548
Irish	36,802
Italian	15,045
Norwegian	5,634
Polish	7,269
Portuguese	39,748
Russian	3,482
Scottish	8,540
Slovak	1,302
Swedish	6,589
Welsh	2,129
West Indian	1,012

African American

The African American population in Hawaii was 27,195 in 1990. This was an increase of 53.76 percent from 17,687 in 1980. The largest concentration of African Americans can be found on the island of Oahu in the city of Honolulu. Large numbers can also be found in and around Pearl Harbor.

Percent of
County Population

☐ 0.00 to 1.99%
☐ 2.00 to 4.99%

Statewide Ethnic Composition

Most of the population of Hawaii, 61 percent, are Asian American. Many are native Hawaiians, but there is also a large number of Chinese, Japanese, Filipinos, and Koreans living on the many islands that make up the Hawaiian chain. Only one-third of the population of Hawaii is white, of which the largest nationality is the Germans.

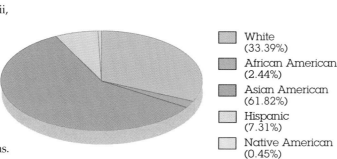

☐ White (33.39%)
☐ African American (2.44%)
☐ Asian American (61.82%)
☐ Hispanic (7.31%)
☐ Native American (0.45%)

Hispanic[††]

The Hispanic population in Hawaii was 81,390 in 1990. This is an increase of 14.21 percent from 71,263 persons in 1980. The highest concentration of Hispanics can be found on the island of Kauai. Other large groups are located in the city of Honolulu as well as in Pearl Harbor.

[††]A person of Mexican, Puerto Rican, Cuban, or other Spanish culture or origin regardless of race.

Percent of
County Population

☐ 3.00 to 9.99%
☐ 10.00 to 24.99%

Education Facts

Total Students 1990: 169,493

Number of School Districts: 1

Expenditure Per Capita on Education 1990: $710

Expenditure Per Capita K–12 1990: $639

Expenditure Per Pupil 1990: $5,008

Total School Enrollment 1990–1991: 171,056

Rank of Expenditures Per Student: 23d in the U.S.

African American Enrollment: 2.6%

Hispanic Enrollment: 2.3%

Asian/Pacific Islander Enrollment: 71.7%

Native American Enrollment: 0.3%

Mean SAT Score 1991 Verbal: 405

Mean SAT Score 1991 Math: 478

Average Teacher's Salary 1992: $34,500

Rank Teacher's Salary: 16th in U.S.

High School Graduates 1990: 10,000

Total Number of Public Schools: 234

Number of Teachers 1990: 8,956

Student/Teacher Ratio: 19.1

Staff Employed in Public Schools: 14,034

Pupil/Staff Ratio: 12.1

Staff/Teacher Ratio: 1.6

Education

Attainment: 82 percent of population 25 years or older were high school graduates in 1989, earning Hawaii a ranking of 11th in the United States; 24 percent of the state's population had completed college; Institutions of Higher Education: The largest universities and colleges in the state include the University of Hawaii, Honolulu (founded 1907), also supports two other four-year campuses. Expenditures per Student: Expenditure increased 77% between 1985 and 1990. Projected High School Graduations: 1998 (12,156), 2004 (12,508); Total Revenues for Education from Federal Sources: $82 million; Total Revenues for Education from State Sources: $540 million; Total Revenues for Education from Local Sources: $538,000; Average Annual Salaries for Public School Principals: N/A; Largest School Districts in State: Hawaii Department of Education Honolulu 169,507 students, 9th in the United States.

Asian American

The Asian American population in Hawaii was 685,238 in 1990. This is an increase of 23.28 percent from 555,845 persons in 1980. Asian Americans by far make up the largest minority group in Hawaii. They can be found in large numbers everywhere. Hawaii is a main stop-off point to and from the far eastern nations. Many Asian groups such as Chinese, Koreans, Filipinos, and Japanese can be found in Hawaii's cities.

Percent of
County Population

☐ 50.0 to 59.9%
☐ 60.0 to 91.9%

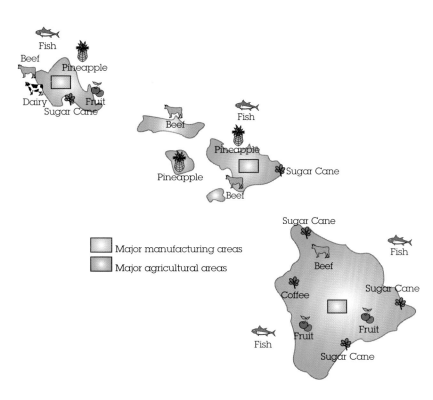

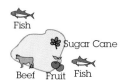

Major manufacturing areas

Major agricultural areas

Transportation

Transportation can be difficult for an island state like Hawaii. Hawaii has to depend on air and sea transportation to move people and goods. Such transportation is expensive, as many Hawaiian islands are quite far apart. Hawaii's major ports include Honolulu on Oahu, Hilo on Hawaii (the island), Kahului on Maui, and Port Allen on the island of Kauai. Hawaii also has several airports located throughout the islands. The busiest airport in Hawaii, however, is Honolulu International Airport.

Hawaii's main islands have a combined total of about 4,000 miles of paved roads and highways, many running along the coast. Rail transportation is almost nonexistent in Hawaii; however, the state does have a few miles of operating railroad track.

Energy and Transportation Facts

Energy. Yearly Consumption: 272 tril. BTUs (residential, 8.5%; commercial, 10.3%; industrial, 24.6%; transportation, 56.3%); Annual Energy Expenditures Per Capita: $1,793; Nuclear Power Plants Located in State: 0; Source of Energy Consumed: Petroleum— 98.2%; Natural Gas— 1.1%; Coal— 0.4%; Hydroelectric Power—0.4%; Nuclear Power—0.0%.

Transportation. Highway Miles: 4,106 (interstates, 44; urban, 1,799; rural, 2,307); Average Yearly Auto Insurance: $974 (1st); Auto Fatalities Rank: 37th; Registered Motor Vehicles: 774,094; Workers in Carpools: 33.9%; Workers Using Public Trans: 7.4%.

Agriculture

Hawaii has 1.7 million farm acres. During the last 40 years, Hawaii's farms have grown larger in size. In 1969, 4,000 farms were found in the state. Today, there are 4,400.

Agriculture adds less than $500 million to the state's gross product annually. The principal commodities in order of marketing receipts are sugar cane, pineapples, greenhouse, and nuts.

Hawaii's leading crop is sugar cane, which produces about 40 percent of the state's farm income. Most of this production is found on the islands of Hawaii and Maui. Pineapples, the next most important crop, are responsible for 21 percent of the farm income. Flowers for leis are grown for export. Other important crops include macadamia nuts, avocados, guavas, papayas, and bananas.

Employment

Employment. Hawaii employed 558,000 people in 1993. Most work in social and personal services (163,600 persons or 29.3% of the workforce). Manufacturing accounts for 3.4% or 19,100 workers. Wholesale and retail trade account for 23.8% or 132,700 workers. Government employs 111,600 workers (20.0%). Construction employs 32,300 workers (8.3%). Transportation and utilities account for 7.4% or 41,100 persons. Agriculture employs 17,300 workers or 3.1%. Finance, real estate, and insurance account for 7.0% or 39,000 workers. Mining employs no people in Hawaii.

Unemployment. Unemployment has decreased to 4.2% in 1993 from a rate of 5.6% in 1985. Today's figure is lower than the national average of 6.8% as shown below.

Housing

Owner Occupied Units: 389,810; Average Age of Units: 25 years; Average Value of Housing Units: $245,300; Renter Occupied Units: 162,820; Median Monthly Rent: $650; Housing Starts: 6,700; Existing Home Sales: 12,500.

Economic Facts

Gross State Product: $26,000,000,000

Income Per Capita: $21,218

Disposable Personal Income: $17,972

Median Household Income: $38,829

Average Annual Pay, 1988: $24,104

Principal Industries: printing, food products, tourism, petroleum products, shipbuilding, stone and clay and glass products

Major Crops: pineapples, sugar cane, flowers, dairy, coffee, papayas, bananas, avocados, taro, sorghum, macadamia nuts, potatoes

Fish: Yellow Fin, Skipjack, Tuna, Scad, Marlin

Livestock: cattle, hogs, broiler chickens

Non-Fuel Minerals: Titanium Oxide, Volcanic Rock, Limestone, Stone, Cement, Sand, Gravel

Organic Fuel Minerals: N/A

Civilian Labor Force: 561,000 (Women: 265,000)

Total Employed: 546,000 (Women: 258,000)

Median Value of Housing: $245,300

Median Contract Rent: $650 per month

Economic Sectors

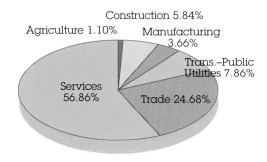

Construction 5.84%
Agriculture 1.10%
Manufacturing 3.66%
Trans.–Public Utilities 7.86%
Services 56.86%
Trade 24.68%

Manufacturing

Manufacturing industries contribute only 5 percent to the Hawaii gross state product. However, it is still an important part of the economy, contributing almost a quarter of a billion dollars a year. In addition, approximately 5 percent of Hawaiiís employees work in manufacturing jobs. Food processing is the stateís largest manufacturing activity. Canned pineapple and refined sugar production dominate the food processing industry, but factories produce dairy products, soft drinks, and bread as well.

Most of Hawaiiís manufacturing enterprises are based in the greater Honolulu vicinity. Besides food processing, the state produces apparel, chemicals, concrete, and stone and glasswares.

Unemployment Rate

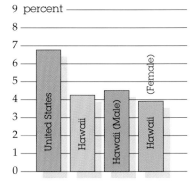

percent

IDAHO
The State of Idaho

Official State Seal

The Great Seal of Idaho was adopted in 1891 based on an 1866 design. The motto *"Esto Perpetua"* (It Is Forever) is printed on a ribbon above an elk's head. The women represents Justice, Liberty, and women's suffrage. The shield stands for agriculture and forestry. A miner stands on the right side of the seal. Two cornucopias and a sheaf of wheat line the bottom.

Legal Holidays

January: New Year's Day—1st, Martin Luther King, Jr., Day—3rd Monday; February: Presidents' Day—3rd Monday; May: Memorial Day—4th Monday; June: Pioneer Day—15th; July: Admission Day—3rd; Independence Day—4th; September: Labor Day—1st Monday; October: Columbus Day—2nd Monday; November: Veterans' Day—11th; Thanksgiving—4th Thursday; December: Christmas—25th.

Official State Flag

This flag of Idaho was adopted in 1907, but was illegal because it was only supposed to have a blue field with "The State of Idaho" written on it. The official who was in charge of the flag added the state seal. This flag was popular and widely used. In 1927 the law was adjusted to accommodate the look of the flag.

Festivals and Events

February: Simplot Games, Pocatello; Winter Carnival, McCall; June: Boise River Festival, Boise; National Old-Time Fiddlers' Contest, Weiser; July: First Security Games of Idaho, Pocatello; August: Art on the Green, Coeur d'Alene; September: Wagon Days, Ketchum.

Idaho Compared to States in Its Region.

Resident Pop. in Metro Areas: 7th; Pop. Percent Increase: 2d; Pop. Over 65: 3d; Infant Mortality: 3d; School Enroll. Increase: 7th; High School Grad. and Up: 5th; Violent Crime: 6th; Hazardous Waste Sites: 5th; Unemployment: 5th; Median Household Income: 6th; Persons Below Poverty: 4th; Energy Costs Per Person: 5th.

Mountain Region

	Population	Capital
Montana	839,000	Helena
Wyoming	470,000	Cheyenne
Idaho	1,099,000	Boise
Nevada	1,389,000	Carson City
Utah	1,860,000	Salt Lake City
Colorado	3,566,000	Denver
Arizona	3,936,000	Phoenix
New Mexico	1,616,000	Santa Fe

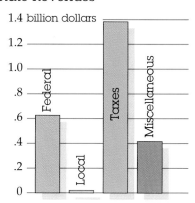

Idaho's Finances

Households: 361,000; Income Per Capita Current Dollars: $16,067; Change Per Capita Income 1980 to 1992: 90.5% (36th in U.S.); State Expenditures: $2,316,000,000; State Revenues: $2,447,000,000; Personal Income Tax: 2 to 8.2%; Federal Income Taxes Paid Per Capita: $1,321; Sales Tax: 5% (prescription drugs exempt).

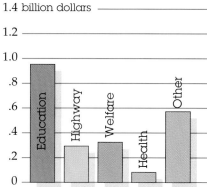

Location, Size, and Boundaries

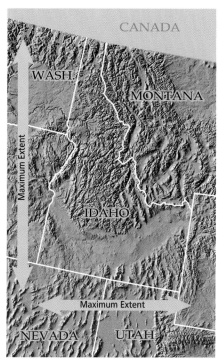

Location. Idaho is located in the northwestern United States in what is known as the Mountain region. It is bounded on four sides by land. The geographic center of Idaho is lat. 44° 15.4' N; long. 114° 57.4' W.

Size. Idaho is the 13th largest state in terms of size. Its area is 83,557 sq. mi. (216,412 km2). Inland water covers 880 sq. mi. (2,279 km2).

Boundaries. Canada, 45 mi. (72 km); Montana, 738 mi. (1,188 km); Wyoming, 170 mi. (274 km); Utah, 153 mi. (246 km); Nevada, 152 mi. (245 km); Oregon 319 mi. (513 km); Washington, 210 mi. (338 km).

Geographic Extent. The north/south extent of Idaho is 479 mi. (771 km). The state extends 305 mi. (491 km) to the east/west.

Facts about Idaho. Origin of Name: Name selected for a portion of the Colorado Territory; Nickname: The Gem State; Motto: "Let it be perpetua" (*Esto Perpetua*); Abbreviations: Ida. (traditional), ID (postal); State Bird: Mountain bluebird; State Tree: Western white pine; State Flower: syringa; State Song: "Here We Have Idaho," words by McKinley Helm and Albert J. Tompkins and music by Sallie Hume-Douglas.

Idaho Compared to Other States. Resident Pop. in Metro Areas: 48th; Pop. Percent Increase: 3d; Pop. Over 65: 34th; Infant Mortality: 29th; School Enroll. Increase: 48th; High School Grad. and Up: 16th; Violent Crime: 40th; Hazardous Waste Sites: 38th; Unemployment: 31st; Median Household Income: 38th; Persons Below Poverty: 17th; Energy Costs Per Person: 35th.

Sources of Information. Tourism, Economy & History: Idaho Department of Commerce, 700 West State Street, Boise, ID 83720. Government: Idaho Legislative, Statehouse, Boise, ID 83720.

Idaho

Legend

⭐ State capitol
⊙ Cities over 35,000 population
○ Other significant cities
● County Seats

🟦 Major cultural attractions
🟦 State Parks
🆆 Welcome Centers
⚲ Major colleges and universities

Scale

0   25   50   75 mi.

25   0   25   50   75   100 km

🟦 Albeni Falls Dam and Reservoir. Camping and water sports. (C-1)

🟦 American Falls Reservoir. Water sports. (P-9)

🟦 Balanced Rock. 40 foot (12 meters) mushroom-shaped rock. (P-5)

🟦 Boise National Forest. Features ghost towns, abandoned mines; winter and water sports. (L-2)

🟦 Caribou National Forest. Mountain ranges, scenic valleys; ghost towns as well as camping. (P-10)

🟦 Challis National Forest. Site of Borah Peak, 12,662 ft (3,859 m), the highest point in the state. (L-5)

🟦 Clearwater National Forest. White pines, streams, and rivers. (F-3)

🟦 Coeur d'Alene. Blue lake with forest and hanging moss. Home of a large population of osprey. (D-1)

🟦 Craters of the Moon National Monument. 83 square miles (215 square kilometers) of craters resembling surface of moon. (N-8)

🟦 Fort Hall. Early pioneer trading settlement dating from 1834. Site of Fort Hall Indian Reservation. (O-10)

🟦 Hells Canyon National Recreation Area. Deepest gorge in North America, 7,900 ft (2,400 m). (I-2)

🟦 Hells Canyon Wilderness Area. Site of the Seven Devils Mountains and many river rapids. (I-2)

🟦 Lake Pend Oreille. The largest lake in state, 180 square miles (470 square kilometers), has water sports and picnic facilities. (C-2)

🟦 Montpelier. An old phosphate mining town and site of part of the old Oregon Trail. (Q-12)

🟦 Old Mission at Cataldo State Park. An Indian mission founded in 1853 by Jesuits. (E-2)

🟦 Priest Lake State Park. Scenic area with camping facilities. (B-1)

🟦 Sawtooth National Forest. Scenic area with alpine mountain lakes and trails. (M-5)

🟦 Sawtooth National Recreation Area. Site of Castle Peak (11,830 ft, 3,610 m) in the White Cloud Mountains. (M-5)

🟦 Sawtooth Wilderness Area. Wilderness area with over 200 lakes and 300 miles (500 kilometers) of scenic trails. (M-5)

🟦 Shoshone Falls. Falls with a 212-foot (65-meter) drop. (P-6)

🟦 Shoshone Ice Cave. Site of a cave 30 feet (9 meters) wide by 40 feet (12 meters) high. (O-6)

🟦 Sun Valley. World-famous resort. Site of many ice skating expositions. (N-6)

🟦 Yellowstone National Park. The oldest and largest national park in the nation with geysers, falls, and hot springs. (K-11)

Major Cities

Boise City	N-2
Caldwell	N-1
Coeur d'Alene	D-1
Idaho Falls	N-10
Lewiston	G-1
Moscow	F-1
Nampa	N-1
Pocatello	P-10
Rexburg	M-11
Twin Falls	P-6

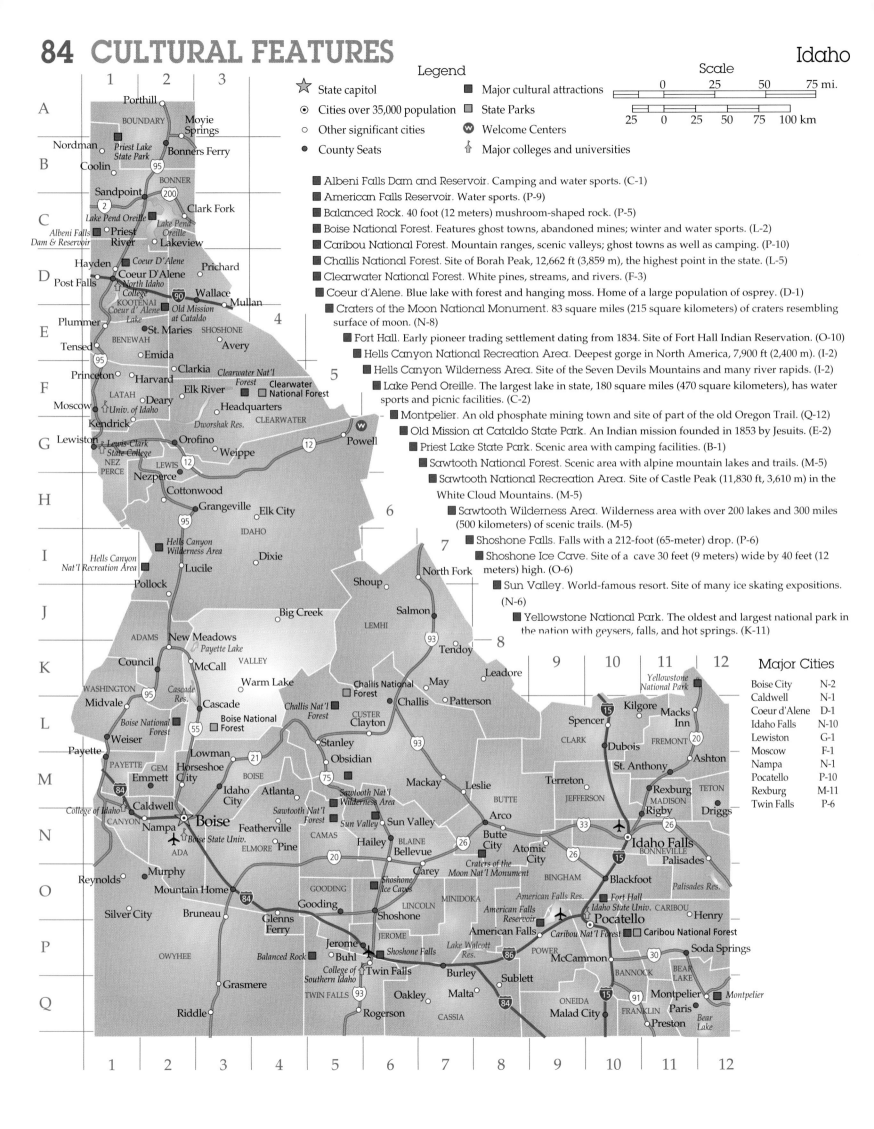

Idaho

Weather Facts

Record High Temperature: 118° F (48° C) on July 27, 1930, at Orofino; Record Low Temperature: -60° F (-51° C) on January 17, 1939, at Island Park; Average January Temperature: 23° F (-5° C); Average July Temperature: 67° F (19° C); Average Yearly Precipitation: 20 in. (51 cm).

Environmental Facts

Air Pollution Rank: 39th; Water Pollution Rank: 36th; Total Yearly Industrial Pollution: 8,244,017 lbs.; Industrial Pollution Rank: 40th; Hazardous Waste Sites: 9; Hazardous Sites Rank: 37th; Landfill Capacity: overextended; Fresh Water Supply: large surplus; Daily Residential Water Consumption: 233 gals. per capita; Endangered Species: Aquatic Species (4)—limpet, Banbury Springs; Birds (3)—crane, whooping; Mammals (3)—bear, grizzly; Other Species (5)—snail, bliss rapids; Plants (2)—four-o'clock, Macfarlane's.

Environmental Quality

Idaho residents generate 750,000 tons of solid waste each year, or approximately 1,500 pounds per capita. Landfill capacity in Idaho will be exhausted in more than 12 years. The state has nine hazardous waste sites. Annual greenhouse gas emissions in Idaho total 17.1 million tons, or 17.0 tons per capita. Industrial sources in Idaho release approximately 8.6 thousand tons of toxins, 106.4 thousand tons of acid precipitation-producing substances, and 1.3 million tons of smog-producing substances into the atmosphere each year.

The state has 86,900 acres within the National Park System; the largest area within the state is Craters of the Moon National Monument. State parks cover just over 43,600 acres, attracting 2.5 million visitors per year.

Idaho spends about 4.2 percent of its budget, or approximately $61 per capita, on environmental and natural resources. Idaho representatives in the U.S. House voted in favor of national environmental legislation 13 percent of the time, while U.S. senators did so 17 percent of the time.

Average Monthly Weather

Boise	Jan	Feb	Mar	Apr	May	Jun	Jul	Aug	Sep	Oct	Nov	Dec	Yearly
Maximum Temperature °F	37.1	44.3	51.8	60.8	70.8	79.8	90.6	87.3	77.6	64.6	49.0	39.3	62.8
Minimum Temperature °F	22.6	27.9	30.9	36.4	44.0	51.8	58.5	56.7	48.7	39.1	30.5	24.6	39.3
Days of Precipitation	12.0	10.3	9.8	8.1	7.8	6.1	2.4	2.6	3.8	6.0	10.2	11.3	90.3

Flora and Fauna

Approximately 40 percent of the state of Idaho is covered by forests. Coniferous (cone-bearing) softwood trees such as the Douglas fir, western larch, and Engelmann spruce inhabit the majority of Idaho's forested areas. Hardwood trees found in Idaho include the quaking aspen and cottonwood. Shrubs, including ocean spray, snowberry, and elderberry, grow in Idaho's mountains and valleys. In addition, the state has several kinds of meadow wildflowers, including buttercup, fireweed, and larkspur.

Wilderness preservation efforts help protect Idaho's wildlife population. Many different species of animals live in Idaho. Several land mammals inhabit both the state's mountains and its rangelands, including moose, elk, mountain goat, cougar, and pronghorn antelope. Bears, including grizzlies, inhabit more remote places in the state. Smaller mammals live throughout Idaho as well, including beavers, muskrats, and raccoons. Idaho's game birds, such as the introduced chukar partridge, primarily nest near rangelands and farms. The Salmon River takes its name from the many salmon that use the river for breeding. In other Idaho rivers, lakes, and streams, one can find steelhead, Kamloops trout, and other salmonids.

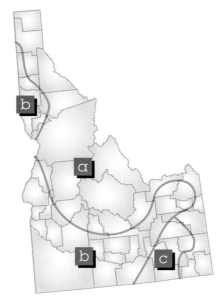

Physical Regions: (a) Rocky Mountains; (b) Columbia Plateau; (c) Basin and Range Region.

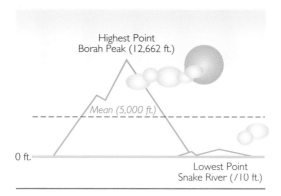

Highest Point
Borah Peak (12,662 ft.)

Mean (5,000 ft.)

0 ft.

Lowest Point
Snake River (710 ft.)

Land Use

Cropland: 33.3%; Pasture: 6.9%; Rangeland: 33.6%; Forest: 20.7%; Urban: 2.4%; Other: 3.1%.

For more information about Idaho's environment, contact the Division of Environment, Department of Health and Welfare, State House, Boise, ID 83720.

Topography

Most of Idaho is covered by mountains. The Rocky Mountain physical region extends over much of northern, eastern, and central Idaho. This area is characterized by rugged mountain ranges interrupted by deep river valleys. Some of the important ranges in this region include the Bitterroot on the border with Montana; the Beaverhead and Lost River mountains and the Lemhi Range in eastern Idaho; and the Clearwater and Salmon River mountains in the central part of the state. The highest point in the state occurs in the Lost River Range; Borah Peak rises to 12,662 ft. (3,859 m) above sea level. The soil is typically cool and moist, colored gray/brown, with low-density amorphous content.

The southern part of the state is dominated by the Snake River Plains in the Columbia Plateau physical region, a semicircular area that sweeps around the mountains to the north. This is a mainly dry area with some farming. Further north along the western border is a plateau area of fertile soils that is well suited to agriculture. The soil is warm and dry with a black, high-organic content surface. South of the Snake River Plains is the Basin and Range physical region. It is a mountainous area running around Idaho's southern fringe. The most prominent mountains are the Wasatch Range in the southeast and the Owyhee Mountains in the southwest. The soil is similar to that described above.

Climate

Although Idaho shares the same latitude as some Great Plains states, it has a milder climate. The winds from the Pacific Ocean bring warm, moist air to Idaho. Mountains help protect the state from harsh weather. Northern Idaho has the state's warmest weather. Average January and July temperatures in Lewiston register 30 degrees F and 75 degrees F. In the capital of Boise, January and July temperatures average 27 degrees F and 75 degrees F.

Idaho's annual average precipitation measures 19 inches, with most of it falling in the winter. The state's desert areas receive only an average of 6 inches of precipitation a year. However, the mountains receive close to 100 inches of annual precipitation. About 60 inches of snow falls in Idaho each year.

Idaho's mountain regions have high summer temperature ranges. Some days have almost a 40-degree F variation between high and low temperature.

Hydrology

The most important river in Idaho is the Snake, one of the longest in the nation at about 1,020 miles (1,642 km). It enters the state from Wyoming and winds its way west through southern Idaho. It then flows north to form part of Idaho's western border with Oregon and Washington, before flowing westward into Washington. The largest tributary of the Snake River is the Salmon, which runs through the central part of the state. Other important rivers include the Payette, the Clearwater, the Boise, and the Selway.

There are several large lakes in Idaho. The largest is Pend Oreille in the north at about 165 sq. miles (427 km). Other sizable lakes in the north include Priest Lake, Coeur d'Alene (a popular resort), and Dworshak Reservoir. Large, mainly man-made lakes are also found in the southern portion of the state, including American Falls Reservoir on the Snake River, and Cascade Reservoir on the Payette.

Idaho's History

Idaho's First People

Idaho was first occupied by humans more than fourteen thousand years ago. These early inhabitants probably subsisted on hunting large game animals, though little is really known about them.

By the time the first whites arrived in Idaho there were six Indian tribes scattered throughout the area. In the south were the Northern Shoshone and the Northern Paiute. The Kutenai, Coeur d'Alene, Pend d'Oreille (or Kalispel), and Nez Perce inhabited the northern part of the state. The large rivers in the region provided these tribes with salmon, which was their food staple, and other fish. They supplemented the food obtained fishing by hunting game and gathering wild roots.

American Exploration

The first known whites to enter the territory that is now Idaho were the individuals in the Lewis and Clark expedition, a U.S.-sponsored trip organized to find a land or water route to the Pacific and gather information on the Indians in the country. This foray into Idaho in 1805 was aided by the Nez Perce Indians, who supplied the expedition with food and canoes and guided them to the Pacific. In 1809, he first trading post was established by the North West Company, and the following year the Missouri Fur Company followed suit. These establishments were set up to capitalize on the beaver furs that attracted white trappers to the area. Soon afterward missionaries started arriving. In 1836, Henry Spalding founded a mission at Lapwai among the Nez Perce.

By 1860, significant numbers of white settlers drawn by mining and the migration of Mormons from Utah had made conflict with the natives of the region inevitable. Treaties establishing reservations for the various tribes were implemented in 1855, but within a few years an increased white presence led to further restrictions on the land set aside for Indians. Some wars between the Indians and

the settlers resulted (most notably the Nez Perce War) which were not resolved until 1878, with a much-reduced land area designated for reservations.

In 1860, gold was discovered at Pierce. This caused a rush of people into the area hoping to make themselves rich through mining. At the time, Idaho was part of the large Washington Territory. By 1862, most of the residents of the Washington Territory were living in Idaho. In 1863, President Lincoln approved an act of Congress and Idaho was made a territory on to itself. This new territory included the future states of Wyoming and Montana. Soon the gold ran low and miners left the area. Shortly after this departure, in the 1880s, lead-silver was discovered in the areas around Hailey and Coeur d'Alene. This caused another rush which solidified the mining industry, and planted the seeds for statehood.

Statehood

The Hudson's Bay Company had control of the area including Idaho in 1840. Six years later, the United States gained control of the Pacific Northwest, including all of Idaho, in a treaty with Great Britain. In 1848, this area officially became the Oregon Territory. Over the next several decades, North Idaho attempted to form a territory with Washington, and Congress approved such a move in 1886, but it was overturned by President Grover Cleveland. Finally in 1890, Idaho was admitted to the Union as the forty-third state. Although Republicans had control of the state government at the time of statehood, this was to be short-lived. A few years later Democrats, with the support of populists, took charge.

About this time there was much labor unrest at the silver mines around the state. In 1892, martial law was declared in northern Idaho mining towns and federal troops were called in to attempt to restore order. Seven years later martial law was once again declared and federal troops once more used to suppress

striking miners. In 1907, legendary labor leader "Big Bill" Haywood was acquitted on charges of assassinating former governor Frank Steunenberg in a case that was related to this violent period of mine labor strife.

Industrialization

Fur trapping is what initially lured whites to the Idaho area in the first decades of the nineteenth century. However, around mid-century the discovery of gold provoked a stampede of settlers, who had previously just passed through along the Oregon Trail en route to the Pacific. In 1880, silver was discovered and a few years later lead-silver at Coeur d'Alene, which would become the leading lead-silver producer in the United States.

After the turn of the century the timber industry was a strong force in the state's economy, as was agriculture. However, agriculture prices dropped in the 1920s, and with the Depression of the 1930s Idaho was in a severe economic slump.

Since World War II, lumber, potatoes, and mining have been the chief industries in the state, supplemented by high-tech firms relocating from California in recent years.

The Mormons

Although the major center of the Mormon religion (or Church of Jesus Christ of Latter-Day Saints) is in Utah, a significant migration of Mormons into Idaho in 1860 has left the state with the second-highest concentration of this sect of any state in the nation (about 29 percent). Founded by Joseph Smith in the 1830s and based on the Book of Mormon and the Bible, the Mormon religion emphasizes revelation, the interconnectedness of temporal and spiritual life, and the importance of spreading the Word. The Mormons' belief in polygamy (the taking of more than one wife) prevented both Utah and Idaho from being admitted to the Union until they renounced polygamy as an act of faith.

Important Events

1805 The Lewis and Clark expedition crosses through Idaho, the first white contact with the state.

1809 North West Company establishes first trading post in Idaho.

1836 First mission established by Henry Spalding.

1842 Oregon Trail is opened.

1855 Treaties creating reservations are established with Nez Perce and other Indian tribes.

1860 Mormons migrate from Utah and establish first white settlement in Idaho at Franklin; gold is first

discovered.

1862 The first newspaper published in Idaho is *The Golden Age* out of Lewiston.

1863 Idaho Territory is created.

1864 Boise becomes the capital of Idaho.

1878 Culmination of Indian wars in Idaho; violent battles with the Nez Perce.

1880 Silver is discovered near Hailey.

1890 Idaho is admitted to the Union as the forty-third state.

1892 Martial law is declared amid mining strikes in northern Idaho.

1899 Martial law again declared in response to mining labor unrest.

1906 Completion of sawmill at Potlatch launches Idaho's timber industry.

1907 "Big Bill" Haywood is acquitted on charges of assassinating former governor Frank Steunenberg.

1915 World's highest dam, Arrowrock, is completed on the Boise River.

1920s Agricultural prices drop setting the stage for a severe

economic slump.

1931 Idaho adopts a state income tax.

1942 Almost ten thousand Japanese-Americans are interned at Hunt.

1959 Completion of Brownlee Dam leaves Idaho with over two million irrigated acres of farmland.

1965 Idaho adopts a state sales tax of 3 percent.

1975 Completion of a waterway linking Lewiston to the Pacific Ocean.

1990 Idaho passes strict anti-abortion bill.

Population Density

Population density for the state of Idaho was 12.2 persons per square mile in 1990 (4.7 per km²). Average U.S. density was 70.3 persons per square mile in 1990 (27.3 per km²). Habitation is most dense around the urban area of Boise. Other dense areas are found in and around Idaho Falls and in the northern counties of the state. Overall, Idaho is a very sparsely populated state.

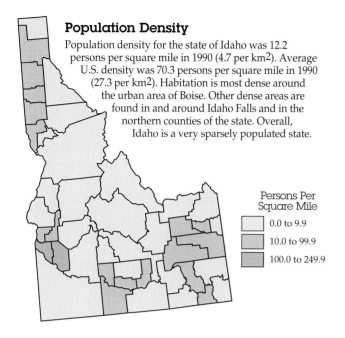

Persons Per Square Mile

- 0.0 to 9.9
- 10.0 to 99.9
- 100.0 to 249.9

Population Projections

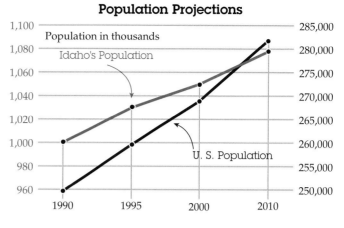

Population in thousands
Idaho's Population
U. S. Population

Population Change

Year	Population
1950	589,000
1960	671,000
1970	718,000
1980	943,935
1990	1,006,749
2000	1,047,000
2010	1,079,000

Period	Change
1950–1970	21.9%
1970–1980	31.5%
1980–1990	6.7%
1990–2000	4.0%

Population Change

The 1990 population figure for the state of Idaho was 1,006,749. This is a 6.65 percent increase from 943,935 in 1980. The next decade will show growth with a population of 1.05 million or a 4.0 percent increase. The area of fastest growth is the county of Blaine located in the center of the state. Other high-change areas include the northern counties and counties located north of Blaine County in the center of the state.

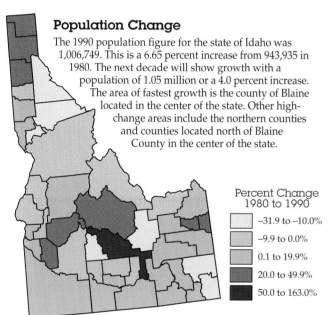

Percent Change 1980 to 1990

- −31.9 to −10.0%
- −9.9 to 0.0%
- 0.1 to 19.9%
- 20.0 to 49.9%
- 50.0 to 163.0%

Population Facts

State Population, 1993: 1,099,000

Rank: 42

Population 2000: 1,047,000 (Rank 43)

Density: 12.2 per sq. mi. (4.7 per km²)

Distribution: 57.4% urban, 42.6% rural

Population Under 5 Years Old: 7.8%

Population Under 18 Years Old: 30.4%

Population Over 65 Years Old: 11.9%

Median Age: 31.5

Number of Households: 361,000

Average Persons Per Household: 2.73

Average Persons Per Family: 3.23

Female Heads of Households: 2.87%

Population That Is Married: 22.27%

Birth Rate: 16.3 per 1,000 population

Death Rate: 7.4 per 1,000 population

Births to Teen Mothers: 12.3%

Marriage Rate: 14.6 per 1,000 population

Divorce Rate: 6.5 per 1,000 population

Violent Crime Rate: 290 per 100,000 pop.

Population on Social Security: 15.5%

Percent Voting for President: 65.2%

Idaho's Famous Citizens

Borah, William E. (1865–1949). Republican U.S. senator from 1907 to 1940. Noted for his influence in foreign policy.

Borglum, Gutzon (1867–1941). Sculptor. Began work in 1927 on the massive presidential stone portraits on Mt. Rushmore.

Boyington, Gregory (Pappy) (1912–1988). Started the *Black Sheep Squadron* of military pilots in World War II.

Brink, Carol Ryrie (1895–1981). Wrote several children's books, including *Anything Can Happen on the River*.

Fisher, Vardis (1895–1968). Writer. Won the Harper Prize for *Children of God*, a historical novel about the Mormons.

Killebrew, Harmon (b. 1936). Hall of Fame baseball player. Led the AL in home runs six times with the Minnesota Twins.

Rainwater, James (1917–1986). Physicist. Won the Nobel Prize for his work on the structure and behavior of the atomic nucleus.

Turner, Lana (1920–1995). Hollywood glamour girl. Starred in such films as *Ziegfeld Girl* and *The Postman Always Rings Twice*.

Wilson, Lawrence (b. 1938). Pro Football Hall of Famer. Defensive back (1960–1972).

Distribution of Income

The per capita income for the state of Idaho (current dollars) was $16,067 in 1992. This is a 90.5 percent increase from $8,433 in 1980. Income is greatest in the county of Clark, which is located in the northeastern part of the state. Other areas include Ada (location of Boise), Blaine, Camas, Power, and Lewis counties. Low-income counties include Franklin and Madison counties.

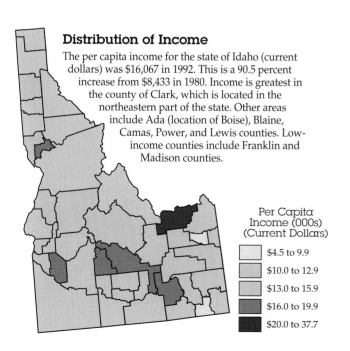

Per Capita Income (000s) (Current Dollars)

- $4.5 to 9.9
- $10.0 to 12.9
- $13.0 to 15.9
- $16.0 to 19.9
- $20.0 to 37.7

Population Profile

Rank. Idaho ranks 42d among U.S. states in terms of population with 1,099,000 citizens.

Minority Population. The state's minority population is 7.9 percent. The state's male to female ratio for 1990 was 99.04 males for every 100 females. It was above the national average of 95.22 males for every 100 females.

Growth. Growing more slowly than the projected national average, the state's population

Government

Capital: Boise (established 1865).

Statehood: Became 43d state on Jul. 3, 1890.

Number of Counties: 44.

Supreme Court Justices: 5, 6-year term.

State Senators: 42, 2-year term.

State Legislators: 84, 2-year term.

United States Senators: 2.

United States Representatives: 2.

Electoral Votes: 4.

State Constitution: Adopted 1889.

is expected to reach 1.07 million by the year 2010 *(see graph above)*.

Older Citizens. The state's population older than 65 was 121,265 in 1990. It grew 29.45% from 93,680 in 1980.

Younger Citizens. The number of children (under 18 years of age) was 308 thousand in 1990. This represents 30.6 percent of the state's population. The state's school aged population was 214 thousand in 1990. It is expected to decrease to 208 thousand by the year 2000. This represents a −2.80% change.

Urban/Rural. 57.4% of the population of the state lives in urban areas while 42.6% live in rural areas.

Largest Cities. Idaho has three cities with a population greater than 35,000. The populations of the state's largest centers are (starting from the most populous) Boise (125,738), Pocatello (46,080), Idaho Falls (43,929), Nampa (28,365), Lewiston (28,082), Twin Falls (27,591), Coeur d'Alene (24,563), Moscow (18,519), Caldwell (18,400), and Rexburg (14,302).

Native American

The Native American population in Idaho was 13,780 in 1990. This was an increase of 32.44 percent from 10,405 in 1980. A large number of these Native Americans can be found on Indian reservations. The largest in the state include Fort Hall Indian Reservation in the southeast and the Western Shoshone Indian Reservation, which shares borders with Nevada in the southwestern portion of the state.

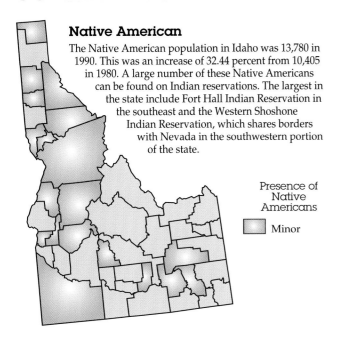

Presence of Native Americans

▢ Minor

Nationalities

African	213
American	43,268
Arab	550
Austrian	1,686
Czech	4,283
Dutch	19,893
English	208,625
Finnish	2,876
German	214,544
Greek	2,053
Hungarian	1,613
Irish	77,852
Italian	16,547
Norwegian	21,843
Polish	7,352
Portuguese	2,005
Russian	2,157
Scottish	24,547
Slovak	1,575
Swedish	34,012
Welsh	10,782
West Indian	303

African American

The African American population in Idaho was 3,370 in 1990. This was an increase of 24.31 percent from 2,711 in 1980. The highest concentrations can be found in Elmore County as well as in Boise and Idaho Falls. Boise has the largest African American community in the state with 730. The next largest concentrations are Pocatello with 395, and Idaho Falls with 256 African American residents.

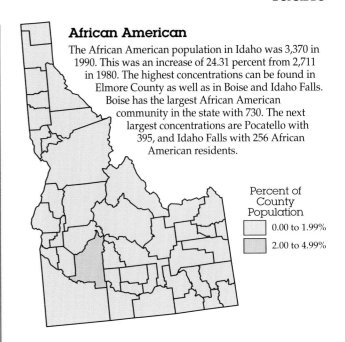

Percent of County Population

▢ 0.00 to 1.99%
▢ 2.00 to 4.99%

Statewide Ethnic Composition

Over 94 percent of the population of the state is white. The largest nationalities are the Germans and the English. The next largest group is the Hispanics, who make up only slightly more than 5 percent of the population. Native Americans are the next largest group, followed by Asian Americans and African Americans.

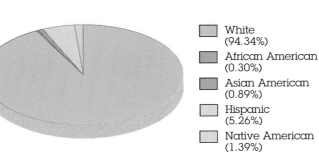

▢ White (94.34%)
▢ African American (0.30%)
▢ Asian American (0.89%)
▢ Hispanic (5.26%)
▢ Native American (1.39%)

Education Facts

Total Students 1990: 214,932

Number of School Districts: 115

Expenditure Per Capita on Education 1990: $668

Expenditure Per Capita K–12 1990: $607

Expenditure Per Pupil 1990: $3,211

Total School Enrollment 1990–1991: 220,840

Rank of Expenditures Per Student: 49th in the U.S.

African American Enrollment: 0.3%

Hispanic Enrollment: 4.9%

Asian/Pacific Islander Enrollment: 0.8%

Native American Enrollment: 1.3%

Mean SAT Score 1991 Verbal: 463

Mean SAT Score 1991 Math: 505

Average Teacher's Salary 1992: $26,300

Rank Teacher's Salary: 46th in U.S.

High School Graduates 1990: 14,000

Total Number of Public Schools: 574

Number of Teachers 1990: 10,987

Student/Teacher Ratio: 20.1

Staff Employed in Public Schools: 17,160

Pupil/Staff Ratio: 12.5

Staff/Teacher Ratio: 1.6

Hispanic[††]

The Hispanic population in Idaho was 52,927 in 1990. This is an increase of 44.55 percent from 36,615 persons in 1980. The Hispanic population is more numerous than the African American population with much higher concentrations in the southern region of the state. Some of the counties with the most dense Hispanic populations are Owyhee, Clark, Canyon, Cassia, Minidoka, Power, and Washington.

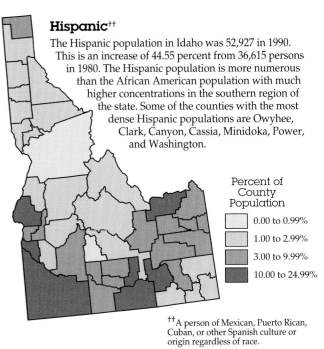

Percent of County Population

▢ 0.00 to 0.99%
▢ 1.00 to 2.99%
▢ 3.00 to 9.99%
▢ 10.00 to 24.99%

[††]A person of Mexican, Puerto Rican, Cuban, or other Spanish culture or origin regardless of race.

Education

Attainment: 77 percent of population 25 years or older were high school graduates in 1989, earning Idaho a ranking of 29th in the United States; 17.1 percent of the state's population had completed college. Institutions of Higher Education: The largest universities and colleges in the state include the University of Idaho, Moscow; Idaho State University, Pocatello; Lewis and Clark State College, Lewiston; Boise State University, Boise. Expenditures per Student: Expenditure increased 78% between 1985 and 1990. Projected High School Graduations: 1998 (11,984), 2004 (9,526); Total Revenues for Education from Federal Sources: $49 million; Total Revenues for Education from State Sources: $370 million; Total Revenues for Education from Local Sources: $161 million; Average Annual Salaries for Public School Principals: N/A.

Asian American

The Asian American population in Idaho was 9,365 in 1990. This is an increase of 46.26 percent from 6,403 persons in 1980. Large concentrations can be found in Elmore County in the central part of the state and in Latah County in the northwestern part of the state. Almost one-third of the Asian American population can be found in the city of Boise.

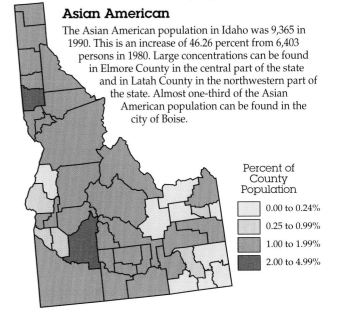

Percent of County Population

▢ 0.00 to 0.24%
▢ 0.25 to 0.99%
▢ 1.00 to 1.99%
▢ 2.00 to 4.99%

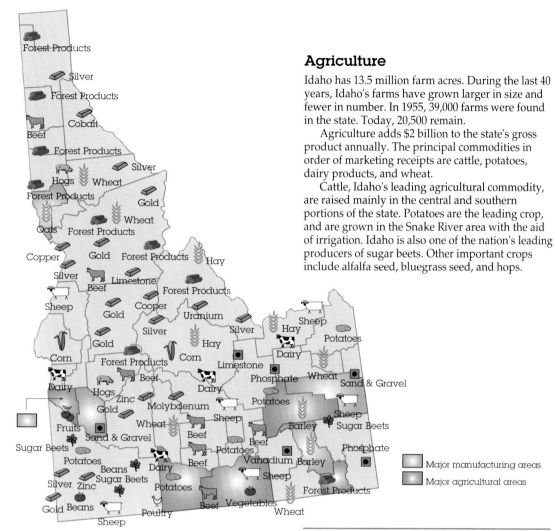

Forest Products
Silver
Forest Products
Cobalt
Beef
Forest Products
Silver
Hogs Wheat
Forest Products
Gold
Wheat
Oats Forest Products
Copper Gold Forest Products Hay
Silver
Beef Limestone
Sheep Copper Uranium
Gold
Silver Silver Hay
Gold Hay
Corn Forest Products Corn Limestone
Dairy
Hogs Zinc
Gold Molybdenum
Fruits Wheat Sheep
Sand & Gravel Beef
Sugar Beets
Potatoes Beef Potatoes
Beans Dairy Beef
Silver Zinc Sugar Beets
Gold Beans Potatoes
Sheep Poultry
Sheep
Hay Potatoes
Dairy
Phosphate Wheat Sand & Gravel
Potatoes
Sheep
Barley Sugar Beets
Beef
Phosphate
Vanadium Barley
Sheep
Beef Vegetables
Forest Products
Wheat

□ Major manufacturing areas
□ Major agricultural areas

Agriculture

Idaho has 13.5 million farm acres. During the last 40 years, Idaho's farms have grown larger in size and fewer in number. In 1955, 39,000 farms were found in the state. Today, 20,500 remain.

Agriculture adds $2 billion to the state's gross product annually. The principal commodities in order of marketing receipts are cattle, potatoes, dairy products, and wheat.

Cattle, Idaho's leading agricultural commodity, are raised mainly in the central and southern portions of the state. Potatoes are the leading crop, and are grown in the Snake River area with the aid of irrigation. Idaho is also one of the nation's leading producers of sugar beets. Other important crops include alfalfa seed, bluegrass seed, and hops.

Transportation

Idaho relies heavily on its roads and highways to transport goods as well as people. The state has approximately 63,000 miles of highways and roads; however, only about half of these are surfaced. Idaho's interstates provide a vital link between the northern and southern parts of the state, for railroad construction has been rendered hopeless due to the mountains in central Idaho.

Idaho does have limited railroad service. Two freight lines carry cargo, while passenger trains reach five Idaho cities. Boise has the state's major airport. The Columbia and Snake rivers, as a result of being dammed, allow barges to travel to the Pacific. Lewiston, on the Idaho-Washington border, is sometimes called the "seaport of Idaho."

Transportation and Energy Facts

Energy. Yearly Consumption: 388 tril. BTUs (residential, 20.9%; commercial, 18.3%; industrial, 37.6%; transportation, 23.2%); Annual Energy Expenditures Per Capita: $1,837; Nuclear Power Plants Located in State: 0; Source of Energy Consumed: Petroleum— 45.5%; Natural Gas— 19.0%; Coal— 4.3%; Hydroelectric Power—31.2%; Nuclear Power—0.0%.

Transportation. Highway Miles: 58,588 (interstates, 612; urban, 3,314; rural, 55,274); Average Yearly Auto Insurance: $402 (44th); Auto Fatalities Rank: 9th; Registered Motor Vehicles: 1,034,290; Workers in Carpools: 16.1%; Workers Using Public Trans: 1.9%.

Housing

Owner Occupied Units: 413,327; Average Age of Units: 25 years; Average Value of Housing Units: $58,200; Renter Occupied Units: 102,432; Median Monthly Rent: $330; Housing Starts: 10,900; Existing Home Sales: 23,400.

Economic Facts

Gross State Product: $16,000,000,000

Income Per Capita: $16,067

Disposable Personal Income: $14,572

Median Household Income: $25,257

Average Annual Pay, 1988: $19,688

Principal Industries: wood products, food products, electrical equipment, chemicals, printing, agribusiness, mobile homes

Major Crops: potatoes, wheat, barley, hay, milk, sugar beets, lumber

Fish: Salmon, Steelhead Trout, Kamloops Trout

Livestock: cattle

Non-Fuel Minerals: Silver, Phosphate, Copper, Lead, Zinc, Cobalt, Garnet, Gold

Civilian Labor Force: 504,000 (Women: 218,000)

Total Employed: 473,000 (Women: 205,000)

Median Value of Housing: $58,200

Median Contract Rent: $330 per month

Economic Sectors

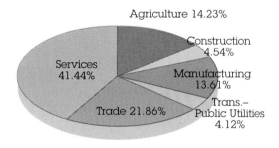

Agriculture 14.23%
Construction 4.54%
Services 41.44%
Manufacturing 13.61%
Trans.– Public Utilities 4.12%
Trade 21.86%

Manufacturing

Idaho's manufacturing sector is relatively new; most industry started up right before World War II. Today, approximately 16 percent of Idaho residents are employed in the manufacturing sector. Over the years, Idaho's manufactured goods have risen in value to almost the same level as its agricultural goods. The state's top three industries are food processing, lumber products, and machinery.

Most of Idaho's factories are located in the south. About 20 different potato processing plants exist. Other food processing establishments process wheat, meat, and beet-sugar. Many lumber companies, including Boise-Cascade, have their headquarters in Boise. Other factories, producing computers, farm equipment, and paper, are also located in the Boise vicinity.

Employment

Employment. Idaho employed 512,000 people in 1993. Most work in wholesale and retail trade (109,500 persons or 21.4% of the workforce). Manufacturing accounts for 13.5% or 69,300 workers. Social and personal services account for 19.0% or 97,500 workers. Government employs 90,400 workers (17.7%). Construction employs 24,600 workers (4.8%). Transportation and utilities account for 4.1% or 20,900 persons. Agriculture employs 46,100 workers or 9.0%. Finance, real estate, and insurance account for 4.4% or 22,700 workers. Mining employs 2,200 people and accounts for only 0.4% of the workforce.

Unemployment. Unemployment has decreased to 6.1% in 1993 from a rate of 7.9% in 1985. Today's figure is lower than the national average of 6.8% as shown below.

Unemployment Rate

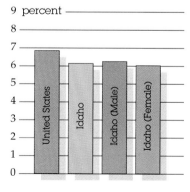

9 percent
8
7
6
5
4
3
2
1
0

United States | Idaho | Idaho (Male) | Idaho (Female)

ILLINOIS
The State of Illinois

Official State Seal

The Great Seal of Illinois is one of three that were used in the state at different times. The most recent was adopted in 1867. Written on a ribbon in the eagle's beak are the phrases "State Sovereignty" and "National Union." During the Civil War the words were reversed so that "National Union" came first. In a semicircle at the bottom is printed the date of Illinois's entrance into the Union.

Legal Holidays

January: New Year's Day—1st, Martin Luther King, Jr., Day—3rd Monday; February: Abraham Lincoln's Birthday—12th; Presidents' Day—3rd Monday; May: Memorial Day—4th Monday; July: Independence Day—4th; September: Labor Day—1st Monday; October: Columbus Day—2nd Monday; November: Veterans' Day—11th; Thanksgiving—4th Thursday; December: Admission Day—3rd; Christmas—25th.

ILLINOIS

Official State Flag

The state flag of Illinois was adopted in 1915. It was the prize winner at a competition organized by the Daughters of the American Revolution. It shows the state seal on a field of white. In 1969 the state name was added to the bottom.

Festivals and Events

January: Clock Tower Jazz Fest, Rockford; February: Galesburg Chocolate Fest, Galesburg; March: Wyatt Earp Birthday Celebration, Monmouth; May: Civil War Days, Mahomet; Dogwood Festival, Quincy; Ducks & Daffodils, Rockford; June: Chicago Peace & Music Festival, Chicago; Dixon Petunia Fest, Dixon; Harvard Milk Day Festival, Harvard; July: Bon Odori Festival, Chicago; Bagelfest, Mattoon; August: Decatur Celebration, Decatur; September: Hog Capital of the World Festival, Kewanee; Marigold Festival, Pekin; Morton Pumpkin Fest, Morton; October: Chocolate Harvest, Mattoon; St. Charles Scarecrow Fest, St. Charles; November: Polish-American Christmas Gala, Chicago; Way of Lights, Belleville; December: Wyatt Earp Christmas Walk, Monmouth.

Illinois Compared to States in Its Region.

Resident Pop. in Metro Areas: 1st; Pop. Percent Increase: 3d; Pop. Over 65: 4th; Infant Mortality: 1st; School Enroll. Increase: 3d; High School Grad. and Up: 3d; Violent Crime: 1st; Hazardous Waste Sites: 3d; Unemployment: 2d; Median Household Income: 1st; Persons Below Poverty: 3d; Energy Costs Per Person: 2d.

East North Central Region

	Population	Capital
Wisconsin	5,038,000	Madison
Michigan	9,478,000	Lansing
Illinois	11,697,000	Springfield
Indiana	5,713,000	Indianapolis
Ohio	11,091,000	Columbus

Illinois's Finances

Households: 4,202,000; Income Per Capita Current Dollars: $21,608; Change Per Capita Income 1980 to 1992: 98.7% (26th in U.S.); State Expenditures: $23,639,000,000; State Revenues: $23,103,000,000; Personal Income Tax: 3%; Federal Income Taxes Paid Per Capita: $2,186; Sales Tax: 6.25%.

State Expenditures

14.0 billion dollars

Education, Highway, Welfare, Health, Other

State Revenues

14.0 billion dollars

Federal, Local, Taxes, Miscellaneous

Location, Size, and Boundaries

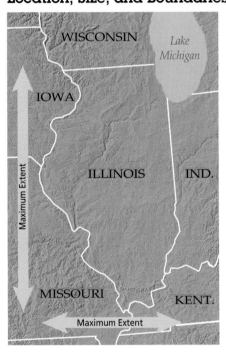

Location. Illinois is located in the East North Central region of the United States. It is bounded on four sides by land and one side by water. The geographic center of Illinois is lat. 40° 0.8' N; long. 89° 18.4' W.

Size. Illinois is the 24th largest state in terms of size. Its area is 56,400 sq. mi. (146,076 km2). Inland water covers 652 sq. mi. (1,689 km2).

Boundaries. Wisconsin, 185 mi. (298 km); Indiana, 397 mi. (639 km); Kentucky, 134 mi. (216 km); Missouri, 367 mi. (591 km); Iowa, 214 mi. (344 km).

Geographic Extent. The north/south extent of Illinois is 381 mi. (613 km). The state extends 211 mi. (340 km) to the east/west.

Facts about Illinois. Origin of Name: From the French spelling and pronunciation of the *Illini* Indian word *Iliniwek* meaning *superior men*; Nickname: The Land of Lincoln; Motto: "State sovereignty, national union"; Abbreviations: Ill. (traditional), IL (postal); State Bird: cardinal; State Tree: white oak; State Flower: native violet; State Song: "Illinois," words by Charles H. Chamberlin and music by Archibald Johnston.

Illinois Compared to Other States. Resident Pop. in Metro Areas: 12th; Pop. Percent Increase: 32d; Pop. Over 65: 27th; Infant Mortality: 6th; School Enroll. Increase: 34th; High School Grad. and Up: 28th; Violent Crime: 4th; Hazardous Waste Sites: 10th; Unemployment: 12th; Median Household Income: 12th; Persons Below Poverty: 26th; Energy Costs Per Person: 24th.

Sources of Information. Tourism/Economy: Illinois Dept. of Commerce and Community Affairs, Illinois Bureau of Tourism, 620 East Adams, Springfield, IL 62701. (Economy: Attn.: Research Office.) Government: Office of the Secretary of State, Communications Dept., Room 474, Centennial Building, Springfield, IL 62756. History: Illinois Historic Preservation Agency, Old State Capitol, Springfield, IL 62701.

Illinois

■ **Cahokia Court House State Memorial.** Historical building, possibly the oldest in Midwest (1737). (M-7)

■ **Chicago Historical Society.** Reference library and museum; includes the Lincoln collection. (C-13)

■ **Chicago Portage National Historic Site.** Part of the famous portage discovered by Marquette and Jolliet and used by American and French pioneers. (C-13)

■ **Early American Museum and Botanical Garden.** Pioneer-era collections and scenic gardens including a waterfall. (H-11)

■ **Elijah Lovejoy Monument.** Pays tribute to the Abolitionist editor. (C-7)

■ **Galena.** Home of Ulysses S. Grant; noted local architecture, includes Old Market House State Memorial. (B-7)

■ **Illinois State Museum.** Natural and social science exhibits. (I-8)

■ **Lincoln Home National Historic Site.** Abraham Lincoln's residence from 1844 to 1861. (I-8)

■ **Lincoln Trail State Memorial.** Figure of Lincoln stands on the site near Lawrenceville where he and family entered state in 1830. (M-13)

■ **Metamora Court House Memorial.** Place where Lincoln practiced law. (F-9)

■ **Oak Park.** Birthplace of author Ernest Hemingway; works of architect Frank Lloyd Wright. (C-13)

■ **Pierre Menard Home State Memorial.** Home of first lieutenant governor. (O-8)

■ **Pullman.** Famous railroad car company built by George M. Pullman in 1890s. (C-13)

■ **Shawneetown State Memorial.** Early gateway to Illinois. (P-12)

■ **Vandalia State House State Memorial.** Capitol building built in 1836. (L-10)

■ **Woodstock.** Old McHenry County Courthouse; Opera House; and the Spring House, built over a mineral spring in 1873. (B-11)

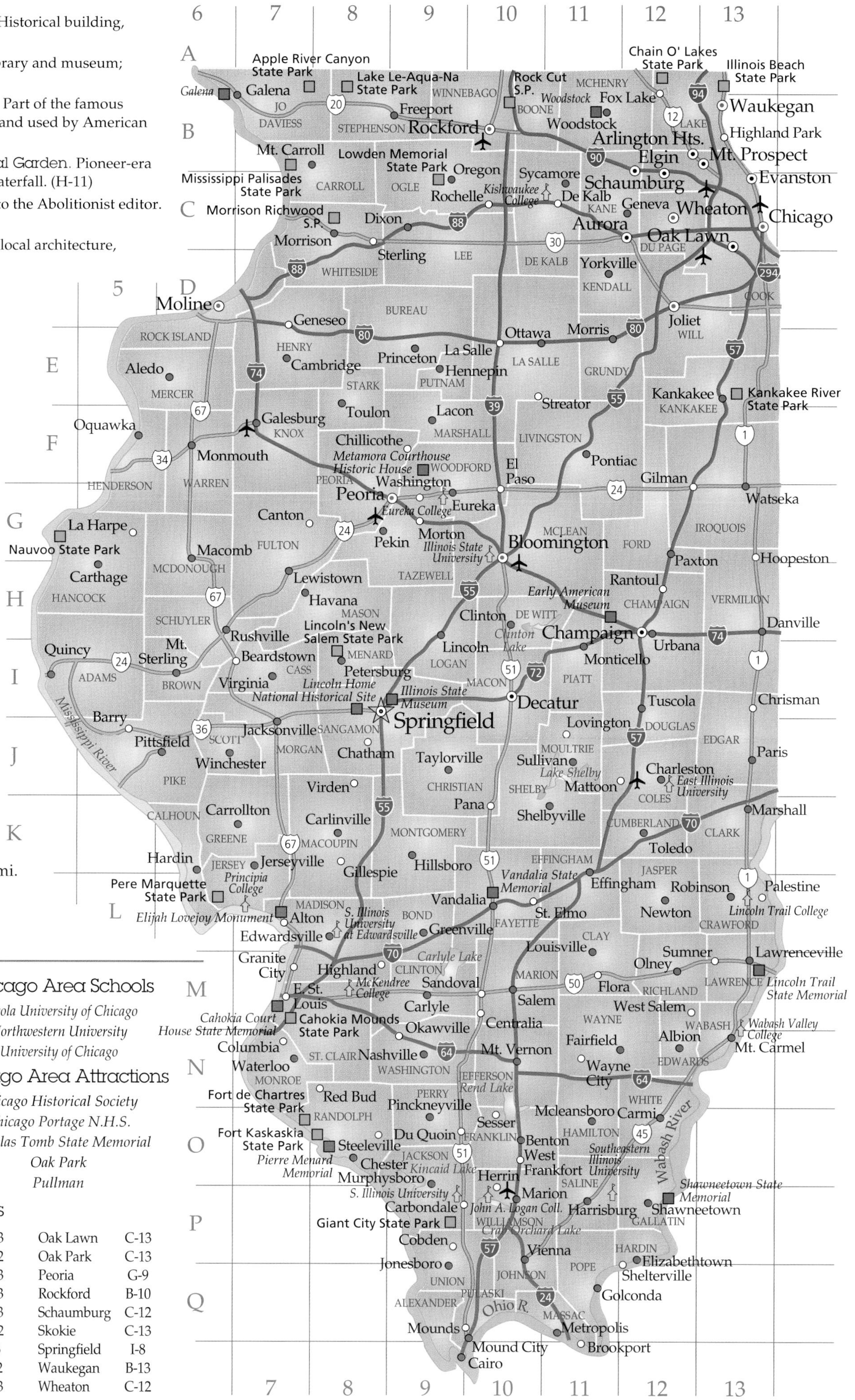

Scale

0   20   40   60 mi.

20 0 20 40 60 80 km

Legend

☆ State capitol

⊙ Cities over 35,000 population

○ Other significant cities

● County Seats

■ Major cultural attractions

□ State Parks

Ⓦ Welcome Centers

⚲ Major colleges and universities

Chicago Area Schools

Loyola University of Chicago
Northwestern University
University of Chicago

Chicago Area Attractions

Chicago Historical Society
Chicago Portage N.H.S.
Douglas Tomb State Memorial
Oak Park
Pullman

Major Cities

Arlington Hts.	B-12	Downers Gr.	C-13	Oak Lawn	C-13
Aurora	C-12	Elgin	C-12	Oak Park	C-13
Berwyn	C-13	Elmhurst	C-13	Peoria	G-9
Bloomington	G-10	Evanston	C-13	Rockford	B-10
Champaign	H-12	Hoffman Est.	C-13	Schaumburg	C-12
Chicago	C-13	Joliet	D-12	Skokie	C-13
Cicero	C-13	Moline	D-6	Springfield	I-8
Decatur	I-10	Mt. Prospect	B-12	Waukegan	B-13
Des Plaines	C-13	Naperville	C-13	Wheaton	C-12

Weather Facts

Record High Temperature: 117° F (47° C) on July 13, 1950, at East St. Louis; Record Low Temperature: -35° F (-37° C) on January 21, 1926, at Mt. Carroll; Average January Temperature: 27° F (-3° C); Average July Temperature: 76° F (24° C); Average Yearly Precipitation: 38 in. (97 cm).

Environmental Facts

Air Pollution Rank: 8th; Water Pollution Rank: 4th; Total Yearly Industrial Pollution: 97,235,574 lbs.; Industrial Pollution Rank: 8th; Hazardous Waste Sites: 37; Hazardous Sites Rank: 10th; Landfill Capacity: adequate; Fresh Water Supply: large surplus; Daily Residential Water Consumption: 170 gals. per capita; Endangered Species: Aquatic Species (7)—fanshell; Birds (4)—eagle, bald; Mammals (2)—bat, gray; Other Species (4)—snail, Iowa pleistocene; Plants (8)—aster, decurrent false.

Environmental Quality

Illinois residents generate 15.0 million tons of solid waste each year, or approximately 2,300 pounds per capita. Landfill capacity in Illinois will be exhausted in 5 to 10 years. The state has 38 hazardous waste sites. Annual greenhouse gas emissions in Illinois total 298.9 million tons, or 25.7 tons per capita. Industrial sources in Illinois release approximately 133.2 thousand tons of toxins, 1.9 million tons of acid precipitation-producing substances, and 4.3 million tons of smog-producing substances into the atmosphere each year.

The state has less than 500 acres within the National Park System. Lincoln Home is a National Historic Site. State parks cover just over 382,200 acres, attracting 34.6 million visitors per year.

Illinois spends approximately 2.3 percent of its budget, or about $34 per capita, on environmental and natural resources. Illinois representatives in the U.S. House voted in favor of national environmental legislation 70 percent of the time, while U.S. senators did so 63 percent of the time.

Average Monthly Weather

Chicago	Jan	Feb	Mar	Apr	May	Jun	Jul	Aug	Sep	Oct	Nov	Dec	Yearly
Maximum Temperature °F	29.2	33.9	44.3	58.8	70.0	79.4	83.3	82.1	75.5	64.1	48.2	35.0	58.7
Minimum Temperature °F	13.6	18.1	27.6	38.8	48.1	57.7	62.7	61.7	53.9	42.9	31.4	20.3	39.7
Days of Precipitation	11.1	9.6	12.4	12.4	11.0	9.9	9.7	9.4	9.5	9.3	10.6	11.5	126.4
Springfield													
Maximum Temperature °F	29.7	35.2	46.5	61.9	72.5	82.1	85.5	83.4	76.7	64.8	48.5	35.4	60.2
Minimum Temperature °F	13.3	18.4	28.1	40.6	50.6	60.2	64.6	62.7	54.5	42.9	30.9	20.2	40.6
Days of Precipitation	9.3	8.3	10.8	11.7	11.3	9.6	8.6	8.2	8.6	7.7	9.1	9.8	113.1

Flora and Fauna

Illinois has considerably less forested land than many other states; forests cover only slightly more than 10 percent of the state's area. The bulk of the trees are located in southern Illinois, and along rivers and streams. Deciduous trees such as hickory, ash, sweet gum, and maple dominate the state's forests. Like other states, Illinois has a wide assortment of wildflowers, including bloodroot, toothwort, and dogtooth violet.

Illinois is a haven for birds of all kinds. Each year, as many as two million wild ducks flock to Illinois to feed and rest along the Illinois River valley. Canadian geese often migrate to southern Illinois for the winter. The state also has its share of mammals, including deer, mink, fox, rabbit, and skunk. Illinois game birds include pheasants and quail, as well as ducks. Fishes of all kinds, such as sunfish, pike, and buffalofish, swim in Lake Michigan, which borders northern Illinois, as well as in the state's rivers, lakes, and streams.

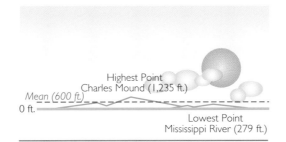

Physical Regions: (a) Central Plains; (b) Shawnee Hills; (c) Gulf Coastal Plain.

Highest Point
Charles Mound (1,235 ft.)
Mean (600 ft.)
0 ft.
Lowest Point
Mississippi River (279 ft.)

Land Use

Cropland: 72.2%; Pasture: 7.7%; Rangeland: 0%; Forest: 9.9%; Urban: 8.1%; Other: 2.1%.

For more information about Illinois's environment, contact the Department of Energy and Natural Resources, 325 W. Adams St., Room 300, Springfield, IL 62704-1892.

Topography

Illinois lies almost entirely within the Central Plains of the United States (the Till Plains physical region). This area is characterized by rolling hills and moist, organically rich, black soils, which makes it very suitable for agriculture. The northeastern corner of the state, around Chicago, is part of the Great Lakes Plains physical region, with elevations not much higher than sea level. Most of the soil is typed as warm and moist rich black clay. Much of the central region of the state is the heart of the Central Plain. It is here that most of the state's agriculture is located, part of the farm belt that stretches across the Midwest from Nebraska to Ohio.

The northwest corner of Illinois is known as the Driftless Area physical region. It is a region of hills and valleys that contains the highest elevation in the state. The peak of Charles Mound stands only 1,235 ft. (376 m) above sea level. Soil is predominantly warm and moist gray/brown clay.

The other part of Illinois that interrupts the flat Central Plains is the Shawnee Hills physical region, located in the southern part of the state. This hilly region supports many orchards. Soil is warm and wet, black, and high in organic content.

The extreme southern portion of the state is part of the coastal plain that extends northward from the Gulf of Mexico.

Climate

The state of Illinois is characterized by great fluctuations in weather, both seasonal and daily. Sometimes temperatures can drop by 20 degrees F in only one hour. Illinois's continental, inland location contributes to these significant climatic changes. Great temperature variation exists between northern and southern Illinois. Temperatures in Chicago average 25 degrees F and 75 degrees F for January and July. Average January and July temperatures in Cairo, on the southern Missouri border, read 38 degrees F and 82 degrees F.

Most of Illinois's precipitation is brought by winds from the Gulf of Mexico. Northern Illinois receives more average rainfall, 45 inches, than the south, which receives 34 inches. Illinois also receives snowfall, with most of it falling in the north.

The city of Chicago benefits from its location next to Lake Michigan. Winds from the lake cool summer heat and warm winter weather.

Hydrology

The longest river in the state is the Illinois, which flows about 282 miles (454 km) from Lake Michigan at Chicago to the Mississippi River just above St. Louis. The Mississippi forms Illinois's entire western boundary with Iowa and Missouri. The Wabash River creates Illinois's southeastern border with Indiana, and the Ohio River forms the southern border with Kentucky. Other important rivers include the Rock in the northwest, the Kaskaskia in the south, and the Sangamon in the central part of the state.

The northeastern border of Illinois is formed by Lake Michigan. Carlyle Reservoir, a man-made lake on the Kaskaskia River, is the largest lake in the state, covering 38 sq. miles (98 sq. km). Other sizable lakes include Shelbyville Reservoir, also on the Kaskaskia; Rend and Crab Orchard lakes in the south; and Fox and Grass lakes in the northeast.

Illinois's History

Illinois's First People

Almost eight thousand years ago, Paleo-Indians occupied Illinois. A few thousand years later, a hunting culture of archaic Indians left evidence of their presence. Woodland Indians appeared by about 1000 B.C. and were skilled potters. They were succeeded by the Middle Mississippi people, the Mound Builders who built earthen temples throughout the southeastern part of the state, including a major one at Cahokia on the Illinois River.

When white men arrived, there were several different tribes scattered about the state. The north was occupied by Kickapoo, Sauk, and Fox and the northeast by Potawatomi and Ottawa. The central part of the state was home to the Kaskaskia, Illinois, and Peoria tribes, while the Cahokia and Tamaroa were settled in the south.

European Exploration

In 1673, Louis Jolliet and Father Jacques Marquette traveled down the Mississippi River and, on their return trip, took the Illinois River to Lake Michigan, becoming the first Europeans to set foot in Illinois. Father Marquette founded a mission two years later near Starved Rock (present-day Ottawa). In 1680, René-Robert Cavelier, Sieur de La Salle, erected Fort Crevecoeur near present-day Peoria and two years later built Fort St. Louis at Starved Rock. However, the first permanent white settlement was constructed by French priests, the Holy Family Mission at Cahokia, near present-day St. Louis. More settlements followed at Kaskaskia and Fort de Chartres.

In 1717, the area became part of the French province of Louisiana and three years later was the seat of French power in the central part of the country. In 1765, as dictated by the Treaty of Paris, France ceded Illinois and surrounding territory to the British. Despite British control, most of the settlers in Illinois remained French. In 1778, during the Revolutionary War, George Rogers Clark captured Kaskaskia and Cahokia from the British and claimed Illinois for Virginia. Virginia ruled the state (minus the French settlers who had fled) until ceding control to the U.S. government in 1784.

Statehood

Three years after the United States took control of Illinois, the state became a part of the newly created Northwest Territory. Next it became a part of the Indiana Territory, created in 1801. In 1809, the Illinois Territory, including Wisconsin, was established with Kaskaskia as the capital. Although the state's population was below the sixty thousand required for statehood, Illinois was accepted into the Union in 1818 as the twenty-first state. Two years later the capital was moved to Vandalia and, finally in 1837, to Springfield.

Like Indiana, Illinois embarked on a massive railroad- and canal-building endeavor that bankrupted the state in the 1830s. Also during this time, with a large influx of white settlers, friction developed with the Indian tribes in the state. The Black Hawk War of 1832 forced some of these tribes out of the state, and the remaining tribes were expelled the following year.

Although Illinois sided with the Union during the Civil War, the state was split and was not considered a haven for blacks on the Underground Railroad. After the war, however, it became the first state to ratify the Thirteenth Amendment abolishing slavery.

Industrialization

The first settlers in Illinois were primarily interested in agriculture, but with the construction of railroads and canals the state situated itself to become a hub of commercial activity in the Midwest. In the second half of the nineteenth century, and especially after the Great Fire of 1871 that leveled Chicago, Illinois' economy boomed. Fueled by steel mills, meat-packing plants, banking, and transportation, by 1890 Illinois had become the third-largest state in population, with Chicago as the country's second-biggest city.

The city of Chicago was founded outside the gates of Ft. Dearborn around 1803. After the construction of the Erie Canal in 1825, Chicago became an important stop in the movement west. The first railroad arrived in the 1850s, and with it came the development of lumbering and the meat-processing industry.

Chicago is a city where vast growth has taken place. The first steel-framework skyscraper was built in Chicago 1884. The Federal Reserve Bank was founded here in 1914. Chicago has the largest harbor in the Great Lakes and one of the nation's busiest airports (Chicago-O'Hare International).

Illinois continued to prosper into the twentieth century, although it was affected like most other states by the Great Depression. Spurred by defense contracts, the state's economy recovered after World War II, and it remains a leading industrial state in the nation.

Nineteenth-Century American Labor

With the large-scale industrialization (mass production of standardized products) of America in the second half of the nineteenth century, workers began to organize for better working conditions and pay, as well as to end some of the rampant abuses (such as child labor). Illinois became central in this struggle with the Haymarket Square Riot of 1886 and the Pullman Strike of 1894. Anarchists gathered in Haymarket Square in Chicago to agitate for an eight-hour workday, but as police were attempting to break up the rally, a bomb went off killing eleven people. Four of the leaders were hanged for inciting riot. In the Pullman Strike, workers were protesting a cut in wages by the Pullman Car Co. and halted rail traffic with their strike. The federal government was eventually called in to halt the strike, and the leaders were arrested.

Important Events

1673 Louis Jolliet and Jacques Marquette travel the Illinois River on their way back up the Mississippi River.

1699 Mission founded at Cahokia becomes first permanent white settlement.

1765 France cedes territory to Britain under Treaty of Paris.

1778 George Rogers Clark claims Illinois for Virginia after defeating British at Kaskaskia.

1784 Virginia cedes Illinois to the United States after the Revolutionary War.

1801 Indiana Territory including Illinois is created.

1809 Illinois Territory including Wisconsin is created.

1818 Illinois is admitted to the Union as the twenty-first state.

1820 Vandalia becomes the state capital.

1833 Last Indian tribes leave the state.

1837 Springfield becomes the state capital.

1860 Abraham Lincoln elected sixteenth President of the United States.

1871 Great Chicago Fire destroys the city, killing over three hundred people.

1894 Federal troops are called in to break up the Pullman Car Co. strike.

1920 Chicago "Black Sox" scandal unearthed, in which eight White Sox players are accused of throwing the 1919 World Series.

1929 St. Valentine's Day Massacre by Al Capone's gang of crosstown rivals leaves seven dead.

1955 Richard Daley elected mayor of Chicago for the first of five terms.

1970 New state constitution is ratified by Illinois voters.

1979 Jane Byrne becomes the first woman mayor of Chicago.

1983 Harold Washington becomes the first black mayor of Chicago.

1988 Chicago Cubs play first night game at Wrigley Field.

1993 Illinois Representative Dan Rostenkowski, chairman of the House Ways and Means Committee, is under threat of being prosecuted for embezzlement.

Population Density

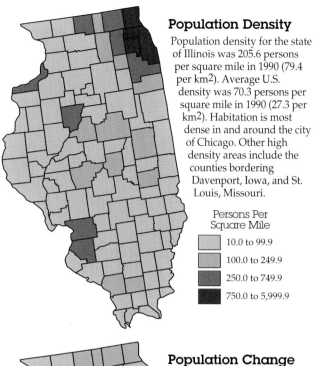

Population density for the state of Illinois was 205.6 persons per square mile in 1990 (79.4 per km2). Average U.S. density was 70.3 persons per square mile in 1990 (27.3 per km2). Habitation is most dense in and around the city of Chicago. Other high density areas include the counties bordering Davenport, Iowa, and St. Louis, Missouri.

Persons Per Square Mile
- 10.0 to 99.9
- 100.0 to 249.9
- 250.0 to 749.9
- 750.0 to 5,999.9

Population Projections

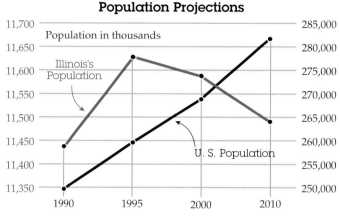

Population in thousands

Illinois's Population

U. S. Population

Population Change

Year	Population
1950	8,712,000
1960	10,086,000
1970	11,128,000
1980	11,427,518
1990	11,430,602
2000	11,580,000
2010	11,495,000

Period	Change
1950–1970	27.7%
1970–1980	2.7%
1980–1990	0.03%
1990–2000	1.3%

Population Change

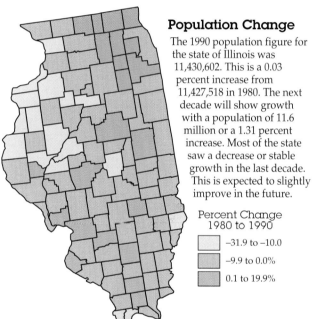

The 1990 population figure for the state of Illinois was 11,430,602. This is a 0.03 percent increase from 11,427,518 in 1980. The next decade will show growth with a population of 11.6 million or a 1.31 percent increase. Most of the state saw a decrease or stable growth in the last decade. This is expected to slightly improve in the future.

Percent Change 1980 to 1990
- –31.9 to –10.0
- –9.9 to 0.0%
- 0.1 to 19.9%

Population Facts

State Population, 1993: 11,697,000

Rank: 6

Population 2000: 11,580,000 (Rank 5)

Density: 205.6 per sq. mi. (79.4 per km²)

Distribution: 84.6% urban, 15.4% rural

Population Under 5 Years Old: 7.7%

Population Under 18 Years Old: 26.0%

Population Over 65 Years Old: 12.6%

Median Age: 32.8

Number of Households: 4,202,000

Average Persons Per Household: 2.65

Average Persons Per Family: 3.23

Female Heads of Households: 4.42%

Population That Is Married: 19.88%

Birth Rate: 17.1 per 1,000 population

Death Rate: 9.0 per 1,000 population

Births to Teen Mothers: 13.1%

Marriage Rate: 8.3 per 1,000 population

Divorce Rate: 3.8 per 1,000 population

Violent Crime Rate: 1,039 per 100,000 pop.

Population on Social Security: 15.4%

Percent Voting for President: 58.9%

Illinois's Famous Citizens

Blair, Bonnie (b. 1964). Speed skater. First American woman to win three gold medals at the Winter Olympics (1988 and 1992).

Goodman, Benny (1909–1986). Jazz clarinetist and orchestra leader. First white big band leader to use black musicians.

Harris, Patricia Roberts (1924–1985). First black woman to hold a cabinet position (secretary of HUD in 1977).

Heston, Charlton (b. 1924). Actor. Won an Academy Award for his role as the title character in *Ben-Hur* in 1959.

Mamet, David (b. 1947). Writes plays with an ear for street language, including *American Buffalo* and *Glengarry Glen Ross*.

Reagan, Ronald Wilson (b. 1911). Elected 40th president of the United States. At 69, he is the oldest person to be sworn into office as president.

Walgreen, Charles R. (1873–1939). Founded the drugstore chain named after him in 1909.

Washington, Harold (1922–1987). Became the first black mayor of Chicago in 1983, battling entrenched machine politicians.

Distribution of Income

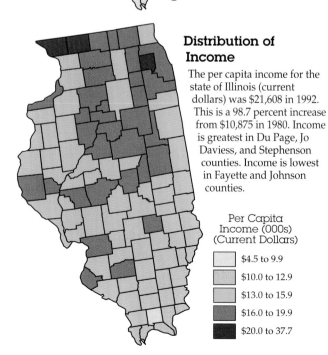

The per capita income for the state of Illinois (current dollars) was $21,608 in 1992. This is a 98.7 percent increase from $10,875 in 1980. Income is greatest in Du Page, Jo Daviess, and Stephenson counties. Income is lowest in Fayette and Johnson counties.

Per Capita Income (000s) (Current Dollars)
- $4.5 to 9.9
- $10.0 to 12.9
- $13.0 to 15.9
- $16.0 to 19.9
- $20.0 to 37.7

Population Profile

Rank. Illinois ranks 6th among U.S. states in terms of population with 11,697,000 citizens.

Minority Population. The state's minority population is 25.4 percent. The state's male to female ratio for 1990 was 94.45 males for every 100 females. It was below the national average of 95.22 males for every 100 females.

Growth. Growing much more slowly than the projected national average, the state's population

Government

Capital: Springfield (established 1839).

Statehood: Became 21st state on Dec. 3, 1818.

Number of Counties: 102.

Supreme Court Justices: 7, 10-year term.

State Senators: 59, 2 or 4-year term.

State Legislators: 118, 2-year term.

United States Senators: 2.

United States Representatives: 20.

Electoral Votes: 22.

State Constitution: Adopted 1970.

is expected to reach 11.49 million by the year 2010 *(see graph above)*.

Older Citizens. The state's population older than 65 was 1,436,545 in 1990. It grew 13.84% from 1,261,885 in 1980.

Younger Citizens. The number of children (under 18 years of age) was 2.9 million in 1990. This represents 25.8 percent of the state's population. The state's school aged population was 1.8 million in 1990. It is expected to increase to 1.86 million by the year 2000. This represents a 3.78% change.

Urban/Rural. 84.6% of the population of the state live in urban areas while 15.4% live in rural areas.

Largest Cities. Illinois has 42 cities with a population greater than 35,000. The populations of the state's largest centers are (starting from the most populous) Chicago (2,783,726), Rockford (139,426), Peoria (113,504), Springfield (105,227), Aurora (99,581), Naperville (85,351), Decatur (83,885), Elgin (77,010), Joliet (76,836), Arlington Heights (75,460), Evanston (73,233), Waukegan (69,392), Schaumburg (68,586), Cicero (67,436), Champaign (63,502), Skokie (59,432), Oak Lawn (56,182), and Oak Park (53,648).

Native American

The Native American population in Illinois was 21,836 in 1990. This was an increase of 14.22 percent from 19,118 in 1980. One-third of the Native American population can be found in the city of Chicago, which has 7,064 Native American residents. The next largest community is Rockford, with only 356 residents of Native American origins.

Presence of Native Americans

- Minor
- Moderate
- Significant

Nationalities

African	17,578
American	319,070
Arab	30,645
Austrian	30,561
Czech	96,400
Dutch	146,599
English	688,434
Finnish	12,865
German	2,613,753
Greek	79,601
Hungarian	40,232
Irish	1,059,510
Italian	543,498
Norwegian	98,256
Polish	717,860
Portuguese	4,310
Russian	104,394
Scottish	101,781
Slovak	73,284
Swedish	233,903
Welsh	29,758
West Indian	16,150

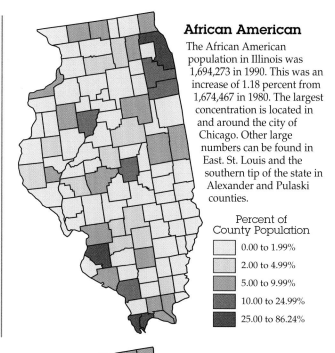

African American

The African American population in Illinois was 1,694,273 in 1990. This was an increase of 1.18 percent from 1,674,467 in 1980. The largest concentration is located in and around the city of Chicago. Other large numbers can be found in East. St. Louis and the southern tip of the state in Alexander and Pulaski counties.

Percent of County Population

- 0.00 to 1.99%
- 2.00 to 4.99%
- 5.00 to 9.99%
- 10.00 to 24.99%
- 25.00 to 86.24%

Statewide Ethnic Composition

Seventy-eight percent of the population of Illinois is white. The top nationalities for this racial group are German, Irish, and Polish. The next largest racial group in the state is the African Americans. Following this, the next largest groups are the Hispanics followed by Asian Americans and Native Americans.

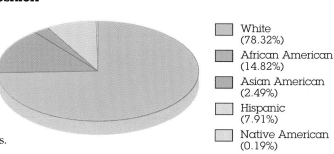

- White (78.32%)
- African American (14.82%)
- Asian American (2.49%)
- Hispanic (7.91%)
- Native American (0.19%)

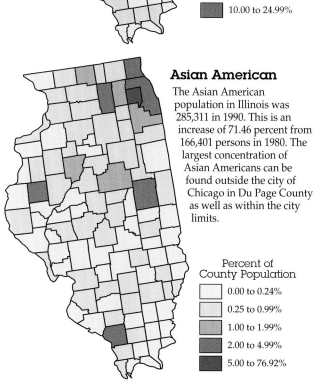

Hispanic[††]

The Hispanic population in Illinois was 904,446 in 1990. This is an increase of 42.30 percent from 635,602 persons in 1980. The largest concentration is located in and around the city of Chicago and the surrounding counties to the north and south.

[††]A person of Mexican, Puerto Rican, Cuban, or other Spanish culture or origin regardless of race.

Percent of County Population

- 0.00 to 0.99%
- 1.00 to 2.99%
- 3.00 to 9.99%
- 10.00 to 24.99%

Education Facts

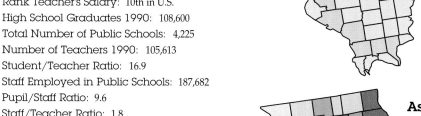

Total Students 1990: 1,797,355

Number of School Districts: 964

Expenditure Per Capita on Education 1990: $728

Expenditure Per Capita K–12 1990: $652

Expenditure Per Pupil 1990: $5,062

Total School Enrollment 1990–1991: 1,784,853

Rank of Expenditures Per Student: 20th in the U.S.

African American Enrollment: 21.9%

Hispanic Enrollment: 9.3%

Asian/Pacific Islander Enrollment: 2.6%

Native American Enrollment: 0.1%

Mean SAT Score 1991 Verbal: 471

Mean SAT Score 1991 Math: 535

Average Teacher's Salary 1992: $36,500

Rank Teacher's Salary: 10th in U.S.

High School Graduates 1990: 108,600

Total Number of Public Schools: 4,225

Number of Teachers 1990: 105,613

Student/Teacher Ratio: 16.9

Staff Employed in Public Schools: 187,682

Pupil/Staff Ratio: 9.6

Staff/Teacher Ratio: 1.8

Education

Attainment: 77 percent of population 25 years or older were high school graduates in 1989, earning Illinois a ranking of 30th in the United States. 21 percent of the state's population had completed college. Institutions of Higher Education: The largest universities and colleges in the state include the University of Illinois, Urbana-Champaign; Southern Illinois University, Carbondale; Northern Illinois University, De Kalb; Northwestern University, Evanston; University of Chicago, Chicago. Expenditures per Student: Expenditure increased 75% between 1985 and 1990. Projected High School Graduations: 1998 (120,751), 2004 (111,955); Total Revenues for Education from Federal Sources: $339 million; Total Revenues for Education from State Sources: $2.4 billion; Total Revenues for Education from Local Sources: $3.7 billion; Average Annual Salaries for Public School Principals: $48,114; Largest School Districts in State: City of Chicago School District #29, 408,201 students, 4th in the United States; School District #46, 26,767, 165th.

Asian American

The Asian American population in Illinois was 285,311 in 1990. This is an increase of 71.46 percent from 166,401 persons in 1980. The largest concentration of Asian Americans can be found outside the city of Chicago in Du Page County as well as within the city limits.

Percent of County Population

- 0.00 to 0.24%
- 0.25 to 0.99%
- 1.00 to 1.99%
- 2.00 to 4.99%
- 5.00 to 76.92%

Transportation

Illinois is well served by many transportation modes. The northern city of Chicago is often considered the transportation center of the United States. It is home to the world's busiest airport, O'Hare International. Also, Chicago has a long history of railroading. Chicago's location along the Great Lakes makes it one of the nation's leading ports.

Illinois as a whole has approximately 135,000 miles of highways and roads. Ten interstates and 22 U.S. highways cross through the state. The Mississippi, Ohio, and Illinois rivers, three major inland waterways, ship goods throughout the Midwest. About 50 Illinois cities receive passenger rail service, and 45 freight lines operate in the state. Midway Airport in Chicago is Illinois's second-busiest airport behind O'Hare.

Energy and Transportation Facts

Energy. Yearly Consumption: 3,513 tril. BTUs (residential, 25.3%; commercial, 18.7%; industrial, 34.7%; transportation, 21.3%); Annual Energy Expenditures Per Capita: $1,863; Nuclear Power Plants Located in State: 13; Source of Energy Consumed: Petroleum— 30.4%; Natural Gas— 27.6%; Coal— 20.8%; Hydroelectric Power—0.0%; Nuclear Power—21.2%.

Transportation. Highway Miles: 136,402 (interstates, 2,053; urban, 32,266; rural, 104,136); Average Yearly Auto Insurance: $534 (26th); Auto Fatalities Rank: 31st; Registered Motor Vehicles: 7,981,725; Workers in Carpools: 17.4%; Workers Using Public Trans: 10.1%.

Employment

Employment. Illinois employed 5.54 million people in 1993. Most work in social and personal services (1,465,500 persons or 26.5% of the workforce). Manufacturing accounts for 16.8% or 932,900 workers. Wholesale and retail trade account for 22.5% or 1,244,600 workers. Government employs 768,200 workers (13.9%). Construction employs 198,300 workers (3.6%). Transportation and utilities account for 5.6% or 309,900 persons. Agriculture employs 110,800 workers or 2.0%. Finance, real estate, and insurance account for 6.9% or 382,200 workers. Mining employs 15,300 people and accounts for only 0.3% of the workforce.

Unemployment. Unemployment has decreased to 7.4% in 1993 from a rate of 9.0% in 1985. Today's figure is higher than the national average of 6.8% as shown below.

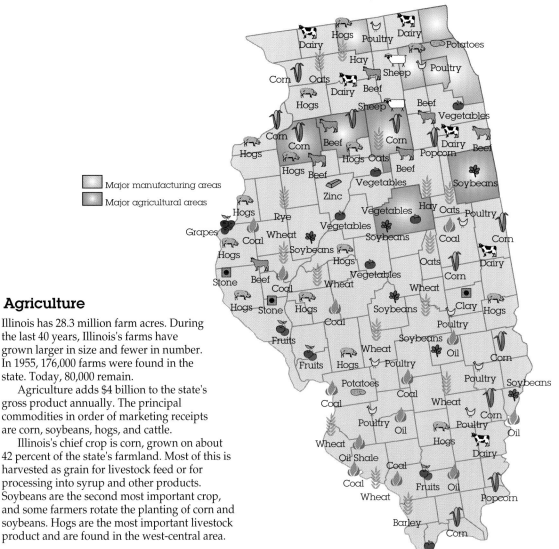

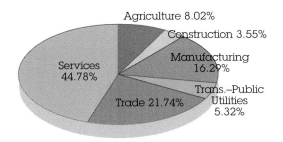

Agriculture

Illinois has 28.3 million farm acres. During the last 40 years, Illinois's farms have grown larger in size and fewer in number. In 1955, 176,000 farms were found in the state. Today, 80,000 remain.

Agriculture adds $4 billion to the state's gross product annually. The principal commodities in order of marketing receipts are corn, soybeans, hogs, and cattle.

Illinois's chief crop is corn, grown on about 42 percent of the state's farmland. Most of this is harvested as grain for livestock feed or for processing into syrup and other products. Soybeans are the second most important crop, and some farmers rotate the planting of corn and soybeans. Hogs are the most important livestock product and are found in the west-central area.

Housing

Owner Occupied Units: 4,506,275; Average Age of Units: 37 years; Average Value of Housing Units: $80,900; Renter Occupied Units: 1,470,362; Median Monthly Rent: $445; Housing Starts: 47,500; Existing Home Sales: 193,900.

Economic Facts

Gross State Product: $256,000,000,000

Income Per Capita: $21,608

Disposable Personal Income: $18,914

Median Household Income: $32,252

Average Annual Pay, 1988: $26,310

Principal Industries: electrical equipment, food products, machinery, chemicals, printing, fabricated metal products, petroleum refining

Major Crops: milk, corn, soybeans, oats, wheat, orchard crops, hay, lumber

Fish: Bass, Carp, Catfish, Perch, Pike, Sunfish

Livestock: cattle, hogs

Non-Fuel Minerals: Peat, crushed stone, sand, gravel

Organic Fuel Minerals: Coal, Petroleum

Civilian Labor Force: 6,029,000 (Women: 2,723,000)

Total Employed: 5,598,000 (Women: 2,546,000)

Median Value of Housing: $80,900

Median Contract Rent: $445 per month

Economic Sectors

Agriculture 8.02%
Construction 3.55%
Manufacturing 16.29%
Trans.–Public Utilities 5.32%
Trade 21.74%
Services 44.78%

Manufacturing

Illinois ranks among the top manufacturing states. The Chicago metropolitan area follows only Los Angeles as the top manufacturing region. About one-fifth of the state gross product comes from this sector. Illinois's leading manufacturing industries include machinery, food processing, electrical equipment, and chemicals. Other industries include the manufacture of transportation equipment, printed materials, fabricated metals, and tires and other rubber goods.

Northern Illinois, especially the Chicago area as well as the Quad Cities of Rock Island, Moline, East Moline, and Davenport, Iowa, is home to many familiar companies. Caterpillar, Sara Lee, Rand McNally, and Motorola all have factories in this region.

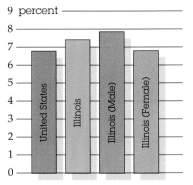

Unemployment Rate

9 percent
8
7
6
5
4
3
2
1
0

United States | Illinois | Illinois (Male) | Illinois (Female)

INDIANA
The State of Indiana

Official State Seal

The Great Seal of Indiana was adopted in 1963 from a design first introduced in 1816. The art depicts a buffalo running away from a wood chopper. This represents the advance of settlement on the frontier. Also included in the background is a depiction of a setting sun over green hills. The date Indiana entered into the Union is printed on the bottom of the seal.

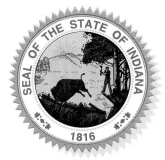

Legal Holidays

January: New Year's Day—1st, Martin Luther King, Jr., Day—3rd Monday; February: Abraham Lincoln's Birthday—12th; Presidents' Day—3rd Monday; Capture of Vincennes—24th; May: Memorial Day—4th Monday; July: Independence Day—4th; September: Labor Day—1st Monday; October: Columbus Day—2nd Monday; November: Veterans' Day—11th; Thanksgiving—4th Thursday; December: Indiana Day—11th; Christmas—25th.

Official State Flag

This flag was adopted in 1917. It was the winner of a statewide contest held in 1916. The nineteen stars represent Indiana's order of admission to the Union. The large star with the state name above it represents Indiana. The torch symbolizes liberty and enlightenment.

Festivals and Events

February: Parke County Maple Fair, Rockville; March: Maple Syrup Festival, Wakarusa; St. Benno Fest, Indianapolis; April: April Fest, Elwood; May: Round the Fountain Art Fair, Lafayette; June: German Fest, Fort Wayne; Mermaid Festival, North Webster; Golden Raintree Festival, New Harmony; World's Largest Garage Sale, South Bend; July: Swiss Days, Berne; Grecian Festival, Merrillville; August: Elwood Glass Fest, Elwod; Popcorn Festival, Van Buren; State Fair, Indianapolis; September: Johnny Appleseed Festival, Fort Wayne; Remembering James Dean Fest, Fairmount; October: Feast of the Hunter's Moon, Lafayette; Riley Fest, Greenfield; Parke County Covered Bridge Fest, Rockville.

Indiana Compared to States in Its Region.

Resident Pop. in Metro Areas: 4th; Pop. Percent Increase: 2d; Pop. Over 65: 3d; Infant Mortality: 3d; School Enroll. Increase: 2d; High School Grad. and Up: 5th; Violent Crime: 4th; Hazardous Waste Sites: 4th; Unemployment: 4th; Median Household Income: 4th; Persons Below Poverty: 4th; Energy Costs Per Person: 1st.

East North Central Region

	Population	Capital
Wisconsin	5,038,000	Madison
Michigan	9,478,000	Lansing
Illinois	11,697,000	Springfield
Indiana	5,713,000	Indianapolis
Ohio	11,091,000	Columbus

Indiana's Finances

Households: 2,065,000; Income Per Capita Current Dollars: $18,043; Change Per Capita Income 1980 to 1992: 95.8% (30th in U.S.); State Expenditures: $11,691,000,000; State Revenues: $12,265,000,000; Personal Income Tax: 3.4%; Federal Income Taxes Paid Per Capita: $1,655; Sales Tax: 5% (food and prescription drugs exempt).

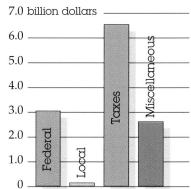

State Expenditures

7.0 billion dollars
6.0
5.0
4.0
3.0
2.0
1.0
0

Education, Highway, Welfare, Health, Other

State Revenues

7.0 billion dollars
6.0
5.0
4.0
3.0
2.0
1.0
0

Federal, Local, Taxes, Miscellaneous

Location, Size, and Boundaries

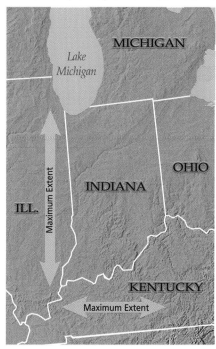

Location. Indiana is located in the East North Central region of the United States. It is bounded on four sides by land with a small coastline along Lake Michigan. The geographic center of Indiana is lat. 39° 53.7' N; long. 86° 16' W.

Size. Indiana is the 38th largest state in terms of size. Its area is 36,291 sq. mi. (93,994 km2). Inland water covers 194 sq. mi. (502 km2).

Boundaries. Lake Michigan, 45 mi. (72 km); Michigan, 99 mi. (159 km); Ohio, 179 mi. (288 km); Kentucky, 848 mi. (1,365 km); Illinois, 357 mi. (575 km).

Geographic Extent. The north/south extent of Indiana is 280 mi. (451 km). The state extends 160 mi. (257 km) to the east/west.

Facts about Indiana. Origin of Name: Meaning "Land of the Indians"; Nickname: The Hoosier State; Motto: "The crossroads of America"; Abbreviations: Ind. (traditional), IN (postal); State Bird: cardinal; State Tree: tuliptree; State Flower: peony; State Song: "On the Banks of the Wabash, Far Away," words and music by Paul Dresser.

Indiana Compared to Other States. Resident Pop. in Metro Areas: 23d; Pop. Percent Increase: 27th; Pop. Over 65: 26th; Infant Mortality: 16th; School Enroll. Increase: 33d; High School Grad. and Up: 31st; Violent Crime: 29th; Hazardous Waste Sites: 11th; Unemployment: 31st; Median Household Income: 24th; Persons Below Poverty: 36th; Energy Costs Per Person: 6th.

Sources of Information. Tourism: Department of Commerce, Tourism and Marketing Division, One North Capitol, Suite 700, Indianapolis, IN 46204. Economy: Department of Commerce, Division of Economic Analysis, One North Capitol, Suite 700, Indianapolis, IN 46204. Government: Legislative Services Agency, State House, Room 302, Indianapolis, IN 46204. History: Secretary of State's Office, State House, Room 201, Indianapolis, IN 46204.

■ Angel Mounds State Memorial. Site of a prehistoric Indian village. (P-6)

■ Chain O' Lakes State Park. Canoeing and boating through eight lakes. (C-12)

■ Corydon. State capital from 1816 to 1825. Restored capitol building. (O-10)

■ French Lick. Vacation resort area with three artesian springs. (N-8)

■ George Rogers Clark National Historical Park. Dedicated to the man who helped take Fort Sackville from the British in 1779. (M-5)

■ Hoosier National Forest. Open to fishing, hiking, camping, hunting, and swimming. (L-9)

■ Indiana Dunes National Lakeshore. Sandy beaches for swimming, fishing, and picnicking. (B-7)

■ Indianapolis Motor Speedway. Built in 1909, site of the Indy 500 automobile race. (I-9)

■ International Friendship Gardens. Sculptured gardens and bird sanctuary. (B-7)

■ James F. D. Lanier State Memorial. Home of the banker who helped finance Indiana during the Civil War. (M-12)

■ Jasper-Pulaski Fish and Wildlife Area. Bluegill, catfish, and carp in small ponds. Also waterfowl hunting. (D-7)

■ Lincoln Boyhood National Memorial. Boyhood home of Abraham Lincoln. (O-7)

■ Lincoln Pioneer Village. Memorial to Abraham Lincoln. (P-7)

■ McCormick's Creek State Park. Indiana's oldest state park. Hiking with canyons and cliffs. (K-8)

■ Parke County Covered Bridges. Self guided tour of 32 wooden covered bridges. (I-6)

■ Pigeon Roost State Memorial. 44-foot monument dedicated to pioneers killed by Indians in 1812. (M-11)

■ Pokagon State Park. Camping, fishing, hiking, and swimming as well as a nature center. (B-13)

■ St. Meinrad Archabbey. Benedictine monastery built in 1852. (O-7)

■ Santa Claus. Famous post office, theme park, toy shops, and more. (O-7)

■ Shakamak State Park. Three man-made lakes for boating and fishing. (K-6)

■ T. C. Steele Memorial. Home and studio of the Indiana artist (1847-1926). (K-8)

■ Tippecanoe Battlefield State Memorial. Site of William Henry Harrison's defeat of the Indians in 1811. (F-8)

■ Versailles State Park. Rolling hills, camping, and a saddlebarn. (L-12)

■ Vincennes. First settlement in Indiana and territorial capital as well as the home of President William Henry Harrison. (M-5)

■ Wawasee Lake. The largest lake in the state. (C-11)

■ Wyandotte Cave. One of world's largest caves. Spelunking tours. (O-9)

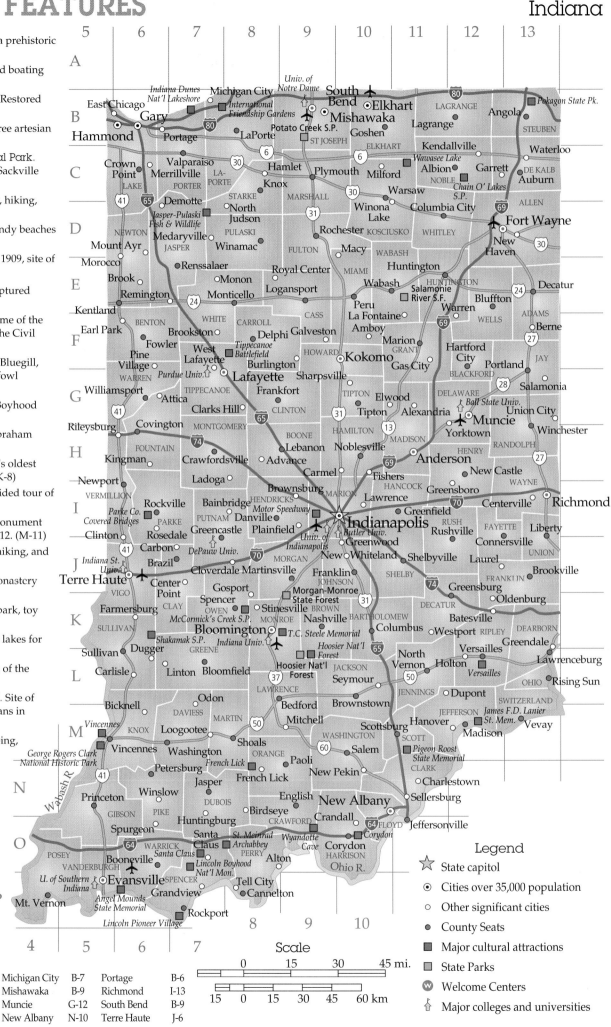

Major Cities

Anderson	H-11	Greenwood	J-10
Bloomington	K-8	Hammond	B-6
Columbus	K-10	Indianapolis	I-10
East Chicago	B-6	Kokomo	F-10
Elkhart	B-10	Lafayette	G-7
Evansville	P-5	Lawrence	I-10
Fort Wayne	D-12	Marion	F-11
Gary	B-6	Merrillville	C-6

Michigan City	B-7	Portage	B-6
Mishawaka	B-9	Richmond	I-13
Muncie	G-12	South Bend	B-9
New Albany	N-10	Terre Haute	J-6

Scale

0   15   30   45 mi.

15   0   15   30   45   60 km

Legend

☆ State capitol

⊙ Cities over 35,000 population

○ Other significant cities

● County Seats

■ Major cultural attractions

□ State Parks

Ⓦ Welcome Centers

⚲ Major colleges and universities

Indiana

Weather Facts

Record High Temperature: 116° F (47° C) on July 13, 1932, at Collegeville; Record Low Temperature: -35° F (-37° C) on February 1, 1947, at Greensburg; Average January Temperature: 28° F (-2° C); Average July Temperature: 75° F (24° C); Average Yearly Precipitation: 41 in. (104 cm).

Environmental Facts

Air Pollution Rank: 6th; Water Pollution Rank: 22d; Total Yearly Industrial Pollution: 120,522,658 lbs.; Industrial Pollution Rank: 4th; Hazardous Waste Sites: 33; Hazardous Sites Rank: 11th; Landfill Capacity: adequate; Fresh Water Supply: large surplus; Daily Residential Water Consumption: 128 gals. per capita; Endangered Species: Aquatic Species (10)—clubshell; Birds (3)—eagle, bald; Mammals (2)—bat, gray; Other Species (4)—butterfly, Karner blue; Plants (2)—clover, running buffalo.

Environmental Quality

Indiana residents generate 4.5 million tons of solid waste each year, or approximately 1,600 pounds per capita. Landfill capacity in Indiana will be exhausted in 5 to 10 years. The state has 35 hazardous waste sites. Annual greenhouse gas emissions in Indiana total 217.1 million tons, or 39.1 tons per capita. Industrial sources in Indiana release approximately 128.4 thousand tons of toxins, 2.5 million tons of acid precipitation-producing substances, and 3.5 million tons of smog-producing substances into the atmosphere each year.

The state has 9,700 acres within the National Park System; the largest area within the state is George Rogers Clark National Historical Park. State parks cover just over 51,700 acres, attracting 10.5 million visitors per year.

Indiana spends approximately less than 1 percent (0.7%) of its budget, or approximately $10 per capita, on environmental and natural resources.

Average Monthly Weather

Indianapolis	Jan	Feb	Mar	Apr	May	Jun	Jul	Aug	Sep	Oct	Nov	Dec	Yearly
Maximum Temperature °F	34.2	38.5	49.3	63.1	73.4	82.3	85.2	83.7	77.9	66.1	50.8	39.2	32.0
Minimum Temperature °F	17.8	21.1	30.7	41.7	51.5	60.9	64.9	62.7	55.3	43.4	32.8	23.7	42.2
Days of Precipitation	11.7	10.1	13.0	12.2	12.1	9.8	9.4	8.7	7.7	8.1	10.3	11.9	125.1
South Bend													
Maximum Temperature °F	30.4	34.1	44.3	58.6	69.9	79.5	82.7	81.0	74.6	63.1	47.8	35.7	58.5
Minimum Temperature °F	15.9	18.6	27.7	38.4	48.1	58.1	62.3	60.8	53.7	43.4	32.8	22.5	40.2
Days of Precipitation	15.5	12.5	14.1	13.1	11.3	10.6	9.4	9.3	9.1	10.1	12.8	15.4	143.3

Flora and Fauna

When white settlers first came to Indiana, the area was approximately 80 percent forested. Today, however, forests cover only 18 percent of the state. Indiana has over 120 native species of trees, the most prevalent being beech, oak, sycamore, and maple trees. Other trees such as the bald cypress, yellow poplar, and Virginia pine also grow in Indiana. Indiana has a varied assortment of other vegetation, ranging from insect-eating plants such as the bladderwort, to prickly pear cactus. The state's wildflowers include asters, pussy willows, peonies, and goldenrod.

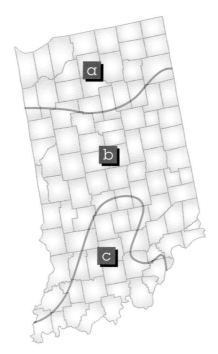

Physical Regions: (a) Great Lakes Plains; (b) Till Plains; (c) Southern Hills and Lowlands.

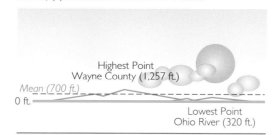

Highest Point
Wayne County (1,257 ft.)
Mean (700 ft.)
0 ft.
Lowest Point
Ohio River (320 ft.)

Land Use

Cropland: 62.5%; Pasture: 9.3%; Rangeland: 0%; Forest: 16.6%; Urban: 7.9%; Other: 3.7%.

For more information about Indiana's environment, contact Natural Resources Commission, Department of Natural Resources, 608 State Office Bldg., Indianapolis, IN 46204.

Indiana's large-animal population has all but disappeared over the years. The white-tailed deer is the only sizable animal left roaming Indiana's forests and grasslands. However, many smaller mammals, including muskrats, woodchucks, opossums, and squirrels, live throughout Indiana. Birds, both game and song, can be found in all parts of the state. The quail is Indiana's most common game bird; the cardinal is the state bird. Several fishes, such as salmon, pickerel, bass, and catfish, live in Indiana rivers and lakes.

Topography

Indiana can be divided into several topographic regions. The Southern Hills and Lowlands physical region of the state is characterized by rough hills and valleys. Many underground caverns are found in the area. The lowest elevation in the state can also be found in the south. The soil is mostly warm and moist, with low organic content and red/yellow coloring.

Most of the rest of Indiana lies within the fertile Central Plains (the Till Plains physical region), a rich agricultural region that sweeps across much of the Midwest. Warm and moist gray/brown clay predominates as the soil in this region. The area does have some gentle hills and valleys, including the highest point in the state (a hill that rises 1,257 ft. [383 m] above sea level). The Plains were swept by glaciers during the last Ice Age, which left them flat and also deposited the minerals that have enriched the soil.

The northwestern area of Indiana, bordering Lake Michigan, is part of the Great Lakes Plains physical region. This is also a fertile low-lying area. Soil type varies from black organic to fine loamy sand, with elevations not much above sea level. Large sand dunes separate the Great Lakes coastal area from the inland region in this corner of the state.

Climate

The continental climate of Indiana causes humid summers and cold, yet moist, winters. As in Illinois, Lake Michigan affects the state's weather. During winter, winds carry lake moisture over the Indiana land. Heavy snowfall results from this pattern. Only minor temperature differences can be seen from north to south. January and July temperatures for South Bend, in the extreme north, average 25 degrees F and 73 degrees F. Evansville and the extreme south register average January and July temperatures of 35 degrees F and 78 degrees F.

Indiana receives lighter rainfall but heavier snowfall in the north. Northern Indiana averages 34 inches of precipitation a year. Along the Ohio River, average precipitation measures 44 inches annually. However, only 10 or so inches of snow fall here annually.

Southern Illinois is prone to both dry spells and flooding conditions. The Ohio River valley especially experiences these two extremes.

Hydrology

The most important river in the state is the Wabash, which begins in northeastern Indiana (near Fort Wayne) and flows southwest. It forms the southwest border with Illinois, just below Terre Haute, finally emptying into the Ohio River. The Ohio forms Indiana's entire southern border with Kentucky. The White River flows southwest from Indianapolis in the central part of the state and empties into the Wabash. Other important rivers are the St. Joseph and the St. Marys, which meet at Fort Wayne; the Kankakee in northwestern Indiana; and the Whitewater and the Laughery in southeastern Indiana.

There are many lakes in the state, especially in the north. The largest of these is Lake Wawasee at about 5 sq. miles (13 sq. km). Other sizable lakes in the north include Huntington Lake, Maxinkuckee Lake, Salamon Lake, and Chapman Lake. In the south are Lake Monroe, Lake Lemon, and others.

Indiana's History

Indiana's First People

As with many other midwestern and southern states, there is much evidence of the ancient Mound Builder civilizations found in Indiana. Several areas, including Mounds State Park and Angel Mound near Evansville, preserve the impressive legacy of these peoples. The Mississippian culture, the last of these groups, has left remains of a large village near Newburgh on the Ohio River.

When the first Europeans arrived, the area was inhabited by descendants of the Woodland culture, tribes that spoke Algonquian languages. The Miami and Potawatomi Indians migrated south and settled in the northern portion of the state, while the Kickapoo and Wea journeyed from areas south of Indiana and settled in the north.

European Exploration

In 1679, Frenchmen led by René-Robert Cavelier, Sieur de La Salle, became the first whites to set foot in Indiana as they explored the Mississippi valley. In the first several decades of the eighteenth century, French settlements were established at Vincennes; at Quiatenon, near present-day Lafayette; and at Fort Miami, near present-day Fort Wayne.

At the end of the French and Indian War in 1763, Britain took control of French Canada and French-controlled American territory including Indiana, although Chief Pontiac resisted giving up some British-claimed villages until 1765. In 1779, American colonel George Rogers Clark captured Vincennes from the British during the Revolutionary War. After the war, Indiana became a U.S. possession as part of what was known as the Northwest Territory (which also included Illinois, Ohio, Michigan, Wisconsin, and part of Minnesota). Congress, under the Ordinance of 1787, set up an organizational structure to govern the territory. In 1811, in response to an Indian uprising, William Henry Harrison and over 1,000 troops attacked and defeated a force of Shawnee Indians lead by The Shawnee Prophet (brother of Chief Tecumseh). Harrison then burned their village and left. As a result, Harrison was made a national hero. British interest in the area continued until Great Britain was finally defeated in the War of 1812.

Statehood

With U.S. control over the Northwest Territory, settlers began to move into the established towns and villages only to be met with resistance on the part of the Indians. In 1791, the Miami Indians inflicted heavy casualties on federal troops near Fort Miami, but were defeated three years later by troops under the command of Gen. Anthony Wayne. The final conflict with Indians in Indiana occurred as the Miami were defeated near Peru in 1812.

In 1800, the Northwest Territory was reorganized as the Indiana Territory with Vincennes as the capital. In 1805, Michigan was detached from the Indiana Territory, and four years after that the territory was reduced to Indiana's present borders with William Henry Harrison as its first governor. In 1816, Indiana was admitted to the Union as the nineteenth state with Croyden as its capital (switched to Indianapolis in 1825).

In 1846, the last Indians (Potawatomi) were forced from the state, and in 1851 a new state constitution excluded blacks from settling in the state. Despite strong sympathies for the Confederate cause, Indiana remained part of the Union during the Civil War. Only one raid took place on Indiana soil during the Civil War. In 1863, Confederate General John Hunt Morgan led raids into Kentucky, Indiana, and Ohio before being captured by Union troops.

Later, Blacks began to make headway in Indiana life and politics. Gary was one of the first cities in the United States to elect a Black mayor (Richard Hatcher) in 1967. The first Black congress member (Katie Hall) was a woman who was elected in 1983.

Indiana was the first state in the Union to provide a state-supported school system. In 1852, the modern school system was founded, and in 1907, high schools were added to the state system.

Industrialization

The completion of a rail link between Indianapolis and Madison in 1847 provided a boost to Indiana's agricultural production, which included hogs, timber, and corn. Indeed, extensive railroad and canal building had so bankrupted the state that the constitution of 1851 required a balanced state budget. After the Civil War, Indiana's economic activity was fueled by manufacturing as well as farming and timber. Some of the industries setting up shop in the state included glass making, leather working, brick making, and brewing. In 1905, U.S. Steel opened its largest plant in what was to become Gary as Indiana became a leading producer of iron and steel. During the 1920s, Indiana lost its car-manufacturing plants (except Studebaker) to Detroit. Today Indiana's economy is still largely split between farming and manufacturing.

New Harmony

This utopian community was originally founded as Harmony, a village on the Wabash River, by George Rapp, who moved his disciples there from Pennsylvania in 1815. Rapp sold the village to Robert Owen, who renamed it New Harmony, in 1824. As with others at the time, Owen wished to establish a secular communitarian society that would treat equality and property in a new way. He wanted the competitive system of capitalism to be replaced by cooperation in which laborers would receive "the value of their work." Unfortunately, overcrowding and confusion of purpose and leadership led to the demise of the experiment after only a few years. After the demise, an intellectual center was established by some of the remaining members.

Important Events

1679 René-Robert Cavelier, Sieur de La Salle, passes through Indiana while exploring the Mississippi valley.

1725 Jesuits found permanent settlement at Vincennes.

1763 Treaty of Paris forces France to cede control of lands including Indiana to Britain.

1779 American George Rogers Clark defeats British at Vincennes.

1787 Creation of the Northwest Ordinance establishes government in this territory.

1800 Indiana Territory created out of Northwest Territory.

1809 Indiana Territory reorganized to reflect present-day boundaries.

1811 William Henry Harrison defeats Shawnee Indians at the Battle of Tippecanoe.

1816 Indiana admitted to the Union as the nineteenth state.

1824 Robert Owen founds utopian colony of New Harmony.

1825 State capital moved to Indianapolis.

1846 Last Indians forced to depart the state.

1851 New constitution forbidding black settlers is adopted.

1853 Wabash and Erie Canal is opened.

1888 Benjamin Harrison is elected twenty-third president of the U.S.

1894 Elwood Haynes tests his one-cylinder horseless carriage in Kokomo.

1905 U.S. Steel opens its largest plant at Gary, founded on the site to house the workers.

1911 First running of the Indianapolis 500.

1937 Devastating floods send Ohio River to its highest level ever.

1949 Indiana achieves complete desegregation of its public schools.

1965 Studebaker automobiles goes out of business in South Bend after sixty-three years.

1988 J. Danforth Quayle elected Vice President of the United States.

1992 An Indiana court convicts boxer Mike Tyson of raping a beauty-pageant contestant.

Population Density

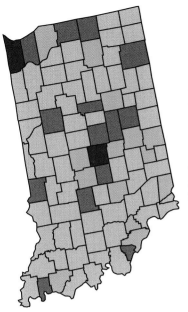

Population density for the state of Indiana was 154.6 persons per square mile in 1990 (59.7 per km2). Average U.S. density was 70.3 persons per square mile in 1990 (27.3 per km2). Habitation is most dense in and around the urban areas of Gary and Indianapolis. The area around Gary is populated with many residents who make their living in the nearby city of Chicago, Ill.

Persons Per Square Mile

- 10.0 to 99.9
- 100.0 to 249.9
- 250.0 to 749.9
- 750.0 to 2,999.9

Population Change

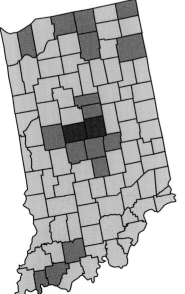

The 1990 population figure for the state of Indiana was 5,544,159. This is a 0.98 percent increase from 5,490,224 in 1980. The next decade will show a loss with a population of 5.5 million or a –0.76 percent decrease. Much of the state saw little growth or even a decease in population in the last decade. The future will bring much of the same.

Percent Change 1980 to 1990

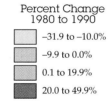

- –31.9 to –10.0%
- –9.9 to 0.0%
- 0.1 to 19.9%
- 20.0 to 49.9%

Distribution of Income

The per capita income for the state of Indiana (current dollars) was $18,043 in 1992. This is a 95.8 percent increase from $9,215 in 1980. Income is greatest in the areas in and around the capital city of Indianapolis. Evansville and South Bend are also areas of higher income.

Per Capita Income (000s) (Current Dollars)

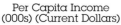

- $10.0 to 12.9
- $13.0 to 15.9
- $16.0 to 19.9
- $20.0 to 37.7

Population Projections

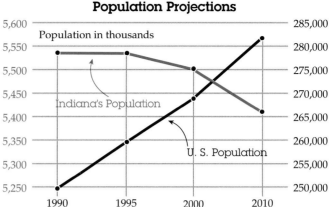

Population in thousands

Indiana's Population

U. S. Population

Population Facts

State Population, 1993: 5,713,000

Rank: 14

Population 2000: 5,502,000 (Rank 14)

Density: 154.6 per sq. mi. (59.7 per km2)

Distribution: 64.9% urban, 35.1% rural

Population Under 5 Years Old: 7.2%

Population Under 18 Years Old: 25.8%

Population Over 65 Years Old: 12.7%

Median Age: 32.8

Number of Households: 2,065,000

Average Persons Per Household: 2.61

Average Persons Per Family: 3.11

Female Heads of Households: 3.93%

Population That Is Married: 21.68%

Birth Rate: 15.6 per 1,000 population

Death Rate: 8.9 per 1,000 population

Births to Teen Mothers: 14.5%

Marriage Rate: 9.6 per 1,000 population

Divorce Rate: N/A

Violent Crime Rate: 505 per 100,000 pop.

Population on Social Security: 16.4%

Percent Voting for President: 55.2%

Population Profile

Rank. Indiana ranks 14th among U.S. states in terms of population with 5,713,000 citizens.

Minority Population. The state's minority population is 10.5 percent. The state's male to female ratio for 1990 was 94.13 males for every 100 females. It was below the national average of 95.22 males for every 100 females.

Growth. The state's population is decreasing and is expected to be 5.4 million by the year 2010.

Government

Capital: Indianapolis (established 1825).

Statehood: Became 19th state on Dec. 11, 1816.

Number of Counties: 92.

Supreme Court Justices: 5, 10-year term.

State Senators: 50, 4-year term.

State Legislators: 100, 2-year term.

United States Senators: 2.

United States Representatives: 10.

Electoral Votes: 12.

State Constitution: Adopted 1851.

Population Change

Year	Population
1950	3,934,000
1960	4,674,000
1970	5,202,000
1980	5,490,224
1990	5,544,159
2000	5,502,000
2010	5,409,000

Period	Change
1950–1970	32.2%
1970–1980	5.5%
1980–1990	1.0%
1990–2000	–0.8%

Indiana's Famous Citizens

Haynes, Elwood (1857–1925). Built an early one-horsepower automobile in 1894. Also discovered several alloys.

Jackson, Michael (b. 1958). His 1983 album *Thriller* is the biggest selling solo album of all time.

Karras, Alex (b. 1935). All-Pro football player with the Detroit Lions (1960–1962).

Letterman, David (b. 1947). Late night talk show host since 1982. Has won the ratings war since Johnny Carson retired.

Morton, Oliver (1823–1877). Governor from 1861 to 1867. Influential as U.S. Senator in ratifying the 15th Amendment.

Porter, Cole (1893–1964). Composer for popular Broadway musicals such as *Kiss Me Kate*, and *Anything Goes*.

Pyle, Ernest Taylor (1900–1945). Journalist. Won a Pulitzer Prize in 1944 for his war stories of ordinary soldiers on the front.

Walker, Madam C. J. (1867–1919). Business-woman. Invented beauty products for black women (to straighten curly hair, etc.).

Wallace, Lewis (1827–1905). Governor of New Mexico Territory and author of *Ben-Hur, a Tale of the Christ*.

Older Citizens. The state's population older than 65 was 696,196 in 1990. It grew 18.93% from 585,384 in 1980.

Younger Citizens. The number of children (under 18 years of age) was 1.4 million in 1990. This represents 26.3 percent of the state's population. The state's school-aged population was 955 thousand in 1990. It is expected to decrease to 944 thousand by the year 2000. This represents a –1.15% change.

Urban/Rural. 64.9% of the population of the state live in urban areas while 35.1% live in rural areas.

Largest Cities. Indiana has 16 cities with a population greater than 35,000. The populations of the state's largest centers are (starting from the most populous) Indianapolis (731,327), Fort Wayne (173,072), Evansville (126,272), Gary (116,646), South Bend (105,511), Hammond (84,236), Muncie (71,035), Bloomington (60,633), Anderson (59,459), Terre Haute (57,483), Kokomo (44,962), Lafayette (43,764), Elkhart (43,627), Mishawaka (42,608), Richmond (38,705), New Albany (36,322), East Chicago (33,982), Michigan City (33,822), Marion (32,618), Columbus (31,802), and Portage (29,060).

Native American

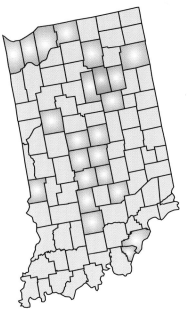

The Native American population in Indiana was 12,720 in 1990. This was an increase of 33.97 percent from 9,495 in 1980. A large percentage of the Native American population in the state resides in Indianapolis. Fort Wayne has the next largest Native American population with 560 residents. Indiana is also home to the Miami tribe.

Presence of
Native Americans

- Minor
- Moderate

Nationalities

African	4,172
American	395,497
Arab	7,032
Austrian	5,050
Czech	8,885
Dutch	105,561
English	511,426
Finnish	2,831
German	1,748,546
Greek	15,705
Hungarian	26,548
Irish	503,122
Italian	83,122
Norwegian	15,417
Polish	129,095
Portuguese	1,650
Russian	11,808
Scottish	67,196
Slovak	28,677
Swedish	41,190
Welsh	22,877
West Indian	2,392

African American

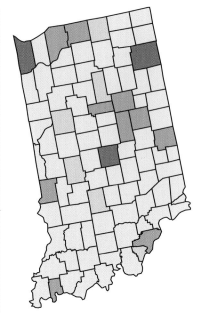

The African American population in Indiana was 432,092 in 1990. This was an increase of 4.25 percent from 414,489 in 1980. The largest number of African Americans is found in the city of Indianapolis. Over 40 percent of the African American population in the state can be found in this city. Large numbers can also be found in Gary and East Chicago.

Percent of
County Population

- 0.00 to 1.99%
- 2.00 to 4.99%
- 5.00 to 9.99%
- 10.00 to 24.99%

Statewide Ethnic Composition

Over 90 percent of the population of Indiana is white. The largest nationalities in this racial group are German, English, and Irish. The next largest group is African Americans, followed by Hispanics, Asians, and Native Americans. Slightly more than one-third of a million people claim to be American and acknowledge no other nationality.

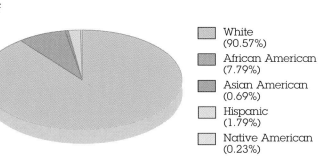

- White (90.57%)
- African American (7.79%)
- Asian American (0.69%)
- Hispanic (1.79%)
- Native American (0.23%)

Hispanic[††]

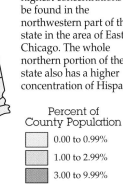

The Hispanic population in Indiana was 98,788 in 1990. This is an increase of 13.49 percent from 87,047 persons in 1980. The highest concentrations can be found in the northwestern part of the state in the area of East Chicago. The whole northern portion of the state also has a higher concentration of Hispanics.

Percent of
County Population

- 0.00 to 0.99%
- 1.00 to 2.99%
- 3.00 to 9.99%

[††]A person of Mexican, Puerto Rican, Cuban, or other Spanish culture or origin regardless of race.

Education Facts

Total Students 1990: 954,165

Number of School Districts: 303

Expenditure Per Capita on Education 1990: $728

Expenditure Per Capita K–12 1990: $639

Expenditure Per Pupil 1990: $4,398

Total School Enrollment 1990–1991: 949,133

Rank of Expenditures Per Student: 35th in the U.S.

African American Enrollment: 10.9%

Hispanic Enrollment: 1.8%

Asian/Pacific Islander Enrollment: 0.6%

Native American Enrollment: 0.1%

Mean SAT Score 1991 Verbal: 408

Mean SAT Score 1991 Math: 457

Average Teacher's Salary 1992: $34,800

Rank Teacher's Salary: 13th in U.S.

High School Graduates 1990: 60,800

Total Number of Public Schools: 1,923

Number of Teachers 1990: 54,236

Student/Teacher Ratio: 17.5

Staff Employed in Public Schools: 107,094

Pupil/Staff Ratio: 8.9

Staff/Teacher Ratio: 2.0

Asian American

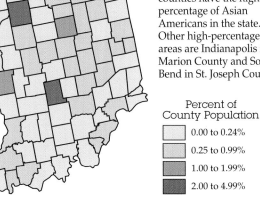

The Asian American population in Indiana was 12,720 in 1990. This is an increase of 33.97 percent from 9,495 persons in 1980. Tippecanoe and Monroe counties have the highest percentage of Asian Americans in the state. Other high-percentage areas are Indianapolis in Marion County and South Bend in St. Joseph County.

Percent of
County Population

- 0.00 to 0.24%
- 0.25 to 0.99%
- 1.00 to 1.99%
- 2.00 to 4.99%

Education

Attainment: 78 percent of population 25 years or older were high school graduates in 1989, earning Indiana a ranking of 26th in the United States; 14 percent of the state's population had completed college. Institutions of Higher Education: The largest universities and colleges in the state include Indiana University, Bloomington; Purdue University, West Lafayette; Ball State University, Muncie; Indiana State University, Terre Haute; University of Southern Indiana, Evansville; University of Notre Dame, South Bend; University of Evansville, Evansville; Butler University, Indianapolis; Valparaiso University, Valparaiso. Expenditures per Student: Expenditure increased 72% between 1985 and 1990. Projected High School Graduations: 1998 (64,444), 2004 (57,757); Total Revenues for Education from Federal Sources: $187 million; Total Revenues for Education from State Sources: $2.1 billion; Total Revenues for Education from Local Sources: $1.4 billion; Average Annual Salaries for Public School Principals: $47,092; Largest School Districts in State: Indianapolis Public Schools, 48,805 students, 69th in the United States; Ft. Wayne Community Schools, 26,767, 130th.

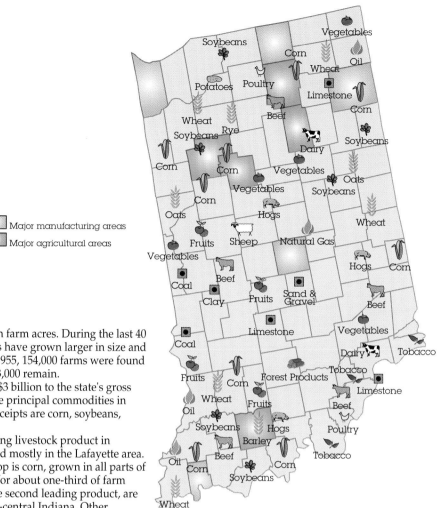

Major manufacturing areas
Major agricultural areas

Agriculture

Indiana has 16 million farm acres. During the last 40 years, Indiana's farms have grown larger in size and fewer in number. In 1955, 154,000 farms were found in the state. Today, 63,000 remain.

Agriculture adds $3 billion to the state's gross product annually. The principal commodities in order of marketing receipts are corn, soybeans, hogs, and cattle.

Hogs are the leading livestock product in Indiana, and are found mostly in the Lafayette area. The most valuable crop is corn, grown in all parts of the state. It accounts for about one-third of farm income. Soybeans, the second leading product, are found mainly in west-central Indiana. Other valuable crops include tomatoes, cucumbers, and potatoes.

Housing

Owner Occupied Units: 2,246,046; Average Age of Units: 34 years; Average Value of Housing Units: $53,900; Renter Occupied Units: 589,881; Median Monthly Rent: $374; Housing Starts: 35,400; Existing Home Sales: 100,800.

Economic Facts

Gross State Product: $105,000,000,000

Income Per Capita: $18,043

Disposable Personal Income: $15,882

Median Household Income: $28,797

Average Annual Pay, 1988: $22,522

Principal Industries: food products, chemicals, primary metals, machinery, electrical equipment, transportation equipment, furniture, pharmaceuticals, housing

Major Crops: corn, soybeans, tobacco, wheat, apples, peaches, spearmint, peppermint, rye, hay, oats

Fish: Bass, Pickerel, Pike, Salmon, Sunfish

Livestock: hogs, beef cattle

Non-Fuel Minerals: Limestone, Building Stone, Clay, Gypsum

Organic Fuel Minerals: Coal

Civilian Labor Force: 2,798,000 (Women: 1,320,000)

Total Employed: 2,632,000 (Women: 1,247,000)

Median Value of Housing: $53,900

Median Contract Rent: $374 per month

Economic Sectors

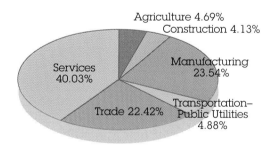

Agriculture 4.69%
Construction 4.13%
Manufacturing 23.54%
Services 40.03%
Transportation–Public Utilities 4.88%
Trade 22.42%

Manufacturing

The state of Indiana has one of the highest percentages of manufacturing of all the states; more people work in manufacturing jobs than in any other industry in the state. Thirty percent of the gross state product comes from manufacturing. Steel and other primary metal production is the leading industry. Other important industries include the manufacture of transportation equipment, electrical equipment, and chemicals.

Northwest Indiana, including cities such as Gary and East Chicago, is one of the world leaders in steel production. In addition, Indiana produces more steel than anywhere else in the United States. Indianapolis manufactures many pharmaceuticals, Indiana's leading chemical product. Other chemical products include resins, soaps, and pesticides.

Transportation

Major transportation arteries of all types cross through Indiana. The first stagecoach route, the National Road, was built in the early 1900s. It is now a part of U.S. Highway 40. Today, Indiana has 92,000 miles of highways and roads; over 90 percent are paved.

Lake Michigan provides Indiana with access to many ports in the United States, as well as other countries. The state's busiest port, the Burns Waterway Harbor, is located in Portage. Smaller Indiana ports can be found along the Ohio River. Indiana has about 30 freight railroads providing service through the state. Furthermore, 20 Indiana cities have passenger rail services. Indianapolis International is Indiana's busiest airport. Others are located in Fort Wayne and South Bend.

Energy and Transportation Facts

Energy. Yearly Consumption: 2,421 tril. BTUs (residential, 18.2%; commercial, 11.2%; industrial, 47.4%; transportation, 23.2%); Annual Energy Expenditures Per Capita: $2,125; Nuclear Power Plants Located in State: 0; Source of Energy Consumed: Petroleum— 30.8%; Natural Gas— 17.8%; Coal— 51.3%; Hydroelectric Power—0.2%; Nuclear Power—0.0%.

Transportation. Highway Miles: 92,054 (interstates, 1,140; urban, 19,109; rural, 72,945); Average Yearly Auto Insurance: $497 (33 d); Auto Fatalities Rank: 31st; Registered Motor Vehicles: 4,515,850; Workers in Carpools: 16.3%; Workers Using Public Trans: 1.3%.

Employment

Employment. Indiana employed 2.78 million people in 1993. Most work in manufacturing (638,700 persons or 23.0% of the workforce). Wholesale and retail trade accounts for 21.9% or 608,300 workers. Social and personal services account for 20.2% or 562,200 workers. Government employs 392,900 workers (14.1%). Construction employs 118,600 workers (4.3%). Transportation and utilities account for 4.8% or 133,600 persons. Agriculture employs 72,300 workers or 2.6%. Finance, real estate, and insurance account for 4.6% or 128,300 workers. Mining employs 6,600 people and accounts for only 0.2% of the workforce.

Unemployment. Unemployment has decreased to 5.3% in 1993 from a rate of 7.9% in 1985. Today's figure is lower than the national average of 6.8% as shown below.

Unemployment Rate

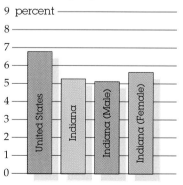

IOWA

The State of Iowa

Official State Seal

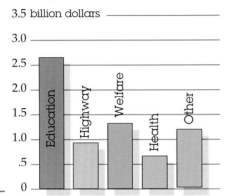

The Great Seal of Iowa was adopted in 1847 after Iowa became a state. The foreground includes a soldier holding an American flag. In the background is the steamship *Iowa* on the Mississippi river. Also included is a typical Iowa farm complete with log cabin, plow, sickle, and rake. An eagle holds in its beak the Iowa state motto printed on a blue ribbon.

Legal Holidays

January: New Year's Day—1st, Martin Luther King, Jr., Day—3rd Monday; February: Abraham Lincoln's Birthday—12th; Presidents' Day—3rd Monday; March: Bird Day—21; May: Memorial Day—4th Monday; July: Independence Day—4th; September: Labor Day—1st Monday; October: Columbus Day—2nd Monday; Youth Honor Day—31st; November: Veterans' Day—11th; Thanksgiving—4th Thursday; December: Christmas—25th; Admission Day—28th.

Official State Flag

The state flag of Iowa was adopted in 1921 after years of debate as to whether a flag other than the U.S. flag was needed. The flag has three vertical stripes of blue, white, and red. On the white stripe is the state name below an eagle holding a blue ribbon with the state motto.

Festivals and Events

January: Bald Eagle Appreciation Days, Keokuk; March: St. Patrick's Day Celebration, Emmetsburg; April: Civil War Reenactment, Keokuk; May: Pella Tulip Time Fest, Pella; June: Grant Wood Art Festival, Stone City-Anamosa; Trek Fest, Riverside; Scandinavian Dager Celebration, Eagle Grove; July: Mississippi Valley Blues Festival, Davenport; Nordic Fest, Decorah; August: Iowa State Fair, Des Moines; National Hobo Convention, Britt; September: Gesundheit, Westphalia; Czech Village Festival, Cedar Rapids; October: Covered Bridge Festival, Madison County; November: Jule Fest, Elk Horn.

Iowa Compared to States in Its Region.

Resident Pop. in Metro Areas: 5th; Pop. Percent Increase: 6th; Pop. Over 65: 1st; Infant Mortality: 5th; School Enroll. Increase: 7th; High School Grad. and Up: 4th; Violent Crime: 4th; Hazardous Waste Sites: 3d; Unemployment: 4th; Median Household Income: 4th; Persons Below Poverty: 4th; Energy Costs Per Person: 5th.

West North Central Region

	Population	Capital
Minnesota	4,517,000	St. Paul
Iowa	2,814,000	Des Moines
Missouri	5,234,000	Jefferson City
North Dakota	635,000	Bismarck
South Dakota	715,000	Pierre
Nebraska	1,607,000	Lincoln
Kansas	2,531,000	Topeka

Iowa's Finances

Households: 1,064,000; Income Per Capita Current Dollars: $18,287; Change Per Capita Income 1980 to 1992: 95.7% (31st in U.S.); State Expenditures: $6,711,000,000; State Revenues: $6,519,000,000; Personal Income Tax: 0.4 to 9.98%; Federal Income Taxes Paid Per Capita: $1,524; Sales Tax: 4% (food and prescription drugs exempt).

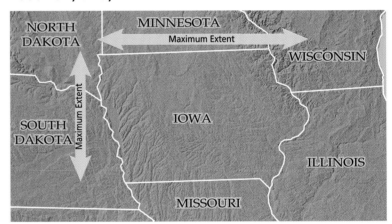

Location, Size, and Boundaries

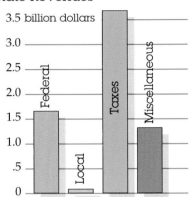

Location. Iowa is located in the West North Central region of the United States. It is bounded on four sides by land. The geographic center of Iowa is lat. 41° 57.7' N; long. 93° 23.1' W.

Size. Iowa is the 25th largest state in terms of size. Its area is 56,290 sq. mi. (145,791 km2). Inland water covers 349 sq. mi. (904 km2).

Boundaries. Minnesota, 264 mi. (425 km); Wisconsin, 93 mi. (150 km); Illinois, 219 mi. (352 km); Missouri, 244 mi. (393 km); Nebraska, 200 mi. (322 km); South Dakota, 131 mi. (211 km).

Geographic Extent. The north/south extent of Iowa is 210 mi. (338 km). The state extends 324 mi. (521 km) to the east/west.

Facts about Iowa. Origin of Name: Indian word meaning "beautiful land" or "one who puts to sleep"; Nickname: The Hawkeye State; Motto: "Our liberties we prize and our rights we will maintain"; Abbreviations: Ia. (traditional), IA (postal); State Bird: Eastern goldfinch; State Tree: oak; State Flower: wild rose; State Song: "The Song of Iowa," words by S. H. M. Byers and sung to the tune of "Dor Tannenbaum."

Iowa Compared to Other States. Resident Pop. in Metro Areas: 40th; Pop. Percent Increase: 39th; Pop. Over 65: 3d; Infant Mortality: 37th; School Enroll. Increase: 45th; High School Grad. and Up: 13th; Violent Crime: 39th; Haz. Waste Sites: 19th; Unemployment: 46th; Med. Household Income: 36th; Persons Below Poverty: 29th; Energy Costs Per Person: 32d.

Sources of Information. Tourism: Tourism Division, Department of Economic Development, 200 East Grand Avenue, Des Moines, IA 50309. Economy, Government & History: Public Information Office, General Assembly, State Capitol, Des Moines, IA 50319.

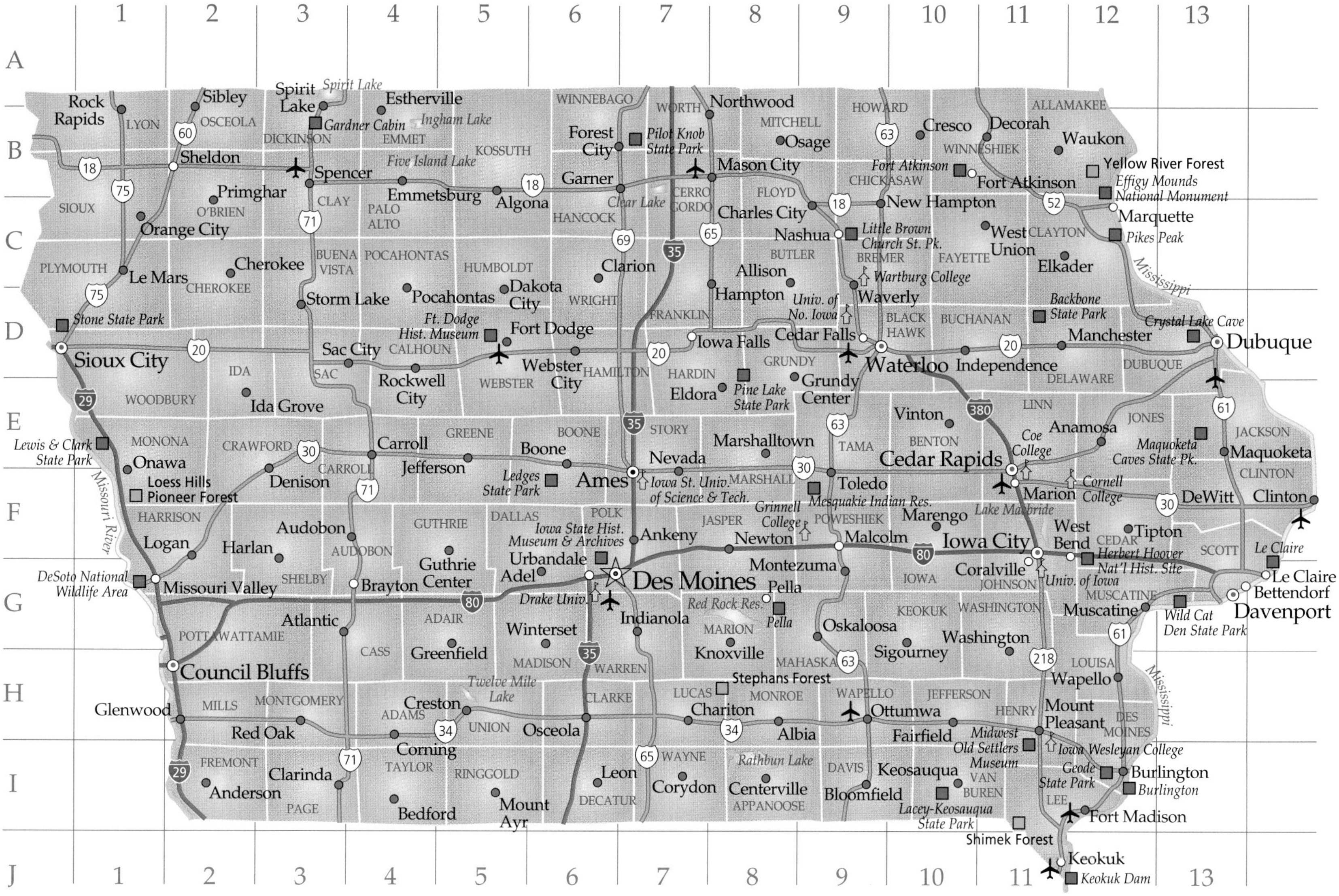

Iowa

Map grid columns 1–13, rows A–J.

Cities and features (map labels):

Rock Rapids, Sibley, Spirit Lake, Spirit Lake, Estherville, WINNEBAGO, Northwood, HOWARD, Cresco, Decorah, ALLAMAKEE
LYON, OSCEOLA, 60, Gardner Cabin, Ingham Lake, WORTH, MITCHELL, 63, WINNESHIEK, Waukon
DICKINSON, EMMET, KOSSUTH, Forest City, Pilot Knob State Park, Osage, Fort Atkinson, Yellow River Forest
Sheldon, 18, Spencer, Five Island Lake, Garner, Garner, Mason City, CHICKASAW, Fort Atkinson, Effigy Mounds National Monument
75, Primghar, 71, Emmetsburg, Algona, 18, Clear Lake, CERRO GORDO, FLOYD, 18, New Hampton, 52, Marquette
SIOUX, O'BRIEN, PALO ALTO, Charles City, Nashua, West Union, CLAYTON, Pikes Peak
Orange City, CLAY, HANCOCK, 65, Allison, Little Brown Church St. Pk., BREMER, FAYETTE, Elkader
PLYMOUTH, Le Mars, Cherokee, POCAHONTAS, HUMBOLDT, Clarion, BUTLER, Hampton, Wartburg College, Backbone State Park, Crystal Lake Cave
CHEROKEE, BUENA VISTA, Storm Lake, Pocahontas, Dakota City, WRIGHT, FRANKLIN, Univ. of No. Iowa, Waverly, BUCHANAN, Manchester, Dubuque
Stone State Park, Ft. Dodge Hist. Museum, Fort Dodge, Iowa Falls, Cedar Falls, BLACK HAWK, 20, DUBUQUE, 61
Sioux City, 20, Sac City, CALHOUN, Webster City, HAMILTON, 20, GRUNDY, Waterloo, Independence, DELAWARE
29, IDA, SAC, Rockwell City, WEBSTER, Eldora, Pine Lake State Park, Grundy Center, Vinton, LINN, Anamosa, JONES
WOODBURY, Ida Grove, GREENE, BOONE, STORY, HARDIN, 63, BENTON, Coe College, Maquoketa Caves State Pk., JACKSON, Maquoketa
Lewis & Clark State Park, MONONA, CRAWFORD, Carroll, Boone, Nevada, Marshalltown, TAMA, Cedar Rapids, 380, Cornell College, CLINTON
Onawa, Loess Hills Pioneer Forest, 30, Jefferson, Ledges State Park, Ames, Iowa St. Univ. of Science & Tech., MARSHALL, Toledo, Mesquakie Indian Res., Marion, 30, DeWitt, Clinton
HARRISON, Denison, CARROLL, 71, DALLAS, Iowa State Hist. Museum & Archives, JASPER, Grinnell College, POWESHIEK, Marengo, Lake Macbride, West Branch, CEDAR, Tipton, SCOTT, Le Claire
Logan, Harlan, Audobon, GUTHRIE, Ankeny, Newton, Malcolm, 80, Iowa City, Herbert Hoover Nat'l Hist. Site, Le Claire
Missouri Valley, SHELBY, AUDUBON, Guthrie Center, Urbandale, Adel, Des Moines, Montezuma, Malcolm, Iowa City, Coralville, Univ. of Iowa, MUSCATINE, Bettendorf
DeSoto National Wildlife Area, Brayton, ADAIR, Drake Univ., Pella, Pella, KEOKUK, WASHINGTON, JOHNSON, Muscatine, Wild Cat Den State Park, Davenport
Atlantic, Winterset, Indianola, Red Rock Res., MARION, Oskaloosa, Washington, 61, 218
POTTAWATTAMIE, CASS, Greenfield, MADISON, WARREN, Knoxville, MAHASKA, Sigourney, LOUISA, Wapello
Council Bluffs, 35, CLARKE, LUCAS, Chariton, MONROE, Stephans Forest, WAPELLO, JEFFERSON, HENRY, Mount Pleasant
Glenwood, MILLS, MONTGOMERY, Creston, ADAMS, Osceola, 34, Albia, Ottumwa, Fairfield, Midwest Old Settlers Museum, Iowa Wesleyan College, DES MOINES
Red Oak, Corning, UNION, 34, 65, WAYNE, DAVIS, Keosauqua, VAN BUREN, Geode State Park, Burlington
29, FREMONT, Clarinda, TAYLOR, RINGGOLD, Leon, Corydon, Centerville, Bloomfield, Rathbun Lake, Lacey-Keosauqua State Park, LEE, Fort Madison
Anderson, PAGE, Bedford, Mount Ayr, DECATUR, APPANOOSE, Shimek Forest, Keokuk, Keokuk Dam

Scale

0 20 40 60 mi.

20 0 20 40 60 80 km

Legend

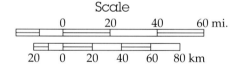

⭐ State capitol   ⬛ Major cultural attractions

⊙ Cities over 35,000 pop.   ◻ State Parks

○ Other significant cities   Ⓦ Welcome Centers

● County Seats   ⛨ Major colleges and universities

Major Cities

Ames	F-7	Davenport	G-13	Mason City	B-8
Ankeny	F-7	Des Moines	G-6	Muscatine	G-12
Bettendorf	G-13	Dubuque	D-13	Newton	F-8
Boone	E-6	Fort Dodge	D-5	Oskaloosa	G-9
Burlington	I-12	Fort Madison	I-12	Ottumwa	H-9
Cedar Falls	D-9	Indianola	G-7	Sioux City	D-1
Cedar Rapids	F-11	Iowa City	F-11	Spencer	B-3
Clinton	F-14	Keokuk	J-11	Urbandale	G-6
Coralville	F-11	Marion	F-11	Waterloo	D-9
Council Bluffs	H-2	Marshalltown	E-8	W. Des Moines	G-6

⬛ **Backbone State Park.** Limestone bluffs and scenic drives. (D-11)

⬛ **Burlington.** In 1838 was the temporary capital of the state. (I-12)

⬛ **Crystal Lake Cave.** Cave with underground streams and lakes. (D-13)

⬛ **DeSoto National Wildlife Refuge.** Wilson Island State Recreation Area. (G-1)

⬛ **Effigy Mounds National Monument.** Prehistoric Indian mounds. (B-12)

⬛ **Fort Atkinson Monument State Park.** Pioneer fort built in 1840 with barracks. (B-10)

⬛ **Fort Dodge Historical Museum.** Replica of fort built in 1850 with pioneer exhibits. (D-5)

⬛ **Gardner Cabin Historic Site.** Restored log cabin built in 1856. (B-3)

⬛ **Geode State Park.** Unusual rock formations. (I-12)

⬛ **Herbert Hoover National Historic Site.** Birthplace of the former president. (F-12)

⬛ **Iowa State Historical Museum and Archives.** Museum of 19th-century farm life. (F-6)

⬛ **Keokuk Dam.** Dam and lock on the Mississippi River. (J-12)

⬛ **Lacey-Keosauqua State Park.** Site of a prehistoric Indian village. (I-10)

⬛ **Le Claire.** Birthplace of William Cody (Buffalo Bill). (F-14)

⬛ **Ledges State Park.** Site of a wildlife research station. (F-6)

⬛ **Lewis and Clark State Park.** Water and winter sports. (E-1)

⬛ **Little Brown Church in the Vale.** Historic church dedicated in 1864. (C-9)

⬛ **Maquoketa Caves State Park.** Caves and natural bridge with 50 foot (15 m) arch. (E-13)

⬛ **Mesquakie Indian Reservation.** Only Indian reservation in Iowa. (F-9)

⬛ **Midwest Old Settlers and Threshers Heritage Museum.** Antique farm equipment and a steam engine collection. (H-11)

⬛ **Pella.** Historical Dutch farm village. (G-8)

⬛ **Pikes Peak State Park.** Site of the famed Bridal Veil Falls. (C-12)

⬛ **Pilot Knob State Park.** Glacial formations. (B-7)

⬛ **Pine Lake State Park.** Site of Indian mounds. (D-8)

⬛ **Stone State Park.** Scenic view of three states. (D-1)

⬛ **Wild Cat Den State Park.** Mill and dam constructed in 1848. (G-13)

Weather Facts

Record High Temperature: 118° F (48° C) on July 19, 1930, at Keokuk; Record Low Temperature: -47° F (-44° C) on January 11, 1908, at Washta; Average January Temperature: 20° F (-7° C); Average July Temperature: 76° F (24° C); Average Yearly Precipitation: 33 in. (84 cm).

Environmental Facts

Air Pollution Rank: 22d; Water Pollution Rank: 19th; Total Yearly Industrial Pollution: 35,419,451 lbs.; Industrial Pollution Rank: 24th; Hazardous Waste Sites: 20; Hazardous Sites Rank: 18th; Landfill Capacity: adequate; Fresh Water Supply: large surplus; Daily Residential Water Consumption: 131 gals. per capita; Endangered Species: Aquatic Species (4)—pearlymussel, Higgins' eye; Birds (4)—eagle, bald; Mammals (1)—bat, Indiana; Other Species (1)—snail, Iowa pleistocene; Plants (6)—bush-clover, prairie.

Environmental Quality

Iowa residents generate 2.3 million tons of solid waste each year, or approximately 1,600 pounds per capita. Landfill capacity in Iowa will be exhausted in more than 12 years. The state has 21 hazardous waste sites. Annual greenhouse gas emissions in Iowa total 68.5 million tons, or 24.2 tons per capita. Industrial sources in Iowa release approximately 26.7 thousand tons of toxins, 373.0 thousand tons of acid precipitation-producing substances, and 1.2 million tons of smog-producing substances into the atmosphere each year.

The state has 1,700 acres within the National Park System; the largest area within the state is Herbert Hoover National Historic Site. State parks cover just over 51,000 acres, attracting 12.1 million visitors per year.

Iowa spends approximately 1.4 percent of its budget, or approximately $31 per capita, on environmental and natural resources. Iowa representatives in the U.S. House voted in favor of national environmental legislation 52 percent of the time, while U.S. senators did so 54 percent of the time.

Average Monthly Weather

Des Moines	Jan	Feb	Mar	Apr	May	Jun	Jul	Aug	Sep	Oct	Nov	Dec	Yearly
Maximum Temperature °F	27.0	33.2	44.2	61.0	72.6	81.8	86.2	84.0	75.7	65.0	47.6	33.7	59.3
Minimum Temperature °F	10.1	15.8	26.0	39.9	51.6	61.4	66.3	63.7	54.4	43.3	29.5	17.6	40.0
Days of Precipitation	7.4	7.3	10.0	10.5	11.2	10.6	9.1	9.2	8.7	7.6	7.0	7.9	106.5

Flora and Fauna

In the past, the majority of Iowa's land consisted of prairies and woodlands. Today, however, much of that land is used for farming. Many types of deciduous trees grow near Iowa's rivers and lakes. Hickory, oak, and walnut trees are all common hardwoods. Other trees include willow and cottonwood, which exist primarily on the edges of rivers and lakes. Fir and white pine, two conifers, grow in the northeastern part of Iowa. Wildflowers bloom in Iowa all year long. Bloodroots and violets are two spring flowers. Other seasonal wildflowers include purple phlox, blooming in summer, and sunflowers, blooming in the fall.

The white-tailed deer is Iowa's only common large animal. However, the state has many other smaller mammals such as bobcats, coyotes, and jackrabbits. Iowa's farmlands are popular nesting grounds for many birds, both native to the state and migratory. Iowa's game birds include pheasant and quail. Lakes and streams throughout the state contain many types of fishes such as crappie, walleye, and bluegill. Both bass and trout live mostly in northeast Iowa waterways.

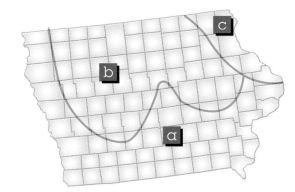

Physical Regions: (a) Dissected Till Plains; (b) Young Drift Plains; (c) Driftless Area.

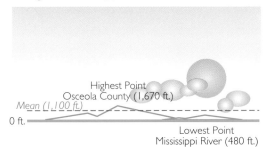

Highest Point
Osceola County (1,670 ft.)
Mean (1,100 ft.)
0 ft.
Lowest Point
Mississippi River (480 ft.)

Land Use

Cropland: 76.4%; Pasture: 10.9%; Rangeland: 0%; Forest: 5.2%; Urban: 4.8%; Other: 2.7%.

For more information about Iowa's environment, contact the Chief Environmental Officer, E. 9th and Grand Aves., Wallace Bldg., Des Moines, IA 50319-0034.

Topography

Almost the entire state of Iowa is part of the Central Plain that is the heart of the Cornbelt that spreads across the Midwest from Nebraska to Ohio. Iowa has the richest topsoil of all these states, making the entire state well suited to agriculture. The northern part of Iowa has particularly fertile soil, warm and moist, predominantly composed of organically rich black clay that is almost completely level. It is located within the Young Drift Plains physical region. Many of the natural lakes in Iowa are found in this area. Most of the natural wetlands that were also a part of the topography in the north have been filled in and turned into farmland. The highest point in the state can be found in the northwest: a hill measuring 1,670 ft. (509 m) above sea level.

The northeastern part of the state, near the Mississippi River, is known as the Driftless Area physical region. This area has rough forest-covered hills, rather than the flat plains of the rest of Iowa. Soil is a warm and moist gray/brown clay. The plains in the southern part of Iowa are located in the Dissected Till Plains physical region, and consist of gentle hills and valleys. Soil is typically warm and moist black organically rich clay. The lowest elevation in the state is also found in this region.

Climate

Iowa, in the middle of the United States, has a continental climate. As a result of high variation in temperature as well as precipitation, the state experiences hot, humid summers and cold winters. Temperatures in the summer can reach over 100 degrees F, and winter temperatures can drop to -10 degrees F. Sioux City, in northwestern Iowa, has average January and July temperatures of 18 degrees F and 74 degrees F. Moving southward, average January and July temperatures measure 24 degrees F and 77 degrees F.

Precipitation varies slightly between northern and southern Iowa. The south receives about 36 inches of annual precipitation, while the north receives an average of 25 inches. Snow often covers northern Iowa between January and March.

Because of Iowa's highly variable precipitation, the state is prone to flooding as well as droughts. One of the worst floods in recent history occurred in 1993.

Hydrology

Iowa's eastern and western borders are formed by two of the largest rivers in the United States. The Mississippi River creates the entire eastern boundary with Wisconsin and Illinois. The Missouri River forms the western boundary with Nebraska, while the Big Sioux forms that portion of the western border shared with South Dakota.

The most important river within the state is the Des Moines, which runs for about 474 miles (763 km). It begins in the central part of the state and flows southeast, draining into the Mississippi River at the border of Iowa, Missouri, and Illinois. Many other rivers contribute to Iowa's important agriculture industry. Some of these are the Wapsipinicon, the Cedar, and the Nisanabotna.

Southern Iowa has several large man-made lakes, including Rathburn Reservoir and Saylorville Reservoir. The north has smaller natural lakes such as Storm Lake and Clear Lake.

Iowa's History

Iowa's First People

Tribes of Paleo-Indians roamed the area of what is now Iowa starting some thirteen thousand years ago. They were hunters but left little evidence of their culture.

From about 1000 B.C. to A.D. 700, people of the Woodland culture (or Temple Mound Builders) occupied much of the Ohio Valley, including Iowa. The Adena, the earlier of these groups, disappeared around A.D. 200, while the Hopewell coexisted for some time with the Adena, outlasting them by some five hundred years. It is not clear where these peoples came from, whether they warred against each other or what eventually befell them. The Mississippian Mound Builder culture, represented by the Oneonta in Iowa, followed the Woodland people. When whites arrived, there were Sioux Indians in the western portion of Iowa, and Iowa and Illinois Indians in the east.

European Exploration

Louis Jolliet and Jacques Marquette, passing through Iowa on a voyage down the Mississippi River in 1673, claimed the territory (as part of the Louisiana Territory) for France. It was more than one hundred years (1788) before Julien Dubuque, a French Canadian trapper, established the first permanent white settlement (a lead-mining town) in Iowa.

In 1762, France had transferred title of the Louisiana Territory to Spain, only to reacquire it in 1800 and sell it to the United States three years later. The United States intended the area that would become Iowa to be future Indian territory. The government relocated the Sauk, Fox, and Winnebago tribes from Wisconsin and Illinois (being settled by white farmers) to these lands. However, the relentless westward drive of white settlement soon encroached on Iowa. After several decades of resistance (led by Sauk chieftain Black Hawk), the Sauk and Fox were forced to abandon their lands in 1832 (after defeat in the Black Hawk War) and move westward. Further cession of Indian lands continued, the last being the transfer of Sioux land to the government in 1851, although some confrontations continued, culminating in the Spirit Lake Massacre of 1857 in which forty-two whites were killed.

Statehood

After Missouri was accepted into the Union in 1821, Iowa's territorial status became uncertain. In 1834 it came under the jurisdiction of Michigan. Two years later it became part of the just-created Territory of Wisconsin, and in 1838 the Territory of Iowa was created with Iowa City as its capital. Robert Lucas, the territorial governor, drafted ambitious plans to extend Iowa's boundaries to include southern Minnesota. Even though this land was not included in the final boundaries of the state, Iowa was admitted to the Union (paired with the slave state of Florida) in 1846. The capital was moved to Des Moines in 1857.

Shortly after its creation as a free state, Iowa became part of the route of the Underground Railroad, transporting escaped slaves from the South through the state to the Mississippi River. During the Civil War, Iowa was a Union state and contributed to the Northern cause.

From its creation until the 1960s, Iowa had been dominated by conservative Republicans in state politics, but Democrats have made strong inroads since then.

Industrialization

With some of the most fertile topsoil in the country, Iowa from the start attracted settlers who were interested in farming. By the second half of the nineteenth century, after forcing Indians off the land, white settlers had developed much of the state for agricultural production. A large percentage of those working the land were commercial farmers, and the vast areas under cultivation testified to the dominant role agriculture played in the state's economy. By the late nineteenth century, corn had become the leading agricultural commodity in Iowa, much of it feed corn for hogs.

This period also saw the development of eastern Iowa as a manufacturing center. The main focus was the production of farm equipment such as tractors. This production also led the way for the mechanization of the farm so as to be able to produce larger quantities of foodstuffs for a growing United States population.

Although agriculture continues to play an important role, manufacturing of machinery, electrical equipment, and other products since World War II has diversified the state's economy. During the late 1970s and early 1980s Iowa farmers suffered with the downturn in the economy. Highly developed areas such as Iowa City, Des Moines, and Cedar Rapids developed as high technology centers, and have made small inroads in improving the local economy. The state has also seen efforts to give the economy a boost through gambling.

Iowa's Agrarian Movements

Many of Iowa's population were rural farmers. Finding themselves at the mercy of railroads, to get their products to market, and government regulation, they (and other farm states) organized an agrarian reform movement in the second half of the nineteenth century. Founded in 1867, the National Grange evolved from a social and educational forum into a political movement partially responsible for laws regulating railroads and grain storage facilities.

In 1876, the national Greenback Party was formed, which took up much of the agenda of the Grange movement and pressed for reforms such as federal regulation of interstate commerce that were of interest to farmers. The Populist Party, founded in 1892, continued this call for reform with agrarian protests against eastern industrialists— control of commerce.

Important Events

1673 Louis Jolliet and Jacques Marquette pass through Iowa on trip down the Mississippi and claim area for France.

1762 France transfers title of Louisiana Territory, including Iowa, to Spain.

1788 Julien Dubuque establishes first permanent white settlement.

1803 Iowa becomes U.S. territory as part of the Louisiana Purchase.

1812 Iowa becomes part of the Missouri Territory.

1824 Sauk and Fox Indians, having been relocated from Wisconsin and Illinois, cede land to Iowa.

1832 Black Hawk War with Indians results in complete takeover of Sauk and Fox lands by the state.

1834 Iowa is placed under the jurisdiction of Michigan, and two years later it becomes part of the Territory of Wisconsin.

1836 *The Dubuque Visitor* becomes the first newspaper in Iowa.

1838 Territory of Iowa is created by the U.S. Congress.

1846 Iowa admitted to the Union as the twenty-ninth state.

1857 Spirit Lake Massacre results in the death of forty-two whites at the hands of the Sioux. As a result, the capital is relocated to Des Moines.

1868 State constitution is amended to enfranchise blacks

1869 Davenport and Council Bluffs are linked by transstate railroad.

1884 State legislature enacts Prohibition Law.

1892 James Weaver is the Populist candidate for president.

1928 Herbert Hoover elected President of the United States as a Republican.

1948 Iowa leads the nation in the production of corn, hogs, poultry, and eggs.

1960 Urban population exceeds rural for the first time.

1982 Unemployment rate of 8.3% is highest since the Great Depression.

1993 Massive flooding of the Missouri and Mississippi Rivers, brought on by heavy spring rains, devastates the state.

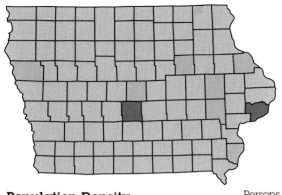

Population Density

Population density for the state of Iowa was 49.7 persons per square mile in 1990 (19.2 per km2). Average U.S. density was 70.3 persons per square mile in 1990 (27.3 per km2). Habitation is most dense around the urban areas of Des Moines and Davenport. Other high density areas include Sioux City, Dubuque, Burlington, and Cedar Rapids.

Persons Per Square Mile
- 10.0 to 99.9
- 100.0 to 249.9
- 250.0 to 749.9

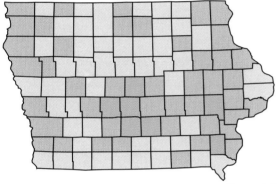

Population Change

The 1990 population figure for the state of Iowa was 2,776,755. This is a –4.7 percent decrease from 2,913,808 in 1980. The next decade will show a loss with a population of 2.5 million or a –8.2 percent decrease. Most of the state with the exception of a few counties around Des Moines have seen a decrease in population in the last decade.

Percent Change 1980 to 1990
- -31.9 to –10.0%
- -9.9 to 0.0%
- 0.1 to 19.9%

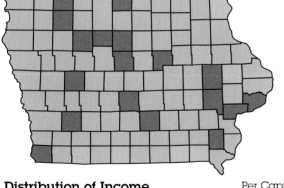

Distribution of Income

The per capita income for the state of Iowa (current dollars) was $18,287 in 1992. This is a 95.7 percent increase from $9,346 in 1980. Income distribution in the state is even with no real high income areas versus low income areas. As can be seen in this map even the cities do not show areas of high incomes as compared with counties with little or no urban areas.

Per Capita Income (000s) (Current Dollars)
- $10.0 to 12.9
- $13.0 to 15.9
- $16.0 to 19.9

Population Projections

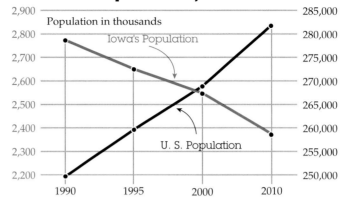

Population in thousands
Iowa's Population
U. S. Population

Population Change

Year	Population
1950	2,621,000
1960	2,756,000
1970	2,832,000
1980	2,913,808
1990	2,776,755
2000	2,549,000
2010	2,382,000

Period	Change
1950–1970	8.1%
1970–1980	2.9%
1980–1990	–4.7%
1990–2000	–8.2%

Population Facts

State Population, 1993: 2,814,000
Rank: 30
Population 2000: 2,549,000 (Rank 31)
Density: 49.7 per sq. mi. (19.2 per km²)
Distribution: 60.6% urban, 39.4% rural
Population Under 5 Years Old: 6.9%
Population Under 18 Years Old: 26.1%
Population Over 65 Years Old: 15.4%
Median Age: 34.0
Number of Households: 1,064,000
Average Persons Per Household: 2.52
Average Persons Per Family: 3.05
Female Heads of Households: 3.07%
Population That Is Married: 22.68%
Birth Rate: 14.2 per 1,000 population
Death Rate: 9.7 per 1,000 population
Births to Teen Mothers: 10.2%
Marriage Rate: 8.7 per 1,000 population
Divorce Rate: 3.9 per 1,000 population
Violent Crime Rate: 303 per 100,000 pop.
Population on Social Security: 18.9%
Percent Voting for President: 65.3%

Population Profile

Rank. Iowa ranks 30th among U.S. states in terms of population with 2,814,000 citizens.

Minority Population. The state's minority population is 4.1 percent. The state's male to female ratio for 1990 was 93.91 males for every 100 females. It was below the national average of 95.22 males for every 100 females.

Growth. The state's population is decreasing and is expected to be 2.4 million by the year 2010.

Government

Capital: Des Moines (established 1857).
Statehood: Became 29th state on Dec. 28, 1846.
Number of Counties: 99.
Supreme Court Justices: 9, 8-year term.
State Senators: 50, 4-year term.
State Legislators: 100, 2-year term.
United States Senators: 2.
United States Representatives: 5.
Electoral Votes: 7.
State Constitution: Adopted 1857.

Iowa's Famous Citizens

Carson, Johnny (b. 1925). Television talk-show host. Took over "The Tonight Show" from Jack Paar in 1962 and reigned for 30 years.

Farmer, Art (b. 1928). Jazz flugelhornist. Played with Clifford Brown, Sonny Rollins, and others, as well as his own Jazztet.

Feller, Bob (b. 1918). Hall of Fame baseball pitcher. Cleveland Indians star pitched 3 no-hitters and 12 one-hitters.

Friedman, Esther Pauline and Pauline Esther (b. 1918). Twins became advice columnists Ann Landers and Abigail Van Buren.

Glaspell, Susan (1876–1948). Writer. Won the Pulitzer Prize for her play *Alison's House* in 1931.

Palmer, Daniel D. (1845–1913). Founder of chiropractic (spinal adjustment). Published *The Science of Chiropractic* in 1906.

Wallace, Henry (1888–1965). Served as vice president of the U.S. (1940–1944) and as secretaries of agriculture and commerce.

Wayne, John (1907–1979). Actor. Known for westerns and war films. Won an Academy Award for his role in the film *True Grit* (1969).

Older Citizens. The state's population older than 65 was 426,106 in 1990. It grew 9.94% from 387,584 in 1980.

Younger Citizens. The number of children (under 18 years of age) was 719 thousand in 1990. This represents 25.9 percent of the state's population. The state's school aged population was 467 thousand in 1990. It is expected to decrease to 430 thousand by the year 2000. This represents a –7.92% change.

Urban/Rural. 60.6% of the population of the state live in urban areas while 39.4% live in rural areas.

Largest Cities. Iowa has nine cities with a population greater than 35,000. The populations of the state's largest centers are (starting from the most populous) Des Moines (193,187), Cedar Rapids (108,751), Davenport (95,333), Sioux City (80,505), Waterloo (66,467), Iowa City (59,738), Dubuque (57,546), Council Bluffs (54,315), Ames (47,198), Cedar Falls (34,298), West De Moines (31,702), Clinton (29,201), Mason City (29,040), Bettendorf (28,132), Burlington (27,208), Fort Dodge (25,894), Marshalltown (25,178), Ottumwa (24,488), Urbandale (23,500), Muscatine (22,881), Marion (20,403), and Ankeny (18,482).

Iowa

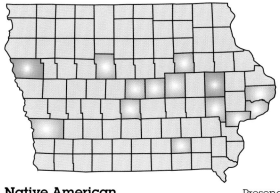

Native American

The Native American population in Iowa was 7,349 in 1990. This was an increase of 16.45 percent from 6,311 in 1980. Many Native Americans can be found living in the one Indian reservation located in the state, the Sac and Fox Indian Reservation. Iowa is named after the Iowa tribe, which is also located in the state.

Presence of Native Americans

Minor

Moderate

Nationalities

African	1,643
American	86,754
Arab	3,200
Austrian	2,637
Czech	40,445
Dutch	109,073
English	229,297
Finnish	1,439
German	1,178,945
Greek	4,844
Hungarian	2,079
Irish	263,514
Italian	29,051
Norwegian	100,866
Polish	18,569
Portuguese	656
Russian	4,492
Scottish	29,792
Slovak	6,740
Swedish	73,172
Welsh	14,421
West Indian	345

Statewide Ethnic Composition

Over 96 percent of the population of Iowa is white. The largest nationalities in this racial group are German, Irish, and English. The next largest group is African Americans, followed by Hispanics, Asians, and Native Americans. Slightly over 86,000 people claim to be American and acknowledge no other nationality.

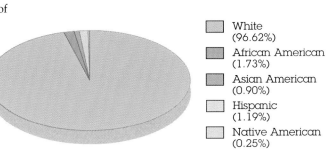

White (96.62%)

African American (1.73%)

Asian American (0.90%)

Hispanic (1.19%)

Native American (0.25%)

Education Facts

Total Students 1990: 478,486	Mean SAT Score 1991 Verbal: 515
Number of School Districts: 431	Mean SAT Score 1991 Math: 578
Expenditure Per Capita on Education 1990: $777	Average Teacher's Salary 1992: $29,200
Expenditure Per Capita K–12 1990: $728	Rank Teacher's Salary: 32d in U.S.
Expenditure Per Pupil 1990: $4,877	High School Graduates 1990: 36,200
Total School Enrollment 1990–1991: 483,652	Total Number of Public Schools: 1,607
Rank of Expenditures Per Student: 25th in the U.S.	Number of Teachers 1990: 30,806
African American Enrollment: 2.7%	Student/Teacher Ratio: 15.7
Hispanic Enrollment: 1.1%	Staff Employed in Public Schools: 56,826
Asian/Pacific Islander Enrollment: 1.3%	Pupil/Staff Ratio: 8.4
Native American Enrollment: 0.3%	Staff/Teacher Ratio: 1.9

Education

Attainment: 83 percent of population 25 years or older were high school graduates in 1989, earning Iowa a ranking of 9th in the United States; 17 percent of the state's population had completed college; Institutions of Higher Education: The largest universities and colleges in the state include the University of Iowa, Iowa City; Iowa State University of Science and Technology, Ames; University of Northern Iowa, Cedar Falls; Drake University, Des Moines; Morningside College, Sioux City; Luther College, Decorah; Coe College, Cedar Rapids; Grinnell College, Grinnell. Expenditures per Student: Expenditure increased 74% between 1985 and 1990. Projected High School Graduations: 1998 (31,055), 2004 (29,731); Total Revenues for Education from Federal Sources: $100 million; Total Revenues for Education from State Sources: $927 million; Total Revenues for Education from Local Sources: $930 million; Average Annual Salaries for Public School Principals: $41,788; Largest School Districts in State: Des Moines Independent Community School District, 29,760 students, 139th in the United States.

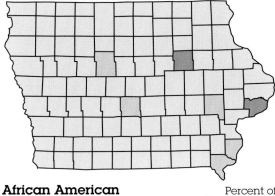

African American

The African American population in Iowa was 48,090 in 1990. This was an increase of 13.88 percent from 42,228 in 1980. The highest percentages can be found in Black County in the northeast and in Davenport in Scott County in the east. Twenty-eight percent of the African Americans in the state reside in Des Moines.

Percent of County Population

0.00 to 1.99%

2.00 to 4.99%

5.00 to 9.99%

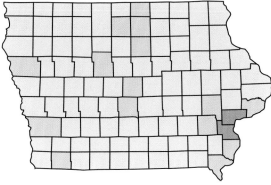

Hispanic[++]

The Hispanic population in Iowa was 32,647 in 1990. This is an increase of 27.85 percent from 25,536 persons in 1980. The highest percentages of Hispanics in the state can be found in Muscatine and Louisa counties just south and west of Davenport. Another 15 percent of the Hispanic population can be found in Des Moines.

Percent of County Population

0.00 to 0.99%

1.00 to 2.99%

3.00 to 9.99%

[++]A person of Mexican, Puerto Rican, Cuban, or other Spanish culture or origin regardless of race.

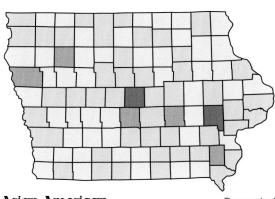

Asian American

The Asian American population in Iowa was 25,476 in 1990. This is an increase of 88.89 percent from 25,476 persons in 1980. High concentrations of Asian Americans can be found in Story and Johnson counties. Eighteen percent of the Asian Americans in the state can be found in Des Moines.

Percent of County Population

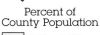

0.00 to 0.24%

0.25 to 0.99%

1.00 to 1.99%

2.00 to 4.99%

Agriculture

Iowa has 33.3 million farm acres. During the last 40 years, Iowa's farms have grown larger in size and fewer in number. In 1955, 193,000 farms were found in the state. Today, 100,000 remain.

Agriculture adds $5 billion to the state's gross product annually. The principal commodities in order of marketing receipts are hogs, corn, cattle, and soybeans.

Iowa is the nation's leading producer of corn, supplying about a fifth of the corn grown in the United States. Much of the corn becomes livestock feed. Hogs are the main livestock product in the state, and Iowa also leads the nation in this category, supplying about a fourth of the hogs raised in the United States. Cattle are also important in the state, and many of the other crops grown (alfalfa, soybeans, etc.) serve as cattle feed.

Transportation

In the early 20th century, Iowa's state government started a massive road-building project. Today, the state has 112,000 miles of highways and roads. Interstates run both north-south and east-west.

Iowa's waterways have always been an important transportation mode. The state has many river ports along the Mississippi River, including Davenport, Burlington, Fort Madison, and Keokuk. The Missouri River is also navigable along the Iowa border, making Iowa the only state bordered by two navigable rivers.

Railroads have operated in Iowa since the mid-19th century. Six different freight lines handle Iowa's cargo. A passenger line serves some larger Iowa cities. Des Moines has the state's busiest airport. However, several small airfields are located throughout the state.

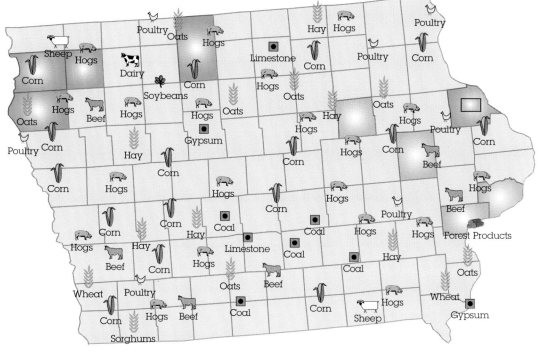

Major manufacturing areas
Major agricultural areas

Energy and Transportation Facts

Energy. Yearly Consumption: 937 tril. BTUs (residential, 23.5%; commercial, 15.6%; industrial, 37.0%; transportation, 24.0%); Annual Energy Expenditures Per Capita: $1,865; Nuclear Power Plants Located in State: 1; Source of Energy Consumed: Petroleum— 32.8%; Natural Gas— 24.9%; Coal— 36.7%; Hydroelectric Power—1.0%; Nuclear Power—4.7%.

Transportation. Highway Miles: 112,586 (interstates, 783; urban, 9,096; rural, 103,490); Average Yearly Auto Insurance: $379 (47th); Auto Fatalities Rank: 23d; Registered Motor Vehicles: 2,705,754; Workers in Carpools: 16.2%; Workers Using Public Trans: 1.2%.

Employment

Employment. Iowa employed 1.49 million people in 1993. Most work in wholesale and retail trade (319,900 persons or 21.5% of the workforce). Manufacturing accounts for 15.8% or 235,800 workers. Social and personal services account for 21.3% or 317,400 workers. Government employs 222,800 workers (15.0%). Construction employs 48,400 workers (3.3%). Transportation and utilities account for 3.8% or 56,600 persons. Agriculture employs 116,100 workers or 7.8%. Finance, real estate, and insurance account for 5.0% or 74,100 workers. Mining employs 2,100 people and accounts for only 0.1% of the workforce.

Unemployment. Unemployment has decreased to 4.0% in 1993 from a rate of 8.0% in 1985. Today's figure is lower than the national average of 6.8% as shown below.

Housing

Owner Occupied Units: 1,143,669; Average Age of Units: 39 years; Average Value of Housing Units: $45,900; Renter Occupied Units: 285,743; Median Monthly Rent: $336; Housing Starts: 12,100; Existing Home Sales: 53,500.

Economic Sectors

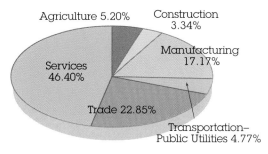

Agriculture 5.20%
Construction 3.34%
Manufacturing 17.17%
Services 46.40%
Trade 22.85%
Transportation–Public Utilities 4.77%

Economic Facts

Gross State Product: $53,000,000,000

Income Per Capita: $18,287

Disposable Personal Income: $16,089

Median Household Income: $26,229

Average Annual Pay, 1988: $19,810

Principal Industries: farm machinery, electrical equipment, food products, printing, transportation equipment, chemicals, publishing

Major Crops: corn, soybeans

Fish: Smallmouth Bass, Trout, Largemouth Bass, Crappies

Livestock: hogs, cattle

Non-Fuel Minerals: Limestone, Shale, Clay, sand, gravel

Organic Fuel Minerals: Coal

Civilian Labor Force: 1,516,000 (Women: 704,000)

Total Employed: 1,447,000 (Women: 676,000)

Median Value of Housing: $45,900

Median Contract Rent: $336 per month

Manufacturing

Iowa's manufacturing sector contributes approximately 21 percent of the state gross product each year. The overwhelming majority of manufacturing activity involves food processing of some sort. Machinery and electrical equipment production rank second and third after food processing.

Iowa's traditional food processing methods have been dramatically changed in the last 20 years. Many cities that were once important to food processing, such as Dubuque, have lost much business. Huge agri-businesses like ConAgra have taken over the industry with more efficient methods. However, Cedar Rapids and Sioux City are still leading cereal and popcorn producers, respectively.

Other important manufacturing cities include Davenport (farm equipment) and Newton (washers and dryers).

Unemployment Rate

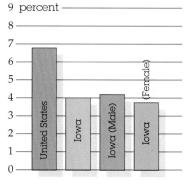

9 percent
8
7
6
5
4
3
2
1
0

United States | Iowa | Iowa (Male) | Iowa (Female)

KANSAS
The State of Kansas

Official State Seal

The Great Seal of Kansas was adopted in 1861 after Kansas achieved statehood. The state motto, *"Ad Astra Per Aspera,"* (To the Stars Through Difficulties), was added to symbolize the difficulties Kansas had in becoming a state. The date of the state's admission is printed along the bottom of the seal. A man plowing a field and a steamboat on a river grace the center of the seal.

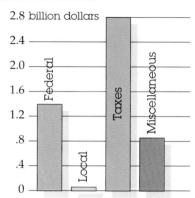

Legal Holidays

January: New Year's Day—1st, Martin Luther King, Jr., Day—3rd Monday; Admission Day—29th; February: Abraham Lincoln's Birthday—12th; Presidents' Day—3rd Monday; May: Memorial Day—4th Monday; July: Independence Day—4th; September: Labor Day—1st Monday; October: Columbus Day—2nd Monday; November: Veterans' Day—11th; Thanksgiving—4th Thursday; December: Christmas—25th.

Official State Flag

The state flag of Kansas has been in existence since 1927. Not many changes have been made since that time. The flag consists of the state seal and state name on a blue background. The official state flower, the sunflower, is included above the state seal.

Festivals and Events

March: Crappiethon USA, Milford Lake; St. Patrick's Day & Celebration, Wichita; April: Sand Creek Folk Life Fest, Newton; May: Wichita River Festival, Wichita; June: Beef Empire Days, Garden City; HutchFest, Hutchinson; July: Zoobalee, Garden City; Mexican Fiesta, Topeka; Mid American Native American Pow Wow, Wichita; August: Pony Express Festival, Hanover; September: Buffalo Bill Days, Leavenworth; Lenexa Spinach Festival, Lenexa; State Fair, Hutchinson; Asian Days Festival, Wichita; October: Apple Festival, Topeka; Oktoberfest, Manhattan; November: Festival of Carols, Topeka; December: Festival of Trees, Topeka.

Kansas Compared to States in Its Region.

Resident Pop. in Metro Areas: 3d; Pop. Percent Increase: 3d; Pop. Over 65: 6th; Infant Mortality: 3d; School Enroll. Increase: 3d; High School Grad. and Up: 3d; Violent Crime: 2d; Hazardous Waste Sites: 4th; Unemployment: 5th; Median Household Income: 2d; Persons Below Poverty: 4th; Energy Costs Per Person: 2d.

West North Central Region

	Population	Capital
Minnesota	4,517,000	St. Paul
Iowa	2,814,000	Des Moines
Missouri	5,234,000	Jefferson City
North Dakota	635,000	Bismarck
South Dakota	715,000	Pierre
Nebraska	1,607,000	Lincoln
Kansas	2,531,000	Topeka

Kansas's Finances

Households: 945,000; Income Per Capita Current Dollars: $19,376; Change Per Capita Income 1980 to 1992: 97.1% (28th in U.S.); State Expenditures: $5,052,000,000; State Revenues: $4,968,000,000; Personal Income Tax: 4.5 to 5.95%; Federal Income Taxes Paid Per Capita: $1,702; Sales Tax: 4.25% (prescription drugs exempt).

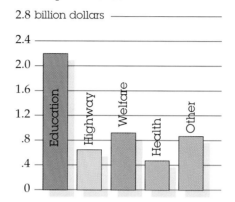

State Expenditures

State Revenues

Location, Size, and Boundaries

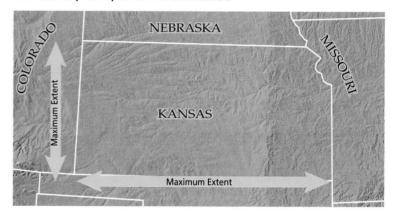

Location. Kansas is located in the West North Central region of the United States. It is bounded on four sides by land. The geographic center of Kansas is lat. 38° 29.9' N; long. 98° 41.9' W.

Size. Kansas is the 14th largest state in terms of size. Its area is 82,264 sq. mi. (213,064 km2). Inland water covers 477 sq. mi. (1,235 km2).

Boundaries. Nebraska, 357 mi. (575 km); Missouri, 244 mi. (393 km); Oklahoma, 411 mi. (661 km); Colorado, 207 mi. (333 km).

Geographic Extent. The north/south extent of Kansas is 208 mi. (335 km). The state extends 411 mi. (661 km) to the east/west.

Facts about Kansas. Origin of Name: After the *Kansa* or *Kaw* Indians, and means *"people of the south wind"*; Nickname: The Sunflower State; Motto: "To the stars through difficulties" (*Ad astra per aspera*); Abbreviations: Kans. or Kan. (traditional), KS (postal); State Bird: Western meadowlark; State Tree: Cottonwood; State Flower: sunflower; State Song: "Home on the Range," words by Brewster Higley and music by Daniel Kelley.

Kansas Compared to Other States. Resident Pop. in Metro Areas: 36th; Pop .Percent Increase: 31st; Pop. Over 65: 13th; Infant Mortality: 32d; School Enroll. Increase: 24th; High School Grad. and Up: 10th; Violent Crime: 30th; Haz. Waste Sites: 33d; Unemployment: 48th; Med. Household Income: 29th; Persons Below Poverty: 29th; Energy Costs Per Person: 8th.

Sources of Information. Tourism/Economy: Kansas Department of Commerce, Travel and Tourism Division, 400 Southwest 8th Street, 5th Floor, Topeka, KS 66603. Government: Division of Legislative Administrative Services, 511 South State House, Topeka, KS 66612. History: Kansas State Historical Society, 120 West 10th Street, Topeka, KS 66612.

■ Atchison. Birthplace of Amelia Earhart. (B-13)

■ Cedar Bluff State Park. Camping and boating. (D-4)

■ Cheyenne Bottoms. Wildlife refuge with hunting and fishing. (E-6)

■ Council Grove. Site of a treaty signed with the Indians to open up the first section of the Santa Fe Trail in 1825. (E-11)

■ Dodge City. Site of Boot Hill cemetery and re-created Dodge City circa 1870. (G-4)

■ Eisenhower Center. Childhood home, museum, and library of the former general and president. (D-9)

■ Fall River State Park. Camping, picnicking, and water sports. (G-11)

■ Fort Hays Historic Site. Fort built in 1865 to protect military roads and guard mail transports. (D-5)

■ Fort Larned National Historic Site. Established in 1859 to guard travelers on the Santa Fe Trail. (F-5)

■ Fort Leavenworth. Established in 1827, contains a federal penitentiary and the post museum. (C-14)

■ Fort Riley. The first territorial capitol (1855). (C-10)

■ Fort Scott National Historic Site. A military post established in 1842. (F-14)

■ Garden City. Site of the Lee Richardson Zoo and the Finney County Wildlife Area. (F-2)

■ Garden of Eden. Man-made art made out of cement, limestone, and wood. (D-6)

■ Hollenburg Pony Express Station. Only remaining original Pony Express station in the U.S. (A-10)

■ John Brown Memorial Park. The site of the log-cabin home of the Abolitionist (1850s). (E-14)

■ Kansas Cosmosphere and Space Center. Center dedicated to space travel. Includes a planetarium and Omnimax Theatre. (F-8)

■ Kanopolis State Park. Camping and boating. (D-7)

■ Kirwin National Wildlife Refuge. Reservoir for boating and swimming. (B-5)

■ Lebanon. Near geographic center of 48 states. (B-7)

■ Little House on the Prairie. Log cabin home of author Laura Ingalls Wilder. (H-12)

■ Meade. Dalton Gang Hideout and the Meade Co. Historical Society Museum. (H-3)

■ Meade's Ranch. Geodetic center of North America. (C-7)

■ Oakley. Site of chalk bluffs and pyramids containing reptilian fossils. (C-2)

■ Neosho State Lake. Artificial lake for boating, swimming, and other water sports. (G-13)

■ Pioneer Adobe House and Museum. Mennonite home built in 1876. (E-10)

■ Rock City. Over 200 sandstone formations. (D-8)

■ Sedgwick County Zoo. Native habitats for birds and animals. (G-9)

■ Shawnee Methodist Mission. Indian mission and school established in 1839. (D-14)

■ Tuttle Creek State Park. Camping, fishing, and picnicking. (C-10)

Land Use

Cropland: 56.6%; Pasture: 4.5%; Rangeland: 32.4%; Forest: 1.3%; Urban: 3.6%; Other: 1.6%.

Environmental Facts

Air Pollution Rank: 25th; Water Pollution Rank: 27th; Total Yearly Industrial Pollution: 27,567,951 lbs.; Industrial Pollution Rank: 27th; Hazardous Waste Sites: 11; Hazardous Sites Rank: 30th; Landfill Capacity: adequate; Fresh Water Supply: surplus; Daily Residential Water Consumption: 158 gals. per capita; Endangered Species: Aquatic Species (2)—madtom, Neosho; Birds (5)—crane, whooping; Mammals (2)—bat, gray; Other Species (1)—beetle, American burying; Plants (2)—milkweed, Mead's.

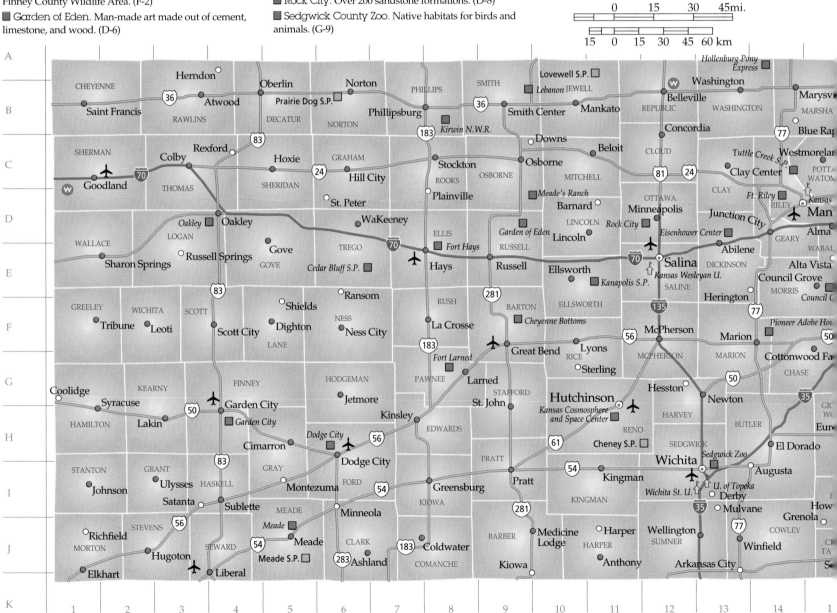

Average Monthly Weather

Topeka	Jan	Feb	Mar	Apr	May	Jun	Jul	Aug	Sep	Oct	Nov	Dec	Yearly
Maximum Temperature °F	36.3	43.0	53.2	66.5	76.0	84.6	89.6	88.5	80.7	69.9	53.8	41.8	65.3
Minimum Temperature °F	15.7	21.9	30.4	42.7	53.2	63.1	67.5	65.6	56.2	44.1	31.5	21.8	42.8
Days of Precipitation	6.1	6.2	8.7	9.7	11.4	10.4	8.6	8.3	7.5	6.7	6.1	6.2	95.9
Wichita													
Maximum Temperature °F	39.8	46.1	55.8	68.1	77.1	87.4	92.9	91.5	82.0	71.2	55.1	44.6	67.6
Minimum Temperature °F	19.4	24.1	32.4	44.5	54.6	64.7	69.8	67.9	59.2	46.9	33.5	24.2	45.1
Days of Precipitation	5.4	5.3	7.6	7.9	10.6	9.3	7.4	7.6	7.7	6.3	4.9	5.6	85.6

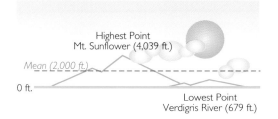

Highest Point
Mt. Sunflower (4,039 ft.)

Mean (2,000 ft.)

0 ft.

Lowest Point
Verdigris River (679 ft.)

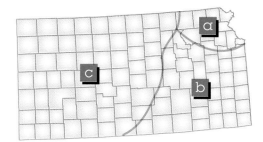

★ State capitol
⊙ Cities over 35,000 population
○ Other significant cities
● County Seats

■ State Parks
Ⓦ Welcome Centers
⚲ Major colleges and universities
■ Major cultural attractions

Physical Regions: (a) Dissected Till Plains; (b) Southeastern Plains; (c) Great Plains.

Major Cities

Arkansas City	J-13
Atchison	C-18
Coffeyville	J-17
Derby	I-13
Dodge City	H-6
El Dorado	H-14
Emporia	F-16
Garden City	E-3
Great Bend	F-9
Hays	E-8
Hutchinson	G-11
Junction City	D-14
Kansas City	D-19
Lawrence	E-18
Leavenworth	C-19
Leawood	D-19
Lenexa	D-19
Liberal	J-4
Manhattan	D-14
McPherson	F-12
Merriam	D-19
Newton	G-13
Olathe	E-19
Ottawa	F-18
Overland Park	D-19
Parsons	J-18
Pittsburg	I-19
Prairie Village	D-19
Salina	E-12
Shawnee	D-19
Topeka	D-17
Wichita	I-13
Winfield	J-13

Climate

The state is characterized by warm summers, but rather cold winters. Winds blow over the plains easily, for no natural barriers exist. Temperature differences in location across the state are only slight. Topeka, more to the north, has average January and July temperatures of 29 degrees F and 80 degrees F. Wichita, farther south, has average January and July temperatures of 32 degrees F and 80 degrees F.

Precipitation varies across Kansas; however, most precipitation falls between April and September. However, summers can be dry because of high evaporation rates. Southeast Kansas receives around 40 inches of annual precipitation, while the west receives an average of only 17 inches.

Kansas weather can change very quickly. When clashing air masses meet on Kansas's plains, all kinds of violent weather, including blizzards, tornadoes, and floods, can occur.

Hydrology

The Missouri River forms the state's northeast boundary with Missouri. The Kansas River flows eastward into the Missouri, draining much of northeastern Kansas. The Arkansas flows through much of the southwestern and south-central portions of the state. Other important rivers include the Solomon, the Smokey Hill, and the Pawnee in north and central Kansas; and the Cottonwood, the Neosho, the Pottawatomie, and the Verdigris in the eastern part of the state.

Kansas has many man-made lakes, created for irrigation projects or for recreation. The largest of these is Milford Lake, on the Republican River. Others include Waconda Lake, on the Solomon River; Turtle Creek and Perry reservoirs on the Kansas; the Toronto and Elk City reservoirs on the Verdigris; and the Center Bluff and Kanopolis reservoirs on the Smokey Hill River.

Flora and Fauna

The state of Kansas is well known for its prairie grasslands; almost 200 different kinds of grasses grow in the state. Eastern Kansas has tall grasses such as bluestem, while the shorter buffalo and blue grama grasses grow in the western part of the state. Trees grow mostly in river valleys, and especially in the eastern part of the state. Some of Kansas's trees include sycamore, pecan, locust, and hackberry. A variety of wildflowers, including clover, verbena, daisies, and thistles, grow in different parts of Kansas. Sunflowers dominate throughout the state.

Herds of buffalo once roamed the Kansas prairies; however, smaller animals currently make up the majority of Kansas wildlife. Coyotes, prairie dogs, muskrats, and opossums all live throughout the state. Antelope are still found on the prairies. Many game birds, such as prairie chickens and geese, also live in Kansas, while songbirds include meadowlarks and crows. Kansas also has quite a large reptile population; in fact, two poisonous snakes, rattlesnakes and copperheads, can be found in the state. Bass and bluegills live in Kansas's rivers, streams, and lakes.

Topography

There are several distinct topographic regions in Kansas. The land rises gradually from east to west across the state. In the northeastern section is the Dissected Till Plains physical region, a fertile area of rolling plains. The Osage Plains and the Flint Hills are found in southeastern Kansas. The Flint Hills are west of the Osage Plains, and are characterized by limestone ridges. The Southeastern Plains physical region contains the Arkansas River Lowlands. These lowlands, which cover the southeast corner of the state, include the lowest elevations in Kansas. The soil is warm, moist, and rich but rather thin, depth being 20 inches or less over bedrock.

The Smokey Hills occupy the central portion of Kansas. Sandstone and limestone formations are found in this area of gently rolling hills. This area is part of the Great Plains that roll westward to the foothills of the Rocky Mountains.

The western part of Kansas is covered by the Great Plains physical region. The Dissected Till Plains run through the northern part of this area, while the High Plains cover the rest of this region. The soil is characterized as warm and dry, colored brown, and high in organic content. Elevations are highest in this area, reaching over 4,000 ft. (1,200 m) above sea level.

Weather Facts

Record High Temperature: 121° F (49° C) on July 17, 1932, at Fredonia; Record Low Temperature: -40° F (-40° C) on February 12, 1901, at Lebanon; Average January Temperature: 31° F (-1° C); Average July Temperature: 78° F (26° C); Average Yearly Precipitation: 28 in. (71 cm).

Environmental Quality

See page 376.

Kansas's History

Kansas's First People

Kansas was first inhabited about ten thousand years ago by Paleo-Indians and later by various other Indian cultures. By the time Europeans arrived in Kansas, it was occupied by several Plains Indian tribes: the Wichita, Osage, Pawnee, and Kansa peoples.

In the seventeenth and eighteenth centuries, other tribes migrated to the Great Plains of Kansas and surrounding territories. The Arapaho and Cheyenne came from the Red River vicinity further north and were involved in the Cheyenne Wars of the Great Plains. The Comanche migrated southeastward from the Great Basin and western Wyoming area. They were great horsemen and warriors and fought the United States in the Great Plains. The Kiowa, from the mountainous regions of upper Missouri river, joined the Comanches in the Comanche Wars against the United States.

European Exploration

In 1541, Francisco Vásquez de Coronado became the first European to enter Kansas in his quest for gold. In 1601, an expedition led by Juan de Oñate fueled Spain's desire for the area's rich lands. However, explorations by the French during the seventeenth century resulted in René-Robert Cavelier, Sieur de La Salle, claiming the area for France in 1682. Over the following several decades, the French set up trading posts in the region and in 1719, Charles Claude du Tisne did further exploring of the territory for the French. Fort Orleans was built at the mouth of the Osage River by the French in 1722. Plains Indians drove them out six years later.

Most of the first half of the eighteenth century witnessed tension between France and Spain over the territory. This tension remained until France ceded the area as part of the Louisiana Territory to Spain at the conclusion of the French and Indian Wars in 1762. France reclaimed the territory in 1800 when the Spanish returned it to them. Three years later

Kansas became a U.S. possession when France sold the Louisiana Territory to the United States for $15 million.

Statehood

The early years of the nineteenth century saw many expeditions organized by the U.S. government to explore its new territories in the West. Most of these passed through Kansas, including the Lewis and Clark expedition in 1804, Zebulon Pike (namesake of Pike's Peak) in 1806, and Stephen Long in 1819, who mistakenly termed the Great Plains region the "Great American Desert."

This characterization of the Plains as an arid wasteland prompted the United States to relocate many of the Indian tribes that were being displaced in other states to Kansas. With the opening of the Sante Fe Trail (much of which lay in Kansas) in 1822 and the Oregon Trail in the 1840s—and especially after thousands of travelers passed through in 1849 during the Gold Rush—the attraction of the land became obvious. By 1854, over two million acres of Indian land was cleared for white settlers, with the Indians being shuttled to Oklahoma.

In 1812, Kansas became part of the Missouri Territory. It remained so until 1854, when the Territory of Kansas was created as part of the Kansas-Nebraska Act.

Violent events took place in Kansas in the 1850s. When Kansas was opened up for settlement conflict soon erupted between southern slave owners and northern abolitionists over the legal status of slavery. The conflict escalated when people from neighboring states such as Missouri entered into Kansas and attempted to influence local elections to suit their needs. Abolitionists refused to reconize these elections and held ones of their own. Violence erupted when proslavery forces sacked the town of Lawrence in 1856. In retaliation, abolitionist John Brown and six men attacked and murdered five

settlers at Pottawatomie Creek. Thus the term "Bleeding Kansas" was born. In the end, over 200 persons had been killed. Finally, in 1861, after a debate as to whether it should be considered a slave or free state, Kansas was admitted to the Union as the thirty-fourth state (a free state).

Industrialization

After the Civil War, with the Sante Fe and Union Pacific railroads crossing the state, settlers began arriving in larger numbers, including immigrants from Germany, Sweden, Russia, and other places. These new settlers took to the land and, buoyed by a particular strain of hardy winter wheat introduced by Russian Mennonites, Kansas's agriculture blossomed. Even the state's dry western fields were put into cultivation as a combination of rainy seasons and dry-farming techniques were used to steadily increase production into the first decades of the twentieth century. Kansas was hit hard by the Depression and the simultaneous effects of the Dust Bowl, but rebounded during World War II as Wichita's aircraft industry helped supply the war effort. Since the war, the aircraft industry and agriculture (especially wheat and cattle) have led the economy.

The Dust Bowl

From 1930 to 1941 the Great Plains of the United States suffered what one scientist called "the worst drought in the climatic history of the country." The western half of Kansas was at the center of this economic and ecological disaster. The region received only marginal rainfall in good years, and with the ever-increasing demand for wheat the land was pushed to its natural limits. The cover vegetation that was subsequently lost exposed the soil, and when the rain stopped and the winds came this soil was simply blown away.

Important Events

1541 Initial European exploration by Spaniard Francisco Vásquez de Coronado.

1682 René-Robert Cavelier, Sieur de La Salle, claims the area for the French.

1722 Fort Orleans established by the French on the Osage River.

1762 France cedes Louisiana Territory, which includes Kansas, to Spain.

1800 Louisiana Territory returned to France by Spain.

1803 Kansas becomes U.S. possession as part of the Louisiana Purchase.

1812 Territory of Missouri, which includes Kansas, is established.

1822 Opening of the Sante Fe Trail.

1827 Fort Leavenworth military installation is opened.

1834 United States establishes Kansas as Indian Country to hold eastern Indians forced out by white settlers.

1854 Kansas-Nebraska Act establishes the Territory of Kansas.

1856 Abolitionist John Brown murders five proslavery settlers in retaliation for the attack on the town of Lawrence.

1861 Kansas admitted into the Union as the thirty-fourth state.

1870s Major migration boosts the state's agriculture.

1880 Prohibition is made part of the state constitution.

1890s Discovery of oil and gas leads to establishment of these industries in the state.

1912 Women are granted suffrage in Kansas.

1930s Kansas becomes part of the Dust Bowl as severe drought lasts throughout the decade.

1948 Kansas repeals state prohibition.

1954 Supreme Court decision *Brown vs. Board of Education of Topeka, Kansas* rules that public school segregation is unconstitutional.

1976 Kansas senator Robert Dole is Republican nominee for Vice President of the United States.

1995 Sen. Dole becomes Senate majority leader for the second time (initially 1985-1987).

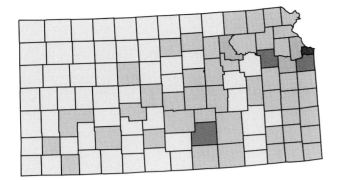

Population Density

Population density for the state of Kansas was 30.3 persons per square mile in 1990 (11.7 per km2). Average U.S. density was 70.3 persons per square mile in 1990 (27.3 per km2). Habitation is most dense around the urban area of Kansas City. Cities such as Wichita, Topeka, and Manhattan also have higher density populations. Most of the population of Kansas is located in the eastern portion of the state.

Persons Per Square Mile

- 0.0 to 9.9
- 10.0 to 99.9
- 250.0 to 749.9
- 750.0 to 1,999.9

Population Projections

Population in thousands
Kansas's Population
U. S. Population

(chart, left axis 2,425–2,600; right axis 250,000–285,000; x-axis 1990, 1995, 2000, 2010)

Population Change

Year	Population
1950	1,905,000
1960	2,183,000
1970	2,249,000
1980	2,363,679
1990	2,477,574
2000	2,529,000
2010	2,564,000

Period	Change
1950–1970	18.1%
1970–1980	5.1%
1980–1990	4.8%
1990–2000	2.1%

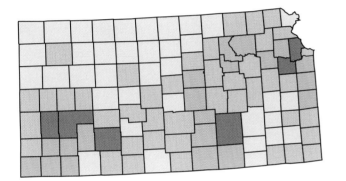

Population Change

The 1990 population figure for the state of Kansas was 2,477,574. This is a 4.82 percent increase from 2,363,679 in 1980. The next decade will show growth with a population of 2.5 million or a 2.08 percent increase. The areas of fastest growth include counties around the major cities such as Kansas City, Wichita, Topeka, and Manhattan. Some western counties also saw significant population increases in the last decade.

Percent Change 1980 to 1990

- −31.9 to −10.0%
- −9.9 to 0.0%
- 0.1 to 19.9%
- 20.0 to 49.9%

Population Facts

State Population, 1993: 2,531,000

Rank: 32

Population 2000: 2,529,000 (Rank 33)

Density: 30.3 per sq. mi. (11.7 per km²)

Distribution: 69.1% urban, 30.9% rural

Population Under 5 Years Old: 7.4%

Population Under 18 Years Old: 26.9%

Population Over 65 Years Old: 13.9%

Median Age: 32.9

Number of Households: 945,000

Average Persons Per Household: 2.53

Average Persons Per Family: 3.08

Female Heads of Households: 3.29%

Population That Is Married: 22.30%

Birth Rate: 15.7 per 1,000 population

Death Rate: 9.0 per 1,000 population

Births to Teen Mothers: 12.3%

Marriage Rate: 9.2 per 1,000 population

Divorce Rate: 5.0 per 1,000 population

Violent Crime Rate: 500 per 100,000 pop.

Population on Social Security: 16.6%

Percent Voting for President: 63.0%

Kansas's Famous Citizens

Cunningham, Glenn (1882–1942). Olympic runner. Set a new world record in 1932 for running the mile. Silver medalist in 1936.

Johnson, Hugh (1882–1942). Directed the national draft while in the military, receiving the Distinguished Service Medal.

Kassebaum, Nancy Landon (b. 1932). U.S. senator since 1978. Daughter of 1936 presidential candidate Alf Landon.

Kelly, Emmett (1898–1979). Invented his famous clown character Weary Willie, a ragged melancholy hobo, in 1933.

Kenton, Stan (1911–1979). Big bandleader. Known for his "Progressive Jazz" band, which utilized dissonance and atonality.

McDaniel, Hattie (1895–1952). Actress. Became the first African-American to win an Academy Award, for Gone with the Wind (1940).

Runyon, Damon (1884–1946). Wrote humorous stories in a slangy style about the New York underworld such as Guys and Dolls.

Sutherland, Earl W. Jr. (1915–1974). Biochemist. Won the Nobel Prize in 1971 for his work on hormonal regulation of the body.

Population Profile

Rank. Kansas ranks 32d among U.S. states in terms of population with 2,531,000 citizens.

Minority Population. The state's minority population is 11.7 percent. The state's male to female ratio for 1990 was 96.18 males for every 100 females. It was above the national average of 95.22 males for every 100 females.

Growth. The state's population is increasing and is expected to be 2.6 million by the year 2010.

Government

Capital: Topeka (established 1861).

Statehood: Became 34th state on Jan. 21, 1861.

Number of Counties: 105.

Supreme Court Justices: 7, 6-year term.

State Senators: 40, 4-year term.

State Legislators: 125, 2-year term.

United States Senators: 2.

United States Representatives: 4.

Electoral Votes: 6.

State Constitution: Adopted 1859.

Older Citizens. The state's population older than 65 was 342,571 in 1990. It grew 11.86% from 306,263 in 1980.

Younger Citizens. The number of children (under 18 years of age) was 662 thousand in 1990. This represents 26.7 percent of the state's population. The state's school aged population was 432 thousand in 1990. It is expected to increase to 440 thousand by the year 2000. This represents a 1.85% change.

Urban/Rural. 69.1% of the population of the state live in urban areas while 30.9% live in rural areas.

Largest Cities. Kansas has 11 cities with a population greater than 35,000. The populations of the state's largest centers are (starting from the most populous) Wichita (304,011), Kansas City (149,767), Topeka (119,883), Overland Park (111,790), Lawrence (65,608), Olathe (63,352), Salina (42,303), Hutchinson (39,308), Leavenworth (38,495), Shawnee (37,993), Manhattan (37,712), Lenexa (34,034), Emporia (25,512), Garden City (24,097), Prairie Village (23,186), Dodge City (21,129), Junction City (20,604), Leawood (19,693), Pittsburg (17,775), Hays (17,767), and Newton (16,700).

Distribution of Income

The per capita income for the state of Kansas (current dollars) was $19,376 in 1992. This is a 97.1 percent increase from $9,829 in 1980. Income is greatest in six counties: Doniphan, Jackson, Linn, Wilson, Haskell, and Wichita. As can be seen in this map, these counties are widely dispersed throughout the state.

Per Capita Income (000s) (Current Dollars)

- $10.0 to 12.9
- $13.0 to 15.9
- $16.0 to 19.9
- $20.0 to 37.7

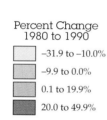
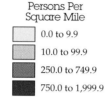
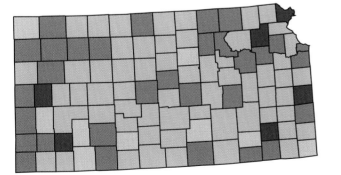

Native American

The Native American population in Kansas was 21,965 in 1990. This was an increase of 23.20 percent from 17,829 in 1980. Many Native Americans can also be found living in the Kickapoo and Potawatomi Indian reservations located in the eastern part of the state. Kansas is also home to the Kansa tribe.

Presence of Native Americans

 Minor

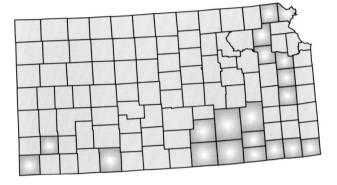

Nationalities

African	2,385
American	118,653
Arab	4,141
Austrian	3,935
Czech	16,717
Dutch	51,932
English	262,237
Finnish	1,065
German	805,458
Greek	2,961
Hungarian	2,247
Irish	220,609
Italian	28,838
Norwegian	13,524
Polish	21,620
Portuguese	961
Russian	8,764
Scottish	34,419
Slovak	5,163
Swedish	51,714
Welsh	14,510
West Indian	1,169

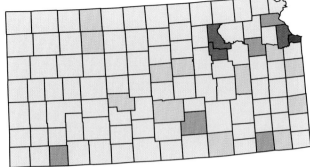

African American

The African American population in Kansas was 143,076 in 1990. This was an increase of 13.23 percent from 126,356 in 1980. The largest concentration of African American population can be found in Kansas City. Other high numbers can be found in Riley and Geary counties in the cities of Manhattan and Junction City.

Percent of County Population

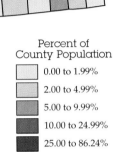

	0.00 to 1.99%
	2.00 to 4.99%
	5.00 to 9.99%
	10.00 to 24.99%
	25.00 to 86.24%

Statewide Ethnic Composition

Over 90 percent of the population of Kansas is white. The largest nationalities in this racial group are German, English, and Irish. The next largest group is African Americans, followed by Hispanics, Asians, and Native Americans. Almost 119,000 people claim to be American and acknowledge no other nationality.

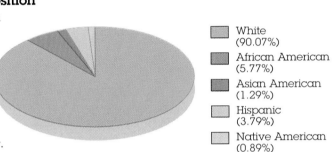

- White (90.07%)
- African American (5.77%)
- Asian American (1.29%)
- Hispanic (3.79%)
- Native American (0.89%)

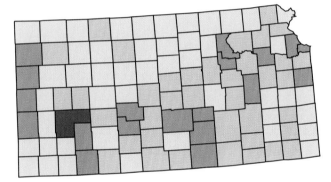

Education Facts

Total Students 1990: 430,864

Number of School Districts: 304

Expenditure Per Capita on Education 1990: $819

Expenditure Per Capita K–12 1990: $725

Expenditure Per Pupil 1990: $5,044

Total School Enrollment 1990–1991: 436,250

Rank of Expenditures Per Student: 21st in the U.S.

African American Enrollment: 8.0%

Hispanic Enrollment: 4.2%

Asian/Pacific Islander Enrollment: 1.4%

Native American Enrollment: 1.0%

Mean SAT Score 1991 Verbal: 493

Mean SAT Score 1991 Math: 546

Average Teacher's Salary 1992: $30,700

Rank Teacher's Salary: 28th in U.S.

High School Graduates 1990: 25,700

Total Number of Public Schools: 1,459

Number of Teachers 1990: 29,083

Student/Teacher Ratio: 15.0

Staff Employed in Public Schools: 50,175

Pupil/Staff Ratio: 8.6

Staff/Teacher Ratio: 1.7

Hispanic[††]

The Hispanic population in Kansas was 93,670 in 1990. This is an increase of 47.89 percent from 63,339 persons in 1980. The highest concentration of Hispanic population can be found in Finney County. The largest cities in the state also have significant Hispanic populations— Wichita, Kansas City, and Topeka.)

[††]A person of Mexican, Puerto Rican, Cuban, or other Spanish culture or origin regardless of race.

Percent of County Population

	0.00 to 0.99%
	1.00 to 2.99%
	3.00 to 9.99%
	25.00 to 97.22%

Education

Attainment: 82 percent of population 25 years or older were high school graduates in 1989, earning Kansas a ranking of 12th in the United States; 22 percent of the state's population had completed college. Institutions of Higher Education: The largest universities and colleges in the state include the University of Kansas, Lawrence; University of Kansas Medical Center, Kansas City; Kansas State University, Manhattan; Wichita State University, Wichita; Washburn University, Topeka; Benedictine College, Atchison. Expenditures per Student: Expenditure increased 79% between 1985 and 1990. Projected High School Graduations: 1998 (41,554), 2004 (37,548); Total Revenues for Education from Federal Sources: $88 million; Total Revenues for Education from State Sources: $765 million; Total Revenues for Education from Local Sources: $930 million; Average Annual Salaries for Public School Principals: N/A; Largest School Districts in State: Wichita School District, 45,835 students, 75th in the United States; Shawnee Mission Public Schools, 29,845 students, 138th.

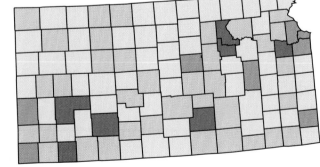

Asian American

The Asian American population in Kansas was 31,750 in 1990. This is an increase of 87.90 percent from 16,897 persons in 1980. The Asian American population is primarily located in urban areas such as Wichita, Kansas City, and Topeka. Twenty-five percent of the Asian American population is located in Wichita.

Percent of County Population

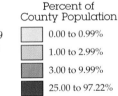

	0.00 to 0.24%
	0.25 to 0.99%
	1.00 to 1.99%
	2.00 to 4.99%

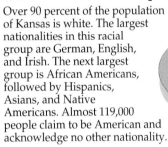

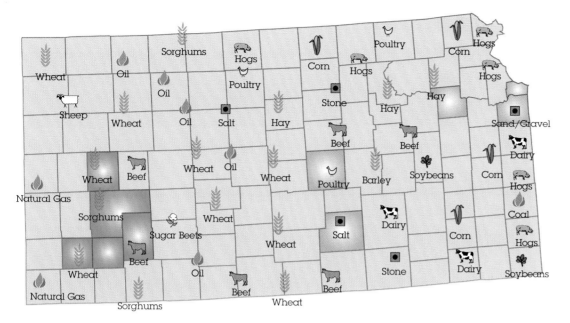

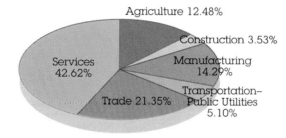

Major manufacturing areas

Major agricultural areas

Transportation

Kansas is one of the leading states in the nation in the total distance covered by roadway. The state has approximately 133,000 miles of roads and highways. The extensive system links farm communities to market centers. Interstate 70 crosses the entire state, from the Colorado line to the Missouri border.

Kansas has two rail centers, Kansas City and Wichita. A passenger rail line serves 7 Kansas cities, and 11 rail lines provide freight service for the state. Wichita also has the busiest airport in Kansas. The Kansas City International Airport, which also serves Kansas, is actually located in Missouri. Smaller airstrips exist around the state. Kansas lacks any significant water transportation routes, although the Missouri River does briefly border the northeast.

Energy and Transportation Facts

Energy. Yearly Consumption: 1,039 tril. BTUs (residential, 18.1%; commercial, 16.4%; industrial, 40.6%; transportation, 24.8%); Annual Energy Expenditures Per Capita: $2,061; Nuclear Power Plants Located in State: 1; Source of Energy Consumed: Petroleum— 35.9%; Natural Gas— 33.9%; Coal— 24.5%; Hydroelectric Power—0.0%; Nuclear Power—5.7%.

Transportation. Highway Miles: 133,655 (interstates, 872; urban, 9,508; rural, 124,147); Average Yearly Auto Insurance: $392 (46th); Auto Fatalities Rank: 31st; Registered Motor Vehicles: 1,920,568; Workers in Carpools: 14.6%; Workers Using Public Trans: 0.7%.

Employment

Employment. Kansas employed 1.25 million people in 1993. Most work in wholesale and retail trade jobs (274,200 persons or 22% of the workforce). Manufacturing accounts for14.6% or 182,400 workers. Government employs 229,700 workers (18.3%). Social and personal services employ 269,300 people (21.5%). Construction and Transportation and utilities each account for 3.7% (46,500 persons) and 5.3% (65,900 persons) of the workforce, respectively. Agriculture employs 65,200 workers or 5.2%. Finance, real estate, and insurance employs 58,100 workers, or 4.6%. Mining employs 8,800 people and accounts for only 0.7% of the work force.

Unemployment. Kansas' unemployment rate of 5% has not changed between 1985 and 1993. Today's figure is lower than the national average of 6.8% as shown below.

Agriculture

Kansas has 47.8 million farm acres. During the last 40 years, Kansas's farms have grown larger in size and fewer in number. In 1955, 120,000 farms were found in the state. Today, 65,000 remain.

Agriculture adds $2 billion to the state's gross product annually. The principal commodities in order of marketing receipts are cattle, wheat, corn, and sorghum grain.

Beef cattle account for about 52 percent of Kansas's farm income. The second largest income producer is wheat, at about 22 percent. The state leads the nation in the production of this crop, with the central portion of the state producing the most. Kansas has about three million irrigated acres, primarily in the western part of the state where corn, hay, wheat, and other crops are grown.

Housing

Owner Occupied Units: 1,044,112; Average Age of Units: 34 years; Average Value of Housing Units: $52,200; Renter Occupied Units: 289,751; Median Monthly Rent: $372; Housing Starts: 11,000; Existing Home Sales: 53,700.

Economic Facts

Gross State Product: $49,000,000,000

Income Per Capita: $19,376

Disposable Personal Income: $16,982

Median Household Income: $27,291

Average Annual Pay, 1988: $21,002

Principal Industries: food products, printing, machinery, transportation equipment, chemicals, coal and gas products

Major Crops: wheat, grain, hay, sorghum, soybeans, corn

Fish: Bass, Bluegills, Catfish, Crappies

Livestock: hogs, cattle

Non-Fuel Minerals: Salt Rock, Helium

Organic Fuel Minerals: Petroleum, Nat. Gas, Coal

Civilian Labor Force: 1,295,000 (Women: 588,000)

Total Employed: 1,238,000 (Women: 563,000)

Median Value of Housing: $52,200

Median Contract Rent: $372 per month

Economic Sectors

Agriculture 12.48%

Construction 3.53%

Services 42.62%

Manufacturing 14.29%

Trade 21.35%

Transportation– Public Utilities 5.10%

Manufacturing

At one time, Kansas had substantial glass and zinc industries; however, these have since left the state. Today, the manufacture of transportation equipment dominates the Kansas economy. Other leading industries include food processing, printed materials, and chemicals.

Over 60 percent of light aircraft in the United States are produced in Kansas. Wichita and the surrounding area produces both commercial and military aircraft. Other transportation equipment, including locomotive and automobile parts, is produced in Kansas City and other areas. The Kansas City area also produces much of the state's chemicals and printed materials. In addition, Kansas ranks high in the nation for flour production, with mills in Hutchinson and Topeka.

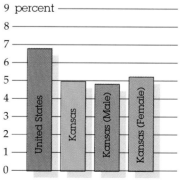

Unemployment Rate

KENTUCKY
The State of Kentucky

Official State Seal

The Great Seal of Kentucky was adopted in 1792 after Kentucky became a state. The seal shows an embrace of two hunters. One is dressed in frontier dress while the other is dressed in more formal garb. This symbolizes Kentucky's relationship with the states to the east. The state motto, "United we stand, divided we fall," encircles the two hunters.

Legal Holidays

January: New Year's Day—1st, Martin Luther King, Jr., Day—3rd Monday; February: Presidents' Day—3rd Monday; May: Memorial Day—4th Monday; June: Admission Day—1st; Confederate Memorial Day—3rd; Boone Day—7th; July: Independence Day—4th; September: Labor Day—1st Monday; October: Columbus Day—2nd Monday; November: Veterans' Day—11th; Thanksgiving—4th Thursday; December: Christmas—25th.

State Flag

The Kentucky state flag was adopted from older military flags. The state seal was included in the design, but was not approved until 1918.

Festivals and Events

February: Dulcibrrr, Falls of Rough; Square Dance Weekend, Jamestown; April: Kentucky Derby Festival, Louisville; May: Maifest, Covington; Spring Ghost Tales, Louisville; International Strange Music Weekend, Carter Caves State Park; June: Festival of Bluegrass, Lexington; Louisville City Fair, Louisville; Summer Sunfest, Covington; August: Battle of Blue Licks Celebration, Mount Olivet; September: Corn Island Storytelling Fest, Louisville; Oktoberfest, Covington; October: Swappin' Meetin', Cumberland; Trigg County Country Ham Festival, Cadiz; Oktoberfest, Covington & Louisville

Kentucky Compared to States in Its Region.

Resident Pop. in Metro Areas: 3d; Pop. Percent Increase: 3d; Pop. Over 65: 3d; Infant Mortality: 4th; School Enroll. Increase: 4th; High School Grad. and Up: 3d; Violent Crime: 3d; Hazardous Waste Sites: 1st; Unemployment: 3d; Median Household Income: 3d; Persons Below Poverty: 2d; Energy Costs Per Person: 3d.

East South Central

	Population	Capital
Kentucky	3,789,000	Frankfort
Tennessee	5,099,000	Nashville
Alabama	4,187,000	Montgomery
Mississippi	2,643,000	Jackson

Kentucky's Finances

Households: 1,380,000; Income Per Capita Current Dollars: $16,534; Change Per Capita Income 1980 to 1992: 105.4% (21st in U.S.); State Expenditures: $9,235,000,000; State Revenues: $9,222,000,000; Personal Income Tax: 2 to 6%; Federal Income Taxes Paid Per Capita: $1,312; Sales Tax: 6% (food and prescription drugs exempt).

State Expenditures

7.0 billion dollars

6.0
5.0
4.0
3.0
2.0
1.0
0

Education, Highway, Welfare, Health, Other

State Revenues

7.0 billion dollars

6.0
5.0
4.0
3.0
2.0
1.0
0

Federal, Local, Taxes, Miscellaneous

Facts about Kentucky. Origin of Name: After a *Cherokee* Indian word possibly meaning *"land of tomorrow,"* and *"Meadowland"*; Nickname: The Bluegrass State; Motto: "United we stand, divided we fall"; Abbreviations: Ky. or Ken. (traditional), KY (postal); State Bird: Kentucky cardinal; State Tree: Kentucky coffeetree; State Flower: goldenrod; State Song: "My Old Kentucky Home" words and music by Stephen Foster.

Kentucky Compared to Other States. Resident Pop. in Metro Areas: 38th; Pop. Percent Increase: 30th; Pop. Over 65: 25th; Infant Mortality: 31st; School Enroll. Increase: 47th; High School Grad. and Up: 49th; Violent Crime: 33d; Hazardous Waste Sites: 20th; Unemployment: 24th; Median Household Income: 45th; Persons Below Poverty: 6th; Energy Costs Per Person: 19th.

Location, Size, and Boundaries

Location. Kentucky is located in the southeastern United States in what is known as the East South Central region. It is bounded on four sides by land. The geographic center of Kentucky is lat. 37° 21.5' N; long. 85° 30.4' W.

Size. Kentucky is the 37th largest state in terms of size. Its area is 40,395 sq. mi. (104,623 km2). Inland water covers 745 sq. mi. (1,930 km2).

Boundaries. Illinois, 131 mi. (211 km); Indiana, 345 mi. (555 km); Ohio, 167 mi. (269 km); West Virginia, 107 mi. (172 km); Virginia, 127 mi. (204 km); Tennessee, 336 mi. (541 km); Missouri, 77 mi. (124 km).

Geographic Extent. The north/south extent of Kentucky is 175 mi. (282 km). The state extends 350 mi. (563 km) to the east/west.

Major Cities

City	Grid	City	Grid
Ashland	C-21	Newport	A-14
Bowling Green	H-9	Nicholasville	E-14
Covington	A-14	Okolona	D-11
Danville	F-13	Owensboro	E-7
Elizabethtown	F-10	Paducah	H-2
Erlanger	A-14	Radcliff	E-10
Florence	A-14	Richmond	E-15
Frankfort	D-13	Shively	D-11
Georgetown	D-14	Winchester	E-15
Glasgow	H-10		
Henderson	E-5		
Hopkinsville	I-5		
Jeffersontown	11-D		
Lexington	D-14		
Louisville	D-11		
Madisonville	G-6		
Middlesborough	J-18		
Murray	J-3		

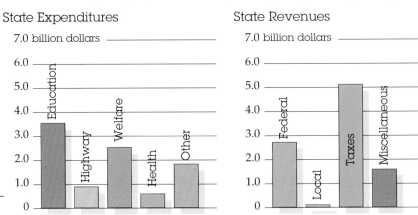

Kentucky

■ Abraham Lincoln Birthplace National Historic Site. 116-acre site honors Lincoln's beginnings including a 56-step memorial, one for each year of his life. (A-10)

■ Ancient Buried City (King Mounds). A museum that features 5 of 40 prehistoric Indian mounds explored; museum. (A-10)

■ Bardstown. Talbott Tavern, the oldest western stagecoach stop in America; My Old Kentucky Home State Park, the inspiration for the famous Stephen Foster song. (A-10)

■ Bowling Green. Confederate capital of Kentucky during the Civil War, now includes five scenic historic areas; home of Western Kentucky University.

■ Covington Landing. One of the largest floating restaurant/entertainment complexes on the inland waterways; offers view of Cincinnati skyline plus dancing, dining, shopping, and entertainment. (A-10)

■ Cumberland Gap National Historical Park. In Kentucky, Virginia, and Tennessee; near Middlesboro; pass used by Daniel Boone and pioneers. (A-10)

■ Danville. Isaac Shelby Cemetery, grave of first governor of Kentucky; Constitution Square State Historic Site, where Kentucky's constitution was drafted in 1792. (A-10)

■ J. B. Speed Art Museum. More than 3,000 works; Sculpture Court, English Renaissance Room, and "The Grange" in Devon. (A-10)

■ Jefferson Davis Monument State Historic Site. 351-foot memorial honoring the president of the Confederacy. (A-10)

■ Land Between the Lakes. 40-mile long peninsula between Barkley and Kentucky lakes; TVA-owned and operated national demonstration area for recreation, environmental education, and resource management. (A-10)

■ Lexington. Lexington-Fayette County is known as the "Horse Capitol of the World" and features numerous horse farms and the American Saddle Horse Museum. (A-10)

■ Louisville Zoo. More than 1,300 exotic animals in naturalistic settings including polar bears and American wildcats. (A-10)

■ Mammoth Cave National Park. World's most extensive cave system features over 330 miles of explored passageways and nearly every type of cave formation. (A-10)

■ Old Governor's Mansion. Oldest official executive residence in the United States; home of 33 Kentucky governors; now the lieutenant governor's residence. (A-10)

■ Perryville Battlefield State Historic Site. Site of the greatest Civil War battle in Kentucky; the South's last serious attempt to gain possession of Kentucky in 1862. (A-10)

■ Shaker Village at Pleasant Hill. Small communal town founded by the Shaker community in 1805; features 30 original buildings on 2,700 scenic acres. (A-10)

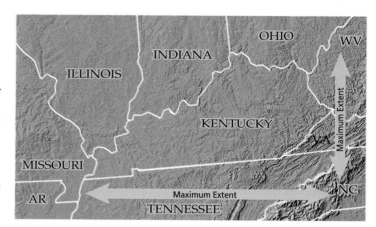

Scale

0   10   20   30mi.

10   0   10   20   30   40 km

Legend

☆ State capitol
⊙ Cities over 35,000 pop.
○ Other significant cities
● County Seats

■ Major cultural attractions
■ State Parks
Ⓦ Welcome Centers
⚲ Major colleges & universities

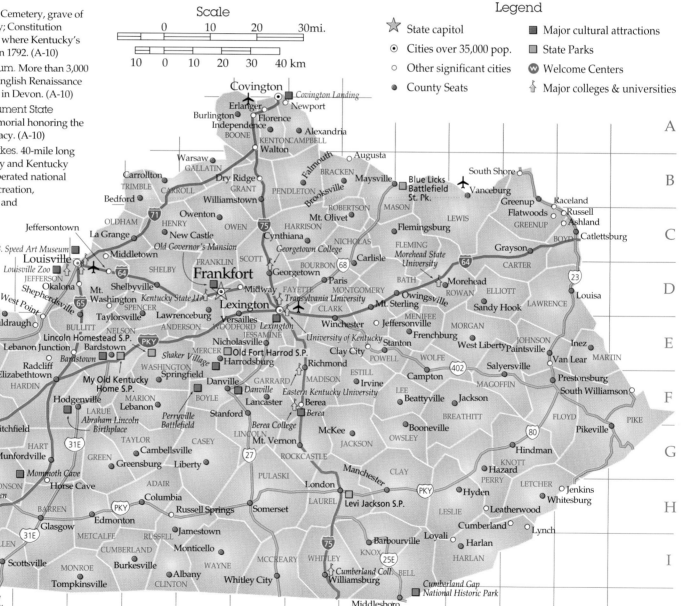

Weather Facts

Record High Temperature: 114° F (46° C) on July 27, 1926, at Greensburg; Record Low Temperature: -34° F (-37° C) on January 27, 1959, at Cynthia; Average January Temperature: 35° F (2° C); Average July Temperature: 76° F (24° C); Average Yearly Precipitation: 47 in. (119 cm).

Environmental Facts

Air Pollution Rank: 18th; Water Pollution Rank: 30th; Total Yearly Industrial Pollution: 40,687,772 lbs.; Industrial Pollution Rank: 22d; Hazardous Waste Sites: 19; Hazardous Sites Rank: 21st; Landfill Capacity: adequate; Fresh Water Supply: large surplus; Daily Residential Water Consumption: 129 gals. per capita; Endangered Species: Aquatic Species (27)—clubshell; Birds (3)—eagle, bald; Mammals (4)—bat, gray; Other Species (1)—snake, northern copperbelly water; Plants (7)—clover, running buffalo.

Environmental Quality

Kentucky residents generate 4.6 million tons of solid waste each year, or approximately 2,400 pounds per capita. Landfill capacity in Kentucky will be exhausted in less than 5 years. The state has 17 hazardous waste sites. Annual greenhouse gas emissions in Kentucky total 109.6 million tons, or 29.4 tons per capita. Industrial sources in Kentucky release approximately 60.3 thousand tons of toxins, 1.2 million tons of acid precipitation-producing substances, and 1.9 million tons of smog-producing substances into the atmosphere each year.

The state has 79,300 acres within the National Park System; the largest area within the state is Mammoth Cave National Park. State parks cover just over 43,000 acres, attracting 27.3 million visitors per year.

Kentucky spends approximately 1.6 percent of its budget, or approximately $32 per capita, on environmental and natural resources.

Average Monthly Weather

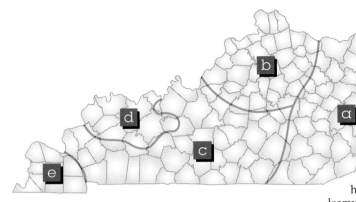

Topography

There are several distinct topographic regions in Kentucky. The Appalachian Plateau physical region, which is part of the Appalachian Mountain system, is the dominant topographical feature of eastern Kentucky. The highest point in the state is found in this region: Black Mountain, near the southeast border, rises 4,139 ft. (1,263 m) above sea level. The soil there is warm and moist, as it is for all of the state, and is predominantly rocky, colored light gray to brown.

In the north-central part of Kentucky is the

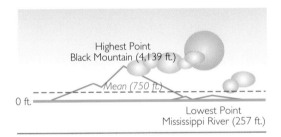

Highest Point
Black Mountain (4,139 ft.)

Mean (750 ft.)

0 ft.

Lowest Point
Mississippi River (257 ft.)

Land Use

Cropland: 24.2%; Pasture: 24.8%; Rangeland: 0%; Forest: 41.9%; Urban: 5.1%; Other: 4%.

For more information about Kentucky's environment, contact the Department of Natural Resources, 691 Teton Trail, Frankfort, KY 40601.

Bluegrass Region. This is an area of gently rolling hills, where most of Kentucky's famous horses are raised. Soil is a gray/brown loamy clay. The south-central area is known as the Pennyroyal physical region, a mostly flat area used for farming. The soil is colored red or yellow and is relatively low in organic content. Between these two regions of central Kentucky lies a narrow region called the Knobs, named for the peculiar sandstone hills that are its primary feature.

The Western Coal Field physical region lies west of the Pennyroyal Region and south of the Ohio River. Much strip-mining has been done in this region of vast coal reserves. Farming is also pursued in this generally flat area where the soil is mostly gray/brown clay.

Climate

The state of Kentucky has a moderate climate, characterized by warm, yet moist, conditions. Summers are usually warm, and winters cool. Kentucky's weather patterns are influenced by the Gulf of Mexico, especially during summer. The western part of the state has slightly higher average temperatures than the east. In the west, in places such as Bowling Green, January and July temperatures average 38 degrees F and 79 degrees F. To the northeast, in Lexington, January and July temperatures average 34 degrees F and 76 degrees F. Much of Kentucky's average 46 inches of precipitation a year falls in spring, the rainiest season. From south to north, precipitation decreases. Southern Kentucky receives the highest average precipitation, about 50 inches a year, while the north averages only 40 inches.

Kentucky is located in a path several storm systems follow. Storms happen year-round; however, most storms occur between March and September.

Hydrology

River systems define a good portion of Kentucky's borders. The Mississippi River forms the western boundary with Missouri. The entire northern border with Indiana and Ohio is defined by the Ohio River. The northeast border is formed by the Big Sandy and Tug Fork rivers. Important rivers within the state include the Kentucky in north-central Kentucky, the Licking in the eastern part of the state, the Cumberland and Rockcastle in the south, and the Green in the west.

There are several large artificial lakes in Kentucky. The largest of these is Cumberland Lake at 74 sq. miles (192 sq. km). Others in south-central and southwestern Kentucky include Green River Reservoir, Rough River Reservoir, Barren River Reservoir, and Nolin Reservoir. Dale Hollow Lake is located on the border with Tennessee. In the east are smaller lakes, such as Buckhorn Reservoir, Dewey Reservoir, and Fishtrap Reservoir.

Lexington	Jan	Feb	Mar	Apr	May	Jun	Jul	Aug	Sep	Oct	Nov	Dec	Yearly
Maximum Temperature °F	39.8	43.7	53.7	65.8	74.9	82.6	85.9	85.0	79.3	67.6	54.1	44.4	64.7
Minimum Temperature °F	23.1	25.4	34.1	44.3	53.6	61.8	65.9	64.8	58.1	45.9	35.7	27.8	45.0
Days of Precipitation	12.3	11.2	12.8	12.2	11.7	10.5	11.2	9.1	8.0	8.1	10.8	11.5	129.5
Louisville													
Maximum Temperature °F	40.8	45.0	54.9	67.5	76.2	84.0	87.6	86.7	80.6	69.2	55.5	45.4	66.1
Minimum Temperature °F	24.1	26.8	35.2	45.6	54.6	63.3	67.5	66.1	59.1	46.2	36.6	28.9	46.2
Days of Precipitation	11.2	10.6	13.0	11.8	11.5	9.9	10.5	8.4	7.9	7.6	10.4	11.3	124.0

Flora and Fauna

Approximately half of Kentucky's land is covered by forests. Furthermore, the state lies within the Eastern Deciduous Forest region. The majority of trees are hardwoods such as yellow poplar, ash, beech, and hickory. Kentucky's softwood trees include red cedar, hemlock, and a variety of pines. A wide assortment of shrubs and flowers grow throughout the state. Common plants include huckleberries, serviceberries, mountain laurel, and wild plums. Plants such as snakeroot and trillium are found in wooded areas. Pennyroyal, a wildflower, blooms in that part of central Kentucky known as the Pennyroyal Region.

Grasses such as bluegrass and fescue grow in most parts of Kentucky.

Most of the wildlife in Kentucky consists of small animals; deer are the only common large mammals. Small animals living in the state include raccoons, rabbits, chipmunks, and woodchucks. Cardinals, crows, American egrets, and blue and white herons are among Kentucky's most common birds. The state also has over 200 kinds of fishes, including rockfish, muskellunge, and walleye.

Kentucky's History

Kentucky's First People

Native American culture can be traced back to more than thirteen thousand years ago in Kentucky, when nomadic hunters roamed the land. They were succeeded much later by the Woodland and Adena people of two to three thousand years ago. The Mississippian culture of Mound Builders (A.D. 700 to about 1650) constructed a major Temple Mound at Kincaid in southwestern Kentucky.

By the time of the arrival of the first Europeans, Kentucky was largely uninhabited, being used solely as the hunting grounds for Shawnee and Cherokee tribes, who made their homes in neighboring states.

European Exploration

Kentucky was first penetrated by white men in 1654 when Col. Abraham Wood led an expedition to chart the area. In 1672, René-Robert Cavelier, Sieur de La Salle, claimed the region of Kentucky as part of the Louisiana Territory for France. It wasn't until 1736 that the French established a settlement in Kentucky, a trading village on the Ohio River.

A British-American surveying team led by Thomas Walker and Christopher Gist explored the area in 1750 and discovered the Cumberland Gap, a passable route through the Cumberland Mountains that would prove valuable for future settlers and explorers. One of these explorers was Daniel Boone. First entering Kentucky in 1767 to tame the wilderness for the purpose of white settlement, Boone founded Fort Boonesborough in 1775 (James Harrod, a Pennsylvanian, had established the first permanent white settlement the year before, Harrodsburg). That year, Judge Richard Henderson attempted to purchase Kentucky for the Transylvania Company in a questionable deal with the Cherokee. The Boonesborough residents submitted to the idea of a representative government under the rule of a Transylvania Company administration as Henderson sought the establishment of a fourteenth colony.

Statehood

Virginia was determined to stop the course of events in Kentucky and, in 1776, created the County of Kentucky to be under its domain. Kentuckians sent representatives to sit in Virginia's House of Burgesses until 1786, when Virginia relinquished its claim to Kentucky in the face of increased settlement in the state. The Cumberland Gap had become the primary route to the Mississippi Valley and many travelers remained in the area. Finally, Kentucky was admitted to the Union in 1792 as the fifteenth state.

The Civil War badly divided Kentucky, as loyalties were split between the Union and Confederate forces. Plantation owners depended on slave labor and thus supported the South, while strong abolitionists such as Henry Clay appealed to those opposed to the institution of slavery, supporters of the North.

Although the Kentucky legislature decided for the Union cause, some thirty thousand men fought for the Confederacy. In the beginning of the war, Confederate forces invaded Kentucky. Most of the fighting ended in 1863, however, when the Confederate army was driven out. During Reconstruction, there was much violence directed toward blacks until the Kentucky legislature passed laws ensuring their civil rights in the 1870s. The state constitution was rewritten in 1792 and again in 1891, the latter document standing as Kentucky's current constitution.

Industrialization

In the late eighteenth and early nineteenth centuries, settlers in Kentucky established an agricultural economy. Whiskey production resulted in the desirable blend known as Bourbon, after Bourbon County. Hemp was another early crop. By the time of the Civil War, tobacco accounted for half of the state's agricultural output. Kentucky also became a leading center for the breeding of Thoroughbred horses, inspiring the creation of the popular Kentucky Derby in 1875.

After the Civil War, coal mines in eastern Kentucky led the way toward a more industrial economy as workers migrated to the cities. The state's fortunes declined in the twentieth century, and Kentucky was particularly hard hit by the Depression in the 1930s.

After World War II, Kentucky did much to modernize itself. An interstate road network was established which allowed access to all parts of the state. Problems with access to higher education were solved with the creation of a regional university system. State parks were updated and the state joined the Appalachian Regional Commission in the mid-1960s. A new tax was established to help clean up areas polluted by coal miners, and a new outlook on the environment was formed. Though tobacco and mining remain important components of Kentucky's economy, manufacturing leads the state today.

Coal

Coal has had a major impact not only on the economy, but on the way of life and the environment of Kentucky. Two coal fields exist in the state, one in western Kentucky and the other in the Appalachian Mountains in the east. At one time coal mining in the state was a very profitable venture. With the development of new technologies the profits have dwindled and many mines were abandoned. A culture of poverty has taken hold in the Appalachian region, one of the poorest rural areas in the country. Despite the War on Poverty of the federal government in the 1960s, as well as state antipoverty programs, the area remains depressed.

The method of extracting coal used most often is surface, or strip mining, in which layers of the earth are removed to expose the beds lying underneath.

Important Events

1654 Kentucky charted by Col. Abraham Wood and others.

1682 Kentucky claimed as part of the Louisiana Territory by France.

1750 Thomas Walker and Christopher Gist discover the Cumberland Gap, a route to be used by many westward travelers.

1774 James Harrod establishes first permanent settlement in the state, Harrodsburg.

1775 Fort Boonesborough founded by Daniel Boone.

1776 Kentucky is declared a county of the state of Virginia.

1783 First whiskey is produced in Kentucky at Louisville.

1786 Kentucky is separated from the state of Virginia.

1792 Kentucky is admitted to the Union as the fifteenth state.

1815 Steamboats provide transportation on the Ohio River.

1828 The character of "Jim Crow" is introduced in Louisville.

1851 Kentucky expels emancipated slaves from the state.

1860 Tobacco accounts for one-half of Kentucky's agricultural output.

1875 First Kentucky Derby horse race is run in Louisville.

1891 The state constitution is rewritten.

1900 Kentucky ranks first in per capita income of all southern states.

1905–1908 Black Patch War sees burning of tobacco warehouses in protest against the tobacco industry.

1937 Fort Knox is established as the repository for the nation's gold.

1940 Kentucky ranks last in the nation in per capita income.

1963 The depressed coal-mining area of Appalachia receives word of national aid.

1976 Mine explosion kills twenty-six people at Black Mountain Mine.

1989 Statewide lottery is established.

1990 Kentucky enacts sweeping school-reform legislation to help improve school performance and alleviate inequalities.

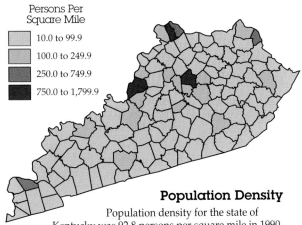

Persons Per Square Mile

- 10.0 to 99.9
- 100.0 to 249.9
- 250.0 to 749.9
- 750.0 to 1,799.9

Population Density

Population density for the state of Kentucky was 92.8 persons per square mile in 1990 (35.8 per km2). Average U.S. density was 70.3 persons per square mile in 1990 (27.3 per km2). Habitation is most dense around the urban and manufacturing areas of Lexington, Louisville, and Cincinnati, Ohio. Other high areas include the cities of Ashland and Paducah. Much of the state is sparsely populated with population densities lower than 100 people per square mile.

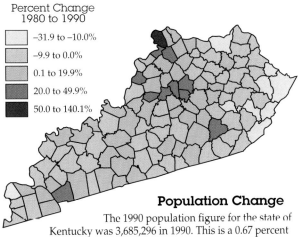

Percent Change 1980 to 1990

- –31.9 to –10.0%
- –9.9 to 0.0%
- 0.1 to 19.9%
- 20.0 to 49.9%
- 50.0 to 140.1%

Population Change

The 1990 population figure for the state of Kentucky was 3,685,296 in 1990. This is a 0.67 percent increase from 3,660,777 in 1980. The next decade will show growth with a population of 3.7 million or a 1.29 percent increase. The areas of fastest growth include Boone County in the north near Cincinnati, Ohio, and the area around Lexington. Other areas include Laurel and Trigg counties. Many counties in the state are losing population, which accounts for the small growth overall.

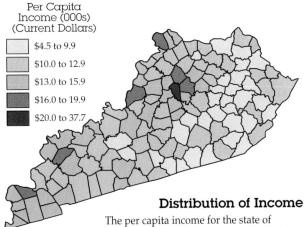

Per Capita Income (000s) (Current Dollars)

- $4.5 to 9.9
- $10.0 to 12.9
- $13.0 to 15.9
- $16.0 to 19.9
- $20.0 to 37.7

Distribution of Income

The per capita income for the state of Kentucky (current dollars) was $16,534 in 1992. This is a 105.4 percent increase from $8,051 in 1980. Income is greatest in the county of Woodford near the city of Lexington. Other high-income areas include the cities of Paducah, Louisville, and Lexington. Many of the low income areas of the state can be found in the Cumberland Mountain region. Here, many coal miners have lost their jobs as mines have cut costs or closed down.

Population Projections

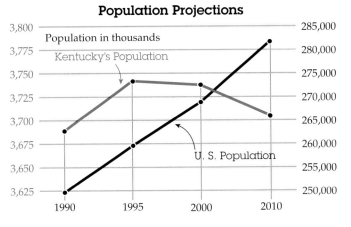

Population in thousands
Kentucky's Population
U. S. Population

Population Change

Year	Population
1950	2,945,000
1960	3,041,000
1970	3,231,000
1980	3,660,777
1990	3,685,296
2000	3,733,000
2010	3,710,000

Period	Change
1950–1970	9.7%
1970–1980	13.3%
1980–1990	0.7%
1990–2000	1.3%

Population Facts

State Population, 1993: 3,789,000

Rank: 24

Population 2000: 3,733,000 (Rank 26)

Density: 92.8 per sq. mi. (35.8 per km2)

Distribution: 51.8% urban, 48.2% rural

Population Under 5 Years Old: 6.9%

Population Under 18 Years Old: 25.7%

Population Over 65 Years Old: 12.7%

Median Age: 33.0

Number of Households: 1,380,000

Average Persons Per Household: 2.60

Average Persons Per Family: 3.08

Female Heads of Households: 4.33%

Population That Is Married: 23.38%

Birth Rate: 14.8 per 1,000 population

Death Rate: 9.5 per 1,000 population

Births to Teen Mothers: 17.5%

Marriage Rate: 13.8 per 1,000 population

Divorce Rate: 5.8 per 1,000 population

Violent Crime Rate: 438 per 100,000 pop.

Population on Social Security: 17.7%

Percent Voting for President: 53.7%

Population Profile

Rank. Kentucky ranks 24th among U.S. states in terms of population with 3,789,000 citizens.

Minority Population. The state's minority population is 8.4 percent. The state's male to female ratio for 1990 was 93.96 males for every 100 females. It was below the national average of 95.22 males for every 100 females.

Growth. Growing slightly faster than the projected national average, the state's population is expected to reach 3.7 million by the year 2010 (see graph above).

Older Citizens. The state's population older than 65 was 466,845 in 1990. It grew 13.91% from 409,828 in 1980.

Younger Citizens. The number of children (under 18 years of age) was 954 thousand in 1990. This represents 25.9 percent of the state's population. The state's school aged population was 623 thousand in 1990. It is expected to decrease to 599 thousand by the year 2000. This represents a –3.85% change.

Urban/Rural. 51.8% of the population of the state live in urban areas while 48.2% live in rural areas.

Largest Cities. Kentucky has five cities with a population greater than 35,000. The populations of the state's largest centers are (starting from the most populous) Louisville (269,063), Lexington-Fayette (225,366), Owensboro (53,549), Covington (43,264), Bowling Green (40,641), Hopkinsville (29,809), Paducah (27,256), Frankfort (25,968), Henderson (25,945), Pleasure Ridge Park (25,131), Ashland (23,622), Jeffersontown (23,221), Valley Station (22,840), Newburg (21,647), and Fort Knox (21,495).

Government

Capital: Frankfort (established 1793).

Statehood: Became 15th state on Jun. 1, 1792.

Number of Counties: 120.

Supreme Court Justices: 7, 8-year term.

State Senators: 38, 4-year term.

State Legislators: 100, 2-year term.

United States Senators: 2.

United States Representatives: 6.

Electoral Votes: 8.

State Constitution: Adopted 1891.

Kentucky's Famous Citizens

Chandler, Albert Benjamin (Happy) (1898–1991). Public official, baseball figure. Elected to two terms as governor (1935-1939, 1955-1959). He became baseball commissioner in 1945. Elected to the National Baseball Hall of Fame in 1982.

Hampton, Lionel (b. 1909?). Musician. Played the vibraphone and the drums in various bands and orchestras. He started his own big band in 1940.

Hines, Duncan (1880–1959). Publisher and author. Collected data on restaurants and compiled them into a book called *Adventures in Good Eating*. His name is now being used for a food company specializing in boxed cake mixes.

Lincoln, Abraham (1809–1865). Elected 16th president of the United States. Presided over a divided nation during the Civil War and was assassinated on April 15, 1865 by John Wilkes Booth.

Lynn, Loretta (b. 1935). Country singer and songwriter. Had a hit single with "I'm a Honky Tonk Girl" in 1960. The motion picture *Coal Miner's Daughter*, released in 1980, is the story of her life.

Kentucky

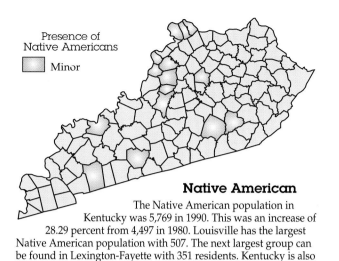

Native American

The Native American population in Kentucky was 5,769 in 1990. This was an increase of 28.29 percent from 4,497 in 1980. Louisville has the largest Native American population with 507. The next largest group can be found in Lexington-Fayette with 351 residents. Kentucky is also home to the Shawnee tribe.

Presence of Native Americans
☐ Minor

Nationalities

African	2,384
American	609,795
Arab	4,159
Austrian	1,895
Czech	2,309
Dutch	46,903
English	424,267
Finnish	964
German	662,049
Greek	3,280
Hungarian	3,662
Irish	436,605
Italian	36,086
Norwegian	4,674
Polish	15,783
Portuguese	903
Russian	4,167
Scottish	44,289
Slovak	3,174
Swedish	10,089
Welsh	12,615
West Indian	1,446

Statewide Ethnic Composition

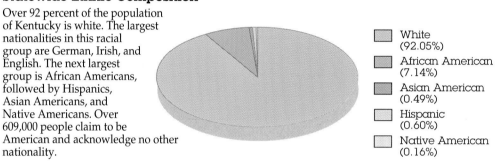

Over 92 percent of the population of Kentucky is white. The largest nationalities in this racial group are German, Irish, and English. The next largest group is African Americans, followed by Hispanics, Asian Americans, and Native Americans. Over 609,000 people claim to be American and acknowledge no other nationality.

☐ White (92.05%)
☐ African American (7.14%)
☐ Asian American (0.49%)
☐ Hispanic (0.60%)
☐ Native American (0.16%)

Education Facts

Total Students 1990: 630,688	Mean SAT Score 1991 Verbal: 473
Number of School Districts: 177	Mean SAT Score 1991 Math: 520
Expenditure Per Capita on Education 1990: $629	Average Teacher's Salary 1992: $30,900
Expenditure Per Capita K–12 1990: $583	Rank Teacher's Salary: 27th in U.S.
Expenditure Per Pupil 1990: $4,390	High School Graduates 1990: 38,500
Total School Enrollment 1990–1991: 630,091	Total Number of Public Schools: 1,385
Rank of Expenditures Per Student: 36th in the U.S.	Number of Teachers 1990: 35,598
African American Enrollment: 9.4%	Student/Teacher Ratio: 17.7
Hispanic Enrollment: 0.2%	Staff Employed in Public Schools: 71,377
Asian/Pacific Islander Enrollment: 0.4%	Pupil/Staff Ratio: 8.8
Native American Enrollment: 0.0%	Staff/Teacher Ratio: 2.0

Education

Attainment: 65 percent of population 25 years or older were high school graduates in 1989, earning Kentucky a ranking of 49th in the United States; 15 percent of the state's population had completed college. Institutions of Higher Education: The largest universities and colleges in the state include the University of Kentucky, Lexington-Fayette; University of Louisville, Louisville; Western Kentucky University, Bowling Green; Eastern Kentucky University, Richmond; Murray State University, Murray; Morehead State University, Morehead; and Kentucky State University, Frankfort. Berea College, Berea. Expenditures per Student: Expenditure increased 65% between 1985 and 1990. Projected High School Graduations: 1998 (45,490), 2004 (46,079); Total Revenues for Education from Federal Sources: $212 million; Total Revenues for Education from State Sources: $1.2 billion; Total Revenues for Education from Local Sources: $421 million; Average Annual Salaries for Public School Principals: $39,823; Largest School Districts in State: Jefferson County School District, 91,353 students, 24th in the United States; Fayette County, 31,191 students, 131st.

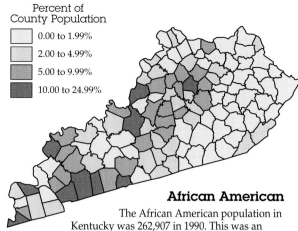

Percent of County Population
☐ 0.00 to 1.99%
☐ 2.00 to 4.99%
☐ 5.00 to 9.99%
☐ 10.00 to 24.99%

African American

The African American population in Kentucky was 262,907 in 1990. This was an increase of 1.40 percent from 259,289 in 1980. The African American population can be found in large numbers throughout the state. Large concentrations are in urban areas such as Lexington and Louisville. Counties with high percentages are located in the southwest portion of the state around Kentucky Lake.

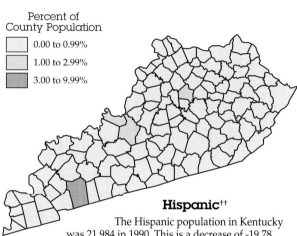

Percent of County Population
☐ 0.00 to 0.99%
☐ 1.00 to 2.99%
☐ 3.00 to 9.99%

Hispanic[††]

The Hispanic population in Kentucky was 21,984 in 1990. This is a decrease of -19.78 percent from 27,406 persons in 1980. The largest percentage of Hispanics can be found in Christian County in the southwestern portion of the state. Other populous areas include Meade and Hardin counties. Many Hispanics make Lexington their home as well.

[††] A person of Mexican, Puerto Rican, Cuban, or other Spanish culture or origin regardless of race.

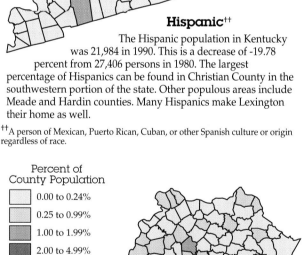

Percent of County Population
☐ 0.00 to 0.24%
☐ 0.25 to 0.99%
☐ 1.00 to 1.99%
☐ 2.00 to 4.99%

Asian American

The Asian American population in Kentucky was 17,812 in 1990. This is an increase of 58.46 percent from 11,241 persons in 1980. Hardin County contains the highest percentage of Asian Americans in the state. Other high-percentage areas include Meade, Christian, and Fayette counties. Twenty percent of the Asian American population lives in the city of Lexington.

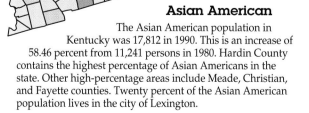

Agriculture

Kentucky has 14.1 million farm acres. During the last 40 years, Kentucky's farms have grown larger in size and fewer in number. In 1955, 193,000 farms were found in the state. Today, 91,000 remain.

Agriculture adds $2 billion to the state's gross product annually. The principal commodities in order of marketing receipts are tobacco, cattle, horses, and dairy products.

Livestock and livestock products account for about 55 percent of Kentucky's farm income. Thoroughbred horses make up about 49 percent of this. They are raised primarily on the bluegrass pastures near Lexington. Tobacco is the state's leading crop, and Kentucky is the nation's second leading supplier. Many of the other crops grown, including corn, barley, and hay, are used as cattle feed.

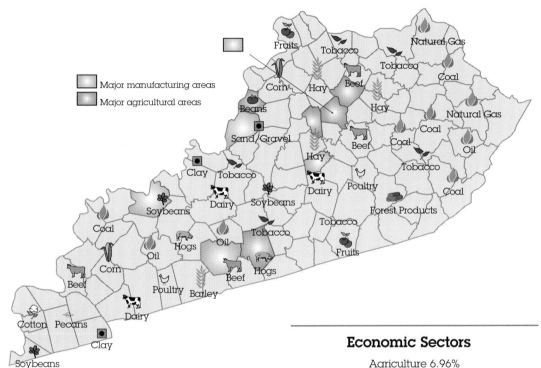

Major manufacturing areas
Major agricultural areas

Housing

Owner Occupied Units: 1,506,845; Average Age of Units: 28 years; Average Value of Housing Units: $50,500; Renter Occupied Units: 392,285; Median Monthly Rent: $319; Housing Starts: 19,400; Existing Home Sales: 83,300.

Economic Facts

Gross State Product: $65,000,000,000

Income Per Capita: $16,534

Disposable Personal Income: $14,664

Median Household Income: $22,534

Average Annual Pay, 1988: $20,730

Principal Industries: machinery, transportation equipment, food products, printing, chemicals, electrical equipment, tobacco products

Major Crops: tobacco, corn, milk, hay, soybeans

Fish: N/A

Livestock: horses, cattle, hogs, poultry

Non-Fuel Minerals: Sand, Gravel, Clay, Stone

Organic Fuel Minerals: Coal, Petroleum, Nat. Gas

Civilian Labor Force: 1,744,000 (Women: 787,000)

Total Employed: 1,615,000 (Women: 729,000)

Median Value of Housing: $50,500

Median Contract Rent: $319 per month

Economic Sectors

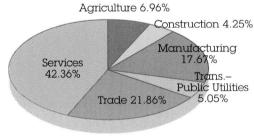

Agriculture 6.96%
Construction 4.25%
Manufacturing 17.67%
Services 42.36%
Trans.– Public Utilities 5.05%
Trade 21.86%

Manufacturing

Like Kansas, Kentucky's leading manufacturing activity is the production of transportation equipment. However, automobile, not aircraft production, is the leading transportation manufacturing activity. Kentucky's other manufacturing industries include chemicals, electrical equipment, and tobacco production. Manufacturing as a whole contributes just under one fourth to the Kentucky state gross product.

Manufacturing takes place all over Kentucky. The Louisville area, in northern Kentucky, is one of the largest truck production centers in the country. Other cities such as Georgetown and Bowling Green have their own automobile parts factories. Louisville and Lexington produce a variety of manufactured goods, from air-conditioning equipment to cigarettes. Furthermore, Kentucky leads the nation in bourbon whiskey production.

Transportation

Earlier in history, many of Kentucky's roads were toll roads. However, a state highway commission organized in 1912 created a system of free roads throughout the state. Today, Kentucky has 69,000 miles of highways and roads, approximately 1,400 of which are freeways. Many of Kentucky's lesser roads pale in comparison to similar roads in neighboring states because of access and general repair.

About 1,600 miles of navigable waterways, including the Mississippi and Ohio rivers, run in and along Kentucky. About 15 freight companies use the 3,300 miles of railroad track in Kentucky. Furthermore, four Kentucky cities are served by passenger rail services. The state has approximately 80 airports, both large and small.

Energy and Transportation Facts

Energy. Yearly Consumption: 1,476 tril. BTUs (residential, 19.0%; commercial, 12.4%; industrial, 43.2%; transportation, 25.5%); Annual Energy Expenditures Per Capita: $1,936; Nuclear Power Plants Located in State: 0; Source of Energy Consumed: Petroleum— 32.8%; Natural Gas— 12.7%; Coal— 52.0%; Hydroelectric Power—2.5%; Nuclear Power—0.0%.

Transportation. Highway Miles: 71,765 (interstates, 763; urban, 10,008; rural, 61,757); Average Yearly Auto Insurance: $473 (38th); Auto Fatalities Rank: 9th; Registered Motor Vehicles: 2,983,220; Workers in Carpools: 19.2%; Workers Using Public Trans: 1.6%.

Employment

Employment. Kentucky employed 1.68 million people in 1993. Most work in social and personal service jobs (363,000 persons or 21.6% of the workforce). Wholesale and retail trade account for 21.4% or 360,000 workers. Government employs 276,400 workers (16.4%). Manufacturing employ 292,400 people (17.4%). Construction accounts for 4.1%, or 69,200 persons. Transportation and utilities accounts for 4.9%, or 82,300 persons. Agriculture employs 64,000 workers or 3.8%. Finance, real estate, and insurance employs 3.7% of the workforce, or 63,100. Mining employs 27,500 people and accounts for only 1.6% of the work force.

Unemployment. Unemployment has decreased to 6.2% in 1993 from a rate of 9.5% in 1985. Today's figure is lower than the national average of 6.8% as shown below.

Unemployment Rate

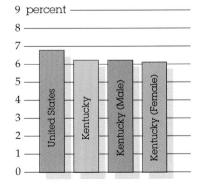

percent

United States
Kentucky
Kentucky (Male)
Kentucky (Female)

LOUISIANA
The State of Louisiana

Official State Seal

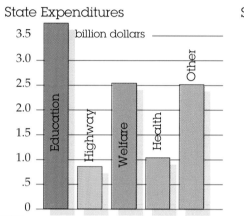

The Great Seal of Louisiana was first adopted in 1902. The seal contains the pelican (the state bird) surrounded by the state motto, "Union, Justice, and Confidence." The words "The State of Louisiana" run around the top of the seal.

Legal Holidays

January: New Year's Day—1st, Battle of New Orleans—8th; Martin Luther King, Jr., Day—3rd Monday; Robert E. Lee's Birthday—19th; February: Presidents' Day—3rd Monday; April: Admission Day—30th; May: Memorial Day—4th Monday; June: Confederate Memorial Day—3rd; July: Independence Day—4th; September: Labor Day—1st Monday; October: Columbus Day—2nd Monday; November: All Saints' Day—1st; Veterans' Day—11th; Thanksgiving—4th Thursday; December: Louisiana Purchase Anniversary —20th; Christmas—25th.

Louisiana's Finances

Households: 1,499,000; Income Per Capita Current Dollars: $15,712; Change Per Capita Income 1980 to 1992: 81.2% (46th in U.S.); State Expenditures: $10,683,000,000; State Revenues: $10,362,000,000; Personal Income Tax: 2 to 6%; Federal Income Taxes Paid Per Capita: $1,292; Sales Tax: 4% (Prescription drugs exempt).

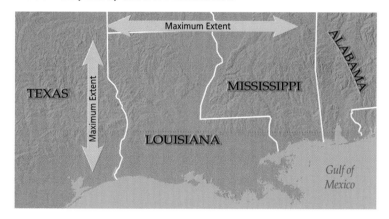

State Expenditures

State Revenues

Official State Flag

The state flag of Louisiana was adopted at the beginning of the Civil War. It has gone through changes since then and was finally legalized in 1912. The pelican, the symbol of self-sacrifice, is included above the state motto, "Union, Justice, and Confidence."

Location, Size, and Boundaries

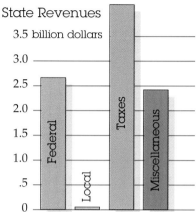

Location. Louisiana is located in the West South Central region of the United States. It is bounded on three of four sides by land with a general coastline along the Gulf of Mexico. The geographic center of Louisiana is lat. 30° 58.1' N; long. 92° 32.2' W.

Size. Louisiana is the 31st largest state in terms of size. Its area is 48,523 sq. mi. (125,675 km2). Inland water covers 3,593 sq. mi. (9,306 km2).

Louisiana touches the Gulf of Mexico along a 397-mile coastline.

Boundaries. Arkansas, 166 mi. (267 km); Mississippi, 596 mi. (959 km); Gulf of Mexico, 397 mi. (639 km); Texas, 327 mi. (526 km).

Geographic Extent. The north/south extent of Louisiana is 236 mi. (380 km). The state extends 237 mi. (380 km) to the east/west.

Festivals and Events

February: Mamou Mardi Gras Festival, Mamou; Black Heritage Festival of Louisiana, Lake Charles; Mardi Gras, New Orleans; April: French Quarter Fest, New Orleans; April/May: New Orleans Jazz & Heritage Festival, New Orleans; May: Breaux Bridge Crawfish Days, Breaux Bridge; Trash Fest, Anacoco; June: Louisiana Peach Festival, Ruston; Blueberry Festival, Mansfield; Jambalaya Festival, Gonzales; July: Bastille Day Celebration; Kaplan; August: Le Cajun Music Awards Festival, Lafayette; September: Alligator Festival, Boutte; Louisiana Shrimp & Petroleum Festival, Morgan City; Louisiana Sugar Cane Festival, New Iberia; October: Gumbo Fest, Bridge City; State Fair, Shreveport; December: Christmas Festival, Natchitoches.

Louisiana Compared to States in Its Region.

Resident Pop. in Metro Areas: 2d; Pop. Percent Increase: 4th; Pop. Over 65: 3d; Infant Mortality: 1st; School Enroll. Increase: 3d; High School Grad. and Up: 3d; Violent Crime: 1st; Hazardous Waste Sites: 2d; Unemployment: 1st; Median Household Income: 3d; Persons Below Poverty: 1st; Energy Costs Per Person: 1st.

West South Central

	Population	Capital
Arkansas	2,424,000	Little Rock
Louisiana	4,295,000	Baton Rouge
Oklahoma	3,231,000	Oklahoma City
Texas	18,031,000	Austin

Facts about Louisiana. Origin of Name: Named after the French king Louis XIV.; Nickname: The Pelican State; Motto: "Union, Justice, and Confidence"; Abbreviations: La. (Traditional), LA (postal); State Bird: brown pelican; State Tree: bald cypress; State Flower: magnolia; State Song: "Give Me Louisiana," words and music by D. Fontane. "You Are My Sunshine," words and music by Jimmy Davis and C. Mitchell.

Louisiana Compared to Other States. Resident Pop. in Metro Areas: 22d; Pop. Percent Increase: 35th; Pop. Over 65: 39th; Infant Mortality: 4th; School Enroll. Increase: 44th; High School Grad. and Up: 43d; Violent Crime: 7th; Hazardous Waste Sites: 28th; Unemployment: 10th; Median Household Income: 47th; Persons Below Poverty: 2d; Energy Costs Per Person: 3d.

Sources of Information. Tourism: Department of Culture, Recreation, and Tourism, P.O. Box 94291, Baton Rouge, LA 70804. Economy: Department of Economic Development, P.O. Box 94185, Baton Rouge, LA 70804. Government/History: Secretary of State, P.O. Box 94125, Baton Rouge, LA 70804.

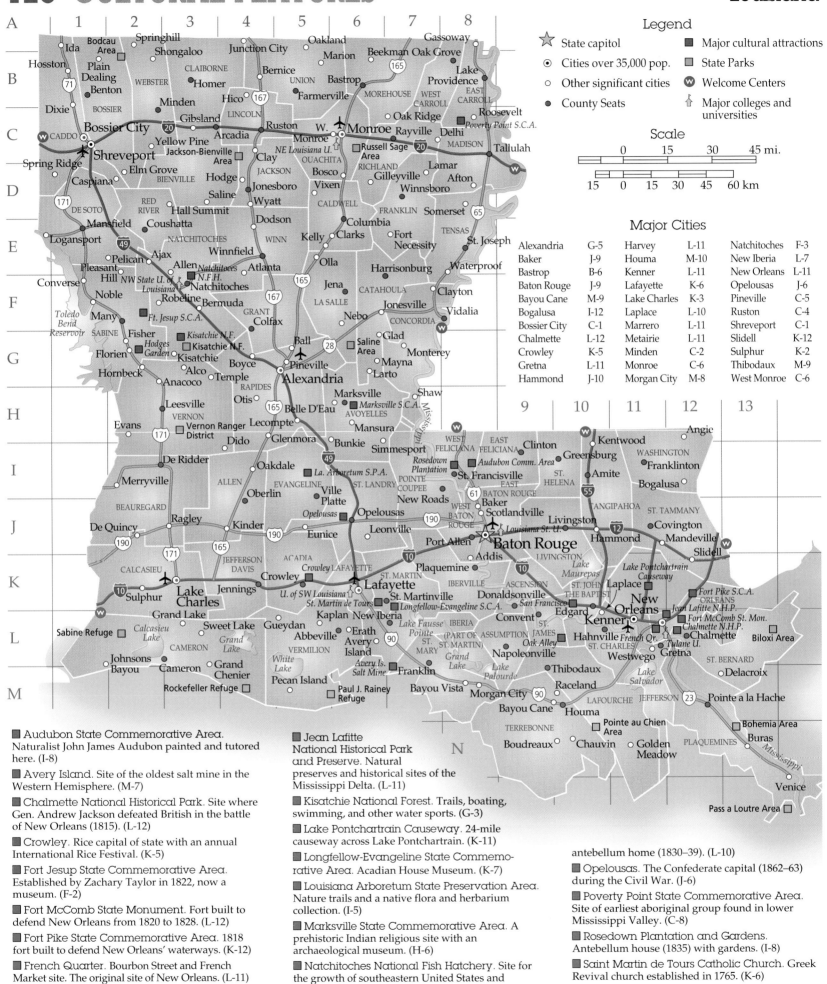

Legend

⭐ State capitol
◉ Cities over 35,000 pop.
○ Other significant cities
● County Seats
■ Major cultural attractions
▫ State Parks
Ⓦ Welcome Centers
⌂ Major colleges and universities

Scale

0 15 30 45 mi.
15 0 15 30 45 60 km

Major Cities

City	Grid	City	Grid	City	Grid
Alexandria	G-5	Harvey	L-11	Natchitoches	F-3
Baker	J-9	Houma	M-10	New Iberia	L-7
Bastrop	B-6	Kenner	L-11	New Orleans	L-11
Baton Rouge	J-9	Lafayette	K-6	Opelousas	J-6
Bayou Cane	M-9	Lake Charles	K-3	Pineville	C-5
Bogalusa	I-12	Laplace	L-10	Ruston	C-4
Bossier City	C-1	Marrero	L-11	Shreveport	C-1
Chalmette	L-12	Metairie	L-11	Slidell	K-12
Crowley	K-5	Minden	C-2	Sulphur	K-2
Gretna	L-11	Monroe	C-6	Thibodaux	M-9
Hammond	J-10	Morgan City	M-8	West Monroe	C-6

■ **Audubon State Commemorative Area.** Naturalist John James Audubon painted and tutored here. (I-8)

■ **Avery Island.** Site of the oldest salt mine in the Western Hemisphere. (M-7)

■ **Chalmette National Historical Park.** Site where Gen. Andrew Jackson defeated British in the battle of New Orleans (1815). (L-12)

■ **Crowley.** Rice capital of state with an annual International Rice Festival. (K-5)

■ **Fort Jesup State Commemorative Area.** Established by Zachary Taylor in 1822, now a museum. (F-2)

■ **Fort McComb State Monument.** Fort built to defend New Orleans from 1820 to 1828. (L-12)

■ **Fort Pike State Commemorative Area.** 1818 fort built to defend New Orleans' waterways. (K-12)

■ **French Quarter.** Bourbon Street and French Market site. The original site of New Orleans. (L-11)

■ **Hodges Garden.** Scenic gardens, greenhouses, and wildlife pastures. (G-2)

■ **Jean Lafitte National Historical Park and Preserve.** Natural preserves and historical sites of the Mississippi Delta. (L-11)

■ **Kisatchie National Forest.** Trails, boating, swimming, and other water sports. (G-3)

■ **Lake Pontchartrain Causeway.** 24-mile causeway across Lake Pontchartrain. (K-11)

■ **Longfellow-Evangeline State Commemorative Area.** Acadian House Museum. (K-7)

■ **Louisiana Arboretum State Preservation Area.** Nature trails and a native flora and herbarium collection. (I-5)

■ **Marksville State Commemorative Area.** A prehistoric Indian religious site with an archaeological museum. (H-6)

■ **Natchitoches National Fish Hatchery.** Site for the growth of southeastern United States and Louisiana fishes for pond stocking. (F-3)

■ **Oak Alley Plantation.** Restored Greek Revival antebellum home (1830–39). (L-10)

■ **Opelousas.** The Confederate capital (1862–63) during the Civil War. (J-6)

■ **Poverty Point State Commemorative Area.** Site of earliest aboriginal group found in lower Mississippi Valley. (C-8)

■ **Rosedown Plantation and Gardens.** Antebellum house (1835) with gardens. (I-8)

■ **Saint Martin de Tours Catholic Church.** Greek Revival church established in 1765. (K-6)

■ **San Francisco Plantation House.** Example of mid-19th century architecture. (K-10)

Louisiana

Weather Facts

Record High Temperature: 114° F (46° C) on August 9, 1932, at Plain Dealing; Record Low Temperature: -16° F (-27° C) on February 13, 1899, at Minden; Average January Temperature: 50° F (10° C); Average July Temperature: 81° F (27° C); Average Yearly Precipitation: 56 in. (142 cm).

Environmental Facts

Air Pollution Rank: 5th; Water Pollution Rank: 1st; Total Yearly Industrial Pollution: 277,878,454 lbs.; Industrial Pollution Rank: 1st; Hazardous Waste Sites: 11; Hazardous Sites Rank: 30th; Landfill Capacity: overextended; Fresh Water Supply: large surplus; Daily Residential Water Consumption: 156 gals. per capita; Endangered Species: Aquatic Species (4)—heelsplitter, inflated; Birds (8)—eagle, bald; Mammals (3)—bear, American black; Other Species (5)—tortoise, gopher; Plants (2)—geocarpon minimum.

Environmental Quality

Louisiana residents generate 3.5 million tons of solid waste each year, or approximately 2,000 pounds per capita. Landfill capacity in Louisiana will be exhausted in more than 12 years. The state has 11 hazardous waste sites. Annual greenhouse gas emissions in Louisiana total 172.9 million tons, or 39.2 tons per capita. Industrial sources in Louisiana release approximately 422.1 thousand tons of toxins, 1.0 million tons of acid precipitation-producing substances, and 3.0 million tons of smog-producing substances into the atmosphere each year.

The state has 6,300 acres within the National Park System. Noteworthy is Jean Laffite National Historical Park. State parks cover just over 36,000 acres, attracting 1.1 million visitors per year.

Louisiana spends approximately 2.6 percent of its budget, or approximately $44 per capita, on environmental and natural resources.

Average Monthly Weather

New Orleans	Jan	Feb	Mar	Apr	May	Jun	Jul	Aug	Sep	Oct	Nov	Dec	Yearly
Maximum Temperature °F	61.8	64.6	71.2	78.6	84.5	89.5	90.7	90.2	86.8	79.4	70.1	64.4	77.7
Minimum Temperature °F	43.0	44.8	51.6	58.8	65.3	70.9	73.5	73.1	70.1	59.0	49.9	44.8	58.7
Days of Precipitation	10.0	9.1	8.9	7.0	7.6	10.7	14.6	13.2	9.8	5.6	7.4	10.0	114.1
Shreveport													
Maximum Temperature °F	55.8	60.6	68.1	76.7	83.5	90.1	93.3	93.2	87.7	78.9	66.8	59.2	76.2
Minimum Temperature °F	36.2	39.0	45.8	54.6	62.4	69.4	72.5	71.5	66.5	54.5	44.5	38.2	54.6
Days of Precipitation	9.2	8.1	9.2	8.6	8.8	7.9	7.9	6.8	6.7	6.6	8.2	9.1	97.1

Flora and Fauna

Overall, the state of Louisiana has approximately 4,500 species of plant life. Many different types of trees live in different parts of the state. Oak and cypress trees, often covered with Spanish moss, grow in interior swampy areas of Louisiana. Hickory and loblolly pine grow in the northwestern part of the state. In the eastern prairies, longleaf pine trees can be found. Smaller dogwood and hackberry trees grow along Louisiana's streams. Wildflowers growing in the state include lilies, orchids, honeysuckle, and jasmine.

Louisiana has a diverse wildlife population as well. Foxes and beavers live in the northwest. Swampy areas are inhabited by wildcats and white-tailed deer. In the state's famous bayous, one can see alligators and nutrias, a rodent similar to the beaver. Over half of all wild geese and ducks in North America spend the winter in Louisiana's coastal marshes. The brown pelican, the state bird, lives there year round. Menhaden and pompano can be found in the Gulf of Mexico. Sunfish, catfish, and freshwater drum, also known as gaspergou, fill Louisiana rivers, streams, and lakes.

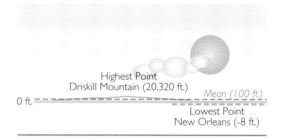

Physical Regions: (a) East Gulf Coastal Plain; (b) Mississippi Alluvial Plain; (c) West Gulf Coastal Plain.

Highest Point
Driskill Mountain (20,320 ft.)
Mean (100 ft.)
0 ft.
Lowest Point
New Orleans (-8 ft.)

Land Use

Cropland: 24.5%; Pasture: 8.6%; Rangeland: 0.9%; Forest: 48.1%; Urban: 5.5%; Other: 12.4%.

For more information about Louisiana's environment, contact the Department of Natural Resources, P.O. Box 94396, Baton Rouge, LA 70804.

Topography

Gulf Coastal terrain covers the entire area of Louisiana, with some distinctive regional variations. The coastal delta section in the south together with the lowlands of the coastal areas has the richest and most fertile soil in the state. The lowest elevation in the state is found here. New Orleans is actually several feet below sea level.

In east-central Louisiana, the East Gulf Coastal Plain physical region is a productive farmland with warm and moist soil that is predominantly gray/brown loamy clay. Paralleling the Mississippi and Red rivers is the Mississippi Alluvial Plain physical region, which consists of a series of ridges. The land on these ridges is known as front land. Soil is warm and wet, dark in color, and ranges from tillable to swamps and marshes. In the western part of the state from the Gulf to the northern border lies the Western Gulf Coastal Plain physical region. It is an area of coastal beaches and marshlands that extend into the interior of the state. Underground deposits of salt form salt domes, which lie underneath this coastal area. As one moves north, the land gradually slopes up to the hills and prairies that characterize the landscape north to the Arkansas border. It is close to this border that the highest point in Louisiana can be found. Driskill Mountain rises 535 ft. (163 m) above sea level. Soil type ranges from red/yellow clay to gray/brown loamy clay that is high in iron and manganese.

Climate

Louisiana has a humid, subtropical climate that is characteristic throughout the state. Both the Gulf of Mexico itself and prevailing southerly winds are responsible for the state's climatic pattern. Although Louisiana's climate is rather uniform across the state, regional temperature variations do exist. The southeast city of New Orleans has average January and July temperatures of 56 degrees F and 83 degrees F. In the northwest, where Shreveport is located, January and July temperatures average 48 degrees F and 83 degrees F as well.

Louisiana's average of 57 inches of precipitation a year makes it one of the wettest states. The southeast corner receives more rainfall, 64 inches, than the northwest, which averages only 46 inches of precipitation a year.

Because of its location, Louisiana is very vulnerable to storms. The coastal areas of the state have been bombarded by hurricanes, lesser tropical storms, and even tornadoes.

Hydrology

The most important river in Louisiana is the Mississippi. It forms the upper two-thirds of the state's border with Mississippi, then flows southeast through Baton Rouge, before emptying into the Gulf of Mexico just beyond New Orleans. The Pearl River forms the rest of the eastern border with Mississippi, while the Sabine River defines much of the western boundary with Texas. The Red River runs from the northwest corner of the state to the central portion. The Atchafalaya flows through the south-central part of Louisiana.

Levees have been built on many of these rivers to prevent flooding, since much of the state's land lies very low (New Orleans is actually below sea level). There are many lakes in Louisiana, including brackish ones in the south. The largest of these is Lake Pontchartrain (above New Orleans) at 630 sq. miles (1,014 sq. km).

Louisiana's History

Louisiana's First People

Native peoples occupied what is now Louisiana as long as ten thousand years ago. The state was never very densely populated by these early tribes of hunter-gatherers and was on the outer fringes of the Adena and Hopewell Mound Builder cultures prevalent in the Southeast from about 1000 B.C. to about A.D. 700. The Hopewell site of Poverty Point, near present-day Marksville, is this culture's greatest lasting achievement in the state.

The Indian tribes occupying Louisiana at the time Europeans arrived were mostly farmers. They consisted of the Caddo (some of whom would later act as scouts for the U.S. Army) in the northwest, the Tunica in the northeast, the primitive Atakapa in the southwest, the Natchez near the Mississippi River, and the Chitimacha in the south-central Atchafalaya Basin

European Exploration

Louisiana was first penetrated by whites in 1519, when Alonso Alvarez de Pineda explored the Mississippi River for the Spanish. In 1541, Hernando de Soto claimed the Mississippi for Spain. However, there was not much further activity in the region until René-Robert Cavelier, Sieur de La Salle, claimed Louisiana for France in 1682. Pierre Le Moyne, Sieur d'Iberville, in 1699 started a colony at Biloxi, but the first permanent settlement in Louisiana was established by Louis Juchereau de St. Denis in 1714 at Natchitoches. Four years later, Jean-Baptiste Le Moyne, Sieur de Bienville, founded New Orleans.

In 1717, France granted a proprietorship to John Law and his Company of the Indies in order to promote development in the region. This was a largely unsuccessful endeavor. In 1731, Louisiana became a French crown colony. It remained so until 1762, when France was forced to cede the entire Louisiana Territory to Spain in the aftermath of the French and Indian Wars. It was also about this time that Acadians (Cajuns) began to migrate to the state from Nova Scotia to escape the British.

In 1800, Spain returned control of the Louisiana Territory to France, and three years later it was acquired by the United States in the Louisiana Purchase.

Statehood

In 1804, the United States divided the newly purchased territory, creating the Territory of Orleans to cover most of present-day Louisiana. Eight years later, on the eve of the War of 1812, Louisiana was admitted to the Union as the eighteenth state. In 1819, the present boundaries were completed with the addition of land west of the Red River and the Florida Parishes.

In 1815, the final battle of the War of 1812 (taking place after the peace treaty had been signed) resulted in the bloody rout of the British at New Orleans. American troops lead by Andrew Jackson were attacked by the British forces led by Major General Sir Edward Pakenham. In the ensuing battle, British troops were forced to retreat under heavy fire from American rifles and cannons. At the conclusion of the battle the British has 2,100 casualties and 300 dead as opposed to only 58 casualties and thirteen dead on the American side. General Pakenham himself was killed in the engagement.

By the time of the Civil War, Louisiana's plantations were heavily dependent on slave labor, and the state seceded from the Union in 1861. New Orleans was captured by Union naval forces under Captain David Farragut on April 26, 1862. This allowed the opportunity for further successes at Vicksburg. Louisiana suffered heavy losses in the war, and the federal government took control of the state in the war's aftermath. Finally, in 1868, Louisiana crafted a new constitution containing civil rights for blacks and was readmitted to the Union.

A brief period of liberalization in state government occurred during Reconstruction, but it was quickly extinguished by plantation owners and other business interests who blocked any political reform until Huey Long was elected governor in 1928.

Industrialization

In the first half of the nineteenth century, cotton and sugar dominated Louisiana's economy, which was quite healthy during this time. The state was badly battered in the Civil War and struggled for decades to regain its economic footing. In the early years of the twentieth century, rice, brought by midwestern farmers to the state, also became an important crop, and the first oil wells were drilled.

Starting with Huey Long's administration in 1928, with massive public works projects like road building, and continuing after World War II with the development of offshore oil wells and soybeans as another agricultural product, Louisiana has rebounded with a strong modern economy. However, depressed oil prices in the 1980s have produced a slump.

Huey Long

In 1928, Huey Long was elected governor of Louisiana and quickly shifted the political balance of power away from the businessmen and politicians who had controlled the state for so long. He increased corporate taxes and created jobs with a massive public works program that included the construction of new highways, bridges, schools, and hospitals. He accomplished this social agenda by taking control of government with an almost dictatorial hand. His reforms launched him into the national spotlight and he was elected to the U.S. Senate in 1930. Dismayed that the New Deal programs did not go far enough, he founded the Share Our Wealth Society in 1934, promoting a redistribution of wealth in America. Intending to run for president in 1936, he was assassinated in 1935.

Important Events

1519 Alonso Alvarez de Pineda is first European to enter Louisiana while exploring the Mississippi.

1682 Louisiana claimed by René-Robert Cavelier, Sieur de La Salle for France.

1699 Settlement established by Pierre Le Moyne, Sieur d'Iberville, at Biloxi.

1714 First permanent settlement is established by Louis Juchereau de St. Denis at Natchitoches.

1718 New Orleans founded by Jean Baptiste Le Moyne, Sieur de Bienville.

1723 New Orleans becomes the capital of Louisiana

1762 France cedes Louisiana to Spain at the end of the French and Indian Wars.

1763 Acadians begin their migration out of Nova Scotia to the area near St. Martinville.

1800 France regains control of Louisiana from the Spanish.

1803 France sells the territory to the United States in the Louisiana Purchase.

1804 Louisiana Territory is partitioned by Congress; present-day Louisiana becomes the Territory of Orleans.

1812 Louisiana is admitted to the Union as the eighteenth state.

1815 Battle of New Orleans is the final battle of the War of 1812.

1838 First Mardi Gras (a pre-Lenten street festival) is held in New Orleans.

1850 Capital of Louisiana is moved to Baton Rouge.

1861 Louisiana secedes from the Union.

1868 Louisiana is readmitted to the Union.

1928 Huey Long elected governor and brings major social reform to the state.

1935 Huey Long, now a U.S. Senator and Presidential candidate, is assassinated.

1956 World's longest bridge (23.8 miles) is constructed over Lake Pontchartrain.

1986 Governor Edwin Edwards is indicted by a federal grand jury on conspiracy charges.

1990 David Duke, a former Ku Klux Klan member, is the Republican nominee for governor, he loses the election.

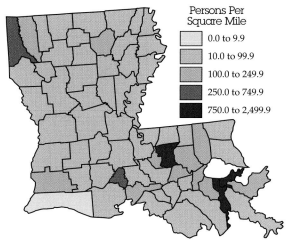

Persons Per Square Mile
- 0.0 to 9.9
- 10.0 to 99.9
- 100.0 to 249.9
- 250.0 to 749.9
- 750.0 to 2,499.9

Population Projections

Population in thousands

Louisiana Population

U. S. Population

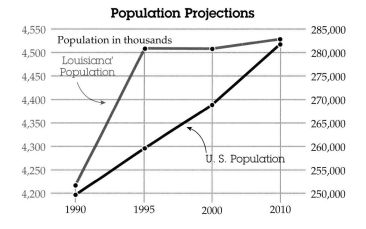

Population Change

Year	Population
1950	2,684,000
1960	3,260,000
1970	3,652,000
1980	4,205,900
1990	4,219,973
2000	4,516,000
2010	4,545,000

Period	Change
1950–1970	36.1%
1970–1980	15.2%
1980–1990	0.3%
1990–2000	7.0%

Population Density

Population density for the state of Louisiana was 96.9 persons per square mile in 1990 (37.4 per km2). Average U.S. density was 70.3 persons per square mile in 1990 (27.3 per km2). Habitation is most dense in and around the urban areas of New Orleans and Baton Rouge. Other high density areas are the cities of Lafayette and Shreveport.

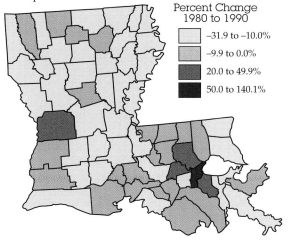

Percent Change 1980 to 1990
- –31.9 to –10.0%
- –9.9 to 0.0%
- 20.0 to 49.9%
- 50.0 to 140.1%

Population Change

The 1990 population figure for the state of Louisiana was 4,219,973. This is a 0.33 percent increase from 4,205,900 in 1980. The next decade will show growth with a population of 4.5 million or a 7.01 percent increase. The areas of fastest growth are the parishes of St. John the Baptist and surrounding parishes, and the parish of Vernon.

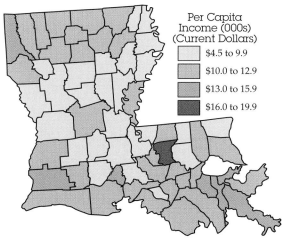

Per Capita Income (000s) (Current Dollars)
- $4.5 to 9.9
- $10.0 to 12.9
- $13.0 to 15.9
- $16.0 to 19.9

Distribution of Income

The per capita income for the state of Louisiana (current dollars) was $15,712 in 1992. This is an 81.2 percent increase from $8,672 in 1980. Income is greatest in the area in and around the capital of Baton Rouge. Other high-income areas are the parishes around New Orleans and Caddo parish, which is the location of Shreveport.

Population Facts

State Population, 1993: 4,295,000

Rank: 21

Population 2000: 4,516,000 (Rank 21)

Density: 96.9 per sq. mi. (37.4 per km²)

Distribution: 68.1% urban, 31.9% rural

Population Under 5 Years Old: 7.9%

Population Under 18 Years Old: 28.9%

Population Over 65 Years Old: 11.2%

Median Age: 31.0

Number of Households: 1,499,000

Average Persons Per Household: 2.74

Average Persons Per Family: 3.28

Female Heads of Households: 5.55%

Population That Is Married: 19.04%

Birth Rate: 17.1 per 1,000 population

Death Rate: 8.9 per 1,000 population

Births to Teen Mothers: 17.6%

Marriage Rate: 9.4 per 1,000 population

Divorce Rate: N/A

Violent Crime Rate: 951 per 100,000 pop.

Population on Social Security: 15.6%

Percent Voting for President: 59.8%

Population Profile

Rank. Louisiana ranks 21st among U.S. states in terms of population with 4,295,000 citizens.

Minority Population. The state's minority population is 34.4 percent. The state's male to female ratio for 1990 was 92.82 males for every 100 females. It was below the national average of 95.22 males for every 100 females.

Growth. Growing slower than the projected national average, the state's population is

Government

Capital: Baton Rouge (established 1882).

Statehood: Became 18th state on Apr. 30, 1812.

Number of Counties: 64 Parishes.

Supreme Court Justices: 7, 10-years.

State Senators: 39, 4-year term.

State Legislators: 105, 4-year term.

United States Senators: 2.

United States Representatives: 7.

Electoral Votes: 9.

State Constitution: Adopted 1974.

Louisiana's Famous Citizens

Gottschalk, Louis Moreau (1829–1869). Pianist and composer. His music was the first to successfully incorporate popular tunes.

Herriman, George (1880–1944). Cartoonist. Introduced his most famous cartoon strip, "Krazy Kat," in 1911.

Lawless, Theodore (1892–1971). Dermatologist. Founded the first clinical lab at Northwestern Medical School.

Lewis, Jerry Lee (b.1935). Rock n roll pianist. Had big hits with "Great Balls of Fire" and "Whole Lot a Shakin' Goin' On."

Marsalis, Wynton (b. 1961). Jazz trumpeter. Has won Grammy Awards for both jazz and classical recordings.

Polk, Leonidas (1806–1864). Episcopalian missionary bishop of the Southwest in the 1830s. Became bishop of Louisiana in 1841.

Prudhomme, Paul (b. 1940). Restaurateur-chef. His cookbooks and shows helped introduce Cajun food to the American public.

White, Edward D. (1845–1921). U.S. senator (1891–1894) and Chief Justice of the Supreme Court from 1910 to 1921.

expected to reach 4.5 million by the year 2010 (see graph above).

Older Citizens. The state's population older than 65 was 468,991 in 1990. It grew 16.01% from 404,279 in 1980.

Younger Citizens. The number of children (under 18 years of age) was 1.2 million in 1990. This represents 29.1 percent of the state's population. The state's school aged population was 791 thousand in 1990. It is expected to decrease to 784 thousand by the year 2000. This represents a –0.88% change.

Urban/Rural. 68.1% of the population of the state live in urban areas while 31.9% live in rural areas.

Largest Cities. Louisiana has 11 cities with a population greater than 35,000. The populations of the state's largest centers are (starting from the most populous) New Orleans (496,938), Baton Rouge (219,531), Shreveport (198,525), Metairie (149,428), Lafayette (94,440), Kenner (72,033), Lake Charles (70,580), Monroe (54,909), Bossier City (52,721), Alexandria (49,188), Marrero (36,671), Chalmette (31,860), New Iberia (31,828), Houma (30,495), Laplace (24,194), Slidell (24,124), and Terrytown (23,787).

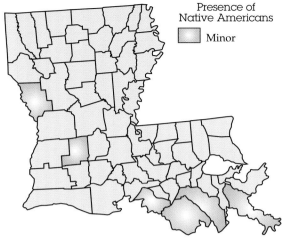

Presence of
Native Americans

Minor

Nationalities

African	7,122
American	280,143
Arab	8,411
Austrian	2,204
Czech	3,424
Dutch	24,837
English	232,151
Finnish	1,177
German	362,269
Greek	4,400
Hungarian	3,738
Irish	303,358
Italian	135,256
Norwegian	6,153
Polish	14,551
Portuguese	1,845
Russian	4,478
Scottish	25,697
Slovak	3,375
Swedish	9,875
Welsh	7,075
West Indian	3,316

Native American

The Native American population in Louisiana was 18,541 in 1990. This was an increase of 44.39 percent from 12,841 in 1980. New Orleans has the largest Native American community in the state with 759 residents. Shreveport is the second largest with 389.

Statewide Ethnic Composition

Over 67 percent of the population of Louisiana is white. The largest nationalities in this racial group are German, Irish, and English. The next largest group is African Americans, who make up over 30 percent of the population. Over 280,000 people claim to be American and acknowledge no other nationality.

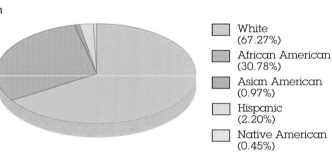

- White (67.27%)
- African American (30.78%)
- Asian American (0.97%)
- Hispanic (2.20%)
- Native American (0.45%)

Education Facts

Total Students 1990: 783,025

Number of School Districts: 66

Expenditure Per Capita on Education 1990: $620

Expenditure Per Capita K–12 1990: $561

Expenditure Per Pupil 1990: $4,041

Total School Enrollment 1990–1991: 779,161

Rank of Expenditures Per Student: 40th in the U.S.

African American Enrollment: 44.1%

Hispanic Enrollment: 1.0%

Asian/Pacific Islander Enrollment: 1.1%

Native American Enrollment: 0.4%

Mean SAT Score 1991 Verbal: 476

Mean SAT Score 1991 Math: 518

Average Teacher's Salary 1992: $27,000

Rank Teacher's Salary: 42d in U.S.

High School Graduates 1990: 37,800

Total Number of Public Schools: 1,536

Number of Teachers 1990: 42,117

Student/Teacher Ratio: N/A

Staff Employed in Public Schools: N/A

Pupil/Staff Ratio: N/A

Staff/Teacher Ratio: N/A

Education

Attainment: 71 percent of population 25 years or older were high school graduates in 1989, earning Louisiana ranking of 43d in the United States; 17 percent of the state's population had completed college. Institutions of Higher Education: The largest universities and colleges in the state include the Louisiana State University, Baton Rouge; Grambling State University, Grambling; Louisiana Tech University, Ruston; McNeese State University, Lake Charles; Tulane University, New Orleans; and Loyola University, New Orleans. Expenditures per Student: Expenditure increased 77% between 1985 and 1990. Projected High School Graduations: 1998 (33,832), 2004 (28,293); Total Revenues for Education from Federal Sources: $248 million; Total Revenues for Education from State Sources: $1.4 billion; Total Revenues for Education from Local Sources: $851 million; Average Annual Salaries for Public School Principals: $34,535; Largest School Districts in State: Orleans Parish School Board, 84,428 students, 27th in the United States; East Baton Rouge Parish School Board, 60,279 students, 54th.

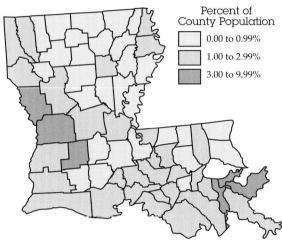

Percent of
County Population

- 5.00 to 9.99%
- 10.00 to 24.99%
- 25.00 to 86.24%

African American

The African American population in Louisiana was 1,299,281 in 1990. This was an increase of 4.91 percent from 1,238,472 in 1980. Louisiana has a large number of African Americans. The highest concentration extends from the northern part of the state along the Mississippi River down through New Orleans to the Gulf.

Percent of
County Population

- 0.00 to 0.99%
- 1.00 to 2.99%
- 3.00 to 9.99%

Hispanic[††]

The Hispanic population in Louisiana was 93,044 in 1990. This is a decrease of -6.14 percent from 99,134 persons in 1980. The largest percentages of Hispanics can be found in and around New Orleans and in counties bordering Texas.

[††]A person of Mexican, Puerto Rican, Cuban, or other Spanish culture or origin regardless of race.

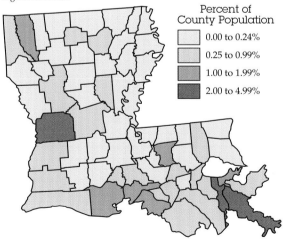

Percent of
County Population

- 0.00 to 0.24%
- 0.25 to 0.99%
- 1.00 to 1.99%
- 2.00 to 4.99%

Asian American

The Asian American population in Louisiana was 41,099 in 1990. This is an increase of 69.95 percent from 24,183 persons in 1980. The largest percentages of Asian Americans can be found in the southeastern portion of the state and in Vernon County on the Texas border.

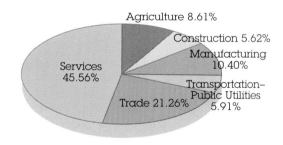

Major manufacturing areas
Major agricultural areas

Agriculture

Louisiana has 8.6 million farm acres. During the last 40 years, Louisiana's farms have grown larger in size and fewer in number. In 1955, 111,000 farms were found in the state. Today, 29,000 remain.

Agriculture adds $1 billion to the state's gross product annually. The principal commodities in order of marketing receipts are cotton, sugar cane, soybeans, and rice.

Crops account for about two-thirds of Louisiana's farm income. Soybeans are the leading crop, grown for livestock feed and for soybean oil. Cotton is produced mainly in the northeastern part of the state, while sugar cane is raised in a region south of Baton Rouge. Rice farms are found in the area between Lake Charles and Lafayette. Other crops include sweet potatoes and strawberries.

Economic Sectors

- Agriculture 8.61%
- Construction 5.62%
- Manufacturing 10.40%
- Transportation–Public Utilities 5.91%
- Trade 21.26%
- Services 45.56%

Manufacturing

Before the 1980s, petroleum products fueled the Louisiana economy. However, today the petroleum industry falls behind chemicals as the leading state manufacturing activity. Louisiana's 3,000 or so manufacturing companies contribute only 13 percent of the annual state gross product. Aside from chemical and petroleum products, the state also produces transportation equipment, processed foods, paper, and wood products.

Manufacturing mostly takes place in Louisiana's cities. Baton Rouge , Shreveport, and New Orleans are all large manufacturing centers. All three cities produce various chemicals, including fertilizers, soap, and drugs. Most petroleum products come from Baton Rouge or Westlake. Coffee, soft drinks, and other processed foods are primarily made in southeastern Louisiana.

Transportation

Historically, Louisiana's waterways have both benefited and hindered transportation. Goods and people moved across the Mississippi River in the past by ferry, but now they move across bridges. The Lake Pontchartrain Causeway, the world's longest bridge, connects New Orleans and St. Tammany Parish. Several other bridges link parts of Louisiana separated by the Mississippi River.

Both rail and road networks are extensive. Approximately 30 freight rail lines operate within the state. A passenger line serves seven Louisiana cities. Also, Louisiana has around 58,000 miles of highways and roads. However, many smaller roads have fallen into disrepair due to government spending cutbacks. Louisiana has many small airports, about 300, scattered across the state. The airport in New Orleans is Louisiana's busiest.

Energy and Transportation Facts

Energy. Yearly Consumption: 3,469 tril. BTUs (residential, 8.5%; commercial, 6.2%; industrial, 63.9%; transportation, 21.5%); Annual Energy Expenditures Per Capita: $3,095; Nuclear Power Plants Located in State: 2; Source of Energy Consumed: Petroleum— 42.6%; Natural Gas— 46.6%; Coal— 6.3%; Hydroelectric Power—0.0%; Nuclear Power—4.4%.

Transportation. Highway Miles: 58,629 (interstates, 869; urban, 12,319; rural, 46,310); Average Yearly Auto Insurance: $724 (10th); Auto Fatalities Rank: 5th; Registered Motor Vehicles: 3,093,511; Workers in Carpools: 20.0%; Workers Using Public Trans: 3.0%.

Employment

Employment. Louisiana employed 1.74 million people in 1993. Most work in social and personal service jobs (409,200 persons or 23.5% of the workforce). Wholesale and retail trade account for 21.9% or 381,700 workers. Government employs 341,300 workers (19.6%). Manufacturing employ 185,600 people (10.7%). Construction employs 96,600 people (5.6%). Transportation and utilities account for 6.1% or 105,300 persons. Agriculture employs 43,500 workers or 2.5% Finance, real estate, and insurance accounts for 77,900 people, or 4.5% of the workforce. Mining employs 45,700 people and accounts for 2.6% of the work force.

Unemployment. Unemployment has decreased to 7.4% in 1993 from a rate of 11.5% in 1985. Today's figure is higher than the national average of 6.8% as shown below.

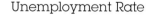

Unemployment Rate

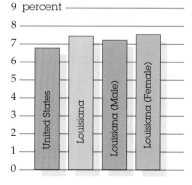

9 percent

- United States
- Louisiana
- Louisiana (Male)
- Louisiana (Female)

Housing

Owner Occupied Units: 1,716,241; Average Age of Units: 26 years; Average Value of Housing Units: $58,500; Renter Occupied Units: 501,319; Median Monthly Rent: $352; Housing Starts: 12,700; Existing Home Sales: 49,300.

Economic Facts

Gross State Product: $79,000,000,000

Income Per Capita: $15,712

Disposable Personal Income: $14,163

Median Household Income: $21,949

Average Annual Pay, 1988: $21,501

Principal Industries: petroleum products, chemicals, paper products, transportation equipment, food products, drugs, fertilizers

Major Crops: cotton, sugar cane, dairy, rice, soybeans, corn, tobacco, hot peppers

Fish: Bass, Catfish, Sunfish, Rays

Livestock: cattle

Non-Fuel Minerals: Sulfur, Salt

Organic Fuel Minerals: Petroleum, Nat. Gas

Civilian Labor Force: 1,933,000 (Women: 888,000)

Total Employed: 1,796,000 (Women: 819,000)

Median Value of Housing: $58,500

Median Contract Rent: $352 per month

MAINE
The State of Maine

Official State Seal

The Great Seal of Maine, adopted in 1820, includes the Maine coat of arms. It contains a depiction of a sailor and a farmer bordered by the state motto, *"Dirigo"* (I Direct or I Guide), and the state name. The star above the state motto is the North Star, which is the star used for navigation by sailors. It was chosen as the state symbol because at that time Maine was the northernmost state in the Union.

Legal Holidays

January: New Year's Day—1st; Martin Luther King, Jr., Day—3rd Monday; February: Presidents' Day—3rd Monday; March: Admission Day—15th; April: Patriot's Day—Third Monday; May: Memorial Day—4th Monday; July: Independence Day—4th; September: Labor Day—1st Monday; October: Columbus Day—2nd Monday; November: Veterans' Day—11th; Thanksgiving—4th Thursday; December: Christmas—25th.

Official State Flag

The state flag of Maine was adopted in 1909. It was originally carried by the state's military during the Civil War. It contains the state coat of arms placed on a blue background. Also included on the coat of arms is the pine tree, which is important commercially in the state.

Festivals and Events

January: Snowdeo, Rangeley; White, White World, Sugarloaf & Kingfield; March: New England Sled Dog Races, Rangeley; April: Fisherman's Festival, Boothbay Harbor (may also be in March); July: Beanhole Bean Festival, Oxford; Maine Potato Blossom Festival, Fort Fairfield; Deering Oaks Family Festival, Portland; August: Indian Day Celebration, Sipayik; Rangeley Lakes Blueberry Fest, Rangeley; The Maine Festival, Brunswick; September: Cumberland Fair, Cumberland; Thomas Point Beach Bluegrass Fest, Brunswick; October: Fryeburg Fair, Fryeburg; December: Christmas Prelude, Kennebunkport.

Maine Compared to States in Its Region.

Resident Pop. in Metro Areas: 5th; Pop. Percent Increase: 2d; Pop. Over 65: 4th; Infant Mortality: 6th; School Enroll. Increase: 4th; High School Grad. and Up: 5th; Violent Crime: 4th; Hazardous Waste Sites: 5th; Unemployment: 4th; Median Household Income: 6th; Persons Below Poverty: 1st; Energy Costs Per Person: 1st.

New England Region

	Population	Capital
Maine	1,239,000	Augusta
New Hampshire	1,125,000	Concord
Vermont	576,000	Montpelier
Massachussetts	6,012,000	Boston
Rhode Island	1,000,000	Providence
Connecticut	3,277,000	Hartford

Maine's Finances

Households: 465,000; Income Per Capita Current Dollars: $18,226; Change Per Capita Income 1980 to 1992: 121.8% (4th in U.S.); State Expenditures: $3,232,000,000; State Revenues: $3,312,000,000; Personal Income Tax: 2.1 to 9.89%; Federal Income Taxes Paid Per Capita: $1,447; Sales Tax: 6% (food and prescription drugs exempt).

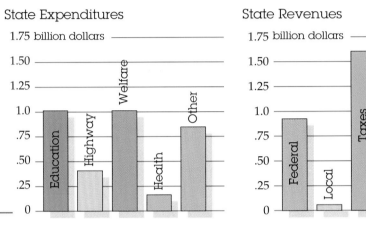

State Expenditures

State Revenues

Location, Size, and Boundaries

Location. Maine is located in the farthest northeastern corner of the United States. in the New England region. It is bounded on three of four sides by land with a general coastline along the Atlantic Ocean in the southeast. The geographic center of Maine is lat. 45° 15.2' N; long. 69° 14' W.

Size. Maine is the 39th largest state in terms of size. Its area is 33,215 sq. mi. (86,027 km2). Inland water covers 2,295 sq. mi. (5,944 km2). Maine touches the Atlantic Ocean along a 228 mile coastline.

Boundaries. Canada, 481 mi. (774 km); Atlantic Ocean, 228 mi. (367 km); New Hampshire, 174 mi. (280 km).

Geographic Extent. The north/south extent of Maine is 322 mi. (518 km). The state extends 207 mi. (333 km) to the east/west.

Facts about Maine. Origin of Name: Means *"mainland"*– used by English explorers to distinguish mainland from offshore islands; Nickname: The Pine Tree State; Motto: Dirigo *"I Direct or I Guide"*; Abbreviations: Me. (traditional), ME (postal); State Bird: chickadee; State Tree: white pine; State Flower: white pine cone and tassel; State Song: "State of Maine Song," words and music by Roger Vinton Snow.

Maine Compared to Other States. Resident Pop. in Metro Areas: 44th; Pop. Percent Increase: 45th; Pop. Over 65: 15th; Infant Mortality: 50th; School Enroll. Increase: 17th; High School Grad. and Up: 18th; Violent Crime: 47th; Haz. Waste Sites: 38th; Unemployment: 23d; Med. Household Income: 26th; Persons Below Poverty: 35th; Energy Costs Per Person: 11th.

Sources of Information. Tourism/History: Maine Publicity Bureau, 97 Winthrop Street, Hollowell, ME 04347. Economy/Government: Maine Dept. of Economic and Community Developement, State House Station 59, Augusta, ME 04333.

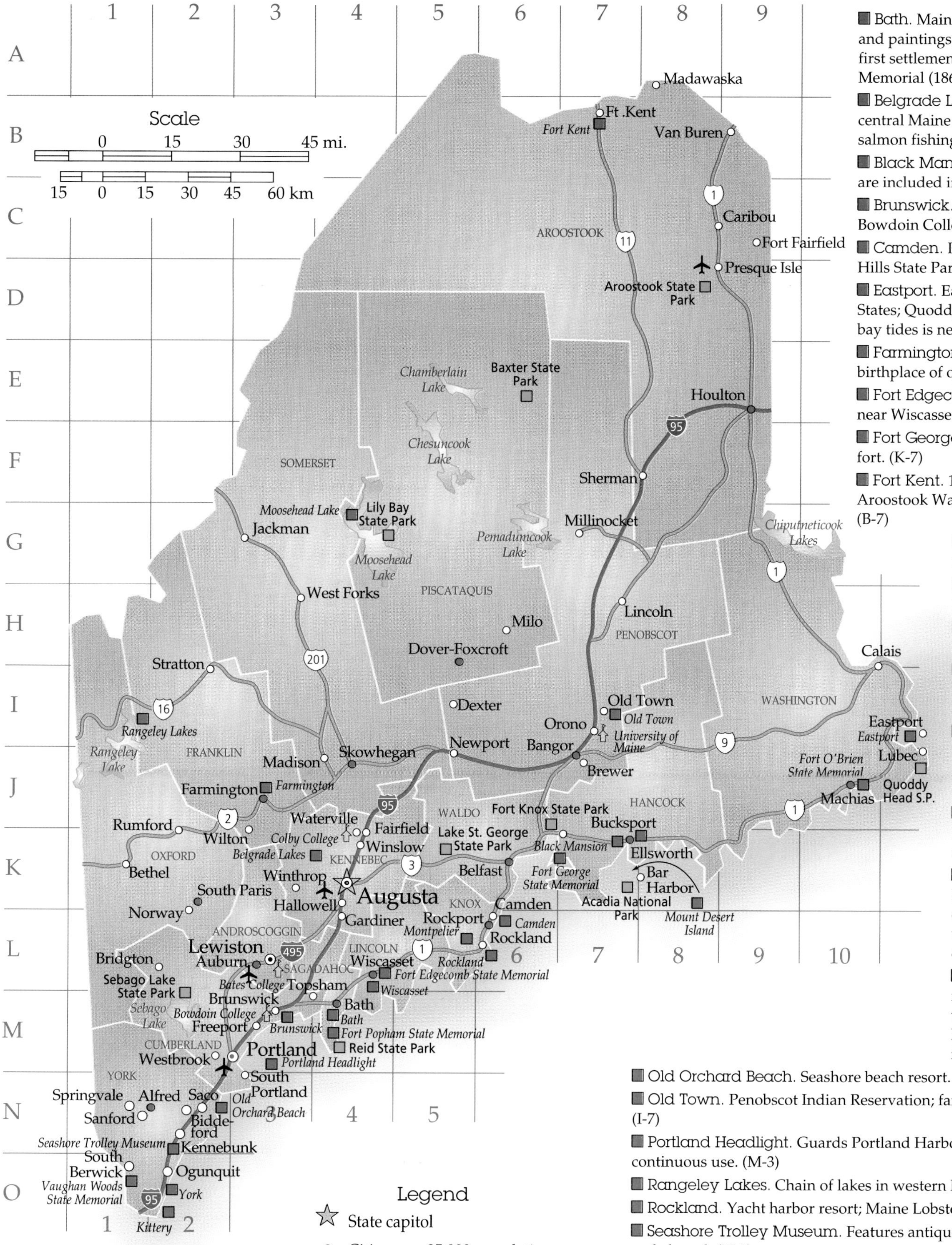
1 2 3 4 5 6 7 8 9
A B C D E F G H I J K L M N O
Scale
0 15 30 45 mi.
15 0 15 30 45 60 km
Madawaska
Ft .Kent
Fort Kent
Van Buren
1
Caribou
Fort Fairfield
AROOSTOOK
11
Presque Isle
Aroostook State Park
Chamberlain Lake
Baxter State Park
Houlton
95
Chesuncook Lake
SOMERSET
Sherman
Moosehead Lake
Lily Bay State Park
Jackman
Millinocket
Pemadumcook Lake
Chiputneticook Lakes
Moosehead Lake
West Forks
PISCATAQUIS
Lincoln
Milo
PENOBSCOT
Dover-Foxcroft
Stratton
201
Calais
Dexter
Old Town
Old Town
WASHINGTON
16
Rangeley Lakes
Orono
University of Maine
Eastport
Eastport
Rangeley Lake
FRANKLIN
Madison
Skowhegan
Newport
Bangor
9
Fort O'Brien State Memorial
Lubec
Brewer
Quoddy Head S.P.
Farmington
Farmington
Machias
95
WALDO
Fort Knox State Park
HANCOCK
1
Rumford
2
Waterville
Fairfield
Bucksport
Wilton
Colby College
Lake St. George State Park
Black Mansion
Ellsworth
OXFORD
Belgrade Lakes
Winslow
KENNEBEC
3
Bethel
Belfast
Fort George State Memorial
Bar Harbor
Winthrop
South Paris
Augusta
Acadia National Park
Hallowell
KNOX
Camden
Mount Desert Island
Norway
Gardiner
Rockport
Camden
ANDROSCOGGIN
Montpelier
Rockland
Lewiston
495
LINCOLN
1
6 7 8 9 10
Bridgton
Auburn
SAGADAHOC
Wiscasset
Rockland
Sebago Lake State Park
Bates College
Topsham
Fort Edgecomb State Memorial
Wiscasset
Brunswick
Bath
Sebago Lake
Bowdoin College
Freeport
Brunswick
Bath
Fort Popham State Memorial
CUMBERLAND
Portland
Reid State Park
Westbrook
Portland Headlight
YORK
South Portland
Springvale
Alfred
Saco
Old Orchard Beach
Sanford
Bidde-ford
3 4 5
Seashore Trolley Museum
Kennebunk
South Berwick
Ogunquit
Vaughan Woods State Memorial
York
95
1 Kittery 2

Legend

- ☆ State capitol
- ⦿ Cities over 35,000 population
- ○ Other significant cities
- ● County Seats
- ■ Major cultural attractions
- □ State Parks
- Ⓦ Welcome Centers
- ⇧ Major colleges and universities

Major Cities

Auburn	L-3	Presque Isle	D-8
Augusta	K-4	Saco	N-2
Bangor	J-7	Sanford	N-1
Biddeford	N-2	S. Portland	N-3
Brunswick	M-3	Waterville	K-4
Lewiston	L-3	Westbrook	M-2
Portland	M-3		

■ Bath. Maine Maritime Museum, ship models and paintings; nearby are Popham Beach, site of first settlement in Maine (1607), Fort Popham Memorial (1861). (M-4)

■ Belgrade Lakes. Chain of lakes in west-central Maine excellent for bass, trout, and salmon fishing. (K-4)

■ Black Mansion. Many original furnishings are included in this 1826 mansion. (K-8)

■ Brunswick. Harriet Beecher Stowe House; Bowdoin College, established in 1794. (M-3)

■ Camden. Popular resort; includes Camden Hills State Park. (L-6)

■ Eastport. Easternmost city in the United States; Quoddy Tidal Power Project to harness bay tides is nearby. (I-11)

■ Farmington. State university; nearby is birthplace of opera star Lillian Nordica. (J-3)

■ Fort Edgecomb State Memorial. 1808 fort near Wiscasset. (L-4)

■ Fort George State Memorial. 1779 British fort. (K-7)

■ Fort Kent. 1839 blockhouse built during Aroostook War over New Brunswick boundary. (B-7)

■ Fort McClary Memorial. 18th-century fort. (O-2)

■ Fort O'Brien State Memorial. 1775 fort. (J-10)

■ Fort Popham State Memorial. 1861 fort. (M-4)

■ John Paul Jones State Memorial. Tribute to soldiers and sailors of Maine. (O-2)

■ Kittery. 1760 Georgian style Lady Pepperrell House; Portsmouth Navy Yard; Old Church, built in 1730. (O-2)

■ Montpelier. Replica of Henry Knox's home, first United States secretary of war. (L-5)

■ Moosehead Lake. Largest lake in state located in west-central Maine, noted for moose watching, hunting, fishing, camping. (G-4)

■ Mount Desert Island. Scenic resorts, including Bar Harbor, with magnificent estates, and Northeast Harbor, with a racing fleet port. (K-7)

■ Old Orchard Beach. Seashore beach resort. (N-2)

■ Old Town. Penobscot Indian Reservation; famous for manufacture of canoes. (I-7)

■ Portland Headlight. Guards Portland Harbor; oldest lighthouse in continuous use. (M-3)

■ Rangeley Lakes. Chain of lakes in western Maine. (I-1)

■ Rockland. Yacht harbor resort; Maine Lobster Festival held in August. (L-6)

■ Seashore Trolley Museum. Features antique streetcars from the United States and abroad. (N-2)

■ Vaughan Woods State Memorial. Features scenic trails near South Berwick. (O-1)

■ Wiscasset. Impressive homes built by sea captains and shipping merchants; now a colony for artists and writers; Maine Art Gallery. (M-4)

■ York. One of oldest English public buildings in the United States is now the Old Gaol Museum, built in 1719. (O-2)

Weather Facts

Record High Temperature: 105° F (41° C) on July 9, 1907, at North Bridgton; Record Low Temperature: -48° F (-44° C) on January 18, 1921, at Van Buren; Average January Temperature: 16° F (-9° C); Average July Temperature: 68° F (20° C); Average Yearly Precipitation: 41 in. (104 cm).

Environmental Facts

Air Pollution Rank: 33d; Water Pollution Rank: 29th; Total Yearly Industrial Pollution: 15,271,414 lbs.; Industrial Pollution Rank: 35th; Hazardous Waste Sites: 9; Hazardous Sites Rank: 37th; Landfill Capacity: overextended; Fresh Water Supply: large surplus; Daily Residential Water Consumption: 126 gals. per capita; Endangered Species: Aquatic Species (1)—sturgeon, shortnose; Birds (4)—eagle, bald; Mammals (1)—cougar, eastern; Plants (3)—lousewort, furbish.

Environmental Quality

Maine residents generate 900,000 tons of solid waste each year, or approximately 1,620 pounds per capita. Landfill capacity in Maine will be exhausted in 5 to 10 years. The state has 9 hazardous waste sites. Annual greenhouse gas emissions in Maine total 20.6 million tons, or 17.1 tons per capita. Industrial sources in Maine release approximately 10.0 thousand tons of toxins, 112.2 thousand tons of acid precipitation-producing substances, and 5.1 million tons of smog-producing substances into the atmosphere each year.

The state has 41,100 acres within the National Park System; the largest area within the state is Acadia National Park. State parks cover just over 72,000 acres, attracting 2.5 million visitors per year.

Maine spends approximately 1.9 percent of its budget, or approximately $33 per capita, on environmental and natural resources. Maine representatives in the U.S. House voted in favor of national environmental legislation 88 percent of the time, while U.S. senators did so 84 percent of the time.

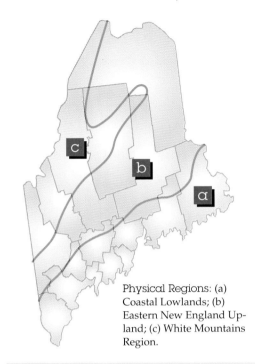

Physical Regions: (a) Coastal Lowlands; (b) Eastern New England Upland; (c) White Mountains Region.

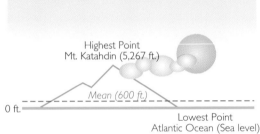

Highest Point
Mt. Katahdin (5,267 ft.)

Mean (600 ft.)

0 ft.

Lowest Point
Atlantic Ocean (Sea level)

Land Use

Cropland: 4.8%; Pasture: 2.1%; Rangeland: 0%; Forest: 86.8%; Urban: 2.6%; Other: 3.7%.

For more information about Maine's environment, contact the Environmental Protection Department, State House 17, Augusta, ME 04333.

Average Monthly Weather

Caribou	Jan	Feb	Mar	Apr	May	Jun	Jul	Aug	Sep	Oct	Nov	Dec	Yearly
Maximum Temperature °F	19.9	22.9	33.5	45.8	60.7	71.0	75.7	73.1	63.9	51.7	38.0	23.9	48.3
Minimum Temperature °F	1.4	3.0	15.1	28.8	39.7	49.6	54.5	51.8	43.2	34.5	24.2	7.5	29.4
Days of Precipitation	14.4	12.3	12.8	13.0	13.3	13.6	13.9	13.2	12.4	12.3	14.5	14.5	160.1
Portland													
Maximum Temperature °F	31.0	33.1	40.5	52.5	63.4	72.8	78.9	77.5	69.6	59.0	47.1	34.9	55.0
Minimum Temperature °F	11.9	12.9	23.7	33.0	42.1	51.4	57.3	55.8	47.7	37.9	29.6	16.7	35.0
Days of Precipitation	11.0	10.0	11.3	12.0	12.5	11.4	9.7	9.5	8.4	9.2	11.6	11.4	128.0

Flora and Fauna

Maine has perhaps the highest percentage of forested land of any of the states—nearly 90 percent. Approximately 18 million acres of land is covered with forests. The majority of these forests are a combination of coniferous spruce and fir trees. However, other trees such as hemlock, birch, beech, and basswood also grow in the state. Shrubs and similar plants can also be found in Maine, some of which include chockberry, shadbush, witch hazel, and blueberry. Maine's wildflowers include buttercups, goldenrods, hepaticas, and mayflowers.

Maine's forests provide habitat for many wildlife species. Large mammals include moose, bear, and deer. An assortment of fur-bearing animals such as lynx, fox, marten, and mink also live in the state's woodlands. Maine has over 300 kinds of birds living within its borders, including owls, sparrows, and chickadees. Birds living in coastal areas include gulls and loons. Bass, perch, and pickerel all live in Maine's inland waterways. Striped bass, flounder, and tuna live off the Maine coast, as do lobsters and other sea life.

Topography

There are several distinct topographic regions in Maine. The southeastern coastal area lies within the Coastal Lowlands physical region that runs up the coast of New England. This area extends from 10 to 30 miles (16 to 48 km) inland, and is characterized by sandy beaches and salt marshes, as well as hundreds of islands just off the coast.

The White Mountains physical region extends from Vermont into the western part of Maine, where these mountains are known as the Longfellow Range. The highest elevations in the state are found here, including many peaks over 4,000 ft. (1,200 m). The highest of these is Mount Katahdin, which rises 5,268 ft. (1,606 m) above sea level.

Extending northeast beyond the White Mountains is the Eastern New England Upland physical region of Maine, which also stretches eastward to the Coastal Plain. This is a region of plateaus that give way to numerous mountain streams and lakes. The fertile Aroostook Plateau, renowned for the potatoes it produces, lies in the northeast section of this area. The soil throughout Maine is extremely homogeneous; it is mostly cool and moist, high in organic, iron, and aluminum content, and predominantly brown.

Climate

Because of its location, Maine has colder weather than much of the United States. Maine lies in the path of frontal systems that blow air from the west. Arctic air also blows over Maine, causing cooler temperatures. Caribou, in northern Maine, has average January and July temperatures of 9 degrees F and 65 degrees F. In a southern, coastal city like Portland, January and July temperatures average 21 degrees F and 69 degrees F.

Maine averages 43 inches of annual precipitation. The coast receives slightly more rainfall (46 inches) than more inland locations (38 inches). Snowfall in Maine can be heavy in some places; northern Maine can receive over 100 inches of snow a year.

Hydrology

The two most important rivers in Maine are the Penobscot and the Kennebec. Both begin in the central part of the state and flow southward. The Penobscot empties into Penobscot Bay, and the Kennebec into the Atlantic Ocean. The St. John River forms part of the northeast boundary with New Brunswick, Canada, and the St. Croix River forms part of the southeastern boundary. The Allagash in the north and the Androscoggin in the southwest are other important rivers in the state.

Maine is dotted with thousands of lakes, the largest being Moosehead Lake at 119 sq. miles (308 sq. km). Moosehead is located in the central part of the state, where most of the largest lakes are. Some others include Eagle Lake, Chamberlain Lake, Millinocket Lake, and Chesuncook Lake. Sebago Lake, in the southwest, is the second largest lake.

Maine's History

Maine's First People

The earliest natives in Maine date from the Archaic era of Indian culture. The Red Paint People occupied the area of Maine and parts of Canada from about 3000 B.C. to 500 B.C. Named for the ground-up red hematite found on their graves (in which they also placed tools and effigies made of bone, slate, and other materials), they were primarily a foraging group. They would subsist on hunting, trapping, and gathering edible plants at a location until the food sources dwindled, then migrate to another location.

At the time of European contact, Maine was inhabited by the Algonquian-speaking Abenaki, who were almost wiped out by smallpox shortly afterward. Also, the Penobscot and Passamaquoddy tribes occupied the central portion of the state.

European Exploration

The Viking Leif Erikson is reputed to have touched Maine's shores in A.D. 1000. Almost five centuries later (1497–1499), John Cabot explored the coastal areas of the region and claimed the territory for England. A competing claim was entered in 1524 by Giovanni da Verrazano, exploring the coastal area for France. It wasn't until 1604 that an attempt was made to establish a settlement in Maine. The French tried on an island in the St. Croix River, but abandoned the site in less than a year. The English launched a similarly failed venture at Sagadahoc in 1607. The first permanent settlement was established by the English in 1622. Ferdinando Gorges and John Mason were granted territory between the Kennebec and Merrimack rivers. This land was divided seven years later at the Piscataqua River, with Gorges taking the area east of the river, chartered as the Province and County of Maine in 1639.

Numerous other settlements sprang up around the same time, including fur-trading posts established by the Plymouth Pilgrims. The French were also busy in the area, setting up missions to convert the Indians. This alliance proved troubling for the British. In 1675, French and Indian attacks on British settlements began the series of intermittent conflicts known as the French and Indian Wars that would last almost a century.

Statehood

In 1652, the Massachusetts Bay Colony annexed the Province of Maine, which protested the act. The dispute was resolved when Massachusetts purchased Maine in 1677, and when Massachusetts was granted a new royal charter in 1691, Maine was designated a district.

The state played an important role during the Revolutionary War, though the British remained in control for the duration of the conflict. After the war, the Continental Congress declared Maine to be one of the three districts of Massachusetts. The British once again occupied the state during the War of 1812, after which serious support for statehood began to arise. In a referendum in 1819, Maine voters overwhelmingly approved such a measure, and the following year the state was admitted to the Union as the twenty-third state (a free state teamed with the slave state of Missouri), with the capital at Portland. In 1832, the capital was moved to Augusta.

Conflict erupted in 1838 with the unsettled boundary between New Brunswick, Canada and Maine. Lumberjacks from New Brunswick entered into the Aroostook Valley angering the local populace. A sort of "war" erupted between the two peoples, and it took President Van Buren to send General Winfield Scott to the area to settle things down. Although no one was killed, this "war" signified a need to settle this boundary dispute. The dispute was eventually settled in the Webster-Ashburton Treaty of 1842 with the United States agreeing to British suggestions.

Industrialization

The first sawmill in Maine was opened in 1623, and the timber industry has played a dominant role in the economy of the state ever since. Fishing in Maine's abundant streams also played a role in the early years of the state's settlement.

After independence, Maine became a center of shipbuilding and its timber industry continued to thrive (trees being by far the state's most abundant natural resource). As the nineteenth century progressed, textile mills and shoemaking factories added an industrial base to the state's economy. Following the Civil War, paper making started to thrive and Maine was well positioned to be a leading supplier of the wood pulp necessary for the production of paper. The remarkable natural scenery in the state also gave rise to a growth in tourism. This mix of industries still dominates Maine today.

Natural Scenic Resources

Situated in the northeastern corner of the United States, Maine possesses a scenic natural beauty that has led the state to develop a concern for conservation issues. More than 80 percent of the land is covered by spruce, fir, pine (the state's nickname is the Pine Tree State), and other forest trees.

Acadia National Park, established in 1916, is the first national park in the east. The largest recreational area in the state is Baxter State Park which consists of over 200,000 acres (80,940 hectares) of protected land.

There are over 5,000 rivers and streams and 2,500 lakes and ponds in addition to the rugged beauty of Maine's coastline. In the 1970s, the state began an effort to conserve the depleted Atlantic salmon stock in inland coastal waterways. Pollution control for the state's water resources is a prime concern, as is overcutting of forest reserves and development of wilderness areas. The concern for acid rain has also lead citizens to seek legislation for controlling and eventually eliminating it.

Important Events

1000 Leif Erikson lands on Maine's northeastern shore.

1497–1499 John Cabot claims Maine for England after exploring the coastal areas.

1524 Giovanni da Verrazano claims Maine for the French after an exploration of the coastal region.

1604 French attempt unsuccessful settlement on island in St. Croix River.

1607 British attempt unsuccessful settlement at Sagadahoc.

1622 Ferdinando Gorges and John Mason granted land between the Kennebec and Merrimack rivers.

1629 Land divided, with territory east of the Piscataqua River becoming Province of Maine.

1652 Massachusetts Bay Colony annexes the Province of Maine.

1677 Massachusetts purchases Maine for six thousand dollars.

1691 Maine becomes a district of Massachusetts under its new charter.

1763 End of French and Indian War leaves almost no Indian population left in the state.

1819 Maine's voters approve a referendum to separate from Massachusetts.

1820 Maine admitted into the Union as the twenty-third state.

1832 Capital of Maine is moved from Portland to Augusta.

1861 Hannibal Hamlin is elected Vice President of the United States.

1957 Maine sends its first Democrat, Edmund Muskie, to the U.S. Senate.

1972 Maine's only nuclear power plant, Maine Yankee, begins operation.

1980 Penobscot and Passamaquoddy Indians settle their lawsuit against the state for return of their ancestral lands for $81.5 million.

1987 Attempt to close down the Maine Yankee Power Plant by voter referendum is defeated for the third time.

1988 Democratic U.S. senator George Mitchell becomes Senate majority leader.

1990 Due to a financial crisis, state offices are shut down and state employees put on furlough.

Population Density

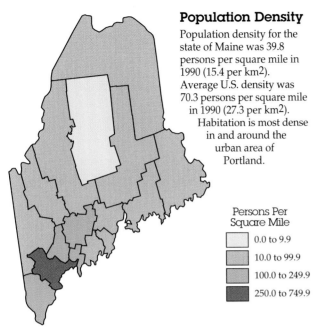

Population density for the state of Maine was 39.8 persons per square mile in 1990 (15.4 per km2). Average U.S. density was 70.3 persons per square mile in 1990 (27.3 per km2). Habitation is most dense in and around the urban area of Portland.

Persons Per Square Mile

	0.0 to 9.9
	10.0 to 99.9
	100.0 to 249.9
	250.0 to 749.9

Population Change

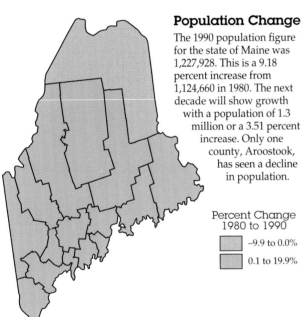

The 1990 population figure for the state of Maine was 1,227,928. This is a 9.18 percent increase from 1,124,660 in 1980. The next decade will show growth with a population of 1.3 million or a 3.51 percent increase. Only one county, Aroostook, has seen a decline in population.

Percent Change 1980 to 1990

	–9.9 to 0.0%
	0.1 to 19.9%

Distribution of Income

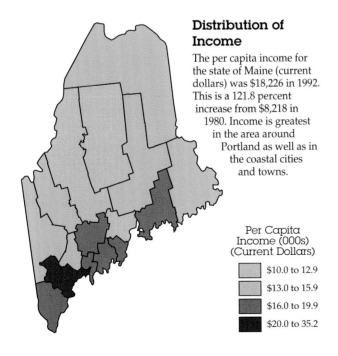

The per capita income for the state of Maine (current dollars) was $18,226 in 1992. This is a 121.8 percent increase from $8,218 in 1980. Income is greatest in the area around Portland as well as in the coastal cities and towns.

Per Capita Income (000s) (Current Dollars)

	$10.0 to 12.9
	$13.0 to 15.9
	$16.0 to 19.9
	$20.0 to 35.2

Population Projections

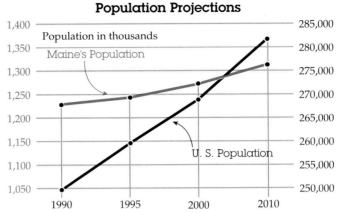

Population in thousands

Maine's Population

U. S. Population

Population Change

Year	Population
1950	914,000
1960	975,000
1970	997,000
1980	1,124,660
1990	1,227,928
2000	1,271,000
2010	1,308,000

Period	Change
1950–1970	9.1%
1970–1980	12.8%
1980–1990	9.2%
1990–2000	3.5%

Population Facts

State Population, 1993: 1,239,000
Rank: 39
Population 2000: 1,271,000 (Rank 41)
Density: 39.8 per sq. mi. (15.4 per km²)
Distribution: 44.6% urban, 55.4% rural
Population Under 5 Years Old: 6.7%
Population Under 18 Years Old: 24.8%
Population Over 65 Years Old: 13.6%
Median Age: 33.9
Number of Households: 465,000
Average Persons Per Household: 2.56
Average Persons Per Family: 3.03
Female Heads of Households: 3.61%
Population That Is Married: 22.03%
Birth Rate: 14.1 per 1,000 population
Death Rate: 9.0 per 1,000 population
Births to Teen Mothers: 10.8%
Marriage Rate: 9.5 per 1,000 population
Divorce Rate: 4.3 per 1,000 population
Violent Crime Rate: 132 per 100,000 pop.
Population on Social Security: 17.7%
Percent Voting for President: 72.0%

Maine's Famous Citizens

Bradley, Milton (1836–1911). Founded the Milton Bradley Company, which popularized board games and croquet in America.

Fuller, Melville Weston (1833–1910). Chief Justice of the U.S. Supreme Court from 1888 to 1910.

Gannett, Henry (1846–1914). Chief geographer of the U.S. Geological Survey (1882-1914) and organizer of the Census Bureau.

Hamlin, Hannibal (1809–1891). Vice president under Abraham Lincoln. Also served as U.S. Senator (1848-1861 and 1865-1881).

Jewett, Sarah Orne (1849–1909). Writer of stories, such as "Deephaven," based on the sea-port town in which she grew up.

Jones, Rufus Matthew (1863–1948). Active in the Quaker movement. Wrote four volumes of the six volume history of the Society of Friends.

Piston, Walter (1894–1976). Composer in the Neoclassical style. His Symphonies 3 and 7 won Pulitzer Prizes.

Smith, Margaret Chase (b. 1897). Elected to the U.S. House in 1940 and to the Senate in 1948, serving until 1973.

Population Profile

Rank. Maine ranks 39th among U.S. states in terms of population with 1,239,000 citizens.

Minority Population. The state's minority population is 2.0 percent. The state's male to female ratio for 1990 was 94.89 males for every 100 females. It was below the national average of 95.22 males for every 100 females.

Growth. Growing more slowly than the projected national average, the state's population is expected to reach 1.3 million by the year 2010 (*see graph above*).

Older Citizens. The state's population older than 65 was 163,373 in 1990. It grew 15.93% from 140,918 in 1980.

Younger Citizens. The number of children (under 18 years of age) was 309 thousand in 1990. This represents 25.2 percent of the state's population. The state's school aged population was 213 thousand in 1990. It is expected to increase to 230 thousand by the year 2000. This represents a 7.98% change.

Urban/Rural. 44.6% of the population of the state live in urban areas while 55.4% live in rural areas.

Largest Cities. Maine has two cities with a population greater than 35,000. The populations of the state's largest centers are (starting from the most populous) Portland (64,358), Lewiston (39,757), Bangor (33,181), Auburn (24,309), South Portland (23,163), Augusta (21,325), Biddeford (20,710), Waterville (17,173), Westbrook (16,121), Saco (15,181), Brunswick (14,683), Presque Isle (10,550), and Sanford (10,296).

Government

Capital: Augusta (established 1832).
Statehood: Became 23d state on Mar. 15, 1820.
Number of Counties: 16.
Supreme Court Justices: 7, 7-year term.
State Senators: 35, 2-year term.
State Legislators: 151, 2-year term.
United States Senators: 2.
United States Representatives: 2.
Electoral Votes: 4.
State Constitution: Adopted 1819.

Native American

The Native American population in Maine was 5,998 in 1990. This was an increase of 37.57 percent from 4,360 in 1980. Many Native Americans in the state of Maine can be found residing in the Passamaquoddy and Penobscot Indian reservations.

Presence of Native Americans

☐ Minor

Nationalities

African	276
American	86,826
Arab	2,382
Austrian	1,126
Czech	1,636
Dutch	8,278
English	279,371
Finnish	4,862
German	75,249
Greek	4,458
Hungarian	2,031
Irish	133,810
Italian	35,807
Norwegian	4,400
Polish	15,682
Portuguese	2,783
Russian	5,326
Scottish	44,372
Slovak	2,054
Swedish	15,147
Welsh	5,592
West Indian	527

African American

The African American population in Maine was 5,138 in 1990. This was an increase of 51.97 percent from 3,381 in 1980. The number of African Americans in the state of Maine is small, with no county having a large percentage.

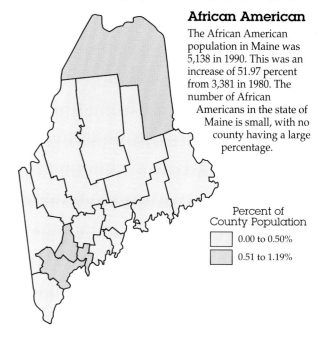

Percent of County Population

☐ 0.00 to 0.50%
☐ 0.51 to 1.19%

Statewide Ethnic Composition

Over 98 percent of the population of Maine is white. The largest nationalities in this racial group are English, Irish, and German. The next largest group is Hispanics, followed by Asians, Native Americans, and African Americans. Over 86,000 people claim to be American and acknowledge no other nationality.

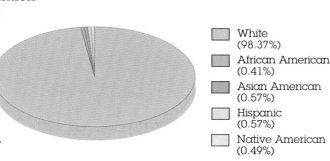

☐ White (98.37%)
☐ African American (0.41%)
☐ Asian American (0.57%)
☐ Hispanic (0.57%)
☐ Native American (0.49%)

Hispanic[††]

The Hispanic population in Maine was 6,829 in 1990. This is an increase of 36.44 percent from 5,005 persons in 1980. The only county with a high percentage of Hispanics is Sagadahoc County in the southwestern portion of the state.

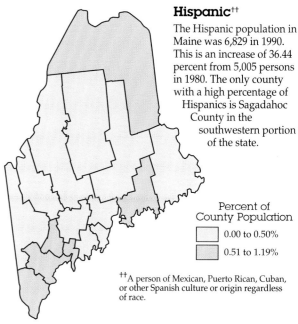

Percent of County Population

☐ 0.00 to 0.50%
☐ 0.51 to 1.19%

[††] A person of Mexican, Puerto Rican, Cuban, or other Spanish culture or origin regardless of race.

Education Facts

Total Students 1990: 213,775

Number of School Districts: 282

Expenditure Per Capita on Education 1990: $974

Expenditure Per Capita K–12 1990: $882

Expenditure Per Pupil 1990: $5,894

Total School Enrollment 1990–1991: 210,200

Rank of Expenditures Per Student: 11th in the U.S.

African American Enrollment: 0.5%

Hispanic Enrollment: 0.2%

Asian/Pacific Islander Enrollment: 0.8%

Native American Enrollment: 0.2%

Mean SAT Score 1991 Verbal: 421

Mean SAT Score 1991 Math: 458

Average Teacher's Salary 1992: $30,100

Rank Teacher's Salary: 30th in U.S.

High School Graduates 1990: 14,200

Total Number of Public Schools: 748

Number of Teachers 1990: 14,908

Student/Teacher Ratio: 14.1

Staff Employed in Public Schools: 26,317

Pupil/Staff Ratio: 8.1

Staff/Teacher Ratio: 1.7

Education

Attainment: 77 percent of population 25 years or older were high school graduates in 1989, earning Maine a ranking of 32d in the United States; 18.5 percent of the state's population had completed college. Institutions of Higher Education: The largest universities and colleges in the state include the University of Maine (founded 1865), Orono; Colby College, Waterville; Bates College, Lewiston; Bowdoin College, Brunswick. Expenditures per Student: Expenditure increased 58% between 1985 and 1990. Projected High School Graduations: 1998 (14,014), 2004 (14,468); Total Revenues for Education from Federal Sources: $52 million; Total Revenues for Education from State Sources: $459 million; Total Revenues for Education from Local Sources: $375 million; Average Annual Salaries for Public School Principals: $35,361.

Asian American

The Asian American population in Maine was 6,683 in 1990. This is an increase of 133.10 percent from 2,867 persons in 1980. The Asian American population is less centralized than that of Hispanics. Asian Americans are the fastest-growing minority group in the state.

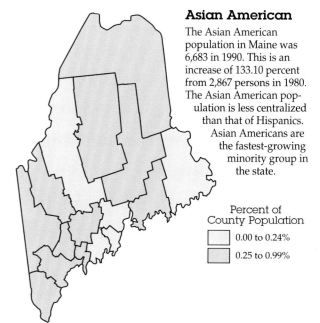

Percent of County Population

☐ 0.00 to 0.24%
☐ 0.25 to 0.99%

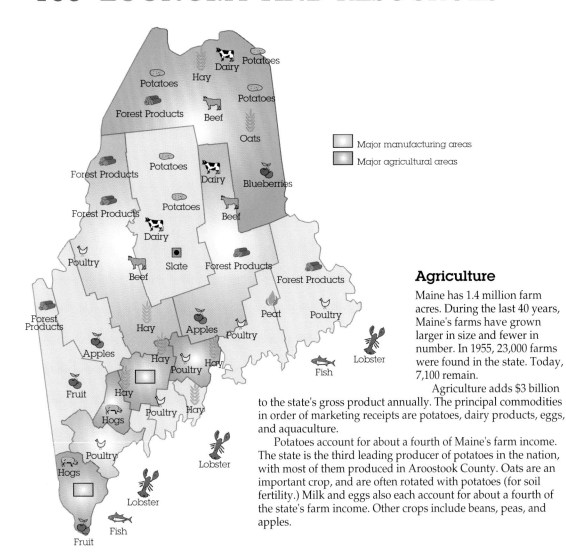

Major manufacturing areas

Major agricultural areas

Transportation

The state of Maine began constructing quality roads around the beginning of the 19th century. Today, the state has approximately 22,000 miles of roads and highways. Maine has two major highways, the Maine Turnpike and Interstate 95.

Maine has several deepwater ports along its coast. Portland is the closest U.S. port to Europe. Other Maine ports include Searsport and Eastport. Maine's first railroad, the Bangor and Old Town, was built in 1836. Today, a handful of railroads still ship freight across Maine. Passenger rail lines serve some larger cities. The state is also connected to Canada on the Via Canada passenger railroad. The Portland International Jetport is Maine's busiest airport. Another major airport can be found at Bangor.

Agriculture

Maine has 1.4 million farm acres. During the last 40 years, Maine's farms have grown larger in size and fewer in number. In 1955, 23,000 farms were found in the state. Today, 7,100 remain.

Agriculture adds $3 billion to the state's gross product annually. The principal commodities in order of marketing receipts are potatoes, dairy products, eggs, and aquaculture.

Potatoes account for about a fourth of Maine's farm income. The state is the third leading producer of potatoes in the nation, with most of them produced in Aroostook County. Oats are an important crop, and are often rotated with potatoes (for soil fertility.) Milk and eggs also each account for about a fourth of the state's farm income. Other crops include beans, peas, and apples.

Energy and Transportation Facts

Energy. Yearly Consumption: 362 tril. BTUs (residential, 21.8%; commercial, 16.0%; industrial, 32.9%; transportation, 29.3%); Annual Energy Expenditures Per Capita: $2,057; Nuclear Power Plants Located in State: 1; Source of Energy Consumed: Petroleum— 63.3%; Natural Gas—1.4%; Coal— 2.5%; Hydroelectric Power—14.4%; Nuclear Power—18.5%.

Transportation. Highway Miles: 22,481 (interstates, 366; urban, 2,479; rural, 20,002); Average Yearly Auto Insurance: $468 (39th); Auto Fatalities Rank: 27th; Registered Motor Vehicles: 978,134; Workers in Carpools: 18.8%; Workers Using Public Trans: 0.9%.

Employment

Employment. Employment. Maine employed 580,000 people in 1993. Most work in social and personal service jobs (134,000 persons or 23.1% of the workforce). Wholesale and retail trade account for 22.4% or 130,100 workers. Government employs 95,000 workers (16.4%). Manufacturing employs 91,100 people (15.7%). Construction employs 20,900 people (3.6%). Transportation and utilities account for 3.8% or 21,900 persons. Agriculture employs 16,300 workers or 2.8%. Finance, real estate, and insurance employ 25,600 workers, or 4.4%. Mining employs 100 people and accounts for less than 1% of the workforce.

Unemployment. Unemployment has increased to 7.9% in 1993 from a rate of 5.4% in 1985. Today's figure is higher than the national average of 6.8% as shown below.

Housing

Owner Occupied Units: 587,045; Average Age of Units: 35 years; Average Value of Housing Units: $87,400; Renter Occupied Units: 133,275; Median Monthly Rent: $419; Housing Starts: 4,100; Existing Home Sales: 11,600.

Economic Facts

Gross State Product: $23,000,000,000 (1989)

Income Per Capita: $18,226

Disposable Personal Income: $16,298

Median Household Income: $27,854

Average Annual Pay, 1988: $20,870

Principal Industries: paper products, transportation equipment, electrical equipment, wood products, leather products, food products, rubber and plastic goods

Major Crops: potatoes, eggs, milk, oats, hay, corn, peas, sugar beets, dry beans,broccoli, apples, blueberries

Fish: Cod, Lobster, Flounder, Mackerel, Pollock, Bass

Livestock: Chickens, Cows

Non-Fuel Minerals: Granite, Limestone, Tourmaline, Brick Clay, Copper, Zinc, Fieldstone, Lead

Organic Fuel Minerals: N/A

Civilian Labor Force: 647,000 (Women: 302,000)

Total Employed: 598,000 (Women: 283,000)

Median Value of Housing: $87,400

Median Contract Rent: $419 per month

Economic Sectors 1992

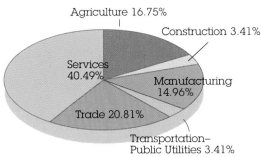

Agriculture 16.75%

Construction 3.41%

Services 40.49%

Manufacturing 14.96%

Trade 20.81%

Transportation–Public Utilities 3.41%

Manufacturing

Most of the value goods Maine produces come from the manufacturing sector. Overall, the number of manufacturing jobs in the state continues to decline, a trend which began in the 1950s. Wood products industries are the second largest concentration, and the most stable manufacturing jobs. Maine's number one manufacturing industry, however, is paper products. Smaller manufacturing industries include electrical equipment, food processing, and footwear.

Several Maine towns across the state, including Millinocket, Bucksport, and Winslow, have paper manufacturing plants. Sawmills and lumber yards can also be found in many parts of the state. Other Maine towns produce outerwear, textiles, and packaged foods (lobster, apples) for shipment elsewhere in the world.

Unemployment Rate

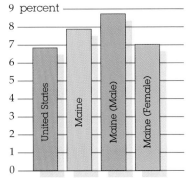

MARYLAND
The State of Maryland

Official State Seal

The Great Seal of Maryland was adopted in 1876. It contains two men supporting the Calvert and Crossland arms of Lord Baltimore. Below the arms is one of the state mottoes, *"Fatti Maschii Parole Femine"* (Manly Deeds, Womanly Words). The other motto, *"Scuto Bonae Voluntatis Tuae Coronasti Nos"* (With Favor Wilt Thou Compass Us as with a Shield), encircles the top of the seal.

Legal Holidays

January: New Year's Day—1st; Martin Luther King, Jr., Day—3rd Monday; February: Abraham Lincoln's Birthday—12th; Presidents' Day—3rd Monday; March: Maryland Day—25th; April: Admission Day—28th; May: Memorial Day—4th Monday; July: Independence Day—4th; September: Labor Day—1st Monday; Defender's Day—12th; National Anthem Day—14th; October: Columbus Day—2d Monday; November: Veterans' Day—11th; Thanksgiving—4th Thursday; Repudiation Day—23rd; December: Christmas—25th.

Official State Flag

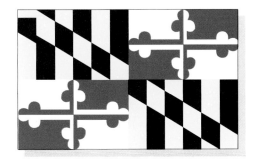

Officially adopted in 1904, the state flag of Maryland contains the family arms of Lord Baltimore. The flag features the arms of both the Crosslands (crosses) and the Calverts (stripes). This flag was revived in the 1880s after not being used since the Revolutionary War.

Festivals and Events

January: Chinese Lunar New Year Celebration, Baltimore; March: Spring Day Celebration, Baltimore; Maple Syrup Demonstration, Thurmont; April: Springfest, Ocean City; May: Preakness Frog Hop, Baltimore; Towsontown Spring Festival, Towson; June: Chicken Clucking Contest, Baltimore; Annapolis Arts Festival, Annapolis; July: Chesapeake Turtle Derby, Baltimore; Hog Calling Contest, Baltimore; August: Autumn Glory Fest, Oakland; Maryland Renaissance Festival, Annapolis; State Fair, Timonium; September: Polka-Motion By-the-Ocean, Ocean City; October: St. Mary's County Oyster Fest, Leonardtown November: Waterfowl Festival, Easton; December: Christmas Madrigal Feast, Emmitsburg.

Maryland Compared to States in Its Region.

Resident Pop. in Metro Areas: 2d; Pop. Percent Increase: 7th; Pop. Over 65: 6th; Infant Mortality: 8th; School Enroll. Increase: 1st; High School Grad. and Up: 1st; Violent Crime: 3d; Hazardous Waste Sites: 7th; Unemployment: 4th; Median Household Income: 1st; Persons Below Poverty: 8th; Energy Costs Per Person: 7th.

South Atlantic Region

	Population	Capital
Delaware	700,000	Dover
Maryland	4,965,000	Annapolis
Washington DC	578,000	—
Virginia	6,491,000	Richmond
West Virginia	1,820,000	Charleston
North Carolina	6,.945,000	Raleigh
South Carolina	3,643,000	Columbia
Georgia	6,917,000	Atlanta
Florida	13,679,000	Tallahassee

Maryland's Finances

Households: 1,749,000; Income Per Capita Current Dollars: $22,974; Change Per Capita Income 1980 to 1992: 112.3% (13th in U.S.); State Expenditures: $11,012,000,000; State Revenues: $11,320,000,000; Personal Income Tax: 2 to 5%; Federal Income Taxes Paid Per Capita: $2,303; Sales Tax: 5% (food and prescription drugs exempt).

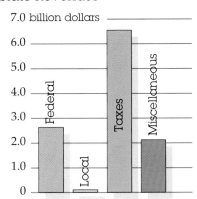

State Expenditures

State Revenues

Location, Size, and Boundaries

Location. Maryland is located in the southern United States in what is known as the South Atlantic region. It is bounded on three of four sides by land with a small coastline along the Atlantic Ocean in the southeast. The geographic center of Maryland is lat. 39° 26.5' N; long. 77° 22.3' W.

Size. Maryland is the 42d largest state in terms of size. Its area is 10,577 sq. mi. (27,395 km2). Inland water covers 686 sq. mi. (1,777 km2).

Maryland touches the Atlantic Ocean along a 31 mile coastline.

Boundaries. Pennsylvania, 196 mi. (316 km); Delaware, 122 mi. (196 km); Atlantic Ocean, 31 mi. (50 km); Virginia, 233 mi. (375 km); District of Columbia, 25 mi. (40 km); West Virginia, 235 mi. (378 km).

Geographic Extent. The north/south extent of Maryland is 126 mi. (203 km). The state extends 199 mi. (320 km) to the east/west.

Facts about Maryland. Origin of Name: After Queen Henrietta Maria, the wife of King Charles I of England; Nickname: The Old Line State; Motto: "Manly deeds, womanly words" (*Fatti maschii parole femine*) ; Abbreviations: Md. (traditional), MD (postal); State Bird: Baltimore oriole; State Tree: white oak; State Flower: black-eyed susan; State Song: "Maryland, My Maryland," words by James Ryder Randall and sung to "O, Tannenbaum."

Maryland Compared to Other States. Resident Pop. in Metro Areas: 7th; Pop. Percent Increase: 22d; Pop. Over 65: 41st; Infant Mortality: 20th; School Enroll. Increase: 2d; High School Grad. and Up: 22d; Violent Crime: 6th; Haz. Waste Sites: 33d; Unemployment: 28th; Med. Household Income: 4th; Persons Below Poverty: 46th; Energy Costs Per Person: 43d.

Sources of Information. Tourism: Dept. of Economic and Employment Development, Office of Tourism Development, 217 East Redwood Street, 9th Floor, Baltimore, MD 21202. Government/History: Office of the Governor, State House, Annapolis, MD 21404.

■ Antietam National Battlefield Site. Civil War battle site in 1862. (B-6)

■ Beltsville. Site of the National Agricultural Research Center. (D-9)

■ Chesapeake and Ohio Canal National Historical Park. Focuses on canals as transportation routes in early America. (A-4)

■ Cross Manor. The oldest brick house in Maryland built in 1643. (G-9)

■ Crystal Grottoes. Rock formations. (B-6)

■ Dans Mountain State Park. Trails and picnicking. (B-2)

■ Elk Neck State Park. Beautiful scenery, picnicking. (B-11)

■ Fort Frederick State Park. Fort built in 1756 during French and Indian War. (B-5)

■ Fort McHenry National Monument and Historic Shrine. The national anthem was inspired and written near this fort. (C-9)

■ Fort Tonoloway State Park. Historic site with a fort. (A-4)

■ Gathland State Park. Monument to the famous Civil War correspondent. (C-6)

■ General Smallwood State Park. The home of Gen. William Smallwood. (F-8)

■ Hampton National Historic Site. 60-acre site with a large 18th-century mansion surrounded by 27 historic structures. (B-9)

■ Ocean City. Seashore resort with boardwalk, swimming, and boating. (G-14)

■ Old St. Paul's Church. Church built in 1692. (C-9)

■ Patapsco Valley State Park. Scenic nature trails. (C-8)

■ Rehoboth Presbyterian (Makemie's) Church. Built in 1705. (H-12)

■ Seton Shrine-White House. Replica of the first parochial school in United States. (A-7)

■ St. Marys City. The first capital of Maryland (1634). (G-10)

■ Third Haven Friends Meeting House. Possibly the oldest frame house of worship in the United States (1682–84). (E-11)

■ Washington Monument State Park. First monument dedicated to George Washington. Located along the Appalachian Trail. (B-6)

■ Wye Oak State Park. Site of a 400-year-old white oak tree that is 95 feet (29 meters) high. (E-11)

Weather Facts

Record High Temperature: 109° F (43° C) on July 3, 1898, in Allegany County; Record Low Temperature: -40° F (-40° C) on January 12, 1908, at Oakland; Average January Temperature: 32° F (0° C); Average July Temperature: 76° F (24° C); Average Yearly Precipitation: 43 in. (109 cm).

Environmental Facts

Air Pollution Rank: 36th; Water Pollution Rank: 24th; Total Yearly Industrial Pollution: 13,002,950 lbs.; Industrial Pollution Rank: 39th; Hazardous Waste Sites: 10; Hazardous Sites Rank: 32d; Landfill Capacity: overextended; Fresh Water Supply: large surplus; Daily Residential Water Consumption: 177 gals. per capita; Endangered Species: Aquatic Species (3)—mussel, dwarf wedge; Birds (3)—eagle, bald; Mammals (2)—bat, Indiana; Other Species (4)—beetle, northeastern beach tiger; Plants (6)—bulrush, northeastern (=barbed bristle).

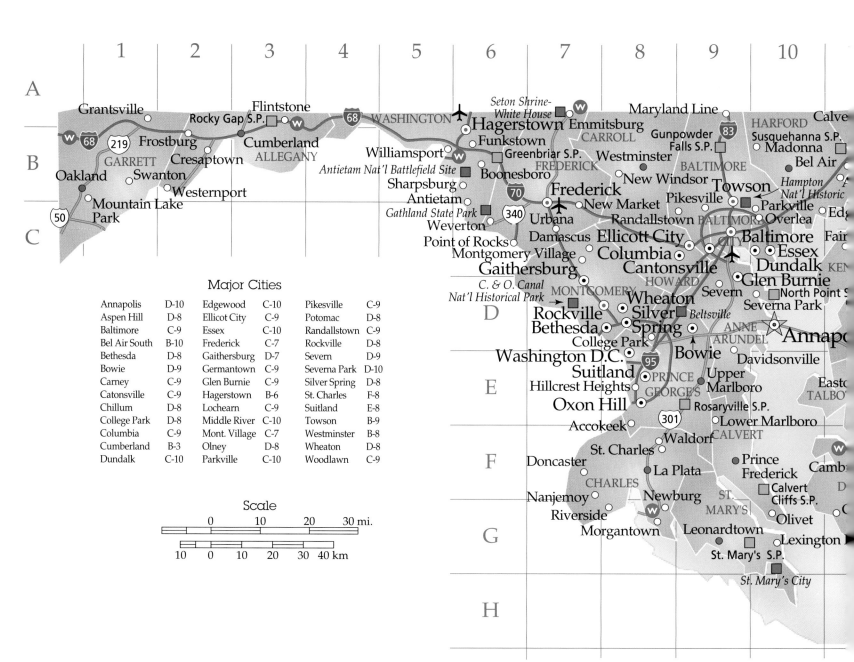

Major Cities

Annapolis	D-10	Edgewood	C-10	Pikesville	C-9
Aspen Hill	D-8	Ellicot City	C-9	Potomac	D-8
Baltimore	C-9	Essex	C-10	Randallstown	C-9
Bel Air South	B-10	Frederick	C-7	Rockville	D-8
Bethesda	D-8	Gaithersburg	D-7	Severn	D-9
Bowie	D-9	Germantown	C-9	Severna Park	D-10
Carney	C-9	Glen Burnie	C-9	Silver Spring	D-8
Catonsville	C-9	Hagerstown	B-6	St. Charles	F-8
Chillum	D-8	Lochearn	C-9	Suitland	E-8
College Park	D-8	Middle River	C-10	Towson	B-9
Columbia	C-9	Mont. Village	C-7	Westminster	B-8
Cumberland	B-3	Olney	D-8	Wheaton	D-8
Dundalk	C-10	Parkville	C-10	Woodlawn	C-9

Scale

0   10   20   30 mi.

10   0   10   20   30   40 km

Maryland

Average Monthly Weather

Baltimore	Jan	Feb	Mar	Apr	May	Jun	Jul	Aug	Sep	Oct	Nov	Dec	Yearly
Maximum Temperature °F	41.0	43.7	53.1	65.1	74.2	82.9	87.1	85.5	79.1	67.7	55.9	45.1	65.0
Minimum Temperature °F	24.3	25.7	33.4	42.9	52.5	61.5	66.5	65.7	58.6	46.1	36.6	27.9	45.1
Days of Precipitation	10.5	9.2	10.6	10.6	11.0	9.3	9.0	9.6	7.5	7.4	9.1	9.1	112.8

Land Use

Cropland: 29.7%; Pasture: 8.5%; Rangeland: 0%; Forest: 39.9%; Urban: 15.5%; Other: 6.4%.

- ★ State capitol
- ⊙ Cities over 35,000 population
- ○ Other significant cities
- ● County Seats
- ■ Major cultural attractions
- ▢ State Parks
- ⓦ Welcome Centers
- ♟ Major colleges and universities

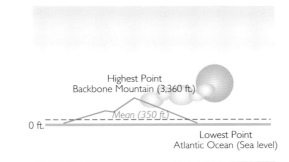

Highest Point Backbone Mountain (3,360 ft.)
Mean (350 ft.)
0 ft.
Lowest Point Atlantic Ocean (Sea level)

Physical Regions: (a) Atlantic Coastal Plain; (b) Piedmont; (c) Blue Ridge; (d) Appalachian Ridge and Valley; (e) Appalachian Plateau.

Topography

There are several distinct topographic regions in Maryland. Eastern Maryland lies in the Atlantic Coastal Plain physical region that extends down the Atlantic seaboard. The Chesapeake Bay divides this area into the Eastern and Western shores, mostly a flat lowland region of beaches and marshes. Soil is classified as warm and moist, as it is throughout the state, and color ranges from white to black.

West of the Coastal Plain is the Piedmont physical region, a fertile section of gentle hills and river valleys that rises gradually toward the northwest. High elevations in this region surpass 1,000 ft. The soil is predominantly clay with color ranging from red/yellow to brown. The Blue Ridge physical region extends from southern Pennsylvania as a narrow strip of mountainous land between the Piedmont and the Appalachian Ridge and Basin physical regions. Soil type is red clay.

The Appalachian Ridge and Valley physical region extends westward from the Blue Ridge. It is an area of mountain ranges and valleys that run in a northeast-southwest direction. The Blue

For more information about Maryland's environment, contact the Department of Environment, 2500 Broening Highway, 2d Floor, Bldg. 30A, Baltimore, MD 21224.

Ridge, including the Catoctin Mountains, forms the eastern edge of this region. In Maryland's northwest corner is the Appalachian Plateau physical region, where the highest elevations in the state are found. Backbone Mountain rises 3,360 ft. (1,024 m) above sea level. The Great Valley, a fertile agricultural area, is the largest valley in the region. The soil in these two western physical regions is a loamy clay with a light surface color.

Environmental Quality

Maryland residents generate 7.2 million tons of solid waste each year, or approximately 3,200 pounds per capita. Landfill capacity in Maryland will be exhausted in 5 to 10 years. The state has 10 hazardous waste sites. Annual greenhouse gas emissions in Maryland total 77.9 million tons, or 16.9 tons per capita. Industrial sources in Maryland release approximately 21.6 thousand tons of toxins, 295.4 thousand tons of acid precipitation-producing substances, and 1.3 million tons of smog-producing substances into the atmosphere each year. The state has 39,700 acres within the National Park System. Noteworthy is Harpers Ferry National Historical Park. State parks cover just over 219,000 acres, attracting 7.8 million visitors per year.

Maryland spends approximately 1.6 percent of its budget, or approximately $32 per capita, on environmental and natural resources.

Climate

Many states' climates differ between the north and south; however, Maryland's climate differs more between the east and west. Altitude also has an effect on climate. Overall, Maryland has a humid climate. However, summers range from hot to somewhat cool, and winters from mild to severe. Along the coastal plain, temperatures for January and July average 39 degrees F and 75 degrees F. In Cumberland, in northwestern Maryland, January and July temperatures only average 29 degrees F and 68 degrees F.

Precipitation falls fairly evenly throughout Maryland; the state receives approximately 43 inches a year. The Baltimore-Washington metropolitan area receives slightly more precipitation than Maryland's Eastern Shore. The majority of Maryland's snowfall occurs in the Appalachian Plateau, where average snowfall totals 78 inches.

Maryland's mountainous western edge has weather patterns more like a midwestern state than an Eastern Seaboard state. There, winter temperatures often remain below freezing.

Hydrology

The Potomac River forms Maryland's western and southwestern border with Virginia and West Virginia. Like most other rivers in the state, it flows into the Chesapeake Bay. The Patuxent is the main river on the Western Shore, flowing southeast into the Bay. Others include the Patapsco and the Gunpowder at Baltimore.

On the Eastern Shore, the principal rivers are the Choptank, the Chester, the Pocomoke, the Nanticoke, and the Wicomico, all flowing southwest into the bay. The Susquehanna enters from Pennsylvania in the north to drain into the Chesapeake.

Maryland has many man-made lakes, although none is of significant size. The largest is Deep Creek Lake in western Maryland. Others include Liberty Lake on the north branch of the Patapsco, and Pretty Boy Reservoir on the Gunpowder.

Chesapeake Bay itself is the largest body of water in the state, as well as being the chief geographical feature. It is about 600 sq. miles (1,554 sq. km).

Flora and Fauna

More than 150 kinds of trees grow in Maryland's forests, which cover between one-third and 40 percent of the state. On the southern Eastern Shore, forests are made up of a mix of Virginia, pitch, and loblolly pines. The western part of the state has predominately an oak-hickory hardwood forest. Other trees growing in Maryland include black locust, beech, and ash. A variety of berries—strawberries, blackberries, and raspberries grow on Maryland's Western Shore. The Eastern Shore mainly has grass-type plants, such as sedges.

Many animals inhabit Maryland, including raccoons, foxes, chipmunks, otters, and white-tailed deer. Bears and bobcats occasionally appear in Maryland's more mountainous areas. Game birds such as grouse, wild turkey, and partridge live in the western part of the state. Many Atlantic migratory birds stop in Maryland. Maryland's inland waters contain catfish and carp. The Chesapeake Bay has a wide assortment of sea life, with fishes such as alewives, rockfish, and sea trout. Other coastal animal life includes diamondback terrapins, crabs, shrimp, and oysters.

12 / 13 / 95 / Elkton / e Grace / Cecilton / 301 / ertown / ANNE'S / ville / ahoe S.P. / Hillsboro / Denton / va / ROLINE / Federalsburg / Salem / Vienna / Bishopville / Hebron / Salisbury 50 / Ocean City / WICOMICO / Ocean City / 13 / WORCESTER / Snow Hill / s Anne / omoke River S.P. / Shad Landing S.P. / SOMERSET / Pocomoke City / ield / Beaverdam

Maryland's History

Maryland's First People

Although the Mound Builder cultures covered much of what is now the central and southeastern United States, some Adena migrants and their Hopewell successors settled in the Chesapeake Bay region (roughly 500 B.C. to A.D. 700).

At the time of European arrival in North America, both Algonquian and Iroquois tribes inhabited the Chesapeake area, including Accomac, Nanticoke, and Wicomico on the Eastern Shore; the Susquehanna, Yacomico, and Piscataway (or Conoy) on the Western Shore; as well as Powhatan, Nottoway, Meherrin, Secotan, Weapemeoc, and Tuscarora in other regions of the state. Both the Algonquian and Iroquois had strong tribal affiliations. The Iroquois often lived communally (they were known as "People of the Longhouse") while the Algonquian lived in wigwams.

European Exploration

In 1524, Giovanni da Verrazano touched down near Chincoteague while exploring the Atlantic coast, and two years later, Spanish explorers entered Chesapeake Bay, naming it Santa María. Capt. John Smith sailed into the bay in 1608, but it was not until 1631 that colonization was attempted as William Claiborne set up a fur-trading post on Kent Island. The following year, George Calvert was granted land north of the Potomac by Charles I of England. His son Cecilius Calvert, Lord Baltimore, led colonists across the Atlantic in 1634 to settle this land that included all of present-day Delaware and parts of Pennsylvania and Virginia. Their first settlement was at St. Mary's.

There was much friction between Catholics and Puritans in the early period of Maryland's colonization. The Calverts were Roman Catholics and had come to the New World to escape religious intolerance at home. William Claiborne at first refused to recognize Lord Baltimore's charter and in 1644 Richard Ingle, a Puritan, captured St. Mary's, forcing Lord Baltimore's temporary exile. Two years later he ousted the rebels and in 1649 had Maryland's assembly pass the Toleration Act granting freedom to practice religion to all Christians. Puritans again took control in 1654 until Oliver Cromwell finally recognized Lord Baltimore's charter in 1657.

Statehood

In 1691, Maryland was declared a crown colony by William and Mary, with the Church of England as the official religion. Proprietorship was handed back to Maryland only when Benedict Leonard Calvert, the fourth Lord Baltimore, embraced Protestantism in 1715.

In 1767, the boundaries between Maryland, Delaware, and Pennsylvania were established by the Mason-Dixon survey. After some initial hesitation, Maryland joined the colonies in revolt against England, becoming the first of the former colonies to adopt a state constitution. In 1788, Maryland was admitted to the Union as the seventh state. Three years later it ceded land along the Potomac River to the federal government for the creation of the District of Columbia.

In 1861, despite strong secessionist sentiment, the Maryland House of Delegates defeated such a legislative move. Abraham Lincoln found it necessary to impose military rule in the state to keep it in the Union fold. The battle of Antietam (Sharpsburg) on September 17, 1862, was a much needed victory for Union troops after crushing defeats in previous battles. Although both sides suffered heavy casualties (22,000 dead), General Robert E. Lee felt it best to withdraw from the area. Union General McClellan was in a wonderful position to attack and possibly destroy Lee's army, but hesitated thereby allowing Lee his escape. Shortly after, McClellan was relieved of his command by Lincoln. Harper's Ferry was an easy victory for Confederate General Stonewall Jackson, and as a result, he captured over 11,000 prisoners. The Confederate troops made it as far as Hagerstown near the Pennsylvania border before being turned back.

In 1867, Maryland adopted its present-day constitution.

Industrialization

Agriculture was dominant in the early period of the state's colonization. Tobacco in the southern and central regions, and later wheat in the western part of the state, were the primary crops by the beginning of the eighteenth century.

After the Civil War, manufacturing became increasingly important as shipbuilding, steel making, textiles, and other industries emerged to lead an economic restructuring of the state.

Today, manufacturing is still the principal source of income, with electronic equipment and metals the leading industries. Baltimore is one of the leading ports in the nation, and fishing (in the Chesapeake—though limited by pollution) and agriculture (chickens and dairy) also contribute to the state's economy.

Chesapeake Bay

The largest bay in the United States, Chesapeake Bay divides Maryland between the Delmarva Peninsula and the mainland. Historically important for the commercial harvesting of crabs, clams, and oysters, the bay has been seriously degraded by pollution. An intensive study by the Environmental Protection Agency has found that the main pollutants come from upstream sources. Phosphorus originates from point sources, mainly sewage treatment plants. Nitrogen comes from non-point sources, primarily pesticide runoff from agricultural lands and storm water runoff from developed urban areas.

Important Events

1524 Giovanni da Verrazano touches down near Chincoteague.

1526 Spanish explorers sail into Chesapeake Bay and name it Santa María.

1608 John Smith explores Chesapeake Bay.

1631 William Claiborne establishes first settlement on Kent Island.

1632 King Charles I grants land north of the Potomac River to George Calvert.

1634 Cecilius Calvert, Lord Baltimore, son of George Calvert, sails overseas and establishes a settlement at St. Mary's.

1644 Puritans capture St. Mary's and rule for two years.

1649 Maryland Assembly passes the Toleration Act, granting religious freedom to all Christians.

1654 Puritans again take control of Maryland's government.

1657 England recognizes Lord Baltimore's charter as legitimate.

1691 Maryland declared a crown colony by William and Mary.

1695 Capital of Maryland is relocated from St. Mary's to Annapolis.

1715 England relinquishes control of Maryland to the Proprietorship of Lord Baltimore IV.

1729 Baltimore is founded.

1767 State boundaries are established under the Mason-Dixon survey.

1776 Maryland adopts a state constitution.

1788 Maryland is admitted to the Union as the seventh state.

1861 Maryland House of Assembly rejects a bill of secession.

1904 Great fire destroys Baltimore.

1968 Spiro T. Agnew, Maryland's governor, is elected Vice President of the United States.

1975 Gov. Marvin Mandel forced to resign amid charges of mail fraud and racketeering.

1993 First African-American Supreme Court justice Thurgood Marshall dies in Bethesda. Six African-American Secret Service agents file a discrimination suit against Denny's restaurants, claiming racial discrimination.

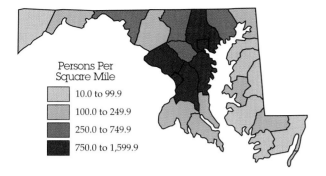

Persons Per
Square Mile

- 10.0 to 99.9
- 100.0 to 249.9
- 250.0 to 749.9
- 750.0 to 1,599.9

Population Density

Population density for the state of Maryland was 489.2 persons per square mile in 1990 (188.9 per km²). Average U.S. density was 70.3 persons per square mile in 1990 (27.3 per km²). Habitation is most dense in the urban corridor spreading from Baltimore to Washington, D.C. One of the most dense regions in the state is the city of Baltimore, which has a population of 736,014.

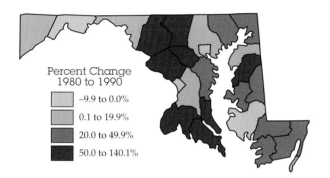

Percent Change
1980 to 1990

- –9.9 to 0.0%
- 0.1 to 19.9%
- 20.0 to 49.9%
- 50.0 to 140.1%

Population Change

The 1990 population figure for the state of Maryland was 4,781,468. This is a 13.39 percent increase from 4,216,975 in 1980. The next decade will show growth with a population of 5.3 million or a 10.30 percent increase. The areas of fastest growth are the suburbs around the cities of Baltimore and Washington, D.C. While the suburbs grow, the cities have lost population in the last decade.

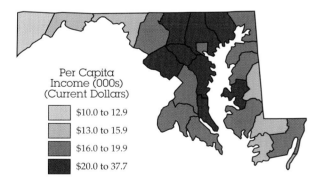

Per Capita
Income (000s)
(Current Dollars)

- $10.0 to 12.9
- $13.0 to 15.9
- $16.0 to 19.9
- $20.0 to 37.7

Distribution of Income

The per capita income for the state of Maryland (current dollars) was $22,974 in 1992. This is a 112.3 percent increase from $10,824 in 1980. Income is greatest in the urban corridor spreading from Baltimore to Washington, D.C. The per capita income radiates out from this point from higher incomes around the cities to lower incomes on the state frontiers.

Population Projections

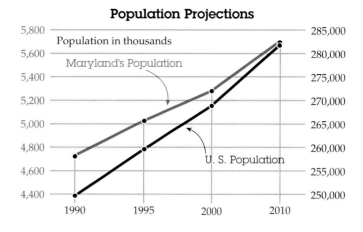

Population in thousands

Maryland's Population

U. S. Population

Population Change

Year	Population
1950	2,343,000
1960	3,113,000
1970	3,938,000
1980	4,216,975
1990	4,781,468
2000	5,274,000
2010	5,688,000

Period	Change
1950–1970	68.1%
1970–1980	7.1%
1980–1990	13.4%
1990–2000	10.3%

Population Facts

State Population, 1993: 4,965,000

Rank: 19

Population 2000: 5,274,000 (Rank 16)

Density: 489.2 per sq. mi. (188.9 per km²)

Distribution: 81.3% urban, 18.7% rural

Population Under 5 Years Old: 7.8%

Population Under 18 Years Old: 25.0%

Population Over 65 Years Old: 11.0%

Median Age: 33.0

Number of Households: 1,749,000

Average Persons Per Household: 2.67

Average Persons Per Family: 3.14

Female Heads of Households: 4.85%

Population That Is Married: 19.84%

Birth Rate: 16.8 per 1,000 population

Death Rate: 8.0 per 1,000 population

Births to Teen Mothers: 10.5%

Marriage Rate: 9.7 per 1,000 population

Divorce Rate: 3.4 per 1,000 population

Violent Crime Rate: 956 per 100,000 pop.

Population on Social Security: 12.9%

Percent Voting for President: 53.4%

Population Profile

Rank. Maryland ranks 19th among U.S. states in terms of population with 4,965,000 citizens.

Minority Population. The state's minority population is 30.7 percent. The state's male to female ratio for 1990 was 96.71 males for every 100 females. It was above the national average of 95.22 males for every 100 females.

Growth. Growing faster than the projected national average, the state's population is

Government

Capital: Annapolis (established 1694).

Statehood: Became 7th state on Apr. 28, 1788.

Number of Counties: 23.

Supreme Court Justices: 7, 10-year term.

State Senators: 47, 4-year term.

State Legislators: 141, 4-year term.

United States Senators: 2.

United States Representatives: 8.

Electoral Votes: 10.

State Constitution: Adopted 1867.

Maryland's Famous Citizens

Blake, Eubie (1883–1983). Jazz pianist and composer. Early originator of ragtime music and composer of "The Charleston Rag."

Bushman, Francis X. (1883–1966). Actor. Started in film in 1911 and became the first big star of silent films.

Chase, Samuel (1741–1811). Signer of the Declaration of Independence and Supreme Court justice (1796–1811).

Clancy, Tom (b. 1947). Writer of military suspense thrillers such as _The Hunt for Red October_ and _Patriot Games_.

Foxx, Jimmy (1907–1967). Hall of Fame baseball player. He is among the top 10 players lifetime in home runs and RBIs.

Hopkins, Johns (1795–1873). Major investor in the Baltimore & Ohio Railroad. He left $7 million to found Johns Hopkins Hospital.

Rous, Peyton (1879–1970). Awarded the Nobel Prize in Medicine in 1966 for his work in discovering a cancer caused by a virus.

Thomas, M. Carey (1857–1935). Educator. She became president of Bryn Mawr College in 1894 and raised women's academic standards.

expected to reach 5.7 million by the year 2010 (_see graph above_).

Older Citizens. The state's population older than 65 was 517,482 in 1990. It grew 30.81% from 395,609 in 1980.

Younger Citizens. The number of children (under 18 years of age) was 1.2 million in 1990. This represents 24.3 percent of the state's population. The state's school aged population was 717 thousand in 1990. It is expected to increase to 839 thousand by the year 2000. This represents a 17.02% change.

Urban/Rural. 81.3% of the population of the state live in urban areas while 18.7% live in rural areas.

Largest Cities. Maryland has 21 cities with a population greater than 35,000. The populations of the state's largest centers are (starting from the most populous) Baltimore (736,014), Silver Spring (76,046), Columbia (75,883), Dundalk (65,800), Bethesda (62,936), Wheaton-Glenmont (53,720), Towson (49,445), Potomac (45,634), Aspen Hill (45,494), Rockville (44,835), Ellicott City (41,396), Germantown (41,145), Essex (40,872), Frederick (40,148), Gaithersburg (39,542), and Bowie (37,589).

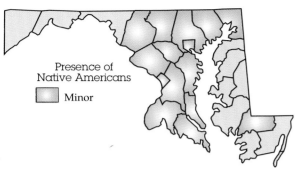

Native American

The Native American population in Maryland was 12,972 in 1990. This was an increase of 45 percent from 8,946 in 1980. Twenty percent of the Native American population can be found residing in the city of Baltimore, which has a Native American population of 2,555. Maryland is also home to the Conoy and Nanticoke tribes.

Presence of Native Americans

☐ Minor

Statewide Ethnic Composition

Over 70 percent of the population of Maryland is white. The largest nationalities in this racial group are German, English, and Irish. The next largest group is African Americans, followed by Asians, Hispanics, and Native Americans. Over 178,000 people claim to be American and acknowledge no other nationality.

Nationalities

African	28,752
American	178,700
Arab	13,080
Austrian	10,929
Czech	15,442
Dutch	39,051
English	438,951
Finnish	3,597
German	945,514
Greek	27,974
Hungarian	15,484
Irish	433,201
Italian	181,930
Norwegian	14,399
Polish	137,064
Portuguese	5,148
Russian	70,966
Scottish	63,585
Slovak	20,891
Swedish	24,329
Welsh	23,580
West Indian	30,110

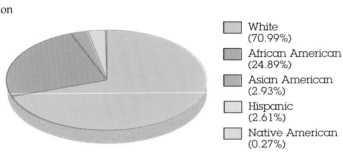

- White (70.99%)
- African American (24.89%)
- Asian American (2.93%)
- Hispanic (2.61%)
- Native American (0.27%)

Education Facts

Total Students 1990: 698,806	Mean SAT Score 1991 Verbal: 429
Number of School Districts: 24	Mean SAT Score 1991 Math: 475
Expenditure Per Capita on Education 1990: $891	Average Teacher's Salary 1992: $39,500
Expenditure Per Capita K–12 1990: $803	Rank Teacher's Salary: 7th in U.S.
Expenditure Per Pupil 1990: $6,184	High School Graduates 1990: 42,000
Total School Enrollment 1990–1991: 715,152	Total Number of Public Schools: 1,217
Rank of Expenditures Per Student: 8th in the U.S.	Number of Teachers 1990: 42,569
African American Enrollment: 32.7%	Student/Teacher Ratio: 16.8
Hispanic Enrollment: 2.1%	Staff Employed in Public Schools: 76,623
Asian/Pacific Islander Enrollment: 3.3%	Pupil/Staff Ratio: 9.1
Native American Enrollment: 0.2%	Staff/Teacher Ratio: 1.8

Education

Attainment: 81 percent of population 25 years or older were high school graduates in 1989, earning Maryland ranking of 19th in the United States; 27.4 percent of the state's population had completed college. Institutions of Higher Education: The largest universities and colleges in the state include the University of Maryland, College Park; Morgan State University, Baltimore City; St. Mary's College of Maryland, St. Mary's City; United States Naval Academy, Annapolis; Johns Hopkins University, Baltimore; Goucher College, Towson; Western Maryland College, Westminster; Mount St. Mary's College, Emmitsburg. Expenditures per Student: Expenditure increased 71% between 1985 and 1990. Projected High School Graduations: 1998 (50,615), 2004 (55,328); Total Revenues for Education from Federal Sources: $173 million; Total Revenues for Education from State Sources: $1.3 billion; Total Revenues for Education from Local Sources: $1.9 billion; Average Annual Salaries for Public School Principals: $48,106; Largest School Districts in State: Baltimore City Public School System, 107,782 students, 16th in the United States; Prince Georges County Public Schools, 106,974, 17th.

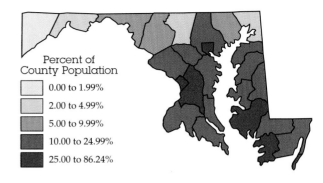

Percent of County Population

- ☐ 0.00 to 1.99%
- 2.00 to 4.99%
- 5.00 to 9.99%
- 10.00 to 24.99%
- 25.00 to 86.24%

African American

The African American population in Maryland was 1,190,000 in 1990. This was an increase of 24.29 percent from 957,418 in 1980. Thirty-seven percent of the African American population resides in the city of Baltimore. Many more can be found around Washington, D.C. Dorchester and Somerset counties also have large percentages of African Americans.

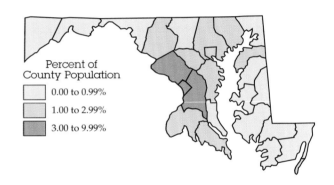

Percent of County Population

- ☐ 0.00 to 0.99%
- 1.00 to 2.99%
- 3.00 to 9.99%

Hispanic[††]

The Hispanic population in Maryland was 125,102 in 1990. This is an increase of 93.22 percent from 64,746 persons in 1980. The highest percentages of Hispanics can be found residing in the counties surrounding Washington, D.C.

[††]A person of Mexican, Puerto Rican, Cuban, or other Spanish culture or origin regardless of race.

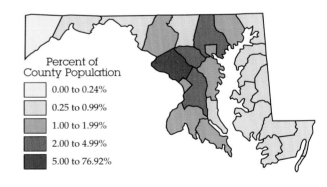

Percent of County Population

- ☐ 0.00 to 0.24%
- 0.25 to 0.99%
- 1.00 to 1.99%
- 2.00 to 4.99%
- 5.00 to 76.92%

Asian American

The Asian American population in Maryland was 139,719 in 1990. This is an increase of 114.76 percent from 65,058 persons in 1980. The largest percentage of Asian Americans can be found in Montgomery County and the corridor between Washington, D.C., and Baltimore.

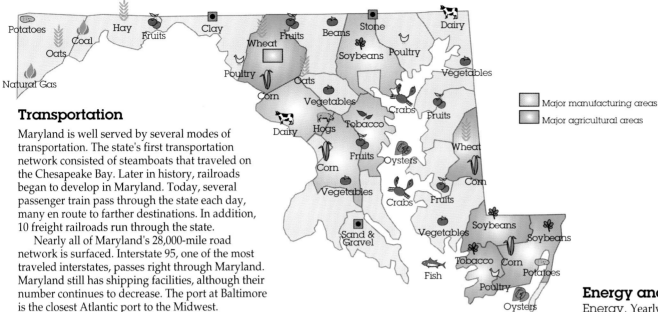

Major manufacturing areas

Major agricultural areas

Transportation

Maryland is well served by several modes of transportation. The state's first transportation network consisted of steamboats that traveled on the Chesapeake Bay. Later in history, railroads began to develop in Maryland. Today, several passenger train pass through the state each day, many en route to farther destinations. In addition, 10 freight railroads run through the state.

Nearly all of Maryland's 28,000-mile road network is surfaced. Interstate 95, one of the most traveled interstates, passes right through Maryland. Maryland still has shipping facilities, although their number continues to decrease. The port at Baltimore is the closest Atlantic port to the Midwest. Baltimore-Washington International Airport serves the entire metropolitan area. Other, smaller airstrips exist throughout the state.

Agriculture

Maryland has 0.65 million farm acres. During the last 40 years, Maryland's farms have grown larger in size and fewer in number. In 1955, 32,000 farms were found in the state. Today, 6,600 remain.

Agriculture adds $1 billion to the state's gross product annually. The principal commodities in order of marketing receipts are broilers, greenhouse, dairy products, and soybeans.

Livestock and livestock products account for about 69 percent of Maryland's farm income. Half of this comes from the production of broilers, raised in the central and southern portions of the Eastern Shore. Milk production is centered in Frederick County. Flowers and ornamental shrubs are produced in Maryland's greenhouses and nurseries. Other crops include tobacco and tomatoes.

Housing

Owner Occupied Units: 1,891,917; Average Age of Units: 30 years; Average Value of Housing Units: $116,500; Renter Occupied Units: 598,309; Median Monthly Rent: $548; Housing Starts: 31,800; Existing Home Sales: 73,400.

Economic Facts

Gross State Product: $99,000,000,000

Income Per Capita: $22,974

Disposable Personal Income: $19,746

Median Household Income: $39,386

Average Annual Pay, 1988: $25,960

Principal Industries: food products, electrical equipment, printing, chemicals, computer software, biotech products

Major Crops: greenhouse products, milk, corn, tobacco, soybeans, peaches, apples

Fish: Crabs, Rockfish, Trout, Carp, Catfish, Bluefish

Livestock: chickens

Non-Fuel Minerals: Sandy Loams, Clay, Granite, Limestone, Talc

Organic Fuel Minerals: Coal, Nat. Gas

Civilian Labor Force: 2,554,000 (Women: 1,185,000)

Total Employed: 2,403,000 (Women: 1,115,000)

Median Value of Housing: $116,500

Median Contract Rent: $548 per month

Economic Sectors

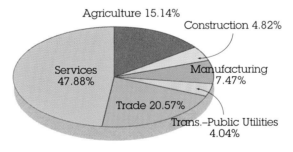

- Agriculture 15.14%
- Construction 4.82%
- Services 47.88%
- Manufacturing 7.47%
- Trade 20.57%
- Trans.–Public Utilities 4.04%

Manufacturing

Although manufacturing in Maryland has declined in recent years, the value of its products has increased. Large shipbuilding and steel plants have decreased in size over the years. However, more advanced industries such as computer software have expanded greatly. Today, electrical products manufacturing leads as Maryland's largest manufacturing activity, followed by food products, chemicals, and printed materials. Communication equipment ranks as the most important type of electrical equipment produced.

Most of the state's manufacturing takes place in the Baltimore-Washington, D.C., metropolitan area, especially of high-technology products. The area also produces a large number of newspapers. Facilities in southern Maryland print many federal government documents.

Energy and Transportation Facts

Energy. Yearly Consumption: 1,215 tril. BTUs (residential, 26.5%; commercial, 14.7%; industrial, 31.2%; transportation, 27.7%); Annual Energy Expenditures Per Capita: $1,657; Nuclear Power Plants Located in State: 2; Source of Energy Consumed: Petroleum— 46.7%; Natural Gas— 16.8%; Coal— 25.5%; Hydroelectric Power—1.4%; Nuclear Power—9.2%.

Transportation. Highway Miles: 29,172 (interstates, 481; urban, 13,574; rural, 15,598); Average Yearly Auto Insurance: $702 (11th); Auto Fatalities Rank: 31st; Registered Motor Vehicles: 3,688,899; Workers in Carpools: 21.7%; Workers Using Public Trans: 8.1%.

Employment

Employment. Maryland employed 2.50 million people in 1993. Most work in social and personal service jobs (665,100 persons or 26.1% of the workforce). Wholesale and retail trade account for 19.9% or 499,200 workers. Government employs 417,200 workers (16.6%). Manufacturing employs 179,500 people (7.2%). Construction employs 119,900 people (4.8%). Transportation and utilities account for 3.9% or 98,400 persons. Agriculture employs 37,600 workers or 1.5%. Finance, real estate, and insurance employ 5.2%, or 129,300 workers. Mining employs 1,200 people and accounts for less than 1% of the workforce.

Unemployment. Unemployment has increased to 6.2% in 1993 from a rate of 4.6% in 1980. Today's figure is lower than the national average of 6.8% as shown below.

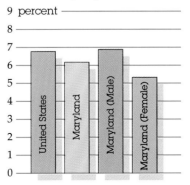

Unemployment Rate

9 percent

- United States
- Maryland
- Maryland (Male)
- Maryland (Female)

MASSACHUSETTS

The Commonwealth of Massachusetts

Official State Seal

The Great Seal of Massachusetts was adopted in 1780. Small details were changed and the seal was standardized in 1898. The coat of arms is included in the center of the seal with the state motto, *"Ense Petit Placidam Sub Libertate Quietem"* (By the Sword We Seek Peace, but Peace Only Under Liberty). Also included is an arm holding a sword that can be found at the top of the seal.

Legal Holidays

January: New Year's Day—1st; Martin Luther King, Jr., Day—3rd Monday; February: Ratification Day—2nd; Presidents' Day—3rd Monday; April: Student Government Day—1st Friday; Patriot's Day—Third Monday; May: Memorial Day—4th Monday; July: Independence Day—4th; August: Liberty Tree Day—14th; Susan B. Anthony Day—26th; September: Labor Day—1st Monday; October: Columbus Day—2nd Monday; November: Veterans' Day—11th; Thanksgiving—4th Thursday; John F. Kennedy Day—28th; December: Forefathers' Day (Plymouth)—21st; Christmas—25th.

Official State Flag

The official state flag of Massachusetts was originally two-sided from 1908 to 1971. Included on a white field is the coat of arms. The arms contain a Native American holding a bow and a white star in the upper left corner. Also included is the state motto.

Festivals and Events

February: Mardi Gras Celebration, Boston; March: Sugartime Special, Boston; April: Boston Marathon; May: Sheep Shearing Fest, North Andover; June: Cape Cod Chowder Fest, Hyannis; July: Bastille Day Celebration, Boston; Pilgrim Wedding, Plymouth Plantation; July/August: Feast of the Blessed Sacrament, New Bedford; September: World Kielbasa Festival, Chicopee; September /October: Massachusetts Cranberry Festival, Eadville Railroad & South Carver; November: Rail-a-Rama, Boston; December: Re-enactment of Boston Tea Party, Boston.

Sources of Information. Tourism: Office of Travel and Tourism, 100 Cambridge Street, 13th Floor, Boston, MA 02202. Economy: Office of Business and Development, 100 Cambridge Street, 13th Floor, Boston, MA 02202. Government: Office of the Secretary of State, Citizen Information Service, 1 Ashburton Place, Room 1611, Boston, MA 02108. History: Office of the Secretary of State, Citizen Information Service, 1 Ashburton Place, Room 1611, Boston, MA 02108.

Location, Size, and Boundaries

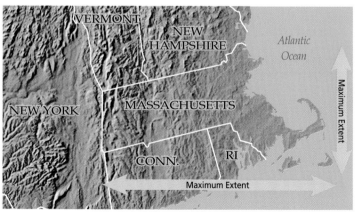

Massachusetts's Finances

Households: 2,247,000; Income Per Capita Current Dollars: $24,059; Change Per Capita Income 1980 to 1992: 125.7% (3d in U.S.); State Expenditures: $17,812,000,000; State Revenues: $18,234,000,000; Personal Income Tax: 6.25 to 12%; Federal Income Taxes Paid Per Capita: $2,295; Sales Tax: 5% (food and prescription drugs exempt).

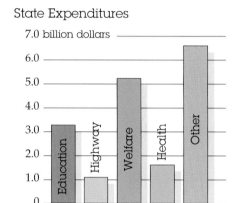

State Expenditures

State Revenues

Location. Massachusetts is located in the northeastern United States in the New England region. It is bounded on three of four sides by land with a general coastline along the Atlantic Ocean in the east. The geographic center of Massachusetts is lat. 42° 20.4' N; long. 72° 1.9' W.

Size. Massachusetts is the 45th largest state in terms of size. Its area is 8,257 sq. mi. (21,386 km2). Inland water covers 431 sq. mi. (1,116 km2). Massachusetts touches the Atlantic Ocean along a 192 mile coast.

Boundaries. Vermont, 41 mi. (66 km); New Hampshire, 94 mi. (151 km); Atlantic Ocean, 192 mi. (309 km); Rhode Island, 46 mi. (74 km); Connecticut, 92 mi. (148 km); New York, 50 mi. (81 km).

Geographic Extent. The north/south extent of Massachusetts is 110 mi. (177 km). The state extends 190 mi. (306 km) to the east/west.

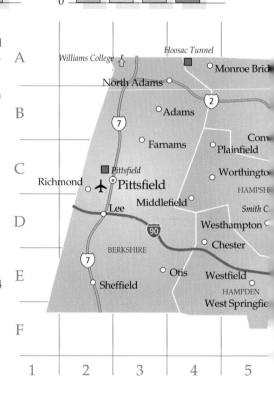

Facts about Massachusetts. Origin of Name: Means *"near the great hill"* or *"place of the great hill,"* refers to the Great Blue Hill south of Boston; Nickname: The Bay State; Motto:"By the sword we seek peace, but peace only under liberty"; Abbreviations: Mass. (traditional), MA (postal); State Bird: chickadee; State Tree: American elm; State Flower: mayflower; State Song: "All Hail to Massachusetts," words and music by Arthur J. Marsh.

Massachusetts Compared to Other States. Resident Pop. in Metro Areas: 3d; Pop. Per. Increase: 49th; Pop. Over 65: 12th; Infant Mortality: 47th; School Enroll. Increase: 13th; High School Grad. and Up: 15th; Violent Crime: 14th; Hazardous Waste Sites: 14th; Unemployment: 6th; Median Household Income: 6th; Persons Below Poverty: 44th; Energy Costs Per Person: 41st.

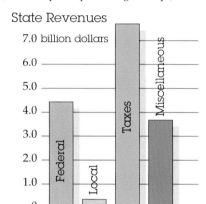

Legend

⭐ State capitol

⊙ Cities over 35,000 pop.

○ Other significant cities

● County Seats

■ Major cultural attractions

▫ State Parks

Ⓦ Welcome Centers

⚲ Major colleges and universities

Massachusetts

Massachusetts Compared to Its Region.

Resident Pop. in Metro Areas: 1st; Pop. Percent Increase: 6th; Pop. Over 65: 3d; Infant Mortality: 4th; School Enroll. Increase: 3d; High School Grad. and Up: 3d; Violent Crime: 1st; Hazardous Waste Sites: 1st; Unemployment: 2d; Median Household Income: 2d; Persons Below Poverty: 4th; Energy Costs Per Person: 5th.

New England Region

	Population	Capital
Maine	1,239,000	Augusta
New Hampshire	1,125,000	Concord
Vermont	576,000	Montpelier
Massachusetts	6,012,000	Boston
Rhode Island	1,000,000	Providence
Connecticut	3,277,000	Hartford

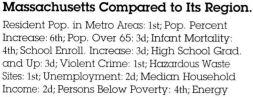

■ Adams National Historic Site. Home of Adams family since 1731. (E-10)

■ Amherst. Home of Emily Dickinson, built in 1813. Also the home of Amherst College, Univ. of Massachusetts (D-4)

■ Concord. Home of Emerson, Thoreau, Hawthorne, the Alcotts. Also the site of the Sleepy Hollow cemetery. (D-9)

■ Dorchester Heights National Historic Site. Site of the American batteries that forced the British to evacuate Boston in 1776. (D-10)

■ Gloucester. Fishing port and resort. (C-11)

■ Harvard. American Indian Museum, and Shaker Museum. (D-10)

■ Lexington. Site of the famous battle of the American Revolution by Minute Men and British troops. (D-9)

■ Marblehead. Summer resort with yachting as a main focus. (C-11)

■ Martha's Vineyard. Summer resort

island with colored cliffs at Gay Head. Also the site of the state lobster hatchery. (I-11, I-12)

■ Minute Man National Historical Park. Historic structures of American Revolution at Lincoln, Lexington, and Concord. (D-9)

■ Nantucket. Summer resort as well as an old whaling port on Nantucket Island. Whaling Museum. (I-14)

■ Pittsfield. Site of the homes of Holmes, Melville, Longfellow, and Hawthorne. Also a popular ski center. (D-1)

■ Plymouth. Vacation resort. Also the site of Plymouth Rock, where the Pilgrims landed in 1620. (F-11)

■ Salem. Site of the infamous witch hunt, House of Seven Gables, and the Hawthorne House (1692). (C-11)

■ Salem Maritime National Historic Site. Authentic historic buildings and structures such as the Salem Custom House and Derby Wharf. (C-11)

■ Sandwich. Production site of popular colored glass from 1825–1888. (G-12)

■ Saugus. The birthplace of the American steel industry with the first producing ironworks in the New World built in the 1640s. (D-10)

■ Walden Pond. Frequented by author and philosopher Henry David Thoreau. (D-9)

■ Woods Hole. Site of the Oceanographic Institution and the United States Marine Biological Laboratories and the United States Bureau of Fisheries Museum and Aquarium. (H-11)

Scale

0 10 20 30 mi.

10 0 10 20 30 40 km

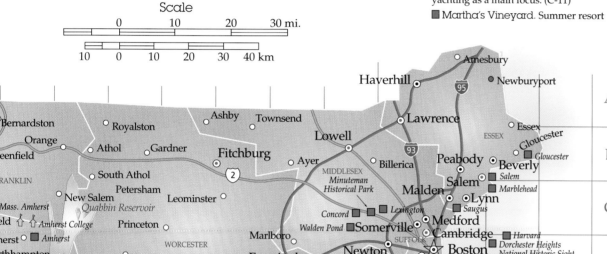

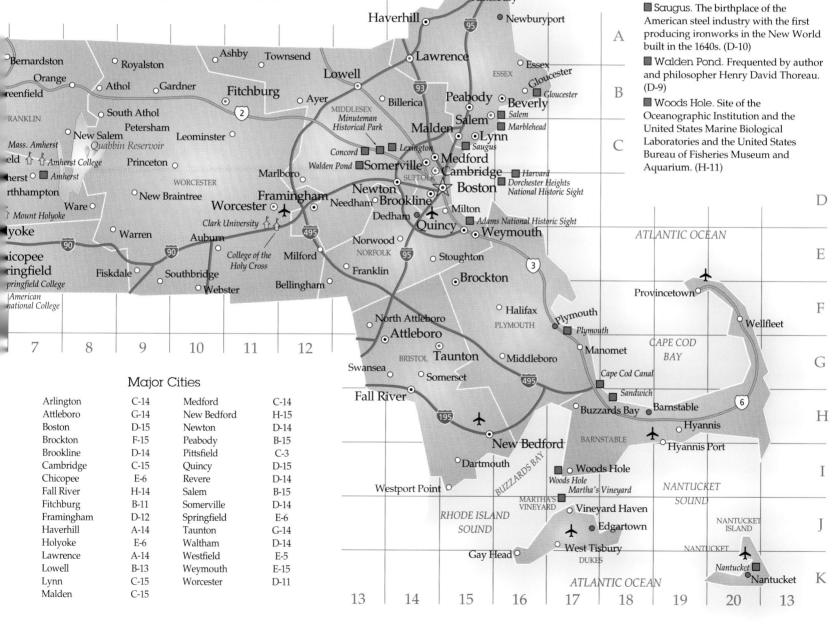

Major Cities

Arlington	C-14	Medford	C-14
Attleboro	G-14	New Bedford	H-15
Boston	D-15	Newton	D-14
Brockton	F-15	Peabody	B-15
Brookline	D-14	Pittsfield	C-3
Cambridge	C-15	Quincy	D-15
Chicopee	E-6	Revere	D-14
Fall River	H-14	Salem	B-15
Fitchburg	B-11	Somerville	D-14
Framingham	D-12	Springfield	E-6
Haverhill	A-14	Taunton	G-14
Holyoke	E-6	Waltham	D-14
Lawrence	A-14	Westfield	E-5
Lowell	B-13	Weymouth	E-15
Lynn	C-15	Worcester	D-11
Malden	C-15		

Weather Facts

Record High Temperature: 107° F (42° C) on August 1, 1971, at New Bedford; Record Low Temperature: -34° F (-37° C) on January 17, 1953, at Birch Hill Dam; Average January Temperature: 26° F (-3° C); Average July Temperature: 70° F (21° C); Average Yearly Precipitation: 45 in. (114 cm).

Environmental Facts

Air Pollution Rank: 31st; Water Pollution Rank: 43d; Total Yearly Industrial Pollution: 14,530,717 lbs.; Industrial Pollution Rank: 37th; Hazardous Waste Sites: 25; Hazardous Sites Rank: 14th; Landfill Capacity: overextended; Fresh Water Supply: large surplus; Daily Residential Water Consumption: 125 gals. per capita; Endangered Species: Aquatic Species (1)—sturgeon, shortnose; Birds (14)—crow, mariana; Mammals (5)—bat, Indiana; Other Species (8)—beetle, northeastern beach tiger; Plants (4)—bulrush, northeastern.

Environmental Quality

Massachusetts residents generate 6.6 million tons of solid waste each year, or approximately 2,200 pounds per capita. Landfill capacity in Massachusetts will be exhausted in less than 5 years. The state has 25 hazardous waste sites. Annual greenhouse gas emissions in Massachusetts total 89.9 million tons, or 15.3 tons per capita. Industrial sources in Massachusetts releases approximately 36.3 thousand tons of toxins, 402.1 thousand tons of acid precipitation-producing substances, and 1.6 million tons of smog-producing substances into the atmosphere each year.

The state has 30,900 acres within the National Park System. Noteworthy is Boston National Historical Park. State parks cover just over 262,000 acres, attracting 12.0 million visitors per year.

Massachusetts spends approximately 1.6 percent of its budget, or approximately $40 per capita, on environmental and natural resources.

Average Monthly Weather

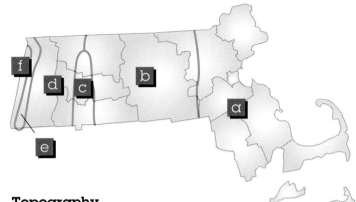

Physical Regions: (a) Coastal Lowlands; (b) Eastern New England Upland; (c) Connecticut Valley Lowland; (d) Western New England Upland; (e) Berkshire Valley; (f) Taconic Mountains.

Topography

There are several distinct topographical regions in Massachusetts. The eastern portion of the state is made up of the Coastal Lowlands physical region, which extends up to 40 miles inland from the coastline, and includes Cape Cod and the islands off the coast. West of the Coastal Lowlands lies the Eastern New England Upland physical region, which is an extension of the White Mountains of New Hampshire. This narrow band, running north to south through the state, has elevations exceeding 1,000 ft. (300 m) in the north. It gradually slopes

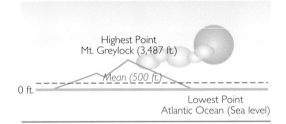

Highest Point
Mt. Greylock (3,487 ft.)

Mean (500 ft.)

0 ft.

Lowest Point
Atlantic Ocean (Sea level)

Land Use

Cropland: 6%; Pasture: 3.7%, Rangeland: 0%; Forest: 60.6%; Urban: 21.9%; Other: 7.8%.

For more information about Massachusetts' environment, contact the Secretary of Environmental Affairs, Room 2000, 100 Cambridge St., Boston, MA 02202.

toward the coastal lowlands in the east, and the Connecticut River Valley to its west.

The Connecticut Valley Lowland physical region is characterized by the Connecticut River. This fertile region, which also runs north to south through Massachusetts, supports much agricultural activity. The western part of Massachusetts is in the Western New England Upland physical region, consisting mainly of the Berkshire Hills, a southern extension of the Green Mountains of Vermont. The Taconic Mountains physical region crosses the extreme northwestern tip of the state. The soil throughout the state is cool and moist, colored brown, and high in organic and iron content.

Climate

Located between eastern Canada and the Middle Atlantic states, Massachusetts has four recognizable seasons. Climate is influenced by both the sea and the many weather systems that pass through the state. Although the coast is generally warmer than the western part of Massachusetts, only slight temperature differences between these two areas exist. Boston, along the coast, has average January and July temperatures of 29 degrees F and 72 degrees F. In Pittsfield, near the Massachusetts-New York border, temperatures average 21 degrees F and 68 degrees F for January and July.

As with temperatures, only slight variation exists in precipitation across Massachusetts. The state itself averages 42 inches of precipitation a year. Western Massachusetts receives slightly more precipitation; however, some of this is in the form of snow.

Although a northern state, Massachusetts is sometimes hit by hurricanes. Two of the most damaging hit in 1944 and 1985.

Hydrology

The Connecticut River is the most important river in the state. It flows south through the west-central portion of the state. Some of its tributaries include the Westfield, the Deerfield, and the Millers. The Housatonic flows through the southwestern part of Massachusetts. The Merrimack enters Massachusetts from New Hampshire in the northeast, then changes course and flows northeastward into the Atlantic Ocean. Its primary tributaries are the Concord and the Nashua, which flow southwest. The Charles, Mystic, and Neponset rivers flow into Boston Bay.

The largest lakes in Massachusetts are man-made. Quabbin Reservoir, in the center of the state, covers about 38 sq. miles (98 sq. km). Others include Wachusett and Barre Falls reservoirs, also in central Massachusetts. Assawompset Pond in the southeastern part of the state is the largest natural lake.

Boston	Jan	Feb	Mar	Apr	May	Jun	Jul	Aug	Sep	Oct	Nov	Dec	Yearly
Maximum Temperature °F	36.4	37.7	45.0	56.6	67.0	76.6	81.8	79.8	72.3	62.5	51.6	40.3	59.0
Minimum Temperature °F	22.8	23.7	31.8	40.8	50.0	59.3	65.1	63.9	56.9	47.1	38.7	27.1	43.9
Days of Precipitation	11.4	10.4	11.7	11.4	11.6	10.6	9.2	10.0	8.6	8.8	10.9	11.5	126.3
Worcester													
Maximum Temperature °F	30.9	32.9	41.1	54.5	65.9	74.4	79.0	77.0	69.4	59.3	46.9	34.7	55.5
Minimum Temperature °F	15.6	16.6	52.2	35.4	45.5	54.8	60.7	59.0	51.3	41.3	32.0	20.1	38.1
Days of Precipitation	11.4	10.8	12.1	11.4	12.2	11.4	9.9	10.1	9.2	8.7	11.8	12.5	131.6

Flora and Fauna

Both deciduous and coniferous forests cover Massachusetts's wooded areas. The state has approximately 60 percent of its land covered by forests. Common deciduous forests, located in the south near the border with Connecticut, include maple, birch, and hickory. Well-known conifers, or cone-bearing trees, including hemlock, spruce, and balsam fir, grow farther north. Many shrubs and other plants exist throughout the state, including mountain laurels, ferns, and rhododendrons. Violets bloom in river valleys during springtime. Mayflowers and trilliums, both wildflowers, mainly grow in western Massachusetts.

Massachusetts is mostly populated with smaller mammals such as muskrats, porcupines, skunks, foxes, and the very small meadow mouse. Larger animals such as deer live throughout Massachusetts, but bobcats and bears continually become harder to find. The state's game birds include pheasant and partridge. Other birds such as gulls and terns live along the Massachusetts shore. Pickerel, trout, bass, perch, and other fish species live in Massachusetts rivers and lakes. Coastal sea life includes lobsters, clams, and oysters.

Massachusetts's History

Massachusetts's First People

Hunter-gatherer tribes roamed Massachusetts thousands of years ago. At the time of European arrival in America, the region was home to several Algonquian-speaking tribes, probably descendants of the Woodland culture that had prevailed farther south. Some of these tribes were the Massachuset in the northeast, the Wampanoag in the southeast, the Nipmuc, Pequot, and Mohegan in the central region, the Pocumtuc in the west, and the Nauset on Cape Cod. For most of these tribes, the wooded forests served as a source of shelter, fuel, and tools, and the animals who dwelled there proved to be the primary source of food. Some also were fishermen (coastal tribes) and farmers.

European Exploration

The Vikings may have encountered the Massachusetts shoreline in 1000, but after the exploration of the coast by John Cabot in 1498, French, Spanish, and Portuguese fishermen began fishing off its shores. The Pilgrims arrived from the Netherlands in 1620 aboard the Mayflower to establish the first permanent white settlement in Massachusetts at Plymouth Rock. They were followed shortly by other colonists from England. The Dorchester Company started a colony at Salem in 1626, and they were joined two years later by the Puritans. A large group of Puritans under John Winthrop then founded the Massachusetts Bay Colony in 1630 with Boston as its capital. Conceived as a Christian commonwealth, the colony was not tolerant of religious dissension; Anne Hutchinson and Roger Williams, among others, were banished for their "heretical" views.

As immigrants moved into the interior of Massachusetts, conflict with the Indians arose. At first helpful to the new white visitors, teaching them how to plant corn and squash, the Indians began to resent the encroachment onto their lands by the white man and their subjection to his laws. As a result of this tension, first the Pequot War in 1637 and finally King Philip's War in 1675–1676 resulted in the permanent defeat of the Indians, including the almost complete extermination of some tribes (the Wampanoag and Nipmuc among them).

Statehood

In 1682, King Charles II canceled Massachusetts's charter as a result of disputes between the monarchy and the colony. In 1689, the colonists set up their own government and three years later were granted a new charter by William and Mary, establishing Plymouth Colony and the Province of Maine as part of Massachusetts under a royal governor. That year (1692) also witnessed the execution of nineteen people by Puritan authorities at the Salem Witch Trials.

The colony prospered through the first half of the eighteenth century. However, with an increase in the demand for taxes from the British Crown, which also wished to limit political autonomy, Massachusetts, along with the other colonies, revolted. The Boston Tea Party of 1773, signifying the colony's protest of "no taxation without representation," resulted in Great Britain's revoking their charter and resuming control of the colony. The Revolutionary War had started.

One of the most famous engagement of the Revolution occurred on the night of April 18, 1775. British General Thomas Gage was in route towards a colonial storehouse in Concord from his base in Boston. He hoped to seize stores of weapons and quickly crush any rebellion. The "Minute Men" were warned, however, by the efforts of Paul Revere's famous ride. General Gage reached his destination and destroyed the supplies, but met resistance from behind every tree and rock. Gage was forced to return to Boston. The Revolution had begun with this "Shot Heard Round the World."

After the war, Massachusetts was admitted to the Union as the sixth state. Massachusetts was a leading abolitionist state and, as such, was strongly Union during the Civil War.

Industrialization

Early economic activity consisted chiefly of fishing and fur trading. With the migration into the interior of the state in the early eighteenth century, lumber and grain mills were established and seaports captured much of the trade between the Old World, America, and the Caribbean.

In the early nineteenth century, textile mills were built in Lowell, Lawrence, and other towns as this industry came to dominate the state's economy for the next one hundred years. Other industries (shipbuilding, shoemaking, metalworking) helped establish Massachusetts as a leading manufacturing state.

Although the state suffered a prolonged decline after the Great Depression, with old industries closing up and moving out, since World War II there has been a resurgence. Led by the computer industry situated around Boston, high-tech industries have revitalized the economy, although there has been a downturn in the early 1990s.

Education

In 1636, Harvard College, later Harvard University, became the first college established in the United States. Since this auspicious beginning, Massachusetts has been a leader in higher education in the nation. Harvard is considered a world-class institution, as well as the top university in America. The Massachusetts Institute of Technology and the New England Conservatory of Music are leading institutions in their respective fields, and other prominent schools include Amherst, Boston University, Smith, Wellesley, Brandeis, and others. Given this important public resource, the state has also spent money to bolster its state universities and community colleges.

Important Events

1000 Probable visit by the Vikings to the Massachusetts coast.

1498 John Cabot explores the Massachusetts coast.

1620 Pilgrims arrive from the Netherlands and establish a colony at Plymouth Rock.

1623 Thanksgiving Day first celebrated by the Pilgrims.

1626 Permanent settlement established at Salem.

1628 Puritans join the settlement at Salem.

1630 Puritans found the Massachusetts Bay Colony with Boston as the capital.

1648 First witch is executed in America at Charlestown.

1675-76 King Philip's War wipes out most of the Indians in the state.

1682 Massachusetts's charter is revoked by England. Later, Colonists set up their own provisional government.

1692 William and Mary grant Massachusetts a new charter.

1765 England imposes the Stamp Act, a tax on publications and documents.

1773 Boston Tea Party to protest taxation results in East India tea being dumped into Boston Harbor.

1775 Revolutionary War begins at Lexington and Concord.

1788 Massachusetts is admitted to the Union as the sixth state.

1796 John Adams elected second President of the United States.

1824 John Quincy Adams elected sixth President of the United States.

1923 Vice President Calvin Coolidge becomes the thirtieth President when President Warren Harding dies.

1950s Computers and electronics shift Massachusetts economy away from heavy industry.

1960 John F. Kennedy elected thirty-fifth President of the United States.

1988 Massachusetts governor Michael Dukakis becomes the Democratic nominee for President of the United States.

1992 Sen. Paul Tsongas (Democrat) puts in his bid for the presidency.

Population Projections

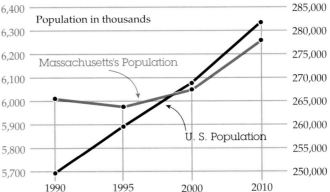

Population in thousands

Massachusetts's Population

U. S. Population

(x-axis: 1990, 1995, 2000, 2010)
(left y-axis: 5,700 · 5,800 · 5,900 · 6,000 · 6,100 · 6,200 · 6,300 · 6,400)
(right y-axis: 250,000 · 255,000 · 260,000 · 265,000 · 270,000 · 275,000 · 280,000 · 285,000)

Population Change

Year	Population
1950	4,691,000
1960	5,160,000
1970	5,706,000
1980	5,737,037
1990	6,016,425
2000	6,087,000
2010	6,255,000

Period	Change
1950–1970	21.6%
1970–1980	0.5%
1980–1990	4.9%
1990–2000	1.2%

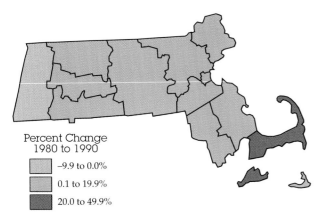

Persons Per Square Mile
- 10.0 to 9.9
- 100.0 to 249.9
- 250.0 to 749.9
- 750.0 to 11,699.9

Population Density

Population density for the state of Massachusetts was 767.6 persons per square mile in 1990 (296.4 per km2). Average U.S. density was 70.3 persons per square mile in 1990 (27.3 per km2). Habitation is most dense in a north-south band in the eastern counties of the state. Within this band are the cities of Boston, Cambridge, and New Bedford.

Percent Change 1980 to 1990
- –9.9 to 0.0%
- 0.1 to 19.9%
- 20.0 to 49.9%

Population Change

The 1990 population figure for the state of Massachusetts was 6,016,425. This is a 4.87 percent increase from 5,737,037 in 1980. The next decade will show growth with a population of 6.1 million or a 1.17 percent increase. The areas of fastest growth are found in the counties of Barnstable and Dukes. The former is the site of Cape Cod National Seashore.

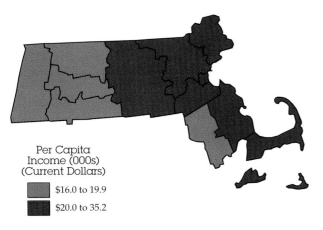

Per Capita Income (000s) (Current Dollars)
- $16.0 to 19.9
- $20.0 to 35.2

Distribution of Income

The per capita income for the state of Massachusetts (current dollars) was $24,059 in 1992. This is a 125.7 percent increase from $10,659 in 1980. The per capita income for Massachusetts is one of the highest in the country. Most of the state enjoys per capita incomes of $20,000 or higher.

Population Facts

State Population, 1993: 6,012,000

Rank: 13

Population 2000: 6,087,000 (Rank 13)

Density: 767.6 per sq. mi. (296.4 per km²)

Distribution: 84.3% urban, 15.7% rural

Population Under 5 Years Old: 7.2%

Population Under 18 Years Old: 23.1%

Population Over 65 Years Old: 13.9%

Median Age: 33.6

Number of Households: 2,247,000

Average Persons Per Household: 2.58

Average Persons Per Family: 3.15

Female Heads of Households: 4.50%

Population That Is Married: 19.45%

Birth Rate: 15.4 per 1,000 population

Death Rate: 8.8 per 1,000 population

Births to Teen Mothers: 8.0%

Marriage Rate: 8.1 per 1,000 population

Divorce Rate: 2.8 per 1,000 population

Violent Crime Rate: 736 per 100,000 pop.

Population on Social Security: 16.5%

Percent Voting for President: 60.2%

Population Profile

Rank. Massachusetts ranks 13th among U.S. states in terms of population with 6,012,000 citizens.

Minority Population. The state's minority population is 12.4 percent. The state's male to female ratio for 1990 was 92.36 males for every 100 females. It was below the national average of 95.22 males for every 100 females.

Growth. Growing much more slowly than the

Government

Capital: Boston (established 1630).

Statehood: Became 6th state on Feb. 6, 1788.

Number of Counties: 14.

Supreme Court Justices: 7, to age 70.

State Senators: 40, 2-year term.

State Legislators: 160, 2-year term.

United States Senators: 2.

United States Representatives: 10.

Electoral Votes: 12.

State Constitution: Adopted 1780.

Massachusetts's Famous Citizens

Bailey, F. Lee (b. 1933). Lawyer. Defense attorney for high-profile clients such as Patty Hearst and O. J. Simpson.

Benchley, Robert (1889–1945). Wrote humorous pieces for magazines such as *Vanity Fair* and drama criticism for *The New Yorker*.

Davis, Bette (1908–1989). Actress. Won Academy Awards for her roles in the films *Dangerous* (1935) and *Jezebel* (1938).

Gibson, Charles Dana (1867–1944). His drawings of young women (Gibson Girls) helped define the ideal of female beauty.

Kennedy, John Fitzgerald (1917–1963). Elected 35th president of the United States. Assassinated in Dallas, Texas in November, 1963.

Morton, William (1819–1868). Pioneered the use of ether as an anesthetic during surgery.

Pinkham, Lydia Estes (1819–1883). Made commercial success of an herbal remedy sold as Mrs. Lydia E. Pinkham's Vegetable Compound.

Wheatley, Phyllis (1753–1784). Poet. Slave whose owners taught her languages and literature and freed her upon their death.

projected national average, the state's population is expected to reach 6.3 million by the year 2010 *(see graph above)*.

Older Citizens. The state's population older than 65 was 819,284 in 1990. It grew 12.77% from 726,531 in 1980.

Younger Citizens. The number of children (under 18 years of age) was 1.4 million in 1990. This represents 22.5 percent of the state's population. The state's school aged population was 829 thousand in 1990. It is expected to increase to 920 thousand by the year 2000. This represents a 10.98% change.

Urban/Rural. 84.3% of the population of the state lives in urban areas while 15.7% live in rural areas.

Largest Cities. Massachusetts has 35 cities with a population greater than 35,000. The populations of the state's largest centers are (starting from the most populous) Boston (574,283), Worcester (169,759), Springfield (156,983), Lowell (103,439), New Bedford (99,922), Cambridge (95,802), Brockton (92,788), Fall River (92,703), Quincy (84,985), Newton (82,585), Lynn (81,245), Somerville (76,210), Lawrence (70,207), and Framingham (64,994).

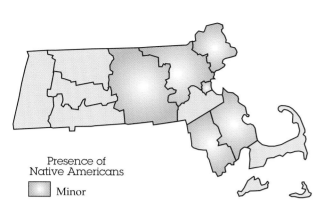

**Presence of
Native Americans**

Minor

Native American

The Native American population in Massachusetts was 12,241 in 1990. This was an increase of 36.07 percent from 8,996 in 1980. Fifteen percent of the Native American population resides in the city of Boston. Massachusetts is named after the Massachuset tribe, which makes its home there.

Statewide Ethnic Composition

Over 89 percent of the population of Massachusetts is white. The largest nationalities in this racial group are Irish, Italian, and English. The next largest group is African Americans, followed by Hispanics, Asian Americans, and Native Americans. Over 161,000 people claim to be American and acknowledge no other nationality.

Nationalities

African	37,924
American	161,269
Arab	35,255
Austrian	12,128
Czech	8,331
Dutch	28,154
English	592,523
Finnish	21,168
German	325,614
Greek	70,049
Hungarian	11,215
Irish	1,136,140
Italian	652,593
Norwegian	18,391
Polish	252,143
Portuguese	241,173
Russian	99,360
Scottish	121,285
Slovak	9,796
Swedish	89,443
Welsh	12,387
West Indian	48,847

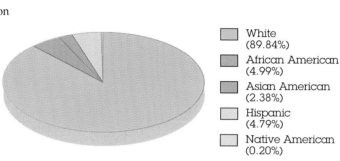

White (89.84%)

African American (4.99%)

Asian American (2.38%)

Hispanic (4.79%)

Native American (0.20%)

Education Facts

Total Students 1990: 825,588

Number of School Districts: 352

Expenditure Per Capita on Education 1990: $826

Expenditure Per Capita K–12 1990: $781

Expenditure Per Pupil 1990: $6,351

Total School Enrollment 1990–1991: 834,159

Rank of Expenditures Per Student: 7th in the U.S.

African American Enrollment: 7.5%

Hispanic Enrollment: 7.4%

Asian/Pacific Islander Enrollment: 3.2%

Native American Enrollment: 0.1%

Mean SAT Score 1991 Verbal: 426

Mean SAT Score 1991 Math: 470

Average Teacher's Salary 1992: $37,300

Rank Teacher's Salary: 9th in U.S.

High School Graduates 1990: 49,700

Total Number of Public Schools: 1,817

Number of Teachers 1990: 59,583

Student/Teacher Ratio: 14.0

Staff Employed in Public Schools: 104,058

Pupil/Staff Ratio: 7.9

Staff/Teacher Ratio: 1.8

Education

Attainment: 81 percent of population 25 years or older were high school graduates in 1989, earning Massachusetts a ranking of 20th in the United States; 28.1 percent of the state's population had completed college. Institutions of Higher Education: The largest universities and colleges in the state include the University of Massachusetts, Amherst; Northeastern University, Boston; Boston University, Boston; Boston College, Chestnut Hill; Brandeis University, Waltham; Massachusetts Institute of Technology, Cambridge; Smith College, Northampton; College of the Holy Cross, Worcester; Wellesley College, Wellesley; Mount Holyoke College, South Hadley; Williams College, Williamstown; Amherst College, Amherst; Harvard College (founded 1636), Cambridge. Expenditures per Student: Expenditure increased 73% between 1985 and 1990. Projected High School Graduations: 1998 (57,769), 2004 (63,579); Total Revenues for Education from Federal Sources: $198 million; Total Revenues for Education from State Sources: $1.9 billion; Total Revenues for Education from Local Sources: $2.4 billion; Average Annual Salaries for Public School Principals: $45,853; Largest School Districts in State: Boston School District, 59,597 students, 55th in the United States.

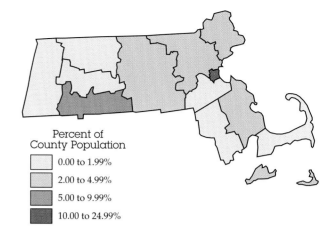

**Percent of
County Population**

0.00 to 1.99%

2.00 to 4.99%

5.00 to 9.99%

10.00 to 24.99%

African American

The African American population in Massachusetts was 300,130 in 1990. This was an increase of 35.79 percent from 221,029 in 1980. The largest percentage of African Americans can be found in the city of Boston. Almost 50 percent of Massachusetts's African American population lives in this city.

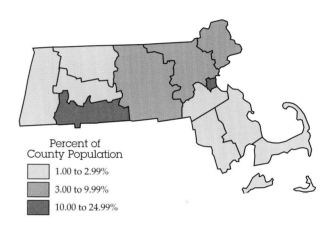

**Percent of
County Population**

1.00 to 2.99%

3.00 to 9.99%

10.00 to 24.99%

Hispanic[++]

The Hispanic population in Massachusetts was 287,549 in 1990. This is an increase of 103.87 percent from 141,043 persons in 1980. The largest percentage of Hispanics can be found in Boston and in Springfield in Hampden County.

[++]A person of Mexican, Puerto Rican, Cuban, or other Spanish culture or origin regardless of race.

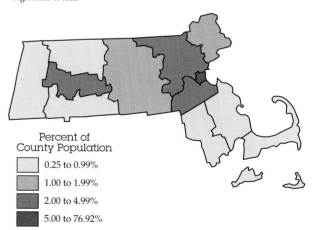

**Percent of
County Population**

0.25 to 0.99%

1.00 to 1.99%

2.00 to 4.99%

5.00 to 76.92%

Asian American

The Asian American population in Massachusetts was 143,392 in 1990. This is an increase of 177.23 percent from 51,723 persons in 1980. The highest percentage of Asian Americans can be found in Boston. Twenty-one percent of the Asian American population is located in this city. Other high-percentage areas are in the surrounding counties.

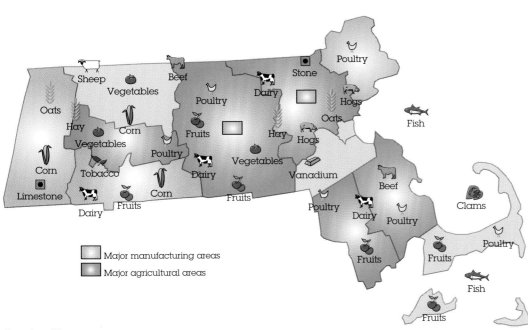

Major manufacturing areas

Major agricultural areas

Agriculture

Massachusetts has 1.0 million farm acres. During the last 40 years, Massachusetts farms have grown larger in size and fewer in number. In 1955, 17,128 farms were found in the state. Today, 7,000 remain.

Agriculture adds $ 1 billion to the state's gross product annually. The principal commodities in order of marketing receipts are greenhouse products, cranberries, hay, and apples.

Greenhouse and nursery products account for about 25 percent of Massachusetts farm income. The state's second leading product is cranberries. Massachusetts produces about half of the nation's supply. The cranberry bogs are found mainly in the marshy coastal areas. Hay is grown as feed for the state's dairy cattle. Other important crops include apples, eggs, and sweet corn.

Housing

Owner Occupied Units: 2,472,711; Average Age of Units: 42 years; Average Value of Housing Units: $162,800; Renter Occupied Units: 910,047; Median Monthly Rent: $580; Housing Starts: 17,300; Existing Home Sales: 66,000.

Economic Facts

Gross State Product: $145,000,000,000 (1989)

Income Per Capita: $24,059

Disposable Personal Income: $20,822

Median Household Income: $36,952

Average Annual Pay, 1988: $28,041

Principal Industries: transportation equipment, scientific instruments, machinery, printing, fabricated metal products, computer manufacturing

Major Crops: milk, cranberries, greenhouse products, apples, hay, sweet corn, eggs

Fish: Bass, Pickerel, Trout, Perch, Lobster, Cod

Livestock: Poultry

Non-Fuel Minerals: Sand, Gravel, Clay, Peat, Granite

Organic Fuel Minerals: N/A

Civilian Labor Force: 3,127,000 (Women: 1,478,000)

Total Employed: 2,847,000 (Women: 1,364,000)

Median Value of Housing: $162,800

Median Contract Rent: $580 per month

Economic Sectors 1992

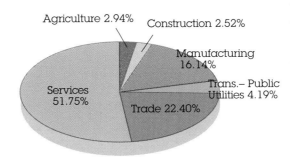

Agriculture 2.94%   Construction 2.52%

Manufacturing 16.14%

Trans.– Public Utilities 4.19%

Services 51.75%

Trade 22.40%

Manufacturing

Traditionally, Massachusetts employed more people in the manufacturing sector than any other state. Even today, manufacturing supplies 15.4 percent of the labor force with jobs; however, the goods produced have changed drastically. Currently, machinery production ranks as the number one industry in Massachusetts. Other items produced in the state include electrical equipment, scientific instruments, and printed material.

Most of Massachusetts' manufacturers are based in the greater Boston vicinity. Digital and Wang, two leading computer manufacturers, have headquarters in the state. Boston also produces goods for the scientific and printing industries. Most of the electrical equipment produced in Massachusetts is made in the northeastern counties of Middlesex and Essex.

Transportation

Much of Massachusetts' transportation occurs by automobile and truck, and therefore on roadways. Massachusetts has an impressive highway network; about 34,000 miles of highways and roads exist throughout the state. Several major highways crisscross Massachusetts, including Interstate 95 and the Massachusetts Turnpike, which goes from Boston to the New York-Massachusetts border.

Over the years, rail service in Massachusetts has dramatically declined. However, 11 railroads maintain freight service for the state. Many Massachusetts cities have passenger rail service as well. Boston is Massachusetts' primary seaport. Fall River, near the Rhode Island border, is another important port, mostly handling petroleum products. The busiest airport in Massachusetts, Logan International, is also one of the world leaders in airport traffic.

Energy and Transportation Facts

Energy. Yearly Consumption: 1,313 tril. BTUs (residential, 28.6%; commercial, 26.0%; industrial, 16.2%; transportation, 29.1%); Annual Energy Expenditures Per Capita: $1,767; Nuclear Power Plants Located in State: 1; Source of Energy Consumed: Petroleum— 62.9%; Natural Gas— 21.6%; Coal— 9.7%; Hydroelectric Power—1.9%; Nuclear Power—3.9%.

Transportation. Highway Miles: 34,323 (interstates, 567; urban, 21,017; rural, 13,306); Average Yearly Auto Insurance: $860 (5th); Auto Fatalities Rank: 50th; Registered Motor Vehicles: 3,663,400; Workers in Carpools: 14.8%; Workers Using Public Trans: 8.3%.

Employment

Employment. Massachusetts employed 2.9 million people in 1993. Most work in social and personal service jobs (951,800 persons or 32.2% of the workforce). Wholesale and retail trade account for 21.8% or 644,000 workers. Government employs 387,400 workers (13.1%). Manufacturing employs 453,500 people (15.4%). Construction employs 80,900 people, or 2.7%. Transportation and utilities account for 4.2% or 123,500 persons. Agriculture employs 32,500 workers or 1.1%. Finance, real estate, and insurance employ 199,300 people, or 6.7%. Mining employs 1,200 people and accounts for less than 1% of the workforce.

Unemployment. Unemployment has increased to 6.9% in 1993 from a rate of 3.9% in 1985. Today, it is higher than the national average of 6.8% as shown below.

Unemployment Rate

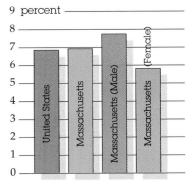

MICHIGAN
The State of Michigan

Official State Seal

The Great Seal of Michigan was first designed in 1835. It includes a shield with a man holding a gun and his hand up in peace. The motto, *"Tuebor"* (I Will Defend), is included on the top of the shield. The state motto, *"Si Quaeris Peninsulam Amoenam, Circumspice"* (If You Seek a Pleasant Peninsula, Look Around You), is placed on a banner at the bottom of the seal.

Legal Holidays

January: New Year's Day—1st, Martin Luther King, Jr., Day—3d Monday; Michigan Statehood Day—26th; February: Presidents' Day—3d Monday; May: Memorial Day—4th Monday; July: Independence Day—4th; September: Labor Day—1st Monday; October: Columbus Day—2nd Monday; November: Veterans' Day—11th; Thanksgiving—4th Thursday; December: Christmas—25th.

Official State Flag

Adopted in 1911, Michigan's flag includes the coat of arms found on the state seal. A moose and elk support the shield. This flag started as a military flag and included the national coat of arms on the other side. The national arms were later dropped from the design.

Festivals and Events

January: Cabin Fever Reliever, Onemaka; February: Perchville USA, Tawas City; March: Ann Arbor Film Festival, Ann Arbor; Snowman Sacrifices, Sault Ste. Marie; Kalamazoo Bach Festival, Kalamazoo; May: Frankenmuth Skyfest, Frankenmuth; Holland Tulip Time Fest, Holland; Kitefest, Kalamazoo; Highland Festival, Alma; June: Bavarian Festival, Frankenmuth; Do Dah Parade, Kalamazoo; Michigan Sugar Festival, Sebewaing; July: Arcadia Daze, Arcadia; Pigeon Farmers' Festival, Pigeon; August: Michigan Fest, East Lansing; Danish Festival, Greenville; September: Carry Nation Fest, Holly; Manistee County Fair, Manistee; October: Ginkgo Fest, Monroe; Red Flannel Fest, Cedar Springs; November: Ann Arbor Winter Art Fair, Ann Arbor

Michigan Compared to States in Its Region.

Resident Pop. in Metro Areas: 2d; Pop. Percent Increase: 5th; Pop. Over 65: 5th; Infant Mortality: 1st; School Enroll. Increase: 1st; High School Grad. and Up: 2d; Violent Crime: 2d; Hazardous Waste Sites: 1st; Unemployment: 1st; Median Household Income: 2d; Persons Below Poverty: 1st; Energy Costs Per Person: 4th.

East North Central Region

	Population	Capital
Wisconsin	5,038,000	Madison
Michigan	9,478,000	Lansing
Illinois	11,697,000	Springfield
Indiana	5,713,000	Indianapolis
Ohio	11,091,000	Columbus

Michigan's Finances

Households: 3,419,000; Income Per Capita Current Dollars: $19,508; Change Per Capita Income 1980 to 1992: 92.1% (33d in U.S.); State Expenditures: $21,840,000,000; State Revenues: $22,079,000,000; Personal Income Tax: 4.6%; Federal Income Taxes Paid Per Capita: $1,826; Sales Tax: 4% (food and prescription drugs exempt).

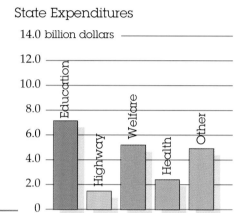

State Expenditures

14.0 billion dollars

Education, Highway, Welfare, Health, Other

State Revenues

14.0 billion dollars

Federal, Local, Taxes, Miscellaneous

Location, Size, and Boundaries

Maximum Extent

Location. Michigan is located in the East North Central region of the United States. It is bounded on four sides by land with coastlines along Lake Superior and Lake Huron. The geographic center of Michigan is lat. 45° 3.7' N; long. 84° 56.3' W.

Size. Michigan is the 23d largest state in terms of size. Its area is 58,216 sq. mi. (150,779 km2). Inland water covers 1,399 sq. mi. (3,623 km2).

Boundaries. Canada, 721 mi. (1,160 km); Ohio, 95 mi. (153 km); Indiana, 126 mi. (203 km) Illinois, 51 mi. (82 km); Wisconsin, 680 mi. (1,094 km).

Geographic Extent. north/south extent is 455 mi. (732 km). The state extends 400 mi. (640 km) to the east/west.

Facts about Michigan. Origin of Name: Named for Lake Michigan, which was called *Michigama "great or large lake"* by the *Chippewa* Indians; Nickname: The Wolverine State; Motto: "If you seek a pleasant peninsula, look about you"; Abbreviations: Mich. (traditional), MI (postal) ; State Bird: robin; State Tree: white pine; State Flower: apple blossom; State Song: (unofficial) "Michigan, My Michigan," words by Douglas M. Malloch.

Michigan Compared to Other States. Resident Pop. in Metro Areas: 16th; Pop. Percent Increase: 37th; Pop. Over 65: 32d; Infant Mortality: 6th; School Enroll. Increase: 29th; High School Grad. and Up: 25th; Violent Crime: 11th; Hazardous Waste Sites: 5th; Unemployment: 5th; Median Household Income: 15th; Persons Below Poverty: 19th; Energy Costs Per Person: 36th.

Sources of Information. Tourism: Travel Bureau, Department of Commerce, P.O. Box 30226, Lansing, MI 48909. Economy/Government: Library of Michigan, Information Services, Box 3007, Lansing, MI 48909. History: Michigan State Archives, 717 West Allegan Street, Lansing, MI 48918.

Michigan

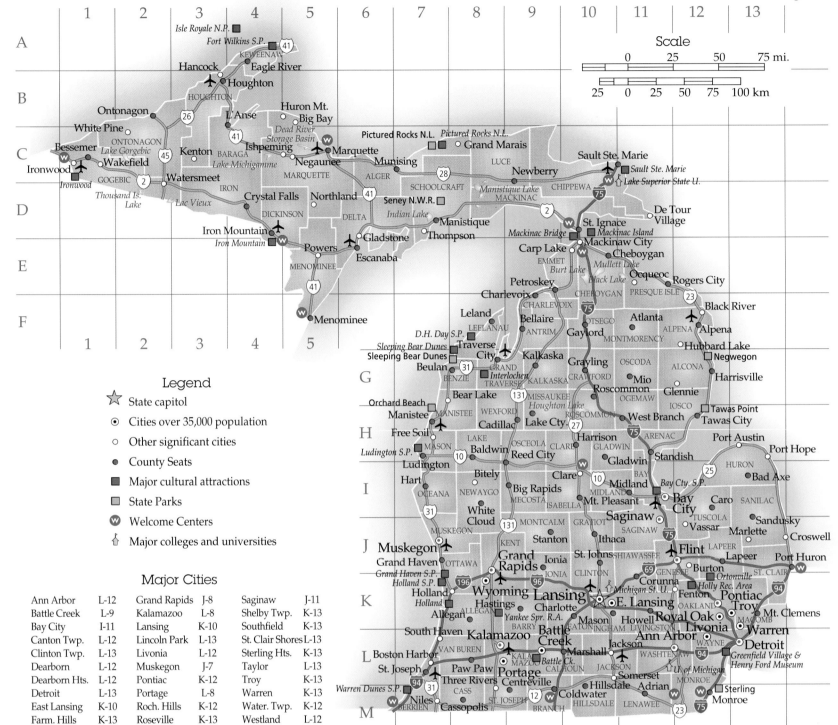

Legend

- ⭐ State capitol
- ⊙ Cities over 35,000 population
- ○ Other significant cities
- ● County Seats
- ■ Major cultural attractions
- ▢ State Parks
- Ⓦ Welcome Centers
- ⬆ Major colleges and universities

Major Cities

City	Grid	City	Grid	City	Grid
Ann Arbor	L-12	Grand Rapids	J-8	Saginaw	J-11
Battle Creek	L-9	Kalamazoo	L-8	Shelby Twp.	K-13
Bay City	I-11	Lansing	K-10	Southfield	K-13
Canton Twp.	L-12	Lincoln Park	L-13	St. Clair Shores	L-13
Clinton Twp.	L-13	Livonia	L-12	Sterling Hts.	K-13
Dearborn	L-12	Muskegon	J-7	Taylor	L-13
Dearborn Hts.	L-12	Pontiac	K-12	Troy	K-13
Detroit	L-13	Portage	L-8	Warren	K-13
East Lansing	K-10	Roch. Hills	K-12	Water. Twp.	K-12
Farm. Hills	K-13	Roseville	K-13	Westland	L-12
Flint	J-12	Royal Oak	K-12	Wyoming	K-8

■ Battle Creek. Cereal factories. (L-9)

■ Bay City State Park. Fishing, scenic views. (I-11)

■ D. H. Day State Park. Camping and beaches. (F-8)

■ Fort Wilkins State Park. Camping and the remains of old United States Army outpost. (A-4)

■ Grand Haven State Park. Camping, fishing, swimming on a lake beach. (J-7)

■ Greenfield Village and Henry Ford Museum. Vintage cars, displays of old America and historic buildings. (L-12)

■ Holland. Tulip center of United States, museum dedicated to the Netherlands. (K-7)

■ Holland State Park. Camping, beaches, and swimming. (K-7)

■ Holly Recreation Area. Winter sports. (K-12)

■ Interlochen Center for the Arts. Site of the national music camp. (G-8)

■ Iron Mountain. Winter sports, skiing, snowmobiling. (E-4)

■ Ironwood. Site of iron mines. Winter sports, skiing, snowmobiling. (C-1)

■ Isle Royale National Park. The largest island in Lake Superior with scenic views. (A-4)

■ Ludington State Park. Camping, fishing, swimming on a lake beach. (H-7)

■ Mackinac Bridge. Bridge that connects Michigan's Upper and Lower peninsulas and is over 5 miles (8 kilometers) long. (D-10)

■ Mackinac Island. Site of Fort Mackinac (1780). (D-10)

■ Ortonville Recreation Area. Fishing, hiking, and scenic views. (K-12)

■ Pictured Rocks National Lakeshore. Site of colored rock formations. America's first national lakeshore. (C-7)

■ Sault Ste. Marie. Canal locks, historic French town on the northeast border with Canada. (C-11)

■ Sleeping Bear Dunes. 35-mile shore area with shifting dunes. (F-8)

■ Warren Dunes State Park. Camping, fishing, swimming on a lake beach. (M-7)

■ Yankee Springs Recreation Area. Deer and small game hunting. (K-8)

Weather Facts

Record High Temperature: 112° F (44° C) on July 12, 1932, at Mio; Record Low Temperature: -51° F (-46° C) on February 8, 1930, at Vanderbilt; Average January Temperature: 20° F (-7° C); Average July Temperature: 70° F (21° C); Average Yearly Precipitation: 33 in. (84 cm).

Environmental Facts

Air Pollution Rank: 10th; Water Pollution Rank: 26th; Total Yearly Industrial Pollution: 77,442,675 lbs.; Industrial Pollution Rank: 10th; Hazardous Waste Sites: 77; Hazardous Sites Rank: 5th; Landfill Capacity: adequate; Fresh Water Supply: large surplus; Daily Residential Water Consumption: 161 gals. per capita; Endangered Species: Aquatic Species (2)—clubshell; Birds (4)—eagle, bald; Mammals (2)—bat, Indiana; Other Species (4)—beetle, Hungerford's crawling water; Plants (7)—fern, American hart's-tongue.

Environmental Quality

Michigan residents generate 11.7 million tons of solid waste each year, or approximately 2,600 pounds per capita. Landfill capacity in Michigan will be exhausted in 5 to 10 years. The state has 79 hazardous waste sites. Annual greenhouse gas emissions in Michigan total 181.5 million tons, or 19.6 tons per capita. Industrial sources in Michigan release approximately 134.4 thousand tons of toxins, 837.7 thousand tons of acid precipitation-producing substances, and 3.7 million tons of smog-producing substances into the atmosphere each year.

The state has 630,200 acres within the National Park System; the largest area within the state is Isle Royale National Park. State parks cover just over 250,000 acres, attracting 25.3 million visitors per year.

Michigan spends approximately 1.4 percent of its budget, or approximately $24 per capita, on environmental and natural resources.

Average Monthly Weather

Michigan	Jan	Feb	Mar	Apr	May	Jun	Jul	Aug	Sep	Oct	Nov	Dec	Yearly
Maximum Temperature °F	30.6	33.5	43.4	57.7	69.4	79.0	83.1	81.5	74.4	62.5	47.6	35.4	58.2
Minimum Temperature °F	16.1	18.0	26.5	36.9	46.7	56.3	60.7	59.4	52.2	41.2	31.4	21.6	38.9
Days of Precipitation	13.1	11.2	13.2	12.5	11.2	10.4	9.2	9.4	9.7	9.6	11.7	13.9	135.0
Marquette													
Maximum Temperature °F	20.1	23.8	33.2	47.4	61.5	70.4	75.3	73.3	63.9	53.4	36.5	24.6	48.6
Minimum Temperature °F	4.1	4.8	13.2	27.4	38.9	48.8	53.8	51.8	44.1	35.2	23.6	11.2	29.7
Days of Precipitation	18.0	13.4	14.7	12.2	10.5	12.3	9.6	13.1	14.5	15.8	15.9	18.5	168.5

Flora and Fauna

Many of Michigan's original forests were cleared with the onset of white settlement, but many species have begun regenerating in old forest locations, and now over half of the state is covered by woodlands. Hardwood trees such as elm, beech, and birch grow in moist soil, while other such as oak and walnut grow in drier conditions. Coniferous forests of hemlock, fir, and other softwood trees can also be found in Michigan. Blackberry, gooseberry, and elder shrubs grow throughout the state. Flowers of Michigan include orange milkweed, chicory, and shooting stars.

Aside from Texas, Michigan has more deer than any other state. Other large animals include black bear and moose. Smaller land mammals in Michigan include badgers, weasels, and squirrels. Geese, grouse, and other game birds live in Michigan as well. Overall, the state is home to hundreds of bird species; the kingfisher and great blue heron are among the most common. Michigan's rivers and lakes are filled with a number of fish species, including pike, perch, and salmon. Other fish such as the herring have become increasingly rare over the years.

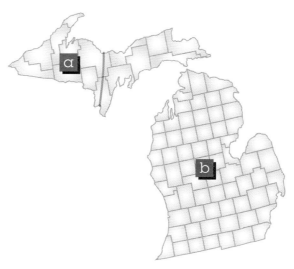

Physical Regions: (a) Superior Upland; (b) Great Lakes Plains.

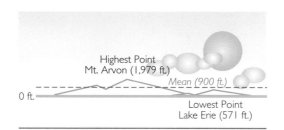

Highest Point
Mt. Arvon (1,979 ft.)
Mean (900 ft.)
0 ft.
Lowest Point
Lake Erie (571 ft.)

Land Use

Cropland: 28.7%; Pasture: 8.3%; Rangeland: 0%; Forest: 46.8%; Urban: 8.9%; Other: 7.3%.

For more information about Michigan's environment, contact the Michigan Department of Natural Resources, Stevens Mason Bldg., P.O. Box 30028, Lansing, MI 48909.

Topography

Michigan is divided into the Upper and Lower Peninsula. Both are covered almost entirely by the Great Lakes Plains physical region. The Lower Peninsula is completely within the Plains. The eastern part of the Lower Peninsula is a lowland area, with the lowest elevations in the state, particularly in the southeast corner along Lake Erie. This generally flat region is well suited to agriculture. Its soil ranges from warm and wet fine loamy sand to cool and moist brown clay. The western and north-central parts of the Lower Peninsula are more hilly and attain elevations of over 1,500 ft. (450 m).

The eastern portion of the Upper Peninsula also lies within the Great Lakes Plains. This area is characterized by swampy low-lying land that is not particularly well suited to agriculture. The western half of the Upper Peninsula is known as the Superior Upland physical region, a hilly territory with a higher elevation than the rest of the state. Low mountain ranges (the Gogebic and the Huron) are found in the northern area. This is where the state's highest point is located; Mount Arvon rises 1,979 ft. (604 m) above sea level. The soil is cool and moist, with color ranging from brown to gray/brown, and high iron and organic content.

Climate

By position alone, Michigan should have a humid continental climate. However, the Great Lakes make Michigan's climate more moist than those of neighboring states. The Great Lakes also bring more cloudiness to Michigan; in the winter, 7 out of 10 days are cloudy. Michigan's Lower Peninsula is usually warmer than its Upper Peninsula. January and July temperatures in Detroit, in the southeast, average 26 degrees F and 74 degrees F. A town like Escanaba, on the Upper Peninsula, has average temperatures of 18 degrees F and 66 degrees F for January and July.

Statewide, Michigan receives 31 inches of annual precipitation. Parts of the northwest and southwest receive slightly more annual precipitation, approximately 36 inches. Snowfall occurs throughout Michigan, with the most falling in the western Upper Peninsula.

Storms of all types (sleet, hail, ice, etc.) are common in Michigan. Occasionally, even tornadoes and blizzards occur.

Hydrology

The longest river in the state is the Grand, which flows west into Lake Michigan near Grand Rapids. It is about 272 miles (438 km) long. Other important rivers in the Lower Peninsula include the Muskegon, the Manastee, and the Kalamazoo in the west, and the Au Sable and Saginaw in the east. Important rivers in the Upper Peninsula include the Whitefish, the Manistique, and the Escanaba.

Most of Michigan's borders are defined by the Great Lakes. Lake Michigan forms the Lower Peninsula's western boundary, while Lake Huron defines the eastern. The southeastern corner has its border marked by Lake Erie and Lake St. Clair, with the Detroit River connecting the two. Lake Superior to the north and Lakes Michigan and Huron to the south help define the Upper Peninsula's borders.

Several large lakes are found in the Lower Peninsula, the largest being Houghton Lake at 29 sq. miles (75 sq. km).

Michigan's History

Michigan's First People

The Paleo-Indian culture of hunters and fishermen may have inhabited the region of Michigan as long as eleven thousand years ago. They would eventually become the earliest users of metals (specifically, copper) in the Western Hemisphere.

Around 500 B.C., representatives of the Mound Builder cultures appeared in the area. The Hopewell peoples were known for their unique earthen burial mounds, a class system with strict division of labor, and a far-flung trading network.

By the time whites arrived in the early seventeenth century, there were several tribes inhabiting mostly the Upper Peninsula of Michigan. The Ojibwa occupied the eastern Upper Peninsula; the Menominee, the central portion of the Upper Peninsula; the Ottawa in the western part of the Lower Peninsula; and the Potawatomi in the southwest.

European Exploration

Etienne Brule was the first European to enter Michigan, exploring the Sault Sainte Marie area of the Upper Peninsula around 1620. He was followed in 1634 by fellow Frenchman Jean Nicolet, who passed through the Straits of Mackinac. The first permanent settlement in Michigan was established by Father Jacques Marquette, who founded a mission at Sault Sainte Marie, and another at St. Ignace a few years later. By the turn of the century, several forts and missions had been established, and in 1701 Antoine de la Mothe, Sieur de Cadillac, founded Fort Pontchartrain at the site of present-day Detroit. The French retained control of Michigan through the first half of the eighteenth century until they were forced to cede the area to the British at the end of the French and Indian War in 1763.

In 1763, several Indian tribes, friendly toward French traders and fearful of what a British presence might bring, revolted against the new rulers. Led by Chief Pontiac of the Ottawa, they seized Forts Michilimackinac and St. Joseph before being beaten back by the British, who after taking control continued the French policy of leaving the region undeveloped (to the benefit of the fur traders dominating the area).

Statehood

During the Revolutionary War, the people of Michigan backed the British, and the Americans were unable to take the territory. Under the Treaty of Paris of 1783, Michigan was granted to the United States, but the British refused to relinquish the territory. After the creation of the Northwest Territory in 1787, the Indians (with the backing of the British) resisted U.S. control. However, by 1796, under Jay's Treaty, the British finally surrendered control of Michigan.

In 1805, the Territory of Michigan was formed, but during the War of 1812, the British captured Fort Mackinac and once again controlled the area until the end of the war. With the completion of the Erie Canal in 1825, settlers began to move into the territory in significant numbers. By 1833, the state had enough population to apply for statehood, and in 1837 was admitted into the Union as the twenty-sixth state. Settlement of a border dispute with Ohio was part of the statehood agreement. Michigan was awarded much of the Upper Peninsula in exchange for the "Toledo Strip," which was granted to Ohio.

Industrialization

Michigan was essentially unsettled fur-trapping country during the seventeenth and eighteenth centuries and the first two decades of the nineteenth century. In the 1830s, the state's land began to be cultivated for such agricultural products as potatoes, wheat, and hops. Mineral deposits were discovered on the Upper Peninsula in the 1840s, and Michigan became a leading producer of copper, iron ore, and salt. In the second half of the nineteenth century, the abundant forest reserves in the state began to be harvested to make Michigan the nation's leading lumber producer.

Around the turn of the century, the development of the automobile industry would come to dominate Michigan's economy. The state suffered a severe slump during the Great Depression but today boasts a mix of industry (mainly autos), agriculture (cherries and blueberries), timber production, and mining (petroleum, gas, and iron ore).

The Auto Industry

In 1886, R. E. Olds produced a steam-driven car in Lansing. The Olds Motor Works in Detroit became the first automobile factory in 1900. By 1903, Henry Ford had founded his Ford Motor Company (also in Detroit), leading the way for Michigan to become the leading producer of automobiles in the world. This was accomplished by Ford's introduction of the Model T, a low-cost, assembly-line-produced car of which fifteen million were manufactured over the next two decades. By 1926, General Motors (founded in 1908) had sales of over a billion dollars. The Depression hurt the industry, but sales rebounded in the 1950s.

The 1930s also brought violence to the automobile industry. In 1935 the United Auto Workers union (UAW) was formed. A series of strikes nearly crippled the automobile industry as the union attempted to win the right to negotiate contracts. World War II saw the refitting of the automobile plants for the war effort. Michigan turned out all types of machinery, tanks, trucks, and airplanes for the war in Europe and the Pacific. After World War II the production of automobiles continued and reached record production levels. The industry's strongest challenge came in the 1970s, when cheaper, better-quality, and more fuel-efficient Japanese imports cornered a large segment of the market.

Important Events

1620 Etienne Brule, a Frenchman, explores the Upper Peninsula near Sault Sainte Marie.

1634 Jean Nicolet explores the Straits of Mackinac.

1668 First permanent settlement is established by Father Jacques Marquette at Sault Sainte Marie.

1701 Fort Pontchartrain founded by Antoine de la Mothe, Sieur de Cadillac, at site of present-day Detroit.

1763 British take control of Michigan from French at conclusion of French and Indian War.

1763 Chief Pontiac leads Indian revolt against British, briefly controlling Forts Michilimackinac and St. Joseph.

1764 British defeat Indians and retake control of Michigan.

1783 British required to give up control of Michigan according to Treaty of Paris ending the Revolutionary War, but refuse to do so.

1796 United States takes control of Michigan under Jay's Treaty.

1805 United States creates Territory of Michigan with Detroit as its capital.

1812 Detroit is captured by the British.

1837 Michigan is admitted into the Union as the twenty-sixth state.

1847 State capital is moved from Detroit to Lansing.

1900 Olds Motor Works becomes the first automobile factory in the United States.

1903 Henry Ford founds the Ford Motor Company in Detroit.

1908 William Durant founds General Motors; Henry Ford introduces the Model T.

1925 Walter Chrysler founds Chrysler Corporation in Detroit.

1963 Michigan's fourth constitution is approved in a referendum.

1973 U.S. Rep. Gerald Ford of Grand Rapids is appointed vice president to replace the resigning Spiro Agnew.

1974 Vice President Gerald Ford succeeds the resigning Richard Nixon to become the first nonelected President of the United States.

1993 Dr. Jack Kevorkian is charged with two deaths under a Michigan law banning assisted suicide.

Michigan

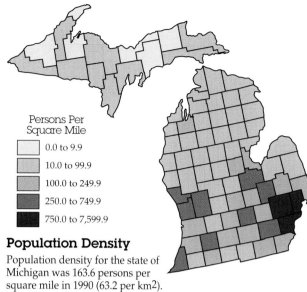

Persons Per Square Mile

- 0.0 to 9.9
- 10.0 to 99.9
- 100.0 to 249.9
- 250.0 to 749.9
- 750.0 to 7,599.9

Population Density

Population density for the state of Michigan was 163.6 persons per square mile in 1990 (63.2 per km2). Average U.S. density was 70.3 persons per square mile in 1990 (27.3 per km2). Habitation is most dense in and around the urban area of Detroit.

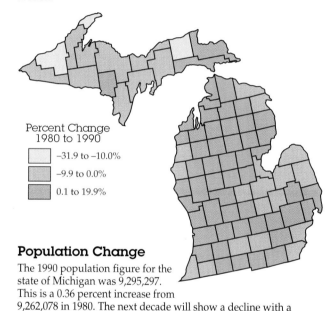

Percent Change 1980 to 1990

- −31.9 to −10.0%
- −9.9 to 0.0%
- 0.1 to 19.9%

Population Change

The 1990 population figure for the state of Michigan was 9,295,297. This is a 0.36 percent increase from 9,262,078 in 1980. The next decade will show a decline with a population of 9.25 million or a −0.49 percent decrease.

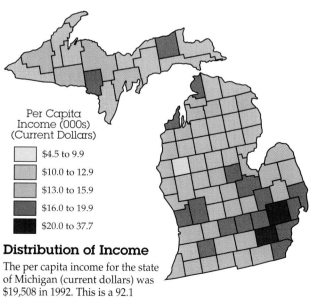

Per Capita Income (000s) (Current Dollars)

- $4.5 to 9.9
- $10.0 to 12.9
- $13.0 to 15.9
- $16.0 to 19.9
- $20.0 to 37.7

Distribution of Income

The per capita income for the state of Michigan (current dollars) was $19,508 in 1992. This is a 92.1 percent increase from $10,154 in 1980. Income is greatest in the counties surrounding Detroit and in the northern peninsula.

Population Projections

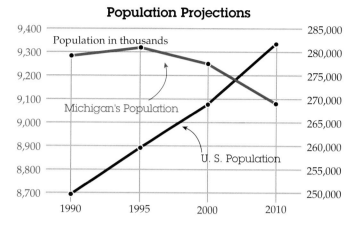

Population in thousands
Michigan's Population
U. S. Population

Population Change

Year	Population
1950	6,372,000
1960	7,834,000
1970	8,890,000
1980	9,262,078
1990	9,295,297
2000	9,250,000
2010	9,097,000

Period	Change
1950–1970	39.5%
1970–1980	4.2%
1980–1990	0.4%
1990–2000	−0.5%

Population Facts

State Population, 1993: 9,478,000

Rank: 8

Population 2000: 9,250,000 (Rank 8)

Density: 163.6 per sq. mi. (63.2 per km²)

Distribution: 70.5% urban, 29.5% rural

Population Under 5 Years Old: 7.7%

Population Under 18 Years Old: 26.6%

Population Over 65 Years Old: 12.2%

Median Age: 32.6

Number of Households: 3,419,000

Average Persons Per Household: 2.66

Average Persons Per Family: 3.16

Female Heads of Households: 4.76%

Population That Is Married: 20.26%

Birth Rate: 16.5 per 1,000 population

Death Rate: 8.5 per 1,000 population

Births to Teen Mothers: 13.5%

Marriage Rate: 8.2 per 1,000 population

Divorce Rate: 4.3 per 1,000 population

Violent Crime Rate: 803 per 100,000 pop.

Population on Social Security: 16.2%

Percent Voting for President: 61.7%

Population Profile

Rank. Michigan ranks 8th among U.S. states in terms of population with 9,478,000 citizens.

Minority Population. The state's minority population is 17.8 percent. The state's male to female ratio for 1990 was 94.36 males for every 100 females. It was below the national average of 95.22 males for every 100 females.

Growth. The state's population is decreasing and is expected to be 9.1 million by the year 2010.

Government

Capital: Lansing (established 1847).

Statehood: Became 26th state on Jan. 26, 1837.

Number of Counties: 83.

Supreme Court Justices: 7, 8-year term.

State Senators: 38, 4-year term.

State Legislators: 110, 2-year term.

United States Senators: 2.

United States Representatives: 16.

Electoral Votes: 18.

State Constitution: Adopted 1963.

Michigan's Famous Citizens

Brown, Olympia (1835–1926). Universalist minister who took up the cause of women's suffrage.

Catton, Bruce (1899–1978). Historian. Wrote a Pulitzer Prize-winning book (*A Stillness at Appomattox*) on the Civil War.

Couzens, James (1872–1936). U.S. senator from 1922 to 1936. Also served as mayor of Detroit and general manager of Ford.

Harris, Julie (b. 1925). Stage and screen actress. Has won four Tony Awards, most recently for *The Belle of Amherst* in 1977.

Hershey, Alfred Day (b.1908). Biologist. Won the Nobel Prize in 1969 for his work on phages, viruses that disintegrate bacteria.

Tomlin, Lily (b. 1939). Actress and comedian. Has won Emmy, Grammy, and Tony awards for TV programs, comedy albums, and stage shows.

Vandenberg, Arthur (1884–1951). U.S. Senator from 1928 to 1951. Important designer of postwar foreign policy in the United States.

Wonder, Stevie (b. 1950). Musician-songwriter. This pop-soul artist has won more than 15 Grammy Awards.

Older Citizens. The state's population older than 65 was 1,108,461 in 1990. It grew 21.51% from 912,258 in 1980.

Younger Citizens. The number of children (under 18 years of age) was 2.5 million in 1990. This represents 26.5 percent of the state's population. The state's school aged population was 1.57 million in 1990. It is expected to increase to 1.6 million by the year 2000. This represents a 1.91% change.

Urban/Rural. 70.5% of the population of the state live in urban areas while 29.5% live in rural areas.

Largest Cities. Michigan has 40 cities with a population greater than 35,000. The populations of the state's largest centers are (starting from the most populous) Detroit (1,027,974), Grand Rapids (189,126), Warren (144,864), Flint (140,761), Lansing (127,321), Sterling Heights (117,810), Ann Arbor (109,592), Livonia (100,850), Dearborn (89,286), Clinton (85,866), Westland (84,724), Kalamazoo (80,277), Southfield (75,728), Farmington Hills (74,652), Troy (72,884), Pontiac (71,166), Taylor (70,811), Saginaw (69,512), St. Clair Shores (68,107), Waterford (66,692), Royal Oak (65,410), and Wyoming (63,891).

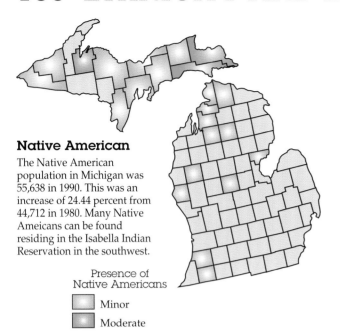

Native American

The Native American population in Michigan was 55,638 in 1990. This was an increase of 24.44 percent from 44,712 in 1980. Many Native Ameicans can be found residing in the Isabella Indian Reservation in the southwest.

Presence of
Native Americans

▢ Minor

▢ Moderate

Nationalities

African	9,917
American	332,467
Arab	65,906
Austrian	14,908
Czech	34,100
Dutch	384,178
English	811,283
Finnish	83,517
German	2,021,618
Greek	35,118
Hungarian	71,135
Irish	692,167
Italian	303,210
Norwegian	42,204
Polish	656,806
Portuguese	2,615
Russian	50,835
Scottish	148,774
Slovak	52,683
Swedish	117,046
Welsh	26,315
West Indian	5,989

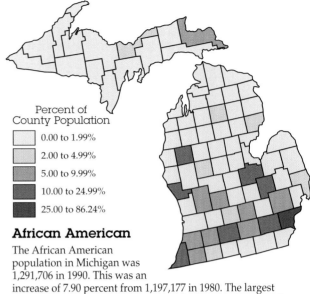

Percent of
County Population

▢ 0.00 to 1.99%
▢ 2.00 to 4.99%
▢ 5.00 to 9.99%
▢ 10.00 to 24.99%
▢ 25.00 to 86.24%

African American

The African American population in Michigan was 1,291,706 in 1990. This was an increase of 7.90 percent from 1,197,177 in 1980. The largest percentage of African Americans can be found in the city of Detroit and in the counties surrounding this city.

Statewide Ethnic Composition

Over 83 percent of the population of Michigan is white. The largest nationalities in this racial group are German, English, and Irish. The next largest group is African Americans, followed by Hispanics, Asian Americans, and Native Americans. Over 332,000 people claim to be American and acknowledge no other nationality.

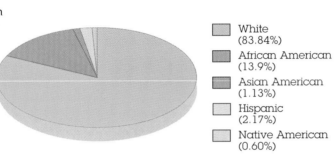

▢ White (83.84%)
▢ African American (13.9%)
▢ Asian American (1.13%)
▢ Hispanic (2.17%)
▢ Native American (0.60%)

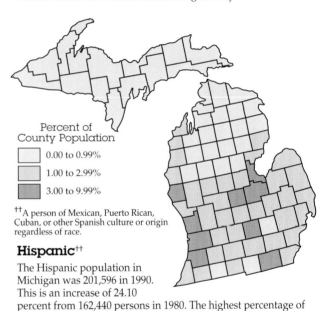

Percent of
County Population

▢ 0.00 to 0.99%
▢ 1.00 to 2.99%
▢ 3.00 to 9.99%

††A person of Mexican, Puerto Rican, Cuban, or other Spanish culture or origin regardless of race.

Hispanic††

The Hispanic population in Michigan was 201,596 in 1990. This is an increase of 24.10 percent from 162,440 persons in 1980. The highest percentage of Hispanics is located in the south-central portion of the state, with very few living in the Upper Peninsula.

Education Facts

Total Students 1990: 1,576,785

Number of School Districts: 561

Expenditure Per Capita on Education 1990: $888

Expenditure Per Capita K–12 1990: $788

Expenditure Per Pupil 1990: $5,257

Total School Enrollment 1990–1991: 1,582,321

Rank of Expenditures Per Student: 18th in the U.S.

African American Enrollment: 17.8%

Hispanic Enrollment: 2.3%

Asian/Pacific Islander Enrollment: 1.2%

Native American Enrollment: 0.9%

Mean SAT Score 1991 Verbal: 461

Mean SAT Score 1991 Math: 519

Average Teacher's Salary 1992: $41,100

Rank Teacher's Salary: 4th in U.S.

High School Graduates 1990: 106,000

Total Number of Public Schools: 3,314

Number of Teachers 1990: 80,321

Student/Teacher Ratio: 19.7

Staff Employed in Public Schools: 170,889

Pupil/Staff Ratio: 9.2

Staff/Teacher Ratio: 2.1

Education

Attainment: 77 percent of population 25 years or older were high school graduates in 1989, earning Michigan a ranking of 31st in the United States; 17.3 percent of the state's population had completed college. Institutions of Higher Education: The largest universities and colleges in the state include the University of Michigan (founded 1817), Ann Arbor ; Michigan State University (founded 1855), East Lansing; Wayne State University, Detroit; Western Michigan University, Kalamazoo; Eastern Michigan University, Ypsilanti; Michigan Technological University, Houghton; Central Michigan University, Mount Pleasant; University of Detroit, Detroit; Calvin College, Grand Rapids. Expenditures per Student: Expenditure increased 71% between 1985 and 1990. Projected High School Graduations: 1998 (111,201), 2004 (108,738); Total Revenues for Education from Federal Sources: $432 million; Total Revenues for Education from State Sources: $2.7 billion; Total Revenues for Education from Local Sources: $4.5 billion; Average Annual Salaries for Public School Principals: $46,712. Largest School Districts in State: Detroit City School District, 175,329 students, 8th in the United States; Flint City School District, 28,701, 145th.

Percent of
County Population

▢ 0.00 to 0.24%
▢ 0.25 to 0.99%
▢ 1.00 to 1.99%
▢ 2.00 to 4.99%

Asian American

The Asian American population in Michigan was 104,983 in 1990. This is an increase of 72.42 percent from 60,888 persons in 1980. Many Asian Americans reside in the counties surrounding the city of Detroit. There is also a presence in the Upper Peninsula in Houghton County.

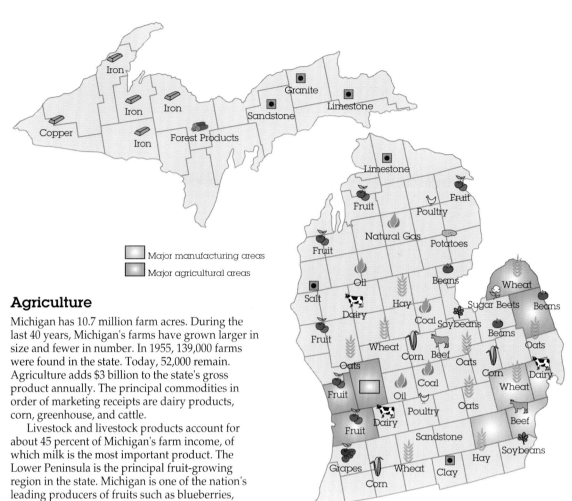

Major manufacturing areas

Major agricultural areas

Agriculture

Michigan has 10.7 million farm acres. During the last 40 years, Michigan's farms have grown larger in size and fewer in number. In 1955, 139,000 farms were found in the state. Today, 52,000 remain. Agriculture adds $3 billion to the state's gross product annually. The principal commodities in order of marketing receipts are dairy products, corn, greenhouse, and cattle.

Livestock and livestock products account for about 45 percent of Michigan's farm income, of which milk is the most important product. The Lower Peninsula is the principal fruit-growing region in the state. Michigan is one of the nation's leading producers of fruits such as blueberries, cantaloupes, peaches, and others. It is also the leading producer of dry beans. Other important crops include asparagus, carrots, and sugar beets.

Housing

Owner Occupied Units: 3,847,926; Average Age of Units: 35 years; Average Value of Housing Units: $60,600; Renter Occupied Units: 966,241; Median Monthly Rent: $423; Housing Starts: 38,600; Existing Home Sales: 170,600.

Economic Facts

Gross State Product: $182,000,000,000 (1989)

Income Per Capita: $19,508

Disposable Personal Income: $17,154

Median Household Income: $31,020

Average Annual Pay, 1988: $26,125

Principal Industries: chemicals, food products, transportation equipment, machinery, fabricated metal products, drugs, furniture, metal processing

Major Crops: milk, corn, hay, beans, sugar beets, cherries, apples, blueberries, dry beans, cucumbers, carrots, mint, grapes, bedding flowers

Fish: Catfish, Chubs, Lake Herring, Trout, Whitefish

Livestock: hogs, cattle, chickens

Non-Fuel Minerals: Iron Ore, Magnesium, Iodine, Limestone, Bromine, Calcium Chloride

Organic Fuel Minerals: Nat. Gas, Petroleum

Civilian Labor Force: 4,543,000 (Women: 2,023,000)

Total Employed: 4,125,000 (Women: 1,851,000)

Median Value of Housing: $60,600

Median Contract Rent: $423 per month

Economic Sectors 1992

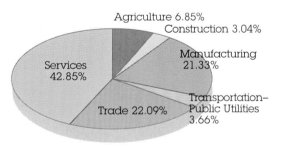

Agriculture 6.85%

Construction 3.04%

Manufacturing 21.33%

Services 42.85%

Trade 22.09%

Transportation–Public Utilities 3.66%

Manufacturing

Michigan is one of the leading manufacturing states in the nation. Michigan's manufacturing sector contributes the highest percentage of any state, 31 percent, to its state gross product. Most of Michigan's industrial workers produce transportation equipment, which is the leading industry. In addition, machinery, processed foods, and fabricated metal products are produced in the state.

Michigan is the nation's leading automobile manufacturer. Several plants are located throughout the state, including in Dearborn, Lansing, and the greater Detroit area. Besides automobiles, Michigan factories produce truck and bus parts, and vehicle accessories such as upholstery and plate glass. Other manufacturing centers include Grand Rapids (fabricated metals) and Battle Creek (food processing).

Transportation

The first paved concrete road in the world was constructed in Michigan in 1909. The current transportation network for the state emphasizes roads and highways. Michigan has approximately 117,000 miles of roadway. Several bridges in the state connect not only Michigan and Canada, but Michigan's Upper and Lower peninsulas as well.

The Great Lakes provide Michigan with several ports. The Great Lakes-St. Lawrence Seaway connects the state with the eastern United States, as well as with other countries. Important ports include Detroit, Alpena, and St. Clair. Major Lower Peninsula cities receive passenger rail service. In addition, about 30 freight rail lines exist throughout Michigan. Detroit and Grand Rapids have the state's two busiest airports.

Energy and Transportation Facts

Energy. Yearly Consumption: 2,754 tril. BTUs (residential, 25.3%; commercial, 16.0%; industrial, 33.7%; transportation, 25.0%); Annual Energy Expenditures Per Capita: $1,786; Nuclear Power Plants Located in State: 5; Source of Energy Consumed: Petroleum— 32.4%; Natural Gas— 30.0%; Coal— 27.0%; Hydroelectric Power—0.2%; Nuclear Power—10.3%.

Transportation. Highway Miles: 117,520 (interstates, 1,240; urban, 28,012; rural, 89,508); Average Yearly Auto Insurance: $661 (16th); Auto Fatalities Rank: 37th; Registered Motor Vehicles: 7,310,552; Workers in Carpools: 12.9%; Workers Using Public Trans: 1.6%.

Employment

Employment. Michigan employed 4.37 million people in 1993. Most work in social and personal service jobs (1 million persons or 23.2% of the workforce). Wholesale and retail trade account for 21.4% or 934,900 workers. Government employs 639,700 workers (14.6%). Manufacturing employs 901,800 people (20.6%). Construction employs 132,500 people, or 3%. Transportation and utilities account for 3.6% or 156,300 persons. Agriculture employs 74,400 workers or 1.7%. Finance, real estate, and insurance employ 4.4%, or 192,400 people. Mining employs 8,700 people and accounts for only 0.2% of the workforce.

Unemployment. Unemployment has decreased to 7% in 1993 from a rate of 9.9% in 1985. Today's figure is higher than the national average of 6.8% as shown below.

Unemployment Rate

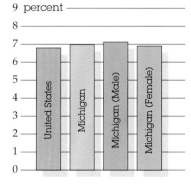

9 percent

MINNESOTA
The State of Minnesota

Official State Seal

The Great Seal of Minnesota was adopted in 1858, modified from an older seal dating from 1849. An engraver's error produced a mirror image of the old seal and this was later accepted. The seal shows a farmer watching a Native American riding a horse in the sunrise. Above this is the state motto, *"L'Etoile du Nord"* (The Star of the North). Also included is the year of statehood.

Legal Holidays

January: New Year's Day—1st; Martin Luther King, Jr., Day—Third Monday; February: Presidents' Day—Third Monday; May: Admission Day—11th; Memorial Day—4th Monday; July: Independence Day—4th; September: Labor Day—First Monday; October: Columbus Day—2nd Monday; November: Veterans' Day—11th; Thanksgiving—4th Thursday; December: Christmas—25th.

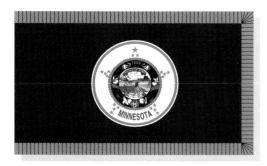

Official State Flag

Adopted in 1893, the Minnesota state flag was originally two-sided. It was changed to one side in 1957, because of the expense of producing it. The North Star is found at the top. At the time of statehood, Minnesota was the northernmost state in the United States.

Festivals and Events

January: Winter Fest, Lake City; St. Paul Winter Carnival, St. Paul; Icebox Days, International Falls; April: Festival of Nations, St. Paul; May: Eagle Creek Rendezvous, Shakopee; Polish Heritage Days, Winona; June: Water Ski Days, Lake City; Danish Days, Minneapolis; July: Woodcraft Fest, Grand Rapids; Sinclair Lewis Days, Sauk Centre; Minneapolis Aquatennial, Minneapolis; August: Minnesota Renaissance Festival, Shakopee (through September); Stiftungfest, Young America; September: Loon Lake Harvest Festival, Aurora; Victorian Fest, Winona; King Turkey Day, Worthington; October: Johnny Appleseed Days, Lake City; November: Santaland, Madison

Minnesota Compared to States in Its Region.

Resident Pop. in Metro Areas: 1st; Pop. Percent Increase: 1st; Pop. Over 65: 7th; Infant Mortality: 7th; School Enroll. Increase: 2d; High School Grad. and Up: 1st; Violent Crime: 5th; Hazardous Waste Sites: 1st; Unemployment: 2d; Median Household Income: 1st; Persons Below Poverty: 5th; Energy Costs Per Person: 7th.

West North Central Region

	Population	Capital
Minnesota	4,517,000	St. Paul
Iowa	2,814,000	Des Moines
Missouri	5,234,000	Jefferson City
North Dakota	635,000	Bismarck
South Dakota	715,000	Pierre
Nebraska	1,607,000	Lincoln
Kansas	2,531,000	Topeka

Minnesota's Finances

Households: 1,648,000; Income Per Capita Current Dollars: $20,049; Change Per Capita Income 1980 to 1992: 100.9% (25th in U.S.); State Expenditures: $12,322,000,000; State Revenues: $12,347,000,000; Personal Income Tax: 6 to 8.5%; Federal Income Taxes Paid Per Capita: $1,824; Sales Tax: 6% (food and prescription drugs exempt).

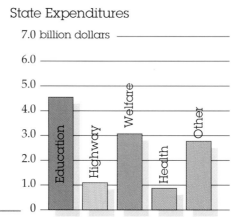
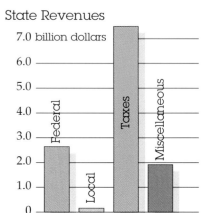

Location, Size, and Boundaries

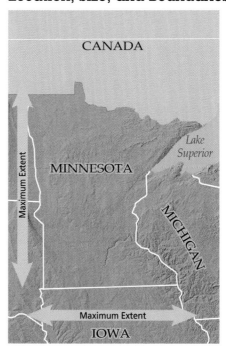

Location. Minnesota is located in the midwestern United States in a region known as the West North Central. It is bounded on four sides by land and one side by water. The geographic center of Minnesota is lat. 46° 1.5' N; long. 95° 19.6' W.

Size. Minnesota is the 12th largest state in terms of size. Its area is 84,068 sq. mi. (217,736 km2). Inland water covers 4,779 sq. mi. (12,378 km2).

Boundaries. Canada, 596 mi. (959 km); Wisconsin, 426 mi. (686 km); Iowa, 263 mi. (423 km); South Dakota, 182 mi. (293 km); North Dakota, 316 mi. (509 km).

Geographic Extent. The north/south extent of Minnesota is 406 mi. (653 km). The state extends 358 mi. (576 km) to the east/west.

Facts about Minnesota. Origin of Name: From two *Sioux* Indian words that mean *"sky-tinted waters"*; Nickname: The Gopher State; Motto: "The star of the north" (*L'Etoile du Nord*); Abbreviations: Minn. (traditional), MN (postal); State Bird: common loon; State Tree: Norway pine; State Flower: pink and white lady's slipper; State Song: "Hail! Minnesota," words by Truman E. Rickard and Arthur E. Upson and music by Truman E. Rickard.

Minnesota Compared to Other States. Resident Pop. in Metro Areas: 26th; Pop. Percent Increase: 23d; Pop. Over 65: 28th; Infant Mortality: 45th; School Enroll. Increase: 20th; High School Grad. and Up: 6th; Violent Crime: 37th; Haz. Waste Sites: 8th; Unemployment: 42d; Med. Household Income: 17th; Persons Below Poverty: 38th; Energy Costs Per Person: 42d.

Sources of Information. Tourism: Minnesota Office of Tourism, 375 Jackson Street, 250 Skyway Level, St. Paul, MN 55101. Government: House of Representatives Information Office, 175 State Office Building, St. Paul, MN 55155. History: Minnesota Hist. Society, 690 Cedar Street, St. Paul, MN 55101.

■ Bunyan House Information Center. Giant statues of the legendary lumberjack and his blue ox. (E-4)

■ Ely. Echo Trail in Superior National Forest; iron mines; and starting point for numerous wilderness canoe trips. (D-10)

■ Grand Portage National Monument. Historic trail and fur-trading post. (C-14)

■ Gunflint Trail. Begins in Superior National Forest near Grand Marais. (D-12)

■ Hibbing. Largest open-pit iron mine in the world. (E-8)

■ Kensington Runestone. Replica of stones believed at one time to have been left by Norsemen. (I-4)

■ Lake Vermillion. Large lake. (D-9)

■ Mendota. Location of oldest house in the state, the Henry H. Sibley House from 1835. (K-8)

■ Mille Lacs Lake. Scenic lake and Indian mounds in central Minnesota. (H-7)

■ Minnesota Museum of Mining. History of Minnesota mining. (E-8)

■ Niagara Cave. Features beautiful underground waterfalls. (N-10)

■ Northfield. Carleton College and St. Olaf College. Site of famous Wild West shootout. (L-8)

■ North Shore Drive. Scenic drive along Lake Superior. (G-9)

■ Northwest Angle. Northernmost point in contiguous United States. (A-4)

■ Pipestone National Monument. Indian peace pipe quarry. (M-2)

■ Red Lake. Largest lake in Minnesota. (D-5)

■ Split Rock Lighthouse. On Lake Superior near Duluth. (F-10)

■ Traverse des Sioux. Ford near St. Peter. (L-6)

■ Two Harbors. Iron-ore docks on Lake Superior. (F-10)

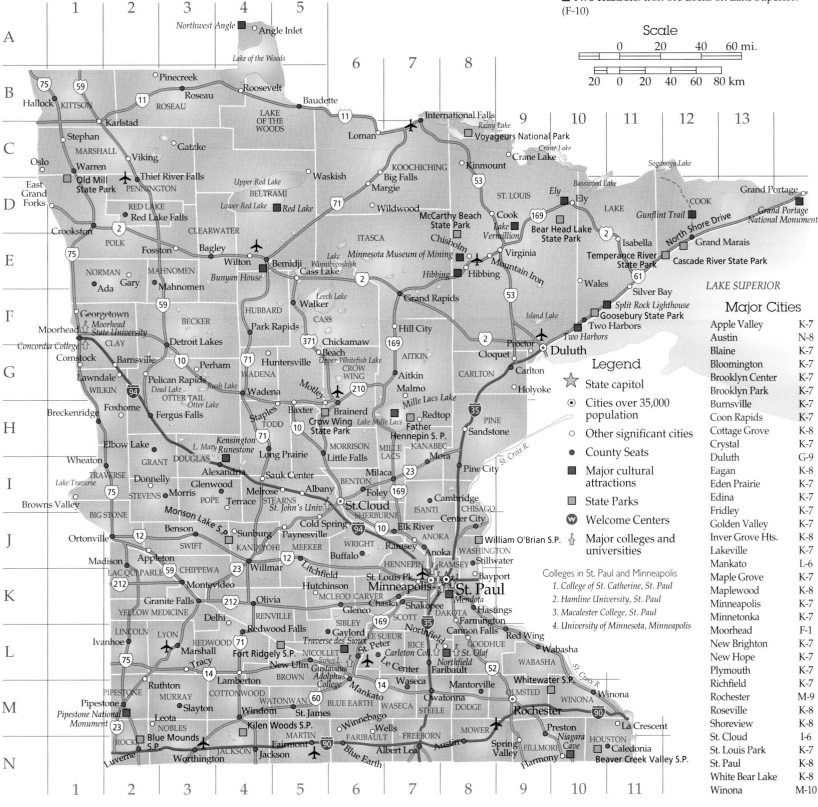

Legend

⭐ State capitol

⊙ Cities over 35,000 population

○ Other significant cities

● County Seats

■ Major cultural attractions

□ State Parks

Ⓦ Welcome Centers

⚑ Major colleges and universities

Colleges in St. Paul and Minneapolis
1. College of St. Catherine, St. Paul
2. Hamline University, St. Paul
3. Macalester College, St. Paul
4. University of Minnesota, Minneapolis

Major Cities

City	Grid
Apple Valley	K-7
Austin	N-8
Blaine	K-7
Bloomington	K-7
Brooklyn Center	K-7
Brooklyn Park	K-7
Burnsville	K-7
Coon Rapids	K-7
Cottage Grove	K-8
Crystal	K-7
Duluth	G-9
Eagan	K-8
Eden Prairie	K-7
Edina	K-7
Fridley	K-7
Golden Valley	K-7
Inver Grove Hts.	K-8
Lakeville	K-7
Mankato	L-6
Maple Grove	K-7
Maplewood	K-8
Minneapolis	K-7
Minnetonka	K-7
Moorhead	F-1
New Brighton	K-7
New Hope	K-7
Plymouth	K-7
Richfield	K-7
Rochester	M-9
Roseville	K-8
Shoreview	K-8
St. Cloud	I-6
St. Louis Park	K-7
St. Paul	K-8
White Bear Lake	K-8
Winona	M-10

162 CLIMATE AND ENVIRONMENT

Minnesota

Weather Facts

Record High Temperature: 114° F (46° C) on July 6, 1936, at Moorhead; Record Low Temperature: -59° F (-51° C) on February 16, 1903, at Pokegama Dam; Average January Temperature: 9° F (-13° C); Average July Temperature: 71° F (22° C); Average Yearly Precipitation: 25 in. (64 cm).

Environmental Facts

Air Pollution Rank: 23d; Water Pollution Rank: 32d; Total Yearly Industrial Pollution: 31,619,094 lbs.; Industrial Pollution Rank: 26th; Hazardous Waste Sites: 42; Hazardous Sites Rank: 8th; Landfill Capacity: adequate; Fresh Water Supply: large surplus; Daily Residential Water Consumption: 152 gals. per capita; Endangered Species: Aquatic Species (2)—mussel, winged mapleleaf; Birds (3)—eagle, bald; Mammals (1)—wolf, gray; Other Species (1)—butterfly, Karner blue; Plants (4)—bush-clover, prairie.

Environmental Quality

Minnesota residents generate 4.0 million tons of solid waste each year, or approximately 1,800 pounds per capita. Landfill capacity in Minnesota will be exhausted in 5 to 10 years. The state has 42 hazardous waste sites. Annual greenhouse gas emissions in Minnesota total 83.1 million tons, or 19.3 tons per capita. Industrial sources in Minnesota release approximately 31.9 thousand tons of toxins, 316.2 thousand tons of acid precipitation-producing substances, and 2.1 million tons of smog-producing substances into the atmosphere each year.

The state has 138,100 acres within the National Park System; the largest area within the state is Voyageurs National Park. State parks cover just over 186,000 acres, attracting 8.0 million visitors per year.

Minnesota spends approximately 1.5 percent of its budget, or approximately $29 per capita, on environmental and natural resources. Minnesota representatives in the U.S. House voted in favor of national environmental legislation 64 percent of the time, while U.S. senators did so 42 percent of the time.

Average Monthly Weather

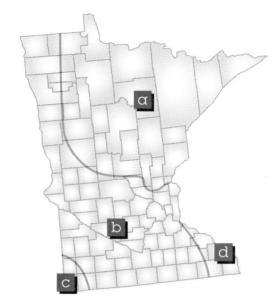

Physical Regions: (a) Superior Upland; (b) Young Drift Plains; (c) Dissected Till Plains; (d) Driftless Area.

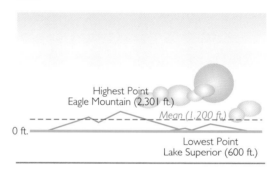

Highest Point Eagle Mountain (2,301 ft.)
Mean (1,200 ft.)
0 ft.
Lowest Point Lake Superior (600 ft.)

Land Use

Cropland: 48.8%; Pasture: 7.3%; Rangeland: 0.3%; Forest: 29.6%; Urban: 4.6%; Other: 9.4%.

For more information about Minnesota's environment, contact the Commissioner of Pollution Control, 520 Lafayette Rd., St. Paul, MN 55155.

Duluth	Jan	Feb	Mar	Apr	May	Jun	Jul	Aug	Sep	Oct	Nov	Dec	Yearly
Maximum Temperature °F	15.5	21.7	31.9	47.6	61.3	70.5	76.4	73.6	63.6	53.0	35.2	21.8	47.7
Minimum Temperature °F	-2.9	2.2	13.9	28.9	39.3	48.2	54.3	52.8	44.3	35.4	21.2	5.8	28.6
Days of Precipitation	11.7	9.7	10.8	10.4	12.2	12.5	11.2	11.5	11.7	9.5	10.9	11.6	133.8
Minneapolis													
Maximum Temperature °F	19.9	26.4	37.5	56.0	69.4	78.5	83.4	80.9	71.0	59.7	41.1	26.7	54.2
Minimum Temperature °F	2.4	8.5	20.8	36.0	47.6	57.7	62.7	60.3	50.2	39.4	25.3	11.7	35.2
Days of Precipitation	8.7	7.4	10.3	10.1	11.3	11.7	9.6	10.0	9.5	8.0	8.4	9.2	114.1

Flora and Fauna

Minnesota's forested land totals just over one-third of the state's area, or around 35 percent. In the north, coniferous forests of pine, spruce, and fir dominate. Between these northern forests and the grasslands to the south, a mix of various hardwood trees such as elm, maple, ash, and black walnut grow. Many types of wildflowers are found throughout Minnesota. Blackberries, raspberries, and wild roses grow in the northern part of the state. Other wildflowers, including blazing stars, prairie phlox, and birds-foot violets, grow in all other regions of Minnesota.

The common white-tailed deer lives virtually all over Minnesota. Moose and bear live in swampy areas in the northern part of the state. Smaller mammals such as gophers, raccoons, minks, and muskrats live throughout Minnesota. Game birds such as ring-necked pheasants and quail live near grain fields. During the summer months, ducks inhabit Minnesota's lake and swamp areas. Over 130 species of fish have been seen in Minnesota's numerous lakes, rivers, and streams. Some of these fishes include pike, trout, walleye, and sunfish.

Topography

Most of Minnesota lies within the Great Plains, with some variations in the different geographical areas of the state. The southeastern corner of the state, near the Mississippi River, is an area of gentle hills interrupted by deep river valleys known as the Driftless Area physical region. The soil of this region is warm and moist gray/brown clay. The Dissected Till Plains physical region, in the southwestern part of the state, is similar to the southeast, with organically richer soil in some areas, which makes this region more suitable for agriculture.

Northern Minnesota has a more varied topography. In the west is the Young Drift Plains physical region, with warm and moist loamy clay soil gray/brown in color. It is drained by the Red River Valley and forms a flat fertile area well suited to agricultural purposes. Much of the landscape of north-central Minnesota is the result of glaciation in the last Ice Age. Lake Agassiz, a huge lake that covered this area, was left behind after the glaciers departed, but it in turn drained away over time. Today it is known as the Superior Uplands physical region and is characterized by flat prairie and rich soil. The soil is typically cool and moist and includes peat bogs and swampland. Upper and Lower Red Lake and other smaller lakes, as well as extensive marshlands, are products of these geological phenomena. The northeast corner of the state includes the Mesabi and Vermillion mountain ranges.

Climate

Minnesota generally has a humid continental climatic type. However, significant variation exists throughout the state. Minnesota can be affected by frontal systems of Arctic air, but also by moist, warm air from the Gulf of Mexico area. Northwest Minnesota has the coldest weather. International Falls, near Canada, has average January and July temperatures of 6 degrees F and 66 degrees F. Around Minneapolis, in a more southeastern location, temperatures for January and July average 15 degrees F and 74 degrees F.

Minnesota's precipitation patterns seem to follow temperature patterns. In the southeast, annual precipitation averages 32 inches. However, in the northwest, precipitation decreases to only 19 inches annually. The state also receives much snowfall, most of it falling in the northeast.

Moorhead, usually having quite cold weather, once recorded Minnesota's highest temperature. On July 6, 1936, the temperature was 114 degrees F.

Hydrology

The most important river in the state is the Mississippi, which has its source in Lake Itasca in north-central Minnesota. It flows through the central portion of the state, and then southeast through Minneapolis-St. Paul to form the southeastern border with Wisconsin. The St. Croix River also defines part of the eastern boundary with Wisconsin. The Red River forms the western border with North Dakota. The Minnesota River flows through the southern part of the state, traveling first southeast, then northeast to drain into the Mississippi at the Twin Cities.

Minnesota has thousands of lakes, some quite large. Red Lake, in the north, is the largest at 442 sq. miles (1,145 sq. km). Other prominent lakes include Mille Lacs Lake at 215 sq. miles (557 sq. km), and Leech Lake at 165 sq. miles (427 sq. km). Lake of the Woods on the northern border with Canada covers more than 1,450 sq. miles (3,755 sq. km).

Minnesota's History

Minnesota's First People

The first inhabitants of Minnesota were Paleo-Indians living at least ten thousand years ago. Around 6000 B.C., the Archaic Indian culture surfaced in the Great Lakes region. These tribes were also migratory, but unlike the Paleo-Indians, had a more diverse source of resources for food and shelter. They hunted small game animals, fished, and gathered wild plants, in addition to using various materials (wood, ivory, copper, and others) to fashion knives, fishhooks, and other tools and containers.

The Woodland culture thrived from around 1000 B.C. to nearly the time of the arrival of the white man. At that time, Minnesota was occupied by the Minnesota Sioux and the Ojibwa.

European Exploration

In 1898, the Kensington Rune Stone was found, which supposedly recounts a visit by the Vikings to the region of Minnesota in 1362. Most scholars, however, discount the authenticity of the document.

It is generally thought that the first Europeans in Minnesota were Pierre Espirit Radisson and Medard Chouart, Sieur des Grosseilliers, who entered Lake Superior in 1660. In 1679, Daniel Greysolon, Sieur du Luth explored the interior, visiting with the Minnesota Sioux at Mille Lacs Lake and claiming the region for France. Seven years later, Nicolas Perrot founded Fort Antoine at Lake Pepin. These men were followed in the years to come by other French and British fur traders, including Pierre Gaultier de Varennes, Sieur de La Vérendrye, who built Fort St. Charles on the banks of the Lake of the Woods as he was searching for a Northwest Passage in 1732.

At the conclusion of the French and Indian War in 1763, France ceded to Great Britain the portion of Minnesota east of the Mississippi River, and to Spain that area west of the Mississippi. The British portion became part of the United States after the Revolutionary War, and the area under Spanish control through the Louisiana Purchase in 1803.

Statehood

The United States established Minnesota's northern boundary in an agreement with the British in 1818, and the following year Fort St. Anthony (later Fort Snelling) was built in this area at the confluence of the Mississippi and Minnesota rivers. It was the first permanent white settlement in the state and served as a center for trade and exploration in the area for many years. In 1837, the Sioux ceded part of central Minnesota to the United States, beginning a process of Indian land transfers to the federal government.

Congress created the Minnesota Territory in 1849, which included parts of North and South Dakota. Two years later, the Sioux gave up a large portion of southern Minnesota, starting an influx of settlers that saw the population grow tenfold by 1857. The next year, Minnesota was admitted to the Union as the thirty-second state with its capital at St. Paul.

Minnesota became the first state to join the Union cause in the Civil War, although no battles were fought there. However, Minnesotans did have their own war with the Sioux. In 1862, a Sioux uprising occurred due to lack of food and supplies for the reservation. The funds for these items were directed towards the war effort. As a result, conflict occurred and five whites were killed. A short war erupted and over 400 settlers were killed. When the Sioux were apprehended over 300 of them were sentenced to death. President Abraham Lincoln stepped in and commuted all but 39 of the sentences. This caused a fervor among the settlers who felt betrayed by the government. Later, the Sioux were expelled from Minnesota.

Industrialization

Until near the middle of the nineteenth century, fur trading was the primary activity of those who came to Minnesota. Beginning in the 1830s, former Indian lands came under the control of the government and settlers were attracted to the area. Farming was practiced by many, and the lumber industry became the primary economic force in the region. When the railroads came through in the 1860s, it enabled farmers to produce goods for markets elsewhere, and by the end of the century, Minnesota was the leading producer of wheat and its flour mills were also among the nation's leaders.

The discovery of iron ore in the 1880s eventually led to Minnesota's becoming a major steel producer in the early twentieth century. U.S. Steel Corporation began producing steel in Duluth in 1915.

The St. Lawrence Seaway opened in 1959 allowing Duluth to become a world port. Today iron ore mining, dairy farming, manufacturing, and transportation are the primary elements in the state's economy.

Democratic-Farmer-Labor Party

The Progressive Movement of the late nineteenth century, which sprang up in the face of hard economic times, was particularly strong in Minnesota, with the Grange movement, the Populist Party, and the Non-Partisan League all registering support in the state. The Farmer-Labor Party grew out of the Non-Partisan League in 1920 and elected two senators and a governor in the next ten years. Floyd Olson, elected governor in 1930, introduced progressive measures, including a graduated income tax.

After Olson's death in 1936, the party declined somewhat, but was revived in a merger with the state Democratic party in 1944. Since World War II, it has produced such national leaders as Hubert Humphrey and Walter Mondale.

Important Events

1660 French explorers Pierre Espirit Radisson and Medard Chouart, Sieur des Grosseilliers, make first European contact with Minnesota.

1679 Daniel Greysolon, Sieur Du Luth, visits Sioux village on Mille Lacs Lake.

1732 Pierre Gaultier de Varennes, Sieur de La Vérendrye, builds Fort St. Charles on the shores of Lake of the Woods.

1763 France cedes territory, including Minnesota, to the British and Spanish at the end of the French and Indian War.

1783 United States takes control of Minnesota east of the Mississippi River from the British.

1803 United States takes control of Minnesota west of the Mississippi River as part of the Louisiana Purchase.

1819 Fort Anthony (later Fort Snelling) is built at the confluence of the Mississippi and Minnesota rivers.

1837 Sioux make first of several land transfers to the United States.

1849 Congress creates the Minnesota Territory.

1858 Minnesota admitted into the Union as the thirty-second state.

1862 Chief Little Crow leads Sioux revolt in which over four hundred whites are killed.

1863 Sioux are driven from Minnesota.

1930 Floyd Olson is elected governor on the Farmer-Labor ticket.

1959 St. Lawrence Seaway is opened.

1964 Hubert Humphrey is elected Vice President of the United States.

1968 Hubert Humphrey is the Democratic nominee for president.

1969 Minnesotan Warren Burger is appointed Chief Justice of the U.S. Supreme Court.

1976 Minnesota senator Walter Mondale is elected Vice President of the United States.

1984 Walter Mondale is the Democratic nominee for President of the United States.

1988 Crippling drought hits the state.

1993 The Mississippi River overflows its banks causing damage.

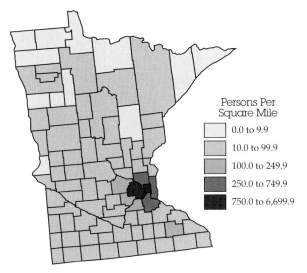

Population Projections

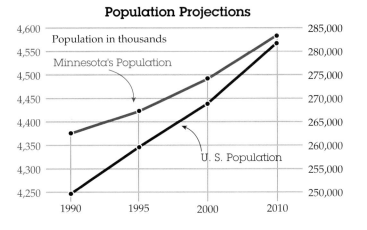

Population in thousands

Minnesota's Population

U. S. Population

Population Change

Year	Population
1950	2,982,000
1960	3,425,000
1970	3,815,000
1980	4,075,970
1990	4,375,099
2000	4,490,000
2010	4,578,000

Period	Change
1950–1970	27.9%
1970–1980	6.8%
1980–1990	7.3%
1990–2000	2.6%

Population Density

Population density for the state of Minnesota was 55.0 persons per square mile in 1990 (21.2 per km2). Average U.S. density was 70.3 persons per square mile in 1990 (27.3 per km2).

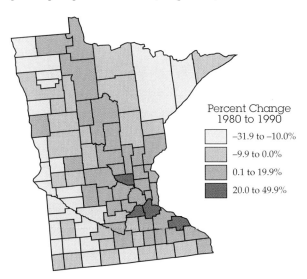

Population Change

The 1990 population figure for the state of Minnesota was 4,375,099 in 1990. This is a 7.34 percent increase from 4,075,970 in 1980. The next decade will show growth with a population of 4.5 million or a 2.63 percent increase.

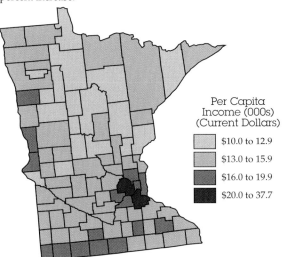

Distribution of Income

The per capita income for the state of Minnesota (current dollars) was $20,049 in 1992. This is a 100.9 percent increase from $9,982 in 1980. The area of highest incomes is found around Minneapolis and St. Paul.

Population Facts

State Population, 1993: 4,517,000

Rank: 20

Population 2000: 4,490,000 (Rank 22)

Density: 55.0 per sq. mi. (21.2 per km²)

Distribution: 69.9% urban, 30.1% rural

Population Under 5 Years Old: 7.5%

Population Under 18 Years Old: 26.9%

Population Over 65 Years Old: 12.5%

Median Age: 22.5

Number of Households: 1,648,000

Average Persons Per Household: 2.58

Average Persons Per Family: 3.13

Female Heads of Households: 3.24%

Population That Is Married: 21.54%

Birth Rate: 15.5 per 1,000 population

Death Rate: 7.9 per 1,000 population

Births to Teen Mothers: 8.0%

Marriage Rate: 7.7 per 1,000 population

Divorce Rate: 3.5 per 1,000 population

Violent Crime Rate: 316 per 100,000 pop.

Population on Social Security: 15.3%

Percent Voting for President: 71.6%

Population Profile

Rank. Minnesota ranks 20th among U.S. states in terms of population with 4,517,000 citizens.

Minority Population. The state's minority population is 6.3 percent. The state's male to female ratio for 1990 was 96.2 males for every 100 females. It was above the national average of 95.22 males for every 100 females.

Growth. Growing much slower than the projected national average, the state's population

Government

Capital: St. Paul (established 1849).

Statehood: Became 32d state on May 11, 1858.

Number of Counties: 87.

Supreme Court Justices: 7 to 9, 6-year term.

State Senators: 67, 4-year term.

State Legislators: 134, 2-year term.

United States Senators: 2.

United States Representatives: 8.

Electoral Votes: 10.

State Constitution: Adopted 1857.

Minnesota's Famous Citizens

Burger, Warren (b. 1907). Served as Chief Justice of the U.S. Supreme Court from 1969 to 1986.

Calvin, Melvin (b. 1911). Chemist. Won the Nobel Prize in 1961 for his work on the process of photosynthesis.

Garland, Judy (1922–1969). Singer-actress. Won a special Academy Award for her role as Dorothy in *The Wizard of Oz* in 1940.

Humphrey, Hubert (1911–1978). Vice president to Lyndon Johnson and presidential nominee in 1968. Served in the Senate for 28 years.

Prince (artist formerly known as) (b. 1959). Musician-songwriter. Had several hit records in the 1980s such as *Purple Rain*.

Schulz, Charles (b. 1922). Introduced his "Peanuts" comic strip (starring Charlie Brown and Snoopy) in 1950.

Sears, Richard Warren (1863–1914). Co-founded Sears, Roebuck, and Company as a mail order business in 1893.

Tyler, Anne (b. 1941). Writes about personal isolation in books such as *The Accidental Tourist*.

is expected to reach 4.6 million by the year 2010 *(see graph above)*.

Older Citizens. The state's population older than 65 was 546,934 in 1990. It grew 14.05% from 479,564 in 1980.

Younger Citizens. The number of children (under 18 years of age) was 1.2 million in 1990. This represents 26.7 percent of the state's population. The state's school aged population was 743 thousand in 1990. It is expected to increase to 791 thousand by the year 2000. This represents a 6.46% change.

Urban/Rural. 69.9% of the population of the state lives in urban areas while 30.1% live in rural areas.

Largest Cities. Minnesota has 18 cities with a population greater than 35,000. The population of the state's largest centers are (starting from the most populous), Minneapolis (368,383), St. Paul (272,235), Bloomington (86,335), Duluth (85,493), Rochester (70,745), Brooklyn Park (56,381), Coon Rapids (52,978), Burnsville (51,288), Plymouth (50,889), St. Cloud (48,812), Minnetonka (48,370), Eagan (47,409), St. Louis Park (43,787), Eden Prairie (39,311), Blaine (38,975), Maple Grove (38,736), and Richfield (35,710).

Minnesota

Presence of
Native Americans

Minor   Moderate

Nationalities

African	5,415
American	66,484
Arab	7,290
Austrian	9,001
Czech	56,010
Dutch	55,573
English	184,127
Finnish	76,267
German	1,630,513
Greek	6,521
Hungarian	6,263
Irish	276,976
Italian	58,120
Norwegian	494,440
Polish	142,302
Portuguese	1,000
Russian	20,031
Scottish	32,207
Slovak	18,566
Swedish	328,573
Welsh	10,069
West Indian	1,518

Native American

The Native American population in Minnesota was 49,909 in 1990. This was an increase of 36.64 percent from 36,527 in 1980. Many are found in the numerous Indian Reservations.

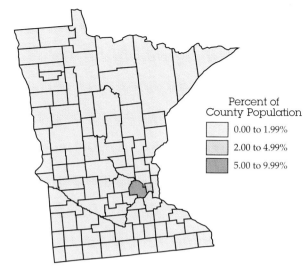

African American

The African American population in Minnesota was 94,944 in 1990. This was an increase of 81.45 percent from 52,325 in 1980. The largest number of African Americans can be found in the Minneapolis area.

Statewide Ethnic Composition

Over ninety-four percent of the population of Minnesota is white. The largest nationalities in this racial group are German, Norwegian, and Swedish. The next largest group are the African Americans followed by the Asians, Hispanics, and Native Americans. Over 66 thousand people claim to be American and acknowledge no other nationality.

White (94.40%)
African American (2.17%)
Asian American (1.78%)
Hispanic (1.23%)
Native American (1.14%)

Percent of County Population
- 0.00 to 1.99%
- 2.00 to 4.99%
- 5.00 to 9.99%

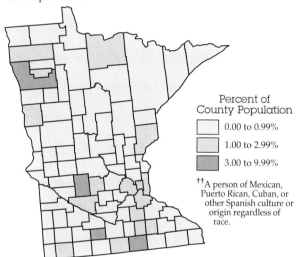

Percent of County Population
- 0.00 to 0.99%
- 1.00 to 2.99%
- 3.00 to 9.99%

††A person of Mexican, Puerto Rican, Cuban, or other Spanish culture or origin regardless of race.

Hispanic††

The Hispanic population in Minnesota was 53,884 in 1990. This is an increase of 67.74 percent from 32,123 persons in 1980. Twenty-one percent of the Hispanics can be found in the city of St. Paul.

Education Facts

Total Students 1990: 39,553

Number of School Districts: 436

Expenditure Per Capita on Education 1990: $933

Expenditure Per Capita K–12 1990: $390

Expenditure Per Pupil 1990: $5,360

Total School Enrollment 1990–1991: 751,913

Rank of Expenditures Per Student: 14th in the U.S.

African American Enrollment: 3.1%

Hispanic Enrollment: 1.2%

Asian/Pacific Islander Enrollment: 2.9%

Native American Enrollment: 1.6%

Mean SAT Score 1991 Verbal: 480

Mean SAT Score 1991 Math: 543

Average Teacher's Salary 1992: $33,700

Rank Teacher's Salary: 19th in U.S.

High School Graduates 1990: 48,200

Total Number of Public Schools: 1,564

Number of Teachers 1990: 43,716

Student/Teacher Ratio: 17.2

Staff Employed in Public Schools: 76,268

Pupil/Staff Ratio: 9.7

Staff/Teacher Ratio: 1.8

Education

Attainment: 85.5 percent of population 25 years or older were high school graduates in 1989, earning Minnesota a ranking of 5th in the United States; 21.5 percent of the state's population had completed college. Institutions of Higher Education: The largest universities and colleges in the state include the University of Minnesota (founded 1851), Minneapolis; Hamline University (founded 1854). Expenditures per Student: Expenditure increased 75% between 1985 and 1990. Projected High School Graduations: 1998 (28,705), 2004 (25,211); Total Revenues for Education from Federal Sources: $140 million; Total Revenues for Education from State Sources: $1.8 billion; Total Revenues for Education from Local Sources: $1.3 billion; Average Annual Salaries for Public School Principals: $47,667 Largest School Districts in State: Minneapolis Special School District, 36,385 students, 108th in the United States; Anoka School District, 33,562, 116th.

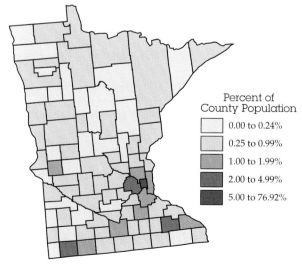

Percent of County Population
- 0.00 to 0.24%
- 0.25 to 0.99%
- 1.00 to 1.99%
- 2.00 to 4.99%
- 5.00 to 76.92%

Asian American

The Asian American population in Minnesota was 77,886 in 1990. This is an increase of 147.97 percent from 31,409 persons in 1980. The largest population can be found in St. Paul.

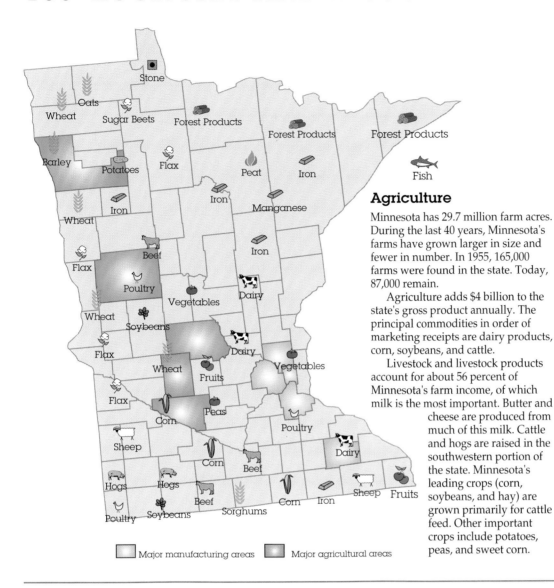

Major manufacturing areas   Major agricultural areas

Agriculture

Minnesota has 29.7 million farm acres. During the last 40 years, Minnesota's farms have grown larger in size and fewer in number. In 1955, 165,000 farms were found in the state. Today, 87,000 remain.

Agriculture adds $4 billion to the state's gross product annually. The principal commodities in order of marketing receipts are dairy products, corn, soybeans, and cattle.

Livestock and livestock products account for about 56 percent of Minnesota's farm income, of which milk is the most important. Butter and cheese are produced from much of this milk. Cattle and hogs are raised in the southwestern portion of the state. Minnesota's leading crops (corn, soybeans, and hay) are grown primarily for cattle feed. Other important crops include potatoes, peas, and sweet corn.

Transportation

Minnesota's many rivers provided transportation for the state's earliest settlers. Today, freight is shipped to ports on the Minnesota, Mississippi, and St. Croix rivers. Lake Superior also handles much of Minnesota's freight transport. The port at Duluth is the busiest freshwater port in the United States.

Minnesota has 131,000 miles of roads and highways across the state. Over 90 percent of these are paved roads. After the Civil War, a large railroad network emerged. Currently, Minnesota has approximately 5,000 miles of track. About 10 Minnesota cities receive rail service. In addition, 12 freight lines ship goods across the state. The Minneapolis-St. Paul International Airport is Minnesota's most active airport. However, smaller airfields can be found throughout the state.

Energy and Transportation Facts

Energy. Yearly Consumption: 1,364 tril. BTUs (residential, 23.8%; commercial, 14.4%; industrial, 35.6%; transportation, 26.2%); Annual Energy Expenditures Per Capita: $1,714; Nuclear Power Plants Located in State: 3; Source of Energy Consumed: Petroleum— 39.6%; Natural Gas— 24.6%; Coal— 23.3%; Hydroelectric Power—2.5%; Nuclear Power—10.1%.

Transportation. Highway Miles: 129,622 (interstates, 913; urban, 14,523; rural, 115,099); Average Yearly Auto Insurance: $566 (22d); Auto Fatalities Rank: 40th; Registered Motor Vehicles: 3,483,830; Workers in Carpools: 15.5%; Workers Using Public Trans: 3.6%.

Employment

Employment. Minnesota employed 2.34 million people in 1993. Most work in social and personal service jobs (614,500 persons or 26.2% of the workforce). Wholesale and retail trade account for 22.9% or 536,500 workers. Government employs 353,700 workers (15.1%). Manufacturing employs 405,400 people (17.3%). Construction employs 79,100 workers (1.1%). Transportation and utilities account for 4.7% or 109,200 persons. Agriculture employs 98,300 workers or 4.2%, as does finance, real estate, and insurance. Mining employs 7,500 people and accounts for only 0.3% of the workforce.

Unemployment. Unemployment has decreased to 5.1% in 1993 from a rate of 6.0% in 1985. Today's figure is lower than the national average of 6.8% as shown below.

Housing

Owner Occupied Units: 1,848,445; Average Age of Units: 32 years; Average Value of Housing Units: $74,000; Renter Occupied Units: 445,865; Median Monthly Rent: $422; Housing Starts: 24,400; Existing Home Sales: 81,800.

Economic Facts

Gross State Product: $93,000,000,000 (1989)

Income Per Capita: $20,049

Disposable Personal Income: $17,255

Median Household Income: $30,909

Average Annual Pay, 1988: $23,961

Principal Industries: paper products, machinery, printing, food products, scientific instruments, fabricated metal products, electrical equipment

Major Crops: corn, soybeans, milk, hay, oats, sugar beets, sunflowers, soybeans, rye, cheese, butter, forest products

Fish: Bass, Northern Pike, Sunfish, Trout, Walleye

Livestock: hogs, cattle

Non-Fuel Minerals: Iron Ore, Granite, Limestone, Sandstone, Sand, Gravel, Taconite

Organic Fuel Minerals: N/A

Civilian Labor Force: 2,431,000 (Women: 1,157,000)

Total Employed: 2,307,000 (Women: 1,110,000)

Median Value of Housing: $74,000

Median Contract Rent: $422 per month

Economic Sectors 1992

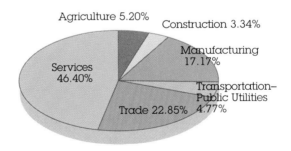

Agriculture 5.20%
Construction 3.34%
Manufacturing 17.17%
Transportation– Public Utilities 4.77%
Trade 22.85%
Services 46.40%

Manufacturing

Minnesota has a sizable manufacturing sector. The production of many different kinds of goods contributes one-fifth of the state gross product. In terms of the value added by manufacture, machinery is Minnesota's leading manufacturing activity. Other manufacturing industries include food production and printed materials. Manufacturing takes place all over Minnesota. Out of all machinery produced in the state, computers are the most important merchandise. Many computer companies have headquarters in Minneapolis, but computers are also made in St. Paul and Duluth. Duluth is also an important meat-packing, as well as publishing, city. Southern Minnesota, especially along the Minnesota River, has most of the canning factories in the state.

Unemployment Rate

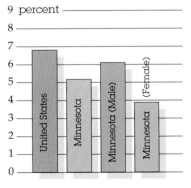

MISSISSIPPI
The State of Mississippi

Official State Seal

The Great Seal of Mississippi was adopted in 1817. It is not unlike the United States coat of arms. It includes an eagle holding arrows and an olive branch. In the center of the eagle is a shield containing the flag of the United States. Around the seal are imprinted the words "The Great Seal of The State of Mississippi."

Legal Holidays

January: New Year's Day—1st; Martin Luther King, Jr., Day—Third Monday; Robert E. Lee Day—18th; February: Presidents' Day—Third Monday; April: Confederate Memorial Day—28th; May: Admission Day—11th; Memorial Day—4th Monday; June: Jefferson Davis's Birthday—1st Monday; July: Independence Day—4th; September: Labor Day—First Monday; October: Columbus Day—2d Monday; November: Veterans' Day—11th; Thanksgiving—4th Thursday; December: Admission Day—10th; Christmas—25th.

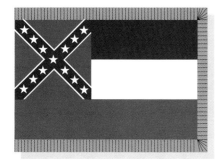

Official State Flag

The Mississippi state flag was adopted in 1894. It contains the Stars and Bars, which was the first flag of the Confederacy. The Stars and Bars are the horizontal red, white, and blue stripes. In the upper left corner is the Confederate battle flag with its distinctive thirteen stars on blue and white stripes on a red field.

Festivals and Events

February: Dixie National Western Fest, Jackson; March: Patty's Party Open House, Jackson; Natchez Spring Pilgrimage, Natchez; April: Oyster Festival, Biloxi; May: Gum Tree Fest, Tupelo; June: Mississippi Broiler Fest, Forest; Oleput Festival, Tupelo; July: Mize Watermelon Fest, Mize; Choctaw Native American Fair, Philadelphia; August: Crop Day, Greenwood; September: Copper Magnolia Fest, Washington; October: Pioneer & Indian Festival, Ridgeland; Natchez Fall Pilgrimage, Natchez; December: Chimneyville Crafts Festival, Jackson; Ethnic Trees of Christmas, Biloxi.

Mississippi Compared to States in Its Region.

Resident Pop. in Metro Areas: 4th; Pop. Percent Increase: 4th; Pop. Over 65: 4th; Infant Mortality: 1st; School Enroll. Increase: 3d; High School Grad. and Up: 4th; Violent Crime: 4th; Hazardous Waste Sites: 4th; Unemployment: 1st; Median Household Income: 4th; Persons Below Poverty: 1st; Energy Costs Per Person: 4th.

East South Central

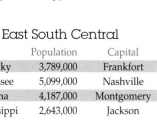

	Population	Capital
Kentucky	3,789,000	Frankfort
Tennessee	5,099,000	Nashville
Alabama	4,187,000	Montgomery
Mississippi	2,643,000	Jackson

Mississippi's Finances

Households: 911,000; Income Per Capita Current Dollars: $14,088; Change Per Capita Income 1980 to 1992: 105.1% (22d in U.S.); State Expenditures: $5,217,000,000; State Revenues: $5,290,000,000; Personal Income Tax: 3 to 5%; Federal Income Taxes Paid Per Capita: $1,001; Sales Tax: 6% (prescription drugs exempt).

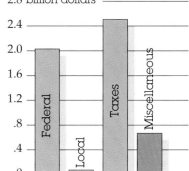

State Expenditures

2.8 billion dollars — Education, Highway, Welfare, Health, Other

State Revenues

2.8 billion dollars — Federal, Local, Taxes, Miscellaneous

Location, Size, and Boundaries

Location. Mississippi is located in the southern United States in what is known as the East South Central region. It is bounded on three of four sides by land with a small coast along the Gulf of Mexico in the southeast. The geographic center of Mississippi is lat. 32° 48.9' N; long. 89° 13' W.

Size. Mississippi is the 32d largest state in terms of size. Its area is 47,716 sq. mi. (123,584 km2). Inland water covers 420 sq. mi. (1,088 km2). Mississippi touches the Gulf of Mexico along a 44–mile coastline.

Boundaries. Tennessee, 119 mi. (192 km); Alabama, 337 mi. (542 km); Gulf of Mexico, 44 mi. (71 km); Louisiana, 307 mi. (494 km); Arkansas, 208 mi. (335 km).

Geographic Extent. The north/south extent is 352 mi. (566 km). The state extends 188 mi. (303 km) to the east/west.

Facts about Mississippi. Origin of Name: Named after an Indian word that translates to "*great water*" or "*father of waters*"; Nickname: The Magnolia State; Motto: "By Valor and Arms" (*Virtute et Armis*); Abbreviations: Miss. (traditional), MS (postal); State Bird: mockingbird; State Tree: magnolia; State Flower: magnolia; State Song: "Go Missis-sip-pi," words and music by Houston Davis.

Mississippi Compared to Other States. Resident Pop. in Metro Areas: 46th; Pop. Percent Increase: 34th; Pop. Over 65: 29th; Infant Mortality: 2d; School Enroll. Increase: 42d; High School Grad. and Up: 50th; Violent Crime: 34th; Hazardous Waste Sites: 47th; Unemployment: 10th; Median Household Income: 50th; Persons Below Poverty: 1st; Energy Costs Per Person: 27th.

Sources of Information. Tourism: Mississippi Division of Tourism, P.O. Box 849, Jackson, MS 39205. Economy, Government & History: Governor, P.O. Box 139, Jackson, MS 39205.

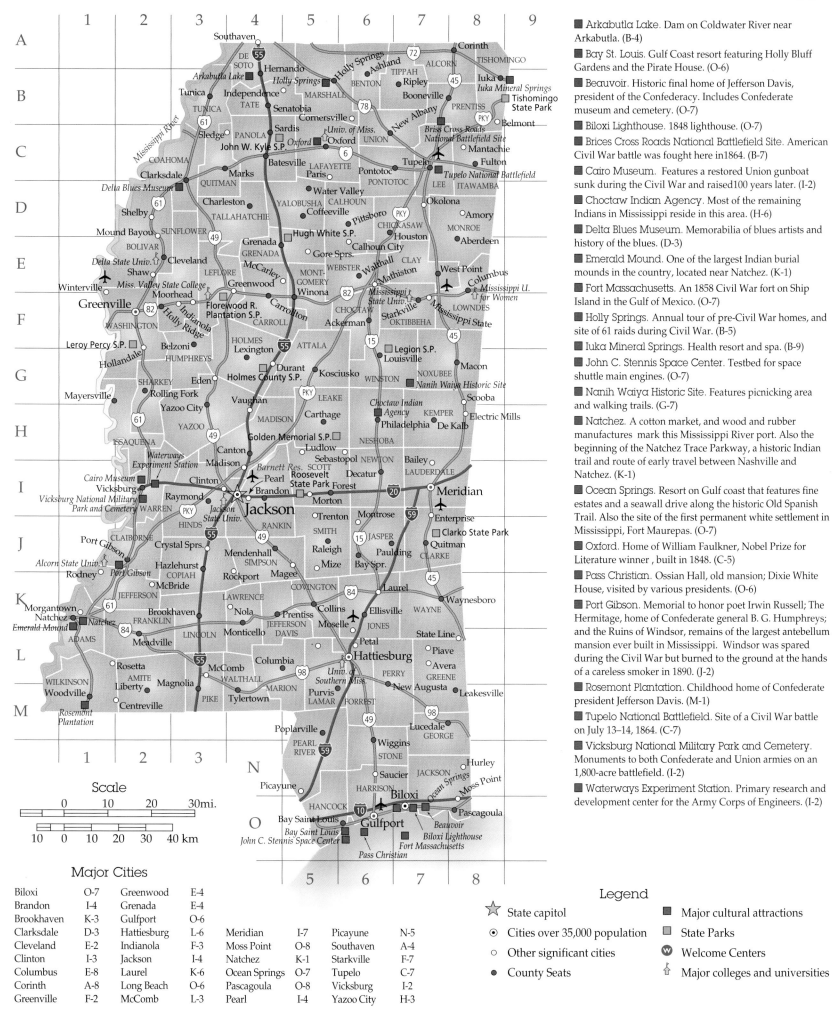

Arkabutla Lake. Dam on Coldwater River near Arkabutla. (B-4)

Bay St. Louis. Gulf Coast resort featuring Holly Bluff Gardens and the Pirate House. (O-6)

Beauvoir. Historic final home of Jefferson Davis, president of the Confederacy. Includes Confederate museum and cemetery. (O-7)

Biloxi Lighthouse. 1848 lighthouse. (O-7)

Brices Cross Roads National Battlefield Site. American Civil War battle was fought here in1864. (B-7)

Cairo Museum. Features a restored Union gunboat sunk during the Civil War and raised100 years later. (I-2)

Choctaw Indian Agency. Most of the remaining Indians in Mississippi reside in this area. (H-6)

Delta Blues Museum. Memorabilia of blues artists and history of the blues. (D-3)

Emerald Mound. One of the largest Indian burial mounds in the country, located near Natchez. (K-1)

Fort Massachusetts. An 1858 Civil War fort on Ship Island in the Gulf of Mexico. (O-7)

Holly Springs. Annual tour of pre-Civil War homes, and site of 61 raids during Civil War. (B-5)

Iuka Mineral Springs. Health resort and spa. (B-9)

John C. Stennis Space Center. Testbed for space shuttle main engines. (O-7)

Nanih Waiya Historic Site. Features picnicking area and walking trails. (G-7)

Natchez. A cotton market, and wood and rubber manufactures mark this Mississippi River port. Also the beginning of the Natchez Trace Parkway, a historic Indian trail and route of early travel between Nashville and Natchez. (K-1)

Ocean Springs. Resort on Gulf coast that features fine estates and a seawall drive along the historic Old Spanish Trail. Also the site of the first permanent white settlement in Mississippi, Fort Maurepas. (O-7)

Oxford. Home of William Faulkner, Nobel Prize for Literature winner , built in 1848. (C-5)

Pass Christian. Ossian Hall, old mansion; Dixie White House, visited by various presidents. (O-6)

Port Gibson. Memorial to honor poet Irwin Russell; The Hermitage, home of Confederate general B. G. Humphreys; and the Ruins of Windsor, remains of the largest antebellum mansion ever built in Mississippi. Windsor was spared during the Civil War but burned to the ground at the hands of a careless smoker in 1890. (J-2)

Rosemont Plantation. Childhood home of Confederate president Jefferson Davis. (M-1)

Tupelo National Battlefield. Site of a Civil War battle on July 13–14, 1864. (C-7)

Vicksburg National Military Park and Cemetery. Monuments to both Confederate and Union armies on an 1,800-acre battlefield. (I-2)

Waterways Experiment Station. Primary research and development center for the Army Corps of Engineers. (I-2)

Scale

```
0    10   20   30mi.
10  0  10  20  30  40 km
```

Major Cities

Biloxi	O-7	Greenwood	E-4
Brandon	I-4	Grenada	E-4
Brookhaven	K-3	Gulfport	O-6
Clarksdale	D-3	Hattiesburg	L-6
Cleveland	E-2	Indianola	F-3
Clinton	I-3	Jackson	I-4
Columbus	E-8	Laurel	K-6
Corinth	A-8	Long Beach	O-6
Greenville	F-2	McComb	L-3

Meridian	I-7	Picayune	N-5
Moss Point	O-8	Southaven	A-4
Natchez	K-1	Starkville	F-7
Ocean Springs	O-7	Tupelo	C-7
Pascagoula	O-8	Vicksburg	I-2
Pearl	I-4	Yazoo City	H-3

Legend

⭐ State capitol

⊙ Cities over 35,000 population

○ Other significant cities

● County Seats

▪ Major cultural attractions

▫ State Parks

Ⓦ Welcome Centers

⚲ Major colleges and universities

Mississippi

Weather Facts

Record High Temperature: 115° F (46° C) on July 29, 1930, at Holly Springs; Record Low Temperature: -19° F (-28° C) on January 30, 1966, at Corinth; Average January Temperature: 45° F (7° C); Average July Temperature: 80° F (27° C); Average Yearly Precipitation: 56 in. (142 cm).

Environmental Facts

Air Pollution Rank: 16th; Water Pollution Rank: 15th; Total Yearly Industrial Pollution: 61,700,338 lbs.; Industrial Pollution Rank: 16th; Hazardous Waste Sites: 2; Hazardous Sites Rank: 47th; Landfill Capacity: adequate; Fresh Water Supply: large surplus; Daily Residential Water Consumption: 135 gals. per capita; Endangered Species: Aquatic Species (6)—mussel, penitent; Birds (5)—crane, Mississippi sandhill; Mammals (1)—bear, Louisiana black; Other Species (8)—snake, eastern indigo; Plants (3)—chaffseed, American.

Environmental Quality

Mississippi residents generate 1.8 million tons of solid waste each year, or approximately 1,400 pounds per capita. Landfill capacity in Mississippi will be exhausted in more than 12 years. The state has 3 hazardous waste sites. Annual greenhouse gas emissions in Mississippi total 51.0 million tons, or 19.5 tons per capita. Industrial sources in Mississippi release approximately 82.1 thousand tons of toxins, 238.2 thousand tons of acid precipitation-producing substances, and 1.3 million tons of smog-producing substances into the atmosphere each year.

The state has 107,500 acres within the National Park System. Noteworthy is Natchez National Historical Park. State parks cover just over 23,000 acres, attracting 3.9 million visitors per year.

Mississippi spends approximately 1.4 percent of its budget, or approximately $20 per capita, on environmental and natural resources. Mississippi representatives in the U.S. House voted in favor of national environmental legislation 28 percent of the time, while U.S. senators did so at no time.

Average Monthly Weather

Jackson	Jan	Feb	Mar	Apr	May	Jun	Jul	Aug	Sep	Oct	Nov	Dec	Yearly
Maximum Temperature °F	56.5	60.9	68.4	77.3	84.1	90.5	92.5	92.1	87.6	78.6	67.5	60.0	76.3
Minimum Temperature °F	34.9	37.2	44.2	52.9	60.8	67.9	71.3	70.2	65.1	51.4	42.3	37.1	52.9
Days of Precipitation	10.7	9.2	10.2	8.3	9.3	8.3	10.4	9.7	8.4	6.2	8.3	10.0	109.0

Flora and Fauna

The state of Mississippi is approximately 55 percent covered by forested areas. Pine trees of all kinds, including, longleaf, slash, and loblolly, grow in an area appropriately called Piney Woods. Pine trees are the most important sources of lumber for the state. Other trees growing in the state include oak and hickory, found in most parts of Mississippi, and pecan, sweet gum, and tupelo, found in alluvial regions. Grasses grow on the state's prairies. Mississippi's flowers include Virginia creepers, crape myrtle, and redbud. The state flower, the magnolia, grows on evergreen trees all over Mississippi.

The majority of Mississippi's wildlife consists of small animals such as squirrels, rabbits, opossums, and foxes. Deer can also be found in the state. Wild doves, wild turkeys, and quail are among Mississippi's common game birds. Other birds such as the mockingbird, Mississippi's state bird, also live in the state. Freshwater fish such as bream (bluegill) and catfish live in Mississippi's rivers and lakes. Speckled trout and mackerel live off the coast, along with other marine life such as crabs and shrimp.

Physical Regions: (a) Mississippi Alluvial Plain; (b) East Gulf Coastal Plain.

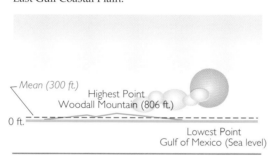

Mean (300 ft.)
Highest Point
Woodall Mountain (806 ft.)
0 ft.
Lowest Point
Gulf of Mexico (Sea level)

Land Use

Cropland: 25.2%; Pasture: 14%; Rangeland: 0%; Forest: 55%; Urban: 4.2%; Other: 1.6%.

For more information about Mississippi's environment, contact the Department of Environmental Quality, Southport Mall, P.O. Box 10631, Jackson, MS 39289.

Topography

Mississippi lies within three topographical regions. The Mississippi River acts as the state's western boundary, and the Mississippi Alluvial Plain physical region is a lowland area that surrounds the river. This region, also known as the Mississippi Delta, is narrow in the southern part of the state. In the north, it widens across a much larger region. The Delta region, fed by the floodwaters of the Mississippi River and its tributaries, has organically rich soils that remain warm and wet year round and is the heart of the cotton-growing region in the South.

East of the Delta lies the East Gulf Coastal Plain physical region, with distinctive red/yellow clay soil that is classed as warm and moist. Most of this area is low-lying hilly terrain. In the southeast is the Piney Woods, with pine forests covering the hills. In the north-central region the Red Clay Hills are found, while in the northeast section of Mississippi the Tennessee River Hills claim the highest elevations in the state. Woodall Mountain rises 806 ft. (246 m) above sea level. The Black Belt physical region, so called for the color of its loamy clay soil, is also found in the northeast.

Climate

The southern state of Mississippi has a subtropical climate, characterized by long, hot summers and short, mild winters. Not much variation exists in temperatures throughout Mississippi, especially in summer. Summer temperatures for Mississippi average 81 degrees F, although parts of the state have higher temperatures. However, thunderstorms and Gulf of Mexico winds bring some relief from the heat. January temperatures have greater fluctuation, with averages of 44 degrees F in the north, by Corinth, and 56 near Biloxi, along the Gulf Coast.

Statewide, Mississippi receives a fair amount of precipitation, about 55 inches a year. The Gulf of Mexico is primarily responsible for Mississippi's higher-than-average precipitation along the coast (66 inches). The northwestern part of the state receives the lightest average annual precipitation (48 inches).

Mississippi has been hit by hurricanes more than once. These storms usually occur in late summer and early fall.

Hydrology

The most important river in the state is the Mississippi, which forms the entire western border of Mississippi with Arkansas and Louisiana. The longest river within the state's borders is the Pearl, which runs for about 475 miles (765 km) through south-central Mississippi before emptying into the Gulf of Mexico. Several rivers flow into the Pascagoula, which also empties into the Gulf of Mexico in the southeast corner of the state. The Big Black River is about 338 miles long (544 km). It flows southwest across the central part of the state, joining the Mississippi below Vicksburg. The Yazoo, the Tallahatchie, and the Big Sunflower are other important rivers in western Mississippi.

There are many man-made lakes in the state. The largest of these is the Ross Barnett Reservoir on the Pearl River above Jackson. Oxbow lakes, such as Beulah Lake, formed when the Mississippi River changes course, are also plentiful.

Mississippi's History

Mississippi's First People

Evidence of human habitation in Mississippi dates back about two thousand years. Around A.D. 700, the Mississippian culture (or Temple Mound Builders) began to flourish in the Southeast and part of the Midwest. These people were farmers, growing corn, squash, and tobacco, as well as craftsmen of clay, marble, and copper into tools and jewelry. The culture was also preoccupied with death, building huge Temple Mounds (the largest covers sixteen acres and stands one hundred feet tall) and imprinting symbols of human sacrifice on pottery and sculpture. The culture disappeared just before the arrival of the white man.

When Europeans did arrive, Mississippi was occupied by several tribes, principally the Chickasaw in the north, the Natchez in the south, and the Choctaw in the central region.

European Exploration

In 1540, Hernando de Soto discovered the Mississippi River and died there in 1542. The area remained unexplored until René-Robert Cavelier, Sieur de La Salle, visited the region in 1682. He claimed the Mississippi Valley for France. In 1699, Pierre Le Moyne, Sieur d'Iberville, built Fort Maurepas, the first permanent white settlement, near present-day Ocean Springs, and in 1716, Jean-Baptiste Le Moyne, Sieur de Bienville, built Fort Rosalie at Natchez. The following year, John Law received a charter from Louis XV for the Mississippi Company, an attempt to commercially develop the area. Many settlers were attracted to the region, though the enterprise lost its charter in 1732.

With the conclusion of the French and Indian War in 1763, Mississippi came under the control of the British. The territory east of the Mississippi River into the Florida panhandle was known as West Florida. Britain controlled this area during the Revolutionary War until the Spanish took it over in 1781. Spain finally ceded this area to the United States in the Treaty of San Lorenzo in 1795.

Statehood

In 1798, Congress created the Mississippi Territory with Natchez as the capital. In 1817, Alabama was split from the Mississippi Territory and organized as the Alabama Territory. That year, Mississippi was admitted to the Union as the twentieth state with Washington as the capital.

After statehood, Mississippi pressured the Chickasaw and Choctaw Indians to cede their lands to the state, which these tribes did in 1832. The cotton industry that was developed on these lands became heavily dependent on slavery, and thus Mississippians' stance in the Civil War became obvious.

In 1861, Mississippi became the second state to secede from the Union. The state was the site of much strategic fighting, with the Battle of Vicksburg (on the Mississippi River) in 1863 being one of the war's most important battles. During this battle, Union troops under the command of General Ulysses S. Grant laid siege to Vicksburg from May 22 to July 4, 1863, before capturing it. This victory opened up a 150-mile stretch of the Mississippi river to Union gunboats, and separated Texas and Arkansas from the rest of the Confederacy. The town of Corinth in north east Mississippi was also another site of Union and Confederate conflict. This town fell in 1862 as a direct result of action at the battle of Shiloh in Tennessee.

After the war, Mississippi was ruled by the Union military before finally being readmitted to the Union in 1870. During Reconstruction, many blacks were elected to office with the encouragement of the ruling Republicans, but when Democrats returned to power in 1875, all such reforms were lost.

Industrialization

As the population of Mississippi began to increase in the early nineteenth century, cotton production quickly emerged as the leading industry in the state, especially with the introduction of Petit Gulf, a Mexican cotton, in 1806. The opening of previously held Indian territories in the 1830s to the cultivation of cotton led to an economic boom in the state. After the Civil War, blacks and many poor whites were subject to the sharecropping system instituted by large plantation owners, a form of economic slavery that assured the planters' continued dominance. In the twentieth century, a boll weevil plague in 1909, a devastating flood of the Mississippi in 1927, and the Great Depression of the 1930s helped make this one-industry state one of the poorest in the nation.

Today, agriculture is more diversified (though cotton remains the top crop), and manufacturing (textiles, furniture) and the service industries also contribute to Mississippi's economy.

Civil Rights

In 1890, Mississippi adopted a new constitution, denying any political rights to blacks and formalizing segregation. The sharecropping system kept blacks in a state of impoverishment, forcing many to leave the state. Their civil rights were violated as well, as evidenced by the more than five hundred lynchings that occurred between 1890 and 1960. This state of affairs did not improve until the modern civil rights struggle, in which Mississippi played a major role.

In 1962, James Meredith, a black student, attempted to enter the University of Mississippi Law School, but his admission was blocked, setting off violent protests. The following year, Medgar Evers, an officer in the NAACP, was murdered in front of his home in Jackson. Following this turmoil and the passage of the Voting Rights Act by Congress, the status of blacks in the state is much improved.

Important Events

1540 Mississippi River discovered by Hernando de Soto.

1682 René-Robert Cavelier, Sieur de La Salle, explores and claims Mississippi Valley region for France.

1699 Fort Maurepas, founded by Pierre Le Moyne, Sieur d'Iberville, becomes first permanent white settlement in the state.

1763 French cede territory to the British at the end of the French and Indian War.

1781 Spanish capture West Florida, containing Mississippi, from the British.

1797 Spanish cede West Florida to the United States under the Treaty of San Lorenzo.

1798 Congress creates the Mississippi Territory, which includes Alabama.

1817 Mississippi is admitted into the Union as the twentieth state.

1822 State capital is moved from Washington to Jackson.

1861 Mississippi becomes the second state to secede from the Union.

1862 Jefferson Davis is inaugurated as the President of the Confederacy.

1863 Major Civil War battle is fought at Vicksburg.

1866–1867 State legislature refuses to ratify antislavery amendments to the Constitution and Mississippi is put under Union military rule.

1870 Mississippi is readmitted to the Union; state elects first black to the U.S. Senate, Hiram Revels.

1890 State constitution denying civil and political rights to blacks is adopted.

1932 Cotton prices plummet and many farms are foreclosed during the Great Depression.

1962 Black student James Meredith is denied admission to University of Mississippi Law School.

1963 NAACP officer Medgar Evers is murdered in Jackson.

1964 Four young civil rights workers are murdered in Philadelphia, Mississippi.

1988 Major drought is worst in the state since the Depression.

1993 African Americans fight to have the Confederate emblem removed from the state flag.

Population Density

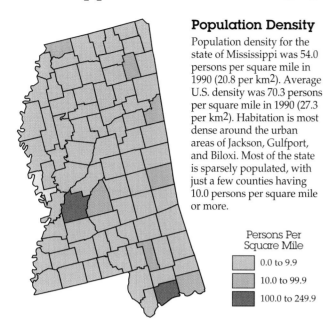

Population density for the state of Mississippi was 54.0 persons per square mile in 1990 (20.8 per km2). Average U.S. density was 70.3 persons per square mile in 1990 (27.3 per km2). Habitation is most dense around the urban areas of Jackson, Gulfport, and Biloxi. Most of the state is sparsely populated, with just a few counties having 10.0 persons per square mile or more.

Persons Per Square Mile

- 0.0 to 9.9
- 10.0 to 99.9
- 100.0 to 249.9

Population Projections

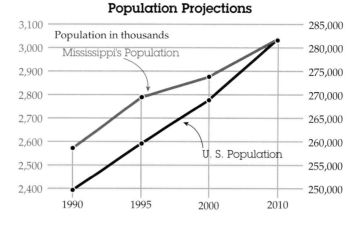

Population in thousands
Mississippi's Population

U. S. Population

Population Change

Year	Population
1950	2,179,000
1960	2,182,000
1970	2,220,000
1980	2,520,638
1990	2,573,216
2000	2,877,000
2010	3,028,000

Period	Change
1950–1970	1.9%
1970–1980	13.6%
1980–1990	2.1%
1990–2000	11.8%

Population Change

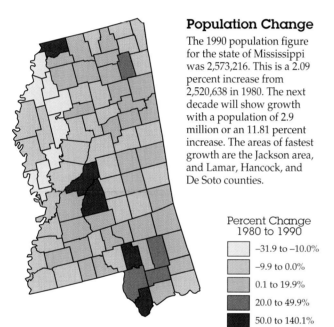

The 1990 population figure for the state of Mississippi was 2,573,216. This is a 2.09 percent increase from 2,520,638 in 1980. The next decade will show growth with a population of 2.9 million or an 11.81 percent increase. The areas of fastest growth are the Jackson area, and Lamar, Hancock, and De Soto counties.

Percent Change 1980 to 1990

- –31.9 to –10.0%
- –9.9 to 0.0%
- 0.1 to 19.9%
- 20.0 to 49.9%
- 50.0 to 140.1%

Population Facts

State Population, 1993: 2,643,000

Rank: 31

Population 2000: 2,877,000 (Rank 29)

Density: 54.0 per sq. mi. (20.8 per km²)

Distribution: 47.1% urban, 52.9% rural

Population Under 5 Years Old: 7.8%

Population Under 18 Years Old: 28.6%

Population Over 65 Years Old: 12.5%

Median Age: 31.2

Number of Households: 911,000

Average Persons Per Household: 2.75

Average Persons Per Family: 3.27

Female Heads of Households: 5.64%

Population That Is Married: 19.36%

Birth Rate: 16.9 per 1,000 population

Death Rate: 9.8 per 1,000 population

Births to Teen Mothers: 21.3%

Marriage Rate: 9.3 per 1,000 population

Divorce Rate: 5.5 per 1,000 population

Violent Crime Rate: 389 per 100,000 pop.

Population on Social Security: 17.7%

Percent Voting for President: 52.8%

Mississippi's Famous Citizens

Andrews, Dana (1909–1992). Actor. Starred in *The Ox-Bow Incident* and *The Best Years of Our Lives*, among others.

Bell, James Thomas (1903–1991). Hall of Fame Negro League baseball player. Starred with the St. Louis Stars from 1922 to 1931.

Faulkner, William (1897–1962). Novelist awarded the 1949 Nobel Prize in Literature and the Pulitzer prize in 1954 .

Lamar, Lucius Quintas Cincinnatus (1825–1893). Served as U.S. senator (1877–1885) and Supreme Court justice (1888–1893).

Meredith, James (b. 1933). First black admitted to University of Mississippi. Attempted halt to his admittance caused riots (1961).

Presley, Elvis Aaron (1935–1977). Dominated popular music from 1956 until his death in 1977; had 45 records that sold more than one-million copies each.

Still, William Grant (1895–1978). Composer and conductor. First African American to conduct a major U.S. symphony orchestra.

Wells-Barnett, Ida Bell (1862–1931). Civil-rights activist in Tennessee and Chicago, where she led antilynching campaigns.

Distribution of Income

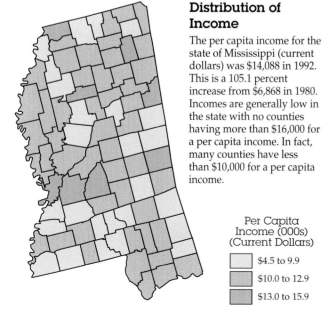

The per capita income for the state of Mississippi (current dollars) was $14,088 in 1992. This is a 105.1 percent increase from $6,868 in 1980. Incomes are generally low in the state with no counties having more than $16,000 for a per capita income. In fact, many counties have less than $10,000 for a per capita income.

Per Capita Income (000s) (Current Dollars)

- $4.5 to 9.9
- $10.0 to 12.9
- $13.0 to 15.9

Population Profile

Rank. Mississippi ranks 31st among U.S. states in terms of population with 2,643,000 citizens.

Minority Population. The state's minority population is 37.0 percent. The state's male to female ratio for 1990 was 91.66 males for every 100 females. It was below the national average of 95.22 males for every 100 females.

Growth. Growing faster than the projected national average, the state's population is expected to reach 3.0 million by the year 2010 (*see graph above*).

Older Citizens. The state's population older than 65 was 321,284 in 1990. It grew 11.03% from 289,357 in 1980.

Younger Citizens. The number of children (under 18 years of age) was 747 thousand in 1990. This represents 29.0 percent of the state's population. The state's school aged population was 496 thousand in 1990. It is expected to increase to 515 thousand by the year 2000. This represents a 3.83% change.

Urban/Rural. 47.1% of the population of the state lives in urban areas while 52.9% live in rural areas.

Largest Cities. Mississippi has six cities with a population greater than 35,000. The population of the state's largest centers are (starting from the most populous), Jackson (196,637), Biloxi (46,319), Greenville (45,226), Hattiesburg (41,882), Meridian (41,036), Gulfport (40,775), Tupelo (30,685), Pascagoula (25,899), Columbus (23,799), Clinton (21,847), Vicksburg (20,908), Clarksdale (19,717), Pearl (19,588), Natchez (19,460), Greenwood (18,906), Laurel (18,827), Starkville (18,458), and Southaven (17,949).

Government

Capital: Jackson (established 1822).

Statehood: Became 20th state on Dec. 10, 1817.

Number of Counties: 82.

Supreme Court Justices: 9, 8-year term.

State Senators: 52, 4-year term.

State Legislators: 122, 4-year term.

United States Senators: 2.

United States Representatives: 5.

Electoral Votes: 7.

State Constitution: Adopted 1890.

Native American

The Native American population in Mississippi was 8,525 in 1990. This was an increase of 24.71 percent from 6,836 in 1980. A large number of the Native Americans living in Mississippi can be found in the Mississippi Choctaw Indian Reservation on the state's eastern border with Alabama.

Presence of Native Americans

- Minor
- Moderate

Nationalities

African	3,535
American	328,276
Arab	3,362
Austrian	710
Czech	1,149
Dutch	19,828
English	198,977
Finnish	921
German	176,523
Greek	1,752
Hungarian	982
Irish	274,554
Italian	25,496
Norwegian	2,619
Polish	7,078
Portuguese	865
Russian	1,234
Scottish	25,395
Slovak	1,583
Swedish	5,312
Welsh	5,164
West Indian	763

African American

The African American population in Mississippi was 915,057 in 1990. This was an increase of 3.15 percent from 887,111 in 1980. Large numbers of African Americans can be found in the counties bordering the Mississippi River and Louisiana. The city of Jackson has the largest community of African Americans in the state.

Percent of County Population

- 2.00 to 4.99%
- 5.00 to 9.99%
- 10.00 to 24.99%
- 25.00 to 86.24%

Statewide Ethnic Composition

Over 63 percent of the population of Mississippi is white. The largest nationalities in this racial group are Irish, English, and German. The next largest group is African Americans, who represent over 35 percent of the population. More people claim to be American than acknowledge any of the other nationalities.

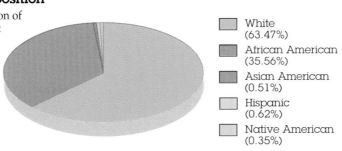

- White (63.47%)
- African American (35.56%)
- Asian American (0.51%)
- Hispanic (0.62%)
- Native American (0.35%)

Hispanic[††]

The Hispanic population in Mississippi was 15,931 in 1990. This is a decrease of -35.58 percent from 24,731 persons in 1980. The largest concentration of Hispanics can be found along the coast of the Gulf of Mexico in Hancock and Harrison counties.

[††]A person of Mexican, Puerto Rican, Cuban, or other Spanish culture or origin regardless of race.

Percent of County Population

- 0.00 to 0.99%
- 1.00 to 2.99%

Education Facts

Total Students 1990: 50,202

Number of School Districts: 152

Expenditure Per Capita on Education 1990: $626

Expenditure Per Capita K–12 1990: $573

Expenditure Per Pupil 1990: $3,322

Total School Enrollment 1990–1991: 500,122

Rank of Expenditures Per Student: 48th in the U.S.

African American Enrollment: 50.6%

Hispanic Enrollment: 0.1%

Asian/Pacific Islander Enrollment: 0.4%

Native American Enrollment: 0.1%

Mean SAT Score 1991 Verbal: 477

Mean SAT Score 1991 Math: 520

Average Teacher's Salary 1992: $24,400

Rank Teacher's Salary: 49th in U.S.

High School Graduates 1990: 27,800

Total Number of Public Schools: 954

Number of Teachers 1990: 27,479

Student/Teacher Ratio: 18.2

Staff Employed in Public Schools: 56,361

Pupil/Staff Ratio: 8.9

Staff/Teacher Ratio: 2.0

Education

Attainment: 68 percent of population 25 years or older were high school graduates in 1989, earning Mississippi a ranking of 46th in the United States; 15.6 percent of the state's population had completed college. Institutions of Higher Education: The largest universities and colleges in the state include the University of Mississippi, Oxford; Mississippi State University, Starkville; University of Southern Mississippi, Hattiesburg; Mississippi University for Women, Columbus; Jackson State University, Jackson; Alcorn State University, Lorman; Delta State University, Cleveland. Expenditures per Student: Expenditure increased 77% between 1985 and 1990. Projected High School Graduations: 1998 (58,519), 2004 (57,048); Total Revenues for Education from Federal Sources: $113 million; Total Revenues for Education from State Sources: $744 million; Total Revenues for Education from Local Sources: $278 million; Average Annual Salaries for Public School Principals: $33,073.

Asian American

The Asian American population in Mississippi was 13,016 in 1990. This is an increase of 76.58 percent from 7,371 persons in 1980. There are three areas where Asian Americans can be found in large numbers: Lafayette, Oktibbeha, and Harrison counties. Other areas include counties along the Mississippi River in the northwest.

Percent of County Population

- 0.00 to 0.24%
- 0.25 to 0.99%
- 2.00 to 4.99%

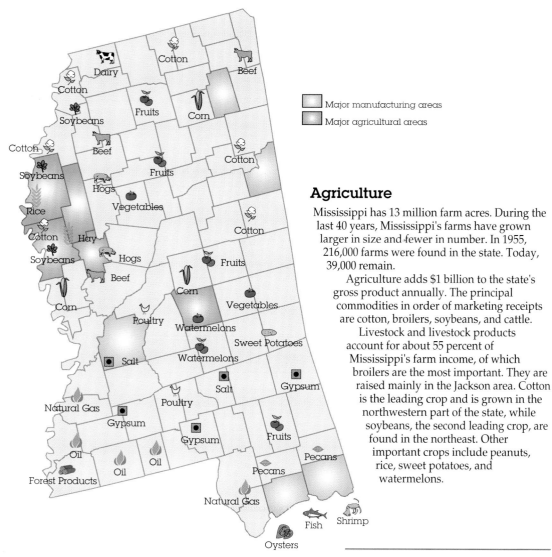

Major manufacturing areas

Major agricultural areas

Transportation

Mississippi's Gulf Coast has several ports that transport many types of goods. Vicksburg, Biloxi, and Pascagoula are all important seaports; Pascagoula receives over 8,000 ships a year. The Tennessee-Tombigbee Waterway connects northeastern Mississippi with Mobile, Alabama. Other river ports in the state include Greenville, Natchez, and Rosedale.

Mississippi's roadway system is one of the best in the South. Approximately 75,000 miles of highways and roads connect all parts of the state. Three railroads, in addition to 18 short lines, move freight across Mississippi on 3,600 miles of railroad track. About 15 Mississippi cities have passenger rail service. Jackson has the only commercial airport in Mississippi. However, airstrips can be found in other parts of the state as well.

Energy and Transportation Facts

Energy. Yearly Consumption: 950 tril. BTUs (residential, 17.8%; commercial, 10.9%; industrial, 37.7%; transportation, 33.5%); Annual Energy Expenditures Per Capita: $1,882; Nuclear Power Plants Located in State: 1; Source of Energy Consumed: Petroleum— 46.6%; Natural Gas— 30.3%; Coal— 11.2%; Hydroelectric Power—0.0%; Nuclear Power—11.6%.

Transportation. Highway Miles: 72,795 (interstates, 685; urban, 7,888; rural, 64,907); Average Yearly Auto Insurance: $519 (28th); Auto Fatalities Rank: 5th; Registered Motor Vehicles: 1,953,973; Workers in Carpools: 23.7%; Workers Using Public Trans: 0.8%.

Agriculture

Mississippi has 13 million farm acres. During the last 40 years, Mississippi's farms have grown larger in size and fewer in number. In 1955, 216,000 farms were found in the state. Today, 39,000 remain.

Agriculture adds $1 billion to the state's gross product annually. The principal commodities in order of marketing receipts are cotton, broilers, soybeans, and cattle.

Livestock and livestock products account for about 55 percent of Mississippi's farm income, of which broilers are the most important. They are raised mainly in the Jackson area. Cotton is the leading crop and is grown in the northwestern part of the state, while soybeans, the second leading crop, are found in the northeast. Other important crops include peanuts, rice, sweet potatoes, and watermelons.

Housing

Owner Occupied Units: 1,010,423; Average Age of Units: 24 years; Average Value of Housing Units: $45,600; Renter Occupied Units: 247,496; Median Monthly Rent: $309; Housing Starts: 10,000; Existing Home Sales: 43,600.

Economic Facts

Gross State Product: $38,000,000,000 (1989)

Income Per Capita: $14,088

Disposable Personal Income: $13,006

Median Household Income: $20,136

Average Annual Pay, 1988: $18,411

Principal Industries: transportation equipment, food products, paper products, furniture, clothing, wood products, electrical equipment

Major Crops: cotton, milk, soybeans, corn, hay, rice, wheat, timber

Fish: Buffalofish, Carp, Catfish

Livestock: chickens, cattle

Non-Fuel Minerals: Clays, Sand, Sandstone, Iron Ore, Lignite, Limestone

Organic Fuel Minerals: Petroleum, Nat. Gas

Civilian Labor Force: 1,183,000 (Women: 557,000)

Total Employed: 1,081,000 (Women: 508,000)

Median Value of Housing: $45,600

Median Contract Rent: $309 per month

Economic Sectors 1992

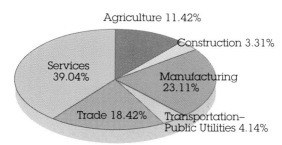

Agriculture 11.42%
Construction 3.31%
Services 39.04%
Manufacturing 23.11%
Trade 18.42%
Transportation–Public Utilities 4.14%

Manufacturing

Mississippi has one of the most diversified manufacturing sectors of any state economy, which employs the majority of Mississippi's workers. Although transportation equipment ranks as the number one manufactured product, several other industries, including electrical equipment, food processing, clothing, and chemicals, are also produced in Mississippi.

Large shipbuilding facilities on the Gulf Coast help make shipbuilding the leading transportation activity. Other industries, such as electrical equipment, are made in more inland cities such as Meridian and Jackson. The northeast part of the state is home to Mississippi's largest clothing manufacturers. Another important industry, food processing, has its roots in cities such as Laurel and Forest.

Employment

Employment. Mississippi employed 1.13 million people in 1993. Most work in manufacturing jobs (254,500 persons or 22.4% of the workforce). Wholesale and retail trade account for 18.4% or 209,000 workers. Government employs 210,100 workers (18.5%). Social and personal services employ 195,600 people (17.2%). Construction employs 39,400 workers, or 3.5%. Transportation and utilities account for 4.0% or 45,700 persons. Agriculture employs 40,900 workers or 3.6%. Finance, real estate, and insurance account for 3.4%, or 38,600 workers. Mining employs 5,200 people and accounts for only 0.5% of the workforce.

Unemployment. Unemployment has decreased to 6.3% in 1993 from a rate of 10.3% in 1985. Today's figure is lower than the national average of 6.8% as shown below.

Unemployment Rate

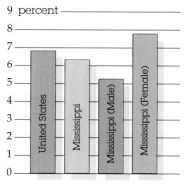

percent

United States
Mississippi
Mississippi (Male)
Mississippi (Female)

MISSOURI
The State of Missouri

Official State Seal

The Great Seal of Missouri was officially used in 1822. It contains two bears supporting a shield. In the shield is the motto, "United We Stand, Divided We Fall." It also contains a grizzly bear, a crescent, and the arms of the United States. Under this shield is a ribbon with the state motto, *"Salus Populi Suprema Lex Esto"* (The Welfare of the People Shall Be the Supreme Law).

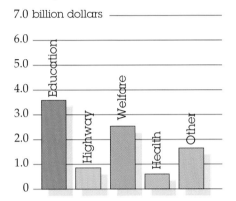

Legal Holidays

January: New Year's Day—1st; Martin Luther King, Jr., Day—Third Monday; February: Abraham Lincoln's Birthday—12th; Presidents' Day—Third Monday; May: Harry S. Truman's Birthday—8th; Admission Day—11th; Memorial Day—4th Monday; July: Independence Day—4th; Tom Sawyer Fence Painting Day (Hannibal)—4th; August: Admission Day—10th; September: Labor Day—First Monday; October: Missouri Day—1st Monday; Columbus Day—2d Monday; November: Veterans' Day—11th; Thanksgiving—4th Thursday; December: Christmas—25th.

Official State Flag

Adopted in 1913, Missouri's flag was created with red, white, and blue stripes to commemorate the Louisiana Purchase of 1803. The state seal coat of arms is placed in the center of the horizontal stripes.

Festivals and Events

January: Elvis Presley Birthday Party, St. Louis; February: Groundhog Run, Kansas City; Midwinter Bluegrass Festival, Hannibal; March: St. Pat's Celebration, Rolla; April: Urban Streams Festival, Springfield; May: St. Louis Storytelling Festival, St. Louis; Lewis & Clark Rendezvous, St. Charles; Valley of Flowers Festival, Florissant; June: Riverfest, Cape Girardeau; July: Tom Sawyer Days, Hannibal; July/August: Ozark Empire Fair, Springfield; August: Festival of the Little Hills, St. Charles; Jour de Fête, Ste. Genevieve; September: Santa-Cali-Gon Days, Independence; Badenfest, St. Louis; October: Autumn Historic Folklife Fest, Hannibal.

Missouri Compared to States in Its Region.

Resident Pop. in Metro Areas: 2d; Pop. Percent Increase: 5th; Pop. Over 65: 5th; Infant Mortality: 2d; School Enroll. Increase: 1st; High School Grad. and Up: 7th; Violent Crime: 1st; Hazardous Waste Sites: 2d; Unemployment: 1st; Median Household Income: 3d; Persons Below Poverty: 2d; Energy Costs Per Person: 6th.

West North Central Region

	Population	Capital
Minnesota	4,517,000	St. Paul
Iowa	2,814,000	Des Moines
Missouri	5,234,000	Jefferson City
North Dakota	635,000	Bismarck
South Dakota	715,000	Pierre
Nebraska	1,607,000	Lincoln
Kansas	2,531,000	Topeka

Missouri's Finances

Households: 1,961,000; Income Per Capita Current Dollars: $18,835; Change Per Capita Income 1980 to 1992: 103.5% (24th in U.S.); State Expenditures: $9,513,000,000; State Revenues: $9,872,000,000; Personal Income Tax: 1.5 to 6%; Federal Income Taxes Paid Per Capita: $1,625; Sales Tax: 4.225% (prescription drugs exempt).

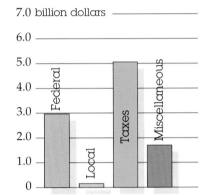

Location, Size, and Boundaries

Location. Missouri is located in the West North Central region of the United States. It is bounded on all sides by land. The geographic center of Missouri is lat. 38° 29.7' N; long. 92° 37.9' W.

Size. Missouri is the 19th largest state in terms of size. Its area is 69,686 sq. mi. (180,487 km2). Inland water covers 691 sq. mi. (1,790 km2).

Boundaries. Iowa, 239 mi. (385 km); Illinois, 360 mi. (579 km); Kentucky, 59 mi. (95 km); Tennessee, 78 mi. (125 km); Arkansas, 331 mi. (553 km); Oklahoma, 35 mi. (56 km); Kansas, 267 mi. (430 km); Nebraska, 69 mi. (111 km).

Geographic Extent. north/south extent is 308 mi. (496 km). The state extends 284 mi. (457 km) to the east and west.

Facts about Missouri. Origin of Name: After the Missouri River, which was most likely named from an Indian word meaning the *"town of the large canoes"*; Nickname: The Show Me State; Motto: "The welfare of the people shall be the supreme law"; Abbreviations: Mo. (traditional), MO (postal); State Bird: bluebird; State Tree: flowering dogwood; State Flower: hawthorn; State Song: "Missouri Waltz," words by J. R. Shannon and music by John V. Eppel.

Missouri Compared to Other States. Resident Pop. in Metro Areas: 27th; Pop. Percent Increase: 38th; Pop. Over 65: 10th; Infant Mortality: 21st; School Enroll. Increase: 18th; High School Grad. and Up: 38th; Violent Crime: 12th; Haz. Waste Sites: 16th; Unemployment: 38th; Med. Household Income: 34th; Persons Below Poverty: 17th; Energy Costs Per Person: 33d.

Sources of Information. Tourism: Div. of Tourism, P.O. Box 1055, Jefferson City, MO 65102. Government: Governor's Office, P.O. Box 720, Capitol Building, Room 217B, Jefferson City, MO 65102.

Missouri

Major Cities

Arnold	F-11	Hannibal	C-9
Ballwin	F-11	Independence	E-3
Belton	E-2	Jefferson City	F-7
Blue Springs	E-3	Joplin	J-3
Cape Girardeau	I-13	Kansas City	E-2
Chesterfield	F-10	Kirksville	F-11
Columbia	E-7	Lee's Summit	E-3
Ferguson	F-11	Liberty	D-3
Florissant	F-11	Maryland Hts.	F-11
Gladstone	E-2	O'Fallon	F-11
Grandview	E-2	Raytown	E-2
		Sedalia	F-5
		Springfield	J-5
		St. Charles	F-11
		St. Joseph	C-2
		St. Louis	F-11
		St. Peters	F-10
		Univ. City	F-11
		Webster Grvs.	F-11

Legend

★ State capitol

⊙ Cities over 35,000 population

○ Other significant cities

● County Seats

■ Major cultural attractions

▢ State Parks

Ⓦ Welcome Centers

⚲ Major colleges and universities

Scale

0 20 40 60 mi.

20 0 20 40 60 80 km

■ Arrow Rock State Historic Site. Historic buildings and the Santa Fe Trail. (E-6)

■ Bagnell Dam. Boating, swimming, and other water sports on a lake created by this dam. (G-6)

■ Battle of Lexington State Historic Site. Site of the Civil War battle, which took place in 1861. (E-4)

■ Branson. Mountain music resort featuring many popular names in country music. (K-5)

■ Bull Shoals Lake. A resort area located in the Ozark Mountains. (K-6)

■ Cape Girardeau. Site of an 18th century trading post (1793). (I-13)

■ Dr. Edmund A. Babler Memorial State Park. Scenic views, camping, and picnicking. (F-10)

■ Excelsior Springs. Health resort with mineral springs. (D-3)

■ Fort Davidson State Historic Site. Site of a Civil War fort. (I-10)

■ George Washington Carver National Monument. Birthplace of the scientist. (J-3)

■ Hannibal. Boyhood home of Mark Twain, with settings of his stories. (C-9)

■ Jefferson City. Capital with many historic 19th-century buildings. (F-7)

■ Lamar. Site of Truman Birthplace Memorial Shrine. (I-3)

■ Mark Twain State Park. Birthplace of Samuel Clemens. (D-8)

■ Onondaga Cave State Park. Caves with camping and picnicking. (G-9)

■ Pershing State Park. Home of World War I hero Gen. John J. Pershing. (C-5)

■ Pilot Knob. Site of the Civil War battle (1864) on a 1,514-foot (461 meter) high hill. (I-10)

■ St. Charles. First state capitol, built in 1814. (F-10)

■ Ste. Genevieve. Oldest town in state, founded in 1735. (G-11)

Weather Facts

Record High Temperature: 118° F (48° C) on July 18, 1936, at Clinton; Record Low Temperature: -40° F (-40° C) on February 13, 1905, at Warsaw; Average January Temperature: 31° F (-1° C); Average July Temperature: 78° F (26° C); Average Yearly Precipitation: 40 in. (102 cm).

Environmental Facts

Air Pollution Rank: 20th; Water Pollution Rank: 20th; Total Yearly Industrial Pollution: 52,396,634 lbs.; Industrial Pollution Rank: 19th; Hazardous Waste Sites: 22; Hazardous Sites Rank: 16th; Landfill Capacity: adequate; Fresh Water Supply: surplus; Daily Residential Water Consumption: 142 gals. per capita; Endangered Species: Aquatic Species (12)—cavefish, Ozark; Birds (4)—eagle, bald; Mammals (2)—bat, gray; Other Species (1)—beetle, American burying; Plants (8)—aster, decurrent false.

Environmental Quality

Missouri residents generate 5.1 million tons of solid waste each year, or approximately 2,000 pounds per capita. Landfill capacity in Missouri will be exhausted in 5 to 10 years. The state has 24 hazardous waste sites. Annual greenhouse gas emissions in Missouri total 112.8 million tons, or 22.0 tons per capita. Industrial sources in Missouri release approximately 97.1 thousand tons of toxins, 1.4 million tons of acid precipitation-producing substances, and 2.3 million tons of smog-producing substances into the atmosphere each year.

The state has 62,700 acres within the National Park System. Noteworthy is Wilson Creek National Battlefield. State parks cover just over 102,000 acres, attracting 15.0 million visitors per year.

Missouri spends approximately 1.5 percent of its budget, or approximately $21 per capita, on environmental and natural resources.

Average Monthly Weather

Kansas City	Jan	Feb	Mar	Apr	May	Jun	Jul	Aug	Sep	Oct	Nov	Dec	Yearly
Maximum Temperature °F	34.5	41.1	51.3	65.1	74.6	83.3	88.5	86.8	78.6	67.9	52.1	40.1	63.7
Minimum Temperature °F	17.2	23.0	31.7	44.4	54.6	63.8	68.5	66.5	58.1	47.0	34.0	23.7	44.4
Days of Precipitation	7.1	7.2	10.0	10.5	11.2	10.2	7.3	9.1	8.2	7.7	7.6	7.5	103.6
St. Louis													
Maximum Temperature °F	37.6	43.1	53.4	67.1	76.4	85.2	89.0	87.4	80.7	69.1	54.0	42.6	65.5
Minimum Temperature °F	19.9	24.5	33.0	45.1	54.7	64.3	68.8	66.6	58.6	46.7	35.1	25.7	45.3
Days of Precipitation	8.3	8.2	11.3	11.0	10.5	9.4	8.5	8.0	8.0	8.4	9.4	9.4	110.4

Flora and Fauna

The vast majority of Missouri's forested areas are located in the southern part of the state. Overall, forests cover approximately one-third of Missouri. Hickory and oak trees can be found in the Ozark region of the state, while sweet gum and bald cypress can be found around the Mississippi Alluvial Plain. The Ozark Plateau, in southwestern Missouri, has more wildflowers growing in it than any other part of the state. Milkweed, sweet William, and hawthorn all grow throughout Missouri. Meadow roses, white snakeroot, and turtleheads blossom on the prairies.

The Mississippi Alluvial Plain is home to mistletoe. Missouri's wildlife population is as plentiful as it is varied. Deer are the most common large mammal living in Missouri, but bears also live within the state's borders. Smaller animals include rabbits, skunks, squirrels, minks, and muskrats. Missouri has many songbirds such as blue jays, cardinals, wood-peckers, and purple finches. Game birds include bobwhite quail and wild turkeys. The rivers, streams, and lakes in Missouri are home to fishes such as jack salmon (or walleye), trout, crappie, and catfish.

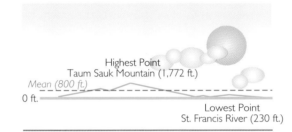

Physical Regions: (a) Dissected Till Plains; (b) Osage Plains; (c) Ozark Plateau; (d) Mississippi Alluvial Plain.

Highest Point
Taum Sauk Mountain (1,772 ft.)
Mean (800 ft.)
0 ft.
Lowest Point
St. Francis River (230 ft.)

Land Use

Cropland: 36.2%; Pasture: 30.3%; Rangeland: 0.1%; Forest: 26.3%; Urban: 5.2%; Other: 1.9%.

For more information about Missouri's environment, contact the Department of Natural Resources, 205 Jefferson St., Office Bldg., P.O. Box 176, Jefferson City, MO 65102.

Topography

There are several distinctive topographic regions in Missouri, all with warm and moist soil. In the north, above the Missouri River, lies the Dissected Till Plains physical region, part of the Central Plains of the United States. This region is characterized by gentle hills and flatlands and has particularly fertile red prairie soil suitable for agriculture. Much of western Missouri is covered by the Osage Plains physical region. This area is similar to the Dissected Till Plains, but the gray/brown soil is less fertile, and the flat prairies are only occasionally interrupted by gentle rolling hills.

Most of southern Missouri is part of the Ozark Plateau physical region that also extends into Arkansas and Oklahoma. This area is comprised of hills and low mountains and slopes from the Plains south to reach elevations of over 1,700 ft. (518 m). The highest point in the state, Taum Sauk Mountain, is found here, rising to 1,772 ft. (540 m) above sea level. This region is also the largest in the state, with red/yellow, low organic content soil. The Mississippi Alluvial Plain physical region, in the southeastern corner of Missouri, is a low-lying area with dark rich fertile soil, fed by the Mississippi River. Much of this region has been drained and is dry and agriculturally productive.

Climate

The state of Missouri has a continental climate. While the summers are hot and humid, winters are generally cold. The lack of major physical features creates a gradual warming temperature pattern from northwest to southeast. Surprisingly, winters in the mountainous Ozark Plateau region are milder than on the lower plains. January temperatures average 14 degrees F in the northwestern part of Missouri, and 30 degrees F in the southeast. A July maximum average temperature of 92 degrees represents the statewide weather pattern.

Overall, Missouri receives an average of 40 inches of annual precipitation. The southeastern corner receives the heaviest precipitation, about 50 inches annually. Lower-than-average precipitation falls in the northwest. The precipitation difference partially affects Missouri's growing season, which is longer in the southeast.

The lack of natural barriers makes it easy for contrasting air masses to clash. When this happens, thunderstorms, and often tornadoes, result.

Hydrology

The Mississippi River forms Missouri's entire eastern boundary with Illinois, Kentucky, and Tennessee. The most important river in the state is the Missouri. It forms the upper half of the western border with Nebraska and Kansas. It then flows eastward and joins the Mississippi at St. Louis. Several rivers in the northern part of the state flow into the Missouri River, including the Grand, the Chariton, and the Platte. Important rivers in southern Missouri include the Osage, the Current, the James, and the Black.

Most of the large lakes in the state are man-made. The largest of these is the Lake of the Ozarks on the Osage River in the central part of the state. It covers about 90 sq. miles (233 sq. km). Others include Stockton, Pomme de Terre, and Taneycomo reservoirs.

Missouri's History

Missouri's First People

The Missouri area was first occupied as long as four thousand years ago. The Woodland Indian culture centered in the Ohio River Valley, and later the Mississippian culture found throughout the Mississippi River Valley, left behind Burial and Temple Mounds as well as tools and crafts of their advanced cultures. The most famous of these Temple Mounds is at Cahokia, Illinois, just across the river from St. Louis.

As whites arrived in Missouri, the Mississippian culture had disappeared and relatively few natives inhabited the region. In the northeast were the Fox, Iliniwek, and Sauk tribes, and in the southwest were the Iowa, Missouri, Osage, and other tribes.

European Exploration

Frenchmen Father Jacques Marquette and Louis Jolliet first encountered the Missouri region on their trip down the Mississippi River in 1673. Nine years later, the French explorer René-Robert Cavelier, Sieur de La Salle, on another exploration of the Mississippi River, claimed the entire Mississippi Valley for France. Later that decade, Louis Armand de Lom d'Arce, Baron de Lahontan, explored the Missouri River, though little development followed these initial forays. Some fur-trading posts and missions were set up, but the first permanent settlement was not established until 1735 at Ste. Genevieve on the Mississippi River.

Although the French ceded control of the territory to Spain in the aftermath of the French and Indian War, French settlers took the lead in developing the area. Pierre Liguest Laclede founded St. Louis in 1764 as a fur-trading and lead mining center (Missouri would soon become the world's leading lead producer). In the 1780s, Spain granted land to American settlers, including slave owners from Kentucky and Tennessee. In 1800, Missouri (as part of the Louisiana Territory) was ceded back to France, and three years later became U.S. territory as part of the Louisiana Purchase.

Statehood

In 1804, the Sauk and Fox Indians ceded lands in northern Missouri to the United States. This would be the first of several land transfers from Indian tribes that virtually eliminated them from the state's population by the 1830s.

Missouri was split from the Louisiana Territory in 1812, and organized as the Missouri Territory (which also included Arkansas, itself organized independently in 1819). A large influx of settlers in the years after 1810 enabled Missouri to reach the requisite population for statehood in 1818. Missouri's desire to be considered a slave state prompted a delay in Congress that was resolved by the Missouri Compromise, which allowed Missouri to remain a slave state but forbade further slavery in the Louisiana Territory north of Arkansas. Consequently, Missouri was admitted into the Union (paired with Maine as a free state) as the twenty-fourth state in 1821.

In the Civil War, despite Missouri's status as a slave state and despite the recent Dred Scott case (in which the Supreme Court upheld the rights of slave owners at the expense of slaves) won by a Missourian, a state convention rebuffed the move for secession.

Industrialization

The early settlement of Missouri revolved around fur trading and, after the discovery of lead in the mid-eighteenth century, lead mining. With settlement in the nineteenth century, agriculture (cotton and cattle) and commerce were important as Missouri became the "Gateway to the West" (Independence, Missouri, was where both the Oregon and Sante Fe trails began).

After the Civil War, with the completion of the transcontinental railroad highlighting Missouri's central location in the nation, industry began to play a role in the state's economy. The urban areas of Kansas City and St. Louis thrived in this atmosphere. Today, agriculture (soybeans and corn), mining (Missouri remains the leading lead producer in the nation), manufacturing (automobiles), and service all contribute to the state's healthy economic mix.

Missouri has a long history of agricultural practices. During the late nineteenth century into the early twentieth century logging companies farmed the prized Ozark and Bootheel timber found in the state. However, these trees were soon depleted and the loggers were forced to move out of the state to other, more plentiful, areas. Cotton farming was also an important agricultural activity. Forests were cleared, swamps were drained, and levees were built to make more land available for the cotton growers.

Missouri has also had its share of environmental problems. In the 1980s, dioxin contamination was discovered in an area near St. Louis called Times Beach. A cleanup program was started in 1991, but it will take years before the area will again be safe.

Gateway to the West

In 1821, the Sante Fe Trail was opened for settlers heading for the Southwest, and in the 1830s the Oregon Trail became the path for settlers traveling to the Northwest. Both trails originated in Independence, Missouri, establishing Missouri as the Gateway to the West. Continuing this tradition several decades later, on April 3, 1860, the Pony Express began delivery of mail between St. Joseph, Missouri, and Sacramento, California, becoming the first regular mail link to the West. Relay riders would convey the mail by horseback, the entire two-thousand-mile journey taking eight days. The service lasted barely more than a year; the invention of the telegraph in 1861 rendered it obsolete.

Important Events

1673 Frenchmen Jacques Marquette and Louis Jolliet pass through Missouri in their exploration of the Mississippi River.

1682 René-Robert Cavelier, Sieur de La Salle claims Mississippi Valley, including Missouri, for France.

1735 First permanent white settlement is established at Ste. Genevieve.

1762 France cedes Missouri to Spain.

1764 Pierre Liguest Laclede founds St. Louis as a fur-trading post and lead-mining town.

1780s Spain allows American settlers into Missouri and grants them land.

1799 Daniel Boone settles in Missouri.

1800 Spain cedes Missouri back to France.

1803 United States takes control of Missouri as part of the Louisiana Purchase.

1808 Missouri Gazette is the first Missouri newspaper, published in St. Louis.

1812 Missouri Territory is created, which includes Arkansas.

1821 Missouri admitted into the Union as the twenty-fourth state under the Missouri Compromise.

1836 Platte Purchase adds six northern counties to the state.

1857 Dred Scott decision handed down by the Supreme Court upholds Dred Scott's status as a slave.

1860 Pony Express mail delivery begins at St. Joseph.

1861 State convention fails to ratify a secession motion.

1905 Joseph Folk is elected governor of Missouri, first in a succession of progressive governors.

1944 Missouri native Harry Truman is elected vice president.

1945 Harry Truman succeeds to the presidency upon the death of Franklin Delano Roosevelt.

1983 Discovery of dioxin at Times Beach is pivotal in national investigation of environmental pollution.

1988 Missouri suffers from extensive drought conditions.

1993 Severe flooding of the Mississippi River causes much dislocation and economic ruin.

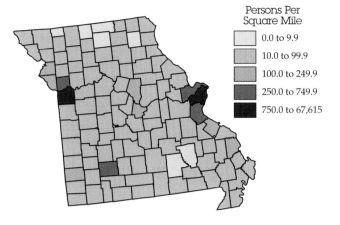

Persons Per Square Mile

- 0.0 to 9.9
- 10.0 to 99.9
- 100.0 to 249.9
- 250.0 to 749.9
- 750.0 to 67,615

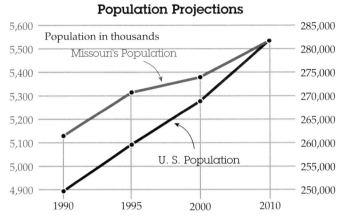

Population Projections

Population in thousands

Missouri's Population

U. S. Population

Population Change

Year	Population
1950	3,955,000
1960	4,326,000
1970	4,688,000
1980	4,916,686
1990	5,117,073
2000	5,383,000
2010	5,521,000

Period	Change
1950–1970	18.5%
1970–1980	4.9%
1980–1990	4.1%
1990–2000	5.2%

Population Density

Population density for the state of Missouri was 74.3 persons per square mile in 1990 (41.8 per km2). Average U.S. density was 70.3 persons per square mile in 1990 (27.3 per km2). Habitation is most dense in and around the urban areas of St. Louis, Kansas City, and Springfield. One low density county is Shannon in the south, which contains the Ozark National Scenic Riverways.

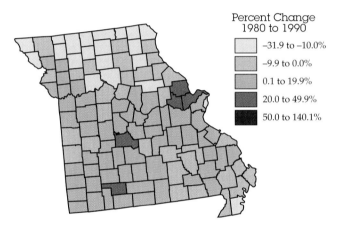

Percent Change 1980 to 1990

- –31.9 to –10.0%
- –9.9 to 0.0%
- 0.1 to 19.9%
- 20.0 to 49.9%
- 50.0 to 140.1%

Population Change

The 1990 population figure for the state of Missouri was 5,117,073. This is a 4.08 percent increase from 4,916,686 in 1980. The next decade will show growth with a population of 5.4 million or a 5.20 percent increase. Fastest growth is located in an area north of St. Louis, Camden county, and Christian County south of Springfield.

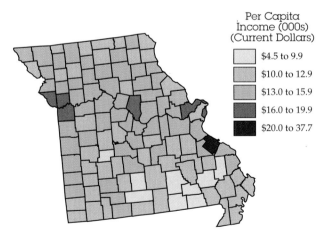

Per Capita Income (000s) (Current Dollars)

- $4.5 to 9.9
- $10.0 to 12.9
- $13.0 to 15.9
- $16.0 to 19.9
- $20.0 to 37.7

Distribution of Income

The per capita income for the state of Missouri (current dollars) was $18,835 in 1992. This is a 103.5 percent increase from $9,256 in 1980. Income is greatest in Ste. Genevieve County, which is located on the Mississippi River south of St. Louis. Other high income areas include the area around Kansas City, Columbia, and St. Louis.

Population Facts

State Population, 1993: 5,234,000

Rank: 16

Population 2000: 5,383,000 (Rank 15)

Density: 74.3 per sq. mi. (41.8 per km²)

Distribution: 68.7% urban, 31.3% rural

Population Under 5 Years Old: 7.3%

Population Under 18 Years Old: 26.0%

Population Over 65 Years Old: 14.1%

Median Age: 33.5

Number of Households: 1,961,000

Average Persons Per Household: 2.54

Average Persons Per Family: 3.08

Female Heads of Households: 4.07%

Population That Is Married: 21.58%

Birth Rate: 15.5 per 1,000 population

Death Rate: 9.8 per 1,000 population

Births to Teen Mothers: 14.4%

Marriage Rate: 9.5 per 1,000 population

Divorce Rate: 5.1 per 1,000 population

Violent Crime Rate: 763 per 100,000 pop.

Population on Social Security: 17.9%

Percent Voting for President: 62.0%

Population Profile

Rank. Missouri ranks 16th among U.S. states in terms of population with 5,234,000 citizens.

Minority Population. The state's minority population is 13.1 percent. The state's male to female ratio for 1990 was 92.9 males for every 100 females. It was below the national average of 95.22 males for every 100 females.

Growth. Growing slower than the projected national average, the state's population is

Government

Capital: Jefferson City (established 1826).

Statehood: Became 24th state on Aug. 10, 1821.

Number of Counties: 114.

Supreme Court Justices: 7, 12-year term.

State Senators: 34, 4-year term.

State Legislators: 163, 2-year term.

United States Senators: 2.

United States Representatives: 9.

Electoral Votes: 11.

State Constitution: Adopted 1945.

Missouri's Famous Citizens

Benton, Thomas Hart (1782–1858). Elected to the U.S. Senate in 1820. Became a strong advocate of Abolition.

Berra, Yogi (b. 1925). Hall of Fame baseball catcher. Won the MVP Award 3 times with the N.Y. Yankees, whom he also managed.

Berry, Chuck (b. 1926). Legendary rock n roller. Famous for his "duck walk" and hits like "Maybellene" and "Johnny B Goode."

Bumbrey, Grace (b. 1937). Opera singer. First black artist to appear at the Bayreuth Festival.

Carver, George Washington (1860–1943). Born into slavery, became head of Tuskeegee Institute's Agriculture Department and make great advances in scientific agriculture.

Cronkite, Walter (b. 1916). As anchorman for "The CBS Evening News" from 1962 to 1981, he lent dignity to American broadcast journalism.

Evans, Walker (1903–1975). Photographer. Documented the conditions of poor farmers during the Great Depression.

Hubble, Edwin (1889–1953). Astronomer. Developed Hubble's Law, the theory that the universe is continually expanding.

expected to reach 5.5 million by the year 2010 (see graph above).

Older Citizens. The state's population older than 65 was 717,531 in 1990. It grew 10.71% from 648,126 in 1980.

Younger Citizens. The number of children (under 18 years of age) was 1.4 million in 1990. This represents 27.1 percent of the state's population. The state's school aged population was 816 thousand in 1990. It is expected to increase to 871 thousand by the year 2000. This represents a 6.74% change.

Urban/Rural. 68.7% of the population of the state live in urban areas while 31.3% live in rural areas.

Largest Cities. Missouri has 15 cities with a population greater than 35,000. The populations of the state's largest centers are (starting from the most populous) Kansas City (435,146), St. Louis (396,685), Springfield (140,494), Independence (112,301), St. Joseph (71,852), Columbia (69,101), St. Charles (54,555), Florissant (51,206), Lee's Summit (46,418), St. Peters (45,779), Joplin (40,961), Blue Springs (40,153), University City (40,087), Chesterfield (37,991), and Jefferson City (35,481).

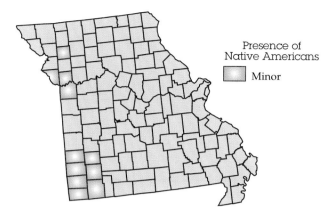

Presence of
Native Americans

Minor

Native American

The Native American population in Missouri was 19,835 in 1990. This was an increase of 33.84 percent from 14,820 in 1980. Eleven percent of the Native American population in the state can be found living in Kansas City. Missouri is also home to the Missouri and Osage tribes.

Statewide Ethnic Composition

Over 83 percent of the population of Missouri is white. The largest nationalities in this racial group are German, Irish, and English. The next largest group is African Americans, followed by Hispanics, Asian Americans, and Native Americans. Over 329,000 people claim to be American and acknowledge no other nationality.

Nationalities

African	6,458
American	329,895
Arab	7,433
Austrian	7,244
Czech	16,975
Dutch	79,903
English	485,785
Finnish	2,176
German	1,527,956
Greek	10,433
Hungarian	8,369
Irish	548,111
Italian	111,344
Norwegian	18,519
Polish	59,572
Portuguese	2,184
Russian	19,406
Scottish	56,837
Slovak	10,575
Swedish	41,378
Welsh	21,295
West Indian	2,288

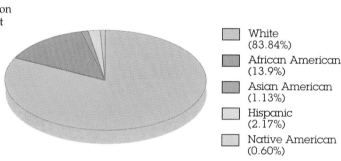

- White (83.84%)
- African American (13.9%)
- Asian American (1.13%)
- Hispanic (2.17%)
- Native American (0.60%)

Education Facts

Total Students 1990: 807,934

Number of School Districts: 543

Expenditure Per Capita on Education 1990: $676

Expenditure Per Capita K–12 1990: $819

Expenditure Per Pupil 1990: $4,479

Total School Enrollment 1990–1991: 810,450

Rank of Expenditures Per Student: 33d in the U.S.

African American Enrollment: 14.9%

Hispanic Enrollment: 0.7%

Asian/Pacific Islanders Enrollment: 0.8%

Native American Enrollment: 0.2%

Mean SAT Score 1991 Verbal: 476

Mean SAT Score 1991 Math: 526

Average Teacher's Salary 1992: $28,900

Rank Teacher's Salary: 35th in U.S.

High School Graduates 1990: 49,200

Total Number of Public Schools: 2,151

Number of Teachers 1990: 51,294

Student/Teacher Ratio: 15.8

Staff Employed in Public Schools: 98,315

Pupil/Staff Ratio: 8.2

Staff/Teacher Ratio: 1.9

Education

Attainment: 76 percent of population 25 years or older were high school graduates in 1989, earning Missouri a ranking of 35th in the United States; 22 percent of the state's population had completed college. Institutions of Higher Education: The largest universities and colleges in the state include the University of Missouri (founded 1841), Columbia; Central Missouri State University, Warrensburg; Northeast Missouri State University, Kirksville; Southwest Missouri State University, Springfield; Southeast Missouri State University, Cape Girardeau; Northwest Missouri State University, Maryville; Washington University and St. Louis University, St. Louis. Expenditures per Student: Expenditure increased 69% between 1985 and 1990. Projected High School Graduations: 1998 (60,880), 2004 (58,721); Total Revenues for Education from Federal Sources: $179 million; Total Revenues for Education from State Sources: $1.2 billion; Total Revenues for Education from Local Sources: $1.6 billion; Average Annual Salaries for Public School Principals: $39,424. Largest School Districts in State: St. Louis City School District, 44,056 students, 78th in the United States; Kansas City School District #33, 34,640, 113th.

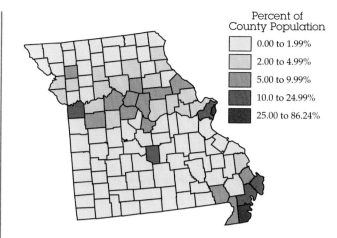

Percent of
County Population

- 0.00 to 1.99%
- 2.00 to 4.99%
- 5.00 to 9.99%
- 10.0 to 24.99%
- 25.00 to 86.24%

African American

The African American population in Missouri was 548,208 in 1990. This was an increase of 6.78 percent from 513,385 in 1980. The two areas with the highest percentage of African Americans in the state are St. Louis and Pemiscot County in the southern part of the state bordering Tennessee.

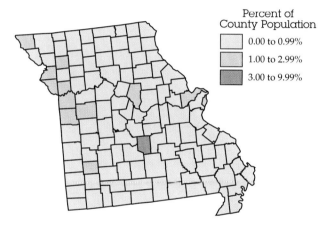

Percent of
County Population

- 0.00 to 0.99%
- 1.00 to 2.99%
- 3.00 to 9.99%

Hispanic[††]

The Hispanic population in Missouri was 61,702 in 1990. This is an increase of 19.45 percent from 51,653 persons in 1980. The county with the highest percentage of Hispanics is Pulaski County, located in the southern part of the state. Many can also be found in and around Kansas City and St. Louis.

[††]A person of Mexican, Puerto Rican, Cuban, or other Spanish culture or origin regardless of race.

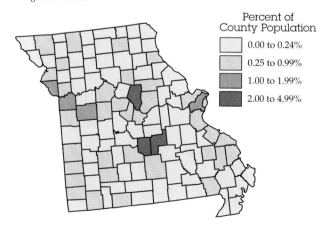

Percent of
County Population

- 0.00 to 0.24%
- 0.25 to 0.99%
- 1.00 to 1.99%
- 2.00 to 4.99%

Asian American

The Asian American population in Missouri was 41,277 in 1990. This is an increase of 72.14 percent from 23,979 persons in 1980. The greatest concentration of Asian Americans in the state can be found in Boone, Pulaski, and Phelps counties. Many can also be found in and around Kansas City and St. Louis.

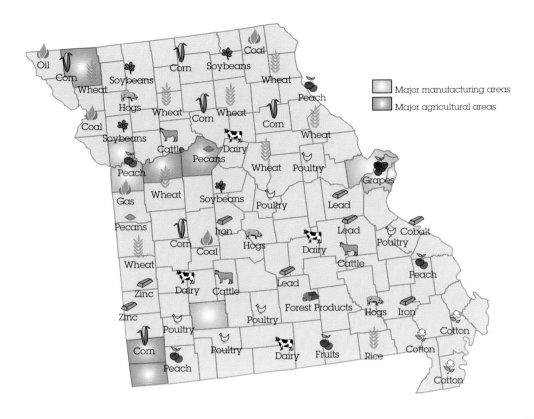

Major manufacturing areas

Major agricultural areas

Transportation

Missouri's central location has made it one of the transportation centers for the United States. The area between St. Louis and Kansas City is one of Missouri's busiest transportation corridors. Air, land, rail, and river traffic all converge in this area.

The port of St. Louis is one of the most heavily used inland ports. Combined, the Mississippi and Missouri rivers have approximately 1,000 miles of commercially navigable waters. The state has around 109,000 miles of highways and roads; 95 percent of these are surfaced. About 20 freight rail lines operate in Missouri; in addition, 10 Missouri cities are served by passenger rail lines. Airports in both St. Louis and Kansas City are among the busiest in the Midwest.

Energy and Transportation Facts

Energy. Yearly Consumption: 1,513 tril. BTUs (residential, 26.4%; commercial, 19.5%; industrial, 22.9%; transportation, 31.3%); Annual Energy Expenditures Per Capita: $1,821; Nuclear Power Plants Located in State: 1; Source of Energy Consumed: Petroleum— 40.6%; Natural Gas— 16.9%; Coal— 34.8%; Hydroelectric Power—0.7%; Nuclear Power—7.0%.

Transportation. Highway Miles: 121,424 (interstates, 1,178; urban, 15,398; rural, 106,026); Average Yearly Auto Insurance: $493 (34th); Auto Fatalities Rank: 19th; Registered Motor Vehicles: 4,004,062; Workers in Carpools: 17.2%; Workers Using Public Trans: 2.0%.

Employment

Employment. Missouri employed 2.48 million people in 1993. Most work in social and personal services (644,100 persons or 26.0% of the workforce). Manufacturing accounts for 16.6% or 411,300 workers. Wholesale and retail trade account for 22.9% or 568,500 workers. Government employs 377,300 workers (15.2%). Construction employs 95,400 workers (3.8%). Transportation and utilities account for 6.2% or 152,900 persons. Agriculture employs 84,400 workers or 3.4%. Finance, real estate, and insurance account for 5.7% or 140,700 workers. Mining employs 4,400 people and accounts for only 0.2% of the workforce.

Unemployment. Unemployment remained the same between 1985 and 1993 at a rate of 6.4%. Today's figure is lower than the national average of 6.8% as shown below.

Agriculture

Missouri has 30.2 million farm acres. During the last 40 years, Missouri's farms have grown larger in size and fewer in number. In 1955, 202,000 farms were found in the state. Today, 106,000 remain. Agriculture adds $2 billion to the state's gross product annually. The principal commodities in order of marketing receipts are cattle, soybeans, hogs, and corn.

Livestock and livestock products account for about 54 percent of Missouri's farm income, of which cattle and hogs are the most important. Much of the cattle raising is concentrated in the southwest. Many of the state's leading crops, such as soybeans, corn, and sorghum, are grown for cattle feed. Other important crops include cotton, hay, wheat, and fruits such as apples, peaches, and grapes.

Housing

Owner Occupied Units: 2,199,129; Average Age of Units: 31 years; Average Value of Housing Units: $59,800; Renter Occupied Units: 585,022; Median Monthly Rent: $368; Housing Starts: 22,100; Existing Home Sales: 106,400.

Economic Facts

Gross State Product: $100,000,000,000 (1989)

Income Per Capita: $18,835

Disposable Personal Income: $16,742

Median Household Income: $26,362

Average Annual Pay, 1988: $22,567

Principal Industries: food products, printing, transportation equipment, fabricated metal products, machinery, chemicals, publishing

Major Crops: corn, hay, soybeans, cotton, winter wheat, alfalfa, rice

Fish: Bass, Bluegill, Crappies, Jack Salmon, Trout

Livestock: hogs, cattle

Non-Fuel Minerals: Lead, Limestone, Magnesium, Nickel, Copper, Silver, Zinc, Dolomite, Cobalt, Granite, Marble

Organic Fuel Minerals: coal

Civilian Labor Force: 2,689,000 (Women: 1,254,000)

Total Employed: 2,511,000 (Women: 1,176,000)

Median Value of Housing: $59,800

Median Contract Rent: $368 per month

Economic Sectors 1992

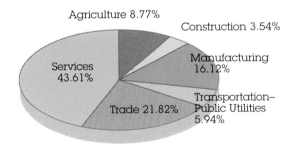

Agriculture 8.77%

Construction 3.54%

Services 43.61%

Manufacturing 16.12%

Trade 21.82%

Transportation–Public Utilities 5.94%

Manufacturing

Like Mississippi, Missouri's leading manufacturing industry is transportation equipment. Overall, manufacturing contributes 23 percent to the state gross product. Aside from transportation equipment, Missouri produces food products, chemicals, electrical equipment, and printed materials.

Out of the state's 7,300-plus factories, over 60 percent are located in the St. Louis and Kansas City metropolitan regions. These two areas produce a variety of goods, including military aircraft, food products, and chemicals. All types of vehicles, from bus bodies to railroad cars, are produced in Missouri. One of the country's largest dairy processing plants is located in Springfield. Much of the nation's beer is brewed in one of the many St. Louis breweries.

Unemployment Rate

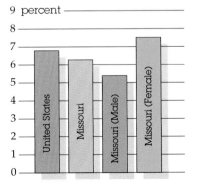

9 percent

8

7

6

5

4

3

2

1

0

United States

Missouri

Missouri (Male)

Missouri (Female)

MONTANA
The State of Montana

Official State Seal

The Great Seal of Montana was adopted by the state legislature in 1893 from an adaptation of an earlier seal created in 1864. One change was the motto, which at one time read *"Oro el Plata,"* but now reads *"Oro y Plata"* (Gold and Silver). A typical Montana scene graces the majority of the seal and includes mountains, the Great Falls, and farming and mining tools.

Legal Holidays

January: New Year's Day–1st; Martin Luther King, Jr., Day—3rd Monday; February: Abraham Lincoln's Birthday—12th; Presidents' Day—3rd Monday; May: Memorial Day—4th Monday; July: Independence Day—4th; September: Labor Day—1st Monday; October: Columbus Day—2nd Monday; November: Admission Day—8th; Veterans' Day—11th; Thanksgiving—4th Thursday; December: Christmas—25th.

Official State Flag

The Montana state flag was adopted in 1905. It was an adaptation of an earlier military flag carried by volunteers in the Spanish-American War in 1898. The flag contains the state name, which was added in 1981 above the scene found on the Great Seal.

Festivals and Events

January: NRA Rodeo Finals, Billings; February: Cabin Fever Winter Fest, Virginia City; April: Helena Railroad Fair, Helena; May: Cherry Blossom Weekend, Bigfork; June: Badlands Native American Celebration, Brockton; Little Bighorn Days, Hardin; July: Mountain Man Rendezvous, Red Lodge; State Fair, Great Falls; North American Native American Days, Browning; August: Mountain Fair, Billings; Festival of Nations, Red Lodge; September: Nordicfest, Libby; Montana State Chokecherry Fest, Lewistown; October: Hunter's Feed, Ennis; Oktoberfest/Thanks Canada, Helena; November: Bald Eagle Migration, Helena; December: Great Falls Christmas Stroll, Great Falls.

Montana Compared to States in Its Region.

Resident Resident Pop. in Metro Areas: 8th; Pop. Percent Increase: 7th; Pop. Over 65: 1st; Infant Mortality: 1st; School Enroll. Increase: 6th; High School Grad. and Up: 4th; Violent Crime: 8th; Hazardous Waste Sites: 6th; Unemployment: 3d; Median Household Income: 8th; Persons Below Poverty: 2d; Energy Costs Per Person: 2d.

Mountain Region

	Population	Capital
Montana	839,000	Helena
Wyoming	470,000	Cheyenne
Idaho	1,099,000	Boise
Nevada	1,389,000	Carson City
Utah	1,860,000	Salt Lake City
Colorado	3,566,000	Denver
Arizona	3,936,000	Phoenix
New Mexico	1,616,000	Santa Fe

Montana's Finances

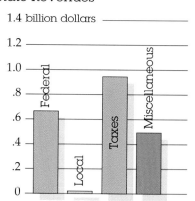

Households: 306,000; Income Per Capita Current Dollars: $16,062; Change Per Capita Income 1980 to 1992: 84.0% (43d in U.S.); State Expenditures: $2,108,000,000; State Revenues: $2,121,000,000; Personal Income Tax: 2 to 11%; Federal Income Taxes Paid Per Capita: $1,268; Sales Tax: N/A.

State Expenditures

1.4 billion dollars
(bars: Education, Highway, Welfare, Health, Corrections)

State Revenues

1.4 billion dollars
(bars: Federal, Local, Taxes, Miscellaneous)

Location, Size, and Boundaries

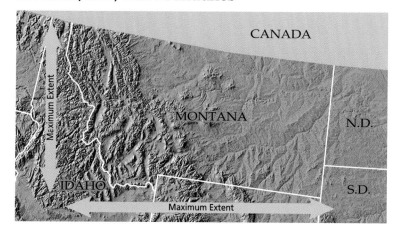

Location. Montana is located in the western United States in what is known as the Mountain region. It is bounded on four sides by land. The geographic center of Montana is lat. 47° 1.9' N; long. 109° 38.3' W.

Size. Montana is the 4th largest state in terms of size. Its area is 147,138 sq. mi. (381,087 km2). Inland water covers 1,551 sq. mi. (4,017 km2).

Boundaries. Canada, 546 mi. (879 km); North Dakota, 212 mi. (341 km); South Dakota, 67 mi. (108 km); Wyoming, 384 mi. (618 km); Idaho, 738 mi. (1,187 km).

Geographic Extent. The north/south extent of Montana is 315 mi. (507 km). The state extends 570 mi. (917 km) to the east/west.

Facts about Montana. Origin of Name: From the Spanish word meaning *"mountainous"*; Nickname: The Treasure State; Motto: "Gold and Silver" (*Oro y Plata*); Abbreviations: Mont. (traditional), MT (postal); State Bird: Western meadowlark; State Tree: ponderosa pine; State Flower: bitterroot; State Song: "Montana," words by Charles C. Cohen and music by Joseph E. Howard.

Montana Compared to Other States. Resident Pop. in Metro Areas: 50th; Pop. Percent Increase: 18th; Pop. Over 65: 18th; Infant Mortality: 24th; School Enroll. Increase: 45th; High School Grad. and Up: 11th; Violent Crime: 46th; Haz. Waste Sites: 41st; Unemployment: 27th; Med. Household Income: 44th; Persons Below Poverty: 10th; Energy Costs Per Person: 10th.

Sources of Information. Tourism: Dept. of Commerce, Montana Promotion Division, 1424 9th Avenue, Helena, MT 59620. Government: Montana Legislative Council, Room 138, State Capitol, Helena, MT 59620. History: Montana Historical Society, 225 North Roberts Street, Helena, MT 59620.

■ **Bannack State Park.** The first territorial capital. Old gold mining town. (H-5)

■ **Big Hole National Battlefield.** Site of the battle with Nez Percé Indians in 1877. (H-5)

■ **Flathead Lake Area.** Skiing, big game hunting, and fishing. (C-4)

■ **Fort Benton.** Fur trading post founded in 1846. (C-9)

■ **Fort Peck Dam.** World's largest hydraulically filled dam. Boating and fishing as well as a museum featuring fossils. (C-16)

■ **Gates of the Mountains.** Cliffs rising 1,200 feet. Wilderness area. (E-7)

■ **Glacier National Park.** Glaciers. Going to the Sun Road. Beautiful scenery. (A-4)

■ **Grasshopper Glacier.** Grasshoppers frozen in ice cliff; 12,799 feet (3,901 meters). (I-10)

■ **Great Falls of the Missouri River.** World's largest springs, discovered by Lewis and Clark in 1805. (D-8)

■ **Hell Creek State Park.** Swimming, boating, and other water sports. (D-15)

■ **Lewis and Clark Caverns State Park.** Formations of stalactites and stalagmites in large caverns. (G-7)

■ **Little Bighorn Battlefield National Monument.** Site of the slaying of Lt. Col. George A. Custer and his troops by the Sioux and Cheyenne Indians on June 25, 1876. (H-15)

■ **Madison Canyon Earthquake Area.** Site of the August 17, 1959 earthquake that created a giant dam. (H-7)

■ **Makoshika State Park.** Colorful badland area formed by erosion. (E-19)

■ **Missouri Headwaters State Park.** Confluence of Jefferson, Madison, and Gallatin rivers forms Missouri River. (G-8)

■ **Museum of the Plains Indian.** Dedicated to Plains Indian lifestyles and artifacts. (B-5)

■ **Museum of the Rockies.** Dinosaur exhibits and other displays about Montana. (G-9)

■ **National Bison Range.** Buffalo, elk, deer, and antelope roam in this scenic area. (D-4)

■ **Richest Hill on Earth.** Silver, gold, copper, and zinc mines with a museum. (G-6)

■ **St. Ignatius Mission.** Pioneer church established in 1854. (D-4)

■ **Virginia City.** Second territorial capital (1865-75). Old gold mining town. (I-17)

■ **Yellowstone National Park.** The largest and oldest national park. Famous geysers, falls, and hot springs. (I-9)

Weather Facts

Record High Temperature: 117° F (47° C) on July 20, 1893, at Glendive; Record Low Temperature: -70° F (-57° C) on January 20, 1954, at Rogers Pass; Average January Temperature: 18° F (-8° C); Average July Temperature: 69° F (21° C); Average Yearly Precipitation: 16 in. (41 cm).

Environmental Facts

Air Pollution Rank: 44th; Water Pollution Rank: 38th; Total Yearly Industrial Pollution: 43,887,973 lbs.; Industrial Pollution Rank: 21st; Hazardous Waste Sites: 8; Hazardous Sites Rank: 39th; Landfill Capacity: overextended; Fresh Water Supply: surplus; Daily Residential Water Consumption: 183 gals. per capita; Endangered Species: Aquatic Species (1)—sturgeon, pallid; Birds (5)—crane, whooping; Mammals (3)—bear, grizzly; Plants (1)—howellia, water.

Land Use

Cropland: 27.2%; Pasture: 4.8%; Rangeland: 56%; Forest: 8%; Urban: 1.5%; Other: 2.5%.

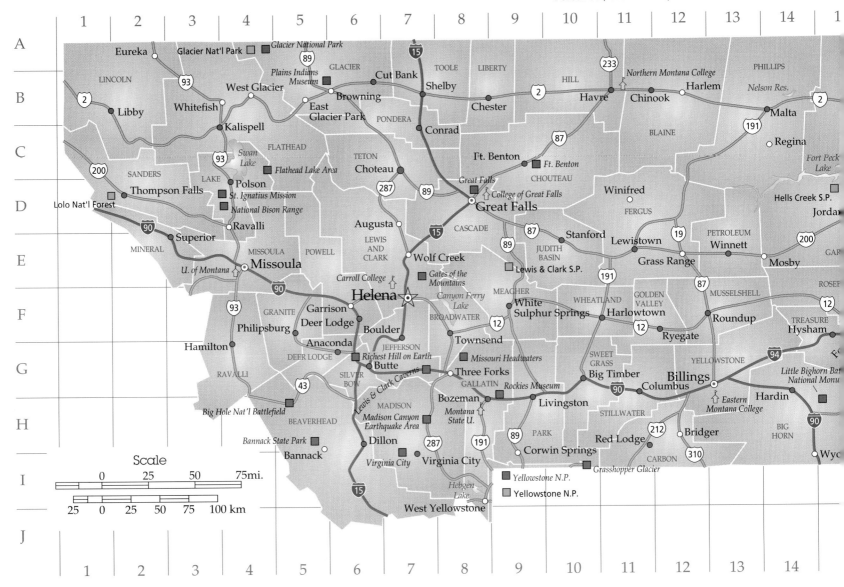

Average Monthly Weather

Helena	Jan	Feb	Mar	Apr	May	Jun	Jul	Aug	Sep	Oct	Nov	Dec	Yearly
Maximum Temperature °F	28.1	36.2	42.5	54.7	64.9	73.1	83.6	81.3	70.3	58.6	42.3	33.3	55.7
Minimum Temperature °F	8.1	15.7	20.6	29.8	39.5	47.0	52.2	50.3	40.8	31.5	20.4	13.5	30.8
Days of Precipitation	7.9	6.7	8.6	8.1	11.1	11.3	7.4	7.6	6.8	5.6	7.0	7.9	95.8

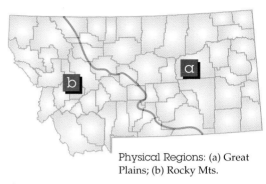

Physical Regions: (a) Great Plains; (b) Rocky Mts.

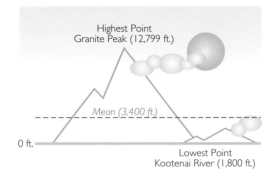

Highest Point
Granite Peak (12,799 ft.)

Mean (3,400 ft.)

0 ft.

Lowest Point
Kootenai River (1,800 ft.)

★ State capitol
⊙ Cities over 35,000 population
○ Other significant cities
● County Seats
■ Major cultural attractions

■ State Parks
Ⓦ Welcome Centers
⚲ Major colleges and universities

Major Cities

Anaconda	G-6
Billings	G-13
Bozeman	H-8
Butte- Silver Bow	G-6
Great Falls	D-8
Havre	B-11
Helena	F-7
Kalispell	C 4
Missoula	E-4

For more information about Montana's environment, contact the Department of Natural Resources and Conservation, 1520 E. 6th Ave., Helena, MT 59620-3201.

Topography

There are two distinct topographic regions in Montana. Much of the eastern and central parts of the state represent the westernmost extension of the Great Plains physical region. This is a region of gently rolling hills interrupted occasionally by small mountain clusters. Numerous river valleys, created by the Missouri and Yellowstone rivers and their tributaries, wind their way through this area. The soil of this region is a dark organic rich loamy clay that varies from warm and dry in the south to cool and moist in the north.

The western part of Montana is dominated by the Rocky Mountain physical region. The Rockies are actually a series of mountain ranges interspersed with river valleys of varying width. Mountain lakes, left behind by retreating glaciers, can also be found in some of these valleys. Some of the mountain ranges to be found here include the Bitteroot, Cabinet, Swan, and Lewis ranges in the northern part of the state; and the Little Belt, Big Belt, Crazy, and Pioneer mountains in the central and southern sections of western Montana. The highest elevation in the state can be found in this area. Granite Peak, which rises 12,799 ft. (3,901 m) above sea level, is located near the southern border with Wyoming. The predominant soil type is cool and moist gray/brown clay.

Environmental Quality

Montana residents generate 600,000 tons of solid waste each year, or approximately 1,500 pounds per capita. Landfill capacity in Montana will be exhausted in 5 to 10 years. The state has 10 hazardous waste sites. Annual greenhouse gas emissions in Montana total 26.4 million tons, or 32.8 tons per capita. Industrial sources in Montana release approximately 17.2 thousand tons of toxins, 147.0 thousand tons of acid precipitation-producing substances, and 1.2 million tons of smog-producing substances into the atmosphere each year.

The state has 1.2 million acres within the National Park System; the largest area within the state is Glacier National Park. State parks cover just over 47,000 acres, attracting 1.6 million visitors per year.

Montana spends approximately 4.3 percent of its budget, or approximately $86 per capita, on environmental and natural resources. Montana representatives in the U.S. House voted in favor of national environmental legislation 25 percent of the time, while U.S. senators did so 25 percent of the time.

Climate

Montana's climate varies considerably statewide. The state can be divided into two distinct climatic regions, because of the Continental Divide. To the west, the climate is cooler in the winter and warmer in the summer. Temperatures in cities such as Missoula average around 20 degrees F in January and 64 degrees F in July. In eastern Montana, cities such as Billings experience January and July average temperatures of 14 degrees F and 71 degrees F respectively.

Overall, Montana receives light precipitation, approximately 14 inches annually. However, some areas in northwestern Montana can be considered arid. On the other hand, the state's western mountain region often receives over 35 inches of precipitation annually.

Although Montana winters can be harsh, Chinook winds occasionally bring relief. These warm, dry winds blow over eastern mountain slopes, melt snow and ice, and allow temporary winter livestock grazing.

Hydrology

The most important river in the state is the Missouri. Its source is where the Gallatin, Jefferson, and Madison rivers meet in southwestern Montana. It flows north past Great Falls, then west across the state and into North Dakota. Significant tributaries include the Milk, the Musselshell, and the Poplar. The Yellowstone River begins in Yellowstone National Park and winds its way northeast through the state, joining the Missouri just over the border in North Dakota. The Powder, Tongue, and Bighorn rivers of southeastern Montana all flow into the Yellowstone. The Clark Fork and Kootenai rivers in northwestern Montana flow westward toward the Pacific Ocean.

Fort Peck Reservoir on the Missouri River is the largest lake in Montana. It is a man-made lake covering about 379 sq. miles (982 sq. km). Other artificial lakes include Canyon Ferry Lake and Tiber Reservoir. Flathead Lake is the largest natural lake, covering 195 sq. miles (505 sq. km).

Flora and Fauna

Forested areas only account for approximately one-fourth of Montana's area. Trees usually growing along the state's river valleys include cottonwood and aspen. Conifer trees such as Douglas fir, tamarack, and spruce grow in moist conditions, and lodgepole pines grow in drier regions. Wildflowers grow throughout Montana, but especially in higher elevations with an alpine climate. Common flowers include asters, dryad, lupine, and primrose. A large portion of the state is covered by grasses such as blue grama and buffalo grasses.

Buffalo once roamed all parts of Montana, but can now only be found in the Flathead Valley as well as other protected areas. The state's numerous large mammals include moose, puma, lynx, elk, and bear; all of these animals live in Montana's mountainous regions. Beavers, muskrats, and minks also live in the mountains. Pronghorn antelope live on the Montana's grassy plains. Grouse, wild geese, and pheasants are all common game birds in Montana. Montana is famous for two kinds of game fish, grayling and trout, which live in the state's cold rivers and lakes.

Montana's History

Montana's First People

People probably migrated to Montana as the glacial period came to an end. According to fragmentary evidence, humans could have first inhabited Montana between ten thousand and four thousand years ago.

The Arapaho, Assiniboin, Atsina, Blackfoot, Cheyenne, and Crow tribes lived on the plains, while the Bannock, Kalispel, Salish, and Shoshone lived in mountainous regions. Other Indians such as the Nez Perce, Sioux, and Mandan hunted within Montana.

European Exploration

As Europeans continuously pushed westward to further their colonization efforts, French trappers probably were the first white explorers to cross into Montana, sometime in the early 1700s. In 1743, Louis-Joseph and François Vérendrye, two traders, reached what they called the "shining mountains," the eastern edge of the northern Rocky Mountains.

In 1803, eastern Montana became American territory as part of the Louisiana Purchase. An expedition led by Meriwether Lewis and William Clark added more of the land included in present-day Montana in 1806. The northwest area of the state was gained by a treaty with Great Britain in 1846. Over its early years, Montana's land had been part of several other states and/or territories, including Idaho, Nebraska, Missouri, the Dakotas, Oregon, and Washington.

In 1807, fur traders started an active trading business in Montana. By 1847, the first permanent settlement existed, an outpost of the American Fur Company. The fur trade dominated Montana's economy until the discovery of gold in 1858 near present-day Drummond.

On the Road to Statehood

Before Montana had its own territory, it was part of the large Idaho Territory, which was created in 1863. However, under the Organic Act, Montana Territory was officially declared by President Abraham Lincoln in May 1864. Montana did not achieve statehood until November 8, 1889, when it became the forty-first state in the Union.

During the territorial period, Montana underwent drastic changes. Native American uprisings began to be a regular occurrence in Montana starting in the early 1860s. While the Sioux, Nez Perce (a tribe living primarily in Idaho and Oregon), and Northern Cheyenne tribes all resisted the reservation movement, the Sioux were the most militant.

The most famous disturbance took place on June 25, 1876. A force of fifteen thousand Sioux and Cheyenne warriors, led by Crazy Horse, defeated seven hundred American soldiers under the command of Maj. Gen. George Custer. The battle, which took place near the Little Bighorn River, has been dubbed the Battle of the Little Bighorn, or Custer's Last Stand.

A year later, the era of organized Indian resistance effectively ended. On October 5, 1877, The military and settlers defeated Chief Joseph and the Nez Perce in a battle near Bear Paw Mountain, near the Canadian border. By the time Montana reached statehood on 1889, most Native Americans had been confined to federal reservations.

Industrialization

The lucrative fur trade dominated Montana's early economy until the discovery of gold. However, in the mid 1860s, livestock developed as the industry leader in Montana.

Ranchers began driving longhorn cattle up from Texas around 1860. By 1866, over a half million cattle could be found grazing on Montana rangelands. The industry expanded even more between 1880 and 1900, when construction began on the Montana portion of the Utah and Northern Railroad system. Besides increasing cattle ranching, the newly built railroad attracted agricultural homesteaders.

Industry flourished in the early twentieth century. The state made great use of its natural resources. Mining continued and dams for hydroelectric power were built. Railroad extensions enabled the processing industries—sugar refining, meat processing, and flour milling—to grow.

Like the rest of the United States, Montana suffered during the Great Depression. Due to the lessening of demand for raw materials, Montana's production of wood products and grains significantly decreased. This decrease, combined with drought, made life difficult. However, the federal government provided relief in the form of federal works projects, including the construction of the massive Fort Peck Dam, completed in 1940. Other projects included park construction, insect control, irrigation, and rural electrification.

Parks, Monuments, and More

Because of the gold and silver found in Montana in its early history, Montana is known as the Treasure State. Montana can also be considered a treasure because of its numerous parks, monuments, and other tourist attractions. Montana is the home of the nation's first national park, Yellowstone, which was established in 1872. In northwestern Montana, Glacier National Park, which has 250 lakes, was established in 1910.

In the 1960s, the state government developed a plan to build more recreation facilities, including campgrounds, parks, and historic sites to attract tourists. Private construction of ski resorts helped extend Montana's tourist season into winter, making it a year-round industry.

Apart from Yellowstone and Glacier National Parks, Montana has eleven national forests and several national monuments.

Important Events

1743 Louis-Joseph and François Vérendrye, two traders, reached what they called the "shining mountains," the eastern edge of the northern Rocky Mountains.

1803 Eastern Montana becomes U.S. territory in the Louisiana Purchase.

1805 Lewis and Clark explore Montana on their way to the West Coast.

1846 Northwestern Montana received by United States from Great Britain under Oregon Treaty.

1847 Fort Benton established by American Fur Company.

1860 The introduction of longhorn cattle to Montana's economy starts with cattle drives from Texas.

1862 Gold discovered at Grasshopper Creek.

1863 Idaho Territory created, includes most of Montana.

1864 President Lincoln establishes Montana Territory in May.

1875 Capital moved from Virginia City to Helena.

1876 Battle of the Little Bighorn ("Custer's Last Stand") fought between Maj. Gen. George Custer's troops and a force of Cheyenne and Sioux warriors.

1877 End of Plains Indian rebellion, Nez Perce surrender to U.S. forces.

1880 Utah and Northern Railroad extends into Montana.

1889 November 8, Montana becomes forty-first state of the Union.

1910 Glacier National Park established by Congress.

1916 Jeanette Rankin becomes first woman in U.S. House of Representatives.

1940 Fort Peck dam completed.

1951 First oil wells in Montana start production.

1960s Tourism plan implemented which builds recreational facilities to attract tourists the state.

1965 Yellowtail Dam construction completed.

1990 Thousands of gallons of gasoline leaks from underground tanks in Paradise Valley.

1991 Native Americans, particularly the Cheyenne, fight to protect their sacred sites from coal miners and railroad developers.

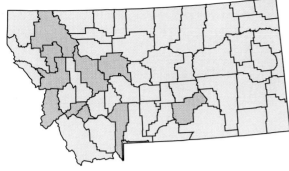

Population Density

Persons Per Square Mile
- 0.0 to 9.9
- 10.0 to 99.9

Population density for the state of Montana was 5.5 persons per square mile in 1990 (2.1 per km2). Average U.S. density was 70.3 persons per square mile in 1990 (27.3 per km2). The state of Montana is one of the most sparsely populated states in the Union. Most of the population and, therefore, most of the density can be found in the cities, such as Great Falls and Helena.

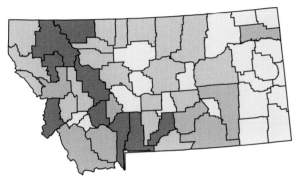

Population Change

Percent Change 1980 to 1990
- −31.9 to −10.0%
- −9.9 to 0.0%
- 0.1 to 19.9%
- 20.0 to 49.9%

The 1990 population figure for the state of Montana was 799,065 in 1990. This is a 1.57 percent increase from 786,690 in 1980. The next decade will show a decline with a population of 794 thousand or a −0.63 percent decrease. The areas of fastest growth are found in the western region of the state in a north-south band. Most of the state, however, suffered a small decline in population in the last decade.

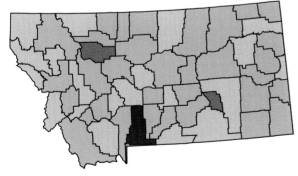

Distribution of Income

Per Capita Income (000s) (Current Dollars)

- $10.0 to 12.9
- $13.0 to 15.9
- $16.0 to 19.9
- $20.0 to 37.7

The per capita income for the state of Montana (current dollars) was $16,062 in 1992. This is an 84.0 percent increase from $8,728 in 1980. Income is greatest in Park County in the south. The northern section of Yellowstone National Park is located south of this county. Another high-income county is Teton in the north. Treasure County in the east also has one of the higher per capita incomes in the state.

Population Projections

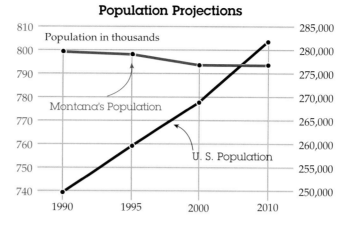

Population in thousands

Montana's Population

U. S. Population

Population Facts

State Population, 1993: 839,000

Rank: 44

Population 2000: 794,000 (Rank 44)

Density: 5.5 per sq. mi. (2.1 per km²)

Distribution: 52.5% urban, 47.5% rural

Population Under 5 Years Old: 7.0%

Population Under 18 Years Old: 27.4%

Population Over 65 Years Old: 13.4%

Median Age: 33.8

Number of Households: 306,000

Average Persons Per Household: 2.53

Average Persons Per Family: 3.08

Female Heads of Households: 3.30%

Population That Is Married: 20.97%

Birth Rate: 14.5 per 1,000 population

Death Rate: 8.6 per 1,000 population

Births to Teen Mothers: 11.5%

Marriage Rate: 8.7 per 1,000 population

Divorce Rate: 5.1 per 1,000 population

Violent Crime Rate: 140 per 100,000 pop.

Population on Social Security: 17.6%

Percent Voting for President: 70.1%

Population Profile

Rank. Montana ranks 44th among U.S. states in terms of population with 839,000 citizens.

Minority Population. The state's minority population is 8.3 percent. The state's male to female ratio for 1990 was 98.13 males for every 100 females. It was above the national average of 95.22 males for every 100 females.

Growth. The state's population is decreasing and is expected to be 794 thousand by the year 2010.

Government

Capital: Helena (established 1875).

Statehood: Became 41st state on Nov. 8, 1889.

Number of Counties: 56.

Supreme Court Justices: 7, 8-year term.

State Senators: 50, 4-year term.

State Legislators: 100, 2-year term.

United States Senators: 2.

United States Representatives: 1.

Electoral Votes: 3.

State Constitution: Adopted 1972.

Population Change

Year	Population
1950	591,000
1960	679,000
1970	698,000
1980	786,690
1990	799,065
2000	794,000
2010	794,000

Period	Change
1950–1970	18.1%
1970–1980	12.8%
1980–1990	1.5%
1990–2000	−0.6%

Montana's Famous Citizens

Cooper, Gary (1901–1961). Actor, best known for his roles in westerns such as *High Noon,* for which he won an Oscar.

Daly, Marcus (1841–1900). Formed his own silver-mining company and founded the mining town of Anaconda.

Guthrie, A.B, Jr. (1901–1991). Wrote about the American West in books such as *The Way West* and *Shane.*

Huntley, Chet (1911–1974). Half of the famous evening news broadcast, "The Huntley-Brinkley Report," which ran 1956-1970.

Lanford, Nathaniel Pitt (1832–1911). Explored Yellowstone National Park and became its first superintendent in 1872.

Loy, Myrna (b. 1905). Actress. Best known for her role as Nora Charles in the *Thin Man* film series starting in 1934.

Mansfield, Mike (b. 1903). Elected to the U.S. Senate in 1952. Served as majority leader from 1961 to 1977.

Plenty Coups (1848–1932). Tribal chief of the Crow Indians. Maintained friendly relations with the U.S. government.

Older Citizens. The state's population older than 65 was 106,497 in 1990. It grew 25.94% from 84,559 in 1980.

Younger Citizens. The number of children (under 18 years of age) was 222 thousand in 1990. This represents 27.8 percent of the state's population. The state's school aged population was 151 thousand in 1990. It is expected to decrease to 144 thousand by the year 2000. This represents a −4.64% change.

Urban/Rural. 52.5% of the population of the state live in urban areas while 47.5% live in rural areas.

Largest Cities. Montana has three cities with a population greater than 35,000. The populations of the state's largest centers are (starting from the most populous) Billings (81,151), Great Falls (55,097), Missoula (42,918), Butte-Silver Bow (33,336), Helena (24,569), Bozeman (22,660), Kalispell (11,917), Orchard Homes (10,317), Anaconda-Deer Lodge County (10,278), and Havre (10,201).

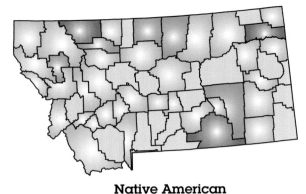

Native American

Presence of Native Americans

Minor

Moderate

Significant

The Native American population in Montana was 47,679 in 1990. This was an increase of 26.73 percent from 37,623 in 1980. Montana has many Indian reservations. The largest include the Crow, Ft. Peck, Blackfeet, Flathead, Ft. Belknap, and Rocky Boys. Most of Montana's Native American population can be found living on these reservations.

Nationalities

African	111
American	24,188
Arab	918
Austrian	3,470
Czech	6,144
Dutch	14,707
English	83,900
Finnish	5,231
German	223,702
Greek	1,431
Hungarian	1,637
Irish	79,599
Italian	14,828
Norwegian	61,423
Polish	10,138
Portuguese	955
Russian	3,510
Scottish	17,155
Slovak	2,506
Swedish	22,248
Welsh	4,534
West Indian	62

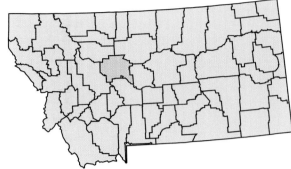

African American

Percent of County Population

0.00 to 1.32%

1.33 to 1.99%

The African American population in Montana was 2,381 in 1990. This was an increase of 37.00 percent from 1,738 in 1980. Most of these African Americans can be found living in the large cities, including Great Falls, Billings, and Helena. The largest African American community can be found in Great Falls, which has an African American population of 531.

Statewide Ethnic Composition

Over 92 percent of the population of Montana is white. The largest nationalities in this racial group are German, English, and Irish. The next largest groups are Native Americans, Hispanics, Asian Americans, and African Americans. Over 24,000 people claim to be American and acknowledge no other nationality.

White (92.74%)

African American (0.25%)

Asian American (0.50%)

Hispanic (1.50%)

Native American (6.01%)

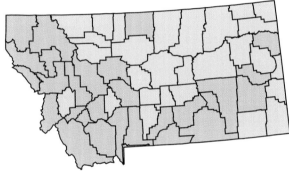

Hispanic[††]

Percent of County Population

0.00 to 0.99%

1.00 to 2.99%

The Hispanic population in Montana was 12,174 in 1990. This is an increase of 22.06 percent from 9,974 persons in 1980. Most of the Hispanic population in located in the southwestern portion of the state as well as in the southern section.

[††]A person of Mexican, Puerto Rican, Cuban, or other Spanish culture or origin regardless of race.

Education Facts

Total Students 1990: 151,265

Number of School Districts: 548

Expenditure Per Capita on Education 1990: $801

Expenditure Per Capita K–12 1990: $733

Expenditure Per Pupil 1990: $4,794

Total School Enrollment 1990–1991: 151,669

Rank of Expenditures Per Student: 28th in the U.S.

African American Enrollment: 0.3%

Hispanic Enrollment: 0.9%

Asian/Pacific Islander Enrollment: 0.5%

Native American Enrollment: 5.5%

Mean SAT Score 1991 Verbal: 464

Mean SAT Score 1991 Math: 518

Average Teacher's Salary 1992: $27,600

Rank Teacher's Salary: 38th in U.S.

High School Graduates 1990: 9,000

Total Number of Public Schools: 758

Number of Teachers 1990: 9,660

Student/Teacher Ratio: 15.7

Staff Employed in Public Schools: 12,543

Pupil/Staff Ratio: 12.1

Staff/Teacher Ratio: 1.3

Education

Attainment: 83.6 percent of population 25 years or older were high school graduates in 1989, earning Montana a ranking of 8th in the United States; 21.1 percent of the state's population had completed college. Institutions of Higher Education: The largest universities and colleges in the state include the University of Montana, Missoula; Montana State University, Bozeman; Eastern Montana College, Billings; Northern Montana College, Havre; Western Montana College, Dillon; and Montana College of Mineral Science and Technology, Butte; Carroll College, at Helena; College of Great Falls, Great Falls; Rocky Mountain College, Billings. Expenditures per Student: Expenditure increased 82% between 1985 and 1990. Projected High School Graduations: 1998 (9,947), 2004 (8,694); Total Revenues for Education from Federal Sources: $49 million; Total Revenues for Education from State Sources: $302 million; Total Revenues for Education from Local Sources: $284 million; Average Annual Salaries for Public School Principals: N/A.

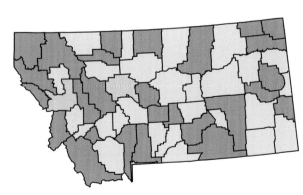

Asian American

Percent of County Population

0.00 to 0.24%

0.25 to 0.99%

1.00 to 1.99%

The Asian American population in Montana was 4,259 in 1990. This is an increase of 45.01 percent from 2,937 persons in 1980. The Asian American population is less centralized than the Hispanic population as can be seen on this map.

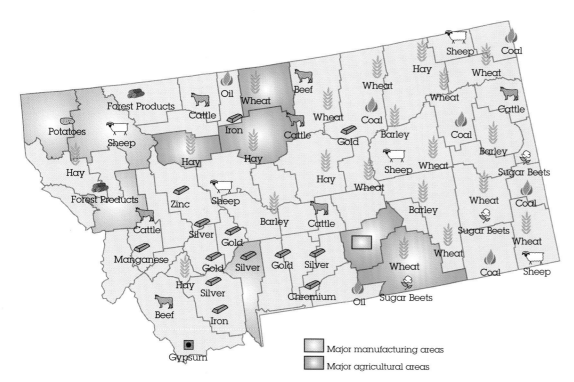

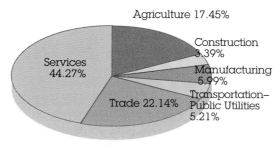

Major manufacturing areas

Major agricultural areas

Agriculture

Montana has 59.9 million farm acres. During the last 40 years, Montana's farms have grown larger in size and fewer in number. In 1955, 33,000 farms were found in the state. Today, 24,500 remain. Agriculture adds $1 billion to the state's gross product annually. The principal commodities in order of marketing receipts are cattle, wheat, barley, and hay.

Livestock and livestock products account for about 59 percent of Montana's farm income, of which beef cattle are the most important. Dairy cattle, sheep, and hogs are also raised on the state's large ranches. Wheat is the leading crop, grown primarily in the northern parts of the state. The Great Falls area grows most of the barley. Other important crops include potatoes and sugar beets.

Housing

Owner Occupied Units: 361,155; Average Age of Units: 29 years; Average Value of Housing Units: $56,600; Renter Occupied Units: 93,906; Median Monthly Rent: $311; Housing Starts: 3,500; Existing Home Sales: 16,200.

Economic Facts

Gross State Product: $14,000,000,000 (1989)

Income Per Capita: $16,062

Disposable Personal Income: $14,064

Median Household Income: $22,988

Average Annual Pay, 1988: $18,648

Principal Industries: food products, wood products, mineral products, chemicals, cement, recreational equipment

Major Crops: wheat, barley, hay, cherries, alfalfa, sugar beets, oats, lumber

Fish: Trout, Grayling

Livestock: cattle, sheep, hogs

Non-Fuel Minerals: Molybdenum, Pallacium, Copper, Gold, Lead, Platinum, Zinc, Barite, Clay

Organic Fuel Minerals: Petroleum, Coal

Civilian Labor Force: 403,000 (Women: 186,000)

Total Employed: 375,000 (Women: 174,000)

Median Value of Housing: $56,600

Median Contract Rent: $311 per month

Economic Sectors 1992

Agriculture 17.45%

Construction 3.39%

Services 44.27%

Manufacturing 5.99%

Transportation-Public Utilities 5.21%

Trade 22.14%

Manufacturing

Montana's manufacturing sector relies heavily on the state's natural resources, as the bulk of Montana's manufactured goods are produced from these resources. Lumber and wood products comprise the greatest percentage of Montana's manufactured products, approximately one third. Aside from natural resource processing, Montana industries include food processing, paper products, and concrete.

Montana has over 70 sawmills, mostly located in the western part of the state. Flathead, Lincoln, and Missoula counties produce much of Montana's lumber. Besides lumber, Montana produces pencils and telephone poles. The food processing and concrete industries are centered in two Montana cities, Billings and Great Falls. Billings also has a large petroleum refinery.

Transportation

Transportation routes in Montana primarily follow three river valleys: the Yellowstone, Missouri, and Clark. Three interstates, the 94, 15, and 90, follow these rivers, respectively. Overall, Montana has approximately 71,000 miles of roads and highways; however, only 60 percent are surfaced roadways.

Railroads have historically carried freight as well as passengers across Montana. The state's first railroad, the Utah & Northern, entered Montana in 1880. Today, the state is served by three freight railroads. Furthermore, 10 cities in Montana receive passenger rail service through Amtrak. Montana does not have any significant water transportation routes. Fort Benton was once served via river, but the Missouri River has since been dammed. Montana's larger airports can be found in Billings.

Energy and Transportation Facts

Energy. Yearly Consumption: 342 tril. BTUs (residential, 17.8%; commercial, 15.2%; industrial, 42.7%; transportation, 24.3%); Annual Energy Expenditures Per Capita: $2,096; Nuclear Power Plants Located in State: 0; Source of Energy Consumed: Petroleum— 29.2%; Natural Gas— 9.5%; Coal— 36.3%; Hydroelectric Power—25.0%; Nuclear Power—0.0%.

Transportation. Highway Miles: 70,357 (interstates, 1,191; urban, 2,348; rural, 68,009); Average Yearly Auto Insurance: $393 (45th); Auto Fatalities Rank: 16th; Registered Motor Vehicles: 906,789; Workers in Carpools: 16.6%; Workers Using Public Trans: 0.6%.

Employment

Employment. Montana employed 401,000 people in 1993. Most work in social and personal services (87,500 persons or 21.8% of the workforce). Manufacturing accounts for 5.7% or 22,900 workers. Wholesale and retail trade account for 21.7% or 87,200 workers. Government employs 74,300 workers (18.5%). Construction employs 13,700 workers (3.4%). Transportation and utilities account for 5.1% or 20,300 persons. Agriculture employs 38,500 workers or 9.6%. Finance, real estate, and insurance account for 3.7% or 14,800 workers. Mining employs 5,700 people and accounts for only 1.4% of the work force.

Unemployment. Unemployment has decreased to 6.0% in 1993 from a rate of 7.7% in 1985. Today's figure is lower than the national average of 6.8% as shown below.

Unemployment Rate

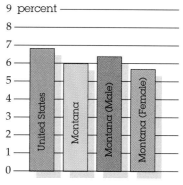

NEBRASKA
The State of Nebraska

Official State Seal

The Great Seal of Nebraska was adopted in 1867. It contains the date of Nebraska's admittance to the Union as well as the state motto, "Equality before the law." A train can be seen in the distance heading toward the Rocky Mountains. A blacksmith hammering on an anvil is placed in the foreground.

Legal Holidays

January: New Year's Day–1st; Martin Luther King, Jr., Day—3rd Monday; February: Abraham Lincoln's Birthday—12th; Presidents' Day—3rd Monday; March: Admission Day—1st; April: Arbor Day—22d; May: Memorial Day—4th Monday; July: Independence Day—4th; September: Labor Day—1st Monday; October: Columbus Day—2nd Monday; November: Admission Day—8th; Veterans' Day—11th; Thanksgiving—4th Thursday; December: Christmas—25th.

Official State Flag

Adopted as a state banner in 1925, the flag of Nebraska was not designated as official until 1963. This present design carries the state seal on a blue background. In World War I, hand-sewn flags with this look were given to troops sent to Europe from Nebraska.

Festivals and Events

January: Winter Festival, Omaha; February: Crane Watch, Kearney; March: Wings Over the Platte, Grand Island; April: Arbor Day Fair/Festival, Nebraska City; May: Lady Vestey Fest, Superior; June: Clarkson Czech Fest, Clarkson; Grundlovfest, Danneborg; July: Blue River Fest, Crete, Klown Karnival, Plainview; August: Cobblestone Fest, Falls City; September: Applejack Festival, Nebraska City; Curtis Fall Fest, Curtis; October: Harvest of Harmony, Grand Island; November: Gingerbread Village, Omaha; December: Christmas on the Prairie, Wahoo.

Sources of Information. Tourism, Government & History: Department of Economic Development, Tourism Division, Box 94666, Lincoln, NE 68509. Economy: Department of Economic Development, Industrial Development Division, Box 94666, Lincoln, NE 68509.

Location, Size, and Boundaries

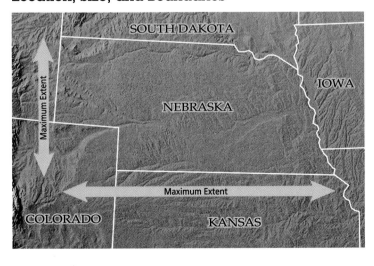

Nebraska's Finances

Households: 602,000; Income Per Capita Current Dollars: $19,084; Change Per Capita Income 1980 to 1992: 112.3% (14th in U.S.); State Expenditures: $3,535,000,000; State Revenues: $3,526,000,000; Personal Income Tax: 2.37 to 6.92%; Federal Income Taxes Paid Per Capita: $1,592; Sales Tax: 5% (food and prescription drugs exempt).

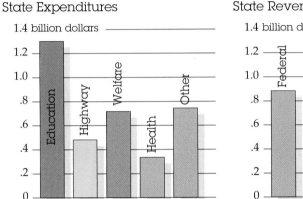

State Expenditures / State Revenues

Nebraska Compared to Other States. Resident Pop. in Metro Areas: 37th; Pop. Percent Increase: 33d; Pop. Over 65: 9th; Infant Mortality: 34th; School Enroll. Increase: 40th; High School Grad. and Up: 8th; Violent Crime: 36th; Hazardous Waste Sites: 33d; Unemployment: 50th; Median Household Income: 37th; Persons Below Poverty: 32d; Energy Costs Per Person: 20th.

Location, Size, and Boundaries

Location. Nebraska is located in the West North Central region of the United States. It is bounded on four sides by land. The geographic center of Nebraska is lat. 41° 31.5' N; long. 99° 51.7' W.

Size. Nebraska is the 15th largest state in terms of size. Its area is 77,227 sq. mi. (200,018 km2). Inland water covers 744 sq. mi. (1,927 km2).

Boundaries. South Dakota, land: 281 mi. (452 km); Missouri River, 140 mi. (225 km); Iowa, 181 mi. (291 km); Missouri, 63 mi. (101 km); Kansas, 355 mi. (571 km); Colorado, 173 mi. (279 km); Wyoming, 139 mi. (224 km).

Geographic Extent. The north/south extent of Nebraska is 205 mi. (330 km). The state extends 415 mi. (668 km) to the east/west.

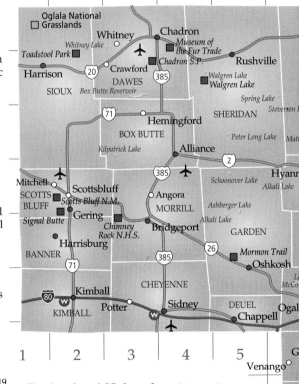

Major Cities

Beatrice	I-18	Lincoln	G-19
Bellevue	F-21	Norfolk	D-17
Columbus	E-17	North Platte	F-9
Fremont	E-19	Omaha	F-21
Grand Is.	G-15	Papillion	F-20
Hastings	H-15	Scottsbluff	D-2
Kearney	H-13		

Facts about Nebraska. Origin of Name: After the *Oto* Indian word *nebrathka*, for the Platte River, meaning *flat water*; Nickname: The Cornhusker State; Motto: "Equality before the law"; Abbreviations: Nebr. or Neb. (traditional), NE (postal); State Bird: Western meadowlark; State Tree: cottonwood; State Flower: goldenrod; State Song: "Beautiful Nebraska," words by Jim Fras and Guy G. Miller and music by Jim Fras.

6

Nebraska Compared to States in Its Region.

Resident Pop. in Metro Areas: 4th; Pop. Percent Increase: 4th; Pop. Over 65: 4th; Infant Mortality: 4th; School Enroll. Increase: 5th; High School Grad. and Up: 2d; Violent Crime: 3d; Hazardous Waste Sites: 4th; Unemployment: 7th; Median Household Income: 5th; Persons Below Poverty: 5th; Energy Costs Per Person: 3d.

West North Central Region

	Population	Capital
Minnesota	4,517,000	St. Paul
Iowa	2,814,000	Des Moines
Missouri	5,234,000	Jefferson City
North Dakota	635,000	Bismarck
South Dakota	715,000	Pierre
Nebraska	1,607,000	Lincoln
Kansas	2,531,000	Topeka

Legend

⭐ State capitol

⊙ Cities over 35,000 population

○ Other significant cities

● County Seats

■ Major cultural attractions

▢ State Parks

Ⓦ Welcome Centers

⚲ Major colleges and universities

■ **Arbor Lodge Historical Park.** Site of the mansion of the founder of Arbor Day, J. Sterling Morton. (H-21)

■ **Ashfall Fossil Beds State Historic Park.** Major deposit site for volcanic ash. Fossilized remains of 10 million year old mammals. (B-15)

■ **Chadron State Park.** Big game and wild turkey seasons. Camping in the Pine Ridge. (B-3)

■ **Chimney Rock National Historic Site.** 300-foot (91 meter) sandstone shaft on the Oregon Trail. (E-3)

■ **Fort Calhoun.** The first United States fort west of the Missouri River (1819). Major stop for the fur trade and western expansion. (E-20)

■ **Fort Kearney State Historical Park.** Important outpost on the Oregon Trail. Re-created buildings such as a stockade and a blacksmith shop. (H-13)

■ **Fort McPherson National Cemetery.** An Army post built in 1863 on the Oregon Trail. Now the only national cemetery in the state. (G-9)

■ **Fort Niobrara National Wildlife Refuge.** Refuge for buffalo, antelope, elk, and Texas longhorn cattle. (A-10)

■ **John Brown's Cave.** Cave and cabin which was used by slaves on the Underground Railway. (H-21)

■ **Lake C. W. McConaughy.** The largest lake on the North Platte River. Camping, boating, and fishing. (F-6)

■ **Museum of the Fur Trade.** Museum dedicated to fur trade. Site of 1841 Bordeaux Trading Post. (A-4)

■ **Oregon and Mormon Trails.** Trails traveled for western expansion. U.S. highways 30 and 26 run parallel to these trails. (G-15) (E-5)

■ **Ponca State Park.** High bluffs overlooking the Missouri River. From Lookout Point three states can be seen. (B-19)

■ **Scotts Bluff National Monument.** A landmark on the Oregon Trail about 800 feet (244 meters) high. (D-2)

■ **Scouts Rest Ranch Historical Park.** The home of William "Buffalo Bill" Cody. (F-9)

■ **Signal Butte.** An Oregon Trail landmark. (D-2)

■ **Toadstool Park.** Site of eroded rocks which resemble large stone mushrooms. (B-2)

■ **Walgren Lake State Recreation Area.** Home of a creature resembling the Loch Ness monster. (B-4)

■ **Willa Cather Home.** Childhood home of the Pulitzer Prize-winning novelist who wrote about pioneers. (I-14)

■ **Winnebago Indian Reservation.** Indian Winter Feast and Medicine dance performed at the annual July powwow. (C-19)

Scale

0	20	40	60 mi.

| 20 | 0 | 20 | 40 | 60 | 80 km |

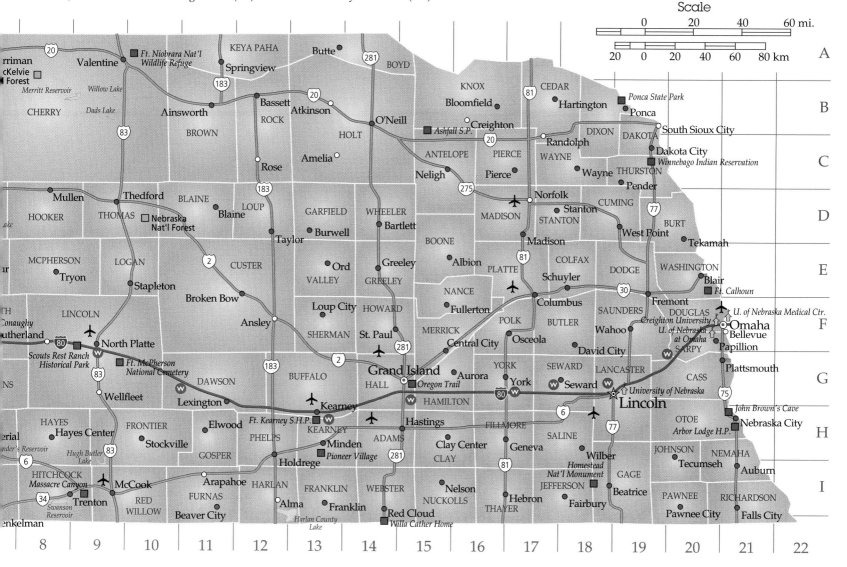

Weather Facts

Record High Temperature: 118° F (48° C) on July 24, 1936, at Minden; Record Low Temperature: -47° F (-44° C) on February 12, 1899, at Camp Clarke; Average January Temperature: 22° F (-6° C); Average July Temperature: 77° F (25° C); Average Yearly Precipitation: 23 in. (58 cm).

Environmental Facts

Air Pollution Rank: 34th; Water Pollution Rank: 33d; Total Yearly Industrial Pollution: 13,130,662 lbs.; Industrial Pollution Rank: 38th; Hazardous Waste Sites: 8; Hazardous Sites Rank: 39th; Landfill Capacity: overextended; Fresh Water Supply: surplus; Daily Residential Water Consumption: 217 gals. per capita; Endangered Species: Aquatic Species (2)—clubshell, southern; Birds (4)—crane, whooping; Mammals (1)—ferret, black-footed; Plants (2)—orchid, western prairie fringed.

Environmental Quality

Nebraska residents generate 1.1 million tons of solid waste each year, or approximately 1,400 pounds per capita. Landfill capacity in Nebraska will be exhausted in more than 12 years. The state has 6 hazardous waste sites. Annual greenhouse gas emissions in Nebraska total 39.6 million tons, or 24.8 tons per capita. Industrial sources in Nebraska release approximately 9.7 thousand tons of toxins, 136.9 thousand tons of acid precipitation-producing substances, and 700 thousand tons of smog-producing substances into the atmosphere each year.

The state has 5,900 acres within the National Park System. Chimney Rock National Historic Site is one of the more noteworthy areas in the state. State parks cover just over 139,000 acres, attracting 9.2 million visitors per year.

Nebraska spends approximately 1.3 percent of its budget, or approximately $17 per capita, on environmental and natural resources.

Average Monthly Weather

North Platte	Jan	Feb	Mar	Apr	May	Jun	Jul	Aug	Sep	Oct	Nov	Dec	Yearly
Maximum Temperature °F	34.2	40.5	47.8	61.5	71.5	81.6	87.8	86.4	77.3	66.7	49.4	39.3	62.0
Minimum Temperature °F	8.3	14.1	21.5	33.6	44.8	55.0	60.6	58.3	46.5	33.7	20.5	12.5	34.1
Days of Precipitation	5.0	5.5	6.9	7.9	10.9	9.3	9.6	7.7	6.7	4.9	4.7	4.4	83.4
Omaha													
Maximum Temperature °F	30.2	37.3	47.7	64.0	74.7	84.2	88.5	86.2	77.5	67.0	50.3	36.9	62.0
Minimum Temperature °F	10.2	17.1	26.9	40.3	51.8	61.7	66.8	64.2	54.0	42.0	28.6	17.4	40.1
Days of Precipitation	6.3	6.6	8.5	9.5	11.6	10.5	8.9	9.1	8.5	6.5	5.5	6.3	97.9

Flora and Fauna

Nebraska has the second lowest percentage of land covered by forests—approximately 2 percent—in the nation. Although the percentage of trees in Nebraska is small, the variety is quite large. Basswood, ash, hackberry, and box elder trees grow in eastern Nebraska, while pine ands cedar trees grow in the western part of the state. Differences also exist among the grasses growing in eastern and western Nebraska. Taller prairie grass grows in the east, while shorter grama grass grows in the west. The chokecherry is one of Nebraska's most common shrubs. Wildflowers bloom through much of the year in Nebraska: evening primroses and violets in the spring, spiderworts in the summer, and sunflowers in the fall.

Small animals dominate the Nebraska wildlife population. Such animals include prairie dogs, badgers, coyotes, and squirrels. Mule deer also live in the state, but other large animals common during the settlement period in the 19th century, such as bison, are all gone. Many game birds, including quail and geese, live throughout Nebraska. Catfish, carp, pike, and perch all live in Nebraska's rivers, streams, and lakes.

Physical Regions: (a) Dissected Till Plains; (b) Great Plains.

Topography

Nebraska lies entirely within the plains. In the east is the Dissected Till Plains physical region, drained by the Missouri River and its tributaries. This lowland area of rolling hills is interspersed with many streams. The fertile, warm, and moist loamy fine sand soil makes this area ideal for agriculture.

Most of Nebraska is covered by the Great Plains physical region with its characteristic warm and moist organically rich brown soil. All of the area east of the Dissected Till Plains falls within this region. The slope of the land rises gradually from east to west

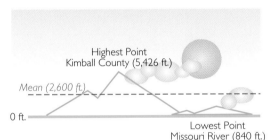

Highest Point
Kimball County (5,426 ft.)

Mean (2,600 ft.)

0 ft.

Lowest Point
Missouri River (840 ft.)

Land Use

Cropland: 42.7%; Pasture: 4.1%; Rangeland: 47.5%; Forest: 1.5%; Urban: 2.6%; Other: 1.6%.

For more information about Nebraska's environment, contact the Department of Environmental Control, 301 Centennial Mall South, Lincoln, NE 68509.

in this vast prairie of flat land, which gives way in the extreme west to the High Plains. This area, close to the Wyoming and Colorado borders, has the highest elevations in the state. The high point reaches 5,426 ft. (1,654 m) above sea level. A section of the Great Plains in the north-central region of the state is known as Sand Hills. This area, covering some 19,000 sq. miles (49,210 sq. km), is a large region of sand dunes held in place by grasses. The abundance of grasses makes this area ideal for grazing. The Badlands of South Dakota reach into Nebraska in the northwest corner of the state.

Climate

As with other landlocked states, Nebraska's climate changes drastically throughout the year. The state's continental climate is characterized by hot summers and cold winters. The mildest weather in Nebraska is in the south-central part of the state, while northeastern Nebraska, where Norfolk is located, has the coldest weather. Temperatures in Nebraska can range from over 100 degrees F to -25 degrees F. However, average January and July temperatures are around 23 degrees F and 76 degrees F.

Nebraska receives little precipitation compared to other states. Northeastern Nebraska receives approximately 36 inches of annual precipitation, while the state's panhandle, in cities like Scottsbluff, only gets around 15 inches a year. Over three-quarters of the state's annual rainfall falls between April and September.

Nebraska's plains topography makes it an ideal target for violent storms. Tornadoes are quite common in the spring months, as are hail and thunderstorms.

Hydrology

The Mississippi River forms the northeastern boundary of Nebraska with South Dakota, and the eastern boundary with Iowa and Missouri. The most important river in Nebraska is the Platte. The North Platte enters the state from Wyoming, and the South Platte from Colorado. They meet near the town of North Platte to form the Platte, which winds its way eastward across central and southern Nebraska before emptying into the Mississippi a bit south of Omaha. The Loup and the Elkhorn are the main tributaries of the Platte, together draining much of northeast Nebraska. The Republican River flows for about 190 mi. (306 km) through the southern part of the state, and the Niobrara flows across much of northern Nebraska.

All of the large lakes in Nebraska are man-made. The largest of these is Lake McConaughy on the North Platte River, covering about 60 sq. mi. (97 sq. km). Others include Swanson Lake on the Republican River, and Hugh Butler Lake.

Nebraska's History

Nebraska's First People

According to archaeological evidence, the area now known as Nebraska has been inhabited by humans for at least twelve thousand years. Nomadic Paleo-Indians roamed the Nebraska prairies during this prehistoric time. Later inhabitants became more settled in one place, and cultivated crops such as corn and beans. Although very little physical evidence is available, it is believed that several groups of people traversed Nebraska's land in these early years.

The Nebraska area was plagued by drought and wind storms before the sixteenth century, forcing many inhabitants to leave. The first Native American tribe to have a recorded existence in Nebraska is the Pawnee. In the sixteenth and seventeenth centuries, other tribes came to Nebraska from the east, some in search of new hunting grounds, others fleeing enemy tribes. Europeans who came to Nebraska later met with numerous other tribes, such as the Arapaho, Ponca, Omaha, Oto, Cheyenne, and Sioux.

Exploration and Settlement

A party of Spanish soldiers, led by Pedro de Villasur, were the first known Europeans to enter the area.

Spain, France, and Mexico struggled for possession of the region that included modern-day Nebraska. However, the United States gained control of Nebraska in 1803, when Thomas Jefferson acquired the territory from France in the Louisiana Purchase. After the purchase, various expeditions were undertaken in the area at Jefferson's request, including those of Lewis and Clark and Stephen Long. Long declared that the land west of the Missouri River, including Nebraska, was unfit for human habitation; famously calling it the "Great American Desert."

White settlement west of the Missouri River was forbidden under the 1834 Indian Intercourse Act, but white Americans could cross the area on the way to the West, and thousands of people did. From 1840 to 1866, over 300,000 people passed through present-day Nebraska on their way west.

The territory of Nebraska was not established until 1854, under the Kansas-Nebraska Act. Nebraska Territory was huge, stretching from Kansas all the way to Canada, and from the Rocky Mountains to the Missouri River. In 1861, the present shape of Nebraska became the new territory boundaries.

Territorial Period and Statehood

Once Nebraska Territory was created, conflicts with Native American tribes flared up. New land for the ever-increasing number of settlers was needed, so Indians were forced to cede most of their land, which had once been protected. By 1890, the Native Americans who remained in Nebraska were moved to reservations.

Settlers came to Nebraska rapidly and in great numbers for four primary reasons. Because of the 1862 Homestead Act, under which the U.S. government granted a homesteader 160 acres of land for a small fee, many farmers were now able to afford to move west. Second, when the Union Pacific Railroad crossed into Nebraska it opened up the territory, making it even more accessible for more people. Third, after the Civil War, many veterans came to Nebraska to settle and take advantage of the open space. Finally, the Burlington Road, which came to Nebraska in the 1860s, promoted immigration to the area using land grants from Congress.

Nebraska was officially admitted to the Union as the thirty-seventh state on March 1, 1867. In the territorial period, Omaha was the capital of Nebraska, but after the granting of statehood legislators moved the capital to Lincoln.

The first state constitution was adopted in 1866, and a second on October 12, 1875, but the document has undergone numerous changes. Nebraska's state government is unique in the fact that, since 1934, it has had a unicameral legislature.

Economic Development

During the time of homesteader settlements, corn was the major crop produced. Today corn is still widely grown, along with soybeans, barley, sorghum, wheat, and rye. Cattle and hog ranching has been conducted since 1859. Overall, more than one-half of the state's population is employed in some industry related to agriculture.

Nebraska's mineral resources are also important to its economy. Petroleum, discovered in the state in 1939, is now the leading mineral produced in Nebraska. Crude oil as well as natural gas can be found in the western panhandle of the state.

Down on the Farm

Although some early Nebraska settlers considered the state a "Great American Desert" as Stephen Long did, others saw it as a "Garden of the World," referring to the fertile agricultural soil.

Farming is a way of life for people live in Nebraska. Over half of the population makes a living from agriculture and it's related industries.

Although farming has existed in Nebraska since the territory was settled, it has greatly expanded since World War II. The size of farms has increased dramatically, yet the number of farms themselves has subsequently decreased.

In recent years, several hardships have affected Nebraska farmers. Because of the national agricultural crisis of the mid-1980s, the state's economy suffered. Banks did not want to finance farms, which were seen as a risky investment. By the late 1980s, however, Nebraska's economy had improved and land values increased. The future for farming in Nebraska looks rather promising.

Important Events

1682 The Sieur de La Salle claims land for France, part of which is present-day Nebraska.

1720 Indians defeat Spanish along the Platte River.

1763 French and Indian War ends; possession of Nebraska shifts from France to Spain.

1803 United States receives part of Nebraska in the Louisiana Purchase.

1804 Lewis and Clark explore Nebraska region.

1820 Missouri Compromise passed; prohibits slavery in Nebraska.

1823 First permanent white settlement established at Bellevue.

1834 The 1834 Indian Intercourse Act prevented white settlement on land west of the Missouri river.

1847 Mormon Trail opened for travel.

1854 The territory of Nebraska established under the Kansas-Nebraska Act.

1861 Nebraska's present boundaries are fixed.

1862 Homestead Act passed; settlement encouraged in Nebraska.

1865 Union Pacific Railroad begins construction in Nebraska.

1866 The first state constitution adopted.

1867 Nebraska becomes thirty-seventh state of the Union on March 1.

1875 State constitution (second) adopted.

1890 The remaining Native Americans are moved to reservations.

1904 Kinkaid Homestead Act passed.

1934 Nebraska legislature adopts a unicameral form.

1948 Strategic Air Command established at Offutt AFB near Omaha.

1968 University of Nebraska college system established.

1980s The economy of the state suffers as a result of the national agricultural crisis.

1989 Omaha becomes the telemarketing capital of the United States as a result of the state's tax breaks and incentives.

1991 Sen. Bob Kerrey (Democrat) decides to run for president and later drops out of the race.

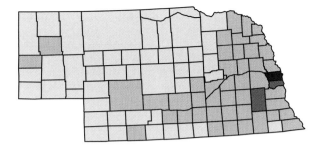

Persons Per Square Mile

- 0.0 to 9.0
- 10.0 to 99.9
- 250.0 to 749.9
- 750.0 to 1,999.9

Population Density

Population density for the state of Nebraska was 20.5 persons per square mile in 1990 (7.9 per km2). Average U.S. density was 70.3 persons per square mile in 1990 (27.3 per km2). Habitation is most dense in and around the urban area of Omaha. The capital, Lincoln, also has a high population density. As you travel west the population density declines until densities of less than 9.0 are found.

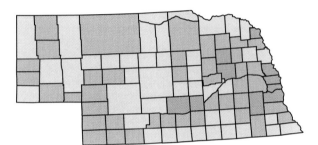

Percent Change 1980 to 1990

- –31.9 to –10.0%
- –9.9 to 0.0%
- 0.1 to 19.9%

Population Change

The 1990 population figure for the state of Nebraska was 1,578,385. This is a 0.55 percent increase from 1,569,825 in 1980. The next decade will show a loss with a population of 1.56 million or a –1.42 percent decrease. Most of the state showed a decrease in population in the last decade. A few cities in the east showed a small increase such as Omaha and Lincoln.

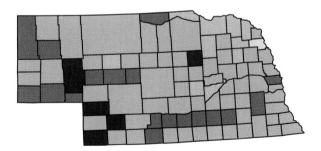

Per Capita Income (000s) (Current Dollars)

- $4.5 to 9.9
- $10.0 to 12.9
- $13.0 to 15.9
- $16.0 to 19.9
- $20.0 to 37.7

Distribution of Income

The per capita income for the state of Nebraska (current dollars) was $19,084 in 1992. This is a 112.3 percent increase from $8,988 in 1980. Incomes of $20,000 or more exist in a few counties located mostly in the western region of the state. This region is an oil-and gas-producing region as well as an agricultural basin growing such crops as sugar beets.

Population Projections

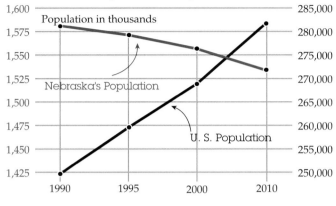

Population Facts

State Population, 1993: 1,607,000

Rank: 37

Population 2000: 1,556,000 (Rank 37)

Density: 20.5 per sq. mi. (7.9 per km2)

Distribution: 66.1% urban, 33.9% rural

Population Under 5 Years Old: 7.4%

Population Under 18 Years Old: 27.3%

Population Over 65 Years Old: 14.1%

Median Age: 33.0

Number of Households: 602,000

Average Persons Per Household: 2.54

Average Persons Per Family: 3.11

Female Heads of Households: 3.18%

Population That Is Married: 22.21%

Birth Rate: 15.4 per 1,000 population

Death Rate: 9.4 per 1,000 population

Births to Teen Mothers: 9.8%

Marriage Rate: 7.7 per 1,000 population

Divorce Rate: 4.0 per 1,000 population

Violent Crime Rate: 335 per 100,000 pop.

Population on Social Security: 17.1%

Percent Voting for President: 63.2%

Population Profile

Rank. Nebraska ranks 37th among U.S. states in terms of population with 1,607,000 citizens.

Minority Population. The state's minority population is 7.6 percent. The state's male to female ratio for 1990 was 95.12 males for every 100 females. It was below the national average of 95.22 males for every 100 females.

Growth. The state's population is decreasing and is expected to be 1.5 million by the year 2010.

Government

Capital: Lincoln (established 1867).

Statehood: Became 37th state on Mar. 1, 1867.

Number of Counties: 93.

Supreme Court Justices: 7, 6-year term.

State Senators: 49, 4-year term.

State Legislators: none.

United States Senators: 2.

United States Representatives: 3.

Electoral Votes: 5.

State Constitution: Adopted 1875.

Population Change

Year	Population
1950	1,326,000
1960	1,417,000
1970	1,488,000
1980	1,569,825
1990	1,578,385
2000	1,556,000
2010	1,529,000

Period	Change
1950–1970	12.2%
1970–1980	5.5%
1980–1990	0.5%
1990–2000	–1.4%

Nebraska's Famous Citizens

Flanagan, Edward Joseph (1886–1948). Priest. Founded the Home for Homeless Boys (which became Boys Town) in 1917.

Fonda, Henry (1905–1982). Actor. Portrayed men of integrity in films such as *The Grapes of Wrath* and *Young Mr. Lincoln*.

Gibson, Bob (b. 1935). Baseball pitcher. Set a NL record with a 1.12 ERA in 1968. Won the Cy Young Award in 1968 and 1970.

Hanson, Howard (1896–1981). Composer and conductor. Director of the Eastman School of Music in Rochester from 1924 to 1964.

La Flesche, Susette (1854–1903). Omaha Indian who fought for Native American rights and wrote their stories.

Morton, J. Sterling (1832–1902). Founder of Arbor Day and U.S. secretary of agriculture (1893–1897).

Nolte, Nick (b. 1942). Actor. Known for his rugged individualism in films such as *Who'll Stop the Rain* and *Lorenzo's Oil*.

Zanuck, Darryl (1902–1979). Co-founded 20th Century Pictures in 1933, which merged with Fox Film two years later.

Older Citizens. The state's population older than 65 was 223,068 in 1990. It grew 8.45% from 205,684 in 1980.

Younger Citizens. The number of children (under 18 years of age) was 429 thousand in 1990. This represents 27.2 percent of the state's population. The state's school aged population was 271 thousand in 1990. It is expected to decrease to 268 thousand by the year 2000. This represents a –1.11% change.

Urban/Rural. 66.1% of the population of the state live in urban areas while 33.9% live in rural areas.

Largest Cities. Nebraska has three cities with a population greater than 35,000. The populations of the state's largest centers are (starting from the most populous) Omaha (335,795), Lincoln (191,972), Grand Island (39,386), Bellevue (30,982), Kearney (24,396), Fremont (23,680), Hastings (22,837), North Platte (22,605), Norfolk (21,476), Columbus (19,480), Scottsbluff (13,711), Beatrice (12,354), Offutt AFB West (10,883), and Papillion (10,372).

Nebraska

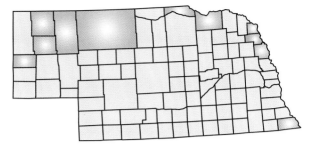

Presence of Native Americans

- ▨ Minor
- ▨ Moderate

Native American

The Native American population in Nebraska was 12,410 in 1990. This was an increase of 36.99 percent from 9,059 in 1980. Two reservations are located in Nebraska. The Santee Sioux Indian Reservation is located in Knox County in the north. The Winnebago/Omaha Indian Reservation is located in Thurston County south of Dakota City.

Nationalities

African	1,316
American	32,107
Arab	2,415
Austrian	1,691
Czech	65,601
Dutch	22,876
English	120,612
Finnish	1,028
German	672,579
Greek	2,468
Hungarian	1,968
Irish	134,010
Italian	23,759
Norwegian	18,297
Polish	41,283
Portuguese	520
Russian	4,808
Scottish	14,628
Slovak	6,278
Swedish	61,510
Welsh	5,610
West Indian	351

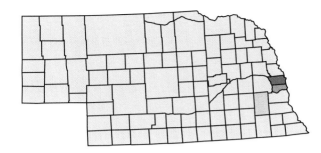

Percent of County Population

- ☐ 0.00 to 1.99%
- ☐ 2.00 to 4.99%
- ☐ 5.00 to 9.99%
- ■ 10.00 to 24.99%

African American

The African American population in Nebraska was 57,404 in 1990. This was an increase of 19.73 percent from 47,946 in 1980. The highest percentage of African Americans can be found in the city of Omaha. Seventy-seven percent of the African Americans living in Nebraska live in that city. Another area with large numbers is the city of Lincoln located in Lancaster County.

Statewide Ethnic Composition

Over 93 percent of the population of Nebraska is white. The largest nationalities in this racial group are German, Irish, and English. The next largest group is African Americans, followed by Hispanics, Asian Americans, and Native Americans. Over 32,000 people claim to be American and acknowledge no other nationality.

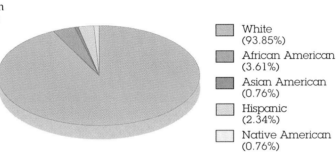

- White (93.85%)
- African American (3.61%)
- Asian American (0.76%)
- Hispanic (2.34%)
- Native American (0.76%)

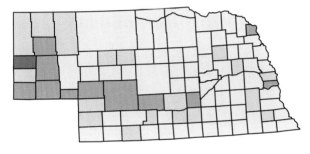

Percent of County Population

- ☐ 0.00 to 0.99%
- ☐ 1.00 to 2.99%
- ☐ 3.00 to 9.99%
- ■ 10.00 to 24.99%

Hispanic[††]

The Hispanic population in Nebraska was 36,969 in 1990. This is an increase of 31.91 percent from 28,025 persons in 1980. The area with the largest percentage of Hispanics is the county of Scotts Bluff in the western panhandle of the state.

[††]A person of Mexican, Puerto Rican, Cuban, or other Spanish culture or origin regardless of race.

Education Facts

Total Students 1990: 27,092

Number of School Districts: 838

Expenditure Per Capita on Education 1990: $652

Expenditure Per Capita K–12 1990: $612

Expenditure Per Pupil 1990: $4,080

Total School Enrollment 1990–1991: 273,002

Rank of Expenditures Per Student: 39th in the U.S.

African American Enrollment: 5.3%

Hispanic Enrollment: 2.3%

Asian/Pacific Islander Enrollment: 1.0%

Native American Enrollment: 1.1%

Mean SAT Score 1991 Verbal: 481

Mean SAT Score 1991 Math: 543

Average Teacher's Salary 1992: $27,200

Rank Teacher's Salary: 40th in U.S.

High School Graduates 1990: 18,800

Total Number of Public Schools: 1,524

Number of Teachers 1990: 18,572

Student/Teacher Ratio: 14.7

Staff Employed in Public Schools: 33,325

Pupil/Staff Ratio: 8.1

Staff/Teacher Ratio: 1.8

Education

Attainment: 82.2 percent of population 25 years or older were high school graduates in 1989, earning Nebraska a ranking of 13th in the United States; 19.7 percent of the state's population had completed college. Institutions of Higher Education: The largest universities and colleges in the state include the University of Nebraska, Lincoln; Nebraska Wesleyan University, Lincoln; Union College, Lincoln; Concordia Teachers College, Seward; Expenditures per Student: Expenditure increased 81% between 1985 and 1990. Projected High School Graduations: 1998 (19,727), 2004 (17,778); Total Revenues for Education from Federal Sources: $75 million; Total Revenues for Education from State Sources: $229 million; Total Revenues for Education from Local Sources: $730 million; Average Annual Salaries for Public School Principals: N/A; Largest School Districts in State: Omaha Public Schools, 41,251 students, 86th in the United States; Lincoln Public Schools, 27,356, 156th.

Percent of County Population

- ☐ 0.00 to 0.24%
- ☐ 0.25 to 0.99%
- ☐ 1.00 to 1.99%
- ■ 2.00 to 4.99%

Asian American

The Asian American population in Nebraska was 12,422 in 1990. This is an increase of 58.44 percent from 7,840 persons in 1980. Two areas in Nebraska have the highest percentage of Asian Americans: Johnson County, located southeast of Lincoln, and Dakota County bordering Sioux City, Iowa, in the northeastern part of the state.

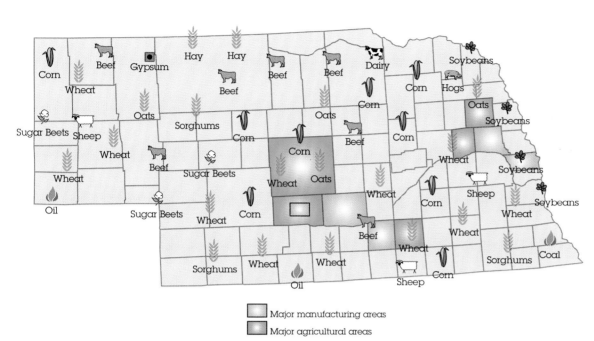

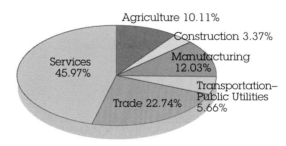

Major manufacturing areas
Major agricultural areas

Agriculture

Nebraska has 47.1 million farm acres. During the last 40 years, Nebraska's farms have grown larger in size and fewer in number. In 1955, 101,000 farms were found in the state. Today, 55,000 remain. Agriculture adds $3 billion to the state's gross product annually. The principal commodities in order of marketing receipts are cattle, corn, hogs, and soybeans.

Livestock and livestock products account for about two-thirds of Nebraska's farm income. Beef cattle graze on the Sand Hills and in the western part of the state. Hogs are found in the Tills Plains, one of the nation's leading hog-producing areas. Corn, the leading crop, is grown mainly for cattle feed. Soybeans are located in the fertile Tills Plains region. Other crops include beans, sugar, and oats.

Housing

Owner Occupied Units: 660,621; Average Age of Units: 35 years; Average Value of Housing Units: $50,400; Renter Occupied Units: 186,632; Median Monthly Rent: $348; Housing Starts: 8,500; Existing Home Sales: 23,200.

Economic Facts

Gross State Product: $31,000,000,000 (1989)

Income Per Capita: $19,084

Disposable Personal Income: $16,992

Median Household Income: $26,016

Average Annual Pay, 1988: $19,372

Principal Industries: food products, machinery, electrical equipment, chemicals

Major Crops: corn, soybeans, wheat, oats, barley, rye, sorghum

Fish: Bass, Carp, Crappies, Catfish, Perch, Pike

Livestock: hogs, cattle

Non-Fuel Minerals: Sand, Gravel, Limestone, Clay

Organic Fuel Minerals: Petroleum, Nat. Gas

Civilian Labor Force: 857,000 (Women: 395,000)

Total Employed: 834,000 (Women: 385,000)

Median Value of Housing: $50,400

Median Contract Rent: $348 per month

Economic Sectors 1992

Agriculture 10.11%
Construction 3.37%
Manufacturing 12.03%
Transportation–Public Utilities 5.66%
Trade 22.74%
Services 45.97%

Manufacturing

Throughout history, Nebraska's manufacturing sector has been closely tied to agriculture, for many industries deal with agricultural products in some way. Recently, the state's manufacturing industries have become more diversified. However, food processing is still the number one manufacturing activity in Nebraska. Machinery and electrical products rank second and third among the state's manufactured products.

Most of Nebraska's food processing takes place in Omaha. Both grain processing and meat packing are important Omaha industries. Food processing also takes place in Dakota City, Grand Island, and Freeport. Other Nebraska towns manufacture farm equipment, the most important machinery product (Gering), and switching devices (Lincoln).

Transportation

Historically, Nebraska has been a well-traveled state. Many national roads cross Nebraska, bringing large numbers of tourists to the state. Nebraska has approximately 96,000 miles of highways and roads. Interstate 80, which runs the east-west length of the state, is Nebraska's most important highway.

Nebraska has also traditionally been a rail center; the first section of the transcontinental railroad originated in Omaha. Currently, three rail lines provide freight service for the state. In addition, five Nebraska cities receive passenger rail service. Although Nebraska is a landlocked state, it does have some water transportation routes. Several cities along the Missouri River serve as river ports. Major ports include Omaha and Nebraska City. Omaha has Nebraska's busiest airport.

Energy and Transportation Facts

Energy. Yearly Consumption: 522 tril. BTUs (residential, 24.3%; commercial, 22.2%; industrial, 25.3%; transportation, 28.2%); Annual Energy Expenditures Per Capita: $1,942; Nuclear Power Plants Located in State: 2; Source of Energy Consumed: Petroleum— 36.0%; Natural Gas— 20.1%; Coal— 26.8%; Hydroelectric Power—1.9%; Nuclear Power—15.2%.

Transportation. Highway Miles: 92,686 (interstates, 481; urban, 5,030; rural, 87,656); Average Yearly Auto Insurance: $352 (49th); Auto Fatalities Rank: 19th; Registered Motor Vehicles: 1,355,050; Workers in Carpools: 14.7%; Workers Using Public Trans: 1.2%.

Employment

Employment. Nebraska employed 830,000 people in 1993. Most work in wholesale and retail trade (92,500 persons or 23.2% of the workforce). Manufacturing accounts for 12.4% or 102,900 workers. Social and personal services account for 22.67% or 187,800 workers. Government employs 74,300 workers (18.5%). Construction employs 149,500 workers (18.0%). Transportation and utilities account for 5.7% or 47,100 persons. Agriculture employs 68,900 workers or 8.3%. Finance, real estate, and insurance account for 6.1% or 50,300 workers. Mining employs 1,400 people and accounts for only 0.2% of the workforce.

Unemployment. Unemployment has decreased to 2.6% in 1993 from a rate of 5.5% in 1985. Today's figure is lower than the national average of 6.8% as shown below.

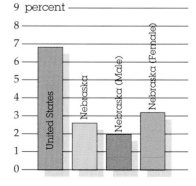

Unemployment Rate

NEVADA
The State of Nevada

Official State Seal

The Great Seal of Nevada was adopted in 1866. Symbols include a plow, mine tunnel, train, and a mill. These symbols represent Nevada's dependence on agriculture and mining. In 1915 a modified version was used on the state flag, because of the great expense needed to reproduce the original.

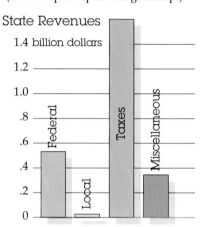

Legal Holidays

January: New Year's Day—1st; Martin Luther King, Jr., Day—3rd Monday; February: Presidents' Day—3rd Monday; May: Memorial Day—4th Monday; July: Independence Day—4th; September: Labor Day—1st Monday; October: Columbus Day—2nd Monday; Admission Day—31st; November: Veterans' Day—11th; Thanksgiving—4th Thursday; December: Christmas—25th.

Official State Flag

The state flag of Nevada was adopted in 1929. It was a design chosen from a contest with a $25 first prize. The flag consists of a silver star surrounded by sagebrush. Above the star are the words "Battle Born." All this is placed in the upper left corner of a blue field.

Festivals and Events

May: City Birthday Celebration, Reno; June: Reno Rodeo, Reno; July: National Hollerin' Contest, Jackpot; Dixieland Jazz Festival, Sparks; National Basque Festival, Elko; August: State Fair, Reno; September: Great High Sierra Chili Cook-Off, Carson City; International Whistle-Off, Carson City; October: North Las Vegas Fair Show, North Las Vegas; December: Las Vegas Mint 400, Las Vegas.

Nevada Compared to States in Its Region.

Resident Pop. in Metro Areas: 2d; Pop Percent Increase: 1st; Pop. Over 65: 4th; Infant Mortality: 5th; School Enroll. Increase: 2d; High School Grad. and Up: 6th; Violent Crime: 2d; Hazardous Waste Sites: 8th; Unemployment: 4th; Median Household Income: 1st; Persons Below Poverty: 8th; Energy Costs Per Person: 3d.

Mountain Region

	Population	Capital
Montana	839,000	Helena
Wyoming	470,000	Cheyenne
Idaho	1,099,000	Boise
Nevada	1,389,000	Carson City
Utah	1,860,000	Salt Lake City
Colorado	3,566,000	Denver
Arizona	3,936,000	Phoenix
New Mexico	1,616,000	Santa Fe

Nevada's Finances

Households: 466,000; Income Per Capita Current Dollars: $20,266; Change Per Capita Income 1980 to 1992: 75.3% (47th in U.S.); State Expenditures: $2,953,000,000; State Revenues: $2,715,000,000; Personal Income Tax: N/A; Federal Income Taxes Paid Per Capita: $2,411; Sales Tax: 5.75% (food and prescription drugs exempt).

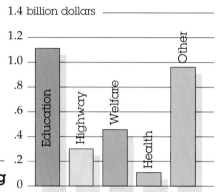

State Expenditures

State Revenues

Location, Size, and Boundaries

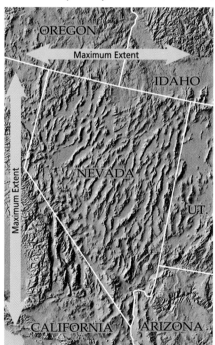

Location. Nevada is located in the western United States in the Mountain region. It is bounded on four sides by land. The geographic center of Nevada is lat. 39° 30.3' N; long. 116° 55.9' W.

Size. Nevada is the 7th largest state in terms of size. Its area is 110,540 sq. mi. (286,298 km2). Inland water covers 651 sq. mi. (1,686 km2).

Boundaries. Oregon, 155 mi. (249.5 km); Idaho, 155 mi. (249.5 km); Utah, 345 mi. (555 km); Arizona, 205 mi. (330 km); California, 628 mi. (998 km).

Geographic Extent. The north/south extent of Nevada is 483 mi. (777 km). The state extends 320 mi. (515 km) to the east/west.

Facts about Nevada. Origin of Name: From the Spanish word meaning "*snow-clad*"; Nickname: The Silver State; Motto: "All for Our Country"; Abbreviations: Nev. (traditional), NV (postal); State Bird: Mountain bluebird; State Trees: bristlecone pine and piñon; State Flower: sagebrush; State Song: "Home Means Nevada," words and music by Bertha Raffetto.

Nevada Compared to Other States. Resident Pop. in Metro Areas: 11th; Pop. Percent Increase: 1st; Pop. Over 65: 40th; Infant Mortality: 32d; School Enroll. Increase: 5th; High School Grad. and Up: 18th; Violent Crime: 17th; Haz. Waste Sites: 50th; Unemployment: 28th; Med. Household Income: 16th; Persons Below Poverty: 38th; Energy Costs Per Person: 14th.

Sources of Information. Tourism: Commission on Tourism, Capitol Complex, Carson City, NV 89710. Economy: Commission on Economic Development, Capitol Complex, Carson City, NV 89710. Government: Legislative Council Bureau, State of Nevada–Capitol Complex, Carson City, NV 89710. History: Commission on Tourism, Capitol Complex, Carson City, NV 89710.

Nevada

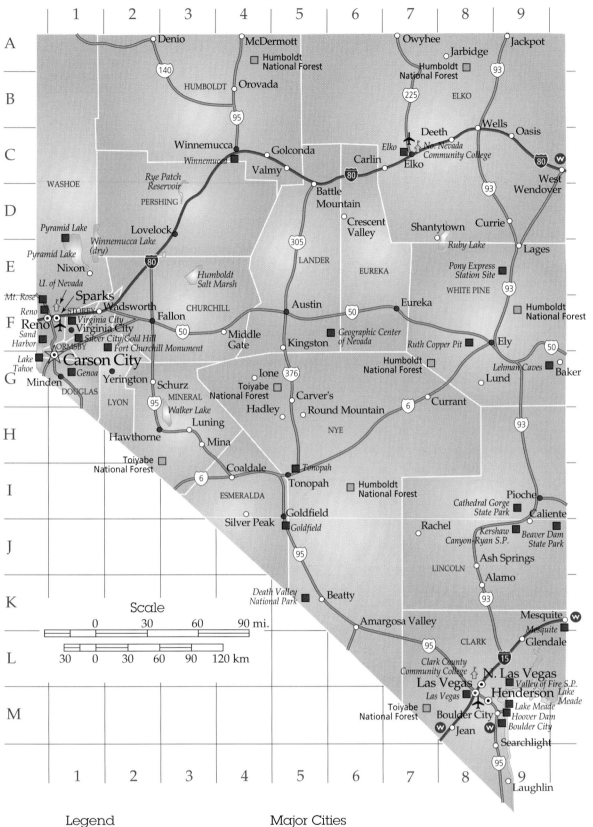

Legend

⭐ State capitol

⊙ Cities over 35,000 population

○ Other significant cities

● County Seats

■ Major cultural attractions

☐ State Parks

Ⓦ Welcome Centers

⚑ Major colleges and universities

Major Cities

Boulder City	M-9	Las Vegas	M-8
Carson City	G-1	N. Las Vegas	L-8
E. Las Vegas	M-8	Reno	F-1
Elko	C-7	Sparks	F-1
Henderson	M-8		

Scale

0   30   60   90 mi.

30   0   30   60   90   120 km

■ Beaver Dam State Park. Scenery, fishing and hunting. (J-9)

■ Boulder City. Built in the 1930s to house the builders of Hoover Dam. Now considered a center for art. (M-9)

■ Cathedral Gorge State Park. Rock formations that look like cathedral spires, also includes areas for camping. (I-9)

■ Death Valley National Park. Scenic desert wasteland. (K-5)

■ Elko. Site of the Cowboy Poetry Gathering and the National Basque Festival. (C-7)

■ Fort Churchill Monument. A military post built in 1860 to protect travelers from Indians. (F-2)

■ Genoa. Site of the pioneer government before the creation of Nevada Territory. (G-1)

■ Geographic Center of Nevada. The center of the state. (F-6)

■ Goldfield. Mining town, once the largest city in the state in 1907. (J-5)

■ Hoover Dam. Forming Lake Mead, this dam is 726 feet (221 meters) high. (M-9)

■ Kershaw Canyon-Ryan State Park. Scenic canyons and camping. (J-9)

■ Lake Mead National Recreation Area. Swimming, fishing, and other water sports. (M-9).

■ Lake Tahoe. Internationally famous resort area with skiing, boating and sitting on the beach . (G-1)

■ Las Vegas. Resort area with gambling, shows, and nightlife. (M-8)

■ Lehman Caves National Monument. Caverns with scenic chambers and tunnels of stalactites and stalagmites; now part of Great Basin National Park. (G-9)

■ Mesquite. Resort town with golfing and western hayrides. (K-10)

■ Mount Rose. Skiing and other winter sports. (F-1)

■ Pony Express Station Site. Site of a Pony Express stop. (E-9)

■ Pyramid Lake. The largest natural lake in Nevada, with fishing and water sports. Named after rock formations that resemble pyramids in the lake. (D-1)

■ Reno. Entertainment, fine hotels, museums, and restaurants. (F-1)

■ Ruth Copper Pit. One of world's largest open-pit mines. (F-8)

■ Sand Harbor. Picnicking, swimming and boating, and other water sports. (F-1)

■ Silver City/Gold Hill. Sister mining cities that developed around the Comstock Lode. Historic buildings and sites. (F-1)

■ Tonopah. Mining camp of the early 1900s which is still producing gold and silver. (I-5)

■ Valley of Fire State Park. 26,000-acre park which gets its name from the red sandstone rock formations. Also includes Indian petroglyphs. (L-9)

■ Virginia City. Site of the Comstock Lode, which was a gold and silver find made in 1859. Was once one of the richest places in the world. Includes the Virginia & Trukee Railroad. (F-1)

■ Winnemucca. Once a fur trapper's trading post, now a resort area with swimming and golf. (C-4)

Nevada

Weather Facts

Record High Temperature: 122° F (50° C) on June 23, 1954, at Overton; Record Low Temperature: -50° F (-46° C) on January 8, 1937, at San Jacinto; Average January Temperature: 31° F (-1° C); Average July Temperature: 74° F (23° C); Average Yearly Precipitation: 21 in. (53 cm).

Environmental Facts

Air Pollution Rank: 48th; Water Pollution Rank: 48th; Total Yearly Industrial Pollution: 3,646,206 lbs.; Industrial Pollution Rank: 44th; Hazardous Waste Sites: 1; Hazardous Sites Rank: 50th; Landfill Capacity: adequate; Fresh Water Supply: impending shortage; Daily Residential Water Consumption: 298 gals. per capita; Endangered Species: Aquatic Species (22)—chub, bonytail; Birds (4)—eagle, bald; Other Species (2)—tortoise, desert; Plants (10)—blazing star, ash meadows.

Environmental Quality

Nevada residents generate 1.0 million tons of solid waste each year, or approximately 2,000 pounds per capita. Landfill capacity in Nevada will be exhausted in more than 12 years. The state has 1 hazardous waste site. Annual greenhouse gas emissions in Nevada total 21.0 million tons, or 19.9 tons per capita. Industrial sources in Nevada release approximately 1.1 thousand tons of toxins, 95.9 thousand tons of acid precipitation-producing substances, and 500 thousand tons of smog-producing substances into the atmosphere each year.

The state has 700,200 acres within the National Park System; the largest area within the state is Great Basin National Park. State parks cover just over 134,000 acres, attracting 2.6 million visitors per year.

Nevada spends approximately 2.6 percent of its budget, or approximately $35 per capita, on environmental and natural resources. Nevada representatives in the U.S. House voted in favor of national environmental legislation 38 percent of the time, while U.S. senators did so 96 percent of the time.

Average Monthly Weather

Las Vegas	Jan	Feb	Mar	Apr	May	Jun	Jul	Aug	Sep	Oct	Nov	Dec	Yearly
Maximum Temperature °F	56.0	62.4	68.3	77.2	87.4	98.6	104.5	101.9	94.7	81.5	66.0	57.1	79.6
Minimum Temperature °F	33.0	37.7	42.3	49.8	59.0	68.6	75.9	73.9	65.6	53.5	41.2	33.6	52.8
Days of Precipitation	3.0	2.6	3.0	1.9	1.4	0.7	2.6	3.0	1.6	1.7	2.0	2.5	25.9

Flora and Fauna

For a predominately desert state, Nevada has a diverse tree population. Juniper and pine trees grow in the state's mountain regions. Other trees growing in Nevada include alders, willows, hemlocks, and cottonwoods. Nevada's desert vegetation varies with latitude. Salt-tolerant iodine bush and soapweed grow in the middle-latitude deserts, while creosote bush grows in deserts to the south. Nevada has meadow areas that bloom with wildflowers such as shooting stars, Indian paintbrush, and violets. Blossoms of the snow can be found in pine-forested areas.

Larger animals such as mule deer and pronghorn antelope are rather scarce in Nevada. However, several small animals such as coyotes, foxes, marmots, and porcupines live throughout the state. Desert animals include a variety of snakes and lizards. Nevada has a game bird population consisting of quail, sage hens, and chukar partridges. Pyramid Lake is home to a number of white pelicans. Nevada's few rivers and lakes contain bass, catfish, trout, and other fish. The cui-ui, once an important food fish, is found only in Pyramid Lake.

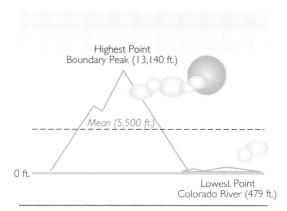

Physical Regions: (a) Columbia Plateau; (b) Sierra Nevada; (c) Basin and Range Region.

Highest Point
Boundary Peak (13,140 ft.)

Mean (5,500 ft.)

0 ft.

Lowest Point
Colorado River (479 ft.)

Land Use

Cropland: 8.7%; Pasture: 2.8%; Rangeland: 77.3%; Forest: 3.5%; Urban: 3.1%; Other: 4.6%.

For more information about Nevada's environment, contact the Division of Environmental Protection, 123 W. Nye Lane, Carson City, NV 89710.

Topography

The Basin and Range physical region is a topographical formation of mountain ranges interrupted by dry basins that covers almost the entire state of Nevada. The mountain ranges in this region are situated in a north-south direction. Some of the more prominent ranges include the Snake, Toana, and Ruby mountains in the eastern part of the state; the Santa Rosa and Toiyabe ranges in the central region; and the Wassuk, Stillwater, Humboldt, and Pine Forest ranges in the west. The highest elevations in the state are found in the southwest region. Boundary Peak, on the California border near Coaldale, which rises 13,140 ft. (4,005 m) above sea level, is the highest. Many bodies of water in the Basin areas contain saltwater, such as Carson Sink and the Humboldt Salt Marsh in the west. In the northwest, in one of the larger basins, lie the Black Rock and Smoke Creek deserts. The soil in this region is almost exclusively warm and dry, colored desert red, and low in organic content. The Columbia Plateau physical region, located in the extreme northeast, has a soil with a thin brown surface layer that has a slightly higher organic content than the desert.

The southwestern corner of the state is crossed by the Sierra Nevada physical region. The area is named for the Sierra Nevada mountain range of California. Also in this region is Lake Tahoe, which lies in both Nevada and California.

Climate

Nevada, directly in the rain shadow of the Sierra Nevada, is the driest state. The mountains prevent moisture from the Pacific Ocean from reaching Nevada. Almost half of Nevada has a desert climate, and the rest of the land has semiarid, with steppe characteristics. Southern Nevada, where Las Vegas is located, has a subtropical climate, where January and July temperatures average 43 degrees F and 86 degrees F. Farther north, around Winnemucca, temperatures for January and July average 30 degrees F and 71 degrees F.

Nevada's average statewide annual precipitation totals only 9 inches. However, the northwestern mountains receive considerably more, around 29 inches a year. Almost all of Nevada's precipitation falls during winter, except in southern Nevada.

Both northern and southern Nevada experience warm, dry weather. Because of their lower elevation and more direct exposure to sunlight, southern deserts have a warmer year-round temperature.

Hydrology

The Colorado River forms the far southeastern boundary of Nevada with Arizona. The Muddy and Virgin rivers flow into the Colorado. Several rivers flow north into Oregon or Idaho, including the Salmon and the Owyhee. The remaining rivers of Nevada drain into the Great Basin, often disappearing during dry seasons. The longest river in Nevada is the Humboldt in the north, which flows westward for about 295 mi. (475 km). Other rivers in the Great Basin include the Reese in central Nevada, and the Walker and Truckee in the west.

Nevada has several large natural lakes. The largest of these is Pyramid Lake, in western Nevada, at 290 sq. mi. (467 sq. km). Lake Tahoe, a bit south of Reno on the California border, is a popular resort. Other sizable lakes include Walker Lake on the Walker River, and Ruby Lake in eastern Nevada.

Nevada's History

Nevada's First People

About twelve thousand years ago, the first inhabitants arrived in the area that is now known as Nevada. As the glacial lakes of the Great Basin, a formation from the Ice Age, receded, fishermen, hunters and gatherers moved into Nevada. One such group, the Lovelock culture, lived in the northwest region of the state around 2000 B.C.

Throughout Nevada, evidence of early human habitation exists. Projectile points, used in hunting, have been found in numerous locations throughout the state. One of the famous sites of early human settlement is the Lost City, also known as the Pueblo Grande de Nevada.

Several different Native American tribes were present in the state until at least the nineteenth century, including the Southern Paiute, Northern Paiute, Shoshone, Gosiute, Mojave, and Washo.

European Exploration

Compared to other states, European explorers came to Nevada quite late. Francisco Garcés, a Spanish priest, was probably the first European to see southern Nevada, arriving in 1775. After Garcés, several other explorers entered the state. Peter Skene Ogden of the British Hudson's Bay Company crossed into northern Nevada in 1825. Jedediah Smith, an American trapper, explored the state between 1826 and 1827.

The land from which Nevada Territory was ultimately carved was acquired from Mexico in 1848 under the Treaty of Guadalupe Hidalgo. Originally, what is now Nevada was part of the Utah Territory. The first permanent white settlement, Mormon Station (now Genoa), was founded in 1850 in western Nevada. Other Mormon settlements sprang up around Mormon Station and in the Las Vegas valley. While the Las Vegas settlement failed, the northwestern farming communities prospered. However, conflict erupted between the

Mormons and miners who had settled in the same area. Most Mormons had left northwestern Nevada by 1857 to resettle in present-day Utah.

Statehood

Nevada Territory was established in 1861, with the 116th meridian serving as the eastern boundary. Three years later, statehood was granted, and the border was extended to the 115th meridian. Carson City has been Nevada's capital since 1861. This rapid transformation from territory to state can be attributed to two distinct events: the Civil War and the discovery of gold. When the Southern states seceded, new free states were able join the Union, for the Southern congressmen had blocked such measures previously. President Lincoln pushed for Nevada's statehood, as it would add another antislavery state to the Union. Second, the 1859 discovery of the Comstock Lode, a huge silver and gold deposit, brought thousands of people to Nevada and established the area as a thriving mining center.

Nevada adopted its constitution in 1864, the same year it achieved statehood; that original amended version continues to govern the state today. Official state boundaries were not devised until January 1867.

Industrialization

With the Comstock Lode's resources depleted by the 1870s, Nevada fell into a twenty-year depression. Despite the efforts of the Silver Party—the political party reigning during Nevada's time of depression—to combat this by increasing the value of silver, the economy of the state did not recover until the early twentieth century, when new silver deposits were found at Tonopah and gold was discovered at the appropriately named Goldfield. In addition, copper reserves were discovered in eastern Nevada during the same period. But once again, the success of mining proved to be short-lived, and Nevada was hit

hard by the Great Depression of the 1930s.

During the 1930s, many public works projects were created, including the impressive Hoover Dam. Legislation passed during this time also legalized gambling in 1931.

In the years following World War II, gambling grew rapidly, becoming the number one tourist attraction. By the end of the 1950s it was the leading industry in Nevada. For twenty years, from 1960 to 1980, Nevada was the fastest-growing state in the country, and this was almost entirely due to the even greater expansion of the gambling industries, centered in Las Vegas and Reno casinos.

The federal government also has a stronghold in Nevada. The state is home to one of the largest testing ranges in the United States, the Nellis Air Force Range and Atomic Energy Commission (AEC) Nuclear Testing Area.

High Rollers and Wedding Bells

Las Vegas is undoubtedly the city most associated with gambling in the United States. It is somewhat humorous to think that such a vice as gambling finds its number-one home in a former area of Mormon settlement. Nonetheless, millions of people flock to Las Vegas to gamble, spend the night in fairy-tale hotels, and of course—get married.

In recent years, several elaborate hotels and casinos have been built in Nevada, including the Luxor, MGM Grand, and Excalibur. These new hotels offer many added attractions besides gambling, making Las Vegas a more family-oriented vacation destination.

Countless couples come to Nevada to marry in one of the state's famous wedding chapels. Some feature drive-through window service, while others offer theme-weddings. Getting married is an all day business in Nevada. Nevada has the highest marriage rate in the United States with 105.6 per 1,000 population. The U.S. average is only 9.3 per 1,000 population.

Important Events

1775 Francisco Garcés explores southern Nevada.

1825 Peter Ogden crosses into Nevada; reaches Humboldt River.

1825 The north and central region is explored by Hudson's Bay Company trappers.

1826 Jedediah Smith, a trapper, explores the area.

1848 The Treaty of Guadalupe Hidalgo at the conclusion of the Mexican War, provides the U.S. with the Nevada territory.

1850 First permanent white settlement, Mormon Station, (now Genoa) founded.

1857 Mormons leave Nevada and resettle in Utah.

1859 Gold and silver discovered in the Comstock Lode.

1861 Nevada Territory established at the 116th meridian.

1864 October 31, Nevada becomes thirty-sixth state in the Union with borders set at the 115th meridian. In the same year, the first transcontinental telegram is sent from Nevada to Washington, D.C., showing support for the Union.

1868 Transcontinental railroad crosses into Nevada.

1875 University of Nevada established, at Élko.

1879 Sutro Tunnel, designed to drain Comstock Lode, completed.

1900 New ore deposits found at Tonopah and Goldfield.

1914 Nevada passes legislation adopting women's suffrage.

1931 Gambling legalized in Nevada. Casinos built in Las Vegas and Reno.

1935 Boulder Dam, now called Hoover Dam, completed.

1951 Atomic testing begins at Yucca Flat.

1959 Gambling is the leading industry.

1988 Congress selects Yucca Mountain as a underground repository for nuclear waste.

1989 Las Vegas and surrounding counties battle for dwindling water supplies.

1990 The state prepares for an infestation of Mormon crickets.

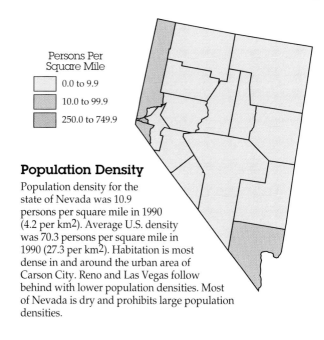

Population Density

Population density for the state of Nevada was 10.9 persons per square mile in 1990 (4.2 per km2). Average U.S. density was 70.3 persons per square mile in 1990 (27.3 per km2). Habitation is most dense in and around the urban area of Carson City. Reno and Las Vegas follow behind with lower population densities. Most of Nevada is dry and prohibits large population densities.

Persons Per Square Mile
- 0.0 to 9.9
- 10.0 to 99.9
- 250.0 to 749.9

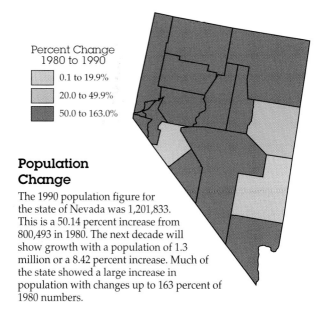

Percent Change 1980 to 1990
- 0.1 to 19.9%
- 20.0 to 49.9%
- 50.0 to 163.0%

Population Change

The 1990 population figure for the state of Nevada was 1,201,833. This is a 50.14 percent increase from 800,493 in 1980. The next decade will show growth with a population of 1.3 million or a 8.42 percent increase. Much of the state showed a large increase in population with changes up to 163 percent of 1980 numbers.

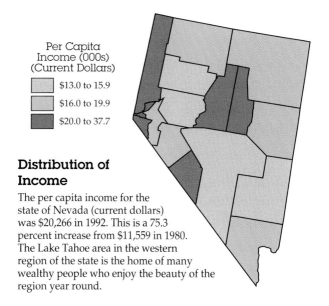

Per Capita Income (000s) (Current Dollars)
- $13.0 to 15.9
- $16.0 to 19.9
- $20.0 to 37.7

Distribution of Income

The per capita income for the state of Nevada (current dollars) was $20,266 in 1992. This is a 75.3 percent increase from $11,559 in 1980. The Lake Tahoe area in the western region of the state is the home of many wealthy people who enjoy the beauty of the region year round.

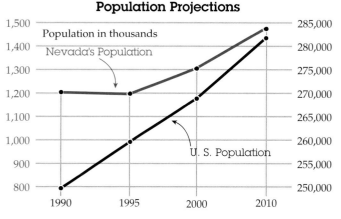

Population Projections

Population in thousands
Nevada's Population
U. S. Population

Population Change

Year	Population
1950	160,000
1960	291,000
1970	493,000
1980	800,493
1990	1,201,833
2000	1,303,000
2010	1,484,000

Period	Change
1950–1970	208.1%
1970–1980	62.3%
1980–1990	50.3%
1990–2000	8.4%

Population Facts

State Population, 1993: 1,389,000

Rank: 38

Population 2000: 1,303,000 (Rank 40)

Density: 10.9 per sq. mi. (4.2 per km²)

Distribution: 88.3% urban, 11.7% rural

Population Under 5 Years Old: 8.0%

Population Under 18 Years Old: 25.5%

Population Over 65 Years Old: 11.0%

Median Age: 33.3

Number of Households: 466,000

Average Persons Per Household: 2.53

Average Persons Per Family: 3.06

Female Heads of Households: 3.95%

Population That Is Married: 19.93%

Birth Rate: 18.0 per 1,000 population

Death Rate: 7.8 per 1,000 population

Births to Teen Mothers: 12.6%

Marriage Rate: 105.6 per 1,000 population

Divorce Rate: 11.4 per 1,000 population

Violent Crime Rate: 677 per 100,000 pop.

Population on Social Security: 13.9%

Percent Voting for President: 50.0%

Nevada's Famous Citizens

Agassi, Andre (b.1970). Tennis player. He was the youngest number-one-ranking American player ever at 18 years old.

Clark, Walter van Tilburg (1909–1971). Author of *The Ox-Bow Incident* and other stories of the western frontier.

Jones, John Percival (1829–1912). U.S. senator (1873–1903). Influential in legislation concerning mining.

McCarran, Patrick (1876–1954). Chief justice of the Nevada Supreme Court (1917–1918) and U.S. senator (1933–1954).

Newlands, Francis (1848–1917). U.S. senator (1903–1917) and co-creator of the Federal Trade Commission in 1914.

Stewart, William Morris (1827–1909). U.S. senator (1864–1875 and 1887–1905) and author of the 15th Amendment.

Sutro, Adolph (1830–1898). Inventor of a tunnel for the Comstock Mines for drainage and transportation.

Winnemucca (1805–1882). Chief of the Northern Paiute tribe.

Winnemucca, Sarah (1844–1891). Interpreter in the Bannock War and lecturer on the plight of her people (the Paiutes).

Population Profile

Rank. Nevada ranks 38th among U.S. states in terms of population with 1,389,000 citizens.

Minority Population. The state's minority population is 21.7 percent. The state's male to female ratio for 1990 was 103.72 males for every 100 females. It was way above the national average of 95.22 males for every 100 females.

Growth. Growing much faster than the projected national average, the state's population is expected to reach 1.5 million by the year 2010 *(see graph above)*.

Older Citizens. The state's population older than 65 was 127,631 in 1990. It grew 94.1% from 65,756 in 1980.

Younger Citizens. The number of children (under 18 years of age) was 297 thousand in 1990. This represents 24.7 percent of the state's population. The state's school aged population was 187 thousand in 1990. It is expected to increase to 211 thousand by the year 2000. This represents a 12.83% change.

Urban/Rural. 88.3% of the population of the state live in urban areas while 11.7% live in rural areas.

Largest Cities. Nevada has nine cities with a population greater than 35,000. The populations of the state's largest centers are (starting from the most populous) Las Vegas (258,295), Reno (133,850), Paradise (124,682), Sunrise Manor (95,362), Henderson (64,942), Sparks (53,367), Spring Valley (51,726), North Las Vegas (47,707), Carson City (40,443), Winchester (23,365), Elko (14,736), Boulder City (12,567), Sun Valley (11,391), and East Las Vegas (11,087).

Government

Capital: Carson City (established 1861).

Statehood: Became 36th state on Oct. 31, 1864.

Number of Counties: 17.

Supreme Court Justices: 5, 6-year term.

State Senators: 21, 4-year term.

State Legislators: 42, 2-year term.

United States Senators: 2.

United States Representatives: 2.

Electoral Votes: 4.

State Constitution: Adopted 1864.

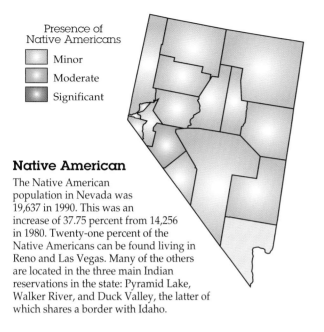

Presence of
Native Americans

- Minor
- Moderate
- Significant

Native American

The Native American population in Nevada was 19,637 in 1990. This was an increase of 37.75 percent from 14,256 in 1980. Twenty-one percent of the Native Americans can be found living in Reno and Las Vegas. Many of the others are located in the three main Indian reservations in the state: Pyramid Lake, Walker River, and Duck Valley, the latter of which shares a border with Idaho.

Statewide Ethnic Composition

Over 84 percent of the population of Nevada is white. The largest nationalities in this racial group are German, Irish, and English. The next largest group is Hispanics, followed by African Americans, Asian Americans, and Native Americans. Over 41,000 people claim to be American and acknowledge no other nationality.

Nationalities

African	1,745
American	41,236
Arab	3,269
Austrian	2,809
Czech	4,550
Dutch	15,945
English	138,545
Finnish	2,355
German	212,400
Greek	5,175
Hungarian	4,607
Irish	115,119
Italian	67,375
Norwegian	15,211
Polish	23,798
Portuguese	6,011
Russian	9,066
Scottish	20,241
Slovak	4,187
Swedish	19,652
Welsh	7,417
West Indian	940

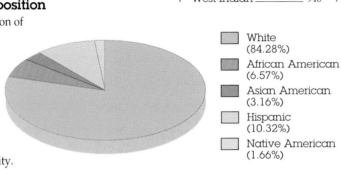

- White (84.28%)
- African American (6.57%)
- Asian American (3.16%)
- Hispanic (10.32%)
- Native American (1.66%)

Education Facts

Total Students 1990: 186,834

Number of School Districts: 17

Expenditure Per Capita on Education 1990: $878

Expenditure Per Capita K–12 1990: $647

Expenditure Per Pupil 1990: $4,677

Total School Enrollment 1990–1991: 201,310

Rank of Expenditures Per Student: 31st in the U.S.

African American Enrollment: 9.2%

Hispanic Enrollment: 9.8%

Asian/Pacific Islander Enrollment: 3.3%

Native American Enrollment: 2.0%

Mean SAT Score 1991 Verbal: 435

Mean SAT Score 1991 Math: 484

Average Teacher's Salary 1992: $33,900

Rank Teacher's Salary: 18th in U.S.

High School Graduates 1990: 9,700

Total Number of Public Schools: 331

Number of Teachers 1990: 9,868

Student/Teacher Ratio: 20.4

Staff Employed in Public Schools: 10,311

Pupil/Staff Ratio: 18.1

Staff/Teacher Ratio: 1.1

Education

Attainment: 84 percent of population 25 years or older were high school graduates in 1989, earning Nevada a ranking of 6th in the United States; 17.2 percent of the state's population had completed college. Institutions of Higher Education: The largest universities and colleges in the state include University of Nevada (founded 1874), Reno; the University of Nevada, Las Vegas; Sierra Nevada College (founded1969), Incline Village. Expenditures per Student: Expenditure increased 62.4% between 1985 and 1990. Projected High School Graduations: 1998 (13,555), 2004 (18,450); Total Revenues for Education from Federal Sources: $25 million; Total Revenues for Education from State Sources: $256 million; Total Revenues for Education from Local Sources: $380 million; Average Annual Salaries for Public School Principals: N/A; Largest School Districts in State: Clarke County School District, 111,460 students, 15th in the United States; Washoe County School District, 36,662, 104th.

Percent of
County Population

- 0.00 to 1.99%
- 2.00 to 4.99%
- 5.00 to 9.99%

African American

The African American population in Nevada was 78,771 in 1990. This was an increase of 53.84 percent from 51,203 in 1980. The largest concentration of African Americans can be found in Mineral County and Las Vegas in Clark County. Thirty-seven percent of the African Americans living in Nevada live in the city of Las Vegas.

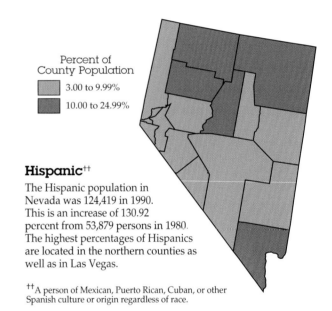

Percent of
County Population

- 3.00 to 9.99%
- 10.00 to 24.99%

Hispanic[††]

The Hispanic population in Nevada was 124,419 in 1990. This is an increase of 130.92 percent from 53,879 persons in 1980. The highest percentages of Hispanics are located in the northern counties as well as in Las Vegas.

[††]A person of Mexican, Puerto Rican, Cuban, or other Spanish culture or origin regardless of race.

Percent of
County Population

- 0.25 to 0.99%
- 1.00 to 1.99%
- 2.00 to 4.99%

Asian American

The Asian American population in Nevada was 38,127 in 1990. This is an increase of 161.84 percent from 14,561 persons in 1980. Many Asian Americans live in Reno as well as in the Lake Tahoe area. Twenty-four percent of the Asian Americans living in Nevada can be found living in Las Vegas.

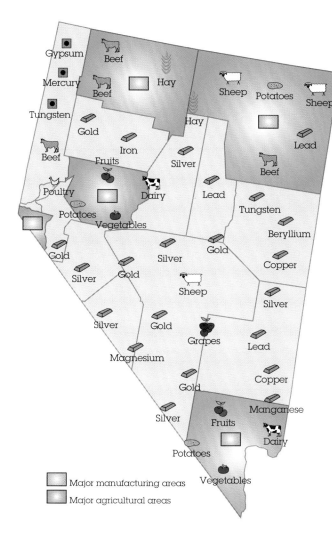

Major manufacturing areas
Major agricultural areas

Housing

Owner Occupied Units: 518,858; Average Age of Units: 18 years; Average Value of Housing Units: $95,700; Renter Occupied Units: 209,175; Median Monthly Rent: $509; Housing Starts: 18,300; Existing Home Sales: 30,500.

Economic Facts

Gross State Product: $28,000,000,000 (1989)

Income Per Capita: $20,266

Disposable Personal Income: $17,711

Median Household Income: $31,011

Average Annual Pay, 1988: $23,083

Principal Industries: printing, food products, machinery, tourism, chemicals, glass products

Major Crops: hay, barley, wheat, potatoes, cotton, oats, alfalfa seed

Fish: Trout, Bass, Carp, Catfish, Crappies

Livestock: cattle, dairy cows, sheep

Non-Fuel Minerals: Copper, Tungsten, Lithium, Gold, Silver, Magnesium, Borates, Clay, Feldspar

Organic Fuel Minerals: N/A

Civilian Labor Force: 649,000 (Women: 287,000)

Total Employed: 614,000 (Women: 273,000)

Median Value of Housing: $95,700

Median Contract Rent: $509 per month

Agriculture

Nevada has 8.9 million farm acres. During the last 40 years, Nevada's farms have grown larger in size and fewer in number. In 1955, 3,000 farms were found in the state. Today, 2,400 remain.

Agriculture adds less than $500 million to the state's gross product annually. The principal commodities in order of marketing receipts are cattle, dairy products, hay, and potatoes.

Livestock ranching accounts for most of Nevada's farm income. Much of the grazing land is rented from the federal government. Most of the beef cattle are shipped to other states for fattening. Hogs and sheep are shipped to meat packers, and wool to textile mills. Virtually all of Nevada's crops are grown on irrigated land. These include hay, alfalfa, and barley.

Economic Sectors 1992

Construction 6.20%
Agriculture N/A
Manufacturing 4.13%
Trans.– Public Utilities 5.25%
Services 63.43%
Trade 20.67%

Manufacturing

Compared to other states, Nevada has a relatively small manufacturing sector, accounting for only 5 percent of the state gross product. Nevada does not really have one major manufacturing industry. However, manufactured products include computers, concrete, chemicals, printed materials, and processed foods.

Nevada has two main manufacturing centers, Las Vegas and Reno. Both of these cities have printing, concrete, and meat-packing factories. The area surrounding Las Vegas has factories that manufacture appliances and neon signs. Computers and other electronic equipment are mostly manufactured in Reno, although Carson City also has computer plants. Most of Nevada's heavy industry is located in Henderson.

Transportation

For a larger state, Nevada does not have an extensive road system at all. Nevada only has approximately 44,000 miles of highways and roads. Furthermore, only about one-third of these roadways are paved. The state has two major interstates: Interstate 15 in southern Nevada and Interstate 80 in the north.

Air travel is important to Nevada's transportation network, especially for the thousands of tourists who come to the state each year. Major airports include McCarran International in Las Vegas, and Reno's Reno-Cannon Airport. Four different rail carriers provide freight service for Nevada. Passenger trains serve four Nevada cities. Nevada does not have any significant water transportation routes, as almost half of Nevada has a desert climate.

Energy and Transportation Facts

Energy. Yearly Consumption: 400 tril. BTUs (residential, 21.5%; commercial, 17.8%; industrial, 26.5%; transportation, 34.3%); Annual Energy Expenditures Per Capita: $1,875; Nuclear Power Plants Located in State: 0; Source of Energy Consumed: Petroleum— 39.1%; Natural Gas— 15.1%; Coal— 40.4%; Hydroelectric Power—5.4%; Nuclear Power—0.0%.

Transportation. Highway Miles: 45,657 (interstates, 545; urban, 4,513; rural, 41,144); Average Yearly Auto Insurance: $673 (14th); Auto Fatalities Rank: 9th; Registered Motor Vehicles: 920,936; Workers in Carpools: 21.1%; Workers Using Public Trans: 2.7%.

Employment

Employment. Nevada employed 692,000 people in 1993. Most work in social and personal services (294,400 persons or 42.5% of the workforce). Manufacturing accounts for 4.3% or 29,500 workers. Wholesale and retail trade account for 19.2% or 133,200 workers. Government employs 88,500 workers (12.8%). Construction employs 45,900 workers (6.6%). Transportation and utilities account for 5.1% or 35,000 persons. Agriculture employs 11,800 workers or 1.7%. Finance, real estate, and insurance account for 4.5% or 30,900 workers. Mining employs 12,600 people and accounts for only 1.8% of the workforce.

Unemployment. Unemployment has decreased to 7.2% in 1993 from a rate of 8.0% in 1985. Today's figure is higher than the national average of 6.8% as shown below.

Unemployment Rate

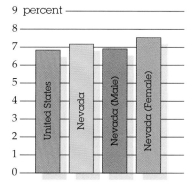

NEW HAMPSHIRE

NEW HAMPSHIRE

The State of New Hampshire

202

Official State Seal

The Great Seal of New Hampshire was adopted in 1931 after an older seal dating from 1784. The 1776 later replaced the original 1784 found on the bottom of the seal. The frigate *Raleigh*, one of the first ships built for the U.S. Navy, is pictured with the United States flag of 1777 on its bow. Around the edges are the words "Seal of the State of New Hampshire."

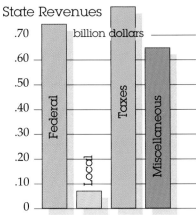

Legal Holidays

January: New Year's Day—1st; Martin Luther King, Jr., Day—3rd Monday; February: Presidents' Day—3rd Monday; April: Fast Day—26th; May: Memorial Day—4th Monday; June: Ratification Day—21st; July: Independence Day—4th; September: Labor Day—1st Monday; October: Columbus Day—2nd Monday; November: Veterans' Day—11th; Thanksgiving—4th Thursday; December: Christmas—25th.

Official State Flag

Adopted in 1909, the New Hampshire state flag was just another version of earlier military flags dating from 1792. The design was altered in 1931 when there were changes made to the state seal. The present flag contains the state seal surrounded by nine stars marking New Hampshire as the ninth state to ratify the Constitution.

Festivals and Events

February: Dartmouth Winter Carnival, Hanover; June: Loudon Camel Classic, Loudon; Monadnock Balloon & Aviation Fest, Keene; July: Sundays in the Garden, Portsmouth; August: Artists in the Park, Wolfeboro; September: Labor Day Festival, Francestown; New Hampshire Highland Games, Lincoln; Riverfest in Manchester, Manchester.

New Hampshire Compared to Its Region.

Resident Pop. in Metro Areas: 4th; Pop. Percent Increase: 4th; Pop. Over 65: 6th; Infant Mortality: 3d; School Enroll. Increase: 1st; High School Grad. and Up: 1st; Violent Crime: 5th; Hazardous Waste Sites: 2d; Unemployment: 3d; Median Household Income: 3d; Persons Below Poverty: 6th; Energy Costs Per Person: 4th.

New England Region

	Population	Capital
Maine	1,239,000	Augusta
New Hampshire	1,125,000	Concord
Vermont	576,000	Montpelier
Massachusetts	6,012,000	Boston
Rhode Island	1,000,000	Providence
Connecticut	3,277,000	Hartford

New Hampshire's Finances

Households: 411,000; Income Per Capita Current Dollars: $22,934; Change Per Capita Income 1980 to 1992: 133.9% (1st in U.S.); State Expenditures: $2,453,000,000; State Revenues: $2,303,000,000; Personal Income Tax: N/A; Federal Income Taxes Paid Per Capita: $2,123; Sales Tax: N/A.

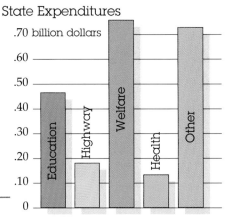

Location, Size, and Boundaries

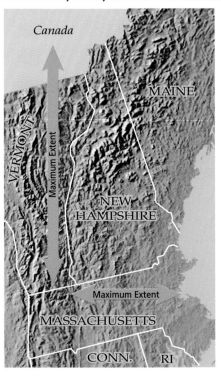

Location. New Hampshire is located in the northeastern United States in the New England region. It is almost completely bounded by land with a small coast along the Atlantic Ocean in the southeast. The geographic center of New Hampshire is lat. 43° 38.5' N; long. 71° 34.3' W.

Size. New Hampshire is the 44th largest state in terms of size. Its area is 9,304 sq. mi. (24,097 km²). Inland water covers 277 sq. mi. (717 km²). New Hampshire touches the Atlantic Ocean along a 13 mile coastline.

Boundaries. Canada, 60 mi. (96 km); Maine, 174 mi. (280 km); Atlantic Ocean, 13 mi. (21 km); Mass., 95 mi. (153 km); Vermont, 213 mi. (343 km).

Geographic Extent. The north/south extent is 180 mi. (290 km). The state extends 93 mi. (150 km) to the east/west.

Facts about New Hampshire. Origin of Name: Named by Capt. John Mason after his home county in England; Nickname: The Granite State; Motto: "Live Free or Die"; Abbreviations: N.H. (traditional), NH (postal); State Bird: purple finch; State Tree: white birch; State Flower: purple lilac; State Song: "Old New Hampshire," words by John F. Holmes and music by Maurice Hoffmann.

New Hampshire Compared to Other States. Resident Pop. in Metro Areas: 34th; Pop. Per. Increase: 47th; Pop. Over 65: 35th; Infant Mortality: 46th; School Enroll. Increase: 1st; High School Grad. and Up: 7th; Violent Crime: 48th; Hazardous Waste Sites: 22d; Unemployment: 12th; Median Household Income: 7th; Persons Below Poverty: 50th; Energy Costs Per Person: 38th.

Sources of Information. Tourism: Office of Vacation Travel, 172 Pembroke Road, P.O. Box 856, Concord, NH 03302. Economy: Department of Resources and Economic Development, 172 Pembroke Road, P.O. Box 856, Concord, NH 03302. Government: Office of Citizen Services, Governor's Office, State House, Concord, NH 03301.

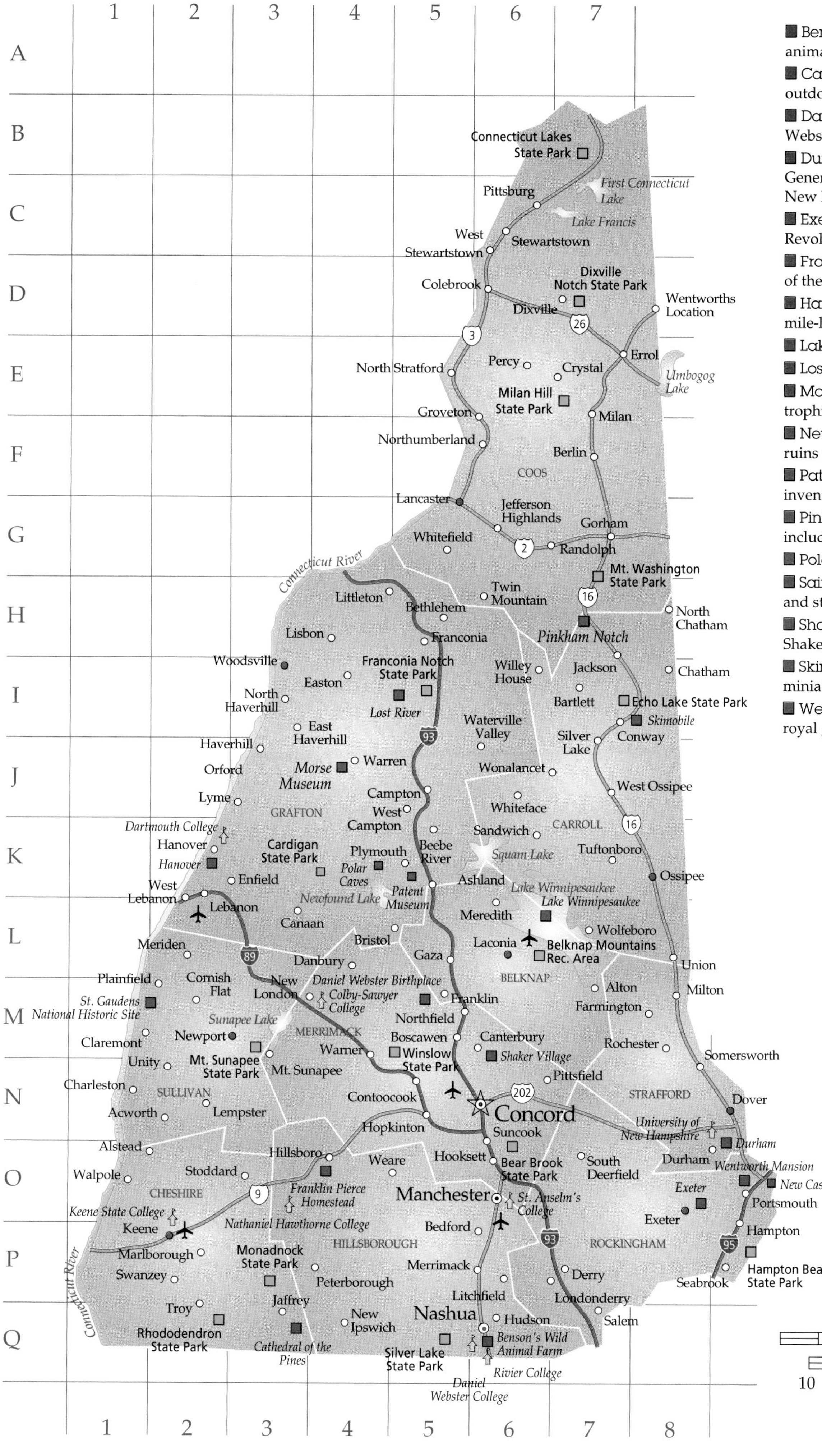

Map Grid

	1	2	3	4	5	6	7
A							
B							
C							
D							
E							
F							
G							
H							
I							
J							
K							
L							

Cultural Features

■ **Benson's Wild Animal Farm.** Breeders of exotic animals for zoos worldwide. (N-5)

■ **Cathedral of the Pines.** World War II memorial and outdoor religious sanctuary. (N-3)

■ **Daniel Webster's Birthplace.** The birthplace of Daniel Webster. (J-4)

■ **Durham.** Home of American Revolution Major General John Sullivan; also the home of the University of New Hampshire. (L-7)

■ **Exeter.** Capital of New Hampshire during American Revolution; Phillips Exeter Academy. (M-7)

■ **Franklin Pierce Homestead.** Home of 14th president of the United States. (L-3)

■ **Hanover.** Dartmouth College, chartered in 1769; 46-mile-long lake created by Wilder Dam nearby. (I-2)

■ **Lake Winnipesaukee.** State's largest lake. (J-5)

■ **Lost River.** Glacial caverns and waterfalls. (G-4)

■ **Morse Museum.** Collection of mounted animals, trophies, and weapons from around the world. (H-3)

■ **New Castle.** Resort at mouth of Piscataqua River; ruins of Fort William and Mary, built around 1630. (L-7)

■ **Patent Museum.** Contains working models of 1836–90 inventions from United States Patent Office. (I-4)

■ **Pinkham Notch.** In White Mountains near Gorham; includes Glen Ellis Falls. (G-5)

■ **Polar Caves.** Frigid caverns. (I-3)

■ **Saint-Gaudens National Historic Site.** Former estate and studios of the famous sculptor. (J-1)

■ **Shaker Village.** Home of remaining members of the Shaker sect. (K-5)

■ **Skimobile.** Scenic ride up Cranmore Mountain in miniature cars. (H-6)

■ **Wentworth-Coolidge Mansion.** Home of the first royal governor of New Hampshire. (L-7)

Major Cities

Berlin	F-7	Lebanon	L-2
Claremont	M-2	Londonderry	P-7
Concord	N-6	Manchester	O-6
Derry	P-7	Nashua	Q-6
Dover	N-9	Portsmouth	O-9
Keene	P-2	Rochester	M-8
Laconia	L-6	Somersworth	N-8

Legend

☆ State capitol

⊙ Cities over 35,000 population

○ Other significant cities

● County Seats

■ Major cultural attractions

□ State Parks

Ⓦ Welcome Center

⚓ Major colleges and universities

Scale

0   10   20   30 mi.

10   0   10   20   30   40 km

Map Labels

Connecticut Lakes State Park
Pittsburg
First Connecticut Lake
Lake Francis
West Stewartstown
Stewartstown
Colebrook
Dixville Notch State Park
Dixville
Wentworths Location
26
North Stratford
Percy
Crystal
Errol
Umbogog Lake
Milan Hill State Park
Groveton
Milan
Northumberland
Berlin
COOS
3
Lancaster
Jefferson Highlands
Gorham
Whitefield
Randolph
2
Mt. Washington State Park
Twin Mountain
16
North Chatham
Littleton
Bethlehem
Pinkham Notch
Lisbon
Franconia
Willey House
Jackson
Chatham
Woodsville
Franconia Notch State Park
Easton
Bartlett
Echo Lake State Park
North Haverhill
Lost River
Waterville Valley
Silver Lake
Skimobile
Conway
Haverhill
East Haverhill
93
Orford
Morse Museum
Warren
Wonalancet
West Ossipee
Lyme
Campton
GRAFTON
West Campton
Whiteface
CARROLL
Sandwich
Tuftonboro
Dartmouth College
Hanover
Cardigan State Park
Plymouth
Beebe River
Squam Lake
16
Hanover
Polar Caves
Ashland
Lake Winnipesaukee
Ossipee
West Lebanon
Enfield
Newfound Lake
Patent Museum
Meredith
Lake Winnipesaukee
Lebanon
Canaan
Bristol
Laconia
Wolfeboro
89
Meriden
Danbury
Gaza
Belknap Mountains Rec. Area
Union
Plainfield
Cornish Flat
New London
Daniel Webster Birthplace
BELKNAP
Alton
Milton
St. Gaudens National Historic Site
Colby-Sawyer College
Franklin
Farmington
Claremont
Sunapee Lake
Northfield
MERRIMACK
Newport
Warner
Boscawen
Canterbury
Rochester
Unity
Mt. Sunapee State Park
Winslow State Park
Shaker Village
Somersworth
Charleston
Mt. Sunapee
Pittsfield
STRAFFORD
Acworth
SULLIVAN
Lempster
Contoocook
202
Dover
Alstead
Hopkinton
University of New Hampshire
Walpole
Stoddard
Weare
Hooksett
Durham
CHESHIRE
9
Franklin Pierce Homestead
Bear Brook State Park
South Deerfield
Durham
Wentworth Mansion
Keene State College
Manchester
St. Anselm's College
Exeter
New Castle
Keene
Nathaniel Hawthorne College
Bedford
Exeter
Portsmouth
Marlborough
HILLSBOROUGH
Hampton
Swanzey
Monadnock State Park
Merrimack
ROCKINGHAM
93
Troy
Jaffrey
Peterborough
Litchfield
Derry
95
Rhododendron State Park
New Ipswich
Nashua
Londonderry
Seabrook
Hampton Beach State Park
Cathedral of the Pines
Silver Lake State Park
Hudson
Salem
Rivier College
Daniel Webster College
Benson's Wild Animal Farm
Connecticut River

Weather Facts

Record High Temperature: 106° F (41° C) on July 4, 1911, at Nashua; Record Low Temperature: -46° F (-43° C) on January 28, 1925, at Pittsburg; Average January Temperature: 19° F (-7° C); Average July Temperature: 67° F (19° C); Average Yearly Precipitation: 43 in. (109 cm).

Environmental Facts

Air Pollution Rank: 38th; Water Pollution Rank: 44th; Total Yearly Industrial Pollution: 6,053,887 lbs.; Industrial Pollution Rank: 41st; Hazardous Waste Sites: 17; Hazardous Sites Rank: 22d; Landfill Capacity: overextended; Fresh Water Supply: large surplus; Daily Residential Water Consumption: 110 gals. per capita; Endangered Species: Aquatic Species (1)—mussel, dwarf wedge; Birds (2)—eagle, bald; Mammals (1)—bat, Indiana; Other Species (1)—butterfly, Karner blue; Plants (3)—cinquefoil, Robbins'.

Environmental Quality

New Hampshire residents generate 1.0 million tons of solid waste each year, or approximately 2,000 pounds per capita. Landfill capacity in New Hampshire will be exhausted in 5 to 10 years. The state has 9 hazardous waste sites. Annual greenhouse gas emissions in New Hampshire total 15.9 million tons, or 14.6 tons per capita. Industrial sources in New Hampshire release approximately 9.6 thousand tons of toxins, 127.8 thousand tons of acid precipitation-producing substances, and 400 thousand tons of smog-producing substances into the atmosphere each year.

The state has 8,600 acres within the National Park System. Noteworthy is Saint-Gaudens National Historic Site. State parks cover just over 29,000 acres, attracting 2.8 million visitors per year.

New Hampshire spends approximately 2.4 percent of its budget, or approximately $31 per capita, on environmental and natural resources. New Hampshire representatives in the U.S. House voted in favor of national environmental legislation 82 percent of the time, while U.S. senators did so 46 percent of the time.

Average Monthly Weather

Concord	Jan	Feb	Mar	Apr	May	Jun	Jul	Aug	Sep	Oct	Nov	Dec	Yearly
Maximum Temperature °F	30.8	33.2	41.9	56.5	68.9	77.7	82.6	80.1	71.9	61.0	47.2	34.4	57.2
Minimum Temperature °F	9.0	11.0	22.2	31.6	41.4	51.6	56.4	54.5	46.2	35.5	27.3	14.5	33.4
Days of Precipitation	10.7	9.6	10.9	11.6	12.0	10.9	10.0	9.9	8.8	8.7	11.5	10.7	125.3

Flora and Fauna

New Hampshire, like other New England states, is heavily forested, with trees covering approximately 80 percent of the land. Birch and maple trees are the most common deciduous trees, although cedar, elm, and other hardwoods also grow in New Hampshire's forests. In the northern mountains, fir and spruce trees prevail. The White Mountains have mostly white pine trees. Shrubs such as sumac, American elder, and blueberry also grow in New Hampshire's forests. Wildflowers are a common sight in New Hampshire as well. Fireweed, daisies, and wild asters are all popular wildflowers.

Northern New Hampshire forests are home to both of the state's two largest animals, moose and black bear. Deer, another large mammal, live throughout the state. Smaller New Hampshire animals include fox, raccoon, skunk, and otter. Bluebirds, sparrows, and other songbirds live in New Hampshire too, along with game birds such as grouse and pheasant. New Hampshire's rivers and lakes have several kinds of trout and bass. Both saltwater fish (cusk, haddock, tuna) and other sea life (clams, lobster, shrimp) live off New Hampshire's coast.

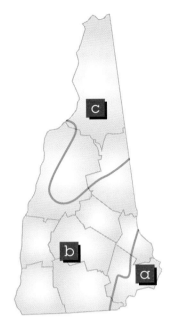

Physical Regions: (a) Coastal Lowlands; (b) Eastern New England Upland; (c) White Mountains Region.

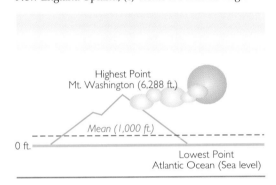

Highest Point
Mt. Washington (6,288 ft.)

Mean (1,000 ft.)

0 ft.

Lowest Point
Atlantic Ocean (Sea level)

Land Use

Cropland: 3.3%; Pasture: 2.3%; Rangeland: 0%; Forest: 81.5%; Urban: 7.5%; Other: 5.4%.

For more information about New Hampshire's environment, contact the Department of Environmental Services, 6 Hazen Drive, Concord, NH 03301.

Topography

There are several distinct topographic regions in New Hampshire. In the southeastern part of the state is the Coastal Lowlands physical region, a narrow band of land that extends up and down the New England coastline, including many beaches.

The Eastern New England Uplands physical region covers much of southern and western New Hampshire. This area includes the Merrimack River Valley in the south-central part of the state, and an area of many lakes east of this valley to the border with Maine. Running down much of the western border is the Connecticut River Valley, with fertile soil suitable for agriculture.

Between the two river valleys lies the White Mountains physical region, part of the northernmost extension of the Appalachian Mountains that reaches into western Maine. Timber from the heavily forested mountains supports a large paper industry in New Hampshire. The highest elevation in the state is in the east: Mt. Washington rises 6,288 ft. (1,917 m) above sea level. This is also the highest peak in the entire northeastern United States. The soil in the state is typically cool and moist, brown, and has high concentrations of organic matter, iron, and aluminum.

Climate

Like that of other New England states, New Hampshire's climate is characterized by short, cool summers and long winters. The climate is a result of the state's latitude, and is affected by elevation and proximity to the coast. Temperatures in Concord for January and July average 21 degrees F and 70 degrees F, respectively. Mean temperatures in the northern mountainous region are usually several degrees cooler.

New Hampshire receives adequate, but varying, precipitation. Mount Washington, in the White Mountains, averages 76 inches of precipitation; however, this is not characteristic of the state. Mean precipitation really only ranges between 36 inches around the town of Hanover, on the Connecticut River, to 42 inches near Durham. Much of the precipitation falls as snow.

New Hampshire's climate directly affects the length of the growing season. In the north, the growing season lasts only 90 days, but in the south, the length increases to 150 days.

Hydrology

The Connecticut River begins in Canada and flows southward, forming almost the entire western boundary of New Hampshire with Vermont. The Salmon Falls and Piscataqua rivers form the southernmost portion of the eastern boundary with Maine. The longest river within the state is the Merrimack, which begins in central New Hampshire and flows southeast into Massachusetts. The Androscoggin begins in the north and flows south, before turning eastward into Maine. Other rivers include the Pemigewasett and Bakers in central New Hampshire, and the Contoocook and Ashuelot in the south.

There are over 1,300 lakes in New Hampshire. The largest of these is Lake Winnipesaukee, covering about 70 sq. mi. (181 sq. km) in the east-central part of the state. Others include Newfound Lake, Winnisquam Lake, and Squam Lake, also in the central region; and Massabesic Lake and Hopkinton Everett Reservoir in the south.

New Hampshire's History

New Hampshire's First People

Humans have lived in the area known now as New Hampshire for at least ten thousand years. There were two main confederacies in the area, the Pennacook (located in the Merrimack and Connecticut valleys, and the Sokoki (located in the White Mountains and Saco Valley).

When the first Europeans arrived in New Hampshire, the Native American population numbered around twelve thousand. Settlements could be found, as far west in the New Hampshire area as the lower Merrimack Valley. However, the population decreased due to disease and fighting with the Europeans. By 1725, most Native Americans had left New Hampshire and headed north.

European Exploration

The earliest known European entry into New Hampshire came in 1603, when Martin Pring, an English captain, sailed along the New Hampshire coast. Two years later, the French explorer Samuel de Champlain visited the same area.

The first permanent white settlement was not established until 1623 at Odiorne Point, near the mouth of the Piscataqua River. Both this and a settlement near present-day Dover were founded on fishing and fur trading, under the authority of the Council of New England, a London-based agency responsible for issuing land grants in the New World. In 1629, Capt. John Mason was granted a parcel of land between the Merrimack and Piscataqua rivers; which he named New Hampshire.

Massachusetts governed New Hampshire on two occasions, first from 1641 until 1670, and again from 1690 until 1692. The official boundary between the two states was not solidified until 1740. As danger of raids diminished and the boundary between the two states was set, the province's population grew. In 1741 under Gov. Benning Wentworth, seventy-five new towns were established.

Statehood

New Hampshire was the first of the original thirteen colonies to create an independent government. Six months before the Declaration of Independence, on January 5, 1776, New Hampshire adopted its own constitution.

During the Revolutionary War, New Hampshire showed strong support for independence. Extensive preparations were made to protect New Hampshire's harbors from British attack. Although no official Revolutionary battles took place on New Hampshire soil, over eighteen thousand men from the state enlisted.

New Hampshire became the ninth state in the Union on June 21, 1788, when it ratified the U.S. Constitution. The state constitution was adopted in 1784, and heavily revised in 1972.

From the time New Hampshire became a state until 1805, the Federalist political party dominated New Hampshire politics. The only exception took place in 1804, when the majority of the state voted for the anti-Federalist Thomas Jefferson.

In June of 1905, at the urging of President Theodore Roosevelt, New Hampshire became a site for world politics when the Treaty of Portsmouth was signed ending the Japanese-Russian War.

Industrialization

Shipbuilding was the first industry in New Hampshire, beginning in the early eighteenth century. By the middle of the 1700s, Portsmouth, the provincial capital, had become a busy commercial port. Throughout the eighteenth and nineteenth centuries, shipbuilding dominated as the chief industry of the state.

As more people moved to the interior of New Hampshire, agriculture became an important economic activity. However, this development was short-lived, as railroad expansion decreased the need for produce to be grown near settlements. Textile

manufacturing soon took over as a leading economic activity. In 1810, the Amoskeag Cotton and Woolen Manufacturing Company sprang up along the Merrimack River, where Manchester now stands. After the Civil War, several improvements in transportation and technology made New Hampshire attractive to a number of new immigrants. The stabilization of industry attracted thousands of immigrants to New Hampshire to work in the new textile factories.

The textile industry reached a high point around 1915, but started to decline after World War I. New Hampshire's old mills in the southern part of the state were not able to compete with the new mills in the southern United States. Industries in northern New Hampshire, primarily paper manufacturing and logging, continued to prosper.

More recently, a number of factors have contributed to the continued urbanization of New Hampshire. Urban sprawl from Boston, interstate highways, and low state taxes have all attracted development to the southern part of the state.

"Live Free or Die"

The phrase "Live Free or Die," which still adorns license plates, is an appropriate motto for New Hampshire. Politically and environmentally, the state reflects an independent attitude. Recycling is one such example of New Hampshire's commitment to the environment. In may towns in the state, recycling trash cans stand beside regular refuse containers, and fines are imposed for failure to use these separate containers. Politically, New Hampshire is also unique, being home to the first presidential primary election every presidential year. Many people believe that whoever wins the primary in New Hampshire will be the next President of the United States.

Important Events

1603 English captain, Martin Pring explores the New Hampshire coast and the Piscataqua River.

1622 Council for New England grants Sir Ferdinando Gorges and Capt. John Mason land later known as New Hampshire.

1623 First settlement near Portsmouth founded by David Thomson.

1629 Captain John Mason acquires land solely for himself; names it New Hampshire.

1641 Four New Hampshire towns place their government under Massachusetts.

1692 New Hampshire becomes a separate province.

1740 Royal decree settles dispute over New Hampshire–Massachusetts border.

1741 Benning Wentworth appointed governor and seventy-five new towns are established.

1759 Indian raids are halted by Robert Roger's Rangers.

1769 Dartmouth College chartered at Hanover.

1774 Colonists seize the British fort at Portsmouth.

1775 The royal governor is driven out of the state.

1776 New Hampshire adopts its own constitution on January 5.

1784 The state constitution adopted.

1788 New Hampshire becomes ninth state of the Union on June 21.

1808 Concord becomes permanent state capital.

1852 Franklin Pierce becomes fourteenth President of the United States.

1905 Treaty of Portsmouth ends Russo-Japanese War.

1911 White Mountain National Forest established.

1915 Textile industry reaches a high point.

1942 Webster-Ashburton Treaty sets New Hampshire-Canada border.

1963 Lottery legalized in New Hampshire.

1972 The state constitution is revised.

1990 Seabrook nuclear power plant turned on after fourteen years of construction.

Population Density

Population density for the state of New Hampshire was 123.7 persons per square mile in 1990 (47.8 per km2). Average U.S. density was 70.3 persons per square mile in 1990 (27.3 per km2). Habitation is most dense around the southeastern section of the state in cities such as Manchester, Portsmouth, and Concord.

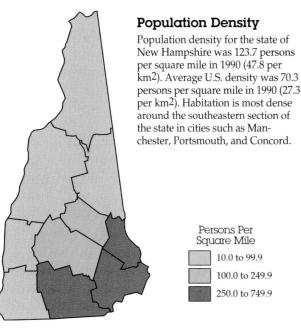

Persons Per
Square Mile

- 10.0 to 99.9
- 100.0 to 249.9
- 250.0 to 749.9

Population Change

The 1990 population figure for the state of New Hampshire was 1,109,252. This is a 20.49 percent increase from 920,610 in 1980. The next decade will show growth with a population of 1.3 million or a 20.17 percent increase. The areas of fastest growth is the southeastern section of the state in cities such as Manchester, Portsmouth, and Concord.

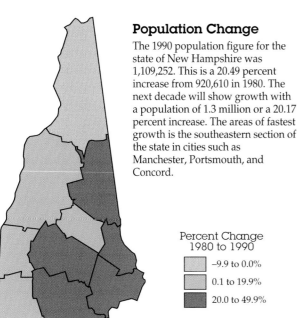

Percent Change
1980 to 1990

- −9.9 to 0.0%
- 0.1 to 19.9%
- 20.0 to 49.9%

Distribution of Income

The per capita income for the state of New Hampshire (current dollars) was $22,934 in 1992. This is a 133.9 percent increase from $9,803 in 1980. Income per capita for the state of New Hampshire is one of the highest in the United States. The counties with the highest income per capita in the state are Hillsborough, Rockingham, Belknap, and Carroll. These counties contain the major cities of the state with the exception of Concord, which is located in Merrimack County.

Per Capita
Income (000s)
(Current Dollars)

- $16.0 to 19.9
- $20.0 to 35.2

Population Projections

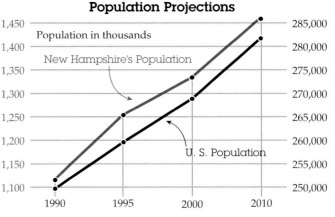

Population in thousands

New Hampshire's Population

U. S. Population

Population Change

Year	Population
1950	533,000
1960	609,000
1970	742,000
1980	920,610
1990	1,109,252
2000	1,333,000
2010	1,455,000

Period	Change
1950–1970	39.2%
1970–1980	24.1%
1980–1990	20.4%
1990–2000	20.2%

Population Facts

State Population, 1993: 1,125,000

Rank: 41

Population 2000: 1,333,000 (Rank 39)

Density: 123.7 per sq. mi. (47.8 per km²)

Distribution: 51.0% urban, 49.0% rural

Population Under 5 Years Old: 7.4%

Population Under 18 Years Old: 25.2%

Population Over 65 Years Old: 11.8%

Median Age: 32.8

Number of Households: 411,000

Average Persons Per Household: 2.62

Average Persons Per Family: 3.09

Female Heads of Households: 3.14%

Population That Is Married: 22.11%

Birth Rate: 15.8 per 1,000 population

Death Rate: 7.7 per 1,000 population

Births to Teen Mothers: 7.2%

Marriage Rate: 9.4 per 1,000 population

Divorce Rate: 4.7 per 1,000 population

Violent Crime Rate: 119 per 100,000 pop.

Population on Social Security: 15.1%

Percent Voting for President: 63.1%

Population Profile

Rank. New Hampshire ranks 41st among U.S. states in terms of population with 1,125,000 citizens.

Minority Population. The state's minority population is 2.7 percent. The state's male to female ratio for 1990 was 96.08 males for every 100 females. It was above the national average of 95.22 males for every 100 females.

Growth. Growing much faster than the

Government

Capital: Concord (established 1808).

Statehood: Became 9th state on Jun. 21, 1788.

Number of Counties: 10.

Supreme Court Justices: 5, to age 70.

State Senators: 24, 2-year term.

State Legislators: 400, 2-year term.

United States Senators: 2.

United States Representatives: 2.

Electoral Votes: 4.

State Constitution: Adopted 1784.

New Hampshire's Famous Citizens

Champney, Benjamin (1817–1907). Leader of a group of landscape painters centered in North Conway.

Chase, Salmon (1808–1873). U.S. senator (1849–1861) and Chief Justice of the U.S. Supreme Court (1864–1873).

French, Daniel Chester (1850–1931). Sculptor. Crafted the seated marble statue at the Lincoln Memorial.

Irving, John (b. 1942). Author of popular offbeat novels such as *The World According to Garp* and *The Hotel New Hampshire*.

Lowe, Thaddeus (1832–1913). Aeronaut. He used balloon flights to study the upper atmosphere.

McAuliffe, S. Christa (1948–1986). First teacher chosen to go into space. She was killed with the Space Shuttle *Challenger* crew.

Parker, Francis (1837–1902). Founder of the Chicago Institute (now the University of Chicago's School of Education).

Stark, John (1728–1822). General. He took part in the defeat of the British at Saratoga, N.Y.

projected national average, the state's population is expected to reach 1.5 million by the year 2010 *(see graph above)*.

Older Citizens. The state's population older than 65 was 125,029 in 1990. It grew 21.43% from 102,967 in 1980.

Younger Citizens. The number of children (under 18 years of age) was 279 thousand in 1990. This represents 25.1 percent of the state's population. The state's school aged population was 177 thousand in 1990. It is expected to increase to 222 thousand by the year 2000. This represents a 25.42% change.

Urban/Rural. 51.0% of the population of the state live in urban areas while 49.0% live in rural areas.

Largest Cities. New Hampshire has three cities with a population greater than 35,000. The populations of the state's largest centers are (starting from the most populous) Manchester (99,567), Nashua (79,662), Concord (36,006), Rochester (26,630), Portsmouth (25,925), Dover (25,042), Keene (22,430), Derry (20,446), Laconia (15,743), Claremont (13,902), Lebanon (12,183), Berlin (11,824), Somersworth (11,249), and Londonderry (10,114).

Native American

The Native American population in New Hampshire was 2,134 in 1990. This was an increase of 59.02 percent from 1,342 in 1980. Most of New Hampshire's Native Americans can be found in the larger urban areas such as Manchester, Nashua, Concord, and Portsmouth.

Presence of Native Americans

Minor

Nationalities

African	439
American	51,026
Arab	3,695
Austrian	1,675
Czech	1,446
Dutch	7,530
English	181,151
Finnish	6,364
German	81,508
Greek	12,985
Hungarian	2,443
Irish	145,467
Italian	56,885
Norwegian	5,244
Polish	32,726
Portuguese	6,192
Russian	7,461
Scottish	34,572
Slovak	1,723
Swedish	15,521
Welsh	3,792
West Indian	878

African American

The African American population in New Hampshire was 7,198 in 1990. This was an increase of 66.47 percent from 4,324 in 1980. Most of New Hampshire's African American population can be found living in urban areas such as Manchester, Nashua, Concord, and Portsmouth.

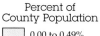

Percent of County Population

0.00 to 0.49%

0.50 to 0.99%

Statewide Ethnic Composition

Over 98 percent of the population of New Hampshire is white. The largest nationalities in this racial group are English, Irish, and German. The next largest group is Hispanics, followed by Asians, African Americans, and Native Americans. Over 51,000 people claim to be American and acknowledge no other nationality.

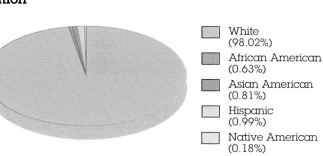

White (98.02%)

African American (0.63%)

Asian American (0.81%)

Hispanic (0.99%)

Native American (0.18%)

Hispanic[++]

The Hispanic population in New Hampshire was 11,333 in 1990. This is an increase of 102.85 percent from 5,587 persons in 1980. The county with the highest percentage of Hispanics is Hillsborough County in the southern region of the state. There are, however, significant numbers of Hispanics living in urban areas such as Manchester (in Hillsborough), Nashua (in Hillsborough), Concord, and Portsmouth.

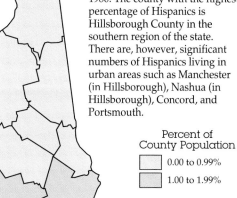

Percent of County Population

0.00 to 0.99%

1.00 to 1.99%

[++]A person of Mexican, Puerto Rican, Cuban, or other Spanish culture or origin regardless of race.

Education Facts

Total Students 1990: 171,696	Mean SAT Score 1991 Verbal: 440
Number of School Districts: 170	Mean SAT Score 1991 Math: 481
Expenditure Per Capita on Education 1990: $827	Average Teacher's Salary 1992: $33,200
Expenditure Per Capita K–12 1990: $731	Rank Teacher's Salary: 22d in U.S.
Expenditure Per Pupil 1990: $5,474	High School Graduates 1990: 12,000
Total School Enrollment 1990–1991: 172,807	Total Number of Public Schools: 444
Rank of Expenditures Per Student: 13th in the U.S.	Number of Teachers 1990: 10,667
African American Enrollment: 0.9%	Student/Teacher Ratio: 16.2
Hispanic Enrollment: 0.9%	Staff Employed in Public Schools: 20,556
Asian/Pacific Islander Enrollment: 1.0%	Pupil/Staff Ratio: 8.4
Native American Enrollment: 0.2%	Staff/Teacher Ratio: 1.9

Education

Attainment: 82.2 percent of population 25 years or older were high school graduates in 1989, earning New Hampshire a ranking of 14th in the United States; 23.5 percent of the state's population had completed college. Institutions of Higher Education: The largest universities and colleges in the state include University of New Hampshire, Durham; Keene State College, Keene; Plymouth State College, Plymouth; Dartmouth College, Hanover; St. Anselm's College, Manchester. Expenditures per Student: Expenditure increased 60.3% between 1985 and 1990. Projected High School Graduations: 1998 (13,714), 2004 (15,282); Total Revenues for Education from Federal Sources: $25 million; Total Revenues for Education from State Sources: $56 million; Total Revenues for Education from Local Sources: $667 million; Average Annual Salaries for Public School Principals: $38,115.

Asian American

The Asian American population in New Hampshire was 9,343 in 1990. This is an increase of 183.12 percent from 3,300 persons in 1980. Asian Americans maintain a higher percentage in Grafton and Hillsborough counties. Like African Americans and Hispanics, Asian Americans have a strong presence in New Hampshire's urban areas.

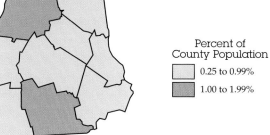

Percent of County Population

0.25 to 0.99%

1.00 to 1.99%

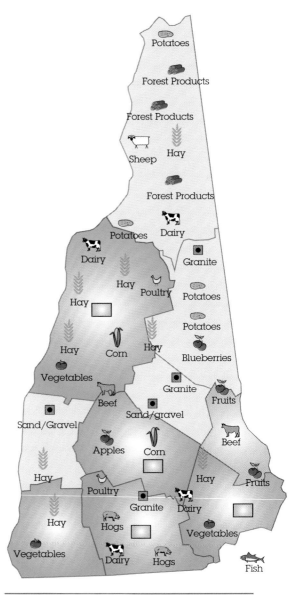

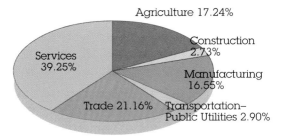

Major manufacturing areas

Major agricultural areas

Housing

Owner Occupied Units: 503,904; Average Age of Units: 27 years; Average Value of Housing Units: $129,400; Renter Occupied Units: 127,782; Median Monthly Rent: $549; Housing Starts: 5,200; Existing Home Sales: 13,600.

Economic Facts

Gross State Product: $25,000,000,000 (1989)

Income Per Capita: $22,934

Disposable Personal Income: $20,889

Median Household Income: $36,329

Average Annual Pay, 1988: $23,600

Principal Industries: scientific instruments, machinery, paper products, plastic products, electrical equipment, printing, shoes, plastics

Major Crops: milk, apples, hay, peaches, corn, maple syrup

Fish: Bluefish, Cod, Flounder, Pollock, Tuna

Livestock: Cattle, Sheep, Horses

Non-Fuel Minerals: Granite, Sand, Gravel, Quartz

Organic Fuel Minerals: N/A

Civilian Labor Force: 634,000 (Women: 288,000)

Total Employed: 589,000 (Women: 269,000)

Median Value of Housing: $129,400

Median Contract Rent: $549 per month

Agriculture

New Hampshire has 0.47 million farm acres. During the last 40 years, New Hampshire's farms have grown larger in size and fewer in number. In 1955, 10,000 farms were found in the state. Today, 2,700 remain.

Agriculture adds less than $500 million to the state's gross product annually. The principal commodities in order of marketing receipts are dairy products, greenhouse, apples, and hay.

Dairy farming accounts for most of New Hampshire's farm income. Many dairy farms are located along the Connecticut River, although they are found throughout the state. The leading crop is hay, used primarily for cattle feed. Potatoes and corn are the most important vegetables, while apples are the leading fruit. Other products include greenhouse goods and maple syrup.

Economic Sectors 1992

Agriculture 17.24%

Construction 2.73%

Services 39.25%

Manufacturing 16.55%

Trade 21.16%   Transportation–Public Utilities 2.90%

Manufacturing

The manufacturing industries of New Hampshire provide over one-quarter, 26 percent, of the state gross product. Also, more than one-quarter of New Hampshire's nonagricultural workers are employed in manufacturing jobs. Machinery is the state's leading industry, but electrical equipment, paper products, and plastics are also produced in New Hampshire factories.

New Hampshire has only one large industrial center in the state. Berlin, north of the White Mountains, produces much of the state's paper goods. However, industry takes place in other parts of New Hampshire as well. The southern New Hampshire towns of Manchester, Merrimack, and Nashua manufacture machinery, computers, military communications equipment, and plastic products.

Transportation

The state of New Hampshire has a more limited transportation network than many other states. The original New Hampshire Turnpike opened in 1796, connecting Portsmouth and Concord. The contemporary New Hampshire Turnpike runs between Massachusetts and Maine, parallel to the coast. Overall, New Hampshire has approximately 16,000 miles of highways and roads. About 225 miles of the highways are part of the Federal Interstate Highway System.

The state's first railroad began operating in 1838. Today, six rail lines provide freight service for New Hampshire. However, Amtrak, the national passenger railroad, serves no New Hampshire cities. Manchester, in southern New Hampshire, has the state's busiest airport. Other airports across the state, including ones in Lebanon and Laconia, serve many passengers.

Energy and Transportation Facts

Energy. Yearly Consumption: 239 tril. BTUs (residential, 28.9%; commercial, 16.7%; industrial, 22.6%; transportation, 31.4%); Annual Energy Expenditures Per Capita: $1,727; Nuclear Power Plants Located in State: 1; Source of Energy Consumed: Petroleum— 49.7%; Natural Gas— 4.9%; Coal— 12.2%; Hydroelectric Power—8.0%; Nuclear Power—25.3%.

Transportation. Highway Miles: 14,913 (interstates, 224; urban, 2,440; rural, 12,473); Average Yearly Auto Insurance: $638 (20th); Auto Fatalities Rank: 47th; Registered Motor Vehicles: 893,647; Workers in Carpools: 15.8%; Workers Using Public Trans: 0.7%.

Employment

Employment. New Hampshire employed 579,000 people in 1993. Most work in social and personal services (136,400 persons or 23.6% of the workforce). Manufacturing accounts for 16.8% or 97,000 workers. Wholesale and retail trade account for 22.2% or 128,300 workers. Government employs 73,600 workers (12.7%). Construction employs 16,800 workers (2.9%). Transportation and utilities account for 3.1% or 17,900 persons. Agriculture employs 8,700 workers or 1.5%. Finance, real estate, and insurance account for 5.1% or 29,800 workers. Mining employs 400 people and accounts for only 0.1% of the workforce.

Unemployment. Unemployment has increased to 6.6% in 1993 from a rate of 3.9% in 1985. Today's figure is lower than the national average of 6.8% as shown below.

Unemployment Rate

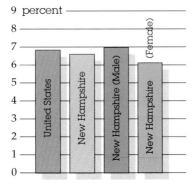

percent

NEW JERSEY
The State of New Jersey

Official State Seal

The Great Seal of New Jersey was adopted in 1776 after some adaptations made by a French artist. The two women supporting the shield represent Liberty and the Roman goddess Ceres. Three plows are placed on the shield to mark New Jersey's agricultural background. The horse's head came from markings found on coins, while the helmet represents sovereignty.

Legal Holidays

January: New Year's Day—1st; Martin Luther King, Jr., Day—3rd Monday; February: Abraham Lincoln's Birthday—12th; Presidents' Day—3rd Monday; March: Crispus Attucks Day—5th; April: Youth Day (New Brunswick)—3rd; May: Memorial Day—4th Monday; July: Independence Day—4th; September: Labor Day—1st Monday; October: Columbus Day—2nd Monday; November: Veterans' Day—11th; Thanksgiving—4th Thursday; December: Ratification Day—18th; Christmas—25th.

Official State Flag

The state flag of New Jersey was adopted in 1896. The state seal is placed on a buff field. This buff field represents the colors found on military uniforms of the New Jersey Continental Line selected by George Washington in 1779. Also included is the state motto, "Liberty and Prosperity."

Festivals and Events

February: Postcard Show, Mt. Laurel; March: Eggsibit, Phillipsburg; Polka Festival, McFee; April: Poe Mystery Weekend, Cape May; May: Cape May Music Fest, Cape May; May in Montclair, Montclair Township; June: Fresh Seafood Festival, Atlantic City; Opera Festival of New Jersey, Lawrenceville; July: Be Nice to New Jersey Week; August: Precanex, Wildwood; Jazz Fest, Willingboro; September: Clownfest, Bloomfield; Wings 'n Water Festival, Stone Harbor; Heritage Days at Holmdel, Holmdel; October: Long Beach Island Chowder Cook-Off, Beach Haven; Victorian Week, Cape May.

New Jersey Compared to Its Region

Resident Pop. in Metro Areas: 1st; Pop. Percent Increase: 2d; Pop. Over 65: 2d; Infant Mortality: 2d; School Enroll. Increase: 1st; High School Grad. and Up: 1st; Violent Crime: 2d; Hazardous Waste Sites: 1st; Unemployment: 2d; Median Household Income: 1st; Persons Below Poverty: 3d; Energy Costs Per Person: 1st.

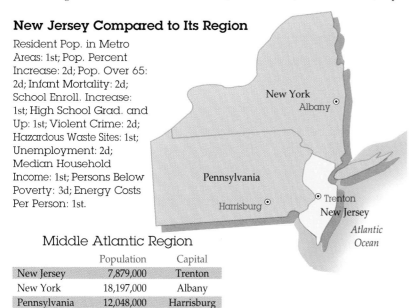

Middle Atlantic Region

	Population	Capital
New Jersey	7,879,000	Trenton
New York	18,197,000	Albany
Pennsylvania	12,048,000	Harrisburg

New Jersey's Finances

Households: 2,795,000; Income Per Capita Current Dollars: $26,457; Change Per Capita Income 1980 to 1992: 127.1% (2d in U.S.); State Expenditures: $24,109,000,000; State Revenues: $23,400,000,000; Personal Income Tax: 2 to 7%; Federal Income Taxes Paid Per Capita: $2,730; Sales Tax: 6% (food and prescription drugs exempt).

State Expenditures

14.0 billion dollars

- Education
- Highway
- Welfare
- Health
- Other

12.0
10.0
8.0
6.0
4.0
2.0
0

State Revenues

14.0 billion dollars

- Federal
- Local
- Taxes
- Miscellaneous

12.0
10.0
8.0
6.0
4.0
2.0
0

Location, Size, and Boundaries

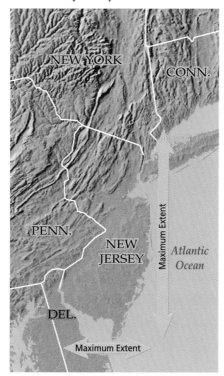

Location. New Jersey is located in the northeastern United States in a region known as the Middle Atlantic. It is bounded on three of four sides by land with a small coastline along the Atlantic Ocean. The geographic center of New Jersey is lat. 40° 4.2' N; long. 74° 33.5' W.

Size. New Jersey is the 46th largest state in terms of size. Its area is 7,836 sq. mi. (20,295 km2). Inland water covers 315 sq. mi. (618 km2). New Jersey touches the Atlantic Ocean along a 130 mile (209 km) coastline.

Boundaries. New York, 108 mi. (174 km); Atlantic Ocean, 130 mi. (209 km); Delaware, 78 mi. (126 km); Pennsylvania, 164 mi. (264 km).

Geographic Extent. The north/south extent is 166 mi. 267 km). The state extends 57 mi. (92 km) to the east/west.

Facts about New Jersey. Origin of Name: Named after the Isle of Jersey in England; Nickname: The Garden State; Motto: "Liberty and Prosperity"; Abbreviations: N.J. (traditional), NJ (postal); State Bird: Eastern goldfinch; State Tree: red oak; State Flower: purple violet; State Song: none.

New Jersey Compared to Other States. Resident Pop. in Metro Areas: 1st; Pop. Per. Increase: 43d; Pop. Over 65: 16th; Infant Mortality: 24th; School Enroll. Increase: 12th; High School Grad. and Up: 26th; Violent Crime: 20th; Hazardous Waste Sites: 1st; Unemployment: 8th; Median Household Income: 3d; Persons Below Poverty: 48th; Energy Costs Per Person: 13th.

Sources of Information. Tourism: The NJ Dept. of Commerce and Economic Development, Division of Travel and Tourism, CN 826, Trenton, NJ 08625. Economy: The NJ Dept. of Commerce and Economic Development, Office of Economic Research, 20 West State Street, Trenton, NJ 08625. Government: Office of Public Information, Office of Legislative Services, State House Annex, Room 123, CN 068, Trenton, NJ 08625.

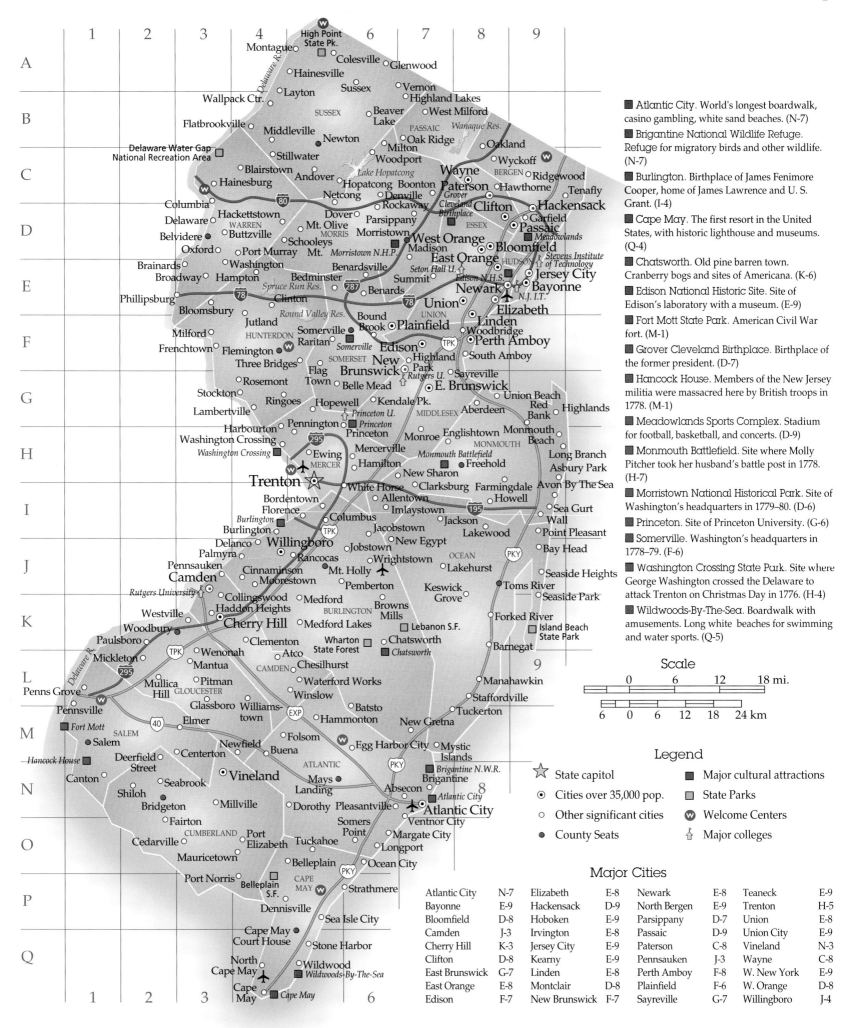

■ **Atlantic City.** World's longest boardwalk, casino gambling, white sand beaches. (N-7)

■ **Brigantine National Wildlife Refuge.** Refuge for migratory birds and other wildlife. (N-7)

■ **Burlington.** Birthplace of James Fenimore Cooper, home of James Lawrence and U. S. Grant. (I-4)

■ **Cape May.** The first resort in the United States, with historic lighthouse and museums. (Q-4)

■ **Chatsworth.** Old pine barren town. Cranberry bogs and sites of Americana. (K-6)

■ **Edison National Historic Site.** Site of Edison's laboratory with a museum. (E-9)

■ **Fort Mott State Park.** American Civil War fort. (M-1)

■ **Grover Cleveland Birthplace.** Birthplace of the former president. (D-7)

■ **Hancock House.** Members of the New Jersey militia were massacred here by British troops in 1778. (M-1)

■ **Meadowlands Sports Complex.** Stadium for football, basketball, and concerts. (D-9)

■ **Monmouth Battlefield.** Site where Molly Pitcher took her husband's battle post in 1778. (H-7)

■ **Morristown National Historical Park.** Site of Washington's headquarters in 1779–80. (D-6)

■ **Princeton.** Site of Princeton University. (G-6)

■ **Somerville.** Washington's headquarters in 1778–79. (F-6)

■ **Washington Crossing State Park.** Site where George Washington crossed the Delaware to attack Trenton on Christmas Day in 1776. (H-4)

■ **Wildwoods-By-The-Sea.** Boardwalk with amusements. Long white beaches for swimming and water sports. (Q-5)

Scale

0   6   12   18 mi.

6   0   6   12   18   24 km

Legend

■ Major cultural attractions
☆ State capitol
□ State Parks
⊙ Cities over 35,000 pop.
Ⓦ Welcome Centers
○ Other significant cities
⚲ Major colleges
● County Seats

Major Cities

City	Grid	City	Grid	City	Grid	City	Grid
Atlantic City	N-7	Elizabeth	E-8	Newark	E-8	Teaneck	E-9
Bayonne	E-9	Hackensack	D-9	North Bergen	E-9	Trenton	H-5
Bloomfield	D-8	Hoboken	E-9	Parsippany	D-7	Union	E-8
Camden	J-3	Irvington	E-8	Passaic	D-9	Union City	E-9
Cherry Hill	K-3	Jersey City	E-9	Paterson	C-8	Vineland	N-3
Clifton	D-8	Kearny	E-9	Pennsauken	J-3	Wayne	C-8
East Brunswick	G-7	Linden	E-8	Perth Amboy	F-8	W. New York	E-9
East Orange	E-8	Montclair	D-8	Plainfield	F-6	W. Orange	D-8
Edison	F-7	New Brunswick	F-7	Sayreville	G-7	Willingboro	J-4

Weather Facts

Record High Temperature: 110° F (43° C) on July 10, 1936, at Runyon; Record Low Temperature: -34° F (-37° C) on January 5, 1904, at River Vale; Average January Temperature: 32° F (0° C); Average July Temperature: 76° F (24° C); Average Yearly Precipitation: 45 in. (114 cm).

Environmental Facts

Air Pollution Rank: 29th; Water Pollution Rank: 34th; Total Yearly Industrial Pollution: 21,441,487 lbs.; Industrial Pollution Rank: 31st; Hazardous Waste Sites: 109; Hazardous Sites Rank: 1st; Landfill Capacity: overextended; Fresh Water Supply: large surplus; Daily Residential Water Consumption: 142 gals. per capita; Endangered Species: Aquatic Species (1)—sturgeon, shortnose; Birds (4)—curlew, Eskimo; Mammals (1)—bat, Indiana; Other Species (1)—turtle, loggerhead sea; Plants (5)—beaked-rush, Knieskern's.

Environmental Quality

New Jersey residents generate 9.5 million tons of solid waste each year, or approximately 2,500 pounds per capita. Landfill capacity in New Jersey will be exhausted in less than 5 years. The state has 109 hazardous waste sites. Annual greenhouse gas emissions in New Jersey total 107.2 million tons, or 13.9 tons per capita. Industrial sources in New Jersey release approximately 86.3 thousand tons of toxins, 513.7 thousand tons of acid precipitation-producing substances, and 2.1 million tons of smog-producing substances into the atmosphere each year.

The state has 34,500 acres within the National Park System. Noteworthy is Morristown National Historic Site. State parks cover just over 293,000 acres, attracting 11.0 million visitors per year.

New Jersey spends approximately 3.6 percent of its budget, or approximately $68 per capita, on environmental and natural resources.

Average Monthly Weather

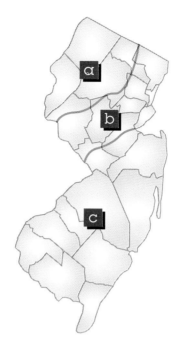

Physical Regions: (a) Highlands; (b) Piedmont; (c) Coastal Plain.

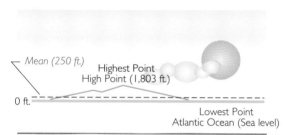

Mean (250 ft.)
Highest Point
High Point (1,803 ft.)
0 ft.
Lowest Point
Atlantic Ocean (Sea level)

Land Use

Cropland: 14.7%; Pasture: 5%; Rangeland: 0%; Forest: 41.4%; Urban: 29.1%; Other: 9.8%.

For more information about New Jersey's environment, contact the Department of Environmental Protection, 401 E. State St., Trenton, NJ 08625.

Atlantic City	Jan	Feb	Mar	Apr	May	Jun	Jul	Aug	Sep	Oct	Nov	Dec	Yearly
Maximum Temperature °F	40.6	42.4	50.3	61.6	71.0	79.6	84.0	82.5	76.7	66.1	55.4	45.0	62.9
Minimum Temperature °F	22.9	23.9	31.6	40.4	49.9	58.8	64.8	63.5	56.4	44.8	35.8	26.6	43.3
Days of Precipitation	10.6	9.8	10.6	10.9	10.2	8.9	8.6	8.6	7.5	7.3	9.4	9.6	112.1
Newark													
Maximum Temperature °F	38.2	40.3	49.1	61.3	71.6	80.6	85.6	84.0	76.9	66.0	54.0	42.3	62.5
Minimum Temperature °F	24.2	25.3	33.3	42.9	53.0	62.4	67.9	67.0	59.4	48.3	39.0	28.6	45.9
Days of Precipitation	11.0	9.6	11.1	10.9	12.0	10.2	10.0	9.3	8.3	7.9	10.3	10.8	121.3

Flora and Fauna

New Jersey's forested land continually decreases as urbanization increases. Today, the state is approximately 40 percent covered by forests. Northern New Jersey hardwood trees include the oak, sweet gum, and yellow poplar. Southern New Jersey, especially the famous Pine Barrens, has several kinds of pine, as well as cedar trees. Queen Anne's lace and goldenrod are two prevalent New Jersey wildflowers. Other common flowers include Virginia cowslips and azaleas. The state flower, the purple violet, grows in wooded areas of New Jersey.

Many smaller mammals inhabit New Jersey, including otters, opossums, foxes, and raccoons. Deer are the only common large animal, but they are monitored by state officials. Both the state's woodlands and its meadows are home to game birds such as wild turkey and ruffed grouse. Wild geese and ducks live on the Atlantic coast and in marshy areas. Many migratory birds stop in New Jersey. Several kinds of fish, including bluefish, pickerel, shad, and weakfish, live in the state's waterways. Other marine life such as crabs and clams can be found off the New Jersey coast.

Topography

There are several distinct topographic regions in New Jersey. Most of southern and eastern New Jersey lies in the Atlantic Coastal Plain physical region, a largely flat area that is barely above sea level. The coastal area has many marshes and popular resort beaches. Much of the eastern region is covered by the Pine Barrens; the sandy soil found there supports mostly short scrub pines and forms a huge aquifer. Inland from the coast, the soil is a warm and moist loamy clay that is high in organic content, making this area suitable for agriculture. This soil type is distributed throughout the state. Northwest of the Coastal Plains is the Piedmont lowlands physical region. Continuing north is the Highlands physical region. This region is notable for its many natural lakes and steep ridges.

In the northwestern part of the state is the Appalachian Valley physical region, consisting of the Kittatinny Mountains and several fertile valleys. The Kittatinny Range is part of the Appalachian Mountains. High Point, the highest elevation in the state, is located in the northwest corner of New Jersey and reaches 1,803 ft. (550 m) above sea level.

Climate

Even though New Jersey is a coastal state, the Atlantic Ocean does not influence climate as much as one might think. Only at the Jersey shore does the ocean affect climate; otherwise, the continental land mass dictates climate. Prevailing westerly winds blow over the state, creating the temperature variations. Northern New Jersey, in places like Newark and Morristown, has average January and July temperatures of 26 degrees F and 70 degrees F. In the south, mean temperatures are higher, 34 degrees F and 76 degrees F, respectively.

Much of New Jersey's 45 inches of annual precipitation falls quite evenly over the entire state; only slight variations exist. The northern part of the state receives more precipitation, almost one-quarter of it being snowfall.

Every part of New Jersey has had extremely variable weather. Both temperatures of over 100 degrees F and below 0 degrees F have been recorded in each county.

Hydrology

The Delaware River forms New Jersey's eastern boundary with Pennsylvania, and the Delaware River and Bay form its southern border. The Hudson River defines New Jersey's northeast boundary with New York, and the Atlantic Ocean forms the rest of the eastern border. The Raritan River, in the north, flows for about 80 miles (129 km) into the Atlantic. The Mullica and Egg Harbor rivers flow southeast into the Atlantic in southern New Jersey. Other rivers in northern New Jersey include the Ramapo, the Passaic, the Musconetcong, and the Hackensack. There are many lakes in the state. The largest is Lake Hopatcong on the Musconetcong River in northern New Jersey. Others include Lake Mohawk and Union Lake.

There are several bays and inlets along New Jersey's Atlantic coast, including Barnegat Bay, Great Bay, Great Egg Inlet, and Hereford Inlet.

New Jersey's History

New Jersey's First People

The Lenni Lenape or Delaware Indians were the first known inhabitants of New Jersey, arriving approximately thirteen thousand years ago. Members of the Algonquian language family, the Lenni Lenape's name means "Original People." The Lenni Lenape primarily relied on agriculture for survival, although they supplemented their diet with freshwater fish. Throughout their history in New Jersey, the population of Lenni Lenape probably never reached over ten thousand.

European Exploration

In 1524, Giovanni da Verrazano became the first European to reach New Jersey, landing at what is now Newark Bay. The Dutch claimed a stake in New Jersey when Henry Hudson, an Englishman sailing under the Dutch flag, sailed along the Jersey shore around Sandy Hook (1609). By 1626 New Netherlands was founded, and several years later, in 1660, the first town, Bergen, was established.

The Dutch colony, situated between the English colonies of New England and Virginia, was a contested area. In March 1664, Charles II, king of England, chartered a large tract of land, including the Dutch claim to New Jersey, to the duke of York. Five months later, a fleet of English ships under the command of Col. Richard Nicolls entered New York Bay to claim their territory. Eleven days later, the Dutch colonial governor, Peter Stuyvesant, formally surrendered to the English, thus ending the Dutch claim.

New Jersey became its own colony in June of 1664, when the territory between the Delaware and Hudson rivers was separated from the area known as New York. Authority over the new colony was granted by the duke of York to his friend Sir George Carteret and Lord John Berkeley. The colony was named New Jersey in honor of Carteret, who had defended the isle of Jersey in the English Civil War.

Europeans drew up treaties between themselves and the Lenni Lenape that proved to be the downfall of the Native Americans. While the Europeans received large parcels of Lenni Lenape land, the Indians received mostly guns and alcohol. This combination of guns, alcohol, and diseases such as smallpox, decimated the Native American population.

In 1758, the first Indian reservation in the United States was established at Brothertown. By 1802, the remaining Native Americans went west.

Revolutionary War and Statehood

The American Revolution divided New Jersey into Revolutionary and Loyalist camps. William Franklin, who was the illegitimate son of the famous Philadelphian Benjamin Franklin, was the state's royal governor from 1763 to 1776, when he departed for England.

New Jersey proved to be important during the American Revolution, because of its strategic location between New York and Philadelphia.

Five major Revolutionary battles were fought on New Jersey soil, the most important being the Battle of Trenton on December 26, 1776, and the Battle of Monmouth on June 28, 1778. George Washington and his troops wintered in New Jersey three times. For a short period after the end of the war, two New Jersey cities served as the national capital. Princeton served as the capital of the United States from June 26, 1783, to November 4, 1783. A year later, Trenton became the capital for scarcely more than a month, from November 1 to December 24, 1784.

The Provincial Congress of New Jersey adopted its state constitution on July 2, 1776. This constitution was in effect until it was amended in 1844. The state became the third state in the Union to adopt the U.S. Constitution in 1787.

Industrialization

New Jersey's first industries were ironworking (established in 1676) and glassblowing. After the Revolutionary War, the ironworking industry nearly collapsed completely. Then in 1791, manufacturing emerged as the leader.

New industry was fueled by the transportation boom, including both canal and railroad construction. These vital transport links provided the raw materials and energy sources manufacturing needed to thrive. The Morris Canal and the Camden & Amboy Railroad, for example, were among the most important transportation links.

By the early 1800s, Paterson, in northern New Jersey, was the country's leading silk manufacturer. The manufacturing trend continued as hat factories, breweries, and paper plants emerged in the Newark area.

Both world wars sparked New Jersey's industrial economy. Both shipbuilding and ammunition manufacturing took place in the state. Today, New Jersey ranks first in the production of pharmaceuticals and second in chemicals.

Beaches and Boardwalks

New Jersey had been advertising itself as a beach resort since 1801, when Cape May started the trend. The travel and tourism industry create a multi-billion dollar industry, providing approximately half a million jobs.

Many people associate the Jersey shore with the resort towns in the southern half of the state, such as Wildwood and Ocean City. However, the northern half of New Jersey also has several beach resorts such as Point Pleasant and Long Branch.

Atlantic City is perhaps the most well-known resort area in New Jersey. In 1870, the first boardwalk was built in Atlantic City. The Miss America pageant, established in 1921, brought much fame to the city and its boardwalk. Atlantic City prospered even more when the state legalized casino gambling in a 1976 referendum.

Important Events

1524 Giovanni da Verrazano explores New Jersey coastline.

1609 Henry Hudson navigates Hudson River.

1614 Cornelius Mey, a Dutch captain, explores Delaware River.

1618 Bergen, a Dutch trading post, is established.

1638 Swedish settlers build forts along Delaware River.

1655 Dutch settlers, lead by Peter Stuyvesant, chase Swedes out of Delaware River settlements.

1660 Bergen becomes the first permanent white settlement.

1664 Peter Stuyvesant surrenders control of the Dutch area to the English.

1676 Colony divided into East and West Jersey.

1702 East and West Jersey reunite after proprietors of both surrender to English crown.

1738 New Jersey separated from New York.

1746 College of New Jersey, now Princeton, is chartered.

1776 Provincial Congress of New Jersey adopts constitution.

1787 New Jersey becomes third state to adopt U.S. Constitution.

1804 Alexander Hamilton killed by Vice President Aaron Burr at a duel in Weehawken.

1844 Second state constitution adopted.

1879 Thomas Edison demonstrates first electric lamp; at Melno Park.

1947 Third state constitution adopted.

1977 Casino gambling is legalized and casinos are built in Atlantic City.

1979 The Pinelands becomes first federal reserve.

1988 New Jersey launches its "Jersey Fresh" campaign to advertise quality of produce.

1993 Republican Christine Todd Whitman becomes governor, defeating incumbent James Florio (Democrat).

1995 Governor Whitman privatizes New Jersey's Division of Motor Vehicles (DMV) under great protest from the DMV worker's union.

1995 Wildwood Indian casino debate begins.

New Jersey

Population Density

Population density for the state of New Jersey was 1,042.0 persons per square mile in 1990 (402.3 per km2). Average U.S. density was 70.3 persons per square mile in 1990 (27.3 per km2). The state of New Jersey has the highest population density in the country. Most of this density can be found in the northern cities bordering New York.

Persons Per Square Mile

- 100.0 to 249.9
- 250.0 to 749.9
- 750.0 to 12,999.9

Population Projections

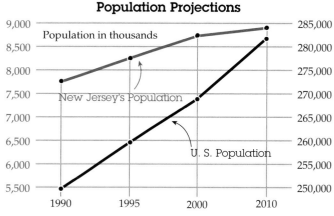

Population in thousands

New Jersey's Population

U. S. Population

Population Change

Year	Population
1950	4,835,000
1960	6,103,000
1970	7,193,000
1980	7,364,823
1990	7,730,188
2000	8,546,000
2010	8,980,000

Period	Change
1950–1970	48.8%
1970–1980	2.4%
1980–1990	5.0%
1990–2000	10.6%

Population Change

The 1990 population figure for the state of New Jersey was 7,730,188. This is a 4.96 percent increase from 7,364,823 in 1980. The next decade will show growth with a population of 8.5 million or a 10.55 percent increase. Much of the state has seen moderate increases in population in the last decade.

Percent Change 1980 to 1990

- –9.9 to 0.0%
- 0.1 to 19.9%
- 20.0 to 49.9%

Population Facts

State Population, 1993: 7,879,000

Rank: 9

Population 2000: 8,546,000 (Rank 9)

Density: 1,042.0 per sq. mi. (402.3 per km²)

Distribution: 89.4% urban, 10.6% rural

Population Under 5 Years Old: 7.4%

Population Under 18 Years Old: 23.9%

Population Over 65 Years Old: 13.6%

Median Age: 34.5

Number of Households: 2,795,000

Average Persons Per Household: 2.70

Average Persons Per Family: 3.21

Female Heads of Households: 4.38%

Population That Is Married: 20.42%

Birth Rate: 15.8 per 1,000 population

Death Rate: 9.1 per 1,000 population

Births to Teen Mothers: 8.4%

Marriage Rate: 7.5 per 1,000 population

Divorce Rate: 3.0 per 1,000 population

Violent Crime Rate: 635 per 100,000 pop.

Population on Social Security: 16.0%

Percent Voting for President: 56.3%

New Jersey's Famous Citizens

Blume, Judy (b. 1938). Award-winning author of fiction for young teens. Her books include *Then Again, Maybe I Won't*.

Livingston, William (1723–1790). Represented New Jersey in the First Continental Congress. First governor of New Jersey.

Moody, John (1868–1958). Created an investment manual on statistical information and private investment.

Newcombe, Don (b. 1926). Baseball pitcher and Rookie of the Year in 1949. He won both the MVP and Cy Young awards in 1956.

Nicholson, Jack (b. 1937). Actor. Known for his irreverence. He won an Academy Award for *One Flew Over the Cuckoo's Nest* (1975).

Stevens, John (1749–1838). He developed several steam-driven engines and worked on the first U.S. patent law.

Streep, Meryl (b. 1949). Actress of a wide range of roles. She won an Academy Award for her role in the film *Sophie's Choice*.

Warwick, Dionne (b. 1941). Pop singer. She popularized Bacharach-David tunes such as "Do You Know the Way to San Jose?"

Distribution of Income

The per capita income for the state of New Jersey (current dollars) was $26,457 in 1992. This is a 127.1 percent increase from $11,648 in 1980. New Jersey is one of the highest income states in the country. Much of the state has a high per capita income with the exception of the far south and Hudson County.

Per Capita Income (000s) (Current Dollars)

- $13.0 to 15.9
- $16.0 to 19.9
- $20.0 to 35.2

Population Profile

Rank. New Jersey ranks 9th among U.S. states in terms of population with 7,879,000 citizens.

Minority Population. The state's minority population is 26.7 percent. The state's male to female ratio for 1990 was 93.52 males for every 100 females. It was below the national average of 95.22 males for every 100 females.

Growth. Growing faster than the projected national average, the state's population is

Government

Capital: Trenton (established 1790).

Statehood: Became 3d state on Dec. 18, 1787.

Number of Counties: 21.

Supreme Court Justices: 7, 7-year term.

State Senators: 40, 2 or 4-year term.

State Legislators: 80, 2-year term.

United States Senators: 2.

United States Representatives: 13.

Electoral Votes: 15.

State Constitution: Adopted 1947.

expected to reach 9.0 million by the year 2010 *(see graph above)*.

Older Citizens. The state's population older than 65 was 1,032,025 in 1990. It grew 20.03% from 859,771 in 1980.

Younger Citizens. The number of children (under 18 years of age) was 1.8 million in 1990. This represents 23.3 percent of the state's population. The state's school aged population was 1.1 million in 1990. It is expected to increase to 1.3 million by the year 2000. This represents a 19.34% change.

Urban/Rural. 89.4% of the population of the state live in urban areas while 10.6% live in rural areas.

Largest Cities. New Jersey has 33 cities with a population greater than 35,000. The populations of the state's largest centers are (starting from the most populous) Newark (275,221), Jersey City (228,537), Paterson (140,891), Elizabeth (110,002), Edison (88,680), Trenton (88,675), Camden (87,492), East Orange (73,552), Clifton (71,742), Cherry Hill (69,319), Brick Township (66,473), Bayonne (61,444), Irvington (59,774), Passaic (58,041), Union City (58,012), Vineland (54,780), and Union (50,024).

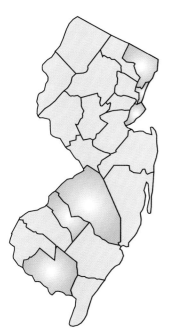

Native American

The Native American population in New Jersey was 14,970 in 1990. This was an increase of 49.28 percent from 10,028 in 1980. Many Native Americans live in the heavily populated urban areas of the northeast. Some also are located in the small Rancocas Indian Reservation located in Burlington County.

Presence of
Native Americans

☐ Minor

Nationalities

African	19,757
American	170,439
Arab	39,304
Austrian	36,214
Czech	21,853
Dutch	87,012
English	412,503
Finnish	5,071
German	991,965
Greek	51,849
Hungarian	88,361
Irish	903,814
Italian	1,191,287
Norwegian	30,039
Polish	443,512
Portuguese	56,928
Russian	167,742
Scottish	81,218
Slovak	74,671
Swedish	41,855
Welsh	22,160
West Indian	60,688

Statewide Ethnic Composition

Over 79 percent of the population of New Jersey is white. The largest nationalities in this racial group are Italian, German, and Irish. The next largest group is African Americans, followed by Hispanics, Asian Americans, and Native Americans. Over 170,000 people claim to be American and acknowledge no other nationality.

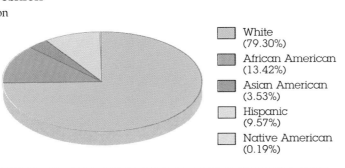

☐ White (79.30%)

☐ African American (13.42%)

☐ Asian American (3.53%)

☐ Hispanic (9.57%)

☐ Native American (0.19%)

Education Facts

Total Students 1990: 1,076,005

Number of School Districts: 603

Expenditure Per Capita on Education 1990: $1,114

Expenditure Per Capita K–12 1990: $1,083

Expenditure Per Pupil 1990: $8,451

Total School Enrollment 1990–1991: 1,082,561

Rank of Expenditures Per Student: 3d in the U.S.

African American Enrollment: 18.5%

Hispanic Enrollment: 11.1%

Asian/Pacific Islander Enrollment: 4.1%

Native American Enrollment: 0.1%

Mean SAT Score 1991 Verbal: 417

Mean SAT Score 1991 Math: 469

Average Teacher's Salary 1992: $41,000

Rank Teacher's Salary: 5th in U.S.

High School Graduates 1990: 68,500

Total Number of Public Schools: 2,264

Number of Teachers 1990: 80,190

Student/Teacher Ratio: 13.5

Staff Employed in Public Schools: 146,617

Pupil/Staff Ratio: 7.3

Staff/Teacher Ratio: 1.8

Education

Attainment: 79.4 percent of population 25 years or older were high school graduates in 1989, earning New Jersey a ranking of 23d in the United States; 25.5 percent of the state's population had completed college. Institutions of Higher Education: The largest universities and colleges in the state include Rutgers University, New Brunswick; Kean, Union, Camden; The New Jersey Institute of Technology, Newark; The University of Medicine and Dentistry of New Jersey, Newark; Princeton University, Princeton; Fairleigh Dickinson University, Rutherford; Seton Hall University, South Orange. Expenditures per Student: Expenditure increased 66% between 1985 and 1990. Projected High School Graduations: 1998 (20,102), 2004 (21,020); Total Revenues for Education from Federal Sources: $293 million; Total Revenues for Education from State Sources: $3 billion; Total Revenues for Education from Local Sources: $3.9 billion; Average Annual Salaries for Public School Principals: $53,056; Largest School Districts in State: Newark City School District, 48,573 students, 70th in the United States; Jersey City School District, 27,788, 152d.

African American

The African American population in New Jersey was 1,036,825 in 1990. This was an increase of 12.10 percent from 924,909 in 1980. Essex County in the north has the highest percentage of African Americans in the state. Cities such as Camden, Trenton, Newark, and Jersey City all have large African American populations.

Percent of
County Population

☐ 0.00 to 1.99%

☐ 2.00 to 4.99%

☐ 5.00 to 9.99%

☐ 10.00 to 24.99%

☐ 25.00 to 86.24%

Hispanic[††]

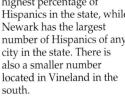

The Hispanic population in New Jersey was 739,861 in 1990. This is an increase of 50.41 percent from 491,883 persons in 1980. Jersey City in Hudson County has the highest percentage of Hispanics in the state, while Newark has the largest number of Hispanics of any city in the state. There is also a smaller number located in Vineland in the south.

†† A person of Mexican, Puerto Rican, Cuban, or other Spanish culture or origin regardless of race.

Percent of
County Population

☐ 1.00 to 2.99%

☐ 3.00 to 9.99%

☐ 10.00 to 24.99%

☐ 25.00 to 97.22%

Asian American

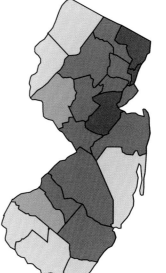

The Asian American population in New Jersey was 272,521 in 1990. This is an increase of 155.89 percent from 106,498 persons in 1980. Asian Americans have a strong presence in New Jersey's cities, especially Jersey City, New Brunswick, and Paterson. They also have a strong presence in most of the counties in the central and upper portion of the state.

Percent of
County Population

☐ 0.25 to 0.99%

☐ 1.00 to 1.99%

☐ 2.00 to 4.99%

☐ 5.00 to 76.92%

New Jersey

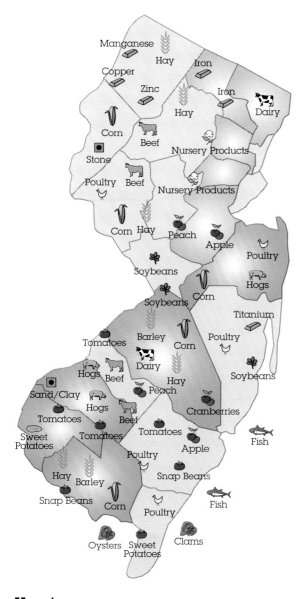

Transportation

New Jersey's position along the Eastern Seaboard makes it an important transportation link for the entire East Coast. The New Jersey road system consists of about 34,000 miles of highways and roads, most of which are paved.

New Jersey's rail lines—both passenger and freight—help move people and goods across the United States. Instate commuter railroads cross almost 500 miles of track.

New Jersey also has several ports along its coast, as well as along the Hudson and Delaware rivers. Newark and Elizabeth are important port cities. A ferry service runs between Cape May, New Jersey, and Lewes, Delaware. Newark has one of the nation's busiest airports, Newark International. Many smaller airports exist all over the state.

Energy and Transportation Facts

Energy. Yearly Consumption: 2,300 tril. BTUs (residential, 21.1%; commercial, 20.9%; industrial, 23.4%; transportation, 34.6%); Annual Energy Expenditures Per Capita: $2,047; Nuclear Power Plants Located in State: 4; Source of Energy Consumed: Petroleum— 59.9%; Natural Gas— 23.7%; Coal— 3.1%; Hydroelectric Power—0.0%; Nuclear Power—13.3%.

Transportation. Highway Miles: 34,286 (interstates, 396; urban, 22,503; rural, 11,783); Average Yearly Auto Insurance: $957 (2d); Auto Fatalities Rank: 45th; Registered Motor Vehicles: 5,591,354; Workers in Carpools: 17.3%; Workers Using Public Trans: 8.8%.

Agriculture

New Jersey has 0.87 million farm acres. During the last 40 years, New Jersey's farms have grown larger in size and fewer in number. In 1955, 23,000 farms were found in the state. Today, 8,400 remain.

Agriculture adds $1 billion to the state's gross product annually. The principal commodities in order of marketing receipts are greenhouse, dairy products, eggs, and peaches.

Greenhouse and nursery products account for most of New Jersey's farm income. Located in northeastern New Jersey for the New York market, these greenhouses produce roses, orchids, lilies, and other ornamental plants. Dairy farms are found mainly in the northwestern part of the state. Many crops are grown in New Jersey, the most important being tomatoes, sweet corn, peaches, blueberries, and cranberries.

Employment

Employment. New Jersey employed 3.70 million people in 1993. Most work in social and personal services (1.01 million persons or 27.4% of the workforce). Manufacturing accounts for 13.9% or 516,200 workers. Wholesale and retail trade account for 22.0% or 815,000 workers. Government employs 566,000 workers (15.3%). Construction employs 114,600 workers (3.1%). Transportation and utilities account for 6.3% or 235,200 persons. Agriculture employs 37,100 workers or 1.0%. Finance, real estate, and insurance account for 6.2% or 228,900 workers. Mining employs 1,800 people and accounts for less than 0.1% of the workforce.

Unemployment. Unemployment has increased to 7.4% in 1993 from a rate of 5.7% in 1985. Today's figure is higher than the national average of 6.8% as shown below.

Housing

Owner Occupied Units: 3,075,310; Average Age of Units: 36 years; Average Value of Housing Units: $162,300; Renter Occupied Units: 973,650; Median Monthly Rent: $592; Housing Starts: 17,300; Existing Home Sales: 139,000.

Economic Facts

Gross State Product: $203,000,000,000 (1989)

Income Per Capita: $26,457

Disposable Personal Income: $23,074

Median Household Income: $40,927

Average Annual Pay, 1988: $29,992

Principal Industries: electrical equipment, chemicals, food products, printing, transportation equipment, telecommunications, pharmaceuticals

Major Crops: dairy, greenhouse products, poultry, winter wheat

Fish: Bass, Bluefish, Crappies, Pike, Salmon, Shad

Livestock: Horses, Chickens, Dairy Cows

Non-Fuel Minerals: Stone, Clay, Gemstones, Peat, Zinc

Organic Fuel Minerals: N/A

Civilian Labor Force: 4,018,000 (Women: 1,806,000)

Total Employed: 3,752,000 (Women: 1,701,000)

Median Value of Housing: $162,300

Median Contract Rent: $592 per month

Economic Sectors 1992

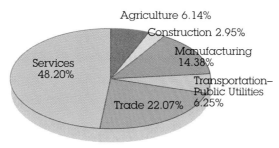

Agriculture 6.14%
Construction 2.95%
Manufacturing 14.38%
Transportation–Public Utilities 6.25%
Trade 22.07%
Services 48.20%

Manufacturing

New Jersey is a leading manufacturing state. The combination of a supportive state tax structure and the presence of foreign businesses makes New Jersey an industrial leader. Each year, New Jersey's manufactured products have a combined added value of over $32 billion. Chemicals and allied goods are the most important products. Other industries include food processing, electrical equipment, and printed materials.

Pharmaceuticals are the most important chemicals produced in New Jersey. Three top pharmaceutical manufacturers have their headquarters in the state. Many of the heavy industrial products are made in northeastern New Jersey. Electrical equipment is also made primarily in this area, and in the southern city of Camden.

Unemployment Rate

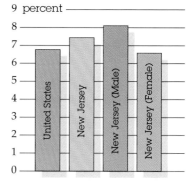

percent

United States
New Jersey
New Jersey (Male)
New Jersey (Female)

NEW MEXICO

The State of New Mexico

Official State Seal

The Great Seal of New Mexico was adopted in 1887 and became the official state seal in 1912 when New Mexico became the forty-seventh state. Included on the seal are the American and Mexican eagles surrounded by the words "The Great Seal of the State of New Mexico." On a ribbon below the eagles is the state motto, *"Crescit Eundo"* (It Grows as It Grows).

Legal Holidays

January: New Year's Day—1st; Admission Day—6th; Martin Luther King, Jr., Day—3rd Monday; February: Abraham Lincoln's Birthday—12th; Presidents' Day—3rd Monday; May: Memorial Day—4th Monday; July: Independence Day—4th; September: Labor Day—1st Monday; October: Columbus Day—2nd Monday; November: Veterans' Day—11th; Thanksgiving—4th Thursday; December: Christmas—25th.

Official State Flag

Adopted in 1925, New Mexico's state flag incorporate an ancient Indian sun symbol. This symbol represents the many sunny days that can be found in the state, while also honoring the Zia Indian Pueblo. The colors symbolize old Spain, which once owned the area.

Festivals and Events

January: Snowmobile Fest, Angel Fire; Winterfest at Angel Fire, Angel Fire; March: San Jose Feast Days, Laguna; May: Traditional Native American Dances, Gallup; June: Fun Flight, Alamogordo; July: Santa Fe Chamber Music Fest, Santa Fe; World's Greatest Lizard Race, Lovington; Freedom Days, Farmington; August: Great American Duck Race, Deming; Intertribal Native American Celebration, Gallup; September: Totah Festival, Farmington; October: Grecian Festival, Albuquerque; Oktoberfest, Angel Fire; Albuquerque International Balloon Fiesta, Albuquerque; November: Electric Light Parade, Lovington.

New Mexico Compared to States in Its Region.

Resident Pop. in Metro Areas: 5th; Pop. Percent Increase: 6th; Pop. Over 65: 5th; Infant Mortality: 1st; School Enroll. Increase: 3d; High School Grad. and Up: 8th; Violent Crime: 1st; Hazardous Waste Sites: 3d; Unemployment: 2d; Median Household Income: 7th; Persons Below Poverty: 1st; Energy Costs Per Person: 4th.

Mountain Region

	Population	Capital
Montana	839,000	Helena
Wyoming	470,000	Cheyenne
Idaho	1,099,000	Boise
Nevada	1,389,000	Carson City
Utah	1,860,000	Salt Lake City
Colorado	3,566,000	Denver
Arizona	3,936,000	Phoenix
New Mexico	1,616,000	Santa Fe

New Mexico's Finances

Households: 543,000; Income Per Capita Current Dollars: $15,353; Change Per Capita Income 1980 to 1992: 88.4% (40th in U.S.); State Expenditures: $4,594,000,000; State Revenues: $4,743,000,000; Personal Income Tax: 1.8 to 8.5%; Federal Income Taxes Paid Per Capita: $1,250; Sales Tax: 5%.

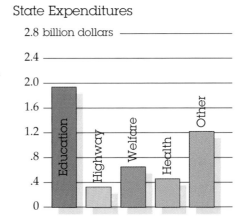

State Expenditures

2.8 billion dollars

2.4
2.0
1.6
1.2
.8
.4
0

Education, Highway, Welfare, Health, Other

State Revenues

2.8 billion dollars

2.4
2.0
1.6
1.2
.8
.4
0

Federal, Local, Taxes, Miscellaneous

Location, Size, and Boundaries

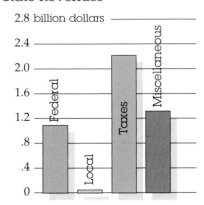

Maximum Extent

Location. New Mexico is located in the southwestern United States in what is known as the Mountain region. It is bounded on four sides by land. The geographic center of New Mexico is lat. 34° 30.1' N; long. 106° 6.7' W.

Size. New Mexico is the 5th largest state in terms of size. Its area is 121,666 sq. mi. (315, 115 km2). Inland water covers 254 sq. mi. (658 km2).

Boundaries. Colorado, 333 mi. (536 km); Oklahoma, 34 mi. (55 km); Texas, 498 mi. (801 km); Mexico, 180 mi. (290 km); Arizona, 389 mi. (626 km).

Geographic Extent. The north/south extent of New Mexico is 391 mi. (629 km). The state extends 352 mi. (566 km) to the east/west.

Facts about New Mexico. Origin of Name: Named by the Spanish in Mexico to refer to land north and west of the Rio Grande; Nickname: The Land of Enchantment; Motto: "It Grows as It Grows" *(Crescit Eundo)*; Abbreviations: N. Mex. or N.M. (traditional), NM (postal); State Bird: roadrunner; State Tree: nut pine; State Flower: yucca flower; State Song: "O, Fair New Mexico," words and music by Elizabeth Garrett.

New Mexico Compared to Other States. Resident Pop. in Metro Areas: 35th; Pop. Per. Increase: 10th; Pop. Over 65: 42d; Infant Mortality: 24th; School Enroll. Increase: 16th; High School Grad. and Up: 33d; Violent Crime: 10th; Hazardous Waste Sites: 32d; Unemployment: 26th; Median Household Income: 40th; Persons Below Poverty: 3d; Energy Costs Per Person: 23d.

Sources of Information. Tourism, Economy & History: Department of Economic Development and Tourism, Joseph M. Montoya State Building, 100 St. Francis Drive, Santa Fe, NM 87503. Government: Legislative Council Service, 334 State Capitol, Santa Fe, NM 87503.

Map Labels

Columns: 1 2 3 4 5 6 7 8 9 10 11

Row A: La Plata · Aztec Ruins Nat'l Monument · Chama · 285 · Vermejo Park · W · Raton · Capulin Mountain National Monument · Des Moines · 64 · Shiprock · Aztec · Navajo Lakes State Pk. · Dulce · Cumbres and Toltec Railroad · Questa · COLFAX

Row B: Shiprock · Farmington · Bloomfield · City of Rocks State Pk. · Tierra Amarilla · Tusas · TAOS · Taos · 64 · Miami · Springer · 25 · UNION · Mount Dora · 64 · 666 · SAN JUAN · RIO ARRIBA · Canjilon · 84 · 68 · Taos · Ranches of Taos · Clayton · 56

Row C: Toadlena · Regina · Cuba · Espanola · Santa Clara · LOS ALAMOS · St. John's College · Santa Fe · Guadalupita · Abbott · Mills · Bueyeros · Hayden · Crystal · 44 · MORA · Levy · HARDING · Mora · Fort Union Nat'l Monument · Solano · Mosquero · Amistad · Chaco Culture National Historical Park · White Horse Lake · Los Alamos · Ponderosa · Bandelier Nat'l Mon · Pecos · Las Vegas · Sabinoso · Conchas Lake · 39 · Gallegos · Nara Visa

Row D: Navajo · MCKINLEY · San Ysidro · SANDOVAL · SANTA FE · Trujillo · Ute Lake · 54 · Logan · Gamerco · Gallup · W · Thoreau · Bernalillo · Rio Rancho · SAN MIGUEL · Conchas Lake State Pk. · Glenrio

Row E: Manuclito · 40 · Bluewater · Grants · Albuquerque · 285 · Rencona · Anton Chico · Colonias · Tucumcari · San Jon · W · Bluewater Lakes State Pk. · Zuni · El Morro · Acomita · University of New Mexico · BERNALILLO · Leyba · Santa Rosa Lake State Pk. · 40 · QUAY · Santa Rosa · GUADALUPE

Row F: El Morro Nat'l Monument · Acoma · Los Lunas · Isleta · VALENCIA · Moriarty · Estancia · Vaughn · 84 · Fence Lake · CIBOLA · Belen · TORRANCE · Yeso · 60 · Fort Sumner · Clovis · Texico · CURRY

Row G: Quemado · Pie Town · Polvadera · Venguita · Mountainair · 54 · Corona · Ramon · DE BACA · Taiban · Oasis State Pk. · W · 60 · 25 · Magdalena · Lemitar · Claunch · Grave of Billy the Kid · Floyd · Portales · CATRON · Aragon · New Mexico Institute of Mining and Technology · Socorro · 285 · ROOSEVELT

Row H: Apache Creek · SOCORRO · 380 · Bingham · LINCOLN · White Oaks · CHAVES · Elkins · 206 · Reserve · Dusty · San Antonio · Carrizozo · 285 · Crossroads · 70

Row I: Glenwood · Monticello · Elephant Butte Lake · Trinity Site (World's First A-Bomb exploded here July 16th, 1945) · Lincoln · Hondo · Roswell · Caprock · Pleasanton · Gila Cliff Dwellings Nat'l Monument · Ruidoso · 380 · Bottomless Lakes State Pk. · Tatum · 180 · SIERRA · Truth or Consequences · Tularosa · International Space Hall of Fame · 285 · Dexter · Lake Arthur · Lovington

Row J: Kingston · Caballo Lake · City of Rocks State Pk. · Elk · Hope · Artesia · 152 · Derry · White Sands National Monument · Alamogordo · 82 · Virden · Bayard · OTERO · Pinon · EDDY · Brantley Lake · 62 · Hobbs · Silver City · Hurley · New Mexico State University · Missile Range · 54 · LEA · 70 · 180 · City of Rocks State Pk. · GRANT

Row K: Lordsburg · Deming · Las Cruces · University Park · Orogrande · Carlsbad · Loving · Eunice · 70 · 10 · Gage · LUNA · White City · 285 · DONA ANA · Anthony · Carlsbad Caverns National Park

Row L: Animas · Hachita · Columbus · Pancho Villa State Pk. · Rodeo · HIDALGO

Scale

0   25   50   75 mi.

25   0   25   50   75   100 km

Legend

☆ State capitol
◉ Cities over 35,000 population
○ Other significant cities
● County Seats
■ Major cultural attractions
□ State Parks
Ⓦ Welcome Centers
⇧ Major colleges and universities

Major Cities

City	Grid	City	Grid
Alamogordo	K-6	Las Cruces	L-5
Albuquerque	E-5	Las Vegas	D-8
Artesia	K-9	Los Alamos	D-5
Carlsbad	L-9	Portales	H-11
Clovis	G-11	Rio Rancho	E-5
Deming	L-3	Roswell	I-9
Farmington	B-2	Santa Fe	D-6
Gallup	D-1	Silver City	K-2
Hobbs	K-11		

Cultural Features

■ **Acoma.** The "sky city," ancient Acoma Indian pueblo on 357-foot mesa; refuge for Indians fleeing Spanish retribution after the 1680 Pueblo Revolt. (F-3)

■ **Aztec Ruins National Monument.** Chacoan outpost from Anasazi times, with reconstructed apartment-style dwellings dating to the 11th century. (A-2)

■ **Bandelier National Monument.** Ancient Indian pueblos and cliff ruins near Los Alamos. (D-5)

■ **Capulin Mountain National Monument.** 1000-foot-tall, symmetrical volcanic cinder cone from a 10,000-year-old eruption. (A-10)

■ **Carlsbad Caverns National Park.** Near Carlsbad; largest known underground chambers. (L-9)

■ **Chaco Culture National Historical Park.** Ruins of Anasazi culture, dating to A.D. 900, included 13 different pueblos and 400 miles of roads connecting 75 outlying communities. (C-2)

■ **Cumbres and Toltec Scenic Railroad.** 64-mile narrow-gauge scenic train ride through Cumbres Pass and Toltec Gorge. (A-5)

■ **El Morro National Monument.** Also known as Inscription Rock; inscriptions of Spanish explorers, wayfarers, and settlers of the Southwest, dating back as far as 1605. (F-2)

■ **Fort Union National Monument.** Near Las Vegas; 19th century fort that guarded the Santa Fe Trail. (D-8)

■ **Gila Cliff Dwellings National Monument.** Abandoned cave homes in face of overhanging cliff. (J-2)

■ **Grave of Billy the Kid.** Near Fort Sumner; outlaw (killed in 1881) is buried in cemetery in Old Fort Sumner. (G-9)

■ **International Space Hall of Fame.** Four-story golden cube containing exhibits of early rocketry experiments and a futuristic space station. (J-9)

■ **Lincoln.** Historic town near Roswell; site of Lincoln County War of 1878; museum featuring war exhibits and Billy the Kid memorabilia. (I-7)

■ **Santa Clara.** Santa Clara Canyon, deep green tree-lined canyon filled with mountain-ringed lakes; Puye Cliff Dwellings, ancestral home carved out of soft volcanic mesa. (D-6)

■ **Shiprock.** Towering rock formation held sacred by Navajo Indians; 7,178 feet above sea level. (B-1)

■ **Taos.** Artists' colony, museums and galleries; 900-year-old Taos Pueblo; Spanish Colonial Martinez Hacienda; home of 19th-century scout Kit Carson. (B-6)

■ **White Sands National Monument.** 230 square miles of glimmering gypsum dunes blown by 15 mile-per-hour winds from Lake Lucero. (K-6)

Weather Facts

Record High Temperature: 116° F (47° C) on June 29, 1918, at Artesia; Record Low Temperature: -50° F (-46° C) on February 1, 1951, at Gavilan; Average January Temperature: 35° F (2° C); Average July Temperature: 75° F (24° C); Average Yearly Precipitation: 13 in. (33 cm).

Environmental Facts

Air Pollution Rank: 46th; Water Pollution Rank: 49th; Total Yearly Industrial Pollution: 20,369,370 lbs.; Industrial Pollution Rank: 32d; Hazardous Waste Sites: 10; Hazardous Sites Rank: 32d; Landfill Capacity: overextended; Fresh Water Supply: impending shortage; Daily Residential Water Consumption: 188 gals. per capita; Endangered Species: Aquatic Species (12)—chub, Chihuahua; Birds (7)—crane, whooping; Mammals (4)—bat, lesser (=Sanborn's) long-nosed; Other Species (3)—rattlesnake, New Mexican ridge-nosed; Plants (13)—cactus, Knowlton.

Environmental Quality

New Mexico residents generate 1.0 million tons of solid waste each year, or approximately 1,300 pounds per capita. Landfill capacity in New Mexico will be exhausted in more than 12 years. The state has 10 hazardous waste sites. Annual greenhouse gas emissions in New Mexico total 54.2 million tons, or 36.0 tons per capita. Industrial sources in New Mexico release approximately 11.0 thousand tons of toxins, 559.8 thousand tons of acid precipitation-producing substances, and 1.2 million tons of smog-producing substances into the atmosphere each year.

The state has 250,300 acres within the National Park System; the largest area within the state is Carlsbad Caverns National Park. State parks cover just over 118,000 acres, attracting 4.3 million visitors per year.

New Mexico spends approximately 1.5 percent of its budget, or approximately $30 per capita, on environmental and natural resources. New Mexico representatives in the U.S. House voted in favor of national environmental legislation 29 percent of the time, while U.S. senators did so 63 percent of the time.

Average Monthly Weather

Albuquerque	Jan	Feb	Mar	Apr	May	Jun	Jul	Aug	Sep	Oct	Nov	Dec	Yearly
Maximum Temperature °F	47.2	52.9	60.7	70.6	79.9	90.6	92.8	89.4	83.0	71.7	57.2	48.0	70.3
Minimum Temperature °F	22.3	25.9	31.7	39.5	48.6	58.4	64.7	62.8	54.9	43.1	30.7	23.2	42.1
Days of Precipitation	4.0	4.0	4.5	3.3	4.4	3.9	8.8	9.4	5.7	4.9	3.4	4.1	60.3

Flora and Fauna

The state of New Mexico is approximately one-fourth covered by forests, occurring almost entirely in the mountain regions. Many different types of trees comprise these forests, including pines, junipers, scrub oaks, and aspens. A variety of grasses grow in the state, including black grama grass in the Lower Sonoran zone in southwestern New Mexico, and blue grama and buffalo grass in the Upper Sonoran area. New Mexico has many desert plants, including cactus, mesquite, and soapweed. Wildflowers such as saxifrages and forget-me-nots grow throughout the state.

Several larger animals live in New Mexico, including mountain lions, black bears, and elk. Other smaller mammals such as badgers, jackrabbits, and prairie dogs also live in the state. Wild turkeys, quail, and other game birds inhabit New Mexico. Many migratory birds either pass through, or spend the winter, in the state. Both black widows and the deadly tarantula spider live in southwestern New Mexico. Two poisonous snakes, rattlesnakes and coral snakes, also live in the state. Perch, trout, and suckers live in New Mexico's rivers and streams.

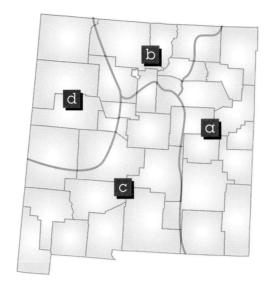

Physical Regions: (a) Great Plains; (b) Rocky Mountains; (c) Basin and Range Region; (d) Colorado Plateau.

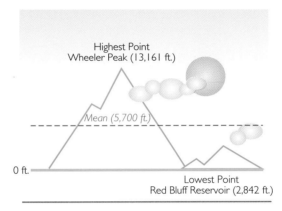

Highest Point
Wheeler Peak (13,161 ft.)

Mean (5,700 ft.)

0 ft.

Lowest Point
Red Bluff Reservoir (2,842 ft.)

Land Use

Cropland: 4.5%; Pasture: 0.4%; Rangeland: 79.7%; Forest: 9.2%; Urban: 1.3%; Other: 4.9%.

For more information about New Mexico's environment, contact the Environmental Improvement Division, P.O. Box 968, Sante Fe, NM 87504-0968.

Topography

There are several distinct topographic regions in New Mexico. The eastern part of the state lies within the westernmost extent of the Great Plains physical region that covers much of the central portion of the United States. The soil is warm and dry, red/brown in color, with high gypsum and clay content. The Rocky Mountains physical region extends from Colorado into the north-central part of New Mexico. The San Juan Mountains and the Sangre de Cristo Range in this area are divided by the Rio Grande River Valley. The highest elevations in the state are found in these ranges. Wheeler Peak, in the Sangre de Cristo Range near Taos, is the highest point in the state, rising 13,161 ft. (4,011 m) above sea level. The soil in this region is cool and moist, and gray/brown in color.

The southern and western portions of the state are in the Basin and Range physical region, an area of scattered mountain ranges and vast arid basins. Some of the mountain ranges in this region are the Guadalupe Mountains in the southeast, which contain the Carlsbad Caverns, an immense network of underground tunnels and chambers; and the San Andres and Black ranges further west. Soil in this region is warm and dry and varies from desert red and low organic content to fertile dark brown loamy clay. The Colorado Plateau physical region covers the northwestern part of the state, with soil similar to the Basin and Range region.

Climate

New Mexico's climatic characteristics can be divided into three different regional climates: desert, semiarid, and mountainous. The desert climate can be found in the western part of the state. The presence of a high-pressure subtropical zone coupled with the lack of a significant source of moisture makes for the desertlike conditions. Temperatures for January and July average 34 degrees F and 74 degrees F; temperatures tend to be higher in the southern part of the state.

New Mexico receives only light precipitation—less than 20 inches a year for the entire state. The northern mountains receive over 20 inches of precipitation, while south-central New Mexico often receives less than 10 inches annually.

Even a warm, dry state like New Mexico receives snowfall. The south receives only 2 inches a year, but the mountains can receive over 300 inches of snow.

Hydrology

The most important river in New Mexico is the Rio Grande. It enters the state from Colorado and flows southwest through the middle of the state, before turning southeast and leaving the state to form the Texas-Mexico border. The Pecos River flows south along much of eastern New Mexico, and then into Texas below Carlsbad. The Canadian River begins in the north and flows southeast, and then east into northern Texas. Other rivers include the Gila and Francisco in the southwest, and the Chaco in the northwest.

Most of the lakes in New Mexico are man-made reservoirs. The largest of these is Elephant Butte Reservoir on the Rio Grande near the town of Truth or Consequences. Others include Lake MacMillan and Alamogordo Reservoir on the Pecos River, and Conchas and Ute reservoirs on the Canadian.

New Mexico's History

New Mexico's First People

Evidence of human existence in New Mexico can be traced back to twenty thousand years ago, when the caves near Albuquerque were inhabited by the Sandia man. This nomadic band of people, like the Folsom and Clovis people, was named for the sites on which their artifacts were discovered. Later in history, around the thirteenth century A.D., more recent Native American tribes came to New Mexico, with the Navajo being the first. The Navajo and Apache were seminomadic tribes, while the Pueblo Indians cultivated several crops.

European Exploration

European explorers came to New Mexico well before the Pilgrims landed at Plymouth Rock in Massachusetts. Although many Spaniards came to New Mexico in the early 1500s, Álvar Nuñez Cabeza de Vaca was probably the first white person to visit the state. In 1540, Francisco Vásquez de Coronado led the first large expedition up the part of the Rio Grande that flows through New Mexico. These early Spanish settlers dominated the area for over two hundred years, only interrupted for a brief period between 1680 and 1683, the years of the Pueblo Revolt. At that time, the Pueblo people temporarily regained control of the region they had dominated long before the arrival of the Europeans.

The first permanent white settlement was established in 1598 at San Juan Pueblo. Another settlement in Santa Fe followed twelve years later in 1610. During its early history, New Mexico was under Spanish colonial rule. The Spaniards did not always treat the native peoples well, and fighting broke out on more than one occasion. In 1821, however, after Mexican independence from Spain, New Mexico became a province of Mexico.

On the Road to Statehood

Mexico controlled New Mexico for approximately twenty-five years, until the United States gained control over the province and claimed it. In 1846, during the Mexican War, Gen. Stephen Kearny marched his troops into Santa Fe and gained possession, thus making New Mexico a part of the United States. The area claimed during the war became an official U.S. territory in 1850. Three years later, under the Gadsden Purchase, the United States secured the strip of land between it and Mexico that now defines the border between the two countries.

The present-day boundaries for New Mexico were set in 1863, with the formation of the Arizona Territory. New Mexico's new territorial status encouraged more traders to travel through the area. The Santa Fe Trail, which was opened in 1821, handled thousands of Americans carrying goods heading from Independence, Missouri, to Santa Fe.

When the transcontinental railroad was finished in the Southwest in 1881, New Mexico became even more accessible to the rest of the country. Statehood, however, did not come to New Mexico until the twentieth century. On January 6, 1912, New Mexico became the forty-seventh state in the Union.

Economic Development

Historically, cattle and sheep ranching have been a part of the New Mexico economy. Even today, agriculture-related industries play a small, yet important part in the economy of the state. Like other western states, New Mexico has rich mineral resources. In fact, the state's diverse mineral resources have enabled it to rank among the top states for mineral production. This trend started when the gold rush invaded New Mexico in the middle of the nineteenth century. Silver was also discovered during this period. Today, however, these metals take a backseat to other minerals such as uranium and copper.

New Mexico also has significant fuel resources. Coal, bituminous and subbituminous, as well as natural gas and petroleum, can be found in different parts of the state.

New Mexico was the site for secret developments and tests during the Second World War. The fist atomic bomb and the first hydrogen bomb were developed by a team of leading scientists including J. Robert Oppenheimer and Albert Einstein in the Los Alamos desert during the early 1940s. These new weapons, which were to be eventually used against Japan dramatically changed the world by ushering in the Atomic Age. The Los Alamos National Scientific Laboratory where the bombs were developed is still dedicated to studying nuclear energy and its uses for defense and industry.

Recently, the New Mexico economy has grown, primarily due to the large number of federal government projects established in the state. The U.S. government employs about one-quarter of the entire workforce in New Mexico and generates almost one-fifth of its total revenue.

New Mexico: State of UFO Controversy

Within the UFO (Unidentified Flying Object) community, New Mexico has been a major center of attention since 1947. In June of that year, a farmer near Roswell reportedly found a "flying saucer" on his ranch. According to the farmer, Max Brazel, alien creatures were present in the crashed saucer. The federal government has denied this whole incident. Indeed, the government admits something crashed at Roswell, but vehemently denies that it was an extra-terrestrial object. The controversy is quite heated between those who believe in UFOs and those who do not. Witnesses reported that they did see alien life forms (although dead due to the crash), while the U.S. Army and other federal officials testified that no such thing existed.

Important Events

1536 Álvar Nuñez Cabeza de Vaca leads an expedition up the Rio Grande river into New Mexico.

1539 Marcos de Niza explores the area looking for gold.

1540 Francisco Vásquez de Coronado leads his expedition up the Rio Grande into the state.

1598 Juan de Oñate claims New Mexico as Spanish territory. The first white settlement established at San Juan Pueblo.

1610 Santa Fe chosen as capital for the territory.

1680 Pueblo Indians regain control of New Mexico.

1776 First part of the Old Spanish Trail, from Santa Fe to Los Ángeles, opens.

1821 Mexico defeats Spain and declares New Mexico a Mexican province.

1821 Trade on the Santa Fe trail with Missouri begins.

1846 United States claims New Mexico as U.S. territory after an invasion by Gen. Stephen Kearny during the Mexican War.

1848 Treaty of Guadalupe Hidalgo grants New Mexico and California to the United States.

1850 New Mexico becomes a U.S. territory.

1853 Gadsden Purchase increases the size of the territory.

1863 Present boundaries are fixed.

1870s Lincoln county war.

1886 Apache raids end as Geronimo surrenders to the United States.

1912 New Mexico becomes the forty-seventh state on January 6.

1916 Pancho Villa raids Columbus.

1945 First atomic bomb tested at White Sands.

1947 "Flying saucer" incident on a ranch in Roswell.

1950 Uranium discovered in state.

1983 Construction begins on a Waste Isolation Plant for disposal of nuclear waste.

1988 State battles record number of grasshoppers.

1993 A deadly flulike virus dubbed the "Four Corners disease" is discovered in New Mexico, Colorado, Arizona, and Texas.

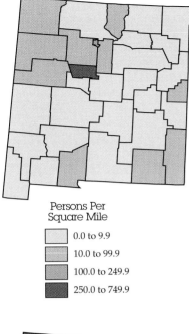

Population Density

Population density for the state of New Mexico was 12.5 persons per square mile in 1990 (4.8 per km2). Average U.S. density was 70.3 persons per square mile in 1990 (27.3 per km2). Habitation is most dense in and around the urban area of Albuquerque. Los Alamos is also an area of high population density. Most of the state has a low population density of 10 persons per mile or less.

Persons Per Square Mile

- 0.0 to 9.9
- 10.0 to 99.9
- 100.0 to 249.9
- 250.0 to 749.9

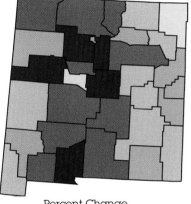

Population Change

The 1990 population figure for the state of New Mexico was 1,515,069. This is a 16.28 percent increase from 1,302,894 in 1980. The next decade will show growth with a population of 2.0 million or a 29.90 percent increase. Much of the state experienced widespread growth in population in the last decade.

Percent Change 1980 to 1990

- −31.9 to −10.0%
- −9.9 to 0.0%
- 0.1 to 19.9%
- 20.0 to 49.9%
- 50.0 to 163.0%

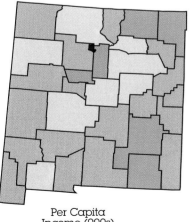

Distribution of Income

The per capita income for the state of New Mexico (current dollars) was $15,353 in 1992. This is an 88.4 percent increase from $8,147 in 1980. Income is greatest in the area of Los Alamos. The state, with the exception of Los Alamos, generally has a low per capita income. Many of the lowest incomes can be found in the numerous Indian reservations located in the state.

Per Capita Income (000s) (Current Dollars)

- $4.5 to 9.9
- $10.0 to 12.9
- $13.0 to 15.9
- $16.0 to 19.9

Population Projections

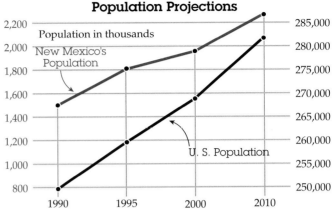

Population in thousands

New Mexico's Population

U. S. Population

Population Change

Year	Population
1950	681,000
1960	954,000
1970	1,023,000
1980	1,302,894
1990	1,515,069
2000	1,968,000
2010	2,248,000

Period	Change
1950–1970	50.2%
1970–1980	27.4%
1980–1990	16.3%
1990–2000	29.9%

Population Facts

State Population, 1993: 1,616,000
Rank: 36
Population 2000: 1,968,000 (Rank 35)
Density: 12.5 per sq. mi. (4.8 per km²)
Distribution: 73.0% urban, 27.0% rural
Population Under 5 Years Old: 8.4%
Population Under 18 Years Old: 29.7%
Population Over 65 Years Old: 10.9%
Median Age: 31.3
Number of Households: 543,000
Average Persons Per Household: 2.74
Average Persons Per Family: 3.26
Female Heads of Households: 4.26%
Population That Is Married: 20.05%
Birth Rate: 18.1 per 1,000 population
Death Rate: 7.0 per 1,000 population
Births to Teen Mothers: 16.3%
Marriage Rate: 8.5 per 1,000 population
Divorce Rate: 4.9 per 1,000 population
Violent Crime Rate: 835 per 100,000 pop.
Population on Social Security: 14.7%
Percent Voting for President: 51.6%

Population Profile

Rank. New Mexico ranks 36th among U.S. states in terms of population with 1,616,000 citizens.

Minority Population. The state's minority population is 50.0 percent. The state's male to female ratio for 1990 was 96.81 males for every 100 females. It was above the national average of 95.22 males for every 100 females.

Growth. Growing much faster than the

Government

Capital: Sante Fe (established 1609).
Statehood: Became 47th state on Jan. 6, 1912.
Number of Counties: 33.
Supreme Court Justices: 5, 8-year term.
State Senators: 42, 4-year term.
State Legislators: 70, 2-year term.
United States Senators: 2.
United States Representatives: 3.
Electoral Votes: 5.
State Constitution: Adopted 1911.

New Mexico's Famous Citizens

Austin, Mary (1868–1934). She wrote about the lives of Indians in the American Southwest in books like *Land of Little Rain*.

Bonney, William (Billy the Kid) (1859–1881). Famous outlaw. He set up base in New Mexico in the late 1860s and killed at least 27 people.

Clark, Ann Nolan (b. 1896). Author of children's books, including *Secret of the Andes* and *Blue Canyon Horse*.

Hilton, Conrad (1887–1979). Opened his first hotel in 1919, and founded the Hilton Hotel chain in 1946.

Lewis, John (b. 1920). Jazz pianist and composer. He took over as leader of the Modern Jazz Quartet in 1952.

Mauldin, Bill (b. 1921). Cartoonist. He published in *Stars and Stripes* during World War II, developing his strip *Willy and Joe*.

Rhodes, Eugene Manlove (1869–1934). Author of realistic western stories based on his experiences as a cowboy.

Unser, Al Sr. (b. 1939). Auto racer. He won the Indianapolis 500 four times.

projected national average, the state's population is expected to reach 2.2 million by the year 2010 (*see graph above*).

Older Citizens. The state's population older than 65 was 163,062 in 1990. It grew 40.68% from 115,906 in 1980.

Younger Citizens. The number of children (under 18 years of age) was 447 thousand in 1990. This represents 29.5 percent of the state's population. The state's school aged population was 308 thousand in 1990. It is expected to increase to 394 thousand by the year 2000. This represents a 27.92% change.

Urban/Rural. 73.0% of the population of the state live in urban areas while 27.0% live in rural areas.

Largest Cities. New Mexico has five cities with a population greater than 35,000. The populations of the state's largest centers are (starting from the most populous) Albuquerque (384,736), Las Cruces (62,126), Santa Fe (55,859), Roswell (44,654), South Valley (35,701), Farmington (33,997), Rio Rancho (32,505), Clovis (30,954), Hobbs (29,115), Alamogordo (27,596), Carlsbad (24,952), Gallup (19,154), Las Vegas (14,753), and North Valley (12,507).

Native American

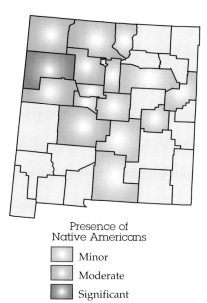

The Native American population in New Mexico was 134,355 in 1990. This was an increase of 26.05 percent from 106,585 in 1980. Many Native Americans live in the large Indian reservations located throughout the state. Some of the largest are the Navajo, Jicarilla, Pueblo, and Mescalero Indian reservations. Many Native Americans also live in the city of Albuquerque.

Presence of Native Americans

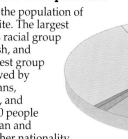

- Minor
- Moderate
- Significant

Nationalities

African	963
American	50,111
Arab	2,606
Austrian	1,952
Czech	3,939
Dutch	15,705
English	130,739
Finnish	1,439
German	177,931
Greek	2,409
Hungarian	2,635
Irish	92,299
Italian	25,430
Norwegian	9,130
Polish	12,826
Portuguese	1,105
Russian	5,182
Scottish	18,045
Slovak	2,824
Swedish	12,897
Welsh	6,300
West Indian	985

African American

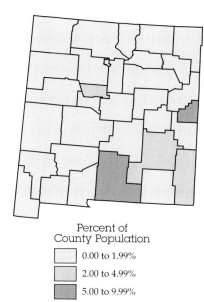

Percent of County Population

- 0.00 to 1.99%
- 2.00 to 4.99%
- 5.00 to 9.99%

The African American population in New Mexico was 30,210 in 1990. This was an increase of 30.94 percent from 23,071 in 1980. Thirty-eight percent of the African American population in New Mexico resides in the city of Albuquerque. Many African Americans also live in Otero and Quay counties.

Statewide Ethnic Composition

Over 75 percent of the population of New Mexico is white. The largest nationalities in this racial group are German, English, and Irish. The next largest group is Hispanics, followed by the Native Americans, African Americans, and Asians. Over 50,000 people claim to be American and acknowledge no other nationality.

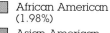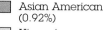

- White (75.64%)
- African American (1.98%)
- Asian American (0.92%)
- Hispanic (38.22%)
- Native American (8.84%)

Hispanic††

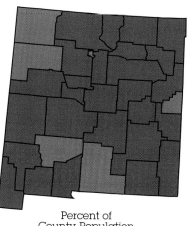

Percent of County Population

- 10.0 to 24.99%
- 25.00 to 97.22%

††A person of Mexican, Puerto Rican, Cuban, or other Spanish culture or origin regardless of race.

The Hispanic population in New Mexico was 579,224 in 1990. This is an increase of 21.37 percent from 477,222 persons in 1980. The state of New Mexico has a large percentage of Hispanics in every county. Many of these people are of Mexican descent. Albuquerque has more Hispanics than any other city in the state.

Education Facts

Total Students 1990: 296,057

Number of School Districts: 88

Expenditure Per Capita on Education 1990: $857

Expenditure Per Capita K–12 1990: $687

Expenditure Per Pupil 1990: $4,446

Total School Enrollment 1990–1991: 283,104

Rank of Expenditures Per Student: 34th in the U.S.

African American Enrollment: 2.2%

Hispanic Enrollment: 44.7%

Asian/Pacific Islander Enrollment: 0.9%

Native American Enrollment: 9.8%

Mean SAT Score 1991 Verbal: 474

Mean SAT Score 1991 Math: 522

Average Teacher's Salary 1992: $26,700

Rank Teacher's Salary: 43d in U.S.

High School Graduates 1990: 14,800

Total Number of Public Schools: 658

Number of Teachers 1990: 15,470

Student/Teacher Ratio: 18.3

Staff Employed in Public Schools: 32,165

Pupil/Staff Ratio: 9.2

Staff/Teacher Ratio: 2.0

Education

Attainment: 74.6 percent of population 25 years or older were high school graduates in 1989, earning New Mexico a ranking of 37th in the United States; 20.6 percent of the state's population had completed college. Institutions of Higher Education: The largest universities and colleges in the state include the University of New Mexico, Albuquerque; New Mexico State University, Las Cruces, New Mexico Highlands University, Las Vegas; Western New Mexico University, Silver City; New Mexico Institute of Mining and Technology, Socorro; New Mexico Military Institute, Roswell; College of Santa Fe and St. John's College, both at Santa Fe. Expenditures per Student: Expenditure increased 74.4% between 1985 and 1990. Projected High School Graduations: 1998 (9,271), 2004 (11,003); Total Revenues for Education from Federal Sources: $781 million; Total Revenues for Education from State Sources: $781 million; Total Revenues for Education from Local Sources: $129 million; Average Annual Salaries for Public School Principals: $36,221; Largest School Districts in State: Albuquerque Public Schools, 86,370 students, 26th in the United States.

Asian American

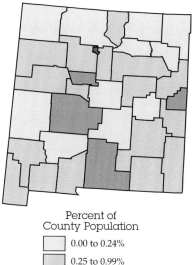

Percent of County Population

- 0.00 to 0.24%
- 0.25 to 0.99%
- 1.00 to 1.99%
- 2.00 to 4.99%

The Asian American population in New Mexico was 14,124 in 1990. This is an increase of 98.43 percent from 7,118 persons in 1980. The county with the highest percentage of Asian Americans is Los Alamos in the northern part of the state. Other large numbers can be found in the city of Albuquerque. In fact, Albuquerque is home to 47 percent of the Asian Americans living in the state.

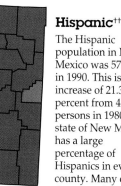

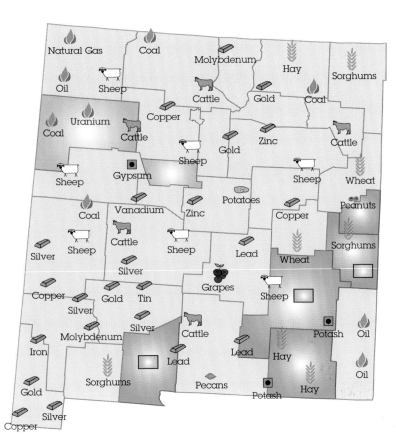

Major manufacturing areas

Major agricultural areas

Transportation

The state of New Mexico is home to the oldest road in the United States, El Camino Real, built in 1581. Another historic route, the Santa Fe Trail, is now paralleled by Interstate 85. Today, New Mexico has approximately 54,000 miles of highways and roads, linking all parts of the state. Interstate 25 is New Mexico's principal north-south route, and Interstate 40 crosses the state from east to west.

New Mexico's first railroad, the Atchison, Topeka, and Santa Fe, began operating in 1878. Currently, five different freight lines serve New Mexico. In addition, five cities receive passenger service. Albuquerque has New Mexico's busiest airport. Outlying cities and towns are connected to Albuquerque by smaller, commuter airlines.

Energy and Transportation Facts

Energy. Yearly Consumption: 588 tril. BTUs (residential, 12.9%; commercial, 16.0%; industrial, 32.1%; transportation, 38.9%); Annual Energy Expenditures Per Capita: $1,927; Nuclear Power Plants Located in State: 0; Source of Energy Consumed: Petroleum— 33.8%; Natural Gas— 32.5%; Coal— 33.5%; Hydroelectric Power—0.3%; Nuclear Power—0.0%.

Transportation. Highway Miles: 61,195 (interstates, 998; urban, 5,828; rural, 55,367); Average Yearly Auto Insurance: $543 (24th); Auto Fatalities Rank: 1st; Registered Motor Vehicles: 1,351,695; Workers in Carpools: 20.3%; Workers Using Public Trans: 1.0%.

Agriculture

New Mexico has 44.2 million farm acres. During the last 40 years, New Mexico's farms have grown larger in size and fewer in number. In 1955, 21,000 farms were found in the state. Today, 13,500 remain.

Agriculture adds $1 billion to the state's gross product annually. The principal commodities in order of marketing receipts are cattle, dairy products, hay, and chili peppers.

Cattle ranching accounts for most of New Mexico's farm income. Beef cattle are found in just about every part of the state, although many are shipped to other states for fattening. The Rio Grande area is home to most of the dairy farms. Hay, the state's leading crop, is grown primarily for cattle feed. Other important crops, grown mainly on irrigated land, include cotton and pecans. New Mexico is the leading producer of chili peppers in the nation.

Employment

Employment. New Mexico employed 700,000 people in 1993. Most work in social and personal services (167,300 persons or 23.9% of the workforce). Manufacturing accounts for 6.1% or 42,500 workers. Wholesale and retail trade account for 21.0% or 147,200 workers. Government employs 159,000 workers (22.7%). Construction employs 35,500 workers (5.1%). Transportation and utilities account for 4.2% or 29,100 persons. Agriculture employs 23,100 workers or 3.3%. Finance, real estate, and insurance account for 3.9% or 27,500 workers. Mining employs 15,800 people and accounts for only 2.3% of the workforce.

Unemployment. Unemployment has decreased to 7.5% in 1993 from a rate of 8.8% in 1985. Today's figure is higher than the national average of 6.8% as shown below.

Housing

Owner Occupied Units: 632,058; Average Age of Units: 23 years; Average Value of Housing Units: $70,100; Renter Occupied Units: 173,081; Median Monthly Rent: $372; Housing Starts: 6,200; Existing Home Sales: 31,000.

Economic Facts

Gross State Product: $25,000,000,000 (1989)

Income Per Capita: $15,353

Disposable Personal Income: $13,709

Median Household Income: $24,087

Average Annual Pay, 1988: $20,275

Principal Industries: printing, electrical equipment, food products, defense–related industries

Major Crops: milk, hay, chiles, pinto beans, lettuce, sorghum, cotton, pecans, peanuts, corn, onions

Fish: Black Bass, Crappies, Pickerel, Salmon, Shad

Livestock: cattle

Non-Fuel Minerals: Potash, Copper, Gold, Gypsum, Molybdenum, Pumice, Uranium

Organic Fuel Minerals: Petroleum, Nat. Gas, Coal

Civilian Labor Force: 715,000 (Women: 319,000)

Total Employed: 665,000 (Women: 298,000)

Median Value of Housing: $70,100

Median Contract Rent: $372 per month

Economic Sectors 1992

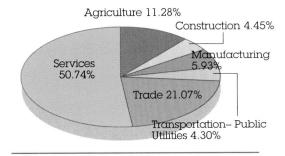

Agriculture 11.28%

Construction 4.45%

Manufacturing 5.93%

Services 50.74%

Trade 21.07%

Transportation– Public Utilities 4.30%

Manufacturing

Only 8 percent of the state gross product comes from the manufacturing sector. In terms of value added by manufacture, electrical equipment production by far leads all manufacturing activities. Other New Mexico manufacturing industries include petroleum refining and printing.

Much of the state's manufacturing takes place in the greater Albuquerque region. Communication equipment ranks as the number one type of electrical equipment produced in New Mexico. Two leading electronics companies, Intel and Honeywell, have large facilities in the Albuquerque area. Mineral processing, petroleum in particular, is concentrated in a few cities, including Gallup and Artesia.

Unemployment Rate

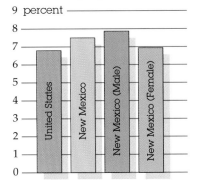

9 percent

NEW YORK
The State of New York

Official State Seal

The Great Seal of New York was adopted in 1778. Liberty and Justice can be seen as the two women holding a shield. The symbols on the shield are mountains with ships on a river. Above the shield are a globe and an eagle. Below the shield is the state motto, *"Excelsior"* (ever upward). "The Great Seal of the State of New York" surrounds the outside of the seal.

Legal Holidays

January: New Year's Day—1st; Martin Luther King, Jr., Day—3rd Monday; February: Abraham Lincoln's Birthday—12th; Presidents' Day—3rd Monday; May: Memorial Day—4th Monday; July: Independence Day—4th; Ratification Day—26th; September: Labor Day—1st Monday; October: Columbus Day—2nd Monday; November: Veterans' Day—11th; Thanksgiving—4th Thursday; December: Christmas—25th.

Official State Flag

The official state flag of New York was adopted in 1896. Slight changes were made to the flag over its one-hundred-year history. For example, the original colors were made to match the uniforms of the New York militia during the Revolution with the addition of a buff field, but in 1902 this field was changed to its present blue.

Festivals and Events

January: Power of Maps, New York City; February: Traditional Ice Harvest, East Meredith; Winter Carnival, Saranac Lake; March: New York Flower Show, New York City; St. Patrick's Day Parade, New York City; April: Polka Weekend, Monticello; May: Albany Tulip Fest, Albany; June: Belmont Stakes, Belmont Park; Frog Jumping Contest, Old Forge; Kool Jazz Festival, New York City; July: July Joygerm Jubilee, Syracuse; August: State Fair, Syracuse; Harlem Week, New York City; September: Antique Engine Jamboree, East Meredith; Mountain Eagle Native American Fest, Hunter; November: Macy's Thanksgiving Day Parade, New York City; New York Marathon, New York City; December: New Year's Eve Celebration, New York City.

New York Compared to Its Region

Resident Pop. in Metro Areas: 2d; Pop. Percent Increase: 3d; Pop. Over 65: 3d; Infant Mortality: 1st; School Enroll. Increase: 3d; High School Grad. and Up: 2d; Violent Crime: 1st; Hazardous Waste Sites: 3d; Unemployment: 1st; Median Household Income: 2d; Persons Below Poverty: 1st; Energy Costs Per Person: 3d.

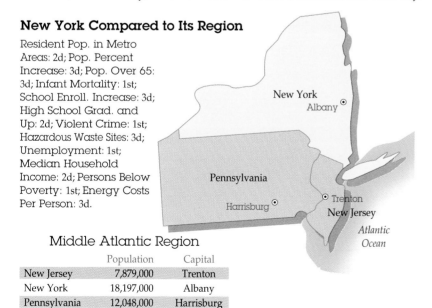

Middle Atlantic Region

	Population	Capital
New Jersey	7,879,000	Trenton
New York	18,197,000	Albany
Pennsylvania	12,048,000	Harrisburg

New York's Finances

Households: 6,639,000; Income Per Capita Current Dollars: $23,534; Change Per Capita Income 1980 to 1992: 115.8% (11th in U.S.); State Expenditures: $60,869,000,000; State Revenues: $60,412,000,000; Personal Income Tax: 4 to 7.875%; Federal Income Taxes Paid Per Capita: $2,291; Sales Tax: 4% (food and prescription drugs exempt).

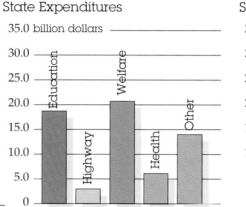

State Expenditures

35.0 billion dollars

(bars: Education, Highway, Welfare, Health, Other)

State Revenues

35.0 billion dollars

(bars: Federal, Local, Taxes, Miscellaneous)

Location, Size, and Boundaries

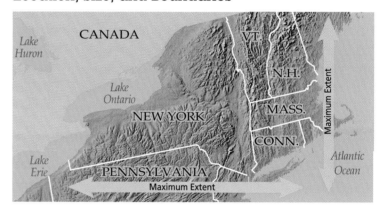

Location. New York is located in the northeastern United States in the Middle Atlantic region. It is bounded on four sides by land with a small coastline along the Atlantic Ocean at New York City extending northeast to the Connecticut border. The geographic center of New York is lat. 42° 57.9' N; long. 76° 1' W.

Size. New York is the 30th largest state in terms of size. Its area is 49,576 sq. mi. (128,402 km2). Inland water covers 1,745 sq. mi. (4,520 km2).

Boundaries. Canada, 445 mi. (716 km); Vermont, 171 mi. (275 km); Mass./Conn., 131.5 mi. (211 km); New Jersey, 92.5 mi. (149 km); Pennsylvania, 344 mi. (554 km).

Geographic Extent. The north/south extent is 310 mi. (499 km). The state extends 320 mi. (515 km) to the east/west.

Facts about New York. Origin of Name: Named for the Duke of York; Nickname: The Empire State; Motto: Excelsior *"ever upward"*; Abbreviations: N.Y. (traditional), NY (postal); State Bird: bluebird; State Tree: sugar maple; State Flower: rose; State Song: "I Love New York," Words and music by Steve Karmen.

New York Compared to Other States. Resident Pop. in Metro Areas: 8th; Pop. Per. Increase: 44th; Pop. Over 65: 22d; Infant Mortality: 16th; School Enroll. Increase: 27th; High School Grad. and Up: 34th; Violent Crime: 2d; Hazardous Waste Sites: 4th; Unemployment: 6th; Median Household Income: 11th; Persons Below Poverty: 20th; Energy Costs Per Person: 50th.

Sources of Information. Tourism: New York State Division of Tourism, 1 Commerce Plaza, Albany, NY 12245. Economy: Department of Economic Development, 1 Commerce Plaza, Albany, NY 12245. Government: Department of State, 162 Washington Avenue, Albany, NY 12231. History: New York State Museum, Room 3099, Cultural Education Center, Albany, NY 12230.

■ Ausable Chasm. Scenic gorge with stone formations created 500 million years ago. (C-14)

■ Cooperstown. Site of the National Baseball Hall of Fame Museum. (H-11)

■ Elmira. Site of Mark Twain's summer home and the National Soaring Museum. (J-7)

■ Federal Hall National Memorial. Site of Washington's inauguration as the first U.S. president in 1789. (N-13)

■ Fire Island National Seashore. Swimming, fishing, and sunning on a barrier island. (N-15)

■ Fort Ticonderoga. Fort built in 1755, used by French, British, and American forces. (E-14)

■ Franklin D. Roosevelt National Historic Site. The birthplace, home, and burial place of the four-term president. (N-13)

■ General Grant National Memorial. Site of the tomb of General and President Ulysses S. Grant. (N-13)

■ Howe Caverns. 160–200-foot underground caverns with an underground lake. (G-10)

■ Kingston. First capital of New York State in 1777 and first settled in 1652. (J-13)

■ Lake Placid. Site of the 1932 and 1980 Winter Olympics. Summer and winter resort. (D-13)

■ Oriskany Battlefield. Site of one of the bloodiest battles of the American Revolution in 1777. (G-10)

■ Sagamore Hill National Historic Site. Home and resting place of Theodore Roosevelt. (M-14)

■ Saratoga National Historical Park. Site of the Battle of Saratoga in 1777. (H-14)

■ Statue of Liberty National Monument. A gift of France located on Liberty Island. Symbol of freedom. (N-13)

■ West Point. Site of the United States Military Academy founded in 1802. (L-13)

Major Cities

Albany	G-13	Hicksville	N-14	Rochester	G-5
Auburn	G-7	Irondequoit	G-5	Rome	G-10
Binghamton	J-9	Jamestown	J-1	Schenectady	G-13
Brentwood	N-14	Levittown	N-14	Syracuse	G-8
Brighton	N-14	Long Beach	N-14	Tonawanda	G-2
Buffalo	H-2	Mt. Vernon	H-2	Troy	G-14
Cheektowaga	N-14	New City	L-13	Utica	G-10
Commack	N-14	New Rochelle	M-13	Valley Stream	N-14
East Meadow	N-14	N.Y. City	N-13	West Babylon	N-14
Elmira	J-7	Niagara Falls	G-2	West Seneca	H-2
Freeport	N-14	N. Tonawanda	G-2	White Plains	M-13
Hempstead	N-14	Oceanside	N-14	Yonkers	M-13

Scale

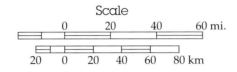

0   20   40   60 mi.

20 0 20 40 60 80 km

☆ State capitol

◉ Cities over 35,000 population

○ Other significant cities

● County Seats

■ Major cultural attractions

□ State Parks

Ⓦ Welcome Centers

⚲ Major colleges and universities

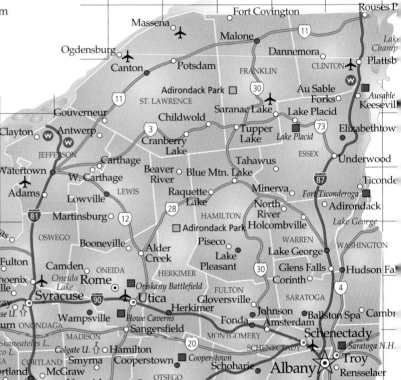

Environmental Quality

New York residents generate 20.0 million tons of solid waste each year, or approximately 2,400 pounds per capita. Landfill capacity in New York will be exhausted in 5 to 10 years. The state has 83 hazardous waste sites. Annual greenhouse gas emissions in New York total 219.0 million tons, or 12.2 tons per capita. Industrial sources in New York release approximately 97.2 thousand tons of toxins, 748.9 thousand tons of acid precipitation-producing substances, and 4.0 million tons of smog-producing substances into the atmosphere each year.

The state has 35,000 acres within the National Park System. Noteworthy is Saratoga National Historical Park. State parks cover just over 255,000 acres, attracting 60.7 million visitors per year.

New York spends less than 1 percent (0.6%) of its budget, or approximately $13 per capita, on environmental and natural resources. New York representatives in the U.S. House voted in favor of national environmental legislation 75 percent of the time, while U.S. senators did so 71 percent of the time.

For more information about New York's environment, contact the Department of Environmental Conservation, 50 Wolf Rd., Albany, NY 12233.

New York

Environmental Facts

Air Pollution Rank: 15th; Water Pollution Rank: 14th; Total Yearly Industrial Pollution: 58,643,927 lbs.; Industrial Pollution Rank: 17th; Hazardous Waste Sites: 84; Hazardous Sites Rank: 4th; Landfill Capacity: adequate; Fresh Water Supply: large surplus; Daily Residential Water Consumption: 167 gals. per capita; Endangered Species: Aquatic Species (2)—mussel, dwarf wedge; Birds (4)—eagle, bald; Mammals (1)—bat, Indiana; Other Species (5)—snail, chittenango ovate amber; Plants (5)—fern, American hart's-tongue.

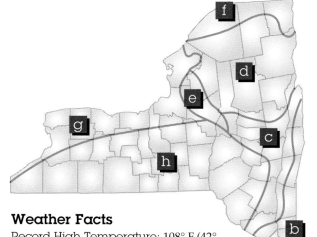

Physical Regions: (a) Atlantic Coastal Plain; (b) New England Upland; (c) Hudson-Mohawk Lowland; (d) Adirondack Upland; (e) Tug Hill Plateau; (f) St. Lawrence Lowland; (g) Erie-Ontario Lowland; (h) Appalachian Plateau.

Topography

There are eight distinct physical regions in New York. New York City and Long Island, at the southeastern tip of New York, lie within the Coastal Plain physical region. Soil in this region is warm and moist with a light-colored surface. The New England Upland physical region runs north along the eastern bank of the Hudson River valley. The soil is similar to that described above. The Hudson-Mohawk Lowland physical region follows the western bank of the Hudson River, then turns northwest to encompass the Mohawk River valley. The soil, typical of most of the state, is cool and moist and high in organic content. Due west of the headwaters of the Mohawk river lies the Tug Hill Plateau physical region. The Adirondack Upland physical region, located in the northeastern part of the state, is dominated by the Adirondack Mountains. The highest elevations in New York are found in the Adirondacks. The highest point is Mt. Marcy, which rises 5,344 ft. (1,629 m) above sea level. The St. Lawrence Lowland physical region extends across the northern border.

The Appalachian Plateau physical region runs along the southern half of the state. Much of the eastern portion of this region is covered by the Catskill Mountains, and is separated from the Adirondacks by the Mohawk River valley. To the east of the Adirondacks and the Catskills is the Hudson

Weather Facts

Record High Temperature: 108° F (42° C) on July 22, 1926, at Troy; Record Low Temperature: -52° F (-47° C) on February 18, 1979, at Old Forge; Average January Temperature: 22° F (-6° C); Average July Temperature: 70° F (21° C); Average Yearly Precipitation: 40 in. (102 cm).

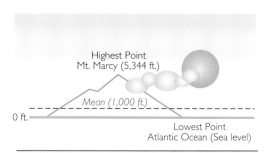

Highest Point
Mt. Marcy (5,344 ft.)

Mean (1,000 ft.)

0 ft.

Lowest Point
Atlantic Ocean (Sea level)

River valley, running most of the length of the eastern border of New York. These fertile river valleys are well suited to agriculture.

The Erie-Ontario Lowland physical region extends along the northwest border of the state, below the St. Lawrence River and east of Lakes Erie and Ontario.

Land Use

Cropland: 19.4%; Pasture: 12.4%; Rangeland: 0%; Forest: 55.9%; Urban: 8.3%; Other: 4%.

Climate

New York's climate fits into the humid continental classification. Because of the influences the Great Lakes and the Atlantic Ocean have on the state, significant variation exists. Three types of air masses—dry continental, warm and humid, and cold and wet—pass over New York's terrain, each creating distinct weather. The central Adirondack Mountains have New York's coldest weather; January temperatures can plummet to -10 degrees F. Long Island, on the Atlantic coast, has a much more temperate winter, with January temperatures averaging around 31 degrees F.

Annual precipitation in New York averages 45 inches, with regional variations. In the Adirondack Mountains as well as Long Island, annual precipitation averages 58 inches. Northern and western New York receive less precipitation, only approximately 32 inches a year.

Snowfall is plentiful in New York. Syracuse, Buffalo, and Rochester usually receive more snowfall than other major cities in the United States.

Average Monthly Weather

Albany	Jan	Feb	Mar	Apr	May	Jun	Jul	Aug	Sep	Oct	Nov	Dec	Yearly
Maximum Temperature °F	30.2	32.7	42.5	57.6	69.5	78.3	83.2	80.7	72.8	61.5	47.8	34.6	57.6
Minimum Temperature °F	11.9	14.0	24.6	35.5	45.4	55.0	59.6	57.6	49.6	39.4	30.8	18.2	36.8
Days of Precipitation	12.1	10.5	11.9	12.1	13.2	11.3	10.3	10.3	9.6	9.0	12.0	12.3	134.4
Buffalo													
Maximum Temperature °F	30.0	31.4	40.4	54.4	65.9	75.6	80.2	78.2	71.4	60.2	47.0	35.0	55.8
Minimum Temperature °F	17.0	17.5	25.6	36.3	46.3	56.4	61.2	59.6	52.7	42.7	33.6	22.5	39.3
Days of Precipitation	19.9	17.1	16.1	14.2	12.3	10.5	9.9	10.6	10.9	11.7	16.0	19.6	168.7

Hydrology

The St. Lawrence River forms New York's northwest boundary with Canada, and Lakes Ontario and Erie constitute much of the rest of the western border. The Hudson is the most important river in the state. It begins in northeastern New York and flows south for about 300 miles (483 km), close to the eastern border, before emptying into the Atlantic Ocean below New York City. The Mohawk is a major tributary of the Hudson, flowing east through midstate for 148 miles (238 km). Other rivers include the Oswego, the Genesee, and the Susquehanna. The Delaware forms part of New York's southern border with Pennsylvania.

New York has thousands of lakes. The largest (excluding the Great Lakes) is Lake Oneida, above Syracuse, covering about 75 sq. mi. (194 sq. km). The Finger Lakes are a series of long narrow lakes in west-central New York, the largest being Lakes Seneca and Cayuga. Lake George is located in northeastern New York.

Flora and Fauna

New York has approximately 130 native tree species. Forests cover close to 60 percent of the state's land. Oak trees are the most common tree in southeastern New York, while coniferous fir and spruce trees dominate farther north in the Adirondack region. Other tree species growing in New York include beech, black cherry, and sugar maple. Apple trees grow along northern waterways such as Lake Champlain. Wildflowers also grow along New York's river valleys; some of these include devil's paintbrush and black-eyed Susans. Several other wildflowers such as

bunchberry, starflower, and goldenthread grow throughout the state.

Many of New York's native animals have become extinct. However, several mammals do remain. Porcupines, squirrels, and foxes all still live in new York. Wildcats and black bears can be found in desolate mountainous areas. Large birds such as eagles and falcons also inhabit New York. Game birds include grouse and wild pheasants. New York's rivers and lakes are home to salmon, sunfish, trout, and many other types of fish. Many fish and shellfish live off New York's coast.

ach S.P.
☐ Montauk○
○Southampton
hogue
nd Nat'l Seashore
at'l Seashore   N

New York's History

New York's First People

Before Europeans came to settle in what is now New York, two families of Native American tribes dominated the landscape. The tribes that were part of the Algonquian language family mainly settled in the area now known as New York City and Long Island. The tribes of the Iroquois family lived primarily in the northern and western parts of the state. By 1570, five tribes, the Cayuga, Mohawk, Oneida, Onondaga, and Seneca, formed a confederation called the League of the Iroquois. A sixth tribe, the Tuscarora, joined the League later, in 1722. Of the two Native American groups, the Iroquois were the dominant group throughout Native history in New York.

European Exploration

The first known European expedition to New York occurred in 1524, when Giovanni da Verrazano sailed up the Hudson River. Nearly a century later, in 1609, the Englishman, Henry Hudson, under a Dutch flag, sailed the Half Moon up the Hudson River as far as present-day Albany. Although Hudson failed to find a northwest passage to the East Indies, he did succeed in staking a claim in the New World.

Throughout the seventeenth century, the Dutch built several forts along the Hudson River, from Manhattan Island to Albany. In 1629, the Dutch West India Company started selling land grants in New Amsterdam (presently New York City).

The Dutch claim to New York ended in 1664, when they were forced to surrender to the British. The new British colony was called New York, in honor of the duke of York. Shortly afterward, New Jersey and Connecticut seceded from the colony.

Revolutionary Period and Statehood

New York played an important part in the French and Indian War and the Revolutionary War. The New York area was in a strategic position during both of these conflicts. The state was situated between the British colony centered around New York City and the settlements of the French to the north in Canada. Many skirmishes of the war were fought on New York soil. When the French were defeated by the British in 1761, much of what now is New York state became part of the colony of New York.

Several of the British tax act committees met in New York, adding to the already mounting anti-British sentiment. Therefore, it should be no surprise that approximately one-third of all Revolutionary War battles took place within New York. Some of the most notable are the battles of Long Island (August 27, 1776), Harlem Heights (September 16, 1776), and White Plains (October 28, 1778). Other battles farther north included Ft. Ticonderoga (July, 1777), Ft. Stanwix (August, 1777), and the surrender of British General John Burgoyne to General Benedict Arnold's forces at Saratoga in the fall of 1777. New York is also home to West Point where Benedict Arnold was located when he attempted to sell information to the British. By May 27, 1776, the colony of New York had decided it had the right to govern itself. Two months later, in July, New York signed the Declaration of Independence. The colony achieved statehood in April 1777, when a state constitution was adopted. The temporary state capital was at Kingston, until Albany was chosen as the permanent capital in 1797. New York was the eleventh state to sign the U.S. Constitution in 1788.

Industrialization

New York in the nineteenth century became a major exporter of agricultural goods. Transportation improvements such as canals and turnpikes which were built during that time aided agricultural endeavors greatly. A short time later, the state also became a major trade and industrial center. By the mid-nineteenth century, New York was the leading state in manufacturing, and after the end of the Civil War, New York's economy developed even more rapidly. The established businesses grew larger, and new growth occurred in many other fields such as commerce, transportation, merchandising, and banking.

Along with this expanding industrialization came a boom in urbanization, as more immigrants flooded into New York City, the largest city in the nation. The combination of big business and big population set the stage for such social ills as corruption, unjust labor conditions, and poor or nonexistent social services. Today, the state of New York is the financial and communications capital of the United States, and is a major world center in these fields as well. Its manufacturing industries also play an important role in the national economy. Finally, tourism gives a boost to New York's economy, as the state plays host to millions of visitors each year.

New York City: "The Big Apple"

New York City is know as the "The Big Apple." Besides having a huge business center, New York City is home to thousands of tourist, entertainment, and cultural attractions.

Millions of people come to New York City to see such sights as the Statue of Liberty, Times Square, and the Empire State Building. New York City also boasts a number of museums, including the Metropolitan Museum of Art, the Museum of Modern Art, and the American Museum of Natural History. Along with the steady stream of tourists, come hopeful actors who flock to legendary Broadway stages in midtown Manhattan. Painters, sculptors, and other artists move to Soho with dreams of opening galleries or showing their works to critics and potential buyers.

Important Events

1524 Giovanni da Verrazano enters New York Harbor and sails up the Hudson.

1570 League of Iroquois formed as recognized by Europeans.

1609 Henry Hudson explores Hudson River, and Champlain explores northen area and the lake which bears his name.

1625 New Netherlands established by the Dutch.

1664 A British fleet seizes and claims Dutch settlement; rename it New York.

1735 Freedom of press secured with Zenger trial victory.

1765 Stamp Act Congress held in New York City.

1775 Ethan Allen captures Fort Ticonderoga from the British.

1776 New York signs Declaration of Independence on May 27.

1785 New York City acts as national capital; until 1790.

1788 New York becomes eleventh state of the Union.

1789 George Washington inaugurated president.

1797 Albany becomes the state capitol.

1802 United States Military Academy founded at West Point.

1825 Erie Canal completed.

1848 First convention for women's rights held in Seneca Falls.

1886 Statue of Liberty dedicated.

1929 Stock market crash which helped usher in the Great Depression.

1931 The Empire State building is completed with 102 stories.

1952 United Nations headquarters completed.

1971 Attica Prison riots kill forty-seven people.

1973 The World Trade Center is completed with 110 stories on both towers.

1987 Panic erupts on Wall Street as Dow Jones average plummets 508 points

1993 The World Trade Center is bombed by terrorists. Six people are killed and one thousand are injured.

1995 Islamic terrorists are tried and convicted for the World Trade Center bombing.

Persons Per Square Mile

▢	0.0 to 9.9
▢	10.0 to 99.9
▢	100.0 to 249.9
▢	250.0 to 749.9
▢	750.0 to 67,615.3

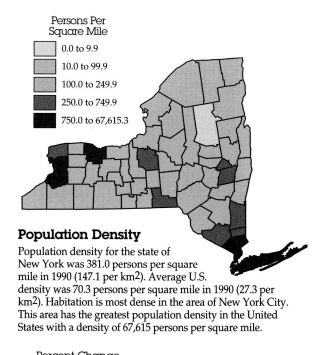

Population Density

Population density for the state of New York was 381.0 persons per square mile in 1990 (147.1 per km2). Average U.S. density was 70.3 persons per square mile in 1990 (27.3 per km2). Habitation is most dense in the area of New York City. This area has the greatest population density in the United States with a density of 67,615 persons per square mile.

Percent Change 1980 to 1990

▢	–31.9 to –10.0%
▢	–9.9 to 0.0%
▢	0.1 to 19.9%
▢	20.0 to 49.9%

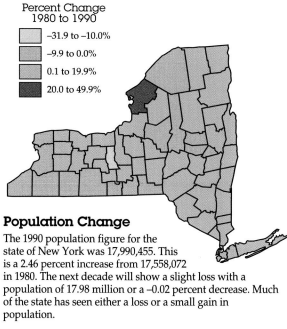

Population Change

The 1990 population figure for the state of New York was 17,990,455. This is a 2.46 percent increase from 17,558,072 in 1980. The next decade will show a slight loss with a population of 17.98 million or a –0.02 percent decrease. Much of the state has seen either a loss or a small gain in population.

Per Capita Income (000s) (Current Dollars)

▢	$10.0 to 12.9
▢	$13.0 to 15.9
▢	$16.0 to 19.9
▢	$20.0 to 35.2

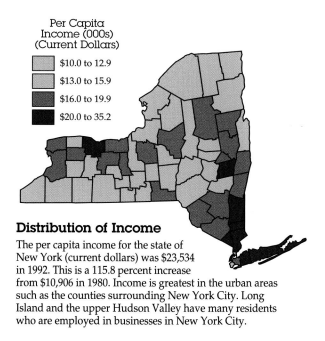

Distribution of Income

The per capita income for the state of New York (current dollars) was $23,534 in 1992. This is a 115.8 percent increase from $10,906 in 1980. Income is greatest in the urban areas such as the counties surrounding New York City. Long Island and the upper Hudson Valley have many residents who are employed in businesses in New York City.

Population Projections

Population in thousands
New York's Population
U. S. Population

(graph with x-axis 1990, 1995, 2000, 2010; left y-axis 17,500–18,200; right y-axis 250,000–285,000)

Population Change

Year	Population
1950	14,830,000
1960	16,838,000
1970	18,268,000
1980	17,558,072
1990	17,990,455
2000	17,986,000
2010	18,139,000

Period	Change
1950–1970	23.2%
1970–1980	–3.9%
1980–1990	2.5%
1990–2000	–0.02%

Population Facts

State Population, 1993: 18,197,000

Rank: 2

Population 2000: 17,986,000 (Rank 3)

Density: 381.0 per sq. mi. (147.1 per km²)

Distribution: 84.3% urban, 15.7% rural

Population Under 5 Years Old: 7.5%

Population Under 18 Years Old: 24.4%

Population Over 65 Years Old: 13.1%

Median Age: 33.9

Number of Households: 6,639,000

Average Persons Per Household: 2.63

Average Persons Per Family: 3.22

Female Heads of Households: 5.11%

Population That Is Married: 18.43%

Birth Rate: 16.5 per 1,000 population

Death Rate: 9.4 per 1,000 population

Births to Teen Mothers: 9.1%

Marriage Rate: 9.4 per 1,000 population

Divorce Rate: 3.2 per 1,000 population

Violent Crime Rate: 1,164 per 100,000 pop.

Population on Social Security: 15.9%

Percent Voting for President: 50.9%

Population Profile

Rank. New York ranks 2d among U.S. states in terms of population with 18,197,000 citizens.

Minority Population. The state's minority population is 32.4 percent. The state's male to female ratio for 1990 was 92.11 males for every 100 females. It was below the national average of 95.22 males for every 100 females.

Growth. Growing slightly faster than the projected national average, the state's population

Government

Capital: Albany (established 1797).

Statehood: Became 11th state on Jul. 26, 1788.

Number of Counties: 62.

Supreme Court Justices: 7, 14-year term.

State Senators: 61, 2-year term.

State Legislators: 150, 2-year term.

United States Senators: 2.

United States Representatives: 31.

Electoral Votes: 33.

State Constitution: Adopted 1894.

New York's Famous Citizens

Cuomo, Mario (b.1932). Governor (1982–1994). Known for his support of liberal causes and his effective public speaking.

Dinkins, David (b. 1927). He was elected as New York City's first African-American mayor in 1989.

Haley, Alex (1921–1992). Author of historical fiction on the struggle of African-Americans in works such as Roots.

Mantle, Mickey (b. 1931–1995). Hall of Fame baseball outfielder. He won the AL MVP in 1956, 1957, and 1962.

Miller, Arthur (b. 1915). Playwright. He explores the individual's search for meaning in works such as Death of a Salesman.

Morgan, J. Pierpont, Jr. (1867–1943). Financier. Headed J. P. Morgan and Company, his father's powerful banking firm.

Roosevelt, Franklin Delano (1882–1945). Elected 32d president of the United States. Presided over the New Deal and the leadership of the nation during World War II.

Roosevelt, Theodore (1858–1919). Elected 26th president of the United States. Hero of the Spanish-American War (1898).

is expected to reach 18.0 million by the year 2010 (see graph above).

Older Citizens. The state's population older than 65 was 2,363,722 in 1990. It grew 9.39% from 2,160,767 in 1980.

Younger Citizens. The number of children (under 18 years of age) was 4.3 million in 1990. This represents 23.7 percent of the state's population. The state's school aged population was 2.6 million in 1990. It is expected to increase to 2.7 million by the year 2000. This represents a 3.27% change.

Urban/Rural. 84.3% of the population of the state live in urban areas while 15.7% live in rural areas.

Largest Cities. New York has 27 cities with a population greater than 35,000. The populations of the state's largest centers are (starting from the most populous) New York (7,322,564), Buffalo (328,123), Rochester (231,636), Yonkers (188,082), Syracuse (163,860), Albany (101,082), Cheektowaga (84,387), Utica (68,637), New Rochelle (67,265), Mount Vernon (67,153), Schenectady (65,566), Tonawanda (65,284), Niagara Falls (61,840), Troy (54,269), Levittown (53,286), Binghamton (53,008), and Irondequoit (52,322).

Native American

The Native American population in New York was 62,651 in 1990. This was an increase of 44 percent from 43,508 in 1980. A large percentage of Native Americans can be found in and around the city of New York. There are also small Indian reservations located in the western part of the state. These include the Tonawanda and the Allegany.

Nationalities

African	64,451
American	468,754
Arab	79,600
Austrian	102,693
Czech	48,329
Dutch	186,762
English	953,639
Finnish	13,759
German	2,098,719
Greek	139,379
Hungarian	115,981
Irish	1,812,735
Italian	2,376,768
Norwegian	56,922
Polish	841,457
Portuguese	34,455
Russian	455,162
Scottish	157,345
Slovak	75,881
Swedish	99,747
Welsh	50,662
West Indian	452,338

Statewide Ethnic Composition

Over 74 percent of the population of New York is white. The largest nationalities in this racial group are Italian, German, and Irish. The next largest group is African Americans, followed by Hispanics, Asian Americans, and Native Americans. Over 468,000 people claim to be American and acknowledge no other nationality.

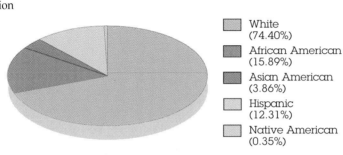

- White (74.40%)
- African American (15.89%)
- Asian American (3.86%)
- Hispanic (12.31%)
- Native American (0.35%)

Education Facts

Total Students 1990: 2,565,841

Number of School Districts: 721

Expenditure Per Capita on Education 1990: $1,091

Expenditure Per Capita K–12 1990: $1,020

Expenditure Per Pupil 1990: $8,680

Total School Enrollment 1990–1991: 2,563,000

Rank of Expenditures Per Student: 1st in the U.S.

African American Enrollment: 20.5%

Hispanic Enrollment: 13.2%

Asian/Pacific Islander Enrollment: 3.9%

Native American Enrollment: 0.3%

Mean SAT Score 1991 Verbal: 413

Mean SAT Score 1991 Math: 468

Average Teacher's Salary 1992: $43,300

Rank Teacher's Salary: 3d in U.S.

High School Graduates 1990: 143,900

Total Number of Public Schools: 3,996

Number of Teachers 1990: 174,354

Student/Teacher Ratio: 14.7

Staff Employed in Public Schools: 345,072

Pupil/Staff Ratio: 7.4

Staff/Teacher Ratio: 2.0

Education

Attainment: 76.7 percent of population 25 years or older were high school graduates in 1989, earning New York a ranking of 34th in the United States; 22.8 percent of the state's population had completed college. Institutions of Higher Education: The largest universities and colleges in the the state include the State University of New York (founded 1948), Albany, Binghamton, Buffalo, and Stony Brook; Columbia University (founded 1754), New York City; City University of New York, including City College and Hunter College; St. John's University, New York City; Fordham University, New York City; Syracuse University, Syracuse; Cornell University, Ithaca; U.S. Military Academy, West Point. Expenditures per Student: Expenditure increased 67% between 1985 and 1990. Projected High School Graduations: 1998 (82,122), 2004 (91,596); Total Revenues for Education from Federal Sources: $775 million; Total Revenues for Education from State Sources: $7.4 billion; Total Revenues for Education from Local Sources: $8.9 billion; Average Annual Salaries for Public School Principals: $50,814; Largest School Districts in State: New York City Public Schools, 930,440 students, 1st in the United States; Buffalo City Schools, 46,689, 72d.

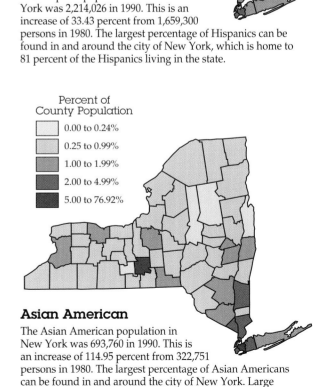

Percent of County Population

- 0.00 to 1.99%
- 2.00 to 4.99%
- 5.00 to 9.99%
- 10.00 to 24.99%

African American

The African American population in New York was 2,859,055 in 1990. This was an increase of 18.84 percent from 2,405,818 in 1980. The largest percentage of African Americans can be found in and around the city of New York. This city is home to 74 percent of the African Americans living in the state.

Percent of County Population

- 0.00 to 0.99%
- 1.00 to 2.99%
- 3.00 to 9.99%
- 10.00 to 24.99%

††A person of Mexican, Puerto Rican, Cuban, or other Spanish culture or origin regardless of race.

Hispanic††

The Hispanic population in New York was 2,214,026 in 1990. This is an increase of 33.43 percent from 1,659,300 persons in 1980. The largest percentage of Hispanics can be found in and around the city of New York, which is home to 81 percent of the Hispanics living in the state.

Percent of County Population

- 0.00 to 0.24%
- 0.25 to 0.99%
- 1.00 to 1.99%
- 2.00 to 4.99%
- 5.00 to 76.92%

Asian American

The Asian American population in New York was 693,760 in 1990. This is an increase of 114.95 percent from 322,751 persons in 1980. The largest percentage of Asian Americans can be found in and around the city of New York. Large numbers can also be found in and around the city of Ithaca.

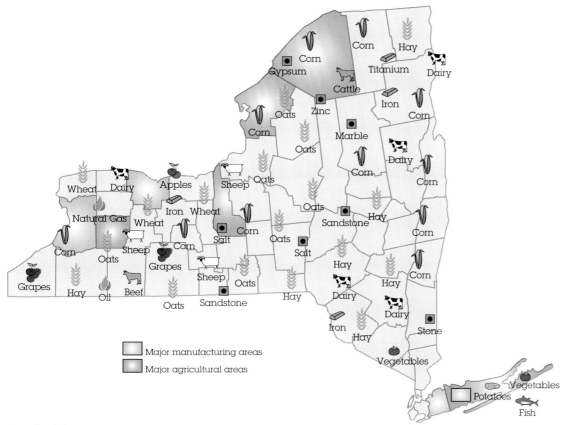

Major manufacturing areas
Major agricultural areas

Agriculture

New York has 8.2 million farm acres. During the last 40 years, New York's farms have grown larger in size and fewer in number. In 1955, 106,000 farms were found in the state. Today, 38,000 remain.

Agriculture adds $3 billion to the state's gross product annually. The principal commodities in order of marketing receipts are dairy products, greenhouse, cattle, and apples.

Livestock and livestock products account for about 72 percent of New York's farm income, with milk being the most important. Dairy farms are found mainly in the northwestern part of the state. More than half the ducks produced in the United States come from Suffolk County. Hay and corn, the state's leading crops, are grown primarily for cattle feed. Other important crops include cabbages, potatoes, corn, and apples.

Housing

Owner Occupied Units: 7,226,891; Average Age of Units: 43 years; Average Value of Housing Units: $131,600; Renter Occupied Units: 3,150,574; Median Monthly Rent: $486; Housing Starts: 26,900; Existing Home Sales: 143,000.

Economic Facts

Gross State Product: $447,000,000,000 (1989)

Income Per Capita: $23,534

Disposable Personal Income: $20,021

Median Household Income: $32,965

Average Annual Pay, 1988: $30,011

Principal Industries: scientific instruments, machinery, printing, chemicals, machinery, photographic equipment, food processing, garment, publishing

Major Crops: dairy, apples, hay, corn, vegetables

Fish: Bluefish, Flounder, Swordfish, Shad

Livestock: Dairy cows

Non-Fuel Minerals: Helium, Iron Ore, Lead, Salt, Zinc, Cement, Stone, Clays

Organic Fuel Minerals: Petroleum

Civilian Labor Force: 8,583,000 (Women: 3,839,000)

Total Employed: 7,967,000 (Women: 3,594,000)

Median Value of Housing: $131,600

Median Contract Rent: $486 per month

Economic Sectors 1992

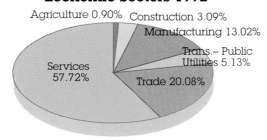

Agriculture 0.90% Construction 3.09%
Manufacturing 13.02%
Trans.– Public Utilities 5.13%
Services 57.72%
Trade 20.08%

Manufacturing

For decades, New York was the nation's leading industrial state; however, California assumed the position in the 1970s. Today, New York still has a strong manufacturing sector. Seven percent of the goods produced in the United States come from New York. While printed materials lead in terms of added manufacture value, the state produces a great variety of goods, from concrete to chemicals.

New York City is the heart of the publishing industry, as well as other industries including clothing and instruments (medical, watches). The northern cities of Buffalo and Syracuse produce surgical instruments and machinery, respectively. Rochester leads the country in photographic and optical equipment production.

Transportation

New York has a varied and extensive transportation system. The state has the world's longest toll superhighway, the 558-mile-long Governor Thomas E. Dewey Thruway. The thruway links several large cities including Syracuse, Buffalo, and Albany.

A state-run waterway, the New York State Barge Canal system, was completed in 1918. The state also has several major ports, including New York City and Buffalo. Passenger rail lines, including Amtrak as well as commuter lines, serve many New York cities. About 35 freight rail lines carry goods through New York. New York City's two major airports, John F. Kennedy International and La Guardia, are two of the busiest in the world. Syracuse and other cities have smaller airports.

Energy and Transportation

Energy. Yearly Consumption: 3,558 tril. BTUs (residential, 26.7%; commercial, 28.5%; industrial, 19.5%; transportation, 25.3%); Annual Energy Expenditures Per Capita: $1,551; Nuclear Power Plants Located in State: 6; Source of Energy Consumed: Petroleum— 47.5%; Natural Gas— 25.6%; Coal— 9.8%; Hydroelectric Power—8.4%; Nuclear Power—8.7%.

Transportation. Highway Miles: 111,686 (interstates, 1,497; urban, 39,063; rural, 72,623); Average Yearly Auto Insurance: $799 (8th); Auto Fatalities Rank: 31st; Registered Motor Vehicles: 9,779,554; Workers in Carpools: 19.3%; Workers Using Public Trans: 24.8%.

Employment

Employment. New York employed 7.98 million people in 1993. Most work in social and personal service jobs (2.40 million persons or 30.2% of the workforce). Wholesale and retail trade account for 19.4% or 1.55 million workers. Government employs 1.42 million workers (17.8%). Manufacturing employs 982,000 people (12.3%). Construction accounts for 3.0% or 238,900 workers. Transportation and utilities account for 5.0% or 401,100 persons. Agriculture employs 95,800 workers or 1.2%. Finance, real estate, and insurance account for 9.1% or 727,700 persons. Mining employs 5,100 people and accounts for only 0.1% of the workforce.

Unemployment. Unemployment has increased to 7.7% in 1993 from a rate of 6.5% in 1985. Today's figure is higher than the national average of 6.8% as shown below.

Unemployment Rate

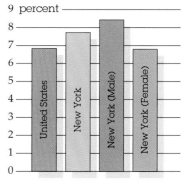

9 percent
8
7
6
5
4
3
2
1
0

United States | New York | New York (Male) | New York (Female)

NORTH CAROLINA
The State of North Carolina

Official State Seal

The Great Seal of North Carolina was adopted in 1893 and has seen some modifications since its inception. The two figures facing each other represent Liberty and Plenty. In the background is a ship on the ocean bordered by mountains on the left. The state motto, *"Esse Quam Videri"* (To Be Rather Than to Seem), is found at the bottom of the seal.

Legal Holidays

January: New Year's Day—1st; Martin Luther King, Jr., Day—3rd Monday; Lee-Jackson Day—18th; February: Presidents' Day—3rd Monday; April: Halifax Independence Day; May: Confederate Memorial Day—10th; Mecklenburg Day—20th; Memorial Day—4th Monday; July: Independence Day—4th; September: Labor Day—1st Monday; October: Columbus Day—2d Monday; November: Veterans' Day—11th; Ratification Day—21st; Thanksgiving—4th Thursday; December: Christmas—25th.

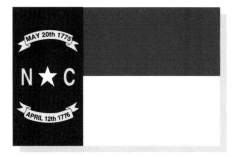

Official State Flag

The North Carolina state flag was adopted in 1861 after the state seceded from the Union. The topmost date is the date of the Mecklenburg Declarations, which asserted America's independence from Great Britain, and the bottom date is when North Carolina voted for independence.

Festivals and Events

February: Zoo Affair, Asheboro; Black American Arts Festival, Greensboro; March: African-American Cultural Festival for Children, Greensboro; April: Blowing Rock Annual Opening Day Trout Derby, Blowing Rock; Fest of Flowers, Asheville; May: Riverspree Fest, Elizabeth City; Winston Cup Race, Charlotte; June: Eastern Music Festival, Greensboro; Micajah, Autryville; July: Bele Chere, Asheville; Folkmoot USA, Waynesville; August: Strange Seafood Exhibit, Beaufort; Cherokee's Bluegrass Fest, Cherokee; September: Everybody's Day Fest, Thomasville; Guilford Native American Assoc. Pow Wow, Guilford; October: Mountain Glory Fest, Marion; November: Wassail Tea, Greensboro; December: Appalachian Potters Market, Marion; Singing Christmas Tree, Greensboro.

Sources of Information. Tourism: Department of Economic and Community Development, Travel and Tourism Division, 430 North Salisbury Street, Raleigh, NC 27603. Economy: Department of Commerce, Industrial Development Division, 430 North Salisbury Street, Raleigh, NC 27603. Government: Secretary of State, Publications Division, 300 North Salisbury Street, Raleigh, NC 27611. History: School Information Program, State Library, 109 East Jones Street, Raleigh, NC 27611.

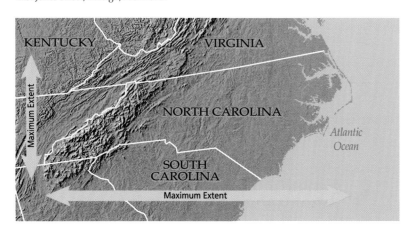

North Carolina's Finances

Households: 2,517,000; Income Per Capita Current Dollars: $17,667; Change Per Capita Income 1980 to 1992: 120.8% (6th in U.S.); State Expenditures: $14,671,000,000; State Revenues: $14,981,000,000; Personal Income Tax: 6 to 7.75%; Federal Income Taxes Paid Per Capita: $1,509; Sales Tax: 4% (prescription drugs exempt).

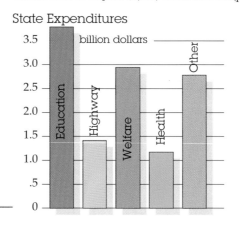

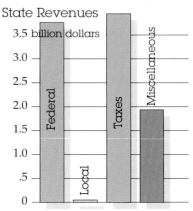

Facts about North Carolina. Origin of Name: After King Charles I of England; Nickname: The Tar Heel State; Motto: "To be, rather than to seem" (*Esse quam videri*); Abbreviations: N.C. (traditional), NC (postal); State Bird: cardinal; State Tree: pine; State Flower: flowering dogwood; State Song: "The Old North State," words by William Gaston and music arrangement by Mrs. E. E. Randolph.

North Carolina Compared to Other States. Resident Pop. in Metro Areas: 32d; Pop. Per. Increase: 17th; Pop. Over 65: 30th; Infant Mortality: 8th; School Enroll. Increase: 15th; High School Grad. and Up: 42d; Violent Crime: 19th; Hazardous Waste Sites: 16th; Unemployment: 36th; Median Household Income: 33d; Persons Below Poverty: 20th; Energy Costs Per Person: 28th.

Location, Size, and Boundaries

Location. North Carolina is located in the southern United States in what is known as the South Atlantic region. It is bounded on three of four sides by land with a general coastline along the Atlantic Ocean in the east. The geographic center of North Carolina is lat. 35° 36.2' N; long. 79° 27.3' W.

Size. North Carolina is the 28th largest state in terms of size. Its area is 52,586 sq. mi. (136,198 km2). Inland water covers 3,788 sq. mi. (9,811 km2). North Carolina touches the Atlantic Ocean along a 301 mile coastline.

Boundaries. Virginia, 320 mi. (515 km); Atlantic Ocean, 301 mi. (484 km); South Carolina, 328 mi. (528 km); Georgia, 68 mi. (109 km); Tennessee, 253 mi. (407 km).

Geographic Extent. The north/south extent of North Carolina is 187 mi. (301 km). The state extends 503 mi. (810 km) to the east/west.

Scale

| 0 | 20 | 40 | 60 mi. |

| 20 | 0 | 20 | 40 | 60 | 80 km |

■ Alamance Battleground State Historic Site. Site where the Regulators were defeated by Royal Governor William Tryon in 1771. (C-11)

■ Bennett Place State Historic Site. Site where Confederate Gen. Joseph E. Johnston surrendered to Gen. William T. Sherman on April 26, 1865. (C-12)

■ Bentonville Battleground State Historic Site. Site where the bloodiest Civil War battle in the state took place on March 19-21, 1865. (D-14)

■ Blowing Rock. Formation which uses air to return rocks tossed from a cliff. (B-6)

■ Bridal Veil Falls. 120-foot (37-meter) falls in Cullasaja River Gorge which can be driven under. (E-2)

■ Cape Hatteras National Seashore Recreational Area. The first national seashore in the country. (E-19)

■ Charlotte Hawkins Brown Memorial. Former secondary school for African Americans run by Charlotte Hawkins Brown for over 50 years. (B-11)

■ Fort Bragg. Site of the 82d Airborne Division War Memorial Museum. (F-12)

■ Fort Fisher State Historic Site. Confederate fort, now a museum centering on naval blockade running during the Civil War. (I-15)

■ Fort Raleigh National Historic Site. Where Sir Walter Raleigh first attempted to start an English settlement in America. (C-19)

■ Great Smoky Mountains National Park. 514,757 acres for fishing, hiking, and camping. Site of Pioneer Homestead and Clingmans Dome. (D-1)

■ Linville Gorge Wilderness Area. Primitive natural environment. Part of the Pisgah National Forest. (C-6)

■ Mount Mitchell State Park. Site of Mount Mitchell, the highest peak in the eastern United States (6,684 feet; 2,037 meters). (C-5)

■ Ocracoke Island. Site of Ocracoke Village and Ocracoke lighthouse, the oldest lighthouse (1823) still in use in the state. (E-19)

■ Orton Plantation. Antebellum mansion built in 1735, with lush gardens. (H-15)

■ Polk Memorial. The birthplace of President James K. Polk. (E-8)

■ Reed Gold Mine State Historic Site. Site of nation's first gold mine (1799) discovered by Conrad Reed. (D-9)

■ Spencer Shops State Historic Site. Museum dedicated to the development of transportation. (C-9)

■ St. Thomas's Episcopal Church. Site of the oldest church building in North Carolina built in 1734. (D-17)

■ Thomas Wolfe Memorial State Historic Site. The site of the board-inghouse home of author Thomas Wolfe. (D-4)

■ Town Creek Indian Mound State Historic Site. Site of a reconstructed Indian temple and mortuary from the 16th century. (E-10)

■ Tryon Palace State Historic Site and Gardens. Buildings built between 1767 and 1770 as a home for Royal Governor William Tryon. (E-17)

■ Wright Brothers National Memorial. Site where Wilbur and Orville Wright made the first flight by powered aircraft on December 17, 1903. (B-19)

North Carolina Compared to Its Region.

Resident Pop. in Metro Areas: 7th; Pop. Percent Increase: 5th; Pop. Over 65: 3d; Infant Mortality: 3d; School Enroll. Increase: 6th; High School Grad. and Up: 6th; Violent Crime: 6th; Hazardous Waste Sites: 3d; Unemployment: 7th; Median Household Income: 6th; Persons Below Poverty: 4th; Energy Costs Per Person: 5th.

South Atlantic Region

	Population	Capital
Delaware	700,000	Dover
Maryland	4,965,000	Annapolis
Washington DC	578,000	—
Virginia	6,491,000	Richmond
West Virginia	1,820,000	Charleston
North Carolina	6,945,000	Raleigh
South Carolina	3,643,000	Columbia
Georgia	6,917,000	Atlanta
Florida	13,679,000	Tallahassee

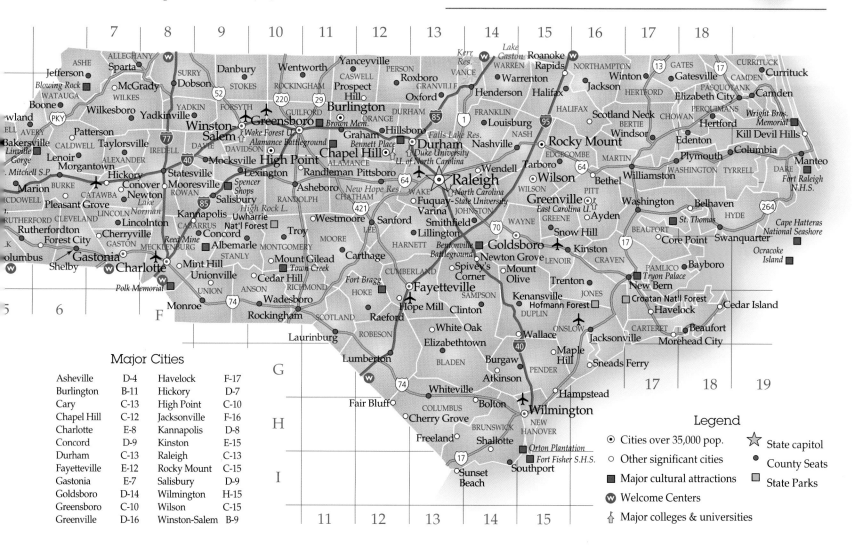

Major Cities

Asheville	D-4	Havelock	F-17
Burlington	B-11	Hickory	D-7
Cary	C-13	High Point	C-10
Chapel Hill	C-12	Jacksonville	F-16
Charlotte	E-8	Kannapolis	D-8
Concord	D-9	Kinston	E-15
Durham	C-13	Raleigh	C-13
Fayetteville	E-12	Rocky Mount	C-15
Gastonia	E-7	Salisbury	D-9
Goldsboro	D-14	Wilmington	H-15
Greensboro	C-10	Wilson	C-15
Greenville	D-16	Winston-Salem	B-9

Legend

⊙ Cities over 35,000 pop. ☆ State capitol
○ Other significant cities ● County Seats
■ Major cultural attractions ☐ State Parks
Ⓦ Welcome Centers
⚲ Major colleges & universities

Weather Facts

Record High Temperature: 109° F (43° C) on July 28, 1940 at Albemarle; Record Low Temperature: -29° F (-34° C) on January 30, 1966 at Mount Mitchell; Average January Temperature: 40° F (4° C); Average July Temperature: 71° F (22° C); Average Yearly Precipitation: 50 in. (127 cm).

Environmental Facts

Air Pollution Rank: 7th; Water Pollution Rank: 25th; Total Yearly Industrial Pollution: 103,583,825 lbs.; Industrial Pollution Rank: 7th; Hazardous Waste Sites: 22; Hazardous Sites Rank: 16th; Landfill Capacity: adequate; Fresh Water Supply: large surplus; Daily Residential Water Consumption: 133 gals. per capita; Endangered Species: Aquatic Species (11)—elktoe, Appalachian; Birds (9)—crane, whooping; Mammals (7)—bat, Indiana; Other Species (1)—spider, spruce-fir moss; Plants (25)—arrowhead, bunched.

Environmental Quality

North Carolina residents generate 6.0 million tons of solid waste each year, or approximately 1,800 pounds per capita. Landfill capacity in North Carolina will be exhausted in more than 12 years. The state has 22 hazardous waste sites. Annual greenhouse gas emissions in North Carolina total 126.5 million tons, or 19.5 tons per capita. Industrial sources in North Carolina release approximately 69.0 thousand tons of toxins, 710.3 thousand tons of acid precipitation-producing substances, and 3.0 million tons of smog-producing substances into the atmosphere each year.

The state has 377,800 acres within the National Park System; the largest area within the state is Great Smoky Mountains National Park. State parks cover just over 173,000 acres, attracting 9.5 million visitors per year.

North Carolina spends 1 percent of its budget, or approximately $15 per capita, on environmental and natural resources.

Average Monthly Weather

Asheville	Jan	Feb	Mar	Apr	May	Jun	Jul	Aug	Sep	Oct	Nov	Dec	Yearly
Maximum Temperature °F	47.5	50.6	58.4	68.6	75.6	81.4	84.0	83.5	77.9	68.7	58.6	50.3	67.1
Minimum Temperature °F	26.0	27.6	34.4	42.7	51.0	58.2	62.4	61.6	55.8	43.3	34.2	28.2	43.8
Days of Precipitation	10.1	9.4	11.2	9.4	11.8	11.2	12.0	12.3	9.5	8.0	9.5	9.6	124.0
Raleigh													
Maximum Temperature °F	50.1	52.8	61.0	72.3	79.0	85.2	88.2	87.1	81.6	71.6	61.8	52.7	70.3
Minimum Temperature °F	29.1	30.3	37.7	46.5	55.3	62.6	67.1	66.8	60.4	47.7	38.1	31.2	47.7
Days of Precipitation	10.0	9.8	10.3	8.9	10.2	9.3	11.2	10.0	7.7	6.9	8.3	8.9	111.6

Flora and Fauna

Because of North Carolina's position in the transition zone between sub-tropical and mid-latitude vegetation, the state has a wide variety of plant life. Forests cover approximately two-thirds of the state. Common trees include cedar, cypress, tupelo, and tulip trees. The Piedmont area is mostly covered with pine trees, a softwood. Flowers start blooming as early as January, when camellias bloom along the North Carolina coast. Other flowers in the state include orchids, rhododendrons, and insect-eating plants such as the Venus fly-trap and sundew.

As in other states, deer populate the entire North Carolina landscape. Small animals also found throughout the state include skunks, foxes, and squirrels. Black bears can be found not only in the mountains, but along the coastal lowlands as well. Many songbirds such as cardinals and wrens claim North Carolina as their home. Several migratory ducks and geese come to the state in winter. North Carolina's rivers and lakes are filled with sunfish, bluegills, and other types of fishes. Marlin and dolphins live off the state's coast.

Topography

There are several distinct topographic regions in North Carolina. The eastern part of the state is covered by the Atlantic Coastal Plain physical region, which extends inland over 100 miles (160 km). The coastal areas are flat, and much of it is swampy. The Outer Banks are narrow stretches of sand that run up and down the coast. The southern part of this region has many sand hills. Most of the interior lowlands have a warm, wet, fertile soil suitable for agriculture. The Piedmont physical region is the hilly area of North Carolina between the flat coastal plains and the mountains in the West. The soil is categorized as warm and moist, and is primarily red/yellow clay.

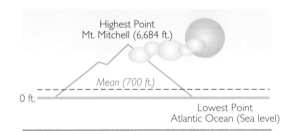

Land Use

Cropland: 22.9%; Pasture: 7%; Rangeland: 0%; Forest: 57.7%; Urban: 8.7%; Other: 3.7%.

For more information about North Carolina's environment, contact Environmental Health and Natural Resources, Archdale Bldg., 512 N. Salisbury St., Raleigh, NC 27604-1148.

Physical Regions: (a) Atlantic Coastal Plain; (b) Piedmont; (c) Mountain Region.

Elevations run from a few hundred ft. above sea level at the fall line with the coastal plain, to about 1,500 ft. (460 m) near the mountains.

The Mountain physical region, in western North Carolina, is dominated by the Appalachian Mountains, with several ranges running through the state. The most important of these is the Blue Ridge Mountains. Others include the Great Smokey and Bald Mountains. The Black Mountains contain the highest elevation in the state. Mt. Mitchell rises 6,684 ft. (2,037 m) above sea level. The soil is similar to that found in the Piedmont.

Climate

North Carolina has a rather mild climate; natural barriers protect the state on both the east and west. The coastal areas of North Carolina stay mild as a result of the warm Gulf Stream off the coast. The Blue Ridge Mountains, in the west, shield some of the colder weather that comes from the north and northwest. However, the western half of the state remains cooler overall. State-wide, temperatures for January and July average 40° F and 76° F. Average temperatures in the mountains are usually several degrees cooler.

North Carolina receives an abundance of precipitation, falling consistently year-round. Between 40 and 80 in. of precipitation falls across the state annually. In the summer, places like Cape Hatteras, along the coast, receive heavier rainfall.

Although North Carolina does not lie directly within usual hurricane territory, these violent storms occasionally reach the state.

Hydrology

One of the longest rivers in the state is the Roanoke, which flows into Ablemarle Sound in northeastern North Carolina. Other rivers that drain into the Atlantic include the Neuse and Tar in central North Carolina, and the Cape Fear and South rivers in the south. In the mountainous west, several rivers flow westward including the Hiwassee, the Little Tennessee, and the Watauga.

It is in the western region that most of the state's lakes lie. These are all man-made lakes. The largest is Lake Norman on the Catawba River in the west-central part of the state. Others include High Rock Lake on the Yadkin, Roanoke Rapids Lake on the Roanoke, and Roxboro Lake on the northern border with Virginia.

North Carolina's eastern border is defined by the Atlantic Ocean, and contains several coastal features. In the north are Curritick, Ablemarle, and Pamlico Sounds. Further south are Raleigh and Onslow Bays, and Cape Fear lies almost at the bottom of the state.

North Carolina's History

North Carolina's First People

Evidence of the first humans who lived in the area known today as the state of North Carolina dates back to around 8,000 B.C. These early peoples were primarily hunters and gatherers, who did not remain in one fixed location for an extended period of time.

Over the years, several different Native American tribes called North Carolina their home. The Tuscarora, Catawba, and Cherokee peoples all lived in North Carolina, although not in the same regions. The Tuscarora lived on the coastal plain until 1713, when they returned to their native New York after being defeated by new European settlers. The Catawba tribe seemed better able to coexist with the white men. The Cherokee, who lived in the Appalachian Mountains, were the last Native American group to be encountered by the Europeans.

European Exploration

The first European to explore any part of North Carolina was Giovanni da Verrazano, who explored the Carolina coast for France. He described the area as one never seen before by "any man, ancient or modern." Two years after Verrazano explored North Carolina, Thucas Vazquez de Ayllon penetrated the coast and set up a temporary colony for Spain near the mouth of what later would be called the Cape Fear River.

North Carolina is home to the first English colony in North America. In 1585, Sir Walter Raleigh, with permission of Queen Elizabeth I, planted a colony on Roanoke Island. Over the years, other settlements were established in North Carolina. The British dominated the area; using a proprietorship system to grant tracts of land. This system lasted from 1663 to 1729. During these years, settlers had a number of problems with the resident, native population of North Carolina. The first permanent incorporated town of Bath was not established until 1706.

Revolutionary Period and Statehood

North Carolina was a British colony until May 1775, when the colonial governor, Josiah Martin, fled the colony. North Carolina was the first colony to officially declare its willingness to fight for independence. The Mecklenburg Resolves, declarations against anything granted by the king of England, were adopted on May 31, 1775. Shortly thereafter, ten regiments and thousands of other soldiers volunteered for the Continental Army.

The first Revolutionary battle fought in North Carolina was on February 22, 1776, at Moore's Creek Bridge. In this year, North Carolina adopted its own state constitution. Whereas North Carolina became the first to declare readiness for independence, it was the second-to-last state to ratify the U.S. Constitution, on November 21, 1789. Three years later, the government located a permanent state capital in Raleigh.

North Carolina continued to be a part of the Union until May 20, 1861, when the state seceded at the onset of the Civil War. Many battles were fought in North Carolina during the Civil War including Averasboro, Bentonville, and Durham Station where Confederate General Joseph E. Johnston surrendered to Union General William Tecumseh Sherman on April 18, 1865. The state again became part of the United States in 1868. As with many of the other Confederate states, its transition back into the Union was not an easy undertaking. Even though slavery was outlawed in all states, many blacks left places such as North Carolina in hopes of better lives in northern states.

Industrialization

The industry boom, which had hit other eastern states in the early 1800s, did not come to North Carolina until 1880. The wave of industrialization, called the First Cotton Mill Campaign, brought several new jobs to the piedmont area of the state. However, workers only prospered slightly, as wages were kept low. The state supported a variety of industries during this time, including tobacco, cotton, and furniture manufacturing. Farming, however, did not fare so well. Heavy debt and low crop prices did not make matters any better for those employed in agriculture.

World War I helped the economy of the state, with the establishment of military bases such as Fort Bragg. In recent years, North Carolina has become a technological center for the country. The cities of the "Research Triangle"—Durham, Raleigh, and Chapel Hill—are home to several large companies specializing in electronics, medicine, and textiles. Farming also remains a significant economic activity for those North Carolinians employed in it, but the numbers of people employed in agricultural projects continues to decline.

North Carolina: Tobacco and Textiles

Tobacco and textiles are two of the top industries in North Carolina. Although North Carolina's industrial base is becoming more diversified, about 35 percent of those people employed in industry work with textiles in some aspect. The reason for this is that textile producers have found that they can run their plants inexpensively in the South where such things as labor costs are cheaper than in the old traditional textile areas of the Northeast.

One may not think of North Carolina as an important agricultural state, but it does rank high in the number, population, and income of farms. This is due in large part to the huge tobacco industry the state supports, which is the leading industry in the state.

On many of the state highways, small stores sell large quantities of these two commodities. Travelers, passing through North Carolina, stop to stock-up on cigarettes, towels, linens, and other textile goods at prices that are lower than in other areas of the country.

Important Events

1524 Giovanni da Verrazano sails along Carolina coast.

1540 Hernando de Soto explores the state's mountainous region.

1585 Roanoke, first English colony, founded by Sir Walter Raleigh. It later failed and returned to England.

1587 Roanoke, second English colony, founded by Sir Walter Raleigh failed and dissapeared. Referred to as the "Lost Colony."

1663 Proprietorship system to grant tracts of land begins.

1706 First town incorporated (Bath).

1712 Separate governors appointed for North and South Carolina.

1713 The Tuscarora peoples are defeated by European settlers and return to New York.

1729 Proprietorship period ends.

1775 Colonial governor, Josiah Martin, flees the colony in May.

1775 Mecklenburg Resolves adopted on May 31. Soldiers swell the ranks of the Continental Army.

1776 North Carolina declares independence from Great Britain on February 22.

1789 North Carolina becomes twelfth state of the Union and ratified the U.S. Constitution on November 21.

1861 Secession from the Union on May 20.

1868 North Carolina readmitted to the Union.

1880 Industrial boom comes to North Carolina as the *First Cotton Mill Campaign.*

1903 First powered airplane successfully flown at Kitty Hawk.

1936 Intracoastal Waterway completed.

1958 The Research Triangle complex is established connecting Durham, Raleigh, and Chapel Hill.

1971 Third state constitution adopted.

1990 Conservative Republican senator Jesse Helms wins a fourth term to Congress by using questionable television ads.

1993 The creation of the mostly African-American Twelfth Congressional District is declared unconstitutional by the U.S. Supreme Court.

Persons Per Square Mile

- 10.0 to 99.9
- 100.0 to 249.9
- 250.0 to 749.9
- 750.0 to 1,299.9

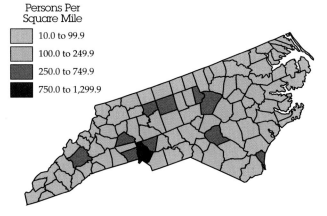

Population Density

Population density for the state of North Carolina was 136.1 persons per square mile in 1990 (52.5 per km2). Average U.S. density was 70.3 persons per square mile in 1990 (27.3 per km2). Habitation is most dense in and around the urban area of Charlotte, North Carolina's most populous city. Other high-density cities in the state include Raleigh, Winston-Salem, and Durham.

Percent Change 1980 to 1990

- −9.9 to 0.0%
- 0.1 to 19.9%
- 20.0 to 49.9%
- 50.0 to 140.1%

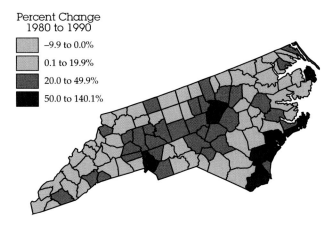

Population Change

The 1990 population figure for the state of North Carolina was 6,628,637. This is a 12.7 percent increase from 5,881,766 in 1980. The next decade will show growth with a population of 7.5 million or a 12.89 percent increase. The areas of fastest growth can be found along North Carolina's coastal region where the fine beaches draw many residents looking for life at the shore. Other high-growth areas are Charlotte and Raleigh.

Per Capita Income (000s) (Current Dollars)

- $10.0 to 12.9
- $13.0 to 15.9
- $16.0 to 19.9
- $20.0 to 37.7

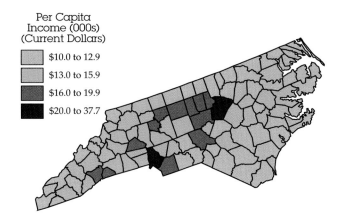

Distribution of Income

The per capita income for the state of North Carolina (current dollars) was $17,667 in 1992. This is a 120.8 percent increase from $8,000 in 1980. Income is greatest in the urban areas. These areas include Charlotte, Raleigh, Winston-Salem, and Durham. Low-income areas are found in the far southern region and the far western regions in the mountainous counties.

Population Projections

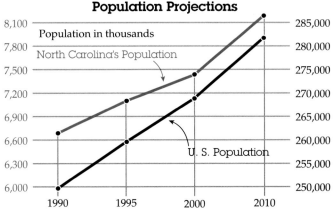

Population in thousands

North Carolina's Population

U. S. Population

Population Change

Year	Population
1950	4,062,000
1960	4,573,000
1970	5,098,000
1980	5,881,766
1990	6,628,637
2000	7,483,000
2010	8,154,000

Period	Change
1950–1970	25.5%
1970–1980	15.4%
1980–1990	12.7%
1990–2000	12.9%

Population Facts

State Population, 1993: 6,945,000

Rank: 10

Population 2000: 7,483,000 (Rank 11)

Density: 136.1 per sq. mi. (52.5 per km²)

Distribution: 50.4% urban, 49.6% rural

Population Under 5 Years Old: 7.2%

Population Under 18 Years Old: 24.3%

Population Over 65 Years Old: 12.4%

Median Age: 33.1

Number of Households: 2,517,000

Average Persons Per Household: 2.54

Average Persons Per Family: 3.03

Female Heads of Households: 4.67%

Population That Is Married: 21.49%

Birth Rate: 15.8 per 1,000 population

Death Rate: 8.6 per 1,000 population

Births to Teen Mothers: 16.2%

Marriage Rate: 7.8 per 1,000 population

Divorce Rate: 5.1 per 1,000 population

Violent Crime Rate: 658 per 100,000 pop.

Population on Social Security: 16.5%

Percent Voting for President: 50.1%

Population Profile

Rank. North Carolina ranks 10th among U.S. states in terms of population with 6,945,000 citizens.

Minority Population. The state's minority population is 25.1 percent. The state's male to female ratio for 1990 was 94.14 males for every 100 females. It was below the national average of 95.22 males for every 100 females.

Growth. Growing much faster than the

Government

Capital: Raleigh (established 1792).

Statehood: Became 12th state on Nov. 21, 1789.

Number of Counties: 100.

Supreme Court Justices: 7, 8-year term.

State Senators: 50, 2-year term.

State Legislators: 120, 2-year term.

United States Senators: 2.

United States Representatives: 12.

Electoral Votes: 14.

State Constitution: Adopted 1970.

North Carolina's Famous Citizens

Brinkley, David (b. 1920). TV journalist. Cohost of "The Huntley-Brinkley Report" (1956–1970).

Daly, Augustin (1838–1899). Playwright. Wrote melodramas, including *Under the Gaslight* and *Saratoga*.

Dare, Virginia (1587–?). First child born in America of English parents.

Duke, James Buchanan (1856–1925). Became president of the American Tobacco Company in 1890.

Gardner, Ava (1922–1990). Actress. Her films include *The Killers* (1946), *The Hucksters* (1947), and *Show Boat* (1951).

Helms, Jesse (b. 1921). Elected to the U.S. Senate in 1972. Known for his extreme right-wing views.

Petty, Richard (b. 1937). Auto racer. He won 7 Daytona 500 races in his career.

Revels, Hiram Rhoades (1822–1901). First African-American member of Congress. Elected to the Senate in 1870.

Travis, Randy (b. 1959). Country singer-songwriter. In 1987, he became the youngest member ever to join the Grand Ole Opry.

projected national average, the state's population is expected to reach 8.2 million by the year 2010 (*see graph above*).

Older Citizens. The state's population older than 65 was 804,341 in 1990. It grew 33.35% from 603,181 in 1980.

Younger Citizens. The number of children (under 18 years of age) was 1.6 million in 1990. This represents 24.2 percent of the state's population. The state's school aged population was 1.1 million in 1990. It is expected to increase to 1.2 million by the year 2000. This represents an 11.81% change.

Urban/Rural. 50.4% of the population of the state live in urban areas while 49.6% live in rural areas.

Largest Cities. North Carolina has 18 cities with a population greater than 35,000. The populations of the state's largest centers are (starting from the most populous) Charlotte (395,934), Raleigh (207,951), Greensboro (183,521), Winston-Salem (143,485), Durham (136,611), Fayetteville (75,695), High Point (69,496), Asheville (61,607), Wilmington (55,530), Gastonia (54,732), Rocky Mount (48,997), Greenville (44,972), and Cary (43,858).

Presence of Native Americans

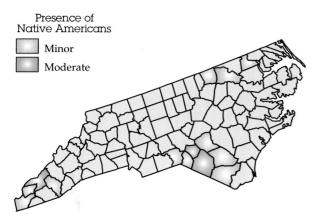

Minor

Moderate

Native American

The Native American population in North Carolina was 80,155 in 1990. This was an increase of 21.80 percent from 65,808 in 1980. Many live in a small Indian reservation located in the far western part of the state called the Cherokee Indian Reservation. Many also live in North Carolina's urban areas such as Charlotte, Raleigh, Durham, and Greensboro.

Statewide Ethnic Composition

Over 75 percent of the population of North Carolina is white. The largest nationalities in this racial group are German, English, and Irish. The next largest group is African Americans, followed by Native Americans, Hispanics, and Asians. Over 787,000 people claim to be American and acknowledge no other nationality.

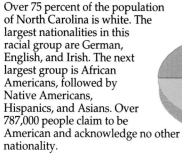

- White (75.55%)
- African American (21.96%)
- Asian American (0.78%)
- Hispanic (1.16%)
- Native American (1.21%)

Nationalities

African	11,110
American	787,800
Arab	8,781
Austrian	4,285
Czech	5,357
Dutch	88,431
English	775,474
Finnish	2,703
German	902,265
Greek	12,662
Hungarian	7,981
Irish	520,713
Italian	78,002
Norwegian	13,084
Polish	39,839
Portuguese	3,326
Russian	11,838
Scottish	124,019
Slovak	7,471
Swedish	22,859
Welsh	20,666
West Indian	5,432

Education Facts

Total Students 1990: 1,080,744

Number of School Districts: 134

Expenditure Per Capita on Education 1990: $737

Expenditure Per Capita K–12 1990: $669

Expenditure Per Pupil 1990: $4,635

Total School Enrollment 1990–1991: 1,082,558

Rank of Expenditures Per Student: 32d in the U.S.

African American Enrollment: 30.4%

Hispanic Enrollment: 0.7%

Asian/Pacific Islander Enrollment: 0.8%

Native American Enrollment: 1.6%

Mean SAT Score 1991 Verbal: 400

Mean SAT Score 1991 Math: 444

Average Teacher's Salary 1992: $29,200

Rank Teacher's Salary: 33d in U.S.

High School Graduates 1990: 64,900

Total Number of Public Schools: 1,952

Number of Teachers 1990: 63,307

Student/Teacher Ratio: 17.1

Staff Employed in Public Schools: 122,470

Pupil/Staff Ratio: 8.8

Staff/Teacher Ratio: 1.9

Education

Attainment: 71.3 percent of population 25 years or older were high school graduates in 1989, earning North Carolina a ranking of 41st in the United States; 18.3 percent of the state's population had completed college. Institutions of Higher Education: The largest universities and colleges in the state include the University of North Carolina (founded 1795), Chapel Hill; North Carolina State University, Raleigh; Duke University, Durham; Wake Forest University, Winston-Salem; Campbell University, Buies Creek. Expenditures per Student: Expenditure increased 73% between 1985 and 1990. Projected High School Graduations: 1998 (64,629), 2004 (68,036); Total Revenues for Education from Federal Sources: $286 million; Total Revenues for Education from State Sources: $2.5 billion; Total Revenues for Education from Local Sources: $974 million; Average Annual Salaries for Public School Principals: $40,539; Largest School Districts in State: Mecklenburg County, 75,903 students, 31st in the United States; Wake County, 62,474 students, 48th.

Percent of County Population

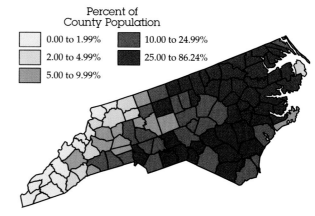

- 0.00 to 1.99%
- 2.00 to 4.99%
- 5.00 to 9.99%
- 10.00 to 24.99%
- 25.00 to 86.24%

African American

The African American population in North Carolina was 1,456,323 in 1990. This was an increase of 10.41 percent from 1,319,054 in 1980. The largest percentages of African American population can be found in a north-south band extending from the northeast through the state and ending on the border with South Carolina. Charlotte in the western section of the state contains the highest number of African Americans.

Percent of County Population

- 0.00 to 0.99%
- 1.00 to 2.99%
- 3.00 to 9.99%

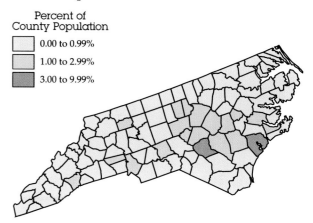

Hispanic[††]

The Hispanic population in North Carolina was 76,726 in 1990. This is an increase of 35.40 percent from 56,667 persons in 1980. Large percentages of Hispanics can be found in Cumberland and Onslow counties as well as in the major cities.

[††]A person of Mexican, Puerto Rican, Cuban, or other Spanish culture or origin regardless of race.

Percent of County Population

- 0.00 to 0.24%
- 0.25 to 0.99%
- 1.00 to 1.99%
- 2.00 to 4.99%

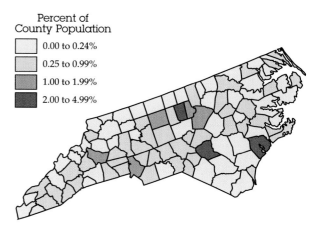

Asian American

The Asian American population in North Carolina was 52,166 in 1990. This is an increase of 137.01 percent from 22,010 persons in 1980. The Asian American pattern is similar to the Hispanic population patterns in the state. Large concentrations can be found in Orange, Cumberland, and Onslow counties as well as in large cities such as Charlotte and Raleigh.

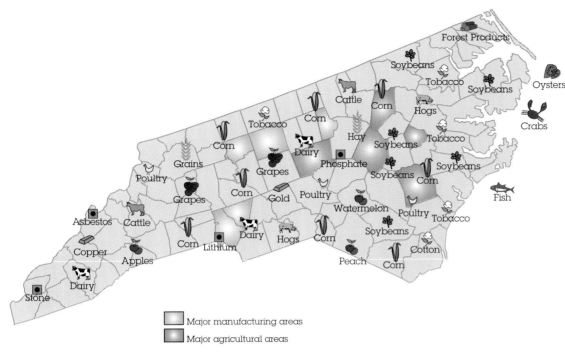

Major manufacturing areas

Major agricultural areas

Transportation

In the past, North Carolina depended on rivers as its primary transportation mode. Today, however, trucks, not river barges, carry most goods shipped in the state. North Carolina has a well-developed road system. The extensive farm-to-market road system is supported by many larger roads and highways. Five interstates pass through North Carolina.

North Carolina still uses rail transportation, although this mode of transport has declined. Passenger rail service reaches seven North Carolina cities. In addition, 25 freight lines provide service through the state. North Carolina's busiest airport is located in Charlotte. Other large airports include ones at Greensboro and Raleigh-Durham. North Carolina has two major ports on the Atlantic Intracoastal Waterway, Wilmington and Morehead City.

Energy and Transportation Facts

Energy. Yearly Consumption: 1,962 tril. BTUs (residential, 23.3%; commercial, 17.3%; industrial, 32.2%; transportation, 27.1%); Annual Energy Expenditures Per Capita: $1,871; Nuclear Power Plants Located in State: 5; Source of Energy Consumed: Petroleum— 40.1%; Natural Gas— 9.5%; Coal— 28.9%; Hydroelectric Power—3.4%; Nuclear Power—18.0%.

Transportation. Highway Miles: 95,582 (interstates, 970; urban, 21,451; rural, 74,131); Average Yearly Auto Insurance: $448 (42d); Auto Fatalities Rank: 5th; Registered Motor Vehicles: 5,306,911; Workers in Carpools: 21.0%; Workers Using Public Trans: 1.0%.

Employment

Employment. North Carolina employed 3.38 million people in 1993. Most work in manufacturing jobs (845,900 persons or 25.0% of the workforce). Wholesale and retail trade account for 21.6% or 729,600 workers. Government employs 529,400 workers (15.6%). Social and personal services employ 688,400 people (20.3%). Construction accounts for 4.5% or 153,300 persons. Transportation and utilities account for 4.6% or 156,300 persons. Agriculture employs 94,700 workers or 2.8%. Finance, real estate, and insurance account for 4.1% or 138,400 workers. Mining employs 3,400 people and accounts for only 0.1% of the workforce.

Unemployment. Unemployment has decreased to 4.9% in 1993 from a rate of 5.4% in 1985. Today's figure is lower than the national average of 6.8% as shown below.

Agriculture

North Carolina has 9.4 million farm acres. During the last 40 years, North Carolina's farms have grown larger in size and fewer in number. In 1955, 268,000 farms were found in the state. Today, 59,000 remain.

Agriculture adds $3 billion to the state's gross product annually. The principal commodities in order of marketing receipts are tobacco, broilers, hogs, and turkeys.

Livestock and livestock products account for about 55 percent of North Carolina's farm income, with broilers being the most important. North Carolina is one of the leading states in the nation in broiler production, which is centered in Alexander, Pitt, Nash, and Wilkes counties. Hogs are the second leading livestock product. Major crops include tobacco, cotton and sweet potatoes.

Housing

Owner Occupied Units: 2,818,193; Average Age of Units: 24 years; Average Value of Housing Units: $65,800; Renter Occupied Units: 777,929; Median Monthly Rent: $382; Housing Starts: 59,800; Existing Home Sales: 185,000.

Economic Facts

Gross State Product: $130,000,000,000 (1989)

Income Per Capita: $17,667

Disposable Personal Income: $15,600

Median Household Income: $26,647

Average Annual Pay, 1988: $21,087

Principal Industries: tobacco products, chemicals, electrical equipment, textiles, food products, machinery

Major Crops: tobacco, sweet potatoes, grapes, apples, pecans, peanuts, tomatoes, corn, cotton

Fish: Marlin, Shellfish, Sturgeon, Bass, Bluegills, Crappies

Livestock: hogs, chicken, turkeys

Non-Fuel Minerals: Feldspar, Gneiss, Limestone, Clay, Granite, Shale, Phosphate, Lithium

Organic Fuel Minerals: N/A

Civilian Labor Force: 3,445,000 (Women: 1,602,000)

Total Employed: 3,246,000 (Women: 1,510,000)

Median Value of Housing: $65,800

Median Contract Rent: $382 per month

Economic Sectors 1992

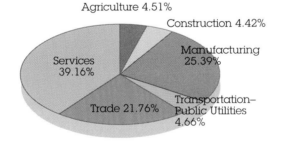

Agriculture 4.51%

Construction 4.42%

Manufacturing 25.39%

Services 39.16%

Trade 21.76%

Transportation– Public Utilities 4.66%

Manufacturing

North Carolina is a leading manufacturing state, ranking sixth overall in industrial output. However, many North Carolina workers receive lower than the average United States wage, for many manufacturing jobs are only semiskilled positions. Tobacco products dominate the state manufacturing sector, but textile, furniture, and electrical equipment production are all important industries as well.

Different areas of North Carolina have their own manufacturing specialties. Factories in Winston-Salem, Greensboro, and Reidsville produce almost half of the cigarettes in the United States. North Carolina has over 1,000 textile plants, many of which are located in Gaston County. The Furniture Capital of America, High Point, is in northern North Carolina.

Unemployment Rate

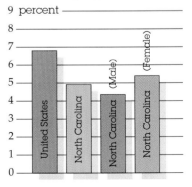

percent

NORTH DAKOTA
The State of North Dakota

Official State Seal

The Great Seal of North Dakota was adopted in 1889. It is based on an earlier seal dating from 1863. A tree surrounded by farming tools and a man on horseback are located in the center of the seal. Lining the inside is the state motto, "Liberty and Union Now and Forever, One and Inseparable." Below this are forty-two stars marking North Dakota's entrance into the United States.

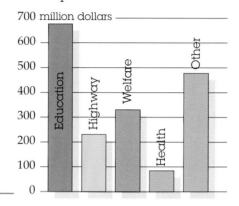

Legal Holidays

January: New Year's Day—1st; Martin Luther King, Jr., Day—3rd Monday; February: Presidents' Day—3rd Monday; May: Memorial Day—4th Monday; July: Independence Day—4th; September: Labor Day—1st Monday; October: Columbus Day—2nd Monday; November: Admission Day—2nd; Veterans' Day—11th; Thanksgiving—4th Thursday; December: Christmas—25th.

Official State Flag

The state flag of North Dakota was adopted in 1911. It came from the flag of the North Dakota National Guard and contains an American eagle holding a banner in its beak with the words *"E Pluribus Unum"* (One from Many). Below this is another banner with the name of the state printed on it.

Festivals and Events

February: Cookbook Festival, Fargo; Muzzleloader's Trade Fair, Jamestown; April: Silent Movie Night, Fargo; May: Dakota Cowboy Poetry Gathering, Medora; June: Hjemkomst Scandinavian Festival, Fargo; Missouri River Expo, Bismarck; July: State Fair, Minot; International Festival of the Arts, Peace Garden; August: Country Jamboree, Fargo; September: Oktoberfest, Bismarck; United Tribes Pow Wow, Bismarck; October: Norsk Hostefest, Minot; Bazaarfest, Fargo; November: Merry Prairie Christmas, Fargo-Moorhead.

North Dakota Compared to States in Its Region.

Resident Pop. in Metro Areas: 6th; Pop. Percent Increase: 7th; Pop. Over 65: 3d; Infant Mortality: 6th; School Enroll. Increase: 6th; High School Grad. and Up: 6th; Violent Crime: 7th; Hazardous Waste Sites: 6th; Unemployment: 3d; Median Household Income: 6th; Persons Below Poverty: 3d; Energy Costs Per Person: 1st.

West North Central Region

	Population	Capital
Minnesota	4,517,000	St. Paul
Iowa	2,814,000	Des Moines
Missouri	5,234,000	Jefferson City
North Dakota	635,000	Bismarck
South Dakota	715,000	Pierre
Nebraska	1,607,000	Lincoln
Kansas	2,531,000	Topeka

North Dakota's Finances

Households: 241,000; Income Per Capita Current Dollars: $16,854; Change Per Capita Income 1980 to 1992: 120.6% (7th in U.S.); State Expenditures: $1,834,000,000; State Revenues: $1,810,000,000; Personal Income Tax: 2.67 to 12%; Federal Income Taxes Paid Per Capita: $1,355; Sales Tax: 5% (food and prescription drugs exempt).

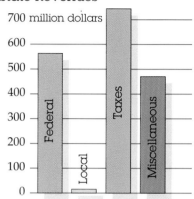

Location, Size, and Boundaries

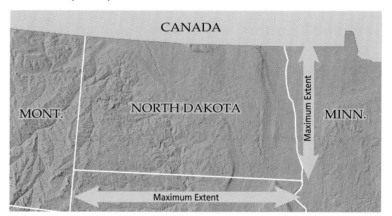

Location. North Dakota is located in the West North Central region of the United States. It is bounded on four sides by land. The geographic center of North Dakota is at lat. 47° 24.7' N; long. 100° 34.1' W.

Size. North Dakota is the 17th largest state in terms of size. Its area is 70,665 sq. mi. (183,022 km2). Inland water covers 1,392 sq. mi. (3,605 km2).

Boundaries. Canada, 310 mi. (499 km); Minnesota, 420 mi. (676 km); South Dakota, 370 mi. (595 km); Montana, 212 mi. (341 km).

Geographic Extent. The north/south extent of North Dakota is 210 mi. (340 km). The state extends 360 mi. (580 km) to the east/west.

Facts about North Dakota. Origin of Name: After the *Sioux* Indians, who called themselves *Dakota* or *Lakota*, meaning *allies* or *friends;* Nickname: The Flickertail State; Motto: "Liberty and union, now and forever, one and inseparable"; Abbreviations: N. Dak. or N.D. (traditional), ND (postal); State Bird: Western meadowlark; State Tree: American elm; State Flower: wild prairie rose; State Song: "North Dakota Hymn," words by James W. Foley and music by C. S. Putnam.

North Dakota Compared to Other States. Resident Pop. in Metro Areas: 43d; Pop. Per. Increase: 50th; Pop. Over 65: 8th; Infant Mort.: 40th; School Enroll. Increase: 41st; High School Grad. and Up: 26th; Violent Crime: 50th; Haz. Waste Sites: 47th; Unemployment: 44th; Med. Household Income: 43d; Persons Below Poverty: 16th; Energy Costs Per Person: 5th.

Sources of Information. Tourism/Economy: Economic Development Commission, Tourism Division, Liberty Memorial Building, Capitol Grounds, Bismarck, ND 58505. Government: Office of the Governor, Director of Constituent Services, State Capitol, Bismarck, ND 58505. History: State Historical Society, Heritage Center, Bismarck, ND 58505.

■ Arrowwood National Wildlife Refuge. Refuge for migratory waterfowl with a chain of lakes. (E-10)

■ Bald Hill Dam. Large dam on the Sheyenne River. (E-11)

■ Burning Coal Vein. Underground lignite coal vein possibly burning since Indian days. (G-1)

■ Camp Arnold Historic Site. Campsite of the Sibley expedition in 1863. (F-12)

■ Camp Hancock State Historic Site. The oldest building in the capital, Bismarck, built in 1872. (F-6)

■ Château de Morés State Historic Site. A French nobleman, the Marquis De Morés, built this château in 1883. (F-1)

■ Crowley Flint Quarry. Quarries used by Indians for making flint arrows and spearheads. (F-4)

■ Dakota Zoo. The largest zoological gardens in the state. (F-6)

■ Double Ditch Indian Village Site. Ruins of Mandan Indian village. (F-6)

■ Fort Abercrombie Historic Park. The first United States military post in the state in 1857. (G-14)

■ Fort Abraham Lincoln State Park. The site of the reconstructed home of General Custer, from which he left to go to fight the battle of the Little Bighorn. (F-6)

■ Fort Buford Historic Site. A fort used between 1866 and 1895. (C-1)

■ Fort Clark Historic Site. Trading post/fort. (E-6)

■ Fort Dilts Historic Site. A fort built out of sod in 1864 for protection from Sioux Indians. (G-1)

■ Fort Ransom State Park. Scenic views and tours of a military post established in 1867. (G-12)

■ Fort Rice State Historic Site. Fort established in 1864. (G-6)

■ Fort Seward State Historic Site. This fort was established in 1872 to protect the Northern Pacific Railway. (F-10)

■ Fort Union Trading Post National Historic Site. A fort built by the American Fur Company in 1829. (C-1)

■ Geographic Center of North America. The center of North America is at this site marked by a monument. (C-8)

■ Sitting Bull State Historic Site. The burial place of the Sioux chief. (H-7)

Environmental Quality

See page 376.

★ State capitol
⊙ Cities over 35,000 pop.
● County Seats
■ Major cultural attractions

▫ State Parks
Ⓦ Welcome Centers
⚲ Major colleges and universities

■ Sullys Hill National Game Preserve. Refuge for buffalo and other range animals. (C-10)

■ Whitestone Hill Battlefield State Historic Site. Site of an Indian and cavalry battle in 1862. (H-10)

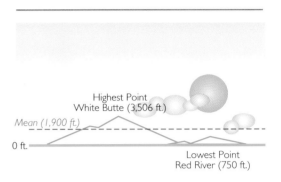

Highest Point
White Butte (3,506 ft.)
Mean (1,900 ft.)
0 ft.
Lowest Point
Red River (750 ft.)

Weather Facts

Record High Temperature: 121° F (49° C) on July 6, 1936, at Steele; Record Low Temperature: -60° F (-51° C) on February 15, 1936, at Parshall; Average January Temperature: 8° F (-13° C); Average July Temperature: 70° F (21° C); Average Yearly Precipitation: 18 in. (46 cm).

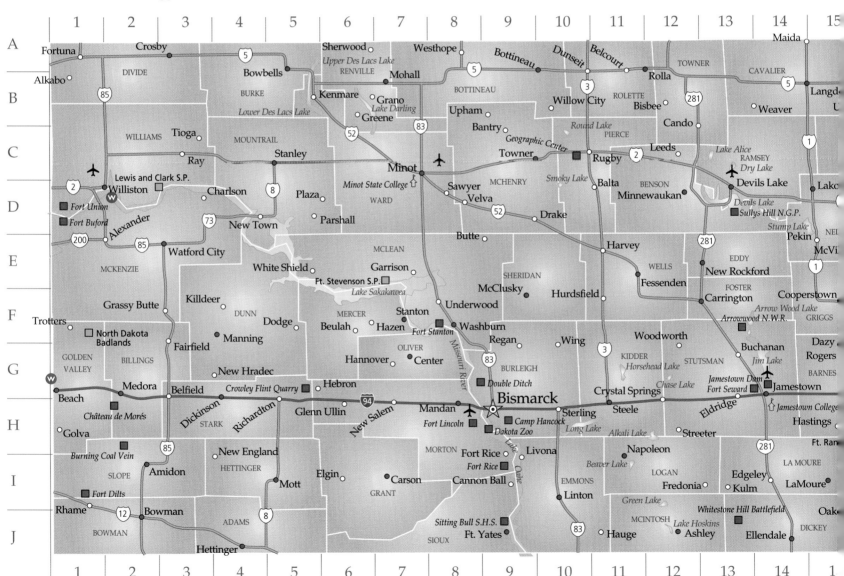

Average Monthly Weather

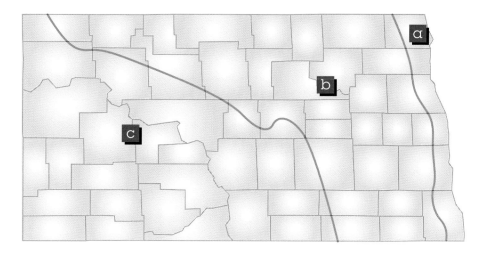

Fargo	Jan	Feb	Mar	Apr	May	Jun	Jul	Aug	Sep	Oct	Nov	Dec	Yearly
Maximum Temperature °F	13.7	20.5	33.2	52.5	68.1	76.9	82.7	81.1	69.8	57.7	37.0	21.3	51.2
Minimum Temperature °F	-5.1	1.5	14.8	31.6	43.0	53.5	58.4	56.4	45.7	34.9	19.4	4.0	29.8
Days of Precipitation	8.6	7.0	7.9	8.1	10.0	10.4	9.6	9.1	8.0	6.5	6.1	8.0	99.4

Physical Regions: (a) Red River Valley; (b) Drift Prarie; (c) Great Plains (Missouri Plateau).

Land Use

Cropland: 66.4%; Pasture: 2.9%; Rangeland: 23.5%; Forest: 1%; Urban: 2.9%; Other: 3.3%.

Scale

0   15   30   45mi.

15   0   15   30   45   60 km

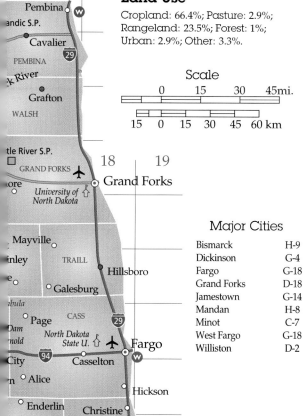

Major Cities

Bismarck	H-9
Dickinson	G-4
Fargo	G-18
Grand Forks	D-18
Jamestown	G-14
Mandan	H-8
Minot	C-7
West Fargo	G-18
Williston	D-2

Topography

North Dakota consists of several varying topographic regions. Along the eastern border of North Dakota is the Red River Valley physical region, an area that was once submerged beneath a glacial lake. This low flat land has extremely fertile soil, classed as cool and moist, that makes it particularly well suited to agriculture.

To the west of the Red River Valley is the Drift Prairie physical region, which covers most of the eastern half of the state. Soil is typically warm and wet with a thick dark organically rich surface layer. The land in this area, which is mainly gentle hills interspersed with valleys and lakes, rises gradually from east to west to reach elevations of over 1,500 ft. (450 m).

The western half of the state is covered by the Great Plains physical region. This highland area is broken by the Missouri River and its surrounding valley called the Missouri Breaks. The soil in this area is cool, moist, dark, and high in organic content. In the southwest part of this region is an area known as the Badlands. It is a long narrow band of land running roughly north to south that contains many unusual rocky formations. The soil is similar to the type found in the the Drift Prairie, but depth to bedrock is 20 inches or less. Various buttes and cones dot the landscape in this area. One of these buttes is the highest elevation in the state: White Butte rises 3,506 ft. (1,069 m).

Environmental Facts

Air Pollution Rank: 47th; Water Pollution Rank: 40th; Total Yearly Industrial Pollution: 1,904,146 lbs.; Industrial Pollution Rank: 48th; Hazardous Waste Sites: 2; Hazardous Sites Rank: 47th; Landfill Capacity: adequate; Fresh Water Supply: surplus; Daily Residential Water Consumption: 138 gals. per capita; Endangered Species: Aquatic Species (1)—sturgeon, pallid; Birds (5)—crane, whooping; Plants (1)—orchid, western prairie fringed.

Climate

The state of North Dakota, in the middle of the continent, has a climate appropriately called continental, with humid continental being more specific. However, one may not think of North Dakota as having a humid climate. Eastern cities such as Fargo experience the humid continental climate, consisting of hot summers with temperatures averaging around 85 degrees F, and cold winters, when temperatures often remain below the freezing mark. The western part of North Dakota is somewhat less humid, and receives less precipitation.

In North Dakota overall, precipitation averages approximately 17 inches a year. However, variation does exist throughout the state. Southwestern North Dakota receives the least amount of precipitation, often less than 15 inches annually.

The entire state is also quite windy. North Dakota's windy days make it an ideal state in which to develop wind energy, an important renewable energy source.

Hydrology

The Red River forms North Dakota's entire eastern boundary with Minnesota, flowing north into Canada. The most important river in the state is the Missouri, which enters North Dakota from the upper western border with Montana, and flows east and then southeast before entering South Dakota in the middle of the state. Several tributaries drain southwest North Dakota, including the Little Missouri, the Knife, the Heart, and the Cannonball. The Souris River in the north-central region flows southeast from Canada, and then loops back up and travels northwest back into Canada. Branches of the Red River in the east include the Forest, the Goose, the Sheyenne, and the Wild Rice. The James River flows through south-central North Dakota.

There are several man-made lakes created by dams for irrigation and hydroelectric projects. The largest of these is Lake Sakakawea on the Missouri River, covering roughly 625 sq. miles (1,619 sq. km), although averaging only 3.5 miles (5.5 km) in width. Devil's Lake in the north-central region is the largest natural lake.

Flora and Fauna

North Dakota has the lowest percentage of its land covered by forests—approximately 1 percent—of any state. Most forests exist around Devil's Lake and in the Turtle Mountains and Pembina Hills. Elm, cottonwood, aspen, and ash trees grow along the Missouri River. Other trees growing in North Dakota include basswood, box elder, oak, and poplar. Most of North Dakota's land is covered with prairie grass: grama and buffalo grass in the southwest, and bluegrass in the northeastern part of the state. Wildflowers such as gaillardias, pasqueflowers, prairie mallows, and beardtongues bloom in the spring and summer.

The common white-tailed deer lives throughout North Dakota. Prairie dogs are abundant in the state's Badlands region. Other animals living in North Dakota include coyotes, bobcats, lynxes, weasels, and flickertail ground squirrels. More waterfowl hatch in North Dakota than in any other state, as many ducks migrate there to breed. Other birds living in the state include Hungarian partridges and pheasants. The rivers, streams, and lakes of North Dakota contain many fishes such as trout, coho salmon, bass, and walleye.

--- **North Dakota's History** ---

North Dakota's First People

People roamed the area now known as North Dakota as far back as fifteen thousand years ago. During this time, hardly any trees grew in North Dakota, as 95 percent of the land was covered with grasses. While these earliest people were primarily hunters, around 1300 B.C. the area was settled by the Mandan tribe, a group of farming people who lived in villages, and who were still around when the first European and American explorers visited present-day North Dakota in the eighteenth and nineteenth centuries, though they were largely decimated by smallpox in the late 1830s.

Although elements of the Sioux and Ojibwa tribes crossed into North Dakota and even lived there for a time, they were more nomadic than the Mandan, being essentially horsemen and buffalo hunters of the Plains. Other Plains tribes, such as the Hidatsa, Arikara, and Cheyenne, also resided in the state at various times.

European Exploration

Overall, European explorers did not come to many of the northern and western states until the 1700s, and North Dakota is no exception to this rule. The Sieur de La Vérendrye, a French explorer, became the first European to travel through North Dakota to a Mandan village in 1738.

As the demand for furs increased, more Europeans came to North Dakota to trap and to trade. The relationship between the native population and the Europeans was reasonably peaceful. Many Native Americans established fur-trading relations with members of the British Hudson's Bay Company. By 1800, the Métis, a people with both European and Indian ancestry, were an established population in the area.

A fur-trading post at Pembina, founded by Alexander Henry in 1801, eventually became the first permanent white settlement in North Dakota in 1812. This was not the first attempt, however, to create a permanent European settlement, as one earlier effort failed.

Territorial Period and Statehood

The United States acquired the land comprising North Dakota in the 1803 Louisiana Purchase. A distinction of territory status for North Dakota did not become recognized until 1861. This territory consisted of both North and South Dakota at the time. The territory was opened to homesteaders two years later on January 1, 1863. Most of the earliest settlers were German, Norwegian, or Canadian farmers.

Many people who came to North Dakota referred to the area as the "Great American Desert." The harsh climate, coupled with a weak transportation system, did not make the territory too desirable to settlers. This trend was somewhat reversed in 1876, when the "bonanza" idea was born. Started on a wheat farm in Casselton by Oliver Dalrymple, a bonanza was a massive gathering of people all working together toward a single crop grown on thousands of acres of land.

The bonanza concept helped boost North Dakota's economy, and the territory began to look more attractive. Soon it had a sufficient population to split the territory into two. As this occurred, statehood was granted, and so on November 2, 1889, North Dakota became the thirty-ninth state in the Union. Its sister state of South Dakota achieved statehood on the same day.

Industry

North Dakota does not have the most favorable climate conditions for agricultural ventures, but nevertheless the state's industries primarily focus on agriculture in one way or another. In addition, mining, manufacturing, and tourism all help contribute to the state's economy.

Settlers as far back as the Mandan tribe have farmed North Dakota land. The bonanza idea of 1876 helped farming to achieve even greater prominence in the state. Today, North Dakota derives one-tenth of its gross state product solely from agriculture. Manufacturing in North Dakota revolves around producing products used for agriculture. Factories that process crops are the most abundant type of manufacturing establishment in the state.

Mining is another important industry in North Dakota. The state ranks first in the entire nation in total number of coal reserves, even though many of these reserves are lignite—low- energy-producing coal. North Dakota became an important producer of crude petroleum when the first reserves were found at Tioga in 1951. Even today, the state still produces a significant amount of the nation's crude supply.

Rich in Tradition

In North Dakota today, both Native Americans and European immigrants keep their own cultural traditions alive. Native American craft products, such as pottery and beadwork, attract many visitors to the state.

Scandinavian traditions remain strong throughout North Dakota. Although none of the fifty Norwegian-language newspapers that were published in 1955 are around today, the language still plays an important role in education. Norwegian language and literature are taught in colleges, and elementary schools.

Combating a Book Problem

One thing North Dakota lacks is adequate library facilities. The majority of the state's population does not live in large towns and cities, where libraries are located. One-fifth of North Dakotans do not have access to a library. To combat problem, county and regional libraries have been established to serve rural populations. Also, bookmobiles travel to smaller villages without permanent public library facilities.

--- **Important Events** ---

1682 La Salle claims area now known as North Dakota.

1738 The Sieur de La Vérendrye travels through North Dakota to a Mandan Indian village.

1800 The Métis become an established population due to intermixing between Europeans and the native population.

1801 Alexander Henry founds a fur-trading post at Pembina.

1803 The United States gains control of half of North Dakota land through the Louisiana Purchase.

1804 Lewis and Clark build Ft. Mandan.

1812 First permanent white settlement established at Pembina.

1818 United States gains control of the other half of North Dakota land from Britain through an agreement.

1832 Missouri river steamboats reach North Dakota.

1837 Mandan tribe plagued by smallpox and largely decimated.

1861 Dakota Territory created which consisted of both North and South Dakota.

1863 Territory opened to homesteaders on January 1.

1871 Northern Pacific Railroad reaches Red River in North Dakota.

1876 Oliver Dalrymple starts the "bonanza" idea on a wheat farm in Casselton.

1881 Sitting Bull, Sioux chief, surrenders at Fort Buford.

1883 Bismarck named territorial capital; replaces Yankton.

1889 North Dakota becomes thirty-ninth state in the Union on November 2.

1912 First to hold a presidential primary.

1915 Nonpartisan League founded.

1933 Moratorium on farm foreclosures goes into effect.

1951 First reserves of crude petroleum discovered at Tioga.

1971 First college of fine arts established at University of North Dakota.

1993 Flooding in Fargo from the Red River causes vast damage.

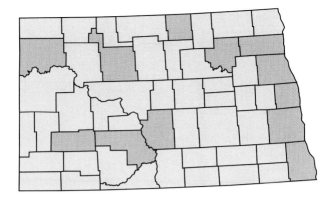

Population Density

Population density for the state of North Dakota was 9.3 persons per square mile in 1990 (3.6 per km2). Average U.S. density was 70.3 persons per square mile in 1990 (27.3 per km2). North Dakota has one of the lowest population densities in the United States with most counties having less than 10.0 people per square mile.

Persons Per Square Mile

- 0.0 to 9.9
- 10.0 to 99.9

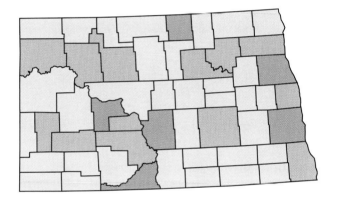

Population Change

The 1990 population figure for the state of North Dakota was 638,800. This is a –2.13 percent decrease from 652,717 in 1980. The next decade will show a loss with a population of 629 thousand or a –1.53 percent decrease. One area that experienced growth during the 1980s was the Standing Rock Indian Reservation.

Percent Change 1980 to 1990

- –31.9 to –10.0%
- –9.9 to 0.0%
- 0.1 to 19.9%

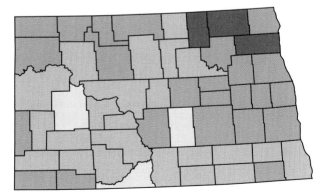

Distribution of Income

The per capita income for the state of North Dakota (current dollars) was $16,854 in 1992. This is a 120.6 percent increase from $7,641 in 1980. Income is greatest in the northeast region of the state in the counties of Towner, Cavalier, and Walsh. Low-income counties include some counties that contain Indian reservations.

Per Capita Income (000s) (Current Dollars)

- $4.5 to 9.9
- $10.0 to 12.9
- $13.0 to 15.9
- $16.0 to 19.9

Population Projections

Population in thousands

North Dakota's Population

U. S. Population

(left axis: 580, 590, 600, 610, 620, 630, 640, 650)
(right axis: 250,000, 255,000, 260,000, 265,000, 270,000, 275,000, 280,000, 285,000)
(x-axis: 1990, 1995, 2000, 2010)

Population Change

Year	Population
1950	620,000
1960	634,000
1970	620,000
1980	652,717
1990	638,800
2000	629,000
2010	611,000

Period	Change
1950–1970	0.0%
1970–1980	5.3%
1980–1990	–2.9%
1990–2000	–0.8%

Population Facts

State Population, 1993: 635,000

Rank: 47

Population 2000: 629,000 (Rank 48)

Density: 9.3 per sq. mi. (3.6 per km2)

Distribution: 53.3% urban, 46.7% rural

Population Under 5 Years Old: 7.1%

Population Under 18 Years Old: 27.0%

Population Over 65 Years Old: 14.6%

Median Age: 32.4

Number of Households: 241,000

Average Persons Per Household: 2.55

Average Persons Per Family: 3.13

Female Heads of Households: 2.74%

Population That Is Married: 22.29%

Birth Rate: 14.5 per 1,000 population

Death Rate: 8.9 per 1,000 population

Births to Teen Mothers: 8.6%

Marriage Rate: 7.3 per 1,000 population

Divorce Rate: 3.6 per 1,000 population

Violent Crime Rate: 65 per 100,000 pop.

Population on Social Security: 17.6%

Percent Voting for President: 67.3%

Population Profile

Rank. North Dakota ranks 47th among U.S. states in terms of population with 635,000 citizens.

Minority Population. The state's minority population is 5.9 percent. The state's male to female ratio for 1990 was 99.25 males for every 100 females. It was above the national average of 95.22 males for every 100 females.

Growth. The state's population is decreasing

Government

Capital: Bismarck (established 1889).

Statehood: Became 39th state on Nov. 2, 1889.

Number of Counties: 53.

Supreme Court Justices: 5, 10-year term.

State Senators: 53, 4-year term.

State Legislators: 106, 2-year term.

United States Senators: 2.

United States Representatives: 1.

Electoral Votes: 3.

State Constitution: Adopted 1889.

North Dakota's Famous Citizens

Dorman, Isaiah (?–1876). African-American soldier and interpreter. He was killed at the Battle of the Little Big Horn.

Eielson, Carl Ben (1897–1929). Aviator. He became the first person to cross the Arctic Ocean by airplane.

Flannagan, John Bernard (1895–1942). Sculptor. He incorporated themes of the life cycle into his work.

Lee, Peggy (b. 1920). Pop-jazz singer. Had numerous hit songs, including Is "That All There Is?" and "Fever."

Maris, Roger (1934–1985). Baseball out-fielder. Set the single season home run record with 61 in 1961 with the New York Yankees.

Miller, John (1843–1908). Member of the Dakota Territorial Council and first governor of the state.

Muench, Aloisius (1889–1962). Became bishop of Fargo in 1935. He later became a cardinal.

Sevareid, Eric (1912–1992). TV commentator for CBS during the Vietnam War and Watergate.

Welk, Lawrence (1903–1992). Big-band leader. Played "Champagne Music."

and is expected to be 611 thousand by the year 2010.

Older Citizens. The state's population older than 65 was 91,055 in 1990. It grew 13.19% from 80,445 in 1980.

Younger Citizens. The number of children (under 18 years of age) was 175 thousand in 1990. This represents 27.5 percent of the state's population. The state's school aged population was 118 thousand in 1990. It is expected to decrease to 110 thousand by the year 2000. This represents a –6.78% change.

Urban/Rural. 53.3% of the population of the state live in urban areas while 46.7% live in rural areas.

Largest Cities. North Dakota has three cities with a population greater than 35,000. The populations of the state's largest centers are (starting from the most populous) Fargo (74,111), Grand Forks (49,425), Bismarck (49,256), Minot (34,544), Dickinson (16,097), Jamestown (15,571), Mandan (15,177), Williston (13,131), and West Fargo (12,287).

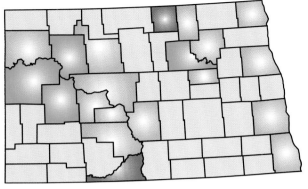

Nationalities

African	186
American	9,994
Arab	771
Austrian	620
Czech	10,726
Dutch	5,234
English	20,223
Finnish	2,490
German	275,630
Greek	411
Hungarian	929
Irish	25,360
Italian	2,662
Norwegian	140,657
Polish	10,716
Portuguese	131
Russian	3,201
Scottish	4,611
Slovak	1,015
Swedish	17,241
Welsh	695
West Indian	119

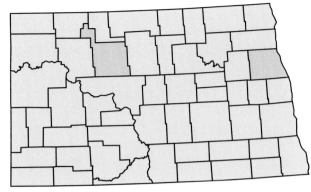

Native American

The Native American population in North Dakota was 25,917 in 1990. This was an increase of 30.20 percent from 19,905 in 1980. Many Indian reservations dot the state, including the Standing Rock, Ft. Berthold, Devil's Lake, and Turtle Mountain Indian reservations.

Presence of Native Americans

- Minor
- Moderate
- Significant

African American

The African American population in North Dakota was 3,524 in 1990. This was an increase of 42.61 percent from 2,471 in 1980. Many African Americans live in the urban areas such as Grand Forks, Minot, Bismarck, and Fargo.

Percent of County Population

- 0.00 to 1.99%
- 2.00 to 4.99%

Statewide Ethnic Composition

Over 94 percent of the population of North Dakota is white. The largest nationalities in this racial group are German, Norwegian, and Irish. The next largest group is Native Americans, followed by Hispanics, African Americans, and Asians. Only 9,994 people claim to be American and acknowledge no other nationality.

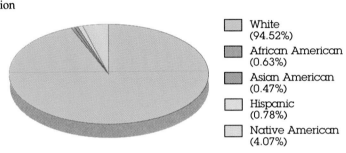

- White (94.52%)
- African American (0.63%)
- Asian American (0.47%)
- Hispanic (0.78%)
- Native American (4.07%)

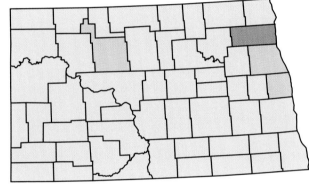

Education Facts

Total Students 1990: 117,816	Mean SAT Score 1991 Verbal: 502
Number of School Districts: 280	Mean SAT Score 1991 Math: 571
Expenditure Per Capita on Education 1990: $672	Average Teacher's Salary 1992: $24,500
Expenditure Per Capita K–12 1990: $610	Rank Teacher's Salary: 48th in U.S.
Expenditure Per Pupil 1990: $3,685	High School Graduates 1990: 7,700
Total School Enrollment 1990–1991: 117,134	Total Number of Public Schools: 679
Rank of Expenditures Per Student: 45th in the U.S.	Number of Teachers 1990: 7,757
African American Enrollment: 0.6%	Student/Teacher Ratio: 15.1
Hispanic Enrollment: 0.6%	Staff Employed in Public Schools: 14,132
Asian/Pacific Islander Enrollment: 0.7%	Pupil/Staff Ratio: 8.3
Native American Enrollment: 6.1%	Staff/Teacher Ratio: 1.8

Hispanic[††]

The Hispanic population in North Dakota was 4,665 in 1990. This is an increase of 19.55 percent from 3,902 persons in 1980. Many Hispanics live in the urban areas such as Grand Forks, Minot, Bismarck, and Fargo.

[††]A person of Mexican, Puerto Rican, Cuban, or other Spanish culture or origin regardless of race.

Percent of County Population

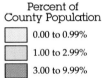
- 0.00 to 0.99%
- 1.00 to 2.99%
- 3.00 to 9.99%

Education

Attainment: 81.1 percent of population 25 years or older were high school graduates in 1989, earning North Dakota a ranking of 16th in the United States; 22.2 percent of the state's population had completed college. Institutions of Higher Education: The largest universities and colleges in the state include University of North Dakota (founded 1883), Grand Forks; North Dakota State University (founded 1890) Fargo; Jamestown College (founded 1884), Jamestown. Expenditures per Student: Expenditure increased 83% between 1985 and 1990. Projected High School Graduations: 1998 (8,218), 2004 (7,486); Total Revenues for Education from Federal Sources: $38 million; Total Revenues for Education from State Sources: $223 million; Total Revenues for Education from Local Sources: $172 million; Average Annual Salaries for Public School Principals: N/A.

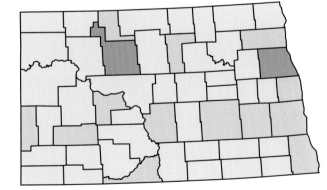

Asian American

The Asian American population in North Dakota was 3,462 in 1990. This is an increase of 57.29 percent from 2,201 persons in 1980. Many Asian Americans can be found living in and around the cities of Minot and Grand Forks.

Percent of County Population

- 0.00 to 0.24%
- 0.25 to 0.99%
- 1.00 to 1.99%

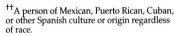

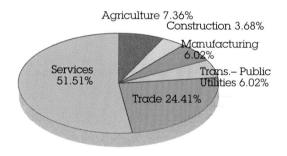

Major manufacturing areas   Major agricultural areas

Agriculture

North Dakota has 40.4 million farm acres. During the last 40 years, North Dakota's farms have grown larger in size and fewer in number. In 1955, 62,000 farms were found in the state. Today, 33,000 remain.

Agriculture adds $1 billion to the state's gross product annually. The principal commodities in order of marketing receipts are wheat, cattle, barley, and sunflowers.

Crops account for about 71 percent of North Dakota's farm income. The state has about 30,000 farms, with cropland and ranchland covering about 90 percent of the state's total land area. Wheat is the leading crop in the state, and North Dakota ranks second only to Kansas in wheat production. The crop is found throughout the entire state.

Housing

Owner Occupied Units: 276,340; Average Age of Units: 30 years; Average Value of Housing Units: $50,800; Renter Occupied Units: 78,484; Median Monthly Rent: $313; Housing Starts: 3,100; Existing Home Sales: 11,800.

Economic Facts

Gross State Product: $11,000,000,000 (1989)

Income Per Capita: $16,854

Disposable Personal Income: $15,297

Median Household Income: $23,213

Average Annual Pay, 1988: $18,132

Principal Industries: machinery, food products, printing, publishing, glass products, oil refining, natural gas processing

Major Crops: wheat, barley, sugar, oats, milk, hay, beets, rye, sunflowers, flaxseed

Fish: Bass, Carp, Catfish, Perch, Trout, Walleye

Livestock: cattle, turkeys, chickens, hogs, sheep

Non-Fuel Minerals: Clay, Sand, Gravel, Sulfur, Corundum

Organic Fuel Minerals: Petroleum, Nat. Gas, Coal

Civilian Labor Force: 317,000 (Women: 146,000)

Total Employed: 304,000 (Women: 140,000)

Median Value of Housing: $50,800

Median Contract Rent: $313 per month

Economic Sectors 1992

Agriculture 7.36%
Construction 3.68%
Manufacturing 6.02%
Trans.– Public Utilities 6.02%
Trade 24.41%
Services 51.51%

Manufacturing

Like Nebraska, North Dakota's manufacturing sector depends on the state's agricultural products. Manufacturing accounts for only 6 percent of the state gross product, one of the lower percentages in the nation. By far, food processing ranks as North Dakota's number one manufacturing activity. However, machinery, petroleum products, and printed materials are also made in the state.

Food processing takes place throughout North Dakota. The Fargo area has several meat-packing plants. Sugar-beet refineries can be found farther north in Hillsboro and Grand Forks. The state capital of Bismarck is home to farm machinery factories, while the nearby city of Mandan has an oil refinery.

Transportation

Although North Dakota is only thinly populated, it has many miles of roadway. Overall, the state has approximately 86,000 miles of highways and roads; however, only about two thirds are surfaced. Two interstates, Interstate 29 and Interstate 94, travel north to south and east to west, respectively.

Traditionally, railroads have been important to North Dakota's transportation network. The first railroad, the Northern Pacific, reached the state in 1872. Today, North Dakota is served by two freight rail lines, the Soo Line and the Burlington Northern. Furthermore, seven North Dakota cities receive passenger rail service. Fargo, on the North Dakota-Minnesota border, has the state's busiest airport. Other cities, such as Grand Forks, Bismarck, and Minot, have significant airports as well.

Energy and Transportation Facts

Energy. Yearly Consumption: 320 tril. BTUs (residential, 16.9%; commercial, 12.5%; industrial, 49.7%; transportation, 20.9%); Annual Energy Expenditures Per Capita: $2,502; Nuclear Power Plants Located in State: 0; Source of Energy Consumed: Petroleum— 20.4%; Natural Gas— 7.5%; Coal— 67.9%; Hydroelectric Power—4.1%; Nuclear Power—0.0%.

Transportation. Highway Miles: 86,648 (interstates, 570; urban, 1,825; rural, 84,823); Average Yearly Auto Insurance: $319 (51st); Auto Fatalities Rank: 40th; Registered Motor Vehicles: 655,335; Workers in Carpools: 15.0%; Workers Using Public Trans: 0.6%.

Employment

Employment. North Dakota employed 305,000 people in 1993. Most work in social and personal services (76,700 persons or 25.1% of the workforce). Wholesale and retail trade account for 24.5% or 74,800 workers. Government employs 67,100 workers (22.0%). Manufacturing jobs employ 19,400 people (6.4%). Construction accounts for 3.8% or 11,700 workers. Transportation and utilities account for 5.9% or 18,000 persons. Agriculture employs 35,700 workers or 11.7%. Finance, real estate, and insurance account for 4.4% or 13,500 workers. Mining employs 3,800 people and accounts for only 1.2% of the workforce.

Unemployment. Unemployment has decreased to 4.3% in 1993 from a rate of 5.9% in 1985. Today's figure is lower than the national average of 6.8% as shown below.

Unemployment Rate

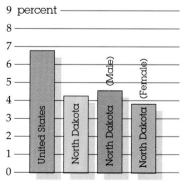

OHIO
The State of Ohio

Official State Seal

The Great Seal of Ohio was adopted at first in 1803. It was later abolished in 1805 and then readopted in 1868. It was later redesigned in 1967 to its present form. The seventeenth state is symbolized on the seal with seventeen rays of light and seventeen arrows bundled up in the foreground. The mountain in the background is Mount Logan and the river is the Scioto River.

Legal Holidays

January: New Year's Day—1st; Martin Luther King, Jr., Day—3rd Monday; February: Presidents' Day—3rd Monday; March: Admission Day—1st; May: Memorial Day—4th Monday; July: Independence Day—4th; September: Labor Day—1st Monday; October: Columbus Day—2nd Monday; November: Veterans' Day—11th; Thanksgiving—4th Thursday; December: Christmas—25th.

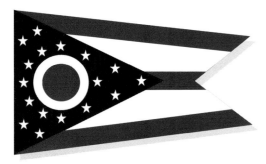

Official State Flag

The state flag of Ohio was adopted in 1902. It is based on a cavalry flag used between 1862 and 1885. The white circle represents the first letter in Ohio's name. The seventeen stars symbolize Ohio's order of admission into the Union.

Festivals and Events

February: Longhorn World Championship Rodeo, Cincinnati; Winter Ski Carnival, Mansfield; April: Spring Floral Fest, Cincinnati; May: Balloonfest, Cincinnati; Israel Festival, Columbus; Utica Old-Fashioned Ice Cream Fest, Utica; June: Columbus Arts Festival, Columbus; Welsh Heritage Days, Rio Grande; July: Annie Oakley Days, Greenville; August: Grecian Festival, Canton; Coshocton Canal Festival, Coshocton; September: Octoberfest, Cincinnati; Popcorn Fest, Marion; October: Paul Bunyan Show, Nelsonville; Circleville Pumpkin Show, Circleville; November: Festival of Lights, Cincinnati.

Ohio Compared to States in Its Region.

Resident Pop. in Metro Areas: 3d; Pop. Percent Increase: 4th; Pop. Over 65: 2d; Infant Mortality: 2d; School Enroll. Increase: 3d; High School Grad. and Up: 4th; Violent Crime: 3d; Hazardous Waste Sites: 4th; Unemployment: 3d; Median Household Income: 5th; Persons Below Poverty: 2d; Energy Costs Per Person: 3d.

East North Central Region

	Population	Capital
Wisconsin	5,038,000	Madison
Michigan	9,478,000	Lansing
Illinois	11,697,000	Springfield
Indiana	5,713,000	Indianapolis
Ohio	11,091,000	Columbus

Ohio's Finances

Households: 4,088,000; Income Per Capita Current Dollars: $18,624; Change Per Capita Income 1980 to 1992: 91.3% (35th in U.S.); State Expenditures: $24,106,000,000; State Revenues: $22,990,000,000; Personal Income Tax: 0.743 to 6.9%; Federal Income Taxes Paid Per Capita: $1,694; Sales Tax: 5% (food and prescription drugs exempt).

State Expenditures

14.0 billion dollars

12.0

10.0

8.0

6.0

4.0

2.0

0

Education, Highway, Welfare, Health, Other

State Revenues

14.0 billion dollars

12.0

10.0

8.0

6.0

4.0

2.0

0

Federal, Local, Taxes, Miscellaneous

Location, Size, and Boundaries

Lake Huron, MICHIGAN, Lake Erie, Maximum Extent, OHIO, W.V, Maximum Extent, KENTUCKY

Location. Ohio is located in the East North Central region of the United States. It is bounded on four sides by land. The geographic center of Ohio is lat. 40° 21.7' N; long. 82° 44.5' W.

Size. Ohio is the 35th largest state in terms of size. Its area is 41,222 sq. mi. (106,765 km2). Inland water covers 247 sq. mi. (640 km2).

Boundaries. Michigan, 70 mi. (113 km); Canada, 205 mi. (330 km); Pennsylvania, 92 mi. (148 km); West Virginia, 277 mi. (446 km); Kentucky, 174 mi. (280 km); Indiana, 179 mi. (288 km).

Geographic Extent. The north/south extent of Ohio is 230 mi. (370 km). The state extends 210 mi. (338 km) to the east/west.

Facts about Ohio. Origin of Name: After the *Iroquois* Indian word meaning *"something great"*—refers to the Ohio River; Nickname: The Buckeye State; Motto: "With God, all things are possible"; Abbreviations: O. (traditional), OH (postal); State Bird: cardinal; State Tree: buckeye; State Flower: scarlet carnation; State Song: "Beautiful Ohio," words by Ballard MacDonald and music by Mary Earl.

Ohio Compared to Other States. Resident Pop. in Metro Areas: 18th; Pop. Per. Increase: 36th; Pop. Over 65: 21st; Infant Mortality: 15th; School Enroll. Increase: 34th; High School Grad. and Up: 30th; Violent Crime: 24th; Hazardous Waste Sites: 11th; Unemployment: 21st; Median Household Income: 25th; Persons Below Poverty: 23d; Energy Costs Per Person: 25th.

Sources of Information. Tourism: Ohio Division of Travel and Tourism, P.O. Box 1001, Columbus, OH 43266. Economy: Department of Development, State Office Tower II, 77 South High Street, Columbus, OH 43215. Government: Secretary of State, 30 East Broad Street, 14th Floor, Columbus, OH 43266. History: Ohio Historical Center, Educational Services Department, 1985 Velma Avenue, Columbus, OH 43211.

Legend

⭐ State capitol

⊙ Cities over 35,000 population

○ Other significant cities

◉ County Seats

◼ Major cultural attractions

☐ State Parks

Ⓦ Welcome Centers

⛫ Major colleges and universities

Major Cities

Akron	D-9	Kettering	H-2
Canton	E-10	Lakewood	C-8
Cincinnati	K-1	Lima	E-2
Cleveland	C-9	Lorain	C-7
Cleveland Hts.	B-9	Mansfield	E-6
Columbus	H-5	Mentor	B-10
Cuyahoga Falls	D-9	Middletown	I-1
Dayton	H-2	Newark	G-7
Elyria	C-8	Parma	C-9
Euclid	B-9	Springfield	H-3
Fairfield	J-1	Toledo	B-4
Hamilton	J-1	Warren	C-11
Huber Hts.	H-2	Youngstown	D-11

◼ **Cuyahoga Valley National Recreation Area.** 33,000-acre area which protects many natural and cultural resources including Native American sites, a 20-mile section of the Ohio and Erie Canal, and other historical sites. (C-9)

◼ **German Village.** Shops, restaurants, outdoor beer gardens, and Brewery District with original architecture. (H-5)

◼ **Harriet Beecher Stowe House.** 1830 home of the author of *Uncle Tom's Cabin*. Cultural and educational center displaying slavery era artifacts. (K-1)

◼ **Holden Arboretum.** 3,100-acre natural woodland museum featuring horticultural displays, gardens, woods, fields, lakes, and ravines. (B-9)

◼ **McKinley Museum of History, Science and Industry.** Audio visual displays and hands-on science experiments. (E-10)

◼ **Millersburg.** Largest Amish population in America. (F-8)

◼ **Mill Creek Park.** 2,500-acre park featuring foot trails, drives, falls, a gorge, formal gardens, and a restored 19th-century grist mill. (D-11)

◼ **Moundbuilders State Memorial.** Includes a circular earthwork 1,200 ft. in diameter, and the Ohio Indian Museum. (G-7)

◼ **Ohio Historical Center.** Museum featuring library, state archives, and historic preservation information. (H-5)

◼ **Ohio River Museum.** Steamboat-era items and scale models of 19th century riverboats. Real steamboat moored alongside museum. (J-9)

◼ **Old West End.** The largest collection of Victorian and Edwardian houses and buildings in Ohio. (B-4)

◼ **Stan Hywet Hall and Gardens.** 65-room Tudor Revival manor house, includes many colorful gardens. (D-9)

◼ **SunWatch Archaeological Indian Village.** 800-year-old Native American village is now a well preserved archaeological site. (H-2)

◼ **United States Air Force Museum.** Over 200 aircraft and thousands of artifacts. (H-2)

◼ **University Circle.** A collection of cultural and educational museums and libraries in a park setting with gardens and a lagoon. (B-9)

Weather Facts

Record High Temperature: 113° F (45° C) on July 21, 1934, at Gallipolis; Record Low Temperature: -39° F (-39° C) on February 10, 1899, at Milligan; Average January Temperature: 27° F (-3° C); Average July Temperature: 73° F (23° C); Average Yearly Precipitation: 39 in. (99 cm).

Environmental Facts

Air Pollution Rank: 4th; Water Pollution Rank: 6th; Total Yearly Industrial Pollution: 118,719,603 lbs.; Industrial Pollution Rank: 5th; Hazardous Waste Sites: 33; Hazardous Sites Rank: 11th; Landfill Capacity: overextended; Fresh Water Supply: large surplus; Daily Residential Water Consumption: 130 gals. per capita; Endangered Species: Aquatic Species (7)—clubshell; Birds (3)—eagle, bald; Mammals (1)—bat, Indiana; Other Species (3)—snake, Lake Erie water; Plants (5)—clover, running buffalo.

Environmental Quality

Ohio residents generate 13.9 million tons of solid waste each year, or approximately 2,600 pounds per capita. Landfill capacity in Ohio will be exhausted in less than 5 years. The state has 33 hazardous waste sites. Annual greenhouse gas emissions in Ohio total 255.2 million tons, or 23.5 tons per capita. Industrial sources in Ohio release approximately 205.6 thousand tons of toxins, 3.3 million tons of acid precipitation-producing substances, and 4.9 million tons of smog-producing substances into the atmosphere each year.

The state has 14,600 acres within the National Park System; the largest area within the state is Hopewell Culture National Park. State parks cover 193,000 acres, attracting 67.2 million visitors per year.

Ohio spends less than 1 percent (0.7%) of its budget, or approximately $12 per capita, on environmental and natural resources.

Average Monthly Weather

Cincinnati	Jan	Feb	Mar	Apr	May	Jun	Jul	Aug	Sep	Oct	Nov	Dec	Yearly
Maximum Temperature °F	37.3	41.2	51.5	64.5	74.2	82.3	85.8	84.8	78.7	66.7	52.6	41.9	63.5
Minimum Temperature °F	20.4	23.0	32.0	42.4	51.7	60.5	64.9	63.3	56.3	43.9	34.1	25.7	43.2
Days of Precipitation	11.9	11.1	13.2	12.4	11.3	10.5	10.0	9.0	7.8	8.3	11.0	12.1	128.7
Cleveland													
Maximum Temperature °F	32.5	34.8	44.8	57.9	68.5	78.0	81.7	80.3	74.2	62.7	49.3	37.5	58.5
Minimum Temperature °F	18.5	19.9	28.4	38.3	47.9	57.2	61.4	60.5	54.0	43.6	34.3	24.6	40.7
Days of Precipitation	16.3	14.3	15.4	14.3	13.1	11.0	10.1	9.7	9.8	11.2	14.5	16.4	156.0

Flora and Fauna

Ohio used to have forests that almost entirely covered the state. Today, however, only 24 percent of its land is forested. The vast majority of Ohio's trees are hardwoods such as black walnut, sycamore, white ash, and tulip trees. The state's plateau region has the most heavily forested areas. Other Ohio plant life includes shrubs like sumac, hawthorn, and viburnum. Wildflowers also grow throughout the state, the most common being toothwort, indigo, anemones, and blue sage.

Ohio's climatic conditions make it possible for a wide variety of wildlife to live in the state. The white-tailed deer is the only common and abundant large mammal, but there are numerous species of small animals such as woodchucks, muskrat, squirrels, cottontail rabbits, and raccoons. Ducks, wild turkeys, and other game birds live all over Ohio. A number of songbirds such as blackbirds, cardinals, and chickadees live among large birds such as the bald eagle. Ohio's most common fish, the black bass, lives in the state's lakes and rivers, as do white bass, walleye, and perch.

Physical Regions: (a) Great Lakes Plains; (b) Till Plains; (c) Appalachian Plateau; (d) Bluegrass Region.

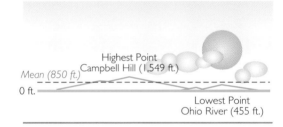

Highest Point Campbell Hill (1,549 ft.)
Mean (850 ft.)
0 ft.
Lowest Point Ohio River (455 ft.)

Land Use

Cropland: 48.8%; Pasture: 9.5%; Rangeland: 0%; Forest: 1%; Urban: 11.4%; Other: 5.3%.

For more information about Ohio's environment, contact the Ohio Environmental Protection Agency, 1800 Watermark Dr., P.O. Box 1049, Columbus, OH 43266.

Topography

There are several distinct topographic regions in Ohio. In the northern part of the state is the Great Lakes Plains physical region that extends southward from the shores of Lake Erie. This area of flat lowlands is a very fertile region well suited to agriculture, with warm and moist soil, colored gray/brown by the high iron and manganese content. The shoreline, a heavily populated area, contains many beaches and ports.

The Till Plains physical region in the western part of the state is the easternmost extension of this fertile farm belt that runs across much of the midwestern United States. Soil type is similar to that found in the Great Lakes Plains. This area is also characterized by rolling hills, one of which is the highest elevation in the state. Campbell Hill, in Logan County, is 1,549 ft. (470 m) above sea level. The lowest elevations in the state occur in the southwest, where the Bluegrass physical region extends north from Kentucky. The soil in this region, as well as in the Allegheny Plateau, is warm and moist with a light surface color due to the crystalline clay in which it was formed.

The eastern half of Ohio is covered by the Allegheny Plateau physical region. Most of this area consists of rugged terrain, with deep valleys interspersed throughout the rough hills. This area is also home to many of Ohio's mineral resources, such as coal and natural gas. The northeastern part of this region has a more gentle terrain.

Climate

Except for a small part along the Ohio River, most of Ohio has a humid continental climate. Because of Ohio's mid-latitude position in the eastern United States, noticeable climatic differences can be seen. Cyclonic prevailing westerly winds contribute partially to these differences. Temperatures vary slightly across Ohio, with northwest cities such as Toledo generally being cooler (27 degrees F in January and 73 degrees F in July) than southeastern cities like Cincinnati, where average January and July temperatures are 35 degrees F and 78 degrees F.

Ohio receives some precipitation year-round. Almost half of the state's annual 38 inches of precipitation falls between May and October, the growing season. Southern Ohio on average receives slightly more precipitation.

Ohio's topography sometimes negatively affects the state's climate. The Appalachian foothills area is prone to creating temperature inversions, resulting in early frosts, and thus, shorter growing seasons.

Hydrology

The Ohio River forms Ohio's southern border with Kentucky, and its southeastern border with West Virginia and Pennsylvania, flowing about 440 miles (707 km) in the state. Lake Erie forms much of the northern border. The Scioto River is the Ohio's main tributary, flowing about 245 miles (395 km) south through the middle of the state. Other tributaries include the Miami in the west and the Muskingum in the east. Important rivers in the north of the state include the Cuyahoga and the Sandusky, which flow into Lake Erie.

Most of the large lakes in Ohio are man-made. The largest of these is Pymatuning Reservoir, on the border with Pennsylvania in the northeast corner of the state, covering about 22 sq. miles (57 sq. km). Grand Lake, in western Ohio, is about 20 sq. miles (52 sq. km). Others include Dillon and Delaware reservoirs in the central part of the state.

Ohio's History

Ohio's First People

The area now known as the state of Ohio has a long history of human settlement. Before more recent Native American tribes came to Ohio, Mound Builders, an early band of people, lived there from about 1000 to 800 B.C. As their name suggests, the Mound Builders constructed huge mounds of land in honor of their dead. Many of these mounds, in addition to other remains, can still be seen today in Ohio.

The Erie people were one of the first native tribes to inhabit Ohio. However, the powerful Iroquois eventually conquered the Erie. Other tribes living in Ohio included the Huron, Ottawa, and Tuscarora in the northern part of the state, the Delaware and Shawnee in the southern areas, and the Miami tribe in the western part of Ohio.

European Exploration

It is not certain which European explorer first crossed into Ohio. Between 1669 and 1670, two explorers came to the area: René-Robert Cavelier, Sieur de La Salle, and Louis Jolliet.

English fur traders came to Ohio in 1685. Other traders from Pennsylvania, Virginia, and the Carolina area came in the early eighteenth century.

After La Salle's expedition, France laid claim to the entire Ohio Valley area. This claim became part of a series of disputes between France and Great Britain. One of the first battles of the French and Indian War, was fought over who controlled Ohio. Virginia, supposedly claiming the area as far back as 1609, also felt Ohio belonged to it. Even Pennsylvania wanted a stake in Ohio, claiming control of an Ohio River fork.

Territorial Period and Statehood

Plans to settle Ohio began in 1785, when the first Land Ordinance passed by the Continental Congress ordered a survey of several land parcels, and their subsequent sale.

In 1786, the Ohio Company of Associates was established to assist New England Revolutionary War veterans in resettlement.

In 1787, the Northwest Ordinance was passed by Congress to create a system of government for the Ohio area, and on July 15 of that year, a territorial government was established. Under this ordinance, Ohio was governed as part of the Northwest Territory. A rapid increase in the number of settlers coming to Ohio soon prompted a movement toward statehood.

With over five thousand males counted in Ohio during the census of 1797, it was guaranteed statehood. In November of 1802, Ohio delegates drew up a plan for statehood, and on March 1, 1803, Ohio became the seventeenth state of the Union. It was the first state to be carved out of the massive Northwest Territory. Chillicothe was chosen as the new state capital. Later, the capital moved to Zanesville, and in 1816, to Columbus.

Ohio's early years as a state were characterized by a sharp increase in population, and a simultaneous increase in industry, trade, and agricultural activities. Soon, many railroad lines crossed through Ohio, helping the state to become known (like Missouri) as the "Gateway to the West."

Industrialization

Ohio's strategic location made it an ideal place for industrialization to occur. The state, located between the already well-established industries of the Eastern Seaboard and the up-and–coming Midwest, proved to be an important crossroads of the United States. The lack of natural boundaries made Ohio an even better corridor for east-to-west trade and travel. Early industries included barrel-making and meat-packing. Cincinnati became the first manufacturing city in Ohio, and today manufacturing contributes one-third of the gross state product.

Canals were the first important means of transportation in Ohio. Completed in 1832, the Ohio and Erie Canal enabled goods to be shipped with greater ease, thus helping Ohio's economy to diversify. Industrialization received a great boost shortly after the Civil War, as more people moved to the state. Ohio today is home to several types of industries, including rubber products, machine parts, chemical products, and electrical machinery. Although many factory workers were laid off in the 1980s due to steel plants closing, new factories continue to open, providing new jobs for displaced workers.

Ohio: A Waterlogged State

The most prevalent natural resource in Ohio is its enormous water supply. Perhaps this is how Ohio received its name, which means "great water" in the Iroquois language. Ohio's water resources are important to the state, and it ranks sixth in the nation in water use. Surface water makes up the bulk of used water, contributing ninety-five percent. Ground water aquifers provide a continuous supply of water, if needed.

Ohio waterways either spill into Lake Erie or the Ohio River. Out of the approximately 3,300 named streams in Ohio, twenty-nine percent of them drain into Lake Erie. Several larger streams and rivers, including the Little Miami, Raccoon, and Mahoning rivers, feed the Ohio River.

As is the case with other major rivers in the United States, the Ohio River is prone to flooding. One of the most recent floods took place in 1990 when rivers and tributaries in the state reached and surpassed one-hundred year flood levels. During this flash flood, seventeen Ohio counties were declared federal disaster areas because of the millons of dollars of damage they sustained. Furthermore, twenty-three people were killed in the small town of Shadyside.

Important Events

1669 René-Robert Cavelier, Sieur de La Salle, and Louis Jolliet first crossed into Ohio.

1685 Fur-traders begin to enter the area.

1763 Treaty of Paris grants Ohio country to England.

1785 The first Land Ordinance is passed by the Continental Congress ordering a survey of some land parcels.

1786 Ohio Company of Associates formed to assist veterans in resettlement, some veterans were defrauded.

1787 Northwest Ordinance passed by Congress to create a system of government.

1788 Marietta, first permanent white settlement, founded.

1794 Battle of Fallen Timbers; British-Indian confederation defeated by Gen. Anthony Wayne.

1803 Ohio becomes seventeenth state in the Union on March 1.

1804 University of Ohio at Athens founded.

1812 Oliver Hazard Perry defeats the British on Lake Erie.

1813 William Henry Harrison invades Canada which ends British incursions.

1816 Columbus becomes capital city.

1825 Law passed requiring counties to finance education.

1832 Ohio and Erie Canal opens.

1851 New state constitution adopted; presently in use.

1869 Ulysses S. Grant becomes first Ohio-born U.S. president.

1903 Wright Brothers develop a more advanced airplane at Dayton.

1937 Great flood of Ohio River causes extensive damage.

1955 Ohio Turnpike completed.

1970 National Guardsmen kill four students at Kent State during an anti-Vietnam War demonstration.

1990 Major flooding causes seventeen counties to be declared federal disaster areas. Twenty-three people are killed in Shadyside as a result of the flood.

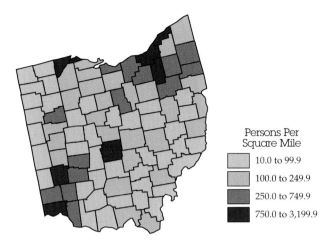

Persons Per Square Mile
- 10.0 to 99.9
- 100.0 to 249.9
- 250.0 to 749.9
- 750.0 to 3,199.9

Population Projections

Population in thousands

Ohio's Population

U. S. Population

(x-axis: 1990, 1995, 2000, 2010)
(left y-axis: 10,200 to 10,900)
(right y-axis: 250,000 to 285,000)

Population Change

Year	Population
1950	7,947,000
1960	9,734,000
1970	10,664,000
1980	10,797,630
1990	10,847,115
2000	10,629,000
2010	10,397,000

Period	Change
1950–1970	34.2%
1970–1980	1.3%
1980–1990	0.5%
1990–2000	–2.0%

Population Density

Population density for the state of Ohio was 264.9 persons per square mile in 1990 (102.3 per km²). Average U.S. density was 70.3 persons per square mile in 1990 (27.3 per km²). Habitation is most dense in and around the urban areas such as Cleveland, Cincinnati, Columbia, Dayton, and Toledo.

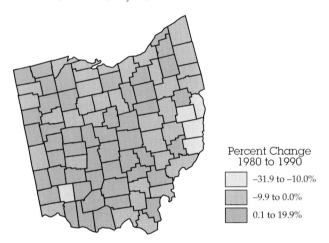

Percent Change 1980 to 1990
- –31.9 to –10.0%
- –9.9 to 0.0%
- 0.1 to 19.9%

Population Change

The 1990 population figure for the state of Ohio was 10,847,115. This is a 0.46 percent increase from 10,797,630 in 1980. The next decade will show a loss with a population of 10.6 million or a –2.01 percent decrease. Much of the state has seen little or no growth in the last decade.

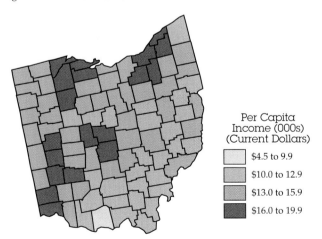

Per Capita Income (000s) (Current Dollars)
- $4.5 to 9.9
- $10.0 to 12.9
- $13.0 to 15.9
- $16.0 to 19.9

Distribution of Income

The per capita income for the state of Ohio (current dollars) was $18,624 in 1992. This is a 91.3 percent increase from $9,738 in 1980. Income is greatest in and around the urban areas of the state. The area of lowest income is Adams County in the southern region of the state.

Population Facts

State Population, 1993: 11,091,000

Rank: 7

Population 2000: 10,629,000 (Rank 7)

Density: 264.9 per sq. mi. (102.3 per km²)

Distribution: 74.1% urban, 25.9% rural

Population Under 5 Years Old: 7.2%

Population Under 18 Years Old: 25.6%

Population Over 65 Years Old: 13.2%

Median Age: 33.3

Number of Households: 4,088,000

Average Persons Per Household: 2.59

Average Persons Per Family: 3.12

Female Heads of Households: 4.41%

Population That Is Married: 21.15%

Birth Rate: 15.4 per 1,000 population

Death Rate: 9.1 per 1,000 population

Births to Teen Mothers: 13.8%

Marriage Rate: 8.7 per 1,000 population

Divorce Rate: 4.7 per 1,000 population

Violent Crime Rate: 562 per 100,000 pop.

Population on Social Security: 16.7%

Percent Voting for President: 60.6%

Population Profile

Rank. Ohio ranks 7th among U.S. states in terms of population with 11,091,000 citizens.

Minority Population. The state's minority population is 13.0 percent. The state's male to female ratio for 1990 was 92.98 males for every 100 females. It was below the national average of 95.22 males for every 100 females.

Growth. The state's population is decreasing and is expected to be 10.4 million by the year 2010.

Government

Capital: Columbus (established 1816).

Statehood: Became 17th state on Mar. 1, 1803.

Number of Counties: 88.

Supreme Court Justices: 7, 6-year term.

State Senators: 33, 4-year term.

State Legislators: 99, 2-year term.

United States Senators: 2.

United States Representatives: 19.

Electoral Votes: 21.

State Constitution: Adopted 1851.

Ohio's Famous Citizens

Grey, Zane (1875–1939). Popular writer of western novels, including *Riders of the Purple Sage.*

Haines, Jesse (Pop) (1893–1978). Hall of Fame baseball pitcher. He played for the St. Louis Cardinals from 1919 to 1937.

Lemay, Curtis (1906–1990). Air Force chief of staff during U.S. entry into the Vietnam War (1961–1965).

Morrison, Toni (b. 1931). Writer about black American life in books such as the Pulitzer Prize-winning *Beloved* (1987).

Peale, Norman Vincent (b. 1898). Author of the best-selling inspirational work *The Power of Positive Thinking* in 1952.

Spielberg, Steven (b. 1937). Film maker. Director of such enormous popular hits as *Jaws* (1975), *E.T.* (1982), and the *Indiana Jones* series (1986–1989).

Tatum, Art (1910–1956). Jazz pianist. Known for his solo improvisations of songs such as "Tea for Two" and "Sweet Lorraine."

Wald, Lillian (1867–1940). Largely responsible for the founding of the world's first public-school nursing program in 1902.

Older Citizens. The state's population older than 65 was 1,406,961 in 1990. It grew 20.31% from 1,169,460 in 1980.

Younger Citizens. The number of children (under 18 years of age) was 2.8 million in 1990. This represents 25.8 percent of the state's population. The state's school aged population was 1.8 million in 1990. It is expected to decrease to 1.7 million by the year 2000. This represents a –1.25% change.

Urban/Rural. 74.1% of the population of the state live in urban areas while 25.9% live in rural areas.

Largest Cities. Ohio has 29 cities with a population greater than 35,000. The populations of the state's largest centers are (starting from the most populous) Columbus (632,910), Cleveland (505,616), Cincinnati (364,040), Toledo (332,943), Akron (223,019), Dayton (182,044), Youngstown (95,732), Parma (87,876), Canton (84,161), Lorain (71,245), Springfield (70,487), Hamilton (61,368), Kettering (60,569), Lakewood (59,718), Elyria (56,746), Euclid (54,875), Cleveland Heights (54,052), Warren (50,793), Mansfield (50,627), Cuyahoga Falls (48,950), and Mentor (47,358).

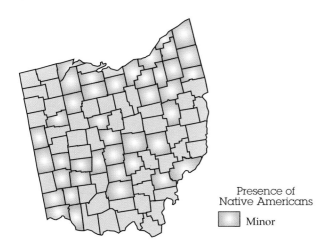

Presence of
Native Americans

☐ Minor

Native American

The Native American population in Ohio was 20,358 in 1990. This was an increase of 33.06 percent from 15,300 in 1980. Many of the Native Americans in Ohio are located in the major cities such as Cleveland, Toledo, Columbus, Akron, and Cincinnati.

Statewide Ethnic Composition

Over 87 percent of the population of Ohio is white. The largest nationalities in this racial group are German, Irish, and English. The next largest group is African Americans, followed by Hispanics, Asian Americans, and Native Americans. Over 540,000 people claim to be American and acknowledge no other nationality.

Nationalities

African	12,383
American	540,991
Arab	35,632
Austrian	18,749
Czech	51,607
Dutch	149,898
English	912,271
Finnish	14,523
German	3,332,856
Greek	40,709
Hungarian	144,002
Irish	977,490
Italian	470,320
Norwegian	19,131
Polish	314,423
Portuguese	3,577
Russian	55,393
Scottish	131,327
Slovak	178,466
Swedish	49,800
Welsh	83,602
West Indian	6,422

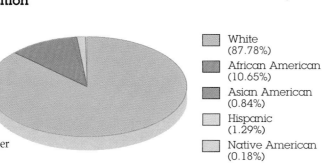

☐ White (87.78%)
☐ African American (10.65%)
☐ Asian American (0.84%)
☐ Hispanic (1.29%)
☐ Native American (0.18%)

Education Facts

Total Students 1990: 1,767,159	Mean SAT Score 1991 Verbal: 450
Number of School Districts: 613	Mean SAT Score 1991 Math: 496
Expenditure Per Capita on Education 1990: $720	Average Teacher's Salary 1992: $33,300
Expenditure Per Capita K–12 1990: $651	Rank Teacher's Salary: 21st in U.S.
Expenditure Per Pupil 1990: $5,269	High School Graduates 1990: 127,800
Total School Enrollment 1990–1991: 1,765,500	Total Number of Public Schools: 3,715
Rank of Expenditures Per Student: 17th in the U.S.	Number of Teachers 1990: 101,466
African American Enrollment: 14.2%	Student/Teacher Ratio: 17.4
Hispanic Enrollment: 1.2%	Staff Employed in Public Schools: 188,155
Asian/Pacific Islander Enrollment: 0.9%	Pupil/Staff Ratio: 9.4
Native American Enrollment: 0.1%	Staff/Teacher Ratio: 1.9

Education

Attainment: 77.6 percent of population 25 years or older were high school graduates in 1989, earning Ohio a ranking of 28th in the United States; 22.2 percent of the state's population had completed college. Institutions of Higher Education: The largest universities and colleges in the state include Ohio University (founded 1804), Athens; Oberlin College (founded 1833), Oberlin; Ohio State University, Columbus; Kent State University, Kent; Miami University, Oxford; Bowling Green State University, Bowling Green; Cleveland State University, Cleveland; University of Cincinnati, Cincinnati; Xavier University, Cincinnati; Case Western Reserve University, Cleveland. Expenditures per Student: Expenditure increased 67% between 1985 and 1990. Projected High School Graduations: 1998 (133,823), 2004 (120,190); Total Revenues for Education from Federal Sources: $338 million; Total Revenues for Education from State Sources: $3.2 billion; Total Revenues for Education from Local Sources: $3 billion; Average Annual Salaries for Public School Principals: $43,912; Largest School Districts in State: Cleveland City School District, 69,799 students, 34th in the United States; Columbus City School District, 63,749 students, 45th.

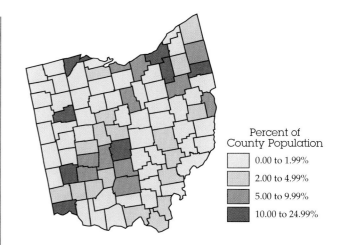

Percent of
County Population

☐ 0.00 to 1.99%
☐ 2.00 to 4.99%
☐ 5.00 to 9.99%
☐ 10.00 to 24.99%

African American

The African American population in Ohio was 1,154,826 in 1990. This was an increase of 7.25 percent from 1,076,742 in 1980. Many of the African Americans in Ohio are located in the major cities such as Cleveland, Toledo, Columbus, Akron, and Cincinnati.

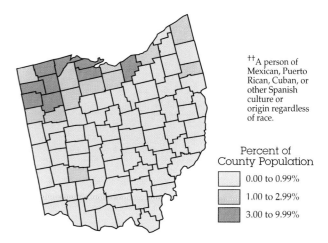

††A person of Mexican, Puerto Rican, Cuban, or other Spanish culture or origin regardless of race.

Percent of
County Population

☐ 0.00 to 0.99%
☐ 1.00 to 2.99%
☐ 3.00 to 9.99%

Hispanic††

The Hispanic population in Ohio was 139,696 in 1990. This is an increase of 16.53 percent from 119,883 persons in 1980. Most of the Hispanics in Ohio reside in the north and northwest corner of the state. There is also a large Hispanic community living in Cleveland.

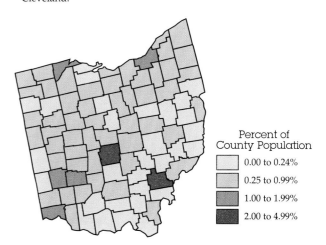

Percent of
County Population

☐ 0.00 to 0.24%
☐ 0.25 to 0.99%
☐ 1.00 to 1.99%
☐ 2.00 to 4.99%

Asian American

The Asian American population in Ohio was 91,179 in 1990. This is an increase of 78.43 percent from 51,100 persons in 1980. There is a large concentration of Asian Americans in the capital, Columbus. There are also large communities located in Athens, Cleveland, Cincinnati, and Toledo.

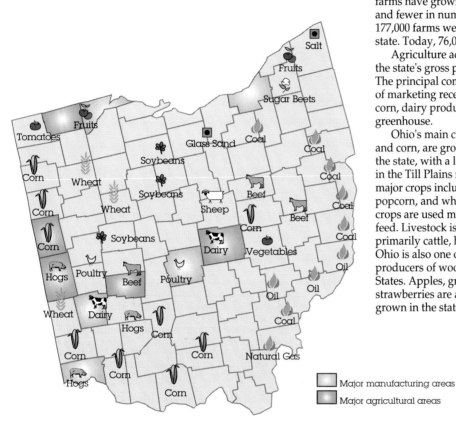

Agriculture

Ohio has 15.2 million farm acres. During the last 40 years, Ohio's farms have grown larger in size and fewer in number. In 1955, 177,000 farms were found in the state. Today, 76,000 remain.

Agriculture adds $3 billion to the state's gross product annually. The principal commodities in order of marketing receipts are soybeans, corn, dairy products, and greenhouse.

Ohio's main crops, soybeans and corn, are grown throughout the state, with a large concentration in the Till Plains region. Other major crops include hay, oats, popcorn, and wheat. These grain crops are used mainly as cattle feed. Livestock is raised in Ohio, primarily cattle, hogs, and sheep. Ohio is also one of the leading producers of wool in the United States. Apples, grapes, and strawberries are among the fruits grown in the state.

Major manufacturing areas
Major agricultural areas

Transportation

Ohio has been traditionally known as the "Gateway to the West," partially because of its well-defined transportation network. Before roads, canals linked Ohio towns. Today, however, the state has approximately 112,000 miles of highways and roads. Many large highways cross Ohio, including the Ohio Turnpike, Interstate 71, and Interstate 70.

Ohio also relies on rail transportation. Four different lines provide freight service. Furthermore, 10 Ohio cities receive passenger rail service. Lake Erie and the rest of the Great Lakes connect Ohio to the Atlantic Ocean via the St. Lawrence River. Important ports of Ohio include Toledo and Cleveland. The Hopkins International Airport, in Cleveland, is the busiest in Ohio.

Energy and Transportation Facts

Energy. Yearly Consumption: 3,687 tril. BTUs (residential, 22.5%; commercial, 15.8%; industrial, 40.4%; transportation, 21.3%); Annual Energy Expenditures Per Capita: $1,928; Nuclear Power Plants Located in State: 2; Source of Energy Consumed: Petroleum— 31.5%; Natural Gas— 23.1%; Coal— 40.8%; Hydroelectric Power—0.1%; Nuclear Power—4.6%.

Transportation. Highway Miles: 113,823 (interstates, 1,573; urban, 31,568; rural, 82,255); Average Yearly Auto Insurance: $503 (32d); Auto Fatalities Rank: 37th; Registered Motor Vehicles: 9,029,829; Workers in Carpools: 13.4%; Workers Using Public Trans: 2.5%.

Employment

Employment. Ohio employed 5.13 million people in 1993. Most work in social and personal jobs (1.27 million persons or 24.9% of the workforce). Wholesale and retail trade account for 22.8% or 1.17 million workers. Government employs 737,100 workers (14.4%). Manufacturing employs 1.04 million people (20.4%). Construction accounts for 3.6% or 183,600 workers. Transportation and utilities account for 4.2% or 213,800 persons. Agriculture employs 97,500 workers or 1.9%. Finance, real estate, and insurance account for 5.0% or 258,700 workers. Mining employs 14,100 people and accounts for only 0.3% of the workforce.

Unemployment. Unemployment has decreased to 6.5% in 1993 from a rate of 8.9% in 1985. Today's figure is lower than the national average of 6.8% as shown below.

Housing

Owner Occupied Units: 4,371,945; Average Age of Units: 36 years; Average Value of Housing Units: $63,500; Renter Occupied Units: 1,293,380; Median Monthly Rent: $379; Housing Starts: 48,100; Existing Home Sales: 179,100.

Economic Facts

Gross State Product: $211,000,000,000 (1989)

Income Per Capita: $18,624

Disposable Personal Income: $16,359

Median Household Income: $28,706

Average Annual Pay, 1988: $23,603

Principal Industries: primary metals, fabricated metal products, transportation equipment, processed foods, electrical equipment, machinery

Major Crops: soybeans, corn, hay, popcorn, barley, red clover, rye, oats, dairy, pulpwood

Fish: Bass, Bluegill, Catfish, Perch, Pike

Livestock: cattle, hogs

Non-Fuel Minerals: Rock Salt, Saltwater Brine, Clay, Limestone, Shudstone

Organic Fuel Minerals: Coal, Oil, Nat. Gas

Civilian Labor Force: 5,440,000 (Women: 2,474,000)

Total Employed: 5,094,000 (Women: 2,330,000)

Median Value of Housing: $63,500

Median Contract Rent: $379 per month

Economic Sectors 1992

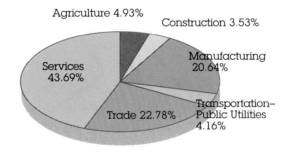

Agriculture 4.93%
Construction 3.53%
Manufacturing 20.64%
Services 43.69%
Trade 22.78%
Transportation– Public Utilities 4.16%

Manufacturing

In its early history, Ohio industry depended on agricultural products. Over the years, however, the manufacturing sector has become much more diversified. Almost 25 percent of Ohio's workforce is employed in manufacturing jobs. The state is among the top in the nation for total value added by the manufacture of goods. Dominant manufacturing industries include transportation equipment, fabricated metal, and machinery.

Ohio produces approximately one-fourth of the trucks in the United States. Toledo, Lorain, and Springfield all have large truck factories. Much of Ohio's fabricated metal products and machine tools come from Cleveland. Cincinnati, in southern Ohio, has machinery (ball bearing) as well as food processing (meat-packing) factories.

Unemployment Rate

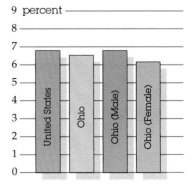

percent — United States, Ohio, Ohio (Male), Ohio (Female)

OKLAHOMA

The State of Oklahoma

Official State Seal

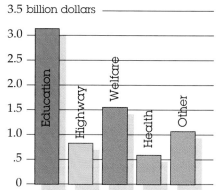

The Great Seal of Oklahoma is made from a design that was created in 1905 for a proposed state called Sequoyah. This Indian state was to encompass five Indian republics. The idea was rejected, however, and the land was added to Oklahoma when it became a state in 1907. The five points on the large star represent the five Indian republics. Forty-five smaller stars surround the larger one.

Legal Holidays

January: New Year's Day—1st; February: Presidents' Day—Third Monday; April: Oklahoma Day—22d; May: Memorial Day—4th Monday; July: Independence Day 4th; September: Native American Day—4th; Labor Day—1st Monday; Cherokee Strip Day—16th; October: Historical Day—10th; Columbus Day 2d Monday; November: Will Rogers Day—4th; Veterans' Day—11th; Admission Day—16th; Thanksgiving—4th Thursday; December: Christmas—25th.

Official State Flag

The state flag of Oklahoma was first adopted in 1911 and included a star on a red field. In 1927 this was changed because it reminded some people of communism. The present design is meant to honor Oklahoma's Indian heritage. Included with an Osage shield are a peace pipe and an olive branch.

Festivals and Events

January: International Finals Rodeo, Tulsa; February: Bullnanza, Guthrie; Hog Calling Contest, Weatherford; Chocolate Festival, Norman; March: Green Country Jazz Festival, Tahlequah; April: Cimarron Territory Celebration, Beaver; Rattlesnake Derby, Magnum; May: Rooster Days, Broken Arrow; Mayfest, Tulsa; June: Santa Fe Trail Daze, Boise City; Sand Plum Fest, Guthrie; July: International Brick & Rolling Pin Throw, Stroud; Peach Festival, Strafford; August: Oklahoma All Night Singing, Konawa; September: Cherokee National Holiday, Tahlequah; State Fair, Oklahoma City; October: Oktoberfest, Tulsa; Sorghum Day Festival, Wewoka; November: Territorial Christmas Celebration, Guthrie.

Oklahoma Compared to States in Its Region.

Resident Pop. in Metro Areas: 3d; Pop. Percent Increase: 2d; Pop. Over 65: 2d; Infant Mortality: 2d; School Enroll. Increase: 2d; High School Grad. and Up: 1st; Violent Crime: 4th; Hazardous Waste Sites: 3d; Unemployment: 4th; Median Household Income: 2d; Persons Below Poverty: 4th; Energy Costs Per Person: 4th.

West South Central

	Population	Capital
Arkansas	2,424,000	Little Rock
Louisiana	4,295,000	Baton Rouge
Oklahoma	3,231,000	Oklahoma City
Texas	18,031,000	Austin

Oklahoma's Finances

Households: 1,206,000; Income Per Capita Current Dollars: $16,198; Change Per Capita Income 1980 to 1992: 74.0% (48th in U.S.); State Expenditures: $7,063,000,000; State Revenues: $6,941,000,000; Personal Income Tax: 0.5 to 7%; Federal Income Taxes Paid Per Capita: $1,371; Sales Tax: 4.5% (prescription drugs exempt).

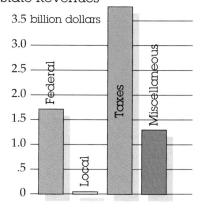

Location, Size, and Boundaries

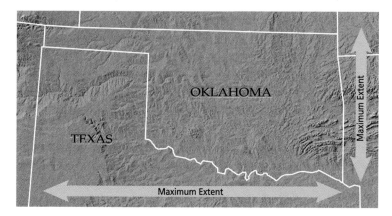

Location. Oklahoma is located in the West South Central region of the United States. It is bounded on four sides by land. The geographic center of Oklahoma is lat. 35° 32.2' N; long. 97° 39.6' W.

Size. Oklahoma is the 18th largest state in terms of size. Its area is 69,919 sq. mi. (181,090 km2). Inland water covers 1,137 sq. mi. (2,945 km2).

Boundaries. Colorado, 58 mi. (93 km); Kansas, 411 mi. (661 km); Missouri, 34 mi. (55 km); Arkansas, 198 mi. (319 km); Texas, 846 mi. (1,361 km); New Mexico, 34 mi. (55 km).

Geographic Extent. The north/south extent is 230 mi. (370 km). The state extends 464 mi. (747 km) to the east/west.

Facts about Oklahoma. Origin of Name: From the Choctaw Indian words *okla* "people" and *homma* "red"; Nickname: The Sooner State; Motto: "Labor Conquers All Things" (*Labor Omnia Vincit*); Abbreviations: Okla. (traditional), OK (postal); State Bird: scissor-tailed flycatcher; State Tree: redbud; State Flower: mistletoe; State Song: "Oklahoma!" words by Oscar Hammerstein II and music by Richard Rodgers.

Oklahoma Compared to Other States. Resident Pop. in Metro Areas: 33d; Pop. Per. Increase: 28th; Pop. Over 65: 17th; Infant Mortality: 22d; School Enroll. Increase: 43d; High School Grad. and Up: 36th; Violent Crime: 23d; Hazardous Waste Sites: 33d; Unemployment: 38th; Median Household Income: 42d; Persons Below Poverty: 9th; Energy Costs Per Person: 17th.

Sources of Information. Tourism: Oklahoma Department of Tourism and Recreation, P.O. Box 60000, Oklahoma City, OK 73146. Government: Office of the Governor, 212 State Capitol, Oklahoma City, OK 73105. History: Oklahoma Historical Society, Historical Building, Oklahoma City, OK 73105.

■ Bitting Springs Mill. Site of a grist mill built in the late 19th century. (E-22)

■ Chickasaw National Recreation Area. Nature walks, nature movies, and wildlife exhibits. (I-16)

■ Custer's Monument. Site of the battle of the Washita in 1868, where George A. Custer defeated the Cheyenne Indians. (F-9)

■ Cypress Tree. A 45-foot (14-meter) in circumference cypress tree, the largest in the state. (K-21)

■ Devil's Den Park. Site of unusual-looking granite boulders, including the Parade of Elephants. (J-17)

■ Dinosaur Quarry. One of the finest collections of dinosaur bones in the United States. (B-1)

■ Fort Gibson. Fort built in 1824 as protection from Plains Indians. The first military post in Oklahoma. (E-20)

■ Guthrie. The first state capital of Oklahoma. Has a historic district listed in the National Register of Historic Districts. (E-15)

■ Murrell Home. Seat in the capital of the Cherokee Nation. (E-21)

■ National Cowboy Hall of Fame and Western Heritage Center. The largest exhibition of western lore in the world honoring the American cowboy. (F-15)

Physical Regions: (a) Ozark Plateau; (b) Prairie Plains; (c) Ouachita Mountains; (d) Sandstone Hills; (e) Arbuckle Mountains; (f) Wichita Mountains; (g) Red River Region; (h) Red Beds Plains; (i) Gypsum Hills; (j) High Plains.

■ Pawnee Bill Museum and Park. Home and memorabilia from Pawnee Bill's Wild West show. (C-16)

■ Sequoyah's Home. The home of the inventor of the Cherokee alphabet. (F-21)

■ Will Rogers Memorial. Museum dedicated to the actor and humorist who appeared in over 70 movies and wrote radio and newspaper columns. (C-19)

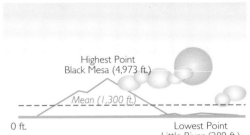

Highest Point
Black Mesa (4,973 ft.)

Mean (1,300 ft.)

0 ft.

Lowest Point
Little River (289 ft.)

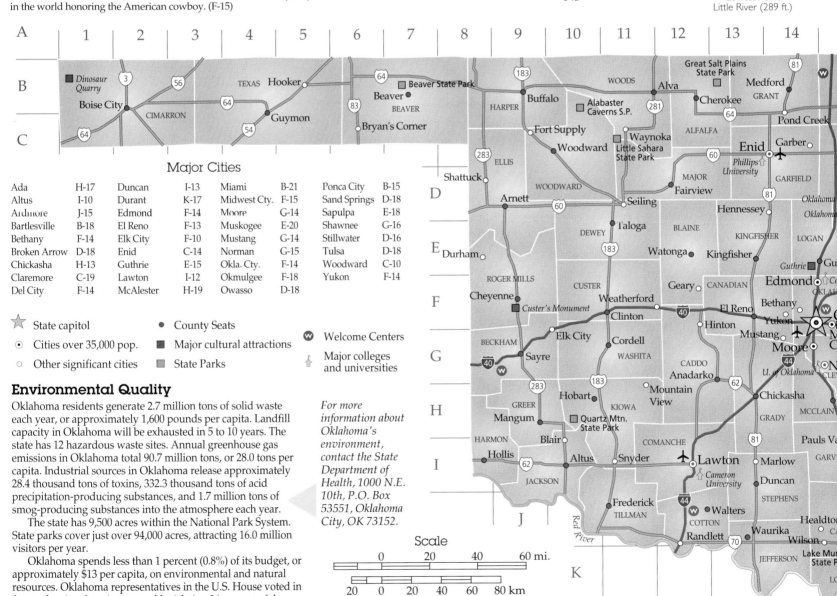

Major Cities

Ada	H-17	Duncan	I-13	Miami	B-21	Ponca City	B-15
Altus	I-10	Durant	K-17	Midwest Cty.	F-15	Sand Springs	D-18
Ardmore	J-15	Edmond	F-14	Moore	G-14	Sapulpa	E-18
Bartlesville	B-18	El Reno	F-13	Muskogee	E-20	Shawnee	G-16
Bethany	F-14	Elk City	F-10	Mustang	G-14	Stillwater	D-16
Broken Arrow	D-18	Enid	C-14	Norman	G-15	Tulsa	D-18
Chickasha	H-13	Guthrie	E-15	Okla. Cty.	F-14	Woodward	C-10
Claremore	C-19	Lawton	I-12	Okmulgee	F-18	Yukon	F-14
Del City	F-14	McAlester	H-19	Owasso	D-18		

☆ State capitol

⊙ Cities over 35,000 pop.

○ Other significant cities

● County Seats

■ Major cultural attractions

▣ State Parks

Ⓦ Welcome Centers

⚲ Major colleges and universities

Environmental Quality

Oklahoma residents generate 2.7 million tons of solid waste each year, or approximately 1,600 pounds per capita. Landfill capacity in Oklahoma will be exhausted in 5 to 10 years. The state has 12 hazardous waste sites. Annual greenhouse gas emissions in Oklahoma total 90.7 million tons, or 28.0 tons per capita. Industrial sources in Oklahoma release approximately 28.4 thousand tons of toxins, 332.3 thousand tons of acid precipitation-producing substances, and 1.7 million tons of smog-producing substances into the atmosphere each year.

The state has 9,500 acres within the National Park System. State parks cover just over 94,000 acres, attracting 16.0 million visitors per year.

Oklahoma spends less than 1 percent (0.8%) of its budget, or approximately $13 per capita, on environmental and natural resources. Oklahoma representatives in the U.S. House voted in favor of national environmental legislation 36 percent of the time, while U.S. senators did so 8 percent of the time.

For more information about Oklahoma's environment, contact the State Department of Health, 1000 N.E. 10th, P.O. Box 53551, Oklahoma City, OK 73152.

Scale

0   20   40   60 mi.

20   0   20   40   60   80 km

Average Monthly Weather

Oklahoma City	Jan	Feb	Mar	Apr	May	Jun	Jul	Aug	Sep	Oct	Nov	Dec	Yearly
Maximum Temperature °F	46.6	52.2	61.0	71.7	79.0	87.6	93.5	92.8	84.7	74.3	59.9	50.7	71.2
Minimum Temperature °F	25.2	29.4	37.1	48.6	57.7	66.3	70.6	69.4	61.9	50.2	37.6	29.1	48.6
Days of Precipitation	5.4	6.4	7.1	7.6	10.0	8.6	6.4	6.5	7.0	6.4	5.2	5.4	81.9
Tulsa													
Maximum Temperature °F	45.6	51.9	60.8	72.4	79.7	87.9	93.9	93.0	85.0	74.9	60.2	50.3	71.3
Minimum Temperature °F	24.8	29.5	37.7	49.5	58.5	67.5	72.4	70.3	62.5	50.3	38.1	29.3	49.2
Days of Precipitation	6.2	7.1	8.1	8.7	10.5	8.9	6.4	6.9	7.3	6.6	6.1	6.5	89.4

Topography

There are no less than eleven distinct topographic regions in Oklahoma. The eastern part of the state is split between the Ozark Plateau physical region, a hilly area that extends into northeastern Oklahoma from Missouri and Arkansas, and the Ouachita Mountains region in the southeast. Between these two areas, and also to their west, lies the Prairie Plains physical region. This low-lying area is dominated by the Arkansas River Valley and its tributaries. West of the Prairie Plains is a gradually rising plain area that covers most of the central portion of the state. Forests cover some of this area, which is broken by two small mountain ranges. In south-central Oklahoma is the Arbuckle Mountains physical region, and in the southwest, the Wichita Mountains region. Running along the southern border of the state is the Red River physical region, a fertile area well suited to agriculture.

The High Plains physical region, in the northwestern part of Oklahoma, around the Panhandle, is a grassy area with the highest elevations in the state. Black Mesa, in the northwest corner, rises to 4,973 ft. (1,516 m) above sea level. Lying due east of the High Plains is the Gypsum Hills physical region.

Still further to the east is the Red Beds Plains physical region. Finally, tucked between the Red Beds Plains and the Prairie Plains is the Sandstone Hills physical region. The soil throughout the state is divided between warm and dry, with reddish color and low organic content, found mostly on the plains, and warm, moist, dark, and fertile along the rivers.

Flora and Fauna

Even in a grassy state like Oklahoma, trees cover approximately one-fifth of the land area. Commercial-quality forests are found in the eastern and southeastern parts of the state. Some valuable trees include elms, hickories, sweet gums, and oaks. The Ouachita region of southeast Oklahoma has predominately forests of hickory and oak as well as oak and pine. Grasslands exist throughout Oklahoma. Short grasses such as buffalo, wire, and grama grasses grow in the northwest. Tall grasses, bluestem and sand grass, grow in the southwest and central parts of the state. Sagebrush and mesquite also grow on Oklahoma's prairies. Wildflowers that bloom in the state include spiderworts, sunflowers, and petunias.

A wide variety of small animals live in different parts of Oklahoma. The plains are home to prairie dogs, coyotes, and armadillos. Deer, rabbits, red foxes, and squirrels live in Oklahoma's forested areas. Oklahoma has a number of species of songbirds including meadowlarks, mockingbirds, and scissor-tailed flycatchers. The state's rivers, streams, and lakes contain several fish species such as paddlefish, drum, catfish, and sunfish.

Land Use

Cropland: 27.2%; Pasture: 17.9%; Rangeland: 34.3%; Forest: 15.3%; Urban: 4.1%; Other: 1.2%.

Climate

From the northwestern panhandle section of Oklahoma to the southeastern region containing the Ouachita Mountains, climate varies from an arid continental climate to a humid, somewhat subtropical climate. The humid regions of eastern Oklahoma merge with the drier, cooler northern and western regions to produce rather pleasant year-round weather, with the temperature averaging 60 degrees F. However, the more mountainous regions in the west experience great temperature ranges, from –10 degrees F in January to almost 100 degrees F in July.

Oklahoma's precipitation varies just as much as its temperature. Panhandle cities like Beaver often receive less than 20 inches of precipitation a year. Conversely, Broken Bow, in the southeast, can receive over 50 inches of annual precipitation. Because of Oklahoma's contrasting climate, the state is occasionally the site of violent weather. Severe thunderstorms, blizzards, and even tornadoes rip through the state from time to time.

Hydrology

The Red River forms most of Oklahoma's southern border with Texas. The Fork River forms the southwest boundary. Important tributaries of the Red include Cache Creek, the Washita River, the Kiamachi River, and Clear Boggy and Muddy Boggy creeks. These streams drain the lower third of Oklahoma. The Arkansas, in the northeastern region, is also an important river. Two of its tributaries, the Cimarron and the Canadian, flow southeastward across central Oklahoma from the Panhandle before emptying into the Arkansas in the east. Smaller streams include the Deep Fork, the Caney, and the Verdigris.

There are many artificial lakes, created by dams, in Oklahoma. The largest of these is Lake Eufaula on the Canadian River in the east-central region, covering about 155 sq. miles (401 sq. km). Other large lakes include Oologah Reservoir on the Verdigris, Lake Texoma on the Red, and Foss and Fort Cobb reservoirs on the Washita.

Weather Facts

Record High Temperature: 120° F (49° C) on July 26, 1943, at Tishomingo; Record Low Temperature: -27° F (-33° C) on January 18, 1930, at Watts; Average January Temperature: 38° F (3° C); Average July Temperature: 83° F (28° C); Average Yearly Precipitation: 32 in. (81 cm).

Environmental Facts

Air Pollution Rank: 26th; Water Pollution Rank: 21st; Total Yearly Industrial Pollution: 26,142,929 lbs.; Industrial Pollution Rank: 29th; Hazardous Waste Sites: 10; Hazardous Sites Rank: 32d; Landfill Capacity: overextended; Fresh Water Supply: surplus; Daily Residential Water Consumption: 173 gals. per capita; Endangered Species: Aquatic Species (6)—cavefish, Ozark; Birds (8)—crane, whooping; Mammals (3)—bat, gray; Other Species (2)—beetle, American burying; Plants (2)—orchid, eastern prairie fringed.

Oklahoma's History

Oklahoma's First People

The first humans came to the area now called Oklahoma at least fifteen thousand years ago. These early inhabitants were a hunting and gathering culture. Evidence of their existence can be found in many caves and other rock shelters scattered mainly throughout the western part of the state.

Native American tribes have also resided in Oklahoma for hundreds of years. The Plains Indians were the primary group of tribes native to the lands of Oklahoma. Soon after the United States acquired territory that included Oklahoma, however, many other tribes were settled in the state.

European Exploration

The first European to explore Oklahoma was the Spanish explorer Francisco Vásquez de Coronado, who crossed into the western part of the state in 1541. French fur traders explored Oklahoma's eastern land a short time later. It was the French who established the first permanent white settlement in Oklahoma in the town now known as Salina in 1817.

Both the Spanish and the French laid claim to Oklahoma. This dispute was resolved in 1803 when the United States received Oklahoma as part of the Louisiana Purchase. The present-day boundaries of the state were essentially set by 1819 under the Adams-Onís Treaty. However, the panhandle part of the state did not officially become a part of the Oklahoma Territory until 1890.

During the early 1800s, several Native American tribes made treaties with the United States that granted the United States land west of the Mississippi River, including parts of Oklahoma. The first such treaty was made by the Osage tribe, which ceded much Oklahoma land to the United States.

Indians, Territorial Period, and Statehood

Under the Indian Removal Act of 1830, Native Americans living east of the Mississippi River were pushed to the western side of the river. Even before this coercive measure, the U.S. government made treaties with various tribes to secure native land in the western part of the country. The first treaty to grant Native Americans land in Oklahoma in exchange for their land in the southeastern region of the United States took place in 1820.

Oklahoma was not originally supposed to be open to white settlers; the land had been reserved for Indian settlements. Pressure from the railroad industry, however, as well as from settlers and even other Native Americans finally persuaded President Benjamin Harrison to open Oklahoma Territory to white settlement in 1889. Under an 1885 law, the United States was required to purchase the land from the Indians.

The Unassigned Lands, areas that were not designated as Native American lands, became popular. As soon as the territory was opened to white settlers, population increased dramatically in only a short period. At first the boom of settlers "sooners" was so great that towns in these Unassigned Lands such as Enid and Oklahoma City became large towns of over five thousand people in a matter of hours.

Under the Organic Act, Oklahoma officially became the Oklahoma Territory on May 2, 1890. As the population increased, so did the pressure for Oklahoma statehood. On November 16, 1907, President Theodore Roosevelt declared Oklahoma the forty-sixth state in the Union. The first capital was located in Guthrie and was moved to Oklahoma City in 1910.

Industrialization

The industrialization period slowly began in Oklahoma when the railroad entered the state.

Prior to 1950, the Oklahoma economy was primarily based on agricultural products such as peanuts, cotton, wheat, livestock, and dairy products. Livestock raising is the leading agricultural venture in the state. Even though Oklahoma farms are generally larger in area than in other regions of the country, their value per acre is noticeably lower.

Oklahoma has historically been a significant producer of minerals. Oil was first obtained in 1859, and since the turn of the century, the state has been a major petroleum producer. Several natural resources, including petroleum and natural gas fields, as well as coal beds, became the dominant components of the state economy around 1950.

Today, petroleum and natural gas production continue to support Oklahoma's economy.

The Dust Bowl and the "Okies"

Oklahoma's population has increased every census since statehood was granted, but with one exception. During the period between 1930 and 1940, thousands of Oklahoma residents left the state, which was considered a "dust bowl" at the time, because of severe drought. Many Oklahoma residents headed westward, often to California. Most of the Oklahoma refugees became migrant labor workers.

The combination of the Great Depression and harsh climatic conditions made life tough in Oklahoma. Many farmers lost their land and had nothing to do. These people who moved out of Oklahoma came to be known as "Okies," taking their name from the state that they fled.

Perhaps the greatest description of the Okie plight can be found in the popular John Steinbeck novel *The Grapes of Wrath*. In the novel, Steinbeck chronicles the struggle of the Joads, an Oklahoma family driven from their home state because of the Depression and dust storms that occurred at the time. This novel helps one to understand how difficult life was for the Okies and others like them due to economic pressure attributable natural and man-made events.

Important Events

1541 Francisco Vásquez de Coronado enters Oklahoma and claims the land for Spain.

1682 La Salle claims land, including Oklahoma, for France.

1762 France gives Spain the Louisiana region, which includes Oklahoma.

1803 Louisiana Purchase grants Oklahoma area to United States.

1817 Salina is established as the first white settlement.

1819 Present boundaries excluding the panhandle is set under the Adams-Onís Treaty.

1820 First treaty with Native American tribes for the exchange of land in Oklahoma for land in the southeastern region of the U.S.

1834 Indian Territory established.

1859 Oil drilled from a well for the first time in Oklahoma.

1866 Five Civilized Tribes give some land from Indian Territory to United States.

1872 First railroad enters Oklahoma.

1889 Oklahoma Territory opened to homesteaders on April 22.

1890 Oklahoma territorial government createdunder the Organic Act; Guthrie named capital. Panhandle is added to the territory.

1907 Oklahoma becomes forty-sixth state in the Union on November 16.

1910 State capital moved to Oklahoma City.

1928 Oklahoma City oil field opens.

1930s "Dust Bowl" hits Oklahoma when severe drought conditions occur.

1959 Prohibition, in effect since statehood, repealed.

1965 National Cowboy Hall of Fame and Western Heritage Center opens.

1986 Karen Silkwood, contaminated by plutonium on the job, paid $1.38 million by her employer, Kerr-McGee.

1991 University of Oklahoma law professor Anita Hill accuses Supreme Court nominee Clarence Thomas of sexual harassment.

1995 Downtown Oklahoma City Federal Building bombed.

Oklahoma

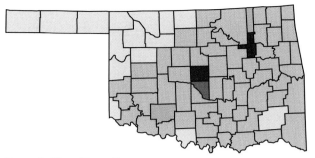

Population Density

Population density for the state of Oklahoma was 45.8 persons per square mile in 1990 (17.7 per km2). Average U.S. density was 70.3 persons per square mile in 1990 (27.3 per km2). Habitation is most dense in and around the two main cities of Oklahoma City and Tulsa. Areas of low population density can be found in the western panhandle.

Persons Per Square Mile

	0.0 to 9.9
	10.0 to 99.9
	100.0 to 249.9
	250.0 to 749.9
	750.0 to 899.9

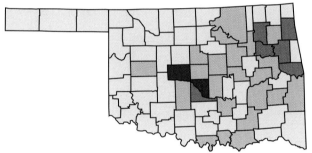

Population Change

The 1990 population figure for the state of Oklahoma was 3,145,585. This is a 3.98 percent increase from 3,025,290 in 1980. The next decade will show growth with a population of 3.4 million or a 7.33 percent increase. The areas of fastest growth are located in the eastern regions of the state east of Tulsa. The most exceptional growth area is the Oklahoma City area.

Percent Change 1980 to 1990

	−31.9 to −10.0%
	0.1 to 19.9%
	20.0 to 49.9%
	50.0 to 140.1%

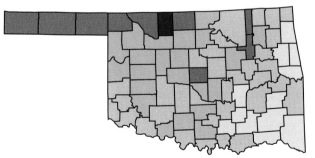

Distribution of Income

The per capita income for the state of Oklahoma (current dollars) was $16,198 in 1992. This is a 74.0 percent increase from $9,308 in 1980. Income is greatest in the panhandle area of the state. This is an area of large gas reserves as well as a site of large deposits of oil. The urban areas also have higher incomes than the surrounding counties. Low–income counties are mainly found in the east.

Per Capita Income (000s) (Current Dollars)

	$4.5 to 9.9
	$10.0 to 12.9
	$13.0 to 15.9
	$16.0 to 19.9
	$20.0 to 37.1

Population Projections

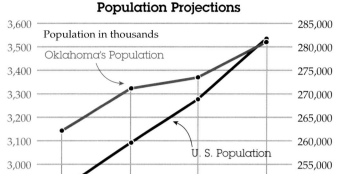

Population Change

Year	Population
1950	2,233,000
1960	2,336,000
1970	2,576,000
1980	3,025,290
1990	3,145,585
2000	3,376,000
2010	3,511,000

Period	Change
1950–1970	15.0%
1970–1980	17.8%
1980–1990	4.0%
1990–2000	7.3%

Population Facts

State Population, 1993: 3,231,000

Rank: 28

Population 2000: 3,376,000 (Rank 28)

Density: 45.8 per sq. mi. (17.7 per km²)

Distribution: 67.7% urban, 32.3% rural

Population Under 5 Years Old: 7.2%

Population Under 18 Years Old: 26.7%

Population Over 65 Years Old: 13.5%

Median Age: 33.2

Number of Households: 1,206,000

Average Persons Per Household: 2.53

Average Persons Per Family: 3.06

Female Heads of Households: 3.99%

Population That Is Married: 22.13%

Birth Rate: 15.1 per 1,000 population

Death Rate: 9.7 per 1,000 population

Births to Teen Mothers: 16.2%

Marriage Rate: 10.3 per 1,000 population

Divorce Rate: 7.7 per 1,000 population

Violent Crime Rate: 584 per 100,000 pop.

Population on Social Security: 17.0%

Percent Voting for President: 59.7%

Oklahoma's Famous Citizens

Albert, Carl (b. 1908). Member of the U.S. House (1947-1977). He also served as Speaker of the House.

Bench, Johnny (b. 1947). Hall of Fame baseball catcher and Rookie of the Year in 1968.

Berryman, John (1914–1972). Poet. He won the Pulitzer Prize in 1965 for his work *77 Dream Songs*.

Gould, Chester (1900–1985). Cartoonist. Created the popular cartoon strip "Dick Tracy" in 1931.

Hinton, S.E. (b. 1950). Writer. She appeals to young readers in books such as *Rumble Fish* and *The Outsiders*.

Jansky, Karl (1905–1950). His discovery of radio interference from space led to the creation of the field of radio astronomy.

Moyers, Bill (b. 1934). Press secretary to Lyndon Johnson and award-winning public television commentator.

Tallchief, Maria (b. 1925). Osage Indian and founder of the Chicago City Ballet.

Population Profile

Rank. Oklahoma ranks 28th among U.S. states in terms of population with 3,231,000 citizens.

Minority Population. The state's minority population is 19.3 percent. The state's male to female ratio for 1990 was 94.80 males for every 100 females. It was below the national average of 95.22 males for every 100 females.

Growth. Growing more slowly than the projected national average, the state's population is expected to reach 3.5 million by the year 2010 *(see graph above)*.

Older Citizens. The state's population older than 65 was 424,213 in 1990. It grew 12.78% from 376,126 in 1980.

Younger Citizens. The number of children (under 18 years of age) was 837 thousand in 1990. This represents 26.6 percent of the state's population. The state's school aged population was 575 thousand in 1990. It is expected to increase to 594 thousand by the year 2000. This represents a 3.3% change.

Urban/Rural. 67.7% of the population of the state live in urban areas while 32.3% live in rural areas.

Largest Cities. Oklahoma has 11 cities with a population greater than 35,000. The populations of the state's largest centers are (starting from the most populous) Oklahoma City (444,719), Tulsa (367,302), Lawton (80,561), Norman (80,071), Broken Arrow (58,043), Edmond (52,315), Midwest City (52,267), Enid (45,309), Moore (40,318), Muskogee (37,708), Stillwater (36,676), Bartlesville (34,256), Ponca City (26,359), Shawnee (26,017), Del City (23,928), Ardmore (23,079), Altus (21,910), and Duncan (21,732).

Government

Capital: Oklahoma City (established 1910).

Statehood: Became 46th state on Nov. 16, 1907.

Number of Counties: 77.

Supreme Court Justices: 9, 6-year term.

State Senators: 48, 4-year term.

State Legislators: 101, 2-year term.

United States Senators: 2.

United States Representatives: 6.

Electoral Votes: 8.

State Constitution: Adopted 1907.

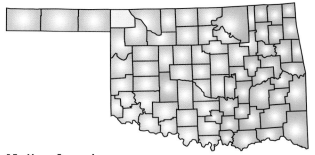

Native American

The Native American population in Oklahoma was 252,420 in 1990. This was an increase of 47.53 percent from 171,092 in 1980. Many of the Native Americans can be found living in the Osage Indian Reservation located in Osage County in the northern section of the state. Oklahoma City and Tulsa also have large Native American communities.

Presence of
Native Americans

Minor

Moderate

Nationalities

African	3,093
American	266,388
Arab	5,958
Austrian	2,154
Czech	13,321
Dutch	73,395
English	304,582
Finnish	1,291
German	566,207
Greek	3,246
Hungarian	2,350
Irish	366,767
Italian	30,149
Norwegian	10,972
Polish	19,476
Portuguese	1,707
Russian	4,793
Scottish	36,945
Slovak	3,890
Swedish	19,269
Welsh	11,790
West Indian	13,268

Statewide Ethnic Composition

Over 82 percent of the population of Oklahoma is white. The largest nationalities in this racial group are German, Irish, and English. The next largest group is Native Americans, followed by African Americans, Hispanics, and Asians. Over 266,000 people claim to be American and acknowledge no other nationality.

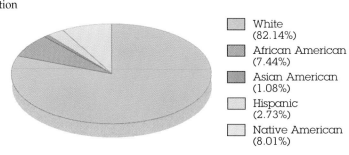

White (82.14%)

African American (7.44%)

Asian American (1.08%)

Hispanic (2.73%)

Native American (8.01%)

Education Facts

Total Students 1990: 57,858

Number of School Districts: 604

Expenditure Per Capita on Education 1990: $683

Expenditure Per Capita K–12 1990: $583

Expenditure Per Pupil 1990: $3,835

Total School Enrollment 1990–1991: 577,000

Rank of Expenditures Per Student: 42d in the U.S.

African American Enrollment: 9.9%

Hispanic Enrollment: 2.6%

Asian/Pacific Islander Enrollment: 1.1%

Native American Enrollment: 11.4%

Mean SAT Score 1991 Verbal: 476

Mean SAT Score 1991 Math: 521

Average Teacher's Salary 1992: $25,300

Rank Teacher's Salary: 47th in U.S.

High School Graduates 1990: 36,200

Total Number of Public Schools: 1,859

Number of Teachers 1990: 35,617

Student/Teacher Ratio: 16.2

Staff Employed in Public Schools: 65,076

Pupil/Staff Ratio: 8.9

Staff/Teacher Ratio: 1.8

Education

Attainment: 75.4 percent of population 25 years or older were high school graduates in 1989, earning Oklahoma a ranking of 36th in the United States; 17.1percent of the state's population had completed college. Institutions of Higher Education: The largest universities and colleges in the state include the University of Oklahoma, Norman; Oklahoma State University, Stillwater; Central State University, Edmond; University of Tulsa, Tulsa. Expenditures per Student: Expenditure increased 71.2% between 1985 and 1990. Projected High School Graduations: 1998 (39,094) , 2004 (38,912); Total Revenues for Education from Federal Sources: $104 million; Total Revenues for Education from State Sources: $1.2 billion; Total Revenues for Education from Local Sources: $494 million; Average Annual Salaries for Public School Principals: $34,375; Largest School Districts: Tulsa City School District, 40,919 students, 89th in the United States; Oklahoma City School District, 38,092 , 101st.

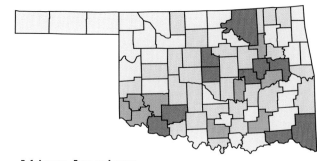

African American

The African American population in Oklahoma was 233,801 in 1990. This was an increase of 14.16 percent from 204,810 in 1980. Thirty percent of the African Americans living in Oklahoma reside in the capital, Oklahoma City. There are also large communities in various pockets around the state such as the four-county Tulsa area.

Percent of County Population

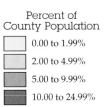

0.00 to 1.99%

2.00 to 4.99%

5.00 to 9.99%

10.00 to 24.99%

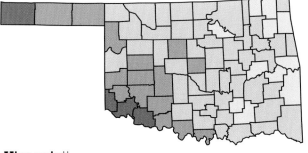

Hispanic[++]

The Hispanic Population in Oklahoma was 86,160 in 1990. This is an increase of 50.05 percent from 57,419 persons in 1980. Most of the Hispanic population lives in counties bordering Texas. The southwest corner of the state and the far western section of the panhandle contain the highest percentage of Hispanics.

Percent of County Population

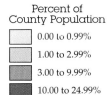

0.00 to 0.99%

1.00 to 2.99%

3.00 to 9.99%

10.00 to 24.99%

[++]A person of Mexican, Puerto Rican, Cuban, or other Spanish culture or origin regardless of race.

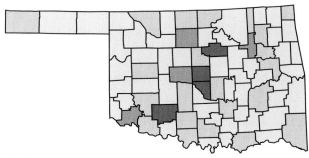

Asian American

The Asian American population in Oklahoma was 33,563 in 1990. This is an increase of 73.91 percent from 19,299 persons in 1980. Most of the Asian Americans are located in Oklahoma City, Lawton, and Stillwater. Thirty-one percent of the Asian American population resides in Oklahoma City.

Percent of County Population

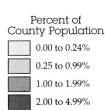

0.00 to 0.24%

0.25 to 0.99%

1.00 to 1.99%

2.00 to 4.99%

Oklahoma

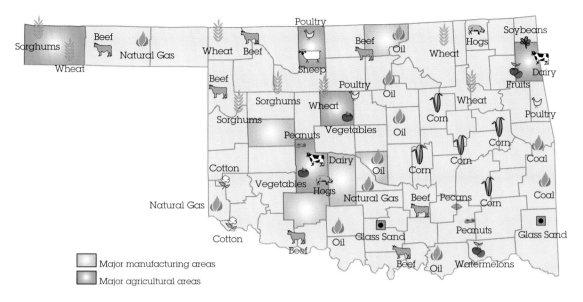

Major manufacturing areas
Major agricultural areas

Transportation

Railroads have proved important in the growth of Oklahoma. The Missouri-Kansas-Texas Railroad, Oklahoma's first, was built in 1870. Today, 15 freight rail lines serve the state; however, no passenger trains stop in Oklahoma.

Oklahoma's extensive road network has replaced much of the state's rail transportation. Oklahoma has approximately 110,000 miles of highways and roads; almost 80 percent are surfaced. Major interstates run both north to south and east to west. Tulsa and Oklahoma City have the state's major airports. Other cities such as Muskogee have airports as well. Oklahoma has one significant water transportation route. The McClellan-Kerr Arkansas River Navigation System links Oklahoma with the Mississippi River, and thus, ultimately, with the Gulf of Mexico.

Energy and Transportation Facts

Energy. Yearly Consumption: 1,283 tril. BTUs (residential, 18.8%; commercial, 14.3%; industrial, 40.1%; transportation, 26.8%); Annual Energy Expenditures Per Capita: $1,888; Nuclear Power Plants Located in State: 0; Source of Energy Consumed: Petroleum— 32.6%; Natural Gas— 43.9%; Coal— 22.0%; Hydroelectric Power—1.4%; Nuclear Power—0.0%.

Transportation. Highway Miles: 112,432 (interstates, 929; urban, 12,281; rural, 100,151); Average Yearly Auto Insurance: $448 (41st); Auto Fatalities Rank: 23d; Registered Motor Vehicles: 2,736,955; Workers in Carpools: 17.7%; Workers Using Public Trans: 0.6%.

Employment

Employment. Oklahoma employed 1.43 million people in 1993. Most work in social and personal services (304,000 persons or 21.2% of the workforce). Manufacturing accounts for 11.7% or 167,900 workers. Wholesale and retail trade account for 20.1% or 287,500 workers. Government employs 270,000 workers (18.9%). Construction employs 41,800 workers (2.9%). Transportation and utilities account for 5.0% or 71,500 persons. Agriculture employs 53,000 workers or 3.7%. Finance, real estate, and insurance account for 4.3% or 61,400 workers. Mining employs 35,500 people and accounts for only 2.5% of the workforce.

Unemployment. Unemployment has decreased to 6.0% in 1993 from a rate of 7.1% in 1985. Today's figure is lower than the national average of 6.8% as shown below.

Agriculture

Oklahoma has 34 million farm acres. During the last 40 years, Oklahoma's farms have grown larger in size and fewer in number. In 1955, 119,000 farms were found in the state. Today, 71,000 remain.

Agriculture adds $2 billion to the state's gross product annually. The principal commodities in order of marketing receipts are cattle, wheat, greenhouse, and broilers.

Oklahoma is one of the nation's leading suppliers of beef, tending over 5 million head of cattle. Many of the cattle are fattened in feed lots to increase their value. Farm-raised catfish is another livestock commodity. The most important crop is winter wheat. Hay, corn, and cotton are other important crops. The eastern and central parts of the state produce peaches and pecans.

Housing

Owner Occupied Units: 1,406,499; Average Age of Units: 26 years; Average Value of Housing Units: $48,100; Renter Occupied Units: 370,654; Median Monthly Rent: $340; Housing Starts: 13,500; Existing Home Sales: 61,500.

Economic Facts

Gross State Product: $52,000,000,000 (1989)

Income Per Capita: $16,198

Disposable Personal Income: $14,344

Median Household Income: $23,577

Average Annual Pay, 1988: $20,968

Principal Industries: rubber products, machinery, transportation equipment, electrical equipment, plastic products, petroleum products

Major Crops: wheat, hay, soybeans, sorghum, corn, peanuts

Fish: Bass, Buffalo Fish, Carp, Catfish, Paddle Fish

Livestock: cattle

Non-Fuel Minerals: Crushed Stone, Iodine, Limestone

Organic Fuel Minerals: Petroleum, Nat. Gas

Civilian Labor Force: 1,517,000 (Women: 686,000)

Total Employed: 1,416,000 (Women: 643,000)

Median Value of Housing: $48,100

Median Contract Rent: $340 per month

Economic Sectors 1992

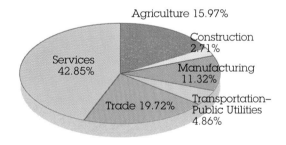

Agriculture 15.97%
Construction 2.71%
Manufacturing 11.32%
Transportation–Public Utilities 4.86%
Trade 19.72%
Services 42.85%

Manufacturing

Oklahoma's manufacturing sector has grown considerably as a result of its advantages. A significant energy supply, willing workforce, and a favorable tax structure all attract large industries to the state. Besides transportation equipment, the leading manufactured product, Oklahoma produces machinery, electrical equipment, and petroleum products.

Oklahoma's manufacturing industries are concentrated in Oklahoma City, and spread to the northeast near the Kansas and Missouri borders. The majority of transportation equipment produced by Oklahoma factories is used by the military. Plants in Tulsa and Lawton manufacture military aircraft and rocket parts, respectively. Oklahoma City produces televisions and computers. Many other cities manufacture goods used in the oil industry.

Unemployment Rate

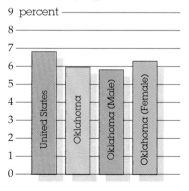

percent

United States
Oklahoma
Oklahoma (Male)
Oklahoma (Female)

OREGON
The State of Oregon

Official State Seal

The Great Seal of Oregon was adopted in 1903. The seal contains many symbols marking the pioneering and natural resource aspects of the state. The wagon, mountains, trees, and a steamer help to symbolize this heritage. The state motto, "The Union," is found below the wagon, while an American eagle is perched above the scene. The date of statehood is printed along the bottom of the seal.

Legal Holidays

January: New Year's Day—1st; February: Abraham Lincoln's Birthday Celebration—1st; Admission Day—14th; Presidents' Day—3d Monday; May: Memorial Day—4th Monday; July: Independence Day 4th; September: Labor Day—1st Monday; October: Columbus Day 2d Monday; November: Veterans' Day—11th; Admission Day—16th; Thanksgiving—4th Thursday; December: Christmas—25th.

Official State Flag

Adopted in 1925, this Oregon flag incorporates the state seal on a blue field. It is also the only state flag that is double-sided. The other side includes a beaver that demonstrates the importance of this animal to the state's economy.

Festivals and Events

January: Whale of a Wine Festival, Gold Beach; February: Oregon Shakespeare Festival (through October), Ashland; Newport Seafood & Wine Fest, Newport; March: Winter Games of Oregon, various locations; April: Pear Blossom Fest, Medford; Hood River Valley Blossom Festival, Hood River; May: Willamette Valley Folk Fest, Eugene; Rhododendron Fest, Florence; June: Oregon Bach Festival, Eugene; Portland Rose Festival, Portland; July: Children's Festival, Jacksonville; Sherwood Robin Hood Festival, Sherwood; August: Hood River Apple Jam, Hood River; State Fair, Salem; September: Pendleton Round-Up, Pendleton; October: Medford Jazz Jubilee, Medford; Hood River Valley Harvest Festival, Hood River; December: Scanfair, Portland; Snowflake Fest, Klamath Falls.

Oregon Compared to States in Its Region.

Resident Pop. in Metro Areas: 4th; Pop. Percent Increase: 3d; Pop. Over 65: 1st; Infant Mortality: 2d; School Enroll. Increase: 5th; High School Grad. and Up: 3d; Violent Crime: 4th; Hazardous Waste Sites: 3d; Unemployment: 1st; Median Household Income: 5th; Persons Below Poverty: 2d; Energy Costs Per Person: 3d.

Pacific Region

	Population	Capital
Washington	5,255,000	Olympia
Oregon	3,032,000	Salem
California	31,211,000	Sacramento
Alaska	599,000	Juneau
Hawaii	1,172,000	Honolulu

Oregon's Finances

Households: 1,103,000; Income Per Capita Current Dollars: $18,202; Change Per Capita Income 1980 to 1992: 84.5% (42d in U.S.); State Expenditures: $6,842,000,000; State Revenues: $7,297,000,000; Personal Income Tax: 5 to 9%; Federal Income Taxes Paid Per Capita: $1,642; Sales Tax: N/A.

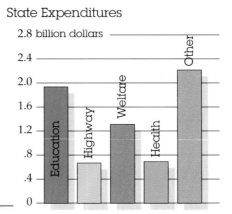

State Expenditures

2.8 billion dollars
2.4
2.0
1.6
1.2
.8
.4
0

Education, Highway, Welfare, Health, Other

State Revenues

2.8 billion dollars
2.4
2.0
1.6
1.2
.8
.4
0

Federal, Local, Taxes, Miscellaneous

Facts about Oregon.

Origin of Name: From the French word *Ouragan*, meaning "*hurricane*"; Nickname: The Beaver State; Motto: "She Flies with Her Own Wings" (*Alis Volat Propriis*); Abbreviations: Ore. or Oreg. (traditional), OR (postal); State Bird: Western meadowlark; State Tree: Douglas fir; State Flower: Oregon grape; State Song: "Oregon, My Oregon," words by J. A. Buchanan and music by Henry B. Murtagh.

Oregon Compared to Other States.

Resident Pop. in Metro Areas: 24th; Pop. Per. Increase: 7th; Pop. Over 65: 14th; Infant Mortality: 34th; School Enroll. Increase: 38th; High School Grad. and Up: 9th; Violent Crime: 28th; Hazardous Waste Sites: 38th; Unemployment: 12th; Median Household Income: 30th; Persons Below Poverty: 25th; Energy Costs Per Person: 39th.

Sources of Information.

Tourism: Oregon Economic Development Department, 775 Summer Street NE, Salem, OR 97310. Government: Secretary of State, Oregon Blue Book, State Capitol, Salem, OR 97310. History: Secretary of State, Oregon Blue Book, State Capitol, Salem, OR 97310.

■ **Abert Rim.** 19 miles (30 kilometers) long basaltic lava formation. One of the highest exposed faults in the United States. (J-10)

■ **Bonneville Dam.** Salmon can be seen swimming over the dam and the lock. (B-7)

■ **Crater Lake National Park.** Lake in the crater of an extinct volcano. (I-6)

■ **Emigrant Springs State Park.** Resting place of Oregon pioneers. (C-13)

■ **Fort Clatsop National Memorial.** Fort where Lewis and Clark set up winter camp in 1805-06. (A-3)

■ **Hart Mountain Antelope Refuge.** Wildlife viewing and camping. (K-11)

■ **Hells Canyon National Recreation Area.** Deepest river gorge in North America with an average depth of 6,600 feet (2,000 meters). (B-17)

■ **John Day Fossil Beds National Monument.** 30-million-year-old fossil beds. (D-10, E-10, E-12)

■ **Lava River Caves State Park.** Site of an old lava flow. (G-7)

■ **Mount Hood.** A dormant volcano and the highest point in the state at 11,239 feet. (C-7)

■ **Multnomah Falls.** Large falls that drop 680 feet (207 meters) into the in Columbia River gorge. (C-6)

■ **Oregon Caves National Monument.** Limestone caves. (K-4)

■ **Oregon Dunes National Recreation Area.** Sand dune formations extend for 44 miles (71 kilometers) with some dunes being over 500 feet high. (G-2)

■ **Oregon Trail.** 1800s pioneers' route from the Mississippi Valley . (G-17)

■ **Seaside.** Ocean resort with swimming and other water sports. Site of a marker showing the end of the Lewis and Clark Trail. (B-2)

■ **Silver Falls State Park.** Site of 14 scenic waterfalls. (D-5)

■ **The Dalles.** Rock canal around rapids of Columbia River gorge. (C-8)

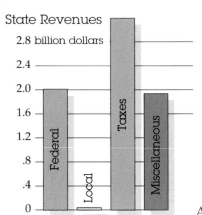

A 1
B
C
D
PACIFIC C
Cape
E
F Cape
G
H Coos
Cape Ara
I
Cape Blanco
Port Orford
J
K Gold
Cape Fer
Broo
L
1

Location, Size, and Boundaries

Location. Oregon is located in the northwestern United States in what is known as the Pacific region. It is bounded on three of four sides by land with a general coast along the Pacific Ocean in the west. The geographic center of Oregon is lat. 43° 52.1' N; long. 120° 58.7' W.

Size. Oregon is the 10th largest state in terms of size. Its area is 96,981 sq. mi. (251,180 km2). Inland water covers 797 sq. mi. (2,064 km2). Oregon touches the Pacific Ocean along a 296 mile coastline.

Boundaries. Washington, 443 mi. (713 km); Idaho, 332 mi. (534 km); Nevada, 153 mi. (246 km); California, 220 mi. (354 km); Pacific Ocean, 296 mi. (477 km).

Geographic Extent. The north/south extent of Oregon is 295 mi. (475 km). The state extends 395 mi. (636 km) to the east/west.

Major Cities

City	Grid	City	Grid
Albany	E-4	Lake Oswego	C-5
Altamont	K-7	McMinnville	D-4
Ashland	K-5	Medford	K-5
Beaverton	C-5	Milwaukie	C-5
Bend	G-8	Oregon City	C-5
Coos Bay	H-2	Pendleton	B-13
Corvallis	E-4	Portland	C-5
Eugene	G-4	Roseburg	I-4
Grants Pass	K-4	Salem	D-4
Gresham	C-5	Springfield	G-4
Hayesville	D-4	Tigard	C-5
Hillsboro	C-4	Tualatin	C-5
Keizer	D-4	West Linn	C-5
Klamath Falls	K-7		

Legend

- ★ State capitol
- ⊙ Cities over 35,000 population
- ○ Other significant cities
- ● County Seats
- ■ Major cultural attractions
- ▣ State Parks
- Ⓦ Welcome Centers
- ⚲ Major colleges & universities

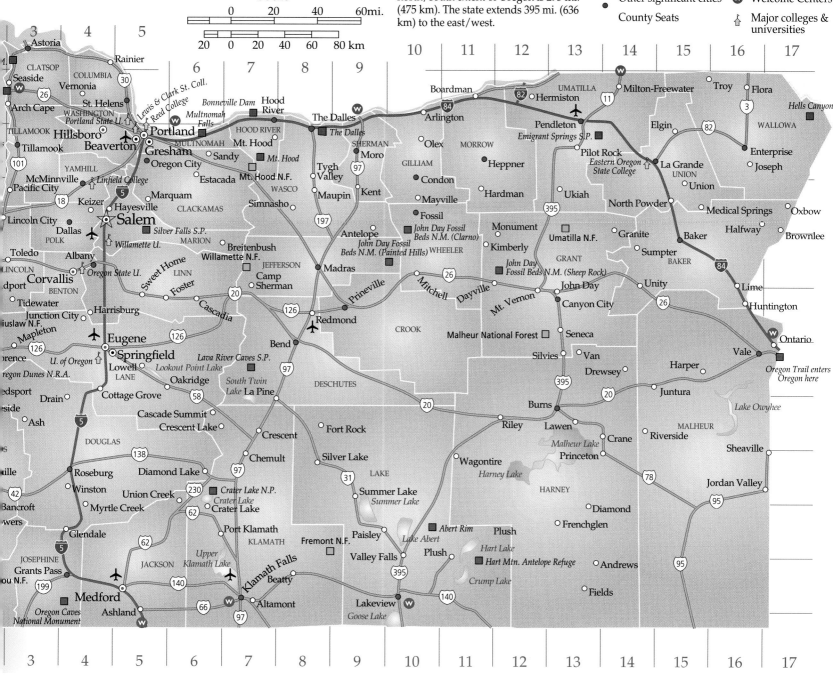

Weather Facts

Record High Temperature: 119° F (48° C) on August 10, 1898, at Pendleton; Record Low Temperature: -54° F (-48° C) on February 9, 1933, at Ukiah; Average January Temperature: 33° F (1° C); Average July Temperature: 67° F (19° C); Average Yearly Precipitation: 28 in. (71 cm).

Environmental Facts

Air Pollution Rank: 30th; Water Pollution Rank: 31st; Total Yearly Industrial Pollution: 19,652,985 lbs.; Industrial Pollution Rank: 33d; Hazardous Waste Sites: 8; Hazardous Sites Rank: 39th; Landfill Capacity: adequate; Fresh Water Supply: large surplus; Daily Residential Water Consumption: 179 gals. per capita; Endangered Species: Aquatic Species (10)—chub, Borax Lake; Birds (7)—eagle, bald; Mammals (1)—deer, Columbian white-tailed; Other Species (1)—butterfly, Oregon silverspot; Plants (7)—checker-mallow, Nelson's.

Environmental Quality

Oregon residents generate 2.4 million tons of solid waste each year, or approximately 1,750 pounds per capita. Landfill capacity in Oregon will be exhausted in more than 12 years. The state has 8 hazardous waste sites. Annual greenhouse gas emissions in Oregon total 38.4 million tons, or 13.9 tons per capita. Industrial sources in Oregon release approximately 18.1 thousand tons of toxins, 30.5 thousand tons of acid precipitation-producing substances and 1.5 million tons of smog-producing substances into the atmosphere each year.

The state has 194,600 acres within the National Park System; the largest area within the state is Crater Lake National Park. State parks cover just over 89,000 acres, attracting 39.8 million visitors per year.

Oregon spends 3 percent of its budget, or approximately $67 per capita, on environmental and natural resources.

For more information about Oregon's environment, contact the Department of Environmental Quality, 811 S.W. 6th Ave., Portland, OR 97204.

Average Monthly Weather

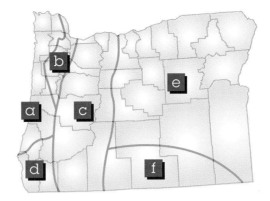

Physical Regions: (a) Coast Range; (b) Willamette Lowland; (c) Cascade Mountains; (d) Klamath Mountains; (e) Columbia Plateau; (f) Basin and Range Region.

Topography

There are several distinct topographic regions in Oregon. At the western extreme lies the Coast Range physical region. Soil is classed as cool and wet, colored gray, and high in organic content. The mountains of the Coast Range, a relatively small formation, rise from the Pacific coastline and run north to south. Valleys, formed by mountain streams,

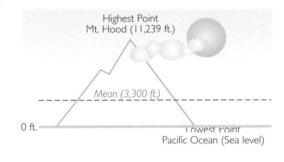

Land Use

Cropland: 15%; Pasture: 6.6%; Rangeland: 31.6%; Forest: 41%; Urban: 3.4%; Other: 2.4%.

cut through the mountains. Just to the east of the Coast Range is the Willamette Lowlands physical region, a fertile agricultural valley with warm and dry black rich soil that is fed by the Willamette River. This valley separates the Coast Range from the Cascade Mountains physical region. The soil found in this region is similar to that found in the Willamette Lowlands. This rugged chain has many high mountains, including some volcanos. The highest point in Oregon can be found here. Mount Hood rises 11,245 ft. (3,427 m) above sea level.

In the southwest corner, where the Coast and Cascade ranges meet, is the Klamath Mountains physical region. The soil of this region, the result of ancient volcanic activity, is warm and moist, with reddish brown color and high organic content. Almost half of the state is included in the Columbia Plateau physical region, which runs from the Snake River at the eastern border west to the Cascade Mountains. This vast area was formed by volcanic outflows of magma that have since been eroded and uplifted to form high forested mountains and spectacular deep canyons. Soil is predominantly warm and dry, and desert red in color.

The Basin and Range physical region, a mostly arid region, covers much of southern Oregon. The soil found in this region is a warm and dry brown clay with a rich dark surface.

Climate

Not only do the Cascade Mountains divide Oregon into different climatic regions; the mountain range itself has varying climatic regions. Along Oregon's coast, in places such as Newport, the climate is humid, yet relatively mild. In the lower altitudes, mean temperatures show little variation between January (45 degrees F) and July (60 degrees F). The Cascade Mountains represent several climates, from year-round snow on the mountain peaks, to wet but mild on mountain slopes. In between these two extremes, various climatic combinations occur. Oregon's precipitation falls in varying amounts across the state. Along the coast, mean precipitation totals 80 inches annually. However, the mountain region receives close to 130 inches of precipitation a year. East of the Cascades, in places like Bend, precipitation may total only 12 inches annually.

Semiarid southeastern Oregon is often called the Oregon Desert. However, only a few small areas have true desert characteristics.

Hydrology

The most important river in Oregon is the Columbia. It flows westward, forming most of Oregon's northern border with Washington before emptying into the Pacific Ocean. Its longest tributary is the Willamette, which flows north to meet the Columbia at Portland, close to the coast. Other important rivers include the Deschutes and the John Day, which drain much of central Oregon. The Snake River forms half of Oregon's eastern border with Idaho. Its main tributaries, the Grande Ronde, the Wallowa, and the Powder, drain most of eastern Oregon. There are also numerous streams in the state, including the Donner und Blitzen and the Silvies in east-central Oregon.

There are several large natural lakes in Oregon. The largest of these is Upper Klamath Lake in the southwest, covering about 90 sq. miles (233 sq. km). Crater Lake, in the Cascade Mountains, is the deepest lake in the United States, with a depth of 1,932 ft. (589 meters).

Pendleton	Jan	Feb	Mar	Apr	May	Jun	Jul	Aug	Sep	Oct	Nov	Dec	Yearly
Maximum Temperature °F	39.4	46.9	53.4	61.4	70.6	79.6	88.9	85.9	77.1	63.7	48.7	42.5	63.2
Minimum Temperature °F	26.3	31.8	34.4	39.2	46.1	52.9	59.6	57.5	50.5	41.3	33.4	29.5	41.8
Days of Precipitation	12.3	10.8	10.9	8.9	7.8	6.6	2.6	3.2	4.4	7.2	11.4	12.6	98.7
Portland													
Maximum Temperature °F	44.3	50.4	54.5	60.2	66.9	72.7	79.5	78.6	74.2	63.9	52.3	46.4	62.0
Minimum Temperature °F	33.5	36.0	37.4	40.6	46.4	52.2	55.8	55.8	51.1	44.6	38.6	35.4	44.0
Days of Precipitation	18.2	16.1	17.2	14.0	11.7	9.1	3.8	4.9	7.9	12.4	17.9	18.7	151.9

Flora and Fauna

Coniferous forests of Douglas fir help contribute to Oregon's rank as the leading timber state. Forests cover approximately one-half of its area, and include both coniferous softwoods such as hemlock and Sitka spruce, and hardwoods such as maple, alder, and cottonwood. The Cascade Mountains and the Coast Range have the heaviest forests. The eastern part of Oregon is largely covered by either grass or plants like sagebrush. Numerous wildflowers bloom throughout Oregon such as the Oregon Grape, partially because of

variation in climate and elevation.

Both large and small animals live in Oregon. Bear, Rocky Mountain and Roosevelt elk, and black-tailed deer live in Oregon's wooded areas. Smaller animals such as bobcats, coyotes, and river otters live throughout the state. Sea otters, sea lions, and seals can be found seasonally along the Pacific coast. Freshwater fish include cutthroat and brook trout; ocean fish include halibut and tuna. Thousands of salmon enter Oregon each year to lay their eggs.

Oregon's History

Oregon's First People

Several Native American tribes, including the Bannock, Chinook, Klamath, Modoc, and Nez Perce, are known to have lived in present-day Oregon for some time. In fact, either these people or their ancestors are thought to have come to Oregon as far back as ten thousand years ago.

Before these tribes settled in Oregon, the physical landscape was primarily made up of a combination of grasslands and forests. However, in order to attract animals, the Indians burned the grasses and trees. Besides hunting game, early Oregon residents gathered foodstuffs from the forest. On the coast, people depended on sea life, including shellfish, salmon, and even seals.

European Exploration

During the 1700s, and even before, many ships made contact with the Oregon coastline; however, no real exploration of the interior was ever done until the early nineteenth century. Before exploration, the people who crossed through Oregon were usually fur traders. The native population welcomed these traders and provided them with furs in exchange for guns, alcohol, and trinkets.

Between 1805 and 1806, Meriwether Lewis and William Clark included Oregon in their famous expedition. While Lewis and Clark did explore part of the state, including the Columbia River area and the northwest coast, the natives living in Oregon provided most of the information about the rest of the area.

Lewis and Clark's expedition provided insight into the Oregon wilderness and peaked the United States' interest in the territory. The British desired the same thing. In the early 1800s, traders and trappers also had an interest in Oregon. The American Fur Company, started by John Jacob Astor, founded Astoria, a fur-trading town, in 1811.

Other than fur traders, the first white settlers did not come until the 1830s. The migration to Oregon increased even more after 1840, when immigrants started to move west.

Territorial Period and Statehood

Oregon's population boom of the mid-nineteenth century acted as a catalyst in the movement toward official territorial status. In 1843, a territorial government was established. At the same time, provisions were made for a system of land ownership to begin. Under this system, a married man was entitled to 640 acres of land.

Beginning in 1841, a large movement of settlers started coming to Oregon from the Mississippi river along a route known as the Oregon Trail.

After a long dispute with Britain, the northern boundary of the Oregon Territory was established at the forty-ninth parallel (1846). In 1850, gold was discovered in southwestern Oregon, attracting even more settlers to the area. Another significant gold discovery was made in 1860 in eastern Oregon.

With the population of Oregon Territory continually increasing, statehood seemed the next logical step. Thus, in 1859, Oregon became the thirty-third state in the Union. Its early years as a state were characterized by increases in many areas. Population increased, as did farming, cattle raising, and railroad building.

Industrialization

In Oregon's early history, agriculture played an important role in economic development. Many people who came to settle in Oregon brought various tools of agriculture with them, such as seeds and livestock. However, the state has limited croplands, and farming eventually declined as a sustainable industry. The arrival of the railroad to Oregon in the 1870s enabled small industries, such as timber, to grow. The railroads provided Oregon products an easier and cheaper route out of the state.

During World War II, the Oregon timber industry began to diversify to accommodate wartime needs. Other industries, specializing in apparel and heavy machinery, developed in the same time period. In the early 1950s, Oregon's electronics industry expanded and improved. In contemporary Oregon, the timber industry, and its related by-product industries, plays a vital role in the Oregon economy, but not without problems. Many people believe that the timber industry is disruptive to the environment. Protests have been conducted against the clearing of Oregon forests, particularly the "old growth" trees.

Oregon: Bike-Friendly State

While some people complain that Oregon is an environmentally unfriendly state, this is not correct. The state of Oregon, and Portland and Eugene in particular, are some of the most bicycle-friendly places in the United States. A combination of state and individual city funds enable Oregon cities incorporate the bicycle into the transportation network. Eugene itself has been rated one of the ten best bicycle-friendly cities, according to Bicycling magazine. The residents of this city see the bicycle as a viable mode of transportation, not only for recreation but for commuting purposes as well. Two examples of Oregon's devotion to the bicycle is the Bicycle Master Plan for the city of Portland, and the Bicycle Advisory Committee of Eugene.

The Bicycle master plan for Portland, which was developed in 1973 included several suggestions on how to make Portland's roadways more accommodating for bicycles. Although some people did protest the plan, Portland still ranks high on the bicycle-friendly meter. The city of Eugene has a Bicycle Advisory committee made up of citizens, technical specialists, and government officials, all working to make their city a nicer and safer place to ride a bicycle.

Important Events

1543 Oregon coast may have been sited by Spanish explorers.

1792 Capt. Robert Gray explores and names Columbia River.

1805–1806 Meriwether Lewis and William Clark explore the Columbia river and northwest coast.

1811 Fur trading post, Astoria, set up by The American Fur Company and John Jacob Astor.

1818 Agreement allows United States and Great Britain to jointly administer land that includes present-day Oregon.

1824–1825 Russia relinquishes claims on Oregon.

1832 The first school in the region is founded at Ft. Vancouver.

1834 The Willamette Valley is settled.

1841 Oregon Trail opens and a large migration of settlers start to enter the area.

1846 The northern boundary of Oregon is set at the forty-ninth parallel.

1848 Oregon Territory established.

1849 Free public school system is established.

1850 Gold is discovered in southwest Oregon.

1859 Oregon becomes thirty-third state in the Union on February 14.

1859 The first railroad is built along the Columbia river.

1860 Other deposits of gold are discovered.

1902 Crater Lake National Park founded.

1912 State adopts women's suffrage as well as other political reforms in the "Oregon System."

1938 Bonneville Dam, on Columbia River, opens.

1957 The Dalles dam is completed.

1971 Oregon passes law requiring cash deposits for cans and bottles.

1990 Oregon's first woman governor, Barbara Roberts, is elected.

1992 Republican Senator Robert Packwood is accused of sexual harassment by ten women over a twenty-year period.

1995 Republican Senator Robert Packwood is asked to resign from the Senate and does so under pressure.

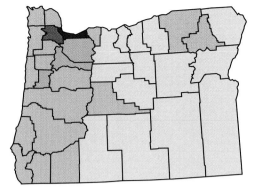

Population Density

Population density for the state of Oregon was 29.6 persons per square mile in 1990 (11.4 per km²). Average U.S. density was 70.3 persons per square mile in 1990 (27.3 per km²). Habitation is most dense in and around the urban area of Portland. Most of the population of the state is located in the western counties bordering the Pacific Ocean.

Persons Per Square Mile
- 0.0 to 9.9
- 10.0 to 99.9
- 100.0 to 249.9
- 250.0 to 749.9
- 750.0 to 1,399.9

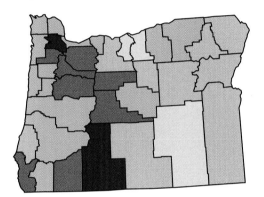

Population Change

The 1990 population figure for the state of Oregon was 2,842,321. This is a 7.95 percent increase from 2,633,105 in 1980. The next decade will show growth with a population of 2.9 million or a 1.22 percent increase. The areas of fastest growth are Washington and Klamath counties. Other fast growing counties can be found mostly in the western regions.

Percent Change 1980 to 1990
- −31.9 to −10.0%
- −9.9 to 0.0%
- 0.1 to 19.9%
- 20.0 to 49.9%
- 50.0 to 163.0%

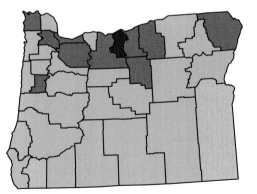

Distribution of Income

The per capita income for the state of Oregon (current dollars) was $18,202 in 1992. This is an 84.5 percent increase from $9,863 in 1980. Income is greatest in Sherman County in the north. Most of the high income areas are located in the northern counties bordering Washington.

Per Capita Income (000s) (Current Dollars)
- $10.0 to 12.9
- $13.0 to 15.9
- $16.0 to 19.9
- $20.0 to 37.7

Population Projections

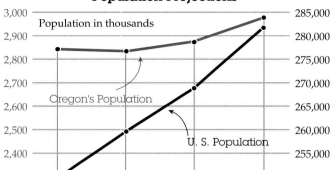

Population Change

Year	Population
1950	1,521,000
1960	1,772,000
1970	2,101,000
1980	2,633,105
1990	2,842,321
2000	2,877,000
2010	2,991,000

Period	Change
1950–1970	38.1%
1970–1980	25.3%
1980–1990	7.9%
1990–2000	1.2%

Population Facts

State Population, 1993: 3,032,000

Rank: 29

Population 2000: 2,877,000 (Rank 30)

Density: 29.6 per sq. mi. (11.4 per km²)

Distribution: 70.5% urban, 29.5% rural

Population Under 5 Years Old: 7.1%

Population Under 18 Years Old: 25.7%

Population Over 65 Years Old: 13.8%

Median Age: 34.5

Number of Households: 1,103,000

Average Persons Per Household: 2.52

Average Persons Per Family: 3.02

Female Heads of Households: 3.58%

Population That Is Married: 21.58%

Birth Rate: 15.1 per 1,000 population

Death Rate: 8.8 per 1,000 population

Births to Teen Mothers: 12.0%

Marriage Rate: 8.8 per 1,000 population

Divorce Rate: 5.5 per 1,000 population

Violent Crime Rate: 506 per 100,000 pop.

Population on Social Security: 17.4%

Percent Voting for President: 65.7%

Population Profile

Rank. Oregon ranks 29th among U.S. states in terms of population with 3,032,000 citizens.

Minority Population. The state's minority population is 9.4 percent. The state's male to female ratio for 1990 was 96.66 males for every 100 females. It was above the national average of 95.22 males for every 100 females.

Growth. Growing more slowly than the projected national average, the state's population is expected to reach 3.0 million by the year 2010 (*see graph above*).

Older Citizens. The state's population older than 65 was 391,324 in 1990. It grew 29.01% from 303,336 in 1980.

Younger Citizens. The number of children (under 18 years of age) was 724 thousand in 1990. This represents 25.5 percent of the state's population. The state's school aged population was 464 thousand in 1990. It is expected to increase to 477 thousand by the year 2000. This represents a 2.8% change.

Urban/Rural. 70.5% of the population of the state live in urban areas while 29.5% live in rural areas.

Largest Cities. Oregon has nine cities with a population greater than 35,000. The populations of the state's largest centers are (starting from the most populous) Portland (437,319), Eugene (112,669), Salem (107,786), Gresham (68,235), Beaverton (53,310), Medford (46,951), Corvallis (44,757), Springfield (44,683), Hillsboro (37,520), Aloha (34,284), Lake Oswego (30,576), Albany (29,462), Tigard (29,344), Powellhurst-Centennial (28,756), Keizer (21,884), Bend (20,469), Milwaukie (18,692), and Altamont (18,591).

Government

Capital: Salem (established 1855).

Statehood: Became 33th state on Feb. 14 1859.

Number of Counties: 36.

Supreme Court Justices: 7, 6-year term.

State Senators: 30, 4-year term.

State Legislators: 60, 2-year term.

United States Senators: 2.

United States Representatives: 5.

Electoral Votes: 7.

State Constitution: Adopted 1857.

Oregon's Famous Citizens

Beard, James (1903–1985). Gastronome and cookbook author. One of the best-known food writers in America in the 20th century.

Cleary, Beverly (b. 1916). Author of books for young readers, including *Ramona the Pest* and *Otis Spofford*.

Graves, Morris Cole (b. 1910). Artist. He produced mystical paintings of birds influenced by Asian cultures.

Markham, Edwin (1852–1940). Poet. He was famous for "The Man With the Hoe."

McLoughlin, John (1784–1857). Helped keep peace with the Indians as a partner in the Northwest Fur Company (1824–1846).

Miller, Joaquin (1827–1913). Poet. Captured the spirit of the West in works such as *Songs of the Sierras*.

Morse, Wayne (1900–1974). Served in the U.S. Senate as a Republican and as a Democrat, supporting labor and farmers.

Reed, John (1887–1920). Journalist and radical. He helped found the Communist Labor Party.

Severinsen, Doc (b. 1927). Bandleader and trumpet player. Headed the Tonight Show Orchestra from 1969 until the early 1990s.

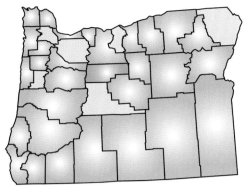

Native American

The Native American population in Oregon was 38,496 in 1990. This was an increase of 29.25 percent from 29,783 in 1980. Many Native Americans can be found in Oregon's cities, such as Portland, Eugene, and Salem. Others live in the Warm Springs Indian Reservation located in Wasco and Jefferson counties.

Presence of Native Americans

- Minor
- Moderate

Nationalities

African	2,158
American	103,352
Arab	4,985
Austrian	5,862
Czech	13,700
Dutch	63,474
English	367,884
Finnish	16,697
German	674,023
Greek	6,682
Hungarian	6,861
Irish	253,347
Italian	57,388
Norwegian	83,574
Polish	30,940
Portuguese	7,743
Russian	18,776
Scottish	66,685
Slovak	5,753
Swedish	79,319
Welsh	20,214
West Indian	982

Statewide Ethnic Composition

Over 92 percent of the population of Oregon is white. The largest nationalities in this racial group are German, English, and Irish. The next largest group is Hispanics, followed by Asian Americans, African Americans, and Native Americans. Over 103,000 people claim to be American and acknowledge no other nationality.

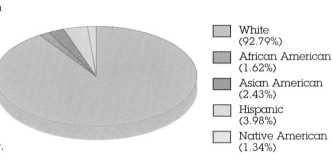

- White (92.79%)
- African American (1.62%)
- Asian American (2.43%)
- Hispanic (3.98%)
- Native American (1.34%)

Education Facts

Total Students 1990: 472,394	Mean SAT Score 1991 Verbal: 439
Number of School Districts: 303	Mean SAT Score 1991 Math: 483
Expenditure Per Capita on Education 1990: $873	Average Teacher's Salary 1992: $34,100
Expenditure Per Capita K–12 1990: $781	Rank Teacher's Salary: 17th in U.S.
Expenditure Per Pupil 1990: $5,291	High School Graduates 1990: 25,200
Total School Enrollment 1990–1991: 484,700	Total Number of Public Schools: 1,190
Rank of Expenditures Per Student: 16th in the U.S.	Number of Teachers 1990: 26,342
African American Enrollment: 2.4%	Student/Teacher Ratio: 18.4
Hispanic Enrollment: 4.0%	Staff Employed in Public Schools: 482,235
Asian/Pacific Islander Enrollment: 2.8%	Pupil/Staff Ratio: 9.8
Native American Enrollment: 1.7%	Staff/Teacher Ratio: 1.9

Education

Attainment: 83.9 percent of population 25 years or older were high school graduates in 1989, earning Oregon a ranking of 7th in the United States, 20.2 percent of the district's population had completed college. Institutions of Higher Education: The largest universities and colleges in the state include University of Oregon, Eugene; Oregon State University, Corvallis; Portland State University, Portland; Lewis and Clark College, Portland; University of Portland, Portland; Willamette University, Salem. Expenditures per Student: Expenditure increased 78% between 1985 and 1990. Projected High School Graduations: 1998 (26,747), 2004 (23,302); Total Revenues for Education from Federal Sources: $133 million; Total Revenues for Education from State Sources: $537 million; Total Revenues for Education from Local Sources: $1.3 billion; Average Annual Salaries for Public School Principals: $40,793; Largest School District: Portland School District, 51,825 students, 62d in the United States; Salem/Keizer School District, 26,930, 162d.

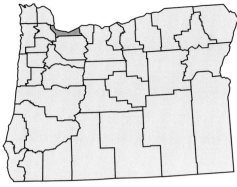

African American

The African American population in Oregon was 46,178 in 1990. This was an increase of 23.29 percent from 37,454 in 1980. The largest concentration of African Americans can be found in the Portland area. Seventy-three percent of the African American population lives in this city.

Percent of County Population

- 0.00 to 1.99%
- 5.00 to 9.99%

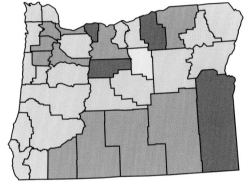

Hispanic[††]

The Hispanic population in Oregon was 112,707 in 1990. This is an increase of 71.16 percent from 65,847 persons in 1980. Many Hispanics can be found living in counties such as Malheur, Jefferson, Hood River, and Morrow.

[††]A person of Mexican, Puerto Rican, Cuban, or other Spanish culture or origin regardless of race.

Percent of County Population
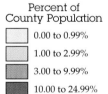
- 0.00 to 0.99%
- 1.00 to 2.99%
- 3.00 to 9.99%
- 10.00 to 24.99%

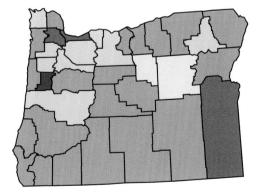

Asian American

The Asian American population in Oregon was 69,269 in 1990. This is an increase of 76.24 percent from 39,303 persons in 1980. The largest percentage of Asian Americans can be found in Benton County. Large communities are also located in the Portland area.

Percent of County Population

- 0.00 to 0.24%
- 0.25 to 0.99%
- 1.00 to 1.99%
- 2.00 to 4.99%
- 5.00 to 76.92%

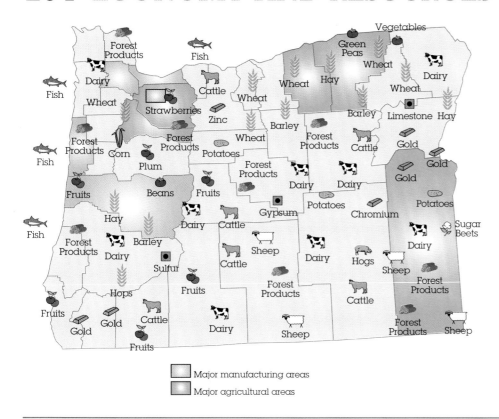

Major manufacturing areas

Major agricultural areas

Agriculture

Oregon has 17.5 million farm acres. During the last 40 years, Oregon's farms have grown larger in size and fewer in number. In 1955, 54,000 farms were found in the state. Today, 37,000 remain.

Agriculture adds $2 billion to the state's gross product annually. The principal commodities in order of marketing receipts are cattle, greenhouse, dairy products, and wheat.

The leading agricultural product in Oregon is

timber, primarily Douglas fir (in the Cascade Mountains) and ponderosa pine (in the Blue Mountains). Beef cattle are raised east of the Cascades, and dairy cattle in the west. Daffodils, irises, and lilies are propagated in Oregon greenhouses. Wheat is the most important crop. Other vegetables (grown in the Willamette Valley) include onions, hops, and peas.

Housing

Owner Occupied Units: 1,193,567; Average Age of Units: 28 years; Average Value of Housing Units: $67,100; Renter Occupied Units: 394,927; Median Monthly Rent: $408; Housing Starts: 19,700; Existing Home Sales: 58,800.

Economic Facts

Gross State Product: $52,000,000,000 (1989)

Income Per Capita: $18,202

Disposable Personal Income: $15,614

Median Household Income: $27,250

Average Annual Pay, 1988: $22,348

Principal Industries: wood products, paper products, food products, scientific instruments, electrical equipment, machinery

Major Crops: timber, milk, wheat, hay, greenhouse products, grass seed, potatoes, sugar beets, barley, fruits

Fish: Salmon, Cod, Halibut, Herring, Sole, Tuna

Livestock: cattle, sheep, dairy cows, poultry

Non-Fuel Minerals: Limestone, Clay, Gemstones, Gold, Nickel, Silver, Talc

Organic Fuel Minerals: Natural Gas, Coal

Civilian Labor Force: 1,508,000 (Women: 660,000)

Total Employed: 1,418,000 (Women: 617,000)

Median Value of Housing: $67,100

Median Contract Rent: $408 per month

Economic Sectors 1992

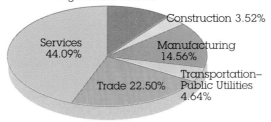

Agriculture 10.62%

Construction 3.52%

Services 44.09%

Manufacturing 14.56%

Trade 22.50%

Transportation–Public Utilities 4.64%

Manufacturing

As in other states, Oregon's manufacturing sector is highly dependent on its natural resources. The majority of the people employed in Oregon work in wood-related industries. Aside from these, Oregon manufacturing industries include food processing, machinery, and electronics.

The majority of Oregon's industries are located in the Willamette River valley region. Many places in western Oregon have wood-processing enterprises, and Oregon leads the country in lumber production. Oregon's frozen-vegetable market is centered in Marion and Umatilla counties. Portland, on the Oregon-Washington border, produces other food products such as bread and soft drinks. A leading electronics company, Tektronix, has its headquarters in Beaverton.

Transportation

The Oregon Trail was Oregon's first major transportation route. Many pioneers used it on their way to the West Coast. Today, the state has about 133,000 miles of highways and roads. Two major interstates, I-84 and I-5, run through Oregon.

Most of the major cities in Oregon, including Portland, Eugene, and Salem, have passenger rail service. In addition, 15 different freight lines run through the state. Although an inland city, Portland is still considered a major ocean port. The Columbia River provides access to the Pacific Ocean. Other Oregon ports include Newport, Coos Bay, and Astoria. The Portland International Airport is one of the busiest on the West Coast. Eugene has the state's second-busiest airport.

Energy and Transportation Facts

Energy. Yearly Consumption: 953 tril. BTUs (residential, 22.0%; commercial, 17.4%; industrial, 29.0%; transportation, 31.6%); Annual Energy Expenditures Per Capita: $1,714; Nuclear Power Plants Located in State: 1; Source of Energy Consumed: Petroleum— 36.3%; Natural Gas— 12.7%; Coal— 3.3%; Hydroelectric Power—46.0%; Nuclear Power—1.6%.

Transportation. Highway Miles: 95,237 (interstates, 727; urban, 9,494; rural, 85,743); Average Yearly Auto Insurance: $535 (25th); Auto Fatalities Rank: 27th; Registered Motor Vehicles: 2,583,405; Workers in Carpools: 17.4%; Workers Using Public Trans: 3.4%.

Employment

Employment. Oregon employed 1.47 million people in 1993. Many work in social and personal services (327,000 persons or 22.2% of the workforce). Manufacturing accounts for 14.4% or 211,000 workers. Wholesale and retail trade account for 22.2% or 327,000 workers. Government employs 233,000 workers (15.9%). Construction employs 54,000 workers (3.7%). Transportation and utilities account for 4.5% or 66,000 persons. Agriculture employs 75,000 workers or 5.1%. Finance, real estate, and insurance account for 6.2% or 91,000 workers. Mining employs 1,700 people.

Unemployment. Unemployment has increased to 7.2% in 1993 from a rate of 5.6% in 1985. Today's figure is higher than the national average of 6.8% as shown below.

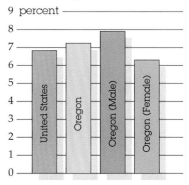

Unemployment Rate

9 percent

PENNSYLVANIA

The State of Pennsylvania

Official State Seal

The Great Seal of Pennsylvania was adopted in 1791. The three symbols—the ship, plow, and wheat—represent the crests of three counties. An olive branch, which symbolizes peace, is paired with a stalk of corn along the bottom. Also included is an American bald eagle. The words "The Seal of the State of Pennsylvania" form a semi-circle around the seal.

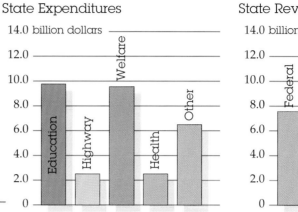

Legal Holidays

January: New Year's Day—1st; February: Abraham Lincoln's Birthday—12th; Admission Day—14th; Presidents' Day—3d Monday; May: Memorial Day—4th Monday; June: Flag Day—14th; July: Independence Day 4th; September: Labor Day—1st Monday; October: Columbus Day 2nd Monday; November: Veterans' Day—11th; Thanksgiving—4th Thursday; December: Ratification Day—12th; Christmas—25th.

Official State Flag

The Pennsylvania state flag was adopted in 1907. The coat of arms from the state seal was used to replace the coat of arms of William Penn. The state motto, "Virtue, Liberty, and Independence," can be found on the ribbon below the two black horses supporting the arms. All are placed on a field of blue.

Festivals and Events

January: Mummer's Day Parade, Philadelphia; February: Groundhog Day Festival, Punxsutawney; Great American Chocolate Festival, Hershey; March: Black Arts Festival, Carlisle; Pennsylvania Maple Fest, Meyersdale; April: Maple Syrup Fest, Beaver; Spring Craft Fair, York; May: Apple Blossom Festival, Gettysburg; Corn Planting Ceremony, Allentown; Rhubarb Festival, Intercourse; June: Pennsylvania Dutch Kutztown Folk Festival, Kutztown; July: Hanover Dutch Festival, Hanover; Pennsylvania Renaissance Faire, Cornwall; August: Roasting Ears of Corn Food Fest, Allentown; Corn Fest, Shippensburg; September: Cabbage Patch Scarecrow Contest, Lahaska; Children's Arts Festival, Doylestown; October: Fall Folk Festival, Fulton County; November: York Yule Fest, York; December: Washington Crossing the Delaware Reenactment, Washington's Crossing; Gettysburg Yuletide Fest, Gettysburg.

Pennsylvania Compared to Its Region

Resident Pop. in Metro Areas: 3d; Pop .Percent Increase: 1st; Pop. Over 65: 1st; Infant Mortality: 1st; School Enroll. Increase: 2d; High School Grad. and Up: 3d; Violent Crime: 3d; Hazardous Waste Sites: 2d; Unemployment: 3d; Median Household Income: 3d; Persons Below Poverty: 2d; Energy Costs Per Person: 2d.

Middle Atlantic Region

	Population	Capital
New Jersey	7,879,000	Trenton
New York	18,197,000	Albany
Pennsylvania	12,048,000	Harrisburg

Pennsylvania's Finances

Households: 4,496,000; Income Per Capita Current Dollars: $20,253; Change Per Capita Income 1980 to 1992: 104.1% (23d in U.S.); State Expenditures: $30,338,000,000; State Revenues: $29,859,000,000; Personal Income Tax: 2.1%; Federal Income Taxes Paid Per Capita: $1,858; Sales Tax: 6% (food and prescription drugs exempt).

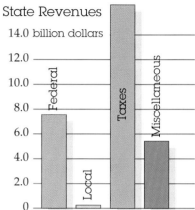

State Expenditures

14.0 billion dollars

12.0

10.0

8.0

6.0

4.0

2.0

0

Education, Highway, Welfare, Health, Other

State Revenues

14.0 billion dollars

12.0

10.0

8.0

6.0

4.0

2.0

0

Federal, Local, Taxes, Miscellaneous

Location, Size, and Boundaries

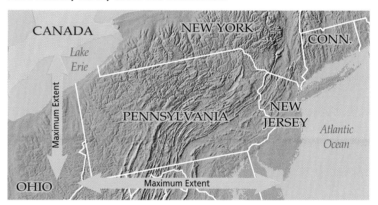

Location. Pennsylvania is located in the northeastern United States in a region known as the Middle Atlantic. It is bounded on four sides by land. The geographic center of Pennsylvania is lat. 40° 53.8' N; long. 77° 44.8' W.

Size. Pennsylvania is the 33rd largest state in terms of size. Its area is 45,333 sq. mi. (117,412 km2). Inland water covers 367 sq. mi. (950 km2).

Boundaries. New York, 327 mi. (526 km); New Jersey, 166 mi. (267 km); Delaware, 25 mi. (40 km); Maryland, 101 mi. (163 km); West Virginia, 81 mi. (130 km); Ohio, 129 mi. (208 km); Lake Erie Shoreline, 51 mi. (82 km).

Geographic Extent. The north/south extent of Pennsylvania is 169 mi. (272 km). The state extends 307 mi. (494 km) to the east/west.

Facts about Pennsylvania. Origin of Name: From *"Penn's Woods"*—named after William Penn, who established the Pennsylvania Colony; Nickname: The Keystone State; Motto: "Virtue, Liberty and Independence"; Abbreviations: Pa. or Penn. (traditional), PA (postal); State Bird: ruffed grouse; State Tree: hemlock; State Flower: mountain laurel; State Song: none.

Pennsylvania Compared to Other States. Resident Pop. in Metro Areas: 9th; Pop. Per. Increase: 41st; Pop. Over 65: 2d; Infant Mortality: 16th; School Enroll. Increase: 25th; High School Grad. and Up: 35th; Violent Crime: 32d; Hazardous Waste Sites: 2d; Unemployment: 12th; Median Household Income: 22d; Persons Below Poverty: 32d; Energy Costs Per Person: 30th.

Sources of Information. Tourism: Pennsylvania Bureau of Travel Marketing, P.O. Box 61, Warrendale, PA 15086. Economy, Government & History: Office of the Chief Clerk, Pennsylvania House of Representatives, House Post Office, Main Capitol Building, Harrisburg, PA 17120.

■ Brandywine Battlefield Historical Park. Headquarters of Washington during Battle of Brandywine in 1777. (J-16)

■ Carlisle. Carlisle Barracks, historic military post; Molly Pitcher's grave. (I-11)

■ Cornwall. Cornwall Iron Furnace, a well preserved ironmaking complex open since 1742. (I-14)

■ Delaware Water Gap National Recreation Area. Scenic area created by Delaware River's flow through gap in the Kittatinny Mountains; attractions include hiking, water sports. (E-18)

■ Fort Necessity National Battlefield. Commemorates George Washington's first battle at the start of the French and Indian War. (K-3)

■ Gettysburg National Military Park and Cemetery. Major Civil War battle; Abraham Lincoln delivered Gettysburg Address at cemetery; Eisenhower National Historic Site nearby. (K-11)

■ Hershey. Famous cocoa and chocolate candy factory; entertainment and resort area. (I-13)

■ Independence National Historical Park. Historic Philadelphia landmarks; Independence Hall, Congress Hall and Liberty Bell Pavilion. (J-18)

■ Lancaster. Scenic farmland countryside; President James Buchanan's home; Farmers' Market; Sturgis Pretzel House; Pennsylvania Farm Museum. (J-14)

■ New Hope. Artists' colony on the Delaware River; Bucks County Playhouse; numerous art galleries; historic Delaware Canal. (H-18)

■ Pennsbury Manor. William Penn's 17th-century plantation features a manor house, outbuildings, animals, and period gardens. (I-19)

■ Philadelphia Museum of Art. Third largest art museum in the United States; features more than 300,000 paintings, sculptures, drawings, prints, decorative arts, furniture, period rooms, and Oriental art. (J-18)

■ Pocono Mountains. Wooded hills and valleys of northeastern Pennsylvania; mountain resorts, skiing, hiking, and other outdoor attractions. (E-17)

■ Valley Forge National Historic Park. Site of Washington's army 1777–1778 winter encampment; replicas of log buildings and cannons. (J-17)

■ Washington Crossing Historical Park. Place near New Hope where Washington and his army crossed the Delaware to take Trenton in 1776. (I-18)

■ York. Nation's capital 1777–1778; site of Colonial Courthouse where Continental Congress met; Quaker Meeting House (1769); numerous farmers' markets. (J-12)

Major Cities

Allentown	G-16	Mt. Lebanon	H-2
Altoona	H-7	Monroeville	H-3
Baldwin	H-2	Murrysville	H-3
Bethel Park	I-2	New Castle	F-1
Bethlehem	G-17	Norristown	I-17
Carlisle	I-11	Penn Hills	H-3
Chester	J-17	Philadelphia	J-18
Drexel Hill	J-17	Pittsburgh	H-2
Easton	G-18	Pottstown	I-16
Erie	A-2	Reading	H-15
Harrisburg	I-12	Scranton	D-16
Hazleton	F-15	Sharon	E-1
Johnstown	I-6	State College	G-9
King of Prussia	J-17	West Chester	J-16
Lancaster	J-14	West Mifflin	H-2
Lebanon	I-13	Wilkes-Barre	E-15
Levittown	I-19	Wilkinsburg	H-2
McCandless	H-2	Williamsport	E-12
McKeesport	H-3	York	J-13

⭐ State capitol   ■ Major cultural attra

⊙ Cities over 35,000 pop.   □ State Parks

○ Other significant cities   Ⓦ Welcome Centers

● County Seats   ⚓ Major colleges and universities

Average Monthly Weather

Philadelphia	Jan	Feb	Mar	Apr	May	Jun	Jul	Aug	Sep	Oct	Nov	Dec	Yearly
Maximum Temperature °F	38.6	41.1	50.5	63.2	73.0	81.7	86.1	84.6	77.8	66.5	54.5	43.0	63.4
Minimum Temperature °F	23.8	25.0	33.1	42.6	52.5	61.5	66.8	66.0	58.6	46.5	37.1	28.0	45.1
Days of Precipitation	10.9	9.4	10.8	10.7	11.3	10.1	9.3	9.0	8.0	7.6	9.5	10.0	116.7
Pittsburgh													
Maximum Temperature °F	34.1	36.8	47.6	60.7	70.8	79.1	82.7	81.1	74.8	62.9	49.8	38.4	59.9
Minimum Temperature °F	19.2	20.7	29.4	39.4	48.5	57.1	61.3	60.1	53.3	42.1	33.3	24.3	40.7
Days of Precipitation	16.3	14.1	15.7	13.6	12.6	11.6	10.5	9.7	9.3	10.7	13.2	16.4	153.6

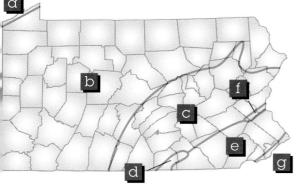

Physical Regions: (a) Erie Lowland; (b) Appalachian Plateau; (c) Appalachian Ridge and Valley; (d) Blue Ridge; (e) Piedmont; (f) New England Upland; (g) Atlantic Coastal Plain.

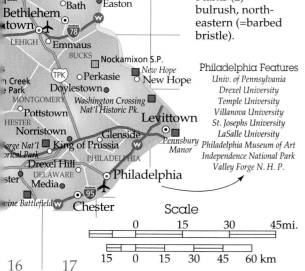

Environmental Facts

Air Pollution Rank: 13th; Water Pollution Rank: 18th; Total Yearly Industrial Pollution: 67,631,003 lbs.; Industrial Pollution Rank: 15th; Hazardous Waste Sites: 97; Hazardous Sites Rank: 2d; Landfill Capacity: adequate; Fresh Water Supply: large surplus; Daily Residential Water Consumption: 156 gals. per capita; Endangered Species: Aquatic Species (2)— clubshell; Birds (3)—eagle, bald; Mammals (3)—bat, Indiana; Plants (2)—bulrush, northeastern (=barbed bristle).

Philadelphia Features
Univ. of Pennsylvania
Drexel University
Temple University
Villanova University
St. Josephs University
LaSalle University
Philadelphia Museum of Art
Independence National Park
Valley Forge N. H. P.

Scale

0   15   30   45mi.

15   0   15   30   45   60 km

16   17

Topography

There are several distinct topographic regions in Pennsylvania. The Atlantic Coastal Plain physical region is in the southeastern corner of the state and runs in a northeast-southwest direction. The soil is warm and moist and has a base red/yellow clay that is relatively low in organic content. Parallel to the Coastal Plain, and further inland, is the Piedmont physical region. This area of gentle rolling hills has rich soil well suited to agriculture.

The Appalachian Ridge and Valley physical region dominates much of central and northeastern Pennsylvania. This area includes the Pocono Mountains. The Susquehanna River valley cuts through much of this area. The Blue Ridge physical region, extending north from Georgia, crosses the central southern border in a narrow finger. The Appalachian Plateau physical region covers most of the northern and western parts of the state. The rugged landscape is divided by steep valleys and contains the highest elevations in Pennsylvania. The highest point is Mt. Davis, which rises 3,213 ft. (979 m) above sea level. The Erie Lowland physical region is a narrow strip that borders Lake Erie in the northwest corner of the state. The soil here is gray/brown in color and glacial in nature. Finally, the New England Upland physical region forms a narrow rectangular ridge that runs between the Piedmont and the Appalachian Ridge and Valley regions with soil similar to the Blue Ridge region.

Weather Facts

Record High Temperature: 111° F (44° C) on July 10, 1936, at Phoenixville; Record Low Temperature: -42° F (-41° C) on January 5, 1904, at Smethport; Average January Temperature: 28° F (-2° C); Average July Temperature: 72° F (22° C); Average Yearly Precipitation: 42 in. (107 cm).

Land Use

Cropland: 20.8%; Pasture: 9%; Rangeland: 0%; Forest: 55.3%; Urban: 10.1%; Other: 4.8%.

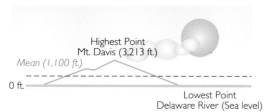

Highest Point
Mt. Davis (3,213 ft.)

Mean (1,100 ft.)

0 ft.

Lowest Point
Delaware River (Sea level)

Climate

As a whole, the state of Pennsylvania has a humid continental climate. However, topographical variations allow for local climatic differences. In Philadelphia, summers are longer and winters milder than in a city like Altoona, which lies in the Appalachian Mountain range. There, summers are short and only mild, whereas winters are longer and often harsh. Temperatures average 25 degrees F in January and 69 degrees in July. Philadelphia and the rest of the southeast average temperatures of 34 degrees F and 77 degrees F for January and July respectively.

Because it is close to the Atlantic Ocean, southeastern Pennsylvania receives more precipitation, approximately 48 inches, than the rest of the state, which averages 42 inches. Northwestern McKean County receives the most snowfall, often 80 inches.

Prevailing westerly winds account for Pennsylvania's great weather fluctuation. High- and low-pressure areas pass over the state, causing unpredictable weather patterns.

Hydrology

The Delaware River forms Pennsylvania's entire eastern boundary with New York and New Jersey. The most important river in the state is the Susquehanna, which with its tributaries drains much of eastern and central Pennsylvania. It enters the state from central New York and flows southeast to Wilkes-Barre. It then turns southwest to Harrisburg before making another turn southeast and flowing into Maryland, where it empties into the Chesapeake Bay. The Juniata is its main tributary. The Allegheny and Monongahela rivers meet at Pittsburgh to form the Ohio River, which flows west into Ohio. The Allegheny drains much of northwestern Pennsylvania, while the Monongahela drains the southwest. The Clarion is an important feeder stream of the Allegheny, while the Youghiogheny is the Monongahela's main tributary.

Most of the large lakes in the state are man-made. The largest of these is Raystown Lake, covering about 12 sq. mi. (31 sq. km).

Flora and Fauna

Sixty percent of Pennsylvania is covered by forests. Pennsylvania's position between northern and southern forests allows mixed hardwood and softwood forests in the northern part of the state. Southeastern Pennsylvania has mixed deciduous hardwood forests of elm, sycamore, and oak. The state's softwood trees include hemlock and pine. Basswood and black cherry trees also grow in Pennsylvania. Wild berry, wild ginger, and wintergreen plants grow statewide. Ferns and greenbriars grow in the west. Spring wildflowers include hepatica and bloodroot.

White-tailed deer live in all parts of Pennsylvania. Black bears live predominantly in the northern forests. Squirrels, moles, beavers, and raccoons live throughout the state. Pennsylvania's game birds include bobwhite quail and woodcock, as well as the ruffed grouse, the state bird. Bobolinks, orioles, and other songbirds also live in the state. Many types of fishes such as brown trout, pickerel, and chub live in Pennsylvania's streams, rivers, and lakes.

Environmental Quality

See page 376.

Pennsylvania's History

Pennsylvania's First People

Native American tribes have lived in Pennsylvania for approximately fifteen thousand years. Tribes belonging to one of two primary language families, Algonquian and Iroquois, were represented in the state. The Susquehanna, an Iroquoian tribe, lived in the Susquehanna River vicinity. Tribes belonging to the Algonquian language family that lived in Pennsylvania included the Delaware (Lenni Lenape), Shawnee, Conoy, and Nanticoke.

Exploration and Early Colonial Period

In the early seventeenth century, the Dutch, British, and Swedish all had claims to Pennsylvania's land. Over the years, all three of these nations ruled Pennsylvania territory at one time or another. However, the Dutch were the first Europeans to explore Pennsylvania's Delaware River coastline in 1614.

The Swedes created the first settlements in Pennsylvania. In 1643, a group of Swedes called the area south of present-day Philadelphia, New Sweden, and established two settlements, one near Tinicum and the other at New Gottenburg, near modern-day Chester.

In 1664, the British claimed Pennsylvania for themselves.

William Penn, a British Quaker, received a land grant from Charles II, king of England, in 1681, to set up a colony in America based on religious freedom. Calling the colony Pennsylvania, meaning Penn's Woods, Penn founded what became the first permanent British colony in the New World.

As a haven of religious tolerance, Pennsylvania attracted many English immigrants. Penn sought to make his colony a "holy experiment"; he established lenient suffrage requirements, granted minimum imprisonment for debts, and implemented the death penalty only under severe circumstances.

Pennsylvania as a colony had relatively amiable relations with the Native Americans living in the area. This helped set the standard of peace between the native peoples and the Europeans who came to their lands. William Penn had treaties with the Lenni Lenape as well as the Iroquois.

Revolutionary Period and Statehood

Pennsylvania could easily be referred to as the "Birthplace of Democracy." As early as 1766, Pennsylvania residents spoke out against British colonial rule. By 1774, Philadelphia, became the military, political, and economic capital of the growing revolutionary movement. Philadelphia was also the site of the First and Second Continental Congresses, held in 1774 and 1775–1776, respectively. The Declaration of Independence, written by Thomas Jefferson, was also signed in Philadelphia on July 4, 1776.

Philadelphia and the rest of Pennsylvania played a vital role in the Revolutionary War. The Continental Army, commanded by George Washington, resided in Valley Forge during the winter and spring of 1777–1778, and several battles were fought on Pennsylvania soil. Philadelphia remained the capital of the breakaway nation during most of the Revolutionary period; except for one brief period when Philadelphia lay in danger.

In 1787, the Constitutional Convention met in Philadelphia to prepare the document that would govern the new nation. Pennsylvania became the second state to ratify the new United States Constitution on December 12, 1787. Philadelphia remained the national capital from 1790 until 1800, when the capital was moved to Washington, D.C.

Industrialization

In 1750, the iron industry was the major economic force in Pennsylvania, and for the rest of the colonies. During the Revolutionary period, Pennsylvania became the center of all industrial growth.

Canals played an important role in the continuation of industrial development in the next century. In 1825, the Schuylkill Canal opened, connecting Philadelphia and Reading. The railroad also helped Pennsylvania industry by enabling goods to be shipped farther and faster.

By the middle of the nineteenth century, Pittsburgh became a dominant industrial center, primarily because of its steel plants. Coal mining and steel production became the backbone of the Pennsylvania economy.

Today, Pennsylvania still has roots in coal and steel, but the economy no longer revolves around manufacturing. As in other parts of the country, the number of jobs in the service sector continually grows. Always a city with a great deal of industry, Philadelphia has now become a city with an agglomeration of medical products companies. In central Pennsylvania, around Lancaster, agriculture plays a key role in the local economy, and contributes as well to the economy of the state.

"Birthplace of Democracy"

Each year, millions of tourists flock to Philadelphia, the City of Brotherly Love, to see where the United States had its beginnings as a nation.

In Philadelphia, one can truly see the "Birthplace of Democracy." Some of the historic sites in the city include Independence Hall, Betsy Ross House, Carpenter's Hall, and of course, the Liberty Bell. Philadelphia is also home to Independence National Historic Park where the founding fathers debated topics that became part of every Americans' history in some of the most historic buildings in the nation. Other sites in Philadelphia include the USS Olympia (Adm. Dewey's flagship during the Spanish-American War), the Philadelphia Zoo (the nation's first zoo), and Benjamin Franklin's grave.

Important Events

1614 The Dutch explore the Delaware River coastline.

1643 Swedes establish a capital for their land claims on Tinicum Island.

1655 The Dutch regain control of the Pennsylvania area.

1664 The British claim the Pennsylvania area.

1681 Charles II of England grants William Penn land; becomes Pennsylvania.

1701 Charter of Privileges established.

1754 French and Indian War begins.

1766 First seeds of discontent when residents speak out against British rule.

1774 First Continental Congress.

1775 Second Continental Congress.

1776 Declaration of Independence adopted.

1777–1778 George Washington and his troops spend the winter at Valley Forge.

1787 Pennsylvania becomes second state of the Union.

1787 The Constitution is signed.

1790 Philadelphia becomes the nation's capitol.

1811 First steamboat tested at Pittsburgh.

1825 Schuylkill Canal opened.

1859 First oil well in the world drilled near Titusville.

1863 Battle of Gettysburg; Confederate army defeated.

1889 Johnstown flood kills hundreds of people.

1920 First commercial radio station, KDKA, begins operation in Pittsburgh.

1959 Nuclear power plant at Shippingport opens.

1969 State constitution is modernized.

1979 Three Mile Island nuclear power plant disaster.

1992 Philadelphia celebrates the five-hundredth anniversary of the discovery of America by Christopher Columbus.

1993 The new multi-million dollar Pennsylvania Convention Center opens in Philadelphia.

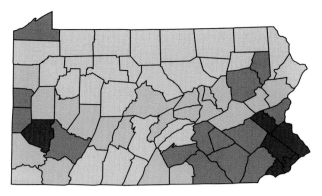

Population Density

Population density for the state of Pennsylvania was 265.1 persons per square mile in 1990 (102.4 per km2). Average U.S. density was 70.3 persons per square mile in 1990 (27.3 per km2). Habitation is most dense in and around the urban areas of Philadelphia and Pittsburgh as well as in all of the southeastern region and Erie County.

Persons Per Square Mile
- 10.0 to 99.9
- 100.0 to 249.9
- 250.0 to 749.9
- 750.0 to 11,699.9

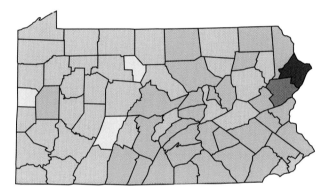

Population Change

The 1990 population figure for the state of Pennsylvania was 11,881,643. This is a –0.1 percent decrease from 11,893,895 in 1980. The next decade will show a decline with a population of 11.5 million or a –3.19 percent decrease. The areas of fastest growth are in the region of the Pocono Mountains located in the northeast.

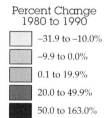

Percent Change 1980 to 1990
- –31.9 to –10.0%
- –9.9 to 0.0%
- 0.1 to 19.9%
- 20.0 to 49.9%
- 50.0 to 163.0%

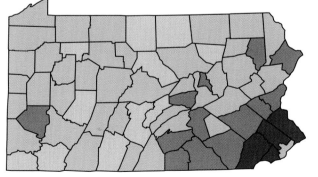

Distribution of Income

The per capita income for the state of Pennsylvania (current dollars) was $20,253 in 1992. This is a 104.1 percent increase from $9,923 in 1980. Income is greatest in the counties surrounding Philadelphia. With few exceptions, as you move farther from the city, the per capita incomes drop.

Per Capita Income (000s) (Current Dollars)
- $10.0 to 12.9
- $13.0 to 15.9
- $16.0 to 19.9
- $20.0 to 35.2

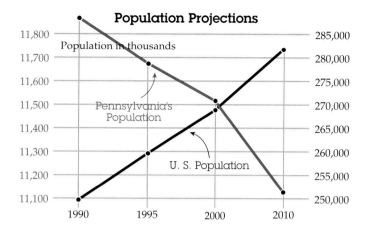

Population Projections

Population in thousands

Pennsylvania's Population

U. S. Population

(left axis: 11,100 – 11,800; right axis: 250,000 – 285,000; years 1990, 1995, 2000, 2010)

Population Change

Year	Population
1950	10,498,000
1960	11,329,000
1970	11,813,000
1980	11,893,895
1990	11,881,643
2000	11,503,000
2010	11,134,000

Period	Change
1950–1970	12.5%
1970–1980	0.7%
1980–1990	–0.1%
1990–2000	–3.2%

Population Facts

State Population, 1993: 12,048,000
Rank: 5
Population 2000: 11,503,000 (Rank 6)
Density: 265.1 per sq. mi. (102.4 per km²)
Distribution: 68.9% urban, 31.1% rural
Population Under 5 Years Old: 6.8%
Population Under 18 Years Old: 23.7%
Population Over 65 Years Old: 15.7%
Median Age: 35.0
Number of Households: 4,496,000
Average Persons Per Household: 2.57
Average Persons Per Family: 3.10
Female Heads of Households: 4.27%
Population That Is Married: 21.06%
Birth Rate: 14.5 per 1,000 population
Death Rate: 10.3 per 1,000 population
Births to Teen Mothers: 10.9%
Marriage Rate: 7.2 per 1,000 population
Divorce Rate: 3.3 per 1,000 population
Violent Crime Rate: 450 per 100,000 pop.
Population on Social Security: 18.9%
Percent Voting for President: 54.3%

Population Profile

Rank. Pennsylvania ranks 5th among U.S. states in terms of population with 12,048,000 citizens.

Minority Population. The state's minority population is 12.4 percent. The state's male to female ratio for 1990 was 92.03 males for every 100 females. It was below the national average of 95.22 males for every 100 females.

Growth. The state's population is decreasing

Government

Capital: Harrisburg (established 1812).
Statehood: Became 2d state on Dec. 12, 1787.
Number of Counties: 67.
Supreme Court Justices: 7, 10-year term.
State Senators: 50, 4-year term.
State Legislators: 203, 2-year term.
United States Senators: 2.
United States Representatives: 21.
Electoral Votes: 23.
State Constitution: Adopted 1968.

Pennsylvania's Famous Citizens

Ayer, Francis Wayland (1848–1923). Advertising innovator. He created such devices as trademarks and slogans.

Babbitt, Milton (b. 1916). Composer in the twelve tone system. He received a Lifetime Achievement Pulitzer Prize in 1982.

Franklin, Benjamin (1706–1790). Civic leader, politician, author, inventor and scientist.

Kelly, Grace (1929–1982). Actress and Princess of Monaco. She won an Academy Award in 1954 for her role in the film The Country Girl.

Selznick, David O. (1902–1965). Film producer of such famous movies as King Kong and Gone with the Wind.

Updike, John (b. 1932). Author of stories about troubled middle-class life, captured in books such as Rabbit Run.

Weissmuller, Johnny (1904–1984). Winner of 3 Olympic gold medals for swimming in 1924, and actor in a dozen Tarzan movies.

Williams, Daniel Hale (1858–1931). He performed the first successful open–heart surgery in 1893.

and is expected to be 11.1 million by the year 2010.

Older Citizens. The state's population older than 65 was 1,829,106 in 1990. It grew 19.48% from 1,530,933 in 1980.

Younger Citizens. The number of children (under 18 years of age) was 2.8 million in 1990. This represents 23.5 percent of the state's population. The state's school aged population was 1.7 million in 1990. It is expected to decrease to 1.6 million by the year 2000. This represents a –0.91% change.

Urban/Rural. 68.9% of the population of the state live in urban areas while 31.1% live in rural areas.

Largest Cities. Pennsylvania has 16 cities with a population greater than 35,000. The populations of the state's largest centers are (starting from the most populous) Philadelphia (1,585,577), Pittsburgh (369,879), Erie (108,718), Allentown (105,090), Scranton (81,805), Reading (78,380), Bethlehem (71,428), Lancaster (55,551), Levittown (55,362), Harrisburg (52,376), Altoona (51,881), Penn Hills (51,430), Wilkes-Barre (47,523), York (42,192), Chester (41,856), State College (38,923), and Bethel Park (33,823).

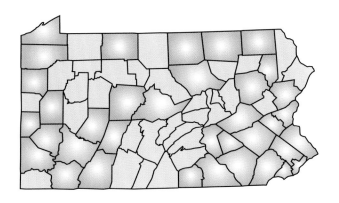

Nationalities

African	13,088
American	309,814
Arab	30,798
Austrian	43,549
Czech	28,356
Dutch	172,084
English	749,786
Finnish	5,471
German	3,485,436
Greek	44,265
Hungarian	92,006
Irish	1,270,330
Italian	1,047,893
Norwegian	18,777
Polish	632,518
Portuguese	9,209
Russian	156,394
Scottish	132,813
Slovak	295,843
Swedish	73,648
Welsh	109,613
West Indian	17,550

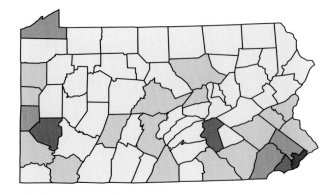

Native American

The Native American population in Pennsylvania was 14,733 in 1990. This was an increase of 34.82 percent from 10,928 in 1980. Twenty-three percent of the Native American population in Pennsylvania lives in or around the city of Philadelphia. Pennsylvania is also home to the Susquehanna and Delaware tribes.

Presence of
Native Americans

☐ Minor

African American

The African American population in Pennsylvania was 1,089,795 in 1990. This was an increase of 4.25 percent from 1,045,318 in 1980. Fifty-eight percent of the African American population in the state lives in the city of Philadelphia. Other large communities can be found in Harrisburg and Pittsburgh.

Percent of
County Population

☐ 0.00 to 1.99%
☐ 2.00 to 4.99%
☐ 5.00 to 9.99%
☐ 10.00 to 24.99%
☐ 25.00 to 86.24%

Statewide Ethnic Composition

Over 88 percent of the population of Pennsylvania is white. The largest nationalities in this racial group are German, Irish, and Italian. The next largest group is African Americans, followed by the Hispanics, Asian Americans, and Native Americans. Over 309,000 people claim to be American and acknowledge no other nationality.

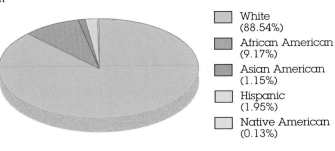

☐ White (88.54%)
☐ African American (9.17%)
☐ Asian American (1.15%)
☐ Hispanic (1.95%)
☐ Native American (0.13%)

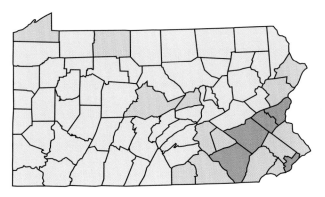

Education Facts

Total Students 1990: 1,655,279

Number of School Districts: 501

Expenditure Per Capita on Education 1990: $789

Expenditure Per Capita K–12 1990: $717

Expenditure Per Pupil 1990: $6,534

Total School Enrollment 1990–1991: 1,667,630

Rank of Expenditures Per Student: 6th in the U.S.

African American Enrollment: 13.1%

Hispanic Enrollment: 2.6%

Asian/Pacific Islander Enrollment: 1.5%

Native American Enrollment: 0.1%

Mean SAT Score 1991 Verbal: 417

Mean SAT Score 1991 Math: 459

Average Teacher's Salary 1992: $38,700

Rank Teacher's Salary: 8th in U.S.

High School Graduates 1990: 109,900

Total Number of Public Schools: 3,276

Number of Teachers 1990: 106,218

Student/Teacher Ratio: 15.7

Staff Employed in Public Schools: 190,175

Pupil/Staff Ratio: 8.7

Staff/Teacher Ratio: 1.8

Hispanic[††]

The Hispanic population in Pennsylvania was 232,262 in 1990. This is an increase of 50.86 percent from 153,961 persons in 1980. Thirty-eight percent of the Hispanics in the state live in Philadelphia.

[††]A person of Mexican, Puerto Rican, Cuban, or other Spanish culture or origin regardless of race.

Percent of
County Population

☐ 0.00 to 0.99%
☐ 1.00 to 2.99%
☐ 3.00 to 9.99%

Education

Attainment: 76.8 percent of population 25 years or older were high school graduates in 1989, earning Pennsylvania a ranking of 33d in the United States; 18.6 percent of the state's population had completed college. Institutions of Higher Education: The largest universities and colleges in the state include Pennsylvania State University, University Park; Temple University, Philadelphia; University of Pittsburgh, Pittsburgh; University of Pennsylvania, Philadelphia; Drexel University, Philadelphia; Carnegie-Mellon University, Pittsburgh; Villanova University, Villanova; Lehigh University, Bethlehem. Expenditures per Student: Expenditure increased 67% between 1985 and 1990. Projected High School Graduations: 1998 (130,177), 2004 (129,396); Total Revenues for Education from Federal Sources: $462 million; Total Revenues for Education from State Sources: $4 billion; Total Revenues for Education from Local Sources: $4.3 billion; Average Annual Salaries for Public School Principals: $42,711; Largest School Districts in State: Philadelphia City School District, 189,451 students, 7th in the United States; Pittsburgh School District, 39,559, 96th.

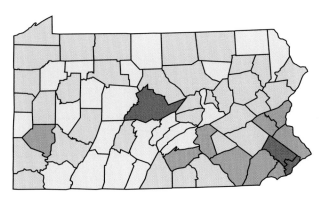

Asian American

The Asian American population in Pennsylvania was 137,438 in 1990. This is an increase of 100.27 percent from 68,625 persons in 1980. Most of the Asian American population can be found in Philadelphia, State College, and Montgomery County.

Percent of
County Population

☐ 0.00 to 0.24%
☐ 0.25 to 0.99%
☐ 1.00 to 1.99%
☐ 2.00 to 4.99%

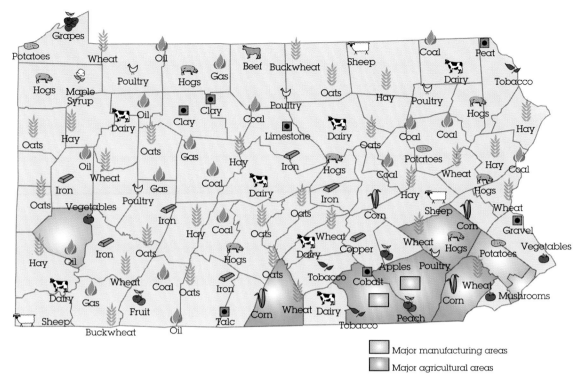

Major manufacturing areas

Major agricultural areas

Transportation

Since the colonial period, Pennsylvania has had an extensive transportation network. The first hard-surfaced roadway in the country, between Philadelphia and Lancaster, was opened in 1794. Pennsylvania's modern road system is very extensive. The turnpike runs not only east to west, but also northward with the Northeast Extension. Water transportation routes can be found throughout Pennsylvania. Pittsburgh, in the west, is considered the center of Pennsylvania's water transportation. Philadelphia is another important port city; large ships can even travel up the Delaware River as far north as Morrisville. Many freight as well as passenger rail lines serve many parts of Pennsylvania. Philadelphia and Pittsburgh have two of the busiest airports in the nation. Harrisburg is an important commuter air hub.

Energy and Transportation Facts

Energy. Yearly Consumption: 3,492 tril. BTUs (residential, 23.5%; commercial, 15.2%; industrial, 37.3%; transportation, 24.0%); Annual Energy Expenditures Per Capita: $1,863; Nuclear Power Plants Located in State: 9; Source of Energy Consumed: Petroleum— 31.9%; Natural Gas— 17.0%; Coal— 35.1%; Hydroelectric Power—0.2%; Nuclear Power—15.8%.

Transportation. Highway Miles: 116,788 (interstates, 1,587; urban, 30,823; rural, 85,965); Average Yearly Auto Insurance: $642 (19th); Auto Fatalities Rank: 27th; Registered Motor Vehicles: 8,179,231; Workers in Carpools: 18.1%; Workers Using Public Trans: 6.4%.

Agriculture

Pennsylvania has 7.9 million farm acres. During the last 40 years, Pennsylvania's farms have grown larger in size and fewer in number. In 1955, 129,000 farms were found in the state. Today, 51,000 remain.

Agriculture adds $3 billion to the state's gross product annually. The principal commodities in order of marketing receipts are dairy products, cattle, greenhouse, and mushrooms.

Livestock and livestock products account for about 72 percent of Pennsylvania's farm income, of which milk is the most important product. Dairy farms are found mainly in the eastern part of the state. The leading crops are corn and hay, grown in the Piedmont region in the southeast. Pennsylvania is the nation's leading producer of mushrooms, most grown near Philadelphia in damp, cool conditions indoors.

Employment

Employment. Pennsylvania employed 11.47 million people in 1993. Most work in social and personal services (1.52 million persons or 27.9% of the workforce). Manufacturing accounts for 17.2% or 940,000 workers. Wholesale and retail trade account for 20.9% or 1.15 million workers. Government employs 707,700 workers (12.9%). Construction employs 197,000 workers (3.6%). Transportation and utilities account for 4.9% or 266,700 persons. Agriculture employs 98,600 workers or 1.8%. Finance, real estate, and insurance account for 5.5% or 303,000 workers. Mining employs 21,600 people and accounts for only 0.4% of the workforce.

Unemployment. Unemployment has decreased to 7.0% in 1993 from a rate of 8.0% in 1985. Today's figure is higher than the national average of 6.8% as shown below.

Housing

Owner Occupied Units: 4,938,140; Average Age of Units: 41 years; Average Value of Housing Units: $69,700; Renter Occupied Units: 1,287,662; Median Monthly Rent: $404; Housing Starts: 39,000; Existing Home Sales: 216,100.

Economic Facts

Gross State Product: $228,000,000,000 (1989)

Income Per Capita: $20,253

Disposable Personal Income: $17,658

Median Household Income: $29,069

Average Annual Pay, 1988: $24,393

Principal Industries: electrical equipment, food products, printing, transportation equipment, fabricated metal products, machinery, chemicals, clothing, oil refining

Major Crops: milk, eggs, greenhouse products, corn, hay, mushrooms, barley, corn, tomatoes, pears, cherries

Fish: Bass, Trout, Carp, Pickerel

Livestock: beef cattle, milk cows, hogs, sheep

Non-Fuel Minerals: Limestone, Clay, Mica, Peat

Organic Fuel Minerals: Coal, Nat. Gas, Petroleum

Civilian Labor Force: 5,933,000 (Women: 2,685,000)

Total Employed: 5,524,000 (Women: 2,521,000)

Median Value of Housing: $69,700

Median Contract Rent: $404 per month

Economic Sectors 1992

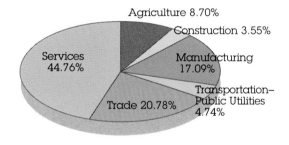

Agriculture 8.70%

Construction 3.55%

Services 44.76%

Manufacturing 17.09%

Transportation–Public Utilities 4.74%

Trade 20.78%

Manufacturing

Pennsylvania has a long history of industry, beginning in colonial times. It is still a leading manufacturing state; however, manufacturing jobs are steadily declining. Today, food processing ranks as the number one manufacturing activity. Chemicals, machinery, and fabricated metals are all important contributors to the state's economy.

Most of Pennsylvania's manufacturing takes place in the southeastern and southwestern parts of the state. Philadelphia is the food processing center of Pennsylvania. Other area industries include clothing, chemical (pharmaceutical), and medical equipment. Pittsburgh, in the southwest, has much of Pennsylvania's heavy industries. Hershey, in south-central Pennsylvania, has the largest chocolate and cocoa processing plants in the world.

Unemployment Rate

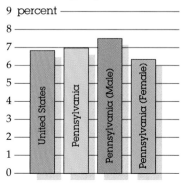

9 percent

United States | Pennsylvania | Pennsylvania (Male) | Pennsylvania (Female)

RHODE ISLAND
The State of Rhode Island

Official State Seal

The Great Seal of Rhode Island was adopted in 1664, before Rhode Island became a state. The anchor in the center of the seal symbolizes hope, and the word "Hope" is printed above it. The printing around the seal, "Seal of the State of Rhode Island and Providence Plantations" represents the official name of the original colony.

Legal Holidays

January: New Year's Day—1st; February: Presidents' Day—3d Monday; May: State Independence Day—4th; Ratification Day—29th; Memorial Day—4th Monday; July: Independence Day—4th; September: Labor Day—1st Monday; October: Columbus Day—2d Monday; November: Veterans' Day—11th; Thanksgiving—4th Thursday; December: Christmas—25th.

Official State Flag

The official state flag of Rhode Island was adopted in 1897. The first flag appeared around 1647 and was legalized as a state flag in 1877. Included on the flag is the anchor, the symbol of hope. The word "Hope" is printed below it. The anchor first appeared on a regimental flag carried by the Second Rhode Island Regiment during the Revolution.

Festivals and Events

January: Newport Yacht Club Frostbite Fleet Race, Newport; Penguin Plunge, Jamestown; February: Newport Music Festival Winter Concert Series, Newport; March: Anniversary—Voters Reject Constitution; May: Gaspee Days, Warwick; June: Big Easy Bash, Escoheag; July: Newport Music Festival, Newport; Children's Party at Green Animals, Newport; September: Cajun & Bluegrass Music Fest, Escoheag; October: Johnny Cake Festival, West Kingston & Usquepaugh; Narragansett Native American Fall Festival, Providence; Oktoberfest, Providence; Columbus Day Festival, Providence; November: Nouveau Beaujolais Tasting, Newport; December: Champagne Tasting, Newport.

Rhode Island Compared to Its Region.

Resident Pop. in Metro Areas: 3d; Pop. Percent Increase: 3d; Pop. Over 65: 1st; Infant Mortality: 1st; School Enroll. Increase: 6th; High School Grad. and Up: 6th; Violent Crime: 3d; Hazardous Waste Sites: 4th; Unemployment: 1st; Median Household Income: 4th; Persons Below Poverty: 3d; Energy Costs Per Person: 6th.

New England Region

	Population	Capital
Maine	1,239,000	Augusta
New Hampshire	1,125,000	Concord
Vermont	576,000	Montpelier
Massachusetts	6,012,000	Boston
Rhode Island	1,000,000	Providence
Connecticut	3,277,000	Hartford

Rhode Island's Finances

Households: 378,000; Income Per Capita Current Dollars: $20,299; Change Per Capita Income 1980 to 1992: 112.0% (15th in U.S.); State Expenditures: $3,331,000,000; State Revenues: $2,849,000,000; Personal Income Tax: N/A; Federal Income Taxes Paid Per Capita: $1,845; Sales Tax: 7% (food and prescription drugs exempt).

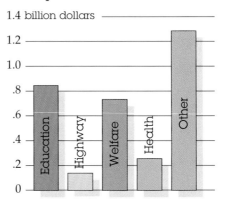

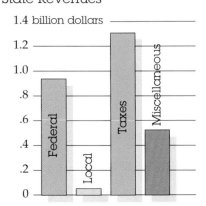

Location, Size, and Boundaries

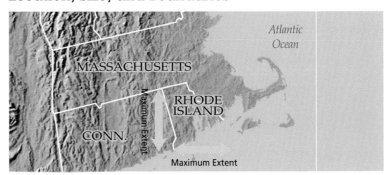

Maximum Extent

Location. Rhode Island is located in the northeastern United States in the New England region. It is bounded on three of four sides by land with a small coast along the Atlantic Ocean in the southeast. The geographic center of Rhode Island is lat. 41° 40.3' N; long. 71° 34.6' W.

Size. Rhode Island is the smallest state in terms of size. Its area is 1,214 sq. mi. (3,144 km2). Inland water covers 165 sq. mi. (427 km2). Rhode Island touches the Atlantic Ocean along a 40 mile coastline.

Boundaries. Massachusetts, 64 mi. (103 km); Atlantic Ocean, 40 mi. (64 km); Connecticut, 56 mi. (90 km).

Geographic Extent. The north/south extent of Rhode Island is 48 mi. (77 km). The state extends 37 mi. (60 km) to the east/west.

Facts about Rhode Island. Official Name: State of Rhode Island and Providence Plantations—refers to the 36 islands and the mainland that make up the state; Nickname: The Ocean State; Motto: "Hope"; Abbreviations: R.I. (traditional), RI (postal); State Bird: Rhode Island red; State Tree: red maple; State Flower: violet; State Song: "Rhode Island," words and music by T. Clarke Brown.

Rhode Island Compared to Other States. Resident Pop. in Metro Areas: 5th; Pop. Per. Increase: 46th; Pop. Over 65: 4th; Infant Mortality: 37th; School Enroll. Increase: 22d; High School Grad. and Up: 40th; Violent Crime: 31st; Hazardous Waste Sites: 28th; Unemployment: 4th; Median Household Income: 13th; Persons Below Poverty: 42d; Energy Costs Per Person: 49th.

Sources of Information. Tourism: Rhode Island Tourism Division, 7 Jackson Walkway, Providence, RI 02903. Economy: Department of Economic Development, 7 Jackson Walkway, Providence, RI 02903. Government: Office of the Secretary of State, Room 217, State House, Providence, RI 02903. History: Office of the Secretary of State, Room 217, State House, Providence, RI 02903.

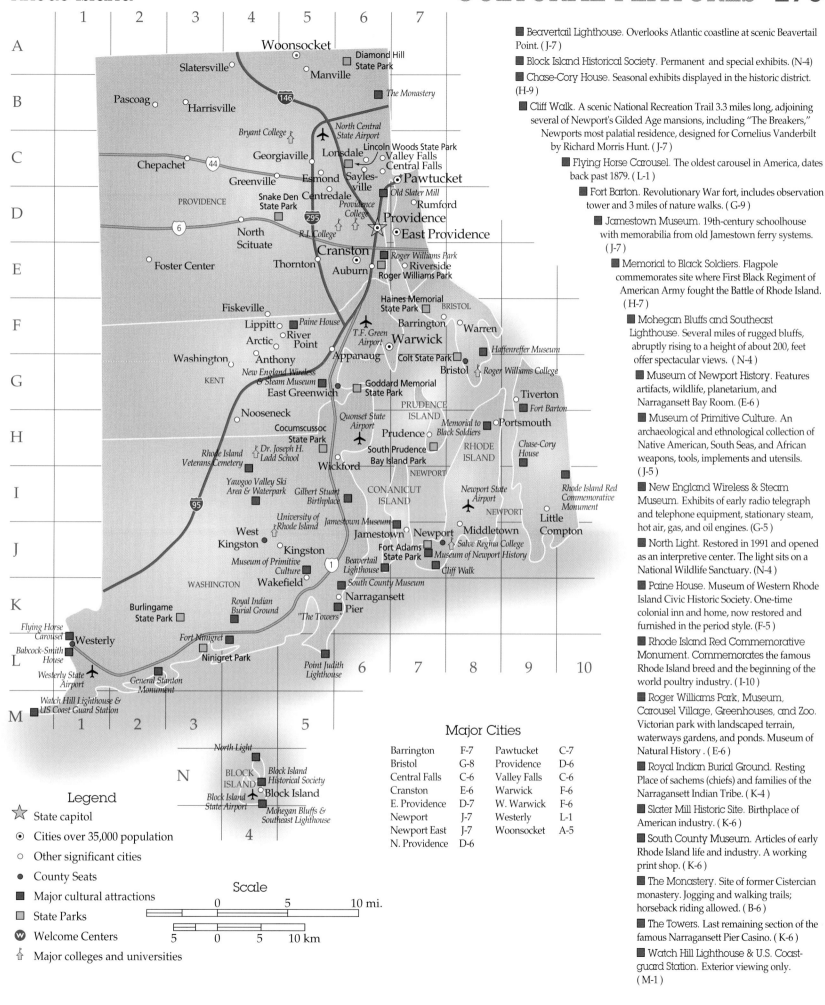

Rhode Island

Woonsocket
Slatersville
Diamond Hill State Park
Manville
Pascoag
Harrisville
146
The Monastery
North Central State Airport
Bryant College
Lincoln Woods State Park
Georgiaville
Lonsdale
Valley Falls
Chepachet
44
Central Falls
Greenville
Esmond
Sayles-ville
Pawtucket
Snake Den State Park
Centredale
Old Slater Mill
PROVIDENCE
Providence College
Rumford
295
Providence
North Scituate
R.I. College
East Providence
6
Foster Center
Cranston
Thornton
Roger Williams Park
Auburn
Riverside
Roger Williams Park
Fiskeville
Haines Memorial State Park
BRISTOL
Lippitt
Paine House
Barrington
Warren
Arctic
River Point
T.F. Green Airport
Warwick
Washington
Anthony
Appanaug
Colt State Park
KENT
New England Wireless & Steam Museum
Haffenreffer Museum
East Greenwich
Goddard Memorial State Park
Bristol
Roger Williams College
Nooseneck
Tiverton
Cocumscussoc State Park
PRUDENCE ISLAND
Fort Barton
Rhode Island Veterans Cemetery
Dr. Joseph H. Ladd School
Quonset State Airport
Prudence
Memorial to Black Soldiers
Portsmouth
Yawgoo Valley Ski Area & Waterpark
Wickford
South Prudence Bay Island Park
RHODE ISLAND
Chase-Cory House
Gilbert Stuart Birthplace
CONANICUT ISLAND
NEWPORT
Rhode Island Red Commemorative Monument
95
University of Rhode Island
Jamestown Museum
Newport State Airport
NEWPORT
West Kingston
Jamestown
Newport
Middletown
Little Compton
Kingston
Fort Adams State Park
Salve Regina College
Museum of Primitive Culture
Beavertail Lighthouse
Museum of Newport History
WASHINGTON
Wakefield
South County Museum
Cliff Walk
Burlingame State Park
Royal Indian Burial Ground
Narragansett Pier
"The Towers"
Flying Horse Carousel
Westerly
Fort Ninigret
Point Judith Lighthouse
Babcock-Smith House
Ninigret Park
Westerly State Airport
General Stanton Monument
Watch Hill Lighthouse & US Coast Guard Station

North Light
BLOCK ISLAND
Block Island Historical Society
Block Island State Airport
Block Island
Mohegan Bluffs & Southeast Lighthouse

Legend

⭐ State capitol
⊙ Cities over 35,000 population
○ Other significant cities
● County Seats
◼ Major cultural attractions
◻ State Parks
Ⓦ Welcome Centers
⚲ Major colleges and universities

Scale

0   5   10 mi.

5   0   5   10 km

Major Cities

Barrington	F-7	Pawtucket	C-7
Bristol	G-8	Providence	D-6
Central Falls	C-6	Valley Falls	C-6
Cranston	E-6	Warwick	F-6
E. Providence	D-7	W. Warwick	F-6
Newport	J-7	Westerly	L-1
Newport East	J-7	Woonsocket	A-5
N. Providence	D-6		

◼ Beavertail Lighthouse. Overlooks Atlantic coastline at scenic Beavertail Point. (J-7)

◼ Block Island Historical Society. Permanent and special exhibits. (N-4)

◼ Chase-Cory House. Seasonal exhibits displayed in the historic district. (H-9)

◼ Cliff Walk. A scenic National Recreation Trail 3.3 miles long, adjoining several of Newport's Gilded Age mansions, including "The Breakers," Newports most palatial residence, designed for Cornelius Vanderbilt by Richard Morris Hunt. (J-7)

◼ Flying Horse Carousel. The oldest carousel in America, dates back past 1879. (L-1)

◼ Fort Barton. Revolutionary War fort, includes observation tower and 3 miles of nature walks. (G-9)

◼ Jamestown Museum. 19th-century schoolhouse with memorabilia from old Jamestown ferry systems. (J-7)

◼ Memorial to Black Soldiers. Flagpole commemorates site where First Black Regiment of American Army fought the Battle of Rhode Island. (H-7)

◼ Mohegan Bluffs and Southeast Lighthouse. Several miles of rugged bluffs, abruptly rising to a height of about 200, feet offer spectacular views. (N-4)

◼ Museum of Newport History. Features artifacts, wildlife, planetarium, and Narragansett Bay Room. (E-6)

◼ Museum of Primitive Culture. An archaeological and ethnological collection of Native American, South Seas, and African weapons, tools, implements and utensils. (J-5)

◼ New England Wireless & Steam Museum. Exhibits of early radio telegraph and telephone equipment, stationary steam, hot air, gas, and oil engines. (G-5)

◼ North Light. Restored in 1991 and opened as an interpretive center. The light sits on a National Wildlife Sanctuary. (N-4)

◼ Paine House. Museum of Western Rhode Island Civic Historic Society. One-time colonial inn and home, now restored and furnished in the period style. (F-5)

◼ Rhode Island Red Commemorative Monument. Commemorates the famous Rhode Island breed and the beginning of the world poultry industry. (I-10)

◼ Roger Williams Park, Museum, Carousel Village, Greenhouses, and Zoo. Victorian park with landscaped terrain, waterways gardens, and ponds. Museum of Natural History. (E-6)

◼ Royal Indian Burial Ground. Resting Place of sachems (chiefs) and families of the Narragansett Indian Tribe. (K-4)

◼ Slater Mill Historic Site. Birthplace of American industry. (K-6)

◼ South County Museum. Articles of early Rhode Island life and industry. A working print shop. (K-6)

◼ The Monastery. Site of former Cistercian monastery. Jogging and walking trails; horseback riding allowed. (B-6)

◼ The Towers. Last remaining section of the famous Narragansett Pier Casino. (K-6)

◼ Watch Hill Lighthouse & U.S. Coast-guard Station. Exterior viewing only. (M-1)

Weather Facts

Record High Temperature: 104° F (40° C) on August 2, 1975, at Providence; Record Low Temperature: -23° F (-31° C) on January 11, 1942, at Kingston; Average January Temperature: 30° F (-1° C); Average July Temperature: 70° F (21° C); Average Yearly Precipitation: 44 in. (112 cm).

Environmental Facts

Air Pollution Rank: 42d; Water Pollution Rank: 41st; Total Yearly Industrial Pollution: 3,452,131 lbs.; Industrial Pollution Rank: 45th; Hazardous Waste Sites: 12; Hazardous Sites Rank: 27th; Landfill Capacity: overextended; Fresh Water Supply: large surplus; Daily Residential Water Consumption: 106 gals. per capita; Endangered Species: Aquatic Species (1)—sturgeon, shortnose; Birds (3)—eagle, bald; Mammals (1)—bat, Indiana; Other Species (1)—beetle, American burying; Plants (2)—gerardia, sandplain.

Environmental Quality

Rhode Island residents generate 1.0 million tons of solid waste each year, or approximately 2,000 pounds per capita. Landfill capacity in Rhode Island will be exhausted in 5 to 10 years. The state has 11 hazardous waste sites. Annual greenhouse gas emissions in Rhode Island total 11.7 million tons, or 11.8 tons per capita. Industrial sources in Rhode Island release approximately 6.8 thousand tons of toxins, 14.9 thousand tons of acid precipitation-producing substances, and 200.0 thousand tons of smog-producing substances into the atmosphere each year.

The state has less than 500 acres within the National Park System. State parks cover just over 8,200 acres, attracting 5.1 million visitors per year.

Rhode Island spends 1.9 percent of its budget, or approximately $36 per capita, on environmental and natural resources. Rhode Island representatives in the U.S. House voted in favor of national environmental legislation 94 percent of the time, while U.S. senators did so 75 percent of the time.

Average Monthly Weather

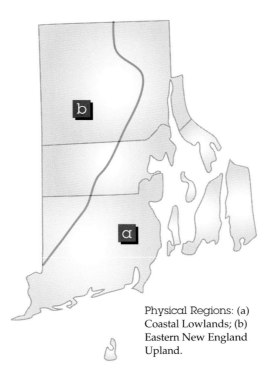

Physical Regions: (a) Coastal Lowlands; (b) Eastern New England Upland.

Mean (200 ft.) Highest Point Jerimoth Hill (812 ft.)

0 ft.

Lowest Point Atlantic Ocean (Sea level)

Land Use

Cropland: 3.3%; Pasture: 5.6%; Rangeland: 0%; Forest: 61.1%; Urban: 24.4%; Other: 5.6%.

For more information about Rhode Island's environment, contact the Department of Environmental Management, 9 Hayes St., Providence, RI 02908.

Block Island	Jan	Feb	Mar	Apr	May	Jun	Jul	Aug	Sep	Oct	Nov	Dec	Yearly
Maximum Temperature °F	37.2	36.9	42.8	51.8	60.7	69.8	76.0	75.8	69.7	60.8	51.5	41.9	56.2
Minimum Temperature °F	25.0	25.1	31.4	38.9	47.6	56.9	63.6	63.8	57.9	48.9	40.2	29.6	44.1
Days of Precipitation	10.0	9.2	10.6	10.2	10.0	8.7	7.3	7.9	7.4	7.8	10.2	11.1	110.3
Providence													
Maximum Temperature °F	36.4	37.7	45.5	47.5	67.6	76.6	81.7	80.3	73.1	63.2	51.9	40.5	59.3
Minimum Temperature °F	20.0	20.9	29.2	38.3	47.6	57.0	63.3	61.9	53.8	43.1	34.8	24.1	41.2
Days of Precipitation	10.9	9.9	11.6	11.1	11.3	10.9	9.0	9.5	8.3	8.5	11.0	12.0	124.0

Flora and Fauna

Rhode Island, the smallest state, has approximately 60 percent of its land covered with forests. Like Pennsylvania, Rhode Island is located between northern and southern forests, and therefore has quite a varied tree population. Paper birch trees, also known as canoe birches, grow in northern Rhode Island. Other trees in the state include oak, maple, poplar, cedar, and hemlock. Several plants such as wild carrots and red deer grass grow throughout Rhode Island. Wildflowers such as cattails grow in the marshy areas near Charleston, and scarlet pimpernels grow in Newport, in southern Rhode Island.

Rhode Island has a smaller mammal population than many other states, but squirrels, rabbits, otters, deer, and a few other animals all live in the state. Several birds live in Rhode Island, especially on Block Island, 10 miles of the coast. Bird species include catbirds, blue jays, barred owls, and shore birds such as ospreys and loons. Partridges, woodcocks, and other game birds also live in the state. Both saltwater (butterfish, flounder) and freshwater (perch, eels) fish swim in Rhode Island waters.

Topography

There are two distinct topographic regions in Rhode Island. The Coastal Lowlands physical region covers eastern Rhode Island. The southeastern part of this region is dominated by Narragansett Bay and the other bays, inlets, and islands that characterize the area. Most of the bays and islands have rocky shorelines, while the remainder of the other coastal areas enjoy sandy beaches. Salt marshes are also found in the coastal areas.

The northwestern portion of Rhode Island lies in the New England Upland physical region. This area of gentle rolling hills slopes gradually up to the northwest corner of the state. The highest elevation in Rhode Island is found here. Jerimoth Hill rises 812 ft. (247 m) above sea level. The soil in both physical regions follows the pattern typical of the New England states in that it is homogeneous in the extreme. It is cool and moist, colored brown, and high in iron and organic content. Rhode Island's land area includes its 36 islands. The largest of these is Aquidneck Island, at about 45 sq. miles (117 sq. km). Block Island, which is roughly 11 sq. miles (28 sq. km) in area, lies about 10 miles (16 km) off Rhode Island's shore in the Atlantic Ocean. The soil on the island is classed as warm and moist with a light gray or brown surface.

Climate

The climate in Rhode Island can be classified as humid continental. However, weather varies across the state through the months. In the capital city of Providence and the surrounding area, winter temperatures average between 38 and 40 degrees F. Near the Massachusetts border, though, the January temperature usually does not rise above 35 degrees F. In the summer, Providence and most of the northern half of the state see temperatures in the 80s, while the coastal areas, including Block Island in Narragansett Bay, only have temperatures in the 70s.

Precipitation across the state as a whole averages around 42 inches annually. However, one spot in the west-central part of the state often receives over 50 inches of precipitation annually.

For a small state, Rhode Island has quite an extensive coastline. Over the years, the state's coast has been bombarded by several hurricanes, often accompanied by tidal waves.

Hydrology

The dominant body of water in Rhode Island is Narragansett Bay. It defines most of the state's eastern border, and has created many of Rhode Island's 38 islands. The most important river in the state is the Blackstone, which flows southeast from Woonsocket near the Massachusetts border in central Rhode Island. It first becomes the Pawtucket River, then the Seekonk. The Seekonk and the Sakonnet in southeastern Rhode Island are really saltwater estuaries of Narragansett Bay. Freshwater rivers in the state include the Pawtuxet and the Ponaganset in central Rhode Island, the Chepachet River in the north, and the Pawcatuck River, which forms Rhode Island's southwestern border with Connecticut.

Many of the largest lakes in the state are man-made. The largest of these is Scituate Reservoir on the Pawtuxet River in the center of the Rhode Island. Others include the Flat River Reservoir and Pascoag Reservoir.

Rhode Island's History

Rhode Island's First People

Approximately ten thousand Native Americans lived on the lands that would become the smallest state in the Union. The Narraganset tribe, a member of the Algonquian language family, made up the majority of the native population; about six thousand Native Americans belonged to the this tribe. The Narragansets lived in the southern part of Rhode Island, around present-day Providence.

In the eastern shore region lived the Wampanoags, a rival tribe. Yet another, but considerably weaker tribe, the Nipmuc people, lived in the northern, more inland regions of Rhode Island. A fourth major group of Native Americans, the Niantics, lived in the southern part of the state. All of the aforementioned tribes hunted, fished, and farmed for survival.

Later in history, the previously feuding Narragansets and Wampanoags joined forces, during King Philip's War in 1675. The warfare hit the Indians hard, and surviving members of both tribes banded together with the Niantics. This fragmented group of native people ultimately assumed the name Narraganset although the Wampanoags still exist in Massachusetts and Connecticut.

European Exploration

Giovanni da Verrazano, a Florentine navigator, was probably the first European to explore Rhode Island. However, another European, Miguel de Cortereal from Portugal, may have sailed along the Rhode Island coast as early as 1511. Verrazano gave Rhode Island its name in 1524, when he compared the terrain to the island of Rhodes in the Mediterranean Sea.

In the 1600s, several traders, primarily Dutch, sailed through the waters off Rhode Island's coast. Later in the century, Rhode Island became a religious haven. Roger Williams, a man exiled from Puritan Boston, founded the first permanent white settlement at Providence in 1636. In the same year, other religious refugees fled Massachusetts. Two of these, William Coddington and John Clarke, obtained a deed from Native Americans for the area known now as Rhode Island, which at that time was called Aquidneck Island. Eight years later, in 1644, the land was renamed Rhode Island.

Meanwhile, Roger Williams had secured a charter for the new colony. He united three settlements—Providence, Portsmouth, and Newport—under one incorporation, "The Incorporation of Providence Plantations in the Narragansett Bay in New England." Although always known for religious freedom, Rhode Island was officially recognized as an area for religious freedom by King Charles II of England in 1663.

Colonial Period and Statehood

Since Rhode Island has an accessible coastline, it benefited greatly from trade in its early years. However, starting in the 1760s, Great Britain imposed restrictions on all colonial trading. Naturally, Rhode Island residents did not agree with such measures, and strong anti-British sentiment began to spread. In 1769, a British ship, ironically named Liberty, was burned by Rhode Islanders in protest against taxes.

When the Revolutionary War began, many residents of Rhode Island signed up for the militia. Rhode Island was also the first colony to officially declare its independence, on May 4, 1776. Throughout the war, Rhode Island towns were the site of many a battle between the Continental Army and British troops.

Although the colony wholeheartedly supported the American Revolution, Rhode Island was the last of the original thirteen colonies to ratify the Constitution. On May 29, 1790, it became the thirteenth state in the Union.

Industrialization

Many diverse industries started to develop in Rhode Island during the middle of the eighteenth century, with textiles and jewelry being two of the earliest and foremost. The textile industry came to Rhode Island in 1790, when Samuel Slater built the first American textile machines; his textile mill in Pawtucket was the first ever cotton mill.

In addition to textile plants, Rhode Island is also home to the jewelry industry.

Many of the textile and other mills were located on the coast, and relied on water power. Other industries relying on water resources—boat building, shipping, fishing, and even whaling—fared well in Rhode Island. These industries carried the state into the twentieth century, but then started to decline. This is especially true of the whaling industry, as new fuels replaced whale oil for illumination.

Today the Rhode Island economy is more service-oriented than in the past. Many of the manufacturing jobs that used to exist in the state are now gone. The number of defense-related jobs, which employed thousands of people have decreased in recent years.

Architecture Across the Ages in Newport

The state of Rhode Island may be the smallest of the fifty United States, but it has a great architectural tradition. In the city of Newport, located on Aquidneck Island in the Narragansett Bay, one can find buildings representing the seventeenth, eighteenth, and nineteenth centuries. From colonial taverns to the summer "cottages" of the wealthy, Newport has it all.

One of the oldest buildings in Newport is the Whitehorse Tavern, built in 1673. These and other buildings such as the Friends Meeting House (1699) and the Touro Synagogue, the oldest in the country (1763), have been restored with financial help from the Doris Duke Foundation, a Newport philanthropy organization. This dedication to preservation enables thousands of tourists who come to Newport to see these rare buildings of our colonial past.

In the nineteenth century, many wealthy Americans built their summer homes in Newport. Many of these summer residences are located along the Cliffs Walk, on the Newport coast. On this three mile long path, one can see the rugged coast of the Atlantic Ocean on one side, and beautiful mansions on the other. The homes were mainly built between 1839 and 1901. Perhaps the most famous of these summer homes is The Breakers, built in 1892. This seventy-room home was built for the wealthy Vanderbilt family.

Important Events

1511 Miguel de Cortereal sails along the Aquidneck Island (Rhode Island) coast.

1524 Giovanni da Verrazano sails into Narragansett Bay.

1636 Providence, first white settlement, founded by Roger Williams.

1644 Aquidneck Island renamed Rhode Island.

1647 Three Rhode Island settlements united under a charter granted to Roger Williams.

1657 Rhode Island provides protection to persecuted Quakers.

1658 Rhode Island provides protection to persecuted Jews from Holland.

1760s Great Britain imposes restrictions on all colonial trade.

1763 The oldest synagogue in the country, Touro Synagogue, is built.

1769 The British ship, Liberty, is burned in response to British taxes.

1774 State prohibits importation of slaves.

1776 Rhode Island is the first to declare independence from British rule on May 4.

1790 On May 29, Rhode Island becomes thirteenth state in the Union.

1790 First cotton mill established at Pawtucket.

1794 The first jewelry business in the United States is founded by Nehemiah and Seril Dodge.

1831 Silver-plating factory is opened.

1842 Dorr's Rebellion. Political movement led by Thomas Wilson Dorr to achieve constitutional reform. Later, it was stopped and Dorr was tried and convicted for treason.

1869 Newport Bridge replaces last major ferry route.

1938 Hurricane/tidal wave combination kills 238 people.

1947 State sales tax adopted.

1973 Naval Air Station at Quonset Point closes.

1985 Narraganset tribe attempts to gain reservation status, but is denied.

1990 The Rhode Island Share and Deposit Indemnity Corporation collapses, preventing over 300,000 bank customers from gaining access to their bank deposits.

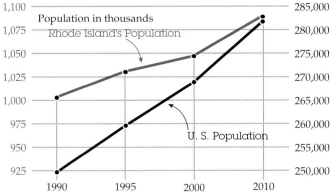

Population Density

Population density for the state of Rhode Island was 960.3 persons per square mile in 1990 (370.7 per km2). Average U.S. density was 70.3 persons per square mile in 1990 (27.3 per km2). Rhode Island is the second most densely populated state in the United States, with New Jersey being the most densely populated.

Persons Per Square Mile

- 250.0 to 749.9
- 750.0 to 4,799.9

Population Projections

Population in thousands
Rhode Island's Population

U. S. Population

Population Change

Year	Population
1950	792,000
1960	855,000
1970	951,000
1980	947,154
1990	1,003,464
2000	1,049,000
2010	1,085,000

Period	Change
1950–1970	20.1%
1970–1980	–0.4%
1980–1990	5.9%
1990–2000	4.6%

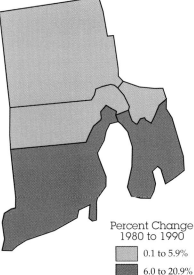

Population Change

The 1990 population figure for the state of Rhode Island was 1,003,464. This is a 5.95 percent increase from 947,154 in 1980. The next decade will show growth with a population of 1.05 million or a 4.54 percent increase. The areas of fastest growth are found in the south around Narragansett Bay.

Percent Change 1980 to 1990

- 0.1 to 5.9%
- 6.0 to 20.9%

Population Facts

State Population, 1993: 1,000,000

Rank: 43

Population 2000: 1,049,000 (Rank 42)

Density: 960.3 per sq. mi. (370.7 per km²)

Distribution: 86.0% urban, 14.0% rural

Population Under 5 Years Old: 7.1%

Population Under 18 Years Old: 23.2%

Population Over 65 Years Old: 15.2%

Median Age: 34.0

Number of Households: 378,000

Average Persons Per Household: 2.55

Average Persons Per Family: 3.11

Female Heads of Households: 4.42%

Population That Is Married: 20.16%

Birth Rate: 15.1 per 1,000 population

Death Rate: 9.5 per 1,000 population

Births to Teen Mothers: 10.5%

Marriage Rate: 8.1 per 1,000 population

Divorce Rate: 3.7 per 1,000 population

Violent Crime Rate: 462 per 100,000 pop.

Population on Social Security: 18.3%

Percent Voting for President: 58.4%

Rhode Island's Famous Citizens

Angell, James (1829–1916). Educator and journalist. He was president of the universities of Vermont and Michigan.

Dorr, Thomas Wilson (1805–1854). Elected governor on the "People's Party" ticket and later convicted of treason.

Eddy, Nelson (1901–1967). Singer and actor. Starred with Jeanette MacDonald in films such as *Rose Marie* and *Maytime*.

Gorham, Jabez (1792–1869). Silversmith and founder of the Gorham Manufacturing Company.

Hopkins, Esek (1718–1802). First commodore of the new Continental Navy in 1775.

Lajoie, Napolean (1875–1959). Hall of Fame baseball player. He hit .422 in 1901, the highest batting average in AL history.

Lovecraft, H. P. (1890–1937). uthor of horror and fantasy fiction stories, originally published in *Weird Tales* magazine.

Perleman, S. J. (1904–1979). Humorist. Writer of scripts for Marx Brothers films and books such as *Westward Ho*.

Woodcock, Leonard (b. 1911). President of the United Auto Workers from 1970 to 1977 and Ambassador to China (1979–1981).

Distribution of Income

The per capita income for the state of Rhode Island (current dollars) was $20,299 in 1992. This is a 112.0 percent increase from $9,576 in 1980. Income is greatest in the eastern counties of Bristol and Newport. Rhode Island has a well developed shellfish and fishing industry.

Per Capita Income (000s) (Current Dollars)

- $16.0 to 19.9
- $20.0 to 35.2

Population Profile

Rank. Rhode Island ranks 43d among U.S. states in terms of population with 1,000,000 citizens.

Minority Population. The state's minority population is 10.7 percent. The state's male to female ratio for 1990 was 92.25 males for every 100 females. It was below the national average of 95.22 males for every 100 females.

Growth. Growing slower than the projected

Government

Capital: Providence (established 1900).

Statehood: Became 13th state on May 29, 1790.

Number of Counties: 5.

Supreme Court Justices: 5, life term.

State Senators: 50, 2-year term.

State Legislators: 100, 2-year term.

United States Senators: 2.

United States Representatives: 2.

Electoral Votes: 4.

State Constitution: Adopted 1986.

national average, the state's population is expected to reach 1.1 million by the year 2010 *(see graph above)*.

Older Citizens. The state's population older than 65 was 150,547 in 1990. It grew 18.61% from 126,922 in 1980.

Younger Citizens. The number of children (under 18 years of age) was 226 thousand in 1990. This represents 22.5 percent of the state's population. The state's school aged population was 136 thousand in 1990. It is expected to increase to 150 thousand by the year 2000. This represents a 10.29% change.

Urban/Rural. 86.0% of the population of the state live in urban areas while 14.0% live in rural areas.

Largest Cities. Rhode Island has six cities with a population greater than 35,000. The populations of the state's largest centers are (starting from the most populous) Providence (160,728), Warwick (85,427), Cranston (76,060), Pawtucket (72,644), East Providence (50,380), Woonsocket (43,877), North Providence (32,090), West Warwick (29,268), Newport (28,227), Bristol (21,625), Central Falls (17,637), Westerly (16,477), Barrington (15,849), and Valley Falls (11,175).

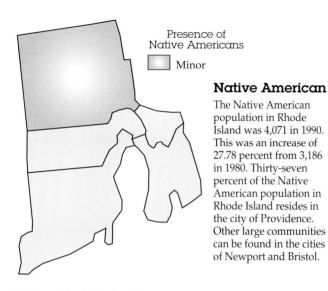

Presence of
Native Americans

▨ Minor

Native American

The Native American population in Rhode Island was 4,071 in 1990. This was an increase of 27.78 percent from 3,186 in 1980. Thirty-seven percent of the Native American population in Rhode Island resides in the city of Providence. Other large communities can be found in the cities of Newport and Bristol.

Nationalities

African	11,888
American	20,994
Arab	4,488
Austrian	1,692
Czech	1,088
Dutch	3,718
English	104,224
Finnish	937
German	48,445
Greek	4,724
Hungarian	1,640
Irish	140,661
Italian	164,509
Norwegian	2,314
Polish	31,298
Portuguese	76,773
Russian	8,930
Scottish	13,875
Slovak	1,441
Swedish	14,056
Welsh	1,501
West Indian	1,971

African American

The African American population in Rhode Island was 38,861 in 1990. This was an increase of 42.03 percent from 27,361 in 1980. Sixty-one percent of the African American population in Rhode Island resides in the city of Providence. Other large communities can be found in the cities of Newport and Bristol.

Percent of
County Population

▢ 0.00 to 1.99%
▨ 2.00 to 4.99%
▨ 5.00 to 9.99%

Statewide Ethnic Composition

Over 91 percent of the population of Rhode Island is white. The largest nationalities in this racial group are Italian, Irish, and English. The next largest group is Hispanics, followed by African Americans, Asian Americans, and Native Americans. Only 21,000 people claim to be American and acknowledge no other nationality.

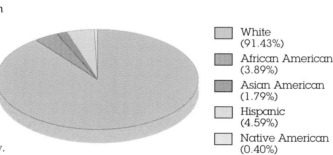

☐ White (91.43%)
☐ African American (3.89%)
☐ Asian American (1.79%)
☐ Hispanic (4.59%)
☐ Native American (0.40%)

Hispanic[††]

The Hispanic population in Rhode Island was 45,752 in 1990. This is an increase of 132.16 percent from 19,707 persons in 1980. Fifty-five percent of the Hispanic population lives in the city of Providence. Other large communities can be found in the cities of Newport and Bristol.

Percent of
County Population

☐ 0.00 to 0.99%
☐ 1.00 to 2.99%
☐ 3.00 to 9.99%

[††]A person of Mexican, Puerto Rican, Cuban, or other Spanish culture or origin regardless of race.

Education Facts

Total Students 1990: 135,729

Number of School Districts: 37

Expenditure Per Capita on Education 1990: $827

Expenditure Per Capita K–12 1990: $806

Expenditure Per Pupil 1990: $6,989

Total School Enrollment 1990–1991: 137,946

Rank of Expenditures Per Student: 4th in the U.S.

African American Enrollment: 6.4%

Hispanic Enrollment: 5.9%

Asian/Pacific Islander Enrollment: 3.2%

Native American Enrollment: 0.4%

Mean SAT Score 1991 Verbal: 421

Mean SAT Score 1991 Math: 459

Average Teacher's Salary 1992: $36,000

Rank Teacher's Salary: 11th in U.S.

High School Graduates 1990: 7,800

Total Number of Public Schools: 294

Number of Teachers 1990: 9,514

Student/Teacher Ratio: 14.5

Staff Employed in Public Schools: 15,184

Pupil/Staff Ratio: 8.9

Staff/Teacher Ratio: 1.6

Education

Attainment: 72.7 percent of population 25 years or older were high school graduates in 1989, earning Rhode Island a ranking of 40th in the United States; 20.2 percent of the state's population had completed college. Institutions of Higher Education: The largest universities and colleges in the state include University of Rhode Island (founded 1892), Kingston; Rhode Island College (founded 1854), Providence; Brown University (founded 1770), Providence; Providence College, Providence; Rhode Island School of Design, Providence. Expenditures per Student: Expenditure increased 62.9% between 1985 and 1990. Projected High School Graduations: 1998 (10,123), 2004 (10,589); Total Revenues for Education from Federal Sources: $30 million; Total Revenues for Education from State Sources: $298 million; Total Revenues for Education from Local Sources: $354 million; Average Annual Salaries for Public School Principals: $42,882.

Asian American

The Asian American population in Rhode Island was 18,325 in 1990. This is an increase of 189.81 percent from 6,323 persons in 1980. Fifty-two percent of the Asian American population lives in the city of Providence. Other large communities can be found in the cities of Newport and Bristol.

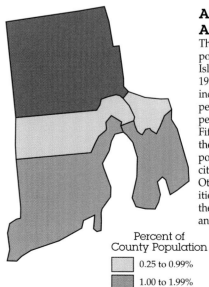

Percent of
County Population

☐ 0.25 to 0.99%
▨ 1.00 to 1.99%
▨ 2.00 to 4.99%

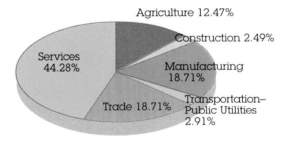

Major manufacturing areas
Major agricultural areas

Agriculture

Rhode Island has 0.06 million farm acres. During the last 40 years, Rhode Island's farms have grown larger in size and fewer in number. In 1955, 2,000 farms were found in the state. Today, 700 remain.

Agriculture adds less than $500 million to the state's gross product annually. The principal commodities in order of marketing receipts are greenhouse, dairy products, eggs, and potatoes.

Greenhouse and nursery products account for about two-thirds of Rhode Island's farm income. Sod, ornamental trees, and shrubs are the primary products. Milk is the second leading agricultural commodity and is produced throughout the state. Potatoes are also important and found mainly in southern Rhode Island. Apples are the most important fruit.

Transportation

Water transport has been important to the state of Rhode Island, especially from the colonial era to the middle of the 19th century. Although not as important as they once were, Providence and Newport are still the major ports for Rhode Island. Rhode Island's network of highways and roads covers only about 6,300 miles. Despite being the smallest state, Rhode Island is served by two major interstates, I-95 and I-295, which goes around Providence.

The first railroad in Rhode Island began running in 1835. Currently, two freight rail lines serve the state. Amtrak and other passenger rail lines serve 10 cities. The city of Warwick is home to Rhode Island's busiest airport, the Theodore Francis Green State Airport.

Energy and Transportation Facts

Energy. Yearly Consumption: 215 tril. BTUs (residential, 27.9%; commercial, 21.4%; industrial, 23.3%; transportation, 27.0%); Annual Energy Expenditures Per Capita: $1,747; Nuclear Power Plants Located in State: 0; Source of Energy Consumed: Petroleum— 61.3%; Natural Gas— 37.3%; Coal— 0.0%; Hydroelectric Power—1.3%; Nuclear Power—0.0%.

Transportation. Highway Miles: 6,120 (interstates, 70; urban, 4,597; rural, 1,523); Average Yearly Auto Insurance: $837 (6th); Auto Fatalities Rank: 48th; Registered Motor Vehicles: 622,025; Workers in Carpools: 15.5%; Workers Using Public Trans: 2.5%.

Employment

Employment. Rhode Island employed 472,000 people in 1993. Most work in social and personal services (135,000 persons or 28.6% of the workforce). Manufacturing accounts for 18.5% or 87,500 workers. Wholesale and retail trade account for 19.7% or 93,200 workers. Government employs 61,400 workers (13.0%). Construction employs 11,900 workers (2.5%). Transportation and utilities account for 3.0% or 14,200 persons. Agriculture employs 6,100 workers or 1.3%. Finance, real estate, and insurance account for 5.3% or 25,200 workers. Mining employs 200 people and accounts for less than 0.1% of the workforce.

Unemployment. Unemployment has increased to 7.7% in 1993 from a rate of 4.9% in 1985. Today's figure is higher than the national average of 6.8% as shown below.

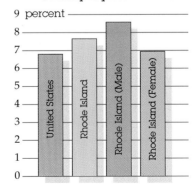

Housing

Owner Occupied Units: 414,572; Average Age of Units: 40 years; Average Value of Housing Units: $133,500; Renter Occupied Units: 152,032; Median Monthly Rent: $489; Housing Starts: 3,000; Existing Home Sales: 11,000.

Economic Facts

Gross State Product: $19,000,000,000 (1989)

Income Per Capita: $20,299

Disposable Personal Income: $17,863

Median Household Income: $32,181

Average Annual Pay, 1988: $23,082

Principal Industries: primary metals, jewelry, silverware, fabricated metal products, rubber, plastics

Major Crops: greenhouse products, potatoes, nursery stock

Fish: Bluefish, Flounder, Bass, Lobster, Clams, Eels

Livestock: Poultry

Non-Fuel Minerals: Granite, Limestone, Sandstone

Organic Fuel Minerals: N/A

Civilian Labor Force: 513,000 (Women: 241,000)

Total Employed: 469,000 (Women: 223,000)

Median Value of Housing: $133,500

Median Contract Rent: $489 per month

Economic Sectors 1992

Agriculture 12.47%
Construction 2.49%
Services 44.28%
Manufacturing 18.71%
Trade 18.71%
Transportation–Public Utilities 2.91%

Manufacturing

Manufacturing has a long history in Rhode Island. Ships were built in the state during the colonial period; however, their manufacturing importance has declined. Today, manufacturing provides 24 percent of the state's gross product. Jewelry production is the state's leading manufacturing industry. Other manufacturing activities include the production of fabricated metal goods and electrical equipment.

Providence, Rhode Island's capital, is one of the largest producers of jewelry, especially costume jewelry, in the United States. Silverware is also produced in Providence. Facilities throughout the state manufacture metal products such as bolts and pipe fittings. Electrical equipment, including radios, is manufactured in Portsmouth.

SOUTH CAROLINA
The State of South Carolina

Official State Seal

The Great Seal of South Carolina was adopted in 1776. It represents South Carolina's struggle for independence. The left shield contains a palmetto tree and an oak. The right shield is a depiction of Hope walking along a weapon-covered beach. The state mottoes, *"Animis Opibusque Parati"* (Prepared in Mind and Resources) and *"Dum Spiro Spero,"* (While I Breathe I Hope).

Legal Holidays

January: New Year's Day—1st; Robert E. Lee's Birthday—19th; February: Presidents' Day—3d Monday; April: Attack on Fort Sumter Anniversary —12th; May: Confederate Memorial Day—10th; Ratification Day—23rd; Memorial Day—4th Monday; June: Jefferson Davis' Birthday—3rd; July: Independence Day 4th; September: Labor Day—1st Monday; October: Columbus Day—2nd Monday; November: Veterans' Day—11th; Thanks-giving—4th Thursday; December: Christmas—25th.

Official State Flag

The official state flag was adopted in 1861 after South Carolina seceded from the Union. The palmetto tree represents a Revolutionary War battle involving a fort built out of palmetto trees. The blue field and the white crescent were present before the addition of the palmetto tree.

Festivals and Events

January: Southeastern Wildlife Exposition, Charleston; March: Canadian American Days Fest, Myrtle Beach; April: Southern Plant/Floral Fest, Florence; May: Greek Spring Festival, Charleston; Hartscapades, Hartsville; Fest-I-Fun, Fort Mill; Low Country Shrimp Fest, McClellanville; June: Pee Dee Summer Jamboree, Florence; Sun Fun Fest, Myrtle Beach; July: A Day in France, Lake City; Hillbilly Day, Mountain Rest; August: South Carolina Peanut Party, Pelion; September: Scottish Games & Highland Gathering, Charleston; Golden Leaf Festival, Mullins; October: Oktoberfest, Walhalla; Fall Fiesta of the Arts, Sumter; Gopher Hill Fest, Ridgeland; November: South Carolina Bluegrass Fest, Myrtle Beach; Christmas Connection, Myrtle Beach.

South Carolina Compared to States in Its Region.

Resident Pop. in Metro Areas: 5th; Pop. Percent Increase: 4th; Pop. Over 65: 5th; Infant Mortality: 2d; School Enroll. Increase: 7th; High School Grad. and Up: 7th; Violent Crime: 2d; Hazardous Waste Sites: 2d; Unemployment: 6th; Median Household Income: 7th; Persons Below Poverty: 2d; Energy Costs Per Person: 4th.

South Atlantic Region

	Population	Capital
Delaware	700,000	Dover
Maryland	4,965,000	Annapolis
Washington DC	578,000	—
Virginia	6,491,000	Richmond
West Virginia	1,820,000	Charleston
North Carolina	6.,945,000	Raleigh
South Carolina	3,643,000	Columbia
Georgia	6,917,000	Atlanta
Florida	13,679,000	Tallahassee

South Carolina's Finances

Households: 1,258,000; Income Per Capita Current Dollars: $15,989; Change Per Capita Income 1980 to 1992: 111.6% (17th in U.S.); State Expenditures: $7,969,000,000; State Revenues: $7,862,000,000; Personal Income Tax: 2.5 to 7%; Federal Income Taxes Paid Per Capita: $1,334; Sales Tax: 5% (prescription drugs exempt).

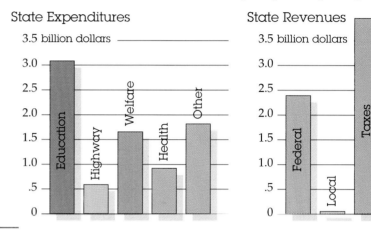

State Expenditures

State Revenues

Location, Size, and Boundaries

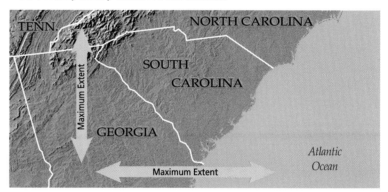

Location. South Carolina is located in the southern United States in what is known as the South Atlantic region. It is bounded on three of four sides by land with a general coast along the Atlantic Ocean in the southeast. The geographic center of South Carolina is lat. 33° 49.8' N; long. 80° 52.4' W.

Size. South Carolina is the 40th largest state in terms of size. Its area is 31,055 sq. mi. (80,433 km2). Inland water covers 830 sq. mi. (2,150 km2). South Carolina touches the Atlantic Ocean along a 187 mile coastline.

Boundaries. North Carolina, 327 mi. (526 km); Atlantic Ocean, 187 mi. (301 km); Georgia, 310 mi. (499 km).

Geographic Extent. The north/south extent is 210 mi. (338 km). The state extends 273 mi. (439 km) to the east/west.

Facts about South Carolina. Origin of Name: After King Charles I of England; Nickname: The Palmetto State; Motto: "Prepared in mind and resources" and "While I breathe, I hope"; Abbreviations: S.C. (traditional), SC (postal); State Bird: cardinal; State Tree: palmetto; State Flower: Carolina jessamine; State Song: "Carolina," words by Henry Timrod and music by Mrs. Anne Custis Burgess.

South Carolina Compared to Other States. Resident Pop. in Metro Areas: 25th; Pop. Per. Increase: 16th; Pop. Over 65: 37th; Infant Mortality: 3d; School Enroll. Increase: 21st; High School Grad. and Up: 43d; Violent Crime: 5th; Haz. Waste Sites: 15th; Unemployment: 35th; Median Household Income: 35th; Persons Below Poverty: 14th; Energy Costs Per Person: 21st.

Sources of Information. Tourism/Government: Division of Tourism, P.O. Box 71, Columbia, SC 29202. History: South Carolina Department of Archives and History, P.O. Box 11669, 1430 Senate Street, Columbia, SC 29211.

Legend

⭐ State capitol
◉ Cities over 35,000 population
○ Other significant cities
● County Seats
■ Major cultural attractions
▪ State Parks
Ⓦ Welcome Centers
⚑ Major colleges and universities

Major Cities

City	Grid	City	Grid	City	Grid
Aiken	G-5	Goose Creek	I-10	N. Augusta	G-4
Anderson	D-2	Greenville	C-3	N. Charleston	I-10
Cayce	F-7	Greenwood	E-4	Orangeburg	G-7
Charleston	J-10	Hanahan	I-10	Rock Hill	B-7
Clemson	C-2	Hilton Head I.	K-8	Simpsonville	C-3
Columbia	E-7	Irmo	E-6	Spartanburg	B-4
Dentsville	E-7	Ladson	I-10	Summerville	I-9
Easley	C-2	Mauldin	C-3	Sumter	F-9
Florence	E-10	Mt. Pleasant	I-10	Taylors	B-3
Gaffney	B-5	Myrtle Beach	F-13	W. Columbia	F-7

■ Andrew Jackson Historical State Park. Site of the birth of President Andrew Jackson. (B-7)

■ Chattooga National Wild and Scenic River. Excellent rapids for whitewater rafting and canoeing. (C-1)

■ Cheraw. Site of many historic buildings including a church built in 1768. (C-10)

■ Congaree Swamp National Monument. Scenic rivers for canoeing. Also includes nature trails. (F-7)

■ Cowpens National Battlefield Site. Revolutionary War battle where Daniel Morgan defeated British troops in 1781. (A-4)

■ Fort Moultrie. Site of the first military victory for the patriots in the American Revolution (1776). (J-10)

■ Fort Sumter National Monument. The site of the first battle of the American Civil War. (J-10)

■ Givhans Ferry State Park. Scenic park with an old Indian path. Also includes fishing and picnicking areas. (I-9)

■ Hunting Island State Park. Sand beaches, surf and beach houses for swimming or sunning. Also has a lighthouse on a barrier island. (K-8)

■ Huntington Beach State Park. Sand beaches and surf for swimming and sunning. Also has a children's playground. (G-12)

■ Kings Mountain State Park. In 1780, the British lost a battle to the Americans at this site during the Revolutionary War. (B-6)

■ Lake Murray. A 41-mile (66-kilometer) reservoir formed by Saluda Dam; that provides fine fishing and boating. (E-6)

■ Lee State Park. Park activities include horseback riding, swimming, boating, and fishing. (E-9)

■ Myrtle Beach State Park. Sand beaches and surf for swimming and sunning. Also includes a fishing pier. (G-13)

■ Oconee State Park. Boating, water skiing, and other water sports. Also has hiking trails. (C-1)

■ Old Dorchester State Park. Site of a colonial town built in the 1690s which is now in ruins. (I-9)

■ Parris Island. The United States Marine Corps Recruit Depot. (K-8)

■ Pleasant Ridge State Park. Boating, water skiing, and other water sports. Also has hiking trails. (B-3)

■ Santee State Park. Lakeside swimming and fishing. (G-8)

■ Sesquicentennial State Park. 150th anniversary memorial to the city of Columbia. (E-7)

■ Table Rock State Park. Camping and picnicking in a scenic environment. (B-2)

Scale

0   15   30   45 mi.

15   0   15   30   45   60 km

Weather Facts

Record High Temperature: 111° F (44° C) on June 28, 1954, at Camden; Record Low Temperature: -20° F (-29° C) on January 18, 1977, at Caesars Head; Average January Temperature: 45° F (7° C); Average July Temperature: 81° F (27° C); Average Yearly Precipitation: 47 in. (119 cm).

Environmental Facts

Air Pollution Rank: 12th; Water Pollution Rank: 23d; Total Yearly Industrial Pollution: 67,924,618 lbs.; Industrial Pollution Rank: 14th; Hazardous Waste Sites: 23; Hazardous Sites Rank: 15th; Landfill Capacity: overextended; Fresh Water Supply: large surplus; Daily Residential Water Consumption: 126 gals. per capita; Endangered Species: Aquatic Species (1)—sturgeon, shortnose; Birds (7)—eagle, bald; Mammals (3)—cougar, eastern; Other Species (2)—snake, eastern indigo; Plants (21)—amaranth, seabeach.

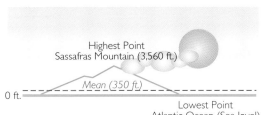

Highest Point
Sassafras Mountain (3,560 ft.)

Mean (350 ft)

0 ft.

Lowest Point
Atlantic Ocean (Sea level)

Average Monthly Weather

Charleston	Jan	Feb	Mar	Apr	May	Jun	Jul	Aug	Sep	Oct	Nov	Dec	Yearly
Maximum Temperature °F	58.8	61.2	68.0	76.0	82.9	87.0	89.4	88.8	84.6	76.8	68.7	61.4	75.3
Minimum Temperature °F	36.9	38.4	45.3	52.5	61.4	68.0	71.6	71.2	66.7	54.7	44.6	38.5	54.2
Days of Precipitation	9.7	8.9	10.1	7.4	8.9	10.9	13.4	12.6	9.5	5.9	7.0	8.4	112.8

Land Use

Cropland: 19%; Pasture: 6.6%; Rangeland: 0%; Forest: 62.3%; Urban: 7.9%; Other: 4.2%.

Flora and Fauna

The state of South Carolina is approximately two-thirds covered with forests. Most of the trees found in the state are hardwoods such as oak, maple, and hickory. Spanish moss often hangs from oak trees. Pine and hemlock, two softwoods, also grow in the state. Subtropical plants such as yucca and palmetto grow along coastal areas of South Carolina. The wild Venus fly-trap grows only in the Carolinas. Other plants growing in the state include azaleas and mountain laurels.

Alligators and black bears live in the southern, swampy areas of South Carolina. White-tailed deer roam throughout the state. South Carolina's smaller animals include fox squirrels, wildcats, and cottontail rabbits. Few states have more different kinds of birds than South Carolina, which has over 450 species. Wild turkeys, quail, ducks, and mourning doves are all represented. An abundance of sea life lives along South Carolina's coast. Sea turtles, bottle-nosed dolphins, and even sperm whales swim offshore. More than 340 kinds of fishes swim in coastal waters; freshwater fish include bream and rockfish.

Topography

There are several distinct topographic regions in South Carolina. The Atlantic Coastal Plain physical region is largely low and flat and occupies the southeastern portion of South Carolina, an area that includes about two-thirds of the state. This region is divided into two distinct subtypes. The outer coastal plain extends from the Atlantic Ocean westward approximately 50 miles inland (80 km). The terrain includes beaches, swamps, and marshland as well as many islands off the coast. The three largest are Pawleyís Island, Edisto Island, and Hilton Head Island. The rest of the region, known as the Inner Coastal Plain, is more hilly and gradually gains elevation as it runs northwest to the Piedmont Plateau. Coastal Plain soil is warm and wet with a thin organically rich surface that varies from light to dark The fall line separates the Coastal Plain and the Piedmont, and denotes where fast-running streams slow as they reach flatter ground.

The Piedmont physical region covers most of the northwestern third of the state. This region continues to rise in a northwest direction, reaching elevations of over 1,200 ft. (370 m) in the west. The soil of the Piedmont is a warm and moist red/yellow clay with a low organic component. In the northwest corner of South Carolina lies the Blue Ridge physical region, a part of the Appalachian Mountains of the eastern United States. These mountains are of relatively modest elevation in South Carolina, the highest point being Sassafras Mountain at 3,560 ft. (1,084 m) above sea level. Blue Ridge soil is similar to that of the Piedmont.

Environmental Quality

South Carolina residents generate 3.9 million tons of solid waste each year, or approximately 2,200 pounds per capita. Landfill capacity in South Carolina will be exhausted in more than 12 years. The state has 23 hazardous waste sites. Annual greenhouse gas emissions in South Carolina total 60.5 million tons, or 17.4 tons per capita. Industrial sources in South Carolina release approximately 42.8 thousand tons of toxins, 360.1 thousand tons of acid precipitation-producing substances, and 1.5 million tons of smog-producing substances into the atmosphere each year.

The state has 21,000 acres within the National Park System. Noteworthy is the Congaree Swamp National Monument. State parks cover just over 78,000 acres, attracting 8.0 million visitors per year.

South Carolina spends 1.2 percent of its budget, or approximately $21 per capita, on environmental and natural resources. South Carolina representatives in the U.S. House voted in favor of national environmental legislation 61 percent of the time, while U.S. senators did so 33 percent of the time.

For more information about South Carolina's environment, contact the Department of Health and Environmental Control, J. Marion Sims Bldg., 2600 Bull St., Columbia, SC 29201.

Physical Regions: (a) Atlantic Coastal Plain; (b) Piedmont; (c) Blue Ridge.

Climate

South Carolina's pleasant weather is the result of its subtropical climate. Summers are generally hot and humid, while winter weather is mild. Charleston, in the south, has mean January and July temperatures of 51 degrees F and 81 degrees F. Meanwhile in Greenville, in northwest South Carolina, January and July temperatures average 42 degrees F and 71 degrees F, respectively. The Gulf Stream of the Atlantic Ocean keeps ocean water temperature relatively warm. During the summer, ocean temperature frequently stays above 80 degrees F. South Carolina's yearly precipitation averages 45 inches. However, the more mountainous northwest averages slightly higher amounts (around 60 inches). Places like Barnwell, in the southwest, receive the lightest precipitation, only about 38 inches a year.

Being a coastal state, South Carolina is occasionally hit by hurricanes. In 1991, Hurricane Hugo caused millions of dollars of damage in the Myrtle Beach vicinity.

Hydrology

Several large rivers flow southeast through the state, emptying into the Atlantic Ocean. The Broad and Saluda rivers drain much of northwest and north-central South Carolina before joining at Columbia to form the Congaree. The Congaree then joins the Wateree, which flows through central South Carolina, at Lake Marion. The Santee then flows out of Lake Marion and into the Atlantic. The next largest river is the Pee Dee in the north. Others include the Edisto and the Salkehatchie in the south. The Savannah River forms South Carolina's southwest border with Georgia.

All of the large lakes in South Carolina are man-made. The largest is Lake Marion, covering about 165 sq. miles (427 sq. km). Others include Lake Moultrie, just southeast of Lake Marion; Lakes Murray and Greenwood on the Saluda; and Lake Keowee in the state's northwest corner.

South Carolina's History

South Carolina's First People

The first humans came to South Carolina approximately eleven thousand years ago. These early inhabitants were a predominantly hunting and gathering society, but later developed agricultural practices sometime around 1000 B.C.

Around A.D. 1000, the Mississippian group of people came to the South Carolina area. The most advanced culture of pre-Columbian people, the Mississippian group constructed a rather complex civilization. They were also Mound Builders, like the similar culture found in Ohio. Despite their high level of society, the Mississippian people disappeared shortly before Europeans came to South Carolina.

By around 1600, some twenty thousand native people from two to three dozen individual tribes could be found living in present-day South Carolina, representing three distinct language families: Iroquoian, Siouan, and Muskogean. Major tribes included the Cherokee, Catawba, and Yamasee peoples. By 1800, virtually all of South Carolina's Native American population had been resettled to the west.

European Exploration

In 1521, the first Europeans, a band of Spaniards from Santo Domingo led by Francisco Gordillo, came to explore South Carolina. In 1526 another group of Spaniards tried to create a settlement at present-day Georgetown, but failed after only nine months. The Spanish did not settle another outpost until 1566, when they founded Santa Elena on Parris Island.

French Protestants, under the guidance of Jean Ribaut, tried to colonize the area around Port Royal in 1562, but this colony also failed.

British influence entered South Carolina when eight Englishmen were granted a charter from King Charles II of England to establish a colony in the New World. The Carolina colony, named after the king, encompassed all of both

of present-day North and South Carolina, as well as part of Georgia. In 1670, the first permanent white settlement, called Charles Town (later Charleston), was founded along the Ashley River.

Colonial Period and Statehood

Even before the American Revolution, South Carolina was reluctant to follow orders from the British colonial government. The Carolina colony was divided into North and South as a result of the upheaval between the Carolinians and the British. In 1729, North and South Carolina became two separate colonies. The border between the two was not finalized until 1815. During the colonial period, the British crown continued to govern both North and South Carolina.

During the Revolutionary War, South Carolina rallied against the British, but did not see full-fledged fighting until 1780, when the British captured Charleston. After that, South Carolina was the site of several small battles.

On May 23, 1788, South Carolina became the eighth state in the Union with the capital remaining at Columbia. Although most of the activity in the state took place along the coast, Columbia was chosen as capital to appease the settlers living in the western piedmont region.

Until the 1820s, the economy and population of South Carolina grew. However, this upward trend soon collapsed. Many South Carolina residents became increasingly dissatisfied with the way the state was governed. The dissatisfaction led to the secession of South Carolina from the United States; it was the first state to do so, on December 20, 1860. The next year the Battle of Fort Sumter commenced the Civil War. South Carolina was readmitted to the Union in 1868.

Industrialization

South Carolina began to prosper as a result of the array of crops grown in the state. In the years before the Revolutionary War, indigo and

rice became increasingly important crops. Trade centered around the port city of Charleston.

Later in the eighteenth century, cotton emerged as an important crop. The introduction of the cotton gin, invented by Eli Whitney, helped the growth of the industry. The success of cotton turned many farmers living in the piedmont into plantation owners who used slave labor to cultivate their labor intensive cash crop.

South Carolina's cotton industry helped support the development of textile mills. Located predominantly in the northwest part of the state, textile mills began to be built in South Carolina around 1880. The textile industry grew rapidly, and by 1940, three-quarters of the South Carolina workforce was employed in the textile trade.

Today, textiles remain an important component of the South Carolina economy. Other industries now located in the state include chemicals, paper products, and food crops.

Myrtle Beach and Hilton Head Island

Golfers flock to South Carolina in every season, and its pleasant climate makes Myrtle Beach a prime location for the sport. The town has many golf courses, ranging from simple par-3 courses to the more exclusive *Dunes* resort golf course. Many professional golfing events are held at Myrtle Beach. Along with golfing, Myrtle Beach is also a popular beach resort where families can go for sun and fun.

Another popular place for golfing in South Carolina is Hilton Head Island where one of the best courses in the country is located. This course, *Harbour Town Golf Links at Sea Pines Plantation*, was designed by Pete Dye and all-time golf great Jack Nicklaus. Here, professionals as well as amateurs play many challenging holes on three courses—*Harbour Town, Sea Marsh, and Ocean Course*, amidst beautiful scenery.

Important Events

1521 Francisco Gordillo, a Spaniard, explores South Carolina.

1526 Spanish set up a settlement at present-day Georgetown, but it fails after nine months.

1562 Jean Ribaut, a French Protestant, colonizes an area around Port Royal, but it fails.

1566 Spanish build Fort San Felipe at Santa Elena on Parris Island.

1670 First permanent white settlement; called Charles Town, established by the British.

1715 Yamasee War. Battles between the Yamasee Indians and colonists.

1729 North and South Carolina divide into two separate colonies.

1731 Township plan concept introduced in South Carolina by Gov. Robert Johnson.

1776 A temporary state constitution is drafted.

1778 A second constitution is drafted.

1780 The British capture Charlestown.

1780 Francis Marion attacks British positions around Charlestown.

1788 South Carolina becomes eighth state in the Union on May 23.

1801 Santee Canal opens.

1852 Charlotte and South Carolina Railroad completed.

1860 South Carolina is the first state to secede from the Union on December 20.

1861 Battle of Fort Sumter, starting Civil War, on April 12.

1868 South Carolina readmitted to the Union.

1876 End of Reconstruction era.

1880 First textile mills are built the state.

1934 Kerr-Smith Tobacco Control Act passed; decreases acreage devoted to tobacco crops.

1988 Worst drought and heat wave in forty years hits South Carolina.

1989 Hurricane severely damages the South Carolina coast.

1991 Republican senator Strom Thurmond is noted as being the oldest member of Congress at eighty-eight.

Population Projections

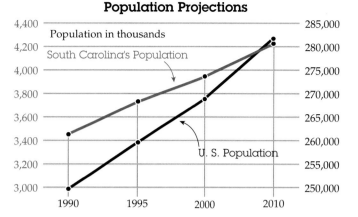

Population in thousands
South Carolina's Population
U. S. Population

	1990	1995	2000	2010

Population Change

Year	Population
1950	2,117,000
1960	2,392,000
1970	2,597,000
1980	3,121,820
1990	3,468,703
2000	3,906,000
2010	4,205,000

Period	Change
1950–1970	22.7%
1970–1980	20.2%
1980–1990	11.1%
1990–2000	12.6%

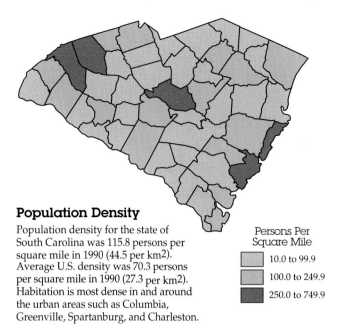

Population Density

Population density for the state of South Carolina was 115.8 persons per square mile in 1990 (44.5 per km2). Average U.S. density was 70.3 persons per square mile in 1990 (27.3 per km2). Habitation is most dense in and around the urban areas such as Columbia, Greenville, Spartanburg, and Charleston.

Persons Per Square Mile
- 10.0 to 99.9
- 100.0 to 249.9
- 250.0 to 749.9

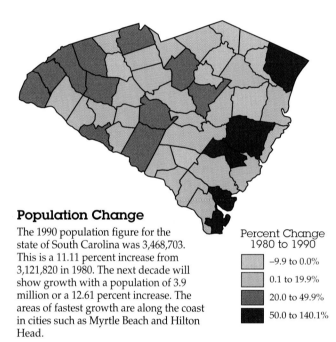

Population Change

The 1990 population figure for the state of South Carolina was 3,468,703. This is a 11.11 percent increase from 3,121,820 in 1980. The next decade will show growth with a population of 3.9 million or a 12.61 percent increase. The areas of fastest growth are along the coast in cities such as Myrtle Beach and Hilton Head.

Percent Change 1980 to 1990
- –9.9 to 0.0%
- 0.1 to 19.9%
- 20.0 to 49.9%
- 50.0 to 140.1%

Population Facts

State Population, 1993: 3,643,000

Rank: 25

Population 2000: 3,906,000 (Rank 24)

Density: 115.8 per sq. mi. (44.5 per km²)

Distribution: 54.6% urban, 45.4% rural

Population Under 5 Years Old: 7.6%

Population Under 18 Years Old: 26.2%

Population Over 65 Years Old: 11.6%

Median Age: 32.0

Number of Households: 1,258,000

Average Persons Per Household: 2.68

Average Persons Per Family: 3.16

Female Heads of Households: 5.08%

Population That Is Married: 20.47%

Birth Rate: 16.8 per 1,000 population

Death Rate: 8.5 per 1,000 population

Births to Teen Mothers: 17.1%

Marriage Rate: 15.7 per 1,000 population

Divorce Rate: 4.5 per 1,000 population

Violent Crime Rate: 973 per 100,000 pop.

Population on Social Security: 15.7%

Percent Voting for President: 45.0%

South Carolina's Famous Citizens

Byars, Betsy (b. 1928). Author of popular children's books including *The Summer of the Swans* and *The Pinballs*.

Frazier, Joe (b. 1944). Boxer. He defeated Muhammad Ali in 1972 to become the heavyweight champion of the world.

Hayne, Robert (1791–1839). U.S. Senator (1822-1832). Elected to the governorship in 1832.

Keyserling, Leon (1908–1987). Economist. He helped draft Social Security plans in 1935.

Mays, Benjamin (1894–1984). President of Morehouse College from 1940 to 1967. He was a voice of moderation in civil rights.

Smalls, Robert (1839–1915). He piloted a Confederate ship carrying slaves to the Union side in Charleston in 1862.

Thurmond, Strom (b. 1902). He was elected to the U.S. Senate in 1954 and still retains the seat.

Townes, Charles (b. 1915). Physicist. He won the Nobel Prize in 1964 for his work in developing a maser (used in atomic clocks).

Turner, Henry McNeal (1834–1915). First African-American army chaplain.

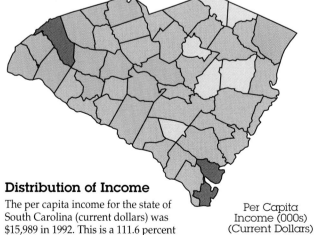

Distribution of Income

The per capita income for the state of South Carolina (current dollars) was $15,989 in 1992. This is a 111.6 percent increase from $7,558 in 1980. Income is greatest in the golfing areas of Beaufort County in the south. This is the home of Hilton Head and Harbor Town. Greenville County in the west is also an area of high incomes.

Per Capita Income (000s) (Current Dollars)
- $4.5 to 9.9
- $10.0 to 12.9
- $13.0 to 15.9
- $16.0 to 19.9

Population Profile

Rank. South Carolina ranks 25th among U.S. states in terms of population with 3,643,000 citizens.

Minority Population. The state's minority population is 31.7 percent. The state's male to female ratio for 1990 was 93.90 males for every 100 females. It was below the national average of 95.22 males for every 100 females.

Growth. Growing much faster than the

Government

Capital: Columbia (established 1790).

Statehood: Became 8th state on May 23, 1788.

Number of Counties: 46.

Supreme Court Justices: 5, 10-year term.

State Senators: 46, 4-year term.

State Legislators: 124, 2-year term.

United States Senators: 2.

United States Representatives: 6.

Electoral Votes: 8.

State Constitution: Adopted 1985.

projected national average, the state's population is expected to reach 4.2 million by the year 2010 *(see graph above).*

Older Citizens. The state's population older than 65 was 396,935 in 1990. It grew 38.15% from 287,328 in 1980.

Younger Citizens. The number of children (under 18 years of age) was 920 thousand in 1990. This represents 26.5 percent of the state's population. The state's school aged population was 620 thousand in 1990. It is expected to increase to 664 thousand by the year 2000. This represents a 7.1% change.

Urban/Rural. 54.6% of the population of the state live in urban areas while 45.4% live in rural areas.

Largest Cities. South Carolina has seven cities with a population greater than 35,000. The populations of the state's largest centers are (starting from the most populous) Columbia (98,052), Charleston (80,414), North Charleston (70,218), Greenville (58,282), Spartanburg (43,467), Sumter (41,943), Rock Hill (41,643), Mount Pleasant (30,108), Florence (29,813), Anderson (26,184), St. Andrews (25,692), Myrtle Beach (24,848), Goose Creek (24,692), and Hilton Head Island (23,694).

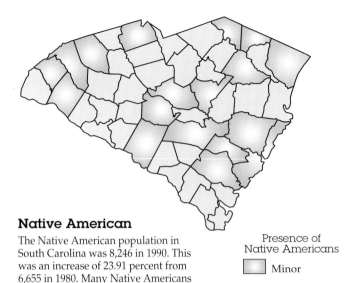

Native American

The Native American population in South Carolina was 8,246 in 1990. This was an increase of 23.91 percent from 6,655 in 1980. Many Native Americans can be found in South Carolina's major cities, such as Charleston, Columbia, Greenville, and Spartanburg.

Presence of Native Americans

☐ Minor

Nationalities

African	5,368
American	363,795
Arab	4,738
Austrian	2,179
Czech	2,798
Dutch	33,683
English	334,658
Finnish	1,276
German	402,001
Greek	6,771
Hungarian	4,071
Irish	313,159
Italian	39,664
Norwegian	5,473
Polish	19,997
Portuguese	1,578
Russian	4,203
Scottish	54,375
Slovak	4,390
Swedish	11,389
Welsh	10,009
West Indian	2,496

African American

The African American population in South Carolina was 1,039,884 in 1990. This was an increase of 9.70 percent from 947,969 in 1980. The counties with the highest percentage of African Americans run north to south through the center of the state, with very few counties having less than 25 percent.

Percent of County Population

■ 5.00 to 9.99%
■ 10.00 to 24.99%
■ 25.00 to 86.24%

Statewide Ethnic Composition

Over 69 percent of the population of South Carolina is white. The largest nationalities in this racial group are German, English, and Irish. The next largest group is African Americans, who make up almost 30 percent of the population. Over 363,000 people claim to be American and acknowledge no other nationality.

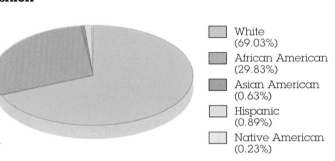

☐ White (69.03%)
☐ African American (29.83%)
☐ Asian American (0.63%)
☐ Hispanic (0.89%)
☐ Native American (0.23%)

Education Facts

Total Students 1990: 616,177

Number of School Districts: 91

Expenditure Per Capita on Education 1990: $678

Expenditure Per Capita K–12 1990: $605

Expenditure Per Pupil 1990: $3,843

Total School Enrollment 1990–1991: 622,618

Rank of Expenditures Per Student: 41st in the U.S.

African American Enrollment: 41.1%

Hispanic Enrollment: 0.3%

Asian/Pacific Islander Enrollment: 0.6%

Native American Enrollment: 0.1%

Mean SAT Score 1991 Verbal: 395

Mean SAT Score 1991 Math: 437

Average Teacher's Salary 1992: $28,300

Rank Teacher's Salary: 37th in U.S.

High School Graduates 1990: 34,000

Total Number of Public Schools: 1,103

Number of Teachers 1990: 36,625

Student/Teacher Ratio: 17.0

Staff Employed in Public Schools: 63,333

Pupil/Staff Ratio: 9.7

Staff/Teacher Ratio: 1.7

Hispanic[††]

The Hispanic population in South Carolina was 30,551 in 1990. This is a decrease of -8.60 percent from 33,426 persons in 1980. Most of the Hispanic population is located in the eastern coastal counties of the state.

Percent of County Population

☐ 0.00 to 0.99%
☐ 1.00 to 2.99%

[††]A person of Mexican, Puerto Rican, Cuban, or other Spanish culture or origin regardless of race.

Education

Attainment: 69.8 percent of population 25 years or older were high school graduates in 1989, earning South Carolina a ranking of 44th the United States; 16.6 percent of the state's population had completed college. Institutions of Higher Education: The largest universities and colleges in the state include University of South Carolina , Columbia; Clemson University, Clemson; Winthrop College, Rock Hill; The Citadel, Charleston; South Carolina State College, Orangeburg; Medical University of South Carolina, Charleston; College of Charleston (founded 1770), Charleston. Expenditures per Student: Expenditure increased 77% between 1985 and 1990. Projected High School Graduations: 1998 (38,734), 2004 (37,902); Total Revenues for Education from Federal Sources: $185 million; Total Revenues for Education from State Sources: $1.2 billion; Total Revenues for Education from Local Sources: $807 million; Average Annual Salaries for Public School Principals: $42,537; Largest School Districts in State: Greenville County School District, 50,876 students, 63d in the United States, Charleston County School District, 42,893, 79th.

Asian American

The Asian American population in South Carolina was 22,382 in 1990. This is an increase of 78.09 percent from 12,568 persons in 1980. The largest percentage of Asian Americans can be found in Williamsburg County in the eastern part of the state.

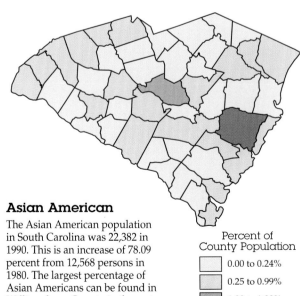

Percent of County Population

☐ 0.00 to 0.24%
☐ 0.25 to 0.99%
☐ 1.00 to 1.99%
■ 2.00 to 4.99%

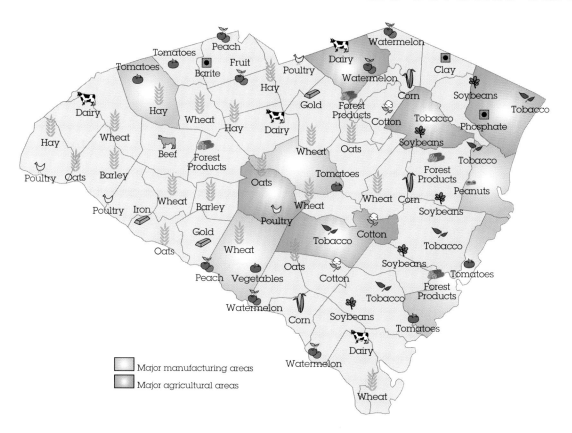

Major manufacturing areas

Major agricultural areas

Transportation

The state of South Carolina has approximately 63,000 miles of roads and highways; almost three-quarters of these are paved. South Carolina has two major interstates: I-95, which runs north to south, and I-26, which goes from northwest to southeast.

Both passenger and freight rail lines serve South Carolina. Amtrak serves five cities with passenger service. Seven different freight lines, including the Seaboard System Railroad and Southern Railway, carry goods. South Carolina has two major seaports, Charleston and Georgetown. The Atlantic Intracoastal Waterway is the primary water transportation route. South Carolina has many airports located throughout the state. Major airports include those located in Charleston and Columbia. The Myrtle Beach jetport handles much of the tourist air traffic.

Energy and Transportation Facts

Energy. Yearly Consumption: 1,209 tril. BTUs (residential, 19.9%; commercial, 13.4%; industrial, 40.9%; transportation, 25.8%); Annual Energy Expenditures Per Capita: $1,921; Nuclear Power Plants Located in State: 7; Source of Energy Consumed: Petroleum— 30.8%; Natural Gas— 10.3%; Coal—22.0%; Hydroelectric Power—2.0%; Nuclear Power—34.9%.

Transportation. Highway Miles: 64,129 (interstates, 810; urban, 10,517; rural, 53,612); Average Yearly Auto Insurance: $528 (27th); Auto Fatalities Rank: 9th; Registered Motor Vehicles: 2,600,929; Workers in Carpools: 22.5%; Workers Using Public Trans: 1.1%.

Employment

Employment. South Carolina employed 1.68 million people in 1993. Most work in manufacturing (373,600 persons or 22.2% of the workforce). Social and personal services account for 19.7% or 332,400 workers. Wholesale and retail trade account for 20.8% or 351,100 workers. Government employs 296,700 workers (17.6%). Construction employs 81,800 workers (4.9%). Transportation and utilities account for 3.9% or 66,300 persons. Agriculture employs 37,100 workers or 2.2%. Finance, real estate, and insurance account for 3.9% or 65,800 workers. Mining employs 1,800 people and accounts for only 0.1% of the workforce.

Unemployment. Unemployment increased to 7.5% from a rate of 6.8% in 1985. Today's figure is higher than the national average of 6.8% as shown below.

Agriculture

South Carolina has 5.1 million farm acres. During the last 40 years, South Carolina's farms have grown larger in size and fewer in number. In 1955, 124,000 farms were found in the state. Today, 24,300 remain.

Agriculture adds $1 billion to the state's gross product annually. The principal commodities in order of marketing receipts are tobacco, broilers, cattle, and soybeans.

Crops and livestock products each account for about 49 percent of South Carolina's farm income, with tobacco being the leading product. Most of the tobacco is produced in the state's northeastern region. The northwest is home to most of the dairy and cattle farms. Soybeans, the second leading crop, are found in most parts of the state. Other important crops include cotton, peaches, hay, and wheat.

Housing

Owner Occupied Units: 1,424,155; Average Age of Units: 23 years; Average Value of Housing Units: $61,100; Renter Occupied Units: 368,861; Median Monthly Rent: $376; Housing Starts: 23,500; Existing Home Sales: 62,200.

Economic Facts

Gross State Product: $60,000,000,000 (1989)

Income Per Capita: $15,989

Disposable Personal Income: $14,318

Median Household Income: $26,256

Average Annual Pay, 1988: $20,439

Principal Industries: rubber and plastic products, machinery, electrical equipment, textiles, chemicals, paper products

Major Crops: tobacco, eggs, milk, wheat, soybeans, cotton, peaches

Fish: Shrimp, Clams, Crab, Oysters, Swordfish

Livestock: chickens, cattle

Non-Fuel Minerals: Kaolin, Limestone, Peat, Mica, Sand, Talc, Topaz, Granite

Organic Fuel Minerals: N/A

Civilian Labor Force: 1,744,000 (Women: 821,000)

Total Employed: 1,635,000 (Women: 772,000)

Median Value of Housing: $61,100

Median Contract Rent: $376 per month

Economic Sectors 1992

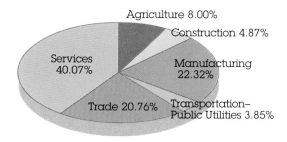

Agriculture 8.00%

Construction 4.87%

Services 40.07%

Manufacturing 22.32%

Trade 20.76%

Transportation– Public Utilities 3.85%

Manufacturing

Manufacturing has traditionally been an important part of South Carolina's economy. In fact, manufacturing employs more workers, 22.2 percent, than any other economic sector. South Carolina, like other southern states, has a large textile industry. Other manufacturing activities include chemical, paper products, and machinery production.

South Carolina is a leading textile producer. Most of the over 400 textile mills in the state are located in the northwest, in cities such as Greenville and Spartanburg. These mills produce a variety of textile goods. Charleston, on the South Carolina coast, produces many of the state's chemicals. Many of South Carolina's paper products come from the northern city of Rock Hill.

Unemployment Rate

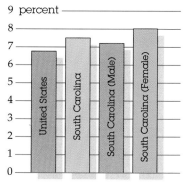

9 percent

8

7

6

5

4

3

2

1

0

United States

South Carolina

South Carolina (Male)

South Carolina (Female)

SOUTH DAKOTA
The State of South Dakota

Official State Seal

The Great Seal of South Dakota was adopted in 1889. Changes in the colors were adopted and legalized in 1961. The state motto, "Under God the People Rule," is placed in the upper edge. The seal is made up of a river with a steamboat running through it. A farmer is seen plowing his fields in the foreground. A smelting furnace is placed in the background.

Legal Holidays

January: New Year's Day—1st; February: Presidents' Day—3d Monday; May: Memorial Day—4th Monday; July: Independence Day 4th; September: Labor Day—1st Monday; October: Columbus Day—2d Monday; Pioneer's Day—13th; November: Admission Day—2d; Veterans' Day—11th; Thanksgiving—4th Thursday; December: Christmas—25th.

Official Flag

This South Dakota flag was adopted in 1909. It was originally double-sided with the state seal on the back side. In 1963 this was changed and the seal was moved to the front and placed in the center of the sun. The state nickname was changed in 1992.

Festivals and Events

January: Black Hills Stock Show/Rodeo, Rapid City; February: National Players Festival, Yankton; March: Schmeckfest, Freeman; May: Black Hills Balloon Rally, Sturgis; June: Czech Days, Tabor; Midsummer Festival, Vermillion; Sodbuster Fest, Webster; July: Gold Discovery Days, Custer; Black Hills Heritage Fest, Rapid City; August: Trainfest, Millbank; German Summerfest, Rapid City; Oahe Days, Pierre; State Fair, Huron; September: Corn Palace Fest, Mitchell; Black Hills Sawdust Fest, Spear-fish; Homesteader Harvest Festival, Brandon; October: Buffalo Round Up, Custer; November: Christmas at the Capitol, Pierre.

South Dakota Compared to States in Its Region.

Resident Pop. in Metro Areas: 7th; Pop. Percent Increase: 2d; Pop. Over 65: 2d; Infant Mortality: 1st; School Enroll. Increase: 4th; High School Grad. and Up: 5th; Violent Crime: 6th; Hazardous Waste Sites: 5th; Unemployment: 6th; Median Household Income: 7th; Persons Below Poverty: 1st; Energy Costs Per Person: 4th.

West North Central Region

	Population	Capital
Minnesota	4,517,000	St. Paul
Iowa	2,814,000	Des Moines
Missouri	5,234,000	Jefferson City
North Dakota	635,000	Bismarck
South Dakota	715,000	Pierre
Nebraska	1,607,000	Lincoln
Kansas	2,531,000	Topeka

South Dakota's Finances

Households: 259,000; Income Per Capita Current Dollars: $16,558; Change Per Capita Income 1980 to 1992: 115.0% (12th in U.S.); State Expenditures: $1,490,000,000; State Revenues: $1,518,000,000; Personal Income Tax: N/A; Federal Income Taxes Paid Per Capita: $1,395; Sales Tax: 4% (prescription drugs exempt).

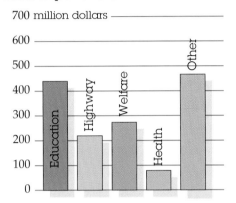

State Expenditures

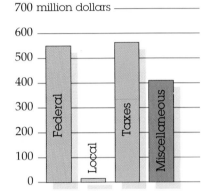

State Revenues

Location, Size, and Boundaries

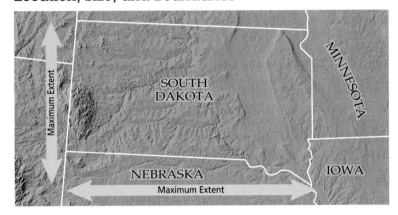

Location. South Dakota is located in the West North Central region of the United States It is bounded on four sides by land. The geographic center of South Dakota is lat. 44° 24.1' N; long. 100° 28.7' W.

Size. South Dakota is the 16th largest state in terms of size. Its area is 77,047 sq. mi. (199,551 km2). Inland water covers 1,092 sq. mi. (2,828 km2).

Boundaries. North Dakota, 361 mi. (581 km); Minnesota, 148 mi. (296 km); Iowa, 143 mi. (230 km); Nebraska, 423 mi. (681 km); Wyoming, 138 mi. (222 km); Montana, 67 mi. (108 km).

Geographic Extent. The north/south extent of South Dakota is 245 mi. (394 km). The state extends 380 mi. (610 km) to the east/west.

Facts about South Dakota. Origin of Name: After the *Sioux* Indians who called themselves *Dakota* or *Lakota*, meaning *"allies"* or *"friends"*; Nickname: The Mount Rushmore State; Motto: "Under God, people rule"; Abbreviations: S.Dak. or S.D. (traditional), SD (postal); State Bird: ring necked pheasant; State Tree: Black Hills spruce; State Flower: American pasqueflower; State Song: "Hail, South Dakota," words and music by Deecort Hammitt.

South Dakota Compared to Other States. Resident Pop. in Metro Areas: 45th; Pop. Per. Increase: 26th; Pop. Over 65: 7th; Infant Mort.: 12th; School Enroll. Increase: 26th; High School Grad. and Up: 24th; Violent Crime: 45th; Haz. Waste Sites: 45th; Unemployment: 49th; Median Household Income: 46th; Persons Below Poverty: 11th; Energy Costs Per Person: 26th.

Sources of Information. Tourism: Department of Tourism, 711 East Wells Avenue, Pierre, SD 57501. Government: Office of the Governor, 500 East Capitol Avenue, Pierre, SD 57501. History: South Dakota State Historical Society, 900 Governor's Drive, Pierre SD 57501.

South Dakota's History

South Dakota's First People

According to archaeological evidence, ancestors of modern man have lived in the South Dakota area for at least twenty-five thousand years. Around A.D. 500, a group of people known as the Mound Builders came to South Dakota and settled along the banks of the Big Sioux River. As their name suggests, a key feature of the Mound Builder culture was the great mounds of earth they constructed. Most scholars believe these huge mounds were in honor of the Mound Builders' dead.

More recent Native Americans began to live in South Dakota around the middle of the thirteenth century. These people, probably ancestors of the Arikara tribe, lived along the Missouri River, and built several fortresses there. These fortresses were huge: capable of holding up to five thousand people.

By the sixteenth century, the Arikara people had appeared in South Dakota. Like their predecessors, the Arikara built fortified settlements. Their villages became the core of their tribal organization, and also served as agricultural and horse-trading centers.

European Exploration

It was the French who first explored the territory containing the eventual state of South Dakota. In 1742, two French brothers, François and Louis Joseph La Vérendrye claimed land for their home country. The French remained in control of South Dakota's land until 1762, when France ceded it to Spain.

Around the time of this exchange of power, many Europeans started to pass through and trade in South Dakota. The rising European presence, coupled with the arrival of another Native American tribe, the Sioux, caused the demise of the Arikara tribe in the late 1700s. Then, after several decades of controlling the territory, Spain gave the land back to France.

But France did not keep their reacquired land for long. In 1803, the United States bought the land encompassing South Dakota as part of the Louisiana Purchase. The South Dakota area gradually filled with fur-trading posts. One such post, Fort Pierre, was founded in 1817. In 1859, following an agreement with the Yankton Sioux people, Yankton became the first permanent white settlement in South Dakota.

Territorial Period and Statehood

The Dakota Territory, containing the future North and South Dakota, was established in 1861. In 1862, a sparse population settled along the Missouri River and its tributaries.

This soon changed after the coming of the railroad and the discovery of gold.

The first railroad line, the Winona & St. Peter Railroad, crossed into South Dakota in early 1871. The discovery of gold came quite accidentally, when Maj. Gen. George Custer led an expedition into the Black Hills.

Tension between the new settlers and the native Sioux increased. Finally, in 1876, the famous Battle of the Little Bighorn occurred in what is now Montana, where General Custer and his troops were defeated by the Sioux, Cheyenne, and Arapaho. This great Native victory was short-lived, however, as the U.S. Army took the offensive in subsequent months. The defeated Native peoples of the Plains were then herded onto government reservations, and resistance was finally crushed in 1890 at the Wounded Knee massacre.

Homesteading had officially begun in 1863, and increasing numbers of homesteaders settled in the Dakota Territory throughout the subsequent decades. With the Indians seemingly under control and more white settlers on the move, the push toward statehood increased. The Democrats in Washington, D.C., were somewhat reluctant to grant statehood, as the territory was mostly Republican. Finally, on November 2, 1889, North and South Dakota separated and achieved statehood, with South Dakota becoming the fortieth state in the Union.

Economic Development

Agriculture has played a large part in the South Dakota economy. Even today, agricultural industries provide employment for thousands of South Dakota residents. However, the mining and manufacturing sectors of the economy have made great gains since the end of World War II.

The production of livestock is the largest component of the agricultural industries in South Dakota. Hogs, lambs, and beef cattle are the top three such animal commodities. South Dakota farmers also grow crops, with wheat, corn, rye, and alfalfa seed among those cultivated.

The United States' largest gold mine, the Homestake Mine, is located in Lead, South Dakota. Besides gold, South Dakota has rich deposits of uranium, discovered in 1951, and plutonium, found in 1953.

The manufacturing realm of the South Dakota economy produces several diverse products such as meat packing which is the leading industry in the state.

Mount Rushmore

Although the state of South Dakota does not have a large population, it does have many scenic attractions. Millions of people visit South Dakota to see attractions such as Mount Rushmore. However, in addition to this well-known tourist destination, South Dakota is home to many lesser-known, hidden historic sites, including ghost towns, old trading posts, and Native American villages.

Mount Rushmore, a national memorial in the Black Hills, is perhaps the most famous South Dakota attraction. On this huge mass of stone, the faces of four former presidents, George Washington, Thomas Jefferson, Abraham Lincoln, and Theodore Roosevelt were carved under the guidance of Gutzon Borglum, an American sculptor. Millions of visitors have come to see these gigantic countenances.

Important Events

1742 South Dakota explored by the La Vérendrye brothers.

1762 France cedes South Dakota land to Spain, but gets it back at the end of the century.

1803 Louisiana Purchase; United States acquires area including South Dakota.

1817 Fort Pierre is founded as a fur-trading post.

1822 John Jacob Astor starts American Fur Company.

1859 First permanent white settlement at Yankton.

1861 Dakota Territory established which includes South and North Dakota.

1862 Yankton becomes the capital of the Dakota territory.

1863 Homesteading officially begins.

1874 Gold rush begins on the Great Sioux Reservation.

1879 "Great Dakota Boom" starts.

1881 Sitting Bull, chief of the Sioux, surrenders at Fort Buford.

1889 The Dakota Territory is separated and South Dakota becomes the fortieth state in the Union on November 2.

1890 Battle of Wounded Knee. The last major clash between federal troops and American Indians.

1904 Pierre is made the state capitol.

1916 Non Partisan League organized.

1922 Proposal for state-operated banks rejected; five years later one-half of South Dakota's banks close.

1927 Mount Rushmore monument begun.

1934 Indian Reorganization Act passed.

1941 Mount Rushmore completed.

1951 Uranium is discovered.

1952 Plutonium is discovered.

1972 Canyon Lake Dam collapses killing over two-hundred people.

1973 Native Americans occupy Wounded Knee for seventy days.

1988 Drought hits state and crops are ruined.

1991 One-hundred-year remembrance of the Battle of Wounded Knee is marked by apologies by Gov. George Mickelson.

■ Badlands National Park. Deep gorges, saw-edged spires, and other striking formations form a beautiful spectacle that covers more than 244,000 acres. (G-3)

■ Black Hills. Black Hills National Forest; features mountain scenery, ghost towns, swimming, horseback riding.

■ Corn Palace. Decorated inside and out with thousands of bushels of native corn, grain, and grasses; site of annual corn festival.

■ Crazy Horse Memorial. Monument to the Native American leader is currently emerging as the fifth granite face in the Black Hills. (F-1)

■ Custer. The oldest town in the Black Hills features the Gold Days of Summer, and Custer State Park nearby. (G-1)

■ Deadwood. Frontier mining town in Black Hills; Adams Memorial Museum features Wild Bill Hickok and Calamity Jane memorabilia. (E-1)

■ Dells of the Sioux. Beautiful gorge near Dell Rapids on the Big Sioux River. (H-14)

■ Devil's Gulch. Deep scenic chasm near Garretson. (H-14)

■ Hot Springs. Warmwater river and mineral springs run year round through the city. Wind Cave National Park is nearby. (H-1)

■ Jewel Cave National Monument. Over 80 miles of passageways feature glittering calcite crystals that line its walls in column, drapery, balloon and other formations. (G-1)

■ Little Town on the Prairie. De Smet is the town made famous by author Laura Ingalls Wilder in her pioneer adventure novels. (E-12)

■ Mount Rushmore National Memorial. 60-foot-high granite sculptures of presidents Washington, Jefferson, Theodore Roosevelt, and Lincoln survey the black hills. (F-1)

■ Petrified Wood Park. Features over 400 unusual petrified wood structures and fossils. (A-4)

■ Sitting Bull's Grave. The great Sioux leader lies buried on a bluff just west of Mobridge beneath a seven-ton granite bust. (B-7)

■ Stratosphere Bowl. Launch site for many hot air balloons near Rapid City. (F-2)

■ Theodore Roosevelt Monument. High above on Mount Roosevelt near Deadwood, offers view of four states. (E-1)

■ Wind Cave National Park. One of America's oldest national parks. Beneath the ground is a 68-mile maze of unusual boxwork. (G-1)

Weather Facts

Record High Temperature: 120° F (49° C) on July 5, 1936, at Gannvalley; Record Low Temperature: -58° F (-50° C) on February 17, 1936, at McIntosh; Average January Temperature: 17° F (-8° C); Average July Temperature: 75° F (24° C); Average Yearly Precipitation: 18 in. (46 cm).

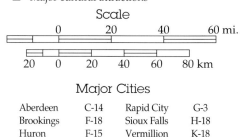

☆ State capitol
⊙ Cities over 35,000 pop.
○ Other significant cities
● County Seats
■ Major cultural attractions

▭ State Parks
Ⓦ Welcome Centers
♟ Major colleges and universities

Scale

```
0        20      40       60 mi.

20   0   20      40    60    80 km
```

Major Cities

Aberdeen	C-14	Rapid City	G-3
Brookings	F-18	Sioux Falls	H-18
Huron	F-15	Vermillion	K-18
Mitchell	H-15	Watertown	D-18
Pierre	F-10	Yankton	J-17

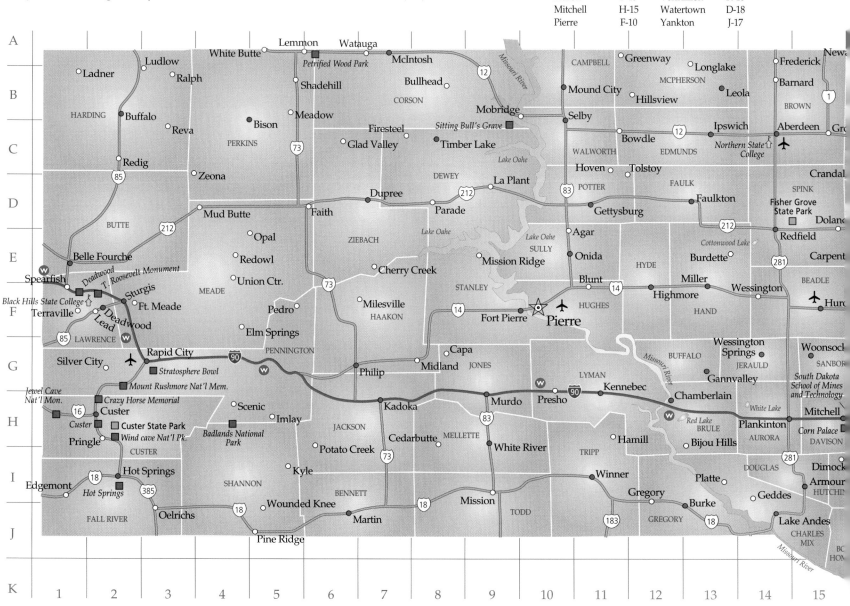

Topography

There are several distinct topographic regions in South Dakota. The eastern portion of the state is covered by the Central Lowlands, which includes two separate physical regions. The Drift Prairie physical region lies to the north and is characterized by gentle rolling hills and many natural lakes. The soil is cool and moist, with a thin dark surface. The Dissected Till Plains physical region, in the southeastern corner of the state, has soil of glacial origin. It is warm and moist soil, colored brown, with a thin black organic surface. The Missouri River bisects the state and separates the Central Lowlands of the east from the Great Plains that cover most of western South Dakota.

The Great Plains physical region occupies the western two-thirds of South Dakota. Much of this area is gentle hills and plains, interrupted by more rugged land features such as ridges, buttes, and canyons. In the southwest corner of the state are the Badlands, an area of severely eroded ridges and gullies that form a rugged landscape. This is the most famous of such areas in the United States. The soil is similar to that found on the Dissected Till Plains. On the western border with

Wyoming, just northwest of the Badlands, is the Black Hills physical region. This is an isolated circular mountain area of steep cliffs and deep valleys. The soil is classed as a cool and moist gray/brown clay. The highest point in the state can be found here: Harney Peak rises 7,242 ft. (2,207 m) above sea level.

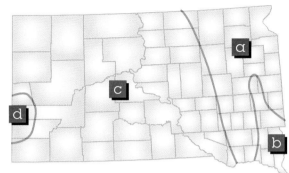

Physical Regions: (a) Drift Prairie; (b) Dissected Till Plains; (c) Great Plains; (d) Black Hills.

Environmental Facts

Air Pollution Rank: 43d; Water Pollution Rank: 45th; Total Yearly Industrial Pollution: 2,966,630 lbs.; Industrial Pollution Rank: 46th; Hazardous Waste Sites: 4; Hazardous Sites Rank: 45th; Landfill Capacity: adequate; Fresh Water Supply: surplus; Daily Residential Water Consumption: 120 gals. per capita; Endangered Species: Aquatic Species (1)—sturgeon, pallid; Birds (5)—crane, whooping; Mammals (1)—ferret, black-footed; Other Species (1)—beetle, American burying; Plants (1)—orchid, prairie fringed.

Environmental Quality

See page 376.

Land Use

Cropland: 39.2%; Pasture: 5.2%; Rangeland: 48.7%; Forest: 1.2%; Urban: 2.4%; Other: 3.3%.

Climate

South Dakota's great distance from any large body of water results in great variations in temperature. Although temperatures can reach over 100 degrees F, the state's low humidity makes such temperatures more bearable. The south has mean January and July temperatures of 22 degrees F and 73 degrees F, while temperatures in the north average 15 degrees F and 68 degrees F.

South Dakota receives low yearly precipitation, around 20 inches for the state. The southeastern corner of South Dakota, where Sioux Falls is located, receives the most annual precipitation, about 26 inches. On the other hand, precipitation in the northwest averages only 12 inches a year. Almost three-quarters of all precipitation falls during the growing season, which averages 130 days.

South Dakota is seemingly always plagued by violent weather. Blizzards often occur during winter, and tornadoes sweep across the land in the spring.

Hydrology

The most important river in the state is the Missouri. It enters from North Dakota in the center of the state and flows southeast, finally making up part of South Dakota's southern border with Nebraska. The Grand, Moreau, Cheyenne, and White rivers are tributaries of the Missouri that drain western South Dakota. The James and the Big Sioux drain much of the eastern part of the state, flowing into the Missouri in the southeast corner of South Dakota. The Big Sioux actually forms part of the state's southeast border with Iowa.

All of the large lakes in the state are man-made. The largest of these is the Oahe Reservoir, on the Missouri river in north-central South Dakota, which is about 250 miles (403 km) long. Others include Lake Sharpe and Lake Francis Case, also on the Missouri, and Houghton Reservoir on the James.

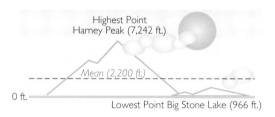

Highest Point Harney Peak (7,242 ft.)

Mean (2,200 ft.)

0 ft.

Lowest Point Big Stone Lake (966 ft.)

Average Monthly Weather

	Jan	Feb	Mar	Apr	May	Jun	Jul	Aug	Sep	Oct	Nov	Dec	Yearly
Rapid City													
Maximum Temperature °F	32.4	37.4	44.2	57.0	68.1	77.9	86.5	85.7	75.4	63.2	46.7	37.4	59.3
Minimum Temperature °F	9.2	14.6	21.0	32.1	43.0	52.5	58.7	57.0	46.4	36.1	23.0	14.8	34.0
Days of Precipitation	6.6	7.2	8.7	9.2	11.7	12.3	9.0	7.9	6.5	4.9	5.7	6.1	95.9
Sioux Falls													
Maximum Temperature °F	22.9	29.3	40.1	58.1	70.5	80.3	86.2	83.9	73.5	62.1	43.7	29.3	56.7
Minimum Temperature °F	1.9	8.9	20.6	34.6	45.7	56.3	61.8	59.7	48.5	36.7	22.3	10.1	33.9
Days of Precipitation	6.1	6.5	8.7	9.2	10.5	10.7	9.4	8.9	8.2	6.1	6.2	6.1	96.8

Flora and Fauna

Only about 4 percent of South Dakota's area is covered by forests. Coniferous trees such as spruce, fir, and pine grow in the Black Hills, a region in western South Dakota. Deciduous hardwood forests of oak, ash, and elm exist all over the state, but especially along rivers and streams. One might not think a northern state like South Dakota would have cacti, but they do grow in the western part of the state. Wildflowers such as larkspurs and forget-me-nots bloom in the Black Hills. Black-eyed Susans and mariposa lilies grow on eastern prairies.

South Dakota is home to more free-roaming buffalo than any other state; approximately 8,000 live with its boundaries. Other South Dakota wildlife includes bighorn sheep, jackrabbits, coyotes, and Rocky Mountain goats. The pheasant is only one of the state's game birds. South Dakota has several species of fishes swimming in its lakes, rivers, and streams. Glacial lakes contain perch, bluegill, and walleye, and the Missouri River contains bass, northern pike, and sauger.

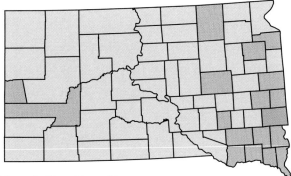

Population Density

Population density for the state of South Dakota was 9.2 persons per square mile in 1990 (3.5 per km2). Average U.S. density was 70.3 persons per square mile in 1990 (27.3 per km2). Habitation is most dense in and around the urban area of Sioux Falls. Rapid City, Aberdeen, and Watertown are also areas of higher density. Most of South Dakota is very sparsely populated.

Persons Per Square Mile

- 0.0 to 9.9
- 10.0 to 99.9
- 100.0 to 249.9

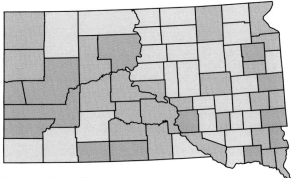

Population Change

The 1990 population figure for the state of South Dakota was 696,004. This is a 0.76 percent increase from 690,768 in 1980. The next decade will show growth with a population of 714 thousand or a 2.59 percent increase. The areas of fastest growth are found in the cities of the state. Many of the counties have experienced little or negative growth in the last decade.

Percent Change 1980 to 1990

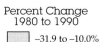

- −31.9 to −10.0%
- −9.9 to 0.0%
- 0.1 to 19.9%

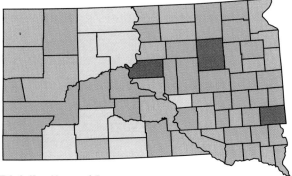

Distribution of Income

The per capita income for the state of South Dakota (current dollars) was $16,558 in 1992. This is a 115.0 percent increase from $7,701 in 1980. Income is greatest in areas such as Sioux City, and Sully and Spink counties. Low incomes can be found in counties where Indian reservations are located. Examples include the Cheyenne and Pine Ridge reservations.

Per Capita Income (000s) (Current Dollars)

- $4.5 to 9.9
- $10.0 to 12.9
- $13.0 to 15.9
- $16.0 to 19.9

Population Projections

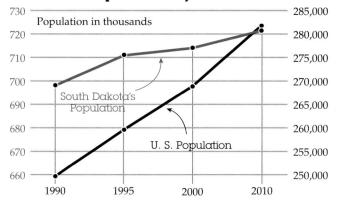

Population in thousands

South Dakota's Population

U. S. Population

Population Facts

State Population, 1993: 715,000

Rank: 45

Population 2000: 714,000 (Rank 46)

Density: 9.2 per sq. mi. (3.5 per km2)

Distribution: 50.0% urban, 50.0% rural

Population Under 5 Years Old: 7.6%

Population Under 18 Years Old: 28.7%

Population Over 65 Years Old: 14.7%

Median Age: 32.5

Number of Households: 259,000

Average Persons Per Household: 2.59

Average Persons Per Family: 3.16

Female Heads of Households: 2.98%

Population That Is Married: 21.91%

Birth Rate: 15.8 per 1,000 population

Death Rate: 9.1 per 1,000 population

Births to Teen Mothers: 10.8%

Marriage Rate: 10.8 per 1,000 population

Divorce Rate: 3.7 per 1,000 population

Violent Crime Rate: 182 per 100,000 pop.

Population on Social Security: 18.5%

Percent Voting for President: 67.0%

Population Profile

Rank. South Dakota ranks 45th among U.S. states in terms of population with 715,000 citizens.

Minority Population. The state's minority population is 8.9 percent. The state's male to female ratio for 1990 was 96.89 males for every 100 females. It was above the national average of 95.22 males for every 100 females.

Growth. Growing much slower than the

Government

Capital: Pierre (established 1889).

Statehood: Became 40th state on Nov. 2, 1889.

Number of Counties: 66.

Supreme Court Justices: 5, 8-year term.

State Senators: 35, 2-year term.

State Legislators: 70, 2-year term.

United States Senators: 2.

United States Representatives: 1.

Electoral Votes: 3.

State Constitution: Adopted 1889.

Population Change

Year	Population
1950	653,000
1960	683,000
1970	668,000
1980	690,768
1990	696,004
2000	714,000
2010	722,000

Period	Change
1950–1970	2.3%
1970–1980	3.4%
1980–1990	0.7%
1990–2000	2.6%

South Dakota's Famous Citizens

Beadle, William Henry Harrison (1838–1915). He became the surveyor-general of the Dakota Territory in 1869.

Brokaw, Tom (b. 1940). TV journalist. He has been anchor of the "NBC Nightly News" program since 1982.

Deloria, Vine, Jr. (b. 1933). Sioux activist. He wrote books on Indian nationalism, including *Custer Died for Your Sins*.

Garland, Hamlin (1860–1940). Author of books depicting farm families on the frontier, including *Main-Traveled Roads*.

Hart, Mary (b. 1951).TV personality. She cohosted the show "Entertainment Tonight."

Lawrence, Ernest (1901–1958). Physicist. He won the Nobel Prize in 1939 for his work on a cyclotron for atoms.

McGovern, George (b. 1922). Democratic presidential nominee in 1972. He also served in the U.S. Senate (1963–1981).

Mills, Billy (b. 1938). He won the Olympic gold medal in the 10,000 meter race in 1964.

Reifel, Benjamin (b. 1906). He became the first Indian elected to Congress from the state in 1960.

projected national average, the state's population is expected to reach 722 thousand by the year 2010 *(see graph above)*.

Older Citizens. The state's population older than 65 was 102,331 in 1990. It grew 12.43% from 91,019 in 1980.

Younger Citizens. The number of children (under 18 years of age) was 198 thousand in 1990. This represents 28.5 percent of the state's population. The state's school aged population was 129 thousand in 1990. It is expected to increase to 133 thousand by the year 2000. This represents a 3.1% change.

Urban/Rural. 50.0% of the population of the state live in urban areas while 50.0% live in rural areas.

Largest Cities. South Dakota has two cities with a population greater than 35,000. The populations of the state's largest centers are (starting from the most populous) Sioux Falls (100,814), Rapid City (54,523), Aberdeen (24,927), Watertown (17,592), Brookings (16,270), Mitchell (13,798), Pierre (12,906), Yankton (12,703), Huron (12,448), and Vermillion (10,034).

Native American

The Native American population in South Dakota was 50,575 in 1990. This was an increase of 11.09 percent from 45,525 in 1980. Many of the Native Americans live in the large Indian reservations located throughout the state. These reservations include the Standing Rock, Cheyenne, Pine Ridge, Rosebud, Lake Traverse, Lower Brule/Crow Creek, and the Yankton.

Presence of Native Americans

◻ Minor
◻ Moderate
◻ Significant

Nationalities

African	310
American	12,546
Arab	975
Austrian	867
Czech	13,305
Dutch	22,698
English	38,052
Finnish	2,376
German	302,793
Greek	621
Hungarian	662
Irish	41,804
Italian	3,706
Norwegian	73,355
Polish	5,411
Portuguese	329
Russian	2,047
Scottish	4,504
Slovak	1,152
Swedish	18,357
Welsh	1,939
West Indian	88

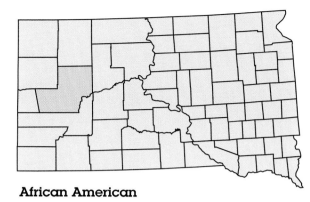

African American

The African American population in South Dakota was 3,258 in 1990. This was an increase of 51.39 percent from 2,152 in 1980. Mead County has the highest percentage of African Americans in the state. Twenty-two percent of the African Americans live in Sioux Falls, which has a community of 733.

Percent of County Population

◻ 0.00 to 1.99%
◻ 2.00 to 4.99%

Statewide Ethnic Composition

Over 91 percent of the population of South Dakota is white. The largest nationalities in this racial group are German, Norwegian, and Irish. The next largest group is Native Americans, followed by Hispanics, African Americans, and Asians. Only 13,000 people claim to be American and acknowledge no other nationality.

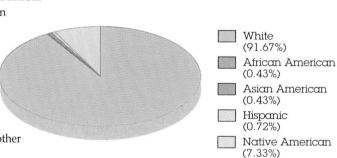

◻ White (91.67%)
◻ African American (0.43%)
◻ Asian American (0.43%)
◻ Hispanic (0.72%)
◻ Native American (7.33%)

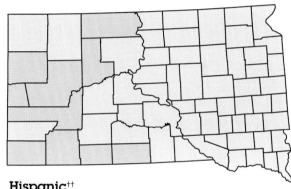

Hispanic[††]

The Hispanic population in South Dakota was 17,803 in 1990. This is an increase of 87.26 percent from 9,507 persons in 1980. The Hispanic population is generally located in the western counties in the state. There is, however, a large Hispanic community in Sioux Falls.

[††]A person of Mexican, Puerto Rican, Cuban, or other Spanish culture or origin regardless of race.

Percent of County Population

◻ 0.00 to 0.99%
◻ 1.00 to 2.99%

Education Facts

Total Students 1990: 127,329

Number of School Districts: 185

Expenditure Per Capita on Education 1990: $618

Expenditure Per Capita K–12 1990: $556

Expenditure Per Pupil 1990: $3,730

Total School Enrollment 1990–1991: 128,635

Rank of Expenditures Per Student: 43d in the U.S.

African American Enrollment: 0.5%

Hispanic Enrollment: 0.6%

Asian/Pacific Islander Enrollment: 0.7%

Native American Enrollment: 7.6%

Mean SAT Score 1991 Verbal: 496

Mean SAT Score 1991 Math: 551

Average Teacher's Salary 1992: $23,300

Rank Teacher's Salary: 50th in U.S.

High School Graduates 1990: 7,700

Total Number of Public Schools: 799

Number of Teachers 1990: 8,299

Student/Teacher Ratio: 15.5

Staff Employed in Public Schools: 14,129

Pupil/Staff Ratio: 9.0

Staff/Teacher Ratio: 1.7

Education

Attainment: 78.3 percent of population 25 years or older were high school graduates in 1989, earning South Dakota a ranking of 25th in the United States; 18.4 percent of the state's population had completed college. Institutions of Higher Education: The largest universities and colleges in the state include University of South Dakota (founded 1862), Vermillion; South Dakota State University (founded 1881), Brookings; South Dakota School of Mines and Technology (founded 1887), Rapid City. Expenditures per Student: Expenditure increased 80% between 1985 and 1990. Projected High School Graduations: 1998 (9,483), 2004 (8,273); Total Revenues for Education from Federal Sources: $47 million; Total Revenues for Education from State Sources: $115 million; Total Revenues for Education from Local Sources: $272 million; Average Annual Salaries for Public School Principals: N/A.

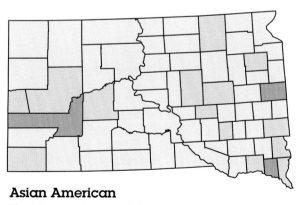

Asian American

The Asian American population in South Dakota was 3,123 in 1990. This is an increase of 71.31 percent from 1,823 persons in 1980. Asian Americans are concentrated in three main areas in the state, in Pennington, Clay, and Brookings counties. There is also a significant Asian American presence in Sioux Falls.

Percent of County Population

◻ 0.00 to 0.24%
◻ 0.25 to 0.99%
◻ 1.00 to 1.99%

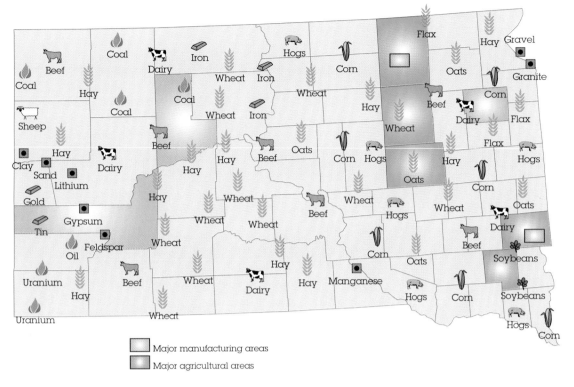

Major manufacturing areas

Major agricultural areas

Transportation

South Dakotans first relied on rivers as a transportation mode. The Missouri River was important in early exploration and settlement of the state. Today, South Dakota's 73,000-mile network of roads and highways is the more important transportation system. Almost all roads are surfaced. Two major interstates, I-29 and I-90, run north to south and east to west, respectively.

Rail service to South Carolina has declined over the years. The first railroad entered the state in 1872. Seven different freight rail lines operate in South Dakota. However, no passenger railroads stop in South Dakota. The largest and busiest airport in the state is located in Sioux Falls, in the southeast. Several smaller airports can be found throughout South Dakota.

Energy and Transportation Facts

Energy. Yearly Consumption: 205 tril. BTUs (residential, 25.9%; commercial, 16.1%; industrial, 25.9%; transportation, 32.7%); Annual Energy Expenditures Per Capita: $1,804; Nuclear Power Plants Located in State: 0; Source of Energy Consumed: Petroleum— 49.3%; Natural Gas— 13.2%; Coal— 17.6%; Hydroelectric Power—20.0%; Nuclear Power—0.0%.

Transportation. Highway Miles: 83,299 (interstates, 678; urban, 1,858; rural, 81,441); Average Yearly Auto Insurance: $333 (50th); Auto Fatalities Rank: 9th; Registered Motor Vehicles: 719,690; Workers in Carpools: 14.0%; Workers Using Public Trans: 0.3%.

Agriculture

South Dakota has 44.2 million farm acres. During the last 40 years, South Dakota's farms have grown larger in size and fewer in number. In 1955, 63,000 farms were found in the state. Today, 34,500 remain.

Agriculture adds $2 billion to the state's gross product annually. The principal commodities in order of marketing receipts are cattle, wheat, hogs, and corn.

Livestock and livestock products account for about two-thirds of South Dakota's farm income. Half of the state is covered with pasture land. Most of the beef cattle are concentrated in the western half. Corn, the leading crop, is grown mainly in the southeastern part of the state. South Dakota is among the leading producers of crops such as wheat, barley, flax seed, hay, oats, and rye.

Housing

Owner Occupied Units: 292,436; Average Age of Units: 34 years; Average Value of Housing Units: $45,200; Renter Occupied Units: 81,179; Median Monthly Rent: $306; Housing Starts: 3,900; Existing Home Sales: 13,700.

Economic Facts

Gross State Product: $11,000,000,000 (1989)

Income Per Capita: $16,558

Disposable Personal Income: $15,082

Median Household Income: $22,503

Average Annual Pay, 1988: $17,131

Principal Industries: food products, scientific instruments, machinery, printing, publishing, lumber, glass products

Major Crops: corn, wheat, hay, sunflowers, milk, rye, flax, alfalfa seed, timber

Fish: Bass, Bluegills, Perch, Walleye, Trout

Livestock: hogs, cattle, lambs, sheep

Non-Fuel Minerals: Gold, Lignite, Clay, Feldspar, Granite, Gypsum, Limestone, Quartz

Organic Fuel Minerals: Petroleum

Civilian Labor Force: 361,000 (Women: 167,000)

Total Employed: 349,000 (Women: 161,000)

Median Value of Housing: $45,200

Median Contract Rent: $306 per month

Economic Sectors 1992

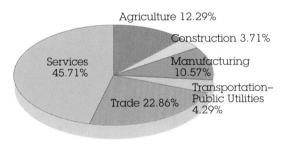

- Agriculture 12.29%
- Construction 3.71%
- Manufacturing 10.57%
- Transportation–Public Utilities 4.29%
- Trade 22.86%
- Services 45.71%

Manufacturing

Over the years, the manufacturing sector of South Dakota's economy has continually expanded. The state has approximately 1,000 manufacturing facilities; however, most employ fewer than 50 people. Food processing, meat packing in particular, is South Dakota's leading manufacturing industry. Others in the state include the manufacture of machinery, medical instruments, and printed materials.

Food-processing plants are located throughout South Dakota. Sioux Falls has the largest meat-packing establishment, in addition to other food-processing factories. Cities such as Rapid City, Aberdeen, and Mitchell process dairy products. Machinery, especially farm and construction equipment, is manufactured primarily in Sioux City and Rapid City.

Employment

Employment. South Dakota employed 347,000 people in 1993. Most work in social and personal services (82,500 persons or 23.8% of the workforce). Manufacturing accounts for 11.3% or 39,300 workers. Wholesale and retail trade account for 23.5% or 81,400 workers. Government employs 66,700 workers (19.2%). Construction employs 13,100 workers (3.8%). Transportation and utilities account for 4.3% or 14,800 persons. Agriculture employs 42,300 workers or 12.2%. Finance, real estate, and insurance account for 5.1% or 17,700 workers. Mining employs 2,500 people and accounts for less than 0.7% of the workforce.

Unemployment. Unemployment has decreased to 3.5% in 1993 from a rate of 5.1% in 1985. Today's figure is lower than the national average of 6.8% as shown below.

Unemployment Rate

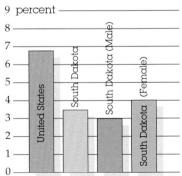

TENNESSEE
The State of Tennessee

Official State Seal

The Great Seal of Tennessee has never been officially adopted, but has been in existence since 1801. The XVI represents Tennessee's status as the sixteenth state in the Union. The agriculture and commerce words and symbols represent Tennessee's dependence on these activities. The 1796 is the year of Tennessee's admission to the Union.

Legal Holidays

January: New Year's Day—1st; February: Presidents' Day—3d Monday; March: Andrew Jackson's Birthday—15th; May: Memorial Day—4th Monday; June: Admission Day—1st; July: Independence Day 4th; September: Labor Day—1st Monday; October: Columbus Day—2d Monday; Pioneer's Day—13th; November: Admission Day—2d; Veterans' Day—11th; Thanksgiving—4th Thursday; December: Christmas—25th

Official State Flag

The flag of Tennessee was adopted in 1905. It was developed by a member of the state National Guard. The three stars represent either Tennessee's being the third state to be admitted to the Union after the original thirteen states or the three U.S. presidents from the state.

Festivals and Events

January: Chocolate Festival, Knoxville; March: Gospel Music, Nashville; April: Good Earth Festival, Chattanooga; Spring Wildflower Pilgrimage, Gatlinburg; Dogwood Arts Fest, Maryville; May: Ramp Festival, Cosby; Memphis in May, Memphis; Pig-Out on the River, Chattanooga; June: Covered Bridge Celebration, Elizabethton; Riverbend Festival, Chattanooga; July: Fiddlers' Jamboree & Craft Fest, Smithville; August: Elvis International Tribute Week, Memphis; Rock City Fairytale Fest, Rock City; September: Belle Meade Plantation Fall Fest, Nashville; Italian Street Fair, Brentwood; Mid-South Fair, Memphis; October: National Storytelling Festival, Jonesborough; Fall Pow Wow & Fest, Mt. Juliet; November: Jubilee, Chattanooga; Smoky Mountain Lights/Winterfest, Gatlinburg; December: Christmas on the River, Chattanooga.

Tennessee Compared to States in Its Region.

Resident Pop. in Metro Areas: 2d; Pop. Percent Increase: 1st; Pop. Over 65: 2d; Infant Mortality: 3d; School Enroll. Increase: 1st; High School Grad. and Up: 1st; Violent Crime: 2d; Hazardous Waste Sites: 2d; Unemployment: 4th; Median Household Income: 1st; Persons Below Poverty: 4th; Energy Costs Per Person: 2d.

East South Central

	Population	Capital
Kentucky	3,789,000	Frankfort
Tennessee	5,099,000	Nashville
Alabama	4,187,000	Montgomery
Mississippi	2,643,000	Jackson

Tennessee's Finances

Households: 1,854,000; Income Per Capita Current Dollars: $17,341; Change Per Capita Income 1980 to 1992: 116.5% (10th in U.S.); State Expenditures: $9,633,000,000; State Revenues: $9,624,000,000; Personal Income Tax: N/A; Federal Income Taxes Paid Per Capita: $1,530; Sales Tax: 5.5% (prescription drugs exempt).

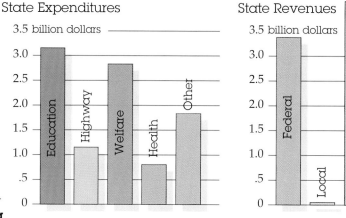

Location, Size, and Boundaries

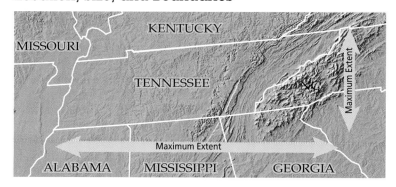

Location. Tennessee is located in the East South Central region of the United States. It is bounded on four sides by land. The geographic center of Tennessee is lat. 35° 47.7' N; long. 86° 37.3' W.

Size. Tennessee is the 34th largest state in terms of size. Its area is 42,244 sq. mi. (109,412 km2). Inland water covers 916 sq. mi. (2,372 km2).

Boundaries. Kentucky, 346 mi. (557 km); Virginia, 127 mi. (204 km); North Carolina, 255 mi. (410 km); Georgia, 75 mi. (121 km); Alabama, 150 mi. (242 km); Mississippi, 123 mi. (198 km); Arkansas, 163 mi. (262 km); Missouri, 67 mi. (108 km).

Geographic Extent. The north/south extent is 110 mi. (180 km). The state extends 430 mi. (690 km) to the east/west.

Facts about Tennessee. Origin of Name: After the *Cherokee* Indian village *Tanasie*; Nickname: The Volunteer State; Motto: "Agriculture and commerce"; Abbreviations: Tenn. (traditional), TN (postal); State Bird: mockingbird; State Tree: tulip poplar; State Flower: iris; State Songs: "Rocky Top," words and music by Boudleaux and Felice Bryant, and "The Tennessee Waltz,"words by Pee Wee King and music by Redd Stewart.

Tennessee Compared to Other States. Resident Pop. in Metro Areas: 31st; Pop. Per. Increase: 20th; Pop. Over 65: 24th; Infant Mort.: 10th; School Enroll. Increase: 28th; High School Grad. and Up: 45th; Violent Crime: 15th; Haz. Waste Sites: 25th; Unemployment: 33d; Median Household Income: 39th; Persons Below Poverty: 12th; Energy Costs Per Person: 16th.

Sources of Information. Tourism: Dept. of Tourist Development, P.O. Box 23170, Nashville, TN 37202. Economy: Dept. of Economic and Community Development, Industrial Research Division, 320 Sixth Avenue North, Nashville, TN 37219. Government: Information Center, Tennessee State Capitol, Nashville, TN 37219. History: Dept. of Tourist Development, P.O. Box 23170, Nashville, TN 37202.

■ Andrew Johnson National Historic Site. Site of two homes and the grave of the former president. (C-21)

■ Beale Street Historic District. Site of night clubs and specialty shops. Home of blues music. (G-1)

■ Casey Jones' Home and Railroad Museum. Home of the railroading man. Exhibits of 19th century railroading including a steam locomotive engine. (E-4)

■ Chickamauga and Chattanooga National Military Park. Site of Civil War battles fought during the fall of 1863 that resulted in over 48,000 casualties. (G-14)

■ Cumberland Gap National Historical Park. Passage used by early settlers through the mountains. Museum and visitors' center. (B-19)

■ Fort Donelson National Battlefield. First major Union victory. Captured by General Ulysses S. Grant in 1862. (B-7)

■ Gatlinburg. Resort area including the Guinness World Records Museum and bluegrass and mountain music. (E-20)

■ Graceland. Home of singer and actor Elvis Presley. (G-1)

■ Grand Ole Opry. Site for live country music. (C-10)

■ Hermitage. Home of President Andrew Jackson. (D-10)

■ James K. Polk Ancestral Home. Built in 1816, was the home of the 11th president. (E-9)

■ Lookout Mountain. National Historic Site. Point Park and the Incline Railway; a steep passenger railway. (G-14)

■ Sam Davis Home. Home of the Confederate spy hanged by Union troops after refusing to reveal the name of his informant. (D-11)

■ Shiloh National Military Park. Site of the battle of Shiloh in 1862, which resulted in over 23,000 casualties. (G-5)

■ Stones River National Battlefield. One of the bloodiest battles in the Appalachians with 23,000 casualties. (E-11)

■ Tennessee State Capitol. Tomb of President James K. Polk and burial spot of architect William Strickland. (D-10)

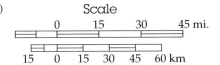

Scale

★ State capitol
⊙ Cities over 35,000 population
○ Other significant cities
● County Seats
■ Major cultural attractions
▢ State Parks
Ⓦ Welcome Centers
⚲ Major colleges and universities

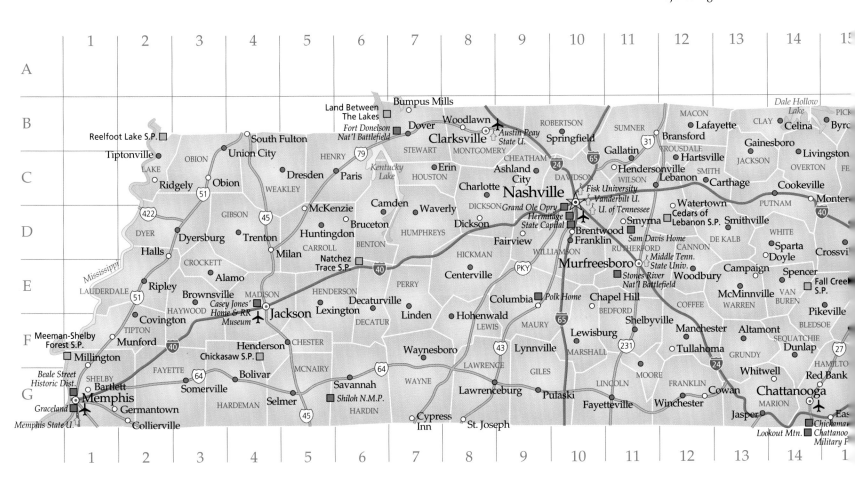

Major Cities

Flora and Fauna

Approximately half of the state of Tennessee is covered by forests. The eastern part of the state has a hardwood and softwood mix, consisting of cherry and oak, both hardwoods, as well as shortleaf pines, a softwood tree. The rest of the state has mostly deciduous hardwood forests. The Nashville Basin contains predominately cedar trees. Other common trees include sycamore, maple, and poplar. Wildflowers such as yellow jasmine, hop clover, passionflower, and dragonroot all grow in Tennessee. Mountain laurel and rhododendron are two common shrubs that grow on Tennessee mountainsides.

Many different forms of wildlife live in all parts of Tennessee. The white-tailed deer is perhaps the most prevalent, living throughout the state. Other animals include muskrats, beavers, skunks, and raccoons. Wild hogs live in more remote locations in the Tennessee mountain regions. Wild turkeys, ducks, and other game birds also live in the state. Songbirds fly all over Tennessee, including such birds as the wood thrush, mockingbird, and robin. The rivers, streams, and lakes in Tennessee contain bass, trout, and walleye.

Weather Facts

Record High Temperature: 113° F (45° C) on August 9, 1930, at Perryville; Record Low Temperature: -32° F (-36° C) on December 17, 1930, at Mountain City; Average January Temperature: 39° F (4° C); Average July Temperature: 79° F (26° C); Average Yearly Precipitation: 51 in. (130 cm).

Environmental Facts

Air Pollution Rank: 2d; Water Pollution Rank: 12th; Total Yearly Industrial Pollution: 130,678,862 lbs.; Industrial Pollution Rank: 3d; Hazardous Waste Sites: 14; Hazardous Sites Rank: 25th; Landfill Capacity: overextended; Fresh Water Supply: large surplus; Daily Residential Water Consumption: 150 gals. per capita; Endangered Species: Aquatic Species (47)—bean, purple; Birds (3)—eagle, bald; Mammals (5)—bat, gray; Other Species (4)—riversnail, Anthony's; Plants (18)—aster, Ruth's golden.

Environmental Quality

See page 376.

Highest Point
Clingmans Dome (6,643 ft.)

Mean (900 ft.)

0 ft.

Lowest Point
Mississippi River (178 ft.)

Land Use

Cropland: 23.3%; Pasture: 20.3%; Rangeland: 0%; Forest: 46.9%; Urban: 6.7%; Other: 2.8%.

Climate

Overall a humid, temperate climate, Tennessee's seasons vary slightly across the state. In western Tennessee, near Memphis, the January and July temperatures of 43 and 80 degrees F reflect a hot summer and mild winter pattern. Eastern Tennessee has mean January and July temperatures of 37 degrees F and 70 degrees F. The middle west region has the shortest summers and most severe winters, although weather is still quite mild.

Tennessee as a whole receives more than adequate precipitation. Apart from the Pacific Northwest, Tennessee's eastern mountains receive the most precipitation in the contiguous United States. The Appalachian Mountains often receive over 60 inches of precipitation annually. Precipitation in Nashville, on the other hand, usually averages 46 inches annually.

Because of the combination of nearly always mild weather and abundant rainfall, Tennessee has a rather long growing season. Both eastern and western Tennessee can have over 200 growing days.

Hydrology

The Mississippi River forms Tennessee's western boundary with Missouri and Arkansas. Its tributaries, the Obion, the Forked Deer, the Hatchie, the Loosahatchie, and the Wolf, drain much of western Tennessee. The Tennessee River enters the state from Kentucky in the northwest and flows south. Some of its main branches are the Big Sandy and Duck rivers. The Cumberland River enters Tennessee just east of where the Tennessee River enters, but turns eastward, flowing through the north-central part of the state, before turning back north and reentering Kentucky. Its tributaries, including the Caney Fork and the Stone, drain much of central Tennessee. The Clinch River runs southwest through eastern Tennessee.

Tennessee has many artificial lakes created by dams built by the Tennessee Valley Authority (TVA). The largest of these is Kentucky Lake on the Tennessee River. Others include Douglas Lake and Watts Bar Lake on the Clinch River.

Topography

There are several distinct topographic regions in Tennessee. All soil in the state is classed as warm and moist. The eastern border of Tennessee lies in the Blue Ridge physical region, and is a part of the Appalachian Mountains system. The soil in this region is predominantly red/yellow clay. The highest elevations in the state are found here. Clingmans Dome, the highest peak, rises to 6,643 ft. (2,025 m) above sea level. Other ranges in this region include the Great Smoky and the Bald Mountains. East of the Blue Ridge is the Appalachian Ridge and Valley physical region. This is a fertile area with rich, brown soils suitable for agriculture. The Great Valley separates the Blue Ridge from the Appalachian Plateau. The Appalachian Plateau physical region is an area of flat ridges and deep valleys. Although the soil is an organically poor red/yellow clay, it is rich in coal and other mineral deposits.

Much of central Tennessee is part of the Highland Rim and Central Basin physical regions. The Central Basin is a low-lying area of gentle hills with rich soils for farming. It is surrounded by the Highland Rim, which is a flat plain at a higher elevation than the Basin. Where the Basin has rich soil, the Rim's soil is a low-organic-content red/yellow clay. The Gulf Coastal Plain physical region, which extends up from the Gulf of Mexico, runs along Tennessee's western border. Soil here is typically gray/brown clay.

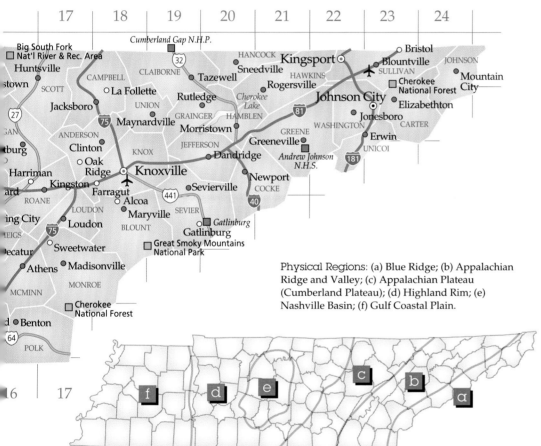

Physical Regions: (a) Blue Ridge; (b) Appalachian Ridge and Valley; (c) Appalachian Plateau (Cumberland Plateau); (d) Highland Rim; (e) Nashville Basin; (f) Gulf Coastal Plain.

Average Monthly Weather

Knoxville	Jan	Feb	Mar	Apr	May	Jun	Jul	Aug	Sep	Oct	Nov	Dec	Yearly
Maximum Temperature °F	46.9	51.2	60.1	71.0	78.3	84.6	87.2	86.9	81.7	70.9	59.1	50.3	69.0
Minimum Temperature °F	29.5	31.7	39.3	48.2	56.5	64.0	68.0	67.1	61.2	48.1	38.4	31.9	48.7
Days of Precipitation	12.4	11.4	12.5	11.0	11.0	10.2	11.4	9.5	8.3	7.8	10.1	10.8	126.4
Memphis													
Maximum Temperature °F	48.3	53.0	61.4	72.9	81.0	88.4	91.5	90.3	84.3	74.5	61.4	52.3	71.6
Minimum Temperature °F	30.9	34.1	41.9	52.2	60.9	68.9	72.6	70.8	61.1	51.3	41.1	34.3	51.9
Days of Precipitation	10.0	9.5	10.8	10.2	9.2	8.5	8.7	7.7	7.2	6.2	8.8	9.6	106.1

Tennessee's History

Tennessee's First People

The first known inhabitants of the state of Tennessee, called Paleo-Indians, probably came to the area about fifteen thousand years ago. Following this group of people were the Archaic, Woodland, and Mississippian cultures.

Next came a group of people called Mound Builders. The Mound Builders received their name for the enormous earthen mounds they erected in honor of their dead. They came to the Tennessee area a little over a thousand years ago.

Following the Mound Builders were the Cherokee, Shawnee, Chickasaw, and Chickamunga tribes. Members of these tribes also constructed mounds in their early history, but this soon ceased. Other tribes residing in Tennessee included the Creek and Yuchi (Uchean) tribes.

The Cherokee dominated the eastern portion and the middle of Tennessee, claiming that land as their hunting grounds. The Shawnee tribe also lived in the middle section of the state. The Chickamunga, a subgroup of the Cherokee, lived more to the south, near where the city of Chattanooga now stands. The third group, the Chickasaw, lived in the western part of Tennessee.

European Exploration

The first European explorers to come to Tennessee were a band of Spaniards. Led by Hernando de Soto, the group moved through some Native American villages in the Tennessee River valley in 1540. One year later, in 1541, de Soto discovered the Mississippi River, near where Memphis now stands.

No other explorers came to Tennessee for over a hundred years. Then, both the English and French claimed parts of the state. Representatives from the two countries explored Tennessee in the same year, 1673. First a pair of Englishmen, James Needham and Gabriel Arthur, explored the Tennessee River valley area. Later in the year, Jacques Marquette, a French priest, and Louis Jolliet from Canada explored the Mississippi River.

Although the French, British, and Spanish all claimed parts of Tennessee, French settlers were the first to move into the area. A French trading post at French Lick was established in 1714, near the settled area called New France.

The French and Indian War, between British and French settlers, started in 1754. Even though the French were severely outnumbered by the British, they still won most of the early skirmishes. By 1763, however, the British had won the war, and subsequently claimed all of the French land east of the Mississippi River.

Tennessee had a significant settler population by 1770. Some of these settlers formed the Watauga Association, a wilderness law-and-order group, in 1772. This group of settlers drew up the first written constitution in North America.

Territorial Period and Statehood

Tennessee did not become a territory in the same way most of the other United States did. The first attempt at starting a territory of some sort came in 1784, after the Revolutionary War, when the state of Franklin was founded. This eastern Tennessee territory was created from the land ceded to the federal government from North Carolina, which had controlled Tennessee's land.

The State of Franklin did not last, however, as North Carolina refused to recognize the independent territory, complete with its own governor. In 1788, Franklin's governor, John Sevier, was arrested, and the territory folded.

Another territorial attempt was made in 1789, when North Carolina ceded some of its western land again to the U.S. government. A new governor, William Blount, was chosen to administer all land south of the Ohio River. The new territory was called Southwest Territory.

This territorial period lasted approximately six years. On June 1, 1796, Tennessee became the sixteenth state in the Union, and Sevier became the first governor of the new state.

Economic Activity

In its early history, Tennessee was primarily an agricultural state. Today, however, only a small percentage of people are employed in agricultural industries. The best agricultural land, the coastal lowlands located near the Mississippi River, grows a number of diverse crops, among them soybeans, tobacco, corn, and wheat are all important crops.

Manufacturing also plays an important role in the Tennessee economy, contributing one-fourth of the gross state product. The manufacturing industries are quite diversified and include chemicals, transportation equipment, electronic equipment, and rubber products. In addition to the traditional factory products, Tennessee has a few automobile assembly lines within its boundaries.

Tennessee is also home to several scientific and energy-related jobs. Ever since the Great Depression, Tennessee has received virtually all of its power from the Tennessee Valley Authority, a Depression-era public works program. Furthermore, the atomic bomb was conceived at Oak Ridge, a Tennessee town that was concealed until after World War II. Today, Oak Ridge continues to support a large national laboratory.

Graceland

There have been thousands of rock-n-roll musicians over the history of the music; however, Elvis Presley is still considered by many to be the "King." Each year, tens of thousands of ardent Elvis fans make a pilgrimage to the home of their late favorite singer. Graceland, located in Memphis, is that place featuring tours and souvenirs commemorating the legenary rock idol.

Important Events

1540 Hernando de Soto move through the Tennessee River Valley.

1541 De Soto and company explores the Mississippi River near Memphis.

1566 Spaniards build a fort near present-day Chattanooga.

1673 British and French explorers come to Tennessee.

1714 French trading post at French Lick is established.

1763 British win the French and Indian War and claim all land east of the Mississippi River, including Tennessee.

1769 First permanent white settlement established in Watauga Valley.

1772 Settlers form the Watauga Association, a law-and-order group.

1784 State of Franklin established, but was not recognized.

1788 Franklin's governor, John Sevier, is arrested, and the territory folds.

1790 Tennessee becomes Southwest Territory.

1796 Tennessee becomes sixteenth state in the Union on June 1.

1829 Andrew Jackson becomes the 7th president of the United States.

1843 Permanent state capital established at Nashville.

1861 Tennessee secedes from Union; last Southern state to do so.

1862 Battle of Shiloh, one of the most costly of the Civil War, is fought.

1863 Confederate defeat at the battles of Chickamauga and Chattanooga.

1866 Tennessee is readmitted to the Union after the Civil War.

1925 Scopes "Monkey Trial" held at Dayton.

1933 Tennessee Valley Authority (TVA) created.

1942 Manhattan Project, to build an atomic bomb, created.

1964 Tennessee Space Institute founded.

1968 Rev. Martin Luther King, Jr., assassinated on April 4 in Memphis.

1973 Elvis Presley dies at Graceland, August 16.

1988 Worst drought in years hits Tennessee.

1993 U.S. Postal Service issues an Elvis Presley commemorative stamp.

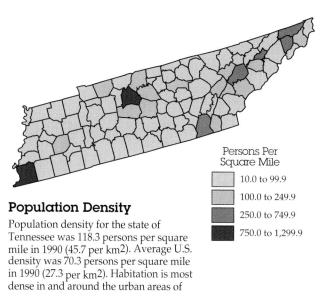

Population Density

Population density for the state of Tennessee was 118.3 persons per square mile in 1990 (45.7 per km2). Average U.S. density was 70.3 persons per square mile in 1990 (27.3 per km2). Habitation is most dense in and around the urban areas of Nashville, Memphis, Knoxville, and Chattanooga.

Persons Per Square Mile
- 10.0 to 99.9
- 100.0 to 249.9
- 250.0 to 749.9
- 750.0 to 1,299.9

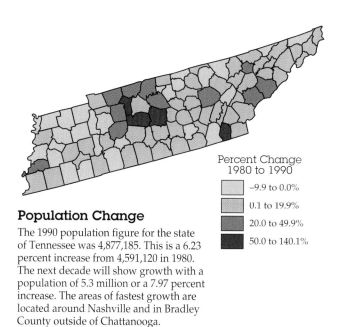

Population Change

The 1990 population figure for the state of Tennessee was 4,877,185. This is a 6.23 percent increase from 4,591,120 in 1980. The next decade will show growth with a population of 5.3 million or a 7.97 percent increase. The areas of fastest growth are located around Nashville and in Bradley County outside of Chattanooga.

Percent Change 1980 to 1990
- –9.9 to 0.0%
- 0.1 to 19.9%
- 20.0 to 49.9%
- 50.0 to 140.1%

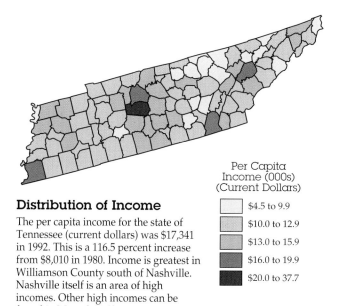

Distribution of Income

The per capita income for the state of Tennessee (current dollars) was $17,341 in 1992. This is a 116.5 percent increase from $8,010 in 1980. Income is greatest in Williamson County south of Nashville. Nashville itself is an area of high incomes. Other high incomes can be found in Memphis, Chattanooga, and Knoxville.

Per Capita Income (000s) (Current Dollars)
- $4.5 to 9.9
- $10.0 to 12.9
- $13.0 to 15.9
- $16.0 to 19.9
- $20.0 to 37.7

Population Projections

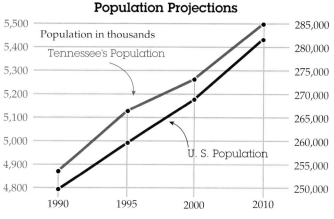

Population in thousands

Tennessee's Population

U. S. Population

Population Change

Year	Population
1950	3,292,000
1960	3,575,000
1970	3,937,000
1980	4,591,120
1990	4,877,185
2000	4,410,000
2010	4,609,000

Period	Change
1950–1970	19.6%
1970–1980	16.6%
1980–1990	6.2%
1990–2000	8.0%

Population Facts

State Population, 1993: 5,099,000

Rank: 17

Population 2000: 5,266,000 (Rank 17)

Density: 118.3 per sq. mi. (45.7 per km²)

Distribution: 60.9% urban, 39.1% rural

Population Under 5 Years Old: 7.0%

Population Under 18 Years Old: 24.8%

Population Over 65 Years Old: 12.7%

Median Age: 33.6

Number of Households: 1,854,000

Average Persons Per Household: 2.56

Average Persons Per Family: 3.05

Female Heads of Households: 4.77%

Population That Is Married: 21.73%

Birth Rate: 15.4 per 1,000 population

Death Rate: 9.5 per 1,000 population

Births to Teen Mothers: 17.6%

Marriage Rate: 13.4 per 1,000 population

Divorce Rate: 6.5 per 1,000 population

Violent Crime Rate: 726 per 100,000 pop.

Population on Social Security: 17.1%

Percent Voting for President: 52.4%

Population Profile

Rank. Tennessee ranks 17th among U.S. states in terms of population with 5,099,000 citizens.

Minority Population. The state's minority population is 17.5 percent. The state's male to female ratio for 1990 was 92.91 males for every 100 females. It was below the national average of 95.22 males for every 100 females.

Growth. Growing slower than the projected national average, the state's population is

Government

Capital: Nashville (established 1826).

Statehood: Became 16th state on Jun. 1, 1796.

Number of Counties: 95.

Supreme Court Justices: 5, 8-year term.

State Senators: 33, 4-year term.

State Legislators: 99, 2-year term.

United States Senators: 2.

United States Representatives: 9.

Electoral Votes: 11.

State Constitution: Adopted 1870.

Tennessee's Famous Citizens

Baker, Howard (b. 1925). He served in the U.S. Senate from 1966 to 1984, the last 4 years as Senate majority leader.

Forrest, Nathan (1821–1877). He became the first grand wizard of the Ku Klux Klan, which he helped found.

Hastie, William (1904–1976). He became the first black judge of the U.S. Circuit Court of Appeals in 1949.

Moore, Grace (1901–1947). Opera singer and actress. She starred in the 1934 film *One Night of Love*.

Parton, Dolly (b. 1946). Country singer-songwriter and actress. She won a Grammy Award in 1978 for the song "Here You Come Again."

Ransom, John Crowe (1888–1974). Poet. He founded the *Kenyon Review* and was known for his literary criticism.

Ross, John (1790–1866). Principal chief of the Cherokee Nation. He had to lead his people on the *Trail of Tears* to Oklahoma.

Terrell, Mary Church (1863–1954). First president of the National Association of Colored Women.

expected to reach 5.5 million by the year 2010 (*see graph above*).

Older Citizens. The state's population older than 65 was 618,818 in 1990. It grew 19.56% from 517,588 in 1980.

Younger Citizens. The number of children (under 18 years of age) was 1.2 million in 1990. This represents 24.9 percent of the state's population. The state's school aged population was 818 thousand in 1990. It is expected to increase to 829 thousand by the year 2000. This represents a 1.34% change.

Urban/Rural. 60.9% of the population of the state live in urban areas while 39.1% live in rural areas.

Largest Cities. Tennessee has nine cities with a population greater than 35,000. The populations of the state's largest centers are (starting from the most populous) Memphis (610,337), Nashville-Davidson (488,374), Knoxville (165,121), Chattanooga (152,466), Clarksville (75,494), Johnson City (49,381), Jackson (48,949), Murfreesboro (44,922), Kingsport (36,365), Germantown (32,893), Hendersonville (32,188), Cleveland (30,354), Columbia (28,583), Oak Ridge (27,310), and Bartlett (26,989).

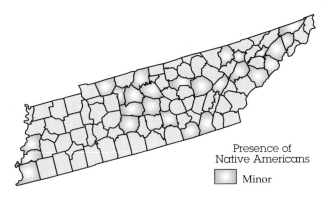

Presence of Native Americans

☐ Minor

Native American

The Native American population in Tennessee was 10,039 in 1990. This was an increase of 44.53 percent from 6,946 in 1980. Twenty-one percent of the Native Americans in Tennessee can be found in Nashville (1,130) and Memphis (960). Tennessee is also the home of the Yuchi tribe.

Nationalities

African	4,584
American	681,522
Arab	5,365
Austrian	2,071
Czech	4,061
Dutch	75,611
English	537,164
Finnish	1,508
German	577,416
Greek	5,832
Hungarian	4,631
Irish	572,665
Italian	51,197
Norwegian	7,766
Polish	23,026
Portuguese	1,155
Russian	7,182
Scottish	69,514
Slovak	4,713
Swedish	17,328
Welsh	17,591
West Indian	3,391

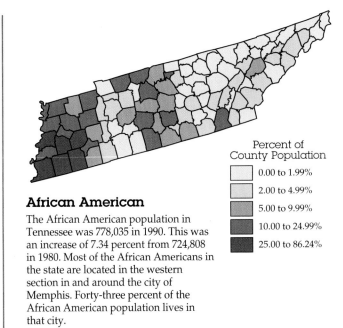

Percent of County Population

☐ 0.00 to 1.99%
☐ 2.00 to 4.99%
☐ 5.00 to 9.99%
☐ 10.00 to 24.99%
☐ 25.00 to 86.24%

African American

The African American population in Tennessee was 778,035 in 1990. This was an increase of 7.34 percent from 724,808 in 1980. Most of the African Americans in the state are located in the western section in and around the city of Memphis. Forty-three percent of the African American population lives in that city.

Statewide Ethnic Composition

Eighty-three percent of the population of Tennessee is white. The largest nationalities in this racial group are German, Irish, and English. The next largest group is African Americans, followed by Hispanics, Asian Americans, and Native Americans. Over 681,000 people claim to be American and acknowledge no other nationality.

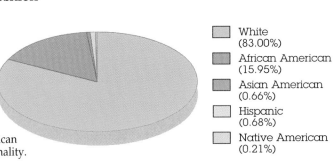

☐ White (83.00%)
☐ African American (15.95%)
☐ Asian American (0.66%)
☐ Hispanic (0.68%)
☐ Native American (0.21%)

Education Facts

Total Students 1990: 81,966	Mean SAT Score 1991 Verbal: 487
Number of School Districts: 141	Mean SAT Score 1991 Math: 528
Expenditure Per Capita on Education 1990: $575	Average Teacher's Salary 1992: $28,600
Expenditure Per Capita K–12 1990: $542	Rank Teacher's Salary: 36th in U.S.
Expenditure Per Pupil 1990: $3,707	High School Graduates 1990: 46,300
Total School Enrollment 1990–1991: 833,590	Total Number of Public Schools: 1,535
Rank of Expenditures Per Student: 44th in the U.S.	Number of Teachers 1990: 43,643
African American Enrollment: 22.3%	Student/Teacher Ratio: 19.1
Hispanic Enrollment: 0.3%	Staff Employed in Public Schools: 86,049
Asian/Pacific Islander Enrollment: 0.7%	Pupil/Staff Ratio: 9.5
Native American Enrollment: 0.1%	Staff/Teacher Ratio: 2.0

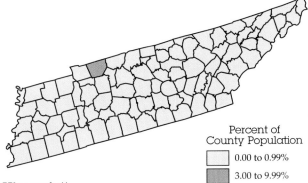

Percent of County Population

☐ 0.00 to 0.99%
☐ 3.00 to 9.99%

Hispanic[††]

The Hispanic population in Tennessee was 32,741 in 1990. This is a decrease of -3.92 percent from 34,077 persons in 1980. The county with the highest percentage of Hispanics is the northern county of Montgomery. The city of Clarksville can be found here. This is also the site of Fort Campbell.

[††]A person of Mexican, Puerto Rican, Cuban, or other Spanish culture or origin regardless of race.

Education

Attainment: 65.4 percent of population 25 years or older were high school graduates in 1989, earning Tennessee a ranking of 48th the United States; 15.7 percent of the state's population had completed college. Institutions of Higher Education: The largest universities and colleges in the state include University of Tennessee, Knoxville; Vanderbilt University, Nashville; University of the South, Sewanee. Expenditures per Student: Expenditure increased 72% between 1985 and 1990. Projected High School Graduations: 1998 (47,829), 2004 (48,499); Total Revenues for Education from Federal Sources: $233 million; Total Revenues for Education from State Sources: $994 million; Total Revenues for Education from Local Sources: $1 billion; Average Annual Salaries for Public School Principals: $38,833; Largest School Districts in State: Memphis City School District, 105,604 students, 19th in the United States; Nashville-Davidson County School District, 67,352, 40th.

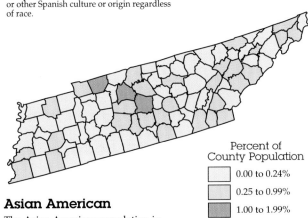

Percent of County Population

☐ 0.00 to 0.24%
☐ 0.25 to 0.99%
☐ 1.00 to 1.99%

Asian American

The Asian American population in Tennessee was 31,839 in 1990. This is an increase of 114.79 percent from 14,823 persons in 1980. The county of Montgomery and Fort Campbell have a high percentage of Asian Americans. Communities can also be found in Nashville and Murfreesboro.

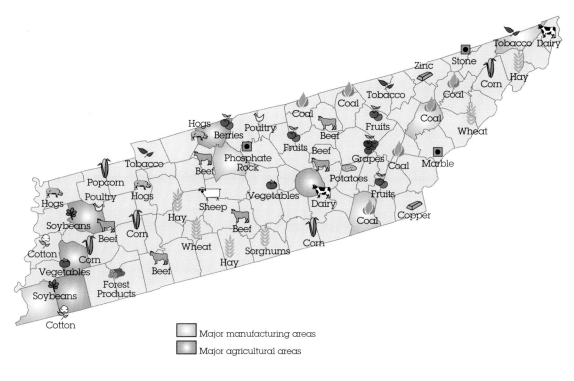

Major manufacturing areas
Major agricultural areas

Transportation

Tennessee's terrain has caused many transportation problems, especially of a financial nature. Building roads and railroads through Tennessee's hills was at first costly. Nevertheless, the state developed a solid transportation network. Tennessee has almost 85,000 miles of highways and roads.

Several rail lines provide freight service to many parts of Tennessee. In addition, passenger lines link Memphis, in the southwest corner of Tennessee, with other regional cities like Chicago and New Orleans. Three rivers—the Mississippi, Tennessee, and Cumberland—provide water transportation routes. The Tennessee-Tombigbee Waterway links the state with Alabama, and ultimately, the Gulf of Mexico. Memphis is not only Tennessee's busiest airport, but also the main terminal for Federal Express. Nashville and Knoxville also have important airports.

Energy and Transportation Facts

Energy. Yearly Consumption: 1,746 tril. BTUs (residential, 21.9%; commercial, 11.5%; industrial, 41.5%; transportation, 25.2%); Annual Energy Expenditures Per Capita: $1,872; Nuclear Power Plants Located in State: 2; Source of Energy Consumed: Petroleum— 34.3%; Natural Gas— 14.2%; Coal— 34.2%; Hydroelectric Power—6.6%; Nuclear Power—10.8%.

Transportation. Highway Miles: 85,144 (interstates, 1,062; urban, 16,314; rural, 68,830); Average Yearly Auto Insurance: $478 (37th); Auto Fatalities Rank: 5th; Registered Motor Vehicles: 4,645,083; Workers in Carpools: 18.4%; Workers Using Public Trans: 1.3%.

Agriculture

Tennessee has 12.4 million farm acres. During the last 40 years, Tennessee's farms have grown larger in size and fewer in number. In 1955, 203,000 farms were found in the state. Today, 86,000 remain.

Agriculture adds $2 billion to the state's gross product annually. The principal commodities in order of marketing receipts are cattle, dairy products, cotton, and tobacco.

Beef cattle, Tennessee's leading agricultural product, are raised mainly in the Nashville Basin and the Great Valley. Hogs are found in the western half of the state. This area is also home to Tennessee's leading crop, soybeans. Cotton is also grown in the west, and tobacco is found in the northeastern and central parts of the state. Hay and corn, found throughout the state, are used primarily as cattle feed.

Housing

Owner Occupied Units: 2,026,067; Average Age of Units: 25 years; Average Value of Housing Units: $58,400; Renter Occupied Units: 568,875; Median Monthly Rent: $357; Housing Starts: 31,200; Existing Home Sales: 120,500.

Economic Facts

Gross State Product: $92,000,000,000 (1989)

Income Per Capita: $17,341

Disposable Personal Income: $15,820

Median Household Income: $24,807

Average Annual Pay, 1988: $21,541

Principal Industries: food products, chemicals, machinery, rubber products, transportation equipment, fabricated metal products, electrical equipment

Major Crops: milk, tobacco, hay, cotton, wheat, soybeans, corn, lumber

Fish: Bass, Crappies, Trout, Walleyes

Livestock: hogs, cattle, horses

Non-Fuel Minerals: Marble, Pyrite, Zinc, Lignite, Barite, Copper, Stone

Organic Fuel Minerals: Coal, Petroleum, Nat. Gas

Civilian Labor Force: 2,416,000 (Women: 1,080,000)

Total Employed: 2,256,000 (Women: 1,009,000)

Median Value of Housing: $58,400

Median Contract Rent: $357 per month

Economic Sectors 1992

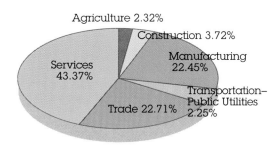

Agriculture 2.32%
Construction 3.72%
Services 43.37%
Manufacturing 22.45%
Transportation– Public Utilities 2.25%
Trade 22.71%

Manufacturing

Tennessee is a leading manufacturing state, producing a wide variety of goods. Approximately 25 percent of the state's gross product comes from manufacturing industries. In terms of value added by manufacture, chemical production is the leading manufacturing activity. Other industries include food processing, machinery, and transportation equipment.

Manufacturing takes place throughout Tennessee; Memphis, Nashville, and the Tri-Cities of Bristol, Kingsport, and Johnson City are all industrial centers. The manufacture of all types of chemicals accounts for 15 percent of Tennessee's manufacturing income. Many food products, including cereals, come from Memphis. Fayetteville and Lewisburg make heating and refrigeration equipment. Large automobile manufacturing plants operate in Smyrna and Spring Hill.

Employment

Employment. Tennessee employed 2.36 million people in 1993. Most work in social and personal services (574,000 persons or 24.3% of the workforce). Manufacturing accounts for 22.4% or 528,300 workers. Wholesale and retail trade account for 22.7% or 534,200 workers. Government employs 361,700 workers (15.3%). Construction employs 94,400 workers (4.0%). Transportation and utilities account for 5.4% or 126,400 persons. Agriculture employs 54,200 workers or 2.3%. Finance, real estate, and insurance account for 4.4% or 103,700 workers. Mining employs 5,300 people and accounts for only 0.2% of the workforce.

Unemployment. Unemployment has decreased to 5.7% in 1993 from a rate of 8.0% in 1985. Today's figure is lower than the national average of 6.8% as shown below.

Unemployment Rate

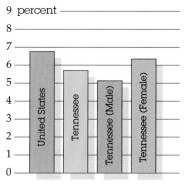

9 percent
8
7
6
5
4
3
2
1
0

United States | Tennessee | Tennessee (Male) | Tennessee (Female)

TEXAS
The State of Texas

Official State Seal

The Great Seal of Texas was first used during the time Texas was a republic. The seal read "The Republic of Texas," and included the wreath of laurel and oak. The star was also present. After Texas joined the Union the seal was changed from "Republic" to "State." The reverse side of the seal contains the flags of the six nations that once ruled over Texas.

Legal Holidays

January: New Year's Day—1st; February: Presidents' Day—3d Monday; Confederate Heroes Day—19th; March: Independence Day—2d; April: San Jacinto Day—21st; May: Memorial Day—4th Monday; June: Emancipation Day—19th; July: Independence Day—4th; August: Lyndon B. Johnson's Birthday—27th; September: Labor Day—1st Monday; October: Columbus Day—2d Monday; November: Father of Texas Day (Austin)—3rd; Veterans' Day—11th; Thanksgiving—4th Thursday; December: Christmas—25th; Admission Day—29th.

Texas's Finances

Households: 6,071,000; Income Per Capita Current Dollars: $17,892; Change Per Capita Income 1980 to 1992: 81.8% (45th in U.S.); State Expenditures: $30,744,000,000; State Revenues: $31,346,000,000; Personal Income Tax: N/A; Federal Income Taxes Paid Per Capita: $1,766; Sales Tax: 6.25% (food and prescription drugs exempt).

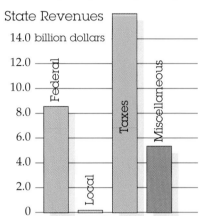

State Expenditures

State Revenues

Official State Flag

Adopted in 1839, this flag contains the lone star that has been present on flags flown over Texas since 1819. The flag contains three stripes, one vertical and two horizontal. The red, white, and blue on the stripes represents Texas's union with the United States.

Festivals and Events

January: Texas Citrus Fiesta, Mission; February: Charro Days, Brownsville; March: Houston Festival, Houston; Waco Wind Fest, Waco; St. Patrick's Day Beard Growing Contest, Shamrock; April: Poteet Strawberry Festival, Poteet; Fiesta San Antonio, San Antonio; May: Springfest, Bryan; Stagecoach Days, Marshall; June: Seaspace, Houston; Juneteenth Blues Festival, Houston; July: Great Texas Mosquito Fest, Clute; Harvest Weekends, Bryan; August: Texas Folklife Fest, San Antonio; Austin Aqua Fest, Austin; September: Pioneer Days, Fort Worth; Native American Pow Wow, Grand Prairie; October: Fireant Fest, Marshall; November: Wonderland of Lights, Marshall; December: Dickens on the Strand, Galveston.

Texas Compared to States in Its Region.

Resident Pop. in Metro Areas: 1st; Pop. Percent Increase: 1st; Pop. Over 65: 4th; Infant Mortality: 3d; School Enroll. Increase: 1st; High School Grad. and Up: 2d; Violent Crime: 2d; Hazardous Waste Sites: 1st; Unemployment: 2d; Median Household Income: 1st; Persons Below Poverty: 3d; Energy Costs Per Person: 2d.

West South Central

	Population	Capital
Arkansas	2,424,000	Little Rock
Louisiana	4,295,000	Baton Rouge
Oklahoma	3,231,000	Oklahoma City
Texas	18,031,000	Austin

Location, Size, and Boundaries

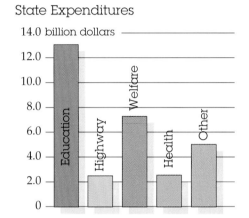

Location. Texas is located in the West South Central region of the United States. It is bounded on three of four sides by land with a general coast along the Gulf of Mexico to the southeast. The geographic center of Texas is lat. 31° 14.6' N; long. 99° 27.5' W.

Size. Texas is the 2d largest state. Its area is 267,338 sq. mi. (692,405 km2). Inland water covers 5,204 sq. mi. (13,478 km2). Texas touches the Gulf of Mexico along a 367 mile coastline.

Boundaries. Oklahoma, 846 mi. (1,362 km); Arkansas, 102 mi. (164 km); Louisiana, 327 mi. (526 km); Gulf of Mexico, 367 mi. (591 km); Mexico, 889 mi. (1,431 km); New Mexico, 498 mi. (801 km).

Geographic Extent. The north/south extent is 773 mi. (1,244 km). The state extends 801 mi. (1,289 km) to the east/west.

Facts about Texas. Origin of Name: From the Indian word *Tejas*; Nickname: The Lone Star State; Motto: "Friendship"; Abbreviations: Tex. (traditional), TX (postal); State Bird: mockingbird; State Tree: pecan; State Flower: bluebonnet; State Song: "Texas, Our Texas," words by Gladys Yoakum Wright and William J. Marsh and music by William J. Marsh.

Texas Compared to Other States. Resident Pop. in Metro Areas: 13th; Pop. Per. Increase: 13th; Pop. Over 65: 46th; Infant Mortality: 37th; School Enroll. Increase: 34th; High School Grad. and Up: 39th; Violent Crime: 9th; Hazardous Waste Sites: 13th; Unemployment: 12th; Median Household Income: 32d; Persons Below Poverty: 8th; Energy Costs Per Person: 4th.

Sources of Information. Tourism: Texas Department of Commerce, Tourism Division, P.O. Box 12728, Austin, TX 78711. Economy: Texas Department of Commerce, P.O. Box 12728, Capitol Station, Austin, TX 78711. Government/History: Staff Services, P.O. Box 12068, Austin, TX 78711.

Weather Facts

Record High Temperature: 120° F (49° C) on August 12, 1936, at Seymour; Record Low Temperature: -23° F (-31° C) on February 8, 1933, at Seminole; Average January Temperature: 46° F (8° C); Average July Temperature: 84° F (29° C); Average Yearly Precipitation: 28 in. (71 cm).

Environmental Facts

Air Pollution Rank: 1st; Water Pollution Rank: 2d; Total Yearly Industrial Pollution: 192,108,234 lbs.; Industrial Pollution Rank: 2d; Hazardous Waste Sites: 29; Hazardous Sites Rank: 13th; Landfill Capacity: adequate; Fresh Water Supply: surplus in East, impending shortage in southwest; Daily Residential Water Consumption: 180 gals. per capita; Endangered Species: Aquatic Species (8)—darter, fountain; Birds (13)—crane, whooping; Mammals (4)—bat, Mexican long-nosed; Other Species (18)—harvestman, bee creek cave; Plants (28)—ambrosia, South Texas.

Land Use

Cropland: 19.5%; Pasture: 10.8%; Rangeland: 58.1%; Forest: 5.8%; Urban: 4.3%; Other: 1.5%.

Environmental Quality

Texas residents generate 17.8 million tons of solid waste each year, or approximately 2,200 pounds per capita. Landfill capacity in Texas will be exhausted in more than 12 years. The state has 29 hazardous waste sites. Annual greenhouse gas emissions in Texas total 459.0 million tons, or 27.3 tons per capita. Industrial sources in Texas release approximately 441.2 thousand tons of toxins, 2.4 million tons of acid precipitation-producing substances, and 9.5 million tons of smog-producing substances into the atmosphere each year.

The state has 1,098,700 acres within the National Park System; the largest area within the state is Big Bend National Park. State parks cover just over 201,000 acres, attracting 24.0 million visitors per year.

Topography

There are several distinct topographic regions in Texas. The Gulf Coastal Plain physical region covers Texas from the Rio Grande in the lower southwest corner of the state to the eastern border with Louisiana. The southern portion of this low-lying region has very rich soil, suitable for agriculture. The

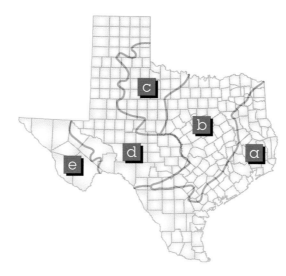

Physical Regions: (a) Gulf Coastal Plains; (b) Prairie Plains; (c) Rolling Plains; (d) Great Plains; (e) Basin and Range Region.

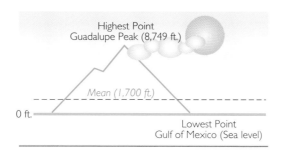

For more information about Texas's environment, contact the Office of Environmental Analysis, Department of Health, 1100 W. 49th St., Austin, TX 78711.

soil is distinctive because it is the only soil in Texas that is classed warm and moist or wet, while the soil in the rest of the state is warm and dry. Soil color in this region ranges from red/yellow to a black mud that cracks in the hot summer sun. A thickly forested area called the Piney Woods reaches into southeastern Texas from Louisiana.

West of the Coastal Plains is thePrairie Plains physical region, with rolling hills and rugged terrain. The soil of the Texas Hill Country, and the Burnet-Llano Basin, is a red clay. The fertile Black Waxy Prairie is also located in this region. The Rolling Plains physical region continues the rolling hilly landscape of the North-Central Plains. The Great Plains physical region is a flat treeless area that extends from the Rolling Plains west into New Mexico and up into the High Plains of the Texas Panhandle. The soil of the Great Plains, as well as that of the Rolling Plains, is reddish brown with an organically rich black surface.

The Basin and Range physical region is located in the far western part of the state below New Mexico. The soil ranges from loamy clay to huge surface deposits of limestone and gypsum. The terrain includes high plains interrupted by various mountain ranges, including the Santiago, Davis, and Guadalupe ranges. The highest point in the state is Guadalupe Peak, which has an elevation of 8,751 ft. (2,667 m).

Climate

Texas's climate ranges from a humid subtropical in the southwest, to a semiarid climate in the northwest. The lower Rio Grande valley has the highest average January and July temperatures, 60 degrees F and 85 degrees F, respectively. At Amarillo, in the northern panhandle, the average July temperature, 79 degrees F, is warm. However, January temperatures average only 35 degrees F. Along the Gulf of Mexico coast, weather is warm, but damp.

Precipitation in Texas decreases as one travels east to west, although the entire state receives some rainfall. Tyler, in east Texas, averages 46 inches of precipitation. However, in El Paso, on the Mexican border, yearly precipitation sometimes does not exceed 10 inches.

The Red River valley, on the Texas-Oklahoma border, is the site of some rather violent weather. Each year, at least 100 tornadoes of various sizes pass through the area, causing much damage.

Hydrology

The Rio Grande forms Texas's southwest border with Mexico, entering from New Mexico and emptying into the Gulf of Mexico. The Red River forms much of Texas's northern border with Oklahoma, while the Sabine defines half of its eastern border with Louisiana. Most of the principal rivers within the state flow southeasterly and empty into the Gulf of Mexico. These include the Colorado, the Brazos, and the Trinity rivers in central and eastern Texas. The Pecos River, in southwest Texas, flows into the Rio Grande. The Canadian River flows east across northern Texas.

Most of Texas's lakes are man-made, created for hydroelectric or irrigation purposes. The largest of these is Toledo Bend on the Louisiana border. Others include Armistad and Falcon reservoirs on the Rio Grande. Texas is also home to many saltwater lakes, including the Sal de Rey and Sal Vieja.

Average Monthly Weather

Dallas-Ft. Worth	Jan	Feb	Mar	Apr	May	Jun	Jul	Aug	Sep	Oct	Nov	Dec	Yearly
Maximum Temperature °F	54.0	59.1	67.2	76.8	84.4	93.2	97.8	97.3	89.7	79.5	66.2	58.1	76.9
Minimum Temperature °F	33.9	37.8	44.9	55.0	62.9	70.8	74.7	73.7	67.5	56.3	44.9	37.4	55.0
Days of Precipitation	6.7	6.5	7.1	7.9	8.78	6.4	4.9	4.6	6.8	6.0	5.8	6.3	77.8
El Paso													
Maximum Temperature °F	57.9	62.7	69.6	78.7	87.1	95.9	95.3	93.0	87.5	78.5	65.7	58.2	77.5
Minimum Temperature °F	30.4	34.1	40.5	48.5	56.6	65.7	69.6	67.5	60.6	48.7	37.0	30.6	49.2
Days of Precipitation	3.9	2.8	2.4	1.7	2.2	3.4	7.8	8.0	5.3	4.1	2.7	3.7	48.1

Flora and Fauna

The popular notion that Texas is nothing but flatland is not too far from the truth. Forested areas make up only 14 percent of the state. Eastern Texas, near Tyler, has a dense forest composed of both softwoods (pine trees) and a variety of hardwoods (magnolia, oak, ash). Other Texas trees include juniper, aspen, pecan, and hickory. Texas has over 500 different types of grasses, such as side oats, growing across the state. Common Texas wildflowers include sunflowers and primroses. Cactus and yucca, two desert plants, grow

in the southwestern part of the state.

As in other states, bison once lived across the Texas plains. Today, however, they are found only in protected areas. Many of Texas's large animals, including black bears and mountain lions, live in the eastern forested areas. Smaller animals living in Texas include armadillos, coyotes, and antelope. Many reptiles, including alligators and snakes, also inhabit the state. Bass, sunfish, and other freshwater fish live in Texas rivers and lakes.

Legend

⭐ State capitol

⊙ Cities over 35,000

○ Other significant cities

● County Seats

■ Major cultural attractions

▢ State Parks

Ⓦ Welcome Centers

⚲ Major colleges and universities

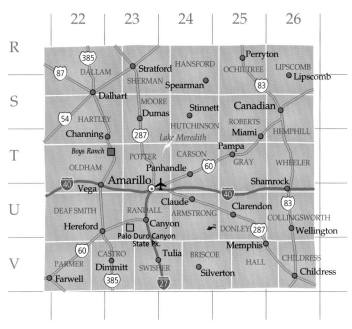

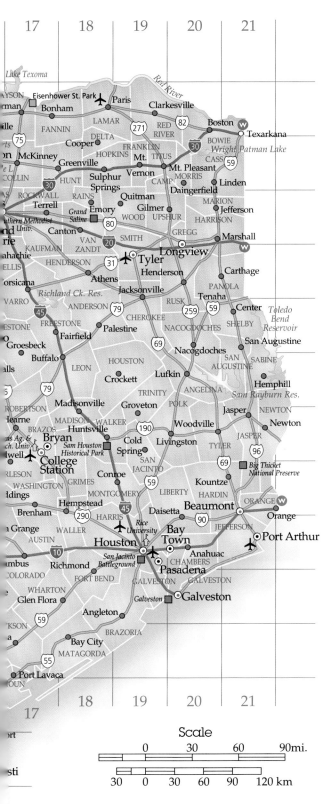

Scale

```
0       30      60      90mi.
```

```
30   0   30    60    90    120 km
```

Major Cities

Abilene	E-12	El Paso	F-1	Mesquite	D-16
Amarillo	U-23	Fort Worth	D-16	Midland	E-8
Arlington	D-16	Galveston	K-20	Odessa	F-7
Austin	I-15	Garland	D-16	Pasadena	J-19
Baytown	J-20	Grand Prairie	D-16	Plano	D-16
Beaumont	I-21	Harlingen	Q-15	Port Arthur	J-21
Brownsville	Q-15	Houston	J-19	Richardson	D-16
Bryan	H-17	Irving	D-16	San Angelo	G-10
Carrollton	D-16	Killeen	G-15	San Antonio	K-14
College Station	H-17	Laredo	O-12	Tyler	E-19
Corpus Christi	N-15	Longview	E-20	Victoria	L-16
Dallas	D-16	Lubbock	B-8	Waco	F-16
Denton	C-16	McAllen	Q-14	Wichita Falls	B-14

■ **Abilene.** Established as a stock shipping point in 1881; Abilene Christian University; Abilene Fine Arts Museum; Fort Phantom Hill. (E-12)

■ **Alamo State Historical Site.** Former Spanish mission that later became a Texas revolution massacre site in 1836. (K-14)

■ **Amistad Dam.** Dam on Rio Grande forms a large reservoir and recreation area. (K-9)

■ **Big Bend National Park.** Along the Rio Grande: diversified landscape includes canyons, volcanic rock formations, floodplains, and deserts. (L-6)

■ **Big Thicket National Preserve.** Vast area of tangled, often impenetrable woods, streams, and marshes; hiking and boating. (I-21)

■ **Boys Ranch.** Successful home for troubled boys; Old Tascosa, former important supply and shipping point for several large ranches, now a ghost town; Boot Hill Cemetery. (T-23)

■ **Caverns of Sonora.** Delicate Crystal formations grow in profusion on ceilings, walls, and floors. (I-10)

■ **Crystal City.** Primary center for packing, processing, and shipping vegetables; famous for its spinach crop; Popeye statue downtown. (L-11)

■ **Eisenhower State Park.** House where President Dwight D. Eisenhower was born in Denison. (B-17)

■ **Fort Davis National Historic Site.** Ruins of frontier outpost established in 1854; popular camping and hiking areas nearby. (I-5)

■ **Fredericksburg.** Settled by immigrant Germans in 1846; many original buildings in traditional German style; birthplace of Admiral Nimitz. (I-13)

■ **Galveston.** Port and seaside resort; 10.4-mile-long seawall protects Galveston Island from damaging storms; seaside attractions. (K-20)

■ **Grand Saline.** One of the largest salt plants in the United States; salt dome under city is 1.5 miles across and 16,000 feet thick. (D-18)

■ **Guadalupe Mountains National Park.** High peaks, deep canyons and diversified plant and animal life; hiking and camping. (F-3)

■ **Highland Lakes.** North of Austin; dams on Colorado River form Austin, Travis, Marble Falls, L. B. Johnson, Inks, and Buchanan lakes. (I-15)

■ **Jersey Lily Saloon.** Rustic saloon, courtroom, and billiard hall of Judge Roy Bean. (J-9)

■ **Johnson City.** Named for pioneer Johnson family; Lyndon B. Johnson National Historical Park; Pedernales Falls State Park. (I-14)

■ **King Ranch.** Largest cattle ranch in continental U.S.; 825,000 acres spread over four counties; several unique breeds of cattle. (O-15)

■ **Laredo.** Nation's largest inland port; port of entry into Mexico on Pan American Highway and Rio Grande. (O-12)

■ **McDonald Observatory.** On Mount Locke; clear air and cloudless nights make ideal site for 82-inch reflecting telescope. (H-4)

■ **Mineral Wells.** Health and pleasure resort famous for medicinal waters; view of Brazos River from nearby Inspiration Point. (D-14)

■ **Missions of San Antonio.** In addition to the Alamo, four other Franciscan missions established in San Antonio; Mission Trail, a driving route connecting the missions. (K-14)

■ **Padre Island National Seashore.** 80-mile stretch of undeveloped beach; one of the last natural seashores in the nation. (O-15)

■ **Palo Duro Canyon State Park.** One of state's largest state parks; scenic canyons and multicolored rock strata; outdoor Pioneer Amphitheater, setting for *Texas* musical drama. (U-23)

■ **Sam Houston Historical Park.** Monument to early history of Houston; restored historic buildings; Museum of Texas History; the Long Row, a reconstructed 1837 shopping strip. (H-18)

■ **San Jacinto Battleground State Historic Park.** Place where Texas won independence from Mexico in 1836, marked by a 570-foot monument; San Jacinto Museum of Texas History. (J-19)

■ **Sierra de Cristo Rey.** Large monument of Christ built on 4,576-foot summit above El Paso where territories of Texas, Mexico, and New Mexico meet. (F-1)

■ **Ysleta del Sur Pueblo.** Oldest community in Texas; visitor program and arts and crafts center run by Tigua Indians. (F-1)

Texas's History

Texas's First People

Human beings have lived in the area of Texas since at least 10,000 B.C. with a second wave of early residents arriving around 500 B.C. According to archaeological evidence, these later people were racially and culturally different from their predecessors.

With the agricultural revolution came another group of ancient people. These Neo-American Indians used the newly developed bow and arrow. Two groups of people, resembling the Pueblo and Mound Building cultures of other areas, lived in the panhandle and eastern parts of Texas, respectively.

Many different Native American tribes lived in the state. The most sophisticated of the tribes was the Caddo from eastern Texas, who lived in villages composed of large wooden buildings and whose culture had a distinct social order. In the southern and coastal parts of Texas lived the Coahuiltecan and Karankawa tribes.

The Plains Native American culture was represented by several individual tribes, including the Tonkawa, Lipan Apache, Comanche, Kiowa, Kiowa-Apache, and Wichita. In the far western edges of Texas, members of the Pueblo culture could be found, although these people soon disappeared.

European Exploration

The Spanish were the first Europeans to explore Texas. The state was first claimed in 1519, when Alonso de Pineda sailed along the Gulf of Mexico coast from Florida to Mexico. Later, another Spaniard, Álvar Núñez Cabeza de Vaca, explored the interior of Texas. In 1540, Francisco Vásquez de Coronado ventured into the western part of Texas. The first European settlement in Texas was established in 1682, at Ysleta, near present-day El Paso. The Spanish went on to set up two missions in 1690, but soon abandoned them.

Texas interested not only Spanish explorers, but French explorers as well. René-Robert Cavelier, the Sieur de La Salle, established Fort St. Louis, on Matagorda Bay, for the French in 1685. However, in 1687, Fort St. Louis was destroyed by Indians.

Republic Period and Statehood

In 1819, Spain was granted control of Texas under the Adams-Onís Treaty Two years later, this area fell under Mexican control when it broke away from Spain. In 1823, Stephen Austin went to Mexico City to persuade the Mexican government to allow settlement in Texas. Mexico granted Stephen Austin's request, and legitimate American settlement began. By 1836, Texas's population was around fifty thousand.

The Texans (being mainly Americans) had more in common with the people of the United States than with Mexico and this caused strained relations with the Mexican government. Furthermore, the language and cultural differences between Mexicans and the Texans, made relations difficult.

In 1836, Texas fought for its independence. The most famous battle occurred at the Alamo, near San Antonio. Here, 187 people, including Davy Crockett, held the Alamo for five days before it fell. The Texans lost this battle, but soon went on to win the war and declare independence.

In 1845, Texas petitioned the United States for statehood, and Congress approved the plan. Passage of the measure was delayed because many northern states did not want another slave state, but on December 29, 1845, Texas became the twenty-eighth state.

During the subsequent Mexican War, the United States gained control of some of Mexico's territories, and much of this new acquisition became part of Texas for a brief time. The state of Texas received $10 million in the Compromise of 1850, when it relinquished its claim to lands that eventually made up parts of New Mexico, Colorado, Wyoming, Oklahoma, and Kansas.

Economic Development

Early in Texas's history, agriculture dominated the economy. As the railroad spread into more parts of the state and technology improved, so did farming. Crops could now be irrigated and transported with greater ease. Most of the state's land is conducive to agriculture of some kind, and today Texas remains a strong agricultural state. Major crops include cotton, sorghum, wheat, and corn. The largest agricultural venture, however, is the beef cattle industry; over thirteen million cattle are located in Texas at any given time.

In 1901, the oil boom began in Texas when crude oil was discovered at Spindletop oil field, located near Beaumont. To develop this rich mineral resource, many drilling fields and refineries were built. The oil industry penetrates several aspects of economic life in Texas. Much of the money used in real estate and construction, for example, comes from the petroleum industry. In addition to oil, Texas supports a huge natural gas industry as well, with the panhandle section of the state being the richest in the resource.

Early on in the twentieth century, manufacturing also contributed to the Texas economy. At first, Texas factories mainly processed raw materials. After World War II manufacturing diversified and expanded. In recent years, Texas factories have produced products such as watches, electrical equipment, chemicals, and aircraft parts.

Dallas: A Day in 1963

On November 22, 1963, millions of Americans witnessed the shooting of President John Fitzgerald Kennedy on live national television. President Kennedy was shot in Dallas, right in front of the Texas Book Depository, as his motorcade proceeded down the street. One man, Lee Harvey Oswald, was charged with the assassination,

Important Events

1519 Alonso de Pineda sails along Texas coast.

1528 Cabeza de Vaca explores the interior of Texas.

1541 Coronado reaches western Texas.

1682 Ysleta, near El Paso, is the first European settlement.

1685 La Salle builds Fort St. Louis near Matagorda Bay.

1690 The Spanish set up two missions, but later abandon them.

1718 Mission San Antonio de Valero founded.

1819 Adams-Onís Treaty grants Spain control over Texas.

1821 Texas becomes a Mexican state.

1823 Stephen Austin asks the Mexican government to allow settlement.

1835 Texas Revolution begins.

1836 Texas declares independence; one year later, United States recognizes the independence.

1836 Battle at the Alamo is fought where over 170 defenders died, including Davy Crockett.

1845 Texas becomes twenty-eighth state in the Union on December 29.

1861 Texas secedes from the Union.

1870 State readmitted to the Union.

1901 Oil boom starts with oil discovery at Spindletop oil field.

1910 First U.S. Army plane flown.

1944 Texas's "white primary" voting law struck down by U.S. Supreme Court.

1963 President John F. Kennedy assassinated in Dallas on November 22.

1963 Texan, Lyndon B. Johnson, becomes 36th president.

1964 Houston Space Center is completed.

1974 Dallas-Fort Worth Regional Airport opens.

1986 Farm Aid II held in Manor to benefit devastated farmers.

1988 Drought disaster declared.

1993 Branch Davidian members perish in fire after a stand-off with federal agents at their Waco compound.

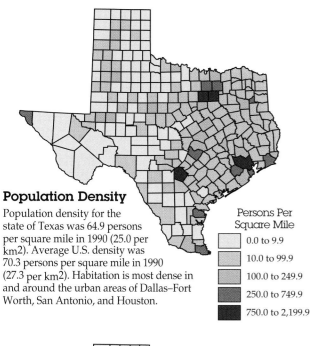

Population Density

Population density for the state of Texas was 64.9 persons per square mile in 1990 (25.0 per km2). Average U.S. density was 70.3 persons per square mile in 1990 (27.3 per km2). Habitation is most dense in and around the urban areas of Dallas–Fort Worth, San Antonio, and Houston.

Persons Per Square Mile
- 0.0 to 9.9
- 10.0 to 99.9
- 100.0 to 249.9
- 250.0 to 749.9
- 750.0 to 2,199.9

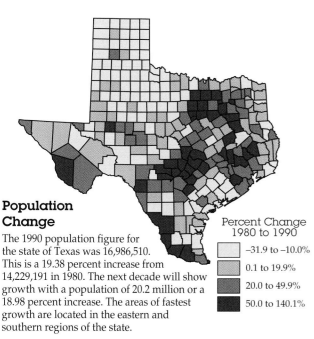

Population Change

The 1990 population figure for the state of Texas was 16,986,510. This is a 19.38 percent increase from 14,229,191 in 1980. The next decade will show growth with a population of 20.2 million or a 18.98 percent increase. The areas of fastest growth are located in the eastern and southern regions of the state.

Percent Change 1980 to 1990
- −31.9 to −10.0%
- 0.1 to 19.9%
- 20.0 to 49.9%
- 50.0 to 140.1%

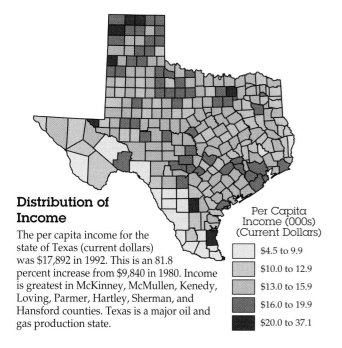

Distribution of Income

The per capita income for the state of Texas (current dollars) was $17,892 in 1992. This is an 81.8 percent increase from $9,840 in 1980. Income is greatest in McKinney, McMullen, Kenedy, Loving, Parmer, Hartley, Sherman, and Hansford counties. Texas is a major oil and gas production state.

Per Capita Income (000s) (Current Dollars)
- $4.5 to 9.9
- $10.0 to 12.9
- $13.0 to 15.9
- $16.0 to 19.9
- $20.0 to 37.1

Population Projections

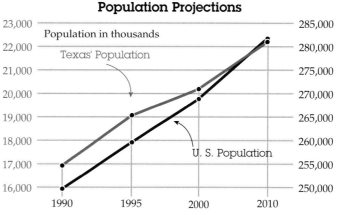

Population in thousands

Texas' Population

U. S. Population

Population Change

Year	Population
1950	7,711,000
1960	9,624,000
1970	11,236,000
1980	14,229,191
1990	16,986,510
2000	20,211,000
2010	22,281,000

Period	Change
1950–1970	45.7%
1970–1980	26.6%
1980–1990	19.4%
1990–2000	19.0%

Population Facts

State Population, 1993: 18,031,000

Rank: 3

Population 2000: 20,211,000 (Rank 2)

Density: 64.9 per sq. mi. (25.0 per km²)

Distribution: 80.3% urban, 19.7% rural

Population Under 5 Years Old: 8.4%

Population Under 18 Years Old: 28.7%

Population Over 65 Years Old: 10.2%

Median Age: 30.8

Number of Households: 6,071,000

Average Persons Per Household: 2.73

Average Persons Per Family: 3.28

Female Heads of Households: 4.13%

Population That Is Married: 20.23%

Birth Rate: 18.6 per 1,000 population

Death Rate: 7.4 per 1,000 population

Births to Teen Mothers: 15.6%

Marriage Rate: 10.7 per 1,000 population

Divorce Rate: 5.5 per 1,000 population

Violent Crime Rate: 840 per 100,000 pop.

Population on Social Security: 13.0%

Percent Voting for President: 49.1%

Population Profile

Rank. Texas ranks 3d among U.S. states in terms of population with 18,031,000 citizens.

Minority Population. The state's minority population is 39.7 percent. The state's male to female ratio for 1990 was 97.05 males for every 100 females. It was above the national average of 95.22 males for every 100 females.

Growth. Growing much faster than the projected national average, the state's population

Government

Capital: Austin (established 1845).

Statehood: Became 28th state on Dec. 29, 1845.

Number of Counties: 254.

Supreme Court Justices: 9, 6-year term.

State Senators: 31, 4-year term.

State Legislators: 150, 2-year term.

United States Senators: 2.

United States Representatives: 30.

Electoral Votes: 32.

State Constitution: Adopted 1876.

Texas' Famous Citizens

Cisneros, Henry (b. 1947). Mayor of San Antonio from 1980 to 1988. He was appointed Secretary of HUD in 1993.

Cliburn, Van (b. 1934). Classical pianist. He won the International Tchaikovsky Competition in 1958.

Eisenhower, Dwight David (1890–1969). Supreme commander of western allied forces in Europe during World War II. Elected 34th president of the United States in 1952.

Hagman, Larry (b. 1931). Actor. Best known for his roles in the TV shows "I Dream of Jeannie" and "Dallas."

Landry, Tom (b. 1924). Football coach. He led the Dallas Cowboys to 5 straight Super Bowls.

Murphy, Audie (1924–1971). War hero and actor. He earned 24 medals in World War II and acted in war films afterward.

Porter, Katherine Anne (1890–1980). Author of short stories such as "Pale Horse, Pale Rider" and "Noon Wine."

Rayburn, Sam (1882–1961). He served in the U.S. House from 1912 to 1961, the last 17 years as Speaker of the House.

is expected to reach 22.2 million by the year 2010 *(see graph above)*.

Older Citizens. The state's population older than 65 was 1,716,576 in 1990. It grew 25.19% from 1,371,161 in 1980.

Younger Citizens. The number of children (under 18 years of age) was 4.8 million in 1990. This represents 28.5 percent of the state's population. The state's school aged population was 3.3 million in 1990. It is expected to increase to 3.7 million by the year 2000. This represents a 10.86% change.

Urban/Rural. 80.3% of the population of the state live in urban areas while 19.7% live in rural areas.

Largest Cities. Texas has 49 cities with a population greater than 35,000. The populations of the state's largest centers are (starting from the most populous) Houston (1,630,553), Dallas (1,006,877), San Antonio (935,933), El Paso (515,342), Austin (465,622), Fort Worth (447,619), Arlington (261,721), Corpus Christi (257,453), Lubbock (186,206), Garland (180,650), Amarillo (157,615), Irving (155,037), Plano (128,713), Laredo (122,899), Pasadena (119,363), Beaumont (114,323), Abilene (106,654), and Waco (103,590).

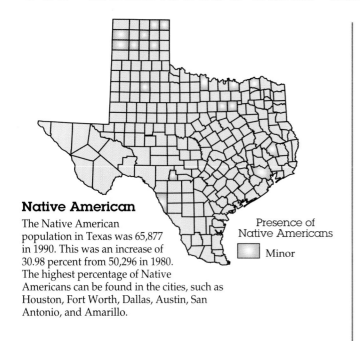

Native American

The Native American population in Texas was 65,877 in 1990. This was an increase of 30.98 percent from 50,296 in 1980. The highest percentage of Native Americans can be found in the cities, such as Houston, Fort Worth, Dallas, Austin, San Antonio, and Amarillo.

Presence of Native Americans

☐ Minor

Nationalities

African	4,584
American	681,522
Arab	5,365
Austrian	2,071
Czech	4,061
Dutch	75,611
English	537,164
Finnish	1,508
German	577,416
Greek	5,832
Hungarian	4,631
Irish	572,665
Italian	51,197
Norwegian	7,766
Polish	23,026
Portuguese	1,155
Russian	7,182
Scottish	69,514
Slovak	4,713
Swedish	17,328
Welsh	17,591
West Indian	3,391

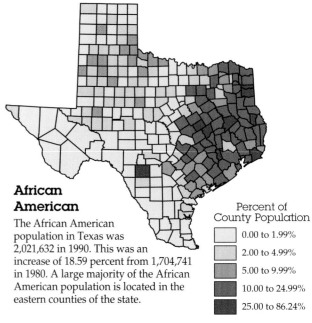

African American

The African American population in Texas was 2,021,632 in 1990. This was an increase of 18.59 percent from 1,704,741 in 1980. A large majority of the African American population is located in the eastern counties of the state.

Percent of County Population

☐ 0.00 to 1.99%
☐ 2.00 to 4.99%
☐ 5.00 to 9.99%
☐ 10.00 to 24.99%
☐ 25.00 to 86.24%

Statewide Ethnic Composition

Over 75 percent of the population of Texas is white. The largest nationalities in this racial group are German, Irish, and English. The next largest group is Hispanics, who make up over 25 percent of the population. Over 681,000 people claim to be American and acknowledge no other nationality.

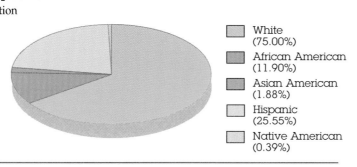

☐ White (75.00%)
☐ African American (11.90%)
☐ Asian American (1.88%)
☐ Hispanic (25.55%)
☐ Native American (0.39%)

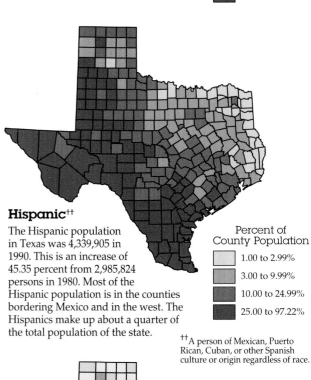

Education Facts

Total Students 1990: 3,328,514	Mean SAT Score 1991 Verbal: 411
Number of School Districts: 1,062	Mean SAT Score 1991 Math: 463
Expenditure Per Capita on Education 1990: $849	Average Teacher's Salary 1992: $29,000
Expenditure Per Capita K–12 1990: $734	Rank Teacher's Salary: 34th in U.S.
Expenditure Per Pupil 1990: $4,326	High School Graduates 1990: 170,000
Total School Enrollment 1990–1991: 3,353,270	Total Number of Public Schools: 5,937
Rank of Expenditures Per Student: 37th in the U.S.	Number of Teachers 1990: 200,795
African American Enrollment: 14.6%	Student/Teacher Ratio: 16.7
Hispanic Enrollment: 33.1%	Staff Employed in Public Schools: 332,948
Asian/Pacific Islander Enrollment: 1.9%	Pupil/Staff Ratio: 10.0
Native American Enrollment: 0.2%	Staff/Teacher Ratio: 1.7

Hispanic[††]

The Hispanic population in Texas was 4,339,905 in 1990. This is an increase of 45.35 percent from 2,985,824 persons in 1980. Most of the Hispanic population is in the counties bordering Mexico and in the west. The Hispanics make up about a quarter of the total population of the state.

Percent of County Population

☐ 1.00 to 2.99%
☐ 3.00 to 9.99%
☐ 10.00 to 24.99%
☐ 25.00 to 97.22%

[††] A person of Mexican, Puerto Rican, Cuban, or other Spanish culture or origin regardless of race.

Education

Attainment: 74.3 percent of population 25 years or older were high school graduates in 1989, earning Texas a ranking of 38th in the United States; 21.7 percent of the state's population had completed college. Institutions of Higher Education: The largest universities and colleges in the state include University of Texas, Austin; Texas A&M University, College Station; Lamar University, Beaumont; University of Houston, Houston; Texas Tech University, Lubbock; Southern Methodist University, Dallas; Texas Christian University, Fort Worth; Baylor University, Waco; Abilene Christian University, Abilene; Rice University, Houston. Expenditures per Student: Expenditure increased 79% between 1985 and 1990. Projected High School Graduations: 1998 (209,371), 2004 (207,630); Total Revenues for Education from Federal Sources: $978 million; Total Revenues for Education from State Sources: $5.6 billion; Total Revenues for Education from Local Sources: $6 billion; Average Annual Salaries for Public School Principals: $43,146; Largest School Districts in State: Houston Independent School District, 191,282 students, 6th in the United States; Dallas Independent School District, 132,256, 11th.

Asian American

The Asian American population in Texas was 319,459 in 1990. This is an increase of 149.36 percent from 128,109 persons in 1980. The highest percentage of Asian Americans can be found in the cities such as Houston, Fort Worth, Dallas, Austin, San Antonio, and Amarillo.

Percent of County Population

☐ 0.00 to 0.24%
☐ 0.25 to 0.99%
☐ 1.00 to 1.99%
☐ 2.00 to 4.99%
☐ 5.00 to 76.92%

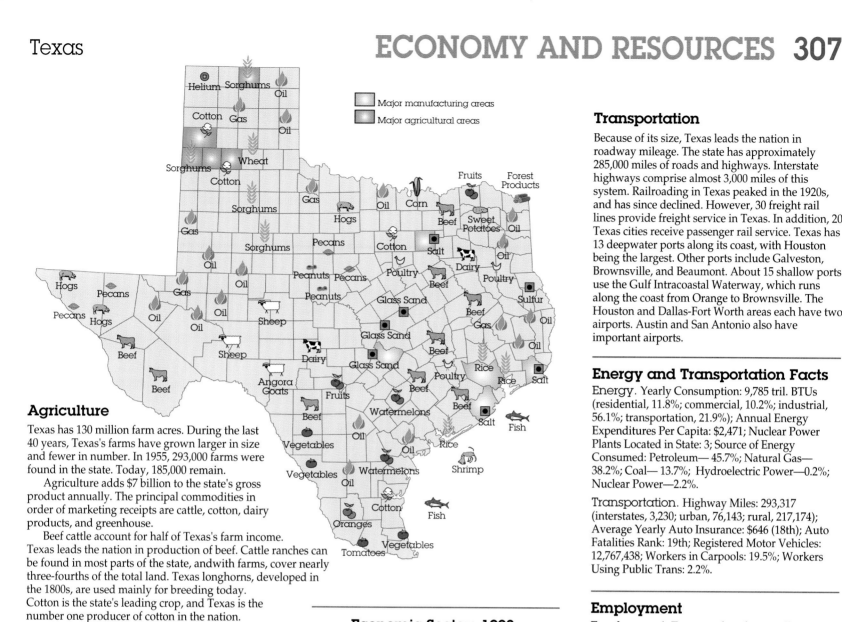

Major manufacturing areas
Major agricultural areas

Agriculture

Texas has 130 million farm acres. During the last 40 years, Texas's farms have grown larger in size and fewer in number. In 1955, 293,000 farms were found in the state. Today, 185,000 remain.

Agriculture adds $7 billion to the state's gross product annually. The principal commodities in order of marketing receipts are cattle, cotton, dairy products, and greenhouse.

Beef cattle account for half of Texas's farm income. Texas leads the nation in production of beef. Cattle ranches can be found in most parts of the state, and with farms, cover nearly three-fourths of the total land. Texas longhorns, developed in the 1800s, are used mainly for breeding today. Cotton is the state's leading crop, and Texas is the number one producer of cotton in the nation.

Housing

Owner Occupied Units: 7,008,999; Average Age of Units: 23 years; Average Value of Housing Units: $59,600; Renter Occupied Units: 2,332,892; Median Monthly Rent: $395; Housing Starts: 85,100; Existing Home Sales: 258,800.

Economic Facts

Gross State Product: $340,000,000,000 (1989)

Income Per Capita: $17,892

Disposable Personal Income: $15,965

Median Household Income: $27,016

Average Annual Pay, 1988: $23,760

Principal Industries: petroleum products, transportation equipment, chemicals, machinery, electrical equipment, cosmetics, drugs, computers, soft drinks, rubber

Major Crops: cotton, watermelons, wheat, corn, sorghum, cabbages, spinach

Fish: Crab, Oysters, Shrimp, Bass, Catfish, Sunfish

Livestock: cattle

Non-Fuel Minerals: Sulfur, Limestone, Lignite, Asphalt, Titanium, Uranium, Marble, Talc

Organic Fuel Minerals: Petroleum, Nat. Gas

Civilian Labor Force: 8,555,000 (Women: 3,818,000)

Total Employed: 7,991,000 (Women: 3,563,000)

Median Value of Housing: $59,600

Median Contract Rent: $395 per month

Economic Sectors 1992

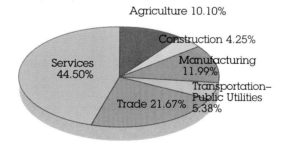

Agriculture 10.10%
Construction 4.25%
Manufacturing 11.99%
Transportation–Public Utilities 5.38%
Trade 21.67%
Services 44.50%

Manufacturing

Prior to World War II, Texas's manufacturing industries centered on raw materials processing. However, since then, the state's manufacturing sector has greatly expanded and diversified. Today, chemicals rank as the number one manufactured product made in Texas. Other manufacturing activities include food processing, electrical equipment, and petroleum products.

Manufacturing takes place throughout Texas. Many people employed in manufacturing live in the Dallas-Fort Worth and Houston areas. The Gulf Coast is home to both the chemical and petroleum refining industries. Petroleum refineries are located in cities like Houston and Beaumont. Food processing takes place in southern Texas, in San Antonio, as well as in Amarillo, in the Texas panhandle.

Transportation

Because of its size, Texas leads the nation in roadway mileage. The state has approximately 285,000 miles of roads and highways. Interstate highways comprise almost 3,000 miles of this system. Railroading in Texas peaked in the 1920s, and has since declined. However, 30 freight rail lines provide freight service in Texas. In addition, 20 Texas cities receive passenger rail service. Texas has 13 deepwater ports along its coast, with Houston being the largest. Other ports include Galveston, Brownsville, and Beaumont. About 15 shallow ports use the Gulf Intracoastal Waterway, which runs along the coast from Orange to Brownsville. The Houston and Dallas-Fort Worth areas each have two airports. Austin and San Antonio also have important airports.

Energy and Transportation Facts

Energy. Yearly Consumption: 9,785 tril. BTUs (residential, 11.8%; commercial, 10.2%; industrial, 56.1%; transportation, 21.9%); Annual Energy Expenditures Per Capita: $2,471; Nuclear Power Plants Located in State: 3; Source of Energy Consumed: Petroleum— 45.7%; Natural Gas— 38.2%; Coal— 13.7%; Hydroelectric Power—0.2%; Nuclear Power—2.2%.

Transportation. Highway Miles: 293,317 (interstates, 3,230; urban, 76,143; rural, 217,174); Average Yearly Auto Insurance: $646 (18th); Auto Fatalities Rank: 19th; Registered Motor Vehicles: 12,767,438; Workers in Carpools: 19.5%; Workers Using Public Trans: 2.2%.

Employment

Employment. Texas employed 8.50 million people in 1993. Most work in social and personal services (1.92 million persons or 22.6% of the workforce). Manufacturing accounts for 11.6% or 987,100 workers. Wholesale and retail trade accounts for 21.2% or 1.8 million workers. Government employs 1.37 million workers (16.2%). Construction employs 350,600 workers (4.1%). Transportation and utilities account for 5.1% or 436,900 persons. Agriculture employs 238,200 workers or 2.8%. Finance, real estate, and insurance account for 5.0% or 427,600 workers. Mining employs 166,200 people and accounts for only 2.0% of the workforce.

Unemployment. Unemployment remained unchanged between 1985 and 1993 at a rate of 7.0%. Today's figure is higher than the national average of 6.8% as shown below.

Unemployment Rate

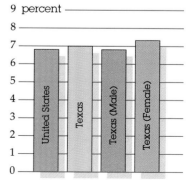

UTAH
The State of Utah

Official State Seal

The Great Seal of Utah is deeply rooted in Mormon life. The beehive in the center of the seal represents the state motto, "Industry." The beehive symbol was also used to represent a name given to Utah by the Mormons, Deseret. This name, which is found in the Book of Mormon, is said to translate to "honeybee." In 1896 the eagle, flags, and dates were added to mark Utah's statehood.

Legal Holidays

January: New Year's Day—1st; Admission Day—4th; February: Abraham Lincoln's Birthday—12th; Presidents' Day—3d Monday; May: Memorial Day—4th Monday; July: Independence Day—4th; Pioneer Day—24th; September: Labor Day—1st Monday; October: Columbus Day—2d Monday; November: Veterans' Day—11th; Thanksgiving—4th Thursday; December: Christmas—25th.

Official State Flag

The Utah state flag was adopted in 1911. It was created by the state Daughters of the American Revolution in 1903. It was originally white on blue, but when a flag was ordered to be given to the battleship *Utah* it was produced in color. This was accepted and made official in 1913.

Festivals and Events

January: Sundance Film Festival, Park City; April: Ute Tribal Bear Dance, Salt Lake City; May: Golden Spike Re-enactment, Promontory; Old Deseret Days, Salt Lake City; June: Summerfest Art Faire, Logan; July: Pioneer Days, State-Wide; Days of '47 Celebration, Salt Lake City; August: Park City Art Festival, Park City; World Folkfest, Springfield; September: Greek Festival, Salt Lake City; Melon Days, Green River; State Fair, Salt Lake City; Viva La Fiesta, Salt Lake City; Southern Utah Folklife Festival, Springdale; November: Dickens Festival, Salt Lake City.

Utah Compared to States in Its Region.

Resident Pop. in Metro Areas: 4th; Pop. Percent Increase: 4th; Pop. Over 65: 8th; Infant Mortality: 6th; School Enroll. Increase: 5th; High School Grad. and Up: 1st; Violent Crime: 7th; Hazardous Waste Sites: 2d; Unemployment: 8th; Median Household Income: 3d; Persons Below Poverty: 7th; Energy Costs Per Person: 7th.

Mountain Region

	Population	Capital
Montana	839,000	Helena
Wyoming	470,000	Cheyenne
Idaho	1,099,000	Boise
Nevada	1,389,000	Carson City
Utah	1,860,000	Salt Lake City
Colorado	3,566,000	Denver
Arizona	3,936,000	Phoenix
New Mexico	1,616,000	Santa Fe

Utah's Finances

Households: 537,000; Income Per Capita Current Dollars: $15,325; Change Per Capita Income 1980 to 1992: 93.0% (32d in U.S.); State Expenditures: $4,057,000,000; State Revenues: $4,060,000,000; Personal Income Tax: 2.55 to 7.2%; Federal Income Taxes Paid Per Capita: $1,282; Sales Tax: 5% (prescription drugs exempt).

State Expenditures
2.8 billion dollars

Education, Highway, Welfare, Health, Other

State Revenues
2.8 billion dollars

Federal, Local, Taxes, Miscellaneous

Location, Size, and Boundaries

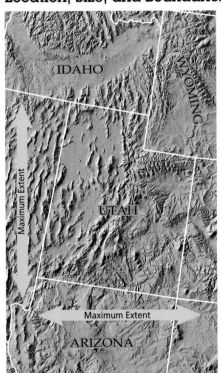

Location. Utah is located in the western United States in what is known as the Mountain region. It is bounded on four sides by land. The geographic center of Utah is lat. 39° 23.2' N; long. 111° 41.1' W.

Size. Utah is the 11th largest state in terms of size. Its area is 84,916 sq. mi. (219,932 km2). Inland water covers 2,820 sq. mi. (7,304 km2).

Boundaries. Idaho, 154 mi. (248 km); Wyoming, 174 mi. (280 km); Colorado, 276 mi. (444 km); Arizona, 277 mi. (446 km); Nevada, 345 mi. (555 km).

Geographic Extent. The north/south extent of Utah is 345 mi. (555 km). The state extends 275 mi. (443 km) to the east/west.

Facts about Utah. Origin of Name: Named by the U.S. Congress after the Ute Indian tribe; Nickname: The Beehive State; Motto: "Industry"; Abbreviations: Ut. (traditional), UT (postal); State Bird: seagull; State Tree: blue spruce; State Flower: sego lily; State Song: "Utah, We Love Thee," words and music by Evan Stephans.

Utah Compared to Other States. Resident Pop. in Metro Areas: 19th; Pop. Per. Increase: 6th; Pop. Over 65: 49th; Infant Mortality: 44th; School Enroll. Increase: 39th; High School Grad. and Up: 2d; Violent Crime: 41st; Hazardous Waste Sites: 26th; Unemployment: 44th; Median Household Income: 20th; Persons Below Poverty: 31st; Energy Costs Per Person: 47th.

Sources of Information. Tourism: Utah Travel Council, Council Hall, Capitol Hill, Salt Lake City, UT 84114. Government: House of Representatives, State Capitol, Salt Lake City, UT 84114. History: Division of State History, 300 Rio Grande, Salt Lake City, UT 84101.

Legend

⭐ State capitol
⊙ Cities over 35,000 population
○ Other significant cities
● County Seats
■ Major cultural attractions
□ State Parks
Ⓦ Welcome Centers
⚑ Major colleges and universities

Scale

0   25   50   75 mi.

25   0   25   50   75   100 km

■ **Alpine Scenic Loop Road.** 20-mile (32-kilometer) scenic driving route around Mount Timpanogos. (E-5)

■ **Alta.** Was once an old mining camp and is now a winter resort. (E-5)

■ **Arches National Park.** The world's largest concentration of natural stone arches. Structures include Balanced Rock and the Fiery Furnace. (I-9)

■ **Bear Lake State Recreation Area.** Scenic lake for boating and other water sports. Also sites for picnicking. (B-6)

■ **Bonneville Salt Flats Speedway.** Site of automobile testing and speed records on a hard natural salt deposit. (D-1)

■ **Brighton.** Mountain resort with summer and winter action. (E-5)

■ **Bryce Canyon National Park.** Large scenic canyonland with colored rock formations. Includes Pink Cliffs of Wasatch limestone. (L-4)

■ **Camp Floyd State Park.** Site of an old stagecoach inn. (E-5)

■ **Canyonlands National Park.** Superior mountain bike trails as well as unusual rock formations. (J-9)

■ **Capitol Reef National Park.** White sandstone domes which resemble the United States Capitol. (J-6)

■ **Cedar Breaks National Monument.** Site of a huge amphitheater-like structure eroded into the cliffs. Hiking trails around brightly colored cliffs. (L-3)

■ **Dinosaur National Monument.** A vast area of dinosaur fossils from the Jurassic Period, including fossilized shark teeth. (E-10)

■ **Flaming Gorge Dam and National Recreation Area.** A 502-foot (153-meter) high dam. Focal point for wildlife watching. (D-9)

■ **Glen Canyon National Recreation Area.** On the Colorado River. Large, deep canyons and sheer cliffs. (L-6)

■ **Golden Spike National Historic Site.** Marks the completion of the first transcontinental railroad on May 10, 1869. (B-3)

■ **Goosenecks of the San Juan State Park.** Picnicking, hiking, and relaxing among a view of a river gorge. (M-8)

■ **Great Salt Lake.** The second saltiest body of water in the world (the Dead Sea being the first), and the largest lake in the state. Boating and other water sports. (D-4)

■ **Hovenweep National Monument.** Ancient Pueblo Indian ruins. (M-10)

■ **Natural Bridges National Monument.** Sipapu, Kachina, and Owachomo are the names of three natural bridges in this monument; Sipapu is the second largest in the world. (L-9)

■ **Rainbow Bridge National Monument.** Site of the largest natural bridge in the world. (M-7)

■ **Timpanogos Cave National Monument.** Limestone caves carved into the mountainsides. (E-5)

■ **Utah Lake.** Boating, fishing, and other water sports. (F-5)

■ **Wasatch Mountain State Park.** Picnicking, hiking, and relaxing. (D-6)

■ **Zion National Park.** One of the oldest national parks in the United States Includes the Great White Throne, the Watchman, and Weeping Rock. (M-2)

Major Cities

City	Grid	City	Grid	City	Grid
American Fork	E-5	Logan	B-5	Salt Lake City	D-5
Bountiful	D-5	Magna	E-5	Sandy	E-5
Brigham City	C-5	Midvale	E-5	South Jordan	E-5
Cedar City	L-2	Murray	E-5	South Ogden	C-5
Centerville	D-5	North Ogden	C-5	Spanish Fork	F-5
Clearfield	C-4	Ogden	C-5	Springville	F-5
Holladay	D-5	Orem	F-5	St. George	M-1
Kaysville	C-4	Pleasant Grove	E-5	Tooele	E-4
Kearns	E-5	Provo	F-5	W. Jordan	E-5
Layton	C-4	Roy	C-4	W. Valley City	D-5

Weather Facts

Record High Temperature: 116° F (47° C) on June 28, 1892, at St. George; Record Low Temperature: -50° F (-46° C) on January 5, 1913, in Utah County; Average January Temperature: 26° F (-3° C); Average July Temperature: 73° F (23° C); Average Yearly Precipitation: 13 in. (33 cm).

Environmental Facts

Air Pollution Rank: 9th; Water Pollution Rank: 42d; Total Yearly Industrial Pollution: 79,206,383 lbs.; Industrial Pollution Rank: 9th; Hazardous Waste Sites: 12; Hazardous Sites Rank: 27th; Landfill Capacity: adequate; Fresh Water Supply: current surplus in east, impending shortage in west; Daily Residential Water Consumption: 284 gals. per capita; Endangered Species: Aquatic Species (8)—chub, bonytail; Birds (4)—crane, whooping; Mammals (2)—ferret, black-footed; Other Species (2)—ambersnail, kanab; Plants (24)—bear-poppy, dwarf.

Environmental Quality

Utah residents generate 1.1 million tons of solid waste each year, or approximately 1,250 pounds per capita. Landfill capacity in Utah will be exhausted in more than 12 years. The state has 12 hazardous waste sites. Annual greenhouse gas emissions in Utah total 42.8 million tons, or 25.3 tons per capita. Industrial sources in Utah release approximately 126.5 thousand tons of toxins, 138.8 thousand tons of acid precipitation-producing substances, and 1.1 million tons of smog-producing substances into the atmosphere each year.

The state has 2,022,700 acres within the National Park System; the largest area within the state is Canyonlands National Park. State parks cover 98,000 acres, attracting 4.9 million visitors per year.

Utah spends 1.8 percent of its budget, or approximately $30 per capita, on environmental and natural resources.

For more information about Utah's environment, contact the State Department of Natural Resources, 1636 W. North Temple, Salt Lake City, UT 84116-3156.

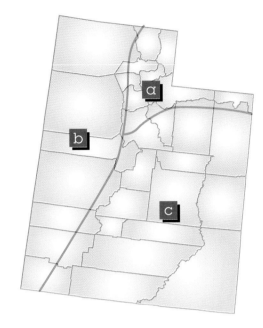

Physical Regions: (a) Rocky Mountains; (b) Basin and Range Region; (c) Colorado Plateau.

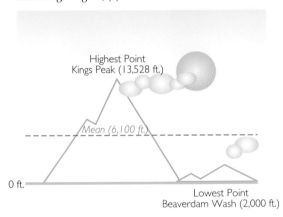

Highest Point Kings Peak (13,528 ft.)

Mean (6,100 ft.)

0 ft.

Lowest Point Beaverdam Wash (2,000 ft.)

Land Use

Cropland: 12.2%; Pasture: 3.4%; Rangeland: 51.7%; Forest: 19.4%; Urban: 2.9%; Other: 10.4%.

Average Monthly Weather

Salt Lake City	Jan	Feb	Mar	Apr	May	Jun	Jul	Aug	Sep	Oct	Nov	Dec	Yearly
Maximum Temperature °F	37.4	43.7	51.5	61.1	72.4	83.3	93.2	90.0	80.0	66.7	50.2	38.9	64.0
Minimum Temperature °F	19.7	24.4	29.9	37.2	45.2	53.3	61.8	59.7	50.0	39.3	29.2	21.6	39.3
Days of Precipitation	9.9	8.8	9.9	9.4	8.1	5.4	4.5	5.6	5.3	6.3	7.8	9.1	90.3

Flora and Fauna

Utah's forested land covers approximately 30 percent of the state. Forests exist primarily in the mountainous parts of Utah. A variety of trees, including firs, spruces, and pines, grow in the higher elevations, while juniper and pine grow at slightly lower elevations. Several plants and shrubs grow in the Utah mountains as well. The oldest tree in the United States, the bristlecone pine, also grows in Utah. Mesquite, greasewood, and cactus all grow in Utah's desert areas. Sagebrush and grasses grow in somewhat more moist conditions.

Large animals such as black bear, lynx, elk, and moose roam the Utah mountains. The mule deer, another large mammal, is the state's most common game animal. Herds of wild mustangs still gallop over Utah's terrain, and a few bison still live in southeast Utah. Smaller animals include badgers, martens, and ringtails. Grouse, geese, and quail all inhabit Utah, and many reptiles and snakes can be found throughout the state. Although Utah does not have many rivers, a number of fishes such as trout, grayling, and whitefish all swim in the state's waters.

Topography

There are three distinct topographic regions in Utah. The northern and northeastern areas of the state are covered by the Rocky Mountain physical region. The soil varies from cool and moist to warm and dry, with a dark organically rich surface. In the northeast corner, the Uinta Range extends westward from Colorado. The highest elevations in the state are found here. The highest is Kings Peak, which reaches 13,528 ft. (4,123 m) above sea level. To the west of this range is the Wasatch Range, which is situated perpendicular to the Uinta Range.

The southern and eastern parts of Utah are covered by the Colorado Plateau physical region. This area is characterized by plateau areas, such as buttes and mesas, cut by the deep river valleys that run through the region. The West and East Tavaputs plateaus are some of the largest in this region. The soil is a warm and dry loamy clay less than 20 inches over bedrock.

The western part of Utah lies in the Basin and Range physical region. The Great Salt Lake Desert, the bed of an ancient lake, comprises much of this region; as a result, the soil is very low in organic content and varies from desert red loamy clay to salt flats. Small ranges and valleys are scattered throughout the area surrounding the desert. The lowest elevations in the state occur in the southwest corner of the region.

Climate

Following Nevada, Utah is the second driest state. Climate changes across the state from a semitropical climate in the southwest to a more continental climate in the northern regions. Temperature variations reflect this climate difference. In the Wasatch Mountains of northeastern Utah, January and July temperatures average 20 degrees F and 60 degrees F. In the southwest, mean January and July temperatures are higher, 39 degrees F and 84 degrees F, respectively.

Although Utah is considered a dry state, some areas receive significant precipitation. The mountains in the north and west often receive over 40 inches of rainfall a year. Some places, like Alta, receive heavy snowfall, sometimes more than 400 inches. Conversely, the Great Salt Lake Desert receives only 5 inches of annual precipitation.

Desert conditions cover about a third of Utah. Besides the Great Salt Lake Desert, Utah has the Sevier and Escalante deserts as well.

Hydrology

The most important river in Utah is the Colorado. It flows southwest through the southeastern part of the state, draining much of central and eastern Utah with its tributaries. Its principal feeder is the Green River, which begins to the north in Wyoming and meets the Colorado in southeastern Utah. Other tributaries include the San Rafael, the Dirty Devil, and the San Juan. In northern Utah, the Bear, Provo, and Weber rivers drain into the Great Salt Lake. The other significant river in Utah is the Sevier in the southwest.

The Great Salt Lake Desert, in northwestern Utah, is the remnant of an enormous freshwater lake from the last Ice Age. This ancient seabed is called Lake Bonneville, of which the Bonneville Salt Flats are a part. Great Salt Lake and Utah Lake now cover part of the old Bonneville lakebed. Great Salt Lake is the largest natural lake west of the Mississippi River, covering over 2,200 sq. miles (5,700 sq. km).

Utah's History

Utah's First People

Utah has been inhabited by human beings since around 9000 B.C. The first known inhabitants, called by scholars the Desert Culture, were primarily hunters and gatherers, as they had no agricultural skills.

Around two thousand years ago a new people emerged, called the Anasazi or Basket Makers. The Anasazi resided in the Colorado Plateau area, and developed agricultural practices and constructed permanent dwellings. Later, around A.D. 700, these people began living in villages. The Anasazi culture reached its peak during the Pueblo period, when these predecessors to the Pueblo Indians lived in cliff dwellings. After A.D. 1300, the culture declined quickly, perhaps as a result of drought, invasion, or a combination of both.

Later, other Native American cultures settled in the Utah area. In the western part of the state lived the Gosiute, a primitive people who dug for food. The Southern Paiute, based in southwest Utah, were also gatherers, but developed great skill at basket weaving. The Ute tribe, located in eastern Utah, were perhaps the most well off of the Utah Native Americans. In the 1600s they acquired horses, and later learned to hunt buffalo while on horseback.

European and American Exploration

Two Franciscan missionaries were the first Europeans to explore Utah. In 1776, Silvestre Velez de Escalante and Francisco Atanasis Dominguez led an expedition into the "northern mystery," the land north of already-established Spanish missions. On this expedition, the two missionaries discovered Utah Lake.

Around 1811-12, fur trappers came to Utah. Two of these trappers, Peter Skene Ogden and Etienne Provost, have cities that bear their names, Ogden and Provo.

The first white person probably to see the Great Salt Lake was Jim Bridger, a mountain man, trapper, and scout. He came to the area in the winter of 1824-25. Soon after Bridger's arrival, southern Utah became a frequently traversed place, as people moved from Santa Fe, New Mexico, to Los Angeles, California on the Old Spanish Trail. In 1844, an Army engineer, John C. Frémont, surveyed the Great Basin area, including parts of Utah.

Mormon Settlement and Statehood

Perhaps the best-known group of people to settle in Utah are the Mormons. This group was started by Joseph Smith in Fayette, New York, in 1830. Mormons officially belong to the Church of Jesus Christ of Latter-Day Saints.

Brigham Young became the Mormon leader in 1844, after Smith and his brother, Hyrum, had been shot to death. Everywhere the Mormons traveled, they were persecuted so, in 1847, Brigham Young and a band of Mormon pioneers traveled westward to what is now Utah. By July 24, 1847, the first Mormons settled around the Great Salt Lake valley. Brigham Young is said to have exclaimed, "This is the place!" upon reaching the Great Salt Lake.

In 1849, the Mormons established a system of government, called the State of Deseret, a name from the Book of Mormon meaning, "honeybee." With Brigham Young as governor, this state covered a great expanse of land from Oregon to Mexico. The United States, however, did not recognize this state; instead, it considered the territory, with much smaller boundaries, the Territory of Utah.

Utah Territory made several attempts to achieve statehood, but these were continually rejected by the federal government. The reason for this rejection was the Mormon practice of polygamy, or the taking of multiple spouses. In 1862, Congress passed a law that prohibited polygamy, and troops were sent to Utah Territory. In 1890, under pressure, the Mormon church officially denounced the practice.

Five years later, in 1895, Utah submitted a new constitution to the federal government, in hopes of finally achieving statehood. A short time later, on January 4, 1896, Utah became the forty-fifth state in the Union.

Industrialization

Utah's industrial period began when the first transcontinental railroad was completed in the state on May 10, 1869, at Promontory Point. Soon after this line was completed, a great railroad building boom started in Utah.

Agricultural techniques improved during this time as new advances made it possible to cultivate thousands of acres that previously were unusable. Crops grown included wheat, barley, and sugar beets. The sugar beet, first planted by Mormons in the 1850s, became so successful a crop that by 1890, a beet-sugar manufacturing plant, Lehi, was opened in the state. Both world wars stimulated manufacturing in Utah. The manufacturing centered around Salt Lake City, and Utah, Cache, and Weber counties. Factories in Utah produce electronics, fabricated metals, and even textiles. The federal government also has a strong presence in Utah; approximately 70 percent of Utah land is owned by the U.S. government.

Utah: Snowboarders' Paradise

Snowboarding, the sport that combines skiing and surfing, has grained immense popularity in recent years. The sport originated in the 1970s; since then, it has changed drastically. For mountain states like Utah, snowboarding's success has proved favorable, as many tourists flock to the Mormon state to ride the waves of snow.

Utah's climate makes it an ideal spot for serious snowboarding. The storms that come from the desert areas of the state bring low-humidity precipitation to the mountains, creating a fine, powdery snow that is perfect for winter sports.

Important Events

1765 Juan María Antonio Rivera leads a trading expedition through southeastern Utah.

1776 Two Franciscan missionaries, Escalante and Dominguez, explore Utah region.

1811–1812 Fur trappers begin to come to Utah.

1824 Jim Bridger stumbles upon Great Salt Lake.

1844 John C. Frémont surveys the Great Basin area.

1847 Brigham Young and his Mormon followers settle in Utah.

1849 Mormons create State of Deseret.

1850 Utah Territory established by Congress.

1850s Sugar beet introduced.

1862 Congress passes a law outlawing polygamy, and troops are sent to Utah.

1869 Transcontinental Railroad completed, May 10, at Promontory Point.

1890 Mormon church officially prohibits polygamy.

1890 Public school system established.

1895 Utah submits a new constitution to the federal government.

1896 Utah becomes forty-fifth state in the Union on January 4.

1902 Newlands Act passed.

1914 Bonneville Salt Flats used for auto racing.

1915 State capitol building completed.

1919 Zion National Park opened.

1922 First Newlands Act of 1902 reclamation project completed.

1928 Bryce Canyon National Park opened.

1951 Uranium boom begins.

1963 Electricity production begins at Flaming Gorge Dam.

1965 Canyonlands National Park created.

1969 Salt Lake City convention center, Salt Palace, opens.

1977 Foreign-trade zone created in Salt Lake City.

1988 Forest fires, due to drought, burn millions of acres.

1992 The bones of the largest known specimen of a velociraptor are found.

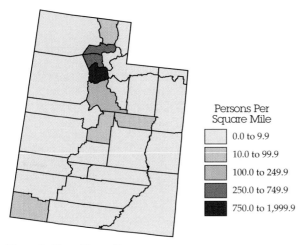

Persons Per Square Mile
- 0.0 to 9.9
- 10.0 to 99.9
- 100.0 to 249.9
- 250.0 to 749.9
- 750.0 to 1,999.9

Population Density

Population density for the state of Utah was 21.0 persons per square mile in 1990 (8.1 per km2). Average U.S. density was 70.3 persons per square mile in 1990 (27.3 per km2). Habitation is most dense in and around the urban area of Salt Lake City. This area extends to include cities such as Ogden and Provo.

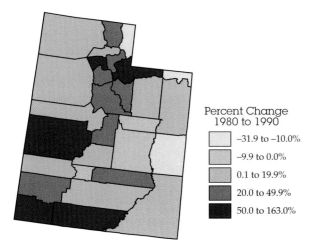

Percent Change 1980 to 1990
- −31.9 to −10.0%
- −9.9 to 0.0%
- 0.1 to 19.9%
- 20.0 to 49.9%
- 50.0 to 163.0%

Population Change

The 1990 population figure for the state of Utah was 1,722,850. This is a 17.92 percent increase from 1,461,037 in 1980. The next decade will show growth with a population of 2.0 million or a 15.56 percent increase. The state experienced widespread growth in the last decade.

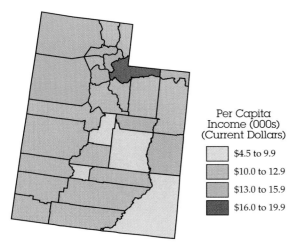

Per Capita Income (000s) (Current Dollars)
- $4.5 to 9.9
- $10.0 to 12.9
- $13.0 to 15.9
- $16.0 to 19.9

Distribution of Income

The per capita income for the state of Utah (current dollars) was $15,325 in 1992. This is a 93.0 percent increase from $7,942 in 1980. Income is greatest in the northern counties, with Summit County having the highest numbers. The western end of Summit County consists of suburbs of Salt Lake City.

Population Projections

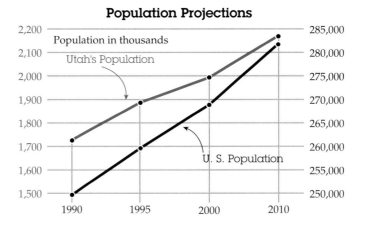

Population in thousands
Utah's Population
U. S. Population

Population Change

Year	Population
1950	689,000
1960	900,000
1970	1,066,000
1980	1,461,037
1990	1,722,850
2000	1,991,000
2010	2,171,000

Period	Change
1950–1970	54.7%
1970–1980	37.1%
1980–1990	17.9%
1990–2000	15.6%

Population Facts

State Population, 1993: 1,860,000

Rank: 34

Population 2000: 1,991,000 (Rank 34)

Density: 21.0 per sq. mi. (8.1 per km²)

Distribution: 87.0% urban, 13.0% rural

Population Under 5 Years Old: 9.7%

Population Under 18 Years Old: 36.1%

Population Over 65 Years Old: 8.8%

Median Age: 26.2

Number of Households: 537,000

Average Persons Per Household: 3.15

Average Persons Per Family: 3.67

Female Heads of Households: 2.85%

Population That Is Married: 20.20%

Birth Rate: 21.1 per 1,000 population

Death Rate: 5.3 per 1,000 population

Births to Teen Mothers: 10.3%

Marriage Rate: 11.0 per 1,000 population

Divorce Rate: 5.1 per 1,000 population

Violent Crime Rate: 287 per 100,000 pop.

Population on Social Security: 11.2%

Percent Voting for President: 65.1%

Population Profile

Rank. Utah ranks 34th among U.S. states in terms of population with 1,860,000 citizens.

Minority Population. The state's minority population is 8.9 percent. The state's male to female ratio for 1990 was 98.69 males for every 100 females. It was above the national average of 95.22 males for every 100 females.

Growth. Growing much faster than the projected national average, the state's population

Government

Capital: Salt Lake City (established 1824).

Statehood: Became 45th state on Jan. 4, 1896.

Number of Counties: 29.

Supreme Court Justices: 5, 10-year term.

State Senators: 29, 4-year term.

State Legislators: 75, 2-year term.

United States Senators: 2.

United States Representatives: 3.

Electoral Votes: 5.

State Constitution: Adopted 1895.

Utah's Famous Citizens

Adams, Maude (1872–1953). Actress. She was most noted for her performances in *Peter Pan*, in which she appeared over 1,500 times.

Browning, John Moses (1855–1926). Inventor. He designed the breech-loading, single-shot rifle and other arms.

Dallin, Cyrus (1861–1944). Sculptor. Captured the nobility of Indians in works such as *The Medicine Man* and *The Scout*.

Haywood, William "Big Bill" (1869–1928). Labor leader. He helped organize the Industrial Workers of the World.

Held, John Jr. (1889–1958). Illustrator and author. He created the "flaming youth" and "flapper" images so popular in the 1920s.

Marriott, J. Willard (1900–1985). He opened the first motel in 1957 and went on to found the Marriott Hotel chain.

Olsen, Merlin (b. 1940). Hall of Fame football player. He played in the Pro-Bowl 14 times, a record.

Redford, Robert (b. 1937). Actor. He won an Academy Award in 1980 for his directorial debut, *Ordinary People*.

is expected to reach 2.2 million by the year 2010 *(see graph above)*.

Older Citizens. The state's population older than 65 was 149,958 in 1990. It grew 37.3% from 109,220 in 1980.

Younger Citizens. The number of children (under 18 years of age) was 627 thousand in 1990. This represents 36.4 percent of the state's population. The state's school aged population was 441 thousand in 1990. It is expected to increase to 496 thousand by the year 2000. This represents a 12.47% change.

Urban/Rural. 87.0% of the population of the state live in urban areas while 13.0% live in rural areas.

Largest Cities. Utah has two cities with a population greater than 35,000. The populations of the state's largest centers are (starting from the most populous) Salt Lake City (159,936), West Valley City (86,976), Provo (86,835), Sandy (75,058), Orem (67,561), Ogden (63,909), Taylorsville-Bennion (52,351), West Jordan (42,892), Layton (41,784), Bountiful (36,659), Logan (32,762), Millcreek (32,230), Murray (31,282), Cottonwood Heights (28,766), St. George (28,502), and Kearns (28,374).

Utah

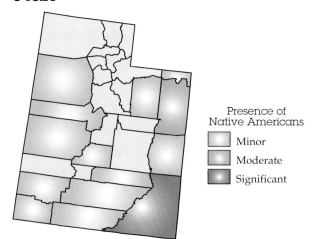

Native American

The Native American population in Utah was 24,283 in 1990. This was an increase of 21.45 percent from 19,994 in 1980. There are three Indian reservations in the state where most of the Native Americans make their homes. These are the Uintah/Ouray, Skull Valley, and Goshute reservations.

Presence of Native Americans

Minor

Moderate

Significant

Nationalities

African	800
American	57,268
Arab	2,131
Austrian	2,428
Czech	2,748
Dutch	34,509
English	584,412
Finnish	2,401
German	211,543
Greek	8,628
Hungarian	1,765
Irish	71,921
Italian	31,089
Norwegian	21,728
Polish	9,342
Portuguese	1,362
Russian	2,542
Scottish	48,569
Slovak	2,784
Swedish	61,781
Welsh	22,573
West Indian	285

Statewide Ethnic Composition

Over 93 percent of the population of Utah is white. The largest nationalities in this racial group are English, German, and Irish. The next largest group is Hispanics, followed by Asian Americans, Native Americans, and African Americans. Over 57,000 people claim to be American and acknowledge no other nationality.

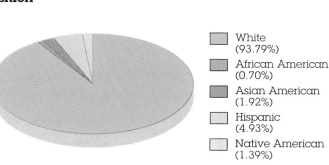

White (93.79%)

African American (0.70%)

Asian American (1.92%)

Hispanic (4.93%)

Native American (1.39%)

Education Facts

Total Students 1990: 437,446	Mean SAT Score 1991 Verbal: 494
Number of School Districts: 40	Mean SAT Score 1991 Math: 537
Expenditure Per Capita on Education 1990: $738	Average Teacher's Salary 1992: $26,500
Expenditure Per Capita K–12 1990: $651	Rank Teacher's Salary: 45th in U.S.
Expenditure Per Pupil 1990: $2,767	High School Graduates 1990: 22,200
Total School Enrollment 1990–1991: 444,732	Total Number of Public Schools: 718
Rank of Expenditures Per Student: 50th in the U.S.	Number of Teachers 1990: 17,933
African American Enrollment: 0.5%	Student/Teacher Ratio: 24.8
Hispanic Enrollment: 3.7%	Staff Employed in Public Schools: 31,351
Asian/Pacific Islander Enrollment: 1.8%	Pupil/Staff Ratio: 14.0
Native American Enrollment: 1.4%	Staff/Teacher Ratio: 1.8

Education

Attainment: 88.2 percent of population 25 years or older were high school graduates in 1989, earning Utah a ranking of 1st in the United States; 24.2 percent of the state's population had completed college. Institutions of Higher Education: The largest universities and colleges in the state include University of Utah, Salt Lake City; Utah State University, Logan; Weber State College, Ogden; Southern Utah State College, Cedar City; Brigham Young University, Provo. Expenditures per Student: Expenditure increased 89% between 1985 and 1990. Projected High School Graduations: 1998 (33,077), 2004 (29,590); Total Revenues for Education from Federal Sources: $73 million; Total Revenues for Education from State Sources: $660 million; Total Revenues for Education from Local Sources: $450 million; Average Annual Salaries for Public School Principals: $39,017; Largest School Districts in State: Granite School District, 77,515 students, 30th in the United States; Jordan School District, 63,605, 46th.

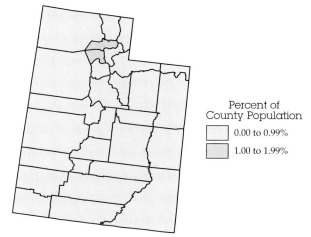

African American

The African American population in Utah was 11,576 in 1990. This was an increase of 19.45 percent from 9,691 in 1980. Twenty-four percent of the African American population in the state lives in Salt Lake City.

Percent of County Population

0.00 to 0.99%

1.00 to 1.99%

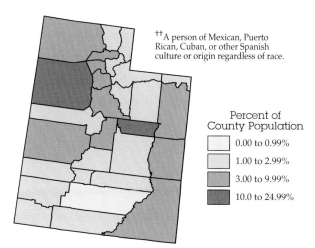

[++]A person of Mexican, Puerto Rican, Cuban, or other Spanish culture or origin regardless of race.

Percent of County Population

0.00 to 0.99%

1.00 to 2.99%

3.00 to 9.99%

10.0 to 24.99%

Hispanic[++]

The Hispanic population in Utah was 84,597 in 1990. This is an increase of 40.29 percent from 60,302 persons in 1980. Tooele and Carbon counties have the highest percentage of Hispanics in the state. Hispanic communities are also present in large numbers in Salt Lake City.

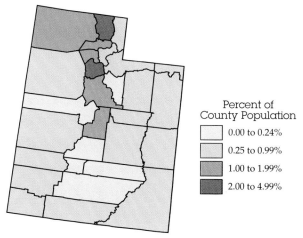

Percent of County Population

0.00 to 0.24%

0.25 to 0.99%

1.00 to 1.99%

2.00 to 4.99%

Asian American

The Asian American population in Utah was 33,371 in 1990. This is an increase of 70.24 percent from 19,602 persons in 1980. Cache County and Salt Lake City have the highest percentage of Asian Americans in the state.

Agriculture

Utah has 11.2 million farm acres. During the last 40 years, Utah's farms have grown larger in size and fewer in number. In 1955, 23,000 farms were found in the state. Today, 13,000 remain.

Agriculture adds less than $500 million to the state's gross product annually. The principal commodities in order of marketing receipts are cattle, dairy products, hay, and turkeys.

Livestock and livestock products account for about three-fourths of Utah's farm income. Beef cattle are raised in the south-central part of the state, as well as east of the Great Salt Lake. Dairy farms can also be found in this area. Most of Utah's crops are found in the north-central part of the state, with hay, used for cattle feed, being the leading crop. Other crops include wheat, barley, corn, and potatoes.

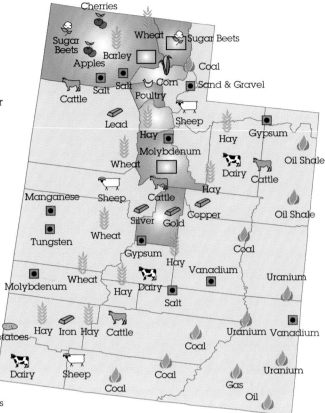

Major manufacturing areas
Major agricultural areas

Housing

Owner Occupied Units: 598,388; Average Age of Units: 24 years; Average Value of Housing Units: $68,900; Renter Occupied Units: 169,793; Median Monthly Rent: $369; Housing Starts: 15,600; Existing Home Sales: 31,200.

Economic Facts

Gross State Product: $28,000,000,000 (1989)

Income Per Capita: $15,325

Disposable Personal Income: $13,355

Median Household Income: $29,470

Average Annual Pay, 1988: $20,874

Principal Industries: food products, scientific instruments, transportation equipment, printing, machinery, glass products, textiles, petroleum products, coal products

Major Crops: milk, hay, cherries, wheat, onions, potatoes, greenhouse products, alfalfa seeds, sugar beets, apples

Fish: Bass, Catfish, Graylings, Perch, White fish

Livestock: cattle, turkeys

Non-Fuel Minerals: Tar Sands, Copper, Gold, Molybdenum, Silver, Clay, Limestone

Organic Fuel Minerals: Coal, Nat. Gas, Petro., Oil Shale

Civilian Labor Force: 805,000 (Women: 358,000)

Total Employed: 765,000 (Women: 340,000)

Median Value of Housing: $68,900

Median Contract Rent: $369 per month

Economic Sectors 1992

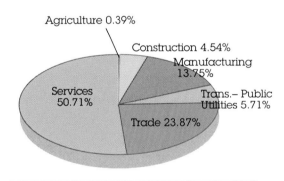

Agriculture 0.39%

Construction 4.54%

Manufacturing 13.75%

Services 50.71%

Trans.– Public Utilities 5.71%

Trade 23.87%

Manufacturing

Utah has a moderate manufacturing sector. The state's manufacturing activities contribute 17 percent to the state gross product. In terms of overall value added by manufacture, machinery is Utah's leading manufacturing industry. However, transportation and electrical equipment, as well as food products, are also manufactured in the state.

The greater Salt Lake City area has many of the manufacturing industries in the state. Webb, Utah, and Cache counties also have a high concentration of factories. Salt Lake County produces almost all of Utah's computing equipment. Logan and Ogden, in the north, are the major dairy-processing centers of the state. Rocket and weapons systems are manufactured in Brigham City.

Transportation

In 1869, the first transcontinental railroad was finished in Promontory, Utah, when the old Union Pacific and Central Pacific lines joined. Today, 10 different railroads, including the Union Pacific and the Denver and Rio Grande Western, provide Utah with freight service. Two Utah cities have passenger rail service.

For a larger state, Utah has only 46,000 miles of highways and roads. However, Utah benefits from having three major interstates cross the state. Interstate 15 runs north to south, and both I-70 and I-80 cross Utah from east to west. The state's largest and busiest airport is the Salt Lake International Airport. Every major western city is no more than two hours away from Salt Lake City by plane.

Energy and Transportation Facts

Energy. Yearly Consumption: 566 tril. BTUs (residential, 19.1%; commercial, 15.7%; industrial, 38.3%; transportation, 27.0%); Annual Energy Expenditures Per Capita: $1,621; Nuclear Power Plants Located in State: 0; Source of Energy Consumed: Petroleum— 29.6%; Natural Gas— 20.3%; Coal— 49.3%; Hydroelectric Power—0.9%; Nuclear Power—0.0%.

Transportation. Highway Miles: 43,270 (interstates, 937; urban, 6,084; rural, 37,186); Average Yearly Auto Insurance: $463 (40th); Auto Fatalities Rank: 27th; Registered Motor Vehicles: 1,252,268; Workers in Carpools: 20.5%; Workers Using Public Trans: 2.3%.

Employment

Employment. Utah employed 875,000 people in 1993. Most work in social and personal services (212,100 persons or 24.2% of the workforce). Manufacturing accounts for 12.6% or 110,500 workers. Wholesale and retail trade account for 21.9% or 191,500 workers. Government employs 159,700 workers (18.3%). Construction employs 39,700 workers (4.5%). Transportation and utilities account for 5.4% or 47,300 persons. Agriculture employs 21,000 workers or 2.4%. Finance, real estate, and insurance account for 4.7% or 41,200 workers. Mining employs only 0.9%, or 8,300 workers.

Unemployment. Unemployment has decreased to 3.9% in 1993 from a rate of 5.9% in 1985. Today's figure is lower than the national average of 6.8% as shown below.

Unemployment Rate

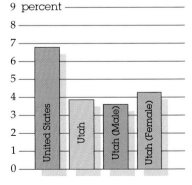

VERMONT

The State of Vermont

Official State Seal

The Great Seal of Vermont was created in 1779. The seal is divided into two sections. The top section contains a tree with fourteen branches, suggesting that Vermont will be the fourteenth state. Also included are a cow, wheat, and a forest. The bottom portion of the seal contains the state name and the state motto, "Freedom and Unity."

Legal Holidays

January: New Year's Day—1st; February: Abraham Lincoln's Birthday—12th; Presidents' Day—3d Monday; March: Town Meeting Day—2nd; Admission Day—4th; May: Memorial Day—4th Monday; July: Independence Day—4th; August: Bennington Battle Day—16th; September: Labor Day—1st Monday; October: Columbus Day—2d Monday; November: Veterans' Day—11th; Thanksgiving—4th Thursday; December: Christmas—25th.

Official State Flag

The first Vermont state flag was adopted in 1804. The flag took its present form in 1923. Between those years the flag went through many changes. One change was the removal of seventeen stars and stripes and the state name from the top.

Festivals and Events

January: Brookfield Ice Harvest, Brookfield; Stowe Winter Carnival, Stowe; April: Vermont Maple Festival, St. Albans; May: Lilac Sunday Festival, Shelburne; Mayfest, Bennington; June: Lake Champlain Balloon Festival, Montpelier; Lake Champlain Discovery Festival, Burlington (through July); July: Vermont Quilt Festival, Northfield; Green Mountain Chew Chew, Bennington; Vermont Lumberjack Roundup, Barton; Swanton Summer Fest, Swanton; Ethnic Heritage Festival, Barre; August: Champlain Valley Fair, Essex Junction; Rockingham Old Home Days, Rockingham; Bread & Puppet Festival, Glover; September: Fall Foliage festival, West Danville; State Fair, Rutland; September/October: Oktoberfest, Stowe; October: Vermont Apple Festival, Springfield; Annual Fall Festival, Newbury; December: Wassail Celebration, Woodstock.

Vermont Compared to States in Its Region.

Resident Pop. in Metro Areas: 6th; Pop. Percent Increase: 1st; Pop. Over 65: 5th; Infant Mortality: 5th; School Enroll. Increase: 5th; High School Grad. and Up: 2d; Violent Crime: 6th; Hazardous Waste Sites: 6th; Unemployment: 4th; Median Household Income: 5th; Persons Below Poverty: 2d; Energy Costs Per Person: 2d.

New England Region

	Population	Capital
Maine	1,239,000	Augusta
New Hampshire	1,125,000	Concord
Vermont	576,000	Montpelier
Massachusetts	6,012,000	Boston
Rhode Island	1,000,000	Providence
Connecticut	3,277,000	Hartford

Vermont's Finances

Households: 211,000; Income Per Capita Current Dollars: $18,843; Change Per Capita Income 1980 to 1992: 120.4% (8th in U.S.); State Expenditures: $1,690,000,000; State Revenues: $1,701,000,000; Personal Income Tax: N/A; Federal Income Taxes Paid Per Capita: $1,629; Sales Tax: 5% (food and prescription drugs exempt).

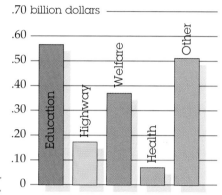

Location, Size, and Boundaries

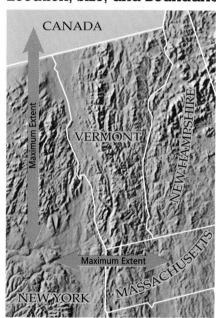

Location. Vermont is located in the northeastern United States in the New England region. It is bounded on four sides by land. The geographic center of Vermont is lat. 43° 55.6' N; long. 72° 40.3' W.

Size. Vermont is the 43rd largest state in terms of size. Its area is 9,609 sq. mi. (24,887 km2). Inland water covers 342 sq. mi. (886 km2).

Boundaries. Canada, 89 mi. (143 km); New Hampshire, 242 mi. (390 km); Massachusetts, 41 mi. (66 km); New York, 189 mi. (304 km).

Geographic Extent. The north/south extent of Vermont is 158 mi. (254 km). The state extends 90 mi. (145 km) to the east/west.

Facts about Vermont. Origin of Name: From the French words *Vert Mont*, Meaning "*Green Mountain*"; Nickname: The Green Mountain State; Motto: Freedom and Unity; Abbreviations: Vt. (traditional), VT (postal); State Bird: hermit thrush; State Tree: sugar maple; State Flower: red clover; State Song: "Hail Vermont," words and music by Josephine Hovey Perry.

Vermont Compared to Other States. Resident Pop. in Metro Areas: 49th; Pop. Per. Increase: 40th; Pop. Over 65: 33rd; Infant Mortality: 49th; School Enroll. Increase: 19th; High School Grad. and Up: 12th; Violent Crime: 49th; Hazardous Waste Sites: 41st; Unemployment: 28th; Median Household Income: 19th; Persons Below Poverty: 41st; Energy Costs Per Person: 29th.

Sources of Information. Tourism: Vermont Travel Division, 134 State Street, Montpelier, VT 05602. Economy: Agency of Development and Community Affairs, 109 State Street, Montpelier, VT 05602. Government: Vermont Legislative Council, 115 State Street, Montpelier, VT 05602. History: Vermont Historical Society, 109 State Street, Montpelier, VT 05602.

Major Cities

Burlington	E-1
Rutland	K-3
S. Burlington	E-1

Scale

0　10　20　30mi.

10　0　10　20　30　40 km

Legend

☆ State capitol

⊙ Cities over 35,000 population

○ Other significant cities

● County Seats

■ Major cultural attractions

□ State Parks

Ⓦ Welcome Centers

⚑ Major colleges and universities

■ Branbury State Park. Relaxing lakeside beach. (I-2)

■ Brighton State Park. Sand beach for sunning. Swimming, fishing, and other water sports. Hiking along nature trails. (C-9)

■ Button Bay State Park. Boating, fishing, and camping on the shores of Lake Champlain. (G-1)

■ Constitution House. Vermont's first constitution was written here in 1777. (L-6)

○ Coolidge Birthplace. The birthplace and boyhood home of the former president. (L-4)

■ Crystal Lake State Park. Sand beach for sunning. Water sports. (C-7)

■ Dorset. 19th century homes. (N-2)

■ Elmore State Park. Campground and site of Elmore Mountain. Sand beach for swimming, fishing, and boating. (E-5)

■ Grand Isle County. Popular summer resort area on a group of islands in Lake Champlain. (B-1)

■ Jamaica State Park. Fishing, boating, and other water sports. (O-4)

■ Lake St. Catherine State Park. Site of Lake St. Catherine. Area for swimming, relaxing, and hiking. (L-1)

■ Manchester. Site for golfing in summer and skiing in winter. (N-2)

■ Marble Exhibit. Exhibits of marble and granite. Site of a marble factory. (K-2)

■ Middlebury. Popular resort area with an annual winter carnival. (H-2)

■ Molly Stark State Park. Picnicking and hiking in this scenic area. (Q-3)

■ Mount Ascutney State Park. Snowmobiling in winter, hiking in summer. (L-5)

■ St. Albans Bay State Park. On Lake Champlain. Water sports. (B-1)

■ Sand Bar State Park. On Lake Champlain. Water sports. (D-1)

■ Smuggler's Notch. Site of a pass used to smuggle goods from Canada in War of 1812. Also a skiing area. (D-3)

■ Weston. A restored pioneer village. (M-4)

■ Wolcott. The last covered railroad bridge in use in Vermont. (D-5)

Map Labels

Lake Memphremagog

Alburg, Highgate Springs, Richford, East Richford, North Troy, Derby Line, Norton, Canaan
Swanton, Berkshire, Jay, Derby Center
Saint Albans, Enosburg, Troy, Newport, Lemington
St. Albans Bay S.P., FRANKLIN, Montgomery Center, Brow: Browington, Island Pond, ESSEX
Grand Isle County, Fairfield, ORLEANS, Orleans, Brighton State Park
North Hero, Bakersfield, Lowell, Barton, Bloomfield
Grand Isle, Georgia Center, Belvidere Center, Crystal Lake State Park, Newark
South Hero, Belvidere Jct., Eden Mills, East Haven
GRAND ISLE, Waterville, Eden, Sheffield
Chimney Corner, Sand Bar S.P., Milton, Fairfax, Cambridge, Johnson, Craftsbury, Wheelock, Guildhall
Westford, Smuggler's Notch, LAMOILLE, North Wolcott, Lyndonville, Lyndon St. College
Colchester, Morrisville, Wolcott, E. Hardwick, Lyndon, N. Concord
St. Michael's College, CHITTENDEN, Underhill Center, Elmore S.P., Hardwick, CALEDONIA
Winooski, Essex Junction, Moscow, Stowe, Woodbury, Danville, N. Concord, Lunenburg
Burlington, U. of Vermont, S. Burlington, Richmond, Waterbury Center, Calais, St. Johnsbury, Concord
Shelburne, Bolton, Worcester, Marshfield
Charlotte, Waterbury, WASHINGTON, Plainfield, East Barnet
Huntington, Vermont College, East Montpelier, Groton, Barnet
Monkton, Montpelier, Barre, Webersterville, Orange, Wells River
Button Bay S.P., Starksboro, Northfield, Williamstown
Vergennes, Bristol, Warren, Norwich U.
Addison, Lincoln, Roxbury, Corinth, Bradford
Middlebury College, South Lincoln, East Granville, Chelsea, ORANGE
Middlebury, Middlebury, Granville, Randolph Center, Ely
Chimney Point, East Middlebury, Randolph, Stafford, Thetford
Branbury S.P., Rochester, East Thetford
Cornwall, Salisbury, Bethel, Sharon
West Cornwall, Green Mountain National Forest, Stockbridge, Royalton, Norwich
ADDISON, Orwell, Brandon, Pittsfield, West Hartford, Wilder
Sudbury, Pittsford, WINDSOR, Hartford, White River Jct.
Benson, Proctor, Marble Exhibit, Sherburne Center, Woodstock
West Haven, Rutland, Bridgewater, Hartland
Fair Haven, West Rutland, Coolidge Birthplace, Plymouth, Hartland
Green Mt. College, Poultney, Wallingford, Constitution House, Windsor
RUTLAND, Ludlow, Tyson, Ascutney State Park
Lake St. Catherine S.P., Tinmouth, Cavendish
Pawlet, Mt. Tabor, Danby, Weston, Springfield
Dorset, Weston, Chester
Green Mountain National Forest, BENNINGTON, Londonderry, Grafton, Rockingham
Manchester Ctr., Manchester, Jamaica S.P., Saxtons River
Arlington, Sunderland, Jamaica, WINDHAM
Shaftsbury, Stratton, Townshend, Westminster
N. Bennington, Newfane, Putney
Green Mountain National Forest, West Dover, Brattleboro
Bennington College, Bennington, Wilmington, Marlboro College
Molly Stark S.P., Marlboro, Vernon
Pownal, Stamford, Jacksonville

Weather Facts

Record High Temperature: 105° F (41° C) on July 4, 1911, at Vernon; Record Low Temperature: -50° F (-46° C) on December 30, 1933, at Bloomfield; Average January Temperature: 18° F (-8° C); Average July Temperature: 69° F (21° C); Average Yearly Precipitation: 39 in. (99 cm).

Environmental Facts

Air Pollution Rank: 49th; Water Pollution Rank: 46th; Total Yearly Industrial Pollution: 870,090 lbs.; Industrial Pollution Rank: 49th; Hazardous Waste Sites: 8; Hazardous Sites Rank: 39th; Landfill Capacity: adequate; Fresh Water Supply: large surplus; Daily Residential Water Consumption: 98 gals. per capita; Endangered Species: Aquatic Species (1)—mussel, dwarf wedge; Birds (2)—eagle, bald; Mammals (1)—bat, Indiana; Plants (2)—bulrush, northeastern (Barbed bristle).

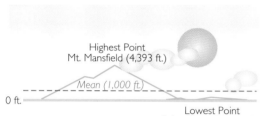

Highest Point
Mt. Mansfield (4,393 ft.)

Mean (1,000 ft.)

0 ft.

Lowest Point
Lake Champlain (95 ft.)

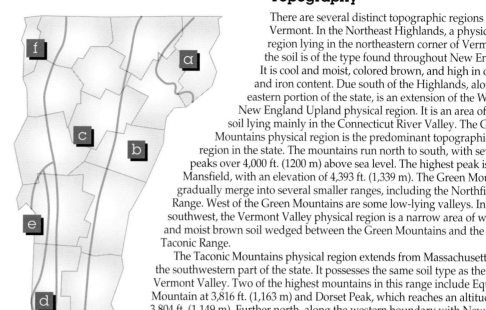

Physical Regions: (a) Northeast Highlands; (b) Western New England Upland; (c) Green Mountains; (d) Vermont Valley; (e) Taconic Mountains; (f) Champlain Valley.

Land Use

Cropland: 11.8%; Pasture: 7%; Rangeland: 0%; Forest: 75.3%; Urban: 3.7%; Other: 2.2%.

Topography

There are several distinct topographic regions in Vermont. In the Northeast Highlands, a physical region lying in the northeastern corner of Vermont, the soil is of the type found throughout New England. It is cool and moist, colored brown, and high in organic and iron content. Due south of the Highlands, along the eastern portion of the state, is an extension of the Western New England Upland physical region. It is an area of fertile soil lying mainly in the Connecticut River Valley. The Green Mountains physical region is the predominant topographic region in the state. The mountains run north to south, with several peaks over 4,000 ft. (1200 m) above sea level. The highest peak is Mt. Mansfield, with an elevation of 4,393 ft. (1,339 m). The Green Mountains gradually merge into several smaller ranges, including the Northfield Range. West of the Green Mountains are some low-lying valleys. In the southwest, the Vermont Valley physical region is a narrow area of warm and moist brown soil wedged between the Green Mountains and the Taconic Range.

The Taconic Mountains physical region extends from Massachusetts into the southwestern part of the state. It possesses the same soil type as the Vermont Valley. Two of the highest mountains in this range include Equinox Mountain at 3,816 ft. (1,163 m) and Dorset Peak, which reaches an altitude of 3,804 ft. (1,149 m). Further north, along the western boundary with New York, is the Champlain Valley. This low-lying region of rolling hills surrounds Lake Champlain and has a warm and moist gray/brown clay-derived soil suitable for agriculture.

Climate

Vermont, located halfway between the equator and the North Pole, lies within the northern temperate zone. The state is characterized as having short, warm summers and long, chilling winters. Temperatures vary as the result of elevation differences as well as inland location. January and July temperatures at Rutland, in middle Vermont, average 21 degrees F and 70 degrees F. Temperatures in the mountains are somewhat cooler, and valleys stay warmer.

Annual rainfall across Vermont varies slightly, with the west receiving around 34 inches, and the east-central region receiving 40 inches. The state receives even more precipitation in the form of snow. Snowfall in the Champlain Valley averages 70 inches, whereas the mountains often receive over 100 inches of snow a year.

Every so often, Vermont feels the effects of the nor'easter weather pattern. Winter low-pressure systems off the Maine coast bring moisture to northern Vermont, causing heavier snowfall.

Hydrology

Vermont's entire eastern border with New Hampshire is formed by the Connecticut River. The longest river within the state is Otter Creek, which flows about 95 miles (153 km) through northwestern Vermont before emptying into Lake Champlain. Other important rivers in the state include the Lamoille, the Missisquoi, and the Winooski, all of which begin east of the Green Mountains and drain into Lake Champlain. Other rivers flow east of the Green Mountains and into the Connecticut River.

Vermont has hundreds of natural lakes, mostly mountain lakes in the northern region. The largest of these, also the largest in New England, is Lake Champlain, which covers roughly 315 sq. miles (816 sq. km). In the north-central region is Lake Memphremagog, Vermont's second largest lake (though the lake lies partly in Quebec). The largest lake entirely within the state is Bomoseen Lake, which is about 3.5 sq. miles (9 sq. km).

Average Monthly Weather

Burlington	Jan	Feb	Mar	Apr	May	Jun	Jul	Aug	Sep	Oct	Nov	Dec	Yearly
Maximum Temperature °F	25.4	27.3	37.7	52.6	66.4	75.9	80.5	77.6	68.8	57.0	43.6	30.3	53.6
Minimum Temperature °F	7.7	8.8	20.8	32.7	44.0	54.0	58.6	56.6	48.7	38.7	29.6	14.9	34.6
Days of Precipitation	14.1	11.5	13.2	12.3	13.6	12.5	11.8	12.5	11.6	11.7	14.2	14.7	153.7

Flora and Fauna

Many different species of trees make up Vermont's forests, which cover approximately three-quarters of the state. This figure is significantly higher than it was a century ago, when forests covered only 30 percent of Vermont. Northern hardwoods such as maple, beech, and basswood grow throughout Vermont. Conifers such as pines, firs, and spruces flourish at elevations over 2,000 feet. Other trees in Vermont include oak and hickory. Ferns grow in mountainous areas as well, and the state's wildflowers include buttercups, lilacs, arbutuses, and pussy willows.

The white-tailed deer is Vermont's most common large animal. However, bears, Canadian lynx, and coyotes also can be found. Occasionally people report mountain lion sightings, although no significant population exists in the state. Moose sometimes cross into Vermont from Canada or other states. Smaller Vermont animals include weasels, shrews, snowshoe rabbits, woodchucks, and raccoons. The partridge and spruce grouse are two game birds found in Vermont. Common songbirds include sparrows and warblers. The state's rivers, streams, and lakes are filled with such fishes as bass, pickerel, and walleye.

Environmental Quality

Vermont residents generate 330,000 tons of solid waste each year, or approximately 1,200 pounds per capita. Landfill capacity in Vermont will be exhausted in 5 to 10 years. The state has 8 hazardous waste sites. Annual greenhouse gas emissions in Vermont total 8.4 million tons, or 15.2 tons per capita. Industrial sources in Vermont release approximately 1.3 thousand tons of toxins, 2.1 thousand tons of acid precipitation-producing substances, and 200.0 thousand tons of smog-producing substances into the atmosphere each year.

The state has 4,100 acres within the National Park System. Noteworthy is Marsh-Billings National Historical Park. State parks cover just over 170,000 acres, attracting 982,000 visitors per year.

Vermont spends 1.9 percent of its budget, or approximately $36 per capita, on environmental and natural resources. Vermont representatives in the U.S. House voted in favor of national environmental legislation 100 percent of the time, while U.S. senators did so 80 percent of the time.

For more information about Vermont's environment, contact the Agency of Natural Resources, 103 S. Main St., Waterbury, VT 05677.

─────────────── **Vermont's History** ───────────────

Vermont's First People

Native Americans belonging to the Algonquian language family dominated the Vermont landscape in its early history. Algonquian tribes such as the Abenaki, Pennacook, and Mahican used the land as hunting grounds, traveling on both waterways and footpaths. These tribes lived in the western part of Vermont rather peacefully until Indians from New York state ventured into Vermont. The Iroquois, a powerful group of Native American tribes, forced the Algonquian tribes to move sometime in the early seventeenth century. Later in the 1600s, Algonquian people moved back into Vermont with the help of the French.

European Exploration

In 1609, Samuel de Champlain explored the area now known as the state of Vermont. He claimed the eastern shores of Lake Champlain for his home country, France. The French built a fort dedicated to Saint Anne in 1666, on the Isle of Motte in Lake Champlain. The Champlain Valley marked the divider between the French influence in Vermont and to the north, and the British interests south of Vermont.

The British came to the Vermont area in 1690. Capt. Jacobus de Warm constructed a trading post on Chimney Point, located near present-day Middlebury. However, the post did not last for very long. In the 1730s, the French came to the area and built a fort at the same location.

The first permanent white settlement was established in 1724 at Fort Dummer, on the Connecticut River, now the site of Brattleboro. It was built by Massachusetts pioneers who feared invasion from both the French and Native Americans.

Throughout the early eighteenth century, the French, British, and American settlers built several forts all through the Champlain valley area.

On the Road to Statehood

In the years before the Revolutionary War, Vermont's land was highly contested. Two of the British royal colonies, New York and New Hampshire, fought for control of Vermont, which was regarded as a territory. Both of these colonies began to make land grants on Vermont soil. Beginning in 1749, New Hampshire governor Benning Wentworth started granting the New Hampshire Grants, and by 1763, 131 grants had been made. One year later, in 1764, New York state granted the same land to other settlers. In 1770, with the land still in dispute, New Hampshire sent a military force called the Green Mountain Boys to drive unwanted settlers from Vermont land.

During the Revolutionary War, the Green Mountain Boys helped the rebelling colonies gain their independence from England. Their assault on Fort Ticonderoga in New York in 1775 has been often referred to as the first offensive of the American Revolution.

As the war raged on, Vermont residents established an independent republic. Residents of the area met in Windsor July 2-8 to draw up a constitution. The one that came out of the meeting looked almost exactly like Pennsylvania's constitution. The republic was officially called the Republic of Vermont, although that name did not gain popularity. People preferred to refer to the republic simply as Vermont. The republic functioned until 1791, when Vermont became a part of the Union as the fourteenth state on March 4.

Industrialization

Vermont's early industrial efforts primarily catered to the Canadian market. Vermont began producing potash and pear ash probably in the late 1700s or very early 1800s. The northward drainage of Lake Champlain made for favorable conditions for these first industries. During the War of 1812, Vermont became a center for smuggling. Goods were

secretly shipped between Vermont and Canada during this time. Meanwhile, in a legal fashion, the United States' first battleship, the Saratoga, was built in Vergennes, Vermont. This battleship helped the nation gain final control over Lake Champlain in 1814, when Americans defeated the British.

The War of 1812 itself, in addition to canal building, can be considered stimulating factors in the growth of the Vermont economy. The economy began to shift southward away from Canada, and more toward the neighboring state of New York. The Champlain Canal from Lake Champlain to the Hudson River helped the emerging wool industry, as well as agriculture, to develop.

Vermont's first agricultural ventures centered around sheep farming. However, in the 1860s dairy farms became the dominant farm type in Vermont. Even today, Vermont ranks as a top state where dairy income is a high percentage of farm income.

In Vermont today, tourism has become a major industry. Each year, thousands of skiers come to Vermont's famous resorts. The first ski areas were built in the 1930s; this led to a winter tourism boom, beginning in the 1960s. In addition to quality skiing facilities, Vermont also has a number of scenic campsites scattered throughout the state.

Bread and Puppet: A Vermont Tradition

Every summer, hundreds of people come to the town of Glover, Vermont, to experience the Bread and Puppet Domestic Resurrection Circus. This weekend-long event usually takes place at the end of August, although festivals have been held at the end of June as well.

The Bread and Puppet Theater was founded in the 1960s in New York City. The theater troupe performed plays of political satire, social commentary, and other controversial topics. In 1975, Bread and Puppet held its first pageant on the Dopp farm in Glover.

─────────────── **Important Events** ───────────────

1609 Samuel de Champlain claims region for France.

1666 Fort St. Anne built by French.

1690 Capt. Jacobus de Warm constructs a trading post on Chimney point.

1724 First permanent white settlement established at Fort Dummer on the Connecticut River.

1749 New Hampshire governor Wentworth begins issuing land grants in Vermont.

1764 New York gains control of Vermont area.

1770 Green Mountain Boys sent to remove unwanted settlers from New York living on Vermont land.

1775 Green Mountain Boys capture Fort Ticonderoga during the Revolutionary War.

1777 Vermont declares itself an independent republic.

1791 Vermont becomes fourteenth state in the Union on March 4.

1805 Montpelier chosen as state capital.

1814 Thomas MacDonough defeats a British fleet on Lake Champlain during the War of 1812.

1834 First electric motor invented in Brandon.

1837 Antislavery rule adopted.

1864 Confederate guerrillas raid St. Albans during the Civil War.

1881 Chester A. Arthur becomes the twenty-first president of the United States.

1923 Calvin Coolidge becomes the thirtieth president of the United States.

1927 Heavy flooding devastates much of state.

1958 First Democratic governor elected in over one hundred years.

1974 Vermont French Cultural Commission founded to promote French language and culture.

1988 Vermont joins eight other states in fight for acid rain controls in the Midwest.

1993 A University of Vermont biochemist, Richard Fishel, with the help of Richard Kolodner from the Dana-Farber Cancer Institute in Boston, is the first to isolate a gene related to colon cancer.

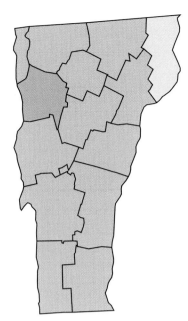

Population Density

Population density for the state of Vermont was 60.8 persons per square mile in 1990 (23.5 per km2). Average U.S. density was 70.3 persons per square mile in 1990 (27.3 per km2). Habitation is most dense in and around the urban area of Burlington. Vermont is a low–density state with few areas of high population. Burlington is Vermont's most populous city with 39,127 residents.

Persons Per
Square Mile

0.0 to 9.9

10.0 to 99.9

100.0 to 249.9

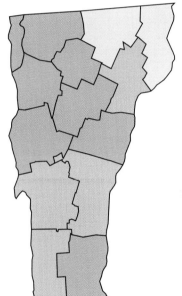

Population Change

The 1990 population figure for the state of Vermont was 562,758. This is a 10.03 percent increase from 511,456 in 1980. The next decade will show growth with a population of 591 thousand or a 5.02 percent increase. The areas of fastest growth are found in counties in the northwest. This area consists of the cities of Burlington and Montpelier.

Percent Change
1980 to 1990

0.1 to 4.9%

5.0 to 10.9%

11.0 to 22.9%

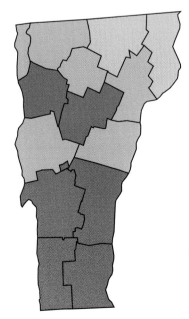

Distribution of Income

The per capita income for the state of Vermont (current dollars) was $18,834 in 1992. This is a 120.4 percent increase from $8,546 in 1980. Income is greatest around urban areas as well as in the southern region of the state. The lowest per capita incomes are found in the north bordering Canada.

Per Capita
Income (000s)
(Current Dollars)

$10.0 to 12.9

$13.0 to 15.9

$16.0 to 19.9

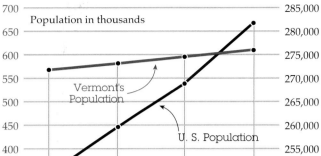

Population Projections

Population in thousands

Vermont's Population

U. S. Population

Population Change

Year	Population
1950	378,000
1960	389,000
1970	446,000
1980	511,456
1990	562,758
2000	591,000
2010	608,000

Period	Change
1950–1970	18.0%
1970–1980	14.6%
1980–1990	10.2%
1990–2000	5.0%

Population Facts

State Population, 1993: 576,000

Rank: 49

Population 2000: 591,000 (Rank 49)

Density: 60.8 per sq. mi. (23.5 per km2)

Distribution: 32.2% urban, 67.8% rural

Population Under 5 Years Old: 7.0%

Population Under 18 Years Old: 25.3%

Population Over 65 Years Old: 12.0%

Median Age: 33.0

Number of Households: 211,000

Average Persons Per Household: 2.57

Average Persons Per Family: 3.06

Female Heads of Households: 3.44%

Population That Is Married: 21.13%

Birth Rate: 14.7 per 1,000 population

Death Rate: 8.2 per 1,000 population

Births to Teen Mothers: 8.5%

Marriage Rate: 10.7 per 1,000 population

Divorce Rate: 4.5 per 1,000 population

Violent Crime Rate: 117 per 100,000 pop.

Population on Social Security: 15.9%

Percent Voting for President: 67.5%

Population Profile

Rank. Vermont ranks 49th among U.S. states in terms of population with 576,000 citizens.

Minority Population. The state's minority population is 1.9 percent. The state's male to female ratio for 1990 was 95.90 males for every 100 females. It was above the national average of 95.22 males for every 100 females.

Growth. Growing slower than the projected national average, the state's population is

Government

Capital: Montpelier (established 1805).

Statehood: Became 14th state on Mar. 4, 1791.

Number of Counties: 237 Towns.

Supreme Court Justices: 5, 6-year term.

State Senators: 30, 2-year term.

State Legislators: 150, 2-year term.

United States Senators: 2.

United States Representatives: 1.

Electoral Votes: 3.

State Constitution: Adopted 1793.

Vermont's Famous Citizens

Aiken, George David (1892–1984). He served in the U.S. Senate from 1941 to 1975. He also served as governor.

Bean, Orson (b. 1928). Actor-comedian. He starred in such plays as *Will Success Spoil Rock Hunter* and *Mr. Roberts*.

Brownson, Orestes A. (1803–1876). Author and religious leader. He was founder and editor of the Boston Quarterly Review.

Davenport, Thomas (1802–1851). Inventor. He built an electric motor in 1834 and patented it 3 years later.

Hunt, William Morris (1824–1879). Architect. He cofounded the American Institute of Architects in 1857.

Kidd, Billy (b. 1943). He became the first American to win an Olympic medal in alpine skiing in 1964.

Power, Hiram (1805–1873). Sculptor. He fashioned portrait busts and statues of U.S. presidents.

Vallee, Rudy (1901–1986). Singer-actor.

Wells, Henry (1805–1878). In 1850, he cofounded the American Express Company and two years later, Wells-Fargo and Company.

expected to reach 608 thousand by the year 2010 *(see graph above)*.

Older Citizens. The state's population older than 65 was 66,163 in 1990. It grew 13.75% from 58,166 in 1980.

Younger Citizens. The number of children (under 18 years of age) was 143 thousand in 1990. This represents 25.4 percent of the state's population. The state's school aged population was 94 thousand in 1990. It is expected to increase to 105 thousand by the year 2000. This represents an 11.7% change.

Urban/Rural. 32.2% of the population of the state live in urban areas while 67.8% live in rural areas.

Largest Cities. Vermont has one city with a population greater than 35,000. The populations of the state's largest centers are (starting from the most populous) Burlington (39,127), Rutland (18,230), and South Burlington (12,809).

Native American

Presence of Native Americans

Minor

The Native American population in Vermont was 1,696 in 1990. This was an increase of 62.92 percent from 1,041 in 1980. Most of the Native Americans living in Vermont live in the urban areas, which include Montpelier, Rutland, and Burlington.

Nationalities

Nationality	Count
African	213
American	32,133
Arab	1,117
Austrian	1,273
Czech	1,316
Dutch	5,648
English	105,185
Finnish	1,492
German	40,041
Greek	1,325
Hungarian	1,830
Irish	62,955
Italian	22,877
Norwegian	2,239
Polish	12,237
Portuguese	1,271
Russian	3,894
Scottish	19,072
Slovak	1,093
Swedish	6,354
Welsh	4,061
West Indian	215

Statewide Ethnic Composition

Over 98 percent of the population of Vermont is white. The largest nationalities in this racial group are English, Irish, and German. The next largest group is Hispanics, followed by Asian Americans, African Americans, and Native Americans. Over 32,000 people claim to be American and acknowledge no other nationality.

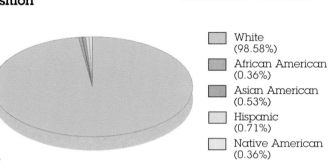

- White (98.58%)
- African American (0.36%)
- Asian American (0.53%)
- Hispanic (0.71%)
- Native American (0.36%)

Education Facts

Total Students 1990: 94,779

Number of School Districts: 276

Expenditure Per Capita on Education 1990: $921

Expenditure Per Capita K–12 1990: $840

Expenditure Per Pupil 1990: $5,740

Total School Enrollment 1990–1991: 96,230

Rank of Expenditures Per Student: 12th in the U.S.

African American Enrollment: 0.4%

Hispanic Enrollment: 0.2%

Asian/Pacific Islander Enrollment: 0.5%

Native American Enrollment: 0.5%

Mean SAT Score 1991 Verbal: 424

Mean SAT Score 1991 Math: 466

Average Teacher's Salary 1992: $33,600

Rank Teacher's Salary: 20th in U.S.

High School Graduates 1990: 6,100

Total Number of Public Schools: 336

Number of Teachers 1990: 6,973

Student/Teacher Ratio: 13.8

Staff Employed in Public Schools: 11,959

Pupil/Staff Ratio: 7.9

Staff/Teacher Ratio: 1.7

Education

Attainment: 82 percent of population 25 years or older were high school graduates in 1989, earning Vermont a ranking of 15th in the United States; 26.7 percent of the state's population had completed college; Institutions of Higher Education: The largest universities and colleges in the state include University of Vermont and State Agricultural College, Burlington; Vermont Technical College, Randolph Center; Middlebury College, Middlebury; Norwich University, Northfield. Expenditures per Student: Expenditure increased 72.4% between 1985 and 1990. Projected High School Graduations: 1998 (7,081), 2004 (7,436); Total Revenues for Education from Federal Sources: $22 million; Total Revenues for Education from State Sources: $165 million; Total Revenues for Education from Local Sources: $307 million; Average Annual Salaries for Public School Principals: $36,898.

African American

The African American population in Vermont was 1,951 in 1990. This was an increase of 64.23 percent from 1,188 in 1980. Most of the African American population can be found in Vermont's major urban areas, including Montpelier, Rutland, and Burlington.

Percent of County Population

- 0.00 to 0.20%
- 0.21 to 0.69%

Hispanic[††]

The Hispanic population in Vermont was 3,661 in 1990. This is an increase of 10.81 percent from 3,304 persons in 1980. Montpelier and the surrounding areas contain the highest percentage of Hispanics in the state.

[††]A person of Mexican, Puerto Rican, Cuban, or other Spanish culture or origin regardless of race.

Percent of County Population

- 0.00 to 0.99%
- 1.00 to 2.99%

Asian American

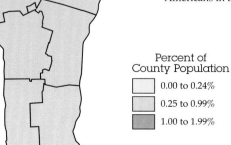

The Asian American population in Vermont was 3,215 in 1990. This is an increase of 102.07 percent from 1,591 persons in 1980. Burlington and the surrounding areas contain the highest percentage of Asian Americans in the state.

Percent of County Population

- 0.00 to 0.24%
- 0.25 to 0.99%
- 1.00 to 1.99%

Vermont

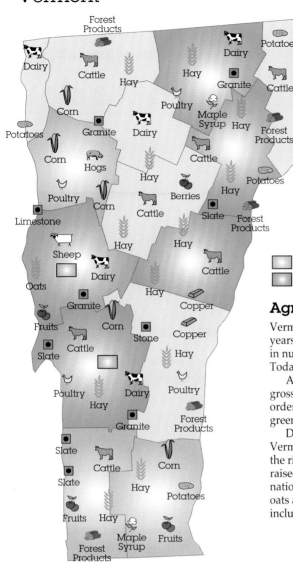

Major manufacturing areas

Major agricultural areas

Transportation

Although no longer used, the first canal in the United States was built in Bellows Falls between 1791 and 1802. Lake Champlain and a system of canals in both northern and southern Vermont provide the state with water transportation routes.

Vermont has approximately 14,000 miles of highways and roads. The two major interstates, I-89 and I-91, are Vermont's major highways. Interstate 91 connects the United States with Canada. Twelve freight rail lines provide service in Vermont. The leading rail line, the Vermont Central, provides important freight service between Canada and the entire Atlantic seaboard. Passenger rail lines serve about seven Vermont cities. Burlington, in the north on Lake Champlain, has the state's busiest airport.

Energy and Transportation Facts

Energy. Yearly Consumption: 132 tril. BTUs (residential, 29.5%; commercial, 18.9%; industrial, 19.7%; transportation, 31.8%); Annual Energy Expenditures Per Capita: $1,930; Nuclear Power Plants Located in State: 1; Source of Energy Consumed: Petroleum— 47.2%; Natural Gas— 4.4%; Coal— 0.0%; Hydroelectric Power—20.8%; Nuclear Power—27.7%.

Transportation. Highway Miles: 14,145 (interstates, 320; urban, 1,314; rural, 12,831); Average Yearly Auto Insurance: $484 (36th); Auto Fatalities Rank: 31st; Registered Motor Vehicles: 464,810; Workers in Carpools: 17.9%; Workers Using Public Trans: 0.7%.

Agriculture

Vermont has 1.5 million farm acres. During the last 40 years, Vermont's farms have grown larger in size and fewer in number. In 1955, 16,000 farms were found in the state. Today, 6,900 remain.

Agriculture adds less than $500 million to the state's gross product annually. The principal commodities in order of marketing receipts are dairy products, cattle, greenhouse, and hay.

Dairy farming accounts for about 81 percent of Vermont's farm income. These farms are found mainly in the river valleys of northern Vermont. Beef cattle are also raised in this region. Vermont is among the leaders in the nation in the production of maple syrup. Hay, corn, and oats are grown as cattle feed. Other important crops include potatoes and apples.

Employment

Employment. Vermont employed 299,000 people in 1993. Most work in social and personal services (73,800 persons or 24.7% of the workforce). Manufacturing accounts for 14.5% or 43,400 workers. Wholesale and retail trade account for 20.1% or 60,000 workers. Government employs 90,400 workers (17.7%). Construction employs 11,300 workers (3.8%). Transportation and utilities account for 3.7% or 11,200 persons. Agriculture employs 12,600 workers or 4.2%. Finance, real estate, and insurance account for 4.0% or 12,100 workers. Mining employs 600 people and accounts for only 0.2% of the workforce.

Unemployment. Unemployment has increased to 5.4% in 1993 from a rate of 4.8% in 1985. Today's figure is lower than the national average of 6.8% as shown below.

Housing

Owner Occupied Units: 271,214; Average Age of Units: 32 years; Average Value of Housing Units: $95,500; Renter Occupied Units: 61,841; Median Monthly Rent: $446; Housing Starts: 2,400; Existing Home Sales: 11,000.

Economic Facts

Gross State Product: $12,000,000,000 (1989)

Income Per Capita: $18,834

Disposable Personal Income: $16,640

Median Household Income: $29,792

Average Annual Pay, 1988: $21,355

Principal Industries: transportation equipment, electrical equipment, paper products, machinery, food products, printing, computer equipment, machine tools

Major Crops: milk, maple syrup, Christmas trees, potatoes

Fish: N/A

Livestock: Beef Cattle, Chickens, Hogs, Turkeys, Horses

Non-Fuel Minerals: Granite, Marble, Talc, Slate, Clay

Organic Fuel Minerals: N/A

Civilian Labor Force: 311,000 (Women: 145,000)

Total Employed: 291,000 (Women: 138,000)

Median Value of Housing: $95,500

Median Contract Rent: $446 per month

Economic Sectors 1992

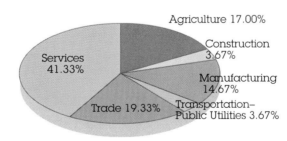

Agriculture 17.00%
Construction 3.67%
Manufacturing 14.67%
Transportation–Public Utilities 3.67%
Trade 19.33%
Services 41.33%

Manufacturing

For a small state, Vermont has a fairly diversified manufacturing sector. Approximately 23 percent of the state gross product comes from manufacturing industries. Vermont's manufacturing factories are small-about three-quarters of them employ fewer than 50 people. Electrical equipment is Vermont's leading manufacturing industry. However, the state also produces fabricated metal products, printed materials, and wood products.

Burlington, in northern Vermont, contains many different manufacturing facilities. Computer equipment, machine guns, and machine tools are all manufactured there. The state's largest book printer and binder is located in Brattleboro, in southern Vermont. Northwestern Vermont, especially Franklin County, has paper mills. Rutland, in the middle of the state, manufactures aircraft parts and business forms.

Unemployment Rate

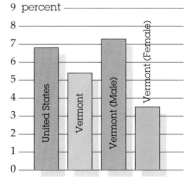

VIRGINIA

The State of Virginia

Official State Seal

This official seal of Virginia first appeared in 1776. Virginia is the only state to have a Greater and a Lesser seal. The only difference between the two is their size. The seals show a depiction of Virtue treading on Tyranny. Below this is the state motto, *"Sic Semper Tyrannis"* (Thus always to tyrants). The reverse side of the seal shows the figures of Liberty, Eternity, and the Roman goddess Ceres.

Legal Holidays

January: New Year's Day—1st; Lee-Jackson Day—18th; February: Presidents' Day—3d Monday; May: Memorial Day—4th Monday; Confederate Memorial Day—Last Monday; June: Ratification Day—25th; July: Independence Day—4th; September: Labor Day—1st Monday; October: Columbus Day: Second Monday; Yorktown Day (Yorktown)—19th; November: Veterans' Day—11th; Thanksgiving—4th Thursday; December: Christmas—25th.

Official State Flag

The state flag was adopted in 1930, but has been in existence since Virginia seceded from the Union in 1861. It contains the state coat of arms, the state motto, and the state name placed in the center of a blue field. It is also required to have a white fringe down the fly edge.

Festivals and Events

February: George Washington Birthday Parade, Alexandria; March: Kite Fest, Lorton; St. Patrick's Day Celebration, Norfolk; Virginia Spring Show, Richmond; April: Shenandoah Apple Blossom Festival, Winchester (through May); May: National Chicken Cooking Contest, Richmond; Country Comeback, Hampton; Norfolk Annual Fitness Fest, Norfolk; June: Conservation Festival, Roanoke; Hampton Jazz Festival, Hampton; Potomac River Fest, Colonial Beach; July: Chincoteague Annual Carnival & Pony Penning, Chincoteague Island; Summerfest, Harrisonburg; August: Roanoke Beach Party, Roanoke; Old Fiddlers' Convention, Galax; September: Blackbeard Pirate Jamboree, Norfolk; Great Peanut Tour, Skippers; Pumpkin Centers Reunion, Dye; October: Children's Fantasy Fest, Norfolk; Virginia Fall Foliage Fest, Waynesboro; November: Virginia Thanksgiving Festival, Charles City County; December: Jamestown Christmas, Williamsburg; Scottish Christmas Walk, Alexandria.

Virginia Compared to Other States. Resident Pop. in Metro Areas: 20th; Pop. Per. Increase: 19th; Pop. Over 65: 43d; Infant Mortality: 11th; School Enroll. Increase: 7th; High School Grad. and Up: 32d; Violent Crime: 35th; Hazardous Waste Sites: 18th; Unemployment: 33d; Median Household Income: 10th; Persons Below Poverty: 38th; Energy Costs Per Person: 34th.

Facts about Virginia. Origin of Name: After Queen Elizabeth I of England, who was known as the *Virgin Queen*; Nickname: Old Dominion; Motto: "Thus always to tyrants" (*Sic semper tyrannis*); Abbreviations: Va. (traditional), VA (postal); State Bird: cardinal; State Tree: flowering dogwood; State Flower: flowering dogwood; State Song: "Carry me back to old Virginia," words and music by James A. Bland.

Sources of Information. Tourism: Division of Tourism, 1021 East Cary Street, Richmond, VA 23219. Economy: Division of Tourism, 1021 East Cary Street, Richmond, VA 23219. Government: Division of Tourism, 1021 East Cary Street, Richmond, VA 23219. History: Division of Tourism, 1021 East Cary Street, Richmond, VA 23219.

Virginia's Finances

Households: 2,292,000; Income Per Capita Current Dollars: $20,629; Change Per Capita Income 1980 to 1992: 109.3% (19th in U.S.); State Expenditures: $12,694,000,000; State Revenues: $13,087,000,000; Personal Income Tax: 2 to 5.75%; Federal Income Taxes Paid Per Capita: $1,981; Sales Tax: 3.5% (prescription drugs exempt).

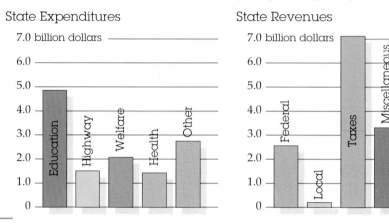

Location, Size, and Boundaries.

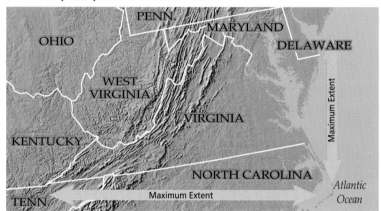

Location. Virginia is in the South Atlantic region of the United States. It is bounded on three of four sides by land with a general coast along the Atlantic Ocean in the east. The geographic center of is lat. 37° 29.3' N; long. 78° 33.8' W.

Size. Virginia is the 36th largest state. Its area is 40,817 sq. mi. (105,716 km2). Inland water covers 1,037 sq. mi. (2,686 km2). Virginia touches the Atlantic Ocean along a 112 mile coastline.

Boundaries. West Virginia, 438 mi. (705 km); Maryland, 233 mi. (375 km); District of Columbia, 12 mi. (19 km); Atlantic Ocean, 112 mi. (180 km); North Carolina, 320 mi. (515 km); Tennessee, 114 mi. (184 km); Kentucky, 127 mi. (204 km).

Geographic Extent. The north/south extent is 200 mi. (320 km). The state extends 440 mi. (710 km) to the east/west.

Legend

⊙ Cities over 35,000 pop.
○ Other significant cities
■ Major cultural attractions
Ⓦ Welcome Centers
⚲ Major colleges & universities
☆ State capitol
● County Seats
▪ State Parks

Scale

0   20   40   60 mi.

20 0 20 40 60 80 km

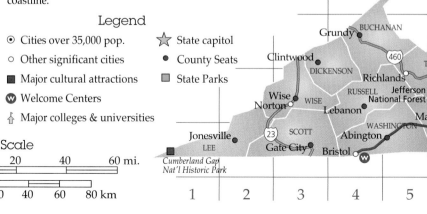

Virginia Compared to Its Region.

Resident Pop. in Metro Areas: 4th; Pop. Percent Increase: 6th; Pop. Over 65: 7th; Infant Mortality: 4th; School Enroll. Increase: 3d; High School Grad. and Up: 3d; Violent Crime: 7th; Hazardous Waste Sites: 4th; Unemployment: 5th; Median Household Income: 3d; Persons Below Poverty: 6th; Energy Costs Per Person: 6th.

South Atlantic Region

	Population	Capital
Delaware	700,000	Dover
Maryland	4,965,000	Annapolis
Washington DC	578,000	—
Virginia	6,491,000	Richmond
West Virginia	1,820,000	Charleston
North Carolina	6,945,000	Raleigh
South Carolina	3,643,000	Columbia
Georgia	6,917,000	Atlanta
Florida	13,679,000	Tallahassee

■ **Appomattox Court House National Historical Park.** Site where Robert E. Lee surrendered to U. S. Grant in 1865. (H-13)

■ **Arlington National Cemetery.** Originally Robert E. Lee's home. Site of the Tomb of the Unknown Soldier. (C-17)

■ **Booker T. Washington National Monument.** The birthplace of the educator and reformer. (H-10)

■ **Colonial National Historical Park.** Site of Jamestown, the first permanent English settlement in the New World. (H-18)

■ **Cumberland Gap National Historical Park.** Mountain pass used by pioneers. Hiking, camping, and seasonal programs. (J-1)

■ **Fredericksburg.** Site of the home of Mary Washington; George Washington's mother, and the James Monroe Museum and Memorial Library. (E-16)

■ **George Washington Birthplace National Monument.** The birthplace of the first president. Includes tours of the mansion and gardens. (E-17)

■ **Jamestown Island and Festival Park.** Site of the first permanent English settlement in America. Living history museum with ships, a fort, and an Indian village. (H-18)

■ **Lee Memorial Chapel Museum.** Burial place of Robert E. Lee. Includes his office and a statue. (G-11)

■ **MacArthur Memorial.** Burial place of Gen. Douglas MacArthur. (I-19)

■ **Manassas National Battlefield Park.** Site of both battles of Bull Run in 1861 and 1862. (C-16)

■ **Mariners' Museum.** Collection of vintage boats and other maritime memorabilia. (I-19)

■ **Monticello.** Home and burial place of President Thomas Jefferson. (F-13)

■ **Mount Vernon.** Home and burial place of George and Martha Washington on the Potomac River. (C-17)

■ **Petersburg National Battlefield.** Site of a ten-month siege during the Civil War. (H-16)

■ **Stratford Hall Plantation.** The estate and birthplace of Robert E. Lee. (E-18)

■ **Williamsburg.** Restored colonial city with a theme park. (H-18)

■ **Woodrow Wilson's Birthplace.** Includes a museum and a restored Greek Revival manse. (E-12)

■ **Yorktown.** Site of the surrender of the British to Washington's forces on October 18, 1781. (H-18)

Major Cities

City	Grid	City	Grid
Alexandria	C-17	Hampton	I-19
Annandale	C-17	Harrisonburg	D-12
Arlington	C-17	Hopewell	H-16
Bailey's Crossroads	C-17	Lake Ridge	D-17
Blacksburg	H-8	Lynchburg	G-12
Bristol	J-4	Manassas	C-16
Cave Spring	H-10	McLean	C-17
Centreville	C-16	Mechanicsville	G-16
Chantilly	C-16	Mount Vernon	C-17
Charlottesville	F-13	Newport News	I-19
Chesapeake	J-19	Norfolk	I-19
Dale City	D-17	Petersburg	H-16
Danville	J-11	Portsmouth	I-19
Fairfax	C-16	Reston	C-16
Franconia	C-17	Richmond	G-16
Fredericksburg	E-16	Roanoke	H-10
		Salem	H-9
		Springfield	C-17
		Staunton	E-12
		Sterling	C-16
		Suffolk	J-18
		Virginia Beach	I-20
		Waynesboro	E-12
		W. Springfield	C-17
		Winchester	B-14
		Woodbridge	D-17

Weather Facts

Record High Temperature: 110° F (43° C) on July 15, 1954, at Balcony Falls; Record Low Temperature: -29° F (-34° C) on February 10, 1899, at Monterey; Average January Temperature: 35° F (2° C); Average July Temperature: 76° F (24° C); Average Yearly Precipitation: 42 in. (107 cm).

Environmental Facts

Air Pollution Rank: 11th; Water Pollution Rank: 13th; Total Yearly Industrial Pollution: 68,365,848 lbs.; Industrial Pollution Rank: 13th; Hazardous Waste Sites: 20; Hazardous Sites Rank: 18th; Landfill Capacity: overextended; Fresh Water Supply: large surplus; Daily Residential Water Consumption: 129 gals. per capita; Endangered Species: Aquatic Species (24)—bean, purple; Birds (4)—eagle, bald; Mammals (7)—bat, gray; Other Species (6)—beetle, northeastern beach tiger; Plants (13)—birch, Virginia round-leaf.

Environmental Quality

Virginia residents generate 9.0 million tons of solid waste each year, or approximately 3,100 pounds per capita. Landfill capacity in Virginia will be exhausted in less than 5 years. The state has 20 hazardous waste sites. Annual greenhouse gas emissions in Virginia total 112.6 million tons, or 18.7 tons per capita. Industrial sources in Virginia release approximately 108.1 thousand tons of toxins, 430.1 thousand tons of acid precipitation-producing substances, and 2.4 million tons of smog-producing substances into the atmosphere each year.

The state has 309,600 acres within the National Park System; the largest area within the state is Shenandoah National Park. State parks cover just over 49,000 acres, attracting 3.9 million visitors per year.

Virginia spends 1.5 percent of its budget, or approximately $25 per capita, on environmental and natural resources.

Average Monthly Weather

Norfolk	Jan	Feb	Mar	Apr	May	Jun	Jul	Aug	Sep	Oct	Nov	Dec	Yearly
Maximum Temperature °F	48.1	49.9	57.5	68.2	75.7	83.2	86.9	85.7	80.2	69.8	60.8	51.9	68.2
Minimum Temperature °F	31.7	32.3	39.4	48.1	57.2	65.3	69.9	69.6	64.2	52.8	43.0	35.0	50.7
Days of Precipitation	10.4	10.4	10.9	10.1	9.9	9.3	11.2	10.5	7.9	7.6	8.1	9.0	115.2
Roanoke													
Maximum Temperature °F	44.8	48.0	56.9	68.2	76.4	83.0	86.7	85.5	79.4	68.6	57.4	47.8	66.9
Minimum Temperature °F	26.2	27.8	35.3	44.3	53.0	60.1	64.6	63.8	57.0	44.9	36.3	28.7	45.2
Days of Precipitation	10.1	9.7	10.9	10.1	11.9	10.0	11.6	10.7	8.4	7.7	9.0	8.8	119.0

Flora and Fauna

The state of Virginia has approximately two-thirds of its land covered by forests. In the eastern Tidewater region, pine trees dominate the landscape. Hardwood trees such as beech and maple mostly grow in the western, more mountainous part of Virginia. The Dismal Swamp, in the southeast near the North Carolina border, supports cypress trees. Morning glories, violets, and other wildflowers grow throughout Virginia. Rhododendron and mountain laurel plants are abundant in western Virginia. Other flowering plants include redbud and flowering dogwood, the state flower.

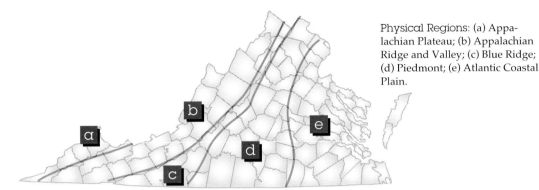

Physical Regions: (a) Appalachian Plateau; (b) Appalachian Ridge and Valley; (c) Blue Ridge; (d) Piedmont; (e) Atlantic Coastal Plain.

Topography

There are five distinct topographic regions in Virginia, all with warm and moist, or wet soil. The eastern part of the state lies in the Atlantic Coastal Plain physical region, also known as the Tidewater. This low-lying flat area, which extends about 100 miles (160 km) inland, contains soil that varies from red/yellow clay with low organic content to dark-surfaced loam, high in concentrations of iron and manganese. The terrain is divided by several rivers

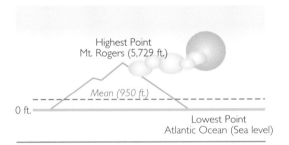

Highest Point
Mt. Rogers (5,729 ft.)

Mean (950 ft.)

0 ft.

Lowest Point
Atlantic Ocean (Sea level)

Land Use

Cropland: 14.5%; Pasture: 14.5%; Rangeland: 0%; Forest: 59.7%; Urban: 7.3%; Other: 4%.

For more information about Virginia's environment, contact the Natural Resources Commission, 9th Street Office Bldg., 202 N. 9th St., Richmond, VA 23219.

Deer, elk, wildcats, and bears are all found in Virginia's wooded areas, and black bears also live around the Dismal Swamp. Smaller animals living in the state include opossums, foxes, squirrels, and raccoons. Game birds such as wild turkeys, woodcocks, ruffed grouse, and doves also call Virginia home, as do such songbirds as the robin, cardinal, and sparrow. The Chesapeake Bay is filled with all types of marine life, including fishes (flounder, mackerel), scallops, oysters, and crabs. Virginia's rivers, streams, and lakes contain alewife, carp, pike, and other freshwater fish.

and inlets. Swampy areas are also found there, the largest being the Dismal Swamp in the southeast.

The central part of the state is covered by the Piedmont physical region. This area of gentle rolling hills gains elevation from about 300 ft. (91 m) near the fall line with the coastal plains to about 1,000 ft. (300 m) at the foot of the Blue Ridge Mountains. Red/yellow clay characterizes the soil found in this region.

Climate

The state of Virginia has a temperate climate, affected by both elevation and distance from the Atlantic Ocean. Moving east to west, temperature decreases as these two indicators increase. Overall, Virginia summers are hot and winters are mild. The Blue Ridge Mountains region, near Roanoke, has average January and July temperatures of 32 degrees F and 68 degrees F. On the tidewater, or coastal plain, temperatures for January and July average 41 degrees F and 78 degrees F.

Statewide, Virginia averages 40 inches of precipitation annually; however, regional variations of precipitation do exist. The Shenandoah Valley, in the northern part of the state, receives the lightest precipitation, only 32 inches annually. The southeastern coast, including Newport News, receives the highest average precipitationæover 50 inches.

Virginia does receive snowfall, but it does not last very long. Even in the mountains, snow is only on the ground approximately 60 days a year.

Hydrology

The Potomac River forms Virginia's northeastern border with Maryland, before emptying into Chesapeake Bay, which defines the state's eastern border. Several rivers flow southeast from the mountains in the west into the Chesapeake. The most important of these is the James, which cuts through the middle of the state. Others farther north include the Pamunkey, the York, and the Rappahannock. The Potomac, Rappahannock, York, and James rivers form a series of peninsulas in Virginia's Tidewater area. Other rivers include the Roanoke in the south-central region, the Shenandoah in the north, and the Clinch in the southwest.

All of the large lakes in Virginia are man-made. The largest of these is the John H. Kerr Reservoir on the Roanoke River at the North Carolina border, covering about 65 sq. miles (168 sq. km). Others include Smith Mountain Lake and Claytor Lake in the southwest.

Virginia's History

Virginia's Earliest People

The land that now makes up the state of Virginia was first inhabited approximately ten thousand years ago. During this time, the inhabitants were probably hunter-gatherers.

In the 1600s, three distinct language groups of Native Americans lived in the Virginia region. In the coastal part of the state lived the Powhatan, a tribe belonging to the Algonquian language family. Members of the Siouan family lived in different parts of Virginia, with the Nahyssan tribe living along the Roanoke River, and the Monacan and Manahoac tribes living in the piedmont region. The third language family, the Iroquoian, was represented by the Susquehanna, Cherokee, and Nottoway tribes. The Susquehanna settled near the Chesapeake Bay, the Cherokee lived in the southwest, and the Nottoway lived in the southeastern part of Virginia.

Exploration and Early Colonial Period

The first settlement in Virginia was a Spanish mission established in 1570, which failed a short time later.

In 1585, the British, under Sir Walter Raleigh, reached Roanoke Island, and a colony was established. The land on the east coast of the United States was named Virginia, after Queen Elizabeth I. This settlement failed by 1591.

In 1606, King James I of England created the Virginia Company of London, in order to colonize America. Colonists from the company settled the first permanent English settlement in America, at Jamestown, on May 14, 1607.

In 1624, the British crown took control of the Jamestown colony, when James I revoked the Virginia Company's charter. Jamestown was not well suited to support an administrative center. So in 1699, the colonial capital was moved to Williamsburg.

In 1700, Virginia had approximately fifty-eight thousand residents, making it the largest colony in North America. As the population increased, settlers began to move away from the Virginia coastline and venture westward into the piedmont.

Revolution, Statehood, and Civil War

By the middle of the eighteenth century Virginia colonists were becoming upset by adverse British government policies. Examples included the Townsend and Stamp Acts passed by the British Parliament during the 1760s and 1770s. Many Virginia residents remained loyal to the British government, although they did want the right to govern themselves. Others, however, voiced strong opposition to British colonial rule. Perhaps the most famous of these patriots was Patrick Henry. In 1775, he delivered his famous "Give me Liberty or give me Death" speech in Richmond.

At the Second Continental Congress in 1775, Virginia moved to declare the colonies "free and independent states." The idea helped inspire Thomas Jefferson to write the Declaration of Independence which was adopted on July 4, 1776. Virginia become the first independent commonwealth a month before, in June 1776, when it adopted its own constitution.

During the Revolutionary War, several battles took place on Virginia soil, including the 1781 British defeat at Yorktown by general Charles Cornwallis to George Washington and his French allies.

The U.S. Constitution was written in 1787, and a year later, Virginia ratified the Constitution and became the tenth state in the Union on June 25.

In 1861, Virginia seceded from the Union and Richmond was made the capital of the Confederate States of America (CSA). Many battles took place on Virginia soil including the first battle at Bull Run (Manassas). On April 9, 1865, the Civil War came to an end when Gen. Robert E. Lee surrendered his Confederate army to Union general Ulysses S. Grant at Appomattox Court House.

Economic Development

In the early 1600s, agriculture dominated the Virginia economy. In 1612, John Rolfe introduced Virginia to the tobacco plant as a commercial crop. Its success as a crop saved the young colony from collapse, and soon, tobacco served as the principal crop. Tobacco fields were maintained by slave labor, although Virginia officially abolished the African slave trade in 1778.

Tobacco continues to be an important crop, accounting for more farm income than any other agricultural crop in the state. However, soybeans, corn, hay, and apples are also grown. Virginia also derives much of its farm income from poultry, cattle, and dairy farming.

Manufacturing developed in the 1840s, but the onset of the Civil War disrupted its progress. However, after the war, manufacturing increased steadily until World War II. Industries in Virginia include electronics, textiles, plastic products, and of course, tobacco products.

Virginia: Military History

Throughout the years, Virginia has played an important role in the course of events that have shaped our United States history. During the American Revolution, several Virginians were at the forefront of the fight for independence. The same is true during the Civil War. Richmond served as the capital of the short-lived Confederate States of America. The outcomes of both the Revolutionary and the Civil War were decided in Virginia: the British and the Confederacy both surrendered their armies on Virginia soil. On October 19, after the Battle of Yorktown, Cornwallis surrendered his troops to Gen. George Washington. On April 9, 1865, the Civil War ended when Gen. Robert E. Lee surrendered his Confederate army to Union general Ulysses S. Grant at Appomattox Court House.

Important Events

1570 Spanish build a mission on York River; proves unsuccessful.

1585 Sir Walter Raleigh reaches Roanoke Island.

1591 The Roanoke Island colony fails.

1607 Jamestown becomes the first permanent English settlement in America on May 14, set up by the Virginia Company of London.

1612 Tobacco crop introduced.

1624 Virginia becomes a royal colony, when James I revokes the Virgin Company's charter.

1699 Capital moves from Jamestown to Willamsburg.

1775 Virginia declares the colonies "free and independent states," at the Second Continental Congress.

1775 George Washington becomes commander of the Continental Army.

1776 Virginia declares its independence from Great Britain in June.

1781 Cornwallis surrenders to Washington at Yorktown.

1788 Virginia becomes tenth state in the Union on June 25.

1792 Kentucky formed out of three western Virginia counties.

1831 Nat Turner's slave insurrection.

1861 Virginia secedes from the Union.

1865 General Lee surrenders Confederate forces at Appomattox; Civil War ends.

1870 Virginia readmitted to the Union.

1912 Woodrow Wilson becomes eighth Virginia resident to become president.

1954 Supreme Court decision banning school segregation meets with much resistance.

1969 First Republican governor elected in the twentieth century.

1971 Revised state constitution adopted.

1990 L. Douglas Wilder, first Black elected governor in the United States.

1993 The Walt Disney Company announces plans to build a historic theme park near Manassas. Plans are soon withdrawn due to protests from local residents and historical groups.

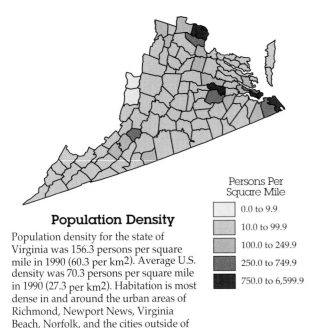

Population Density

Population density for the state of Virginia was 156.3 persons per square mile in 1990 (60.3 per km2). Average U.S. density was 70.3 persons per square mile in 1990 (27.3 per km2). Habitation is most dense in and around the urban areas of Richmond, Newport News, Virginia Beach, Norfolk, and the cities outside of Washington, D.C.

Persons Per Square Mile

	0.0 to 9.9
	10.0 to 99.9
	100.0 to 249.9
	250.0 to 749.9
	750.0 to 6,599.9

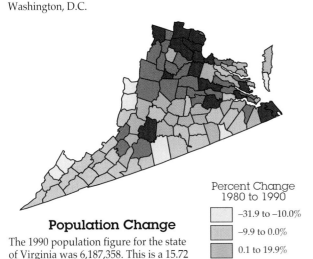

Population Change

The 1990 population figure for the state of Virginia was 6,187,358. This is a 15.72 percent increase from 5,346,818 in 1980. The next decade will show growth with a population of 6.9 million or a 11.15 percent increase. The northeast region of the state experienced tremendous growth over the last decade with growth rates of over 50 percent.

Percent Change 1980 to 1990

	−31.9 to −10.0%
	−9.9 to 0.0%
	0.1 to 19.9%
	20.0 to 49.9%
	50.0 to 140.1%

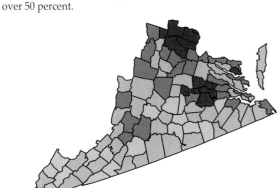

Distribution of Income

The per capita income for the state of Virginia (current dollars) was $20,629 in 1992. This is a 109.3 percent increase from $9,857 in 1980. Income is greatest in the counties outside Washington, D.C. Another node of high incomes is found around the city of Richmond.

Per Capita Income (000s) (Current Dollars)

	$10.0 to 12.9
	$13.0 to 15.9
	$16.0 to 19.9
	$20.0 to 37.7

Population Projections

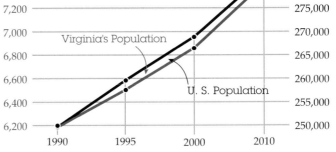

Population in thousands

Virginia's Population

U. S. Population

Population Change

Year	Population
1950	3,319,000
1960	3,986,000
1970	4,659,000
1980	5,346,818
1990	6,187,358
2000	6,877,000
2010	7,410,000

Period	Change
1950–1970	40.4%
1970–1980	14.8%
1980–1990	15.7%
1990–2000	11.2%

Population Facts

State Population, 1993: 6,491,000

Rank: 12

Population 2000: 6,877,000 (Rank 12)

Density: 156.3 per sq. mi. (60.3 per km2)

Distribution: 69.4% urban, 30.6% rural

Population Under 5 Years Old: 7.3%

Population Under 18 Years Old: 24.5%

Population Over 65 Years Old: 10.9%

Median Age: 32.6

Number of Households: 2,292,000

Average Persons Per Household: 2.61

Average Persons Per Family: 3.09

Female Heads of Households: 4.12%

Population That Is Married: 21.05%

Birth Rate: 16.1 per 1,000 population

Death Rate: 7.8 per 1,000 population

Births to Teen Mothers: 11.7%

Marriage Rate: 11.5 per 1,000 population

Divorce Rate: 4.4 per 1,000 population

Violent Crime Rate: 373 per 100,000 pop.

Population on Social Security: 13.6%

Percent Voting for President: 52.8%

Virginia's Famous Citizens

Beatty, Warren (b. 1937). Actor. He won an Academy Award in 1981 for his direction of the film *Reds*.

Falwell, Jerry (b. 1933). Clergyman. He founded the Moral Majority in 1979 to bring Christian influence into politics.

Glasgow, Ellen (1873-1945). Author. She won the Pulitzer Prize for her novel *In This Our Life* in 1942.

Johnston, Joseph E. (1807–1891). Member of the U.S. House from 1879 to 1881. He also served as Commissioner of Railroads.

Maclaine, Shirley (b. 1934). Actress. Her films include *The Apartment* (1960) and *Terms of Endearment* (1983).

Styron, William (b. 1925). Author. He won the Pulitzer Prize for his novel *The Confessions of Nat Turner* in 1968.

Tarkenton, Fran (b. 1940). Hall of Fame football player.

Washington, George (1732–1799). Elected first president of the United States. Hero of the American Revolution and the father of the country.

Wilder, Douglas (b. 1931). He became the first black ever elected governor in 1989.

Population Profile

Rank. Virginia ranks 12th among U.S. states in terms of population with 6,491,000 citizens.

Minority Population. The state's minority population is 24.2 percent. The state's male to female ratio for 1990 was 96.21 males for every 100 females. It was above the national average of 95.22 males for every 100 females.

Growth. Growing faster than the projected national average, the state's population is expected to reach 7.4 million by the year 2010 (*see graph above*).

Older Citizens. The state's population older than 65 was 664,470 in 1990. It grew 31.5% from 505,304 in 1980.

Younger Citizens. The number of children (under 18 years of age) was 1.5 million in 1990. This represents 24.3 percent of the state's population. The state's school aged population was 1.0 million in 1990. It is expected to increase to 1.2 million by the year 2000. This represents a 16.12% change.

Urban/Rural. 69.4% of the population of the state live in urban areas while 30.6% live in rural areas.

Largest Cities. Virginia has 21 cities with a population greater than 35,000. The populations of the state's largest centers are (starting from the most populous) Virginia Beach (393,069), Norfolk (261,229), Richmond (203,056), Arlington (170,936), Newport News (170,045), Chesapeake (151,976), Hampton (133,793), Alexandria (111,183), Portsmouth (103,907), Roanoke (96,397), Lynchburg (66,049), Burke (57,734), Danville (53,056), Suffolk (52,141), Annandale (50,975), and Reston (48,556).

Government

Capital: Richmond (established 1780).

Statehood: Became 10th state on Jun. 25, 1788.

Number of Counties: 95.

Supreme Court Justices: 7, 12-year term.

State Senators: 40, 4-year term.

State Legislators: 100, 4-year term.

United States Senators: 2.

United States Representatives: 11.

Electoral Votes: 13.

State Constitution: Adopted 1970.

Virginia

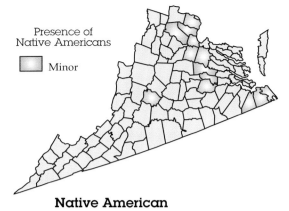

Presence of
Native Americans

☐ Minor

Native American

The Native American population in Virginia was 15,282 in 1990. This was an increase of 54.88 percent from 9,867 in 1980. Norfolk, Virginia Beach, Roanoke, Charlottesville, and Richmond are areas with large Native American populations. The largest Native American community can be found in Virginia Beach, with 1,384.

Nationalities

African	15,401
American	578,291
Arab	21,587
Austrian	9,423
Czech	11,496
Dutch	64,943
English	777,357
Finnish	4,507
German	920,112
Greek	19,799
Hungarian	15,630
Irish	532,181
Italian	145,753
Norwegian	23,173
Polish	75,449
Portuguese	7,630
Russian	29,360
Scottish	105,196
Slovak	19,373
Swedish	34,067
Welsh	29,795
West Indian	9,982

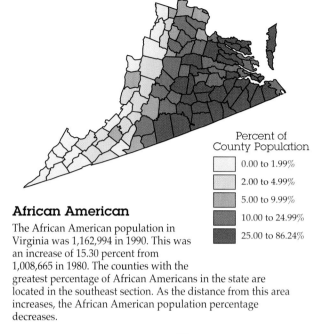

African American

The African American population in Virginia was 1,162,994 in 1990. This was an increase of 15.30 percent from 1,008,665 in 1980. The counties with the greatest percentage of African Americans in the state are located in the southeast section. As the distance from this area increases, the African American population percentage decreases.

Percent of County Population

☐ 0.00 to 1.99%
☐ 2.00 to 4.99%
☐ 5.00 to 9.99%
☐ 10.00 to 24.99%
☐ 25.00 to 86.24%

Statewide Ethnic Composition

Over 77 percent of the population of Virginia is white. The largest nationalities in this racial group are German, English, and Irish. The next largest group is African Americans, followed by Hispanics, Asian Americans, and Native Americans. Over 578,000 people claim to be American and acknowledge no other nationality.

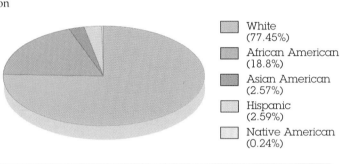

☐ White (77.45%)
☐ African American (18.8%)
☐ Asian American (2.57%)
☐ Hispanic (2.59%)
☐ Native American (0.24%)

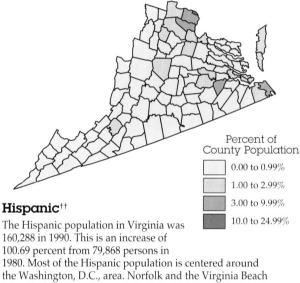

Percent of County Population

☐ 0.00 to 0.99%
☐ 1.00 to 2.99%
☐ 3.00 to 9.99%
☐ 10.0 to 24.99%

Hispanic[††]

The Hispanic population in Virginia was 160,288 in 1990. This is an increase of 100.69 percent from 79,868 persons in 1980. Most of the Hispanic population is centered around the Washington, D.C., area. Norfolk and the Virginia Beach area also have large Hispanic populations.

[††]A person of Mexican, Puerto Rican, Cuban, or other Spanish culture or origin regardless of race.

Education Facts

Total Students 1990: 985,346

Number of School Districts: 136

Expenditure Per Capita on Education 1990: $852

Expenditure Per Capita K–12 1990: $752

Expenditure Per Pupil 1990: $5,335

Total School Enrollment 1990–1991: 998,463

Rank of Expenditures Per Student: 15th in the U.S.

African American Enrollment: 23.7%

Hispanic Enrollment: 1.0%

Asian/Pacific Islander Enrollment: 2.6%

Native American Enrollment: 0.1%

Mean SAT Score 1991 Verbal: 424

Mean SAT Score 1991 Math: 466

Average Teacher's Salary 1992: $31,900

Rank Teacher's Salary: 24th in U.S.

High School Graduates 1990: 61,300

Total Number of Public Schools: 1,779

Number of Teachers 1990: 62,796

Student/Teacher Ratio: 15.9

Staff Employed in Public Schools: 120,203

Pupil/Staff Ratio: 8.2

Staff/Teacher Ratio: 1.9

Education

Attainment: 74.3 percent of population 25 years or older were high school graduates in 1989, earning Virginia a ranking of 39th in the United States; 27.3 percent of the state's population had completed college. Institutions of Higher Education: The largest universities and colleges in the state include College of William and Mary (founded 1693), Williamsburg; University of Virginia (founded 1819), Charlottesville; Virginia Polytechnic Institute, Blacksburg; Virginia Commonwealth University, Richmond; Old Dominion University, Norfolk; Virginia State University, Petersburg; University of Richmond, Richmond. Expenditures per Student: Expenditure increased 68.1% between 1985 and 1990. Projected High School Graduations: 1998 (79,792), 2004 (92,311); Total Revenues for Education from Federal Sources: N/A; Total Revenues for Education from State Sources: N/A; Total Revenues for Education from Local Sources: N/A; Average Annual Salaries for Public School Principals: $42,667; Largest School Districts in State: Fairfax County Public Schools, 126,713 students, 12th in the United States; Virginia Beach City Public Schools, 68,348, 36th.

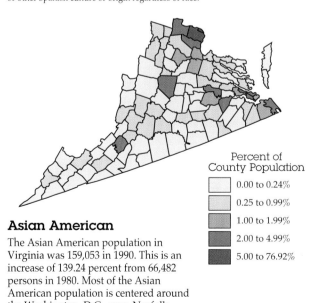

Percent of County Population

☐ 0.00 to 0.24%
☐ 0.25 to 0.99%
☐ 1.00 to 1.99%
☐ 2.00 to 4.99%
☐ 5.00 to 76.92%

Asian American

The Asian American population in Virginia was 159,053 in 1990. This is an increase of 139.24 percent from 66,482 persons in 1980. Most of the Asian American population is centered around the Washington, D.C., area. Norfolk, Virginia Beach, Roanoke, Charlottesville, and Richmond are also areas with large Asian American populations.

Major manufacturing areas
Major agricultural areas

Transportation

The first toll road in the United States, the Little River Turnpike, was built between Alexandria and Snicker's Gap in the late 18th century. Virginia's roads and highways today have a mileage of approximately 55,000 miles. Two Virginia interstates, I-95 and I-81, are two of the most used north-south interstates in the country.

Virginia has had rail service since the origin of railroading. Today, 13 different rail lines provide freight service, while passenger lines serve 17 Virginia cities. The Chesapeake Bay and the Potomac and James rivers are important water transportation routes. Major port cities include Norfolk, Newport News, and Alexandria. The Washington, D.C., metropolitan area has two major airports, Washington National and Dulles International, both located in Virginia.

Energy and Transportation Facts

Energy. Yearly Consumption: 1,848 tril. BTUs (residential, 22.8%; commercial, 20.8%; industrial, 25.2%; transportation, 31.3%); Annual Energy Expenditures Per Capita: $1,758; Nuclear Power Plants Located in State: 4; Source of Energy Consumed: Petroleum— 48.3%; Natural Gas— 11.8%; Coal—23.2%; Hydroelectric Power—0.0%; Nuclear Power—16.6%.

Transportation. Highway Miles: 68,429 (interstates, 1,106; urban, 15,581; rural, 52,848); Average Yearly Auto Insurance: $503 (31st); Auto Fatalities Rank: 45th; Registered Motor Vehicles: 5,238,706; Workers in Carpools: 21.9%; Workers Using Public Trans: 4.0%.

Agriculture

Virginia has 8.6 million farm acres. During the last 40 years, Virginia's farms have grown larger in size and fewer in number. In 1955, 136,000 farms were found in the state. Today, 43,000 remain.

Agriculture adds $2 billion to the state's gross product annually. The principal commodities in order of marketing receipts are cattle, broilers, dairy products, and tobacco.

Livestock and livestock products account for most of Virginia's farm income. Beef cattle, the leading product, are found in the western part of the state. Rockingham County produces most of the milk, chicken, and turkeys in the state. Tobacco, the leading crop, is grown in the Piedmont region and in the far western part of the state. Virginia's vegetables, including sweet potatoes and tomatoes, are grown near the Chesapeake Bay.

Housing

Owner Occupied Units: 2,496,334; Average Age of Units: 25 years; Average Value of Housing Units: $91,000; Renter Occupied Units: 746,163; Median Monthly Rent: $495; Housing Starts: 44,600; Existing Home Sales: 104,200.

Economic Facts

Gross State Product: $136,000,000,000 (1989)

Income Per Capita: $20,629

Disposable Personal Income: $18,010

Median Household Income: $33,328

Average Annual Pay, 1988: $23,804

Principal Industries: tobacco products, transportation equipment, chemicals, electrical equipment, food products, textiles, furniture

Major Crops: tobacco, milk, hay, corn, apples, soybeans

Fish: Flounder, Bass, Carp, Perch, Mackerel, Shad

Livestock: chickens, cattle

Non-Fuel Minerals: Basalt, Granite, Limestone, Marble, Lead, Sandstone, Soapstone, Kyanite

Organic Fuel Minerals: Coal

Civilian Labor Force: 3,306,000 (Women: 1,567,000)

Total Employed: 3,113,000 (Women: 1,473,000)

Median Value of Housing: $91,000

Median Contract Rent: $495 per month

Economic Sectors 1992

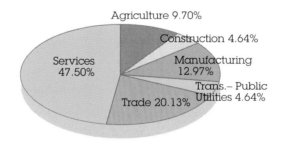

Agriculture 9.70%
Construction 4.64%
Manufacturing 12.97%
Trans.– Public Utilities 4.64%
Trade 20.13%
Services 47.50%

Manufacturing

Virginia's manufacturing industry developed in the mid-19th century; however, the Civil War prevented any growth during that time. During the last 50 years, Virginia has expanded its manufacturing sector. Currently, chemical production is the state's leading manufacturing activity. Tobacco products, processed foods, and electrical equipment are also important to Virginia's economy.

Several cities throughout the state contain manufacturing facilities. The city of Richmond represents many different manufacturing industries. Most of Virginia's cigarettes come from large factories in Richmond. Chemicals, especially synthetic fibers, are made in Richmond, Hopewell, and Williamsburg. Food processing takes place across Virginia. Portsmouth and Newport News, in the south, have shipbuilding facilities.

Employment

Employment. Virginia employed 3.20 million people in 1993. Most work in social and personal services (796,700 persons or 24.8% of the workforce). Manufacturing accounts for 12.6% or 404,700 workers. Wholesale and retail trade account for 20.2% or 648,400 workers. Government employs 598,100 workers (18.6%). Construction employs 153,200 workers (4.8%). Transportation and utilities account for 4.7% or 149,300 persons. Agriculture employs 64,200 workers or 2.0%. Finance, real estate, and insurance account for 4.9% or 156,600 workers. Mining employs 12,600 people and accounts for only 0.4% of the workforce.

Unemployment. Unemployment has decreased to 5.0% in 1993 from a rate of 5.6% in 1985. Today's figure is lower than the national average of 6.8% as shown below.

Unemployment Rate

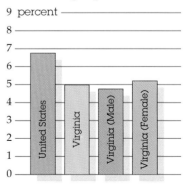

WASHINGTON
The State of Washington

Official State Seal

The Great Seal of Washington first appeared in 1889, but was very different from the present seal. It was changed because it was found to be too difficult to engrave. The state legislature decided to add a portrait of George Washington and write the words "The Seal of the State of Washington" around the outer edge. The date of statehood was also added at this time.

Legal Holidays

January: New Year's Day—1st, Martin Luther King, Jr., Day—3d Monday; February: Abraham Lincoln's Birthday—12th; Presidents' Day—3d Monday; May: Memorial Day—4th Monday; July: Independence Day—4th; September: Labor Day—1st Monday; October: Columbus Day—2d Monday; November: Admission Day—11th; Veteran's Day—11th; Thanksgiving—4th Thursday; December: Christmas—25th.

Official State Flag

The state flag of Washington was adopted in 1923. Created by the Daughters of the American Revolution in 1915, it is the only state flag with a green field, which symbolizes Washington as the Evergreen State.

Festivals and Events

January: Ski-Jumping Tournament, Leavenworth; April: Crabfeed & Auction, Bainbridge Island; Trade Fair, Seattle; Daffodil Festival, Puyallup; May: Irrigation Festival, Sequim; Apple Blossom Festival, Wenatchee; Rhododendron Festival, Port Townsend; Blossom Time Festival, Bellingham; June: Lummi Stommish Water Carnival, Bellingham; Timber Bowl Celebration, Darington; Kelso Hilander Summer Festival, Kelso; July: Pacific International Yachting Association Regatta, Seattle; Toppenish Native American Pow Wow, Toppenish; August: Stockader Days, Vancouver; September: Western Washington State Fair, Puyallup; Wooden Boat Festival, Port Townsend; November: Northwest Art Festival, Seattle; Seattle Boat Show, Seattle.

Washington Compared to States in Its Region.

Resident Pop. in Metro Areas: 2d; Pop.Percent Increase: 2d; Pop. Over 65: 2d; Infant Mortality: 4th; School Enroll. Increase: 3d; High School Grad. and Up: 2d; Violent Crime: 3d; Hazardous Waste Sites: 2d; Unemployment: 1st; Median Household Income: 4th; Persons Below Poverty: 3d; Energy Costs Per Person: 4th.

Pacific Region

	Population	Capital
Washington	5,255,000	Olympia
Oregon	3,032,000	Salem
California	31,211,000	Sacramento
Alaska	599,000	Juneau
Hawaii	1,172,000	Honolulu

Washington's Finances

Households: 1,872,000; Income Per Capita Current Dollars: $20,398; Change Per Capita Income 1980 to 1992: 90.4% (37th in U.S.); State Expenditures: $14,724,000,000; State Revenues: $13,434,000,000; Personal Income Tax: N/A; Federal Income Taxes Paid Per Capita: $2,138; Sales Tax: 6.5% (food and prescription drugs exempt).

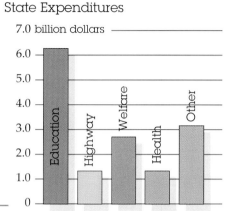

State Expenditures

State Revenues

Location, Size, and Boundaries

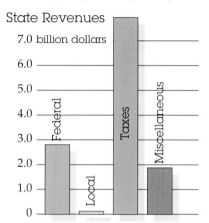
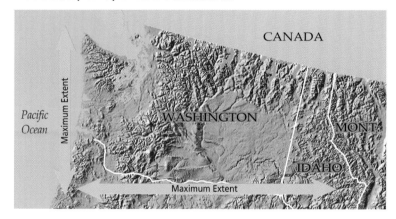

Location. Washington is located in the northwest Pacific region of the United States. It is bounded on three of four sides by land with a general coastline along the Pacific Ocean in the west. The geographic center of Washington is lat. 47° 20' N; long. 120° 16.1' W.

Size. Washington is the 20th largest state in terms of size. Its area is 68,192 sq. mi. (176,617 km2). Inland water covers 1,622 sq. mi. (4,201 km2). Washington touches the Pacific Ocean along a 157 mile coastline.

Boundaries. Canada, 286 mi. (460 km); Idaho, 213 mi. (343 km); Oregon, 443 mi. (713 km); Pacific Ocean, 157 mi. (253 km).

Geographic Extent. The north/south extent is 240 mi. (390 km). The state extends 360 mi. (580 km) to the east/west.

Facts about Washington. Origin of Name: Named in honor of George Washington; Nickname: The Evergreen State; Motto: "Alki" (Indian word for *"bye and bye"*); Abbreviations: Wash. (traditional), WA (postal); State Bird: willow goldfinch; State Tree: Western hemlock; State Flower: coast rhododendron; State Song: "Washington, My Home," words and music by Helen Davis.

Washington Compared to Other States. Resident Pop. in Metro Areas: 15th; Pop. Per. Increase: 4th; Pop. Over 65: 36th; Infant Mort.: 43d; School Enroll. Increase: 14th; High School Grad. and Up: 4th; Violent Crime: 27th; Haz. Waste Sites: 7th; Unemployment: 12th; Median Household Income: 14th; Persons Below Poverty: 34th; Energy Costs Per Person: 40th.

Sources of Information. Tourism: Dept. of Trade and Econ. Development, Tourism Development Division, 101 General Administration Bldg., Olympia, WA 98504.

■ **American Camp Site.** Camp set up in 1859 on San Juan Island that was involved in a boundary dispute with Britain. (B-4)

■ **Coulee Dam National Recreation Area.** Site of the Grand Coulee Dam on Franklin D. Roosevelt Lake. (D-13)

■ **English Blockhouse.** Site of an English camp on San Juan Island set up in 1860. (C-4)

■ **Fort Columbia.** Military fort established in 1895. (I-2)

■ **Fort Okanogan.** Early trading posts for western travelers. (D-12)

■ **Fort Simcoe.** Fort built for protection against Indians in 1856–1857. (H-9)

■ **Fort Vancouver National Historic Site.** Fort built in 1825 for the Hudson's Bay Company. (J-5)

■ **Gardiner Cave.** Cave with large limestone formations. (A-17)

■ **Ginkgo Petrified Forest Museum.** Museum dedicated to informing the public about the Petrified Forest. (G-11)

■ **Hood Canal Floating Bridge.** One of world's longest floating bridges. (D-5)

■ **Illahee State Park.** White sand beaches for bathing and tanning. (E-5)

■ **Indian Rock Paintings.** Site of ancient Indian rock paintings. (H-10)

■ **Mount Baker.** Mountain 10,750 feet (3,277 meters) high. (C-7)

■ **Mount Rainier National Park.** Site of glaciers on an ancient volcano. (G-7)

■ **Mount St. Helens National Volcanic Monument.** Site of the 1980 volcanic eruption which caused widespread damage. (I-6)

■ **Olympic National Park.** Site of Mount Olympus. (D-3)

■ **Peace Arch State Park.** Symbol representing the peaceful relationship between Canada and the United States. (A-5)

■ **St. Paul's Mission.** Site of a Jesuit mission built in 1847. (B-13)

■ **Stonehenge Memorial.** Site of a replica of Stonehenge. (J-9)

■ **Whitman Mission National Historic Site.** Site of the mission of Marcus Whitman (1836). (I-14)

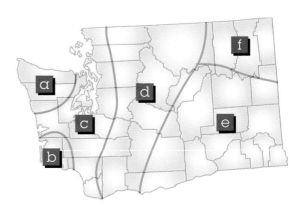

Physical Regions: (a) Olympic Mountains; (b) Coast Range; (c) Puget Sound Lowland; (d) Cascade Mountains; (e) Columbia Plateau; (f) Rocky Mountains.

Major Cities

Auburn	F-6	Everett	D-6	Lakewood	F-5	Richland	I-13
Bellevue	E-6	Federal Way	F-6	Longview	I-4	Seattle	E-6
Bellingham	B-5	Fircrest	F-5	Lynnwood	D-6	Spokane	E-17
Bothell	E-6	Inglewood	E-7	Mercer Island	E-6	Tacoma	F-5
Bremerton	E-5	Kennewick	I-13	Olympia	G-5	Vancouver	J-5
Fairwood	E-6	Kent	F-6	Parkland	F-5	Wenatchee	E-10
Edmonds	D-6	Kirkland	E-6	Redmond	E-6	White Center	E-6
				Renton	E-6	Yakima	H-10

Scale

0 20 40 60 mi.

20 0 20 40 60 80 km

Topography

There are several distinct topographic regions in Washington. The southwestern corner of the state is covered by the Coast Range physical region, which extends north from Oregon. The Willapa Hills, overlooking Willapa Bay, are the most important physical feature of this region. Soil in the Coast Range is cool and wet, colored gray, and very high in organic content.

Located in the northwest corner, with the Pacific Ocean to the west and the Strait of Juan de Fuca to to the north, is the Olympic Mountains physical region. This territory is some of the wildest in North America, with several areas that have never been explored. Soil is similar to that found in the Coast Range. The Puget Sound Lowland physical region lies between the Coast Range and the Cascade Mountains. Puget Sound, a very large saltwater bay that is almost entirely surrounded by land, is the central feature of this region. Soil type varies from cool and wet former

tundra, to warm and moist clay that is high in organic content. East of the lowland is the Cascade Mountains physical region, mainly consisting of a rugged range of mostly dormant volcanoes. One of these, Mt. St. Helens, erupted in 1980, causing much damage and loss of life. Many high peaks are found in this range. The highest in the state is Mt Rainier, which rises 14,410 ft. (4,392 m) above sea level. Soil is cool and moist, colored reddish brown with a large concentration of ash.

The Columbia Plateau physical region covers much of the state east of the Cascades. It was formed by an ancient lava flow and is dissected by many river valleys. Some of these valleys, such as the Yakima River Valley, have rich soils and are well suited to agriculture. The Rocky Mountains physical region is situated in Washington's northeast corner. The main rivers that drain this region are the mighty Columbia and its tributary, the Okanogan River.

Climate

Washington divides nicely into two distinct climatic regions: a western moist, temperate zone, and an eastern drier, continental zone. The rain shadow effect of the Cascade Mountains is responsible for this phenomenon; temperatures are affected accordingly. In Seattle, January and July temperatures only vary slightly between 41 degrees F and 66 degrees F respectively. However, in Spokane, near the Idaho border, average January and July temperatures range from 25 degrees F to 72 degrees F.

Moisture from the Pacific Ocean brings significant precipitation to western Washington. Because of the mountains, this moisture seldom reaches eastern Washington. Therefore, some of central Washington is semidesert. Precipitation ranges from over 125 inches on the Olympic Peninsula to only 6 inches near Richland.

Snow accumulation varies just as much as rainfall. While coastal areas receive 5 inches on average, the Cascades often receive well over 100 inches of snow in winter.

Weather Facts

Record High Temperature: 118° F (48° C) on August 5, 1961, at Ice Harbor Dam; Record Low Temp-erature: -48° F (-44° C) on December 30, 1968, at Winthrop; Average January Temperature: 31° F (-1° C); Average July Temperature: 66° F (19° C); Average Yearly Precipitation: 29 in. (74 cm).

Land Use

Cropland: 25.9%; Pasture: 4.7%; Rangeland: 18.6%; Forest: 42.2%; Urban: 5.3%; Other: 3.3%.

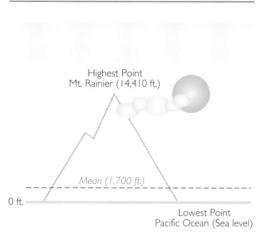

Highest Point
Mt. Rainier (14,410 ft.)

Mean (1,700 ft.)

0 ft.

Lowest Point
Pacific Ocean (Sea level)

Hydrology

The most important river in Washington, and one of the longest in the United States, is the Columbia, flowing for over 1,000 miles (1,610 km) in the state. It enters Washington from Canada in the northeast and travels generally south through the central part of the state, before turning west to form much of Washington's southern border with Oregon on its way to the Pacific Ocean. Some of its tributaries include the Pend Oreille, the Sanpoil, the Okanogan, and the Methow in the north. The Snake River, in southeastern Washington, is the state's second longest river. Several rivers in the west flow into Puget Sound, including the Skagit, the Cedar, and the Puyallup.

The largest lake in Washington is Franklin D. Roosevelt Lake, created by the Grand Coulee Dam on the Columbia, covering about 125 sq. miles (324 sq. km). There are also many glacial lakes in Washington in the northwest, including Lake Whatcom and Lake Sammamish.

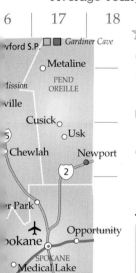

6   17   18

<table>
<thead>
<tr><th></th><th></th></tr>
</thead>
<tbody>
<tr><td>★</td><td>State capitol</td></tr>
<tr><td>⊙</td><td>Cities over 35,000 population</td></tr>
<tr><td>○</td><td>Other significant cities</td></tr>
<tr><td>●</td><td>County Seats</td></tr>
<tr><td>■</td><td>Major cultural attractions</td></tr>
<tr><td>□</td><td>State Parks</td></tr>
<tr><td>Ⓦ</td><td>Welcome Centers</td></tr>
<tr><td>⚲</td><td>Major colleges and universities</td></tr>
</tbody>
</table>

Average Monthly Weather

Seattle-Tacoma	Jan	Feb	Mar	Apr	May	Jun	Jul	Aug	Sep	Oct	Nov	Dec	Yearly
Maximum Temperature °F	43.9	48.8	51.1	56.8	64.0	69.2	75.2	73.9	68.7	59.5	50.3	45.6	58.9
Minimum Temperature °F	34.3	36.8	37.2	40.5	46.0	51.1	54.3	54.3	51.2	45.3	39.3	36.3	43.9
Days of Precipitation	18.6	15.8	17.2	13.7	10.4	9.1	5.0	6.3	9.3	13.1	17.9	19.3	155.6
Spokane													
Maximum Temperature °F	31.3	39.0	46.2	56.7	66.1	74.0	84.0	81.7	72.4	58.3	41.4	34.2	57.1
Minimum Temperature °F	20.0	25.7	29.0	34.9	42.5	49.3	55.3	54.3	46.5	36.7	28.5	23.7	37.2
Days of Precipitation	14.1	11.4	11.6	8.6	9.2	7.7	4.3	5.0	5.9	7.5	12.6	15.1	112.9

Flora and Fauna

The Pacific Northwest state of Washington is over half covered with forests. Western Washington has several conifers such as hemlock, Douglas fir, Sitka spruce, and red cedar. In the eastern part of the state, common softwoods include western larch, lodgepole pine, and ponderosa (western yellow) pine. Deciduous trees such as maple, birch, and alder also grow in Washington. Plant life varies greatly because of climate and elevation differences. Goldenrod and lupine bloom in fields, while rare wildflowers grow in mountain climates. Western dogwood and rhododendron also grow in Washington.

Washington is home to four species of deer: the

elk, Colombian black-tailed deer, mule deer, and common white-tailed deer. Other large animals include black bears and cougars. Many small animals such as bobcats, beavers, and martens also live in the state. Washington's game bird population is made up of wild ducks, pheasants, and two kinds of grouse. Oysters, clams, and saltwater fish such as halibut and cod live off Washington's coast. The state's freshwater fish include cutthroat and rainbow trout, grayling, and whitefish.

Environmental Quality

See page 376.

Environmental Facts

Air Pollution Rank: 28th; Water Pollution Rank: 7th; Total Yearly Industrial Pollution: 26,522,151 lbs.; Industrial Pollution Rank: 28th; Hazardous Sites: 49; Hazardous Sites Rank: 7th; Landfill Capacity: adequate; Fresh Water Supply: large surplus; Daily Residential Water Consumption: 191 gals. per capita; Endangered Species: Aquatic Species (2)—salmon, Chinook (snake river spring/summer); Birds (7)—eagle, bald; Mammals (4)—bear, grizzly; Other Species (1)—butterfly, oregon silverspot; Plants (3)—checker-mallow, Nelson's.

Washington's History

Washington's First People

The first humans probably came to the Washington region more than ten thousand years ago, according to extensive archaeological evidence. Places such as Marmes Cave, near North Bonneville, have yielded significant insight into these ancient peoples.

In the coastal areas west of the Cascade Mountains lived the Chinook, Puyallup, Clatsop, Nooksack, Clallam, and Nisqually tribes. These people lived primarily on salmon and other types of fish. Artifacts recovered from the coastal areas suggest that these natives constructed masks, tools, and other items from wood.

Other Native American tribes lived in the interior of the state. These tribes included the Nez Perce, Cayuse, Colville, Spokane, Yakima, and Okanagan. These people were primarily nomadic hunters who lived in tepees made of animal skin. Like Plains tribes farther east, the plateau Indians of interior Washington relied on horses to support their nomadic lifestyle.

European and American Exploration

In 1775, the Spanish navigator Bruno Heceta reached the mouth of the Columbia River. His party made the first landing on Washington soil, near the site of present-day Point Grenville. As a result of this expedition, Spain lay claim to the Washington area.

British explorers were also interested in Washington. The first Englishman to come to the Pacific Northwest was Capt. James Cook, who in 1778 saw most of the Washington coast, although inclement weather prevented further exploration. A few years later, in 1792, another British explorer, George Vancouver, surveyed the Puget Sound and Strait of Georgia region.

Around the same time, Americans began to explore Washington's land. Robert Gray, an American captain, rediscovered the Columbia River in 1792 and claimed that area for the United States. In 1805, the famous duo of Lewis and Clark explored along the Columbia River all the way to the Pacific Ocean.

With all this exploration came settlement. At first, the settlers who came to Washington were fur traders. The fur industry dominated Washington's economy throughout the early 1800s, with many fur companies establishing outposts in the state.

After the fur traders came missionaries. In 1836, Americans established a settlement near the present town of Walla Walla. The first permanent American settlement was made at Tumwater, on the Puget Sound, in 1845. The large increase in both American and British settlement caused a controversy between the two countries over borders. In 1846, the forty-ninth parallel was set as the border between British-controlled Canada and the United States.

Territorial Period and Statehood

As early as 1853, a proposal was made to establish a territory out of Washington land. The Columbia Territory proposal was passed by Congress in March, 1853, and Olympia was chosen as the capital. The territory was named Washington in honor of the first president of the United States. Parts of Idaho and Montana were included in this territory.

At first, settlement in the territory remained somewhat slow. This changed in the 1860s, however, when gold was discovered in nearby Oregon and British Columbia. The town of Walla Walla in eastern Washington became the chief supplier for gold prospectors, and the eastern part of the state began to develop rapidly. In 1863, the Territory of Idaho was created, and part of eastern Washington Territory was broken off to join the new territory. Washington's permanent boundaries were established in 1872.

The dawn of the railroad helped Washington towns like Seattle, Tacoma, and Spokane to emerge as industrial centers. As Washington's population increased, statehood for the territory seemed inevitable. So, on October 1, 1889, citizens of the territory approved a constitution. On November 11, 1889, Washington became the forty-second state in the Union.

Economic Development

Throughout its history, the state of Washington has relied upon its natural resources to provide industries for the state. In the 1860s, lumbering became Washington's first large industry. Lumber mills were scattered all around the Puget Sound area. Even today, Washington's timber industries remain an important feature of the state's economy, serving both national and international markets.

The discovery of gold also helped spark economic activity in Washington. The first gold deposits were found in 1855, attracting prospectors as well as settlers. However, the state did not start to become populated until the railroad came through in 1883.

During World War I, Washington's industrial base shifted in order to accommodate wartime demands. Shipbuilding became an important industry at this time and expanded even further during World War II. Large-scale shipbuilding and military aircraft factories were built. In addition to aerospace products, Washington factories produce nonelectrical machinery, paper products, and printing and publishing materials.

One State, Two Climatic Regions

When many people think of Washington state, they think rain. However, not all Washington residents have to carry their umbrellas everywhere they go. The state has two major climatic regions, one wet and one dry, separated from each other by the Cascade Mountains. The combination of prevailing westerly winds and the "rain shadow" effect of the great mountain range produces this climatic dichotomy.

Important Events

1775 Spanish explorer Bruno Heceta reaches Washington.

1778 Capt. James Cook explores the Washington coast.

1792 George Vancouver surveys Puget Sound and the Strait of Georgia.

1792 American captain Robert Gray "rediscovers" Columbia River.

1805 Lewis and Clark explore the Columbia River.

1810 North West Company, a fur trading group, established near Spokane.

1818 United States and Great Britain jointly occupy Oregon region, including Washington.

1836 Americans settle and area near Walla Walla.

1845 Tumwater, on the Puget Sound, becomes the first American settlement.

1846 Treaty between United States and Great Britain sets Canadian border at forty-ninth parallel.

1853 Washington Territory created in March.

1855 The first gold deposits are found.

1863 Part of Washington given to Idaho territory.

1872 Permanent boundaries are established.

1883 The first railroad enters the area.

1889 Washington becomes forty-second state in the Union on November 11.

1928 Capitol building at Olympia completed.

1937 Bonneville Power Administration starts operations.

1944 First plutonium produced in Richland.

1950 Tacoma Narrows Bridge completed.

1964 Columbia River Treaty of 1961 receives final approval from United States and Canada.

1974 Spokane World's Fair, Expo '74, held.

1989 Logging in some areas of the state is halted because of a threat to the northern spotted owl.

1980 Mount St. Helens, in the Cascades, erupts.

1988 The state is struck with multiple forest fires.

1990 The northern spotted owl is declared a threatened species.

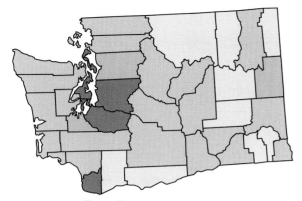

Population Density

Population density for the state of Washington was 73.1 persons per square mile in 1990 (28.2 per km2). Average U.S. density was 70.3 persons per square mile in 1990 (27.3 per km2). Habitation is most dense around the urban areas of Seattle and Tacoma. Clark County in the south has a high density as well. This county is just over the border from the city of Portland, Oregon.

Persons Per Square Mile
- 0.0 to 9.9
- 10.0 to 99.9
- 100.0 to 249.9
- 250.0 to 749.9

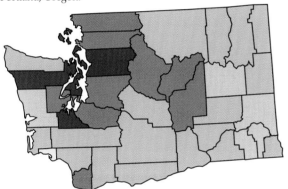

Population Change

The 1990 population figure for the state of Washington was 4,866,692. This is a 17.78 percent increase from 4,132,156 in 1980. The next decade will show growth with a population of 5.0 million or a 2.55 percent increase. The areas of fastest growth surround Washington's major cities of Seattle and Tacoma.

Percent Change 1980 to 1990
- –9.9 to 0.0%
- 0.1 to 19.9%
- 20.0 to 49.9%
- 50.0 to 163.0%

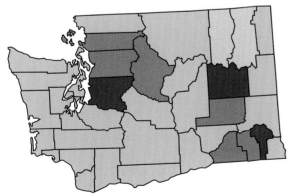

Distribution of Income

The per capita income for the state of Washington (current dollars) was $20,398 in 1992. This is a 90.4 percent increase from $9,857 in 1980. Income is greatest in and around the Seattle area. Garfield and Lincoln counties also have some of the highest per capita incomes in the state.

Per Capita Income (000s) (Current Dollars)
- $10.0 to 12.9
- $13.0 to 15.9
- $16.0 to 19.9
- $20.0 to 37.7

Population Projections

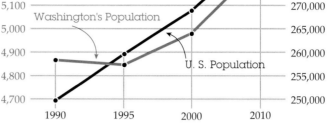

Population in thousands

Washington's Population

U. S. Population

Population Change

Year	Population
1950	2,379,000
1960	2,855,000
1970	3,413,000
1980	4,132,156
1990	4,866,692
2000	4,991,000
2010	5,282,000

Period	Change
1950–1970	43.5%
1970–1980	21.1%
1980–1990	17.8%
1990–2000	2.5%

Population Facts

State Population, 1993: 5,255,000

Rank: 15

Population 2000: 4,991,000 (Rank 18)

Density: 73.1 per sq. mi. (28.2 per km²)

Distribution: 76.4% urban, 23.6% rural

Population Under 5 Years Old: 7.6%

Population Under 18 Years Old: 26.4%

Population Over 65 Years Old: 11.7%

Median Age: 33.1

Number of Households: 1,872,000

Average Persons Per Household: 2.53

Average Persons Per Family: 3.06

Female Heads of Households: 3.61%

Population That Is Married: 21.15%

Birth Rate: 16.3 per 1,000 population

Death Rate: 7.6 per 1,000 population

Births to Teen Mothers: 10.8%

Marriage Rate: 10.0 per 1,000 population

Divorce Rate: 5.9 per 1,000 population

Violent Crime Rate: 523 per 100,000 pop.

Population on Social Security: 14.5%

Percent Voting for President: 59.9%

Population Profile

Rank. Washington ranks 15th among U.S. states in terms of population with 5,255,000 citizens.

Minority Population. The state's minority population is 13.5 percent. The state's male to female ratio for 1990 was 98.40 males for every 100 females. It was above the national average of 95.22 males for every 100 females.

Growth. Growing more slowly than the

Government

Capital: Olympia (established 1889).

Statehood: Became 42d state on Nov. 11, 1889.

Number of Counties: 39.

Supreme Court Justices: 9, 6-year term.

State Senators: 49, 4-year term.

State Legislators: 98, 2-year term.

United States Senators: 2.

United States Representatives: 9.

Electoral Votes: 11.

State Constitution: Adopted 1889.

Washington's Famous Citizens

Boeing, William (1881–1956). He founded the Boeing Airline Company to construct aircraft in 1916.

Brattain, Walter (1902–1987). Physicist. He won the Nobel Prize in 1956 for his work on the invention of the transistor.

Carlson, Chester (1906–1968). He received a patent for a process to become known as xerography in 1940.

Elway, John (b. 1960). Football player. He helped the Denver Broncos reach the Super Bowl 3 times (1987, 1988, 1990).

Hendrix, Jimi (1942–1970). Rock guitar player. He incorporated dissonance and feedback into his ground breaking guitar playing.

McCarthy, Mary (1912–1989). Author and critic. She wrote drama criticism for the *Partisan Review* from 1937 to 1948.

Wainwright, Jonathan (1883–1953). Military officer. He was given the Medal of Honor after being held prisoner by the Japanese.

Yamasaki, Minoru (1912–1986). Architect. He designed the World Trade Center in New York City.

projected national average, the state's population is expected to reach 5.3 million by the year 2010 (*see graph above*).

Older Citizens. The state's population older than 65 was 564,115 in 1990. It grew 30.71% from 431,562 in 1980.

Younger Citizens. The number of children (under 18 years of age) was 1.2 million in 1990. This represents 25.5 percent of the state's population. The state's school aged population was 812 thousand in 1990. It is expected to increase to 836 thousand by the year 2000. This represents a 2.96% change.

Urban/Rural. 76.4% of the population of the state live in urban areas while 23.6% live in rural areas.

Largest Cities. Washington has 17 cities with a population greater than 35,000. The populations of the state's largest centers are (starting from the most populous) Seattle (516,259), Spokane (177,196), Tacoma (176,664), Bellevue (86,874), Everett (69,961), Federal Way (67,554), Lakewood (58,412), Yakima (54,827), Bellingham (52,179),Vancouver (46,380), East Hill-Meridian (42,696), Kennewick (42,155), Renton (41,688), Kirkland (40,052), and Bremerton (38,142).

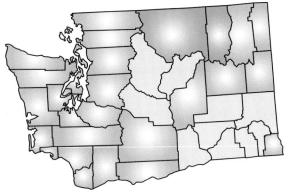

Native American

The Native American population in Washington was 81,483 in 1990. This was an increase of 33.07 percent from 61,233 in 1980. Many Native Americans live in the Indian reservations located around the state. These reservations include the Yakima, Spokane, Colville, and Quinault.

Presence of Native Americans

- ⬜ Minor
- ⬜ Moderate

Nationalities

African	5,455
American	171,350
Arab	7,047
Austrian	11,374
Czech	19,676
Dutch	101,194
English	561,397
Finnish	31,388
German	1,053,459
Greek	14,109
Hungarian	10,403
Irish	416,507
Italian	108,796
Norwegian	232,000
Polish	61,202
Portuguese	8,602
Russian	25,127
Scottish	110,840
Slovak	11,834
Swedish	166,984
Welsh	33,446
West Indian	2,856

Statewide Ethnic Composition

Over 88 percent of the population of Washington is white. The largest nationalities in this racial group are German, English, and Irish. The next largest group is Hispanics, followed by Asian Americans, African Americans, and Native Americans. Over 171,000 people claim to be American and acknowledge no other nationality.

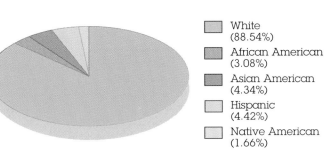

- ⬜ White (88.54%)
- ⬜ African American (3.08%)
- ⬜ Asian American (4.34%)
- ⬜ Hispanic (4.42%)
- ⬜ Native American (1.66%)

Education Facts

Total Students 1990: 810,232

Number of School Districts: 296

Expenditure Per Capita on Education 1990: $966

Expenditure Per Capita K–12 1990: $738

Expenditure Per Pupil 1990: $5,042

Total School Enrollment 1990–1991: 840,554

Rank of Expenditures Per Student: 22d in the U.S.

African American Enrollment: 4.1%

Hispanic Enrollment: 5.2%

Asian/Pacific Islander Enrollment: 5.3%

Native American Enrollment: 2.4%

Mean SAT Score 1991 Verbal: 433

Mean SAT Score 1991 Math: 480

Average Teacher's Salary 1992: $34,800

Rank Teacher's Salary: 14th in U.S.

High School Graduates 1990: 46,600

Total Number of Public Schools: 1,858

Number of Teachers 1990: 41,819

Student/Teacher Ratio: 20.1

Staff Employed in Public Schools: 72,517

Pupil/Staff Ratio: 11.2

Staff/Teacher Ratio: 1.8

Education

Attainment: 88.2 percent of population 25 years or older were high school graduates in 1989, earning Washington a ranking of 2d in the United States; 24.1 percent of the state's population had completed college. Institutions of Higher Education: The largest universities and colleges in the state include University of Washington, Seattle; Washington State University, Pullman; Evergreen State College, Olympia; Seattle University, Seattle. Expenditures per Student: Expenditure increased 73% between 1985 and 1990. Projected High School Graduations: 1998 (56,523), 2004 (67,177); Total Revenues for Education from Federal Sources: $193 million; Total Revenues for Education from State Sources: $2.4 billion; Total Revenues for Education from Local Sources: $597 million; Average Annual Salaries for Public School Principals: $44,965; Largest School Districts in State: Seattle, 40,781 students, 90th in the United States; Tacoma, 29,343, 142d.

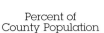

African American

The African American population in Washington was 149,801 in 1990. This was an increase of 41.85 percent from 105,604 in 1980. Most of the African American population in the state of Washington is located in the Seattle-Tacoma area. Over half of the African American population lives in this area.

Percent of County Population

- ⬜ 0.00 to 1.99%
- ⬜ 2.00 to 4.99%
- ⬜ 5.00 to 9.99%

Hispanic[††]

The Hispanic population in Washington was 214,570 in 1990. This is an increase of 78.78 percent from 120,016 persons in 1980. The highest percentage of Hispanics can be found in Adams and Franklin counties. There are also large numbers in the Seattle-Tacoma area.

[††]A person of Mexican, Puerto Rican, Cuban, or other Spanish culture or origin regardless of race.

Percent of County Population

- ⬜ 0.00 to 0.99%
- ⬜ 1.00 to 2.99%
- ⬜ 3.00 to 9.99%
- ⬜ 10.00 to 24.99%
- ⬜ 25.00 to 97.22%

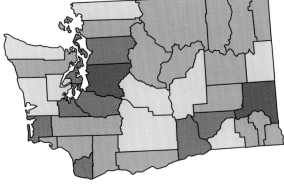

Asian American

The Asian American population in Washington was 210,958 in 1990. This is an increase of 100.08 percent from 105,438 persons in 1980. The highest percentage of Asian Americans can be found in the Seattle-Tacoma area. There are also large numbers in Whitman County.

Percent of County Population

- ⬜ 0.25 to 0.99%
- ⬜ 1.00 to 1.99%
- ⬜ 2.00 to 4.99%
- ⬜ 5.00 to 76.92%

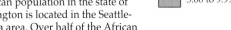
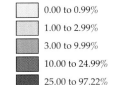

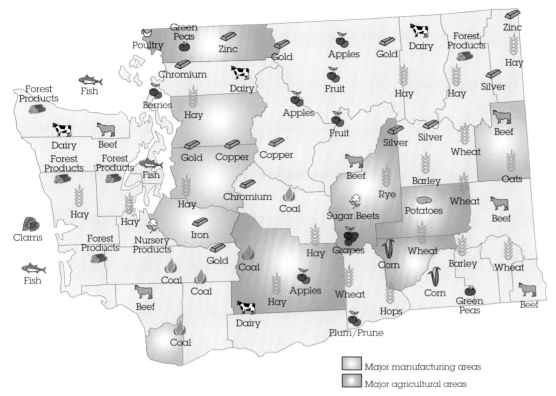

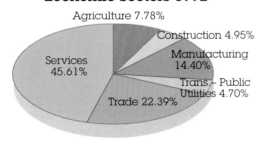
Major manufacturing areas
Major agricultural areas

Agriculture

Washington has 16 million farm acres. During the last 40 years, Washington's farms have grown larger in size and fewer in number. In 1955, 65,000 farms were found in the state. Today, 36,000 remain.

Agriculture adds $4 billion to the state's gross product annually. The principal commodities in order of marketing receipts are apples, cattle, dairy products, and wheat.

Washington ranks second in the nation in the production of timber, its leading agricultural product. Douglas fir and western hemlock are the primary trees harvested. Washington is the nation's leader in the production of hops, used for brewing beer. Wheat, the leading crop, is grown in the eastern part of the state. Washington also leads the nation in the production of apples, including the Red and Golden Delicious varieties.

Housing

Owner Occupied Units: 2,032,378; Average Age of Units: 26 years; Average Value of Housing Units: $93,400; Renter Occupied Units: 687,032; Median Monthly Rent: $445; Housing Starts: 38,700; Existing Home Sales: 97,000.

Economic Facts

Gross State Product: $97,000,000,000 (1989)

Income Per Capita: $20,398

Disposable Personal Income: $18,038

Median Household Income: $31,183

Average Annual Pay, 1988: $23,942

Principal Industries: food products, paper products, transportation equipment, chemicals, printing, publishing, shipbuilding

Major Crops: apples, timber, milk, wheat, pears, plums, cherries, grapes, hops

Fish: Cod, Flounder, Halibut, Salmon, Crabs, Oysters, Clams

Livestock: cattle, poultry

Non-Fuel Minerals: Gold, Magnesite, Lead, Zinc, Clay, Limestone, Barite, Copper, Olivine

Organic Fuel Minerals: Coal

Civilian Labor Force: 2,498,000 (Women: 1,131,000)

Total Employed: 2,340,000 (Women: 1,071,000)

Median Value of Housing: $93,400

Median Contract Rent: $445 per month

Economic Sectors 1992

Agriculture 7.78%
Construction 4.95%
Services 45.61%
Manufacturing 14.40%
Trans. – Public Utilities 4.70%
Trade 22.39%

Manufacturing

The state of Washington does not depend on natural resources for its manufactured products as much as one might think. Instead, the production of transportation equipment leads Washington's manufacturing sector. Other industries in the state include shipbuilding, food processing, paper products, and nonelectrical machinery. Overall, 17 percent of the state gross product comes from manufacturing industries.

Commercial aircraft provides the bulk of transportation equipment produced in Washington. Boeing, a leading aircraft manufacturer, is Washington's single largest employer, with factories in Seattle, Auburn, Renton, and Kent. The Puget Sound area has one of the largest shipyards on the Pacific Coast. Western Washington has most of the state's wood-processing plants.

Transportation

Washington's transportation network is quite extensive. The state has several water transportation routes with many ports. The ports of Seattle and Tacoma are the leading Puget Sound ports. The Washington Ship Canal, a man-made waterway, goes through Seattle, connecting Lake Union and Lake Washington with Puget Sound. Inland ports along the Columbia River include Vancouver and Longview.

Washington has approximately 86,000 miles of highways and roads. The state has the longest railroad tunnel in the country, the 7.8-mile-long Cascade Tunnel. About 13 Washington cities receive passenger rail service. Furthermore, 15 freight rail lines serve Washington. The Seattle-Tacoma International Airport is among the busiest in the world. Spokane, near the Idaho border in eastern Washington, also has a large airport.

Energy and Transportation Facts

Energy. Yearly Consumption: 1,965 tril. BTUs (residential, 19.8%; commercial, 15.0%; industrial, 35.6%; transportation, 29.6%); Annual Energy Expenditures Per Capita: $1,714; Nuclear Power Plants Located in State: 1; Source of Energy Consumed: Petroleum— 38.9%; Natural Gas— 8.9%; Coal—4.5%; Hydroelectric Power—45.5%; Nuclear Power—2.3%.

Transportation. Highway Miles: 79,413 (interstates, 762; urban, 17,025; rural, 62,388); Average Yearly Auto Insurance: $588 (21st); Auto Fatalities Rank: 40th; Registered Motor Vehicles: 4,465,843; Workers in Carpools: 16.6%; Workers Using Public Trans: 4.5%.

Employment

Employment. Washington employed 2.49 million people in 1993. Most work in social and personal services (579,100 persons or 23.3% of the workforce). Wholesale and retail trade accounts for 21.9% or 544,500 workers. Manufacturing accounts for 13.7% or 562,200 workers. Government employs 392,900 workers (14.1%). Construction employs 118,600 workers (4.3%). Transportation and utilities account for 4.8% or 340,200 persons. Agriculture employs 92,100 workers or 3.7%. Finance, real estate, and insurance account for 4.9% or 120,900 workers. Mining employs 3,200 people and accounts for only 0.1% of the workforce.

Unemployment. Unemployment has decreased to 7.5% in 1993 from a rate of 8.1% in 1985. Today's figure is higher than the national average of 6.8% as shown below.

Unemployment Rate

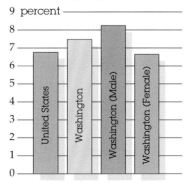

WEST VIRGINIA
The State of West Virginia

Official State Seal

The Great Seal of West Virginia was adopted in 1863. It includes the date of statehood along with a farmer and a miner. Two rifles and a liberty hat are placed below them. The state motto, *"Montani Semper Liberi"* (Mountaineers Are Always Free), is included along the bottom of the seal. This motto represents the time when the state separated itself from the rest of Virginia.

Legal Holidays

January: New Year's Day—1st, Martin Luther King, Jr. Day—3d Monday; February: Abraham Lincoln's Birthday—12th; Presidents' Day—3d Monday; May: Memorial Day—4th Monday; June: West Virginia Day—20th; July: Independence Day—4th; September: Labor Day—1st Monday; October: Columbus Day—2nd Monday; November: Veterans' Day—11th; Thanksgiving—4th Thursday; December: Christmas—25th.

Official State Flag

The state flag of West Virginia was first displayed in 1904 in the Louisiana Purchase Exposition. The flag was originally two-sided, with the state flower on one side and the arms on the other. In 1929 this was changed, and the state flower appeared with the coat of arms on the front.

Festivals and Events

February: Winter Ski Carnival, Davis; March: White Water Weekend, Petersburg; Black Cultural Festival, Charleston; April: Music Festival, Wheeling; Creative Arts Festival, Charleston; May: Woodchopping Festival, Webster Springs; May Music Festival, Charleston; June: Strawberry Festival, Buchannon; Folk Festival, Glenville; July: Rhododendron Festival, Webster Springs; August: Appalachian Arts & Crafts Festival, Beckley; West Virginia State Fair, Lewisburg; State Dairy Cattle Show, Jackson's Mill; September: Oglebay Park Horse Show, Wheeling; Preston County Buckwheat Festival, Kingwood; Tomato Festival, Berkeley Springs; Ohio River Regatta, New Martinsville; October: All West Virginia Boat Racing Championships, Charles-ton; Black Walnut Festival, Spencer; November: Tobacco Festival, Huntington; Apple Harvest Festival, Martinsburg.

West Virginia Compared to States in Its Region.

Resident Pop. in Metro Areas: 8th; Pop. Percent Increase: 8th; Pop. Over 65: 2d; Infant Mortality: 6th; School Enroll. Increase: 8th; High School Grad. and Up: 8th; Violent Crime: 8th; Hazardous Waste Sites: 8th; Unemployment: 1st; Median Household Income: 8th; Persons Below Poverty: 1st; Energy Costs Per Person: 1st.

South Atlantic Region

	Population	Capital
Delaware	700,000	Dover
Maryland	4,965,000	Annapolis
Washington DC	578,000	—
Virginia	6,491,000	Richmond
West Virginia	1,820,000	Charleston
North Carolina	6.,945,000	Raleigh
South Carolina	3,643,000	Columbia
Georgia	6,917,000	Atlanta
Florida	13,679,000	Tallahassee

West Virginia's Finances

Households: 689,000; Income Per Capita Current Dollars: $15,065; Change Per Capita Income 1980 to 1992: 89.0% (39th in U.S.); State Expenditures: $4,396,000,000; State Revenues: $4,559,000,000; Personal Income Tax: 3 to 6.5%; Federal Income Taxes Paid Per Capita: $1,189; Sales Tax: 6% (prescription drugs exempt).

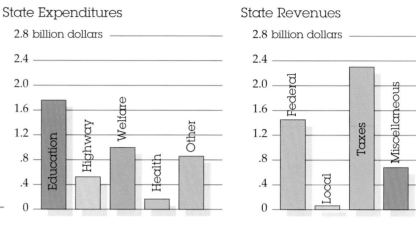

State Expenditures — 2.8 billion dollars: Education, Highway, Welfare, Health, Other

State Revenues — 2.8 billion dollars: Federal, Local, Taxes, Miscellaneous

Location, Size, and Boundaries

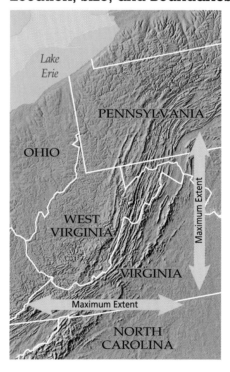

Location. West Virginia is located in the eastern United States in the South Atlantic region. It is bounded on four sides by land. The geographic center of West Virginia is lat. 38° 35.9' N; long. 80° 42.2' W.

Size. West Virginia is the 41st largest state in terms of size. Its area is 24,181 sq. mi. (62,629 km2). Inland water covers 111 sq. mi. (287 km2).

Boundaries. Ohio, 277 mi. (446 km); Pennsylvania, 119 mi. (191 km); Maryland, 235 mi. (378 km); Virginia, 438 mi. (705 km); Kentucky, 111 mi. (179 km).

Geographic Extent. The north/south extent of West Virginia is 237 mi. (381 km). The state extends 265 mi. (426 km) to the east/west.

Facts about West Virginia. Origin of Name: Was part of Virginia until the Civil War; Nickname: The Mountain State; Motto: "Mountaineers are always free" (*Montani semper liberi*); Abbreviations: W. Va. (traditional), WV (postal); State Bird: cardinal; State Tree: sugar maple; State Flower: rhododendron; State Song: "The West Virginia Hills," words by Ellen King and music by James A. Bland.

West Virginia Compared to Other States. Resident Pop. in Metro Areas: 41st; Pop. Per. Increase: 42d; Pop. Over 65: 5th; Infant Mort.: 14th; School Enroll. Increase: 50th; High School Grad. and Up: 48th; Violent Crime: 44th; Haz. Waste Sites: 44th; Unemployment: 1st; Median Household Income: 49th; Persons Below Poverty: 4th; Energy Costs Per Person: 7th.

Sources of Information. Tourism: West Virginia Division of Tourism and Parks, 2101 Washington Street East, Charleston, WV 25305. Economy: Community and Industrial Development, Building 6, Room B-504, Capitol Complex, Charleston, WV 25305. History: West Virginia Division of Culture and History, Cultural Center, State Capitol, Charleston, WV 25305.

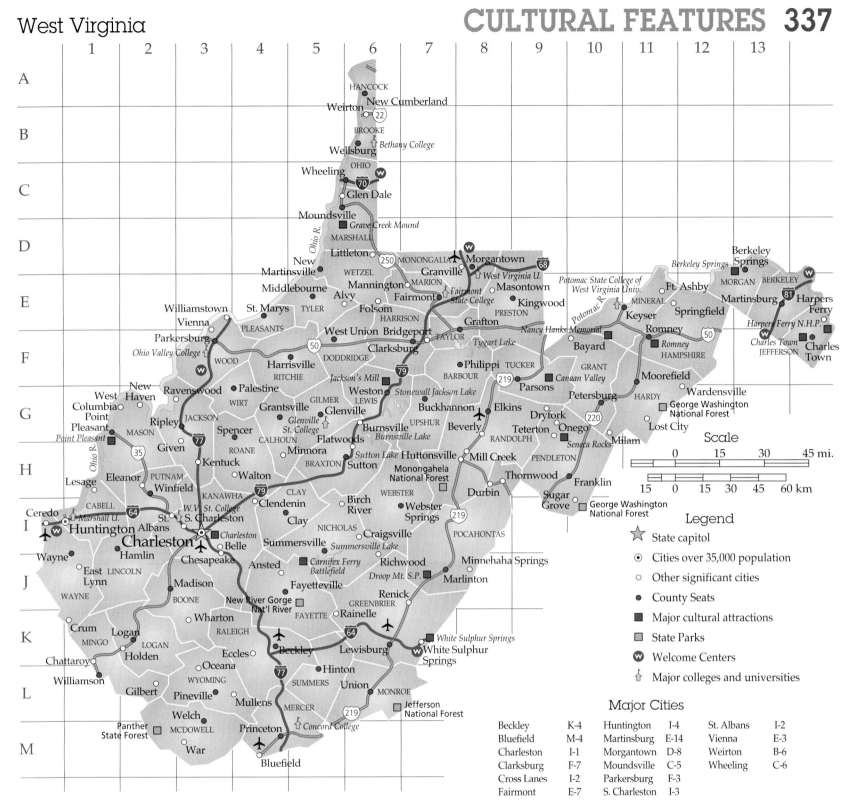

Legend

⭐ State capitol

⊙ Cities over 35,000 population

○ Other significant cities

● County Seats

■ Major cultural attractions

▢ State Parks

Ⓦ Welcome Centers

⛨ Major colleges and universities

Major Cities

Beckley	K-4	Huntington	I-4	St. Albans	I-2
Bluefield	M-4	Martinsburg	E-14	Vienna	E-3
Charleston	I-1	Morgantown	D-8	Weirton	B-6
Clarksburg	F-7	Moundsville	C-5	Wheeling	C-6
Cross Lanes	I-2	Parkersburg	F-3		
Fairmont	E-7	S. Charleston	I-3		

■ Berkeley Springs. Health resort with mineral springs. Golfing, museums, and Festivals. (D-13)

■ Canaan Valley Resort State Park. Cross-country and downhill skiing. (F-9)

■ Carnifex Ferry Battlefield State Park. Site of a battle during the American Civil War (1861). Annual battle reenactment in October. (I-5)

■ Charleston. Sternwheel Regatta Festival, historic buildings, and museums. (I-3)

■ Charles Town. Named after George Washington's brother. John Brown was hanged here in 1859. Antebellum homes and landmarks. (F-14)

■ Droop Mountain Battlefield State Park. Site of a bloody Civil War battle fought on November 6, 1863. Also the state's first park. (J-7)

■ Grave Creek Mound. The largest conical Indian burial mound in the United States, said to be over 2,000 years old. (D-5)

■ Harpers Ferry National Historical Park. Arsenal for George Washington and stopping place for Lewis and Clark. Site of John Brown's raid in October 1859. (F-14)

■ Jackson's Mill. Boyhood home of Civil War general Stonewall Jackson. (F-6)

■ Nancy Hanks Memorial. The birthplace of Abraham Lincoln's mother. Her family settled here in the early 1780s on Saddle Mountain. (F-10)

■ Point Pleasant. The possible first battle of the American Revolution in 1774 between Virginia troops and British-incited Mingo and Shawnee Indians. (G-1)

■ Romney. Town that changed hands more than 50 times during the Civil War. (F-11)

■ Seneca Rocks. 900 foot sandstone pinnacles popular with rock climbers. (G-9)

■ White Sulphur Springs. Spa in use since the Revolutionary War days. Reenactment of the Battle of Dry Creek. Home of the National Fish Hatchery and the first organized golf club in the United States. (K-7)

Weather Facts

Record High Temperature: 112° F (44° C) on July 10, 1936, at Martinsburg; Record Low Temperature: -37° F (-38° C) on December 30, 1917, at Lewisburg; Average January Temperature: 33° F (1° C); Average July Temperature: 72° F (22° C); Average Yearly Precipitation: 45 in. (114 cm).

Environmental Facts

Air Pollution Rank: 27th; Water Pollution Rank: 16th; Total Yearly Industrial Pollution: 24,805,864 lbs.; Industrial Pollution Rank: 30th; Hazardous Waste Sites: 5; Hazardous Sites Rank: 44th; Landfill Capacity: overextended; Fresh Water Supply: large surplus; Daily Residential Water Consumption: 115 gals. per capita; Endangered Species: Aquatic Species (5)—clubshell; Birds (2)—eagle, bald; Mammals (6)—bat, gray; Other Species (1)—salamander, Cheat Mountain; Plants (5)—bulrush, northeastern (barbed bristle).

Flora and Fauna

West Virginia, in the heart of the Appalachian Mountains, has a large portion, 80 percent, of its land covered by forests. The Appalachian oak and cherry are the two most important deciduous hardwood trees. West Virginia's higher elevations and its river gorges have such conifers as hemlock, white pine, and red spruce. Wildflowers bloom in West Virginia from early in spring to late in autumn. Hepatica and bloodroot bloom in spring, and black-eyed Susans and asters bloom in fall. Other plants in the state include azaleas, dogwoods, white-blossomed hawthorn, and crab apple trees.

Large animals such as black bears and white-tailed deer live in mountainous regions of West Virginia. A number of smaller mammals, including skunks, minks, rabbits, and gray and red foxes also live in the state's wooded areas. Many of West Virginia's fishes such as perch and trout live mainly in mountain streams. However, recently they have started to move to valley rivers as well. Other lakes, rivers, and streams in the state also contain walleye and bass.

Average Monthly Weather

Charleston	Jan	Feb	Mar	Apr	May	Jun	Jul	Aug	Sep	Oct	Nov	Dec	Yearly
Maximum Temperature °F	41.8	45.4	55.4	67.3	76.0	82.5	85.2	84.2	78.7	67.7	55.6	45.9	65.5
Minimum Temperature °F	23.9	25.8	34.1	43.3	51.8	59.4	63.8	63.1	56.4	44.0	35.0	27.8	44.0
Days of Precipitation	15.5	13.7	14.8	13.9	13.3	11.4	12.8	10.9	9.4	9.6	12.0	14.0	151.2

Environmental Quality

West Virginia residents generate 2.5 million tons of solid waste each year, or approximately 2,600 pounds per capita. Landfill capacity in West Virginia will be exhausted in less than 5 years. The state has 5 hazardous waste sites. Annual greenhouse gas emissions in West Virginia total 95.5 million tons, or 51.1 tons per capita. Industrial sources in West Virginia release approximately 33.3 thousand tons of toxins, 1.2 million tons of acid precipitation-producing substances, and 1.3 million tons of smog-producing substances into the atmosphere each year.

The state has 3,200 acres within the National Park System. Noteworthy is Harpers Ferry National Historical Park. State parks cover just over 149,000 acres, attracting 8.3 million visitors per year.

West Virginia spends 1.7 percent of its budget, or approximately $30 per capita, on environmental and natural resources. West Virginia representatives in the U.S. House voted in favor of national environmental legislation 50 percent of the time, while U.S. senators did so 58 percent of the time.

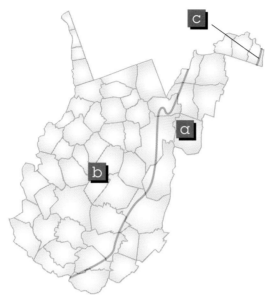

Physical Regions: (a) Appalachian Ridge and Valley; (b) Appalachian Plateau; (c) Blue Ridge.

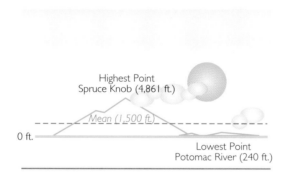

Highest Point Spruce Knob (4,861 ft.)

Mean (1,500 ft.)

0 ft.

Lowest Point Potomac River (240 ft.)

Land Use

Cropland: 7.4%; Pasture: 13.3%; Rangeland: 0%; Forest: 73.6%; Urban: 3.7%; Other: 2%.

For more information about West Virginia's environment, contact the Department of Natural Resources, 1900 Kanawha Blvd. E., Charleston, WV 25305.

Topography

Most of West Virginia lies within the Appalachian Mountain system. The easternmost tip of West Virginia is crossed by the Blue Ridge physical region. This area contains several fertile river valleys suitable for farming. Directly to the west is the Appalachian Ridge and Valley physical region, with warm and moist soil of the red/yellow clay variety that is low in organic content. In this area, the Allegheny Mountains of the Appalachian chain run in a northeast-southwest direction. The highest elevations in the state are found in this region. The highest peak is Spruce Knob, which rises 4,861 ft. (1,482 m) above sea level.

The Ridge and Valley Region gives way to the Appalachian Plateau physical region at the Allegheny Front, a high and rugged escarpment that separates the two regions. The Appalachian Plateau covers most of West Virginia and is an area of rough flat land, cut by numerous river valleys. Several of the largest of these lowland valleys are located in the southwestern part of the state around the Ohio and Kanawha rivers. The soil of the Plateau is classified as warm and moist, brown in color, with a lighter surface of crystalline clay. Coal and other mineral resources are abundant. Many of the mountain peaks exceed 4,000 ft. (1,200 m).

Climate

The Ohio River forms West Virginia's western border with Ohio, flowing for over 270 miles (435 km). The Kanawha is its main tributary. This and other feeder streams such as the Little Kanawha, the New, the Elk, and the Guyandotte, drain much of the state. The Big Sandy and the Tug Fork flow along West Virginia's southwest border with Kentucky. In the north, the Monongahela flows into Pennsylvania, draining, with its tributaries, the West Fork and the Cheat, much of the north-central region. In the panhandle, the Potomac forms West Virginia's northern border with Maryland, and drains much of this region. All of the large lakes in the state are man-made reservoirs, built for hydroelectric or drinking water purposes. Some of these include Summersville and Sutton reservoirs in the central region of the state, East Lynn Reservoir in the southwest, and Tygart Lake in the north.

Hydrology

The Ohio river forms West Virginia's western border with Ohio, flowing for over 270 miles (435 km). The Kanawha is its main tributary. This, and other branches such as the Little Kanawha, the New, the Elk, and the Guyandotte, drain much of the state The Big Sandy and the Tug Fork flow along West Virginia's southwest border with Kentucky. In the north, the Monogahela flows into Pennsylvania. It drains, with its tributaries, the West Fork and the Cheat, much of the north-central region. In the panhandle, the Potomac forms West Virginia's northern border with Maryland, and drains much of this region.

All of the large lakes in the state are man-made reservoirs, built for hydroelectric or drinking water purposes. Some of these include Summersville and Sutton Reservoirs in the central region of the state; East Lynn Reservoir in the southwest; and Tygart Lake in the north.

West Virginia's History

West Virginia's First People

The first people probably arrived in the area of West Virginia over three thousand years ago. Evidence unearthed around the Ohio and Kanawha rivers reveals that ancient peoples made campsites in these areas and left behind piles of shells in their villages.

The mound-building people of the Adena culture also occupied the West Virginia region. One of the largest of their mounds, the Grave Creek Mound, is located in Moundsville, in the northern panhandle of the state.

Later, other Native American groups also inhabited West Virginia, including the Delaware (Lenni Lenape), Cherokee, Conoy, Susquehanna, and Shawnee. Though these tribes hunted on West Virginia ground, none of them claimed it as their permanent territory.

European Exploration

The land included in West Virginia was originally part of the Virginia colony. In 1606, King James I of England granted a charter to the London Company to establish a colony in North America. That colony originally extended from present-day South Carolina to Pennsylvania.

The first white man to come to the area of West Virginia was John Lederer, a German explorer. He reached the Blue Ridge crest around 1669. In 1671, two explorers, Robert Fallam and Thomas Batts, came to West Virginia in search of transportation routes and hunting grounds.

The first settlers did not arrive until 1726, when Morgan Morgan from Delaware built a cabin near Bunker Hill. Soon after, many settlers came to West Virginia looking for religious freedom. A group of Germans came from Pennsylvania and established New Mecklenburg, now called Shepherdstown. Many of these pioneers were farmers who settled in West Virginia's eastern panhandle.

In 1763, George III, king of England, refused to let colonists go to West Virginia until they made peace treaties with the Native Americans. However, many Scotch-Irish, Germans, Dutch, and other settlers ignored this royal decree.

On the Road to Statehood

Besides the physical boundary of the Allegheny Mountains, lifestyle and economic differences kept western Virginia settlers apart from their counterparts in the east.

In 1776, West Virginia settlers demanded their own representative government by sending out a petition to the Continental Congress. However, the beginning of the Revolutionary War halted this early attempt at freedom.

After the war, the gap between east and west widened. The eastern residents controlled all state affairs, and thus represented their own interests. Slavery was a major sticking point with the eastern plantation owners supporting slavery, and the westerners disapproving of it. In 1859, John Brown led an unsuccessful raid on the national arsenal at Harpers Ferry. Following the raid, the state of Virginia voted to secede from the Union and join the Confederacy. The western counties, which were Union supporters, seceded from Virginia and established their own government, named the Restored Government of Virginia.

In August of 1861, the western counties approved a plan for a new state called Kanawha, a Native American word meaning "place of white stone," referring to the rich salt deposits of the region. In November, 1861, the counties wrote a constitution in Wheeling, and residents changed the name of the potential state to West Virginia. The new constitution was approved by voters in April 1862, but it was not until a year later that President Lincoln declared West Virginia a part of the United States. On June 20, 1863, West Virginia became the thirty-fifth state in the Union.

Industrialization

Ever since the 1700s, mining has been the chief industry in West Virginia. In 1742, John Peter Salley discovered coal near the town of Racine. Shortly after the discovery, an iron furnace was built at Kings Creek in the northern panhandle.

Industrialization did not fully develop in West Virginia, until the post-Civil War era. Petroleum and gas wells, coal mines, and railroads were constructed at this time. The West Virginia branch of the United Mine Workers of America (UMW) was established in 1890.

Mining is not without its dangers. One of the worst mine disasters occurred in 1907, when 361 people were killed in an explosion at Monogah.

Besides coal, West Virginia has an abundance of several other natural resources, including petroleum, natural gas, salt, clay, and gravel. Mineral production overall accounts for most of the gross state product.

In recent years the West Virginia economy has diversified. Chemical production and metal products are the leading industries in the manufacturing sector. Trade, commerce, and other service-oriented activities round out the economic profile.

West Virginia: The Mountain State

The state of West Virginia has been nicknamed the "Mountain State." The state can be divided into three regions—the Blue Ridge, Appalachian Ridge and Valley region, and the Appalachian Plateau—all containing rugged terrain.

The Blue Ridge region covers the smallest portion of West Virginia, located on the edge of the state's eastern panhandle border with Virginia. The Appalachian Ridge and Valley region covers the eastern part of the state.

The Appalachian Plateau makes up the final, and largest, land region in West Virginia, covering the entire western part of the state.

Important Events

1609 James I of England grants area including West Virginia to Virginia colony.

1669 John Lederer explores West Virginia region.

1671 Robert Fallam and Thomas Batts enter the area searching for transportation routes.

1726 Morgan Morgan becomes first white settler in West Virginia when he builds a cabin at Bunker Hill.

1742 Coal discovered along the Coal River near Racine.

1763 George III forbads settlement in West Virginia until peace treaties are made with the Indians.

1776 West Virginia settlers petition the Continental Congress for their own government.

1784 Mason and Dixon Line settled as Pennsylvania-Virginia border.

1788 West Virginia enters the United States, but as part of Virginia.

1794 Peter Tarr constructs the first iron furnace west of the Alleghenies at King's Creek.

1815 Gas discovered near Charleston.

1859 John Brown's raid on Harper's Ferry.

1861 Western Virginia counties form Restored Government of Virginia.

1862 West Virginia adopts a new constitution in April.

1863 West Virginia becomes thirty-fifth state in the Union on June 20.

1872 West Virginia adopts a new constitution.

1890 Establishment of the West Virginia branch of the UnitedMine Workers of America (UMW).

1896 Rural free mail delivery begins.

1931 West Virginia becomes leading producer of bituminous coal.

1967 Bridge over Ohio River collapses, killing at least forty people.

1972 Buffalo Creek Dam fails and kills over one hundred people.

1988 Major oil spill pollutes Ohio and Monongahela rivers.

1990 A nine-month, sometimes violent, strike by the United Mine Workers ends.

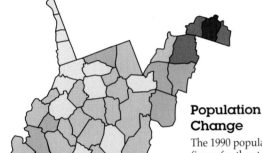

Population Density

Population density for the state of West Virginia was 74.5 persons per square mile in 1990 (28.7 per km2). Average U.S. density was 70.3 persons per square mile in 1990 (27.3 per km2). Habitation is most dense in the panhandle of the state. This area contains the city of Wheeling, which is the third most populous city in the state.

Persons Per Square Mile

0.0 to 9.9	100.0 to 249.9
10.0 to 99.9	250.0 to 749.9

Population Projections

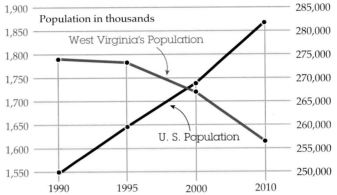

Population in thousands
West Virginia's Population
U. S. Population

(Left axis: 1,550–1,900 | Right axis: 250,000–285,000 | Years: 1990, 1995, 2000, 2010)

Population Change

Year	Population
1950	2,006,000
1960	1,853,000
1970	1,751,000
1980	1,949,664
1990	1,793,477
2000	1,722,000
2010	1,617,000

Period	Change
1950–1970	–12.7%
1970–1980	11.4%
1980–1990	–8.1%
1990–2000	–4.0%

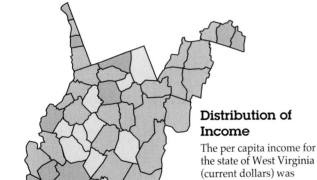

Population Change

The 1990 population figure for the state of West Virginia was 1,793,477. This is a –8.01 percent decrease from 1,949,664 in 1980. The next decade will show a loss with a population of 1.7 million or a –3.99 percent decrease. West Virginia has suffered from the decline in the coal mining industry in the last decade.

Percent Change 1980 to 1990

–31.9 to –10.0%	20.0 to 49.9%
–9.9 to 0.0%	50.0 to 140.1%
0.1 to 19.9%	

Population Facts

State Population, 1993: 1,820,000
Rank: 35
Population 2000: 1,722,000 (Rank 36)
Density: 74.5 per sq. mi. (28.7 per km²)
Distribution: 36.1% urban, 63.9% rural
Population Under 5 Years Old: 6.0%
Population Under 18 Years Old: 24.2%
Population Over 65 Years Old: 15.2%
Median Age: 35.4
Number of Households: 689,000
Average Persons Per Household: 2.55
Average Persons Per Family: 3.05
Female Heads of Households: 4.10%
Population That Is Married: 22.64%
Birth Rate: 12.6 per 1,000 population
Death Rate: 10.8 per 1,000 population
Births to Teen Mothers: 17.8%
Marriage Rate: 7.2 per 1,000 population
Divorce Rate: 5.3 per 1,000 population
Violent Crime Rate: 191 per 100,000 pop.
Population on Social Security: 20.7%
Percent Voting for President: 50.6%

West Virginia's Famous Citizens

Buck, Pearl (1892–1973). Nobel and Pulitzer prize-winning author.

Delany, Martin (1812–1885). Author and abolitionist. In 1852, he wrote the first proposal for black nationalism.

Jarvis, Anna (1864–1948). She started a campaign to establish Mother's Day in 1907 (finally declared in 1915).

Knight, John S. (1894–1948). Publisher. He began buying newspapers in 1937 to start the Knight-Ridder empire.

Lorentz, Pare (1905–1992). Film producer and director. He developed the United States Film Service to produce government films.

Reno, Jesse Lee (1823–1862). Army officer. He led troops in the Civil War battles at Antietam and Bull Run.

Retton, Mary Lou (b. 1968). Gymnast. She won four medals at the 1984 Summer Olympics in Los Angeles.

Vance, Cyrus (b. 1917). Secretary of State under Jimmy Carter. He also served as secretary of the army under John F. Kennedy.

Yeager, Charles (Chuck) (b. 1923). United States Air Force test pilot; first person to fly faster than the speed of sound.

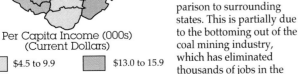

Distribution of Income

The per capita income for the state of West Virginia (current dollars) was $15,065 in 1992. This is an 89.0 percent increase from $7,972 in 1980. Incomes for the state are low in comparison to surrounding states. This is partially due to the bottoming out of the coal mining industry, which has eliminated thousands of jobs in the last decade.

Per Capita Income (000s) (Current Dollars)

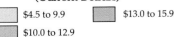

$4.5 to 9.9	$13.0 to 15.9
$10.0 to 12.9	

Population Profile

Rank. West Virginia ranks 35th among U.S. states in terms of population with 1,820,000 citizens.

Minority Population. The state's minority population is 4.2 percent. The state's male to female ratio for 1990 was 92.45 males for every 100 females. It was below the national average of 95.22 males for every 100 females.

Growth. The state's population is decreasing

Government

Capital: Charleston (established 1885).
Statehood: Became 35th state on Jun. 20, 1863.
Number of Counties: 55.
Supreme Court Justices: 5, 12-year term.
State Senators: 34, 4-year term.
State Legislators: 100, 2-year term.
United States Senators: 2.
United States Representatives: 3.
Electoral Votes: 5.
State Constitution: Adopted 1872.

and is expected to be 1.6 million by the year 2010.

Older Citizens. The state's population older than 65 was 268,897 in 1990. It grew 13.04% from 237,868 in 1980.

Younger Citizens. The number of children (under 18 years of age) was 444 thousand in 1990. This represents 24.7 percent of the state's population. The state's school aged population was 318 thousand in 1990. It is expected to decrease to 285 thousand by the year 2000. This represents a –10.38% change.

Urban/Rural. 36.1% of the population of the state live in urban areas while 63.9% live in rural areas.

Largest Cities. West Virginia has two cities with a population greater than 35,000. The populations of the state's largest centers are (starting from the most populous) Charleston (57,287), Huntington (54,844), Wheeling (34,882), Parkersburg (33,862), Morgantown (25,879), Weirton (22,124), Fair-mont (20,210), Beckley (18,296), Clarksburg (18,059), Martinsburg (14,073), South Charleston (13,645), Bluefield (12,756), St. Albans (11,194), Cross Lanes (10,878), Vienna (10,862), and Moundsville (10,753).

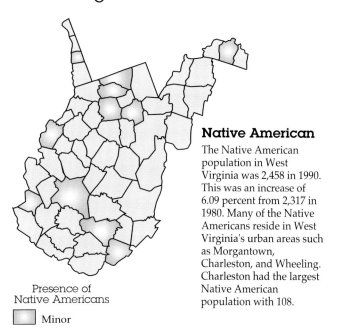

Native American

The Native American population in West Virginia was 2,458 in 1990. This was an increase of 6.09 percent from 2,317 in 1980. Many of the Native Americans reside in West Virginia's urban areas such as Morgantown, Charleston, and Wheeling. Charleston had the largest Native American population with 108.

Presence of Native Americans

Minor

Nationalities

African	674
American	268,036
Arab	4,491
Austrian	1,353
Czech	1,705
Dutch	39,132
English	197,483
Finnish	282
German	376,655
Greek	3,613
Hungarian	6,346
Irish	198,692
Italian	54,112
Norwegian	1,580
Polish	22,049
Portuguese	319
Russian	3,198
Scottish	22,160
Slovak	7,220
Swedish	4,085
Welsh	9,421
West Indian	494

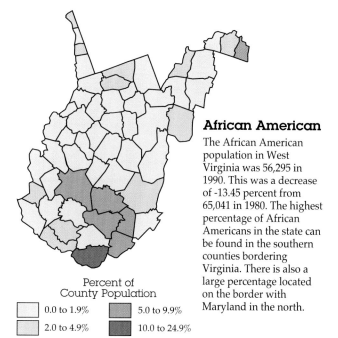

African American

The African American population in West Virginia was 56,295 in 1990. This was a decrease of -13.45 percent from 65,041 in 1980. The highest percentage of African Americans in the state can be found in the southern counties bordering Virginia. There is also a large percentage located on the border with Maryland in the north.

Percent of County Population

- 0.0 to 1.9%
- 2.0 to 4.9%
- 5.0 to 9.9%
- 10.0 to 24.9%

Statewide Ethnic Composition

Over 96 percent of the population of West Virginia is white. The largest nationalities in this racial group are German, Irish, and English. The next largest group is African Americans, followed by Hispanics, Asian Americans, and Native Americans. Over 268,000 people claim to be American and acknowledge no other nationality.

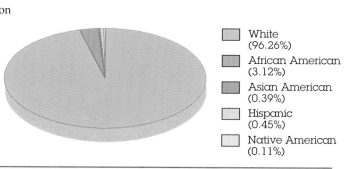

- White (96.26%)
- African American (3.12%)
- Asian American (0.39%)
- Hispanic (0.45%)
- Native American (0.11%)

Hispanic[††]

The Hispanic population in West Virginia was 8,489 in 1990. This is a decrease of -33.19 percent from 12,707 persons in 1980. There are a few counties with a higher-than-average percentage of Hispanics. Such counties include Summers, Harrison, and Jefferson.

[††]A person of Mexican, Puerto Rican, Cuban, or other Spanish culture or origin regardless of race.

Percent of County Population

- 0.0 to 0.9%
- 1.0 to 2.9%

Education Facts

Total Students 1990: 32,754

Number of School Districts: 55

Expenditure Per Capita on Education 1990: $725

Expenditure Per Capita K–12 1990: $678

Expenditure Per Pupil 1990: $4,695

Total School Enrollment 1990–1991: 323,021

Rank of Expenditures Per Student: 30th in the U.S.

African American Enrollment: 3.9%

Hispanic Enrollment: 0.2%

Asian/Pacific Islander Enrollment: 0.4%

Native American Enrollment: 0.0%

Mean SAT Score 1991 Verbal: 441

Mean SAT Score 1991 Math: 485

Average Teacher's Salary 1992: $27,400

Rank Teacher's Salary: 39th in U.S.

High School Graduates 1990: 22,100

Total Number of Public Schools: 1,035

Number of Teachers 1990: 21,392

Student/Teacher Ratio: 15.1

Staff Employed in Public Schools: 39,407

Pupil/Staff Ratio: 8.3

Staff/Teacher Ratio: 1.8

Education

Attainment: 68 percent of population 25 years or older were high school graduates in 1989, earning West Virginia a ranking of 45th in the United States; 11.1 percent of the state's population had completed college. Institutions of Higher Education: The largest universities and colleges in the state include West Virginia University, Morgantown; Marshall University, Huntington; West Virginia State College, Institute; Salem College, Salem, West Virginia Wesleyan College, Buckhannon. Expenditures per Student: Expenditure increased 60% between 1985 and 1990. Projected High School Graduations: 1998 (19,373), 2004 (15,427); Total Revenues for Education from Federal Sources: $103 million; Total Revenues for Education from State Sources: $853 million; Total Revenues for Education from Local Sources: $312 million; Average Annual Salaries for Public School Principals: N/A; Largest School Districts in State: Kanawha County School District, 35,005 students, 112th in the United States.

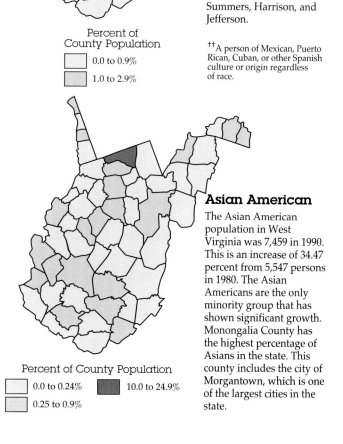

Asian American

The Asian American population in West Virginia was 7,459 in 1990. This is an increase of 34.47 percent from 5,547 persons in 1980. The Asian Americans are the only minority group that has shown significant growth. Monongalia County has the highest percentage of Asians in the state. This county includes the city of Morgantown, which is one of the largest cities in the state.

Percent of County Population

- 0.0 to 0.24%
- 0.25 to 0.9%
- 10.0 to 24.9%

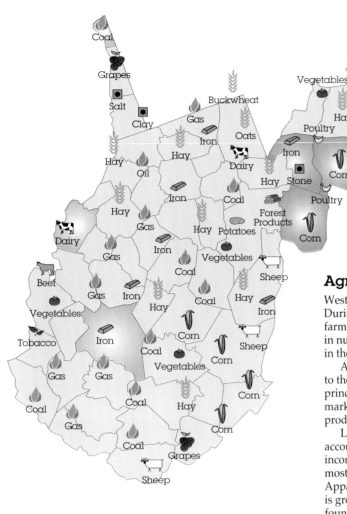

Major manufacturing areas

Major agricultural areas

Agriculture

West Virginia has 3.7 million farm acres. During the last 40 years, West Virginia's farms have grown larger in size and fewer in number. In 1955, 69,000 farms were found in the state. Today, 20,000 remain.

Agriculture adds less than $500 million to the state's gross product annually. The principal commodities in order of marketing receipts are cattle, broilers, dairy products, and turkeys.

Livestock and livestock products account for most of West Virginia's farm income. Cattle and dairy farms are found mostly in the river valleys of the Appalachian Plateau. Hay, the leading crop, is grown primarily as cattle feed. Tobacco is found in the Ohio River Valley, and corn is found there and in the Potomac River Valley. Apples are grown in the fertile Shenandoah Valley.

Transportation

Many of West Virginia's transportation routes follow river valleys. Throughout West Virginia, about 500 miles of waterways are navigable. Three rivers in the state–the Monongahela, Ohio, and Kanawha–transport goods.

Many West Virginia settlements originally developed along railroad lines built in the late 19th century. Today, 13 freight rail lines transport goods throughout the state. In addition, 10 West Virginia cities receive passenger rail service. Because of the terrain, West Virginia does not have a well-developed roadway system. About three-quarters of the 37,000 miles of roads and highways throughout West Virginia are paved. West Virginia has two major airports: one in Charleston, the capital, and one close to Huntington, near the Kentucky and Ohio borders.

Energy and Transportation Facts

Energy. Yearly Consumption: 783 tril. BTUs (residential, 16.5%; commercial, 11.1%; industrial, 54.0%; transportation, 18.4%); Annual Energy Expenditures Per Capita: $2,081; Nuclear Power Plants Located in State: 0; Source of Energy Consumed: Petroleum— 24.0%; Natural Gas— 9.7%; Coal— 65.4%; Hydroelectric Power—0.9%; Nuclear Power—0.0%.

Transportation. Highway Miles: 34,919 (interstates, 550; urban, 3,090; rural, 31,829); Average Yearly Auto Insurance: $557 (23d); Auto Fatalities Rank: 4th; Registered Motor Vehicles: 1,272,907; Workers in Carpools: 21.7%; Workers Using Public Trans: 1.1%.

Employment

Employment. West Virginia employed 702,000 people in 1993. Most work in social and personal services (166,500 persons or 23.7% of the workforce). Manufacturing accounts for 11.8% or 82,900 workers. Wholesale and retail trade account for 21.2% or 148,600 workers. Government employs 132,500 workers (18.9%). Construction employs 48,400 workers (3.3%). Transportation and utilities account for 5.5% or 38,700 persons. Agriculture employs 13,300 workers or 1.9%. Finance, real estate, and insurance account for 3.6% or 25,000 workers. Mining employs 26,100 people and accounts for only 3.7% of the workforce.

Unemployment. Unemployment has decreased to 10.8% in 1993 from a rate of 13.0% in 1985. Today's figure is higher than the national average of 6.8% as shown below.

Housing

Owner Occupied Units: 781,295; Average Age of Units: 33 years; Average Value of Housing Units: $47,900; Renter Occupied Units: 168,341; Median Monthly Rent: $303; Housing Starts: 4,300; Existing Home Sales: 45,700.

Economic Facts

Gross State Product: $28,000,000,000 (1989)

Income Per Capita: $15,065

Disposable Personal Income: $13,526

Median Household Income: $20,795

Average Annual Pay, 1988: $21,356

Principal Industries: stone, clay, primary metals, chemicals, glass products

Major Crops: hay, milk, apples, peaches, timber

Fish: N/A

Livestock: chickens, cattle

Non-Fuel Minerals: Clay, Dolomite, Sandstone, Shale, Salt, Gravel, Sand, Limestone

Organic Fuel Minerals: Coal, Nat. Gas, Petroleum

Civilian Labor Force: 783,000 (Women: 326,000)

Total Employed: 701,000 (Women: 296,000)

Median Value of Housing: $47,900

Median Contract Rent: $303 per month

Economic Sectors 1992

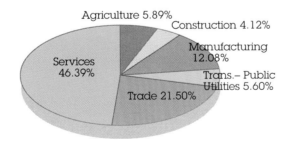

Agriculture 5.89%
Construction 4.12%
Manufacturing 12.08%
Services 46.39%
Trans.– Public Utilities 5.60%
Trade 21.50%

Manufacturing

West Virginia's manufacturing sector contributes approximately 14 percent to the state gross product each year. The production of chemicals ranks as West Virginia's number one manufacturing activity. Other industries in the state include primary and fabricated metals, glass, pottery, and textiles. All these products have a combined total value of $6 billion a year.

Most chemical production takes place in the Ohio and Kanawha river valleys, in cities such as Parkersburg and Charleston. Farther north along the Ohio River, in Wheeling, steel mills can be found. Various West Virginia cities and towns, including Huntington and Salem, produce glassware. Most of the pottery produced in West Virginia comes from Hancock County.

Unemployment Rate

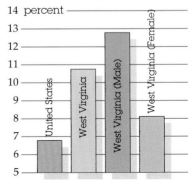

14 percent
13
12
11
10
9
8
7
6
5

United States
West Virginia
West Virginia (Male)
West Virginia (Female)

WISCONSIN The State of Wisconsin

Official State Seal

The Great Seal of Wisconsin was adopted in 1851 and modifications were made in 1881. The coat of arms contains a plow, a pick and shovel, an arm and hammer, and an anchor. The shield is supported by a sailor and a yeoman. Below them are lead ingots representing Wisconsin's natural resources. The state motto, "Forward," is found above a picture of a badger.

Legal Holidays

January: New Year's Day—1st, Martin Luther King, Jr., Day—3d Monday; February: Presidents' Day—3d Monday; May: Memorial Day—4th Monday; Wisconsin Day—29th; July: Independence Day—4th; September: Labor Day—1st Monday; October: Columbus Day—2d Monday; November: Veterans' Day—11th; Thanksgiving—4th Thursday; December: Christmas—25th.

Official State Flag

In 1887 the Wisconsin state flag was accidentally abolished when a law was repealed. A new state flag was adopted in 1913. The coat of arms is placed on a blue field. The state name and the date of statehood were added in 1981, and are placed above and below the coat of arms.

Festivals and Events

January: Lakeside Winter Celebration, Fond du Lac; February: Winter Carnival, Iola; March: Curling Matches, Stevens Point, Wauwatosa; March/April: Smelt Carnival, Marinette; May: Cherry Blossom Festival, Door County; June: Dairy Month; National Musky Festival, Hayward; July: Fiesta Italiana, Milwaukee; Frog Derby, Dousman; Circus Parade, Milwaukee; August: Germanfest, Milwaukee; September: Cheese Days (even-numbered years), Madison; Cedarburg Wine & Harvest Festival, Cedarburg; William Tell Pageant, New Glarus; Cranberry Festival, Wisconsin Rapids; Kraut & Wiener Day, Waterloo; October: Oktoberfest, La Crosse; Welsh Song Festival, Cambria; Christmas Tree Festival, Ogema; Fall Flyaway, Fond du Lac; November/December: Wisconsin Cheese Festival, statewide.

Wisconsin Compared to States in Its Region.

Resident Pop. in Metro Areas: 5th; Pop. Percent Increase: 1st; Pop. Over 65: 1st; Infant Mortality: 4th; School Enroll. Increase: 1st; High School Grad. and Up: 1st; Violent Crime: 5th; Hazardous Waste Sites: 2d; Unemployment: 5th; Median Household Income: 3d; Persons Below Poverty: 4th; Energy Costs Per Person: 5th.

East North Central Region

	Population	Capital
Wisconsin	5,038,000	Madison
Michigan	9,478,000	Lansing
Illinois	11,697,000	Springfield
Indiana	5,713,000	Indianapolis
Ohio	11,091,000	Columbus

Wisconsin's Finances

Households: 1,822,000; Income Per Capita Current Dollars: $18,727; Change Per Capita Income 1980 to 1992: 91.6% (34th in U.S.); State Expenditures: $12,258,000,000; State Revenues: $12,107,000,000; Personal Income Tax: 4.9 to 6.93%; Federal Income Taxes Paid Per Capita: $1,672; Sales Tax: 5% (food and prescription drugs exempt).

State Expenditures

7.0 billion dollars

Education, Highway, Welfare, Health, Others

State Revenues

7.0 billion dollars

Federal, Local, Taxes, Miscellaneous

Location, Size, and Boundaries

Location. Wisconsin is located in the East North Central region of the United States. It is bounded on two sides by land. The geographic center of Wisconsin is lat. 44° 26' N; long. 89° 45.8' W.

Size. Wisconsin is the 26th largest state in terms of size. Its area is 56,154 sq. mi. (145,439 km2). Inland water covers 1,690 sq. mi. (4,377 km2).

Boundaries. Michigan, 680 mi. (1,094 km); Illinois, 182 mi. (293 km); Iowa, 91 mi. (146 km); Minnesota, 426 mi. (686 km).

Geographic Extent. The north/south extent of Wisconsin is 320 mi. (515 km). The state extends 295 mi. (475 km) to the east/west.

Facts about Wisconsin. Origin of Name: An Indian word that has several possible meanings including *"homeland," "wild rice country,"* and *"gathering of the waters"*; Nickname: The Badger State; Motto: "Forward"; Abbreviations: Wis. (traditional), WI (postal); State Bird: robin; State Tree: sugar maple; State Flower: wood violet; State Song: "On, Wisconsin!," words by J. S. Hubbard and Charles D. Rosa and music by William T. Purdy.

Wisconsin Compared to Other States. Resident Pop. in Metro Areas: 28th; Pop. Per. Increase: 25th; Pop. Over 65: 20th; Infant Mortality: 36th; School Enroll. Increase: 29th; High School Grad. and Up: 21st; Violent Crime: 42d; Haz. Waste Sites: 9th; Unemployment: 42d; Median Household Income: 21st; Persons Below Poverty: 36th; Energy Costs Per Person: 43d.

Sources of Information. Tourism: Wisconsin Department of Development, Tourism Development, 123 West Washington Avenue, P.O. Box 7970, Madison, WI 53707. Economy, Government & History: Office of the Governor, State Capitol, Box 7863, Madison, WI 53707.

Wisconsin

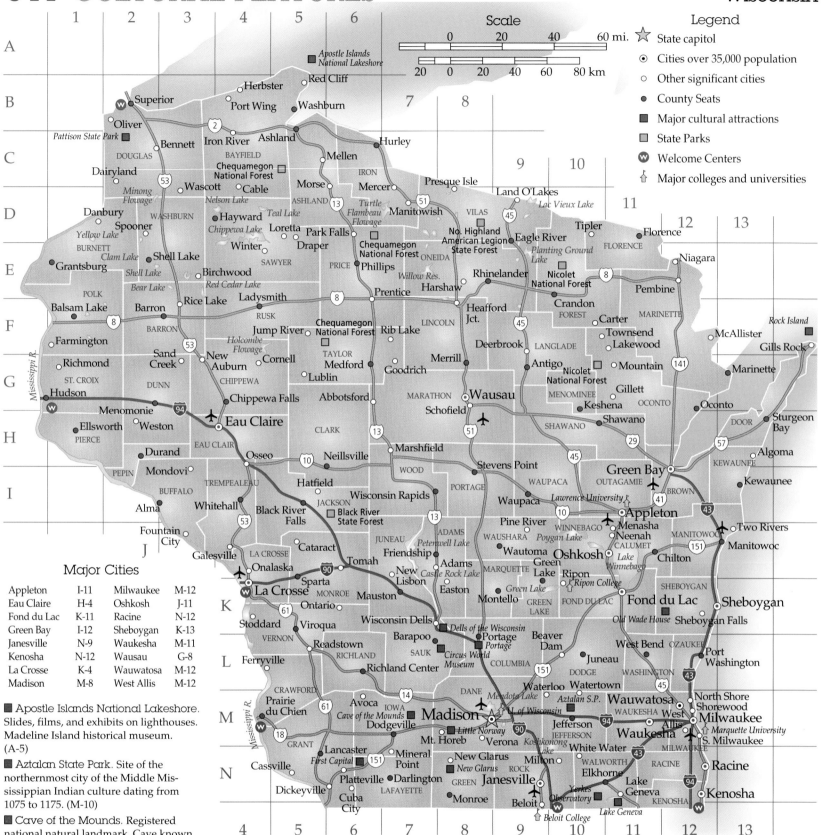

Scale

0   20   40   60 mi.

20 0 20 40 60 80 km

Legend

☆ State capitol
⊙ Cities over 35,000 population
○ Other significant cities
● County Seats
■ Major cultural attractions
▨ State Parks
Ⓦ Welcome Centers
⚲ Major colleges and universities

Major Cities

Appleton	I-11	Milwaukee	M-12
Eau Claire	H-4	Oshkosh	J-11
Fond du Lac	K-11	Racine	N-12
Green Bay	I-12	Sheboygan	K-13
Janesville	N-9	Waukesha	M-11
Kenosha	N-12	Wausau	G-8
La Crosse	K-4	Wauwatosa	M-12
Madison	M-8	West Allis	M-12

■ Apostle Islands National Lakeshore. Slides, films, and exhibits on lighthouses. Madeline Island historical museum. (A-5)

■ Aztalan State Park. Site of the northernmost city of the Middle Mississippian Indian culture dating from 1075 to 1175. (M-10)

■ Cave of the Mounds. Registered national natural landmark. Cave known for the variety of color. (M-7)

■ Circus World Museum. Big Top Shows, magic shows, and tours. Baraboo is the birthplace of the Ringling Bros. Circus. (L-8)

■ Dells of the Wisconsin. Seven-mile stretch of the Wisconsin River with boat tours, water shows, fishing, golf, and museums. (K-8)

■ First Capitol State Park. The state's smallest state park and its first territorial Capitol built in 1836. (N-6)

■ Lake Geneva. One time summer retreat of President Calvin Coolidge. Summer and winter

resort with golf, swimming, and hiking. (N-11)

■ Little Norway. Farmstead built by Norwegian settlers in 1856. (M-8)

■ New Glarus. Swiss community settled in 1845. (N-8)

■ Old Wade House. Stagecoach inn built in 1850. (K-11)

■ Pattison State Park. Site of Big Manitou Falls the state's highest waterfall (165 ft.). (C-2)

■ Portage. Site of the Old Indian Agency House (1832), and the Fort Winnebago Surgeon's Quarters (1828). (L-8)

■ Rock Island State Park. Site of the Potawatomi Lighthouse, the first lighthouse (1837) on Lake Michigan. (F-14)

■ Yerkes Observatory. The world's largest refracting telescope. (N-10)

Wisconsin

Weather Facts

Record High Temperature: 114° F (46° C) on July 13, 1936, at Wisconsin Dells; Record Low Temperature: -54° F (-48° C) on January 24, 1922, at Danbury; Average January Temperature: 15° F (-9° C); Average July Temperature: 71° F (22° C); Average Yearly Precipitation: 31 in. (79 cm).

Environmental Facts

Air Pollution Rank: 19th; Water Pollution Rank: 28th; Total Yearly Industrial Pollution: 39,215,139 lbs.; Industrial Pollution Rank: 23d; Hazardous Waste Sites: 39; Hazardous Sites Rank: 9th; Landfill Capacity: adequate; Fresh Water Supply: large surplus; Daily Residential Water Consumption: 137 gals. per capita; Endangered Species: Aquatic Species (2)—mussel, winged mapleleaf; Birds (4)—eagle, bald; Mammals (1)—wolf, gray; Other Species (2)—butterfly, Karner blue; Plants (6)—bush-clover, prairie.

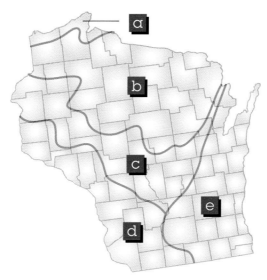

Physical Regions: (a) Lake Superior Lowland; (b) Northern Highland; (c) Central Plain; (d) Western Upland; (e) Eastern Ridges and Lowlands.

Average Monthly Weather

Madison	Jan	Feb	Mar	Apr	May	Jun	Jul	Aug	Sep	Oct	Nov	Dec	Yearly
Maximum Temperature °F	24.5	30.0	40.8	57.5	69.8	78.8	82.8	80.6	72.3	61.1	44.1	30.6	56.1
Minimum Temperature °F	6.7	11.0	21.5	34.1	44.2	53.8	58.3	56.3	47.8	37.8	26.0	14.1	34.3
Days of Precipitation	10.0	8.0	10.8	11.3	11.3	10.3	9.5	9.5	9.4	8.9	9.4	9.9	118.3
Milwaukee													
Maximum Temperature °F	26.0	30.1	39.2	53.5	64.8	75.0	79.8	78.4	71.2	59.9	44.7	32.0	54.6
Minimum Temperature °F	11.3	15.8	24.9	35.6	44.7	54.7	61.1	60.2	52.5	41.9	29.9	18.2	37.6
Days of Precipitation	11.1	9.6	11.8	12.0	11.8	10.7	9.5	9.2	9.1	8.9	10.3	11.0	125.0

Topography

There are several distinct topographic regions in Wisconsin. In the southwestern part of the state lies the Western Upland physical region. Sandstone and limestone formations as well as steep slopes and winding ridges make this one of the most scenic areas of Wisconsin.

The Eastern Ridges and Lowlands physical region contains gentle rolling hills with rich soil suitable for farming, especially in the east off the shores of Lake Michigan. The soil, a warm and moist gray/brown clay, is common to the Western Upland and the Eastern Ridges regions. The Central Plain physical region is a semicircular plain that covers much of central Wisconsin. The soil of this region is warm and moist loamy fine sand. Most of this region was glaciated during the last Ice Age. The Wisconsin

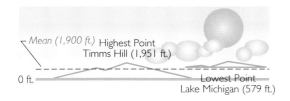

Mean (1,900 ft.) Highest Point
Timms Hill (1,951 ft.)

0 ft.

Lowest Point
Lake Michigan (579 ft.)

Land Use

Cropland: 35.6%; Pasture: 9.3%; Rangeland: 0%; Forest: 41%; Urban: 5.9%; Other: 8.2%.

For more information about Wisconsin's environment, contact the Department of Natural Resources, P.O. Box 7921, Madison, WI 53707.

Dells, a scenic gorge carved by the Wisconsin River, is located in the southwestern section of the region, where the glaciers did not reach. Due north of the Central Plain and running across Wisconsin from west to east is the Northern Highland physical region. Soil is cool and moist and is brown due to high iron and organic content. This area is a vacation destination with its heavily forested hills and hundreds of small lakes. This region also has the highest elevations in the state. The highest point is Timms Hill, which rises 1,952 ft. (595 m) above sea level. The Lake Superior Lowland physical region is predominantly a flat plain, with sandy beaches lining the shoreline. It terminates 5 to 20 miles inland from the lake at a steep headland. Soil is cool, and moist.

Environmental Quality

Wisconsin residents generate 3.6 million tons of solid waste each year, or approximately 1,550 pounds per capita. Landfill capacity in Wisconsin will be exhausted in more than 12 years. The state has 40 hazardous waste sites. Annual greenhouse gas emissions in Wisconsin total 99.9 million tons, or 20.6 tons per capita. Industrial sources in Wisconsin release approximately 48.4 thousand tons of toxins, 545.2 thousand tons of acid precipitation-producing substances, and 2.0 million tons of smog-producing substances into the atmosphere each year.

The state has 66,400 acres within the National Park System. State parks cover just over 117,000 acres, attracting 12.3 million visitors per year.

Wisconsin spends 1.7 percent of its budget, or approximately $35 per capita, on environmental and natural resources.

Flora and Fauna

Most of Wisconsin's forested areas consist of relatively new trees, both hardwood and softwood. Overall, wooded areas cover 42 percent of the state's land. Deciduous hardwood trees include yellow birch, aspen, oak, and elm, and softwoods include tamarack, hemlock, and balsam fir. The majority of forests lie in the North Highland and Central Plain regions of Wisconsin. Many shrubs, including wild black currants, Juneberries, and blueberries grow throughout Wisconsin. Wisconsin's landscape is especially colorful during the fall, because of wildflowers such as goldenrod and fireweed. Furthermore, Wisconsin has over 20 kinds of violets growing across the state.

Wildlife such as black bears, wolves, snowshoe hares, porcupines, and otters live mostly in northern Wisconsin. Recently, coyotes have begun to inhabit the state. Other animals found throughout Wisconsin include white-tailed deer, gophers, and chipmunks. Birds, including songbirds such as nuthatches and robins, and game birds such as jacksnipes and woodcocks, live throughout Wisconsin. Many migratory waterfowl pass through Wisconsin, including Canada geese. The state's rivers, streams, and lakes contain pickerel, sturgeon, trout, walleye, and other game fish.

Climate

Wisconsin has a humid continental climate, characterized by mild summers but long, cold winters. While this holds true for most of the inland areas, the coasts of Lake Superior and Lake Michigan provide cooler summers and milder winters. Some variation exists in temperatures across Wisconsin. A city like Milwaukee, in southern Wisconsin, has average January and July temperatures of 24 degrees F and 75 degrees F. Farther north, near Rhinelander, average January and July temperatures register at 7 degrees F and 60 degrees F.

Wisconsin receives an average of 30 inches of precipitation annually, with only slight differences across the state. A part of northern Wisconsin, near Hurley, receives the most precipitation, about 38 inches annually. Much of this area has a higher elevation.

Although Wisconsin does not receive significant precipitation, thunderstorms are a frequent occurrence during the summer. Their presence has much to do with the Great Lakes.

Hydrology

Two rivers make up most of Wisconsin's western boundary. The St. Croix forms part of the northwest border with Minnesota before flowing into the Mississippi, which forms the rest of the western border with Minnesota and Iowa. The Wisconsin River, in the southwest, is the longest river within the state, flowing for about 425 miles (684 km) before emptying into the Mississippi. Other tributaries of the Mississippi, which drain much of western Wisconsin, are the Black, the LaCrosse, and the Chippewa. Smaller rivers flow in eastern Wisconsin, including the Oconto and Peshtigo, which flow into Green Bay; and the Plauer and the Wolf, which drain into interior lakes.

Wisconsin has thousands of natural lakes. By far the largest of these is Lake Winnebago in the east, covering about 215 sq. miles (557 sq. km). Other sizable lakes include Koshkonong and Geneva in the south, and Poygan and Shawano farther north.

Wisconsin's History

Wisconsin's First People

Humans have inhabited Wisconsin since the end of the last Ice Age, approximately fourteen thousand years ago. These hunters followed large game animals such as the mastodon, caribou, and elk.

About six thousand years ago, another group of people came to Wisconsin. These people were called the Old Copper Indians, since they made tools out of copper.

The next group of people to live in Wisconsin were Paleo-Indians called Mound Builders. The Woodland, Hopewell, and Effigy cultures are all considered Mound Builder groups. Perhaps the most famous mound left by these ancient people in Wisconsin is one near Madison, which is in the shape of a bird.

By A.D. 1000, the Native American tribes with which Europeans first made contact began settling in Wisconsin. Tribes that lived in the state included the Fox, Winnebago, Huron, Illinois, Ojibwa, Potawatomi, and Sioux. Many of these tribes lived in villages, often of up to one hundred people.

Exploration and Early Settlement

The first European to explore Wisconsin was Jean Nicolet of France. In 1634, while trying to find a passage to China, he arrived in the Green Bay area. Until 1763, the Wisconsin region was under nominal French control. Many explorers crossed into Wisconsin during that period, and several fur-trading outposts, mainly French, were established in the area.

In 1660, Jesuit missionaries started a crusade to convert the Wisconsin Native Americans, including the Winnebago, Ojibwa, Fox, and Sauk tribes, to Christianity. This effort, however, proved mostly unsuccessful.

British control of Wisconsin lasted only twenty years, because the United States acquired the region in 1783, following the Revolutionary War. The British did not withdraw from Wisconsin, however, until after the War of 1812. The United States' grasp on

Wisconsin was firmly established in 1816, when the government built two forts, Fort Howard at Green Bay and Fort Crawford at Prairie du Chien.

Territorial Period and Statehood

At first Wisconsin land was part of three different states' territories at separate periods. Starting in 1800 and ending in 1809, Wisconsin was part of Indiana Territory. Then from 1809 to 1818, Illinois Territory controlled Wisconsin. Finally, between 1818 and 1836, the region was administered as part of the territory of Michigan.

The southwestern corner of Wisconsin was the first area to be settled by Americans, in the 1820s. Pioneers came from neighboring states to mine for lead, iron ore, and other minerals. The resulting increase in population prompted the U.S. Congress to create a separate Wisconsin territory on April 20, 1836, with Henry Dodge as the first governor. Originally, Belmont was chosen as the territorial capital. Madison replaced Belmont as the governmental seat in 1838.

Minnesota and Iowa were originally part of Wisconsin Territory. However, in 1838, Iowa became its own territory. A third of present-day Minnesota continued to be a part of Wisconsin until 1848.

In 1848, Wisconsin achieved statehood. On May 29 of that year, Wisconsin became the thirtieth state in the Union. The present state boundaries were set at this time.

Economic Development

In early Wisconsin history, agriculture dominated the state economy. From around 1840 until well after the end of the Civil War, Wisconsin was the nation's leading producer of wheat. However, in the late 1800s, Wisconsin agriculture diversified and other industries, including dairying, gained in importance.

Today, the state of Wisconsin is one of the largest producers of dairy products. It supplies

40 percent of the cheese and 20 percent of the butter to the American market. In addition to cheese and butter, Wisconsin dairy products include ice cream and milk of all kinds (condensed, evaporated, and malted).

Overall, however, it is not dairying that is Wisconsin's most important industry, but rather manufacturing. Approximately one-fourth of the gross state product is derived from manufacturing ventures of some kind. Many other Wisconsin industries contribute to the great importance of manufacturing. Several factories process agricultural and forest products, while others produce metal products, farm machinery, turbines, and power cranes.

The southeastern corner of Wisconsin, and the city of Milwaukee in particular, is the industrial hub of Wisconsin. Milwaukee, moreover, has earned the nickname of Beer Capital of the United States, as it is a leading beer-brewing city.

Wisconsin: State of "Firsts"

Wisconsin can lay claim to several "firsts" of American history. Some of these "firsts" include the Republican party, which was founded in February 1854. In 1856, kindergarten was started by Mrs. Carl Schurz, of Watertown, who assembled the first ever pre-grade school class. At first, kindergarten, a German word, was intended for German-speaking children. However, Mrs. Schurz's idea caught on, and kindergarten became an established part of the American educational system.

The Ringling Bros. and Barnum & Bailey Circus is perhaps the most famous circus in the world, and it all began in Wisconsin in 1884. The founding members of the circus, the Ringling brothers, had their first "big top" performance in Baraboo. From its origins in south-central Wisconsin to its many variations in the rest of the world, the circus continues to be a popular event.

Important Events

1634 Jean Nicolet explores Wisconsin, near Green Bay.

1660 Jesuit missionaries enter Wisconsin and try to convert the Indians.

1689 Nicholas Perrot claims Wisconsin area for France.

1701 First permanent settlement established at Green Bay.

1763 France grants Wisconsin area to Great Britain.

1783 Wisconsin region becomes part of the United States.

1816 Last British troops leave the area.

1816 United States builds Fort Howard and Fort Crawford.

1836 Wisconsin Territory created on April 20.

1838 Madison becomes the capitol.

1848 Wisconsin becomes thirtieth state in the Union on May 29.

1854 Republican party is born.

1856 Kindergarten is introduced to the school system.

1857 First railroad crosses into Wisconsin.

1867 Typewriter invented in Milwaukee.

1882 First hydroelectric plant in the nation built at Appleton.

1884 Ringling Bros. and Barnum & Bailey Circus conducts its first performance in Baraboo.

1918 Wisconsin is first state to use numbers for labeling highway systems.

1932 First unemployment compensation act in the United States passed in Wisconsin legislature.

1964 Wisconsin is first state to have congressional districts appointed by the state supreme court.

1965 State hit with strong tornadoes causing damage in nineteen counties.

1973 Menominee County dissolved; Native Americans come under federal control again, after twelve years of autonomy.

1984 Law passed protecting employees who report wrongdoing by their coworkers.

1993 The discovery of a chemical in the brain that triggers a craving for fat is announced in a medical conference in Milwaukee.

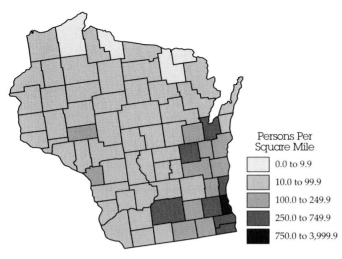

Population Density

Population density for the state of Wisconsin was 90.1 persons per square mile in 1990 (34.8 per km2). Average U.S. density was 70.3 persons per square mile in 1990 (27.3 per km2). Habitation is most dense in and around the urban area of Milwaukee. This area includes the cities of Racine, Sheboygan, and Kenosha.

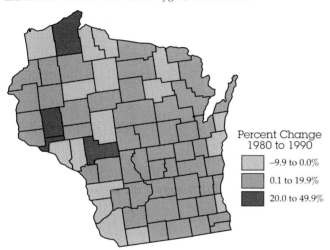

Population Change

The 1990 population figure for the state of Wisconsin was 4,891,769. This is a 3.95 percent increase from 4,705,767 in 1980. The next decade will show a loss with a population of 4.8 million or a –2.2 percent decrease. Bayfield, Dunn, Pepin, and Jackson counties have grown the most over the last decade.

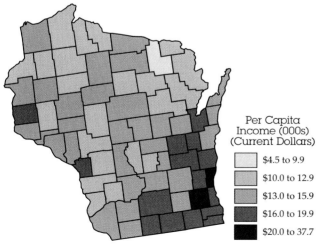

Distribution of Income

The per capita income for the state of Wisconsin (current dollars) was $18,727 in 1992. This is a 91.6 percent increase from $9,772 in 1980. Income is greatest in the counties surrounding Milwaukee. Most of the highest incomes can be found in this region.

Population Projections

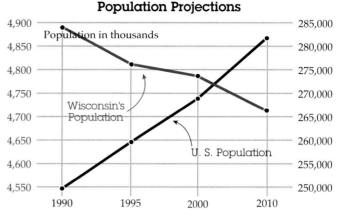

Population in thousands

Wisconsin's Population

U. S. Population

Population Change

Year	Population
1950	3,435,000
1960	3,962,000
1970	4,429,000
1980	4,705,767
1990	4,891,769
2000	4,784,000
2010	4,713,000

Period	Change
1950–1970	28.9%
1970–1980	6.3%
1980–1990	4.0%
1990–2000	–2.2%

Population Facts

State Population, 1993: 5,038,000

Rank: 18

Population 2000: 4,784,000 (Rank 19)

Density: 90.1 per sq. mi. (34.8 per km²)

Distribution: 65.7% urban, 34.3% rural

Population Under 5 Years Old: 7.2%

Population Under 18 Years Old: 26.6%

Population Over 65 Years Old: 13.3%

Median Age: 32.9

Number of Households: 1,822,000

Average Persons Per Household: 2.61

Average Persons Per Family: 3.14

Female Heads of Households: 3.57%

Population That Is Married: 21.42%

Birth Rate: 14.9 per 1,000 population

Death Rate: 8.7 per 1,000 population

Births to Teen Mothers: 10.2%

Marriage Rate: 8.4 per 1,000 population

Divorce Rate: 3.6 per 1,000 population

Violent Crime Rate: 277 per 100,000 pop.

Population on Social Security: 17.2%

Percent Voting for President: 69.0%

Wisconsin's Famous Citizens

Gillette, King Camp (1855–1932). He invented a disposable steel razor and founded the Gillette Safety Razor Company in 1901.

Heiden, Eric (b. 1958). Speed skater. He won gold medals in all 5 speed-skating categories at the 1980 Winter Olympics.

Kennan, George (b. 1904). Historian and diplomat. He was ambassador to the Soviet Union and to Yugoslavia.

King, Frank (1883–1969). Cartoonist. He created the famous comic strip "Gasoline Alley" in 1919.

Liberace (1919–1987). Entertainer-pianist. His concerts were elaborately choreographed affairs with outrageous costumes, etc.

Rehnquist, William H. (b. 1924). He has served on the U.S. Supreme Court since 1972, as Chief Justice since 1986.

Tracy, Spencer (1900–1967). Actor. He starred in several films with Katharine Hepburn and won consecutive Oscars (1937–1938).

Wilder, Thornton (1897–1975). Playwright. He won Pulitzer Prizes for his plays *Our Town* and *The Skin of Our Teeth*.

Population Profile

Rank. Wisconsin ranks 18th among U.S. states in terms of population with 5,038,000 citizens.

Minority Population. The state's minority population is 8.8 percent. The state's male to female ratio for 1990 was 95.76 males for every 100 females. It was above the national average of 95.22 males for every 100 females.

Growth. The state's population is decreasing and is expected to be 4.7 million by the year 2010.

Government

Capital: Madison (established 1848).

Statehood: Became 30th state on May 29, 1848.

Number of Counties: 72.

Supreme Court Justices: 7, 10-year term.

State Senators: 33, 4-year term.

State Legislators: 99, 2-year term.

United States Senators: 2.

United States Representatives: 9.

Electoral Votes: 11.

State Constitution: Adopted 1848.

Older Citizens. The state's population older than 65 was 651,221 in 1990. It grew 15.42% from 564,197 in 1980.

Younger Citizens. The number of children (under 18 years of age) was 1.3 million in 1990. This represents 26.4 percent of the state's population. The state's school aged population was 783 thousand in 1990. It is expected to increase to 787 thousand by the year 2000. This represents a 0.51% change.

Urban/Rural. 65.7% of the population of the state live in urban areas while 34.3% live in rural areas.

Largest Cities. Wisconsin has 18 cities with a population greater than 35,000. The populations of the state's largest centers are (starting from the most populous) Milwaukee (628,088), Madison (191,262), Green Bay (96,466), Racine (84,298), Kenosha (80,352), Appleton (65,695), West Allis (63,221), Waukesha (56,958), Eau Claire (56,856), Oshkosh (55,006), Janesville (52,133), La Crosse (51,003), Sheboygan (49,676), Wauwatosa (49,366), Fond du Lac (37,757), Wausau (37,060), Beloit (35,573), Brookfield (35,184), New Berlin (33,592), Greenfield (33,403), Manitowoc (32,520), Superior (27,134), and Menomonee Falls (26,840).

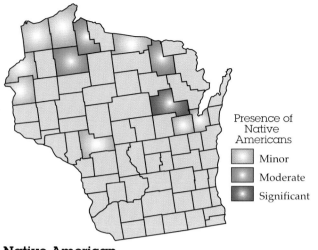

Nationalities

Nationality	Count
African	3,419
American	76,673
Arab	5,086
Austrian	14,059
Czech	59,855
Dutch	86,556
English	211,729
Finnish	23,288
German	2,209,701
Greek	10,382
Hungarian	13,577
Irish	281,309
Italian	96,719
Norwegian	257,345
Polish	325,320
Portuguese	1,104
Russian	18,251
Scottish	29,922
Slovak	26,263
Swedish	88,121
Welsh	13,415
West Indian	1,994

Presence of Native Americans

- Minor
- Moderate
- Significant

Native American

The Native American population in Wisconsin was 39,387 in 1990. This was an increase of 28.91 percent from 30,553 in 1980. Many of the Native Americans living in the state live on Indian reservations such as the Bad River, Menominee, and Oneida.

Statewide Ethnic Composition

Over 92 percent of the population of Wisconsin is white. The largest nationalities in this racial group are German, Polish, and Irish. The next largest group is African Americans, followed by Hispanics, Asian Americans, and Native Americans. Over 76,000 people claim to be American and acknowledge no other nationality.

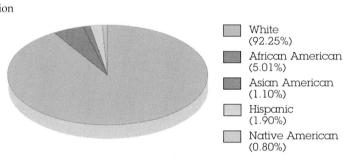

- White (92.25%)
- African American (5.01%)
- Asian American (1.10%)
- Hispanic (1.90%)
- Native American (0.80%)

Education Facts

Total Students 1990: 782,905	Mean SAT Score 1991 Verbal: 481
Number of School Districts: 429	Mean SAT Score 1991 Math: 542
Expenditure Per Capita on Education 1990: $887	Average Teacher's Salary 1992: $35,200
Expenditure Per Capita K–12 1990: $811	Rank Teacher's Salary: 12th in U.S.
Expenditure Per Pupil 1990: $5,946	High School Graduates 1990: 55,800
Total School Enrollment 1990–1991: 790,900	Total Number of Public Schools: 2,019
Rank of Expenditures Per Student: 10th in the U.S.	Number of Teachers 1990: 49,742
African American Enrollment: 8.6%	Student/Teacher Ratio: 15.9
Hispanic Enrollment: 2.4%	Staff Employed in Public Schools: 83,561
Asian/Pacific Islander Enrollment: 1.8%	Pupil/Staff Ratio: 9.4
Native American Enrollment: 1.3%	Staff/Teacher Ratio: 1.7

Education

Attainment: 81.1 percent of population 25 years or older were high school graduates in 1989, earning Wisconsin a ranking of 17th in the United States; 18.9 percent of the state's population had completed college. Institutions of Higher Education: The largest universities and colleges in the state include University of Wisconsin, Madison; Marquette University, Milwaukee; Lawrence University, Appleton; Beloit College, Beloit; Ripon College, Ripon. Expenditures per Student: Expenditure increased 73% between 1985 and 1990. Projected High School Graduations: 1998 (62,177), 2004 (59,308); Total Revenues for Education from Federal Sources: $154 million; Total Revenues for Education from State Sources: $1.5 billion; Total Revenues for Education from Local Sources: $1.9 billion; Average Annual Salaries for Public School Principals: $42,949; Largest School Districts in State: Milwaukee School District, 91,819 students, 23d in the United States.

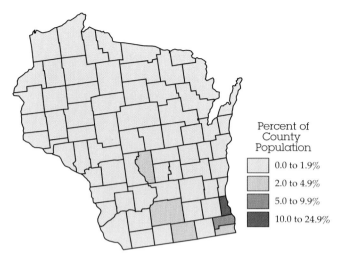

Percent of County Population

- 0.0 to 1.9%
- 2.0 to 4.9%
- 5.0 to 9.9%
- 10.0 to 24.9%

African American

The African American population in Wisconsin was 244,539 in 1990. This was an increase of 33.50 percent from 183,169 in 1980. Milwaukee and the surrounding counties have the highest percentages of African Americans in the state.

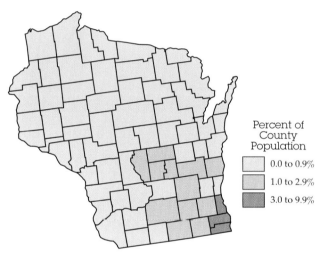

Percent of County Population

- 0.0 to 0.9%
- 1.0 to 2.9%
- 3.0 to 9.9%

Hispanic[††]

The Hispanic population in Wisconsin was 93,194 in 1990. This is an increase of 47.99 percent from 62,972 persons in 1980. Milwaukee and the surrounding counties have the highest percentages of Hispanics in the state.

[††]A person of Mexican, Puerto Rican, Cuban, or other Spanish culture or origin regardless of race.

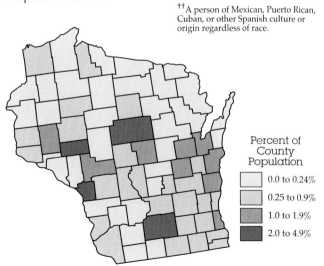

Percent of County Population

- 0.0 to 0.24%
- 0.25 to 0.9%
- 1.0 to 1.9%
- 2.0 to 4.9%

Asian American

The Asian American population in Wisconsin was 53,583 in 1990. This is an increase of 150.12 percent from 21,423 persons in 1980. The highest percentages of Asian Americans can be found in Marathon County as well as in the cities.

Agriculture

Wisconsin has 17.1 million farm acres. During the last 40 years, Wisconsin's farms have grown larger in size and fewer in number. In 1955, 154,000 farms were found in the state. Today, 79,000 remain.

Agriculture adds $4 billion to the state's gross product annually. The principal commodities in order of marketing receipts are dairy products, cattle, corn, and hogs.

The production of milk accounts for about 62 percent of Wisconsin's farm income. The primary dairy farm region is found between Green Bay and Monroe. Cattle and hog farms are found in the state's southwestern section. Hay, corn, and oats are all harvested primarily as livestock feed. Wisconsin is the nation's leader in the production of beets, green peas, and snap beans. Wisconsin also ranks among the leading cranberry producers.

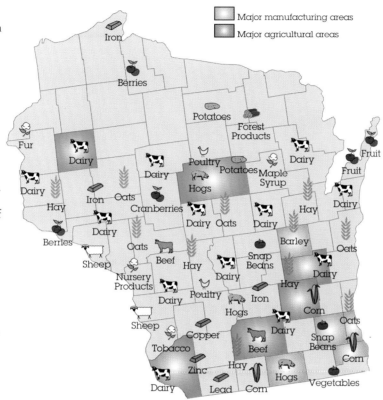

Housing

Owner Occupied Units: 2,055,774; Average Age of Units: 35 years; Average Value of Housing Units: $62,500; Renter Occupied Units: 582,371; Median Monthly Rent: $399; Housing Starts: 30,600; Existing Home Sales: 94,600.

Economic Facts

Gross State Product: $94,000,000,000 (1989)

Income Per Capita: $18,727

Disposable Personal Income: $16,351

Median Household Income: $29,442

Average Annual Pay, 1988: $21,838

Principal Industries: paper products, food products, machinery, fabricated metal products, electrical equipment

Major Crops: milk, cheese, corn, hay, oats, barley, soybeans, wheat, tobacco, potatoes, peas, beans, carrots, cherries, apples, cucumbers

Fish: Bass, Pickerel, Pike, Sturgeon, Trout

Livestock: cattle, hogs

Non-Fuel Minerals: Dolomite, Granite, Iron Ore, Sulfide, Copper, Zinc, Peat, Quartzite

Organic Fuel Minerals: N/A

Civilian Labor Force: 2,592,000 (Women: 1,194,000)

Total Employed: 2,453,000 (Women: 1,136,000)

Median Value of Housing: $62,500

Median Contract Rent: $399 per month

Economic Sectors 1992

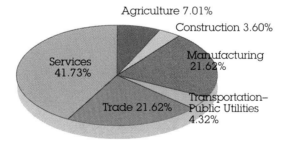

Agriculture 7.01%
Construction 3.60%
Manufacturing 21.62%
Services 41.73%
Trade 21.62%
Transportation–Public Utilities 4.32%

Manufacturing

Wisconsin has a significant and important manufacturing sector. Approximately 28 percent of the state gross product is derived from manufacturing activities. Machinery is Wisconsin's most important manufacturing industry. However, the food processing, paper products, and electrical equipment industries also contribute to the state economy.

Most of Wisconsin's industrial activity takes place in the southeastern part of the state. The Milwaukee metropolitan region is a great center of machinery production for the entire United States. Food processing factories are scattered throughout Wisconsin, in cities like Madison and Cudahy. The Fox and Wisconsin river valleys contain most of Wisconsin's paper mills. Fort Howard, a leading paper manufacturer, is headquartered in Green Bay.

Transportation

The present practice of highway numbering originated in Wisconsin in 1917, when it became the first state to adopt such a system. Today, Wisconsin has approximately 108,000 miles of highways and roads.

As in other states, rail travel in Wisconsin has declined in recent years. However, 6 freight rail lines still provide service to the state, and 10 Wisconsin cities receive passenger service. Wisconsin's position on the Great Lakes makes it a busy port area. Important ports include Milwaukee, Superior, and Green Bay. Lake Michigan and Green Bay are linked by a canal. The Mississippi River has traditionally been an important water route, and remains so even today. Milwaukee is home to Wisconsin's busiest airport. Green Bay and Madison also have large airports.

Energy and Transportation Facts

Energy. Yearly Consumption: 1,412 tril. BTUs (residential, 25.6%; commercial, 17.1%; industrial, 33.3%; transportation, 24.0%); Annual Energy Expenditures Per Capita: $1,645; Nuclear Power Plants Located in State: 3; Source of Energy Consumed: Petroleum— 35.0%; Natural Gas— 24.3%; Coal— 29.7%; Hydroelectric Power—2.3%; Nuclear Power—8.6%.

Transportation. Highway Miles: 110,371 (interstates, 638; urban, 14,841; rural, 95,530); Average Yearly Auto Insurance: $492 (35th); Auto Fatalities Rank: 40th; Registered Motor Vehicles: 3,734,711; Workers in Carpools: 15.4%; Workers Using Public Trans: 2.5%.

Employment

Employment. Wisconsin employed 2.59 million people in 1993. Most work in social and personal services (595,100 persons or 23.0% of the workforce). Manufacturing accounts for 21.6% or 559,100 workers. Wholesale and retail trade accounts for 21.4% or 553,000 workers. Government employs 360,400 workers (13.9%). Construction employs 93,000 workers (3.6%). Transportation and utilities account for 4.4% or 113,300 persons. Agriculture employs 119,100 workers or 4.6%. Finance, real estate, and insurance account for 5.0% or 130,600 workers. Mining employs 2,300 people and accounts for only 0.1% of the workforce.

Unemployment. Unemployment has decreased to 4.7% in 1993 from a rate of 7.2% in 1985. Today's figure is lower than the national average of 6.8% as shown below.

Unemployment Rate

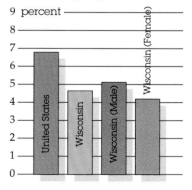

WYOMING The State of Wyoming

Official State Seal

The Great Seal of Wyoming was adopted in 1893. One side of the seal contains a cowboy and a miner leaning up against two pillars. A woman stands on a pedestal between the two pillars. On these pillars are written products the state creates. The banner that reads "Equal Rights" marks Wyoming's fight for women's suffrage.

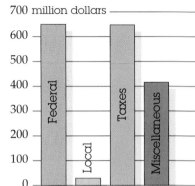

Legal Holidays

January: New Year's Day—1st, Martin Luther King, Jr., Day—3d Monday; February: Presidents' Day—3d Monday; May: Memorial Day—4th Monday; July: Independence Day—4th; Statehood Day—10th; September: Labor Day—1st Monday; October: Columbus Day—2nd Monday; November: Veterans' Day—11th; Thanksgiving—4th Thursday; December: Wyoming Day—10th; Christmas—25th.

Official State Flag

The state flag of Wyoming was adopted in 1917. It was created by a contest winner in 1916. The state seal is placed on a buffalo. A red and white border surrounds a blue field. The red border represents the blood of pioneers, the white represents purity, and the blue represents fidelity and justice.

Festivals and Events

January: Horse-drawn sleigh races, Jackson & Thayne; February: Cowboy State Games Winter Sports Fest, Cheyenne; March: Celebrity Ski Extravaganza, Jackson; April: Pole, Pedal, Paddle, Jackson; May: Old West Days, Jackson; June: Days of '49, Greybull; Woodchoppers Jamboree, Encampment; July: Frontier Days, Cheyenne; Jubilee Days, Laramie; Rawhide Pageant, Lusk; August: Native American Pageant, Thermopolis; Fine Arts Festival, Jackson Hole; Gift of the Waters, Thermopolis; September: Wyoming State Fair, Douglas; Evanston Cowboy Days, Evanston; Fall Arts Fest, Jackson; Oktoberfest, Worland; October: Western Square Dance Festival, Laramie.

Wyoming Compared to States in Its Region.

Resident Pop. in Metro Areas: 6th; Pop. Percent Increase: 8th; Pop. Over 65: 6th; Infant Mortality: 4th; School Enroll. Increase: 8th; High School Grad. and Up: 3d; Violent Crime: 5th; Hazardous Waste Sites: 7th; Unemployment: 7th; Median Household Income: 5th; Persons Below Poverty: 5th; Energy Costs Per Person: 1st.

Mountain Region

	Population	Capital
Montana	839,000	Helena
Wyoming	470,000	Cheyenne
Idaho	1,099,000	Boise
Nevada	1,389,000	Carson City
Utah	1,860,000	Salt Lake City
Colorado	3,566,000	Denver
Arizona	3,936,000	Phoenix
New Mexico	1,616,000	Santa Fe

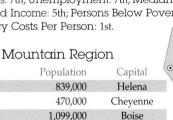

Wyoming's Finances

Households: 169,000; Income Per Capita Current Dollars: $17,423; Change Per Capita Income 1980 to 1992: 53.4% (50th in U.S.); State Expenditures: $1,725,000,000; State Revenues: $1,723,000,000; Personal Income Tax: N/A; Federal Income Taxes Paid Per Capita: $1,742; Sales Tax: 3% (prescription drugs exempt).

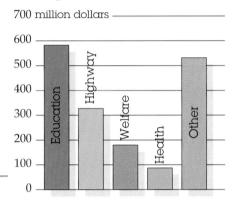

State Expenditures — 700 million dollars (Education, Highway, Welfare, Health, Other)

State Revenues — 700 million dollars (Federal, Local, Taxes, Miscellaneous)

Location, Size, and Boundaries

Location. Wyoming is located in the northwestern United States in what is known as the Mountain region. It is bounded on four sides by land. The geographic center of Wyoming is lat. 42° 58.3' N; long. 107° 40.3' W.

Size. Wyoming is the 9th largest state in terms of size. Its area is 97,914 sq. mi. (253,597 km2). Inland water covers 711 sq. mi. (1,841 km2).

Boundaries. Montana, 384 mi. (618 km); South Dakota, 137 mi. 221 km); Nebraska, 140 mi. (225 km); Colorado, 260 mi. (418 km); Utah, 174 mi. (280 km); Idaho, 174 mi. (280 km).

Geographic Extent. The north/south extent of Wyoming is 265 mi. (426 km). The state extends 365 mi. (587 km) to the east/west.

Facts about Wyoming. Origin of Name: After a *Delaware Indian* word meaning "*upon the great plain*"; Nickname: The Equality State; Motto: "Equal Rights"; Abbreviations: Wyo. (traditional), WY (postal); State Bird: meadowlark; State Tree: cottonwood; State Flower: indian paintbrush; State Song: "Wyoming," words by Charles E. Winter, music by G. E. Knapp.

Wyoming Compared to Other States. Resident Pop. in Metro Areas: 47th; Pop. Per. Increase: 21st; Pop. Over 65: 44th; Infant Mortality: 30th; School Enroll. Increase: 49th; High School Grad. and Up: 5th; Violent Crime: 38th; Haz. Waste Sites: 46th; Unemployment: 40th; Median Household Income: 31st; Persons Below Poverty: 26th; Energy Costs Per Person: 2d.

Sources of Information. Tourism: Division of Tourism and State Marketing, I-25 and College Drive, Cheyenne, WY 82002. History: Historical and Archaeological Resources, Barrett Building, Cheyenne, WY 82002.

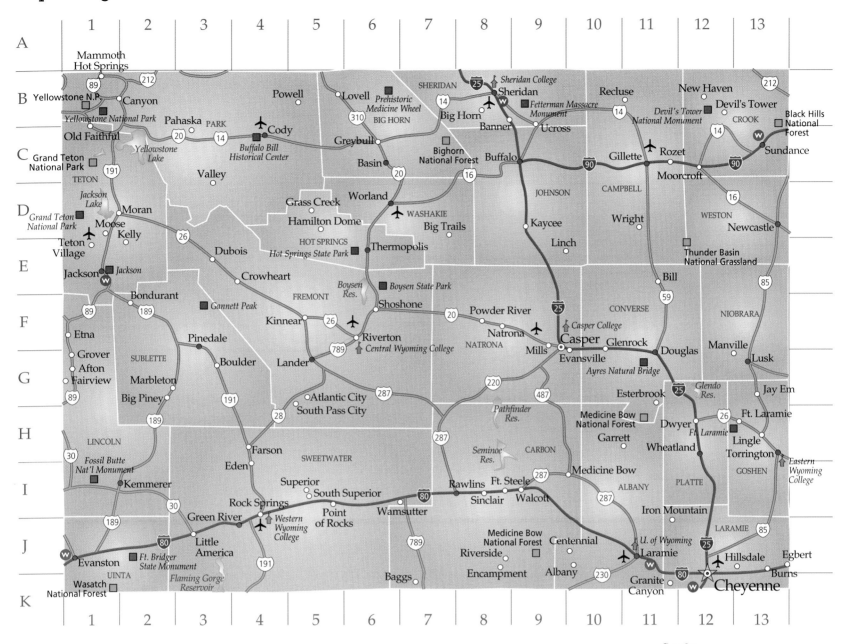

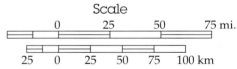

■ **Ayres Natural Bridge.** 30 feet (9 meters) high, 50 feet (15 meters) wide, red sandstone natural arch over La Prele Creek. (G-11)

■ **Boysen State Park.** Surrounded by the Wind River Indian Reservation. Fishing, water sports, and beach. (E-6)

■ **Buffalo Bill Historical Center.** Display of western Americana including the Buffalo Bill Museum, the Whitney Gallery, and the Plains Indian Museum. (C-4)

■ **Devils Tower National Monument.** The first national monument, dedicated September 24, 1906. A 1,280 foot volcanic-rock column. (B-12)

■ **Fetterman Massacre Monument.** Site where Brevet Lt. Col. William Fetterman and his troops were ambushed by the Sioux Indians on December 21, 1866. (B-9)

■ **Fort Bridger State Monument.** Built in 1842 by trapper Jim Bridger. Became the second most important outfitting point (Ft. Laramie being the first) on the way to the Pacific Coast. (J-2)

■ **Fort Laramie National Historic Site.** The most important fur-trading post and military post on the Oregon Trail. (H-13)

■ **Fossil Butte National Monument.** Beds of fossile marine life on the surface of the butte. The newest national monument in the state, dedicated October 23, 1972. (I-1)

■ **Gannett Peak.** The highest point in the state rising 13,804 feet. (F-3)

■ **Grand Teton National Park.** Dedicated in 1929 and later enlarged in 1950 with the addition of Jackson Hole National Monument. 500 square miles of mountain and lake country with more than 60 species of mammals and 100 species of birds. (D-1)

■ **Hot Springs State Park.** Site of the world's largest single mineral hot spring. (E-6)

■ **Jackson.** Resort town with skiing and sleigh rides in winter. (E-1)

■ **Prehistoric Medicine Wheel.** A 70-foot-diameter mountaintop shrine made by prehistoric sun worshipers. (B-6)

■ **Yellowstone National Park.** Spanning three states this park is the oldest and largest (3,472 square miles) national park in the country, dedicated in 1872. There are more than 10,000 thermal features including geysers, falls, and hot springs. There is also an abundance of wildlife with more than 60 species of mammals and 200 species of fish. (B-1)

Scale

0   25   50   75 mi.

25   0   25   50   75   100 km

Major Cities

Casper	F-9	Green River	J-4
Cheyenne	J-12	Laramie	J-11
Evanston	J-1	Rock Springs	I-4
Gillette	C-11	Sheridan	B-8

Legend

☆ State capitol

⊙ Cities over 35,000 population

○ Other significant cities

● County Seats

■ Major cultural attractions

▢ State Parks

Ⓦ Welcome Centers

⚲ Major colleges and universities

Weather Facts

Record High Temperature: 114° F (46° C) on July 12, 1900, at Basin; Record Low Temperature: -63° F (-53° C) on February 9, 1933, at Moran; Average January Temperature: 20° F (-7° C); Average July Temperature: 68° F (20° C); Average Yearly Precipitation: 14 in. (36 cm).

Environmental Facts

Air Pollution Rank: 45th; Water Pollution Rank: 39th; Total Yearly Industrial Pollution: 2,449,553 lbs.; Industrial Pollution Rank: 47th; Hazardous Waste Sites: 3; Hazardous Sites Rank: 46th; Landfill Capacity: overextended; Fresh Water Supply: surplus; Daily Residential Water Consumption: 206 gals. per capita; Endangered Species: Aquatic Species (1)—dace, Kendall warm springs; Birds (3)—crane, whooping; Mammals (3)—bear, grizzly; Other Species (1)—toad, Wyoming.

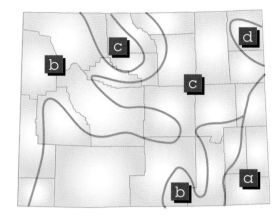

Physical Regions: (a) Great Plains; (b) Rocky Mountains; (c) Intermontane Basins; (d) Black Hills.

Land Use

Cropland: 7.3%; Pasture: 2.8%; Rangeland: 82.2%; Forest: 3%; Urban: 1.6%; Other: 3.1%.

Flora and Fauna

Forested areas only account for approximately one-sixth of Wyoming's land. The majority of the state, around 80 percent, is covered with either a variety of grasses or desert-type shrubs. Wyoming's forests, found along streams and in mountain areas, consist mainly of coniferous trees such as Engelmann spruce, Douglas fir, and lodgepole and ponderosa pine. Wyoming's dry areas have cacti, greasewood, and sagebrush. Grasslands, which cover 40 percent of the land, is composed of wheat grass, bluegrass, and tufted fescues. Wildflowers bloom in the state's mountain areas and include arnica, evening star, sour dock, five-finger, and forget-me-not.

Black, brown, and grizzly bears all live in Wyoming, although the grizzly bear has become endangered. Other large animals include mule deer, moose, mountain lion, and pronghorn antelope. Bison herds live in two national parks, Yellowstone and Grand Teton. Wyoming is also home to otters, weasels, prairie dogs, and other smaller animals. Bald and golden eagles, two large birds, also live in Wyoming. The state's game birds include sage hens, wild turkeys, and pheasants.

Average Monthly Weather

Cheyenne	Jan	Feb	Mar	Apr	May	Jun	Jul	Aug	Sep	Oct	Nov	Dec	Yearly
Maximum Temperature °F	37.3	40.7	43.6	54.0	64.6	75.4	83.1	80.8	72.1	61.0	46.5	40.4	58.3
Minimum Temperature °F	14.8	17.9	20.6	29.6	39.7	48.5	54.6	52.8	43.7	34.0	23.1	18.2	33.1
Days of Precipitation	5.7	6.3	9.4	9.5	11.9	10.8	10.7	9.8	7.4	5.6	6.0	5.6	98.6

Topography

The Rocky Mountain physical region, containing no fewer than twelve separate mountain ranges, dominates the topography of Wyoming. The mountains run generally in a northwest to southeast direction, cover much of the state, and define the Continental Divide. Some of the mountain ranges include the Wyoming, Teton, Gros Ventre, Snake River, and Absaroka, located along the western border, while the Goshen and Laramie ranges rise in the southeast. The central portion of the state contains the Big Horn Range in the north and the Medicine Bow Range in the south. The average elevation in the state, 6,700 ft. (2,042 m), is the second highest in the United States, behind only Colorado. Among this group of sky-scraping mountains, Gannett Peak, in the Wind River Range, is the tallest at 13, 804 ft. (4,207 m). The soil of the mountains is typically cool and

moist, dark and rich, and less than 20 inches in depth. Situated between the mountains and winding throughout the state is the Intermontane Basins physical region. Many of the basins are named for the mountains that surround them, and are predominantly dry flatlands on which low grasses grow. The soil of the basins is a warm and dry desert red clay with a thin dark surface. The Great Plains physical region extends into Wyoming at the southeastern corner of the state. This is cattle range country, but irrigation on some farms has made the organically rich, warm and dry soil agriculturally productive.

Located in the extreme northeastern corner is the Black Hills physical region. Approximately 30 percent of this physical region lies in Wyoming, with the rest across the border in South Dakota. The soil of the Black Hills is similar to that found in the Rocky Mountains, cool and moist, dark, and thin.

Climate

Both high elevation and an inland location make Wyoming's climate dry and cool. The state can be divided into arid, semiarid, steppe, and alpine climates. Most of Wyoming's land is a combination of steppe and semiarid conditions. Arid conditions exist in the western half of the state, and especially in the Red Desert of the Great Divide Basin. January and July temperatures range from 22 degrees F and 71 degrees F in Casper, to 12 degrees F and 59 degrees F in Yellowstone National Park.

Although Wyoming's average statewide precipitation is only about 12 inches, some variation does exist. The mountainous regions receive the most precipitation, mainly in the form of snowfall, and often over 250 inches.

Southern Wyoming sometimes experiences the ground blizzard phenomenon. If dry snow is on the ground and afternoon winds are blowing, a swirling, blinding mass of snow appears, usually against a clear blue sky.

Environmental Quality

Wyoming residents generate 550.0 thousand tons of solid waste each year, or approximately 2,200 pounds per capita. Landfill capacity in Wyoming will be exhausted in more than 12 years. The state has 3 hazardous waste sites. Annual greenhouse gas emissions in Wyoming total 54.8 million tons, or 114.4 tons per capita. Industrial sources in Wyoming release approximately 16.9 thousand tons of toxins, 306.5 thousand tons of acid precipitation-producing substances, and 700.0 thousand tons of smog-producing substances into the atmosphere each year.

The state has 2,392,400 acres within the National Park System; the largest area within the state is Yellowstone National Park. State parks cover just over 125,000 acres, attracting 2.0 million visitors per year.

Wyoming spends 7.7 percent of its budget, or approximately $267 per capita, on environmental and natural resources.

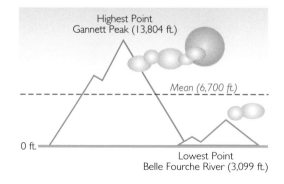

Highest Point
Gannett Peak (13,804 ft.)

Mean (6,700 ft.)

0 ft.

Lowest Point
Belle Fourche River (3,099 ft.)

For more information about Wyoming's environment, contact the Environmental Quality Department, 122 W. 25th St., 4th Floor, Herschler Bldg., Cheyenne, WY 82002.

Hydrology

There are several major river systems in Wyoming. In the southeast, the Platte River flows north out of Colorado and turns southeast around Casper, before entering into Nebraska. It drains this region, along with its tributaries, the Sweetwater, the Medicine Bow, and the Laramie. Major tributaries of the Missouri River, which itself does not flow through the state, drain much of northern Wyoming. The most prominent of these is the Bighorn, in the central part of the state. To the east are the Powder and the Belle Fourche. The principal river in the southwest is the Green, which flows south into Utah, where it meets the Colorado River. The Yellowstone River drains the northwest corner, and the Snake has its beginnings in Wyoming before flowing west into Idaho.

Wyoming has many natural lakes. The largest of these is Yellowstone Lake in Yellowstone National Park. There are also several large man-made lakes, including Boysen Reservoir on the Bighorn River, and Glendo Reservoir on the Platte.

Wyoming's History

Wyoming's First People

According to archaeological evidence, people have lived in Wyoming for approximately eleven thousand years. However, there is little information on these ancient Native Americans.

Later in Wyoming's history, modern Native Americans came to settle in the area. One feature that attracted several tribes to Wyoming was the great herds of buffalo that roamed across the prairies.

In the early 1800s, Wyoming became home to many different Native American tribes. The first tribes to come to Wyoming were the Ute, Blackfoot, Crow, Arapaho, Flathead, and Cheyenne. In the middle of the nineteenth century, the Sioux tribe also came to Wyoming from the north and east. All of these tribes were primarily hunters, relying on buffalo and other game animals for food.

European and American Exploration

Possibly, the first Europeans to cross into Wyoming were French fur traders, arriving sometime in the 1700s. However, the land was not officially explored until after 1800. The first white explorer came to Wyoming in 1805. A French-Canadian named François Antoine Larocque who entered the state to trade with the Native Americans.

In 1807, John Colter, a fur trapper, became the first white man to explore the western part of Wyoming. During his journey, he discovered the geyser and hot springs area that is now a part of Yellowstone National Park.

In 1812, a group of traders traveled from western to eastern Wyoming through a mountain pass called South Pass. Although they did not realize it at the time, this route would prove most important in the migration of pioneers to Wyoming as well as to the rest of the West. Three separate trails went through South Pass: the Oregon Trail to the Pacific Northwest, the Mormon Trail to Utah, and the California Trail to California. Over the years,

South Pass was crossed by many famous people, including Brigham Young, leader of the Mormons, and Capt. John C. Frémont. After Frémont made his survey of Wyoming, the U.S. Congress decided to build forts along the Oregon Trail to protect settlers.

Most of the earliest settlers who came to Wyoming were fur trappers who traded with Native Americans. Between 1825 and 1840, fur trapping and trading was the basis of the economy in the area. In 1825, William Henry Ashley established the first fur-trading rendezvous, an annual tradition that lasted until 1840. Each year, white and Native American fur trappers met to trade their fur pelts, stock up on supplies, and socialize.

Territorial Period and Statehood

The first motions towards territorial status occurred unsuccessfully in 1865. During its history, Wyoming has been part of several other territories, including the Dakota, Oregon, Utah, and Idaho territories.

In July, 1868, Congress passed an act creating Wyoming Territory from the Dakota Territory. President Ulysses S. Grant appointed John Campbell as the first territorial governor.

Wyoming had a progressive atmosphere, because on December 10, 1869, women were granted the right to vote. By 1870, women were also allowed to serve on juries. Furthermore, the first female justice of the peace, Esther Morris of South Pass City, hailed from Wyoming.

The population of Wyoming continued to grow during the territorial years, partly due to the Union Pacific Railroad's presence in the state. As more people came to settle in Wyoming, the push toward statehood increased. Wyoming achieved statehood on July 10, 1890, and became the forty-fourth state in the Union.

Economic Development

Fur trading dominated the Wyoming

economy from the early to middle nineteenth century. However, in 1833, the mineral industry came to Wyoming. The first oil was discovered in the Wind River Basin. Although the oil discovery was important, it did not create a stir again until later in the century.

In 1842, gold was found near South Pass, and prospectors started coming to southern Wyoming. Many gold boom towns such as South Pass City and Atlantic City sprang up during this time.

The interest in Wyoming oil was renewed in 1883, when the first successful well, located at Dallas Field, started producing petroleum. After this rediscovery, the mineral industry took off. Currently, there are over ten thousand oil wells and at least nine hundred natural gas wells in Wyoming.

Wyoming is also a leading producer of uranium. It was first discovered in Wyoming in 1918 in the Silver Cliff mine at Lusk.

The Wyoming economy also relies rather heavily on tourists. Yellowstone, the nation's oldest national park, attracts tens of thousands of visitors each year. In addition, tourists visit several other parks and monuments, including Grand Teton National Park, and the Devils Tower National Monument.

Yellowstone: The First National Park

Yellowstone became the United States' first national park on March 1, 1872, when it was created by an act of Congress. The U.S. government had decided to set aside the Yellowstone area and give it this special status in order to protect it against exploitation by private interests. Although the majority of Yellowstone's nearly three million acres lie within Wyoming's borders, the park spills over into neighboring Idaho and Montana.

Considered one of the greatest wildlife refuges in the world, Yellowstone is home to hundreds of species of plants such as the beautiful fireweed and animals such as grizzly bear, elk, bison, and white pelicans.

Important Events

1805 François Antoine Larocque enters the state to trade furs with the Indians.

1807 John Colter discovers geysers that will become part of Yellowstone National Park.

1812 Robert Stuart leads the first party through South Pass.

1825 William Henry Ashley establishes the first fur-trading rendezvous.

1833 Oil discovered near Wind River Mountains.

1843 Fort Bridger established.

1863 Bozeman Trail opened.

1867 Union Pacific Railroad enters Wyoming.

1867 Cheyenne founded.

1868 Wyoming Territory created in July.

1869 Women granted the right to vote on December 10.

1872 Yellowstone becomes first national park on March 1.

1888 State capitol building completed.

1890 Wyoming becomes forty-fourth state in the Union on July 10.

1902 Shoshone National Forest established, which is the first national forest in the United States.

1906 Devils Tower made nation's first national monument.

1925 Nellie Tayloe Ross becomes first woman governor in nation.

1929 Grand Teton National Park created.

1951 Uranium discovered in many parts of Wyoming.

1954 Titanium deposits discovered.

1960 First intercontinental missile

base opens near Cheyenne.

1966 Bighorn Canyon National Recreation Area established.

1974 Jim Bridger power plant begins operations.

1983 Amtrak discontinues passenger rail service through Wyoming.

1988 Forest fires ravage lands in Wyoming.

1991 Black Hills Indian tribes fight to protect their sacred sites from being turned into a tourist attraction.

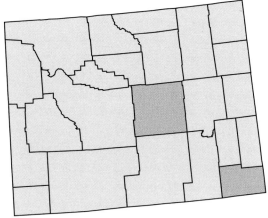

Population Density

Population density for the state of Wyoming was 4.7 persons per square mile in 1990 (1.8 per km2). Average U.S. density was 70.3 persons per square mile in 1990 (27.3 per km2). Wyoming is the second lowest state in terms of density.

Persons Per Square Mile
- 0.0 to 9.9
- 10.0 to 99.9

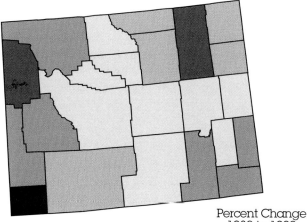

Population Change

The 1990 population figure for the state of Wyoming was 453,588. This is a –3.40 percent decrease from 469,557 in 1980. The next decade will show growth with a population of 489 thousand or a 7.81 percent increase.

Percent Change 1980 to 1990
- –31.9 to –10.0%
- –9.9 to 0.0%
- 0.1 to 19.9%
- 20.0 to 49.9%
- 50.0 to 163.0%

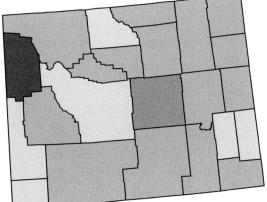

Distribution of Income

The per capita income for the state of Wyoming (current dollars) was $17,423 in 1992. This is a 53.4 percent increase from $11,356 in 1980. Teton County has the highest incomes in the state. Natrona County, home to Casper, is also high.

Per Capita Income (000s) (Current Dollars)
- $10.0 to 12.9
- $13.0 to 15.9
- $16.0 to 19.9
- $20.0 to 37.7

Population Projections

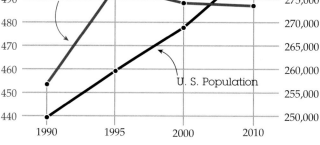

Population in thousands

Wyoming's Population

U. S. Population

Population Change

Year	Population
1950	291,000
1960	331,000
1970	334,000
1980	469,557
1990	453,588
2000	489,000
2010	487,000

Period	Change
1950–1970	14.8%
1970–1980	40.7%
1980–1990	–3.4%
1990–2000	7.7%

Population Facts

State Population, 1993: 470,000

Rank: 50

Population 2000: 489,000 (Rank 50)

Density: 4.7 per sq. mi. (1.8 per km²)

Distribution: 65.0% urban, 35.0% rural

Population Under 5 Years Old: 7.3%

Population Under 18 Years Old: 29.6%

Population Over 65 Years Old: 10.7%

Median Age: 32.0

Number of Households: 169,000

Average Persons Per Household: 2.63

Average Persons Per Family: 3.16

Female Heads of Households: 3.08%

Population That Is Married: 22.22%

Birth Rate: 15.4 per 1,000 population

Death Rate: 7.1 per 1,000 population

Births to Teen Mothers: 13.6%

Marriage Rate: 10.3 per 1,000 population

Divorce Rate: 6.6 per 1,000 population

Violent Crime Rate: 310 per 100,000 pop.

Population on Social Security: 13.9%

Percent Voting for President: 62.3%

Population Profile

Rank. Wyoming ranks 50th among U.S. states in terms of population with 470,000 citizens.

Minority Population. The state's minority population is 9.2 percent. The state's male to female ratio for 1990 was 100.2 males for every 100 females. It was way above the national average of 95.2 males for every 100 females.

Growth. Growing more slowly than the projected national average, the state's population

Government

Capital: Cheyenne (established 1869).

Statehood: Became 44th state on July 10, 1890.

Number of Counties: 23.

Supreme Court Justices: 5, 8-year term.

State Senators: 30, 4-year term.

State Legislators: 64, 2-year term.

United States Senators: 2.

United States Representatives: 1.

Electoral Votes: 3.

State Constitution: Adopted 1889.

Wyoming's Famous Citizens

Arnold, Thurman (1891–1969). Lawyer and author. Wrote several books and served as an assistant attorney general.

Gowdy, Curt (b. 1919). Sportscaster. He broadcast for the Boston Red Sox for 15 years and for the NFL in the 1960s.

Laramie, Jacques (1785–1821). Fur trapper who explored the river named after him.

Moonlight, Thomas (1833–1899). Served as secretary of state for Kansas and, in 1888, became territorial governor of Wyoming.

Morris, Esther (1814–1902). She was justice of the peace in South Pass City and a promoter of women's suffrage.

Rinehart, Mary Roberts (1876–1958). Author of mystery novels such as *The Circular Staircase* and *The Door*.

Ross, Nellie Tayloe (1876–1977). First woman in the United States to serve as a state governor, and also the first woman to head the United States Mint.

Spotted Tail (1833–1881). Sioux Indian chief who attempted compromise as a method of keeping peace with whites.

is expected to reach 487 thousand by the year 2010 (*see graph above*).

Older Citizens. The state's population older than 65 was 47,195 in 1990. It grew 26.9% from 37,175 in 1980.

Younger Citizens. The number of children (under 18 years of age) was 136 thousand in 1990. This represents 29.9 percent of the state's population. The state's school aged population was 96 thousand in 1990. It is expected to remain level at 96 thousand by the year 2000. This represents a 0.0% change.

Urban/Rural. 65.0% of the population of the state live in urban areas while 35.0% live in rural areas.

Largest Cities. Wyoming has two cities with a population greater than 35,000. The populations of the state's largest centers are (starting from the most populous) Cheyenne (50,008), Casper (46,742), Laramie (26,687), Rock Springs (19,050), Gillette (17,635), Sheridan (13,900), Green River (12,711), and Evanston (10,903).

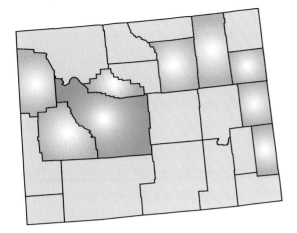

Native American

The Native American population in Wyoming was 9,479 in 1990. This was an increase of 15.71 percent from 8,192 in 1980. Many Native Americans in the state live at the Wind River Reservation.

Presence of Native Americans

 Minor

Moderate

Nationalities

African	155
American	18,105
Arab	219
Austrian	1,266
Czech	2,787
Dutch	7,897
English	67,261
Finnish	1,506
German	124,174
Greek	1,342
Hungarian	931
Irish	37,833
Italian	8,526
Norwegian	11,665
Polish	6,530
Portuguese	643
Russian	1,486
Scottish	10,674
Slovak	1,824
Swedish	12,767
Welsh	3,180
West Indian	56

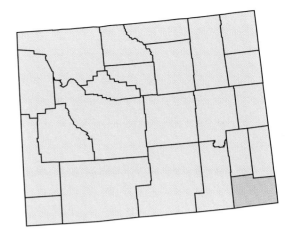

African American

The African American population in Wyoming was 3,606 in 1990. This was an increase of 10.28 percent from 3,270 in 1980. Cheyenne is the home of a majority of the African Americans in the state.

Percent of County Population

- 0.00 to 1.9%
- 2.0 to 2.9%

Statewide Ethnic Composition

Over 94 percent of the population of Wyoming is white. The largest nationalities in this racial group are German, English, and Irish. The next largest group is Hispanics, followed by Native Americans, African Americans, and Asian Americans. Only 18,000 people claim to be American and acknowledge no other nationality.

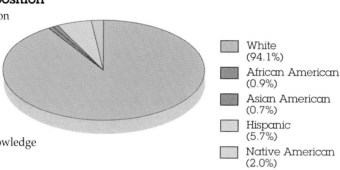

- White (94.1%)
- African American (0.9%)
- Asian American (0.7%)
- Hispanic (5.7%)
- Native American (2.0%)

Education Facts

Total Students 1990: 97,172

Number of School Districts: 49

Expenditure Per Capita on Education 1990: $1,149

Expenditure Per Capita K–12 1990: $1,010

Expenditure Per Pupil 1990: $5,255

Total School Enrollment 1990–1991: 98,210

Rank of Expenditures Per Student: 19th in the U.S.

African American Enrollment: 0.9%

Hispanic Enrollment: 5.9%

Asian/Pacific Islander Enrollment: 0.6%

Native American Enrollment: 1.9%

Mean SAT Score 1991 Verbal: 466

Mean SAT Score 1991 Math: 514

Average Teacher's Salary 1992: $30,400

Rank Teacher's Salary: 29th in U.S.

High School Graduates 1990: 5,800

Total Number of Public Schools: 404

Number of Teachers 1990: 6,773

Student/Teacher Ratio: 14.5

Staff Employed in Public Schools: 13,421

Pupil/Staff Ratio: 7.2

Staff/Teacher Ratio: 2.0

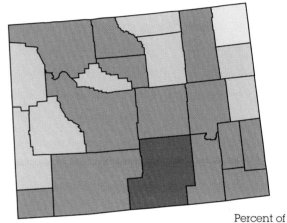

Percent of County Population

- 0.00 to 0.9%
- 1.0 to 2.9%
- 3.0 to 9.9%
- 10.0 to 24.9%

Hispanic[††]

The Hispanic population in Wyoming was 25,751 in 1990. This is an increase of 5.11 percent from 24,499 persons in 1980. Carbon County has the greatest percentage of Hispanics in the state.

[††]A person of Mexican, Puerto Rican, Cuban, or other Spanish culture or origin regardless of race.

Education

Attainment: 85.6 percent of population 25 years or older were high school graduates in 1989, earning Wyoming a ranking of 4th in the United States; 21.9 percent of the state's population had completed college. Institutions of Higher Education: The largest universities and colleges in the state include University of Wyoming, (founded 1887),Laramie. Expenditures per Student: Expenditure increased 104% between 1985 and 1990. Projected High School Graduations: 1998 (5,404), 2004 (4,764); Total Revenues for Education from Federal Sources: $22 million; Total Revenues for Education from State Sources: $279 million; Total Revenues for Education from Local Sources: $267 million; Average Annual Salaries for Public School Principals: N/A.

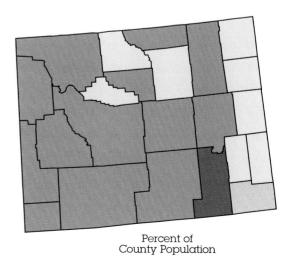

Asian American

The Asian American population in Wyoming was 2,806 in 1990. This is an increase of 43.68 percent from 1,953 persons in 1980. Albany County is the site of the greatest percentage of this ethnic group.

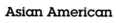

Percent of County Population

- 0.00 to 0.24%
- 0.25 to 0.99%
- 1.00 to 1.99%
- 2.00 to 4.99%

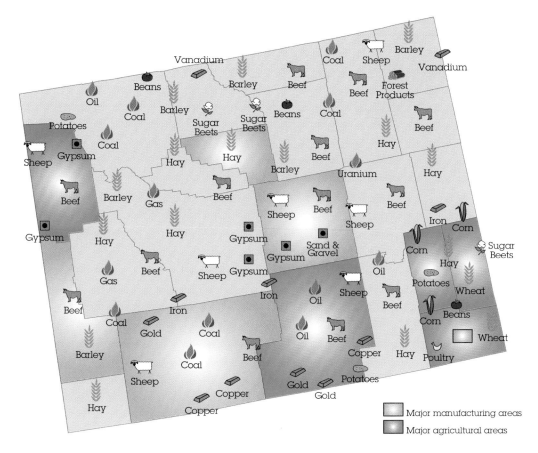

Major manufacturing areas
Major agricultural areas

Agriculture

Wyoming has 34.8 million farm acres. During the last 40 years, Wyoming's farms have grown larger in size and fewer in number. In 1955, 11,000 farms were found in the state. Today, 9,300 remain.

Agriculture adds less than $500 million to the state's gross product annually. The principal commodities in order of marketing receipts are cattle, sugar beets, hay, and sheep.

Beef cattle account for about two-thirds of Wyoming's farm income. They are raised mainly in the eastern part of the state. Grazing pastures cover half of the state's land. Wyoming is third in the nation in the production of sheep and wool. Hay, the leading crop, is grown solely for cattle feed. Certified seed potatoes are grown in Goshen and Laramie counties.

Housing

Owner Occupied Units: 203,411; Average Age of Units: 24 years; Average Value of Housing Units: $61,600; Renter Occupied Units: 51,450; Median Monthly Rent: $333; Housing Starts: 1,800; Existing Home Sales: 10,900.

Economic Facts

Gross State Product: $11,000,000,000 (1989)

Income Per Capita: $17,423

Disposable Personal Income: $15,607

Median Household Income: $27,096

Average Annual Pay, 1988: $20,591

Principal Industries: petroleum products, chemicals, tourism

Major Crops: wheat, hay, beans, potatoes, sugar beets, barley

Fish: N/A

Livestock: cattle, sheep

Non-Fuel Minerals: Benonite, Clay, Sodium Carbonate, Uranium, Gold, Gypsum, Limestone

Organic Fuel Minerals: Coal, Petroleum

Civilian Labor Force: 240,000 (Women: 105,000)

Total Employed: 228,000 (Women: 100,000)

Median Value of Housing: $61,600

Median Contract Rent: $333 per month

Economic Sectors 1992

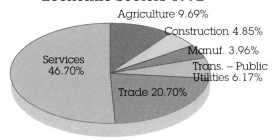

Agriculture 9.69%
Construction 4.85%
Manuf. 3.96%
Trans. – Public Utilities 6.17%
Trade 20.70%
Services 46.70%

Manufacturing

Manufacturing in Wyoming contributes only 3 percent to the gross state product, a lower figure than any other state. All manufactured goods produced in Wyoming have a combined added value by manufacture of only $400 million; this is also lower than any other state. Wyoming's leading manufacturing activities are ones related to chemical production. Other manufacturing industries include petroleum refining, paper products, and machinery.

Factories in Cheyenne and Basin produce fertilizer, Wyoming's chief chemical product. Oil refineries are located in many parts of the state, including Casper, Sinclair, and La Barge. Sawmills can also be found throughout Wyoming, especially in Cheyenne, Afton, and Laramie.

Transportation

Wyoming is sparsely populated, and probably has fewer roads because of this. Overall, Wyoming has approximately 38,000 miles of highways and roads, but only around 60 percent are surfaced. Wyoming's interstates include I-80, which crosses the southern part of the state, and I-25 and I-90, both in the east.

Union Pacific handles most of Wyoming's rail freight, but the Burlington Northern and Chicago and Northwestern rail lines provide service as well. Passenger rail service to Wyoming was discontinued in 1983. Wyoming's busiest airport is located in Casper. Other important airports are located in Cheyenne and the Riverton-Lander area. An unusual, yet important part of Wyoming's transportation network are its high-voltage transmission lines, which carry electricity.

Energy and Transportation Facts

Energy. Yearly Consumption: 391 tril. BTUs (residential, 9.2%; commercial, 10.2%; industrial, 60.4%; transportation, 19.9%); Annual Energy Expenditures Per Capita: $3,245; Nuclear Power Plants Located in State: 0; Source of Energy Consumed: Petroleum— 17.1%; Natural Gas— 15.2%; Coal— 66.5%; Hydroelectric Power—1.2%; Nuclear Power—0.0%.

Transportation. Highway Miles: 39,022 (interstates, 913; urban, 2,489; rural, 36,533); Average Yearly Auto Insurance: $366 (48th); Auto Fatalities Rank: 19th; Registered Motor Vehicles: 482,815; Workers in Carpools: 18.3%; Workers Using Public Trans: 1.4%.

Employment

Employment. Wyoming employed 226,000 people in 1993. Most work in government jobs (57,200 persons or 25.3% of the workforce). Manufacturing accounts for 4.2% or 9,500 workers. Wholesale and retail trade account for 21.2% or 47,900 workers. Social and personal services account for 42,900 workers (19.0%). Construction employs 12,200 workers (5.4%). Transportation and utilities account for 6.4% or 14,500 persons. Agriculture employs 13,600 workers or 6.0%. Finance, real estate, and insurance account for 4.7% or 41,200 workers. Mining employs 7.8%, or 17,700 workers.

Unemployment. Unemployment has decreased to 5.4% in 1993 from a rate of 7.1% in 1985. Today's figure is lower than the national average of 6.8% as shown below.

Unemployment Rate

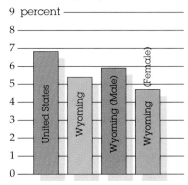

PUERTO RICO

Facts about Puerto Rico. Abbreviation: PR (postal); Capital: San Juan; Population: 3,522,037; Median Age: 28.4; Population Density: 1,027.9 per sq. mi. (642.3 per km²); Males per 100 Females: 93.9; Number of Households: 1,054,924; Average Persons Per Household: 3.31; High School Graduates: 410,559; Total Employed: 934,736; Unemployment Rate: 20.4; Median Income: $9,988; Birth Rate: 18.9; Death Rate: 7.4; Public Elem. & Sec. School Enrollment: 642,392; Public Elem. & Sec. School Teachers: 37,291; Expenditures per Pupil: $1,779; Number of Farms: 20,245; Farm Cuerdas*: 886,846; Total Industry Establishments (Minus Agriculture): 35,742.   *one cuerda=.97 acre.

In 1952 the island of Puerto Rico was made an autonomous part of the United States. The official name is the Commonwealth of Puerto Rico, or *Estado Libre Asociado de Puerto Rico.*

Location. Puerto Rico is located south and east of Florida in the Caribbean Sea. It is the easternmost island in the chain called the Greater Antilles. Puerto Rico is approximately 1,000 mi. from Miami in the continental United States. The geographic center of Puerto Rico is lat. 18° 13.8' N; long. 66° 28.8' W.

Size. Puerto Rico's area is approximately 3,500 sq. mi. (9,100 km2).

Geographic Extent. The north/south extent of Puerto Rico averages 35 mi. (530 km). The island extends 112 mi. (186 km) east/west.

VIRGIN ISLANDS

Facts about Virgin Islands. Abbreviation: VI (postal); Capital: Charlotte Amalie; Population: 101,809; Median Age: 28.2; Population Density: 760.9 per sq. mi. (475.9 per km²); Males per 100 Females: 93.6; Number of Households: 32,020; Average Persons Per Household: 3.14; High School Graduates: 14,021; Total Employed: 44,267; Unemployment Rate: 6.7; Median Income: $24,036; Birth Rate: 22.3; Death Rate: 4.7; Public Elem. & Sec. School Enrollment: 22,346; Public Elem. & Sec. School Teachers: 1,581; Expenditures per Pupil: $5,368; Number of Farms: 267; Farm Acres: 17,785; Total Industry Establishments (Minus Agriculture): 2,604.

The Virgin Islands of the United States were bought from Denmark in 1917. The people living on the islands are United States citizens and have an elected governor and legislature.

Location. The U.S. Virgin Islands are located south and east of Florida in the Caribbean Sea 40 miles (64 km) east of Puerto Rico. The geographic center of the U.S. Virgin Islands is lat. 17° 40.0' N; long. 64° 45.0' W.

Size. The U.S. Virgin Islands are made up of three large islands and have an area of approximately 136 sq. mi. (352 km2).

Geographic Extent. The approximate north/south extent of the U.S. Virgin Islands is 45 mi. (72 km). The islands extends approximately 35 mi. (56 km) to the east/west.

GUAM

Facts about Guam. Abbreviation: GU (postal); Capital: Agana; Population: 133,152; Median Age: 25.0; Population Density: 637.1 per sq. mi. (396.3 per km²); Males per 100 Females: 114.0; Number of Households: 31,373; Average Persons Per Household: 3.97; High School Graduates: 22,220; Total Employed: 52,144; Unemployment Rate: 3.8; Median Income: $31,178; Birth Rate: 28.8; Death Rate: 3.9; Public Elem. & Sec. School Enrollment: 28,244; Public Elem. & Sec. School Teachers: 1,699; Expenditures per Pupil: $4,326; Number of Farms: 351; Farm Acres: 13,134; Total Industry Establishments (Minus Agriculture): 1,490.

The island of Guam was first occupied by the United States in the early 1900s with the construction of a naval station. In 1950 the island of Guam became a United States territory administered by appointed governors until 1970 when elections were held.

Location. Guam is located in the Pacific Ocean approximately 1,500 miles (2,400 km) east of the Philippines, and is the southernmost island in the Northern Marianas. The geographic center of Guam is approximately lat. 13° 21.0' N; long. 144° 52.0' E.

Size. Guam's area is approximately 209 sq. mi. (541 km2).

Geographic Extent. The north/south extent of Guam averages 6 mi. (11.4 km). The island extends 30 mi. (48 km) east/west.

AMERICAN SAMOA & NORTHERN MARIANA ISLANDS

Facts about American Samoa & Northern Mariana Islands. Abbreviation: AS (postal), MP (postal); Capital: Pago Pago (AS), Saipan (MP); Population: 46,773 (AS), 43,345 (MP); Median Age: 20.9 (AS), 27.4 (MP); Population Density: 607.4 per sq. mi. (379.7 per km²) (AS), 235.6 per sq. mi. (151.3 per km²) (MP); Males per 100 Females: 105.6 (AS), 111.0 (MP); Number of Households: 6,607 (AS), 6,873 (MP); Average Persons Per Household: 7.00 (AS), 4.63 (MP); High School Graduates: 6,253 (AS), 8,659 (MP); Total Employed: 13,461 (AS), 25,965 (MP); Unemployment Rate: 5.1 (AS), 2.3 (MP); Median Income: $15,979 (AS), $21,275 (MP).

Location. American Samoa is located 1,800 miles (2,900 km) northeast of New Zealand in the south-central Pacific Ocean. The Northern Marianas are located in the Pacific Ocean approximately 1,500 miles (2,400 km) east of the Philippines. The geographic center of American Samoa is approximately lat. 14° 26.0' S; long. 170° 5.0' W. The geographic center of the Northern Marianas is approximately lat. 18° 0.0' N; long. 144° 58.0 E.

Size. American Samoa's area is 77 sq. mi. (199 km2). The Northern Marianas's area is 179 sq. mi. (286 km2).

Geographic Extent. The north/south extent of the Northern Marianas averages 600 mi. (1,140 km).

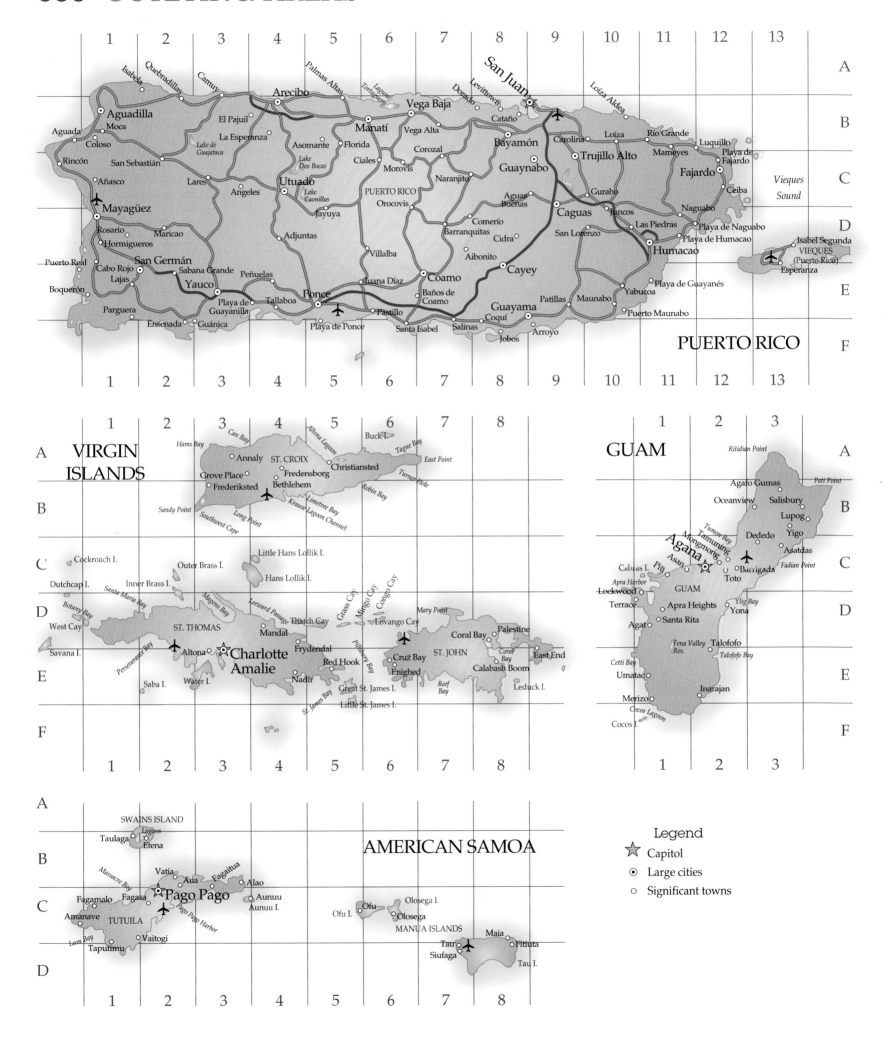

STATE FAST FACTS
& METRO FAST FACTS

	State Population	Population Per Sq. Mile	Population Per Sq. Km	Pct. Pop. Under 5 yrs.	Pct. Pop. Under 18 yrs.	Pct. Pop. Over 65 yrs.
Alabama	4,187,000	79.6	30.7	7.2	26	13
Alaska	599,000	1	0.4	9.7	31.5	4.3
Arizona	3,936,000	32.3	12.5	8.4	27.3	13.4
Arkansas	2,424,000	45.1	17.4	7.1	26.2	14.9
California	31,211,000	190.8	73.7	9	27.3	10.5
Colorado	3,566,000	31.8	12.3	7.6	26.2	10
Connecticut	3,277,000	678.4	262	7.3	23.5	13.9
Delaware	700,000	340.8	131.6	7.5	25	12.3
District of Columbia	578,000	9884.4	3841.1	7	19.9	13.1
Florida	13,679,000	239.6	92.5	7	23	18.4
Georgia	6,917,000	111.9	43.2	7.9	26.7	10.1
Hawaii	1,172,000	172.5	66.6	7.8	25.3	11.4
Idaho	1,099,000	12.2	4.7	7.8	30.4	11.9
Illinois	11,697,000	205.6	79.4	7.7	26	12.6
Indiana	5,713,000	154.6	59.7	7.2	25.8	12.7
Iowa	2,814,000	49.7	19.2	6.9	26.1	15.4
Kansas	2,531,000	30.3	11.7	7.4	26.9	13.9
Kentucky	3,789,000	92.8	35.8	6.9	25.7	12.7
Louisiana	4,295,000	96.9	37.4	7.9	28.9	11.2
Maine	1,239,000	39.8	15.4	6.7	24.8	13.6
Maryland	4,965,000	489.2	188.9	7.8	25	11
Massachusetts	6,012,000	767.6	296.4	7.2	23.1	13.9
Michigan	9,478,000	163.6	63.2	7.7	26.6	12.2
Minnesota	4,517,000	55	21.2	7.5	26.9	12.5
Mississippi	2,643,000	54	20.8	7.8	28.6	12.5
Missouri	5,234,000	74.3	41.8	7.3	26	14.1
Montana	839,000	5.5	2.1	7	27.4	13.4
Nebraska	1,607,000	20.5	7.9	7.4	27.3	14.1
Nevada	1,389,000	10.9	4.2	8	25.5	11
New Hampshire	1,125,000	123.7	47.8	7.4	25.2	11.8
New Jersey	7,879,000	1042	402.3	7.4	23.9	13.6
New Mexico	1,616,000	12.5	4.8	8.4	29.7	10.9
New York	18,197,000	381	147.1	7.5	24.4	13.1
North Carolina	6,945,000	136.1	52.5	7.2	24.3	12.4
North Dakota	635,000	9.3	3.6	7.1	27	14.6
Ohio	11,091,000	264.9	102.3	7.2	25.6	13.2
Oklahoma	3,231,000	45.8	17.7	7.2	26.7	13.5
Oregon	3,032,000	29.6	11.4	7.1	25.7	13.8
Pennsylvania	12,048,000	265.1	102.4	6.8	23.7	15.7
Rhode Island	1,000,000	960.3	370.7	7.1	23.2	15.2
South Carolina	3,643,000	115.8	44.5	7.6	26.2	11.6
South Dakota	715,000	9.2	3.5	7.6	28.7	14.7
Tennessee	5,099,000	118.3	45.7	7	24.8	12.7
Texas	18,031,000	64.9	25	8.4	28.7	10.2
Utah	1,860,000	21	8.1	9.7	36.1	8.8
Vermont	576,000	60.8	23.5	7	25.3	12
Virginia	6,491,000	156.3	60.3	7.3	24.5	10.9
Washington	5,255,000	73.1	28.2	7.6	26.4	11.7
West Virginia	1,820,000	74.5	28.7	6	24.2	15.2
Wisconsin	5,038,000	90.1	34.8	7.2	26.6	13.3
Wyoming	470,000	4.7	1.8	7.3	29.6	10.7

	Population White (1,000)	Pop. African Am. (1,000)	Pop. Native American (1,000)	Pop. Asian & Pac. Is. (1,000)	Population Hispanic (1,000)	Percent Minority Pop.
Alabama	2,976	1,021	17	22	25	26.8
Alaska	415	22	86	20	18	26.5
Arizona	2,963	111	204	55	688	28.9
Arkansas	1,945	374	13	13	20	17.8
California	20,524	2,209	242	2,846	7,688	43.6
Colorado	2,905	133	28	60	424	19.6
Connecticut	2,859	274	7	51	213	16.6
Delaware	535	112	2	9	16	20.9
District of Columbia	180	400	1	11	33	73.3
Florida	10,749	1,760	36	154	1,574	27.2
Georgia	4,600	1,747	13	76	109	30
Hawaii	370	27	5	685	81	72.1
Idaho	950	3	14	9	53	7.9
Illinois	8,953	1,694	22	285	904	25.4
Indiana	5,021	432	13	38	99	10.5
Iowa	2,683	48	7	25	33	4.1
Kansas	2,232	143	22	32	94	11.7
Kentucky	3,392	263	6	18	22	8.4
Louisiana	2,839	1,299	19	41	93	34.4
Maine	1,208	5	6	7	7	2
Maryland	3,394	1,190	13	140	125	30.7
Massachusetts	5,405	300	12	143	288	12.4
Michigan	7,756	1,292	56	105	202	17.8
Minnesota	4,130	95	50	78	54	6.3
Mississippi	1,633	915	9	13	16	37
Missouri	4,486	548	20	41	62	13.1
Montana	741	2	48	4	12	8.3
Nebraska	1,481	57	12	12	37	7.6
Nevada	1,013	79	20	38	124	21.7
New Hampshire	1,087	7	2	9	11	2.7
New Jersey	6,130	1,037	15	273	740	26.7
New Mexico	1,146	30	134	14	579	50
New York	13,385	2,859	63	694	2,214	32.4
North Carolina	5,008	1,456	80	52	77	25.1
North Dakota	604	4	26	3	5	5.9
Ohio	9,522	1,155	20	91	140	13
Oklahoma	2,584	234	252	34	86	19.3
Oregon	2,637	46	38	69	113	9.4
Pennsylvania	10,520	1,090	15	137	232	12.4
Rhode Island	917	39	4	18	46	10.7
South Carolina	2,407	1,040	8	22	31	31.7
South Dakota	638	3	51	3	5	8.9
Tennessee	4,048	778	10	32	33	17.5
Texas	12,775	2,022	66	319	4,340	39.7
Utah	1,616	12	24	33	85	8.9
Vermont	555	2	2	3	4	1.9
Virginia	4,792	1,163	15	159	160	24.2
Washington	4,309	150	81	211	215	13.5
West Virginia	1,726	56	2	7	8	4.2
Wisconsin	4,513	245	39	54	93	8.8
Wyoming	427	4	9	3	26	9.2

	Males/ 100 Females	Median Age	Number of Households (1,000)	Persons Per Household	Persons Per Family	Pct. Female Heads
Alabama	92	33	1,507	2.62	3.13	4.98
Alaska	111.4	29.4	189	2.8	3.33	3.31
Arizona	97.6	32.2	1,369	2.62	3.16	3.88
Arkansas	93.1	33.8	891	2.57	3.06	4.21
California	100.2	31.5	10,381	2.79	3.32	4.01
Colorado	98.1	32.5	1,282	2.51	3.07	3.78
Connecticut	94	34.4	1,230	2.59	3.1	4.27
Delaware	94.1	32.9	247	2.61	3.09	4.4
District of Columbia	87.4	33.5	250	2.26	3.15	8
Florida	93.8	36.4	5,135	2.46	2.95	4.24
Georgia	94.3	31.6	2,367	2.66	3.16	5.09
Hawaii	103.6	32.6	356	3.01	3.48	3.38
Idaho	99	31.5	361	2.73	3.23	2.87
Illinois	94.5	32.8	4,202	2.65	3.23	4.42
Indiana	94.1	32.8	2,065	2.61	3.11	3.93
Iowa	93.9	34	1,064	2.52	3.05	3.07
Kansas	96.2	32.9	945	2.53	3.08	3.29
Kentucky	94	33	1,380	2.6	3.08	4.33
Louisiana	92.8	31	1,499	2.74	3.28	5.55
Maine	94.9	33.9	465	2.56	3.03	3.61
Maryland	96.7	33	1,749	2.67	3.14	4.85
Massachusetts	92.4	33.6	2,247	2.58	3.15	4.5
Michigan	94.4	32.6	3,419	2.66	3.16	4.76
Minnesota	96.2	22.5	1,648	2.58	3.13	3.24
Mississippi	91.7	31.2	911	2.75	3.27	5.64
Missouri	92.9	33.5	1,961	2.54	3.08	4.07
Montana	98.1	33.8	306	2.53	3.08	3.3
Nebraska	95.1	33	602	2.54	3.11	3.18
Nevada	103.7	33.3	466	2.53	3.06	3.95
New Hampshire	96.1	32.8	411	2.62	3.09	3.14
New Jersey	93.5	34.5	2,795	2.7	3.21	4.38
New Mexico	96.8	31.3	543	2.74	3.26	4.26
New York	92.1	33.9	6,639	2.63	3.22	5.11
North Carolina	94.1	33.1	2,517	2.54	3.03	4.67
North Dakota	99.3	32.4	241	2.55	3.13	2.74
Ohio	93	33.3	4,088	2.59	3.12	4.41
Oklahoma	94.8	33.2	1,206	2.53	3.06	3.99
Oregon	96.7	34.5	1,103	2.52	3.02	3.58
Pennsylvania	92	35	4,496	2.57	3.1	4.27
Rhode Island	92.3	34	378	2.55	3.11	4.42
South Carolina	93.9	32	1,258	2.68	3.16	5.08
South Dakota	96.9	32.5	259	2.59	3.16	2.98
Tennessee	92.9	33.6	1,854	2.56	3.05	4.77
Texas	97.1	30.8	6,071	2.73	3.28	4.13
Utah	98.7	26.2	537	3.15	3.67	2.85
Vermont	95.9	33	211	2.57	3.06	3.44
Virginia	96.2	32.6	2,292	2.61	3.09	4.12
Washington	98.4	33.1	1,872	2.53	3.06	3.61
West Virginia	92.5	35.4	689	2.55	3.05	4.1
Wisconsin	95.8	32.9	1,822	2.61	3.14	3.57
Wyoming	100.2	32	169	2.63	3.16	3.08

	Pct. Population that is Married	Birth Rate Per 1,000	Death Rate Per 1,000	Pct. Births to Teen Mothers	Marriage Rate Per 1,000	Divorce Rate Per 1,000
Alabama	21.24	15.7	9.7	18.2	10.5	6.1
Alaska	19.29	21.6	4	9.7	10.8	5.5
Arizona	20.4	18.8	7.9	14.2	10.2	6.9
Arkansas	22.43	15.5	10.5	19.7	14.8	6.9
California	18.38	20.6	7.2	11.6	7.9	4.3
Colorado	20.95	16.2	6.6	11.3	9.4	5.5
Connecticut	20.83	15.2	8.4	8.2	8.6	3.2
Delaware	20.71	16.7	8.7	11.9	8.2	4.4
District of Columbia	10.4	19.5	12	17.8	7.9	4.5
Florida	21.58	15.4	10.4	13.9	10.9	6.3
Georgia	20.17	17.4	8	16.7	9.8	5.5
Hawaii	18.99	18.5	6.1	10.5	16.1	4.6
Idaho	22.27	16.3	7.4	12.3	14.6	6.5
Illinois	19.88	17.1	9	13.1	8.3	3.8
Indiana	21.68	15.6	8.9	14.5	9.6	(NA)
Iowa	22.68	14.2	9.7	10.2	8.7	3.9
Kansas	22.3	15.7	9	12.3	9.2	5
Kentucky	23.38	14.8	9.5	17.5	13.8	5.8
Louisiana	19.04	17.1	8.9	17.6	9.4	(NA)
Maine	22.03	14.1	9	10.8	9.5	4.3
Maryland	19.84	16.8	8	10.5	9.7	3.4
Massachusetts	19.45	15.4	8.8	8	8.1	2.8
Michigan	20.26	16.5	8.5	13.5	8.2	4.3
Minnesota	21.54	15.5	7.9	8	7.7	3.5
Mississippi	19.36	16.9	9.8	21.3	9.3	5.5
Missouri	21.58	15.5	9.8	14.4	9.5	5.1
Montana	20.97	14.5	8.6	11.5	8.7	5.1
Nebraska	22.21	15.4	9.4	9.8	7.7	4
Nevada	19.93	18	7.8	12.6	105.6	11.4
New Hampshire	22.11	15.8	7.7	7.2	9.4	4.7
New Jersey	20.42	15.8	9.1	8.4	7.5	3
New Mexico	20.05	18.1	7	16.3	8.5	4.9
New York	18.43	16.5	9.4	9.1	9.4	3.2
North Carolina	21.49	15.8	8.6	16.2	7.8	5.1
North Dakota	22.29	14.5	8.9	8.6	7.3	3.6
Ohio	21.15	15.4	9.1	13.8	8.7	4.7
Oklahoma	22.13	15.1	9.7	16.2	10.3	7.7
Oregon	21.58	15.1	8.8	12	8.8	5.5
Pennsylvania	21.06	14.5	10.3	10.9	7.2	3.3
Rhode Island	20.16	15.1	9.5	10.5	8.1	3.7
South Carolina	20.47	16.8	8.5	17.1	15.7	4.5
South Dakota	21.91	15.8	9.1	10.8	10.8	3.7
Tennessee	21.73	15.4	9.5	17.6	13.4	6.5
Texas	20.23	18.6	7.4	15.6	10.7	5.5
Utah	20.2	21.1	5.3	10.3	11	5.1
Vermont	21.13	14.7	8.2	8.5	10.7	4.5
Virginia	21.05	16.1	7.8	11.7	11.5	4.4
Washington	21.15	16.3	7.6	10.8	10	5.9
West Virginia	22.64	12.6	10.8	17.8	7.2	5.3
Wisconsin	21.42	14.9	8.7	10.2	8.4	3.6
Wyoming	22.22	15.4	7.1	13.6	10.3	6.6

	Pct. Population on Social Security	Pct. Voting for President	School Age Population (1,000)	Percent Urban	Percent Rural	Pct. Pop. in Metro Areas
Alabama	17.7	55.2	722	60.4	39.6	67.1
Alaska	6.1	65.4	112	67.5	32.5	41.1
Arizona	16.2	54.1	615	87.5	12.5	84.7
Arkansas	19.9	53.8	434	53.5	46.5	44.2
California	12.3	49.1	4,890	92.6	7.4	96.8
Colorado	12.8	62.7	573	82.4	17.6	81.5
Connecticut	16.2	63.8	476	79.1	20.9	95.7
Delaware	15.9	55.2	99	73	27	83
District of Columbia	13.1	49.6	84	100	0	100
Florida	20.6	50.2	1,817	84.8	15.2	92.9
Georgia	13.7	46.9	1,145	63.2	36.8	66.9
Hawaii	13.3	41.9	174	89	11	75.5
Idaho	15.5	65.2	214	57.4	42.6	29.4
Illinois	15.4	58.9	1,800	84.6	15.4	83.8
Indiana	16.4	55.2	955	64.9	35.1	71.5
Iowa	18.9	65.3	467	60.6	39.4	43.2
Kansas	16.6	63	432	69.1	30.9	53.8
Kentucky	17.7	53.7	623	51.8	48.2	47.6
Louisiana	15.6	59.8	791	68.1	31.9	73.5
Maine	17.7	72	213	44.6	55.4	36.1
Maryland	12.9	53.4	717	81.3	18.7	92.8
Massachusetts	16.5	60.2	829	84.3	15.7	96.2
Michigan	16.2	61.7	1,572	70.5	29.5	82.8
Minnesota	15.3	71.6	743	69.9	30.1	68.8
Mississippi	17.7	52.8	496	47.1	52.9	30.1
Missouri	17.9	62	816	68.7	31.3	68.2
Montana	17.6	70.1	151	52.5	47.5	23.9
Nebraska	17.1	63.2	271	66.1	33.9	49.9
Nevada	13.9	50	187	88.3	11.7	84.4
New Hampshire	15.1	63.1	177	51	49	59.4
New Jersey	16	56.3	1,096	89.4	10.6	100
New Mexico	14.7	51.6	308	73	27	55.6
New York	15.9	50.9	2,571	84.3	15.7	91.8
North Carolina	16.5	50.1	1,084	50.4	49.6	65.2
North Dakota	17.6	67.3	118	53.3	46.7	40.3
Ohio	16.7	60.6	1,766	74.1	25.9	81.4
Oklahoma	17	59.7	575	67.7	32.3	59.4
Oregon	17.4	65.7	464	70.5	29.5	69.8
Pennsylvania	18.9	54.3	1,654	68.9	31.1	84.9
Rhode Island	18.3	58.4	136	86	14	93.5
South Carolina	15.7	45	620	54.6	45.4	69.5
South Dakota	18.5	67	129	50	50	31.7
Tennessee	17.1	52.4	818	60.9	39.1	65.5
Texas	13	49.1	3,315	80.3	19.7	83.4
Utah	11.2	65.1	441	87	13	77.5
Vermont	15.9	67.5	94	32.2	67.8	26.9
Virginia	13.6	52.8	1,005	69.4	30.6	77.1
Washington	14.5	59.9	812	76.4	23.6	82.9
West Virginia	20.7	50.6	318	36.1	63.9	41.7
Wisconsin	17.2	69	783	65.7	34.3	68.1
Wyoming	13.9	62.3	96	65	35	29.6

	Pct. One-Parent Families	Pct. High School Grads. or Higher	Hazardous Waste Sites	Per. Cap. Income (Current $)	Med. House-hold Income	Pct. Persons Below Poverty
Alabama	24.3	66.9	12	$16,220	$23,597	18.3
Alaska	23	86.6	7	$21,603	$41,408	9
Arizona	25.5	78.7	10	$17,119	$27,540	15.7
Arkansas	22.9	66.3	12	$15,439	$21,147	19.1
California	25.1	76.2	95	$21,278	$35,798	12.5
Colorado	23.6	84.4	17	$20,124	$30,140	11.7
Connecticut	22.5	79.2	15	$26,979	$41,721	6.8
Delaware	24.3	77.5	19	$21,451	$34,875	8.7
District of Columbia	54.7	73.1	0	$26,360	$30,727	16.9
Florida	26.4	74.4	55	$19,397	$27,483	12.7
Georgia	25.9	70.9	13	$18,130	$29,021	14.7
Hawaii	19.2	80.1	2	$21,218	$38,829	8.3
Idaho	18.6	79.7	9	$16,067	$25,257	13.3
Illinois	24	76.2	37	$21,608	$32,252	11.9
Indiana	22.1	75.6	33	$18,043	$28,797	10.7
Iowa	18.9	80.1	21	$18,287	$26,229	11.5
Kansas	19.9	81.3	10	$19,376	$27,291	11.5
Kentucky	21.6	64.6	19	$16,534	$22,534	19
Louisiana	28.7	68.3	12	$15,712	$21,949	23.6
Maine	21.6	78.8	9	$18,226	$27,854	10.8
Maryland	25.4	78.4	10	$22,974	$39,386	8.3
Massachusetts	23.9	80	26	$24,059	$36,952	8.9
Michigan	26.6	76.8	77	$19,508	$31,020	13.1
Minnesota	19.6	82.4	42	$20,049	$30,909	10.2
Mississippi	29	64.3	2	$14,088	$20,136	25.2
Missouri	22.9	73.9	23	$18,835	$26,362	13.3
Montana	21.5	81	8	$16,062	$22,988	16.1
Nebraska	18.9	81.8	10	$19,084	$26,016	11.1
Nevada	26.6	78.8	1	$20,266	$31,011	10.2
New Hampshire	18.2	82.2	17	$22,934	$36,329	6.4
New Jersey	21.6	76.7	108	$26,457	$40,927	7.6
New Mexico	26.1	75.1	11	$15,353	$24,087	20.6
New York	27.5	74.8	83	$23,534	$32,965	13
North Carolina	24.2	70	23	$17,667	$26,647	13
North Dakota	16.9	76.7	2	$16,854	$23,213	14.4
Ohio	23.8	75.7	33	$18,624	$28,706	12.5
Oklahoma	22.7	74.6	10	$16,198	$23,577	16.7
Oregon	24	81.5	9	$18,202	$27,250	12.4
Pennsylvania	21.7	74.7	98	$20,253	$29,069	11.1
Rhode Island	23.8	72	12	$20,299	$32,181	9.6
South Carolina	25.5	68.3	24	$15,989	$26,256	15.4
South Dakota	19.1	77.1	4	$16,558	$22,503	15.9
Tennessee	24.1	67.1	14	$17,341	$24,807	15.7
Texas	22.6	72.1	29	$17,892	$27,016	18.1
Utah	16.7	85.1	13	$15,325	$29,470	11.4
Vermont	21.8	80.8	8	$18,834	$29,792	9.9
Virginia	21.5	75.2	22	$20,629	$33,328	10.2
Washington	23.7	83.8	50	$20,398	$31,183	10.9
West Virginia	20.2	66	5	$15,065	$20,795	19.7
Wisconsin	21.2	78.6	40	$18,727	$29,442	10.7
Wyoming	20	83	3	$17,423	$27,096	11.9

	Energy Expend. Per Person	Total Students	Total School Districts	Educ. Expend. Per Capita	Educ. Expend. Per Cap. (K-12)	Expend. Per Pupil
Alabama	$2,076	723,343	129	624	550	3,648
Alaska	$3,869	109,280	54	1,568	1,321	6,952
Arizona	$1,786	607,615	238	867	631	4,196
Arkansas	$2,014	43,496	329	621	558	3,419
California	$1,634	4,771,978	1,074	811	750	4,826
Colorado	$1,592	562,755	176	787	716	4,702
Connecticut	$1,865	461,560	166	1,129	1,067	8,455
Delaware	$2,138	97,808	19	835	782	6,016
District of Columbia	$1,787	81,301	1	945	884	8,221
Florida	$1,620	1,772,349	67	787	654	5,003
Georgia	$1,990	1,126,535	186	796	729	4,852
Hawaii	$1,973	169,493	1	710	639	5,008
Idaho	$1,810	214,932	115	668	607	3,211
Illinois	$1,963	1,797,355	964	728	652	5,062
Indiana	$2,204	954,165	303	728	639	4,398
Iowa	$1,860	478,486	431	777	728	4,877
Kansas	$2,146	430,864	304	819	725	5,044
Kentucky	$1,987	630,688	177	629	583	$4,390
Louisiana	$3,235	783,025	66	620	561	4,041
Maine	$2,076	213,775	282	974	882	5,894
Maryland	$1,654	698,806	24	891	803	6,184
Massachusetts	$1,755	825,588	352	826	781	6,351
Michigan	$1,806	1,576,785	561	888	788	5,257
Minnesota	$1,717	39,553	436	933	390	5,360
Mississippi	$1,928	50,202	152	626	573	3,322
Missouri	$1,850	807,934	543	$676	$819	4,479
Montana	$2,111	151,265	548	801	733	4,794
Nebraska	$1,981	27,092	838	652	612	4,080
Nevada	$2,017	186,834	17	878	647	4,677
New Hampshire	$1,777	171,696	170	827	731	5,474
New Jersey	$2,071	1,076,005	603	1,114	1,083	8,451
New Mexico	$1,966	296,057	88	857	687	4,446
New York	$1,531	2,565,841	721	1,091	1,020	8,680
North Carolina	$1,899	1,080,744	134	737	669	4,635
North Dakota	$2,475	117,816	280	672	610	3,685
Ohio	$1,945	1,767,159	613	720	651	$5,269
Oklahoma	$1,992	57,858	604	683	583	3,835
Oregon	$1,765	472,394	303	873	781	5,291
Pennsylvania	$1,872	1,655,279	501	789	717	6,534
Rhode Island	$1,581	135,729	37	827	806	6,989
South Carolina	$1,977	616,177	91	678	605	3,843
South Dakota	$1,938	127,329	185	618	556	3,730
Tennessee	$1,993	81,966	141	575	542	3,707
Texas	$2,549	3,328,514	1,062	849	734	4,326
Utah	$1,599	437,446	40	738	651	2,767
Vermont	$1,876	94,779	276	921	840	5,740
Virginia	$1,827	985,346	136	852	752	5,335
Washington	$1,759	810,232	296	966	738	5,042
West Virginia	$2,185	32,754	55	725	678	4,695
Wisconsin	$1,654	782,905	429	887	811	5,946
Wyoming	$3,371	97,172	49	1,149	1,010	5,255

	Total Enrollment	Pct. African Am. Enrollment	Pct. Hispanic Enrollment	Pct. Asian Enrollment	Pct. Native Am. Enrollment	Avg. Teacher's Salary
Alabama	726,158	35.7	0.2	0.5	0.7	$27,000
Alaska	112,161	4.5	1.9	3.6	22.4	$44,700
Arizona	636,500	4.1	23.7	1.5	6.6	$31,200
Arkansas	436,460	24	0.4	0.6	0.2	$26,600
California	4,950,474	8.7	33	10.4	0.8	$40,200
Colorado	569,792	5.1	16.1	2.2	0.9	$33,100
Connecticut	472,970	12.5	9.7	2	0.2	$47,000
Delaware	99,658	26.9	2.6	1.5	0.1	$34,500
District of Columbia	80,694	90.7	4.6	0.9	0	$41,300
Florida	1,861,592	23.8	11.9	1.4	0.2	$31,100
Georgia	1,151,687	37.9	0.6	0.8	0.1	$29,500
Hawaii	171,056	2.6	2.3	71.7	0.3	$34,500
Idaho	220,840	0.3	4.9	0.8	1.3	$26,300
Illinois	1,784,853	21.9	9.3	2.6	0.1	$36,500
Indiana	949,133	10.9	1.8	0.6	0.1	$34,800
Iowa	483,652	2.7	1.1	1.3	0.3	$29,200
Kansas	436,250	8	4.2	1.4	1	$30,700
Kentucky	630,091	9.4	0.2	0.4	0	$30,900
Louisiana	779,161	44.1	1	1.1	0.4	$27,000
Maine	210,200	0.5	0.2	0.8	0.2	$30,100
Maryland	715,152	32.7	2.1	3.3	0.2	$39,500
Massachusetts	834,159	7.5	7.4	3.2	0.1	$37,300
Michigan	1,582,321	17.8	2.3	1.2	0.9	$41,100
Minnesota	751,913	3.1	1.2	2.9	1.6	$33,700
Mississippi	500,122	50.6	0.1	0.4	0.1	$24,400
Missouri	810,450	14.9	0.7	0.8	0.2	$28,900
Montana	151,669	0.3	0.9	0.5	5.5	$27,600
Nebraska	273,002	5.3	2.3	1	1.1	$27,200
Nevada	201,310	9.2	9.8	3.3	2	$33,900
New Hampshire	172,807	0.9	0.9	1	0.2	$33,200
New Jersey	1,082,561	18.5	11.1	4.1	0.1	$41,000
New Mexico	283,104	2.2	44.7	0.9	9.8	$26,700
New York	2,563,000	20.5	13.2	3.9	0.3	$43,300
North Carolina	1,082,558	30.4	0.7	0.8	1.6	$29,200
North Dakota	117,134	0.6	0.6	0.7	6.1	$24,500
Ohio	1,765,500	14.2	1.2	0.9	0.1	$33,300
Oklahoma	577,000	9.9	2.6	1.1	11.4	$25,300
Oregon	484,700	2.4	4	2.8	1.7	$34,100
Pennsylvania	1,667,630	13.1	2.6	1.5	0.1	$38,700
Rhode Island	137,946	6.4	5.9	3.2	0.4	$36,000
South Carolina	622,618	41.1	0.3	0.6	0.1	$28,300
South Dakota	128,635	0.5	0.6	0.7	7.6	$23,300
Tennessee	833,590	22.3	0.3	0.7	0.1	$28,600
Texas	3,353,270	14.6	33.1	1.9	0.2	$29,000
Utah	444,732	0.5	3.7	1.8	1.4	$26,500
Vermont	96,230	0.4	0.2	0.5	0.5	$33,600
Virginia	998,463	23.7	1	2.6	0.1	$31,900
Washington	840,554	4.1	5.2	5.3	2.4	$34,800
West Virginia	323,021	3.9	0.2	0.4	0	$27,400
Wisconsin	790,900	8.6	2.4	1.8	1.3	$35,200
Wyoming	98,210	0.9	5.9	0.6	1.9	$30,400

	Mean SAT Scores Verbal	Mean SAT Scores Math	Total Schools	Total Teachers	Students Per Teacher	Pupil Per Staff
Alabama	476	515	1,292	40,119	18.1	9.1
Alaska	439	481	495	6,676	16.8	8.1
Arizona	442	490	1026	33,677	18.9	9.9
Arkansas	482	523	1,097	25,674	17	8.8
California	415	482	7,433	221,003	22.4	11.4
Colorado	453	506	1,337	32,375	17.6	9.3
Connecticut	429	468	983	36,105	13.1	8
Delaware	428	464	170	6,077	16.4	9
District of Columbia	405	435	184	6,022	13.4	7.7
Florida	416	466	2,505	109,505	17	8.6
Georgia	400	444	1,732	62,934	18.3	8.9
Hawaii	405	478	234	8,956	19.1	12.1
Idaho	463	505	574	10,987	20.1	12.5
Illinois	471	535	4,225	105,613	16.9	9.6
Indiana	408	457	1,923	54,236	17.5	8.9
Iowa	515	578	1,607	30,806	15.7	8.4
Kansas	493	546	1,459	29,083	15	8.6
Kentucky	473	520	1,385	35,598	17.7	8.8
Louisiana	476	518	1,536	42,117	N/A	N/A
Maine	421	458	748	14,908	14.1	8.1
Maryland	429	475	1,217	42,569	16.8	9.1
Massachusetts	426	470	1,817	59,583	14	7.9
Michigan	461	519	3,314	80,321	19.7	9.2
Minnesota	480	543	1,564	43,716	17.2	9.7
Mississippi	477	520	954	27,479	18.2	8.9
Missouri	476	526	2,151	51,294	15.8	8.2
Montana	464	518	758	9,660	15.7	12.1
Nebraska	481	543	1,524	18,572	14.7	8.1
Nevada	435	484	331	9,868	20.4	18.1
New Hampshire	440	481	444	10,667	16.2	8.4
New Jersey	417	469	2,264	80,190	13.5	7.3
New Mexico	474	522	658	15,470	18.3	9.2
New York	413	468	3,996	174,354	14.7	7.4
North Carolina	400	444	1,952	63,307	17.1	8.8
North Dakota	502	571	679	7,757	15.1	8.3
Ohio	450	496	3,715	101,466	17.4	9.4
Oklahoma	476	521	1,859	35,617	16.2	8.9
Oregon	439	483	1,190	26,342	18.4	9.8
Pennsylvania	417	459	3,276	106,218	15.7	8.7
Rhode Island	421	459	294	9,514	14.5	8.9
South Carolina	395	437	1,103	36,625	17	9.7
South Dakota	496	551	799	8,299	15.5	9
Tennessee	487	528	1,535	43,643	19.1	9.5
Texas	411	463	5,937	200,795	16.7	10
Utah	494	537	718	17,933	24.8	14
Vermont	424	466	336	6,973	13.8	7.9
Virginia	424	466	1,779	62,796	15.9	8.2
Washington	433	480	1,858	41,819	20.1	11.2
West Virginia	441	485	1,035	21,392	15.1	8.3
Wisconsin	481	542	2,019	49,742	15.9	9.4
Wyoming	466	514	404	6,773	14.5	7.2

ALASKA

	Population	Pct. White	Pct. African Amer.	Pct. Native Amer.	Pct. Asian & Pac. Is.	Pct. Hispanic	65+ Years
Anchorage, AK	226,338	80.7	6.4	6.4	4.8	4.1	3.6
Fairbanks, AK	30,843	72.3	12.9	9.1	3.2	0.7	5.0
Juneau, AK	26,751	80.6	1.0	12.9	4.3	2.7	5.1

ALABAMA

	Population	Pct. White	Pct. African Amer.	Pct. Native Amer.	Pct. Asian & Pac. Is.	Pct. Hispanic	65+ Years
Auburn, AL	33,830	79.9	16.3	0.2	3.4	0.9	5.6
Bessemer, AL	33,497	41.4	58.4	0.1	0.1	0.2	17.5
Birmingham, AL	265,968	36	63.3	0.1	0.6	0.4	14.8
Decatur, AL	48,761	82.4	16.5	0.3	0.6	0.8	12
Dothan, AL	53,589	71.5	27.3	0.3	0.8	0.7	12.7
Florence, AL	36,426	82.1	17.1	0.3	0.4	0.5	16.6
Gadsden, AL	42,523	70.8	28.2	0.1	0.7	0.4	20.3
Hoover, AL	39,788	95.2	3.3	0.1	1.2	0.9	9.8
Huntsville, AL	159,789	72.6	24.4	0.5	2.1	1.2	10
Mobile, AL	196,278	59.6	38.9	0.2	1	1	13.7
Montgomery, AL	187,106	56.5	42.3	0.2	0.7	0.8	11.7
Prichard, AL	34,311	20.1	79.4	0.4	0	0.3	11.2
Tuscaloosa, AL	77,759	62.8	35.5	0.1	1.3	0.8	11.7

ARIZONA

	Population	Pct. White	Pct. African Amer.	Pct. Native Amer.	Pct. Asian & Pac. Is.	Pct. Hispanic	65+ Years
Chandler, AZ	90,533	85.2	2.6	1.2	2.4	17.3	5
Flagstaff, AZ	45,857	79.6	2.5	9.2	1.4	15.2	4.3
Glendale, AZ	148,134	85	3	0.9	2.1	15.5	7.9
Mesa, AZ	288,091	90.1	1.9	1	1.5	10.9	12.4
Peoria, AZ	50,618	86.9	2.2	0.6	1.4	15.5	14.9
Phoenix, AZ	983,403	81.7	5.2	1.9	1.7	20	9.7
Scottsdale, AZ	130,069	96	0.8	0.6	1.2	4.8	16.3
Sierra Vista, AZ	32,983	77.4	12	0.6	5.2	11.8	7.3
Sun City, AZ	38,126	99.6	0.2	0.1	0.1	0.5	84.6
Tempe, AZ	141,865	86.8	3.2	1.3	4.1	10.9	6.6
Tucson, AZ	405,390	75.2	4.3	1.6	2.2	29.3	12.6
Yuma, AZ	54,923	73	3.8	1.1	1.7	35.6	12

CALIFORNIA

	Population	Pct. White	Pct. African Amer.	Pct. Native Amer.	Pct. Asian & Pac. Is.	Pct. Hispanic	65+ Years
Alameda, CA	76,459	69.9	6.7	0.7	19.2	9.1	11.8
Alhambra, CA	82,106	40.9	2	0.4	38.1	36.1	13
Altadena, CA	42,658	49	38.8	0.5	4.2	14.1	11.9
Anaheim, CA	266,406	71.4	2.5	0.5	9.4	31.4	8.4
Antioch, CA	62,195	85.4	2.6	1.1	4.8	15.6	7.6
Apple Valley, CA	46,079	86.8	3.9	1	2.5	12.6	9.9
Arcadia, CA	48,290	71.5	0.8	0.4	23.4	10.7	16.1
Arden-Arcade, CA	92,040	89.1	3.9	1	4	6.9	16
Azusa, CA	41,333	66	3.8	0.7	6.6	53.4	6.9
Bakersfield, CA	174,820	72.7	9.4	1.1	3.6	20.5	9.2
Baldwin Park, CA	69,330	55.6	2.4	0.7	12.3	70.8	5.6
Bell, CA	34,365	42	1	0.8	1.4	86.1	6.5
Bell Gardens, CA	42,355	38.2	0.5	1.2	1.3	87.5	4.2
Bellflower, CA	61,815	69.8	6.3	0.9	10.1	23.9	10.8
Berkeley, CA	102,724	62.1	18.8	0.6	14.8	8.4	11
Beverly Hills, CA	31,971	91.3	1.7	0.2	5.5	5.4	20.3
Brea, CA	32,873	87	1.1	0.4	6.2	15.4	9.3
Buena Park, CA	68,784	70.9	2.5	0.7	14.4	24.5	8
Burbank, CA	93,643	82.6	1.7	0.5	6.8	22.6	14.5
Camarillo, CA	52,303	86.3	1.6	0.5	6.3	12.1	16.7
Campbell, CA	36,048	83.6	2	0.6	9.5	10.6	9.3
Carlsbad, CA	63,126	89.8	1.2	0.5	3.2	13.8	13.1
Carmichael, CA	48,702	92.3	2.2	0.8	3.2	5	13.7
Carson, CA	83,995	34.7	26.1	0.6	25	27.9	8
Castro Valley, CA	48,619	85.9	2.9	0.5	8.6	9.2	15
Cerritos, CA	53,240	42.3	7.4	0.3	45.2	12.5	5.7
Chico, CA	40,079	89.5	1.8	1.1	4	8.7	9
Chino, CA	59,682	67.3	9.8	0.5	3.4	36.2	5
Chula Vista, CA	135,163	67.7	4.6	0.6	8.9	37.3	11.7
Citrus Heights, CA	107,439	91.2	2.3	1.1	3.3	6.9	9.6
Claremont, CA	32,503	82.2	5	0.4	8.5	10.3	12.4
Clovis, CA	50,323	83.2	1.7	1.4	5.5	16.3	7.9
Colton, CA	40,213	58.2	8.7	0.9	4.3	49.7	6.6
Compton, CA	90,454	10.6	54.8	0.3	1.9	43.7	5.7
Concord, CA	111,348	84	2.4	0.7	8.7	11.5	9.5
Corona, CA	76,095	75.9	2.8	0.8	7.1	30.4	5.8
Costa Mesa, CA	96,357	84.3	1.3	0.5	6.6	20	8.2
Covina, CA	43,207	80.3	4.1	0.5	7.6	25.6	10.8
Culver City, CA	38,793	69.2	10.4	0.6	12	19.8	13.3
Cupertino, CA	40,263	74.4	0.9	0.3	23	4.9	8.8
Cypress, CA	42,655	79.2	2	0.5	13.7	13.5	7.5
Daly City, CA	92,311	39.5	7.7	0.4	43.8	22.4	10.5
Dana Point, CA	31,896	89.6	0.6	0.6	2.3	13.9	10
Danville, CA	31,306	91.6	0.8	0.3	6.5	4.1	8.4
Davis, CA	46,209	79.7	3	0.7	13.2	7.4	6.2
Diamond Bar, CA	53,672	63.7	5.7	0.4	24.9	17	4.2
Downey, CA	91,444	72.5	3.4	0.6	8.8	32.3	13.4
E. Los Angeles, CA	126,379	42.2	1.4	0.4	1.3	94.7	7.6
El Cajon, CA	88,693	87.4	2.9	1	2.8	14	10.9
El Centro, CA	31,384	60	4.5	0.7	2.5	65.3	8
El Monte, CA	106,209	62.2	1	0.6	11.8	72.5	6.4
El Toro, CA	62,685	85.6	1.8	0.4	9.2	10.3	6.9
Encinitas, CA	55,386	89.4	0.6	0.4	2.9	15.2	9.1
Escondido, CA	108,635	85.2	1.5	0.8	3.7	23.4	13
Fairfield, CA	77,211	68.2	13.8	1	10.7	13.2	6.4
Florence-Graham, CA	57,147	20.4	24	0.3	0.4	77.2	5.5
Fontana, CA	87,535	67.7	8.7	0.9	4.5	36.1	5.5
Fountain Valley, CA	53,691	78.2	0.9	0.6	17.7	8.1	7.3
Fremont, CA	173,339	70.6	3.8	0.7	19.4	13.3	6.7
Fresno, CA	354,202	59.2	8.3	1.1	12.5	29.9	10.1
Fullerton, CA	114,144	74.7	2.2	0.5	12.2	21.3	10.2
Garden Grove, CA	143,050	67.3	1.5	0.6	20.5	23.5	8.7
Gardena, CA	49,847	32.2	23.5	0.5	33.2	23.1	10.9
Gilroy, CA	31,487	68.2	1.2	0.7	4	47.3	7.7
Glendale, CA	180,038	74	1.3	0.3	14.1	21	13.3
Glendora, CA	47,828	88.5	1.1	0.5	5.6	15.2	10.6
Hacienda Hts., CA	52,354	59.1	2.1	0.6	27.3	32	7.7
Hawthorne, CA	71,349	42.3	28.3	0.5	11	31.1	7.3
Hayward, CA	111,498	61.8	9.8	1	15.5	23.9	10.7
Hemet, CA	36,094	90.9	0.7	0.9	1.2	14.9	42.1
Hesperia, CA	50,418	85.7	2.5	0.9	1.4	19	11.3
Highland, CA	34,439	73.1	11	1.1	4.8	22.8	6.6
Huntington Bch., CA	181,519	86.1	0.9	0.6	8.3	11.2	8.3
Huntington Park, CA	56,065	31.2	1.1	0.5	1.8	91.9	5.6
Indio, CA	36,793	54.5	4	0.8	1.6	68.1	8.1
Inglewood, CA	109,602	17.4	51.9	0.4	2.5	38.5	6.8
Irvine, CA	110,330	77.9	1.8	0.2	18.1	6.3	5.8
La Habra, CA	51,266	76.6	0.9	0.7	4.1	33.9	10.7
La Mesa, CA	52,931	90.2	3	0.5	3.1	9.8	18.3
La Mirada, CA	40,452	81.2	1.4	0.6	8.2	25.9	11.4
La Puente, CA	36,955	63.9	3.5	0.6	7.8	74.9	6
Laguna Hills, CA	46,731	91.1	1	0.3	6.3	5.8	39.6
Laguna Niguel, CA	44,400	88.5	1.4	0.3	7.8	7.8	6.9
Lakeside, CA	39,412	94	0.7	0.8	1.4	9.3	10
Lakewood, CA	73,557	81.1	3.7	0.7	9.4	14.6	12.1
Lancaster, CA	97,291	79.4	7.4	0.9	3.7	15.2	7.9
Livermore, CA	56,741	89.4	1.5	0.7	4.6	9.8	7.1
Lodi, CA	51,874	89.3	0.3	0.9	4.7	16.9	15.7
Lompoc, CA	37,649	70.5	7.8	1.3	5.4	26.8	8.5
Long Beach, CA	429,433	58.4	13.7	0.6	13.6	23.6	10.8
Los Angeles, CA	3,485,398	52.8	14	0.5	9.8	39.9	10
Lynwood, CA	61,945	24	23.7	0.4	2.2	70.3	5.1
Manhattan Beach, CA	32,063	93.5	0.6	0.3	4.4	5.1	8.6
Manteca, CA	40,773	89.5	1.5	1.2	3.5	17.8	8.2
Martinez, CA	31,808	87.7	3.3	0.8	5.7	8.4	9
Merced, CA	56,216	61.7	6.9	0.9	15.2	29.9	9
Milpitas, CA	50,686	52.1	5.9	0.9	34.7	18.6	4.9
Mission Viejo, CA	72,820	90.3	0.9	0.3	6.3	7.7	7.9
Modesto, CA	164,730	80.6	2.7	1	7.9	16.3	10.5
Monrovia, CA	35,761	69.7	10.1	0.5	4.5	28.5	10.8
Montebello, CA	59,564	47	1	0.5	15.1	67.6	11.9
Monterey, CA	31,954	86.6	2.9	0.6	7.3	7.8	12.9
Monterey Park, CA	60,738	26.7	0.6	0.3	57.5	31.3	13.8
Moreno Valley, CA	118,779	67.4	13.8	0.7	6.6	22.9	4
Mountain View, CA	67,460	72.7	5	0.6	14.7	16	9.8
N. Highlands, CA	42,105	77.8	10	1.5	6.7	9.3	8.7
Napa, CA	61,842	90.3	0.4	0.8	2.1	15.2	14.9
National City, CA	54,249	40.9	8.5	0.7	17.7	49.6	9.4
Newark, CA	37,861	68.6	4.3	0.6	15.9	22.9	5.3
Newport Beach, CA	66,643	95.8	0.3	0.3	2.9	4	15.5

	Population	Pct. White	Pct. African Amer.	Pct. Native Amer.	Pct. Asian & Pac. Is.	Pct. Hispanic	65+ Years
Norwalk, CA	94,279	55.8	3.2	0.9	12.4	47.9	8.6
Novato, CA	47,585	89.6	2.8	0.5	5	7.3	9.8
Oakland, CA	372,242	32.5	43.9	0.6	14.8	13.9	12
Oceanside, CA	128,398	74.7	7.9	0.7	6.1	22.6	14
Ontario, CA	133,179	64.6	7.3	0.7	3.9	41.7	6.4
Orange, CA	110,658	83	1.4	0.5	7.9	22.8	8.7
Oxnard, CA	142,216	58.7	5.2	0.8	8.6	54.4	7.7
Pacifica, CA	37,670	76.3	5.2	0.7	13.6	13.5	7.4
Palm Springs, CA	40,181	83.2	4.5	0.7	3.3	18.7	25.8
Palmdale, CA	68,842	75.7	6.4	0.9	4.4	22	4.8
Palo Alto, CA	55,900	84.9	2.9	0.3	10.4	5	15.5
Paramount, CA	47,669	48.2	10.7	0.7	5.8	60.8	6.2
Pasadena, CA	131,591	57.3	19	0.4	8.1	27.3	13.2
Petaluma, CA	43,184	92.1	1.3	0.6	3.3	9.2	11.6
Pico Rivera, CA	59,177	58.8	0.7	0.6	3.2	83.2	9.6
Pittsburg, CA	47,564	58.6	17.6	0.8	12.2	23.7	7.7
Placentia, CA	41,259	76.2	1.9	0.5	8.2	24.7	7.2
Pleasant Hill, CA	31,585	89.3	1.4	0.6	7	6.6	11.7
Pleasanton, CA	50,553	90.7	1.4	0.4	5.8	6.7	5.4
Pomona, CA	131,723	57	14.4	0.6	6.7	51.3	7
Poway, CA	43,516	89.9	1.4	0.5	6.2	6.9	7
Ran. Cucamonga, CA	101,409	78.6	5.9	0.6	5.4	20	5.1
Rancho Cordova, CA	48,731	78.9	10.1	1.1	7.3	7.8	8
Rancho Palos Ver., CA	41,659	76.2	1.9	0.2	20.5	5.3	12
Redding, CA	66,462	92.6	1.1	2.2	3.3	4	14.5
Redlands, CA	60,394	79.6	3.8	0.7	4.4	19	11.9
Redondo Beach, CA	60,167	87	1.6	0.5	6.8	11.5	7.2
Redwood City, CA	66,072	82.8	3.6	0.5	6.3	24.1	11.5
Rialto, CA	72,388	57.9	20.4	0.9	3.5	31.5	6.6
Richmond, CA	87,425	36.2	43.8	0.6	11.8	14.5	11.3
Riverside, CA	226,505	70.8	7.4	0.8	5.2	26	8.9
Rohnert Park, CA	36,326	89.2	2.6	1	4.8	8.9	7.5
Rosemead, CA	51,638	35.4	0.6	0.5	34.3	49.7	9
Roseville, CA	44,685	91.5	0.9	1	3.3	10.8	11.3
Rowland Heights, CA	42,647	53.8	5.2	0.4	29.3	29.7	6.8
S. San Francisco, CA	54,312	61.5	4	0.7	24.6	27.1	11.4
Sacramento, CA	369,365	60.1	15.3	1.2	15	16.2	12.1
Salinas, CA	108,777	54.6	3	0.9	8.1	50.6	8.3
San Bernardino, CA	164,164	60.6	16	1	4	34.6	10
San Bruno, CA	38,961	71.6	4.1	0.8	17.9	18.6	10.5
San Buenaventura, CA	92,575	86.1	1.7	1.1	2.7	17.6	12.5
San Clemente, CA	41,100	91.6	0.7	0.4	2.7	12.9	13
San Diego, CA	1,110,549	67.1	9.4	0.6	11.8	20.7	10.2
San Dimas, CA	32,397	81.7	3.8	0.5	8.6	17.3	9.4
San Francisco, CA	723,959	53.6	10.9	0.5	29.1	13.9	14.6
San Gabriel, CA	37,120	48	1.1	0.5	32.4	36.3	13.4
San Jose, CA	782,248	62.8	4.7	0.7	19.5	26.6	7.2
San Leandro, CA	68,223	74.1	5.8	0.7	13.8	15.2	19.3
San Luis Obispo, CA	41,958	88.7	1.9	0.8	5.1	9.4	12.2
San Marcos, CA	38,974	84.7	1.5	0.8	2.9	27.5	14.7
San Mateo, CA	85,486	78.6	3.6	0.4	13.3	15.5	16.3
San Rafael, CA	48,404	83.5	2.9	0.3	5.5	14.4	13.9
San Ramon, CA	35,303	87.1	2	0.3	9	5.8	4.3
Santa Ana, CA	293,742	68	2.6	0.5	9.7	65.2	5.6
Santa Barbara, CA	85,571	77.7	2.2	0.9	2.3	31.5	16.2
Santa Clara, CA	93,613	73.7	2.6	0.5	18.6	15.2	10
Santa Clarita, CA	110,642	87.3	1.5	0.6	4.2	13.4	6.3
Santa Cruz, CA	49,040	85.9	2.3	0.9	4.6	13.6	10.1
Santa Maria, CA	61,284	61.6	2.2	0.9	6.1	45.7	12
Santa Monica, CA	86,905	82.8	4.5	0.4	6.4	14	16.5
Santa Rosa, CA	113,313	89.4	1.8	1.2	3.4	9.5	16.3
Santee, CA	52,902	91.1	1.7	0.8	3	10.7	8.3
Seaside, CA	38,901	52.7	23.5	1	13.5	17.4	5.4
Simi Valley, CA	100,217	88.2	1.5	0.6	5.5	12.7	5.3
So. Sacramento, CA	31,903	51.9	18.8	1.8	12.8	25.2	10
South Gate, CA	86,284	41.6	1.7	0.4	1.6	83.1	7.3
South Whittier, CA	49,514	67.2	1.2	0.7	4.2	51.8	7.8
Spring Valley, CA	55,331	73.6	8.5	0.8	7.9	18.9	8.4
Stockton, CA	210,943	57.5	9.6	1	22.8	25	10.5
Sunnyvale, CA	117,229	71.6	3.4	0.5	19.3	13.2	10.4
Temple City, CA	31,100	71.9	0.6	0.4	19.5	18.8	14.9
Thousand Oaks, CA	104,352	90.4	1.2	0.4	4.8	9.6	9
Torrance, CA	133,107	73	1.5	0.4	21.9	10.1	11.9
Tracy, CA	33,558	86.3	2.5	1	4.6	24.3	8.1
Tulare, CA	33,249	65.6	6.2	1.1	2.5	33.8	10.7
Turlock, CA	42,198	82.5	1.2	0.9	4.4	21	12.5
Tustin, CA	50,689	73.2	5.7	0.5	10.4	20.7	7.5
Union City, CA	53,762	43.9	8.6	0.6	33.4	25.1	7.1
Upland, CA	63,374	78.9	5.3	0.5	7	17.5	9.2
Vacaville, CA	71,479	78.8	8.9	1	3.8	15.9	6.8
Vallejo, CA	109,199	50.5	21.2	0.7	23	10.8	10.9
Victorville, CA	40,674	73.1	9.6	1.1	3.7	23	11.6
Visalia, CA	75,636	74.8	1.5	1	6.4	25.1	11.1
Vista, CA	71,872	80.7	4.5	0.8	4	24.8	12.2
Walnut Creek, CA	60,569	90.6	1	0.3	6.7	4.7	22.8
Watsonville, CA	31,099	55.1	0.7	1	5.6	60.9	12.6
West Covina, CA	96,086	59.8	8.5	0.5	17.2	34.6	8.7
West Hollywood, CA	36,118	90.2	3.4	0.4	3.1	8.7	18.3
Westminster, CA	78,118	69.6	1.1	0.6	22.5	19.1	9.4
Whittier, CA	77,671	73.4	1.3	0.6	3.3	39	13.9
Willowbrook, CA	32,772	11	55.2	0.2	0.6	44.6	9.6
Woodland, CA	39,802	77.5	1.3	1.3	3.1	26.2	11.2
Yorba Linda, CA	52,422	85.7	1.1	0.4	10.1	9.4	5
Yucaipa, CA	32,824	92.6	0.5	0.9	1	11	24

COLORADO

	Population	Pct. White	Pct. African Amer.	Pct. Native Amer.	Pct. Asian & Pac. Is.	Pct. Hispanic	65+ Years
Arvada, CO	89,235	94.3	0.6	0.5	2	7.4	7.6
Aurora, CO	222,103	82.4	11.4	0.6	3.8	6.6	6.8
Boulder, CO	83,312	92.5	1.3	0.5	3.9	4.8	7.8
Colorado Sp., CO	281,140	85.9	7	0.8	2.4	9.1	9.2
Denver, CO	467,610	72.1	12.8	1.2	2.4	23	13.9
Fort Collins, CO	87,758	93.3	1	0.5	2.4	7.1	7.7
Greeley, CO	60,536	89.1	0.7	0.6	1	20.4	11.2
Lakewood, CO	126,481	93.2	1	0.7	1.9	9.1	10.5
Littleton, CO	33,685	96.1	0.9	0.6	1.4	5.2	12.1
Longmont, CO	51,555	92.7	0.4	0.7	1.2	11.1	9.9
Loveland, CO	37,352	94.9	0.3	0.5	0.7	6.8	13
Pueblo, CO	98,640	83	2.2	0.8	0.6	39.5	16
Southglenn, CO	43,087	96.5	0.8	0.3	1.9	3.1	6.8
Thornton, CO	55,031	89.7	1.3	0.9	1.7	16.9	5.3
Westminster, CO	74,625	90.6	1	0.6	3.7	11.5	4.8

CONNECTICUT

	Population	Pct. White	Pct. African Amer.	Pct. Native Amer.	Pct. Asian & Pac. Is.	Pct. Hispanic	65+ Years
Bridgeport, CT	141,686	58.5	26.6	0.3	2.3	26.5	13.6
Bristol, CT	60,640	96	2.1	0.2	0.8	2.7	13.6
Danbury, CT	65,585	86.8	6.6	0.2	3.9	7.7	11.6
East Hartford, CT	50,452	86.8	8.4	0.2	2.2	6	15.6
Hartford, CT	139,739	40	38.9	0.3	1.4	31.6	9.9
Meriden, CT	59,479	89.7	4.3	0.2	0.7	13.7	14.7
Middletown, CT	42,762	85.4	11.1	0.2	1.9	3.3	12
Milford , CT	48,168	96.8	1.5	0.1	1	2.3	13.9
New Britain, CT	75,491	81.6	7.6	0.2	1.8	16.3	16.9
New Haven, CT	130,474	53.9	36.1	0.3	2.4	13.2	12.3
Norwalk, CT	78,331	79.3	15.5	0.1	1.6	9.4	12.6
Norwich, CT	37,391	91.3	5.3	0.6	1.1	3.1	15.7
Shelton, CT	35,418	97.1	1	0.2	1.3	2.5	12.6
Stamford, CT	108,056	76.3	17.8	0.1	2.6	9.8	13.3
Stratford, CT	49,389	90.1	7.9	0.1	0.8	3.6	19.7
Torrington, CT	33,687	96.7	1.7	0.2	1.2	1.1	18.6
Trumbull, CT	32,000	96.8	1.3	0.1	1.7	1.8	15.6
Waterbury, CT	108,961	79.6	13	0.3	0.7	13.4	16.5
West Hartford, CT	60,110	94	2.2	0.1	2.8	3.1	22.1
West Haven, CT	54,021	84.1	12.4	0.2	2	3.6	14.8

DELAWARE

	Population	Pct. White	Pct. African Amer.	Pct. Native Amer.	Pct. Asian & Pac. Is.	Pct. Hispanic	65+ Years
Dover, DE	27,630	65.5	30.9	4.7	1.9	2.8	10.5
Newark, DE	25,098	90.3	5.7	1.4	3.5	1.4	8.5
Wilmington, DE	71,529	42.1	52.4	0.2	0.4	7.1	14.8

DISTRICT OF COLUMBIA

	Population	Pct. White	Pct. African Amer.	Pct. Native Amer.	Pct. Asian & Pac. Is.	Pct. Hispanic	65+ Years
Washington, DC	606,900	29.6	65.8	0.2	1.8	5.4	12.8

FLORIDA

	Population	Pct. White	Pct. African Amer.	Pct. Native Amer.	Pct. Asian & Pac. Is.	Pct. Hispanic	65+ Years
Altamonte Sps., FL	34,879	89.9	5.9	0.3	1.8	8.5	9.6

	Population	Pct. White	Pct. African Amer.	Pct. Native Amer.	Pct. Asian & Pac. Is.	Pct. Hispanic	65+ Years
Boca Raton, FL	61,492	94.4	2.9	0.1	1.9	5.6	21.5
Boynton Beach, FL	46,194	77.7	20.1	0.1	0.6	6.8	30.3
Bradenton, FL	43,779	82.9	14.4	0.2	0.6	5.4	28.5
Brandon, FL	57,985	93	3.8	0.3	1.7	6.9	7.7
Cape Coral, FL	74,991	97.5	1	0.2	0.6	3.7	22
Carol City, FL	53,331	38.9	54.5	0.2	0.6	36	5.9
Clearwater, FL	98,784	89.1	9	0.2	1	2.9	25.6
Coral Gables, FL	40,091	93	3.4	0.1	1.7	41.8	17.4
Coral Springs, FL	79,443	93.1	3.5	0.2	2.1	7.1	7
Davie, FL	47,217	92.8	3.9	0.2	1.7	10	9
Daytona Beach, FL	61,921	67.4	30.7	0.2	1.1	2.5	21.4
Deerfield Beach, FL	46,325	81.6	16.7	0.1	0.8	3.9	36.3
Delray Beach, FL	47,181	72	26.3	0.1	0.7	6.1	31.7
Deltona, FL	50,828	93.8	3.3	0.3	0.7	10.1	18.6
Dunedin, FL	34,012	98.1	1.1	0.2	0.4	1.8	33.3
Fort Lauderdale, FL	149,377	69.6	28.1	0.2	0.9	7.2	17.8
Fort Myers, FL	45,206	64.2	32.2	0.2	0.8	7.7	16.1
Fort Pierce, FL	36,830	53.7	42.4	0.3	0.5	6.4	19.2
Gainesville, FL	84,770	73.4	21.4	0.2	3.9	4.4	9.4
Hialeah, FL	188,004	89.9	1.9	0.1	0.5	87.6	14
Hollywood, FL	121,697	88.2	8.5	0.2	1.3	11.9	23.1
Jacksonville , FL	635,230	71.9	25.2	0.3	1.9	2.6	10.6
Kendale Lakes, FL	48,524	88.8	3.2	0.1	2.4	63.6	8.5
Kendall, FL	87,271	89.9	4.7	0.1	3	31.4	9.4
Lakeland, FL	70,576	78.1	20.2	0.2	0.9	3.3	22.9
Largo, FL	65,674	97.6	1	0.2	0.8	1.9	32.4
Lauderhill, FL	49,708	58.6	38.5	0.1	1.5	6.8	21.3
Margate, FL	42,985	93.1	3.7	0.2	1.5	7.7	30.4
Melbourne, FL	59,646	87.4	9.5	0.3	2.1	3.5	17
Merritt Island, FL	32,886	92.4	5.4	0.4	1.3	2.8	15.3
Miami, FL	358,548	65.6	27.4	0.2	0.6	62.5	16.6
Miami Beach, FL	92,639	88.3	5.2	0.2	1.2	46.8	30.1
Miramar, FL	40,663	79.3	15.7	0.2	2.3	17.3	9.7
N. Miami Beach, FL	35,359	71.6	21.8	0.2	3.4	22.1	19.9
North Miami, FL	49,998	62.4	31.9	0.2	2.4	24.6	15.1
Ocala, FL	42,045	74.9	23.8	0.3	0.6	2.2	20.8
Olympia Heights, FL	37,792	93.3	0.9	0.1	1.3	79.2	14.5
Orlando, FL	164,693	68.8	26.9	0.3	1.6	8.7	11.4
Palm Bay, FL	62,632	89.3	7.5	0.3	1.8	5.3	11.4
Palm Harbor, FL	50,256	98.5	0.4	0.2	0.6	2.1	23.1
Panama City, FL	34,378	75.5	21.8	0.6	1.7	1.3	17
Pembroke Pines, FL	65,452	91.3	5.3	0.2	2	11.5	19.4
Pensacola, FL	58,165	65.7	31.9	0.5	1.6	1.6	16.4
Pine Hills, FL	35,322	72.2	22.8	0.3	2.1	8.4	8.8
Pinellas Park, FL	43,426	96.1	1	0.3	1.9	3.3	23.1
Plantation, FL	66,692	90.7	6.2	0.1	1.8	8.1	14.4
Pompano Beach, FL	72,411	70	28.5	0.1	0.6	5.4	25.2
Port Charlotte, FL	41,535	94.1	4.4	0.2	1	3.5	33.4
Port Orange, FL	35,317	97.7	1	0.3	0.8	2	22.6
Port St. Lucie, FL	55,866	94.2	3.8	0.2	0.9	4	17.2
Sanford, FL	32,387	68.8	28.5	0.4	0.9	4.9	12.9
Sarasota, FL	50,961	82	16.2	0.2	0.7	4.7	25.2
Spring Hill, FL	31,117	97.7	1.3	0.1	0.4	4	33.5
St. Petersburg, FL	238,629	78	19.6	0.2	1.7	2.6	22.2
Sunrise, FL	64,407	89.3	7.4	0.1	1.9	8.6	23
Tallahassee, FL	124,773	68.2	29.1	0.2	1.8	3	8.8
Tamarac, FL	44,822	96	2.3	0.1	0.9	5.4	47.6
Tamiami, FL	33,845	92.5	0.8	0.1	0.7	82.6	9.4
Tampa, FL	280,015	70.9	25	0.3	1.4	15	14.6
Titusville, FL	39,394	87.3	11	0.4	0.8	2.8	15.9
Town 'n' Country, FL	60,946	90.5	4.3	0.2	2.1	17.9	9
West Little River, FL	33,575	27.7	68	0.1	0.3	29.4	8.1
West Palm Beach, FL	67,643	63.4	32.6	0.1	0.9	14.2	18.2

GEORGIA

	Population	Pct. White	Pct. African Amer.	Pct. Native Amer.	Pct. Asian & Pac. Is.	Pct. Hispanic	65+ Years
Albany, GA	78,122	44.2	55	0.2	0.4	0.8	10.8
Athens, GA	45,734	66.4	29.6	0.1	3.3	1.6	10.2
Atlanta, GA	394,017	31	67.1	0.1	0.9	1.9	11.3
Augusta, GA	44,639	43	56	0.2	0.6	0.8	18.8
Columbus, GA	178,681	58.9	38.1	0.3	1.4	3	10.8
East Point, GA	34,402	31.6	66.3	0.2	0.7	1.9	11.6
Macon, GA	106,612	47.1	52.2	0.1	0.4	0.6	14.6

	Population	Pct. White	Pct. African Amer.	Pct. Native Amer.	Pct. Asian & Pac. Is.	Pct. Hispanic	65+ Years
Marietta, GA	44,129	76.3	20.5	0.3	1.8	3.2	10.4
Martinez, GA	33,731	89.6	6.2	0.2	3.7	1.4	5.3
Roswell, GA	47,923	92.2	4.9	0.1	1.8	2.7	6.9
Sandy Springs, GA	67,842	89.6	7.6	0.1	1.6	2.9	9.8
Savannah, GA	137,560	46.8	51.3	0.2	1.1	1.4	13.8
South Augusta, GA	55,998	48.2	48.8	0.3	1.9	2	8.4
Valdosta, GA	39,806	55.2	43.5	0.2	0.9	1.1	10.8
Warner Robins, GA	43,726	72.7	25	0.3	1.4	1.8	8.2

HAWAII

	Population	Pct. White	Pct. African Amer.	Pct. Native Amer.	Pct. Asian & Pac. Is.	Pct. Hispanic	65+ Years
Hilo, HI	37,808	26.6	0.6	0.6	70.2	8.5	14.6
Honolulu, HI	365,272	26.7	1.3	0.3	70.5	4.6	16
Kailua, HI	36,818	57.7	1.4	0.5	39.1	5.5	10.8
Kaneohe, HI	35,448	31.2	1.2	0.4	65.6	6.9	10.9
Waipahu, HI	31,435	11.6	2	0.5	83.8	11.5	10.5

IOWA

	Population	Pct. White	Pct. African Amer.	Pct. Native Amer.	Pct. Asian & Pac. Is.	Pct. Hispanic	65+ Years
Ames, IA	47,198	89.9	2.4	0.1	6.9	1.6	6.8
Cedar Falls, IA	34,298	96.9	1.1	0.2	1.4	0.8	11.1
Cedar Rapids, IA	108,751	95.5	2.9	0.2	1	1.1	13.2
Council Bluffs, IA	54,315	97.8	0.8	0.3	0.4	2.4	13.7
Davenport, IA	95,333	89.1	7.9	0.4	1	3.5	12.7
Des Moines, IA	193,187	89.2	7.1	0.4	2.4	2.4	13.4
Dubuque, IA	57,546	98.4	0.6	0.1	0.6	0.6	16
Iowa City, IA	59,738	91.1	2.5	0.2	5.6	1.7	6.6
Sioux City, IA	80,505	92.6	2.3	2	1.5	3.3	14.7
Waterloo, IA	66,467	86.6	12.1	0.2	0.7	0.8	15.7
West Des Moines, IA	31,702	96.3	1.3	0.1	1.6	1.9	10.6

IDAHO

	Population	Pct. White	Pct. African Amer.	Pct. Native Amer.	Pct. Asian & Pac. Is.	Pct. Hispanic	65+ Years
Boise City, ID	125,738	96.4	0.6	0.6	1.6	2.7	11.9
Idaho Falls, ID	43,929	95.3	0.6	0.6	1.2	4.2	10.3
Pocatello, ID	46,080	94.1	0.9	1.4	1.3	4.5	10.9

ILLINOIS

	Population	Pct. White	Pct. African Amer.	Pct. Native Amer.	Pct. Asian & Pac. Is.	Pct. Hispanic	65+ Years
Addison Village, IL	32,058	87.9	1.7	0.1	5.9	13.4	6.7
Alton, IL	32,905	75.6	23.1	0.5	0.3	1.1	17.3
Arlington Heights, IL	75,460	94.8	0.6	0.1	3.7	2.7	12.2
Aurora, IL	99,581	74.1	11.9	0.2	1.3	23	8.6
Belleville, IL	42,785	92.1	6.8	0.2	0.6	1.3	19
Berwyn, IL	45,426	95.6	0.1	0.1	1.7	7.9	21.4
Bloomington, IL	51,972	90.9	6.7	0.2	1.5	1.6	12
Bolingbrook, IL	40,843	76.8	15.6	0.3	5	5.9	3.5
Buffalo Grove, IL	36,427	94.2	1	0.1	4.4	2	5.5
Calumet City, IL	37,840	73.3	23.7	0.1	0.6	6.4	15.5
Carol Stream, IL	31,716	88.4	3.4	0.2	5.8	5.7	5.2
Champaign, IL	63,502	80.7	14.2	0.2	4.1	1.9	8.2
Chicago, IL	2,783,726	45.4	39.1	0.3	3.7	19.6	11.9
Chicago Heights, IL	33,072	55	35.1	0.2	0.3	15	12.6
Cicero, IL	67,436	75.2	0.2	0.4	1.6	37	13.7
Danville, IL	33,828	78.3	19.1	0.2	1.1	2.1	17.5
De Kalb, IL	34,925	88.9	4.7	0.1	4.5	4.1	6.9
Decatur, IL	83,885	82.5	16.7	0.1	0.5	0.5	16.1
Des Plaines, IL	53,223	92	0.6	0.1	4.7	6.6	15.4
Downers Grove , IL	46,858	93.2	1.7	0.1	4.2	2.4	12.2
East St. Louis, IL	40,944	1.6	98.1	0.1	0.1	0.4	10.8
Elgin, IL	77,010	77.8	7.3	0.2	3.5	18.9	10.5
Elk Grove Village, IL	33,429	91.5	0.8	0.1	6.8	3.6	7.2
Elmhurst, IL	42,029	95.9	0.4	0.1	3	2.7	14.3
Evanston, IL	73,233	70.6	22.9	0.2	4.8	3.7	12.4
Galesburg, IL	33,530	88.6	8.4	0.2	0.9	3.8	18
Glenview, IL	37,093	91	0.8	0.1	7.4	2.4	12.8
Granite City, IL	32,862	98.4	0.2	0.4	0.5	1.8	15.3
Hanover Park, IL	32,895	85.5	3.6	0.2	7.4	11	3
Hoffman Estates , IL	46,561	87.2	2.9	0.2	8	5.5	4.3
Joliet, IL	76,836	69.2	21.6	0.2	1	12.7	14.5
Lombard, IL	39,408	93.4	1.3	0.1	4.4	2.8	12.7
Moline, IL	43,202	94.1	2	0.2	0.9	6.8	16
Mount Prospect, IL	53,170	90.2	1.1	0.1	6.4	6.4	11.9
Naperville, IL	85,351	92.6	2.1	0.1	4.8	1.8	5.6
Normal , IL	40,023	92.4	5	0.1	1.9	1.5	6.3
North Chicago, IL	34,978	56.7	34.4	0.5	3.6	9.2	5.2

	Population	Pct. White	Pct. African Amer.	Pct. Native Amer.	Pct. Asian & Pac. Is.	Pct. Hispanic	65+ Years
Northbrook, IL	32,308	93	0.2	0	6.4	1.6	14.6
Oak Lawn, IL	56,182	98.3	0.1	0.1	1.1	2.4	20.2
Oak Park, IL	53,648	77	18.3	0.1	3.3	3.6	11.5
Orland Park, IL	35,720	95.4	0.4	0.1	3.6	2.3	9.9
Palatine, IL	39,253	94.2	0.9	0.1	3.2	3.6	8.9
Park Ridge, IL	36,175	97.4	0.1	0.1	2.2	1.3	19
Pekin, IL	32,254	99.2	0.1	0.2	0.4	0.6	15.6
Peoria, IL	113,504	76.5	20.9	0.2	1.7	1.6	14.4
Quincy, IL	39,681	94.9	4.1	0.2	0.5	0.4	20.2
Rock Island, IL	40,552	80.7	17.2	0.2	0.6	3.8	17.3
Rockford, IL	139,426	81.1	15	0.3	1.5	4.2	14.7
Schaumburg, IL	68,586	90.6	2.1	0.1	6.5	2.7	7.3
Skokie, IL	59,432	81.2	2.2	0.1	15.6	4.1	20.7
Springfield, IL	105,227	85.6	13	0.2	1	0.8	14.9
Tinley Park, IL	37,121	96.2	1.6	0.1	1.4	2.5	8.9
Urbana, IL	36,344	75.7	11.4	0.2	11.7	2.7	9
Waukegan, IL	69,392	64.3	19.8	0.4	3.1	23.7	11
Wheaton, IL	51,464	93	2.5	0.1	3.8	2	9.3

INDIANA

	Population	Pct. White	Pct. African Amer.	Pct. Native Amer.	Pct. Asian & Pac. Is.	Pct. Hispanic	65+ Years
Anderson, IN	59,459	84.9	14.2	0.3	0.4	0.6	16.1
Bloomington, IN	60,633	91.2	4	0.2	4	1.6	6.9
Columbus, IN	31,802	95.4	2.5	0.2	1.6	0.9	14
East Chicago, IN	33,892	38	33.6	0.2	0.2	47.8	13.2
Elkhart, IN	43,627	84	14	0.4	0.8	2	13.2
Evansville, IN	126,272	89.6	9.5	0.2	0.6	0.6	17.2
Fort Wayne, IN	173,072	80.5	16.7	0.3	1	2.7	13.3
Gary, IN	116,646	16.3	80.6	0.2	0.2	5.7	11.4
Hammond, IN	84,236	84.8	9.2	0.2	0.4	11.8	14.3
Indianapolis, IN	731,327	75.8	22.6	0.2	0.9	1.1	11.4
Kokomo, IN	44,962	89.5	8.9	0.3	0.7	1.7	13.6
Lafayette, IN	43,764	95.8	2.1	0.3	1.1	1.7	13.2
Marion, IN	32,618	82.6	14.8	0.4	0.7	3.2	16.6
Michigan City, IN	33,822	75.8	22.5	0.3	0.7	1.8	13.9
Mishawaka, IN	42,608	97.1	1.6	0.4	0.7	1.1	14.8
Muncie, IN	71,035	89.1	9.5	0.3	0.7	0.9	13.3
New Albany, IN	36,322	93.2	6.2	0.2	0.3	0.5	16.5
Richmond, IN	38,705	89.6	9.2	0.3	0.6	0.7	16.6
South Bend, IN	105,511	76	20.9	0.4	0.9	3.4	16.8
Terre Haute, IN	57,483	88.6	9.4	0.4	1.1	1.3	16.9

KANSAS

	Population	Pct. White	Pct. African Amer.	Pct. Native Amer.	Pct. Asian & Pac. Is.	Pct. Hispanic	65+ Years
Hutchinson, KS	39,308	91.5	4.1	0.6	0.4	5.4	16.6
Kansas City, KS	149,767	65	29.3	0.7	1.2	7.1	13
Lawrence, KS	65,608	87.1	4.9	3	3.9	3	7
Leavenworth, KS	38,495	79.8	15.8	0.7	2	4.7	9.7
Lenexa, KS	34,034	94.6	2.4	0.4	2	1.7	5.8
Manhattan, KS	37,712	90.1	5	0.5	3.3	2.8	8.1
Olathe, KS	63,352	94.3	3	0.4	1.7	1.8	5.2
Overland Park, KS	111,790	95.4	1.8	0.3	1.9	2	9.9
Salina, KS	42,303	93.1	3.5	0.5	1.2	2.7	14.4
Shawnee, KS	37,993	94.9	2.1	0.4	1.7	2.6	7.1
Topeka, KS	119,883	84.7	10.6	1.3	0.8	5.8	14.7
Wichita, KS	304,011	82.3	11.3	1.2	2.6	5	12.4

KENTUCKY

	Population	Pct. White	Pct. African Amer.	Pct. Native Amer.	Pct. Asian & Pac. Is.	Pct. Hispanic	65+ Years
Bowling Green, KY	40,641	86.4	12.2	0.2	1.1	0.7	13.1
Covington, KY	43,264	91.5	7.7	0.2	0.4	0.7	14.3
Lexington-Fayette, KY	225,366	84.5	13.4	0.2	1.6	1.1	9.9
Louisville, KY	269,063	69.2	29.7	0.2	0.7	0.7	16.6
Owensboro, KY	53,549	93	6.4	0.1	0.3	0.4	15

LOUISIANA

	Population	Pct. White	Pct. African Amer.	Pct. Native Amer.	Pct. Asian & Pac. Is.	Pct. Hispanic	65+ Years
Alexandria, LA	49,188	49.6	49.3	0.2	0.7	1	14.3
Baton Rouge, LA	219,531	53.9	43.9	0.1	1.7	1.6	11.5
Bossier City, LA	52,721	79.3	18.1	0.4	1.5	2.6	8.9
Chalmette, LA	31,860	97.7	0.3	0.3	1.1	4.9	11.7
Kenner, LA	72,033	77.4	18.1	0.3	1.7	10.1	6.6
Lafayette, LA	94,440	70.8	27.2	0.2	1.3	1.7	9.5
Lake Charles, LA	70,580	57.3	41.6	0.2	0.5	1.1	13.2
Marrero, LA	36,671	51.9	45	0.5	1.9	2.9	9.3
Metairie, LA	149,428	91.6	4.9	0.2	1.8	6.2	14.1

	Population	Pct. White	Pct. African Amer.	Pct. Native Amer.	Pct. Asian & Pac. Is.	Pct. Hispanic	65+ Years
Monroe, LA	54,909	43.3	55.6	0.1	0.8	0.8	13.4
New Iberia, LA	31,828	64.2	33.3	0.2	2	2.3	12.4
New Orleans, LA	496,938	34.9	61.9	0.2	1.9	3.5	13
Shreveport, LA	198,525	54.3	44.8	0.2	0.5	1.1	13.7

MASSACHUSETTS

	Population	Pct. White	Pct. African Amer.	Pct. Native Amer.	Pct. Asian & Pac. Is.	Pct. Hispanic	65+ Years
Arlington, MA	44,630	95.2	1.3	0.1	3	1.7	17.8
Attleboro, MA	38,383	95.5	1	0.2	2.4	2.9	12.1
Beverly, MA	38,195	97.6	0.9	0.1	1	1.1	15
Boston, MA	574,283	62.8	25.6	0.3	5.3	10.8	11.5
Braintree, MA	33,836	97.4	0.6	0.1	1.6	0.9	17.1
Brockton, MA	92,788	80.2	13	0.3	1.7	6.3	12.4
Brookline, MA	54,718	87.4	3.1	0.1	8.4	2.9	15.4
Cambridge, MA	95,802	75.3	13.5	0.3	8.4	6.8	10.5
Chelmsford, MA	32,388	96.1	0.5	0.1	3.1	1	9.7
Chicopee, MA	56,632	95.4	1.8	0.1	0.6	3.6	17.2
Everett, MA	35,701	93.5	3.2	0.3	1.8	3.8	16.4
Fall River, MA	92,703	97.2	1	0.1	1.3	1.7	18.1
Fitchburg, MA	41,194	89.4	3.4	0.2	2.6	9.6	15.4
Framingham, MA	64,994	90.1	3.7	0.2	2.9	8.1	12.3
Haverhill, MA	51,418	94.9	2	0.2	0.8	5.3	14.2
Holyoke, MA	43,704	73.1	3.6	0.2	0.8	31.1	16.8
Lawrence, MA	70,207	65	6.4	0.5	1.9	41.6	12.6
Leominster, MA	38,145	93.1	2.3	0.2	1.6	8.3	13
Lowell, MA	103,439	81.1	2.4	0.2	11.1	10.1	12.1
Lynn, MA	81,245	83.1	8.1	0.3	3.7	9.1	15.1
Malden, MA	53,884	89.4	4.2	0.2	5.2	2.6	15.3
Marlborough, MA	31,813	94.8	1.8	0.2	1.9	4.2	11.2
Medford, MA	57,407	93.4	4.1	0.1	2	1.7	16.8
New Bedford, MA	99,922	87.6	4.1	0.4	0.4	6.7	17.4
Newton, MA	82,585	92.8	2.1	0.1	4.6	2	14.9
Peabody, MA	47,039	96.8	1.2	0	1.1	2.9	14.1
Pittsfield, MA	48,622	95.5	3.1	0.2	0.8	1.1	17.3
Quincy, MA	84,985	91.7	1.1	0.2	6.6	1.4	16.7
Revere, MA	42,786	93.2	1.4	0.2	3.7	3.8	17
Salem, MA	38,091	93	2.7	0.3	1.4	6.7	15.2
Somerville, MA	76,210	88.7	5.6	0.1	3.7	6.3	12.3
Springfield, MA	156,983	68.6	19.2	0.2	1	16.9	13.7
Taunton, MA	49,832	95.3	2	0.2	0.5	4.7	14.1
Waltham, MA	57,878	91.4	3.1	0.1	3.6	5.6	13.1
Watertown, MA	33,284	96.1	1.3	0.1	2.2	2	17.1
Westfield, MA	38,372	96.5	0.9	0.1	0.8	4.1	13.8
Weymouth, MA	54,063	97.6	1	0.1	0.9	1	13.8
Woburn, MA	35,943	96.6	1	0.2	1.5	2.3	12.7
Worcester, MA	169,759	87.1	4.5	0.3	2.8	9.6	16.1

MARYLAND

	Population	Pct. White	Pct. African Amer.	Pct. Native Amer.	Pct. Asian & Pac. Is.	Pct. Hispanic	65+ Years
Annapolis, MD	33,187	64.9	33	0.2	1.3	1.5	12.2
Aspen Hill, MD	45,494	73.3	14.5	0.4	9.2	7.8	8.8
Baltimore, MD	736,014	39.1	59.2	0.3	1.1	1	13.7
Bethesda, MD	62,936	89.3	3	0.1	6.6	5.9	18.5
Bowie, MD	37,589	91.4	5.7	0.3	2.3	2.2	6.3
Catonsville, MD	35,233	88.7	9.3	0.2	1.7	1	20.4
Chillum, MD	31,309	21.5	69.1	0.3	3.7	9.8	10
Columbia, MD	75,883	75.8	18.5	0.2	4.8	2.5	4.7
Dundalk, MD	65,800	92.9	6.1	0.4	0.4	0.9	16.1
Ellicott City, MD	41,396	88.2	5.2	0.1	6.2	1.4	8.8
Essex, MD	40,872	90	8.4	0.4	0.9	1.3	12.2
Frederick, MD	40,148	84.3	12.8	0.3	1.9	2.1	12.1
Gaithersburg, MD	39,542	72.2	12.9	0.4	10.2	9.3	6.4
Germantown, MD	41,145	80.4	12.1	0.3	5.6	5.1	2
Glen Burnie, MD	37,305	86.3	11.3	0.3	1.7	1.3	10.9
Hagerstown, MD	35,445	92.5	6.3	0.1	0.7	0.8	16
Montgomery, MD	32,315	78.7	11.3	0.3	6.6	7.3	4.9
Oxon H.-Glassm., MD	35,794	18.2	77.9	0.3	2.8	1.9	4.9
Parkville, MD	31,617	85.2	12.7	0.1	1.7	1.2	18.2
Potomac, MD	45,634	84.4	3.7	0.1	11.1	5.4	8.5
Rockville, MD	44,835	79.2	8.3	0.3	9.8	8.6	10.5
Silver Spring, MD	76,046	65.2	22.7	0.3	5.5	13	14.4
Suitland-Silver H., MD	35,111	13.6	84.3	0.3	1.3	1.4	5.8
Towson, MD	49,445	93.7	4	0.1	2	1.3	23.3
Wheat'n-Glenm't, MD	53,720	67	16.2	0.3	11.1	12.1	11.9

	Population	Pct. White	Pct. African Amer.	Pct. Native Amer.	Pct. Asian & Pac. Is.	Pct. Hispanic	65+ Years
Woodlawn, MD	32,907	70	24.5	0.2	4.9	1.5	11.1

MAINE

	Population	Pct. White	Pct. African Amer.	Pct. Native Amer.	Pct. Asian & Pac. Is.	Pct. Hispanic	65+ Years
Bangor, ME	33,181	97.1	0.9	0.7	1	0.6	13.6
Lewiston, ME	39,757	98.2	0.7	0.2	0.7	0.7	16.4
Portland, ME	64,358	96.6	1.1	0.4	1.7	0.8	15

MICHIGAN

	Population	Pct. White	Pct. African Amer.	Pct. Native Amer.	Pct. Asian & Pac. Is.	Pct. Hispanic	65+ Years
Allen Park, MI	31,092	98	0.5	0.2	0.7	3.2	20.3
Ann Arbor, MI	109,592	82	9	0.4	7.7	2.6	7.2
Battle Creek, MI	53,540	80.7	16.5	0.6	1.3	1.8	14.4
Bay City, MI	38,936	93.6	2.4	0.8	0.4	5.6	15.4
Bloomfield, MI	42,137	91.7	2.4	0.1	5.6	1.3	13.4
Canton, MI	57,047	92.9	2	0.3	4.5	1.4	4.8
Clinton, MI	85,866	95.4	3	0.3	1.1	1.2	10.8
Dearborn, MI	89,286	97.6	0.6	0.3	0.9	2.8	18
Dearborn Heights, MI	60,838	97.3	0.5	0.4	1.3	2.3	16.8
Detroit, MI	1,027,974	21.6	75.7	0.4	0.8	2.8	12.2
East Detroit, MI	35,283	98.7	0.2	0.4	0.6	0.8	18.8
East Lansing, MI	50,677	84.6	6.9	0.3	7	2.5	4.5
Farmington Hills, MI	74,652	93.9	1.9	0.2	3.8	1.2	11.8
Flint, MI	140,761	49.6	47.9	0.7	0.5	2.9	10.7
Garden City, MI	31,846	98.6	0.2	0.4	0.5	1.5	9.9
Grand Rapids, MI	189,126	76.4	18.5	0.8	1.1	5	13.1
Jackson, MI	37,446	80.2	17.7	0.6	0.4	2.5	14.1
Kalamazoo, MI	80,277	77.3	18.8	0.6	1.9	2.7	10.9
Kentwood, MI	37,826	91.3	5.6	0.4	2	2	9.6
Lansing, MI	127,321	73.9	18.6	1	1.8	7.9	9.6
Lincoln Park, MI	41,832	97.3	0.9	0.5	0.4	3.8	14.4
Livonia, MI	100,850	98	0.3	0.2	1.3	1.3	13.1
Madison Heights, MI	32,196	95.9	0.9	0.5	2.4	1.2	11.6
Midland, MI	38,053	95.6	1.7	0.4	1.9	1.7	11.9
Muskegon, MI	40,283	69.9	27.1	1	0.3	3.5	14.7
Novi, MI	32,998	96	0.8	0.3	2.6	1.1	8
Pontiac, MI	71,166	51.3	42.2	0.8	1.4	8	8.7
Port Huron, MI	33,694	90.1	6.8	0.8	0.6	3.5	13.9
Portage, MI	41,042	94.3	2.8	0.4	2.1	1.4	8.5
Redford, MI	54,387	98.1	0.7	0.4	0.6	1.5	16.5
Rochester Hills, MI	61,766	95	1.4	0.2	3.2	1.4	8.7
Roseville, MI	51,412	97.3	1	0.5	1.1	1.2	13.7
Royal Oak, MI	65,410	97.9	0.5	0.2	1.1	1.1	15.7
Saginaw, MI	69,512	52.3	40.3	0.5	0.4	10.5	11.9
Shelby, MI	48,655	98	0.3	0.3	1.2	1	7.4
Southfield, MI	75,728	67.9	29.1	0.3	2.4	1.7	17
St. Clair Shores, MI	68,107	98.7	0.2	0.3	0.6	0.9	18.6
Sterling Hgts, MI	117,810	96.3	0.4	0.2	2.9	1.1	9.2
Taylor, MI	70,811	93.2	4.2	0.6	1.3	2.8	8
Troy, MI	72,884	91.5	1.3	0.2	6.8	1.3	8.4
Warren, MI	144,864	97.3	0.7	0.5	1.3	1.1	14.9
Waterford, MI	66,692	96.9	1.1	0.6	0.7	2.3	9.7
West Bloomfield, MI	54,843	92.5	2	0.1	5.2	1.2	9.8
Westland, MI	84,724	94.7	3.3	0.6	1	1.9	10.8
Wyoming, MI	63,891	93.5	2.7	0.5	1.5	3.5	9.7

MINNESOTA

	Population	Pct. White	Pct. African Amer.	Pct. Native Amer.	Pct. Asian & Pac. Is.	Pct. Hispanic	65+ Years
Apple Valley, MN	34,598	96.7	0.9	0.2	1.9	1	2.6
Blaine, MN	38,975	97.2	0.3	0.8	1.4	1	3.1
Bloomington, MN	86,335	94.7	1.6	0.3	3.1	0.9	10.3
Brooklyn Park, MN	56,381	90.6	4.9	0.6	3.4	1.2	3.3
Burnsville, MN	51,288	94.8	2.3	0.3	2.3	1	3.9
Coon Rapids, MN	52,978	97.3	0.5	0.8	1.1	0.9	4.6
Duluth, MN	85,493	95.9	0.9	2.1	0.9	0.6	17.1
Eagan, MN	47,409	93.7	2.4	0.3	3.1	1.3	2.1
Eden Prairie, MN	39,311	96.4	1.1	0.2	2.1	0.7	3.3
Edina, MN	46,070	97.2	0.7	0.1	1.7	0.7	20.4
Mankato, MN	31,477	96.3	0.7	0.3	2.3	1.1	10.9
Maple Grove, MN	38,736	97.1	0.9	0.3	1.6	0.8	2.4
Minneapolis, MN	368,383	78.4	13	3.3	4.3	2.1	13
Minnetonka, MN	48,370	97.1	0.9	0.2	1.6	0.8	9.8
Moorhead, MN	32,295	95.3	0.5	1.4	1.1	2.8	11.1
Plymouth, MN	50,889	95.7	1.6	0.4	2	1	5
Richfield, MN	35,710	93.5	2.6	0.6	2.8	1.1	16.9

	Population	Pct. White	Pct. African Amer.	Pct. Native Amer.	Pct. Asian & Pac. Is.	Pct. Hispanic	65+ Years
Rochester, MN	70,745	94.2	1	0.3	4.1	1.2	11
Roseville, MN	33,485	95.1	1.6	0.3	2.6	1.1	16.8
St. Cloud, MN	48,812	96.8	1	0.6	1.3	0.6	10.2
St. Louis Park, MN	43,787	95.3	1.9	0.4	2.1	1	16.1
St. Paul, MN	272,235	82.3	7.4	1.4	7.1	4.2	13.7

MISSOURI

	Population	Pct. White	Pct. African Amer.	Pct. Native Amer.	Pct. Asian & Pac. Is.	Pct. Hispanic	65+ Years
Blue Springs, MO	40,153	95.6	2.4	0.4	1.1	1.6	5.9
Cape Girardeau, MO	34,438	90.2	8	0.2	1.3	0.6	14.6
Chesterfield, MO	37,991	93.7	2.4	0.1	3.6	1.2	9.2
Columbia, MO	69,101	85.1	9.9	0.3	4.1	1.3	8.7
Florissant, MO	51,206	95	4.1	0.2	0.5	1	13.9
Independence, MO	112,301	96.2	1.4	0.6	1	2	14.4
Jefferson City, MO	35,481	88.8	10.1	0.3	0.5	0.8	15.8
Joplin, MO	40,961	95	2.1	1.9	0.6	1.2	17.2
Kansas City, MO	435,146	66.8	29.6	0.5	1.2	3.9	12.9
Lee's Summit, MO	46,418	96.9	1.7	0.3	0.6	1	10.9
Oakville, MO	31,750	98.7	0.2	0.1	0.7	0.9	6.5
Springfield, MO	140,494	95.7	2.5	0.7	0.9	1	15.2
St. Charles, MO	54,555	95.9	2.8	0.3	0.7	1	9.9
St. Joseph, MO	71,852	95	3.6	0.3	0.4	2.2	17.1
St. Louis, MO	396,685	50.9	47.5	0.2	0.9	1.3	16.6
St. Peters, MO	45,779	96.4	2.2	0.2	1	1.1	4.5
University City, MO	40,087	49.1	48.2	0.1	2.2	1.1	13.9

MISSISSIPPI

	Population	Pct. White	Pct. African Amer.	Pct. Native Amer.	Pct. Asian & Pac. Is.	Pct. Hispanic	65+ Years
Biloxi, MS	46,319	74.6	18.6	0.3	5.7	2.8	11.4
Greenville, MS	45,226	39.8	59.6	0.1	0.4	0.6	12.3
Gulfport, MS	40,775	69.9	28.6	0.3	0.9	1.5	14.4
Hattiesburg, MS	41,882	58.2	40.4	0.1	1.1	1	12.7
Jackson, MS	196,637	43.6	55.7	0.1	0.5	0.4	11.6
Meridian, MS	41,036	54	45.4	0.1	0.4	0.6	16.5

MONTANA

	Population	Pct. White	Pct. African Amer.	Pct. Native Amer.	Pct. Asian & Pac. Is.	Pct. Hispanic	65+ Years
Billings, MT	81,151	94.6	0.5	3.2	0.6	3.1	13.6
Butte-Silver Bow, MT	33,336	97.3	0.1	1.6	0.4	2.4	17
Great Falls, MT	55,097	93.1	1	4.6	0.8	1.7	14.5
Missoula, MT	42,918	95.5	0.3	2.4	1.4	1.3	12.3

NORTH CAROLINA

	Population	Pct. White	Pct. African Amer.	Pct. Native Amer.	Pct. Asian & Pac. Is.	Pct. Hispanic	65+ Years
Asheville, NC	61,607	79.1	19.8	0.3	0.6	0.9	20.1
Burlington, NC	39,498	76.3	22.6	0.2	0.8	0.6	17.2
Camp Lejeune, NC	36,716	67.6	24.7	0.7	2	8.4	0
Cary, NC	43,858	89.8	5.5	0.3	3.8	1.6	4.4
Chapel Hill, NC	38,719	82.3	12.5	0.3	4.3	1.6	8.6
Charlotte, NC	395,934	65.6	31.8	0.4	1.8	1.4	9.8
Durham, NC	136,611	51.7	45.7	0.2	2	1.2	11.3
Fayetteville, NC	75,695	57.6	38.3	1.3	1.5	3.1	10.7
Fort Bragg, NC	34,744	60.9	29.1	0.9	2.6	10.3	0.1
Gastonia, NC	54,732	74	24.9	0.2	0.7	0.5	14.4
Goldsboro, NC	40,709	50.3	47.4	0.3	1.3	1.5	11
Greensboro, NC	183,521	63.9	33.9	0.5	1.4	1	11.8
Greenville, NC	44,972	64.2	34.1	0.2	1.2	0.8	8.7
High Point, NC	69,496	68.1	30.2	0.5	0.9	0.8	14.1
Raleigh, NC	207,951	69.2	27.6	0.3	2.5	1.4	8.8
Rocky Mount, NC	48,997	49.6	49.6	0.2	0.4	0.5	13.1
Wilmington, NC	55,530	64.9	33.9	0.3	0.6	0.9	15.9
Wilson, NC	36,930	52.4	46.9	0.1	0.3	0.7	13.8
Winston-Salem, NC	143,485	59.5	39.3	0.2	0.8	0.9	14.2

NORTH DAKOTA

	Population	Pct. White	Pct. African Amer.	Pct. Native Amer.	Pct. Asian & Pac. Is.	Pct. Hispanic	65+ Years
Fargo, ND	74,111	97.1	0.4	1.1	1.3	0.7	10.1
Grand Forks, ND	49,425	95.5	0.8	2.3	1.1	1.2	9.2
Minot, ND	34,544	95.8	1.1	2.1	0.8	0.8	13.9

NEBRASKA

	Population	Pct. White	Pct. African Amer.	Pct. Native Amer.	Pct. Asian & Pac. Is.	Pct. Hispanic	65+ Years
Grand Island, NE	39,386	96	0.3	0.3	1.3	4.8	14.6
Lincoln, NE	191,972	94.5	2.4	0.6	1.7	2	10.9
Omaha, NE	335,795	83.9	13.1	0.7	1	3.1	12.9

NEW HAMPSHIRE

	Population	Pct. White	Pct. African Amer.	Pct. Native Amer.	Pct. Asian & Pac. Is.	Pct. Hispanic	65+ Years
Concord, NH	36,006	98.2	0.6	0.3	0.7	1	14

	Population	Pct. White	Pct. African Amer.	Pct. Native Amer.	Pct. Asian & Pac. Is.	Pct. Hispanic	65+ Years
Manchester, NH	99,567	97	1	0.2	1.1	2.1	13.7
Nashua, NH	79,662	95.2	1.6	0.2	1.9	3	10.1

NEW JERSEY

	Population	Pct. White	Pct. African Amer.	Pct. Native Amer.	Pct. Asian & Pac. Is.	Pct. Hispanic	65+ Years
Atlantic City, NJ	37,986	35.4	51.3	0.5	4	15.3	19.2
Bayonne, NJ	61,444	90.4	4.7	0.1	1.8	9.5	18.7
Belleville, NJ	34,213	86.1	3.7	0.2	6	10.1	14.6
Bloomfield, NJ	45,061	89.1	4.3	0.1	5	5.1	18
Brick Township, NJ	66,473	97.8	0.6	0.1	0.8	2.6	17.3
Camden, NJ	87,492	19	56.4	0.4	1.3	31.2	8.4
Cherry Hill, NJ	69,319	89.8	3.2	0.1	6.1	2	14.1
Clifton, NJ	71,742	92.8	1.4	0.1	3.5	6.8	20.9
East Brunswick, NJ	43,548	88.1	2.2	0.1	9.1	2.9	8.7
East Orange, NJ	73,552	7.2	89.9	0.4	0.6	4.1	11.5
Edison, NJ	88,680	79.5	5.6	0.1	13.7	4.3	10.7
Elizabeth, NJ	110,002	65.5	19.8	0.3	2.7	39.1	12.1
Ewing, NJ	34,185	78.7	18.3	0.1	1.8	2.7	16.8
Fort Lee, NJ	31,997	77.2	1.3	0.1	20.3	5.6	20.1
Hackensack, NJ	37,049	66.4	24.8	0.2	3.7	15.1	14.3
Hoboken, NJ	33,397	79	5.5	0.2	4.4	30.1	11.1
Irvington, NJ	59,774	22.6	69.9	0.2	2.2	10.6	9.4
Jersey City, NJ	228,537	48.2	29.7	0.3	11.4	24.2	11.1
Kearny, NJ	34,874	90.5	1.2	0.2	4.7	17.1	13.3
Linden, NJ	36,701	76.8	20	0.1	1.5	7.4	19.3
Montclair, NJ	37,729	65.5	31	0.2	2.3	3.3	15.2
New Brunswick, NJ	41,711	57.4	29.6	0.3	4	19.3	9.3
Newark, NJ	275,221	28.6	58.5	0.2	1.2	26.1	9.3
North Bergen, NJ	48,414	84.2	2.1	0.2	4.8	41.2	15.1
North Brunswick, NJ	31,287	80	11.1	0.2	6.8	5.8	9.2
Parsipp'ny-Troy, NJ	48,478	85.1	3.6	0.1	10.1	4.2	9
Passaic, NJ	58,041	45.3	20.6	0.5	7.1	50	10.4
Paterson, NJ	140,891	41.2	36	0.3	1.4	41	9.6
Pennsauken, NJ	34,733	80.5	14.7	0.4	1.8	4.9	15.8
Perth Amboy, NJ	41,967	59.8	11.8	0.4	1.6	55.5	13.8
Plainfield, NJ	46,567	26.5	65.7	0.5	1.1	15	9.9
Sayreville , NJ	34,986	93.1	3.2	0.1	3	4	12.3
Teaneck, NJ	37,825	66.6	26.2	0.2	5.6	6.3	14.5
Trenton, NJ	88,675	42.2	49.3	0.3	0.7	14.1	12.7
Union, NJ	50,024	86.5	9.4	0.1	3.3	4.5	21.6
Union City, NJ	58,012	74.7	5.1	0.2	2.1	75.6	10
Vineland, NJ	54,780	73	11.5	0.3	0.9	23.6	14.1
Wayne, NJ	47,025	95	1.1	0.1	3.1	3.1	13.2
West New York, NJ	38,125	76.7	4	0.4	1.9	73.3	13.7
West Orange, NJ	39,103	87.6	5.7	0.1	5.6	4.4	18.9
Willingboro, NJ	36,291	39.7	56.1	0.3	1.9	5.3	6.9

NEW MEXICO

	Population	Pct. White	Pct. African Amer.	Pct. Native Amer.	Pct. Asian & Pac. Is.	Pct. Hispanic	65+ Years
Albuquerque, NM	384,736	78.2	3	3	1.7	34.5	11.1
Farmington, NM	33,997	77.1	0.8	13.8	0.4	16	8.7
Las Cruces, NM	62,126	88.2	1.9	0.9	1.1	46.9	11.3
Rio Rancho, NM	32,505	84.1	2.6	2.1	1.2	21.8	12
Roswell, NM	44,654	81.7	2.6	0.7	0.6	36.5	16
Santa Fe, NM	55,859	81.2	0.6	2.2	0.6	47.4	12.8
South Valley, NM	35,701	61.4	1.3	1.7	0.4	72.5	9.2

NEVADA

	Population	Pct. White	Pct. African Amer.	Pct. Native Amer.	Pct. Asian & Pac. Is.	Pct. Hispanic	65+ Years
Carson, NV	40,443	90.7	1.7	2.7	1.4	7.7	14.9
Henderson, NV	64,942	91.4	2.7	1	2	8.1	8.3
Las Vegas, NV	258,295	78.4	11.4	0.9	3.6	12.5	10.3
North Las Vegas, NV	47,707	45.2	37.4	1	2.4	22.2	6.8
Paradise, NV	124,682	86.5	4.9	0.6	4	10.5	12.7
Reno, NV	133,850	86.1	2.9	1.4	4.9	11.1	11.8
Sparks, NV	53,367	88.4	2.4	1.4	4.5	8.6	9.3
Spring Valley, NV	51,726	89.3	3.1	0.5	5.1	6.9	9.1
Sunrise Manor, NV	95,362	81.1	9.7	1	4.2	9.9	9.5

NEW YORK

	Population	Pct. White	Pct. African Amer.	Pct. Native Amer.	Pct. Asian & Pac. Is.	Pct. Hispanic	65+ Years
Albany, NY	101,082	75.5	20.6	0.3	2.3	3.1	15.3
Auburn, NY	31,258	91.9	6.8	0.3	0.5	2.2	18.3
Binghamton, NY	53,008	91.9	4.9	0.3	2.1	1.8	19.1
Brentwood, NY	45,218	73	13.4	0.4	2	34.7	7
Brighton, NY	34,455	92.1	3	0.1	4.3	1.6	19.7

	Population	Pct. White	Pct. African Amer.	Pct. Native Amer.	Pct. Asian & Pac. Is.	Pct. Hispanic	65+ Years
Buffalo, NY	328,123	64.7	30.7	0.8	1	4.9	14.8
Cheektowaga, NY	84,387	98.3	1.1	0.1	0.4	0.5	18.7
Commack, NY	36,124	96.1	0.6	0	2.9	2.5	8.5
East Meadow, NY	36,909	90.3	5	0.1	3.5	3.9	13.2
Elmira, NY	33,724	85.4	12.3	0.3	0.6	2.7	15
Freeport, NY	39,894	56.5	32.3	0.4	1.3	21.2	10.4
Hempstead, NY	49,453	32.4	58.8	0.5	1.7	19.1	8.5
Hicksville, NY	40,174	93.8	0.8	0.1	4.4	4.9	14.8
Irondequoit, NY	52,322	97.4	1.3	0.2	0.6	1.4	23.3
Jamestown, NY	34,681	94.9	2.6	0.5	0.5	3	17.2
Levittown, NY	53,286	97.4	0.3	0.1	1.8	4.1	10.8
Long Beach, NY	33,510	87	7.8	0.3	1.7	10.8	18.6
Mount Vernon, NY	67,153	39.8	55.3	0.4	1.8	7.8	14.9
N. Tonawanda, NY	34,989	98.9	0.2	0.3	0.4	0.8	14.5
New City, NY	33,673	92.4	2.7	0.1	4.2	3.6	7.1
New Rochelle, NY	67,265	76	18.1	0.1	2.9	10.8	17.3
New York, NY	7,322,564	52.3	28.7	0.4	7	24.4	13
Niagara Falls, NY	61,840	82.2	15.6	1.6	0.3	1.2	19.2
Oceanside, NY	32,423	97.3	0.4	0.1	1.4	3.9	12.9
Rochester, NY	231,636	61.1	31.5	0.5	1.8	8.7	12.1
Rome, NY	44,350	89.4	8	0.2	1.3	3.9	13.7
Schenectady, NY	65,566	88.6	8.7	0.3	1.1	2.7	17.1
Syracuse, NY	163,860	75	20.3	1.3	2.2	2.9	14.9
Tonawanda, NY	65,284	97.9	0.7	0.2	1	0.8	20
Troy, NY	54,269	88.3	7.6	0.2	3	2.1	14
Utica, NY	68,637	86.7	10.5	0.3	1.1	3.4	19.4
Valley Stream, NY	33,946	94.9	0.4	0	3.6	4.5	17.1
West Babylon, NY	42,410	88.1	9.9	0.2	1	4.7	11
West Seneca, NY	47,866	98.8	0.4	0.2	0.4	0.6	14.9
White Plains, NY	48,718	73.7	19	0.2	3.1	14.2	15.5
Yonkers, NY	188,082	76.2	14.1	0.2	3	16.7	16.4

OHIO

	Population	Pct. White	Pct. African Amer.	Pct. Native Amer.	Pct. Asian & Pac. Is.	Pct. Hispanic	65+ Years
Akron, OH	223,019	73.8	24.5	0.3	1.2	0.7	14.9
Beavercreek, OH	33,626	96.3	0.9	0.2	2.3	1	9.1
Boardman, OH	38,596	98.1	1.1	0.1	0.6	0.9	19.3
Canton, OH	84,161	80.7	18.2	0.5	0.3	1.1	16.4
Cincinnati, OH	364,040	60.5	37.9	0.2	1.1	0.7	13.9
Cleveland, OH	505,616	49.5	46.6	0.3	1	4.6	14
Cleveland Hgts, OH	54,052	60.2	37.1	0.2	2.1	1.1	12.8
Columbus, OH	632,910	74.4	22.6	0.2	2.4	1.1	9.2
Cuyahoga Falls, OH	48,950	98.1	1.1	0.1	0.6	0.4	15.3
Dayton, OH	182,044	58.4	40.4	0.2	0.6	0.7	13.1
East Cleveland, OH	33,096	5.3	93.7	0.1	0.7	0.6	10.5
Elyria, OH	56,746	85	13.7	0.2	0.5	1.5	11.8
Euclid, OH	54,875	82.9	16	0.1	0.9	0.8	22.2
Fairfield, OH	39,729	95	3.3	0.1	1.4	0.7	8.5
Findlay, OH	35,703	95.9	1.3	0.2	0.8	3.4	13.6
Garfield Heights, OH	31,739	84.4	14.8	0.1	0.5	0.8	19.4
Hamilton, OH	61,368	91.9	7.3	0.2	0.4	0.5	14.2
Huber Heights, OH	38,696	90.7	6.9	0.2	1.7	1.5	5.9
Kettering, OH	60,569	97.8	0.7	0.1	1.2	0.8	16.9
Lakewood, OH	59,718	97.5	0.8	0.2	1	1.5	13.5
Lancaster, OH	34,507	98.8	0.5	0.2	0.4	0.5	15.7
Lima, OH	45,549	74.5	24	0.2	0.5	1.5	14.4
Lorain, OH	71,245	78.2	13.8	0.4	0.3	16.9	13.4
Mansfield, OH	50,627	80.7	18.1	0.2	0.6	0.9	15
Marion, OH	34,075	94.7	4.2	0.3	0.5	0.8	13
Mentor, OH	47,358	98.6	0.3	0.1	0.9	0.6	9.4
Middletown, OH	46,022	88.3	11	0.1	0.4	0.4	14.5
Newark, OH	44,389	96	3.2	0.2	0.4	0.7	15.1
North Olmsted, OH	34,204	97.1	0.7	0.1	1.7	1.2	12.9
Parma, OH	87,876	97.9	0.7	0.1	1.1	0.9	19.1
Springfield, OH	70,487	81.6	17.4	0.2	0.5	0.6	15.4
Strongsville, OH	35,308	96.6	0.8	0.1	2.4	1	7.9
Toledo, OH	332,943	77	19.7	0.3	1	4	14.4
Upper Arlington, OH	34,128	97.3	0.3	0.1	2.3	0.7	18.7
Warren, OH	50,793	77.9	21.3	0.2	0.3	0.7	16.9
Youngstown, OH	95,732	59.3	38.1	0.2	0.3	4	18.2

OKLAHOMA

	Population	Pct. White	Pct. African Amer.	Pct. Native Amer.	Pct. Asian & Pac. Is.	Pct. Hispanic	65+ Years
Bartlesville, OK	34,256	88.6	3.3	6.4	1.1	1.8	16.7

	Population	Pct. White	Pct. African Amer.	Pct. Native Amer.	Pct. Asian & Pac. Is.	Pct. Hispanic	65+ Years
Broken Arrow, OK	58,043	91.7	3.1	3.6	.1	2.1	5.5
Edmond, OK	52,315	91.8	3.1	2.5	.2	1.8	7
Enid, OK	45,309	91	4.4	2.3	1.3	2.1	15.8
Lawton, OK	80,561	70.8	19.3	3.3	3.3	6.3	9.2
Midwest City, OK	52,267	77.1	16.3	3.9	1.7	2.7	11.3
Moore, OK	40,318	90.2	1.8	5.3	1.3	3.4	5
Muskogee, OK	37,708	69	18.9	11	0.5	1.5	18.6
Norman, OK	80,071	87.5	3.6	4.8	3.2	2.4	8.2
Oklahoma City, OK	444,719	74.8	16	4.2	2.4	5	11.9
Stillwater, OK	36,676	87.6	3.7	3.4	4.6	1.8	8.2
Tulsa, OK	367,302	79.3	13.6	4.7	1.4	2.6	12.7

OREGON

	Population	Pct. White	Pct. African Amer.	Pct. Native Amer.	Pct. Asian & Pac. Is.	Pct. Hispanic	65+ Years
Aloha, OR	34,284	90.7	0.7	0.7	6.4	3.8	5
Beaverton, OR	53,310	89.4	1	0.5	7.7	3.3	9.1
Corvallis, OR	44,757	89.1	1.2	0.7	8	2.8	9.4
Eugene, OR	112,669	93.4	1.3	0.9	3.5	2.7	12.7
Gresham, OR	68,235	93.8	1.1	1	2.7	3.3	10
Hillsboro, OR	37,520	88.6	0.5	0.6	2.2	11.2	8.7
Medford, OR	46,951	94.8	0.3	1.2	1.2	5.1	17.4
Portland, OR	437,319	84.6	7.7	1.2	5.3	3.2	14.6
Salem, OR	107,786	91.2	1.5	1.6	2.4	6.1	14.5
Springfield, OR	44,683	95.4	0.7	1.5	1.5	2.9	10.8

PENNSYLVANIA

	Population	Pct. White	Pct. African Amer.	Pct. Native Amer.	Pct. Asian & Pac. Is.	Pct. Hispanic	65+ Years
Allentown, PA	105,090	86.2	5	0.2	1.3	11.7	16.9
Altoona, PA	51,881	98	1.5	0.1	0.3	0.4	18.6
Bethel Park, PA	33,823	98.1	1	0.1	0.8	0.5	13.6
Bethlehem, PA	71,428	87.6	2.9	0.1	1.7	13	17.2
Chester, PA	41,856	32	65.2	0.2	0.4	3.8	13.9
Erie, PA	108,718	86.1	12	0.2	0.5	2.4	16.1
Harrisburg, PA	52,376	42.6	50.6	0.3	1.8	7.7	13
Lancaster, PA	55,551	70.9	12.2	0.2	2	20.6	12.2
Levittown, PA	55,362	97.4	1.4	0.1	0.8	1.2	11.1
Mount Lebanon, PA	33,362	97.7	0.5	0	1.7	0.8	18.4
Penn Hills, PA	51,430	83.9	15.5	0.1	0.4	0.5	16.3
Philadelphia, PA	1,585,577	53.5	39.9	0.2	2.7	5.6	15.2
Pittsburgh, PA	369,879	72.1	25.8	0.2	1.6	0.9	17.9
Reading, PA	78,380	78.6	9.7	0.1	1.4	18.5	16.6
Ross Township, PA	33,482	97.9	1.1	0	0.9	0.4	18.5
Scranton, PA	81,805	97.2	1.6	0.1	0.9	0.7	21.9
State College, PA	38,923	88.5	3.4	0.1	7.3	2	4.7
Wilkes-Barre, PA	47,523	96.1	2.9	0.1	0.6	0.7	21
Williamsport, PA	31,933	92.3	6.7	0.2	0.5	0.8	15
York, PA	42,192	72.5	21.3	0.2	1.1	7.7	13.5

RHODE ISLAND

	Population	Pct. White	Pct. African Amer.	Pct. Native Amer.	Pct. Asian & Pac. Is.	Pct. Hispanic	65+ Years
Cranston, RI	76,060	95.1	2.4	0.2	1.8	2	18.6
East Providence, RI	50,380	92.1	4.4	0.5	0.6	1.7	18.9
North Providence, RI	32,090	97.1	1	0.1	1.2	1.8	18.7
Pawtucket, RI	72,644	89.3	3.6	0.3	0.6	7.2	16.3
Providence, RI	160,728	69.9	14.8	0.9	5.9	15.5	13.6
Warwick, RI	85,427	98	0.8	0.2	0.8	1	16.8
Woonsocket, RI	43,877	93.3	2.6	0.2	3	2.6	16.2

SOUTH CAROLINA

	Population	Pct. White	Pct. African Amer.	Pct. Native Amer.	Pct. Asian & Pac. Is.	Pct. Hispanic	65+ Years
Charleston, SC	80,414	57.2	41.6	0.1	0.9	0.8	12.8
Columbia, SC	98,052	53.7	43.7	0.3	1.4	2	11.8
Greenville, SC	58,282	63.6	35.2	0.1	0.8	1	15.9
North Charleston, SC	70,218	62.7	34.3	0.5	1.6	2.5	5.9
Rock Hill, SC	41,643	60.4	38.1	0.4	0.8	0.6	12.4
Spartanburg, SC	43,467	53.1	45.6	0.1	0.9	0.8	15.3
Sumter, SC	41,943	59.8	38.2	0.3	1.2	1.6	10.4

SOUTH DAKOTA

	Population	Pct. White	Pct. African Amer.	Pct. Native Amer.	Pct. Asian & Pac. Is.	Pct. Hispanic	65+ Years
Rapid City, SD	54,523	88.2	1.3	8.9	1	2.2	11.5
Sioux Falls, SD	100,814	96.8	0.7	1.6	0.7	0.6	11.7

TENNESSEE

	Population	Pct. White	Pct. African Amer.	Pct. Native Amer.	Pct. Asian & Pac. Is.	Pct. Hispanic	65+ Years
Chattanooga, TN	152,466	65	33.7	0.2	1	0.6	15.3
Clarksville, TN	75,494	75	20.9	0.4	2.2	3.9	7.1
Germantown, TN	32,893	95.2	1.9	0.2	2.7	0.8	5.4
Hendersonville, TN	32,188	96.7	2.3	0.2	0.6	0.8	8.3
Jackson, TN	48,949	59.1	40.3	0.1	0.4	0.5	15.5
Johnson City, TN	49,381	93.1	5.9	0.2	0.7	0.6	15.9
Kingsport, TN	36,365	94.8	4.4	0.1	0.6	0.3	20
Knoxville, TN	165,121	82.7	15.8	0.2	1	0.7	15.4
Memphis, TN	610,337	44	54.8	0.2	0.8	0.7	12.2
Murfreesboro, TN	44,922	82.3	14.5	0.2	2.8	0.8	9.9
Nashville, TN	488,374	73.8	24.3	0.2	1.4	0.9	11.4

TEXAS

	Population	Pct. White	Pct. African Amer.	Pct. Native Amer.	Pct. Asian & Pac. Is.	Pct. Hispanic	65+ Years
Abilene, TX	106,654	82.4	7	0.4	1.3	15.5	11.8
Amarillo, TX	157,615	82.7	6	0.8	1.9	14.7	12
Arlington, TX	261,721	82.6	8.4	0.5	3.9	8.9	5
Austin, TX	465,622	70.6	12.4	0.4	3	23	7.4
Baytown, TX	63,850	73	12	0.3	0.8	23.2	9.7
Beaumont, TX	114,323	55	41.3	0.2	1.7	4.3	13.8
Bedford, TX	43,762	92.8	2.6	0.4	2.5	4.6	4.7
Brownsville, TX	98,962	84.8	0.2	0.1	0.3	90.1	8.7
Bryan, TX	55,002	69.9	17.2	0.2	1.5	19.8	9.8
Carrollton, TX	82,169	83.1	4.9	0.4	6.8	10.2	3.4
College Station, TX	52,456	83	6.3	0.2	6.5	8.9	2.8
Corpus Christi, TX	257,453	76.1	4.8	0.4	0.9	50.4	10.1
Dallas, TX	1,006,877	55.3	29.5	20.5	2.2	20.9	9.7
Denton, TX	66,270	82	9.5	0.5	2.8	9	8.1
Duncanville, TX	35,748	82.5	12.1	0.3	2.1	6.7	6.8
El Paso, TX	515,342	76.9	3.4	0.4	1.2	69	8.7
Euless, TX	38,149	86.5	4.6	0.6	5.1	7.9	4
Fort Hood, TX	35,580	54.9	33.9	0.8	3.5	12.4	0.1
Fort Worth, TX	447,619	63.8	22	0.4	2	19.5	11.2
Galveston, TX	59,070	61.5	29.1	0.2	2.3	21.4	13.5
Garland, TX	180,650	79.7	8.9	0.5	4.5	11.6	5.5
Grand Prairie, TX	99,616	75.8	9.7	0.8	3	20.5	6.4
Haltom City, TX	32,856	89.8	1.3	0.7	4.8	8.5	12
Harlingen, TX	48,735	80.1	0.8	0.2	0.4	71	13.2
Houston, TX	1,630,553	52.7	28.1	0.3	4.1	27.6	8.3
Hurst, TX	33,574	93.4	2.6	0.5	1.2	5.2	8.9
Irving, TX	155,037	78.7	7.5	0.6	4.6	16.3	5.4
Killeen, TX	63,535	58.1	30.1	0.5	5.8	14	4
Kingwood, TX	37,397	95.2	1.3	0.2	1.9	4.4	3.2
Laredo, TX	122,899	70.8	0.1	0.2	0.4	93.9	8.2
Lewisville, TX	46,521	88.6	4.6	0.6	1.9	8.7	4.5
Longview, TX	70,311	76.6	19.9	0.4	0.6	4.1	13
Lubbock, TX	186,206	77.6	8.6	0.3	1.4	22.5	9.8
McAllen, TX	84,021	70.9	0.3	0.2	0.7	77	10.4
Mesquite, TX	101,484	87.2	5.8	0.5	2.6	8.8	5.3
Midland, TX	89,443	79.8	9.1	0.4	1	21.3	9.4
Missouri City, TX	36,176	60.6	29.4	0.3	6.3	9.2	4.1
N. Richland Hills, TX	45,895	93.6	1.8	0.5	1.6	5.8	6.8
Odessa, TX	89,699	75.4	6	0.5	0.7	31.1	10.1
Pasadena, TX	119,363	83.7	1	0.5	1.6	28.8	7.7
Pharr, TX	32,921	70.2	0.1	0.2	0.1	88.4	11.4
Plano, TX	128,713	88.5	4.1	0.3	4	6.2	3.6
Port Arthur, TX	58,724	49.3	42.2	0.3	4.8	8.2	17.1
Richardson, TX	74,840	86.8	4.7	0.3	6.6	4.3	7.5
San Angelo, TX	84,474	78.8	4.8	0.4	1.1	28	13.1
San Antonio, TX	935,933	72.2	7	0.4	1.1	55.6	10.5
Sherman, TX	31,601	83.2	12.6	0.9	0.8	4.4	16.4
Spring, TX	33,111	88.7	5.8	0.4	1.3	9.4	3
Temple, TX	46,109	72.8	17.1	0.4	0.9	13.7	16.4
Texarkana, TX	31,656	63	35.9	0.4	0.5	1.1	17.1
Texas City, TX	40,822	67.1	25.1	0.4	1.1	15.9	11.3
Tyler, TX	75,450	66.1	28.2	0.3	0.5	8.9	14.8
Victoria, TX	55,076	76.9	7.9	0.3	0.4	37.9	11.4
Waco, TX	103,590	67.6	23.1	0.3	0.9	16.3	14.9
Wichita Falls, TX	96,259	80.4	11.2	0.7	1.8	10	12.6

UTAH

	Population	Pct. White	Pct. African Amer.	Pct. Native Amer.	Pct. Asian & Pac. Is.	Pct. Hispanic	65+ Years
Bountiful, UT	36,659	98.2	0.1	0.3	0.9	1.6	10.8
Layton, UT	41,784	92.7	2.1	0.7	2.3	5.6	4.5
Logan, UT	32,762	91.4	0.6	1.3	5.1	3.1	8.8
Millcreek, UT	32,230	93.2	1.1	1	2.7	5.6	13
Murray, UT	31,282	95.8	0.7	0.5	1.5	4.2	10.3

City	Population	Pct. White	Pct. African Amer.	Pct. Native Amer.	Pct. Asian & Pac. Is.	Pct. Hispanic	65+ Years
Ogden, UT	63,909	87.4	2.7	1.1	1.8	12	14.6
Orem, UT	67,561	96.4	0.1	0.8	1.5	3	6.2
Provo, UT	86,835	94.1	0.3	1.1	2.7	4.2	6.5
Salt Lake City, UT	159,936	87	1.7	1.6	4.7	9.7	14.5
Sandy, UT	75,058	97.1	0.2	0.3	1.7	2.5	3.5
Taylorsville, UT	52,351	93.6	0.7	0.6	2.9	5.6	4.3
West Jordan, UT	42,892	94	0.3	0.6	1.9	6.5	2.7
West Valley City, UT	86,976	90.8	0.8	1.1	4	7.1	4.2

VIRGINIA

City	Population	Pct. White	Pct. African Amer.	Pct. Native Amer.	Pct. Asian & Pac. Is.	Pct. Hispanic	65+ Years
Alexandria, VA	111,183	69.1	21.9	0.3	4.2	9.7	10.3
Annandale, VA	50,975	82.7	3.8	0.2	11.2	6.9	10
Arlington, VA	170,936	76.6	10.5	0.3	6.8	13.5	11.4
Blacksburg, VA	34,590	87.4	4.3	0.1	7.7	1.8	4.2
Burke, VA	57,734	85.5	4.1	0.2	9	4.6	2.6
Charlottesville, VA	40,341	76.1	21.2	0.1	2.3	1.2	12.2
Chesapeake, VA	151,976	70.7	27.4	0.3	1.2	1.3	8.5
Dale City, VA	47,170	76.6	17.5	0.4	4	5.3	1.9
Danville, VA	53,056	62.7	36.6	0.1	0.5	0.5	18.7
Hampton, VA	133,793	58.4	38.9	0.3	1.7	2	9.6
Lynchburg, VA	66,049	72.5	26.4	0.2	0.8	0.7	16.4
McLean, VA	38,168	88.3	1.7	0.2	9.2	4.2	13.9
Newport News, VA	170,045	62.6	33.6	0.3	2.3	2.8	9.3
Norfolk, VA	261,229	56.7	39.1	0.4	2.6	2.9	10.5
Petersburg, VA	38,386	26.6	72.1	0.2	0.8	1.2	15
Portsmouth, VA	103,907	51.2	47.3	0.3	0.8	1.3	13.9
Reston, VA	48,556	81.8	11	0.2	5.3	5.2	6.1
Richmond, VA	203,056	43.4	55.2	0.2	0.9	0.9	15.4
Roanoke, VA	96,397	74.6	24.3	0.2	0.7	0.7	17.1
Suffolk, VA	52,141	54.7	44.6	0.2	0.4	0.6	12.9
Tuckahoe, VA	42,629	92.7	4.7	0.1	2.2	1.3	15.6
Virginia Beach, VA	393,069	80.5	13.9	0.4	4.3	3.1	5.9
Burlington, VT	39,127	96.8	1	0.3	1.5	1.2	10.6

WASHINGTON

City	Population	Pct. White	Pct. African Amer.	Pct. Native Amer.	Pct. Asian & Pac. Is.	Pct. Hispanic	65+ Years
Auburn, WA	33,102	92.4	1.4	2.1	3	3.1	11.6
Bellevue, WA	86,874	86.5	2.2	0.4	9.9	2.5	10.4
Bellingham, WA	52,179	93.8	0.8	1.8	2.8	2.4	14.1
Bremerton, WA	38,142	83.9	7.1	1.7	5.3	4.8	13.6
E. Hill-Meridian, WA	42,696	88.9	2.5	0.8	6.6	2.9	5.6
Everett, WA	69,961	91.7	1.7	1.7	3.9	2.8	13
Federal Way, WA	67,554	86.7	4	0.9	7.2	3.3	6.2
Kennewick, WA	42,155	89.9	1.1	0.8	2	8.7	9.1
Kent, WA	37,960	89.2	3.8	1.4	4.4	3.9	6.5
Kirkland, WA	40,052	92.8	1.5	0.6	4.3	2.4	9.6
Lakewood, WA	58,412	74.5	12.7	1.4	9.5	5.5	10.7
Longview, WA	31,499	94.7	0.5	1.5	2.1	2	15.5
Olympia, WA	33,840	92	1.2	1.2	4.8	2.6	14.5
Redmond, WA	35,800	91.1	1.3	0.5	6.3	2.5	6.9
Renton, WA	41,688	83.5	6.6	1.2	7.7	3	10.5
Richland, WA	32,315	93	1.4	0.7	3.3	3.3	12.6
Seattle, WA	516,259	75.3	10.1	1.4	11.8	3.6	15.2
Spokane, WA	177,196	93.3	1.9	2	2.1	2.1	16.2
Tacoma, WA	176,664	78.1	11.4	2	6.9	3.8	13.7
Vancouver, WA	46,380	92.3	2.3	1.3	3.2	3	16.3
Yakima, WA	54,827	82.5	2.4	2	1.3	16.3	16.4

WISCONSIN

City	Population	Pct. White	Pct. African Amer.	Pct. Native Amer.	Pct. Asian & Pac. Is.	Pct. Hispanic	65+ Years
Appleton, WI	65,695	96.6	0.2	0.4	2.4	0.9	11.9
Beloit, WI	35,573	81.8	15.7	0.3	1.2	1.9	13.4
Brookfield, WI	35,184	96.9	0.4	0.2	2.4	0.7	12.6
Eau Claire, WI	56,856	95.1	0.4	0.6	3.8	0.6	12.7
Fond du Lac, WI	37,757	97.8	0.3	0.5	0.8	1.5	16.3
Green Bay, WI	96,466	94.2	0.5	2.5	2.3	1.1	12.6
Greenfield, WI	33,403	97.6	0.4	0.4	1	2	17.1
Janesville, WI	52,133	98.1	0.6	0.2	0.8	1.1	11.9
Kenosha, WI	80,352	89.8	6.4	0.4	0.6	5.9	13.5
La Crosse, WI	51,003	93.8	0.7	0.4	4.9	0.9	15.7
Madison, WI	191,262	90.7	4.2	0.4	3.9	2	9.3
Manitowoc, WI	32,520	96.4	0.2	0.5	2.5	1.1	19.8
Milwaukee, WI	628,088	63.4	30.5	0.9	1.9	6.3	12.4
New Berlin, WI	33,592	98.4	0.2	0.2	1	0.8	8.5

City	Population	Pct. White	Pct. African Amer.	Pct. Native Amer.	Pct. Asian & Pac. Is.	Pct. Hispanic	65+ Years
Oshkosh, WI	55,006	96.3	0.8	0.5	2.2	0.8	14.1
Racine, WI	84,298	76.4	18.4	0.3	0.5	8.1	13.1
Sheboygan, WI	49,676	94.4	0.2	0.4	3.9	2.5	17
Waukesha, WI	56,958	95.4	0.6	0.3	1.3	5.9	9.8
Wausau, WI	37,060	93.1	0.1	0.7	6	0.7	17.3
Wauwatosa, WI	49,366	97.3	1.2	0.2	1	1	19.8
West Allis, WI	63,221	98.2	0.3	0.5	0.6	1.5	17.9

WEST VIRGINIA

City	Population	Pct. White	Pct. African Amer.	Pct. Native Amer.	Pct. Asian & Pac. Is.	Pct. Hispanic	65+ Years
Charleston, WV	57,287	84.1	14.2	0.2	1.3	0.6	18.4
Huntington, WV	54,844	92.5	6.7	0.1	0.5	0.5	19.9
Parkersburg, WV	33,862	97.7	1.7	0.2	0.3	0.3	19.9
Wheeling, WV	34,882	94.7	4.5	0.1	0.7	0.3	21.9

WYOMING

City	Population	Pct. White	Pct. African Amer.	Pct. Native Amer.	Pct. Asian & Pac. Is.	Pct. Hispanic	65+ Years
Casper, WY	46,742	96.5	0.9	0.5	0.5	3.9	11.4
Cheyenne, WY	50,008	89.6	3.1	0.7	1.2	11.8	12

Kansas
Environmental Quality

Kansas residents generate 1.6 million tons of solid waste each year, or approximately 1,200 pounds per capita. Landfill capacity in Kansas will be exhausted in more than 12 years. The state has 11 hazardous waste sites. Annual greenhouse gas emissions in Kansas total 70.8 million tons, or 28.4 tons per capita. Industrial sources in Kansas release approximately 67.4 thousand tons of toxins, 399.6 thousand tons of acid precipitation-producing substances, and 1.3 million tons of smog-producing substances into the atmosphere each year.

The state has 700 acres within the National Park System. Noteworthy is Fort Larned National Historic Site. State parks cover just over 36,000 acres, attracting 4.1 million visitors per year.

Kansas spends approximately 1.2 percent of its budget, or approximately $19 per capita, on environmental and natural resources. Kansas representatives in the U.S. House voted in favor of national environmental legislation 63 percent of the time, while U.S. senators did so 25 percent of the time.

For more information about Kansas's environment, contact the State Department of Health and Environment, Landon St. Bldg., 901 SW Jackson St., Topeka, KS 66612.

North Dakota
Environmental Quality

North Dakota residents generate 450,000 tons of solid waste each year, or approximately 1,400 pounds per capita. Landfill capacity in North Dakota will be exhausted in more than 12 years. The state has 2 hazardous waste sites. Annual greenhouse gas emissions in North Dakota total 43.5 million tons, or 65.2 tons per capita. Industrial sources in North Dakota release approximately 107.0 thousand tons of toxins, 308.3 thousand tons of acid precipitation-producing substances, and 400.0 thousand tons of smog-producing substances into the atmosphere each year.

The state has 71,300 acres within the National Park System; the largest area within the state is Theodore Roosevelt National Park. State parks cover just over 18,000 acres, attracting 5.9 million visitors per year.

North Dakota spends 2.3 percent of its budget, or approximately $49 per capita, on environmental and natural resources. North Dakota representatives in the U.S. House voted in favor of national environmental legislation 38 percent of the time, while U.S. senators did so 42 percent of the time.

For more information about North Dakota's environment, contact the Department of Environmental Enforcement, Department of Health, Bismarck, ND 58505.

Pennsylvania
Environmental Quality

Pennsylvania residents generate 9.2 million tons of solid waste each year, or approximately 1,640 pounds per capita. Landfill capacity in Pennsylvania will be exhausted in less than 5 years. The state has 97 hazardous waste sites. Annual greenhouse gas emissions in Pennsylvania total 254.6 million tons, or 21.2 tons per capita. Industrial sources in Pennsylvania release approximately 114.1 thousand tons of toxins, 1.8 million tons of acid precipitation-producing substances, and 4.4 million tons of smog-producing substances into the atmosphere each year.

The state has 40,900 acres within the National Park System, the most famous area being Independence National Historical Park in Philadelphia. State parks cover just over 281,000 acres, attracting 36.3 million visitors per year.

Pennsylvania spends 1.5 percent of its budget, or approximately $24 per capita, on environmental and natural resources. Pennsylvania representatives in the U.S. House voted in favor of national environmental legislation 62 percent of the time, while U.S. senators did so 54 percent of the time.

For more information about Pennsylvania's environment, contact the Secretary of Environmental Resources, 9th Floor, Fulton Bldg., P.O. Box 2063, Harrisburg, PA 17120.

South Dakota
Environmental Quality

South Dakota residents generate 750,000 tons of solid waste each year, or approximately 2,100 pounds per capita. Landfill capacity in South Dakota will be exhausted in more than 12 years. The state has 3 hazardous waste sites. Annual greenhouse gas emissions in South Dakota total 16.1 million tons, or 22.6 tons per capita. Industrial sources in South Dakota release approximately 1.5 thousand tons of toxins, 53.6 thousand tons of acid precipitation-producing substances, and 500.0 thousand tons of smog-producing substances into the atmosphere each year.

The state has 183,300 acres within the National Park System; the largest area within the state is Badlands National Park. State parks cover just over 91,000 acres, attracting 5.9 million visitors per year.

South Dakota spends 1.9 percent of its budget, or approximately $30 per capita, on environmental and natural resources. South Dakota representatives in the U.S. House voted in favor of national environmental legislation 75 percent of the time, while U.S. senators did so 63 percent of the time.

For more information about South Dakota's environment, contact the Department of Water and Natural Resources, Joe Foss Office Bldg., Pierre, SD 57501.

Tennessee
Environmental Quality

Tennessee residents generate 3.9 million tons of solid waste each year, or approximately 1,600 pounds per capita. Landfill capacity in Tennessee will be exhausted in more than 12 years. The state has 14 hazardous waste sites. Annual greenhouse gas emissions in Tennessee total 110.2 million tons, or 22.5 tons per capita. Industrial sources in Tennessee release approximately 146.9 thousand tons of toxins, 1.3 million tons of acid precipitation-producing substances, and 2.4 million tons of smog-producing substances into the atmosphere each year.

The state has 266,400 acres within the National Park System; the largest area within the state is Cumberland Gap National Historical Park. Great Smoky Mountains National Park, half of which is located in North Carolina, is the largest park associated with the state. State parks cover just over 166,000 acres, attracting 27.0 million visitors per year.

Tennessee spends 1.3 percent of its budget, or approximately $17 per capita, on environmental and natural resources. Tennessee representatives in the U.S. House voted in favor of national environmental legislation 54 percent of the time, while U.S. senators did so 75 percent of the time.

For more information about Tennessee's environment, contact the Department of Conservation, 701 Broadway, Customs House, Nashville, TN 37234-0435.

Washington
Environmental Quality

Washington residents generate 5.2 million tons of solid waste each year, or approximately 2,200 pounds per capita. Landfill capacity in Washington will be exhausted in more than 12 years. The state has 45 hazardous waste sites. Annual greenhouse gas emissions in Washington total 76.7 million tons, or 16.5 tons per capita. Industrial sources in Washington release approximately 20.8 thousand tons of toxins, 196.1 thousand tons of acid precipitation-producing substances, and 2.7 million tons of smog-producing substances into the atmosphere each year.

The state has 1,912,700 acres within the National Park System; the largest area within the state is Olympic National Park. State parks cover just over 114,000 acres, attracting 46.8 million visitors per year.

Washington spends 2.6 percent of its budget, or approximately $53 per capita, on environmental and natural resources. Washington representatives in the U.S. House voted in favor of national environmental legislation 57 percent of the time, while U.S. senators did so 71 percent of the time.

For more information about Washington's environment, contact the Department of Ecology, Mail Stop P.V. 11, Olympia, WA 98504.